ARTIFICIAL INTELLIGENCE
APPLICATIONS AND INNOVATIONS

IFIP – The International Federation for Information Processing

IFIP was founded in 1960 under the auspices of UNESCO, following the First World Computer Congress held in Paris the previous year. An umbrella organization for societies working in information processing, IFIP's aim is two-fold: to support information processing within its member countries and to encourage technology transfer to developing nations. As its mission statement clearly states,

> IFIP's mission is to be the leading, truly international, apolitical organization which encourages and assists in the development, exploitation and application of information technology for the benefit of all people.

IFIP is a non-profitmaking organization, run almost solely by 2500 volunteers. It operates through a number of technical committees, which organize events and publications. IFIP's events range from an international congress to local seminars, but the most important are:

• The IFIP World Computer Congress, held every second year;
• Open conferences;
• Working conferences.

The flagship event is the IFIP World Computer Congress, at which both invited and contributed papers are presented. Contributed papers are rigorously refereed and the rejection rate is high.

As with the Congress, participation in the open conferences is open to all and papers may be invited or submitted. Again, submitted papers are stringently refereed.

The working conferences are structured differently. They are usually run by a working group and attendance is small and by invitation only. Their purpose is to create an atmosphere conducive to innovation and development. Refereeing is less rigorous and papers are subjected to extensive group discussion.

Publications arising from IFIP events vary. The papers presented at the IFIP World Computer Congress and at open conferences are published as conference proceedings, while the results of the working conferences are often published as collections of selected and edited papers.

Any national society whose primary activity is in information may apply to become a full member of IFIP, although full membership is restricted to one society per country. Full members are entitled to vote at the annual General Assembly, National societies preferring a less committed involvement may apply for associate or corresponding membership. Associate members enjoy the same benefits as full members, but without voting rights. Corresponding members are not represented in IFIP bodies. Affiliated membership is open to non-national societies, and individual and honorary membership schemes are also offered.

ARTIFICIAL INTELLIGENCE APPLICATIONS AND INNOVATIONS

3rd IFIP Conference on Artificial Intelligence Applications and Innovations (AIAI) 2006, June 7-9, 2006, Athens, Greece

Edited by

Ilias Maglogiannis
University of the Aegean, Greece

Kostas Karpouzis
ICCS/NTUA, Greece

Max Bramer
University of Plymouth, United Kingdom

 Springer

Artificial Intelligence Applications and Innovations
Edited by I. Maglogiannis, K. Karpouzis, and M. Bramer

p. cm. (IFIP International Federation for Information Processing, a Springer Series in Computer Science)

ISSN: 1571-5736 / 1861-2288 (Internet)

ISBN 978-1-4419-4168-8   e-ISBN 978-0-387-34224-5
eISBN: 10: 0-387-34224-9
Printed on acid-free paper

9 8 7 6 5 4 3 2 1
springer.com

Contents

vi

Foreword

It is our pleasure to welcome you to the Proceedings of AIAI 2006, the 3rd IFIP Conference on Artificial Intelligence Applications & Innovations being held from 7th till 9th of June, in Athens, Greece. Artificial Intelligence applications build on a rich and proven theoretical background to provide solutions to a wide range of real life problems. The ever expanding abundance of information and computing power enables researchers and users to tackle highly interesting issues for the first time, such as applications providing personalized access and interactivity to multimodal information based on user preferences and semantic concepts or human-machine interface systems utilizing information on the affective state of the user. The purpose of the 3rd IFIP Conference on Artificial Intelligence Applications and Innovations (AIAI) is to bring together researchers, engineers and practitioners interested in the technical advances and business and industrial applications of intelligent systems. AIAI 2006 is focused on providing insights on how AI can be implemented in real world applications.

The response to the 'Call for Papers' was overwhelming, attracting submissions from 23 countries. The task of the Technical Program Committee was very challenging putting together a Program containing 87 high quality contributions. The collection of papers included in the proceedings offer stimulating insights into emerging applications of AI and describe advanced prototypes, systems, tools and techniques. AIAI Proceedings will interest not only academics and researchers, but IT professionals and consultants by examining technologies and applications of demonstrable value.

Eight (8) Special Sessions dedicated to specific AI applications are affiliated within the AIAI 2006 conference:

- Adaptive Learning Systems Engineering (organized by Symeon Retalis, Andreas Papasalouros and Kostas Siassiakos)
- Advances in Artificial Intelligence for Integrated Surveillance and Monitoring Systems (organized by Dimitris Vergados and Christos Anagnostopoulos)

- Computational Intelligence in Software Engineering (organized by Andreou Andreas and Efstratios Georgopoulos)
- Computational Intelligence in Medical Imaging (organized by Efthyvoulos Kyriacou and Ilias Maglogiannis)
- Digital Rights Management Techniques and Interoperability of Protection Tools (organized by Sofia Tsekeridou)
- Emerging Multimodal Interfaces (organized by John Soldatos, Dimitris Tzovaras and Kostas Karpouzis)
- Intelligent Analysis of Medical and Biological Data (organized by Vasileios Megalooikonomou and Despina Kontos)
- Semantics in Multimedia Analysis and Natural Language Processing (organized by Anastasios Delopoulos, Vangelis Karkaletsis, George Paliouras and Manolis Wallace)

The wide range of topics and high level of contributions will surely guarantee a very successful conference. We express our special thanks to all who have contributed to the organization and scientific contents of this conference, first to the authors of the papers, then to the special session organizers and finally to the reviewers and members of the Program and Organization Committees.

June, 2006   AIAI 2006 Conference Chairs:

Ilias Maglogiannis, University of Aegean, Greece,

Kostas Karpouzis, ICCS/NTUA, Greece,

Max Bramer, University of Portsmouth, UK

Acknowledgments

AIAI 2006 conference is co-organized by the Department of Information and Communications Systems Engineering of the University of Aegean and Athens Information Technology (AIT). AIAI 2006 is the official conference of WG12.5 "Artificial Intelligence Applications" working group of IFIP TC12 the International Federation for Information Processing Technical Committee on Artificial Intelligence (AI).

Conference General Chairs

Ilias Maglogiannis, University of Aegean, Greece
Kostas Karpouzis, NTUA, Greece
Max Bramer, University of Portsmouth, UK

Organizing Committee Chairs

Manolis Wallace, University of Indianapolis, Athens Campus, Greece
Lazaros Polymenakos, Athens Information Technology, Greece

Publicity Chair

Constantine D. Spyropoulos, NCSR Demokritos, Greece

Technical Program Committee

Program Committee Chairs

Ilias Maglogiannis, University of Aegean, Greece
John Soldatos, AIT, Greece
John Debenham, University of Technology, Australia

Program Committee Members

Olusola Abidogun, University of the Western Cape, South Africa
Christos Anagnostopoulos, University of Aegean, Greece
Ioannis Anagnostopoulos, University of Aegean, Greece
Andreou Andreas, University of Cyprus, Cyprus
Grigorios Beligiannis, University of Patras, Greece
Zdzislaw Bubnicki, Wroclaw University of Technology, Poland
Luigia Carlucci Aiello, University di Roma La Sapienza, Italy
Weiqin Chen, University of Bergen, Norway
Anastasios Delopoulos, Aristotle University of Thessaloniki, Greece
Yves Demazeau, CNRS/IMAG Institute, France
Christos Douligeris, University of Piraeus, Greece
Efstratios Georgopoulos, Technological Educational Institute of Kalamata, Greece
Starhes Hadjieftymiades, University of Athens, Greece
Timo Honkela, Helsinki University of Technology, Finland
Achilles Kameas, Hellenic Open University, Greece
Vangelis Karkaletsis, NCSR Demokritos, Greece
Stefanos Kollias, National Technical University of Athens, Greece
Despina Kontos, Temple University, USA
George Kormentzas, University of Aegean, Greece
Dimitris Kosmopoulos, NCSR Demokritos, Greece
Efthyvoulos Kyriacou, University of Cyprus, Cyprus
Daoliang Li, China Agricultural University, China
Filia Makedon, Department of Computer Science, Dartmouth College, USA
Yannis Manolopoulos, Aristotle University Thessaloniki, Greece
Kinshuk, Massey University, New Zealand
Vasileios Megalooikonomou, Temple University, USA
Eunika Mercier-Laurent, KIM, France
Alex Nanopoulos, Aristotle University Thessaloniki, Greece
Nikos Nikolaidis, Aristotle University of Thessaloniki, Greece

Daniel O'Leary, University of Southern California, USA
Geroge Papakonstantinou, National Technical University of Athens, Greece
Andreas Papasalouros, National Technical University of Athens, Greece
Constantinos Pattichis, University of Cyprus, Cyprus
Aristodemos Pnevmatikakis, Athens Information Technology, Greece
Lazaros Polymenakos, Athens Information Technology, Greece
Symeon Retalis, University of Piraeus, Greece
Angelos Rouskas, University of Aegean, Greece
Pierre-Yves Schobbens, University of Namur, Belgium
Kostas Siassiakos, University of Piraeus, Greece
Harry Skiannis, NCSR Demokritos, Greece
Derek Sleeman, University of Aberdeen, UK
Costas Spyropoulos, NCSR Demokritos, Greece
Andreas Stafylopatis, NTUA, Greece
Dimitris Stamoulis, University of Athens, Greece
Olga Stepankova, Czech Technical University in Prague, Czech Republic
Kostas Stergiou, University of Aegean, Greece
Vagan Terziyan, MIT Department, University of Jyvaskyla, Finland
Panayiotis Tsanakas, National Technical University of Athens, Greece
Sophia Tsekeridou, University of Thrace, Greece
Dimitris Vergados, University of Aegean, Greece
George Vouros, University of Aegean, Greece
Manolis Wallace, University of Indianapolis, Athens Campus, Greece
Michalis Xenos, Hellenic Open University, Greece
Ioannis Zaharakis, Computer Technology Institute (CTI), Greece

Local Ordinal Classification

Sotiris B. Kotsiantis
Educational Software Development Laboratory
Department of Mathematics
University of Patras, Greece
sotos@math.upatras.gr

Abstract. Given ordered classes, one is not only concerned to maximize the classification accuracy, but also to minimize the distances between the actual and the predicted classes. This paper offers an organized study on the various methodologies that have tried to handle this problem and presents an experimental study of these methodologies with the proposed local ordinal technique, which locally converts the original ordinal class problem into a set of binary class problems that encode the ordering of the original classes. The paper concludes that the proposed technique can be a more robust solution to the problem because it minimizes the distances between the actual and the predicted classes as well as improves the classification accuracy.

1 Introduction

Ordinal classification can be viewed as a bridging problem between the two standard machine-learning tasks of classification and regression. In ordinal classification, the target values are in a finite set (like in classification) but there is an ordering among the elements (like in regression, but unlike classification).

Although Machine Learning (ML) algorithms for ordinal classification are rare, there are a number of statistical approaches to this problem. However, they all rely on specific distributional assumptions for modeling the class variable and also assume a stochastic ordering of the input space [9]. The ML community has mainly addressed the issue of ordinal classification in two ways. One is to apply classification algorithms by discarding the ordering information in the class attribute [2]. The other is to apply regression algorithms by transforming class values to real numbers [9]. This paper proposes a local ordinal technique that locally converts the original ordinal problem into a set of binary problems encoding the ordering of the original classes. Experimental results show that this technique minimizes the distances between the actual and the predicted class, as well as improves the prediction accuracy.

Please use the following format when citing this chapter:

Kotsiantis, Sotiris, 2006, in IFIP International Federation for Information Processing, Volume 204, Artificial Intelligence Applications and Innovations, eds. Maglogiannis, I., Karpouzis, K., Bramer, M., (Boston: Springer), pp. 1–8

This paper is organized as follows: the next section discusses the different techniques that have been presented for handling ordinal classification problems. In section 3, we describe the proposed technique. In Section 4, we present the experimental results of our methodology using different distribution algorithms and compare these results with those of other approaches. In the final section of the paper we discuss further work and some conclusions.

2   Techniques for Dealing with Ordinal Problems

Classification algorithms can be applied to ordinal prediction problems by discarding the ordering information in the class attribute. However, some information that could improve the performance of a classifier is lost when this is done.

The use of regression algorithms to solve ordinal problems has been examined in [9]. In this case each class needs to be mapped to a numeric value. However, if the class attribute represents a truly ordinal quantity, which, by definition, cannot be represented as a number in a meaningful way, there is no upright way of devising an appropriate mapping and this procedure is ad hoc.

Another approach is to reduce the multi-class ordinal problem to a set of binary problems using the one-against-all approach [2]. In the one-against-all approach, a classifier is trained for each of the classes using as positive examples the training examples that belong to that class, and as negatives all the other training examples. The estimates given by each binary classifier are then coupled in order to obtain class probability membership estimates for the multi-class problem [2].

A more sophisticated approach that enables classification algorithms to make use of ordering information in ordinal class attributes is presented in [7]. Similarly with previous method, this method converts the original ordinal class problem into a set of binary class problems that encode the ordering of the original classes. However, to predict the class value of an unseen instance this algorithm needs to estimate the probabilities of the m original ordinal classes using $m - 1$ models. For example, for a three class ordinal problem, estimation of the probability for the first ordinal class value depends on a single classifier: Pr(*Target* < *first value*) as well as for the last ordinal class: Pr(*Target* > *second value*). Whereas, for class value in the middle of the range, the probability depends on a pair of classifiers and is given by

Pr(*Target* > *first value*) * (1 − Pr(*Target* > *second value*)).

3   Proposed Technique

The proposed technique is based on the previous referred sophisticated technique [7]; however, we do not apply this technique globally but locally. If all training instances are taken into account when classifying a new test case, the classifier works as a global method, while when the nearest training instances are taken into account, the classifier works as a local method, since only data local to the area around the testing instance contribute to the classification.

Generally, local methods have significant advantages when the probability measure defined on the space of symbolic features for each class is very complex, but can still be described by a collection of less complex local approximations [1]. The proposed algorithm builds the required number of classifiers for each point to be estimated, taking into account only a subset of the training points. This subset is chosen on the basis of the preferable distance metric between the testing point and the training point in the input space.

In other words, the proposed technique consists of the four steps in Fig. 1.

1. Determine a suitable distance metric.
2. Find the k nearest neighbors using the selected distance metric.
3. Estimate the probabilities of the m original ordinal classes with m − 1 models using as training instances these k instances
4. The estimates given by each binary classifier are then coupled in order to obtain class probability membership estimates

Fig. 1. Local Ordinal Technique

The proposed ensemble has some free parameters such as the distance metric. In our experiments, we used the most well known -Euclidean similarity function- as distance metric. We also used k=50 since about this size of instances is appropriate for a simple algorithm to built a precise model [6].

A key feature of our method is that it does not require any modification of the underlying learning algorithm; it is applicable as long as the classifier produces class probability estimates. In the following section, we empirically evaluate the performance of our approach with the other well known techniques.

4 Experiments

To test the hypothesis that the above method improves the generalization performance on ordinal prediction problems, we performed experiments on real-world ordinal datasets donated by Dr. Arie Ben David (http://www.cs.waikato.ac.nz/ml/weka/). We also used well-known datasets from many domains from the UCI repository [3]. However, the used UCI datasets represented numeric prediction problems and for this reason we converted the numeric target values into ordinal quantities using equal-size binning. This unsupervised discretization method divides the range of observed values into three equal size intervals. The resulting class values are ordered, representing variable-size intervals of the original numeric quantity. This method was chosen because of the lack of numerous benchmark datasets involving ordinal class values.

All accuracy estimates were obtained by averaging the results from 10 separate runs of stratified 10-fold cross-validation. It must be mentioned that we used the free available source code for most algorithms by the book [11]. In the following we present the empirical results obtained using Decision Stump (DS) [8], RepTree [11] and Naïve Bayes (NB) [5] algorithms as base learners. All of them produce class probability estimates.

Table 1 shows the results for the DS algorithm applied (a) without any modification of DS, (b) in conjunction with the ordinal classification method presented in Section 2 (Ordinal DS), (c) in conjunction with the multiclass classification method presented in Section 2 (Multiclass DS) and (d) using the proposed technique (Local Ordinal DS).

In Table 1, for each data set the algorithms are compared according to classification accuracy (the rate of correct predictions) and to mean absolute error:

$$\frac{|p_1 - a_1| + |p_2 - a_2| + ... + |p_n - a_n|}{n}$$

where p: predicted values and a: actual values. Moreover, in Table 1, we represent as "v" that the specific algorithm performed statistically better than the proposed method according to t-test with p<0.05. Throughout, we speak of two results for a dataset as being "significant different" if the difference is statistical significant at the 5% level according to the corrected resampled t-test [10], with each pair of data points consisting of the estimates obtained in one of the 100 folds for the two learning methods being compared. On the other hand, "*" indicates that proposed method performed statistically better than the specific algorithm according to t-test with p<0.05.

As one can observe from the aggregated results in Table 1, the proposed technique is more accurate than the remaining approaches from 2% to 5%. Moreover, it manages to minimize the distances between the actual and the predicted classes. The reduction of the mean absolute error is about 27% compared to the Ordinal DS and 30% compared to the simple DS, while it exceeds the 138% compared to the Multiclass DS. It must be also mentioned that the proposed method is statistically more accurate and has statistically less mean absolute error than the remaining methods in numerous datasets.

Similarly, Table 2 shows the results for the NB algorithm applied (a) without any modification of NB, (b) in conjunction with the ordinal classification method presented in Section 2 (Ordinal NB), (c) in conjunction with the multiclass classification method presented in Section 2 (Multiclass NB) and (d) using the proposed technique (Local Ordinal NB).

As one can see from the aggregated results in Table 2, the proposed technique is more accurate in classification accuracy than the remaining techniques from 2% to 5%. Furthermore, it minimizes the distances between the actual and the predicted classes. In detail, the reduction of the mean absolute error is about 25% compared to the Ordinal NB and 17% compared to simple NB, while it overcomes the 158% compared to Multiclass NB. It must be also stated that the proposed method is statistically more accurate and has statistically less mean absolute error than the remaining methods in a lot of datasets.

Similarly, Table 3 shows the results for the RepTree algorithm applied (a) without any modification of RepTree, (b) in conjunction with the ordinal classification method presented in Section 2 (Ordinal RepTree), (c) in conjunction with the multiclass classification method presented in Section 2 (Multiclass RepTree) and (d) using the proposed technique (Local Ordinal RepTree).

As one can notice from the aggregated results in Table 3, the proposed technique is more accurate in classification accuracy than the remaining techniques from 1% to 2%. What is more, it minimizes the distances between the actual and the predicted classes since the reduction of the mean absolute error is about 15% compared to the Ordinal RepTree and simple RepTree, while it overcomes the 138% compared to Multiclass RepTree. The proposed method is also statistically more accurate and has statistically less mean absolute error than the remaining methods in many datasets.

Table 1. Results for DS algorithm

Dataset		Local Ordinal DS	Multiclass DS	Ordinal DS	DS
auto93	accuracy	80.90	80.57	79.59	81.32
	MeanError	0.14	0.34*	0.18	0.18
autoHorse	accuracy	95.24	91.17	89.63*	91.17
	MeanError	0.04	0.30*	0.09*	0.09*
autoMpg	accuracy	79.67	79.76	78.01	79.61
	MeanError	0.14	0.35*	0.20*	0.21*
autoPrice	accuracy	88.11	89.80	89.80	86.05
	MeanError	0.09	0.31*	0.10	0.13*
bodyfat	accuracy	97.57	99.12	99.12	91.98*
	MeanError	0.02	0.29*	0.01	0.10*
cleveland	accuracy	70.32	71.63	71.14	71.93
	MeanError	0.21	0.37*	0.26*	0.26*
Cloud	accuracy	84.69	87.72	83.43	84.51
	MeanError	0.11	0.32*	0.13	0.14*
Cpu	accuracy	98.09	97.76	97.76	98.24
	MeanError	0.01	0.28*	0.02	0.02
Era	accuracy	25.69	22.08*	24.13	21.81*
	MeanError	0.18	0.20*	0.18*	0.19*
Esl	accuracy	65.53	44.48*	53.72*	43.03*
	MeanError	0.09	0.20*	0.13*	0.16*
fishcatch	accuracy	97.35	92.37*	92.37*	90.56*
	MeanError	0.03	0.30*	0.07*	0.10*
housing	accuracy	79.58	74.81	75.77	70.39*
	MeanError	0.15	0.36*	0.23*	0.28*
hungarian	accuracy	79.06	81.78	81.78	81.78
	MeanError	0.15	0.34*	0.20*	0.20*
Lev	accuracy	61.79	43.86*	49.03*	42.40*
	MeanError	0.20	0.31*	0.25*	0.26*
lowbwt	accuracy	57.25	61.80	61.90	61.90
	MeanError	0.30	0.39*	0.31	0.31
pharynx	accuracy	68.98	73.85	73.85	73.85
	MeanError	0.25	0.37*	0.25	0.25
servo	accuracy	89.72	83.36*	83.24*	83.36*
	MeanError	0.09	0.31*	0.13*	0.12*
Strike	accuracy	98.85	99.06	99.06	99.06
	MeanError	0.01	0.27*	0.01	0.01
swd	accuracy	56.11	51.38*	54.56	51.80*
	MeanError	0.26	0.36*	0.29*	0.30*

Veteran	accuracy	90.45	91.26	90.80	91.26
	MeanError	0.10	0.31*	0.11	0.11
AVERAGE	accuracy	78.25	75.88	76.43	74.80
	MeanError	0.13	0.31	0.16	0.17

Table 2. Results for NB algorithm

Dataset		Local Ordinal NB	Multiclass NB	Ordinal NB	NB
auto93	accuracy	84.36	76.28	74.01	76.18
	MeanError	0.10	0.33*	0.17*	0.16
autoHorse	accuracy	95.14	91.06	90.87	90.67*
	MeanError	0.03	0.29*	0.06*	0.06*
autoMpg	accuracy	82.56	80.65	70.11*	78.89
	MeanError	0.12	0.32*	0.20*	0.15*
autoPrice	accuracy	90.31	91.51	91.45	90.25
	MeanError	0.07	0.30*	0.06	0.07
bodyfat	accuracy	88.96	79.64*	77.22*	81.34*
	MeanError	0.08	0.32*	0.16*	0.13*
cleveland	accuracy	72.45	74.82	75.51	73.31
	MeanError	0.19	0.34*	0.18	0.19
Cloud	accuracy	90.30	91.70	92.04	89.95
	MeanError	0.07	0.30*	0.07	0.08
Cpu	accuracy	97.81	97.56	94.87	97.56
	MeanError	0.01	0.28*	0.04*	0.02
Era	accuracy	23.25	24.73	25.07	24.88
	MeanError	0.18	0.20*	0.18	0.18
Esl	accuracy	67.37	66.84	54.65*	67.52
	MeanError	0.09	0.19*	0.12*	0.10*
fishcatch	accuracy	97.42	89.92*	88.13*	90.10*
	MeanError	0.02	0.30*	0.08*	0.07*
housing	accuracy	81.44	74.76*	56.15*	73.14*
	MeanError	0.13	0.34*	0.29*	0.19*
hungarian	accuracy	81.17	83.95	83.95	83.95
	MeanError	0.13	0.31*	0.12v	0.12v
Lev	accuracy	59.95	56.24*	57.95	56.12*
	MeanError	0.20	0.31*	0.23*	0.23*
lowbwt	accuracy	60.10	58.79	58.52	59.53
	MeanError	0.29	0.39*	0.30	0.30
pharynx	accuracy	70.17	71.09	71.13	70.52
	MeanError	0.24	0.36*	0.25	0.25*
servo	accuracy	87.59	87.24	86.48	87.12
	MeanError	0.10	0.31*	0.12*	0.12*
Strike	accuracy	99.19	99.06	99.06	99.05
	MeanError	0.01	0.27*	0.02*	0.02*
swd	accuracy	50.17	57.31v	56.01v	56.77v
	MeanError	0.27	0.35*	0.26v	0.26v
Veteran	accuracy	89.31	88.48	88.70	86.88
	MeanError	0.09	0.32*	0.12*	0.13*
AVERAGE	accuracy	78.45	77.08	74.59	76.69
	MeanError	0.12	0.31	0.15	0.14

Table 3. Results for RepTree algorithm

Dataset		Local Ordinal RepTree	Multiclass RepTree	Ordinal RepTree	RepTree
auto93	accuracy	82.41	79.73	80.14	80.06
	MeanError	0.14	0.35*	0.20*	0.19*
autoHorse	accuracy	94.45	92.34	94.01	93.17
	MeanError	0.05	0.29*	0.07	0.07
autoMpg	accuracy	81.68	81.34	80.66	80.41
	MeanError	0.14	0.34*	0.17*	0.17*
autoPrice	accuracy	88.86	87.99	88.35	87.81
	MeanError	0.09	0.31*	0.10	0.11
bodyfat	accuracy	96.78	98.88	98.88	98.80
	MeanError	0.03	0.27*	0.01v	0.01v
cleveland	accuracy	71.08	71.73	68.39	71.36
	MeanError	0.21	0.36*	0.26*	0.24*
Cloud	accuracy	86.32	88.54	87.78	88.70
	MeanError	0.12	0.31*	0.11	0.10
Cpu	accuracy	98.04	97.00	96.95	97.29
	MeanError	0.01	0.28*	0.04*	0.03*
Era	accuracy	25.68	19.24*	26.20	26.60
	MeanError	0.18	0.20*	0.18	0.18
Esl	accuracy	66.08	60.59*	62.65	62.37
	MeanError	0.10	0.19*	0.11	0.11*
fishcatch	accuracy	96.71	94.88	94.05	94.70
	MeanError	0.03	0.28*	0.05	0.04
housing	accuracy	80.43	79.51	79.03	78.65
	MeanError	0.16	0.34*	0.18	0.18
hungarian	accuracy	78.62	78.70	78.46	78.46
	MeanError	0.17	0.34*	0.19	0.19
Lev	accuracy	63.16	60.43*	60.79	59.87*
	MeanError	0.20	0.31*	0.20	0.21*
lowbwt	accuracy	56.87	58.89	58.47	58.63
	MeanError	0.32	0.40*	0.34	0.33
pharynx	accuracy	69.79	65.06*	65.01 *	65.31*
	MeanError	0.28	0.40*	0.34*	0.34*
servo	accuracy	93.31	91.42	92.71	90.72
	MeanError	0.06	0.30*	0.07	0.08*
Strike	accuracy	98.97	99.21	99.21	99.21
	MeanError	0.01	0.27*	0.01	0.01
swd	accuracy	56.99	57.45	57.68	56.46
	MeanError	0.27	0.35*	0.26	0.27
Veteran	accuracy	89.20	91.26	91.19	90.90
	MeanError	0.11	0.31*	0.11	0.12
AVERAGE	accuracy	78.77	77.71	78.03	77.97
	MeanError	0.13	0.31	0.15	0.15

5   Conclusion

This paper is devoted to the problem of learning to predict ordinal (i.e., ordered discrete) classes. The local ordinal classification method discussed in this paper is applicable in conjunction with any learning algorithm that can output class probability estimates. According to our experiments in synthetic and real ordinal data sets, it manages to minimize the distances between the actual and the predicted classes, without harming but actually improving the classification accuracy in conjunction with DS, RepTree and NB algorithms. Drawing more general conclusions from these experimental data seems unwarranted. Our results so far show that the proposed methodology for predicting ordinal classes can be naturally derived from classification algorithms, but more extensive experiments will be needed to establish the precise capabilities and relative advantages of this methodology.

For large datasets, the benefit of local ordinal models is somewhat offset by the cost of storing and querying the training dataset for each test set instance. For this reason, in a following project we will focus on the problem of reducing the size of the stored set of instances while trying to maintain or even improve generalization performance by avoiding noise and over-fitting. In [4], numerous instance selection methods that can be combined with the proposed technique can be found.

References

1. C. G. Atkeson, A.W. Moore, S. Schaal, Locally weighted learning. Artificial Intelligence Review 11 (1997) 11–73.
2. E. L. Allwein, R. E. Schapire, Y. Singer, Reducing multiclass to binary: A unifying approach for margin classifiers. Journal of Machine Learning Research 1 (2000) 113–141.
3. C.L. Blake, C.J. Merz, UCI Repository of machine learning databases. Irvine, CA: University of California, Department of Information and Computer Science. [http://www.ics.uci.edu/~mlearn/MLRepository.html] (1998).
4. H. Brighton, C. Mellish, Advances in Instance Selection for Instance-Based Learning Algorithms, Data Mining and Knowledge Discovery, 6 (2002) 153–172.
5. P. Domingos, M. Pazzani, On the optimality of the simple Bayesian classifier under zero-one loss. Machine Learning, 29 (1997) 103-130.
6. E. Frank, M. Hall, B. Pfahringer, Locally weighted naive Bayes. Proc. of the 19th Conference on Uncertainty in Artificial Intelligence. Acapulco, Mexico. Morgan Kaufmann (2003).
7. E. Frank, M. Hall, A simple approach to ordinal prediction, L. De Raedt and P. Flach (Eds.): ECML 2001, LNAI 2167, (2001) 145-156, Springer-Verlag Berlin.
8. W. Iba, P. Langley, Induction of one-level decision trees. Proc. of the Ninth International Machine Learning Conference (1992). Aberdeen, Scotland: Morgan Kaufmann.
9. S. Kramer, G. Widmer, B. Pfahringer, M. DeGroeve, Prediction of ordinal classes using regression trees. Fundamenta Informaticae (2001).
10. C. Nadeau, Y. Bengio, Inference for the Generalization Error. Machine Learning 52(3): 239-281 (2003).
11. I. Witten, E. Frank, Data Mining: Practical Machine Learning Tools and Techniques with Java Implementations, Morgan Kaufmann, San Mateo (2000).

Using Genetic Algorithms and Decision Trees for *a posteriori* Analysis and Evaluation of Tutoring Practices based on Student Failure Models

Dimitris Kalles and Christos Pierrakeas
Hellenic Open University, Laboratory of Educational Material and
Educational Methodology, Sachtouri 23, 26222, Patras, Greece
{kalles, pierrakeas}@eap.gr

Abstract. Many students who enrol in the undergraduate program on informatics at the Hellenic Open University (HOU) fail the introductory course exams and drop out. We analyze their academic performance, derive short rules that explain success or failure in the exams and use the accuracy of these rules to reflect on specific tutoring practices that could enhance success.

1 Introduction

The Hellenic Open University's (HOU) primary goal is to offer university-level education using distance learning methods and to develop the appropriate material and teaching methods to achieve this goal. The HOU offers both undergraduate and postgraduate studies and its courses were initially designed and first offered in 1998 following the distance learning methodology of the British Open University. The HOU was founded in 1992 and currently (2005) nearly 25,000 students are enrolled.

The undergraduate programme in informatics is heavily populated, with more than 2,000 enrolled students. About half of them currently attend junior courses on mathematics, software engineering, programming, databases, operating systems and data structures. A key observation is that substantial failure rates are consistently reported at the introductory courses.

Such failures skew the academic resources of the HOU system towards filtering the input rather than polishing the output, from a quantitative point of view. Even though this may be perfectly acceptable from an educational, political and administrative point of view, we must analyse and strive to understand the mechanism and the reasons of failure. This could significantly enhance the ability of HOU to fine-tune its tutoring and admission policies without compromising academic rigour.

Please use the following format when citing this chapter:
Kalles, Dimitris, Pierrakeas, Christos, 2006, in IFIP International Federation for Information Processing, Volume 204, Artificial Intelligence Applications and Innovations, eds. Maglogiannis, I., Karpouzis, K., Bramer, M., (Boston: Springer), pp. 9–18

There are two key educational problems that have been identified as being core aspects of these failures. The first is that these courses are heavy on mathematics and adult students have not had many opportunities to sharpen their mathematical skills since high-school graduation (which has typically occurred at about 10 years prior to enrolling at HOU). The second is that the lack of a structured academic experience may have rendered dormant one's general learning skills and attitudes.

Our approach to investigating this problem uses increasingly rudimentary technology for data analysis. We use genetic algorithms to derive short decision trees that explain student failure [1, 2].

In this paper we expand that work by investigating differences in the accuracy of the induced models. We focus on short models that are easier to communicate among peers and question whether these differences might be attributed to the versatility of the tutoring practices. The results support our intuition about which practices better smooth out the disadvantages that arise due to some students' special circumstances. These results are now used as supporting data when we attempt to convince fellow tutors of the potential of some specific tutoring practices.

This paper is structured in three subsequent sections. In the next section, we briefly review the problem of predicting student performance at large, and the related techniques we have been using at HOU. We then single out three modules which have clearly different policies in dealing with students who have failed an exam and devise a set of experiments to observe whether these policies can be evaluated by a machine learning model. Finally, we argue about the ability to carry out these experiments at a larger scale and discuss the potential implications of our findings from an educational point of view.

2 Background

The work reported in this paper is part of an effort to analyze data at an institutional level, so we first briefly cover some essential background. We first present the application domain, then we present some key aspects of the technology used and, finally, we summarize the results obtained to date.

2.1 Operational issues

The educational philosophy of Open Universities around the world is to promote "life long education" and to provide adults with "a second educational chance" [3]. The method used is known as "distance learning" education, hence the widely used acronym ODL standing for Open-and-Distance-Learning.

In open and distance learning, dropout rates are definitely higher than those in conventional universities. Relatively recently, the Open Learning journal published a volume on issues on student retention in open and distance learning, where similarities and differences across systems is discussed, highlighting issues of institutions, subjects and geographic areas [4].

The vast majority (up to 98%) of registered students in the "Informatics" program, upon being admitted at HOU, selects the module "Introduction to

Informatics" (INF10). Following that, and according to university recommendations, they will typically select the modules "Fundamental Software Engineering" (INF11) and "Mathematics" (INF12). These modules are the most heavily populated and serve as test-beds for experimentation.

A module is the basic educational unit at HOU. It runs for about ten months and is the equivalent of about 3-4 conventional university semester courses. A student may register with up to three modules per year. For each module, a student is expected to attend five plenary class meetings throughout the academic year (a class contains about thirty students). Each meeting is about four hours long and may be structured along tutor presentations, group-work and review of assigned homework. Furthermore, each student must turn in some written assignments (typically four or six), which contribute towards the final grade, before sitting a written exam.

We have embarked on an effort to analyze the performance of high-risk students [1, 2, 5]. Key demographic characteristics of students (such as age, sex, residence etc), their marks in written assignments and their presence or absence in plenary meetings may constitute the training set for the task of explaining (and predicting) whether a student would eventually pass or fail a specific module. It is important to mention that the great majority of students dropped out after failing to deliver the first one or two written assignments. It is, thus, reasonable to assert that predicting a student's performance can enable a tutor to take early remedial measures by providing more focused coaching, especially in issues such as priority setting and time management.

2.2 Summarizing the technology: decision trees and genetic algorithms

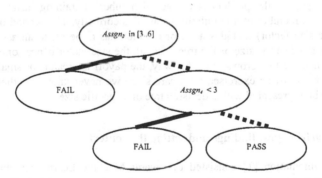

Fig. 1. A sample decision tree

A decision tree [6] for the failure analysis problem could look like the one in Figure 1. In essence, it conveys the information that a mediocre grade at an assignment, turned in at about the middle (in the time-line) of the module (containing 4 assignments altogether), is an indicator of possible failure at the exams, whereas a non-mediocre grade refers the alert to the last assignment. An excerpt of a training set that could have produced the above tree could be the one shown in Table 1.

Table 1. A sample decision tree training set

Assgn$_1$	Assgn$_2$	Assgn$_3$	Assgn$_4$	Exam
...	...	...	...	...
4.6	7.1	3.8	9.1	PASS
9.1	5.1	4.6	3.8	FAIL
7.6	7.1	5.8	6.1	PASS
...	...	...	...	...

Genetic algorithms can directly evolve binary decision trees [7] that explain and/or predict the success/failure patterns of junior undergraduate students. To do so, we evolve populations of trees according to a fitness function that allows for fine-tuning decision tree size vs. accuracy on the training set. At each time-point (in genetic algorithms dialect: *generation*) a certain number of decision trees (*population*) is generated and sorted according to some criterion (*fitness*). Based on that ordering, certain transformations (*genetic operators*) are performed on some members of the population to produce a new population. This is repeated until a predefined number of generations is reached (or no further improvement is detected).

These concepts form the basis of the GATREE system [8], which was built using the GAlib toolkit [9]. A mutation may modify the test attribute at a node or the class label at a leaf. A cross-over may exchange parts between decision trees. The   GATREE   fitness   function   is:

$$fitness(Tree_i) = CorrectClassified_i^2 * \frac{x}{size_i^2 + x}.$$

The first part of the product is the actual number of training instances that a decision tree (a member of a population) classifies correctly. The second part of the product (the size factor) includes a factor x which has to be set to an arbitrary big number. Thus, when the size of the tree is small, the size factor is near one, while it decreases when the tree grows big. This way, the payoff is greater for smaller trees. Of course, this must be exercised with care since we never know whether a target concept can be represented with a decision tree of a specific size.

2.3 Summarizing past findings and setting the context

Initial experimentation [1] consisted of several Machine Learning techniques to predict student performance with reference to the final examination. The WEKA toolkit [10] was used and the key finding, also corroborated by our tutoring experience, is that success in the initial written assignments is a strong indicator of success in the examination. A surprising finding was that demographics were not important.

Follow-up experimentation [2] using the GATREE system [8] initially produced significantly more accurate and shorter decision trees. That stage confirmed the qualitative validity of the original findings (also serving as result replication) and set the context for experimenting with accuracy-size trade offs. That experimentation spanned three academic years, covered the three introductory modules INF10, INF11 and INF2, and validated that genetic induction of decision trees could indeed produce very short and accurate trees that could be used for explaining failures.

We have already documented that drop-out is a significant issue in ODL universities. What is most important, however, is that drop-out usually occurs early in the studies. Failure on a senior year course should simply postpone graduation as the fundamental commitment to studying has been already made. However, failure in a junior course, and for the HOU case, this refers to the INF10, INF11 and INF12 modules, can contribute to a decision to drop out both because the learning investment is not yet large enough to warrant a certain attitude of persistence and because the student may not have had the time to familiarize oneself with the distance learning mode of education (which, given time, allows one to dovetail studying more effectively with other activities).

By regulations, a student who fails a module examination can sit the exam on the following academic year. Such students are only assigned to student groups for examination purposes and the group tutor is responsible for marking their papers only; we thus refer to them as "virtual" students (should they fail their exam for a second year, they must take the module afresh, in which case they are conventionally assigned to a group and cease to be virtual).

Virtual students are not entitled to attending plenary sessions, and to having their assignments graded by the group tutor (as a matter of fact they are not even requested to submit assignments). In practice this regulation may be relaxed by a tutor, who may opt to extend an invitation to attend some plenary sessions to these virtual students usually. Usually, all tutors of a module will either accept or decline to relax the regulation. Of course, there is no focused follow-up of the progress of virtual students, as opposed to the case with typical students.

Any attempt to address these realities involves a political decision that must necessarily take into account the university's administrative regulations.

One step taken by tutors of the INF10 and INF11 modules is to hold a plenary marking session of tutors for each module after an examination, and to discuss variations in individual marking styles based on a predefined assignment of points to exam questions. This is especially important for problems that involve design or prose argumentation. We note that this practice is not widespread within HOU.

A further ad hoc step taken (during the 2003-4 academic year) by the INF11 tutors was to group all virtual students in one group and assign one experienced tutor to that group, as opposed to the usual practice of distributing virtual students across tutors. These students were fully supported by an asynchronous discussion forum and by synchronous virtual classrooms. The tutor did neither hold a physical meeting nor correct any assignments. This was in line with the HOU regulations and, coincidentally, served as a convenient constraint on the "degrees of freedom" of the educational experiment.

We now establish interesting indicators on the effectiveness of these approaches.

3 The experimental environment

We use GATREE for all experiments (even the basic version allows for unlimited experimentation with the x parameter in the fitness function, essentially treating x as an accuracy-vs.-size bias "knob").

For all experiments we used the default settings for the genetic algorithm operations (cross-over probability at 0.99, mutation probability at 0.01, error rate at 0.95 and replacement rate at 0.25). All experiments were carried out using 10-fold cross-validation, on which all averages are based. Because the data sets are reasonably large, ranging from 500 to 1000 student records, and because 10-fold cross-validation is a widely acceptable testing methodology, we opt to not report standard deviations. The experiments were made with a generations/population:150/150 configuration.

All data refer to the 2003-4 academic year. They do not differentiate between typical and virtual students.

Our methodology is the following: we attempt to use the student data sets to develop success/failure models represented as decision trees. We then use the differences between the models derived when we omit some attributes to reflect on the importance of these attributes. The results are then used to comment on alternative educational policies for dealing with virtual students.

We first try to deal with the issue whether we might be able to obtain an overall (typical and virtual students included) model that deals with explaining (and, ultimately, predicting) exam success, across the three modules that have three distinct policies.

The first experimental session attempted to produce short decision trees that could be used to explain the failure model of students in each module. For this, the x knob was set to 1000 (the minimum possible value). For each module, four (4) experimental batches were conducted and the results are shown in Table 3.

Table 2. Results for x=1000, gen/pop:150/150 GATREE decision trees

Data Set	Accuracy (in %)	Size (in nodes)
INF10: Basic	78.20	3
INF10: Basic_T	78.20	3
INF10: Basic_Y	82.58	6
INF10: Basic_TY	82.02	6
INF11: Basic	82.82	5
INF11: Basic_T	82.05	5
INF11: Basic_Y	81.28	6
INF11: Basic_TY	81.54	6
INF12: Basic_T	62.37	6
INF12: Basic_T	63.39	6
INF12: Basic_Y	67.97	6
INF12: Basic_TY	68.81	6

A few words on notation are in order (which apply for all experimental sessions reported in this paper). The *Basic* version of the training set consists of all student records, where the only available attributes are the assignment grades and the class attribute is the *pass/fail* flag. The *Basic_T* version of the training set includes the tutor as an attribute, whereas the *Basic_Y* version includes as an attribute the year of first sitting the exam for that module. The *Basic_TY* version includes both additions. The gen/pop configuration refers to the number of generations and the population size.

The first observation is that the basic model for INF10 simply has a root and two leaves! A slightly larger model, which also tests on the year, is enough to increase sizeably the explanation accuracy.

A casual first observation of the above findings seems to suggest that the tutor attribute is relatively not important (note that we acknowledge that we do not report our results with statistical significance, but we have opted to focus on educated selections of experiments that can demonstrate easily observable trends).

A further observation is that the INF11 module demonstrates a clear "smoothing" of model accuracies across the various versions of its training set. We take this to be a first indication of the success of the INF11 approach to virtual students as it essentially conveys the information that the failure explanation must be traced solely to academic performance (i.e. assignments).

Very short trees may be very concise to communicate but might lack the representational power to detect delicate regularities in the data. We have thus followed-up the experimental results above with increasing x to 10000 to allow for larger trees to be generated. However, for space reasons, we will directly jump to the case where this "tweaking" of the x knob, was accompanied by larger-scale experimentation in terms of generations and populations as well.

The results are shown in Table 4. (Note that we have dropped the reporting of model sizes as they were very close to the ones reported for the shorter experiments.)

Table 4. Results for gen/pop:300/300 GATREE decision trees

Data Set	Accuracy, $x = 1000$ (in %)	Accuracy, $x = 10000$ (in %)
INF10: Basic	78.20	77.42
INF10: Basic_T	78.20	77.30
INF10: Basic_Y	83.60	84.61
INF10: Basic_TY	83.37	83.60
INF11: Basic	82.05	79.74
INF11: Basic_T	81.28	80.26
INF11: Basic_Y	82.31	84.36
INF11: Basic_TY	81.03	83.33
INF12: Basic	62.54	65.08
INF12: Basic_T	63.73	64.07
INF12: Basic_Y	70.51	72.03
INF12: Basic_TY	70.68	73.05

The results are very interesting, to say the least.

Starting from the INF11 module, we see that the short trees are indeed excellent as far as consistency goes. When we go to larger trees, the year attribute creates a performance gap that was not evident before.

This has a two-fold interpretation. On one hand, the larger trees now produced seem to be less well-fitted than the smaller ones (note the accuracy reduction for non-year-inclusive data-sets). This could well be an indication of over-fitting. On the other hand, it suggests that the year attribute has importance; this would concur well with the explanation that students who have failed to pass through the examination filter may be unlikely to have confidence to pursue their studies actively.

Is this finding contradicting the shorter experiments? One needs to examine the results for the other modules to glimpse at the (negative) answer.

First, we observer that for INF12, the year attribute remains a top contributor to the model. For INF10 and INF11 short trees again suggest that the year attribute is less important than for INF12, quite markedly so for INF11, where the year attribute is essentially suppressed. For larger trees, both for INF10 and INF11, the importance of the year attribute seems to rise but at the expense of an overall reduction trend for the *Basic* models. This lends weight to the over-fitting argument but still is plausible, as we said above, since one cannot easily wipe out the *a priori* disadvantage of virtual students.

However, we also note that the increase in accuracy for the INF10 models that use the year attribute is easily seen to be less that the corresponding accuracy for the INF12 models. This observation combined with the observation that the average accuracies for INF10 are also larger than the average accuracies for INF12 may be also interpreted as an indicator that the plenary "marking" session of INF10 helps trim out potential grading inconsistencies. Of course, this may be also a contributor to the underlying quality of the INF11 models, but at the resolution level we are working, we cannot easily confirm or refute the level of this contribution.

Summarising, the importance of the year attribute is only evident for larger trees for the modules that employ the post-exam plenary marking session. Still, that rising importance is clearly less evident than in the INF12 module. Moreover, that evidence is still less proclaimed for the INF11 module that employs a further approach to dealing with virtual students.

4 Conclusions – Focusing on the application domain

We believe that, as of yet, we do not need to experiment with still larger trees, larger populations and more generations, just like we have so argued before [2]. We have observed that large trees give easily rise to the over-fitting phenomenon and that relatively few generations and reasonably small populations could deliver directly usable results. Furthermore, a small accurate model is a very important tool at the hands of a tutor, to assist in the task of continuously monitoring a student's performance with reference to the possibility of passing the final exam. Our setting of parameter x in the accuracy-size trade-off in this paper again confirms this view.

We intend to continue favouring GATREE compared to other software for the particular data analysis tasks, because it incurs a less steep learning curve on the part of a user. However, we have used other software as (simply) another way of replicating the results in the data sets that we have used [2].

We cannot yet answer whether the approach of the INF11 tutors is an approach that would have had replicable educational results in the other modules. The most obvious reason is that exact replication of the above experiments is impossible. Had we wanted to experiment with INF11 approach in INF10, we cannot hope to ever again observe the given set of students and their assignment to groups within modules, as well as the given set of tutors and their assignment to groups. This is one of the reasons that we progressively narrowed down our experiments: we started at only one undergraduate programme, then focused on the most junior and well-subscribed modules, then singled out the two ones that demonstrated one difference only at the policy level.

Having taken these careful steps, we believe that, when one focuses on limiting drop-out, the presented analysis suggest that the effective smoothing-out of the year-and-tutor factors in the success-failure model should benefit from a purely educational decision: by assigning an experienced tutor to directly deal with virtual students. The other alternative, which is to train all tutors to be more active in discussion fora and more proficient in virtual classroom techniques, may be a grand goal with far-reaching benefits, but could demand a substantial mentality shift of the tutors and substantial vocational training resources, entailing significant political decisions.

Are the conclusions and the advice too strong? We think not, taking into account that differences are in the order of several percentage points, with consistent standard deviations, whereas individual performances are in the order of 70% (and not, for example, 95%, where a few percentage points might be less important). Moreover, the validity of the results is strengthened by the fact that we have conducted the experiment in the most controlled of environments. An obvious extension of this work is to try to see whether differences are more or less pronounced in less controlled environments (for example, in senior year modules, where the student population is drawn from more than one academic admission stage).

This observation then sets the context for the wider goal of this research. We investigate the building an "early warning and reaction system" for students with "weak" performance. This research has also operational and political aspects, besides the obvious technical ones.

From both an operational and technical viewpoint, one must set a scheme to validate the performance of a model based on subsequent years' statistics and not simply on cross-validation testing. It is important to note that the approach is self-contained in the sense that it can be readily applied to data available at the university registry.

Deploying this scheme as an organization-wide process would also lend support to our preference for short models. We believe that a small accurate model is a very important tool at the hands of a tutor, to assist in the task of continuously monitoring a student's performance with reference to the possibility of passing the final exam. A small model is easier to communicate among peers, easier to compare with competing ones and can have wider applicability.

Political issues are much subtler, of course, and we have already pin-pointed one.

A sensitive point is that it would be unwise to simply consider the higher or lower overall *absolute* accuracy rate of (any) model in one module as an indicator of success of an approach, at least at this early stage of the research. It is for this reason that in the experiments described above we never pit one module's accuracy against another module's accuracy; besides referring to different student populations (including differences in population sizes), a module also refers to different tutors and to another scientific field.

We believe that such an approach would distract us from our goal. What is more important, we claim, is to detect and observe the trends within the module itself and try to understand what actions need to be taken at the module level.

In [2] we argued that using a system like GATREE and an approach like the one documented above to produce and operationally use success/failure models raises the fundamental question of whether we measure the performance of actors (students or tutors) or the performance of the system at large (the ODL system implemented in HOU). We also conjectured that it is the latter alternative that has the most potential from an educational point of view.

Given that we have successfully used raw data (student records) to *a posteriori* justify an educational policy, as opposed to compute an individual student model *per se*, we believe that this conjecture is now better founded.

References

1. Kotsiantis, S., Pierrakeas, C., & Pintelas, P. (2004). Predicting students' performance in distance learning using Machine Learning techniques. Applied Artificial Intelligence, 18:5, 411-426.
2. Kalles, D., & C. Pierrakeas (2005). Analyzing student performance in distance learning with genetic algorithms and decision trees (accepted for publication in the journal: Applied Artificial Intelligence).
3. Keegan, D. (1993). Theoretical Principles of Distance Education. Routledge, London.
4. Open Leaning (2004). Special issues on "Student retention in open and distance learning". 19:1, http://www.tandf.co.uk/journals/titles/02680513.asp.
5. Xenos, M., Pierrakeas, Ch. & Pintelas, P. (2002). A survey on student dropout rates and dropout causes concerning the students in the Course of Informatics of the Hellenic Open University. Computers & Education, 39, 361-377.
6. Mitchell, T. (1997). Machine Learning. McGraw Hill.
7. Koza, J.R. (1991). Concept formation and decision tree induction using the genetic programming paradigm. Parallel problem solving from nature. Berlin: Springer Verlag.
8. Papagelis, A., & Kalles, D. (2001). Breeding decision trees using evolutionary techniques. In Proceedings of the International Conference on Machine Learning, Williamstown, Massachusetts.
9. Wall, M. (1996). GAlib: A C++ Library of Genetic Algorithm Components. M.I.T. http://lancet.mit.edu/ga/.
10. Witten, I., & Frank, E. (2000). Data mining: practical machine learning tools and techniques with Java implementations. San Mateo, CA: Morgan Kaufmann

Exploiting Decision Trees in Product-based Fuzzy Neural Modeling to Generate Rules with Dynamically Reduced Dimensionality

Minas Pertselakis and Andreas Stafylopatis
National Technical University of Athens,
School of Electrical and Computer Engineering,
9 Iroon Polytechneioy Str., Zografou, 15780, Greece
mper@cslab.ntua.gr, andreas@cs.ntua.gr

Abstract. Decision trees are commonly employed as data classifiers in various research fields, but also in real-world application domains. In the fuzzy neural framework, decision trees can offer valuable assistance in determining a proper initial system structure, which means not only feature selection, but also rule extraction and organization. This paper proposes a synergistic model that combines the advantages of a subsethood-product neural fuzzy inference system and a CART algorithm, in order to create a novel architecture and generate fuzzy rules of the form "IF - THEN IF", where the first "IF" concerns the primary attributes and the second "IF" the secondary attributes of the given dataset as defined by our method. The resulted structure eliminates certain drawbacks of both techniques and produces a compact, comprehensible and efficient rulebase. Experiments in benchmark classification tasks prove that this method does not only reduce computational cost, but it also maintains performance at high levels, offering fast and accurate processing during real-time operations.

1 Introduction

Neuro-fuzzy modeling involves two stages: Parameter Identification and Structure Identification. The former is concerned with the adjustment of system parameters, such as the membership functions, the antecedent and consequent weights and so on, while the latter is related to finding a suitable number of rules, a feature selection scheme and a proper partition of the feature space, which usually is applied as an initialization technique in order to improve learning [1].

For structure identification the literature offers several heuristic but practical and systematic approaches, realized either by unsupervised learning and clustering (fuzzy

Please use the following format when citing this chapter:

Pertselakis, Minas, Stafylopatis, Andreas, 2006, in IFIP International Federation for Information Processing, Volume 204, Artificial Intelligence Applications and Innovations, eds. Maglogiannis, I., Karpouzis, K., Bramer, M., (Boston: Springer), pp. 19–26

c-means, k-means, etc) or supervised techniques, such as the CART-ANFIS combination [2]. However, the problem of structure identification in fuzzy modeling is by no means solved; there are many issues in practice remain to be addressed; the "curse of dimensionality" and finding the optimum number of rules being the most significant.

Decision trees as classification tools have a solid statistic foundation and offer advantages that make them suitable for high-dimensional data [3]. They are considered to be a nonparametric method and are capable of handling datasets with missing values or possible errors. Decision trees are also characterized by their ability to identify features with the most information, which may lead to dimensionality reduction, if exploited. However, decision tree algorithms suffer from certain drawbacks. They use the "divide and conquer" method and partition the feature space into mutually exclusive regions, thus they tend to perform well if few highly relevant attributes exist, but less so if many complex interactions are present. Moreover, decision trees show over-sensitivity to the training set due to their greedy behavior and their "generalization" capabilities are low. Noise and irrelevant attributes may very well affect their performance.

The combination of decision trees and neuro-fuzzy systems constitutes a solid approach to fuzzy modeling. This derives from the fact that decision trees offer a fast and efficient way to produce distinct rules and select relevant inputs, thus producing a roughly correct and compact structure. On the other hand, neuro-fuzzy networks demonstrate the ability to adapt and operate in both numeric and linguistic environments, they can refine the rules by learning from data and increase the "generalization" abilities of the system. In the special case where the neuro-fuzzy model incorporates a fuzzy product operator to aggregate activities at a rule node, the associations between attributes can be estimated and exploited.

Our approach suggests the use of a CART algorithm [4] to induce a top-down tree structure, where each path to a terminal node represents a rule. To "fuzzify" these rules we convert the resulted partitions of the *primary* feature's space into clusters. The clusters (rules) that show low reliability, as indicated by the decision tree, undergo a novel process, where the fuzzy c-means (FCM) clustering method is applied on the related patterns using only the *secondary* features, if any, so as to create two new rules on the same feature-space region. The resulted rulebase is implemented in a subsethood product neuro-fuzzy architecture and a gradient descent learning procedure is employed in order for the rules to be fine-tuned. Experiments in benchmark classification tasks show that the rules extracted by this method, not only reduce computational cost, while keeping performance at high levels, but offer also high interpretability due to the fact that both decision trees and neural fuzzy systems generate easily comprehensible rules.

The paper is divided in the following sections: Section 2 describes the methodology of rulebase generation based on the CART algorithm, whereas in Section 3 we present the architecture and functionality of the subsethood-product neuro-fuzzy model. Experimental results can be found in Section 4, while useful deductions and plans for future research conclude the paper in Section 5.

2 Rule Generation using Decision Trees

It has been shown in various comparative studies that most decision tree algorithms fit into a simple algorithmic framework, whereas the differences concentrate on the tree growing criteria and the ways trees are pruned [3].

To construct an appropriate decision tree for our purposes, we utilize the CART algorithm which first grows the tree extensively based on a training data set, and then prunes the tree back based on a minimum cost-complexity principle [4]. To grow the classification tree, we employ the *Twoing* impurity function, which, at each node t selects a split that minimizes the following expression:

$$\frac{p_l p_r}{4} \left[\sum_j p_j(t_l) p_j(t_r) \right]^2 , \tag{1}$$

where p_l and p_r are the percentages of cases in the splitting node t that branch left and right, $p_j(t_l)$ and $p_j(t_r)$ are the probabilities of a data point in class j, given that the data set comes from the left and right children, respectively. The justification of the twoing rule can be found in the CART monograph [4]. The cost-complexity measure, as shown in several studies, tends to over-pruning, which creates smaller trees, but less accurate [5], [6]. This is desirable in our methodology since the resulted rules will be fine-tuned later on.

Our approach in structure identification involves two successive stages; the initial generation of the rulebase and the propagation of the less capable rules into a subsequent layer for further evaluation.

2.1 Phase 1: Generation of Initial Rulebase

Once the decision tree is constructed, we consider each path that leads to a leaf to represent a Rule. However, the rules created by a decision tree, as noted above, are crisp and partition the data space into mutually exclusive regions. Therefore, we need to convert these rules into a form that conforms to the multivariate concept.

Instead of partitioning, we introduce a cluster analysis approach. We define a cluster C by a center k, which is the mean value of the patterns that belong to the resulted partition (crisp rule) of the feature-space, and a spread σ, which represents the respective standard deviation. Since the cluster analysis approach is multivariate by definition, whereas the decision tree is univariate at each split, we assign random values, within the feature limits, to those attributes that do not take part in the specific crisp rule as defined by the tree. At this point, we should add some definitions that will be used extensively throughout the paper.

The attributes that participate in this procedure, that is the features the decision tree *as a whole* has selected to use, will be called *primary* attributes for the purposes of this paper. Those attributes that do not take part in the constructed decision tree, are called *secondary* attributes. If the total number of attributes of the dataset is N, then the number of the primary attributes is always $M \leq N$. In a high dimension problem it is usually M<<N.

Consequently, the rules that involve only the primary attributes compose the Primary Rule set, while the rules that are formed by the secondary attributes form the Secondary Rule set. The following step of our method deals with the latter type of rules.

2.2 Phase 2: Rule Bisection and Propagation

This second phase evaluates the resulted rules and performs certain actions on them, if required. More explicitly, the clusters that include very few patterns (1-2) are ignored, since those patterns are regarded as outliers, while the rules produced by phase 1 that present low classification reliability according to a reliability criterion subject to further processing. The proposed reliability measure R is an extension of the method suggested in [7], where the reliability criterion is the difference between the two greatest output values. In our approach, the difference value is normalized to enhance the consistency of the result. This extended measure can be formulated for a classifier as follows:

$$R = (Y_{win1} - Y_{win2}) * Y_{win1} \tag{2}$$

where Y_{win1} is the classification output of the leaf node for the class with the greatest value and Y_{win2} is the classification output for the class with the second greatest value.

If this confidence criterion is below a certain threshold, then the system considers the current rule insufficient and fires up the process of rule bisection. For this reason, we execute the FCM clustering algorithm requesting 2 clusters on the patterns that constitute the particular rule-cluster, but only on the attributes that do not take part in the tree structure; the *secondary* attributes. If there is none, then we perform the same clustering procedure with all the attributes of the problem, but this is not usually the case in tasks of high dimension.

In other words, we force the terminal node of the tree to "grow" two new multivariate leaves based on the less informative, according to the tree, features. These new rules aim to find a better solution (clustering) in the selected data space by exploiting all those attributes, $K = N - M$, that the tree have omitted. This leads to a novel system structure with enhanced abilities that will be discussed in detail in the next section.

2.3 Example of Rule Generation Procedure

As a simple example, we use the iris data set. The iris data set consists of 150 four-dimensional patterns, therefore $N=4$, which are categorized into three subspecies of the Iris flower, namely *Iris setosa*, *Iris versicolor*, and *Iris virginica*. The four features represent the sepal length, sepal width, petal length, and petal width measurements on the Iris flower. The generated tree is shown in figure 1.

It is apparent that the decision tree, as a whole, requires only two out of the four attributes to produce this result, namely petal length (PL) and petal width (PW), which implies that $M=2$. Therefore, we assume that all generated clusters are described by these two attributes, even if some of the paths contain only one attribute (like that path leading to node 1), in which case we fill in a random value within the limits that characterize the missing feature (e.g. the petal width feature for node 1).

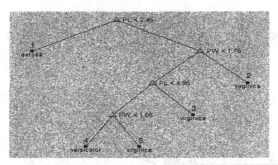

Fig. 1. Example of a decision tree for the Iris data using the CART algorithm

During the second phase, the leaf node 5 is removed due to its low population and leaf node 3 is split, since it presents low reliability, into two new rules defined by the secondary attributes of the dataset, which are the sepal length and width. The system results with 4 primary rules and 2 secondary rules as its initial structure.

3   System Architecture and Operational Details

The proposed system follows the paradigm of [8], as in the numeric inputs are fuzzified using feature-specific Gaussian fuzzy sets and linguistic inputs are presented as is. The antecedent and consequent weights are represented as Gaussian fuzzy connections of the network. The model employs a mutual subsethood-based activation spread and a product aggregation operator, bounded between zero and one, which works in conjunction with volume defuzzification in a gradient descent learning framework. In addition, human expert knowledge can be embedded directly in the form of fuzzy "IF-THEN" rules.

Using the product operator, instead of the more common fuzzy *min* operator for activity aggregation offers certain important advantages. It does not ignore information regarding the dimension of the input and provides a better estimate of the joint strength of the features involved. It is also capable of better discrimination, since it can clearly differentiate between inputs and weight vectors over a wide range of spreads. This approach leads to high performance and economy in parameters, but it also carries a significant drawback. In problems where the dimensionality of the feature space is large, the product operator produces values very close to zero, given that each factor assumes values between zero and one. Theoretically, if the dimension is set beyond a certain finite number, the value of which depends on the computing device, the product operator will underflow and equate to zero. Therefore, there is an upper limit on the dimension a subsethood product based system can handle and this is one of the issues our approach addresses with its dimensionality reduction capabilities.

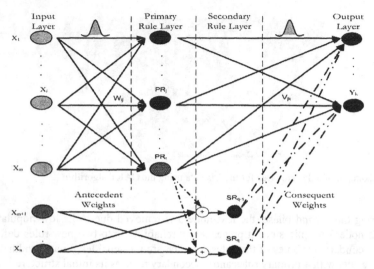

Fig. 2. System architecture. The less reliable primary rule PRr propagates its firing strength to the next layer when it is required, where the secondary attributes form two secondary rules.

The architecture of the proposed neural fuzzy model that constitutes the main difference from previous similar works is presented in figure 2. Fuzzy weights w_{ij} from input nodes i to rule nodes j are modeled by the center w_{ij}^c and spread w_{ij}^σ of a Gaussian fuzzy set and denoted by $w_{ij}=(w_{ij}^c, w_{ij}^\sigma)$. In a similar fashion, consequent fuzzy weights from rule nodes j to output nodes k are denoted by $v_{jk} = (v_{ij}^c, v_{ij}^\sigma)$. The spread of the i-th fuzzified input element is denoted as x_i^σ, while x_i^c is obtained as the crisp value of the i-th input feature element. The net value of the transmitted signal along the fuzzy connections is quantified by the extent of overlap between the two fuzzy sets, known as *mutual subsethood*. All mutual subsethood expressions, gradient descent learning and weight updating equations are omitted, due to lack of space, but can be found in [8].

In our approach, two rule layers exist; the Primary rule layer and the Secondary rule layer. Only one of the two is active at any given time and thus, only the weights that fan-in and out of the activated layer are updated. This behavior could also be depicted as two different networks.

During normal operation the Primary rule layer is responsible for the output. If an unreliable rule obtains the maximum value over all Primary rules then the secondary rule layer is activated. When that occurs, we sum up the product of all mutual subsethoods of the primary attributes that lead to the Primary rule in question and the product of mutual subsethoods of the secondary attributes that are directed to the secondary rule. We are forced to follow this approach due to the nature of the product operator that requires the same number of factors in order to produce comparable values and the same order of magnitude for a balanced weight update. Thus, if z_{rq} is the firing strength of rule PR_r, then the activation strength z_q of rule SR_q is given by:

$$z_q = z_{rq} + \prod_{i=m+1}^{n} E_{iq} \cdot \qquad (3)$$

The output y_k over the k classes is determined using standard volume based centroid defuzzification and its expression for our system is:

$$y_k^p = \frac{\prod_{j=1}^{Q(p)} z_j v_{jk}^c v_{jk}^\sigma}{\prod_{j=1}^{Q(p)} z_j v_{jk}^\sigma}, \qquad (4)$$

where Q(p) is the total number of rules that affect the result for the given pattern p. This robust and flexible structure scheme consolidates a new architecture in fuzzy modeling that enjoys the benefits of the dynamically reduced dimensionality.

4 Experimental Results

We test the performance of the system on 2 datasets, namely the Ionosphere data and the Pima Indians Diabetes data, both of which can be found at the UCI repository[1]. The Ionosphere data set includes 351 records of 34 attributes each that were collected by a radar system in Goose Bay, Labrador. The values are categorized in 2 classes labelled Good and Bad. The Pima Indians diabetes data set, on the other hand, consists of 768 patterns of 8 attributes taken from the National Institute of Diabetes and Digestive and Kidney Diseases. The classes are of binary form denoting positive and negative results in diabetes tests.

For our experiments we split the dataset into a training set and a testing set dividing the patterns in a rough 40% - 60% ratio, respectively. In each experiment, we extract an initial rule base using the CART algorithm as described in section 2 and train the fuzzy-neural network for 100 epochs with a fixed learning rate of 0.001. The results presented in Table 1 show the average of 10 such experiments.

Table 1. Experimental Results and testing accuracy comparison to other known methods[2]. The numbers in parenthesis in the Primary Rules field denote the number of unreliable rules.

Datasets	Our Approach	Accuracy of other known methods

---

[1] Available at http://www.ics.uci.edu/~mlearn/MLRepository.html
[2] Available at http://www.phys.uni.torun.pl/kmk/projects/datasets.html

	Attributes (Primary/Total)	Prim. Rules	Sec. Rules	Accuracy (%)	SVM	MLP+BP	CART	kNN, k=1
Pima Indians	6/8	15 (6)	12	**78.25**	77.6	76.4	72.8	71.9
Ionosphere	6/34	7 (1)	2	**94.4**	93.2	96	88.9	92.1

5   Conclusions - Future Work

This paper describes a novel methodology of rulebase generation and configuration by exploiting the decision trees' unique properties of feature selection and structure identification combined with a clustering technique. We first convert the crisp partitions created by the CART algorithm into clusters, each defined by a hyper-ellipsoid that takes into account only the primary, as selected by the tree, features. The rules-clusters that are considered insufficient according to a reliability measure are bisected by the FCM algorithm and propagate to a secondary network layer, where only the secondary attributes participate.

In other words, our system generates rules of the form "IF-THEN IF" where the first "IF" concerns the primary attributes and the more distinct regions of the dataset, while the second "IF" employs the secondary attributes in order to search for a better partitioning in the more "fuzzy" areas of the problem at hand. These rules are then fine-tuned by a fuzzy neural network that employs a product aggregating operator that estimates the joint strength of all inputs in contrast to the more common fuzzy *min* approach.

Further work on the same field includes the use of different algorithms to split the rules of low reliability, such as the execution of a new decision tree at each node that performs poorly and the exploitation of different aggregation operators, such as the harmonic mean, besides the inner product for rule activation. Various alternatives concerning the reliability measure is also an issue under consideration.

References

1. J.-S. R. Jang, C. -T. Sun, E. Mizutani, *Neuro-Fuzzy and Soft Computing: a computational approach to learning and machine intelligence* (Prentice-Hall, Inc., 1997)
2. J.-S. R. Jang, Structure determination in fuzzy modeling: a fuzzy CART approach, *In proc. of IEEE Int. Conf. on Fuzzy Systems,* Orlando, Florida (1994)
3. L. Rokach, O. Maimon, Top-Down Induction of Decision Trees Classifiers – A survey, *IEEE trans. on Systems, Man and Cybernetics,* **35**(4), 476-487 (2005)
4. L. Breiman, J.H. Friedman, R. A. Olshen, and C. J. Stone, *Classification and Regression Trees* (Wadsworth, Inc., Belmont, California, 1984)
5. J. R. Quinlan, Simplifying decision trees, *Int. J. Man-Machine Studies,* **27,** 221-234 (1987)
6. F. Esposito, D. Malerba, and G. Semerato, A comparative analysis of methods for pruning decision trees, *IEEE Trans. Pattern Anal. Mach. Intell.,* **19**(5), 476-492 (1997)
7. L. P. Cordella, P. Foggia, C. Sansone, F. Tortorella, M. Vento, Reliability Parameters to Improve Combination Strategies in Multi-Expert Systems, *Pattern Analysis and Application,* **2,** 205-214 (1999)
8. S. Paul, S. Kumar, Subsethood- Product Fuzzy Neural Inference System (SuPFuNIS), *IEEE Trans. Neural Networks,* **13**(3), 578–599 (2002)

Retraining the Neural Network for Data Visualization

Viktor Medvedev, Gintautas Dzemyda
Institute of Mathematics and Informatics
Akademijos str. 4, LT-08663 Vilnius, LITHUANIA
{Viktor.m, Dzemyda}@ktl.mii.lt

Abstract. In this paper, we discuss the visualization of multidimensional data. A well-known procedure for mapping data from a high-dimensional space onto a lower-dimensional one is Sammon's mapping. The algorithm is oriented to minimize the projection error. We investigate an unsupervised backpropagation algorithm to train a multilayer feed-forward neural network (SAMANN) to perform the Sammon's nonlinear projection. Sammon mapping has a disadvantage. It lacks generalization, which means that new points cannot be added to the obtained map without recalculating it. The SAMANN network offers the generalization ability of projecting new data, which is not present in the original Sammon's projection algorithm. Retraining of the network when the new data points appear has been analyzed in this paper.

1   Introduction

Feature extraction is the process of mapping the original features into fewer features, which preserve the main information of the data structure. Feature extraction for exploratory data projection enables high-dimensional data visualization for better data structure understanding and for cluster analysis [4]. Furthermore, when the dimensionality of the projection space is two-dimensional the structure of the original dataset can be inspected visually and conclusions on clustering tendencies can be straightforwardly drawn.

The problem of data projection is defined as follows: given a set of high dimensional data points, project them to a low-dimensional space so that the result configuration would perform better than the original data in further processing such as clustering, classification, indexing and searching [3, 5]. Data projection has important applications in pattern analysis, data mining, and neural science. The visual inspection of the data can provide a deeper insight into the data, since clustering tendencies or a low intrinsic dimensionality in the data may become apparent from the projection. In general, this projection problem can be formulated

Please use the following format when citing this chapter:

Medvedev, Viktor, Dzemyda, Gintautas, 2006, in IFIP International Federation for Information Processing, Volume 204, Artificial Intelligence Applications and Innovations, eds. Maglogiannis, I., Karpouzis, K., Bramer, M., (Boston: Springer), pp. 27–34

as mapping a set of n vectors from an d-dimensional space onto an m-dimensional space, with $m<d$.

A large number of approaches for data projection are available in pattern recognition literature [2, 3]. A well-known method to project data is Principal Component Analysis (PCA) which provides mean-square optimized linear projection of data. Another classic method is the Multi-Dimensional Scaling (MDS) that works with inter-point distances and gives a low-dimensional configuration that represents the given distances best. One of the popular MDS-type projection algorithms is Sammon's method [9]. It is a simple but useful nonlinear projection technique that attempts to create a two-dimensional configuration of points in which interpattern distances are preserved. Sammon's mapping is an iterative nonlinear procedure.

The problem of finding the right configuration in a low-dimensional space is an optimization problem: we are interested in obtaining such a configuration that some stress function yields minimum. In general, this optimization problem is difficult because of the very high dimensionality of the parameter space. The stress function is optimal when all the original distances d_{ij}^{*} are equal to the distances of the projected points d_{ij}. However, this is not likely to happen exactly.

The finding a projected map usually starts from the initial configuration of points (e.g. randomly chosen), and then the stress is calculated. Next, the configuration is improved by shifting around all points in small steps to approximate better and better the original distances (thus decreasing the stress). This process is reiterated, until the map corresponding to a (local) minimum of the stress is found.

Mao and Jain [7] have suggested a neural network implementation of Sammon's mapping. A specific backpropagation-like learning rule has been developed to allow a normal feedforward artificial neural network to learn Sammon's mapping in an unsupervised way, called SAMANN. As an alternative to SAMANN's unsupervised learning rule, one could also train a standard feedforward artificial neural network, using supervised backpropagation on a previously calculated Sammon's mapping. Although it requires much more computation, as it involves two learning phases (one for Sammon's mapping, one for the neural network), it should perform at least as well as SAMANN [8].

In Mao and Jain's implementation the network is able to project new patterns after training – a property Sammon's mapping does not have. A drawback of using SAMANN is that the original dataset has to be scaled for the artificial neural network to be able to find a correct mapping, since the neural network can only map to points in the sigmoid's output interval, $(0,1)$. This scaling is dependent on the maximum distance in the original dataset. It is therefore possible that a new pattern, shown to the neural network, will be mapped incorrectly, when its distance to a pattern in the original dataset is larger than any of the original interpattern distances. Another drawback of using SAMANN is that it is rather difficult to train and it is extremely slow.

In this paper, we proposed two strategies for retraining the neural network that realizes multidimensional data visualization.

2 A Neural Network for Sammon's Projection

Sammon's nonlinear mapping is an iterative procedure to project high-dimensional data into low-dimensional configurations. Sammon used a steepest descent method (diagonal Newton method) for optimization.

Suppose that we have n data points, $X_i = (x_{i1}, x_{i2} \ldots, x_{id})$, $i = 1, \ldots, n$, in a d-space and, respectively, we define n points, $Y_i = (y_{i1}, y_{i2} \ldots, y_{im})$, $i = 1, \ldots, n$, in a m-space ($m < d$). The pending problem is to visualize these d-dimensional vectors $X_i, i = 1, \ldots, d$ onto the plane R^2. Let d_{ij}^* denote the distance between X_i and X_j in the input space, and d_{ij} denote the distance between the corresponding points Y_i and Y_j in the projected space. The Euclidean distance is frequently used. The projection error measure E is as follows:

$$E = \frac{1}{\sum\limits_{\substack{i,j=1 \\ i<j}}^{n} d_{ij}^*} \sum\limits_{\substack{i,j=1 \\ i<j}}^{n} \frac{(d_{ij}^* - d_{ij})^2}{d_{ij}^*} \tag{1}$$

E is commonly referred to as Sammon's stress. It is a measure of how well the interpattern distances are preserved when the patterns are projected from a higher-dimensional space to a lower-dimensional space. The stress equal to 0 indicates a lossless mapping. The steepest descent procedure may be used to search for a minimum of E. Sammon's stress is designed so that short distances contribute more to the value of E. In the process of minimizing E, therefore, the mapping gives a greeter priority to the preservation of short distances rather than the long ones. That is why the mapping is capable of unfolding high dimensional data manifolds. Though the algorithm also considers long distances, however, it may fail to unfold strongly twisted patterns.

Sammon's algorithm involves a large amount of computations. Since, $n(n-1)/2$ distances have to be computed for every step within an iteration, the algorithm soon becomes impractical for a large number of patterns. Sammon's algorithm does not provide an explicit function governing the relationship between patterns in the original space and in the configuration (projected) space. Therefore, it is impossible to decide where to place the new d-dimensional data in the final m-dimensional configuration created by Sammon's algorithm. Sammon's algorithm has no generalization capability. In order to project new data, one has to run the program again on pooled data (old data and new data) [4].

SAMANN network for two-dimensional projection is given in Figure 1. It is a feedforward neural network where the number of input units is set to be the feature space dimension d, and the number of output units is specified as the extracted feature space dimension m. They have derived a weight updating rule for the multilayer perceptron neural network that minimizes Sammon's stress, based on the gradient descent method. The general updating rule for all the hidden layers, $l = 1, \ldots, L-1$ and for the output layer ($l = L$) is:

$$\Delta \omega_{jk}^{(l)} = -\eta \frac{\partial E_{\mu\nu}}{\partial \omega_{jk}^{(l)}} = -\eta(\Delta_{jk}^{(l)}(\mu) y_j^{l-1}(\mu) - \Delta_{jk}^{(l)}(\nu) y_j^{l-1}(\nu)) \tag{2}$$

where ω_{jk} is the weight between the unit j in the layer $l-1$ and the unit k in the layer l, η is the learning rate, $y_j^{(l)}$ is the output of the jth unit in the layer l, and μ and ν are two patterns. The $\Delta_{jk}^{(l)}$ are the errors accumulated in each layer and backpropagated to a preceding layer, similarly to the standard backpropagation. The sigmoid activation function whose range is $(0.0, 1.0)$ is used for each unit. However, in the neural network implementation of Sammon's mapping the errors in the output layer are functions of the interpattern distances. In each learning step, the artificial neural network is shown by two points. The outputs of each neuron are stored for both points. The distance between the neural network output vectors can be calculated and an error measure can be defined in terms of this distance and the distance between the points in the input space. From this error measure a weight update rule can be derived. Since no output examples are necessary, this is an unsupervised algorithm.

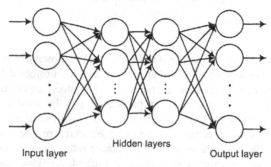

Fig. 1. SAMANN network for two-dimensional projection

The SAMANN Unsupervised Backpropagation Algorithm [7] is as follows:
1. Initialize the weights randomly in the SAMANN network.
2. Select a pair of patterns randomly, present them to the network one at a time, and evaluate the network in a feedforward fashion.
3. Update the weights in the backpropagation fashion starting from the output layer.
4. Repeat steps 2-3 a number of times.
5. Present all the patterns and evaluate the outputs of the network; compute Sammon's stress; if the value of Sammon's stress is below a prespecified threshold or the number of iterations (from steps 2-5) exceeds the prespecified maximum number, then stop; otherwise, go to step 2.

The rate, at which artificial neural networks learns, depends upon several controllable factors. Obviously, a slower rate means that a lot more time is spent in accomplishing the learning to produce an adequately trained system. At the faster learning rates, however, the network may not be able to make the fine discriminations possible with a system that learns more slowly. When the learning rate is very small, the weight adjustments tend to be very small. Thus, if η is small when the algorithm is initialized, the network will probably take an unacceptably long time to converge.

3 Strategies for Retraining of the SAMANN Network

After training the SAMANN network, a set of weights of the neural network are fixed. A new vector shown to the network is mapped into the plane very fast and quite exactly without any additional calculations. However, while working with large data amounts there may appear a lot of new vectors, which entails retraining of the SAMANN network after some time. That is why two strategies for retraining the neural network that realizes multidimensional data visualization have been proposed and then analysis made. Retraining of the network has to be efficient and the training algorithm has to converge rapidly. It has been established that training of the SAMANN neural network requires much calculations, therefore we strive to obtain new weights and a precise data projection as soon as possible.

The strategies of the neural network retraining data are as follows:

1. The SAMANN network is trained by N_1 initial vectors, a set of weights ω_1 is obtained, then the visualization error $E(N_1)$ is calculated and vector projections are localized on the plane. After the emergence of N_2 new vectors, the neural network is retrained with all the N_1+N_2 vectors, and after each iteration the visualization error $E(N_1+N_2)$ is calculated and the computing time is measured. The new set of SAMANN network weights ω_2 is found.

2. The SAMANN network is trained by N_1 initial vectors, a set of weights ω_1 is obtained, and the visualization error $E(N_1)$ is calculated. Since in order to renew the weights ω, a pair of vectors μ and ν is simultaneously provided for the neural network, the neural network is retrained with $2*N_2$ vectors at each iteration: at each step of training one vector is taken from the primary dataset and the other from the new one. After each iteration the visualization error $E(N_1+N_2)$ is calculated and the computing time is measured. The new set of network weights ω_2 is found.

Two datasets have been used in the experiments:

1. Iris Dataset (Fisher's iris dataset) [10]. A real dataset with 150 random samples of flowers from iris species setosa, versicolor, and virginica. From each species there are 50 observations of sepal length, sepal width, petal length, and petal width in cm. The iris flowers are described by 4 attributes.

2. 300 randomly generated vectors $X_i = (x_{i1},...,x_{in}) \in R^n$ (three spherical clusters with 100 vectors each, n=5):

$$x_{ij} \in [0,0.2],\ i=1,...,100;\ j=1,...,5,\ \sqrt{\sum_{j=1}^{n}(0.1-x_{ij})^2} \leq 0.1$$

$$x_{ij} \in [0.4,0.6],\ i=101,...,200;\ j=1,...,5,\ \sqrt{\sum_{j=1}^{n}(0.5-x_{ij})^2} \leq 0.1$$

$$x_{ij} \in [0.8,1],\ i=201,...,300;\ j=1,...,5,\ \sqrt{\sum_{j=1}^{n}(0.9-x_{ij})^2} \leq 0.1$$

These two datasets were divided into two parts: the primary dataset and the set of new vectors. The first part is used for primary training of the SAMANN network, while the new part together with the primary dataset – for retraining the network.

In the analysis of strategies for the network retraining, a particular case of the SAMANN network was considered: a feedforward artificial neural network with one hidden layer and two outputs (d=2). In each case, the same number (n_2=20$)$ of neurons of the hidden layer was taken and the set of initial weights was fixed in advance. To visualize the initial dataset, the following parameters were employed: the number of iterations M=10000, the training parameter $\eta = 10$; to visualize the set of new vectors: the training parameter was $\eta = 1$, and the number of iterations depended on the strategy chosen. One iteration in our research means showing all pairs of samples to the neural network once.

In the Iris dataset, 50 vectors were used for retraining. In the randomly generated set, 90 vectors were used for retraining: 30 vectors for the different clusters.

When calculating, the time of algorithm performance was measured. Figure 2 and Figure 3 demonstrate the results of calculation. Only the results of retraining the SAMANN network with the new vectors are indicated in the figures. The first strategy yield good results, however retraining of the network is slow. The best visualization results are obtained by taking points for network retraining from the primary dataset and the new dataset (second strategy). The second strategy enables us to attain good visualization results in a very short time as well as to get smaller visualization errors and to improve the accuracy of projection as compared to other strategies (Figure 3 illustrates this fact best in the experiment with the dataset of random numbers). The proposed second strategy makes it possible to reduce the duration of calculation a great deal in case there are considerably less new vectors than the initial ones.

Figures 4a and 4b illustrate mapping results of the iris dataset in two different cases: (1) the network has been trained by 150 vectors (Figure 4a); (2) the network has been trained by 100 vectors and retrained using the second strategy (Figure 4b). The interlocation of points is similar in the figures. This indicates a good quality of the retraining. Very high similarity of Figures 4a and 4b leads to the idea of possibility to minimize the training time consumption via dividing the training process into two subprocesses: (1) training of the network by a part of the data vectors; (2) retraining of the network by the remaining part of the dataset.

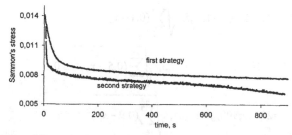

Fig. 2. Dependence of the projection error on the computing time for the Iris dataset

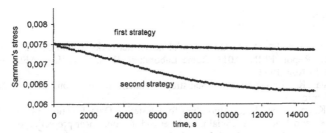

Dependence of the projection error on the computing time for randomly generated vectors

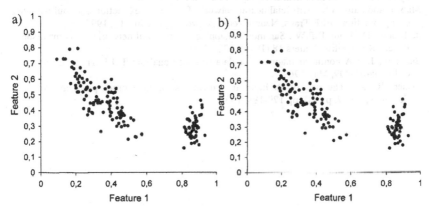

Fig. 4. Mapping results of the Iris dataset: a) training by 150 vectors; b) training by 100 vectors and retraining by 50 vectors

4 Conclusions

Mapping problem usually is formulated as an optimization one. The experiments were carried out both on artificial and real data. Retraining of the SAMANN network when the new data points appear and the ability of network generalization to visualize new data have been analyzed.

Two strategies for retraining the neural network that visualizes multidimensional data have been proposed and investigated. It is important that retraining of the neural network were efficient and the training algorithm were faster convergent, therefore effort was put to obtain a new set of weights in a shorter time. The experiments have shown that it is expedient to take one vector from the primary dataset and the other from the new one at every step of training. This strategy yields smaller visualization errors faster.

References

1. Anderson, D. and McNeill, G.: Artificial neural networks technology. DACS State-of-the-Art Report ELIN: A011, Rome Laboratory, RL/C3C Griffiss AFB, NY 13441-5700, 20 Aug. 1992.
2. Fugunaga, K.: Introduction to Statistical Pattern Recognition, 2nd ed. New-York: Academic, 1990.
3. Jain, A.K. and Dubes, R.C.: Algorithms for Clustering Data. Prentice-Hall, 1988.
4. Jain, A.K. and Mao, J.: Artificial neural network for nonlinear projection of multivariate data, Neural Networks, 1992. IJCNN., International Joint Conference on Volume 3, 7-11 June 1992 Page(s):335 - 340 vol.3.
5. Jain, A.K., Duin, R., and Mao, J.: Statistical pattern recognition: A review. IEEE Trans. Pattern Analysis and Machine Intelligence, 22(1):4–37, Jan. 2000.
6. Lerner, B., Gutterman, H., Aladjem, M., Dinstein, I. and Romem, Y.: Feature extraction by neural network nonlinear mapping for pattern classification.
7. Mao, J. and Jain, A.K.: Artificial neural networks for feature extraction and multivariate data projection, IEEE Trans. Neural Networks, vol.6, pp. 296-317, 1995.
8. de Ridder, D., Duin, R.P.W.: Sammon's mapping using neural networks: A comparison. Pattern Recognition Letters 18 (1997), 1307-1316.
9. Sammon, J.J.: A nonlinear mapping for data structure analysis. IEEE Trans. Computer, C-18(5):401-409, May 1969.
10. Fisher, R. A.: The use of multiple measurements in taxonomic problem. Annual Eugenics, vol. 7, part II, pp 179-188, 1936.

Rule-Based Adaptive Navigation for an Intelligent Educational Mobile Robot

Mihaela M. Oprea

University Petroleum-Gas of Ploiesti, Department of Informatics,
Bd. Bucuresti nr. 39, Ploiesti, 100680, Romania, mihaela@upg-ploiesti.ro

Abstract. The paper presents a hybrid adaptation method that combines a knowledge-based approach with reinforcement learning and a simulated annealing technique, and is applied in the navigation of an educational mobile robot. The experimental results of simulations showed a good behaviour of the robot when doing an adaptive navigation in a dynamic environment by using the proposed hybrid method.

1 Introduction

The improvement of a navigation system performances can be achieved by using different artificial intelligence (AI) techniques such as knowledge-based approaches [11], adaptation methods [2], genetic algorithms, genetic programming [1] and so on. Moreover, the navigation task in a dynamic and uncertain world is a key challenge for mobile robotics [5], [15]. In this paper it is proposed a hybrid adaptation method for the navigation of an educational mobile robot that works in a dynamic environment. The hybrid adaptation method combines a knowledge-based approach with a reinforcement learning technique (RL) and a simulated annealing technique (SA). Our research work involves the application of such a hybrid method in educational mobile robotics for two main types of navigation experiments: simulations and real-world experiments that use a toy mobile robot, ROBO, developed at University of Ploiesti. In our experiments we have considered indoor environments such as offices and homes.

The paper is organized as follows. Section 2 describes the robot navigation task. The intelligent educational mobile robot system is presented in section 3. The architecture of the system as well as the ontology with its associated knowlede base, and adaptation method are detailed. Some experiments and preliminary results are discussed in section 4. The last section concludes the paper and highlights some future work.

Please use the following format when citing this chapter:

Oprea, Mihaela, 2006, in IFIP International Federation for Information Processing, Volume 204, Artificial Intelligence Applications and Innovations, eds. Maglogiannis, I., Karpouzis, K., Bramer, M., (Boston: Springer), pp. 35–43

2 Robot navigation task

The navigation task has to direct the robot to a given location, avoiding obstacles. Its input is a path plan. Basically, navigation is the process of finding clear paths, avoiding collisions with obstacles and calculating the robot's current velocity and orientation. A plan for the navigation problem is a path through the world from the initial state (start state) to the goal state (final state). Usually, the initial state include the complete map of the world. During navigation some unexpected situations may arise, and the robot cannot follow the plan, so it needs to replan starting from the current position as the new start position. In real-time systems it is necessary to tradeoff the quality of a plan against the computational cost of planning, and it is necessary to interleave planning and execution, to combine reactive with deliberative capabilities. Several classes of planning algorithms are used in robot navigation [11]: cell decomposition methods, skeletonization methods, online algorithms, bounded-error planning methods, landmark-based navigation methods.

3 The intelligent educational mobile robot system

For academic and research purposes we have developed an intelligent educational mobile robot system, ROBO, that has a virtual implementation for simulations and a physical implementation for real-world experiments. The robot is used as a testbed for the study of different AI and machine learning techniques teached at the courses of Artificial Intelligence and Intelligent Agents to different categories of students, undergraduate, masterate, and postgraduate. In this section we shall focus on the architecture of the system, on the domain knowledge base and its associated ontology, and on the adaptation method.

3.1 The architecture

The architecture of the intelligent educational mobile robot is composed by the following subsystems: the reactive subsystem (RS), the navigation subsystem (NS), the planning subsystem (PS), the adaptation subsystem (AS), and a knowledge base (KB). Figure 1 shows this architecture.

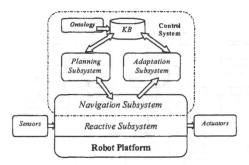

Fig. 1. The architecture of the intelligent educational mobile robot.

The reactive subsystem performs collision avoidance and in collaboration with NS path following. It consists of several processes for perception and action. For example, RS will include the basic four actions (move forward, turn left, turn right, move backward) and sensors related processes. Basically, RS contains a set of behaviours for coordinating perception and action. The navigation subsystem, which works together with RS, performs the robot positioning and path following and has to deal with sensor and actuator uncertainty. The control system is composed by the planning subsystem, the adaptation subsystem and the knowledge base, including also the ontology used. The planning subsystem computes the optimal path that connect the starting position and the destination position. In the planning process several rules from KB are used. The adaptation subsystem will help the robot when unexpected obstacles occur, suggesting solutions to various situations. The main adaptive method used is reinforcement learning [14]. Also, a simulated annealing technique is used in order to help the robot moving out from deadlock locations. The knowledge base contains facts and rules that could be used in both planning, and adaptation processes during the mobile robot navigation.

3.2 The ontology

Built on a particular domain of knowledge, an ontology [4] contains the terminological primitives of the domain structured in a set of concepts (terms) which represent the objects of the domain, and a set of relations between these concepts. All the concepts related to a mobile robot navigation (i.e. directly related to the robot and its environment) were grouped in an ontology named OntoRobotic. Each term is defined, characterized by its properties, constraints, and classified in a hierarchy of classes that form the ontology tree. Figure 2 shows a part from the ontology tree. Example of terms used are: ROBOT, SENSOR, ACTUATOR, INFRARED, ODOMETER, WHEEL, ENVIRONMENT, BEHAVIOUR, DOOR, OBSTACLE AVOIDANCE. Some relations between different concepts are: close-to, next-to, closed, open, front, back, left, right etc.

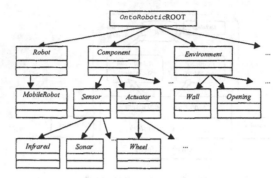

Fig. 2. The ontology tree (selection).

The ontology `OntoRobotic` was developed in Protégé [10], an ontology editing environment based on Java. Starting from the ontology it is generated a knowledge base specific to the mobile robot navigation tasks.

3.3 The knowledge base

The knowledge base contains the knowledge that is used in the navigation task. The knowledge representation method used is the production rule form, i.e. *if-then* rules. KB includes rules generated from the `OntoRobotic` ontology as well as rules that are directly connected with typical situations that may arise during robot navigation.

Examples of rules:

Situation: *moving toward object O*
Rule NTO15 (Robo next to the object O)
if *distance* (Robo, O) < Th^{NT} **then**
    * move back with the distance Δd
    call *obstacle_avoidance*;

Rule CTO16 (Robo close to the object O)
if *distance* (Robo, O) < Th^{CT} **then**
    call *obstacle_avoidance*;
        where the relation between the two thresholds, Th^{NT} and Th^{CT} is $Th^{NT} > Th^{CT}$.

Situation: *crossing doors*
Rule CD5
if *door* (D_2, Open) **then**
    if *Prob* (D_1, Closed) < Th^D **then**
        return Path_B;
return Path_A;
where *Prob*(D=Closed) represents the probability that door D is closed and Th^D is a threshold that is chosen by taking into account the initial values for the probabilities regarding the state of doors that could be crossed by the robot.

Situation: *obstacle avoidance*
Rule OA10
if RoboState(Robo, obstacle_avoidance) **then**
    * follow the obstacle and keep moving toward the goal or try to turn left or right
    if RoboState(Robo,blocked) **then**

* apply a simulated annealing technique (SA), i.e. move the robot in a certain
direction (chosen as given by SA) in order to move out from the deadlock;

The knowledge base includes also a group of rules related to different adaptation situations. In the next subsection we shall focus on the reinforcement learning technique that is used by the educational mobile robot system.

3.4 The adaptation method

The successful applications of reinforcement learning technique to navigation tasks (see e.g. [3], [12], [16]) has determined us to use as adaptation method a reinforcement learning technique. The basic concept behind reinforcement learning technique is that if an action is followed by a satisfactory response, then the tendency to produce that action is stengthened, i.e. reinforced. The learning system receives state information about the environment by means of its sensors, and this state information is used by a reasoning process to determine the action to be taken in the given state. The goal of the learning task is to associate with each state the best action to be selected such that the reward from the environment is maximized [7].

The combination of the navigation and learning methods reported in [8] and [9] had generated the hybrid adaptation method that is used by our educational mobile robot. The reinforcement learning technique was adapted to ROBO and it is briefly presented. Let's consider that a mobile robot RoboS has to find the optimal path in a grid world. The actions set A is composed by the following operators: *move_north, move_south, move_est, move_west, move_NE, move_NW, move_SE, move_SW, hold*. The action *hold* means that the robot will stay at the current location. The goal of RoboS is to learn moves that quickly takes it to its respective goal destination without colliding with the obstacles (static or dynamic) that are or arise in the environment. As the robot knows its current position and the goal position, it can recognize if it moves to or away from the destination. The feedback comes from the robot's sensors via the embedded adaptation subsystem. Thus, the robot R receives a feedback, *feedback(R)*, based on its movement as given by relation (1).

$$feedback(R) = \begin{cases} 1, & \text{move toward R's goal} \\ -1, & \text{move away from R's goal} \\ 0, & \text{no change} \\ fc(R, O), & \text{a collision arise} \end{cases} \tag{1}$$

The feedback is 1 in case the robot moves toward its goal. If it moves away from its goal, the feedback is −1. In case there is no change of the distance between the robot and the goal, the feedback is 0. If a collision arise between the robot R and an obstacle O, then it is used the collision function, $fc(R, O)$ given by relation (2).

$$fc(R, O) = \begin{cases} -4, & \text{lateral collision} \\ -4, & \text{possible frontal collision} \\ -8, & \text{frontal collision} \end{cases} \tag{2}$$

When the robot is located next to an obstacle, it is very likely to produce a collision. Figure 3 shows the three types of possible collisions.

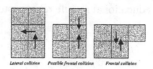

Lateral collision   Possible frontal collision   Frontal collision

Fig. 3. The possible collisions.

4 Preliminary experimental results

The current research work involves two types of experiments, simulations, and real world experiments in indoor environments with the educational robot system, ROBO, developed in the Department of Informatics, University of Ploiesti. The toy mobile robot ROBO (presented in Figure 4) has three sensors, two collision sensors, and one IR sensor. So far, it was studied the application of the hybrid adaptation method in a simulated environment in which a simulated mobile robot is doing navigation tasks. In this section we shall present the simulation results.

Fig. 4. The educational toy robot ROBO.

Experiment 1 (no map use *versus* map use in the navigation task):

The first set of experiments considered an analysis of behaviour-based navigation (with no map of the environment) and an A*-like navigation (with a topological map of the environment). Let's consider the navigation scenario presented in Figure 5. We assume that the mobile robot has 16 sonar sensors arranged in a ring and the following set of possible actions are allowed:

wall_following (go_forward, go_backward*), turn_left* ($\pm90^0$, $\pm45^0$), *turn_right* ($\pm90^0$, $\pm45^0$), *avoid_obstacle*

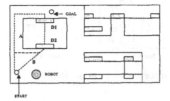

Fig. 5. Path planning – a door is closed.

Two existing planning methods are analysed on different situations that simulate a dynamic and uncertain world in which the robot has to do its mission. Both methods use sensor model (actually, sensor fusion) that include the possibility of failure. The first method A will make a behaviour-based planning that has no map of the world, but instead it has a knowledge base that include *if-then* rules (with uncertainty factors) that characterize different behaviours, given a policy to the planner. The second method B, similar with that described in [13], uses a topological map and an A* algorithm to generate several paths that will be used in conjunction with some behaviours by the replanning algorithm. A complete set of behaviours is developed, considering all the possible situations that may arise (including the worst cases). In order to reduce the complexity (i.e. the number of behaviours) we have made a partition of the possible situations. Figure 5 shows the experimental results obtained for the case in which door D_2 is closed. Method A will give the solution Path A (the best solution in that particular case), while method B will give path B, much longer than path A. In this case method A worked better than method B. A possible solution is to extend the behaviour set with a number of negative behaviours [16] that will be used by the planning/replanning algorithm of method B. Critical situations such as closing a door, blocking at an obstacle avoidance are managed by special rules that exists in the knowledge base of the navigation system. These rules will lead to better solutions. The method will give the safest or the shortest path according with the needs of the navigaton task. This specification, shortest or safest path, will be used to choose the admissible heuristic function for the A* algorithm. The modified version of method B gave a reliable and robust navigation in the case of a simulation of the navigation task with a mobile robot that moves around in a simulated dynamic and uncertain environment.

Experiment 2 (the use of reinforcement learning):

Let's consider the scenario from Figure 6, where a moving object will lock the first attempt of the robot movement, that of going in the north direction. Two solutions could be adopted. In case of the second solution (use of RL&SA), as the obstacle will move into the room, it will clear the way of the robot to its destination, and the robot will take the best decision. The path will be determined by the following sequence of operators {*move_south, hold, hold, move_north,...*}, while simultaneously, the moving obstacle will do the sequence of actions {*move_SW, move_west, hold*}. Therefore, the lessons learned during adaptation (i.e. to hold one one or two times) help the robot to have a better behaviour, that of choosing solution 2.

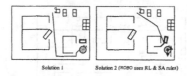

Solution 1   Solution 2 (ROBO uses RL & SA rules)

Fig. 6. Example of a navigation scenario – two solutions.

During experiment 2 we have analysed the Q-learning performance in terms of the average number of steps followed in the robot navigation task. The experimental results obtained are averaged over 50 runs. In order to attain convergence we have set the number of trials at 1000. As shown in Figure 7 the average number of steps is acceptable. Graphic 1 shows the average number of steps in the robot navigation task, in case the system parameters setting is $\beta=0.3$, $\gamma=0.5$, while graphic 2 corresponds to the system parameters $\beta=0.4$, $\gamma=0.7$.

Fig. 7. The performance of Q-learning.

5 Conclusion and future work

The inclusion of an adaptation capability in the architecture of a mobile robot can improve the robot navigation tasks in terms of time and path length. In this paper we have presented a hybrid adaptation method that combines a knowledge based approach with a reinforcement learning technique and a simulated annealing technique. The adaptation method was applied to an intelligent educational mobile robot. The control system of the mobile robot has a knowledge base that includes knowledge under the form of facts and production rules that specify the robot behaviour in certain situations such as obstacle avoidance, crossing doors, U-shaped traps. Basically, the robot guidance during navigation is realized by the rules from the knowledge base that apply also simulated annealing techniques and/or reinforcement learned behaviour rules by taking into account the current state of the mobile robot navigation. The simulations made so far showed a good performance of the hybrid adaptation method in a dynamic and uncertain world. As a future work, we shall analyse the use of the hybrid adaptation method in a real-world indoor environment navigation made by the educational toy mobile robot, ROBO.

References

1. Dain, R. A.: Developing Mobile Robot Wall-Following Algorithms Using Genetic Programming. *HTR Labs*. *Technical Report* (1998).
2. Fukuda, T., Kubota, N.: Learning, Adaptation and Evolution of Intelligent Robotic System, *Proceedings of the IEEE Int. Symposium on Intelligent Control*, Maryland, USA (1998) 2-7.
3. Goldberg, D., Mataric, M.: Reward Maximization in a Non-Stationary Mobile Robot Environment. *Proc. of the 4th Int. Conf. on Autonomous Agents*. Barcelona (2000) 92-99.
4. Gruber, T. R.: A translation approach to portable ontology specifications. *Knowledge Acquisition*, **5**(2) (1993) 199-220.
5. Iocchi, L., Lukasiewicz, T., Nardi, D., Rosati, R.: Reasoning about Actions with Sensing under Qualitative and Probabilistic Uncertainty. *Proceedings of the 16th European Conference on Artificial Intelligence*. Valencia, Spain (2004) 818-822.
6. Latombe, J.-C.: *Robot Motion Planning*. Kluwer Academic Publishers, Boston (1991).
7. Mitchell, T.: *Machine Learning*. McGraw-Hill. Boston (1997).
8. Oprea, M.: Path Planning in a Robot Navigation System. Proceedings of 16th IJCAI99 Workshop PLAN-2 *Scheduling and Planning meet Real-time Monitoring in a Dynamic and Uncertain World*. Stockholm. (1999) 65-70.
9. Oprea, M.: Reinforcement Learning Applied in Mobile Robot Path Planning. *Proceedings of the 15th Int. Conf. on Control Systems and Computer Science CSCS15*. Bucharest. Romania. Politehnica Press (2005) 447-451.
10. Protégé: http://protégé.stanford.edu (2000).
11. Russell, S., Norvig, P.: *Artificial Intelligence - A Modern Approach*, Prentice Hall, New Jersey (1995).
12. Santana, H., Corruble, V., Ratitch, B.: Multi-Agent Patrolling with Reinforcement Learning. *Proeedings of the 3rd Int. Joint Conf. On Autonomous Agents & Multi Agent Systems*. ACM Press. Vol. 3. New York, USA (2004) 1122-1129.
13. Simmons, R., Goodwin, R., Haigh, K. Z., Koenig, S., O'Sullivan, J.: A Layered Architecture for Office Delivery Robots. *Proceedings of Autonomous Agents'97*, Marina Del Rey, USA (1997) 245-252.
14. Sutton, R., Barto, A.: *Reinforcement Learning: An Introduction*. Cambridge USA (1998).
15. Wolf, D, Sukhatme, S.: Online Simultaneous Localization and Mapping in Dynamic Environments. *Proceed. of the IEEE Int. Conf. Robotics and Automation*. (2004) 1301-1307.
16. Yamaguchi, T., Masubuchi, M., Tanaka, Y., Yachida, M.: Reinforcement Learning for a Real Robot in a Real Environment. *Proc. of ECAI'96*, Budapest, Hungary (1996) 694-698.

BRWM: A relevance feedback mechanism for web page clustering

Ioannis Anagnostopoulos[1], Christos Anagnostopoulos[2],
Dimitrios D. Vergados[1] and Ilias Maglogiannis[1]
1 Department of Information and Communication
Systems Engineering,
University of the Aegean,
Karlovassi 83200, Samos – GREECE
2 Department of Cultural Technology and Communication
University of the Aegean,
Mytiline 81100, Lesvos – GREECE

Abstract. This paper describes an information system, which classifies web pages in specific categories according to a proposed relevance feedback mechanism. The proposed relevance feedback mechanism is called Balanced Relevance Weighting Mechanism – BRWM and uses the proportion of the already relevant categorized information amount for feature classification. Experimental measurements over an e-commerce framework, which describes the fundamental phases of web commercial transactions verified the robustness of using the mechanism on real data. Except from revealing the accomplished sequences in a web commerce transaction, the system can be used as an assistant and consultation tool for classification purposes. In addition, BRWM was compared with a similar relevance feedback mechanism from the literature over the established corpus of Reuters-21578 text categorization test collection, presenting promising results.

1 Introduction

This paper presents an algorithm, which clusters web pages that offer commercial services, according to an e-commerce framework and under the basic concepts from the field of information retrieval. The paper is organized as follows. The next section presents an overview of several e-commerce/business frameworks, while it analyses the model is used for the purposes of this work. Section 3 describes some basic information retrieval procedures and mechanisms made in order to conceptually represent the web transactions and phases. The next section presents the main parts and procedures of an information system, which identifies commercial services on the web according to the followed e-commerce framework

Please use the following format when citing this chapter:

Anagnostopoulos, Ioannis, Anagnostopoulos, Christos, Vergados, Dimitrios, Maglogiannis, Ilias, 2006, in IFIP International Federation for Information Processing, Volume 204, Artificial Intelligence Applications and Innovations, eds. Maglogiannis, I., Karpouzis, K., Bramer, M., (Boston: Springer), pp. 44–52

and a proposed relevance feedback mechanism. In parallel, the algorithm is evaluated over an established text categorization test collection from the information retrieval literature and is compared with a similar relevance feedback algorithm. Finally, the paper ends with the results derived over the followed e-commerce framework as well as with a discussion over the potential applications of the presented work.

Table 1. Transaction phases and types of e-commerce pages according to the BMF

Transaction Phase - PT	e-commerce page type	web pages (per type)	web pages (per PT)
Knowledge	Query engines homepages	322	1305
	Directory pages	339	
	Product information pages	365	
	Registration pages	279	
Intention	Product catalogue pages	372	777
	Order – Payment pages	405	
Contracting	Terms and conditions pages	387	387
Settlement	Settlement monitoring pages	313	1355
	Digital delivery pages	364	
	Contact and complaint forms	358	
	After sales support pages	320	

2   The web transactions framework

Numerous different frameworks for the analysis of web commerce/business models have already been proposed in the literature. These frameworks are generally using different approaches to identify, classify and analyse commercial activities [1], [2], [3], [4], [5], [6], [7]. Among the above-mentioned models, the Business Media Framework (BMF) was used for the purposes of our work [1]. This taxonomy relates and interprets the components of the general media model in the business context, thus providing a means for the design and management of business communities. The framework distinguishes four distinct views and four transaction phases of a web commercial transaction. The community view deals with the aspects relevant for modelling the community, such as its organisational structure and shared roles, the protocols, the interests and values behind it, as well as its languages. The implementation view describes the specified community design, such as the community view specifications, the data structures and the business processes on the services offered by the service layer. The transaction view provides the generic interaction or communication services such as the signalling intentions, the contracting and agreement on contracts and or the performance of the transaction in the settlement of contracts. Finally, the infrastructure view provides communication and coordination mechanisms for relating agents of the transaction view as well as the agents taking the roles modelled in the community view, as defined in the implementation view [1].

In parallel BMF also distinguishes four transaction phases. In the knowledge phase a common logical space between agents is being established and information about the transaction is gathered and processed. The intention phase includes services for analysing and activating information acquired in the knowledge phase. In the contracting phase a "contract" is being negotiated between agents while the settlement phase refers to the settlement of the "contract" aforementioned, which actually means the realisation of the web transaction. The distinction of these four phases identifies the structural changes that electronic commerce has brought to traditional commerce methods. Table 1 presents the four phases and the amount of the collected web pages, which were used as the training material. The total sample set consists of 3824 e-commerce pages of several extension formats. These web pages were collected and validated by experts according to BMF. As a result, each web page depicted in Table 1 corresponds to one e-commerce type and one transaction phase. However, a respective data sample that consist of 2134 web pages and do not describe commercial transactions (web pages irrelative to web commerce transactions), was collected automatically using a meta-search engine tool. This tool collects randomly web pages from specified search engine directories and its functions are described in [8].

3   Feature selection

This section describes the feature extraction procedure for the training sample. The training sample consists of twelve classes from which, eleven of them correspond to the BMF transaction phases (knowledge, intention, contracting, settlement) and one class correspond to web pages that do not offer commercial services. Common information filtering techniques such as stop lists, character filters and suffix-stripping methods were initially used for reducing the large amount of the indexed terms. The Information Gain (IG) technique was adopted for feature selection. This technique measures the statistical dependencies between a term and the categorised class based on the entropy. Thus, terms with small information gain are discarded [9]. Rather than evaluating the entropy of a term distribution among a set of documents as is done for the signal-to-noise ratio technique, in the specific technique the entropy of the class distribution is taken under consideration. More specifically, let C denote a random variable used for observing the k possible class labels for the training documents.

$$Entropy(C) = -\sum_{i=1}^{k} P(c_i) log P(c_i) \qquad (1)$$

In IG, entropy measures the homogeneity of the training set D^* with respect to the class distribution which governs C according to Equation 1, where $P(c_i) = (n_{c_i}/n)$, denotes the probability of observing a training document with category c_i and $0log0$ is defined to be zero for all entropy evaluations. Based on this interpretation of entropy, the discriminative power of a particular index term can be measured as follows. Let t and $\bar{t}$ denote the presence and absence of term t, respectively, and T be a binary random variable taking on the values t and $\bar{t}$. The conditional entropy of the random class variable C given T is defined according to

Equation 2, where $P(t)=(n(t)/n)$ and $P(\bar{t})=(n(\bar{t})/n)$ denote the proportions of training documents in which term t is present and absent, respectively. The conditional probabilities are estimated by $P(c_i|t)=(n_{c_i}(t)/n(t))$ and $P(c_i|\bar{t})=(\bar{n}_{c_i}(t)/\bar{n}(t))$. Finally, the Information Gain of term t is defined from Equation 3, as the expected reduction in entropy caused by partitioning the set of training examples D according to the presence or absence of term t. However, by using elementary probability calculus, Equation 3 can be transformed to Equation 4, where the probabilities that a class c_i and a term t do or do not co-occur can be derived from the probabilities introduced as $P(c_i,t)=(n_{c_i}(t)/n)$ and $P(c_i,\bar{t})=(n_{c_i}(\bar{t})/n)$ respectively.

$$Entropy(C\,|\,T) = P(t)Entropy(C\,|\,t) + P(\bar{t})Entropy(C\,|\,\bar{t}) =$$
$$= -P(t)\sum_{i=1}^{k} P(c_i\,|\,t)\log P(c_i\,|\,t) - P(\bar{t})\sum_{i=1}^{k} P(c_i\,|\,\bar{t})\log P(c_i\,|\,\bar{t}) \qquad (2)$$

$$Gain(t) = Entropy(C) - Entropy(C\,|\,T) \qquad (3)$$

$$Gain(t) = \sum_{i=1}^{k} P(c_i,t)\log\frac{P(c_i,t)}{P(c_i)P(t)} + \sum_{i=1}^{k} P(c_i,\bar{t})\log\frac{P(c_i,\bar{t})}{P(c_i)P(\bar{t})} \qquad (4)$$

Using the IG technique, 1063 terms were finally selected in order to compose the vector that represents web pages (Web Page Vector – WPV). The WPV characterize a web page by assigning a unique profile of weight values that depend on the importance of each term in the tested web page. In other words, weights are assigned to terms as statistical importance indicators. If m distinct terms are assigned for content identification, a web page is conceptually represented as an m-dimensional vector, named WPV. Equation 5, highlights the lnc formula used for the weighting mechanism, which is based on the SMART system as described in [10]. Web Page Vector is defined as $WPV_i = \{w_{i1}, w_{i1}, ..., w_{ik}\}$, while the weight of term k in the ith web page is normalized using the cosine length of the vector, where l equals to 1063 and corresponds to the total amount of the used terms.

$$w_{ik}^{sv} = (log(tf_{ik})+1)\cdot(\sum_{k=1}^{1063}[log(tf_{ik})+1]^2)^{-1/2} \qquad (5)$$

4 System architecture

Based on the above information filtering techniques, the proposed system relatively classifies web pages in twelve categories. It compares the content of the web pages with dynamic profiles, which are similarity indicators for the twelve categories (type of web pages). In order to relatively classify web pages, the proposed system uses similarity threshold values between the WPVs and the descriptor vectors. Each threshold is a minimum value dedicated to assign a category label to a tested web page. Thus, web pages with scores above these thresholds are considered to belong to the respective categories, while those with lower scoring values do not. In order to define the respective threshold values we used half of the validated web pages and the PCut thresholding strategy [11], [12].

According to this method for each category c_j, the method sorts the tests documents by score assigning a positive decision to each of the k_j top-ranking documents, where $k_j = P(c_j) \times x \times m$ is the number of documents assigned to c_j and $P(c_j)$ is the prior probability for an arbitrary document that is member of category c_j. The PCut strategy is parameterized by x (fine-tuning parameter), which reflects the average number of documents where the system assigns to a category, m is the number of categories, n represents the number of documents in the validation set and assuming that one scoring value is produced by the classifier for each web page-category pair.

4.1 The proposed relevance feedback mechanism

The scoring mechanism is performed by calculating the scalar product according to Equation 6, where the more this value increases, the more similar the vectors are. The denominator normalizes the similarity comparisons between WPV_i and D where w_{ik}^{WPV} is the weight of term k in WPV_i, and p_{jk}^{D} corresponds to the ltc weighting scheme of term k in each descriptor vector D_j as defined in Equation 7. This weighting scheme uses cosine normalization of logarithmic term frequency by the inverse document frequency.

$$(WPV_i, D_j) = \frac{|WPV_i \cap D_j|}{\sqrt{|WPV_i|} \cdot \sqrt{|D_j|}} = \sum_k w_{ik}^{WPV} \times p_{jk}^{D} \qquad (6)$$

$$p_{jk}^{D} = (log(tf_{jk}) + 1) \cdot log(N/n_k) \cdot (\sum_{k=1}^{1065}[(log(tf_{jk}) + 1) \cdot log(N/n_i)]^2)^{-1/2} \qquad (7)$$

After web page classification, the system automatically re-weights the terms of each descriptor vector. The re-weighting is calculated according to a proposed modification of the Rocchio's type for relevance feedback, called Balanced Relevance Weighting Mechanism - BRWM and is defined from Equation 8.

$$D_{j_{new}} = D_{j_{old}} + c\left(1 + \frac{n_{rel}}{n_{rel} + n_{irr}}\right)\sum_{r=1}^{n_{rel}} \frac{WPV_r}{n_{rel}} - c'\left(1 - \frac{n_{rel}}{n_{rel} + n_{irr}}\right)\sum_{n=1}^{n_{irr}} \frac{WPV_n}{n_{irr}} \qquad (8)$$

In the above equation, D_{new} and D_{old} are the re-calculated descriptor vector and the initial descriptor vector, n_{rel} and n_{irr} stands for the amount of the already recognized relevant and irrelevant pages in respect to a specific category, WPV_r and WPV_n are the relevant and the irrelevant web page vectors, while c and c' are fine tuning constants. BRWM re-weights query terms by adding the weights from the actual occurrence of those query terms in the relevant web pages, and subtracting the weights of those terms occurring in the irrelevant web pages. The contribution of the web pages that are not related to a specific information area is to modify the weighting of the terms coming from relevant web pages.

4.2 Evaluation of BRWM

Before the evaluation of the system with real data, we measured the accuracy of BRWM over an established text collection and we compared the results with a similar relevance feedback algorithm (Findsim), which was tested over the same text collection [13], [14]. In particular, we used the corpus of Distribution 1.0 of

Reuters-21578 text categorization test collection. This collection consists of 21578 documents selected from Reuters newswire stories. The documents of this collection are divided into training and test sets. Each document has five category tags, namely, *EXCHANGES, ORGS, PEOPLE, PLACES,* and *TOPICS.* Each category consists of a number of topics that are used for document assignment. This evaluation is restricted to the *TOPICS* category. In particular, we used the Modified Apte split of Reuters-21578 corpus that consist of 9603 training documents, 3299 test documents and 8676 unused documents. The training set was reduced to 7775 documents as a result of screening out training documents with empty value *of TOPICS* category. There are 135 topics in the *TOPICS* category, with 118 of these topics occurring at least once in the training and test documents. The experiment took place with all of these 118 topics despite the fact that three topic categories with no occurrence of training set automatically degrade the performance of the system.

In contrast to information retrieval systems, in text categorization systems a retrieval output is not appeared. Instead, a number of topics occur and for each topic the document collection is partitioned into training and test cases. The training set contains only positive examples of a topic. In this sense, the training set is not a counterpart of the retrieval output due to the fact that there are not any negative examples. However, a training set for a topic that consists of positive and negative examples can be constructed, under the assumption that any document considered as positive example for the other topics and not in the set of positive examples of the topic at hand is a candidate for being a negative example of this topic. Table 2 presents the ten most frequent topics in the category TOPICS of the Reuters collection as well as the respective amounts of the training and testing sets. The maximum number of positive examples per topic in the corpus is 2877 and the average is 84. The size and especially the quality of the training set is an important issue in generating an induction rule set. In the experiment that took place the training set for each topic consist of all the positive samples, while the negative samples were selected from other topics. The size of the selected negative samples was fixed at the 50% of the positives examples. Finally, the Information Gain technique was used since this was the feature selection mechanism used in the compared studies of [13], [14], [15]. According to these papers it was concluded that that the precision or the accuracy of the rules with the Information Gain metric was 3% better than that of rules with CHI metric χ^2. Table 2 also depicts the experimental results deriving from the comparison between BRWM and Findsim over the Reuters-21578 corpus. The comparison is made over the first ten topics and over all the topics of the collection (in average values) and the results are measured in terms of the breakeven point in the precision-recall diagrams of each topic. Precision is defined as the fraction of retrieved web pages, which are relevant to a specific category, while recall is the fraction of relevant web pages, which have been retrieved in respect to the twelve categories. The break-even point is defined as the point where precision is equal to recall.

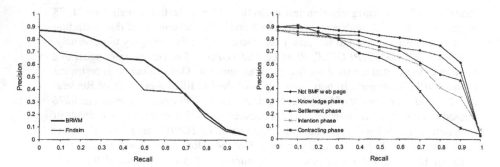

Fig. 1 . Precision-Recall diagrams over: (a) Reuters-21578 corpus, topic "Money-fx", category TOPICS, (b) BMF test sample (average values)

Table 2. Training/Testing sets for the category TOPICS and compared results (breakeven point values) over the Reuters-21578 corpus

Training set	Testing set	Topic of category TOPICS	Findsim	BRWM
2877	1087	Earn	92.9%	90.2%
1650	719	Acq	64.7%	80.6%
538	179	Money-fx	46.7%	56.7%
433	149	Grain	67.5%	63.5%
389	189	Crude	70.1%	68.3%
369	118	Trade	65.1%	60.3%
347	131	Interest	63.4%	67.8%
197	89	Wheat	68.9%	64.7%
212	71	Ship	49.2%	54.1%
182	56	Corn	48.2%	55.3%
		Average top 10	63.7%	66.2%
		Average all	61.7%	64.8%

Topics Earn and Acq were distinguished better among the rest ones on the tested corpus, especially for BRWM. In particular, the breakeven point for the topic Earn was measured above 90% for both algorithms, while for the rest first ten topics the breakeven points presented some fluctuations. However, these fluctuations were expected since the amounts of the training sets are not equal according the Modified Apte split of the collection.

Breakeven point values (in percent) are computed on top 10 topics and on overall 118 topics. In particular, the breakeven point values over the first ten topics were measured equal to 66.2% for BRWM and 63.7% for Findsim, while for the whole collection equal to 64.8% and 61.7% respectively, as presented in Table 2. The results indicated that BRWM presented a better performance in relation to Findsim. Figure 1a presents the precision-recall diagrams of the two compared algorithms in topic "Money-fx" for the category TOPICS. In the precision-recall diagram, labels a and b highlight the breakeven point values that correspond to BRWM and Findsim.

Table 3. Results over the BMF data set

web page type	Break-even point	web page type	Break-even point
Query engines homepages	77.6%	Terms and conditions pages	58.8%
Directory pages	72.8%	Settlement monitoring pages	81.3%
Product information pages	71.2%	Digital delivery pages	77.9%
Registration pages	76.9%	Contact and complaint forms	78.6%
Product catalogue pages	62.6%	After sales support pages	80.4%
Order – Payment pages	68.8%	Not BMF web pages	81.8%

5 Results and discussion

This section presents the results derived from the BRWM algorithm over the rest half amount of the validated BMF data set of Table 1. In particular, Table 3 presents the break-even point values for the eleven type of e-commerce web pages that correspond to the four transaction phases as well as for the web pages that do not offer commercial services (totally twelve categories). According to these values, Figure 1b presents the average precision-recall diagrams for the web pages that correspond to the knowledge, intention, contracting and settlement BMF transaction phase as well as to the page that do not correspond to either of these phases.

The breakeven point for the not BMF related web pages was measured at 81.8%, while for the BMF web pages the average break-even points were measured at 74.6%, 79.6%, 65.7% and 58.8% (knowledge, settlement, intention and contracting phase respectively). Similarly with the tests made over the Reuters-21578 corpus, these variations were expected due to the fact that the amounts of the training sets are not equal among the respective transactions phases of the BMF.

Under the fact that each web page corresponds to one e-commerce type and one transaction phase of the Business Media Framework and this framework analyse an e-commerce model into a series of concurrent sequences, the proposed web information system algorithm can be used in order to identify and classify commercial services and transactions on the web. However, except for classification purposes, the system can be exploited for quantifying e-commerce ontologies and roles. In other words, the system can be either used locally in commercial servers for monitoring customer behaviour directly through local information, or it can be launched independently to a portal, in order to survey and measure commercial activities, services and transactions on the web.

References

1. Klose M., Lechner U., 'Design of Business Media - An integrated Model of Electronic Commerce', In: Haseman, W.D.; Nazareth, D.L. (eds.), Proceedings of the Fifth Americas Conference on Information Systems (AMCIS'99), pp. 115-117, Milwaukee, WI, August 13-15, 1999.
2. Mahadevan B., 'Business Models for Internet-Based ECommerce: An Anatomy', California Management Review, Vol.42, No.4, 2000.

3. Timmers P., '*Business Models for Electronic Markets*', In: Gadient Y., Schmid B. F., Selz D., EM - Electronic Commerce in Europe, EM - Electronic Markets, Vol. 8, No. 2, July 1998.
4.   Lawrence E., Corbitt B., Tidwell A., Fisher J., Lawrence J., 'Internet Commerce Digital Models for Business', John Wiley & Sons, Brisbane, 1998.
5. Selz S., 'Web Assessment: A model for the Evaluation and the Assessment of Successful Electronic Commerce Applications', International Journal of Electronic Markets 7(3).
6. Schmid B.F., Lindemann, M.A, 'Elements of a reference model for electronic markets', Proceedings of the Thirty-First Hawaii International Conference on System Sciences, vol.4, pp. 193-201, 1998.
7. Schmid, B., 'What is new about the Digital Economy', Electronic Markets, vol.11, no.1, 04/2001.
8. Anagnostopoulos I., Psoroulas I., Loumos V. and Kayafas E., Implementing a customised meta-search interface for user query personalisation, IEEE 24th International Conference on Information Technology Interfaces, ITI 2002 pp. 79-84, June 24-27, 2002, Cavtat/Dubrovnik, CROATIA.
9. Yang Y and Pedersen J (1997) A comparative study on feature selection in text categorization. In: Proceedings of the 14th International Conference in Machine Learning, ICML'97, pp. 412 – 420, , 1997, Nashville, TN, USA.
10. Buckley C, Salton G and Allan J (1993) Automatic retrieval with locality information using SMART. In: Proceedings of the 1st Text REtrieval Conference (TREC-1), pp. 59-72, 1993, Gaithersburg, MD, USA.
11. Lewis D., An evaluation of phrasal and clustered representations on a text categorisation task, 15th Annual International ACM Conference on Research and Development in Information Retrieval (SIGIR 92), pp.37-50, 1992.
12. Yang Y., An evaluation of statistical approaches to text categorization, Journal of Information Retrieval, 1(1/2), pp.67-88, 1999.
13. Dumais S, Platt J, Heckerman D and Sahami M, Inductive learning algorithms and representations for text categorization. In: Proceedings of the 7th international conference on Information and knowledge management, ACM Press 1998, Location, pp. 148-155.
14. Alsaffar A, Deogun J and Sever H, Optimal queries in information filtering. Lecture Notes in Artificial Intelligence (LNCS Series), 1932:435-443.
15. Sever H, Gogur A and Tolun M., Text Categorization with ILA. Lecture Notes in Computer Science – LNCS, 2869:300-307.

Bagged Averaging of Regression Models

S. B. Kotsiantis, D. Kanellopoulos, I. D. Zaharakis

Educational Software Development Laboratory
Department of Mathematics
University of Patras, Greece
sotos@math.upatras.gr, dkanellop@teipat.gr, jzaharak@cti.gr

Abstract. Linear regression and regression tree models are among the most known regression models used in the machine learning community and recently many researchers have examined their sufficiency in ensembles. Although many methods of ensemble design have been proposed, there is as yet no obvious picture of which method is best. One notable successful adoption of ensemble learning is the distributed scenario. In this work, we propose an efficient distributed method that uses different subsets of the same training set with the parallel usage of an averaging methodology that combines linear regression and regression tree models. We performed a comparison of the presented ensemble with other ensembles that use either the linear regression or the regression trees as base learner and the performance of the proposed method was better in most cases.

1 Introduction

Several algorithms have been proposed for the design of ensemble of regression models [4]. Mechanisms that are used to make ensemble of regression models include: i) Using different subset of training data with a single machine learning method, ii) Using different training parameters with a single learning method, iii) Using different machine learning methods.

Even though many algorithms of ensemble creation have been proposed, there is as yet no obvious picture of which method is best. One notable successful adoption of ensemble learning in a distributed scenario is the meta-learning framework. It offers a way to mine regression models from homogeneously distributed data. In this approach, supervised learning techniques are first used to build regression models at local data sites; then meta-level models are generated using the locally learned concepts. This paper explores an efficient method for constructing ensembles that can take place in a distributed way. The idea is simple: use different subsets of the same training set with the parallel usage of an averaging methodology at each site that combines a linear regression model [6] and a regression tree algorithm [10].

Please use the following format when citing this chapter:

Kotsiantis, Sotiris, Kanellopoulos, Dimitris, Zaharakis, Ioannis, 2006, in IFIP International Federation for Information Processing, Volume 204, Artificial Intelligence Applications and Innovations, eds. Maglogiannis, I., Karpouzis, K., Bramer, M., (Boston: Springer), pp. 53–60

Using averaging methodology, we expect to obtain better results because both theory and experiments show that averaging helps most if the errors in the individual regression models are not positively correlated [9]. In fact, the comparison with other ensembles that use either the linear regression or regression tree algorithm on 30 standard benchmark datasets showed that the proposed ensemble had on the average better performance.

Section 2 presents the most well-known methods for building ensembles, while section 3 discusses the proposed ensemble method. Experiment results and comparisons of the presented combining method in a number of datasets with other ensembles that also use as base learner either the regression tree or the linear regression model are presented in section 4. We conclude in Section 5 with summary and further research topics.

2   Ensembles of Regression Models

Bagging [2] is a ``bootstrap" ensemble method that creates individuals for its ensemble by training each regression model on a random redistribution of the training set. Each regression model's training set is generated by randomly drawing, with replacement, N examples - where N is the size of the original set; many of the original examples may be repeated in the resulting training set while others may be left out. After the construction of several regression models, averaging the predictions of each regression model performs the final prediction. Breiman [2] made the important observation that instability (responsiveness to changes in the training data) is a prerequisite for bagging to be effective.

Another method that uses different subset of training data with a single data mining method is the boosting approach [5]. Boosting is similar in overall structure to bagging, except that it keeps track of the performance of the learning algorithm and concentrates on instances that have not been correctly learned. Instead of choosing the t training instances randomly using a uniform distribution, it chooses the training instances in such a manner as to favor the instances that have not been accurately learned. After several cycles, the prediction is performed by taking a weighted average of the predictions of each regression model, with the weights being proportional to each regression model's performance on its training set. Additive Regression is a practical version of the boosting approach [7].

Another approach for building ensembles of regression models is to use a variety of learning algorithms on all of the training data and combine their predictions. When multiple regression models are combined using averaging methodology, we expect to obtain good results based on the belief that the majority of experts are more likely to be correct in their decision when they are close in their opinions [9].

Stacked generalization [3], or Stacking, is a more sophisticated approach for combining predictions of different learning algorithms. Stacking combines multiple regression models to induce a higher-level regression model with improved performance. In detail, the original data set constitutes the level zero data and all the base regression models run at this level. The level one data are the outputs of the base regression models. A learning algorithm is then used to determine how the outputs of the base regression models should be combined, using as input the level one data.

3 Proposed Methodology

Bagging uses an averaging technique which is unable to take into account the heterogeneity of the instance space. When majority of the base regression models give a wrong prediction for a new instance then the average value will result in a wrong prediction [8]. The problem may consist in discarding base regression models that are highly accurate in a restricted region of the instance space because this accuracy is swamped by their inaccuracy outside the restricted area. It may also consist in the use of regression models that are accurate in most of the space but still unnecessarily confuse the whole committee in some restricted areas of the space. To overcome this problem we have suggested the bagged averaging using two learning algorithms: the linear regression (LR) model and a regression tree (RT) algorithm. There is a reason that makes us believe the one method acts as a complement to the other. Perlich et al. [12] have proved that the corresponding classification models: logistic regression and decision trees act as a complement to each other. The algorithm is briefly described in Fig. 1.

MODEL GENERATION

Let n be the number of instances in the training data.

For each of t iterations (t=10 in our experiments):
- Sample n instances with replacement from training data.
- Built two regression models (LR, RT) from the sample
- Store the resulting models.

APPLICATION PHASE

For each of the t models:

Predict value of instance by averaging the two learning algorithms (LR, RT)

Return the average value of the predicted values.

Fig. 1. The proposed ensemble

As it is well known, Regression Trees produce decision trees with numeric output for leaf nodes rather than categorical output. M5 is one of the most well-known algorithms for regression tree induction [13] and for this reason it was used for our model.

It has been observed that for bagging, an increase in committee size (sub-regression models) usually leads to a decrease in prediction error, but the relative impact of each successive addition to a committee is ever diminishing. Most of the effect of each technique is obtained by the first few committee members [11]. For this reason, we used 10 sub-regression models for the proposed algorithm.

It must be also mentioned that the proposed ensemble is easily distributed and parallelized. The computations required to obtain the regression models in each bootstrap sample are independent of each other. Therefore we can assign tasks to each processor in a balanced manner. By the end each processor has obtained a part of the Bagged Averaging ensemble. In the case we use the master-slave parallel programming technique, the method starts with the master splitting the work to be done in small tasks and assigning them to each slave (LR and RT regression models). Then the master performs an iteration in which if a slave returns a result (this means it finished its work) then the master assigns it another task if there are still tasks to be executed. Once all the tasks have been carried out the master process obtains the results and orders the slaves to finish since there are not more tasks to be carried out. This parallel and distributed execution of the presented ensemble achieves almost linear speedup.

4   Comparisons and Results

For the comparisons of our study, we used 30 well-known datasets mainly from domains from the UCI repository [1]. These datasets cover many different types of problems having discrete, continuous and symbolic variables.

The most well known measure for the degree of fit for a regression model to a dataset is the correlation coefficient. If the actual target values are $a_1, a_2, ...a_n$ and the predicted target values are: $p_1, p_2, ... p_n$ then the correlation coefficient is given by the formula:

$$R=\frac{S_{PA}}{\sqrt{S_P S_A}} \text{ where } S_{PA}=\frac{\sum_i (p_i-\bar{p})(a_i-\bar{a})}{n-1}, \ S_P=\frac{\sum_i (p_i-\bar{p})^2}{n-1}, \ S_A=\frac{\sum_i (a_i-\bar{a})^2}{n-1}.$$

In order to calculate the regression models' correlation coefficient, the whole training set was divided into ten mutually exclusive and equal-sized subsets and for each subset the regression model was trained on the union of all of the other subsets. Then, cross validation was run 10 times for each algorithm and the average value of the 10-cross validations was calculated (10x10 cross-validation). It must be mentioned that we used the free available source code for the most algorithms by [14].

In the following tables, we represent with "v" that the proposed ensemble (Bagged Averaging) looses from the specific ensemble. That is, the specific algorithm performed statistically better than the proposed according to t-test with p<0.05. Furthermore, in Tables, "*" indicates that Bagged Averaging performed statistically better than the specific ensemble according to t-test with p<0.05. In all the other cases, there is no significant statistical difference between the results (Draws).

In the last rows in all tables one can see the aggregated results in the form (a/b/c). In this notation "a" means that the proposed ensemble is significantly more accurate than the compared algorithm in a out of 30 datasets, "c" means that the proposed ensemble is significantly less accurate than the compared algorithm in c out of 30 datasets, while in the remaining cases (b), there is no significant statistical difference between the results. In the following Tables, we also present the average correlation coefficient of all tested dataset for each ensemble.

For both Bagging and Boosting, much of the reduction in error appears to have occurred after ten to fifteen regression models. But boosting continues to measurably improve their test-set error until around 25 regression models [11]. For this reason, we used 25 sub-regression models for our experiments. Firstly, we compare the presented methodology with bagging and boosting version of LR (using 25 sub-regression models). Secondly, we compare the presented methodology with bagging and boosting version of M5 (using 25 sub-regression models). In the last rows of the Table 1 one can see the aggregated results.

Table 1. Comparing Bagged Averaging ensemble with bagging and boosting version of LR and M5

	Bagged Averaging	Bagging LR	Bagging M5	Boosting LR	Boosting M5
auto93.names	0.81	0.79*	0.80	0.83v	0.80
autoHorse.names	0.95	0.95	0.89*	0.95	0.91*
autoMpg.names	0.93	0.93	0.91*	0.93	0.91*
autoPrice.names	0.90	0.89*	0.89*	0.89*	0.91v
baskball	0.59	0.61v	0.51*	0.62v	0.44*
bodyfat.names	0.99	0.99	0.97*	0.99	0.97*
breastTumor	0.29	0.29	0.26*	0.30	0.18*
cholesterol	0.20	0.20	0.19	0.19*	0.06*
cleveland	0.71	0.72v	0.66*	0.71	0.63*
cloud	0.92	0.93v	0.85*	0.93v	0.86*
cpu	0.96	0.96	0.89*	0.95	0.92*
echoMonths	0.70	0.70	0.70	0.71v	0.69
elusage	0.89	0.87*	0.85*	0.86*	0.85*
fishcatch	0.96	0.97v	0.91*	0.97v	0.96
housing	0.89	0.85*	0.88*	0.85*	0.89
hungarian	0.69	0.71v	0.63*	0.72v	0.61*
lowbwt	0.79	0.79	0.79	0.79	0.78*
meta	0.44	0.40*	0.43	0.38*	0.25*
pbc	0.60	0.59	0.52*	0.60	0.50*
pollution	0.76	0.75	0.68*	0.76	0.67*
pwLinear	0.89	0.87*	0.86*	0.86*	0.90v
quake	0.07	0.06*	0.07	0.06*	0.01*
sensory	0.45	0.38*	0.48v	0.39*	0.45
servo	0.87	0.85*	0.85*	0.85*	0.84*
sleep	0.66	0.65	0.60*	0.62	0.57*
stock	0.97	0.93 *	0.97	0.93 *	0.99 v
strike	0.52	0.53v	0.49*	0.53v	0.47*
triazines	0.43	0.37 *	0.48	0.38 *	0.44
veteran	0.45	0.46	0.39*	0.48v	0.34*
wisconsin	0.36	0.34 *	0.30 *	0.33 *	0.24 *
W-D-L		*6/12/12*	*1/8/21*	*8/10/12*	*3/6/21*
Average correlation coefficient	*0.69*	*0.68*	*0.66*	*0.68*	*0.63*

The presented ensemble has significantly higher correlation coefficient than bagging LR in 12 out of the 30 datasets, while it has significantly lower correlation coefficient in 6 datasets. At this point, it must be also mentioned that the proposed ensemble and the bagging version of LR with 25 sub-regression models need similar training times (more detailed evaluation in quantitative terms will be presented in a future paper). In addition, the presented ensemble has significantly higher correlation coefficient than boosting LR in 12 out of the 30 datasets, whilst it has significantly lower correlation coefficient in 8 datasets.

Moreover, the presented ensemble has significantly higher correlation coefficient than bagging regression tree algorithm –M5– in 21 out of the 30 datasets, while it has significantly lower correlation coefficient in one dataset. In addition, the presented ensemble has significantly higher correlation coefficient than boosting M5 in 21 out of the 30 datasets whilst it has significantly lower correlation coefficients in 3 datasets.

To sum up, on the average the presented ensemble has higher correlation coefficient than the other well-known ensembles that use only the LR algorithm about 2%. Moreover, on the average the performance of the presented ensemble is more accurate than the other well-known ensembles that use only the M5 algorithm from 5% to 8%. What is more, the presented ensemble needed much less time for training than bagging and boosting version of M5 algorithm (more detailed evaluation in quantitative terms will be presented in a future paper).

Subsequently, we compare the presented methodology with other well-known ensembles that use either LR or M5 as base regression models. We compare the proposed methodology with:

- Stacking methodology [3]. We used LR, M5 as base regression models and LR as meta-level regression model.
- Averaging methodology using LR, M5 as base regression models [9]

In the last rows of the Table 2 one can see the aggregated results. The presented ensemble has significantly higher correlation coefficient than averaging in 12 out of the 30 datasets, whilst it has significantly lower correlation coefficient in 3 datasets. It must be also mentioned that on the average the performance of the presented ensemble is more accurate than averaging about 2%.

Similarly, the proposed ensemble has significantly higher correlation coefficient than Stacking in 10 out of the 30 datasets, while it has significantly lower correlation coefficient in 7 datasets. The average relative correlation coefficient improvement of the proposed ensemble is about 2% better in relation to Stacking.

To sum up, the presented methodology of combining LR and M5 algorithms could be an off-the self method-of-choice for a regression task where there is no a priori knowledge available about the domain and the primary goal is to develop an regression model with lowest possible error.

5 Conclusions

It is known that if we are only concerned for the best possible correlation coefficient, it might be difficult or impossible to find a single regression model that performs as well as a good ensemble of regression models. In this study, we built an ensemble of regression models using two different learning methods: the Linear Regression and the M5 algorithm.

Table 2. Comparing Bagged Averaging ensemble with Stacking and Averaging ensembles

	Bagged Averaging	Averaging	Stacking
auto93.names	0.81	0.84v	0.83v
autoHorse.names	0.95	0.95	0.95
autoMpg.names	0.93	0.93	0.93
autoPrice.names	0.90	0.90*	0.90*
baskball	0.59	0.59	0.61v
bodyfat.names	0.99	0.98*	0.99
breastTumor	0.29	0.28	0.28
cholesterol	0.20	0.18*	0.15*
cleveland	0.71	0.68*	0.71
cloud	0.92	0.91*	0.93
cpu	0.96	0.95*	0.94*
echoMonths	0.70	0.71v	0.71v
elusage	0.89	0.89	0.87*
fishcatch	0.96	0.96	0.97v
housing	0.89	0.89	0.89
hungarian	0.69	0.67*	0.72v
lowbwt	0.79	0.79	0.79
meta	0.44	0.42*	0.36*
pbc	0.60	0.59*	0.60
pollution	0.76	0.74	0.74
pwLinear	0.89	0.89	0.89
quake	0.07	0.06*	0.04*
sensory	0.45	0.43*	0.42*
servo	0.87	0.87	0.86*
sleep	0.66	0.64	0.61*
stock	0.97	0.97	0.98 v
strike	0.52	0.51*	0.52
triazines	0.43	0.45	0.45
veteran	0.45	0.46v	0.47v
wisconsin	0.36	0.35	0.31 *
W-D-L		*3/15/12*	*7/13/10*
Average correlation coefficient	*0.69*	*0.68*	*0.68*

While ensembles provide very accurate regression models, too many regression models in an ensemble may limit their practical application. To be feasible and competitive, it is important that the learning algorithms run in reasonable time. In our method, we limit the number of sub-regression models to 20. It was proved after a number of comparisons with other ensembles, which use either M5 or LR as base models, that the Bagged Averaging methodology gives better correlation coefficient in most cases. In a future research project we will also examine the product rule for combining LR and RT. In addition, more experiments based on varying number of sub-regression models are needed for the proposed approach.

Accessing and analyzing data from a ubiquitous computing device offer many challenges. For example, ubiquitous data mining (UDM) introduces additional cost due to communication, computation, security, and other factors. For the proposed method, a learning algorithm can take the form of a software agent in order the proposed model to be used in a ubiquitous environment. Of course, some problems such as agent interaction, cooperation, collaboration, negotiation and organizational behavior should earlier be solved. These are the research topics we are currently working on and hope to report our findings in the near future.

References

1. C.L. Blake, C.J. Merz, UCI Repository of machine learning databases. Irvine, CA: University of California, Department of Information and Computer Science (1998). [http://www.ics.uci.edu/~mlearn/MLRepository.html]
2. L. Breiman, Bagging Predictors. Machine Learning, 24(3) (1996) 123-140.
3. L. Breiman, Stacked Regression. Machine Learning, 24 (1996):49-64.
4. T.G. Dietterich, Ensemble methods in machine learning. In Kittler, J., Roli, F., eds.: Multiple Classifier Systems. LNCS Vol. 1857, Springer (2001) 1–15
5. N. Duffy, D. Helmbold, Boosting Methods for Regression, Machine Learning, 47, (2002) 153–200.
6. J. Fox, Applied Regression Analysis, Linear Models, and Related Methods, ISBN: 080394540X, Sage Pubns (1997).
7. J. Friedman, Stochastic Gradient Boosting, Computational Statistics and Data Analysis 38 (2002) 367-378.
8. Y. Grandvalet, Bagging Equalizes Influence, Machine Learning, Volume 55(3) (2004) 251 – 270.
9. N.L. Hjort, G. Claeskens, Frequentist Model Average Estimators, Journal of the American Statistical Association, 98 (2003) 879-899.
10. Y. Morimoto, H. Ishii, S. Morishita, Efficient Construction of Regression Trees with Range and Region Splitting, Machine Learning, 45(3) (2001) 235-259.
11. D. Opitz, R. Maclin, Popular Ensemble Methods: An Empirical Study, Artificial Intelligence Research, 11 (1999): 169-198, Morgan Kaufmann.
12. C. Perlich, F. J. Provost, J. S. Simonoff, Tree Induction vs. Logistic Regression: A Learning-Curve Analysis. Journal of Machine Learning Research 4 (2003) 211-255
13. Y. Wang, I. H. Witten, Induction of model trees for predicting continuous classes, In Proc. of the Poster Papers of the European Conference on ML, (1997) 128–137.
14. I. Witten, E. Frank, Data Mining: Practical Machine Learning Tools and Techniques with Java Implementations, Morgan Kaufmann, San Mateo (2000).

Appendix: Acknowledgements

The Project is Co-Funded by the European Social Fund & National Resources - EPEAEK II.

Argument-based User Support Systems using Defeasible Logic Programming

Carlos I. Chesñevar[1], Ana G. Maguitman[2], and Guillermo R. Simari[3]

[1] Artificial Intelligence Research Group – Department of Computer Science
Universitat de Lleida – C/Jaume II, 69 – E-25001 Lleida, SPAIN – Email: cic@eps.udl.es
[2] Computer Science Department – Indiana University
Bloomington, IN 47405-7104, USA – Email: anmaguit@cs.indiana.edu
[3] Department of Computer Science and Engineering – Universidad Nacional del Sur
Alem 1253, (8000) Bahía Blanca, ARGENTINA – Email: grs@cs.uns.edu.ar

Abstract. Over the last few years, argumentation has been gaining increasing importance in several AI-related areas, mainly as a vehicle for facilitating rationally justifiable decision making when handling incomplete and potentially inconsistent information. In this setting, user support systems can rely on argumentation techniques to automatize reasoning and decision making in several situations such as the handling of complex policies or managing change in dynamic environments. This paper presents a generic argument-based approach to characterize user support systems, in which knowledge representation and inference are captured in terms of Defeasible Logic Programming, a general-purpose defeasible argumentation formalism based on logic programming. We discuss a particular application which has emerged as an instance of this approach oriented towards providing user decision support for web search.

Keywords: argumentation, logic programming, user support systems, knowledge engineering

1 Introduction and motivations

Critics and recommender systems (commonly known under the general term *user support systems*) have evolved in the last years as specialized tools to assist users in a plethora of computer-mediated tasks by providing guidelines or hints [8]. Most critics and recommenders are based on machine learning and information retrieval algorithms. The resulting systems typically provide suggestions based on *quantitative* evidence (i.e. measures of similarity between objects or users), whereas the inference process which led to these suggestions is commonly unknown (i.e. 'black-box' metaphor). Although the effectiveness of existing critics and recommenders is remarkable, they still have serious limitations as they are unable to perform qualitative inference on the suggestions they offer and are incapable of dealing with the defeasible nature of users' preferences. A solution for this problem can be provided by integrating existing user support technologies with appropriate inferential mechanisms for qualitative reasoning.

Please use the following format when citing this chapter:

Chesñevar, Carlos, Maguitman, Ana, Simari, Guillermo, 2006, in IFIP International Federation for Information Processing, Volume 204, Artificial Intelligence Applications and Innovations, eds. Maglogiannis, I., Karpouzis, K., Bramer, M., (Boston: Springer), pp. 61–69.

In this context, *defeasible argumentation* frameworks [1, 10] constitute an interesting alternative, as they have matured in the last decade to become a sound setting to formalize commonsense, qualitative reasoning. In the last few years, particular attention has been given to extensions of logic programming as a suitable framework for formalizing argumentation in a computationally attractive way. One of such approaches that has been considerably successful is *Defeasible Logic Programming* (DeLP) [5], a general-purpose argumentation formalism based on logic programming.

This paper presents a generic approach to characterize *argument-based user support systems, i.e.* user support systems in which recommendations are provided on the basis of arguments. We describe a particular real-world application which emerged as an instance of this approach oriented towards providing suitable decision support in the context of web search.

2 Defeasible Logic Programming: overview

Defeasible logic programming (DeLP) [5] is a general-purpose defeasible argumentation formalism based on logic programming, intended to model inconsistent and potentially contradictory knowledge.[1] A defeasible logic program is a set $\mathcal{P} = (\Pi, \Delta)$ of Horn-like clauses, where Π and Δ stand for sets of *strict* and *defeasible* knowledge, resp. The set Π of strict knowledge involves *strict rules* of the form $P \leftarrow Q_1, \ldots, Q_k$ and *facts* (strict rules with empty body), and it is assumed to be *non-contradictory*.[2] The set Δ of defeasible knowledge involves *defeasible rules* of the form $P \prec Q_1, \ldots, Q_k$, which stands for "$Q_1, \ldots Q_k$ *provide a tentative reason to believe P.*" Strict and defeasible rules in DeLP are defined in terms of *literals P, Q_1, Q_2, ...* A literal is an atom or the strict negation ($\sim$) of an atom.

Deriving literals in DeLP results in the construction of *arguments*. An argument $\mathcal{A}$ for a literal Q (denoted $\langle \mathcal{A}, Q \rangle$) is a (possibly empty) set of ground defeasible rules that together with the set Π provide a SLD-like proof for a given literal Q, satisfying the additional requirements of *non-contradiction (i.e.,* an argument should not involve contradictory information) and *minimality (i.e.,* the set of defeasible information used should be minimal). Note that arguments are obtained by a mechanism similar to the usual query-driven SLD derivation from logic programming, performed by backward chaining on *both* strict and defeasible rules; in this context a negated literal $\sim P$ is treated just as a new predicate name *no_P*. As a program $\mathcal{P}$ represents incomplete and tentative information, *conflicting* arguments may arise. An argument $\langle \mathcal{B}, R \rangle$ is a *counterargument* for another argument $\langle \mathcal{A}, Q \rangle$ if if there exists a sub-argument $\langle \mathcal{C}, L \rangle$ of $\langle \mathcal{A}, Q \rangle$ *(i.e.,* $\mathcal{C} \subseteq \mathcal{A}$) such that there exists a literal $P \in \mathcal{P}$ verifying both $\Pi \cup \{L, R\} \vdash P$ and $\Pi \cup \{L, R\} \vdash \neg P$. Intuitively, this means that both arguments cannot be accepted simultaneously as they their joint acceptance leads to contradictory conclusions. A preference criterion among arguments " $\succeq$ " is used to determine when

---

[1] For space reasons, we will restrict ourselves to a basic set of definitions and concepts which make this paper self-contained. For more details, see [5, 1].
[2] Contradiction stands for deriving two complementary literals wrt strict negation (P and $\sim P$) or default negation (P and not P).

an argument is a *defeater* for another argument. An argument $\langle \mathcal{B}, R \rangle$ *defeats* another argument $\langle \mathcal{A}, Q \rangle$ if $\langle \mathcal{B}, R \rangle$ is a counterargument for $\langle \mathcal{A}, Q \rangle$ and $\langle \mathcal{B}, R \rangle \succeq \langle \mathcal{A}, Q \rangle$.

However, as defeaters are arguments, they may on its turn be defeated by other arguments, which could on their turn be defeated by other arguments, and so on. This prompts a recursive *dialectical* process rooted in a given argument $\langle \mathcal{A}_0, Q_0 \rangle$, considering all their defeaters, defeaters for such defeaters, and so on. The process can be characterized in a tree-like structure called *dialectical tree* $\mathcal{T}_{\langle \mathcal{A}_0, Q_0 \rangle}$, in which nodes are arguments, the root node is the original argument at issue, and every children node defeats its parent node. Every path in a dialectical tree is a sequence $[\langle \mathcal{A}_0, Q_0 \rangle, \langle \mathcal{A}_1, Q_1 \rangle, \langle \mathcal{A}_2, Q_2 \rangle, \ldots, \langle \mathcal{A}_n, Q_n \rangle]$ that can be thought of as an exchange of arguments between two parties, a *proponent* (evenly-indexed arguments) and an *opponent* (oddly-indexed arguments).[3] Each $\langle \mathcal{A}_i, Q_i \rangle$ is a defeater for the previous argument $\langle \mathcal{A}_{i-1}, Q_{i-1} \rangle$ in the sequence, $i > 0$. A path is *won* by the proponent if its length is odd (*i.e.*, the last argument in the path was given by the proponent, and no defeater followed it); otherwise the path is *lost*. An argument $\langle \mathcal{A}_0, Q_0 \rangle$ is *warranted* iff every path in $\mathcal{T}_{\langle \mathcal{A}_0, Q_0 \rangle}$ is won. Given a DeLP program $\mathcal{P} = (\Pi, \Delta)$, a query Q_0 wrt $\mathcal{P}$ is solved by computing the preceding tree-like structure. Three answers are distinguished: YES (there is at least one warranted argument $\mathcal{A}_0$ for Q_0); NO (there is at least one warranted argument $\mathcal{A}_0$ for $\sim Q_0$); UNDECIDED (none of the previous cases hold).

3 Argument-based User Support Systems using DeLP

Our proposal is to model users' preference criteria in terms of a DeLP program built on top of a traditional content-based search engine. Figure 1(left) presents the basic architecture of a generic argument-based user support system based on DeLP. In this setting users preferences and background knowledge can be codified as facts and rules in a DeLP program. These facts and rules can come from different sources. For example, user's preferences could be entered explicitly by the user or could be inferred by the system (e.g., by monitoring the user's behavior.) Additional facts and rules could be obtained from other repositories of structured (e.g., databases) and semistructured data (e.g., the Web.)

We will distinguish particular subsets in a DeLP program, representing different elements in a user support system. For example, a DeLP program could take the form $\mathcal{P} = \mathcal{P}_{user} \cup \mathcal{P}_{pool} \cup \mathcal{P}_{domain}$, where sets $\mathcal{P}_{user}$ and $\mathcal{P}_{pool}$ represent preferences and behavior of the active user and the pool of users, respectively. In the case of the active user, his/her profile can be encoded as facts and rules in DeLP. In the case of the pool of users, rule induction techniques are in order[4] resulting in defeasible rules characterizing trends and general preference criteria (e.g., *normally if a given user likes X then she also likes Y*). The set $\mathcal{P}_{domain}$ represents the domain (background) knowledge, encoded using facts and rules in DeLP. Either proactively or upon a user's request, an argument-based user support system triggers the search for suggestions. If needed, the collected results could be codified as facts and added to the DeLP program. Finally,

---

[3] Under certain constraints (e.g. avoiding cycles), all paths in a dialectical tree can be guaranteed to be finite. For details see [5].

[4] An approach for inducing defeasible rules from association rules can be found in [6].

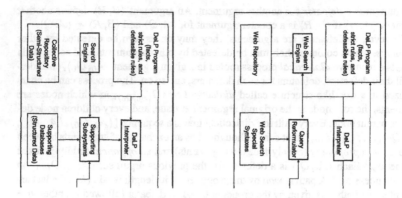

Fig. 1. A Generic Argument-Based User Support System based on DeLP (left); The ARGUENET Framework as a particular instance for argument-based web search (right)

a DeLP interpreter is in charge of performing the qualitative analysis on the program and to provide the final suggestions to the user.

Given the program $\mathcal{P}$, a user's request is transformed into suitable DeLP queries, from which different *suggestions* are obtained. For the sake of simplicity, we will assume in our analysis that user suggestions will be DeLP terms associated with a distinguished predicate name *rel* (which stands for *relevant* or *acceptable as a valid suggestion*). Using this formalization, suggestions will be classified into three sets, namely: (a) S^w (warranted suggestions): those suggestions s_i for which there exists at least one warranted argument supporting $rel(s_i)$ based on $\mathcal{P}$; (b) S^u (undecided suggestions): those suggestions s_i for which there is no warranted argument for $rel(s_i)$, neither there is a warranted argument for $\sim rel(s_i)$ on the basis of $\mathcal{P}$, and (c) S^d (defeated suggestions): those suggestions s_i such that there is a warranted argument supporting $\sim rel(s_i)$ on the basis of $\mathcal{P}$. Given a potential suggestion s_i, the existence of a warranted argument $\langle \mathcal{A}_1, rel(s_i) \rangle$ built on the basis of the DeLP program $\mathcal{P}$ will allow to conclude that s_i should be presented as a final suggestion to the user. If results are presented as a ranked list of suggestions, then warranted suggestions will be more relevant than those which are undecided or defeated. Note that the above classification has a direct correspondence with the doxastic attitudes associated with answers to DeLP queries.

4 ARGUENET: Argument-based User Support for Web Search

Next, we will present a concrete instantiation of an argument-based user support system: a recommendation tool for web search queries called ARGUENET [2]. In this context, the intended user support aims at providing an enriched web search engine which categorizes results, and where the user's needs correspond to strings to be searched

ALGORITHM Recommend_on_Query
INPUT: Query q, DeLP program $\mathcal{P} = \mathcal{P}_{user} \cup \mathcal{P}_{pool} \cup \mathcal{P}_{domain}$
OUTPUT: List L_{new} {*recommendation results wrt $\mathcal{P}'$*}
Let $L = [s_1, s_2, \ldots s_k]$ be the output of solving q
wrt content-based search engine SE
{*L is the list of (the first k) results obtained from query q via SE* }
$\mathcal{P}_{search} = \{$facts encoding $info(s_1), info(s_2) \ldots info(s_k)\}$
{*$info(s_i)$ stands for features associated with result s_i* }
$\mathcal{P}' := $ **Revise** $(\mathcal{P} \cup \mathcal{P}_{search})$.
{**Revise** *stands for a belief revision operator to ensure consistency in $\mathcal{P}'$* }
Initialize S^w, S^u, and S^d as empty sets.
{*S^w, S^u, and S^d stand for the set of results s_i's which are warranted as
relevant, undecided and warranted as non-relevant, respectively* }
FOR EVERY $s_i \in L$
  DO
    Solve query $rel(s_i)$ using DeLP program $\mathcal{P}'$
    IF $rel(s_i)$ is warranted **THEN** add s_i to S^w
    ELSE
      IF $\sim rel(s_i)$ is warranted **THEN** add s_i to S^d
      ELSE add s_i to S^d
Return Recommendation $L_{new} = [s_1^w, s_2^w, \ldots, s_{j1}^w, s_1^u, s_2^u, \ldots, s_{j2}^u, s_1^d, \ldots, s_{j3}^d]$

Fig. 2. Algorithm for solving queries ARGUENET

on the web. The search engine is a conventional search engine (e.g., GOOGLE). Final recommendation results for a query q are prioritized according to domain background knowledge and the user's declared preferences. Figure 1(right) illustrates the architecture of an argument-based news recommender system.

Given a user query q, it will be given as an input to a traditional content-based web search engine, returning a list of search results L. If required, the original query q could be suitably re-formulated in order to improve the quality of the search results to be obtained. In the list L we can assume that s_i is a unique name characterizing a piece of information $info(s_i)$, in which a number of associated features (meta-tags, filename, URL, etc.) can be identified. We assume that such features can be identified and extracted from $info(s_i)$ by some specialized tool, as suggested by Hunter [7] in his approach to dealing with structured news reports. Such features will be encoded as a set $\mathcal{P}_{search}$ of new DeLP facts, extending thus the original program $\mathcal{P}$ into a new program $\mathcal{P}'$. A special operator Revise deals with possible inconsistencies found in $\mathcal{P}_{search}$ with respect to $\mathcal{P}'$, ensuring $\mathcal{P} \cup \mathcal{P}_{search}$ is not contradictory.[5] Following the algorithm shown in Fig. 2 we can now analyze L in the context of a new DeLP program $\mathcal{P}' = \mathcal{P} \cup Facts$, where $Facts$ denotes the set corresponding to the collection discussed above and $\mathcal{P}$ corresponds to domain knowledge and the user's preferences about the search domain.[6] For each s_i, the query $rel(s_i)$ will be analyzed in light of the new program $\mathcal{P}'$. Elements in the original list L of content-based search results will be classified into three sets of warranted, undecided, and defeated results. The final output presented to the user will be a sorted list L' in which the elements of L are

---

[5] For example, contradictory facts may be found on the web. A simple belief revision criterion is to prefer the facts with a newer timestamp over the older ones.
[6] In this particular context, note that $\mathcal{P} = \mathcal{P}_{domain} \cup \mathcal{P}_{user}$.

$$rel(X) \prec author(X, A), trust(A).$$
$$\sim rel(X) \prec author(X, A), trust(A), outdated(X).$$
$$trust(A) \prec not\ faked\_news(A).$$
$$\sim rel(X) \prec address(X, Url), biased(Url).$$
$$biased(Url) \prec thailandian(Url).$$
$$biased(Url) \prec japanese(Url).$$
$$\sim biased(Url) \prec domain(Url, D), D = "jpt.jp".$$
$$rel(X) \leftarrow author(X, bob\_beak).$$
$$oudated(X) \leftarrow date(X, D), getdate(Today),$$
$$(Today - D) > 100.$$
$$thailandian(X) \leftarrow [\text{Computed elsewhere}]$$
$$japanese(X) \leftarrow [\text{Computed elsewhere}]$$
$$domain(Url, D) \leftarrow [\text{Computed elsewhere}]$$
$$getdate(T) \leftarrow [\text{Computed elsewhere}]$$
$$faked\_news(chin\_yao\_lin) \leftarrow$$

$author(s_1, chin\_yao\_lin).$
$address(s_1, "jpt.jp/...").$
$date(s_1, 20031003).$
$author(s_2, jen\_doe).$
$address(s_2, "news.co.uk/...").$
$date(s_1, 20001003).$
$author(s_3, jane\_truth).$
$address(s_3, "jpt.jp/...").$
$date(s_3, 20031003).$
$author(s_4, bob\_beak).$
$address(s_4, "mynews.com/...").$
$date(s_4, 20031003).$

Fig. 3. (a) DeLP program modeling preferences of a journalist; (b) Facts encoded from original web search results

ordered according to their epistemic status with respect to $\mathcal{P}'$. Fig. 2 outlines a high level algorithm, which will be exemplified in the case study shown next.

Example 1. Consider a journalist who wants to search for news articles about recent outbreaks of bird flu. A query q containing the terms *news, bird,* and *flu* will return thousands of search results. Our journalist may have some implicit knowledge to guide the search, such as: (1) she always considers relevant the newspaper reports written by Bob Beak; (2) she usually considers relevant the reports written by trustworthy journalists; (3) Reports written by trustworthy journalists which are out of date are usually not relevant; (4) Knowing that a journalist has not faked reports provides a tentative reason to believe he or she is trustworthy. By default, every journalist is assumed to be trustworthy. (5) Japanese and Thailandian newspapers usually offer a biased viewpoint on bird flu outbreaks; (6) The *"Japanese Times"* (http://jpt.jp) is a Japanese newspaper which she usually considers non biased; (7) Chin Yao Lin is known to have faked a report. Such rules and facts can be modelled in terms of a DeLP program $\mathcal{P}$ shown in Fig. 3(a). Note that some rules in $\mathcal{P}$ rely on "built in" predicates computed elsewhere and not provided by the user.[7]

For the sake of example, suppose that the above query returns a list of search results $L=[s_1, s_2, s_3, s_4]$. Most of these results will be associated with XML or HTML pages, containing a number of features (e.g. author, date, URL, etc.). Such features can be encoded as discussed before in a collection of DeLP facts as shown in Fig. 3(b). We can now analyze s_1, s_2, s_3 and s_4 in the context of the user's preference theory about the search domain by considering the DeLP program $\mathcal{P}'=\mathcal{P}\cup Facts$, where $Facts$ denotes the set corresponding to the collection of facts in Fig. 3(b). For each s_i, the query $rel(s_i)$ will be analyzed wrt this new program $\mathcal{P}'$.

Consider the case for s_1. The search for an argument for $rel(s_1)$ returns the argument $\langle \mathcal{A}_1, rel(s_1) \rangle$: s_1 should be considered relevant since it corresponds to a newspaper article written by Chin Yao Lin who is considered a trustworthy author (note that every journalist is considered to be trustworthy by default.) In this case we have the argument[8] $\mathcal{A}_1=\{$ $rel(s_1) \prec author(c_1, chin\_yao\_lin), trust(chin\_yao\_lin) ; trust(chin\_yao\_lin) \prec not\ faked\_news(chin\_yao\_lin)$ }. Search for defeaters for argument $\langle \mathcal{A}_1, rel(s_1) \rangle$ will result in a defeater $\langle \mathcal{A}_2, \sim rel(s_1) \rangle$: s_1 is not relevant as it comes from a Japanese newspaper,

---

[7] E.g., determining the country of origin corresponding to a specific web domain can be found querying Internet directory services such as WHOIS.

[8] For the sake of clarity, semicolons separate elements in an argument $\mathcal{A} = \{e_1 ; e_2 ; \ldots; e_k \}$.

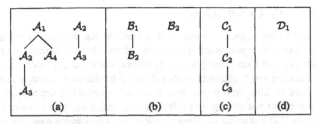

Fig. 4. Dialectical trees associated with (a) $\langle \mathcal{A}_1, rel(s_1) \rangle$ and $\langle \mathcal{A}_2, \sim rel(s_1) \rangle$; (b) $\langle \mathcal{B}_1, rel(s_2) \rangle$ and $\langle \mathcal{B}_2, \sim rel(s_2) \rangle$; (c) $\langle \mathcal{C}_1, rel(s_3) \rangle$ and (d) $\langle \mathcal{D}_1, rel(s_4) \rangle$

which is assumed to be biased about bird flu. In this case we have the argument $\mathcal{A}_2 = \{ \sim rel(c_1) \prec address(c_1, "jpt.jp..."), biased ("jpt.jp...") ; biased("jpt.jp...") \prec japanese ("jpt.jp...") \}$. Note that we also have an argument $\langle \mathcal{A}_3, \sim biased("jpt.jp...") \rangle$ which defeats $\langle \mathcal{A}_2, \sim rel(s_1) \rangle$: Usually articles from the "Japanese Times" are not biased. In this case we have $\mathcal{A}_3 = \{ \sim biased("jpt.jp...") \prec domain("jpt.jp...", "jpt.jp"), ("jpt.jp" = "jpt.jp") \}$. Finally, another defeater for $\langle \mathcal{A}_1, rel(s_1) \rangle$ is found, namely $\langle \mathcal{A}_4, faked\_news(chin\_yao\_lin) \rangle$, with $\mathcal{A}_4 = \emptyset$. No other arguments need to be considered. The resulting dialectical tree rooted $\langle \mathcal{A}_1, rel(s_1) \rangle$ is shown in Fig 4a (left). Not all paths have odd length, and hence $\langle \mathcal{A}_1, rel(s_1) \rangle$ is not warranted. Carrying out a similar analysis for $\sim rel(s_1)$ results in the dialectical tree shown in Figure 4a (right). A similar situation results. There are no other candidate arguments to consider; hence s_1 is deemed as *undecided*.

The case of s_2 is analogous. The argument $\langle \mathcal{B}_1, rel(s_2) \rangle$ can be built, with $\mathcal{B}_1 = \{ rel(s_2) \prec author(s_2,), trust(jen\_doe) ; trust(jen\_oldie) \prec not \ faked\_ \ news \ (jen\_doe) \}$. This argument is defeated by $\langle \mathcal{B}_2, \sim rel(s_2) \rangle$, with $\mathcal{B}_2 = \{ \sim rel(s_2) \prec author(s_2, jen\_doe), trust(jen\_doe), outdated(s_2) ; trust(jen\_doe) \prec not \ faked\_news(jen\_doe) \}$. There are no more arguments to consider, and $\langle \mathcal{B}_1, rel(s_2) \rangle$ is deemed as non warranted ((Fig. 4b (left)). The analysis of $\sim rel(s_2)$ results in a single argument. Thus, its associated dialectical tree has a single node $\langle \mathcal{B}_2, \sim rel(s_2) \rangle$, the only possible path has an odd length, and it is *warranted*.

Following the same line of reasoning used in the case of s_1 we can analyze the case of s_3. An argument $\langle \mathcal{C}_1, rel(s_3) \rangle$ can be built supporting the conclusion $rel(s_3)$ (a newspaper article written by Jane Truth is relevant as she can be assumed to be a trustworthy author). A defeater $\langle \mathcal{C}_2, \sim rel(s_3) \rangle$ will be found: s_1 is not relevant as it comes from a Japanese newspaper, which by default is assumed to be biased about bird flu. But this defeater in its turn is defeated by a third argument $\langle \mathcal{C}_3, biased(s_3) \rangle$. The resulting dialectical tree for $\langle \mathcal{C}_1, rel(s_3) \rangle$ is shown in Fig. 4c (left)). The original argument $\langle \mathcal{C}_1, rel(s_3) \rangle$ can be thus deemed as *warranted*. Finally let us consider the case of s_4. There is an argument $\langle \mathcal{D}_1, rel(s_4) \rangle$ with $\mathcal{D}_1 = \emptyset$, as $rel(s_4)$ follows directly from the strict knowledge in $\mathcal{P}$. Clearly, there is no defeater for an empty argument (as no defeasible knowledge is involved). Hence $rel(s_4)$ is *warranted* (see dialectical tree in Fig. 4d).

Applying the criterion given in the algorithm shown in Fig. 2, the initial list of search results $[s_1, s_2, s_3, s_4]$ will be shown as $[s_3, s_4, s_1, s_2]$ (as $\langle \mathcal{C}_1, rel(s_3) \rangle$ and $\langle \mathcal{D}_1, rel(s_4) \rangle$ are warranted, $\langle \mathcal{A}_1, rel(s_3) \rangle$ is undecided and $\langle \mathcal{B}_2, \sim rel(s_2) \rangle$ is warranted (i.e., s_2 is warranted to be a non-relevant result).

5 Related work. Conclusions

Several kinds of user support systems that operate on top of Internet services have been proposed over the past years. In the case of web-based recommender systems (e.g. SurfLen [4], and Quickstep [9], among others) the usual approach involves taking into account the user's interests –either declared by the user or conjectured by the system– to rank or filter web pages. However such approaches differ from our proposal in that they do not attempt to perform a *qualitative* analysis to warrant recommendations. In [12] a number of interesting *argument assistance tools* are presented. Even though there is a sound logical framework underlying this approach, the focus is rather restricted to legal reasoning, viewing the application of law as dialectical theory construction and evaluating alternative ways of representing argumentative data. In contrast, our analysis is oriented towards characterizing more generic argument-based user support systems.

In this paper we have presented a novel approach towards the development of user support systems by enhancing recommendation technologies through the use of qualitative, argument-based analysis. In particular, we have shown that DeLP is a suitable computational tool for carrying on such analysis in a real-world application for intelligent web search, providing thus a tool for higher abstraction when dealing with users' information needs. Preliminary experiments on the use of ARGUENET were performed on the basis of a prototype. However, it must be remarked that these initial experiments only serve as a "proof of concept" prototype, as thorough evaluations are still being carried out. As performing defeasible argumentation is a computationally complex task, an abstract machine called JAM (Justification Abstract Machine) has been specially developed for an efficient implementation of DeLP [5], allowing to solve queries and computing dialectical trees very efficiently. The JAM provides an argument-based extension of the traditional WAM (Warren's Abstract Machine) for PROLOG. A full-fledged implementation of DeLP is available online,[9] including facilities for visualizing arguments and dialectical trees. Several other features leading efficient DeLP implementations have also been recently studied, in particular those related to comparing conflicting arguments by *specificity* [11] as a syntax-based preference criterion and pruning dialectical trees to speed up the argumentative inference procedure [3].

Current trends in user support system technologies show clearly that the combination of quantitative and qualitative analysis of user preferences will play a major role in the future. In this context, we think that defeasible argumentation techniques will constitute a powerful tool to make inference in user support systems more reliable and and user-friendly. Our approach intends to be a first step to reach this long-term goal.

Acknowledgements: This research work was supported by Projects TIC2003-00950, TIN 2004-07933-C03-03, by Ramón y Cajal Program (MCyT, Spain) by CONICET (Argentina), and by Agencia Nacional de Promoción Científica y Tecnológica (PICT 2002 No. 13.096).

---

[9] See http://lidia.cs.uns.edu.ar/DeLP

References

1. C. Chesñevar, A. Maguitman, and R. Loui. Logical Models of Argument. *ACM Computing Surveys*, 32(4):337–383, December 2000.
2. C. Chesñevar, A. Maguitman, and G. Simari. Argument-Based Critics and Recommenders: A Qualitative Perspective on User Support Systems. *Data and Knowledge Engineering (to appear)*, 2005.
3. C. Chesñevar, G. Simari, and L. Godo. Computing dialectical trees efficiently in possibilistic defeasible logic programming. *LNAI Springer Series Vol. 3662 (Proc. of the 8th Intl. Conf. on Logic Programming and Nonmonotonic Reasoning LPNMR 2005)*, pages 158–171, September 2005.
4. Xiaobin Fu, Jay Budzik, and Kristian J. Hammond. Mining navigation history for recommendation. In *Intelligent User Interfaces*, pages 106–112, 2000.
5. A. García and G. Simari. Defeasible Logic Programming: An Argumentative Approach. *Theory and Practice of Logic Programming*, 4(1):95–138, 2004.
6. G. Governatori and A. Stranieri. Towards the application of association rules for defeasible rules discovery. In *Legal Know. & Inf. Sys.*, pages 63–75. JURIX, IOS Press, 2001.
7. Anthony Hunter. Hybrid argumentation systems for structured news reports. *Knowledge Engineering Review*, pages 295–329, 2001.
8. Joseph A. Konstan. Introduction to recommender systems: Algorithms and evaluation. *ACM Trans. Inf. Syst.*, 22(1):1–4, 2004.
9. S. Middleton, D. DeRoure, and N. Shadbolt. Capturing knowledge of user preferences: Ontologies in recommender systems. In *Proc. ACM K-CAP'01*, Canada, 2001. ACM Press.
10. H. Prakken and G. Vreeswijk. Logical Systems for Defeasible Argumentation. In D. Gabbay and F.Guenther, editors, *Handbook of Phil. Logic*, pages 219–318. Kluwer, 2002.
11. F. Stolzenburg, A. García, C. Chesñevar, and G. Simari. Computing Generalized Specificity. *JANCL*, 13(1):87–113, 2003.
12. Bart Verheij. Artificial argument assistants for defeasible argumentation. *Artif. Intell.*, 150(1-2):291–324, 2003.

Knowledge Modelling Using The UML Profile

Mohd Syazwan Abdullah [1,2], Richard Paige[2], Ian Benest[2], and Chris
Kimble[2]
[1] Faculty of Information Technology, UUM, 06010 Sintok, Kedah,
Malaysia
[2]Department of Computer Science, University of York,
Heslington, York, YO10 5DD, United Kingdom
[1]pathma @uum.edu.my
[2]{syazwan, paige, idb, kimble} @cs.york.ac.uk

Abstract. This paper discusses platform independent conceptual modeling of a
knowledge intensive application, focusing on the use of knowledge-based
systems (KBS) in the context of model-driven engineering. An extension to
the Unified Modeling Language (UML) for knowledge modeling is presented
based on the profiling extension mechanism of UML. The UML profile
discussed in this paper has been successfully captured in a Meta-Object-
Facility (MOF) based UML tool – the eXecutable Modeling Framework
(XMF). The example is that of modeling a knowledge-based system for the
Ulcer Clinical Practical Guidelines (CPG) Recommendations. It demonstrates
the use of the profile, with the prototype system implemented in the Java
Expert System Shell (JESS).

1 Introduction

Knowledge-based systems (KBS) were developed for managing codified knowledge
in the field of Artificial Intelligence (AI). Widely known as expert systems, these
were originally created to emulate the human expert reasoning process [1] and is one
of the successful inventions that has been derived from AI technologies. KBS are
developed using knowledge engineering (KE) techniques [2], which are similar to
those used in software engineering (SE), but have an emphasis on knowledge rather
than on data or information processing.

Central is the conceptual modelling of the system during the analysis and design
stages of the development process; this is widely known as knowledge modelling.
Many knowledge engineering methodologies have been developed with an emphasis
on the use of models, for example: CommonKADS [3]. KBS continue to evolve as
the need to have a stable technology for managing knowledge grows. Their current

Please use the following format when citing this chapter:

Abdullah, Mohd Syazwan, Paige, Richard, Benest, Ian, Kimble, Chris, 2006, in IFIP International
Federation for Information Processing, Volume 204, Artificial Intelligence Applications and
Innovations, eds. Maglogiannis, I., Karpouzis, K., Bramer, M., (Boston: Springer), pp. 70–77

role as an enabler for knowledge management (KM) initiatives has led to greater appreciation of this technology [4, 5]. It has matured from a non-scalable technology to one that can be adopted for managing the knowledge used in demanding commercial applications; it is a tool that is widely accepted by industry [6, 7]. Because it is a maturing technology, the Object Management Group (OMG), which governs object-oriented software modelling standards, has started a standardisation process [8] for knowledge-based engineering services and production rule representation (PRR).

This paper is organized as follows: Section 2 describes and discusses knowledge modelling issues in designing KBS. Section 3 explains the rationale for having an extension to UML for modelling knowledge. Section 4 gives an overview of the UML extension mechanism, while section 5 presents the knowledge modelling profile. Section 6 describes a case study that illustrates how the profile can be used to develop a KBS. Section 7 concludes and indicates future directions for the work.

2 Knowledge Modelling

The *knowledge-level* principle, popularised by [9] for KE purposes, requires that knowledge be modelled at a conceptual level independent of the implementation formalism. Knowledge modelling is similar to that of conceptual modelling, which is widely used to refer to implementation-independent models in SE; both the terms are used inter-changeably in the KE domain. The *knowledge-level* principle is fundamental to the process of conceptualisation for problem solving [10] and is used in KE for the explicit representation of the real world problem that is to be solved by the proposed system [11].

While knowledge about the domain is usually addressed through the use of ontologies, the independent reasoning process is specified with Problem Solving Methods (PSM) [5]. Both ontologies and PSM provide components that are reusable across domains and tasks [12] enabling KBS to be designed, built and deployed quickly. Ontologies are formal declarative representations of the domain knowledge; that is, they are sets of objects with describable relationships [13]. Thus an ontology used for knowledge modelling defines the content-specific knowledge representation elements such as domain-dependent classes, relations, functions and object constants [14]. PSM however describe the reasoning-process (generic inference patterns) at an abstract level, which is independent of the representation formalism (e.g. rules, frames, etc.) [12]. PSM have influenced the leading KE frameworks such as Task Structures, Rôle-Limiting Methods, CommonKADS, Protégé, MIKE, VITAL and others [12]. PSM can be considered to be design patterns in KE for KBS development [3].

It is commonly agreed by researchers [15] that conceptual modelling is an important stage in any software system construction. However, both SE and KE communities have developed different modelling techniques that are now almost unrelated [16] as a result of the fundamental computational difference between them in solving the same problem [17]. As a result, although both field's ultimate goal is to build software systems, the different experiences are difficult to interchange [17].

Nevertheless, most KE modelling notations are derived from the SE field as these are better established.

3   UML Extensibility Mechanism

The OMG's Model Driven Architecture (MDA) – a model-driven engineering framework – provides integration with, and interoperability between, different models developed using standards [18] such as the UML. The growth of MDA will fuel the demand for more meta-models to cater for domain specific modelling requirements [18]. The development of a profile, by constructing a meta-model, will enable it to be integrated into the MDA space. Integration with MDA is important for this knowledge modelling language since it cannot exist in isolation. The UML is a general-purpose modelling language [18] that can be used in very different application domains. It can be enhanced to model domains that are not currently supported, by extending the modelling features of the language in a controlled and systematic fashion. The OMG [19] has defined two mechanisms for extending UML: profiles and meta-model extensions and this work adopts the current UML 2.0 standard.

4   Knowledge Modelling Profile

The work presented in this paper adopts the XMF approach [20] in designing the knowledge modelling profile as the OMG only specifies how profiles should be constituted and not how to design them. By adopting the XMF approach, the profile development is structured into well-defined stages that are easy to follow and methodologically sound. The XMF is a newly developed object-oriented meta-modelling language, and is an extension to existing standards defined by OMG. The XMF approach to creating a profile can be divided into three steps: the derivation of an abstract syntax model of the profile concepts, a description of the profile's semantics, and the presentation of the profile's concrete syntax (not discussed here) if this is different from UML diagrams. Details of the XMF approach and the profile development stages can be found in [20]. XMF was adopted in the original design [21], but since XMF is not MOF compliant, UML tools were not able to support the resulting profile.

Profiles are sometimes referred to as the "lightweight" extension mechanism of UML [22]. A profile contains a predefined set of Stereotypes, TaggedValues, Constraints, and notation icons that collectively specialize and tailor the UML to a specific domain or process. The main construct in the profile is the stereotype that is purely an extension mechanism. In the model, it is marked as <<stereotype>> and has the same structure (attributes, associations, operations) as defined by the meta-model that is used for its description. Nevertheless, the usage of stereotypes is restricted, as changes in the semantics, structure, and the introduction of new concepts to the meta-model are not permitted [23]. In the case of knowledge modelling, the existing constructs of UML are sufficient in representing the KBS concepts.

The Profile Concept

The concepts that underpin the profile are those taken from the existing BNF definition of the CommonKADS Conceptual Modelling Language (CML) [3], providing a well-defined and well-established set of domain concepts. Most of these elements are generally those adopted in the KBS literature and are widely used for representing the concepts of KBS in the KE domain. These knowledge modelling concepts are itemised in Table 1 and the abstract syntax model of the profile is shown in Figure 1 on the next page.

Table 1. Main Knowledge Modelling Concepts

Modelling Concept	Description
Concept (class)	Class that represents the category of things
FactBase/Working Memory	Collection of information/fact that will be matched against the rule
Inference	The lowest level of functional decomposition consisting of primitive reasoning steps
Transfer Function	Transfers information between the reasoning agent and external entities (system, user)
Task	Defines the reasoning function
Task Method	Describes the realization of the task through subfunction decomposition
Static Knowledge Role	Specifies the collection of domain knowledge that is used to make the inference
Dynamic Knowledge Role	Run-time inputs and outputs of inferences
Rule Type	Categorization and specification of knowledge
Rule	Expressions that involve an attribute value of a concept
Knowledge Base	Collection of data stores that contains instances of domain knowledge types

Model Extension

The knowledge modelling profile concept extends the existing meta-models of UML by defining the profile's abstract syntax. There are three places where the profile can be viewed as an extension to UML and these are: Class, Named Element and Constraints, all of which are central to the core UML meta-model and are also found in UML. The knowledge modelling concept class enables the concept to inherit all the features of a class and allows it to specify attributes and constraints on the attribute values. Other concepts such as inference, task, task method, dynamic role, static role, and the transfer function are also viewed as a subclass of the UML Class and inherit its features. This allows operations relating to objects to be expressed through the static role and at the same time allows these elements to specify attributes. Such operations are: an execute inference call from the task method, the execution of the inference process and access to knowledge in the knowledge base. Knowledge base is a subclass of the UML class. It has a 'content' slot for specific tables. This is a natural choice for a subclass as the knowledge base is actually a collection of tables grouped together in order to store rule type instances. The profile's tuple concept is also extended from Class. Constraint class is a subclass of the UML meta-model that incorporates profile concepts such as axioms and rule type expressions. All these concepts need the ability to express constraints and this class allows for this. Rule Type is subclassed from the UML Named Element, which allows rules to be identified using a name. All the associations described in the profile are extensions of the UML association class. However, they are not shown in the profile, as it would clutter the diagram.

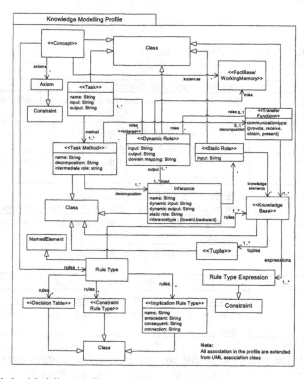

Fig. 1. Knowledge Modeling Profile

6   Case Study - Clinical Practice Guideline Recommendations

The Clinical Practice Guideline (CPG) Recommendations are guidelines that contain statements, which are graded according to the following three levels of evidence: (I) generally consistent findings in a majority of multiply acceptable studies; (II) either based on a single acceptable study, or weak or inconsistent findings in multiply acceptable studies; (III) limited scientific evidence that does not meet all the criteria of acceptable studies of good quality. The guideline contains recommendations for assessment of leg ulcers, management of venous leg ulcers, cleansing, removal of debris, dressing and contact sensitivity, education and training, and quality assurance categories. A knowledge-based system for educational purposes was designed and developed based on the listing of recommendations in terms of: (a) evidence strength; (b) evidence strength and category; (c) category alone. Figure 2 shows how the profile was used to represent part of the CPG case study.

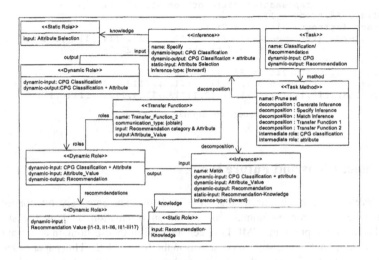

Fig. 2. CPG case study model

The profile here only concentrates on showing the task of making recommendations (*considered as a classification task-type*) based on the user-selected criteria. The task is executed by the method "prune set" which is carried out by several inferences and intermediate roles. For the matching process to provide recommendations, different sets of rules are used depending on the criteria selected by the user. To arrive at a recommendation, the inference would need to access the knowledge or rules from the knowledge base, which will be provided by the static role. The corresponding facts are gathered from the dynamic role that takes user inputs and the CPG recommendations from the factbase.

The case study was implemented as a prototype system in JESS, which is based on the popular CLIPS program [24]. Because of the declarative nature of expert system shells, the concepts of the profile cannot be directly matched to a JESS metamodel entirely. This is due to the fact that some of the JESS elements could not be directly mapped to the profile and future work will improve these mappings. However, the knowledge modelling profile was very useful in understanding the KBS requirements for the CPG recommendations. Given below is a sample Jess program that lists recommendations based on the following evidence strength (in the actual recommendation each has a brief explanation rather than the ID shown as I1, II2, III4 and so on):

If evidence.strength = I Then Recommendation = {I1, I2, I3, I4}

If evidence.strength = II Then Recommendation = {II1, II2, II3, II4, II5, II6}
If evidence.strength = III Then Recommendation = {III1, III2, III3, III4, III5,.... to III19}

```
Sample program code of Jess for the CPG Recommendations
(  defrule strength-I                              \
   ( user (strength ?i&:(= ?i 1)))
 => assert   (recommendation I1 , I2 , I3 , I4)
                    (explanation "Strength equals 1"))))
(  defrule f strength-II
   ( user (strength ?i&:(= ?i 2)))
 => (assert   (recommendation II1 ,  II2 ,  II3 ,  II4 ,II5 ,II6)
                    (explanation "Strength equals 2"))))
(  defrule strength-III
   ( user (strength ?i&:(= ?i 3)))
 => (assert   (recommendation II1 ,  III2 ,  III3 ,  III4 ,III5 ,III6
,III7,  III8,III9,III10,III11,III12,III13,III14,III15,III16,III17)

         (explanation "Strength equals 3 "))))
```

7   Conclusions and Future Work

KBS development is similar to that of SE where they both rely on conceptual modelling of the problem domain to provide an orientation on how the system should address the problem. UML has been adopted in the SE domain as a standard for modelling, but there is still no consensus in the field of KE. This paper describes an extension to UML using the profile mechanism for knowledge modelling that allows KBS to be designed using an object-oriented approach. The profile has been successfully tested on several case studies involving KBS design and development from scratch and in re-engineering an existing KBS. The future work in this area involves improving the mapping of the profile to a specific inference engine meta-model. It is expected that Jess in the first instance, will help assess not only the utility of the profile for building realistic KBS, but also the utility of XMF for capturing the meta-models and building the transformations.

References

1.   Giarratano, J.C. and G.D. Riley, *Expert Systems: Principles and Programming*. 4 ed. 2004, Boston, Massachusetts: Course Technology - Thomson.
2.   Studer, R., Benjamins, R.V. and Fensel, D. *Knowledge Engineering: Principles and Methods*. Data & Knowledge Engineering, 1998. **25**: p. 161-197.
3.   Schreiber, G., Akkermans, H., Anjewierden, A., deHoog, R., Shadbolt, N. de Velde, W.V., and Wielinga, B. *Knowledge Engineering and Management: The CommonKADS Methodology*. 1999, Massachusetts: MIT Press.
4.   Ergazakis, K., Metaxiotis, K., and Psarras, I. *Knowledge Management in Enterprises: A Research Agenda*. Intelligent Systems in Accounting, Finance and Management, 2005. **13** (1): p. 17-26.
5.   Studer, R., Decker, S., Fensel, D., and Staab, S. *Situation and Perspective of Knowledge Engineering*, in *Knowledge Engineering and Agent Technology*.

IOS Series on Frontiers in Artificial Intelligence and Applications., J. Cuena, et al., Editors. 2000, IOS Press: Amsterdam.

6. Liebowtiz, J., *If You Are A Dog Lover, Build Expert System; If You Are A Cat Lover, Build Neural Networks.* Expert Systems With Applications, 2001. **21**: p. 63.

7. Preece, A., *Evaluating Verification and Validation Methods in Knowledge Engineering*, in *Micro-Level Knowledge Management*, R. Roy, Editor. 2001, Morgan-Kaufman: San Francisco. p. 123-145.

8. Tabet, S., Wagner, G., Spreeuwenberg, S., Vincent, P., Jacques, G., de Sainte Marie, C., Pellant, J., Frank, J., and Durand, J . *OMG Production Rule Representation - Context and Current Status*, in *W3C Workshop on Rule Languages for Interoperability.* 2005. Washington, D.C., USA.

9. Newell, A., *The Knowledge Level.* Artificial Intelligence, 1982. **18**: p. 87-127.

10. Gómez, A., Moreno, A., Pazos, J., and Sierra-Alonso, A. *Knowledge maps: An essential technique for conceptualisation.* Data & Knowledge Engineering, 2000. **33**(2): p. 169-190.

11. Juristo, N. and A.M. Moreno, *Introductory paper: Reflections on Conceptual Modelling.* Data & Knowledge Engineering, 2000. **33**(2): p. 103-117.

12. Gomez-Perez, A. and V.R. Benjamins. *Overview of Knowledge Sharing and Reuse Components: Ontologies and Problem-Solving Methods.* in *IJCAI-99 Workshop on Ontologies and Problem-Solving Methods (KRR5).* 1999. Stockholm, Sweden, p. 1-1 - 1-15.

13. Gruber, T.R., *Toward Principles For The Design Of Ontologies Used For Knowledge Sharing.* 1993, Stanford University.

14. Kende, R., *Knowledge Modelling in Support of Knowledge Management.* Lecture Notes in Artificial Intelligence, 2001. **2070**: p. 107-112.

15. Naumenko, A. and A. Wegmann. *A Metamodel for the Unified Modeling Language.* in *UML 2002.* 2002. Dresden, Germany.: Springer, Berlin, p. 2-17.

16. Cuena, J. and M. Molina, *The Role Of Knowledge Modelling Techniques In Software Development: A General Approach Based On A Knowledge Management Tool.* Int. Journal of Human-Computer Studies, 2000. **52**: p. 385-421.

17. Juristo, N., *Guest editor'.* Knowledge Based System, 1998. **11**(2): p. 77-85.

18. Muller, P.-A., Studer, P., and Bezivin. J. *Platform Independent Web Application Modeling.* In The Sixth International Conference On The Unified Modeling Language (UML 2003). 2003: Springer, p. 220-233.

19. OMG, *Unified Modeling Language specification (version 1.4).* 2001.

20. Clark, T., Evans, A., Sammut, P., and Willians, J. *Metamodelling for Model-Driven Development (draft): To be published.* http://albini.xactium.com. 2005.

21 Abdullah, M.S., Evans, A., Paige, R., Benest, I., and Kimble, C. Modelling Knowledge Based Systems Using the eXecuta ble Modelling Framework (XMF), in Cybernetic and Intelligent Systems (CIS) 2004. IEEE Press, p 1053-1059.

22. OMG, *Requirements for UML Profile.* 1999, Object Management Group: Framingham, MA, U.S.A. p. 8.

23. Perez-Martinez, J.E., *Heavyweight Extensions To The UML Metamodel To Describe The C3 Architectural Style.* ACM SIGSOFT Software Engineering Notes, 2003. **28**(3), p. 5-5.

24. Friedman-Hill, E., Jess in Action: Rule-Based System in Java. 2003, Manning.

Optimized Multi-Domain Secure Interoperation using Soft Constraints

Petros Belsis, Stefanos Gritzalis, Sokratis K. Katsikas
Laboratory of Information and Communication Systems Security
Department of Information and Communication Systems Engineering
University of the Aegean, Karlovasi, Samos, Greece
{pbelsis, sgritz, ska}@aegean.gr

Abstract. Building coalitions between autonomous domains and managing the negotiation process between multiple security policies in a multi-domain environment is a challenging task. The negotiation process requires efficient modeling methods for the determination of secure access states and demands support from automated tools aiming to support administrators and to minimize human intervention; thus making the whole process more efficient and less error-prone. In this paper we define a framework that enables the representation of policy merging between autonomous domains, as a constraint satisfaction problem, while remaining neutral in regard to the policy language. Role and permission hierarchies are modeled using the constraint programming formalism. Policy mappings are utilized in order to enable cross-organizational role assignment. Further optimization on policy mappings is achieved by casting the problem to a partially ordered multi-criteria shortest path problem.

1. Introduction

With the proliferation of Internet based technologies and the advances in networked systems we have witnessed a raising necessity for flexible access control schemes over distributed environments. Many approaches attempt to provide support for authorization decisions within a single domain framework. Powerful languages have also emerged [7][6], able to express different policies; still their applicability has been enforced on a single domain basis. In many collaborating environments coalitions between autonomous domains are formed to enable mutual sharing of resources and applications, in order to achieve a common goal. Security considerations can rise in magnitude in collaborative environments where different information systems form coalitions, sharing resources and applications. The nature of the coalitions can be dynamic, meaning that domains may join or leave at any moment, or that role and permission determination policy updates reflect in

Please use the following format when citing this chapter:

Belsis, Petros, Gritzalis, Stefanos, Katsikas, Sokratis, 2006, in IFIP International Federation for Information Processing, Volume 204, Artificial Intelligence Applications and Innovations, eds. Maglogiannis, I., Karpouzis, K., Bramer, M., (Boston: Springer), pp. 78–85

necessary updates in the global policy. Member domains of the coalition perform common operations over shared resources. Access to shared resources must be consistent with the individual policies of coalition members. Secure interoperation should retain two basic principles [1]:

- Autonomy principle: if access is permitted within an individual system it should also be permitted under secure interoperation.
- Security principle: if access is not permitted within an individual system, it must not be permitted under secure interoperation.

We are investigating the problem of enabling coalition formation between autonomous domains. We propose a flexible way to enable cooperation between separate Role Based Access Control (RBAC) oriented policies and through the policy mappings we enable assignment of roles to users belonging to different domains [2]. In order to facilitate the coalition management and to make it less error-prone human intervention has to be reduced by the use of automated tools [3]. We also utilize a powerful mathematical framework based on constraint satisfaction, to which the formalization of the problem can be cast. Under this framework and through the concept of policy mappings, we transform the aforementioned problem to a partially ordered multi-criteria shortest path problem, which can be guided using soft constraints. Among the contributions of this paper are the following:

- Secure interoperation is enabled through the concept of policy mappings, while by modeling the different policies using soft constraints we allow for the determination of additional role mappings, leading thus to the creation of optimal solutions.
- We allow for the execution of actions over the shared resources for roles that have not been explicitly mapped to other roles by the administrator; therefore, we introduce a way to determine automated mappings, avoiding at the same time violations of role hierarchy constraints.

The rest of the paper is organized as follows: after a brief introduction in section 1, section 2 presents the formalism principles and their applicability to security models, section 3 presents related work and a brief comparison with our approach, while section 4 concludes the paper and provides the directions of our future work.

2. Problem Formulation

2.1 The RBAC model

The basic notions behind the RBAC [4] models are users, roles, and permissions. A user represents a human entity or an autonomous agent. A role is associated with a post in an organization assigned to the execution of a specific task, while a collection of permissions are assigned to each role, enabling the fulfillment of the obligations associated with such a task. To extend the support for the least privilege principle (that allows to a user the minimum privileges necessary to fulfill a task), sessions are introduced.

A complete RBAC model includes the following variables and functions:

- The sets U (users), R (roles), P (permissions) and S (sessions)
- User to role assignment $UA \subseteq U \times R : U \rightarrow 2^R$

- Permission to role assignment PA⊆P×R: R→2^P
- A mapping of sessions to a single user assignment US: S→U
- A mapping from sessions to the set of roles associated with each session S→2^R
- A partial ordering RH⊆R×R, represented by the symbol: ≥, which defines role hierarchy. $R_1 \geq R_2$ implies that R_1 inherits permissions from R_2.

RBAC is a dominant security model due to its flexibility and due to the fact that it reflects organizational hierarchy; moreover, its parameters can be easily codified. For this purpose, several RBAC security policy representation languages have emerged, ranging from formal, graphically annotated to expressive full-scale policy management systems with software tools support.

We do not intend to create a new policy representation language. Our work focuses on enabling the coalition of autonomous systems, where each one retains its own security policy. In fact, there is no restriction that all the domains should follow the same policy language; the only requirement being adherence to the RBAC principles.

Given the fact that permissions are a set of Boolean constraints associated with a given role, we can consider policy representation as a set of Boolean constraints. Multi-domain policy merging can then be cast to a condition of joint satisfaction of a constraint-programming problem. In our approach, the administrators of each domain codify the policies. We do not also consider the case where domains for any reason would attempt to conceal policy related information, as in the case where policies contain sensitive information. For example in the case where ministries cooperate there is no danger that policy disclosure would result in potential danger, since all the parties are cooperating on the basis of a common target. Our approach intends to reduce the administrator's involvement overhead by proposing access states that satisfy the pre-specified preferences of each domain.

2.2 Soft constraint satisfaction

Constraint programming is an emerging technology in the area of artificial intelligence [10]. A constraint satisfaction problem (CSP) includes a set of problem variables, a domain of possible values and a set of constraints defined over these variables. Semiring based CSPs or SCSPs [10] are an extension of CSPs where the constraints are defined over an appropriate semiring. We will mainly adopt the notation introduced in [10], [11]. A semiring is a tuple <A,+,*,0,1> where

- A is a set with **0,1** ∈A
- + the additive operation is closed, commutative and associative over A with **0** as the absorbing element
- *, the multiplicative operation is closed and associative over A with **1** as its identity element and **0** as its absorbing element
- * distributes over +

A constraint semiring (c-semiring) is a tuple <A,+,*,0,1> where the idempotency of the additive operation defines a partial ordering such as $a \leq_s b$ iff a+b=b. Additionally * is intensive, that is, $\forall a,b \in A \Rightarrow a * b \leq_s a$.

A semiring-based constraint system is a tuple <S,D,V> where S is a semiring, D is a finite set and V is an ordered set of variables. A constraint over such a system is a tuple <def,con> where con$\subseteq$V is the type of constraint and def contains the value of the constraint. Thus def assigns a value from the semiring to each combination of values of the variables in con. This value can be a probability, a cot, a preference etc. A SCSP then is a tuple <C,v> where v$\subseteq$V and C is a set of constraints.

Given two constraints <def_1,con_1> and <def_2,con_2> over the above constraint system, their combination is defined as <def,con>=<def_1,con_1> $\otimes$ <def_2,con_2> where Con=$con_1 \cup con_2$, where $\cup$ is the union operation over sets, def=$def_1(t \downarrow^{con_2}_{con_1}) * def_2(t \downarrow^{con_2}_{con_1})$ where $t \downarrow^{con_i}_{con_i}$ denotes the part of the tuple t corresponding to variables in con_1. The $\otimes$ operation is commutative and associative, since the * operation is. Moreover, since * is monotone over $\leq$s, adding constraints will not increase the value associated with any tuple t.

For a given constraint system CS=<S,D,V> where c= <def,con> a constraint over CS, and a set I of variables with I $\subseteq$V, the projection of c over I, c$\Downarrow_I$ is the constraint <def',con'> over CS with con'=I$\cap$con, where $\cap$ is the intersection operation over sets and def'(t')= $\sum\limits_{\{t | t \downarrow^{con}_{I \cap con} = t'\}} def(t)$. The solution sol(P) of a constraint problem P=<C,con> over a constraint system CS is defined as sol(P)= $(\otimes C)\Downarrow_{con}$. The optimum level of consistency oLevel(P) is obtained if we first obtain the solution and then projects it over the empty set of variables. Typically the oLevel(P) yields an estimation of how much the solution satisfies the constraints of the problem.

2.3 Modeling RBAC policies using soft-constraints

2.3.1 RBAC hierarchies' representation using soft constraints

We can consider two partial orders in an RBAC system [5]: the hierarchy of roles and the hierarchy of permissions. An example of a role hierarchy in a medical domain is given in Figure 1a. Figure 1b shows an example of permissions hierarchy, adjusted to the UNIX permissions representation. Privileges are hierarchically assigned, so that ancestor roles are assigned additional privileges than their descendant roles. A suitable choice of semirings for a multi-domain policy representation can be as follows:

The role hierarchy can be represented by the role semiring: < R,$+_R$, $*_R$, R_0, R_∞>, where

- R is the set of roles in the system
- The $+_R$ operation is defined as: ($R_1 +_R R_2$) is the highest common descendant of roles R_1 and R_2 in role hierarchy
- The $*_R$ operation is defined as the common ancestor of roles R_1 and R_2 in role hierarchy
- R_∞, R_0 are the roles with maximum and minimum privileges. For example in the hierarchy of Fig 1a for the roles in a hospital the Ward Managers have fewer privileges than Hospital Manager, while the least privileges are assigned to nurses.

Next we consider the permission hierarchy and we define the appropriate semiring $<P,+_P,*_P,P_\infty,P_0>$, where

- P is the set of permissions in the system
- The +P operation is defined as: $(P1+P\ P2)$ is the highest permission between P1 and P2
- The *P is defined as the lowest permission
- P_∞, P0 are highest and lowest permission in the hierarchy respectively.

One solution to the problem, adopted in [5] could be to use the SCSP induced by the domain's assignments of permissions to local roles to find the permissions associated with this particular assignment P_1 of local roles to global roles. Then the SCSP P_2 describing the access rights over the shared workspace is being built. If P_1 dominates P_2 then solution is achieved. Among the limitations of this method we can recognize the fact that no roles are considered as critical and that a possible assignment of permissions to local roles could violate several restrictions defined by the local policies, resulting in a security violation as described in Section 1 for the resulting global policy.

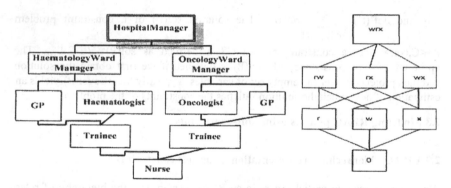

Fig. 1.a (left): An example of a role hierarchy for a medical domain. 1b (right): Example of a permissions hierarchy (adopted from [5])

The above method can be utilized as a recommendation in order to facilitate the administrator's overhead when attempting to merge the local policies. We will expand the applicability of this framework to support the correspondence of roles from one domain to the other, when these roles are not explicitly mapped. At the same time we avoid hierarchy violations during this policy merging process.

2.3.2 Formulating role mappings as a soft constraints multi-criteria shortest path problem

Consider the case where we have two different role hierarchies (Fig 1a). We can represent the roles in this hierarchy by considering a graph G=(N,E) where the roles are represented as nodes in the graph and we assign a weight to each arc e $\in$E from node p to node q (p,q $\in$N). This weight can be a pair of values, associated with the level of each role in the hierarchy (a parameter that defines how important is a role in the organizational hierarchy) and the criticality associated with each role. Now this example may be modeled by two semirings. For the first parameter, we can define a semiring $<N, +, min^*, 0, +\infty>$ where min^* defines the minimum difference considering the result is positive, and $+$ with the classical meaning. For the first parameter of the label, related with the criticality, we define a semiring $<N, +, min, 0, +\infty>$, where min and $+$ are defined with the classical meaning. Consider now the following scenario: According to the technique mentioned in the previous paragraph some of the roles are merged and a number of mappings are established. Now in the case where a role from one domain needs to be assigned the permissions for a role in another domain, we can formalize the problem so as when there is not a direct established mapping from one role in the domain to the other, the system will find (if there exists) the optimal path without additional action to be taken by the domain's administrators. The system simply queries for the target role's permissions. Then we just have to find the shortest path from role p to role v. The cost is measured always counting the parameters assigned to each role. The sole check that needs to be performed, is that there is no hierarchy violation, since the difference from the source to the intermediate roles is not negative at any stage of the path resolution procedure. Of importance is also the discovery of paths where the right-hand (second) terms have minimal differences, implying a similarity in their criticality.

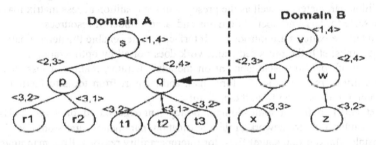

Fig. 2. Example of a role mapping and role hierarchy representation with costs

The problem can be formulated into a Soft Constraint Logic Programming (SCLP) [12] [10] program, which works over an appropriate semiring. In order to find a path that does not violate hierarchy constraints, we calculate the differences between the first values in the pair assigned to each node. We only allow positive differences, meaning that the target role has to be lower in the hierarchy (we consider the different hierarchies and the positions at the same depth as equivalent, independent of the domain to which they belong). Additionally we want to calculate minimal differences based on the second value, so that the criticality of the assigned path is minimal. In the example of Fig. 2, let us consider that a user assigned to role v wants to access some shared resources, which originally demand access rights of role q on the Domain A. There is a direct mapping from role u to role q. The SCLP program will work as follows: v:- c_{vu}, u c_{vu}:-$<1,7>$, The first term of c_{vu} is calculated by subtracting the hierarchy differences (considering they are positive)

$$\sum_{i}^{i,j:neighbours} \sum_{j,i \in J} (x_i - x_j),$$ while the second term $\{min[\sum_{i}^{i,j:neighbours} \sum_{j} (y_i + y_j)]\}$ is based

on the sum of the criticalities which can be set arbitrarily, to hinder administrators from activating these intermediate roles unnecessarily. Accordingly, for transition from u to q we have, u:- c_{uq} ,q c_{uq} :-<0,7>. Additionally, we can pose different restrictions, or there is the case that the role assignment is not allowed since there will be some violation of the hierarchy, or that there does not exist mapping. In this case there are two options: either the request is denied either the demand is resolved based on the administrator's intervention, who should create a new appropriate mapping. By modeling the network as described, we enable policy merging to a high extent, retaining hierarchy related restrictions and thus enabling a secure and scalable solution for the problem of secure interoperation.

3. Related work and Discussion

The problem of enabling the establishment of a multi-domain coalition is a challenging one and attracts lately considerable research focus due to the impact and benefits related with its realization.

In [3] a negotiation language is introduced, based on the RCL2000 [6] RBAC policy language. All the language statements have an equivalent in Restricted First Order Predicate Logic (RFOPL) statements. This framework is flexible, though the number of coalition parameters as well as the presence of the coalition access matrix makes it hard to scale for large number of domains and large number of resources.

In [8] interface policies are introduced. Interface policies enable the determination of role mappings; still the proposed framework does not allow optimization and poses the burden of coalition establishment on the administrator, making it less flexible. Additionally there is no specific formalism and support from tools to facilitate the formation of the coalition from the beginning.

Joshi et al.[9], define a multi-domain policy language based on their X-RBAC model. Under this framework, role codification parameters are stored in XML (eXtensible Markup Language) files, for interoperability reasons. Role mappings are manually specified in separate files, demanding a lot of human effort in order to set up the coalition. There is no support yet from automated tools while updates to local policies are difficult to reflect in the global policy.

In [5] a negotiation scheme, which utilizes soft constraints, is being introduced. We extend this model by incorporating the notion of policy mappings that enable cross-organizational role assignment and by retaining at the same time the basic principles of security and autonomy under secure interoperation. Additionally, in our approach, by modeling role hierarchies using the graph approach and assigning weights to roles we enable the determination of optimal paths and additional policy mappings not explicitly stated by domain's administrators, without violating role hierarchy restrictions and by activating the minimum number of critical roles. Under this prism, our framework proves to be more flexible by incorporating more parameters in the role determination process and allowing optimization by codifying the domain's preferences as soft constraints.

4. Conclusions

We have expressed the negotiation problem between autonomous domains as a constraint satisfaction problem. Interoperation is achieved through role mappings, which can be established as a solution to the constraint satisfaction problem. In order to enable role additional assignments not explicitly stated by the administrators, without violation of security constraints, we cast the problem of role assignment to a multi-criteria shortest path problem. Our solution is scalable and can be used as a support tool for the coalition responsible administrators.

Future work can address issues like negotiating policies when there is no established mutual trust between the domains and thus policy exposure would result to some domains attempting to gain advantage over others.

References

1. Gong L. and Qian X. "The complexity and composability of secure interoperation". In *Proceedings of the Symposium on Security and Privacy*, pages 190–200, Oakland, CA. IEEE Press, 1994.
2. Belsis P., Gritzalis S., Katsikas S., "A scalable Security Architecture enabling coalition formation between autonomous domains". To appear In *"Proceedings of the IEEE ISSPIT International Conference on Signal Processing and Information Technology"*, December 2005 Athens, Greece.
3. Khurana H., Gligor V. D. and Linn J., "Reasoning about Joint Administration of Coalition Resources", In *Proc. of IEEE International Conference on Distributed Computing Systems (ICDCS)*, pp.429-439, Vienna, Austria, July 2002, IEEE press..
4. Sandhu R., Ferraiolo D., and Kuhn R. "The NIST model for role-based access control: towards a unified standard". In *Proceedings of the Fifth ACM Workshop on Role-Based Access Control (RBAC'00)*, pages 47–63, 2000, ACM press.
5. Bharadwaj V. and Baras J. "Towards automated negotiation of access control policies", In *Proceedings of the 4th IEEE International workshop on Policies for distributed Systems and Networks (POLICY 03), pp. 77-86, IEEE press*
6. Ahn G-J. and Sandhu R., "Role-based Authorization Constraints Specification", *ACM Trans. on Inf. System Security*, pages 207-226, Vol. 3, No. 4, Nov. 2000.
7. Organization for the Advancement of Structured Information Standards (OASIS), XACML Extensible access control markup language specification 2.0, OASIS Standard, (available at http://www.oasis-open.org) (Accessed May 2005).
8. Belokolsztolszki A., Eyers D., Moody K., "Policy Contexts: Controlling Information Flow in Parameterised RBAC", In *Proc. of the 4th International Workshop on Policies for Distributed Systems and Networks (POLICY'03)*, IEEE Press, pp. 99-110.
9. Joshi J.B.D., Bhatti R., Bertino E., Ghafoor A., "Access Control Language for Multi-Domain Environments", *IEEE Internet Computing*, Nov. 2004, pp. 40-50, IEEE press.
10. Bistarelli S., "Semirings for Soft Constraint Solving and Programming", Springer Lecture Notes in Computer Science, Vol. 2962, 2004.
11. Bistarelli S., Montanari U., Rossi F. "Semiring-Based Constraint Logic Programming: Syntax and Semantics, , in *ACM Transactions of Programming. Languages and Systems (TOPLAS)*, ACM Press, Pages: 1 - 29 Vol. 23, issue 1, 2001
12. Bistarelli S., Montanari U. and Rossi F. "Semiring-based Constraint Solving and Optimization", in *Journal of the ACM*, vol.44, n.2, pp. 201-236, March 1997.

Learning context models for the recognition of scenarios

Sofia Zaidenberg, Oliver Brdiczka, Patrick Reignier and James Crowley
Laboratoire GRAVIR
655, avenue de l'Europe
38334 Saint-Ismier Cedex, France
{Zaidenberg, Brdiczka, Reignier, Crowley}@inrialpes.fr

Abstract. This paper addresses the problem of automatic learning of scenarios. A ubiquitous computing environment must have the ability to perceive its occupants and their activities in order to recognize a context and to provide appropriate services. A context (a scenario) can be modeled as a temporal sequence of situations. Hard coding contexts by hand is a complex task. Our goal is to learn these context models based on a set of videos showing actors playing predefined scenarios. Once these models are learned, we can use them to classify new scenarios. Hidden Markov Models (HMMs) are particularly well suited for problems with a strong temporal structure; they are easily adaptable to variability of input and robust to noise. But two problems need to be addressed: how many HMMs do we need for all possible scenarios and how many states for each HMM. We propose in this paper an approach based on an incremental algorithm addressing these two problems. Under the best conditions we obtained the minimal error rate of 1.96% (2 errors in 102 validation entries).

1   Introduction

The goal of Ubiquitous computing is to build a computerized space serving human activities. This computerized space has to take into account the multiplicity of the platforms and to *perceive the context* for a better comprehension and anticipation of the user's needs.

A context can be defined as a temporal sequence of situations [2]. A situation is a set of entities playing roles. For example, a lecture scenario can be defined as a set of four situations: persons entering a room *followed by* an alternation of lecturer speaking and someone in the audience asking a question, *followed by* attendees

Please use the following format when citing this chapter:

Zaidenberg, Sofia, Brdiczka, Oliver, Reignier, Patrick, Crowley, James, 2006, in IFIP International Federation for Information Processing, Volume 204, Artificial Intelligence Applications and Innovations, eds. Maglogiannis, I., Karpouzis, K., Bramer, M., (Boston: Springer), pp. 86–97

leaving the room. Specifying a context manually can be a difficult task. The goal here is to let the system automatically learn the context model from a training set of videos.

The contexts we want to learn are: *walking, browsing, fainting, leaving bags behind, meeting, walking together and splitting up, two people fighting*. The videos are part of the CAVIAR project and can be found on the project web site [1].

The Caviar project defines a hierarchy of perceptual components (see Fig. 1). It goes from low level images analysis to high level context interpretation. Each video is associated with an XML file describing for each frame the entities with their position, movement, role and situation. Groups of entities are detected as well, and described by the same elements (movement, role and situation). These files (called *Ground Truth*) have been created manually. They can be used to validate low level perceptual components or, in our case, to replace them as they were not available at the beginning of the project.

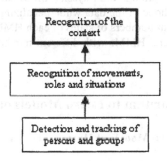

Fig. 1. Hierarchy of components for the perception of context

2 Related Work

The problem of recognizing human activities from videos using machine learning techniques is widely addressed. We can distinguish probabilistic approaches from deterministic ones. Most of the existing works in the probabilistic area use Hidden Markov Models (HMMs) because of their adequacy for temporally correlated sequential data. The study undertaken by [7] relates to the modeling of interactions for the automatic analysis of multimodal group actions in meetings. They first deal with individual actions and then model the interactions by HMMs. Group actions in meeting were as well studied by [14] who proposed a two layer HMM framework. A lot of work has been done to detect usual and unusual activities [1], [4], [5], [6], [13], [15]. Other probabilistic methods have been undertaken: [12] models sequential activities by *Propagation Networks* which can take into account parallel activities. An alternative to HMM methods are *Context-free Grammars* used by [3], [8], [9]. There is no learning in this case and the model is predefined.

---

[1] European CAVIAR project/IST 2001 37540: http://homepages.inf.ed.ac.uk/rbf/CAVIAR/

All these methods, as they are presented, are not quite appropriate for our problem because we do not deal directly with videos but we have higher level information like the movement or the role of entities at every frame. For instance, we know that at a particular frame, a person is "*walking*" (her movement) and is a "*fighter*" (her role).

However, our activities have a temporal structure and we need the model to integrate variability of input. We also need robustness to noise because of the perception algorithms providing our input. These constraints point us to probabilistic methods, and precisely to HMMs.

When using HMMs, well-defined training algorithms, such as Baum-Welch [10], do exist, however the number of states of each HMM must be given "by hand". Some work has been done to optimize the number of states of each HMM in a classification system: [16] propose for instance to set the length of the model to a fraction of the average number of observations of the sequences used to learn the HMM. This fraction is chosen by measuring the recognition rate with different values. A classical model selection criterion is the Bayesian Information Criterion [11] (*BIC*), which maximizes the likelihood of the data while penalizing large-size models. Our method as well tries different numbers of states of each HMM. However our method is exhaustive: we keep several HMMs with different numbers of states (see section 3.3.1).

3 An Incremental Algorithm to Learn Models of Scenarios

3.1. An Approach to Learn Models of Human Activity

Our training set is composed of videos where main actors are playing a predefined scenario. However, secondary actors may be present and play a different scenario. Thus we separate different individuals for each video and label their activity.

To learn the context models, we first classically split the video set into two separate sets: the training and the validation set. To learn the training set, we have considered two approaches: a *supervised* one and an *unsupervised* one. In the first case, we identify five different scenarios and we assign a number of individuals to each scenario. A model is then learned for each scenario in order to represent the assigned individuals. This manual method was tested but, as it will be clear in section 4, results obtained are not as good as with the unsupervised method. Thus, only this last method will be detailed in the following.

In the second case, we use an automatic and *incremental* algorithm (see section 3.3 below) to learn the necessary number of models. We consider each person and compute a "score" of the person's activity on each existing model and compare it to a fixed threshold in order to see if we already have a model that describes this activity. If so, we re-learn that model including this activity. Else, we create a new model learned with the person's activity.

3.2. Feature Extraction from the Ground Truth

The input of an HMM is a sequence of observations. These observations are triplets per frame and entity. They are given by the *Ground Truth* (see Fig. 2). For practical reasons, we transform these triplets into numbers with no information loss [2].

```
<movement evaluation="1.0">walking</movement>
<role evaluation="1.0">walker</role>
<situation evaluation="1.0">moving</situation>
```

Fig. 2. A quote from the XML description of a video.

Table 1. Numbering of all existing values of movements, roles and situations

– "movement": 4 different values – "role": 7 different values – "situation": 4 different values

walking	1		walker	1		moving	1
inactive	2		browser	2		browsing	2
active	3		none	3		inactive	3
running	4		fighter	4		none	4
			leaving group	5			
			leaving victim	6			
			leaving object	7			

Each symbol is first transformed into a number (Table 1). By enumeration, the 3-vector is then transformed into a unique number: the HMM observation. For instance the triplet [walking, browser, moving] becomes [1, 2, 1] and then it becomes the code 5.

3.2.1. Normalizing the Sequences

An observation sequence is the series of observation codes of one entity through all video frames. These sequences are the inputs of our system.

The "score" of a sequence for an HMM is computed using the *Viterbi* algorithm. This "score" corresponds to the probability for a sequence to be generated by this HMM. The order of magnitude of this probability varies with the length of the sequence. If we add an observation to a sequence (for instance, an entity walking during 20 frames instead of 19), the context might not change, however probabilities on the various HMMs will.

As explained in section 3.3, we need to compare the absolute value (the "score") of different sequences on a same HMM. To be able to make this comparison, we must normalize the length of all the sequences. We have chosen a size of 100 observations, which seemed reasonable and much less than the original size of se-

---

[2] In particular, it is easier with the Java HMM library we are using, called *Jahmm*: http://www.run.montefiore.ulg.ac.be/~francois/software/jahmm/

quences[3]. Here is an example on a schematic sequence of the activity "browsing", which consists of alternating the punctual actions "walking" and "browsing" (the punctual action "browsing" means consulting an information desk):

168×"walking"	+	174× "brows-ing"	+	168× "walk-ing"	=	510 observa-tions
⇩		⇩		⇩		⇩
33× "walking"	+	34× "browsing"	+	33× "walking"	=	100 observa-tions

We change the scale of the sequence without changing its aspect and the proportions of the different observations.

3.3. Automatic Choice of the Models to Learn

Persons with the same activity can produce very different observation series. Having just one HMM for each scenario means that this single HMM must be able to learn all those differ-ent observation series. At the same time, there are videos where the activity of a person is not very clear (for instance, someone coming near an information desk and slowing down in front of it: is it a browsing or just a walking by scenario?).

To overcome those problems, we have decided to let the system auto-organize the number of HMMs that are needed and how the videos will be grouped in terms of activities.

The incremental algorithm is described by Fig. 3 and is composed of the following steps:

1) **Initialization:** We create an initial HMM learned on one sequence randomly chosen. This first model is the starting point of the following loop.
2) **Loop on the sequences of the learning set:** We consider every sequence from the learning set at a time and apply the following steps:
   a) We evaluate the current sequence on each existing HMM using the Viterbi algorithm. We choose the HMM with the highest probability to have generated the sequence.
   b) If this maximal probability of "generation" is greater than a threshold[4], we assign the current sequence to the chosen HMM and we learn it again on the sequences it already had, plus the newly added sequence.
   c) If this maximal probability is less than the threshold, this means that there is no HMM that describes well enough the activity of the current sequence. This sequence represents a new scenario. We create a new HMM and learn it with the current sequence only. This new HMM is then integrated into the learning loop on the same basis as the other HMMs.

This algorithm lets the machine decide which and how many models to create. In the section 4.1 we will compare this method with the manual one.

---

[3] The average length of sequences is near 500. Sequences are that long because of numerous repetitions of attributes (movements or roles of entities do not change very often, they are stable).

[4] This threshold is set by hand, but we tested the influence of this choice in section **Error! Reference source not found.**.

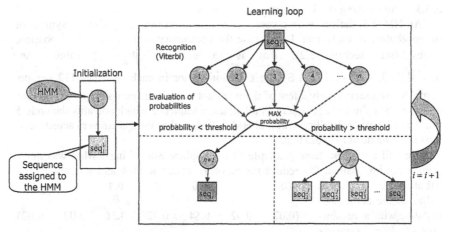

Fig. 3. Schema of the learning algorithm

3.3.1. Automatic Choice of the Number of States

One limitation of the HMMs is that we have to choose the number of states for each model. To avoid under fitting or over-fitting problems if the number of states is too low or too high, we learn several HMMs with different numbers of states for the same scenario. This method lets the machine decide and spares us a decision we might not be able to make correctly. We call this set of HMMs learned on the same sequences but with different numbers of states, a class.

In our experiments a class is composed of HMMs whose number of states varies between 1 and 8. We can count the number of sequences choosing each particular HMM and notice that some of them are never chosen and some are chosen more frequently then others. We could a posteriori decide to delete the unused HMMs and even to keep only the most popular one of each class. This would be similar to [16] where the authors choose the number of states of each HMM in order to maximize the global recognition rate. In our case there is no limitation in us-ing the exhaustive method.

3.3.2. Cross-Validation

In order to evaluate the quality of our models, we use *cross-validation*. We sepa-rate randomly our 147 sequences into two subsets:

– **A training set** composed of 30% of the sequences and used only to learn the models;

– **A validation set** composed of 70% of the sequences and used only to validate the models.

Because this partition has a huge influence on the resulting models, we repeat the whole process n times with a different random partition of the Ground Truth sequences each time.

3.3.3.   Smoothing the Emission Probabilities

An HMM is defined with a vector of emission probabilities of every symbol of its vocabulary in each state. In our case the vocabulary is composed of all possible codes (see section 3.2), that is to say $M = \|V\| = 112$ symbols, and $V = \{1, 2, 3, \cdots, 111, 112\}$. So the emission vector in each state has 112 components, but in practice only few of them are not zero. If the emission probability for a symbol, say the code 5, is zero in all states, a sequence which contains the code 5 will have a zero probability with that HMM. This makes the system very sensitive to noise and we need to avoid that.

We will apply the same principle as in "Laplace Smoothing": what was never seen is not impossible. We reduce the non-zero values to 90% and we equally distribute the collected value on the zeros. For instance with a vocabulary of $M = 7$ symbols we would perform the transformation opposite.

$$(0 \quad\quad 0 \quad\quad \mathbf{0.6} \quad\quad 0 \quad\quad \mathbf{0.4} \quad\quad 0 \quad\quad 0)$$
$$\Downarrow \quad\quad\quad\quad\quad \Downarrow$$
$$(0.02 \quad 0.02 \quad \mathbf{0.54} \quad 0.02 \quad \mathbf{0.36} \quad 0.02 \quad 0.02)$$

With this modification, a noisy sequence will still have a chance to be correctly classified. This also means that we will never have the probability 0, but the order of the probabilities for one sequence on all the HMMs will not change because of this smoothing.

3.3.4.   Adding Information about Groups of Persons

The Ground Truth contains labels about groups of persons at each frame. These groups are labeled like the objects, with movement, role and situation attributes. We also have the infor-mation about who are the group members. We tested two methods taking this into account.

The first method consists in adding a boolean attribute of membership to each object at each frame. The codes are now based on the vector of attributes [movement, role, situa-tion, group], for instance [walking, browser, moving, 0].

But the Ground Truth contains hand made labels . A real tracker will not always be able to distinguish persons who are too close, within a group. When the tracker gets confused between persons, it will assign the attributes of the group to each member. We also made this substitu-tion in order to test this case and compare the results with the first method (see section 4.1).

3.3.5.   Consequence of the Incremental Algorithm: the Labeling of the Models

Using the learned models for classification

Once the models learned, to classify a new entry the system will compare it to every model. Each model will compute a "score" as response to the entry. The output of the classification is the model or the class which had the best score and which correspond the best to the entry.

Evaluation of the classification output

To evaluate the results of our method we need a quality criterion: the percentage of misclassified validation sequences. Our output is a class of HMMs. To know if the activity represented by this class corresponds to the activity of the sequence, we need a label for the sequence and one for the class. We already have labels of sequences, but how to label a class which was automatically created?

We get the label, which represents the scenario or activity modeled by the class, by looking at the labels of the sequences used to learn its HMMs. These labels are composed of key words like "walking", "waiting" or "fighting". A label can contain several key words when the activity is not clear or if there are two activities in the sequence. We count the number of times each key word appears in the labels and we keep the most frequent ones. So the labels of classes are also composed of several key words, which imply that the created classes may overlap.

Fig. 4. A frame from the testing scenarios

4. Tests and Results

To realize the following tests we used the validation set described in section 3.3.2. Fig. 4 shows a frame from the CAVIAR scenarios used in this work where a person is reading an information desk. His role is therefore "browser".

4.1 Evaluation of the Incremental Algorithm and of the Additional Group Information

We tested 6 combinations of possibilities to compare the reference method where we define 5 classes by hand, and the incremental algorithm where classes are automatically created. In both cases we tested the two methods described in section 3.3.4 taking into account the information about groups of persons.

The results in Table 3 show that the automatic method where the machine organizes itself produces better results than when we choose the scenarios to learn by hand. Besides, the infor-mation about groups of individuals seems not to improve the results.

We can notice that the standard deviation of the results on different random partitions is quite high. For instance in the test number 5, executed on 20 random partitions, the average er-ror percentage is 10.44%, and the standard deviation is 5.40% (over 102 validation sequences). This is explained by the dependence of our method on the ordering of the training data.

Table 2. The tests executed on 20 random partitions (for tests 4, 5 and 6).

Test number	Method to create the classes		Groups of individuals		
	Supervised	Unsupervised	Ignored	Boolean attr.	Replace by group attrs.
1	×		×		
2	×			×	
3	×				×
4		×	×		
5		×		×	
6		×			×

Table 3. The results obtained on different tests

Type of result	Test 1	Test 2	Test 3	Test 4	Test 5	Test 6
Minimal PE[5] on validation sequences	11,65%[6]	13,40%	12,12%	1,96%	1,96%	1,96%
Minimal PE on learning sequences	0,00%	0,00%	0,00%	0,00%	0,00%	0,00%
Average PE on validation sequences	11,65%	13,40%	12,12%	8,77%	10,44%	10,44%
Average PE on learning sequences	0,00%	0,00%	0,00%	3,89%	4,11%	4,00%
SD[7] of errors on validation sequences	11,65%	13,40%	12,12%	4,50%	5,40%	4,10%
SD of errors on learning sequences	0,00%	0,00%	0,00%	3,29%	2,63%	2,94%

4.2. Robustness to Noise

The labels of the *Ground Truth* are made by hand; therefore they do not contain noise. But in the real application of the system, the sensors and perception algorithms below our context recognition tool (Fig. 1) will add noise to the data. For the moment, we do not have the possibility to test our approach on real data, thus we measured the robustness to noise by adding simulated random noise [8].

The results on Fig. 5 below show that when the models are learned on clean data, the system can recognize validation sequences with noise. But when the learning set contains more than 30% of noise, the system cannot recognize clean data. When the percentage of noise is over 30%, the sequences do not have a consistent

---

[5] percentage of errors

[6] Tests 1, 2 and 3 have been executed only once, thus the minimal and average percentages, as well as the standard deviation, have no meaning here. They only do for tests 4, 5 and 6, executed on 20 random partitions of the data set.

[7] Standard deviation

[8] Random noise is not the same as problems that are to face with real low level features, but it gives us an estimation of our method's robustness.

structure anymore and the HMMs memorize sequence more than learn a generalized model. In fact, the number of classes increases extensively (Fig. 6). However, the system is robust up to 30% of noise.

Table 4. The tests executed to measure the robustness to noise

		Learning	
		Clean	Noisy
Validation	Clean	Test CC	Test NC
	Noisy	Test CN	Test NN

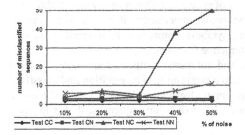

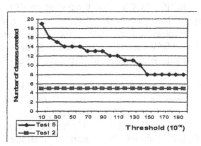

Fig. 1. The number of errors on validation sequences with 10% to 50% of noise.

Fig. 2. The number of classes created with 10% to 50% of noise.

4.3. Tuning the Threshold

Tuning the threshold is a way to influence the number of created classes. When the threshold grows, the number of classes grows (Fig. 8). These classes are more specialized and bring out slight differences between scenarios. When the threshold decreases, the added classes are scarcer and each class is more general and explains different sequences. We measured the variations of the number of errors and the number of classes with the variation of the threshold. The results below (Fig. 7 and Fig. 8) admit to choose the value of the threshold depending on error rate and number of classes.

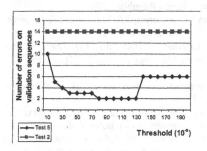

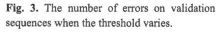

Fig. 3. The number of errors on validation sequences when the threshold varies.

Fig. 4. The number of classes created when the threshold varies.

5. Conclusions and Future Work

We proposed a method capable to automatically acquire the needed number of models representing scenarios of a given training set. The strong point of our method is its degree of automatism. Not only the number of HMMs and the sequences attributed to them are determined automatically. The number of states of each HMM does not need to be specified by hand either. It is easy to add more data and to learn new scenarios.

This approach can be categorized as a *semi-supervised* method. Model creation is completely automatic, the only parameter being a threshold controlling the number of models to create. However, labeling of sequences, that is to say the attribution of a scenario to each individual from a video, is supervised as it is done by a human operator. This step consists in attaching symbols, semantics, to numeric data. In order to avoid that, we could add an "interactive feedback".

In the end we obtained a complete and automatic method, comprising all the necessary steps, from XML conversion into observations to recognition and classification of sequences, while passing by automatic learning of HMMs. Under the best conditions, our tests resulted in 2 errors on 102 validation sequences, that is to say an error rate of 1.96%.

References

[1] R. Bodor, B. Jackson and N. Papanikolopoulos, "Vision-Based Human Tracking and Activity Recognition", *in* 'Proc. of the 11th Med. Conf. on Control and Automation', 2003.

[2] J.L. Crowley, J. Coutaz, G. Rey and P. Reigner, "Perceptual components for context awareness", *in* 'International conference on ubiquitous computing', 2002.

[3] Y.A. Ivanov and A.F. Bobick, "Recognition of Visual Activities and Interactions by Stochastic Parsing", *in* 'IEEE Trans. on Pattern Analysis and Machine Intelligence', 2000.

[4] P. Lichodzijewski, A. Zincir-Heywood and M. Heywood, "Dynamic Intrusion Detection Using Self Organizing Maps", *in* '14th ACITSS', 2002.

[5] G. Ma and X. Lin, "Typical Sequences Extraction and Recognition", *in*, Computer Vision in HCI: ECCV 2004 Workshop on HCI, Prague, Czech Republic, 2004.

[6] D. Mahajan, N. Kwatra, S. Jain, P. Kalra and S. Banerjee, "A Framework for Activity Recognition and Detection of Unusual Activities", *in* 'ICCVGIP', 2004.

[7] I. McCowan, D. Gatica-Perez, S. Bengio, G. Lathoud, M. Barnard and D. Zhang, "Automatic Analysis of Multimodal Group Actions in Meetings", *in* 'IEEE Trans. PAMI' , 2005.

[8] D. Minnen, I. Essa and T. Starner, "Expectation grammars: leveraging high-level expectations for activity recognition", *in* 'CVPR', 2003.

[9] D. Moore and I. Essa, "Recognizing multitasked activities using stochastic context-free grammar", *in* 'CVPR Workshop on Models vs Exemplars in Computer Vision', 2001.

[10] L.R. Rabiner, "A Tutorial on Hidden Markov Models and Selected Applications in Speech Recognition", *in* A. Waibel & K.-F. Lee, ed., 'Readings in Speech Recognition', 1990.

[11] G. Schwarz, "Estimating the dimension of a model", *in* 'Ann. Statist.', pp. 461-464, 1978.

[12] Y. Shi, Y. Huang, D. Minnen, A.F. Bobick and I.A. Essa, "Propagation Networks for Recognition of Partially Ordered Sequential Action", *in* 'CVPR (2)', 2004.

[13] N. Vaswani, A.R. Chowdhury and R. Chellappa, "Activity recognition using the dynamics of the configuration of interacting objects", *in* 'CVPR', 2003.

[14] D. Zhang, D. Gatica-Perez, S. Bengio, I. McCowan and G. Lathoud, "Multimodal Group Action Clustering in Meetings", *in* 'ACM 2nd Intern. Workshop on Video Surveillance and Sensor Networks in conj. with 12th ACM International Conference on Multimedia', 2004.

[15] H. Zhong, J. Shi and M. Visontai, "Detecting Unusual Activity in Video", 'CVPR', 2004.

[16] M. Zimmermann and H. Bunke, "Hidden Markov Model Length Optimization for Handwriting Recognition Systems", *in* 'IWFHR', 2002.

MDA-Based Architecture of a Description Logics Reasoner

Nenad Krdžavac[1], Dragan Đurić[2], Vladan Devedžić[2]
1Faculty of Electrical Engineering, University of Belgrade,
Bulevar Kralja Aleksandra 73, 11 000 Belgrade, Serbia and Montenegro
nenadkr@galeb.etf.bg.ac.yu
2FON - School of Business Administration,
Dept. of Information Systems and Technologies, Univ. of Belgrade
POB 52 Jove Ilica 154, 11000 Belgrade, Serbia and Montenegro
dragandj@gmail.com, devedzic@fon.bg.ac.yu

Abstract. The paper presents the architecture and design of a description logics (DLs) reasoner based on the Model Driven Architecture (MDA) methodology. The architecture relies on OMG's description logics metamodel, tableau metamodel, and model transformations using a language for model transformation. We show an example of DLs knowledge base using UML notation in context of MDA. The idea can be easily applied to implementation of a first-order logic theorem prover. The paper does not discuss implementation details of reasoning algorithms and the reasoner performance.

1 Introduction

Almost every software project needs an analysis of the range of problems that the software being developed should solve [13]. One way is to specify and build the system using modeling tools. For example, a modeling tool such as UML supports full development life-cycle of such software: design, implementation, deployment, maintenance, evaluation, and integration with other systems [16]. Model Driven Architecture (MDA) is an approach to IT system specification that separates the specification of functionality from the specification of implementation on a specific technology platform [10].

The basic notations in description logics (DL) are concepts (unary predicate) and roles (binary predicates) [2]. One of the most important constructive properties of DLs is their reasoning services, which can be applied for reasoning with ontologies. Some publicly available implementations of DLs reasoners [7], [6], [15] can reason

Please use the following format when citing this chapter:

Krdzavac, Nenad, Djuric, Dragan, Devedzic, Vladan, 2006, in IFIP International Federation for Information Processing, Volume 204, Artificial Intelligence Applications and Innovations, eds. Maglogiannis, I., Karpouzis, K., Bramer, M., (Boston: Springer), pp. 98–105

with ontologies, but the authors of those reasoners did not implement their reasoners using advanced model engineering techniques (such as MDA) and current software engineering standards.

The goal of this paper is to describe the architecture of a description logics reasoner in an MDA environment, and some benefits of using that methodology to implementant that kind of software. We suggest possible applications of such description logics reasoners as plug-ins to intelligent systems (we exemplify it by the AIR system [5]), or in intelligent analysis of students' solutions in Web-based intelligent tutoring systems (ITS).

In section 2, we describe basic concepts of Model Driven Architecture (MDA) and refer to basic research papers where readers can find useful information about that methodology. Section 3 is the main section in this paper and describes the architecture of a description logic reasoner. That section also explains some benefits of using MDA in the implementation of the reasoner. We show a method for implementing the reasoning algorithms for description logics based on the Atlas Transformation Language (ATL) [8] that is an alternative to OMG's standard [14] for model transformations. Within the scope of section 3, we describe basic concepts of description logics and give example of a DL based knowledge base in DL syntax and in UML notation.

2   Model Driven Architecture

Model Driven Architecture (MDA) is defined as a realization of model-engineering principles proposed by Object Management Group (OMG) [11]. According to [3], there are a few central properties of the MDA:
1.   Four layer architecture and relationships among them (see Fig. 1).
2.   Transformation among the models on the same layers M1 and M2
3.   XML-based standard for sharing metadata, called XMI

The top-most layer (M3) is called meta-meta model layer and OMG has defined a standard at this layer as well - MOF (Meta Object Facility). According to [10], MOF is the language intended for defining meta-models at M2 layer.

MOF defines a set of reflective APIs consisting of reflective interfaces. Java Metadata Interfaces (JMI) is a realization of the standard called JSR040 [4], and JMI defines Java programming interfaces for manipulating MOF-based models and metamodels [4]. JMI interfaces allow users to create, update, and access instances of metamodels using Java language.

In terms of MDA, a metamodel makes statements about what can be expressed in the valid models described in a certain modeling language. Examples of a metamodels are UML metamodel (Fig. 1) and OMG's Description Logics metamodel (Fig. 2) [13]. The next layer is the model layer (M1) – the layer where we develop real-world models. In terms of UML, it means classes and relationships among them. MDA layers are called linguistic layers, but the concepts from the same linguistic layer belong to different ontological layers [1].

There is an XML-based standard for sharing metadata that can be used for all of the MDA's layers. This standard is called XML Metadata Interchange –XMI [12] (Fig. 1).

The object-oriented paradigm uses the terms *"instanceOf"* and *"inherits"* to describe relations between classes and objects. Model engineering uses the terms *"representedBy"* and *"conformantTo"* [3] to establish relations between the models in MDA layers (see Fig. 1). Model-based engineering and object technologies in software development can be viewed as complementary approaches [3].

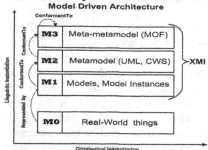

Fig. 1. Four layer architecture of MDA (see [3])

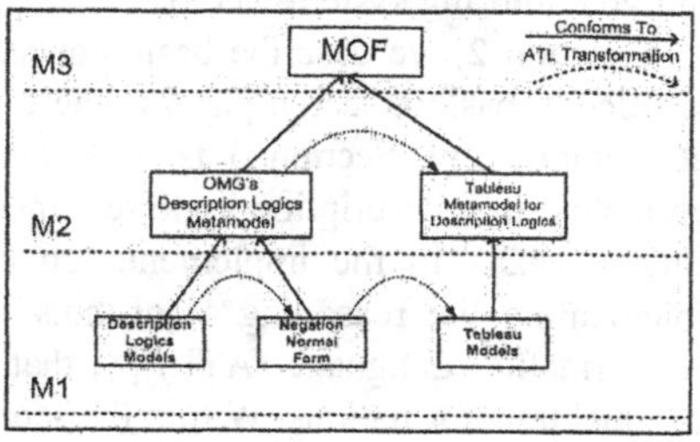

Fig. 2. Architecture of a Description Logic Reasoner

3   MDA-based Architecture of a Reasoner

Our DL reasoner is based on the DLs metamodel, proposed by OMG consortium (www.omg.org) [13], and on the tableau metamodel (Fig. 2).

Some publicly available DL reasoners are successfully implemented in object-oriented technology [15], or in the LISP programming language [6], [7] for very expressive description logics. The authors of such reasoners did not follow software engineering standards, i.e. they did not describe the models of the reasoners in the standard UML notation. The advantage of using such modeling tools is in supporting the full life cycle of software: design, implementation, deployment, maintenance, evaluation and integration. UML supports MDA concepts of software development. Implementation of a MDA-based reasoner includes a few steps:

1. Building the tableau metamodel for description logics;
2. Implementating the repository for OMG's DLs metamodel and the tableau metamodel;
3. Implementating the reasoning algorithms using model transformation.

The tableau metamodel can be built using UML. The tableau algorithm uses a tree (T) to represent the model being constructed [7], hence the Composite design pattern can be used in describing the tableau metamodel.

3.1 UML Model of Description Logics Knowledge Bases

The basic notations in description logics (DL) are concepts (unary predicate) and roles (binary predicates). Specific description logic is mainly characterized by a set of constructors that provides to build more complex concepts (concept expressions) and role expressions [2]. A knowledge base (KB) developed using DL consists of two components, TBox and ABox. Reasoning in description logics (such as satisfiability) is based on tableaux algorithm [7]. A plenty of details in the field of description logics and reasoning can be found at [2].

There are two ways to represent a DL-based knowledge base:

1. Using UML language to describe a model that conforms to DLs metamodel (Fig. 2)
2. Using the definition of the knowledge base and syntax of DLs languages.

Example describes a TBox of family relationships. The first part of the example describes family relationships using DL notations, but the second one describes them in UML and represents a UML model that conforms to DL metamodel proposed by OMG [13].

Example1: Suppose that nouns *Human*, *Male* and *Parent* are atomic concepts and *hasChild* is an atomic role, than means that every Male is Human but not vice versa (Formula 1). Concept definition represents all Fathers that have only male children (Formula 2).

$$\text{Male} \sqsubseteq \text{Human} \qquad\qquad (1)$$

$$\text{Father=Male} \sqcap \forall \text{hasChild.Male} \qquad\qquad (2)$$

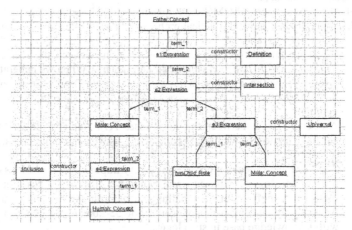

Fig. 3. The "Father" model in the MDA technological space [Online]. Available: http://www.gentleware.com/index.php

The same knowledge base can be expressed using UML language but in MDA environment, Fig. 3. The model shown in Fig. 3 belongs to the M1 layer of the 4-layer MDA (Fig. 2 and Section 3) and conforms to the OMG's DL metamodel.

The semantics (Tarski style) of formulas (1), (2), and semantics of DL model (Fig. 2 and Fig. 3) are the same. According to OMG's ODM proposal [13], the concepts Father, Male and Parent, represented in Fig. 3 in UML notation, are instances of the metaclass Concept. Term_1 and Term_2 are association ends in association relation between the metaclasses Term and Expression. Term_1 represents dyadic constructor, but Term_2 represents monadic constructor [13].

3.2   Implementation of the Repository for Description Logics and Tableau Metamodels

The repository is used for storing and retrieving the models that conform to both DLs and tableau metamodels. It is built using the Metadata Repository (MDR) for NetBeans project (www.mdr.netbeans.org) and Java metadata interfaces (JMI). According to [4], the JMI specification defines Java mappings for MOF. The repository provides standard services for creating, accessing, updating, deleting and validating metadata. There are a few steps in implementing the repository for both metamodels:

1. Converting the UML metamodels into MOF metamodels;
2. Generating JMI interfaces for both metamodels;
3. Instantiating the models in the repository. Imported models conform to both metamodels (Fig. 2).

Using Poseidon for UML tool (www.gentleware.com), the metamodels can be saved in the XMI format. The **uml2mof.jar** tool (www.mdr.netbenas.org) can be used to generate MOF metamodels.

In spite of all the advantages of OMG's DL metamodel [13] and the defined tableau metamodel, there are also several practical problems related to the implementation of the repository for both metamodels:

1. Association ends of the composition relation between the metaclasses *Assertion* and *Instance* [13] have the same name. When we generate JMI interfaces in the association proxy interface we find objects that for different metaclasses have the same name, so we have to change them manually.
2. Association ends between the metaclasses *Term* and *Expression* [13] do not have names, so we have to name them, as we could not generate JMI interfaces.
3. The DL meta-model cannot support a very important class of DLs called description logics with concrete domain [2], as it does not have metaclasses defined in their definitions of both syntax and semantics. Accordingly, the meta-model would not be able to support reasoning with a knowledge base in such logics.
4. During the generation of JMI interfaces all the OCL constraints were ignored and we had to implement the constraints manually.

There are a few advantages of using the MDA methodology to implement the reasoner, wrt. classical object-oriented programming or LISP programming language:

1. Automatic transformation of the model-driven system, from higher-level abstract models to object-oriented models, to a running system.

The metamodels are built using UML. MDR NetBeans Explorer (www.mdr.netbeans.org) enables generating JMI interfaces according to JSR040 [4] standard. These interfaces allow for handling the models at the M1 level (Fig. 2). It cannot be done using object-oriented methodology or LISP programming.

2. Some publicly available reasoners [15] implemented in object-oriented technology used ontology parsers. In our implementation, parsers are not used.

3. Reasoning algorithms, such as checking for consistency, are implemented using data structures like trees or hash tables [15]. In this solution, tableau can be represented using XMI.

Tableau model can be described using XML Metadata Interchange. XMI has a tree structure - every tableau model is a tree [2]. Because of this similarity, it is easy to describe a tableau model (which conforms to the tableau metamodel) using XMI. JMI interfaces generated for tableau metamodel are used for creating, accessing, updating, deleting and validating tableau models according to JSR040 standard [4].

4. Existing publicly available reasoners [7], [6] may not be integrated in today's intelligent metamodeling frameworks, like AIR [5] or intelligent web-based education systems as plug-ins, especially if such a reasoner should be plugged into the Eclipse Modeling Framework (EMF) (www.eclipse.org).

5. Suitability for making further extensions of the reasoner.

Reasoners like PELLET [15] or FACT [7] are YES/NO sort of software. Their reasoning algorithm for consistency answers only Yes or No when checking the consistency of ontology. It is difficult to use them that way in, e.g., intelligent analysis of the semantics of students' solutions in intelligent web-based educational systems [9]. Using JMI interfaces, generated from the tableau metamodel, the tableau model may be analyzed to find useful information about the students' solutions in cases when the students give wrong answers.

3.3 Implementation of the Reasoning Algorithms

A transformation from one model to another is the key technology in the MDA paradigm [3]. OMG proposed a standard [14] for model transformation. Three vital subjects of the proposal that ensure the full realization of MDA are:

1. **Queries:** Take as input a model, and select specific elements from that model.
2. **Views:** Represent models that are derived from other models.
3. **Transformations:** Take as input a model and update it or create a new model.

The Atlas Transformation Language (ATL) [8] is an answer to the **OMG's QVT RFP** [14]. A plenty of useful details about the language is described in [8]. This section describes only some benefits of using such a language for implementing the reasoning algorithms. Some of these advantages are:

1. ATL can be integrated in the Eclipse Modeling Framework (EMF) (www.eclipse.org/gmt) as a plug-in.

ATL is a declarative and hybrid language. The syntax of the language can be integrated into a Java-based environment. It means that the reasoning rules for description logics can be written directly in some Java environment using the expressive power of the language. In the EMF environment, the ATL code can be run and debugged.

2. A transformation model in ATL is a set of transformation rules and Boolean operations.

Reasoning algorithms, based on the tableau for description logics, are based on a set transformation rules [7], including Boolean operations. The ATL language supports set and Boolean operations. The syntax and semantics of the language are described in [8].

3. During the generation of JMI interfaces, all OCL constraints were ignored. We have to implement them manually.

The ATL language is implemented with respect to the OCL standard.

4. ATL is compatible with JMI interfaces.

ATL transformation model is first read using the ATL parser and loaded into Java meta-data repository which is based on a JMI compliant repository. The generated JMI interfaces for both metamodels can be integrated into the ATL language and help in the implementation of the reasoning rules. The interfaces support extension of the rules for very expressive description logics. Although mainly intended to deal with MDA models (based on MOF meta-models and accessible via XMI or JMI), the EMF framework with integrated ATL should also handle other kinds of models from different technological spaces (e.g. Java programs, XML documents, DBMS artifacts, etc.) [8]. This is important in case of using the reasoner in other platforms like intelligent metamodeling frameworks, especially in case of using such a reasoning machine to reason on UML models (not UML diagrams).

The first step in implementing the reasoning algorithms is bridging the DL metamodel and the tableau metamodel at the M2 level (Fig. 2), using the ATL language. At the M1 level (Fig. 2), the DL model in negation normal form must be transformed into the tableau model according to the reasoning expansion rules [7].

4 Conclusion and Future Works

The paper proposed the architecture of a description logic reasoner based on the OMG's DL metamodel. We also proposed a method for implementation of reasoning algorithms for description logics using the ATL language. Such an implementation methodology for the reasoner is flexible in practical uses of the reasoner in today's intelligent metamodeling framework or web-based intelligent tutoring systems. In the future we will try to test our reasoner in various Semantic Web applications.

References

1. Atkinson C., Kuhne T., Model-Driven Development, A Metamodeling Foundation, *IEEE Software* **20** 5 (2003) 36-41
2. Baader F., Calvanese D., D. McGuinness, Nardi D., Patel-Schneider P., The Description Logic Handbook-Theory, Implementation and Application, Cambridge University Press (2003)
3. Bezivin J., In Search of Basic Principles for Model Drive Architecture, *The European Journal for The Informatics Professional,* **5** 2 (2004)
4. Dirckze R., (spec. leader): Java Metadata Interface (JMI) API Specification ver. 1.0 (2002) [Online]. Available: http://jcp.org/aboutJava/communityprocess/final/jsr040/
5. Djuric D., Gasevic D., Damjanovic V., AIR-A Platform for Intelligent Systems, In Proceedings of AIAI 2004: First IFIP International Conference on Artificial Intelligence Applications and Innovations, Toulouse France (2004)
6. Haarslev V., Moller R., RACER Systems Description, *Lecture Notice in Computer Science* **20083** (2001)
7. Horrocks I., Optimising Tableaux Decision Procedures for Description Logics, PhD Thesis, University of Manchester (1997)
8. Jouault F., Kurtev I., Transforming Models with ATL, In Proc. of the Model Transformations in Practice Workshop at MoDELS, Jamaica (2005). Available: http://sosym.dcs.kcl.ac.uk/events/mtip/submissions/jouault_kurtev__transforming_models _with_atl.pdf
9. Krdzavac N., Gasevic D., Devedzic V., Description Logic Reasoning in Web-based Education Environment, In Proceedings of the Workshop on Adaptive Hypermedia and Collaborative Web-based Systems (4th International Conference on Web Engineering), Munich, Germany (2004)
10. Meta Object Facility (MOF) Specification, v1.4, [Online]. Available: http://www.omg.org/docs/formal/02-04-03.pdf
11. Mukerji J., Miler J., MDA Guide Version. 1.0.1, [Online]. Available: http://www.omg.org/docs/omg/03-06-01.pdf
12. OMG XMI Specification, ver. 1.2, OMG Document Formal/02-01-01 (2002) [Online.] Available: http://www.omg.org/cgi-bin/doc?formal/2002-01-01.pdf
13. Ontology Definition Metamodel, Preliminary Revised Submission to OMG RFP ad/2003-03-40 1 (2004) [Online]. Available: http://codip.grci.com/odm/draft
14. Request for Proposal: MOF 2.0 Query / Views /Transformations RFP, OMG Document: ad/2002-04-10 (2002) [Online]. Available: http://www.omg.org/docs/ad/02-04-10.pdf
15. Sirin E., Parsia B., An OWL DL Reasoner, Proceedings on International Workshop on Description Logics (DL2004), British Columbia, Canada 6. - 8. June (2004)
16. Soley R., MDA, An Introduction, [Online]. Available: http://www.omg.org. (2004)

Incremental guideline formalization with tool support

Radu Serban[1], Anna Puig-Centelles[2], Annette ten Teije [1]
[1] Department of Artificial Intelligence,
Vrije Universiteit, Amsterdam, The Netherlands
{serbanr,Annette}@cs.vu.nl
[2] Departament d' Enginyeria i Ci'encia dels Computadors,
Universitat Jaume I, Castellon, Spain
apuig@lsi.uji.es

Abstract. Guideline formalization is recognized as an important component in improving computerized guidelines, which in turn leads to better informedness, lower inter-practician variability and, ultimately, to higher quality healthcare. By means of a modeling exercise, we investigate the role of guideline formalization tools which use two different knowledge transformation principles in producing re-usable knowledge objects useful for representing medical processes and performing updates of medical guidelines. We give a general evaluation of usefulness and state the main requirements for tools that reuse medical knowledge and support authoring of guidelines.

1 Introduction

In recent years, medical guidelines and protocols have become the main instruments for disseminating best practices in clinical medicine. They promote safe practices, reduce inter-clinician practice variations and support decision-making in patient care while containing the costs, therefore leading to improvement of the quality and consistency of healthcare. Concerns for quality, consistency and uniformity of care stimulated the elaboration of a guideline development process for producing computerized evidence-based guidelines. Guideline formalization has been recognized as an essential component in this process, which leads to higher quality computerized guidelines. *Guidelines* set out what should happen, when, and by whom in the care process, and *guideline formalization* is the medical knowledge-driven transformation process by which an informal guideline text is translated into an equivalent but more formal representation, suitable for simulation and verification of properties. The resulting formal specification is tested with respect to requirements for medical processes, such as avoiding critical conditions, asserting the desired ordering of events, or describing how a desired situation can be reached.

Please use the following format when citing this chapter:

Serban, Radu, Puig-Centelles, Anna, Teije, Annette Ten, 2006, in IFIP International Federation for Information Processing, Volume 204, Artificial Intelligence Applications and Innovations, eds. Maglogiannis, I., Karpouzis, K., Bramer, M., (Boston: Springer), pp. 106–118

The potential flaws discovered result in criticism for the part of the guideline that generated the faulty specification.

Currently, the knowledge transformation employed for guideline formalization cannot be performed in one step, due to the complexity of the modeling knowledge required. Even worse, there are no rules for recognizing and transforming frequently encountered medical situations described in narrative medical text into their formal representation. Therefore, the knowledge engineers who perform the formalization cannot effectively apply such rules when similar guidelines are formalized, but rather have to rediscover them from scratch. Recent research on guideline formalization ([5, 6, 7, 10]) propose to solve this problem by making explicit and grouping together the different types of knowledge employed by the knowledge engineers in the formalization process and maintaining a mapping between the textual representation and the formal representation of the medical knowledge. This structuring of medical knowledge according to formal methods techniques ([15]) can then be used in the different phases of the, by now, standardized process of guideline formalization. Tracking of faulty fragments throughout the formalization phases enables guideline improvement.

There are very few tools that currently support a *step-wise knowledge refinement and knowledge tracking methodology for guideline formalization*. We selected two general purpose document management tools which employ different principles for structuring and transformation of knowledge, which makes them suitable for implementing this methodology: the Document Exploration and Linking Tool/Add-ons (DELT/A, formerly known as Guideline Mark-up Tool, or GMT [1, 4, 5]) and Stepper ([2, 3, 6, 7, 8]). Both tools allow the user to define mappings between fragments of two XML documents, providing the necessary support for guideline developers in transforming informal guidelines into more formal representations. Other tools for similar purposes exist, see GEM-Cutter ([9, 10]), or the DeGeL-related tools ([10, 11]), but they focus on other dimensions of guideline development process or do not provide the same flexibility in choosing the target representation model. Our objective is to study the role of refinement and tracking of knowledge objects in producing flexible executable representations of a procedural guideline. By means of a modeling exercise, we investigate the role of these tools, or rather their underlying principles, in producing re-usable knowledge objects which are useful when representing medical processes and performing updates of medical guidelines. We compare the two tools from a knowledge modeler's perspective, according to criteria such as the effectiveness of the model produced, the quality of the representation and the reusability of modeling knowledge across scenarios. We provide a general evaluation of usefulness of the two tools from a reusability perspective and state the main requirements for tools that reuse medical knowledge and support authoring of guidelines.

In the remainder of our paper, we summarize our experiments on applying guideline formalization using Stepper and DELT/A, and provide a preliminary validation of the resulting models. We compare the quality and effectiveness of both transformation tools with respect to producing formal specifications in ASBRU ([14]), an executable plan-oriented language for representing medical protocols. We also explore whether integration of their most useful features is possible.

Both tools were applied on an evidence-based guideline for treatment of breast cancer [12], which provides complex practical situations, suitable to be modeled. We compare the complexity of the transformation process and the quality of the executable model generated by DELTA/A and Stepper, which is given by the number and the complexity of ASBRU plans produced using that tool. Then we summarize the advantages and disadvantages of each tool and the lessons learned from using these tools in guideline formalization.

In DELT/A one typically defines links between parts of two documents which express the same content but in different representation languages. The formalization process is an iterative refinement of various fragments of the text, resulting in an incremental building of an executable model and in mapping increasingly larger narrative fragments to pieces of the model built. As in other mapping and linking approaches, the same transformation step is repeated until no new elements can be formalized.

Stepper uses a multiple-step approach in which the guideline is decomposed into fragments corresponding to a relatively independent set of propositions. These fragments are further split into basic components which can be used to construct an element at the next level of representation of the guideline. Some of these simple transformations can partly be automated and executed independently. Guideline formalization can be viewed as a process consisting of several pipelined refinement steps, performed once for each relevant source fragment, in which only elements produced by the previous refinement step are used.

2   The Step-by-Step Methodology for Guideline Formalization

Stepper ([2,3]) is a tool designed for document formalization based on the idea of multiple-step refinement, in which the focus of each step is to transform the knowledge in the source document into a more formal representation in the destination document. In each subsequent step, the destination document of the previous steps becomes the new source document. The destination element of the last step is typically a formal or executable representation of the original guideline.
A transformation step is described by three components:
1. The schema of the target representation language is a DTD document defining the elements allowed in the target representation
2. The transformation rules file specifies actions (such as, selection, iteration, grouping or splitting) allowed for creating elements in the target representation by using elements in the source file. The Rules file can be created and edited in the Rules editor, which is an integrated module of Stepper.
3. The target representation is an XML file in which elements allowed by the target representation schema are inserted, when the rules for transformation can be applied on the source document received as input.
   The guideline formalization supported by Stepper is actually a gradual refinement of the original text into a set of elements that are closer to the formal representation than the original representation. By manually adjusting the types of refinement performed in each step of the formalization and by building a rules file, a

part of the knowledge necessary for performing the guideline formalization task is made explicit. Later, it can be reused for subsequent transformations.

Stepper uses a step-by-step approach for guideline formalization ([2]), transforming the guideline document from the bottom to the top, in a Document-Centric fashion. The goal of the transformation is to preserve the domain-specific and procedural knowledge conveyed by the guideline, while removing the unnecessary bits. This approach differs from the more predominating Model-Centric approach to guideline formalization, in which a compact conceptual model of the guideline is formulated by the domain expert and gradually converted to a fully operational representation.

There are 3 typical steps used in the step-by-step methodology:

1. Split the guideline text into components that contain procedural knowledge and components that contain definitions of concepts; ignore other parts of the guideline;
2. Group together the procedural knowledge elements associated with the same episode, and the definitions they use, making up scenarios;
3. Based on definitions, combine the scenarios produces in previous step into an executable representation of the guideline.

We have customized this process for medical scenarios that have to be translated into ASBRU:

1. Isolate **narrative structures**, i.e. text describing procedural aspects of the guideline
2. Mark up **medical categories**, i.e. medical concepts connected to the procedural aspects
3. Identify **control structures**, i.e. patterns of control that match the selected procedural fragments
4. Sketch a **preliminary ASBRU** representation, i.e. fragments of executable language that can be mapped to procedural fragments using medical categories and control structures
5. Refine it into the **final ASBRU** representation, i.e. the executable form, obtained by refining the preliminary ASBRU elements through reviewing the control structures and the medical definitions.

The essential change compared to the standard three-step approach of Stepper consists of isolating two types of elements in the "Narrative structures": those which correspond to concepts in the medical vocabulary are obtained by semantic annotation of the narrative fragments using medical thesauri; those describing procedural knowledge are identified using a set of linguistic markers, such as "A {following/after} B", "A {consists of} B", "{if} A {then} B". These elements are then mapped to control blocks of the type "execute action A; then execute action B" or "if condition A is true then execute action B". From these structures a skeleton in the target representation language (in our case, ASBRU) is built. The last step accounts for refining the ASBRU skeleton and integrate its components into an executable representation.

3 Document Linking and Mapping

DELT/A ([1]) is a flexible general purpose tool that facilitates linking and mapping between two XML documents, but has been designed to support guideline formalization ([4]). By viewing knowledge refinement as a particular case of mapping between knowledge components, the linking feature provided by DELT/A supports translation of plain text guidelines into more formal representations. The user defines links between the original guideline and the formal representation, and has the possibility to see how each element in the original guideline translates into the formal representation, and which part of the original text a formal element is obtained from. The tool provides a plugin for translating guidelines into ASBRU as the main formal guideline representation language. The tool is flexible enough to support virtually any knowledge representation formalism for which a DTD has been defined. The existing version of the tool supports validation of an XML against its DTD, multiple and overlapping links between elements of two XML files, evaluation of XPath expressions, filtering and highlighting of XML elements.

The guideline formalization process is captured in DELT/A by having several one-to-one mappings between text fragments in the medical guideline and elements of the target model, which in fact define one-to-many (decomposition) or many-to-one (aggregation) relations. The step-wise refinement approach of Stepper can be emulated in DELT/A, by defining intermediate representations and mappings between pairs of these intermediate representations. Visualization support for tracing the transformation of one knowledge object across several refinement levels is simpler than in Stepper (which provides a cross-level view of one element), but this is due to the fact that guideline formalization in DELT/A is seen as a cascade process in which knowledge is preserved and the decisions in modeling are only taken based on the elements in the immediately preceding representation, not based on elements from several preceding representations, as in Stepper.

DELT/A allows the use of macros, written in an XML-based macro language, which provide the same functionality as the transformation rules in Stepper – a standard refinement of one source element through several rewriting steps. A macro is a hierarchically ordered group of XML elements that are conceptually connected and are often used together. It can be seen as a template, which captures the most frequently used transformations for one source element and can be reused during authoring of guidelines.

4 Defining knowledge transformations

We evaluated the suitability of DELT/A and Stepper tools in clinical guideline formalization, by comparing the ease of use and the quality of the ASBRU executable model generated for a few specific scenarios. One additional object of our investigation was the balance between the domain-specific knowledge and the modeling specific knowledge which is required to perform the formalization of a narrative medical text. We have implemented the knowledge transformation process using the means provided by these tools and studied the gain in effectiveness and quality of representation when this process was repeated for a similar document.

DELT/A and Stepper are both document-centric approaches. Due to the stepwise refinement method used by Stepper, the quality of the target representation (level of detail, presence of complex control structures) depends more heavily on the choice of the intermediate steps taken for refinement. DELT/A can be used to produce quicker a prototype if the mapping between text and elements of the executable language is trivial, because the linking of source and destination elements can be done in one step. However, DELT/A should be regarded as operating at a lower level of conceptualization than Stepper. From this perspective, DELT/A is less semantics-aware than Stepper. Using only one-step for transforming text guidelines into a specification in an executable guideline language (such as ASBRU), as DELT/A does, is difficult. DELT/A is not aware of the different types of control components embedded in one another, while in Stepper this distinction can be made with the right design of refinement steps. However, due to the separation of mapping from semantics, DELT/A gains in flexibility, and there are very few things that Stepper can do which cannot be emulated by using DELT/A macros. Even a multiple step knowledge transformation can be emulated successfully in DELT/A, therefore the two tools can produce comparable results. We want to evaluate which features make them produce better results, which knowledge transformation rules are commonly applied when using them both and whether lessons can be learned about which of these features can be combined when building new applications with similar goals.

Two guidelines written in English were selected for formalization, as they capture recent, clinically relevant, multi-disciplinary, evidence-based material, including recommendations based on expert consensus and based on clinical trials and literature review:
1. the SIGN Scottish [13] guideline for treatment of breast cancer in women.
2. the CBO Dutch ([12]) guideline for treatment of breast cancer.

By analyzing two different guidelines we can assess the differences in the complexity and quality of the transformation with different input text. The parameters that define the quality of the transformation are:
1. the number of anomalies in the guideline knowledge found using the tool;
2. how easy it is to produce an element of the executable model from a source element;
3. the time spent to transform all relevant source elements into executable elements;
4. the quality of the executable model generated (i.e., whether the resulting ASBRU model contains sufficient information to allow simulation of the medical process modeled).

Two narrative chapters were extracted from the SIGN guideline and formalized, first in Stepper, then in DELT/A. Both results could be validated in DELT/A against the DTD of ASBRU. Subsequently, one chapter from the CBO_BC guideline has been formalized, first in DELT/A then in Stepper, using the background knowledge and the project structure collected in the first project (SIGN guideline). This order was chosen to see whether knowledge of the transformation process can be transferred between the two tools and between two different projects of the same tool. This is motivated by the need to investigate the reusability of formalization knowledge acquired in each tool.

4.1. Knowledge Transformations in Stepper

We defined a guideline refinement scenario consisting of 5 transformation steps: Guideline Document (Source) → Narrative Structures → Medical Categories → Control Structures → ASBRU Elements → Final ASBRU representation. This refinement scheme corresponds to decomposition of linguistic structures that make up the original (plain) text of the guideline, according to three dimensions:

a. narrative categories (e.g., definitions, conclusions, recommendations)
b. detailed conceptual (domain-specific, i.e., medical) categories (medical interventions, drugs, symptoms, diagnostic)
c. control structures: action sequencing, decomposition, synchronization and then reconstruction of the formal representation starting from control structure elements.

Narrative Structures are elements such as: definition, recommendation, conclusion, background fragment (containing explanations, evidence supporting a particular treatment), goal statements (expressing medical intentions), procedural fragments (detailing how the procedures are to be done, in which order, what components they have), recommendations, references to literature or to other parts of the document, medical statements. In the subsequent steps we distinguish several refinement procedures applied to each type of element, and focus on the more "formalizable" elements, such as procedural fragments, conclusions, recommendations.

Medical Categories are elements intended to reveal the knowledge composition of the narrative-control structures. Text fragments that have a well-established structure are further decomposed into categorized terms that belong to medical categories. Extracting medical categories from each narrative structure corresponds to a semantic tagging of the text fragments. Medical representation contains the following medical concepts: med_concept | med_goal | med_factor | lab_parameter | med_action | drug | body_part | disease | time_spec | op_relation | med_reference

The transformation from the narrative structures into control ones can take place directly if this step is skipped, but this semantic tagging potentially reveals knowledge gaps that have to be filled in using background knowledge. For instance, it can be detected that a sentence describing a medical action does not refer to which body part it is to be applied, or which drug it uses.

The next step is to extract the elements that describe different programming-like control structures, using a list of words that describe decomposition, aggregation, ordering of actions, temporal constraints and repetition. The Control Representation contains one of these elements: action-goal | condition-action | action-group | scenario | causal-rel | concept-def | ref-to | action-effect | cycle | iteration | action-time | action-effect.

We selected this transformation step, as each of the programming-like structures has a quite different translation in terms of the formal representation language chosen by us, namely ASBRU.

ASBRU Elements step includes all elements of the formal representation of the guideline in ASBRU. However, the resulting ASBRU set of plans does not include yet optimizations, such as, having a minimal number of plans, unique variable names, disjoint variable and plan names, etc used. The last transformation step, from ASBRU elements to Final ASBRU representation, is a refinement and optimization step.

The Preliminary ASBRU and Final ASBRU representations have the same schema, allowing all ASBRU constructs: local and global variable definitions, plans, effects of plans, intentions and plans and termination and completion conditions for plans.

Rules for transformations necessary for guideline formalization were produced on-the-fly, based on the type of knowledge encountered in the chapters analyzed. After the first chapter of the reference guideline was processed, a few knowledge transformation rules were created.

For instance, for processing of the following text fragment:

Definition: Locoregionally advanced breast cancer is used to describe breast cancer which is unresectable on the basis of the classic unresectability criteria: oedema of the skin (peau d'orange), ulceration, satellite skin nodules, etc.

we added the following transformation rules:

Narrative.rules:

    Text → One-to-one (Definition) → Definition

Medical.rules:

    Definition → Decomposition (D_Definition2List) →
    Seletion([MedConcept;OpRelation;Disease;OpRelation;Iteration(0,5,Med_
    Symptom)])

Control.rules:

    Selection([MedConcept;OpRelation;Disease;OpRelation;BodyPart]) →
    Aggregation (A_List2ConceptDef) → Concept-Def

Pre-asbru.rules:

    1. Concept-Def → One-to-One (O_ConceptDef2ContextDef) →
        Plan-library\Domain-Defs\Domain\Context-Def
    2. Concept-Def → One-to-One (O_ConceptDef2VarDef) →
        Plan-library\Plans\Plan-Group\Plan\Value-Def\Variable-Def

Asbru.rules:

    Plan-library\Plans\Plan-Group\Plan\Value-Def\Variable-Def →
    One-to-One (O_VarDef2ContextDef) →
    Plan-library\Domain-Defs\Domain\Context-Def

Based on the usage patterns observed in the transformation process, we adjusted the elements of the transformation, for instance by partitioning the original "Background" element (class) in the "Narrative" representation into two elements: "Definition" and "Procedural Fragment". In the example above, we created the transformation rules allowing for two options for transforming a concept definition ("ConceptDef" element at "Control" level) into different elements at the "ASBRU" level: a definition of a variable that is going to be used at the level of one plan (Variable-Def), or a definition of a context that will be used by several plans. The role of the definition will likely become clear only after all ASBRU plans have been defined, and the dependencies between plans and the variables have been established. Therefore, this transformation of a variable definition into a context definition can take place only in the last refinement step ("ASBRU elements" → "Final ASBRU").

By counting how many elements of each type and which rules were used most often in the formalization of the first chapter of the SIGN guideline, we were able to eliminate the less generic and infrequently-used rules and to select the most frequent ones as transformation patterns.

The formalization of the subsequent chapters took much less time, due to the fact that the elements of the intermediate representation and the transformation rules defined in the formalization of the first chapter were re-used. The time spent for formalization using the Stepper tool has been reduced considerably, when enough transformation rules defined in the first phase could be applied in the second phase. By simulating the Stepper transformations in an application that performs semantic tagging of text and applies automatically the transformation steps (for a given order of the refinement steps, and for a given set of elements and transformation rules), we are able to measure the time spent for formalization. On the other hand, the quality of the resulting formal representation in ASBRU is not as high as that of a manual formalization.

For estimating this quality of the resulting ASBRU representations, we used the following criteria:
1. The number of ASBRU plans generated should be as low as possible;
2. Each plan should have the body part and activation conditions defined
3. Each plan should be executed by another plan, or references to its corresponding medical actions must exist in the background narrative description this plan was generated from.

4.2. Knowledge transformations in DELT/A

Two chapters of the SIGN guideline were formalized in DELT/A separately, in two steps. The initial target representation file was initially empty, and new ASBRU elements were added as they were recognized in the source document. The mappings used the reference ASBRU DTD specification and a set of DELT/A macros built for Text-to-ASBRU transformations.

The formalization was incremental in the sense that different parts of the guideline could be transformed independently and later further refined, based on additional knowledge produced in the transformation. Creation of macros took place in parallel with the formalization, so that, after the first chapter was formalized, the most frequently encountered transformations were stored as DELT/A macros. Therefore, the second chapter was formalized using additional background knowledge acquired in the formalization process of the first chapter. As result, the knowledge engineer produced a more finely-grained and complex model than that of the first model built.

Formalization in DELT/A produced better qualitative representations than Stepper, within a time frame comparable with the one spent in Stepper for the same input. For small and finely structured knowledge objects, the possibility to track directly a formal element to its context in the source document was essential in obtaining a detailed formal representation. This feature was more prominent in

DELT/A, where there was only one formalization step to perform, while the cross-level visualization feature in Stepper helped towards this goal, but involved additional actions.

4.3. Comparing the effectiveness of guideline formalization tools

We formalized the same guideline text extracted from two guidelines in each of the tools, then we cross-validated the results obtained with each tool, with the help of the other tool.

We noticed that in DELT/A more ASBRU plans can be identified than in Stepper, as the transformation process is more direct and the original information is not lost in transformation. This is why we used an independent mark-up of the guideline text to verify that all the relevant parts of text have been processed with both tools. The evaluation has been done based on the several criteria, discussed below.

4.3.1. Ease of use. We evaluated how easy is to set up a refinement scenario and to perform the guideline formalization without previous training. With Stepper it is conceptually clearer to set up a refinement scenario because it is aware of knowledge refinement and splits the guideline transformation process into logical steps. It makes guideline formalization easy without previous training because knowledge is processed at different levels of abstraction or even by different categories of people (medical experts, knowledge engineers, guideline developers). In DELT/A defining the refinement scenario takes more time, but using the macros in formalization is relatively easier than applying the transformation rules in Stepper.

4.3.2. Richness of transformation. The granularity of the elements used during guideline knowledge refinement and the types of transformation rules that can be described determine how expressive the transformation is. In Stepper, the granularity of the elements resulting from transformation is finer than the one used in DELT/A, therefore potentially the formalization in Stepper can capture more formalization knowledge than DELT/A. In Stepper more complex transformation rules can be defined than in DELT/A, such as selection of elements, aggregation of several elements of different types, iteration, and repetition of a particular processing.

4.3.3. Quality of the resulting executable model. It depends on the granularity and complexity of the executable model obtained through transformation. With Stepper, the transformation is a composition of several aspect-oriented transformations at different conceptual levels. This compositionality ensures a more refined result, compared to the more direct knowledge transformation (in one step) in DELT/A. However, DELT/A copes better with changing knowledge, as it does not depend on a long knowledge refinement chain and the changes can be applied faster.

4.3.4. Visualization support. To evaluate how intuitive and easy to use is the visualization support in the two tools, we looked at how easy is to navigate, whether focus on particular parts of guideline is possible while others are hidden, whether several regions of the guideline can be analyzed concurrently, compared, etc. Stepper provides a very convenient cross-level view of an element, which indicates the transformation tree that produced that element, including the order of transformations that have been applied. Different perspectives are given to the modeler, to focus on particular components of the model which is built. In DELT/A, the graphical representation is replaced by a tree-like textual view in which particular language constructs and XPath expressions can be input and matching elements highlighted. However, the focus is on document structure, and does not look from modeller's perspective. The order of modeling steps is not captured. However, from an extensibility perspective, DELT/A is more powerful, as it comes with a set of plugins that can be extended / rewritten to generate graphical representations, though this is not directly supported by the tool itself.

4.3.5. Support for explanation and reasoning. Both tools provide an explicit visualization support for explaining the guideline transformations. Traceability of the steps performed (step history) and connecting the guideline parts with a particular semantics are important in having a better support for understanding the modeling. The Stepper tool provides a feature called "Cross level view" that gives a graphical representation of the transformations done for obtaining a particular element, while DELT/A keeps a counter for recording the order of transformations. However, DELT/A provides a set of views, filters, search and XSLT transformation features which make it potentially richer from an explanation and reasoning perspective.

4.3.6. Facilitating re-usability and modularity of knowledge. An essential feature common to the two tools is the support offered for re-using the transformation steps capturing guideline modeling decisions in other situations, with a minimum of change. In Stepper, the fine granularity of the knowledge captured by the transformation rules allows several complex transformations to be realized by composing several basic transformations. These transformation rules used in each step of the formalization are defined and customized by the knowledge engineer and kept separately in a rules file, in order to be re-used in other translations [4].

5 Conclusions

We compared the implementations of two knowledge transformation principles for guideline formalization, embodied by two of the very few tools that can be used in practice for improving the quality and effectiveness of guideline formalization. The two applications discussed, DELT/A and Stepper, were designed for different purposes: Stepper is a multi-step, customizable document transformation tool, designed for step-by-step knowledge refinement, while DELT/A is a multi-purpose, macro-based, document mapping tool. They have a lot of common, as well as complementary, features, compatible input and output formats (XHTML, XML, DTD) and one common method – cross-document mapping.

The results obtained by formalizing the guidelines with these tools represent valid representations in the target ASBRU language, but still require additional adjustments in order to be executable by an ASBRU interpreter. This indicates that either the text formalized did not contain sufficient procedural knowledge, or the information lost during transformation affected the quality of the ASBRU representation generated. However, the positive impact of the structured guideline development process that these tools implement, on the effectiveness and the quality of the guideline representations generated cannot be dismissed. In the future, separation of domain knowledge from modeling knowledge and maintenance of guideline modeling rules as re-usable components will lead to libraries of pre-compiled transformations that can be imported, tested and applied to specific categories of documents.

The features discussed here represent a few steps in this direction. The refinement process proposed by Stepper and the use of DELT/A macros reduce significantly the time spent in formalization of a guideline for which a guideline formalization process has been configured. Also, the possibility to track a formal element back to its original context in the source document is decisive for a quick understanding of modeling steps and consequently for a better quality of the representation.

As result of our comparison, several requirements can be listed for a guideline formalization tool that would combine their most useful features:

1. execution of multiple, logically independent, **knowledge refinement steps**, which can be traversed both forward (source-to-target) and backward (target-to-source). Stepper supports **visual tracing of the refinement steps**, while in DELT/A a refinement scenario consists of multiple transformations, each involving a pair of documents, and can be reviewed in a pair-wise fashion;
2. **knowledge visualization support** for analyzing the origin, semantic category, importance and precision of data chunks; currently, the history file and the cross-level view in Stepper provide such support, but it can be included in a more natural way as plugin for DELT/A;
3. the **use of macros** (present in DELT/A, absent in Stepper), i.e. the most frequently used transformation rules by which elements in the source representation are transformed into target representation elements;
4. possibility to **customize and iterate the refinement process**, by allowing destination elements of the current step to be included among the source elements of this step; currently, both Stepper and DELT/A support this process
5. **modeling decision support**: user assistance for viewing, editing, summarizing and visualizing available transformations, **support for validation** (checking consistency of an XML file versus its DTD, filtering and highlighting of missing links, etc); DELT/A provides a comprehensive support for this, in Stepper tool new elements can be inserted at the right place in an XML file only in accordance to the DTD schema of the target representation language;
6. **support for semantic tagging and ontologies** in the refinement process, including script support for reporting, refactoring and transformation of parts of the edited documents; Stepper promotes XSL for automating the knowledge transformation, but so far DELT/A has more advanced features concerning the interactive transformation and refactoring of the medical knowledge fragments.

The design principles proposed by the Stepper methodology for guideline formalization provide useful insights for structured guideline development process. For implementation purposes, DELT/A tool is more effective and can be extended more straightforwardly. However, both tools provide many useful and complementary features, which can be reconciled by an application supporting guideline formalization through an incremental refinement of knowledge.

References

1. Votruba, P - Structured Knowledge Acquisition for ASBRU. TR, Vienna University of Technology
2. Ruzicka, M.; Svatek V. - Step-by-Step Mark-Up of Medical Guideline Documents, International Journal of Medical Informatics, vol 70, number 2-3, July 2003, pp 329-335
3. Ruzicka, M.; Svatek V. - An interactive approach to rule-based transformation of XML documents, Proc. DATAKON2003, Brno, The Czech Republic, October 2003, pp. 1-10
4. Votruba, P.; Miksch, S.; Kosara. R.: Tracing the Formalization Steps of Textual Guidelines, in Kaiser, K.; Miksch, S. and Tu, S. (eds.): Computer-based Support for Clinical Guidelines and Protocols. Proc. Symposium on Computerized Guidelines and Protocols (CGP 2004), volume 101, Studies in Health Technology and Informatics. IOS Press, 172-176, 2004.
5. Votruba, P.; Miksch, S.; Kosara, R.: Linking Clinical Guidelines with Formal Representations, in Dojat, M.; Keravnou, E.; Barahona, P. (eds.): Proceedings of the 9th Conference on Artificial Intelligence in Medicine in Europe (AIME 2003), Springer, Berlin, pp. 152-157, 2003.
6. Svátek, V.; Kroupa, T.; Ruzicka, M. - Guide-X – a Step-by-Step, Markup-Based Approach to Guideline Formalisation. Leipzig 13.11.2000–14.11.2000. In: HELLER, B; LOFFLER, M; MUSEN, M; STEFANELLI, M. (eds). Computer-Based Support for Clinical Guidelines and Protocols. Proceedings of EWGLP 2000. Amsterdam : IOS Press, 2001, s. 97–114. ISBN 1-58603-193-7.
7. Ruzicka, M. - XML Knowledge Block Transformation (XKBT). Online at http://euromise.vse.cz/stepper/xkbt
8. Ruzicka M.; Svatek V. Mark–up based analysis of narrative guidelines with the Stepper tool. Proc. Symposium on Computerized Guidelines and Protocols (CGP-04), Praha 2004. IOS Press.
9. A. Agrawal and R. N. Shiffman, Using GEM-encoded guidelines to generate Medical Logic Modules. AMIA 2001.
10. Y. Shahar - A Hybrid Framework for Representation and Use of Clinical Guidelines, in Proc. AMIA 2002, San Antonio, Texas 2002.
11. Shahar, Y; Young, O; Shalom, E; Mayaffit, A.; Moskovitch, R; Hessing, A; Galperin, M - DeGeL: A Hybrid, Multiple-Ontology Framework for Specification and Retrieval of Clinical Guidelines. Proc. of the 9th Conf. on AI in Medicine—Europe (AIME) '03, Cyprus, Oct. 2003, Springer-Verlag Heidelberg, pp. 122 - 131.
12. CBO. Guideline for the Treatment of Breast Carcinoma. CBO, 2002. PMID: 12474555.
13. Scottish Intercollegiate Guidelines Network. Breast Cancer in Women, SIGN#29. SIGN, 1998.
14. Johnson, P.; Miksch, S.; Shahar, Y. - Asbru: A task-specific, intention-based, and time-oriented language for representing skeletal plans. In Pierret-Golbreich C.; Filby I.; Wijngaards N.; Motta, E.; Harmelen, F.v. (eds), Proceedings of the 7th Workshop on Knowledge Engineering: Methods and Languages (KEML-97), 1997.
15. Balser, M.; Coltell, O.; van Croonenborg, J.; Duelli, C.; van Harmelen, F.; Jovell, A.; Lucas, P.; Marcos, M.; Miksch, S.; Reif, W.; Rosenbrand, K.; Seyfang, A.; ten Teije, A. , Proc. Symposium on Computerized Guidelines and Protocols (CGP-04), Prague, Apr. 2004. URL: www.protocure.org.

Accessing data in the semantic web:
An intelligent data integration and
navigation approaches

Mourad Ouziri
CRIP5 – René Descartes University
45, rue des Saints-Pères
75270 Paris Cedex 06, France
mourad.ouziri@univ-paris5.fr
http://www.math-info.univ-paris5.fr/crip5/Pageperso.php?numperson=369

Abstract. We present an original navigation approach to explore data in the framework of the semantic web. Before navigation, data are represented and integrated by jointly using Topic Maps and description logics. Our navigation approach improves the traditional web navigation with two specificities. First, the navigation paths are semantic instead of structural links. Second, it is a subject-centric instead nothing-centric. These two facilities increase the efficiency of information retrieval in the Web. They are implemented in an adaptive interface, which browses, gradually, data as a concept map with rest to user navigation.

1 Introduction

The Web presents a huge amount of heterogeneous collections of data. Application developments, such as e-health, e-business and digital libraries, require access to multiple sources in order to get complete and consistent information. Two many search modes can be used to search information in the Web, query language and navigation. In the first mode [1], user must be expert of the query language and know partial or complete data structure to formulate a query. Considering the number of datasources, query formulation is a fastidious task. Navigation is the most search mode used because it is natural, intuitive and does not require learning any query language syntax.

However, navigation is not efficient in huge collection of data, because it causes the well-known concept of *lost in hyperspace*. That is, user often takes progressively non relevant navigation paths. After some navigation steps, he is confronted to nondesired information space. In this situation, user does not know how to continue the navigation. For example, in e-health doctors may want to get information about a

Please use the following format when citing this chapter:

Ouziri, Mourad, 2006, in IFIP International Federation for Information Processing, Volume 204, Artificial Intelligence Applications and Innovations, eds. Maglogiannis, I., Karpouzis, K., Bramer, M., (Boston: Springer), pp. 119–128

patient. Than, they start search by selecting the given patient from a Web page giving all patients. They navigate from the given patient by following the examination link to get patient exams. In most cases, this Web page presents exaninations of all patients. After that, doctor follows navigation to get practitioners who made the examinations. Suppose that doctor would obtain result of an exam made by a known practitioner. Therefore, doctor selects the given practitioner and navigates to the Web page giving exam results. In traditional navigation, results given in this Web page should be related to all exams made by the given pratitioner for all his patients.

Moreover, when there are many navigation paths from a page, doctor may follow bad navigation paths. Addition of these mistakes brings doctor to nondesired Web pages. Unfortenatly, there is no reverse navigation to reach the nearest Web page previously navigated in order to restart more relevant navigation paths.

In this paper, we propose to integrate data about a defined-domain application and explore the integrated data space using a subject-oriented navigation. Web data are distributed and heterogeneous. To deal with distribution, we use a distributed knowledge representation, Topic Maps, to construct a conceptual graph upon the distributed data of the Web. To deal with heterogeneity, we use description logics to merge data according to their descriptions.

Then, the integrated data is used by a navigation interface. This interface adapts the integrated data to the user profile and allows exploring data in an efficient navigation mode.

2   Related Works

In order to assist user during navigation, navigation interfaces become more and more adaptive. In the context of the Web, these navigation interfaces implement the so-called adaptive hypermedia navigation. Many adaptive hypermedia conception techniques are proposed [2],[3]. These modeling techniques are based on data modeling, navigation structure modeling and abstract interface modeling.

The idea of adaptive hypermedia navigation consists to couple together the domain model and the user model using an adaptivity engine [4]. The domain model represents concepts and their associations of the application domain. The user model represents user objectives, preferences, goals and backgrounds. Adaptation is made by the adaptivity engine using rules [5]. These rules have the form: If event Then action.

Some adaptation rules are executed before presenting the document and others are executed after presenting the document. The rules of the first class are useful to select the document fragments to be shown or hidden and to define the order of these fragments and their visualization specificities. The rules of the second class are mainly used to update the user profile according to this action.

According to [5], hypermedia adaptation is performed at two levels: content adaptation and navigation adaptation. The content adaptation consists to include only pertinent fragments in the presented document, which are organized according to user preferences and goals. In AVANTI system [6], a document fragment can be described using a visual description or acoustic description. For visually handicapped persons, the fragment is presented using acoustic description. As in ELM-ART II [7], the navigation adaptation consist to reorder, annotate, colour according to pertinence of referenced document, desactivated or removed if the referenced document is not pertinent, the hyperlinks of the presented document.

In [16], adaptation is made into two steps: query preview and query refinement. In the first step, the interface presents only some attributes, which are used by the user to specify the so-called *query preview* in order to select only parts on universe of data containing pertinent information. In the second step, the interface presents more attributes, which are used to formulate a *refinement query* evaluated over the data resulted from the first step.

3 Background

3.1 An overview of Topic Maps

Topic Maps [9] is a paradigm used to formalize and organize human knowledge to make creation and retrieval easier in computer processing. It is also used as a mechanism for representing and optimizing resources access. As semantic networks, Topic Maps builds a structured semantic link network on these resources [10].

A topic map[1] is built with topics in a networked form. A topic can be anything that is a subject regardless whether it exists or not. It is the formal representation of any subject, abstract or real, in a computer system such as a person, John, the earth, etc.

Topics can be linked together by associations expressing some given semantics. Topic Maps applications define the nature of the associations. Thus, semantic information or knowledge is specified by the association and especially by topic roles. In Topic Maps, associations can be defined regardless of occurrences. Associations are used to express knowledge between topics and not between occurrences. Topics and associations represent the abstract part of a topic map. The concrete part is represented by occurrences. Occurrences are resources linked to topics. A topic occurrence can be any information that is specified as relevant to a given topic. An example of a topic map represented in XTM [14] (XML for Topic Maps) is shown in Fig. 1.

In the topic map of the Figure 1, Peter and Johanna are represented by topics peter-id and johanna-id, which are associated by the association reified by the topic examination. Each topic of an association plays a role. The topic peter-id is the doctor in the association examination and Johanna-id is the patient in the same association. We note that, generally associations express most important knowledge.

In Topic Maps, anything is a topic. Concepts, objects, associations and roles are represented by topics. In the previous example, individuals Peter and Johanna are represented by topics, the association is an instance of a topic, roles are topics

---

[1] topic map (t, m in tiny) references a knowledge base structured with respect to the Topic Maps formalism (T, M in capital letters)

referenced using PSI (Public Subject Indicator). PSI is a URI to a public topic
maintained (as an ontology) apart from the topic map.

```
<topicMap  xmlns:xlink="http://www.w3.org/1999/xlink">
   <topic id="peter-id">                      /* topics of the topic map */
      <instanceOf><subjectIndicatorRef
xlink:href="http://www.xx.com/onto.daml#human"/></instanceOf>
         <topname><basename>Dr. Peter</basename></topname>
   </topic>
   <topic id="Johanna-id">
      <instanceOf><subjectIndicatorRef
xlink:href="http://www.xx.com/onto.daml#woman"/></instanceOf>
         <topname><basename>Ms. Johanna</basename></topname>
   </topic>
   <topic id="exam-id"> <topname><basename>examination</basename></topname> </topic>
   <association>                        /* topic associations of the topic map */
      <instanceOf> <topicRef="# exam -id"/></instanceOf>
      <member>
            <topicRef="#peter-id"/>
            <roleSpec><subjectIndicatorRef
xlink:href="http://www.xx.com/onto.daml#doctor"/></roleSpec>
      </member>
      <member>
            <topicRef="#Johanna-id"/>
            <roleSpec><subjectIndicatorRef
xlink:href="http://www.xx.com/onto.daml#patient"/></roleSpec>
      </member>
   </association>
</topicMap>
```

Fig. 1. An example of a topic map representing part of a knowledge base in medicine

3.2 An overview of Description Logics

DLs [12] are logics developed to represent complex hierarchical structures and make
reasoning facilities over these structures. DLs are used to build ontologies for
semantic Web [13]. A DL is composed of two parts: abstract knowledge (TBox) and
concrete knowledge (ABox). Concrete knowledge represents a set of facts, which are
expressed by assertions over individuals. Abstract knowledge is expressed using
concepts and roles. Concepts are unary predicates, which represent an abstraction of
individuals. Roles are binary predicates. They represent relations between concepts.

The abstract knowledge is expressed over concepts and roles by using
constructors. Syntax and semantic of some DLs constructors are given in the table 1.
Constructors semantic is given by means of an interpretation $I = (\Delta^I, \cdot^I)$, where,

- Δ^I is a nonempty set which represents the individuals of the concrete knowledge
- $\cdot^I$ is an interpretation function defined as:
  - $\cdot^I (C) = C^I \subseteq \Delta^I$ for each concept C
  - $\cdot^I (R) = R^I \subseteq \Delta^I \times \Delta^I$ for each role R

We consider that C is a concept description and R is a role description. Thus, the
syntax and semantic of the DL constructors are given in [12].

DL knowledge is expressed in a ABox as set of descriptions. A description is defined using the previous constructors. The following ABox knowledge base represents the knowledge expressed using Topic Maps in Figure 1.

Table 1. An example of a TBox representing part of a medical knowledge base

```
doctor ≐ human ⊓ ∀ name.String ⊓ ∀ specialty.String ⊓∀ exam.patient
patient ≐ human ⊓ ∀ name.String ⊓ ∀ natioinality.String ⊓
         ∀ exam⁻¹.doctor ⊓≥1 exam⁻¹⊓ ∀ child.Human
patient_having_child ≐ patient ⊓ ≥1 child
specialist ≐ doctor ⊓ ≥1 specialty
```

peter : doctor	johanna : patient
(peter,'cardiologist'):specialty	(peter,johanna):exam

We have,
$$\Delta^I = \{peter, johanna\},$$
$$Doctor^I = \{peter\}, \quad Patient^I = \{johanna\}$$
$$exam^I = \{(peter,johanna)\}$$
$$specialty^I = \{(peter,'cardiologist')\}$$

DLs provide powerful reasoning facilities on conceptual part (TBox) and others on individuals (ABox). The significant ones are:

- *Subsumption* (⊑): based on concept descriptions, this reasoning allows to explicit subsumption between two concepts. From the example of table 1, the following subsumptions are automatically computed:
  $$specialist \sqsubseteq doctor, \quad patient\_having\_child \sqsubseteq patient$$
- *Realisation*: it consists to affect an individual of the ABox to the most appropriate concept in the TBox. Using the assertion (peter,'cardiologist'):specialty, the realization reasoning infers that peter is a specialist, that is
  $$peter:specialist$$

4 Data integration using Topic Maps and Description Logics

Data representation and integration are important and fundamental tasks to access data in homogeneous and coherent manner. On the Web, data are represented using semistructured HTML or XML models. For HTML documents, data integration consists to link HTML-documents among them using hyperlinks. This is a static and rigid approach. To explore data, Web-documents are navigated by following structural hyperlinks. This is not efficient because hyperlinks are structural and do not consider semantic relationships among documents. XML-based data integration is realized either by a query language for querying multiple XML documents using one single query [18] or by providing a uniform view of multiple XML documents [21]. In order to integrate XML documents, a mechanism to identify multiple instances of a same real object is proposed in [20].

Semistructured data models, OEM [15] and XML, are used in the data integration process [17],[19]. However, using only XML for data integration is not suitable, especially when need data semantics. That is, XML does not give any semantic about tags.

The suitability of description logics for data integration is illustrated in some projects, namely the SIMS [22] and PICSEL [11]. In these systems, datasources are linked together and with the global schema by knowledge expressed manually.

We present an integration process that combines Topic Maps and description logics to make a semantic data integration. First, data sources are represented using Topic Maps in order to track distributed knowledge. However, Topic Maps does not deal with constraints. TMCL [8] is only on specification stage. Secondly, we use description logics in order to track constraints. Constraints are useful in data integration. They are used by description logic reasoning to deduce implicit relations between concepts. The integration process is shown in the following figure:

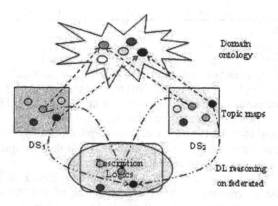

Fig. 2. . Using Topic Maps, description logic and ontology for data integration

The datasources DS_1 and DS_2 are represented using Topic Maps. Two datasource types are considered, namely relational databases and XML documents. For relational databases, topics represent tables and table attributes. For XML documents, topics represent tags. In the topic map of Fig.3, the table (or tag) person and its address attribute (sub-tag) are both represented by topics. These topics are connected to the ontological concepts that they represent using the subjectIndicatorRef tag.

So, semantic integration based on Topic Maps is natural. It consists to merge topics referencing the same ontological concept into one topic in the federated topic map.

```
<topic name=person>                    /*a relational table or an XML tag */
  <subjectIdentity>
    <subjectIndicatorRef xlink:href=http://www.ont.org/PSI/medicalOntology.daml# human"/>
  </subjectIdentity>
</topic>
<topic name=address>                   /*a table attribute or a sub-tag */
  <subjectIdentity>
    <subjectIndicatorRef xlink:href=http://www.ont.org/PSI/medicalOntology.daml#address"/>
  </subjectIdentity>
</topic>
```

Fig. 3. Representing tables/tags and attributes/sub-tags by topics

Then, the federated topic map is used by description logic reasoning in order to provide a consistent federated topic map by computing automatically implicit relations between concepts. Consider that the datasources DS_1 and DS_2 contains the two descriptions:

DS_1 : person $\doteq \forall$ name.String $\sqcap \forall$ address.String $\sqcap$ ...

DS_2 : patient $\doteq$ human $\sqcap \forall$ disease.String $\sqcap \geq 1$ disease

As traditional logics, description logics are not able to make reasoning on distributed knowledge bases. Without consideration of Topic Maps, especially the subjectIdentity of topics, DL reasoning does not infer any relation between person and patient. That is, person $\sqcap$ patient $\sqsubseteq \varnothing$. Semantically, this is not correct.

Consider now that person is human through the subjectIdentity tag of the topic map. That is,

DS_1 : human $\doteq \forall$ name.String $\sqcap \forall$ address.String $\sqcap$ ...

DS_2 : patient $\doteq$ human $\sqcap \forall$ disease.String $\sqcap \geq 1$ disease $\sqcap$ ...

Therefore, DL reasoning infers that patient $\sqsubseteq$ person, which makes semantic connection between the datasources DS_1 and DS_2.

5 Subject-oriented navigation approach

The navigation interfaces on the Web become increasingly intelligent because they automatically adapt the visualized information for each user. Whereas fundamental element of these interfaces is the user profile [5], we present in this section a new approach called subject-oriented navigation, which adapts navigation according to user search.

Subject-oriented navigation. A subject-oriented navigation is based on the notion of subject. A subject is a user-defined object on which a search session is centered. That is, all needed information is related to the subject. Thus, the interface presents only relevant information to the user-defined subject. In the medical domain, patient-oriented navigation allows to get information about a patient, a patient record. In e-business, user would navigate to get all information about a product.

Conceptual schema exactly cardinalized. The federated topic map is visualized as concept card (see fig. 4) that represents at the same time the data and the conceptual schema. So, the concept card is a conceptual schema which represents the real data. Exact cardinalities are showed for the associations. A concept exists in the concept card only when it has relevant instances to the user. Based on this purpose, user query determines the structure and the content of the visualized concept card.

Adaptive interface. The interface that implements the subject-oriented navigation is adaptive, dynamic and progressive. The interface does not present the entire concept card at once because it is not efficient to search information in a huge volume of data. It progressively presents the concept card with the user navigation in order to adapt the content and the structure of the visualized concept card to the user needs. Indeed, as explained before, the conceptual graph visualized represents data. When the data is selected by user, the visualized concept card adapts its structure consequently. Considering the example of the Figure 4, the user selects the patient Paul in the concept card 4(left). So, the interface reconstructs a concept card centred on the patient Paul and the new cardinalities are recalculated. Paul is examined only once by a physician (Medecin in Figure 4), so the cardinality is adjusted. In the federative topic map, there are no results for this patient. Thus, the concept Result (connected to the topic Medecin) is removed from the concept card 4(right).

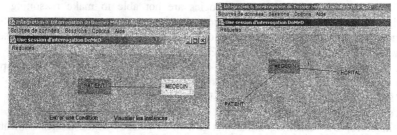

Fig. 4. The left screen gives an example of a conceptual card and the right one shows a concept card obtained after user restriction and navigation to the topic Medecin in the left screen

6 Conclusion

Compared to the traditional web navigation (see Figure 5), the subject-oriented navigation is more adaptive and presents only pertinent data and navigation paths, at each navigation step. Consider that the user wants to get prescriptions of the patient John examined by the doctor Peter. He follows the path Patient, Exam, Doctor and Prescription.

At each step of the user navigation, the interface presents only pertinent data according to the user needs. It presents John's exams, doctors who examined John, and finally John's prescriptions made by Dr. Peter.

If we simulate the same navigation path using traditional approach, useless information could be presented in the html documents presented to the user at each step of the web navigation. That is, at the third step of the navigation, the doctor.html document can not present only the doctors who examined John but presents, therefore, all the doctors stored in the Web pages. At the final step, the prescriptions.html document contains all the prescriptions made by the doctor Peter for all his patients.

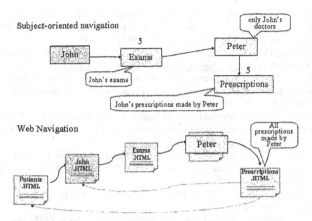

Fig. 5. Our subject navigation approach compared to the traditional navigation on the Web

References

1. Florescu, D., Levy, A., Mendelzon, A.: Database Techniques for the World-Wide Web: A Survey. *Sigmod Records*, vol. 27, n° 3, (1998) 59-74
2. Schwabe, D., Rossi, G., Barbosa, S.D.J.: Systematic Hypermedia Application Design with OOHDM. Proc. of the 7th ACM Conference on HyperText, 1996, p. 116-129
3. Garzotto, F., Paolini, P., Schwabe, D.: HDM - a model-based approach to hypermedia application design. *ACM Transactions on Information Systems* 11 (1993) 1-26
4. Brusilovsky, P.: Methods and techniques of adaptive hypermedia. *In User Modeling and User Adapted Interaction*, vol. 6, n° 2-3, (1996) 87-129
5. De Bra, P., Brusilovsky, P., Houben, G.: Adaptive hypermedia: From Systems to Framework. *ACM Computing Surveys*, (1999) vol. 31, n° 4
6. Stephanidis, C., Paramythis, A., Sfyrakis, M., Stergiou, A., Maou, N., Leventis, A., Paparoulis, G., Karagianidis, C.: Adaptable and Adaptive User Interfaces for Disabled Users in AVANTI Project. *In 5th International Conference on Intelligence in Services and Networks (IS&N '98), Technology for Ubiquitous Telecom Services, Antwerp, Belgium*, p. 153-166
7. Weber, G., Specht, M.: User modeling and adaptive navigation support in WWW-based tutoring systems. *In proceedings of the 6th Int. Conf. on User Modeling, UM97, Vienna, new-York*, (1997) 289-300
8. Moore, G., Nishikawa, M.: The Topic Map Constraint Language. ISO/IEC 13250 (2003). Available at http://www.isotopicmaps.org/tmc
9. Sigel, A., (2000). Towards knowledge organization with Topic Maps. *XML Europe 2000, Palais des congrès Paris*, 12-16 June 2000
10. Fresse, E., (2000). Using Topic Maps for the representation, management and discovery of knowledge. *XML Europe 2000, Palais des congrès Paris*, 12-16 June 2000
11. Goasdoué, F., Lattes, V., Rousset, M.C.: The Use of CARIN Language and Algorithms for Information Integration: The PICSEL Project. International *Journal of Cooperative Information Systems (IJCIS)*, vol. 9, n° 4, (2000) 383-401
12. Borgida, A.: Description Logics in data management. *IEEE Trans. on Knowledge and Data Engineering*, vol. 7, n° 5, (1995) 671-682

13.Horrocks, I., Patel-Schneider, P.F., van Harmelen, F.: Reviewing the Design of DAML+OIL: An Ontology Language for the Semantic Web. *Proc. of 18ᵗʰ National Conference on Artificial Intelligence, AAAI-02,* (2002) 792-797

14.Pepper, S., Moore, G.: XML Topic Maps (XTM) 1.0. *TopicMaps.Org Authoring Group, Aug. 2001. Available at: http://www.topicmaps.org/xtm/index.html*

15.Goldman, R. , Chawathe, S., Crespo, A., McHugh, J. A Standard Textual Interchange Format for the Object Exchange Model (OEM). *Department of Computer Science, Stanford University, California, USA, (1996) 5 p.*

16.Doan, K., Plaisant, C., Shneiderman, B. and Bruns, T.: Interface and Data Architecture for Query Preview *in Networked Information Systems. ACM Transactions on Information Systems,* 1999, vol. 17, n° 3, p. 320-341

17.Papakonstantinou, Y., Garcia-Moulina, H., Widom, J. Object Exchange Across Heterogeneous Information Sources. *Proceedings of IEEE International Conference on Data Engineering,* (1995) 251-260

18.Cohen, S., Mamou, J., Kanza, Y., Sagiv, Y.: XSEarch: A Semantic Search Engine for XML. *VLDB (2003)* 45-56

19.Gardarin, G., Mensch, A., Tomasic, A.: An Introduction to the e-XML Data Integration Suite. *Proceedings of EDBT (2002)* 297-306

20.de Brum Saccol, D., Heuser, C.A.: Integration of XML Data. *Proceedings of EEXTT (2002)* 68-80

21.Camillo, S.D., Heuser, C.A., Mello, R.S.: Querying Heterogeneous XML Sources through a Conceptual Schema. *Proceedings of ER (2003)* 186-199

22.Arens, Y., Chee, C., Hsu, C., Knoblock, C.: Retrieving and Integrating Data from Multiple Information Sources. *In Journal of Intelligent and Cooperative Information Systems,* vol. 2, n°2, (1993) 127-158

An Expert System Delivery Environment
for the World Wide Web

Max Bramer
School of Computing, University of Portsmouth, Lion Terrace,
Portsmouth PO1 3HE, United Kingdom
max.bramer@port.ac.uk
http://www.tech.port.ac.uk/~bramerm/

Abstract. AdviceWeb is a delivery environment aimed at enabling a wide
range of high-quality rule-based advisory expert systems to be created and
made available free of charge to users via the world wide web. Applications
have a uniform 'look and feel', do not require any special software to use and
are fully integrated with other sources of information on the web. A rapid
application development facility is provided which automatically converts
modules written in a simple scripting language into rules and questions for a
production rule interpreter running on the AdviceWeb server.

1 Introduction

Rule-based Expert Systems were one of the most visible and most successful
manifestations of Artificial Intelligence in the 1980s and 1990s, with many
successful applications built, often with substantial commercial value.

The explosive growth of the World Wide Web in the last few years, combined
with the much greater availability of personal computers and relatively high-
bandwidth communications in both homes and offices has led to a widespread
demand for (and expectation of) reliable information on any topic provided free of
charge on request, delivered in a uniform way by a standard web browser.

Given this background it may seem surprising that there are very few Expert
Systems available on the web. Most of the information available is static, and thus
the same for all users. Information tailored to the needs of an individual (if only in a
very basic fashion) is provided on sites run by retailers, bookshops, auction
companies, travel companies and the like, where basic information provided by the
user is matched against large databases of information about available products,
holidays etc. The reasoning used by such systems is too shallow and the databases
too volatile to justify calling them Expert Systems. However, the popularity of such

Please use the following format when citing this chapter:

Bramer, Max, 2006, in IFIP International Federation for Information Processing, Volume 204,
Artificial Intelligence Applications and Innovations, eds. Maglogiannis, I., Karpouzis, K., Bramer,
M., (Boston: Springer), pp. 129–136

sites with Internet users suggests that there could be a high demand for advisory systems on more complex topics that are personalised to the individual, rather than simply extracts from textbooks or general guidance applicable to everyone.

Even if the Expert Systems developed in past years were still available, were all free of charge and could be ported to a PC environment, they would still suffer from the problems that each one would require a separate download of files to a user's PC, they would all have different interfaces and experience gained from using one system would not make it any easier to use another.

The AdviceWeb project (www.adviceweb.org) aims to provide a delivery environment for rule-based advisory expert systems on a wide range of topics to anyone with a standard web browser. Use of the system can be anonymous. There is no need to register, no charge for users and no advertising. There are additional facilities available to registered users, but registration is free and requires only a name and email address to be given, both of which can be anonymised by those concerned about their privacy.

The systems all have a common 'look and feel' designed to appear natural for those already familiar with web-based applications and a standard interface, so that experience gained with using the facilities for one application will automatically transfer to any other application.

A major design aim has been to provide facilities for those who are not computer specialists to develop modules in a straightforward fashion without using any web development tools. Modules are written in a simple scripting language using only a standard text editor and are then uploaded to the AdviceWeb server using a standard web browser. The uploading process automatically invokes a translation program to convert the script into the rules and questions needed for the corresponding expert system module. When the user runs a module a production rule interpreter (written in the server side language PHP) is automatically invoked. This leads to a set of web pages being generated automatically and displayed as a frameset in the user's web browser. The user sees a sequence of such web pages, each with an accompanying question to be answered and supporting information. The sequence of questions is not fixed. Each question depends on the answers previously given.

It is hoped that the relatively little effort involved for the subject specialist to create quite an elaborate rule-based advisory expert system of this kind will encourage accredited module writers, known as *Advice Providers*, to develop not just one system but a suite of systems on a topic of interest. Advice Providers are envisaged as professional bodies or government agencies, rather than commercial companies.

2 AdviceWeb: Basic Use

One of the design aims of the AdviceWeb system is that it should be possible for the module writer, known as the Advice Provider, to construct a module with the minimum of effort and prior training. Ideally Advice Providers should be domain experts not programmers or AdviceWeb specialists.

To this end modules are not written as sequences of web pages, although that is the form in which they are presented to users. Modules are written in a simple scripting language called AWSL (AdviceWeb Scripting Language). AWSL was originally based on the scripting language for the SPSS flowcharting package *allClear 3.5* but has been extended with many additional facilities using tags in a similar way to HTML. Scripts are written using a text editor such as NotePad and are uploaded to the AdviceWeb server using a standard web browser.

Figure 1 shows a very basic but complete AWSL script for a simple application concerning a possible tax concession for providing a welfare service in the UK. The example leaves out many features of the scripting language, which will be explained later, but is sufficient for purposes of illustration at this stage.

```
Are you providing welfare?
    (Yes)
    Is service available to all distressed people?
        (Yes)
        Is the service subsidised > 15% below cost?
            (Yes)
            Is it your policy to subsidise the service?
                (Yes)
                Concession applies
                (No)
                -lab1
                Concession does not apply
            (No)
            > lab1
        (No)
        > lab1
    (No)
    > lab1
```
Fig. 1. A Basic AdviceWeb Script

The script consists of a sequence of questions and answers. The AdviceWeb system (and the reader) can tell which answers are associated which each question by the indentation of the lines. As well as questions and answers there are lines of text, such as "Concession applies", which are called *advice*. The –lab1 line signifies a label named lab1. The >lab1 lines signify 'jump to label lab1'.

A script file is uploaded to the AdviceWeb server and converted to an AdviceWeb *module* simply by completing an onscreen form in a standard web browser. Completing this form enables the Advice Provider to associate further information with the module, including its name, short and long descriptions and optionally the URLs of a home webpage and a Frequently Asked Questions page.

The uploading process automatically invokes the AdviceWeb script converter, which checks the script for syntactic errors, such as questions with only one answer or jumps with no associated labels. Syntactically valid scripts are automatically converted into rule and question files which together comprise the AdviceWeb module that is stored on the server. Modules are written in a special production rule language which will not be described here.

When a user runs a module the associated rules and questions, together with the user's answers are processed by a forward chaining production rule interpreter, which automatically generates a set of web pages and displays them as a frameset in the user's web browser.

The user sees a sequence of web pages, each one asking a question and requesting an answer, either from a list of multiple-choice options or by entering a value (name, annual salary etc.). Instead of answering the question the user can choose to undo any number of previously answered questions or to restart the module. As the consultation session progresses a cumulative set of 'Advice Notes' is built up to take away. None of the AdviceWeb screens are pre-stored. They are all generated automatically from the script files and other information provided during uploading. Many of the screens have additional information to help answer questions and/or links to other (pre-stored) web pages, e.g. on a company or advice bureau website. The intention is that the advice given is justified by links to regulations, legislation, codes of practice, guidance notes and the like.

3   Associating Further Information With Questions and Advice

The following sample consultation illustrates some of the facilities available in AdviceWeb and how the Advice Provider can make use of them by augmenting the basic kind of script shown in Figure 1 using a markup notation.

The example module chosen is DPA, which gives advice on the disciplinary procedures for a fictitious university.

The module is started by selecting it from a menu of available modules. The startup screen is shown as Figure 2 (all screenshots have been converted to black and white for this paper).

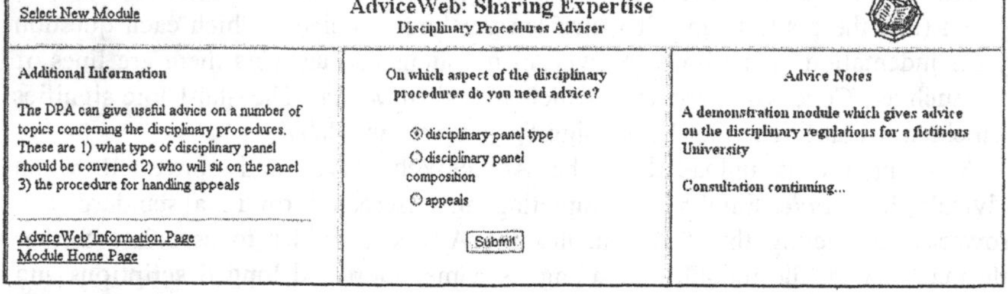

Select New Module	**AdviceWeb: Sharing Expertise** Disciplinary Procedures Adviser	
Additional Information The DPA can give useful advice on a number of topics concerning the disciplinary procedures. These are 1) what type of disciplinary panel should be convened 2) who will sit on the panel 3) the procedure for handling appeals AdviceWeb Information Page Module Home Page	On which aspect of the disciplinary procedures do you need advice? ⊙ disciplinary panel type ○ disciplinary panel composition ○ appeals [Submit]	**Advice Notes** A demonstration module which gives advice on the disciplinary regulations for a fictitious University Consultation continuing...

Fig. 2. Startup Screen for Disciplinary Procedures Adviser Module

The module's initial question is "On which aspect of the disciplinary procedures do you need advice?". Selecting the answer 'disciplinary panel type' and pressing the Submit button produces Figure 3.

The figure shows three vertical frames. From left to right these are the *Information Window*, the *Question Window* and the *Advice Notes Window*, respectively. The framesets for each module have a uniform style, layout, colour scheme etc. so familiarity gained by the user with one module is readily transferred to others. All questions and where applicable a multiple-choice list of possible answers appear in the middle window. Any additional information relating to a question is displayed in the Information Window, together with links to the module home page, FAQ page and search engine, if they exist, and a link to the system information page, which contains a list of the modules available to the user.

Fig. 3. DPA Example – Illustrating Additional Information and Web Link

This screen again illustrates Additional Information associated with a question. In this case there is also a hot link to 'HSR 3.1.1'.

> Is he or she facing the possibility of suspension prior to the hearing? *INF* A student is suspended when they are not allowed to attend lectures or exams. A Student may be suspended by the Vice-Chancellor. See HSR 3.1.1||When a student is suspended prior to a hearing a major disciplinary panel must be convened within 10 days of the start of the suspension *REF* HSR 3.1.1** section3.htm#Disciplinary Machinery

Fig. 4. Example of a Question Augmented with Markup

Figure 4 shows the markup needed in the AWSL script to produce this effect when the question is asked. The question 'Is he or she facing the possibility of suspension prior to the hearing?' is followed by an *information tag* *INF*, followed by the information itself (the two vertical bars signify two new lines).

This is followed by a *reference tag* *REF*, followed by a *reference string*, in this case HSR 3.1.1, followed by a URL 'section3.htm#Disciplinary Machinery'.

The reference string gives the text of the hot link in the information window. Any number of references can be associated with a question. Although absolute URLs are permitted, relative addresses are generally used. Any URL that does not begin with http:// is automatically prefixed by a 'webstem' chosen by the Advice Provider when the script is uploaded to the AdviceWeb server.

Returning to the example given in Figure 3, answering 'unknown' leads to Figure 5. The paragraph numbered 3 in the Advice Notes window gives not only advice but two hot links to sections of the disciplinary regulations. Clicking on these will produce the text of the relevant part of the regulations to justify the advice given.

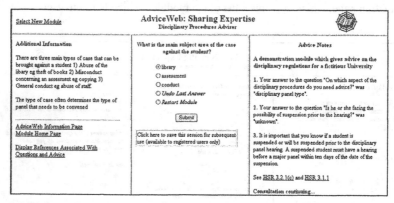

Fig. 5. DPA Example – Advice Notes with Web Links

The marked up advice text from the AWSL script file is shown in Figure 6. The advice text is followed by two reference tag + reference string + URL combinations. Any number of references can be associated with an advice text.

> It is important that you know if a student is suspended or will be suspended prior to the disciplinary panel hearing. A suspended student must have a hearing before a major panel within ten days of the date of the suspension.||See HSR 3.2.1(c) and HSR 3.1.1 *REF* HSR 3.2.1(c)**section3.htm#Major Panels *REF* HSR 3.1.1**section3.htm#Disciplinary Machinery

Fig. 6. Example of Advice Text with Markup

As a consultation progresses a references page is generated giving a cumulative list of the references displayed in the information and advice notes windows. Registered users can save an uncompleted consultation session at any point (for example if they have to break off midway or need to find out information from some other source before continuing). Saved sessions are date and time stamped and can be loaded whenever the module is started in future. When a session is completed registered users have the option to have the Advice Notes of their consultation, including all associated web references, sent to them by email. Unregistered users can simply cut and paste the Advice Notes into a word processor and print off a copy.

4 Additional Facilities

4.1 Using Variables in Advice Modules

An important feature of many Expert Systems is the ability to read in and output variables, as well as performing arithmetic on numerical variables. AdviceWeb has facilities to do all of these. Figure 7 shows a question with a multiple-choice answer augmented so that the answer is assigned to a variable, followed by an instruction to ask the user to input a value and assign it to a variable. A line of the latter kind can be used anywhere a piece of advice would be valid, but is treated as a question.

What is the VAT rate? *VAR* vrate
INPTEXT What is your annual salary? *VAR* y

Fig. 1. Examples of AWSL Script Lines that Refer to Variables

Both questions use the *variable tag* *VAR*. Any or all of the variable, information and reference tags can be associated with any question.

A value can also be assigned to a variable by a LET instruction, which can be placed anywhere a piece of advice would be valid. Arithmetic expressions of any complexity can be used. The value of a variable or an arithmetic expression can be output in a piece of advice. Figure 8 illustrates both of these.

LET z = (x+y)/3+z-y-4.2+2*q
Your profit of [x] pounds will incur a tax liability of [(x-allowance)*rate] pounds

Fig. 2. LET Instructions and Advice Using Variables

4.2 Fine-Tuning Modules

Another desirable feature of an Expert System delivery environment aimed at Advice Providers who are not computer specialists is the ability to fine-tune a module without having to upload it again for every change. AdviceWeb allows Advice Providers who run their own modules to make changes to them onscreen while they are running.

Whenever a module is run by the Advice Provider who uploaded it, an 'Edit' hotlink or button is placed next to the 'Additional Information' line on the information window, the text of the question in the question window and every piece of advice in the advice notes window.

Taking the example shown in Figure 5 for illustration, clicking on either of the 'Edit' links provided for the Advice Provider in the leftmost two columns produces an 'edit form' in the middle column, as shown in Figure 9.

This enables the wording of the question to be adjusted, the additional information to be changed (or deleted) and references to be added if required.

Clicking on the 'Edit' button, which can be seen in the advice window will give another edit screen, which enables the wording of the advice to be modified and the associated references to be changed or deleted.

This onscreen editing facility makes it straightforward to carry out minor maintenance of modules. Advice Providers who prefer not to use the information and reference tag facilities described in Section 3 do not have to do so, as the necessary information and web links can be provided onscreen instead.

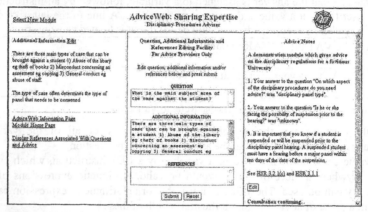

Fig. 9. Example of Onscreen Editing for a Question (Advice Providers Only)

4.3 Linking Modules

Two of the design aims of AdviceWeb are that it should be possible to create substantial systems without significant programming skills and that Advice Providers should find it realistic to develop a suite of modules, not just one.

Both of these aims point to the need for a facility to link modules to each other, thus allowing tasks to be decomposed into smaller subtasks and standard modules to be developed for use in more than one application.

An AWSL script can include a call to another module. This can be placed anywhere a piece of advice would be valid. The AdviceWeb rule interpreter distinguishes between occurrences of the same variable and label names in different modules.

5   Current Status

The AdviceWeb system is fully implemented and currently undergoing trials. A range of test modules has successfully been created by automatic conversion from AWSL script files. The largest group of modules links together approximately 20 modules written independently for related tasks. Feedback from developmental testing has been favourable. Further modules are being developed and Advice Providers are currently being sought for the live system.

A Formally Specified Ontology Management API as a Registry for Ubiquitous Computing Systems

Alexander Paar[1], Jürgen Reuter[1]
John Soldatos[2], Kostas Stamatis[2], Lazaros Polymenakos[2]
[1]Institute for Program Structures and Data Organization (IPD),
Universität Karlsruhe (TH), Am Fasanengarten 5, 76128 Karlsruhe,
Germany
alexpaar@acm.org, reuter@ipd.uka.de
http://www.ipd.uka.de/Tichy
[2]Athens Information Technology
19,5 km Markopoulou Peania, Ave.
jsol@ait.edu.gr, ksta@ait.edu.gr, lcp@ait.edu.gr
http://www.ait.edu.gr

Abstract. Recently, several standards have emerged for ontology markup languages that can be used to formalize all kinds of knowledge. However, there are no widely accepted standards yet that define APIs to manage ontological data. Processing ontological information still suffers from the heterogeneity imposed by the plethora of available ontology management systems. Moreover, ubiquitous computing environments usually comprise software components written in a variety of different programming languages, which makes it even more difficult to establish a common ontology management API with programming language agnostic semantics. We implemented an ontological Knowledge Base Server, which can expose the functionality of arbitrary off-the-shelf ontology management systems via a formally specified and well defined API. A case study was carried out in order to demonstrate the feasibility of our approach to use an ontological Knowledge Base Server as a registry for ubiquitous computing systems.

1 Introduction

With the recent emergence of Semantic Web technologies like RDF(S) [1], DAML+OIL [2], and their common Description Logics (DL) [3] based successor OWL [4] numerous ontologies have been developed to conceptualize a plethora of domains of discourse [5]. This paper introduces an approach to model a ubiquitous

Please use the following format when citing this chapter:

Paar, Alexander, Reuter, Jürgen, Soldatos, John, Stamatis, Kostas, Polymenakos, Lazaros, 2006, in IFIP International Federation for Information Processing, Volume 204, Artificial Intelligence Applications and Innovations, eds. Maglogiannis, I., Karpouzis, K., Bramer, M., (Boston: Springer), pp. 137–146

computing domain of discourse with the Web Ontology Language OWL. This effort was carried out in course of the CHIL research project [6], which builds non-intrusive services aiming to introduce computers into the loop of humans. In order to implement such services, a semantic middleware is being developed that fuses information provided by numerous perceptual components. Each perceptual component (e.g. image and speech recognizers, body trackers, etc.) contributes to the common domain of discourse. The Web Ontology Language OWL was used to replace previous domain models based on particular programming languages.

The CHIL software environment comprises perceptual components written in a variety of different programming languages. In contrast, existing ontology management systems typically provide only very limited connectivity with respect to natively supported programming languages and remoting protocols. The CHIL Knowledge Base Server [7] was developed to adapt off-the-shelf ontology management systems to a formally specified and well defined API. The Knowledge Base Server remedies three major shortcomings of existing ontology management systems. First, a number of programming languages are natively supported providing programming language specific client libraries. Second, almost arbitrary remoting protocols can be hosted in order to greatly improve connectivity compared to the majority of existing APIs that can only be used locally. Third, in contrast to existing ontology management APIs, the Knowledge Base Server interface specification relies on formally specified semantics. The latter feature is a main difference to related work on interface specifications of ontology management APIs such as the DIG protocol, the FaCT system or off-the-shelf ontology management systems such as Jena or Protégé.

The DIG protocol [8], which is a simple API for a general Description Logics system, is one representative of a class of interface definitions that consist of simple mechanisms to *tell* and *ask* DL knowledge bases. These mechanisms follow foundational aspects that have been well-studied over time [9]. Many previous frame-oriented knowledge representation systems such as the Generic Frame Protocol [10] and OKBC (Open Knowledge Base Connectivity) [11] also embody such distinctions. The DIG specification merely defines an XML schema that has to be used along with HTTP as the underlying communication protocol. There is no specific support for a particular programming language. Also, the KRSS specification [12], which is an earlier approach to define a number of tell- and ask operations that a DL system should implement, was tightly bound to the LISP [13] syntax, which may not be adequate for programmers who prefer other languages. Note also that other DIG 1.0 implementations (such as the FaCT reasoner [14, 15]), require further application server software. In [16] a CORBA interface to the FaCT system is proposed. Beyond the fact that CORBA may not be an appropriate remoting technology in today's service oriented- and XML based computing environments, the authors in [16] acknowledge that "*the CORBA IDL does not support the definition of the kinds of recursive data types that may be required for the representation of DL concepts and roles*". This is why an XML based workaround was devised to pass ontological concepts and roles as single data items. Previous approaches to augment DL knowledge base interfaces with remoting capabilities include the wines- [17] and stereo [18] configuration demonstration systems.

Stanford University's Protégé [19], HP Labs' Jena [20], and Karlsruhe University's KAON [21] are all representatives for off-the-shelf ontology management systems, which do not rely on rigid formal semantics for their APIs specification. Moreover, none of these systems supports several programming languages and remoting protocols in order to cope with highly heterogeneous distributed computing environments (such as ubiquitous/pervasive computing environments).

Building on the advantages and merits of the Knowledge Base Server, this paper introduces a formal specification of an ontology management API for the Web Ontology Language OWL using a combination of the Z notation and Description Logics terminology. Moreover, it presents a case study that demonstrates the usefulness of a programming language agnostic remotable ontology management API in the domain of ubiquitous computing. The rest of the paper is structured as follows. Section 2 illustrates – for the most part by example – how the CHIL Knowledge Base Server API was formally specified using a combination of the Z notation and Description Logics terminology. A case study on the use of the CHIL Knowledge Base Server as a registry for a ubiquitous computing system is presented in Section 3. An overview of ongoing- and future work is given in Section 4, which includes also concluding remarks.

2 The CHIL Knowledge Base Server API

Based on the terminology for Description Logics as proposed in [3], formal specifications were devised for methods of the CHIL Knowledge Base Server interfaces IAskingTBox, IAskingABox, ITellingTBox, and ITellingABox for asking and telling the ABox and TBox of an OWL DL based knowledge base, respectively.[1] This formal specification was developed in order to make it possible to consistently adapt off-the-shelf ontology management systems. In particular, ambiguities had to be resolved that may be caused by informal specifications like *"This method returns all super classes of the given class"*. In such cases it mostly remains unclear if the result set will contain the OWL top level concept http://www.w3.org/2002/07/owl#Thing or not.

With a more rigid specification, it would be clear if in an adapter class the top level concept from the result set of an adapted method had to be removed in case the underlying ontology management system yields it. In addition, a more formal specification is machine readable, such that result sets could be validated according to the specification.

For the formal specification of the Knowledge Base Server API, we use the Z notation [22, 23]. Since the API is specific to Description Logics, we added to the Z

---

[1] Java interface definitions and documentation can be found under *www.semantic-software.org*

notation the syntax and semantics of Description Logics as proposed in [3]. Additionally, the semantics of the ' ⊑'-sign, which in Z denotes a sub-bag relation, was over-written, such that it stands for the subsumption relation as defined by Description Logics.

In subsequent paragraphs we provide four examples on how methods from the Knowledge Base Server interfaces (IAskingTBox, IAskingABox, ITellingTBox, and ITellingABox) were formally specified.

The method listDirectSubClasses(String owlClass) from the IAskingTBox interface, which returns all classes that are directly subsumed by the given class owlClass, was defined as follows.

```
┌─ listDirectSubClasses ──────────────────────────────────────
│  Ξ KnowledgeBase
│  owlClass? : String
│  subClasses! : ℙString
│ ────────────────────────────────────────────────────────────
│  subClasses! = { X.toString() | X ⊑owlClass? ∧∀X,Y.Y ⊑X ⇒X ≡Y }
└──────────────────────────────────────────────────────────────
```

Fig. 1. Z notation of method listDirectSubClasses

```
┌─ listPropertyValuesOfIndividual ────────────────────────────
│  Ξ KnowledgeBase
│  role? : String
│  individual? : String
│  values! : ℙString
│ ────────────────────────────────────────────────────────────
│  values! = { val.toString() | ∃role?.D ∧∃val.(individual?, val) ∈role?$^I$ ∧val ∈D$^I$ }
└──────────────────────────────────────────────────────────────
```

Fig. 2. Z notation of method listPropertyValuesOfIndividual

```
┌─ addClass ──────────────────────────────────────────────────
│  Δ KnowledgeBase
│  class? : String
│  superClass? : String
│ ────────────────────────────────────────────────────────────
│  class?  ∈ KnowledgeBase
│  superClass?  ∈ KnowledgeBase
│  KnowledgeBase'=  KnowledgeBase ∪{ class? ⊑superClass? }
└──────────────────────────────────────────────────────────────
```

Fig. 3. Z notation of method addClass

The method listPropertyValuesOfIndividual(String role, String individual), which is defined in the IAskingABox interface, yields all values of role R of individual IND. The result set returned by this method was defined as depicted above.

The interface ITellingTBox comprises methods that can be used to modify the set of terminological axioms, which are defined in a knowledge base. The method addClass(String class, String superClass) adds a class class, which is subsumed by class superClass, to the ontology. Accordingly, the axiom class ⊑superClass where class^I ⊆superClass^I is added to the knowledge base as shown in Fig. 3.

The method addPropertyValueOfIndividual(String role, String individual, String value), which is defined in the ITellingABox interface, can be used to add a role assertion as depicted in Fig. 4.

```
┌─ addPropertyValueOfIndividual ─────────────────────────────────────────┐
│                                                                          │
│  Δ KnowledgeBase                                                         │
│  role? : String                                                          │
│  individual? : String                                                    │
│  value? : String                                                         │
│  ──────────────────────────────────────────────────────────────────     │
│  role? ∈ KnowledgeBase                                                   │
│  individual? ∈ KnowledgeBase                                             │
│  KnowledgeBase'=  KnowledgeBase ∪{ role?(individual?, value?) }          │
│              where (individual?$^I$, value?$^I$) ∈role?$^I$              │
└──────────────────────────────────────────────────────────────────────────┘
```

Fig. 4. Z notation of method addPropertyValueOfIndividual

3 Case Study: The Knowledge Base Server as a Registry for Ubiquitous Computing Systems

The CHIL Knowledge Base Server provides directory services for ubiquitous context-aware computing services. Context-aware services acquire and process information about their surrounding environment, which allows them to execute service logic based not only on input explicitly provided by end users, but also based on information that is derived implicitly. Implicit information is usually derived based on a rich collection of casually accessible, often invisible sensors. Sensor information is processed by middleware components in order to derive elementary context information. Perceptive interfaces and recognition algorithms process audiovisual streams and extract context relating to the identity and location of people and objects. Accordingly, information fusion algorithms can be used to recognize more complex contextual states, which are often characterized as *situations*. Identification of contextual states provides a basis for triggering service logic [24].

Service logic is likely to comprise a rich set of invocations to soft-computing services, including commands to sensors and actuating devices. Thus, non-trivial ubiquitous applications consist of a rich set of sensors, middleware for controlling sensors and actuating devices, perceptual interfaces deriving context cues from sensor streams, as well as information fusion components identifying complex contextual states.

These hardware and middleware components are characterized by extreme diversity in terms of functionality, underlying technologies and vendors. Moreover, ubiquitous computing environments are very dynamic in the sense that sensors, devices, computing resources, and services are likely to dynamically join or leave [24]. Managing heterogeneity and dynamism is crucial to facilitate application development and deployment. Key to dealing with diversity and dynamic environments is a directory service maintaining and providing information about all sorts of components.

While several approaches to directory services middleware exist, the Knowledge Base Server supported by an ontology management system has clear advantages over conventional technologies. Technologies such as UPnP (Universal Plug n' Play), SLP (Service Location Protocol) and UDDI (Universal Description, Discovery and Integration) provide mechanisms for registering and discovering resource and services. However, these mechanisms are not particularly tailored to the range of information and components that are essential to ubiquitous computing services. For example, UDDI and SLP are merely service oriented, while UPnP is very much device oriented. Furthermore, the context-aware, human-centric, pervasive nature of ubiquitous computing services, asks for intelligence in answering queries. Intelligence lies in the ability to infer information from existing sets of meta-data according to current context and user intention. As an example, given the number of different sensors in a smart space, a particular situation model or service may need to acquire a reference to the best-view camera for a particular situation e.g., the camera facing the door for recognizing a person entering a room. Thus, the main benefit of such a knowledge base is its semantic power in knowledge conceptualization.

The Knowledge Base Server has been adopted as a core component of the CHIL architecture [24]. This architecture provides the structuring principles for the CHIL services and mandates that semantic middleware components, sensors, devices, services and resources are registered to the Knowledge Base Server. Sensors, actuators, and devices register their status and capabilities to the Knowledge Base Server upon their bootstrapping. Perceptual components can then discover the sensor streams required for their operation and accordingly register themselves with the Knowledge Base Server. CHIL perceptual technologies comprise a rich collection of 2D-visual components, 3D-visual perceptual components, acoustic components, audio-visual components, as well as output perceptual components like multimodal speech synthesis and targeted audio.

Situation models, which are higher level components of the context-aware semantic middleware, are registered with the Knowledge Base Server as well. Situation models define combinations of perceptual component values towards identifying complex contextual states. Prior to registering themselves they acquire information on perceptual components.

Following the registration of semantic middleware components, the knowledge base provides 'yellow pages' services to middleware elements that need to interact with these components. Also, service logic implementation can leverage the knowledge base 'registry' to acquire binding on sensors, actuating devices and other resources entailed in service logic development. Thus, the Knowledge Base Server acts as an intelligent registry that provides information about components. Information includes a component's physical location in the network, its vendor, its functionality (i.e. the kind of ontological information it can provide), and its operational status.

As already outlined the expressive power of the underlying ontology management system is clearly manifested in cases where there is a need to access information that must/can be inferred rather than being readily available. As a characteristic example consider the query: 'provide a list of cameras facing the door', which the ontology management system can answer even in cases when the camera properties do not explicitly contain information about its relative orientation to the door.

Apart from the semantic capabilities of the CHIL Knowledge Base Server, other benefits of the particular implementation come into foreground in view of the architecture depicted in Fig. 5, in particular.

Platform independence: Given the large number of smart rooms, technology providers and services in CHIL, it is vital to have several ways to access the CHIL Knowledge Base Server. Indeed, in the scope of CHIL services, several components implemented in different languages and running on different operating systems need to access the Knowledge Base Server.

Independency from particular ontology management systems: Similarly to platform independence, the ability to use different ontology management systems proved to be essential since different smart room providers are likely to opt for different ontology management platforms.

The architecture depicted in Fig. 5 has been implemented in one of the CHIL smart rooms, namely the Athens Information Technology (AIT). Early instantiations of this architecture relied on hard-coded communication between hardware and middleware components. The introduction of the Knowledge Base Server has greatly facilitated integration. This is evident in the scope of the 'memory jog' implementation, which is a non-obtrusive service providing pertinent information and assistance in the scope of meetings, lectures, seminars and presentations [25]. The 'Memory Jog' uses the registration services of the knowledge base to dynamically discover and invoke audio- and vision based person tracking components.

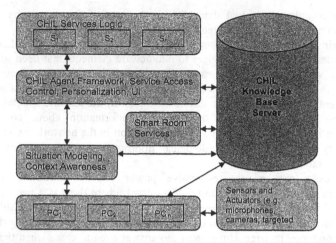

Fig. 5. The CHIL Knowledge Base Server as part of the CHIL semantic middleware

4 Conclusions and Future Work

We developed and implemented a pluggable architectural model for an ontological knowledge base server, which can be used to adapt off-the-shelf ontology management systems. Based on XML Schema Definition and on a combination of the Z notation and formal Description Logics terminology, a programming language independent API was defined. The API supports forwarding of exception information to clients in order to provide programmers with as much information as possible without being restricted to one particular programming language. The well defined ontology management API proved to be suitable both for developing auxiliary Eclipse plug-ins (e.g. for ontology visualization) and for accessing the Knowledge Base Server from a variety of perceptual components. Our case study, conducted in course of the CHIL project, showed that in order to benefit from common type systems defined by OWL ontologies, it is absolutely crucial to improve the connectivity of ontology management systems with a view to: (a) increasing their application scope and (b) to support a variety of different programming languages. The Knowledge Base Server proved to be a reliable backend for a semantic middleware that incorporates more than fifty (50) image- and speech recognition based perceptual components.

Current work on evolving the Knowledge Base Server is focused on further developing auxiliary Eclipse plug-ins that foster the integration of ontology engineering tasks in the software development process. In terms of using the Knowledge Base Server we envision additional applications, beyond the use of the Knowledge Base Server as a directory service. These include using the Knowledge

Base Server for inter-agent communication through establishing appropriate communication ontologies, as well as exploiting the Knowledge Base Server for reasoning on the whole range of concepts of the CHIL ontology. This could obviate the need for developing higher level context abstractions (e.g., Situation Models outlined in Section 3).

Acknowledgements

This work is part of the FP6 CHIL project (FP6-506909), partially funded by the European Commission under the Information Society Technology (IST) program. The authors acknowledge valuable help and contributions from all partners of the project.

References

1. W3C Recommendation: RDF Primer, http://www.w3.org/TR/rdf-primer/ (2004)
2. DARPA's Information Exploitation Office: DAML+OIL, http://www.daml.org/2001/03/daml+oil-index.html (2001)
3. Baader, F., Calvanese, D., McGuiness, D., Nardi, D., Patel-Schneider, P.: The Description Logic Handbook, Cambridge University Press (2003)
4. W3C Recommendation: OWL Web Ontology Language Overview, http://www.w3.org/TR/owl-features/ (2004)
5. DARPA's Information Exploitation Office: DAML Ontology Library, http://www.daml.org/ontologies/ (2004)
6. Information Society Technology (IST) program FP6-506909, Computers in the Human Interaction Loop CHIL, http://chil.server.de/ (2004)
7. Paar, A., Reuter, J., Schaeffer, J.: A Pluggable Architectural Model and a Formally Specified Programming Language Independent API for an Ontological Knowledge Base Server, Australasian Ontology Workshop, Sydney, Australia (2005)
8. Bechhofer, S.:The DIG Description Logic Interface: DIG/1.0, University of Manchester, Oxford Road, Manchester M13 9PLA (2002)
9. Levesque, H.J.: Foundations of a functional approach to knowledge representation, Artificial Intelligence, 23 (1984) 155-212
10. Chaudhri, V.K., Farquhar, A., Fikes, R., Karp, P.D., and Rice, J.: The Generic Frame Protocol 2.0, Technical Report, Artificial Intelligence Center, SRI International, Menlo Park, CA (USA) (1997)
11. Chaudhri, V.K., Farquhar, A., Fikes, R., and Karp, P.D.: Open Knowledge Base Connectivity 2.0, Technical Report KSL-09-06, Stanford University KSL (1998)
12. Patel-Schneider, P.F., and Swartout, B.: Description-logic knowledge representation system specification from the KRSS group of the ARPA knowledge sharing effort, Technical report, AI Principles Research Department, AT&T Bell Laboratories (1993)
13. Graham, P.: ANSI Common LISP, Prentice Hall (1995)
14. Horrocks, I.: The FaCT system, Proc. of the 2nd Int. Conf. on Analytic Tableaux and Related Methods (TABLEAUX), volume 1397 of Lecture Notes in Artificial Intelligence (1998) 307-312

15. Horrocks, I.: FaCT and iFaCT, Proc. of the 1999 Description Logic Workshop (DL'99), CEUR Electronic Workshop Proceedings (1999) 133-135
16. Bechhofer, S., Horrocks, I., Patel-Schneider, P.F., and Tessaris, S.: A proposal for a Description Logic interface, Proc. of the 1999 Description Logic Workshop (DL'99), 33-36, CEUR Electronic Workshop Proceedings (1999)
17. Brachman, R.J., McGuinness, D.L., Patel-Schneider, P.F., Resnick, L.A., and Borgida, A.: Living with CLASSIC: When and how to use KL-ONE-like language, Principles of Semantic Networks, Morgan Kaufmann, Los Altos (1991) 401-456
18. McGuiness D.L., Resnick, L.A., and Isbell, C.: Description Logic in practice: A CLASSIC application, Proc. of the 14th Int. Joint Conf. on Artificial Intelligence (IJCAI) (1995) 2045-2046
19. Stanford University School of Medicine: Protégé knowledge acquisition system, http://protege.stanford.edu/ (2003)
20. HP Labs: Jena 2 - A Semantic Web Framework, http://www.hpl.hp.com/semweb/jena.htm (2004)
21. KAON 2, Universität Karlsruhe (TH), Germany, http://kaon2.semanticweb.org/ (2005)
22. Spivey, J.M.: The Z Notation: A Reference Manual, Prentice-Hall International Series in Computer Science Prentice Hall; 2nd edition (1992)
23. ISO/IEC, Information Technology – Z Formal Specification Notation – Syntax, Type System and Semantics, ISO/IEC 13568:2002 (2002)
24. Soldatos J., Pandis I., Stamatis K., Polymenakos L., Crowley J., 'A Middleware Infrastructure for Autonomous Context-Aware Computing Services', accepted for publication to the Computer Communications Magazine, special Issue on Emerging Middleware for Next Generation Networks (2005).
25. Soldatos, J., Polymenakos, L., Pnevmatikakis, A., Talantzis, F., Stamatis, K., Carras, M.: Perceptual Interfaces and Distributed Agents supporting Ubiquitous Computing Services. In: The Proc. of the Eurescom Summit 2005 (2005) 43–50.
26. Pandis I., Soldatos J., Paar A., Reuter J., Carras M., Polymenakos L., 'An Ontology-based Framework for Dynamic Resource Management in Ubiquitous Computing Environments', in the Proc. of the 2nd International Conference on Embedded Software and Systems, Northwestern Polytechnical University of Xian, P. R. China, December 16-18. (2005).

Intelligent Configurable Electronic Shop Platform based on Ontologies and 3D Visualization

N. Karatzoulis[1], I. Tsampoulatidis[1], I. Maglogiannis[2], I. Zormpas[3],
D. Tzovaras[1] and M. G. Strintzis[1,4]

1 Informatics & Telematics Institute
1st Km Thermi-Panorama Road, PO Box 361,
GR-57001 Thermi-Thessaloniki, Greece
{nkaratz, itsam, tzovaras}@iti.gr

2 Dept. of Information and Communication Systems Engineering
University of the Aegean
{imaglo}@aegean.gr

3 Horama S.A.
{izor}@horama.com

4 Electrical and Computer Engineering Department
Aristotle University of Thessaloniki
GR-54006 Thessaloniki, Greece
strintzi@eng.auth.gr

Abstract. Although on-line shops have become very popular lately, there are still some sectors of industry, such as clothing and furniture, where the on-line shop concept has not penetrated the market yet. The main reason for that is the diversity of the specific sectors, the mentality of the market players and the lack of user friendly environments, where the customer could actually "see" the products. This paper presents an Intelligent Configurable Electronic Shop Platform, based on Ontologies and 3D Visualization, that aims at enabling a suitable representation of products with the most realistic possible visualization outcome. The platform, designed for the furniture sector, includes all the practicable electronic commerce variants and its on-line product configuration process is controlled by an ontology that was created using the OWL Web Ontology Language.

Please use the following format when citing this chapter:

Karatzoulis, Nikolaos, Tsampoulatidis, Ioannis, Maglogiannis, Ilias, Zormpas, Ioannis, Tzovaras, Dimitrios, Strintzis, Michael, 2006, in IFIP International Federation for Information Processing, Volume 204, Artificial Intelligence Applications and Innovations, eds. Maglogiannis, I., Karpouzis, K., Bramer, M., (Boston: Springer), pp. 147–155

1   Introduction

This paper presents an intelligent and user-friendly e-commerce solution, by adopting additional technologies such as a configuration utility supported by an intelligent help desk system and 3D visualization in a virtual reality environment. The focus of this paper is on the furniture sector, however the intention is that the system to be developed will be suitable for manufacturers, suppliers, and wholesalers, from other sectors, such as clothing, bicycles etc. The conception of the system is as generalised as possible, in order to facilitate the transfer to other industrial sectors.

The technical contribution of this paper is to present how to: (i) integrate and develop a product Visualization Tool capable of handling different media types (2D and 3D), (ii) introduce a novel configuration module, which is capable of integrating different functionalities, input and output devices and (iii) provide enhanced work-flow mechanisms and tools for an easy integration into modern legacy systems (ERPs).

The described platform, called hereafter INCOVIS platform, has been designed for furniture products that can be configured on-line. The main modules of the INCOVIS platform are the **Intelligent Configurator Module** (and its ontology structure) and the **3D Visualization Module**. These two modules combined, comprise an advanced 3D Shop system that offers different products to customers, based on their demand and not on a fixed product line.

The paper is structured as following: in section 2 the intelligent configurator module is presented, with special focus on its architecture and ontology structure. In section 3 the 3D visualization module is analysed and in section 4 the e-shop solution and its integration with existing ERPs, is discussed. Finally, section 5 presents some experimental results and concludes the paper.

2   Intelligent Configurator Module and Ontology

The Intelligent Configurator module is a web based application that allows the user to assembly furniture products based on the available furniture parts that are being stored in the systems repository maintained by the furniture manufacturer. Figure 1 displays the Units of the Configurator module.

The Assembly Unit allows the user to insert individual 3D objects to the scene that can consist of a fully functional furniture product. The user can compose the desired product according to his/her needs by selecting the object's parts. The object and the texture selection processes are being controlled by the restriction mechanisms that are generated from the system Ontology [1, 2, 3]. The main functionalities of the Assembly Unit are the following: (i) Insertion of 3D object parts, (ii) Selection of texture and (iii) Assembly process based on rules (i.e. price limit).

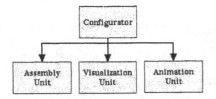

Fig. 1. The Units of the Configurator Module

The purpose of the Visualization Unit is to record and store the 3D object assembly steps in real-time. The assembly consequence is being stored in the 3D animation repository for future reproduction.

The Animation Unit allows the reproduction of the products assembly processes that are being stored in the animation system repository. In the Animation Unit the user can control the viewpoints and the playback of the loaded product assembly process. The web interface of the Configurator Module is depicted in Figure 2.

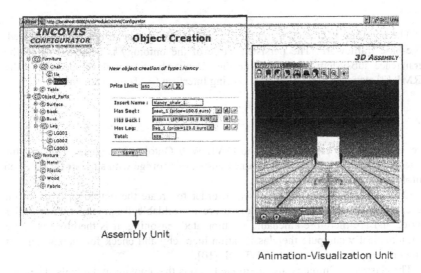

Fig. 2. The web interface of the Configurator

2.1 Configurator Architecture

The Configurator is implemented (Figure 3) using Java programming language. The system runs on Apache Jakarta Tomcat [4] as Java Servlet and it is based on the Jena framework [5], which is a Java framework for building Semantic Web applications.

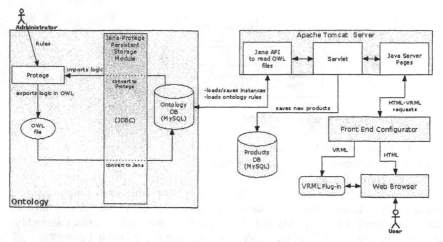

Fig. 3. Configurator Architecture

The ontology is created using the Protégé [6], which is an open source knowledge-base framework. The persistent store of the ontology is achieved using the persistence subsystem of Jena, while the 3D visualization is developed using the VRML [7] standard and External Authoring Interface (EAI) mechanisms.

2.2   Ontology Development

The ontology was created using the OWL Web Ontology Language [8], and the Protégé OWL-Plugin [9], which is an extension of Protégé with support for the Web Ontology Language (OWL).

OWL-DL profile which was used in order to create the ontology, is based on Description Logics. Description Logics are a decidable fragment of First Order Logic2 and are therefore amenable to automated reasoning. It is therefore possible to automatically compute the classification hierarchy and check for inconsistencies in an ontology that conforms to OWL-DL [10].

The classes in Ontology are interpreted as sets that contain individuals. They are described using formal descriptions that state precisely the requirements for membership of the class. For example, the class "Chair" contains all the individuals that are chairs in the INCOVIS domain. The taxonomy of the classes is being achieved using the superclass-subclass model hierarchy.

Table 1. Example of the class hierarchy of the class "Chair" and an example of an Object Type Property for the individual "chair_1".

Class Model	Object Type Property

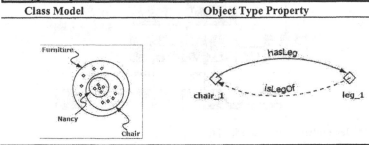

There are two types of properties supported by our ontology a) Data Type Properties and b) Object Type Properties. These OWL Properties represent relationships between two individuals.

In OWL, properties are used to create restrictions. In our ontology the restrictions were used to restrict the individuals that belong to a class. We used the universal quantifier ∀ restrictions to constrain the relationships along a given property to individuals that are members of a specific class. For example, the universal restriction ∀ hasBack back_1 describes the individuals all of whose hasBack relationships are members of the class Back.

Cardinality restrictions were used to define the order in which the individual object parts should appear during the 3D assembly process (i.e. real-time animation). The cardinality restrictions provided the way to describe the class of individuals that have at least, at most or exactly a specified number of relationships with other individuals or datatype values.

The hasValue restrictions, denoted by the symbol ∋, were used to describe the set of individuals that have at least one relationship along a specified property to a specific individual. For example, when we wanted to predefine the dimensions of an individual object part we used a hasValue restriction (dimensions ∋ "40-50-80").

2.3   Ontology Reasoning

Ontology reasoning is achieved using the Jena OWL reasoner (Figure 4). The Jena OWL reasoner could be described as an instance-based reasoner that works by using rules to propogate the if- and only-if- implications of the OWL constructs on instance data. Reasoning about classes is done indirectly - for each declared class a prototypical instance is created and elaborated. The sub-class and sub-property lattices are cached using the embedded OWL reasoner. Each domain, range, sub-property and sub-class declaration is eagerly translated into a single query rewrite rule. The result of a query applied to the graph will be the union of the results from applying the query plus all the rewritten versions of the query to the underlying graph [11].

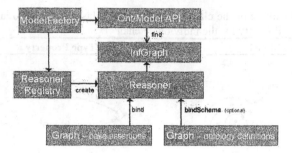

Fig. 4. The Jena Inference API layering [12]

3   3D Visualization Module

The 3D Visualization Module is realized on the Visualization and Animation Units. The structure of the individual 3D scenes supported by the 3D Visualization Module can be seeing at Figure 5.

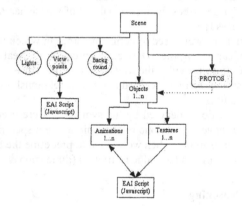

Fig. 5. The 3D scene structure of the 3D Visualization Module

The 3D scene contains the viewpoints, the lighting of the 3D world, the background, the 3D objects and the object functionalities (interactions) that are created dynamically according to the ontology specifications. The user interaction with the 3D scene is achieved by the use of predefined VRML Protos. For every 3D object that is inserted in the 3D scene, an animation representing its assembly process is dynamically generated.

4 The e-shopping platform in practice

The use of the INCOVIS platform "brings" advantages for both suppliers and buyers regarding (i) the cutback of transaction costs, (ii) the use of automated supply procedures, (iii) economy of scale, (iv) wide access on both local and international markets, (v) dynamic real-time price mechanisms/modules and (vi) the use of compatible/expandable technologies.

The requirements of the described INCOVIS platform for furniture products that together with the Intelligent Configurator Module and the 3D Visualization Module comprise the advanced 3D Shop system are:

• search and present all the available products, based on multi-criteria search engines

• group products into multilevel categories (set by the e-shop administrator)

• make offers/ sales and promote them

• update both the product catalogue and all items' availability (set by the e-shop administrator)

• create/use shop baskets (by the end buyers)

• provide several convenient pay/ receive methods

• provide a secure e-payment credit card transaction (with the use of HTTPS and SSL protocols).

However, the efficiency and overall quality of an e-commerce service depends "heavily" on its automatic connection with the existing ERP (Enterprise Resource Planning) system for the catalogue, prices, stock and product update. In order to integrate all the available ERP data with the e-shop database, a powerful staging mechanism is developed and securely transfers all necessary data. This staging process uses a smart "track changes" algorithm, to enhance the update speed.

There are two staging processes, Real Time Staging and Off Line Staging (that uses an automated batch process). The characteristics of the two staging "methods" are compared in the following table.

Table. 2 Staging Procedures Comparison

	Real Time Staging	Off Line Staging
Data Update	(+) All data are updated at all times	(-) All data are updated at specifically defined time periods
Infrastructure	(-) Reliable, high speed, technical infrastructure is necessary, available on a 24x7x365 basis	(+) Not so advanced technical infrastructure is necessary
Security	(-) The system can be secure but certain "protective" actions must be taken	(+) Security is obvious

The previous table shows that a real time staging procedure should be followed only if the nature of the commodity traded imposes the constant database update. In our case an every day off line procedure is chosen for both security and convenience reasons.

Yet, if we try to deduct a general case example we must note that each company's and product's needs, concerning the use of an e-market, are different; therefore the connectivity solutions (between an e-shop and an ERP) provided vary depending on: (i) the ERP used (it can be a widely used international ERP such as SAP, Oracle Applications, etc. or it can be a custom made system that fits to specific needs), (ii) the transaction volume and the form of the data transferred, (iii) the importance of the information transferred (regarding time, safety etc. aspects), (iv) the use of unilateral or bilateral communication and (v) whether it is an on-line or a batch transfer of data.

5   Experimental results and Conclusions

E-commerce services offered through a B2C (business to consumer) or B2B (business to business) system, provide the necessary infrastructure for real time e-business and an added value package of services that guarantee faster and more efficient buy and sell transactions, access to a broadened database of buyers/suppliers and business opportunities through the development of new partnerships.

In conclusion, in this paper we presented an interactive and user-friendly e-commerce solution for the furniture sector, but appropriate for other sectors as well. A furniture company called DIFROS S.A. has been the end-user responsible for using and testing the INCOVIS platform, so a number of its furniture products were integrated in the platform for evaluation and testing purposes (Figure 6). The evaluation procedure showed that the INCOVIS platform presented furniture products realistically and could be efficiently used as an on-line tool for their sales.

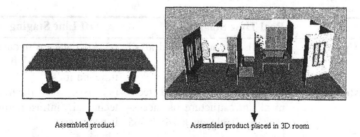

Assembled product   Assembled product placed in 3D room

Fig. 6. The 3D product visualization in the INCOVIS platform

Finally, the main contribution is that it our approach adopts additional technologies such as an intelligent configurator module and a 3D visualization environment aiming at enabling a suitable representation of products in order to achieve the most realistic possible visualization and simulate an up to close shopping procedure.

Acknowledgment. Authors acknowledge the support given by the National General Secretariat of Research and Technology (http://www.gsrt.gr) to the INCOVIS project (http://www.incovis.gr) for carrying this research.

References

1. I. Kompatsiaris, V. Mezaris, and M. G. Strintzis, Multimedia content indexing and retrieval using an object ontology, Multimedia Content and the Semantic Web: Methods, Standards and Tools, G. Stamou and S. Kollias (Editors), ISBN 0-470-85753-6, Wiley, pp. 339-371 (May 2005).

2. I.Tsampoulatidis, G.Nikolakis, D.Tzovaras and M.G.Strintzis, Ontology Based Interactive Graphic Environment for Product Presentation, in Proc. CGI 2004, pp.644 - 647, Heraklion, Crete, Greece (June 2004).

3. V.Mezaris, I.Kompatsiaris, M.G.Strintzis, An Ontology Approach to Object-Based Image Retrieval, Proc. IEEE International Conference on Image Processing (ICIP 2003), Barcelona, Spain, vol. II, pp. 511-514 (September 2003).

4. Apache Jakarta; http://jakarta.apache.org/.

5. Jena, A Semantic Web Framework for Java; http://jena.sourceforge.net/.

6. Protégé, An Ontology Editor and Knowledge-base Framework; http://protege.stanford.edu.

7. Web 3D Consortium, VRML Standard; http://www.web3d.org/x3d/vrml/.

8. Protégé OWL Plugin ; http://protege.stanford.edu/plugins/owl/.

9. The OWL Web Ontology Language; http://www.w3.org/TR/owl-features/.

10. M. Horridge, H. Knublauch, A. Rector, R. Stevens, and C. Wroe, A Practical Guide To Building OWL Ontologies Using The Protégé-OWL Plugin and CO-ODE Tools, Edition 1.0, The University of Manchester (August 2004).

11. J. Carroll, I. Dickinson, C. Dollin, D. Reynolds, A. Seaborne, and K. Wilkinson, Jena: Implementing the Semantic Web Recommendations, Digital Media Systems Laboratory,HP Laboratories Bristol (2003).

12. Jena 2 Inference Support; http://jena.sourceforge.net/inference/.

Adapting User Interfaces to the User Interaction Requirements in Real Time

Martín González, Marcos González, Jorge Manrubia
The Human Communication and Interaction Research Group (HCI-RG) –
Department of Computer Science, University of Oviedo, Spain
martin@uniovi.es, {marcosgonzalezgallego, Jorge_manrubia}@yahoo.es

Abstract. User interfaces are commonly designed to match the requirements of the so-called 'typical user' who represents an abstract generalization of each user of an application. In systems employed by different kinds of users (such as Web systems), the identification of the requirements of their users is very difficult, if not impossible. Our proposal is to avoid the construction of interactive dialogs during the design stage, building them dynamically once the specific cognitive, perceptual and motor requirements of the current user of the system are known: that is, during the execution stage.

1 Introduction

Traditional design of user centered interfaces is based on the identification and definition of the users of the application. Some design guidelines recommend the identification and understanding of the users as the first step to start the design of the product. This design principle shows that only once the requirements of the users have been identified, an interface that effectively satisfies their needs can be designed.

However, the quest for the typical user is opposite to the individuality and diversity that makes up some much of our identity. If the design of the interaction mechanisms of an application aims to make interfaces accessible for all the users, it shouldn't rely on abstract generalizations [1].

The identification of the typical user of applications targeted to different kinds of users is almost impossible without falling in serious misconceptions. Maybe is it possible to describe the typical user of Microsoft Office? Is it possible to identify the typical user of generic Web sites (such as Google), visited by thousands of different users everyday? For some authors such as [2], the answer to those questions is definitely 'no' as 'there is no average user'. For him, 'either compromises must be

Please use the following format when citing this chapter:

Gonzalez, Martin, Gonzalez, Marcos, Manrubia, Jorge, 2006, in IFIP International Federation for Information Processing, Volume 204, Artificial Intelligence Applications and Innovations, eds. Maglogiannis, I., Karpouzis, K., Bramer, M., (Boston: Springer), pp. 156–162

made or multiple versions of the system must be created' in order to satisfy the specific interaction requirements of every user.

2 Low Level Adaptive Systems

Designing different interfaces for each kind of user can be extremely costly. Furthermore, this approach causes excessive development costs when maintaining versions across multiple platforms [3]. A much cheaper solution is the development of a unique user interface able to be adapted to each type of user. Literature includes several references to techniques designed to adapt user interfaces.

Several systems and prototypes generate adapted contents depending on the information stored in general user models. Techniques for the presentation of adaptive content usually include conditional inclusion, contents removing and transformation of contents. Kobsa et al [4] developed and adaptive learning framework tailored to the student's presumed level of familiarity with the subject. This system was called KN-AHS (KoNstanz Adaptive Hypertext System).

Weber and [5] developed another adaptive learning system in the form of an adaptive interactive textbook called ELM-ART. This system was able to learn from the student's actions, performing visual adaptive annotation of links based on the actions performed in previous sessions. Another important adaptive learning system is AHA [6] (De Bra and Calvi, 1998). This system not only learns from user actions but also from tests.

In the EU-funded AVANTI project ([7]; [4]), a web-based information system was developed providing universal access to disabled and elderly users. This project represented an important attempt in the use of techniques for the adaptive presentation in order to satisfy the needs of each individual user, including a broad spectrum of users with perceptual and motor disabilities.

PERSONA [1] is an ambitious (and never implemented) proposal for an adaptive user interface management system based on agents called 'tailors'. Each 'tailor' includes a collection of similar components that perform the same tasks within the user interface, but which are specifically designed for one specific kind of users.

Working on the highest levels of the user interface, these adaptive systems do not pay much attention to the syntactical and lexical levels of the interface responsible for the configuration of the interactive objects (size, color, etc.) and how these objects are going to be accessed by the user [8]. The main handicap in the management of the user model in some of these systems is their data acquisition algorithm, which is based on periodical updates. However, a continuous observation of the user behavior could highly increase the amount of features that could be adapted in the user interface, as well as the global accuracy of the system.

3 The Architecture of GADEA

GADEA tries to emulate the behavior of a human expert in Human-Computer Interaction designing all the interactive dialogs required to establish an effective communication between the application and the specific user.

This emulated expert selects the most suitable interaction style available for the target platform (Web-based or standalone applications), adapting the appearance, contents and access mode of each dialog to the user requirements. The result is a multimodal communication channel [9] containing a combination of visual and aural interactive dialogs.

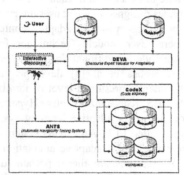

Fig. 1. GADEA uses three main modules: DEVA, ANTS and CodeX. The User Model is shared by ANTS and DEVA. While ANTS is in charge of keeping it updated, DEVA uses it to create user-tailored interactive dialogs.

The architecture of GADEA is based on a two layer design (see figure 1). The upper layer constitutes the user interface's front-end; containing two modules: DEVA (*Dialog Expert eValuator for Adaptation*) and ANTS (*Automatic Navigability Testing System*). The lower layer manages the interaction between the first layer (the user interface) and the application(s); containing one module: CodeX (*Code eXplorer*).

3.1 CodeX (Code eXplorer)

When the user launches the application, CodeX inspects the application's binary code using computational reflection in order to obtain the list of user processes registered by the programmers at the design stage. Those user processes are the actions available to interact with the application. This list is sent to DEVA, which includes the processes in the application's menus. If the user selects a menu option, DEVA will send a notification to CodeX in order to execute the corresponding method.

Whenever a user process requires information from the user, the programmer must design at least one interactive dialog for that process. These dialogs are data containers built at the design stage but filled by the user at the execution time. For example, if an application requires to know the user favorite color, the corresponding interactive dialog will include a data object filled with the color request message (something like 'What is your favorite color?'), and an empty data object for the user favorite color that will be filled with the data provided by the user at execution time.

3.2   DEVA (Dialog Expert Valuator for Adaptation)

When CodeX executes a user process including an interactive dialog, this dialog is sent to DEVA which will convert this data container into a visual or aural display (depending on the kind of user, it could generates a combination of both). This display uses interactive objects (buttons, text fields, menus, etc.) to interact with the user, filling the information included in the data container with the information provided by the user. The conversion algorithm uses general human-computer interaction guidelines which are adapted to the interaction requirements of the current user of the application using the information stored in the user model.

Depending on the requirements of the current user, DEVA selects the most suitable communication channel (for instance, aural channels for blind users) inserting the most suitable interactive objects (for example, certain disabled users cannot use popup menus, radio buttons or checkboxes) and suitably configuring each of them (for instance, short-sighted users require bigger objects).

In the first step, the interactive objects are selected a search algorithm that obtains the list of the interactive objects compatible with the data object's configuration, evaluating each of them according to cognitive criteria. In our previous example, the list of interactive objects than may be used to get information about the favorite color of the user includes at least a popup menu and a text field (among many others). Any of these interactive objects may accomplish the task. However, DEVA would select a text field object for visually disabled users and pop-up menus for users who prefer a mouse-based interaction (see Figure 2 and Figure 3). The scoring method for the search algorithm is based on the 'Keystroke Model' developed by [10] and redeveloped by [11].

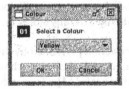

Fig. 2. Interactive dialog created by DEVA when the user prefers a mouse-based interaction or has good pointing skills.

The second step is to design the dialog's layout. We make use of orientation metaphors ([12] cited by [13]) mapping the vertical attribute of any location of the visual space to the 'up is more' and 'down is less' metaphors [13].

The last step defines the size, shape, color, etc. of every interactive object selected. This task is performed using a fuzzy logic engine powered by more than fifty different rules based on state of the art Human-Computer Interaction guidelines as well as on the data stored in the user model.

Once the user has finished the interaction process with the dynamically generated dialog, the dialog is converted into a data container again (including the information provided by the user during the interaction process) which is sent again to CodeX for a further processing by the application.

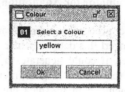

Fig. 3. . Interactive dialog created by DEVA when the user prefers a text-based interaction or has good typing skills.

4.1   ANTS (Automatic Navigability Testing System).

At the same time that the user interacts with the generated dialogs, his actions are continuously recorded and analyzed on the fly by the third module of GADEA: ANTS. The result of this analysis is included in the user model, keeping it updated and therefore, increasing the adaptation accuracy of the system.

Part of the information required to perform the adaptation proposed is provided explicitly by the user when registering in the system. This information includes the user's age, list of user's disabilities (short-sighted user, deaf user, etc.), visual precision (obtained using a simple test), whether the user is lefty or right handed, preferences for an specific kind of interaction (mouse or keyboard) and so on.

Other information required is obtained by a small army of data-gathering agents, which keeps track of the user behavior in every available interactive dialog displayed at execution time. The design metaphor of ANTS is based on the life of a community of ants. The ants (agents) depart from their anthill (a server), looking for food (the information) in every picnic available (interactive dialogs). Once the ant has got the food, it comes back to the anthill and carefully stores the food in one of the available warehouses (the user model).

The ants keep track of every action performed by the user in every user process, creating an abstract navigation model similar to those employed by the Object Oriented Hypermedia Design Model [14]. This navigation model is used to determine the landmarks, routes and mental models [15] employed by the users when they execute the user processes; obtaining the user's expertise degree when working with the application [16].

Some agents are able to analyze the data collected, determining the user's precision in the performance of certain tasks. For example, this system has agents specialized in analyzing the user typing skills (based on the Salthouse's regularities [17]) or the visual form recognition skills (based on Sternberg's regularities 1969, [18]).

5 Testing the System with Real Users

In order to test the precision of this adaptation model, we performed several tests for each feature of the system. As a paradigmatic example of such kind of tests, we are going describe the tests applied to the chromatic adaptation algorithm of GADEA.

Five basic interactive dialogs were created to test this feature (labeled from v1 up to v5.). Each dialog displayed a different text message. Next, volunteers participating in the tests were grouped depending on their visual precision into five groups labeled from A to E. Finally, GADEA generated an adapted version of each dialog for each group.

The results obtained were successful for users of the groups B and C (adults with normal-low and normal-high visual precision) since the average of the selections performed by the volunteers always favored the versions designed by GADEA for their groups. In the case of the group B an average of 84% of the selections favored the version designed by our system for users of that group. This proportion was a little bit higher for the group C (91.42%).

Results for groups D (teenagers with excellent visual precision) and E (adults with high visual precision) reached 70% and 76% respectively. The worst results were obtained by the group A (elderly people with low visual precision) since only 53.33% of the versions developed by GADEA were selected as the most suitable.

This experiment showed that, although relative powerful, the chromatic adaptation algorithm requires finer tuning for certain kind of users (especially for elderly people). Such kind of tests also revealed themselves as a powerful tool to measure the accuracy of the adaptive algorithms of our system.

6 Conclusions and Future Work

We have presented a user interface management system which provides full support for the automatic generation of the lexical and syntactical level of the interface. Since these levels are designed dynamically at execution time (once the real user requirements are known) this strategy prevents the design of interactive dialogs based on misconceptions about the users.

Tasks assigned to the designers are limited to the semantic and conceptual levels of the interface, designing the interchange of information between their programs and the user instead of how that information is displayed. This strategy simplifies the amount of work to be done by the programmers.

Several improvements may be done in this basic open adaptation framework. Our tests showed that the usefulness of the system depends on the precision of adaptation algorithms as well as on the precision of the information stored in the user model. The inclusion of new adaptation features to the system is relatively easy. It requires the addition of new rules to the fuzzy inference engine and (if required) new data-gathering agents to obtain updated information about the input parameters used in the rule. However, each new feature added to the system requires a careful testing process to obtain valid results.

7   References

1. C. Reynolds, A Critical Examination of Separable User Interface Management Systems: Constructs for Individualisation. ACM SIGCHI. (1997) 29(3).
2. B. Schneiderman, Designing the user Interface. Reading, MA: Addison-Wesley. (1987).
3. G. Calvary, J. Coutaz, D. Thevenin, Q. Limbourg, N. Souchon, L. Bouillon, M. Florins, J. Vanderdonckt, Plasticity of User Interfaces: A Revised Reference Framework, Proceedings of the First International Workshop on Task Models and Diagrams for User Interface Design. (2002) 127 – 134.
4. Kobsa, J. Koenemann, W. Pohl, Personalized Hypermedia presentation techniques for improving online customer relationships. The Knowledge Engineering Review. (2001) 111-155.
5. G. Weber, P. Brusilovsky, ELM-ART: An adaptive versatile system for Web-based instruction. *International Journal of Artificial Intelligence in Education* 12 (4), Special Issue on Adaptive and Intelligent Web-based Educational Systems. (2001) 351-384.
6. P. De Bra, L. Calvi, AHA: a Generic Adaptive Hypermedia System. Proceedings of the 2nd Workshop on Adaptive Hypertext and Hypermedia HYPERTEXT'98, Pittsburgh, USA. (1998).
7. J. Fink, A. Kobsa, A. Nill, Adaptable and Adaptive Information Provision for All Users, Including Disabled and Elderly People. New Review of Hypermedia and Multimedia 4. (1998) 163-188.
8. J. Foley, W. C. Kim, S. Kovacevic, K. Murray, UIDE, An Intelligent User Interface Environment. Intelligent User Interfaces. Frontier Series. ACM Press. (1991).
9. W. Wahlster; User and Dialog Models for Multimodal Communication. Intelligent User Interfaces. Frontier Series. ACM Press. (1991).
10. S. Card, K. Stuart, T. Moran, P. Thomas, A. Newell. The Psychology of Human-Computer Interaction. Lawrence Erlbaum Associates (1983).
11. Newell, A. Unified Theories of Cognition. Harvard University Press. Cambridge, Massachusetts. (1990).
12. G. Lakoff; M. Johnson; Metaphors We Live By. Chicago: University of Chicago Press (1980).
13. E. Shulz; M. Van Alphen; W. Rasnake, Discovering User-generated Metaphors through Usability Testing. Proceedings of the Second International Conference on Cognitive Technology. Aizu, Japan (1997).
14. D. Schwabe, G. Rossi, Abstraction, Composition and Lay-Out Definition Mechanism in OOHDM. Proceedings of the ACM Workshop on Effective Abstractions in Multimedia. San Francisco, California. (1995).
15. S. Jul, G. W. Furnas, Navigation in Electronic Worlds: a CHI'97 Workshop. SIGCHI Bulletin Vol. 29, No. 4, October 1997, ACM Press. (1997).
16. S. Karn, S. Keith; J. Perry, J. Thomas, M. J. Krolczyk, Testing for Power Usability: a CHI 97 Workshop. ACM SIGCHI Bulletin Vol . 29, No. 4, October 1997 (1997).
17. T. Salthouse, Perceptual, Cognitive and Motoric Aspects of Transcription Typing. Psychological Bulletin (1986).
18. S. Sternberg, Memory Scanning: New Findings and Current Controversies. Quarterly Journal of Experimental Psychology (1974).

On supporting young students in visual logic modeling

Christos Fidas[1,2], Nikolaos Avouris[2], Vassilis Komis[2], Panagiotis Politis[3]
[1] Instance Ltd, Scientific Park of Patras, 26500 Rio Patras, Greece
fidas@instance.gr
[2] University of Patras, 26500 Rio Patras, Greece
{komis, avouris}@upatras.gr
[3]University of Thessaly, Volos, Greece,
ppol@uth.gr

Abstract. Logic reasoning presents notable difficulties for young children. This paper presents Logic Model Creator (LMC), a new environment that supports building and exploration of intuitive visual representation of logic models by young children. LMC logic models are structured as hypothesis, decision and / or counter decision components. These models are built using visual entities which represent the learning concepts of a specific domain. In this paper we focus on the architecture of LMC and the basic functionality of the environment. In particular we describe the the dynamic creation of equivalent logic models according to the so-called Reference Logic Model, constructed by the students' tutor. Furthermore an assessment module which provides immediate advice to the student in order to help them create a valid logic model is presented. Through experimentation it is demonstrated that the users of LMC can have rich interaction and assessment while exploring decision making logic constructs.

1 Introduction

The importance of using models of phenomena, activities or systems in learning has been widely recognized [1]. A number of software tools have been developed during the last years that support learning through modeling. These software environments mostly concern mathematical models of physical phenomena [2], while other modeling activities have also been proposed, like creation of concept maps, modeling of ecological and other complex phenomena [3], etc. A special case of modeling tools and activities relate to modeling logical propositions or logical constructs, proposed by scientists from science education and psychology fields [1]. Their purpose is to support children's reasoning and help them have access to decision making reasoning in a progressive way [4]. The reasoning of the students

Please use the following format when citing this chapter:

Fidas, Christos, Avouris, Nikolaos, Komis, Vassilis, Politis, Panagiotis, 2006, in IFIP International Federation for Information Processing, Volume 204, Artificial Intelligence Applications and Innovations, eds. Maglogiannis, I., Karpouzis, K., Bramer, M., (Boston: Springer), pp. 163–170

engaged in logical modeling involves studying and exploring logical propositions that are represented in visual form. Through them it can be deduced how the value of a concept or object property has an effect on other properties, which may in turn, affect other parts of the model.

Logic Models Creator (LMC) is a new learning environment which supports logic modeling activities for students of 11 to 16 years old. LMC is a derivative of the decision support component of an earlier modeling environment, ModelsCreator version 2.0 (MCv2), originally built as a tool to be used for qualitative and semi-quantitative reasoning with real world concepts [5]. The original Decision Support component of ModelsCreator included a validation and model diagnosis module described in [6]. The limitations of that module have been tackled in LMC, as discussed in this paper. The logic propositions that can be built and explored with LMC meet the requirements of many curriculum subject matters, like mathematics, science etc., permitting interdisciplinary use of the logic modeling process. LMC puts great emphasis on visualization of the modeling entities, their properties and their relations. Visualization is crucial in supporting the reasoning development of young students and favors the transition from reasoning over objects to reasoning with abstract concepts [7]. This feature is extended also to the simulation of executable models allowing their validation through representation of the phenomenon itself in a visual way and not in an abstract mathematical relation or logical proposition, as it is usually the case. In fig. 1 an example of a model built using LMC is shown. On the left the hypothesis is visualized and on the right hand side the conclusion of the logical proposition. In this example the conditions are tested for deciding to prepare an application for hosting a child over the holiday season by a family.

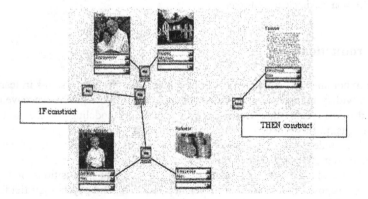

Fig. 1. An example of an LMC logic model

An important aspect of LMC, as with the original MCv2, is its open character regarding the ability provided to the teachers in creating new logical domains (i.e. new subject matters) as well as new primitive entities which are needed for the creation of the logic models.

In the rest of this paper we present first the architecture and basic functionality of the LMC environment for the teacher and the student. We describe an example of use of LMC by groups of young students and discuss the implications of this environment in current teaching practice.

2 Architecture of the Logic Models Creator (LMC) environment

Let M an LMC model, like the one presented in figure 1. This model can be represented as follows: $M = \{ E_i, i=1, ..., k, R_j, j=1,..., l, A_m, m=1, ..., n \}$

Where Ei represents the node entity i of the model, Aj a property of a given entity, R a relationship connecting them. Examples are Entity=House, Attribute=Size. The relations which connect entities' attributes belong to the following set: AND, THEN, OR, AND, ELSE and NOT. Through them logical constructs can be built by the users using direct manipulation in the activity space. Using such an environment, one may construct expressions of arbitrary complexity.

The equivalent logical expression that can be built is:

Proposition = *IF* Construct *THEN* Construct

| *IF* Construct *THEN* Construct *ELSE* Construct

Construct = (Construct *AND* Construct) | (Construct *OR* Construct) | *NOT*(Construct)

| Attribute=Value

In this section an insight into the architecture of LMC system is given. An overview of the system architecture is provided in figure 2, presenting the main user categories and functionalities of the system described in this paper. A modular approach has been followed, in order to reduce the complexity of the design. The aim of each module is to provide specific services to the modules with which it is connected, isolating the details of the construction of these services.

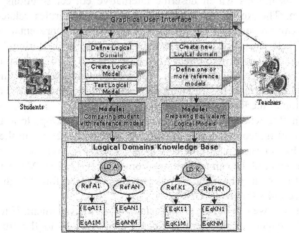

Fig. 2. System architecture of LMC

The system considers two basic user categories a) the students and b) the teachers who interact with the visual environment in order to accomplish specific tasks. While the main task of the students is to build and check the correctness of their logical models the main task of the teachers is to create new logical domains and define the reference models.

In the following some typical interaction scenarios of teachers and students with LMC are described in order to demonstrate the functionality of the architecture.

2.1 Teacher: Creation of a new logical domain

An important aspect of LMC is its open character regarding the ability provided to the teachers of creating new logical domains (i.e. new subject matters) as well as new primitive entities which are needed for the creation of the logical models. As a consequence, the educational environment brings additional value since it can adapt easily to the educational needs of different curriculum domains. Each logical domain represents one or more logical problems which describes decision making concepts that the students must explore. For each logical problem the teacher can create entities which describe verbally and visually the concepts included in the problem domain. Each entity may include a set of a attributes which describe specific characteristics of the entity. Some of them might be irrelevant to the problem at hand. Furthermore to each attribute of an entity can be assigned one more possible value. These values belong to a set which is defined in the creation phase of an entity.

2.2 Teacher: Defining a reference model

In the frame of a logical domain a teacher can define more than one Reference Model against which the students constructs will be subsequently tested. We consider these as models which describe alternative correct solutions to a given logical problem. The Reference Model should not violate rules related with the syntax of logical propositions of LMC. The knowledge representation used for expressing the Reference Model has been a matter of discussion during development of LMC and the previous environment MC. As discussed in [6], a first attempt was to express the Reference Model through Prolog statements, however this approach produced rigid logical models. An alternative proposed here is to use Truth Tables for representation of the Reference Model.

So for each Reference Model in LMC a teacher must complete a Truth Table which contains all the combinations of different events that exists in the Reference Model. If the hypothesis graph connects a set of $\{G1,...,GN\}$ events of different attributes and each attribute can take values from a set $\{G11,...,G1 M)$ than the whole set of different states in which the hypothesis graph can be found is the Cartesian product $Gif = \{G1M \times G2M \times ...GNM\}$

In a similar way we can define the decision part of the statement. If it connects a set of $\{1,...,M\}$ events of different attributes then we add to the truth table M columns which will be associated with values by the teacher. These values of the attributes in the decision graph depend on the values of the attributes of the hypothesis graph.

A truth table (see figure 3) is produced which contains the combinations of the hypothesis graph (according to the reference model of the teacher) and the values of the decision/counter decision graph according to the values of the hypothesis graph.

In fig.3 the user interface of a Truth Table filling phase is shown. While the combinations of the hypothesis graph are filled automatically by the system the values of the attributes in the decision part must be filled by the teacher. After the teacher has finished the completion of the values the system produces logical equivalent propositions for each logical sentence in the Truth Table as described in the following.

Combinations of the hypothesis graph				Conclusion values			
	GII	*G2I*		*GNI*			
...							
G₁ₕ × G₂ₕ × ...Gₙₕ	*G1M*	*G2M*		*GNM*			

Fig. 3. Completion of the Truth Table values for definition of a Reference Model

2.3 Preparing equivalent logical models

As mentioned in section 2.2, every entity is defined by a closed set of attributes and each attribute can take a value from a closed set. This way, if an attribute N is defined by M different states it can take a value from a closed set of M values $M=\{V_{AN1},V_{AN2},...,V_{ANM}\}$. Furthermore if we consider that in a logical sentence of the Truth Table an attribute N has taken a specific value K that belongs in M, then we can deduce that: $V_{NK} \Leftrightarrow NOT(M-K)$

i.e. attribute N has taken value K is equivalent with the fact: attribute N has not taken all the other values that exist in M except K, which in fact can be a way the students can express themselves while solving a logic problem.

At first the hypothesis, decision and counter decision graphs are considered. Equivalent graphs are produced according to the above approach. If $l_{if}=\{l_1,...,l_N\}$ is the set of equivalent hypothesis graphs, $l_{then}=\{l_1,...,l_k\}$ is the set of equivalent decision graphs and $l_{else}=\{l_1,...,l_j\}$ is the set of counter decision graphs then the whole set L of equivalent logical models is the Cartesian product of l_{if}, l_{then} and l_{else} :
$L=\{l_{IF} \times l_{THEN} \times l_{ELSE}\}$

2.4 Student: Defining a logical domain

In order to evaluate a model the student has to specify first the logical problem in a logical domain. The logical domain module informs the active logical domain module about the logical problem that has been selected by the student. The active logical domain module gets form the knowledge base the set of all correct logical models that describe the selected logical problem.

The knowledge base consists of the logical domains, the logical problems, the Reference Models defined by the teachers and the equivalent Logical Models deduced by the system as described in section 2.3. Each logical problem can have one or more Reference Models. Furthermore each Reference Model can have one ore more equivalent Logical Models, created automatically by the system using the above approach. Each logical model in set L (all the correct models for the logical problem) is saved in and expressed internally in the form of logical propositions: *Logical Proposition= If (Hypothesis graph) Then (Decision graph) Else (Counter decision part).*

After the logical domain has been specified the student can create and test the correctness of his logical models. First the translation module is activated in order to translate the students model from the graphical into textual representation similar with the representation of the logical models in the knowledge base. The validation module compares the student model with the models in the knowledge base of the active logical domain and provides to the user the appropriate feedback.

2.5 Student: Validation of a student model and providing feedback

We consider that a logical problem consists of a set of correct logical models L $L=\{l1,...,lN\}$. The purpose of the system is to support the student with appropriate feedback in order to build a model that is equal to a correct logical model in the knowledge base of the active logical domain. To attain this aim, the system creates and displays messages using a relevance factor.

In the case that the student model is equal to a model in set L a message is produced in order to inform the student about the correctness of his model. In any other case the system has diagnosed that the student model has no equal model in set L, it sttempts to find a model in set L which is similar with the students model. With the aim to achieve this goal the validation module scores each model in set L regarding with the student model using the following equation.

$$score= f_{Entities}+f_{attributes}+f_{attributeValues}+f_{Realtions}$$

where

- $f_{Entities}$ =(Student.Correct.Entities/Total.Needed.Entities)
- $f_{attributes}$ =(Student.Correct.Attributes/Total.Needed.Attributes)
- $f_{attributeValues}$ =(Student.Correct.AttributesValues/Total.Needed.AttributesValues)
- $f_{Realtions}$ =(Student.Correct.Relations/Total.Needed. Relations)

The logical model with the highest score is defined as the closest logical model to the developed student model. The validation module specifies the feedback message provided to the student according to the level of similarity between the student and the closest model.

The validation module of LMC checks the level of similarity in (a) the Entities level (b) the Attributes level (c) the Attributes values level and (d) the Relations level and provides the student with appropriate feedback messages in order to support and scaffold the modelling process. In cases where the semantics of the modeling problem render some artifact (e.g., entity, attribute or relationship) more important that another counterpart, the (maximization of the value of the) formula described above may not give the most appropriate result. In such cases allowing the teacher to tune a weighted version could be preferable.

3 Case study of use of LMC

In a recent case study, that involved use of LMC, a pair of two 11-year old students (a boy and a girl) of the final year of a primary school of the city of Volos, in Greece were asked to explore a logical model under the supervision of their teacher. The model is based on a scenario of a dog that is in conduct with a live wire and received an electric shock. The children were asked to investigate the conditions under which they could safely rescue the dog. The mode includes attributes like Material of the *stick* to touch the dog, Material of the *shoes* of the child, Material and condition of the *floor* (see figure 4). The teacher asked the students to investigate various alternatives and to check the validity of the model. The session that lasted one hour was recorded and subsequently analyzed using a dialogue annotation scheme.

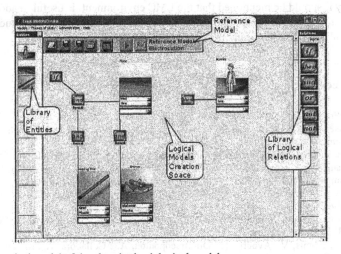

Fig. 4. A typical model of the electric shock logical model

An interesting finding of the study was that the two children were engaged in dialogue with the LMC environment and discussed their own experiences related to the subject domain. They investigated for instance the conducting capability of materials like plastic and rubber in relation to the shoes and inferred that plastic is insulating material, as in cables of household electric appliances. One of the children recalled that her grandmother received a strong shock when she touched a bare live cable. The messages received by LMC were considered relevant and supported the specific task. The children seemed to trust the software environment when they engaged in dialogue with it and expressed their wish to further interact with models in other subject domains. Despite the fact that the children of this age group were lacking strong conceptual models of the domain, they managed to reason about it with the support of LMC.

4 Conclusions

In this paper we described the Logical Model Creator (LMC), an innovative environment that permits building and exploring Logic Propositions. The architecture of LMC and the user interface were presented in this paper. The concept of the Reference Model is used for diagnosing the validity of logic models built by students of 11 to 16 years old. A Truth Table is used as interface component for permitting to the teacher to define the valid states of the Reference Model. This is based on all possible values of the Entity Attributes in the "if graph" of the Model. Through this Table the teacher can specify all possible accepted states of the entities of the *decision* and *counter decision graph* of the model. In a case study, involving primary school students, it was found that the environment was intuitive to use and explore, while the messages received by the environment were considered useful in the specific domain.

Finally it should be mentioned that the LMC environment, is useful in addition to exploring models in various subject matters, for introducing young students in concepts of logic, like Boolean operators and IF-THEN-ELSE constructs.

References

1. Bliss J. From Mental Models to Modelling, in H. Mellar, J. Bliss, R. Boohan, J. Ogborn, C.Tompsett (Eds). Learning with Artificial Worlds: Computer Based Modelling in the Curriculum, The Falmer Press, London, 1994.
2. Teodoro, V. D.: Learning with Computer-Based Exploratory Environments in Science and Mathematics. In S. Vosniadou, E. De Corte, H. Mandl (Eds.), Technology -Based Learning Environments, NATO ASI Series, Vol. 137, Berlin: Springer Verlag. (1994) 179-186
3. Soloway E., Guzdial M., Hay K.E., (1994). Learner Centred Design: The challenge for HCI in the 21"Century, *Interactions*, Vol. 1. No 2, April, pp. 36-48
4. Ogborn J. (1990). A future for modelling in science education, Journal of Computer Assisted Education, Oxford, Blackwell Scientific
5. Fidas, C., Komis, V., Avouris, N., Dimitracopoulou, A. : Collaborative Problem Solving using an Open Modelling Environment. In G. Stahl (ed.), Proc. CSCL 2002, Boulder, Colorado, USA, Lawrence Erlbaum Associates, Inc., (2002) 654-655
6. Partsakoulakis I., Vouros G.. Helping Young Students Reach Valid Decisions Through Model Checking. Proc. 3td ETPE Conf., pp. 669-678, Rhodes, Greece, 2002.
7. Teodoro V.D. Modellus: Using a Computational Tool to Change the Teaching and Learning of Mathematics and Science, in "New Technologies and the Role of the Teacher" Open University, Milton Keynes, UK, 1997.

Attentional Model for Perceiving Social Context in Intelligent Environments

Jérôme Maisonnasse, Nicolas Gourier, Oliver Brdiczka, Patrick Reignier

PRIMA, GRAVIR-IMAG

INRIA Rhône-Alpes,

38349 St. Ismier.

France

Abstract. This paper presents a novel approach to detect interaction groups in intelligent environments. To understand human activity, we must identify human actors as well as their interpersonal links. Interaction detection is a good cue to address activity of user groups. An attentional model is derived from gravitational model and cognitive psychology approaches. Whereas determining locally users'. focus of attention is a difficult task, this model exploits contextual elements such as position, speed and saliency of objects in the scene to estimate shared attention. The attentional model shows promising results on simulated scenarios where unexpected events occur.

1 Introduction

Human activity recognition is a growing field of research. Recent progress in computer multimodal perception promises new developments in the field of ambient applications and pervasive systems. Such systems aim at offering services by taking into account the current user's activity in a specific situation. In intelligent environments, more and more devices are able of perceiving user activity and proposing appropriate services. Addressing the right user at the right moment is essential. We must detect potential users and their connection while doing an activity. This aspect of human activity is neglected by most studies, in which groups are predefined and unchanging. It appears important to explicit relations between different users and to detect interactions between them. Interaction configuration group is the best detector of activity presence in a scene. Indeed, when a participant is in immediate physical contact with another, they contribute to the same global definition of the situation [5]. Delimiting who is concerned by an activity is a difficult operation. Psychology studies show that human activity is more unexpected than we perceive. Limits between different activities are fuzzy when users share the

Please use the following format when citing this chapter:

Maisonnasse, Jerome, Gourier, Nicolas, Brdiczka, Oliver, Reignier, Patrick, 2006, in IFIP International Federation for Information Processing, Volume 204,Artificial Intelligence Applications and Innovations, eds. Maglogiannis, I., Karpouzis, K., Bramer, M., (Boston: Springer), pp. 171–178

same physical space [7]. Outside laboratory conditions, activity evolves in relation to exte
rnal factors which can not be expected. Identification of the current group configuration of users is necessary to connect activity. The dynamics of group configuration, i.e. the split and merge of interaction groups, allows us to perceive relevant evolution of current activities. Determining user focus of attention is a difficult task. Focus of attention is an intern cognitive task which can not be perceived directly. This perception must be estimated from external observations.

We propose an attentional model to dynamically detect interaction group. An interaction between people occurs when we suppose that they share the same information [11]. A cognitive explanation of how people share information is their ability to product a mutual intelligibility of current situation. Perception of current situation is defined by enabled shared resources in a physical, social and cultural environment, more or less stabilized [10]. In this paper, we model available contextual element in intelligent environment to compute mutual intelligibility. From these results, we analyze focus of attention of users, and detect where interactions take place.

2. Related Work

Based on the idea that social world is organized and understandable in the way action is produced, computer sciences attempt to extract invariant features to describe activity. Most computer vision based research in human activity recognition is focused on data processing issues. Many approaches extract a structured representation of user activity from sensory input data [8]. Visual, acoustic and temporal aspects of activity are concerned. Human activity is cut into a sequence of relevant features from observation in relation to a particular activity. Some approaches are very close to input data. These systems work like a black box learning activity from specific observations. Some systems build higher-level representations of activity. Extracted features are used to match some learned concept representing activity [3]. Relations between detected entities are interpreted as semantic relationships. In the second case, the main issue is to identify entities and concepts describing a specific situation or action. Relation detection then depends on concept and entity recognition. However, interactions between users are an implicit data and almost studies do not consider only one group.

It seems important to explicit interaction between users. A first approach has been applied successfully to speech event detection [2]. It could be completed with other modalities. Psychology offers relevant models to understand how people could interact in relation of contextual element. In order to estimate how attention focus is placed on space, we propose a cognitive model. To compute this model, some relevant and available features are used in intelligent environment. Almost every device could give some information about their internal state and their action in direction of users. For example, when an user is receiving an email or his telephone is ringing, this device will send a message to our system about their actions.

However, understanding what humans do when they execute actions is more difficult. User based approaches are exponentially complex and computationally expensive for this problem. For this reason, we implement an attentional model based on context. This approach requires fewer features from users and objects and is psychologically plausible.

3. Role of Context in production of Mutual Intelligibility

To explain the way in which agents are able to communicate, it is necessary to admit that they share mutual knowledge. Theory of mutual knowledge has a characteristic to produce a regression at infinity. But this theory cannot be integrated into a cognitive explanation of production and comprehension of communicative acts. Sperber and Wilson developed a weaker but empirically more adequate concept, the mutual manifestness. For Sperber and Wilson, "a fact is manifest to an individual at a given time if and only if this individual is able at this time to represent this fact mentally and to accept his representation as being true or probably true [11]. In other words, a fact is manifest when it has the characteristic to be perceptible or deduced by an agent at a given time. A fact can thus be manifest without being known. However, some facts can be more manifest than others. To model this, we associate a degree of salience to each fact. The salience is a function of the perceptual and cognitive capacities of the individual, and of his physical environment. For example, let us suppose that a telephone is ringing in a room where an individual A is sitting at an open window and that at the same time a car is passing in a street. In this case, it will be strongly manifest for A that telephone rang, but less clear that a car passed. Thus, because of the difference of salience between the ringing telephone and the car noise, the fact "telephone is ringing" is more manifest, i.e. has more chance to be perceived or deduced than the fact "a car passed". Sperber and Wilson define the cognitive environment as whole facts which are manifest for a given individual. A shared cognitive environment indicates all the facts which are manifest to several individuals. From the example of telephone by imagining that another individual B is in the same part as A. In this case, by supposing that they have same perceptual capacities, it is manifest for A and B which telephone is ringing. This means simply that they are able to perceive or deduce the same fact, and not that they share a belief, a knowledge, or a representation concerning this fact. The Mutual Cognitive Environment (ECM) indicates a shared cognitive environment in which identity of individuals who have access to this environment is manifest. A and B share a cognitive environment which includes all facts and especially their co-presence. As they share the same environment, they can establish an interaction in relation to their common perception of contextual events. This definition is more precise than Dey's definition of context as "any information that can be used to characterize the situation of entities" [4]. Dey does not precise how user information is selected. We define context as the whole set of objects which are manifest for an individual and capable to modify his interpretation of the situation.

3.1 Focus, Nimbus and Spatial Metaphor

In spatial metaphor, localization contributes to structure interactions between users. By considering their interpersonal distance, in virtual space, users adapt their cooperation situation. Space is inhabited by objects which might represent people, information or other computer artefacts. Cooperation for distant users need to be restored by contextualizing space of work and by giving users a mean to control their interaction. "Objects in space are responsible for controlling interactions on the basis of quantifiable levels of awareness between them. Awareness between objects is manipulated via focus and nimbus, subspaces within which an object chooses to direct either its presence or its attention" [9]. Initially, focus and nimbus are defined as follows:

"   -   The more an object is within your focus, the more aware you are of it
    -   The more an object is within your nimbus, the more aware it is of you"[1].

In spatial metaphor, there are objects which manage their awareness by manipulating focus and nimbus subspaces. To define how many objects can interact, we evolve awareness levels from a combination of nimbus and focus configuration. "The level of awareness that A has of object B in medium M is some function of A's focus in M in relation to B's nimbus in M" [1]. Level of awareness defines whether objects may be strongly or weakly aware of each other. This model describes how to quantify level of awareness but not how to compute dynamically focus and nimbus. Indeed, in computer supported co-operative work (CSWC) applications, computing focus and nimbus do not present interest because focus and nimbus are parameters controlled by users as input data. We need a specific model to compute focus direction from contextual elements observation. On the basis of cognitive model, the attractiveness notion of a salient object leads us to another field of research where distance and salience object is useful to understand how objects influence each others.

3.2 Gravitational Model

The first Law of Universal Gravitation has been formulated by Isaac Newton in the 17th Century. Any two objects in the Universe exert gravitational force on each other, with the universal form (1). This force is proportional to the product of their masses and inversely proportional to the square of the separation between the two objects. An example is shown in Figure 1.

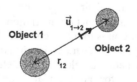

Fig. 1. Object 1 attracts Object 2

$$\vec{F}_{1\to2} = -\vec{F}_{2\to1} = -G\frac{m_1.m_2}{r_{12}^2}\vec{u}_{1\to2} \quad (1)$$

where $\vec{F}_{1\to2}$ is the gravitational force exerted by object 1 on object 2, $G = 6.67.10^{-11} \ N.m^2.kg^{-2}$ is the universal gravitational constant, m_1 and m_2 are the masses of the two objects, r_{12} is the distance between the two objects and $\vec{u}_{1\to2}$ is a unitary vector between the two objects. By considering N objects in the Universe, the force exerted on each object i is equal to the sum of gravitational forces exerted by the N-1 other objects (2):

$$\vec{F}_{\to i} = \sum_{\substack{j=1 \\ j\neq i}}^{N} \vec{F}_{j\to i} = \sum_{\substack{j=1 \\ j\neq i}}^{N} -G\frac{m_j.m_i}{r_{ij}^2}\vec{u}_{j\to i} \quad (2)$$

The Fundamental Principle of Dynamics (3) enounces that the derivative of the quantity of movement of an object i is equal to the sum of the forces exerted on this object. By supposing that the mass m_i of the object is constant, we can compute the acceleration of this object (4). The acceleration a_i of object i stands for the attraction of other objects on object i. In particular, it reflects the fact that objects with little masses are more attracted by objects with bigger masses than objects with bigger masses towards objects with little masses.

$$\frac{d(m_i.\vec{v}_i)}{dt} = \vec{F}_{\to i} \quad (3) \qquad \vec{a}_i = \sum_{\substack{j=1 \\ j\neq i}}^{N} -G\frac{m_j}{r_{ij}^2}\vec{u}_{j\to i} \quad (4)$$

In this work, we compute a likelihood interaction as the cue of a shared activity between co-presence users. An attentional model can identify when people share same resources, on the basis of proxemic information and contextual element salience. We have interpreted this cognitive model by transposing some relevant concept from gravitational model.

4. Social awareness as activity detector tool

Focus of a person is defined by attention direction which is the combination of its external and internal factors. External factors of a person are determined by the attraction of the person, objects or artefacts towards its environment. We adapt the gravitational model to simulate persons' attraction towards other persons or objects. Each person or object has a salience m. The salience corresponds to the mass in the gravitational model and derivates the concept of nimbus in spatial metaphor. We suppose that salience is invariant, which allows computing the attraction vector of each person towards the people and the objects in the environment using the gravitational model. The salience could be defined on perceptive, social or situation features.

Internal factors of a person are determined by the person's current goal or current activity, regardless of its environment. Cues of internal factor of a person are for example current speed and gaze direction. Internal factors can also be represented by a vector. For the moment, we just take into account the current speed. Both external and internal factors vectors are combined so that the influence of external factors decreases exponentially with the internal awareness, as shown by Figure 2. For our application, the influence of the attraction becomes negligible when the speed is higher than the top speed v_{max} of human running of 4 m/s. We compute the attention vector as a linear combination of internal and external factors, as in (5).

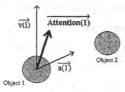

Fig. 2. Attention vector of object 1

$$\overrightarrow{Attention\,(i)} = \lambda \cdot e^{-2\frac{\|v(i)\|}{v_{max}}} \cdot \overrightarrow{a(i)} + \mu \cdot \overrightarrow{v(i)} \quad (5)$$

We consider the interaction area as ellipse constructed as follows; the position of the person is a focus of the ellipse and its addition with the attention vector gives us the center of ellipse. The area of the interaction is called interaction capacity. The interaction capacity is the maximum interaction area which human can act. To calculate the interaction capacity, we consider that two people speaking together at an interpersonal distance of 1.5 meters [6] are in full interaction, and their interaction ellipses recovers fully, as in Figure 6. We define the attention point of a person as the other focus of his interaction ellipse. Beyond a maximal distance of 6 meters, we consider that few social interactions occur, and the great axis reaches its maximum. This prevents us from having too slim ellipse. A fact is salient when it modifies the direction of an interaction ellipse. To determine social interactions and shared activities, we consider ellipses overlaps, as shown in Figures 4 and 5. The use of ellipses reflects the fact that the person stays aware of his surrounding and that the perception field reduces when the attention increases, and that the attention decreases on the opposite direction. In particular, when a person is alone in an empty environment, the attention vector is null, the two foci are equal to his position and his interaction ellipse becomes a circle. This reflect the fact that the person has his attention all around him, as in Figure 3.

Figure 3. Person 0 alone in an empty room

Figure 4. Person 1 close of an salience object 0

Figure 5. Two persons attracted each other.

Figure 6. Two persons in full attraction.

5. Application of the model to social awareness

In this section, we present a simulation which demonstrates the capacities of our attentional model to detect shared activities. Imagine an office environment where three persons (A, B, C) are working at their personal computer (0,1,2). Each person is attracted by his personal task materialized by computer interaction as shown in figure 7. Suddenly, person A starts to speak. The noise produced by his voice is perceptible for all people. Then B and C, attracted by this perception, move their attention focus from their computer to person A, as in Figure 8. When A stops speaking, a person D enters in the room and begins to speak. All persons move their attention to the newcomer, as in Figure 9. Person D gives his directives and exits the room, when the telephone is ringing. All persons lead their attention to telephone, but persons A and C have more probability to interact in relation to distance which separates them, as shown in Figure 10. The scenario described above illustrate how a system could identify where attention is lead on elements of context. The more attention they share, the stronger is their likelihood to interact.

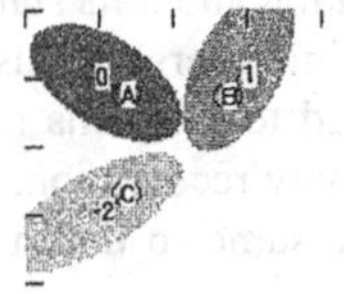

Figure 7. Three persons A, B, C work on their computer 0,1,2

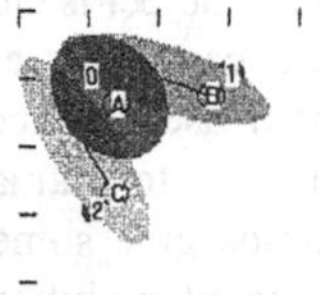

Figure 8. Two persons B, C are attracted by a third person A.

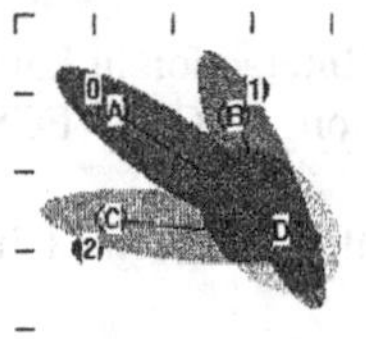

Figure 9. Three persons A, B, C are attracted by a newcomer D who speaks loud

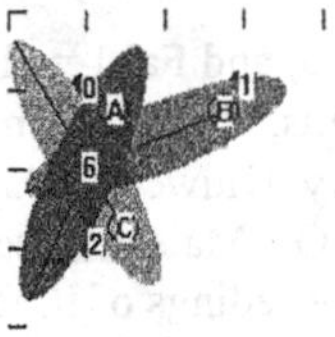

Figure 10. Three persons A, B, C are attracted by the telephone ringing.

Difficulties to use this model come from the choice of parameters for salience for each object. We have developed this model on the basis of a kind of type relation between parameter value and interaction strength. The salience follows an exponential scale. Other parameters could be used for the specification of a particular object salience. For these scenarios, we use parameters indicated in Figure 11.

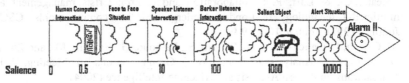

Fig. 3. Salience of right entities on the left entities

6. Conclusion

We propose a new perception tool to recognize human interaction in intelligent environments. On the basis of proxemic information and salience of contextual objects, we attempt to explicit social relationship to determine whether interactions occur or not. When one interaction is detected, we suppose that users have possibility to define or modify their current activity by articulating their respective actions in relation to new appearing fact. Here, we insist on the importance of context in activity production, and explicit mechanism to improve recognition performance.

This approach is based on context evaluation. Human activity is not represented by a sequence of sensory features by describing an entity at t moment, but integrates the relation between entities and the whole elements present in context which could affect his activity. The main difficulty is to identify objects and evaluate their salience. When the object is electronic, it can give information about its status and an a priori salience can be affected. The task of identifying users' status is more difficult, except if users are equipped of sensors. We need to plug this model to a complete architecture to evaluate real gain for human activity recognition. However, simulated scenarios give some interesting results, and presume to detect activities and theirs unexpected evolutions.

7. References

1. Benford, S.D, and Fah1èn, L. E. : A Spatial Model of Interaction in Large Virtual Environments, Proc. Third European Conference on CSCW (ECSCW'93), Milano, Italy, Kluwer (1993).
2. Brdiczka, O., Maisonnasse J., Reignier P. : Automatic detection of Interaction Groups, Proceedings of ICMI 2005, (2005) 32-36.
3. Crowley, J.L. and Reignier, P. : Dynamic Composition of Process Federations for Context Aware Perception of Human Activity, International Conference on Integration of Knowledge Intensive Multi-Agent Systems, KIMAS'03 (2003) .
4. Dey, A., Abowd, G., and Salber, D. : A conceptual framework and a toolkit for supporting the rapid prototyping of context-aware applications. Human-Computer Interaction (2001) 16 (2-4).
5. Goffman, E. : The presentation of self in every day life. Doubleday, New York: Doubleday (1959) (French traduction, 1973, Paris: Éditions Minuit).
6. Hall, E.,T. : The Hidden Dimension. Garden City, N.Y.: Doubleday (1966).
7. Heath, C., & Luff, P. : Collaboration and control: Crisis management and multimedia technology in London Underground line control rooms. CSCW Journal (1992) Volume 1(1), 69-94.
8. McCowan, I., Gatica-Perez, D., Bengio, S., Lathoud, G., Barnard, M., and Zhang, D.: Automatic Analysis of Multimodal Group Actions in Meeting, IEEE Transactions on Pattern Analysis and Machine Intelligence (2004).
9. Rodden, T.: Populating the Application: A Model of Awareness for Cooperative Applications, Computer Supported Cooperative Work '96, Cambridge MA USA, (1996).
10. Salembier, P., Theureau, J., Zouinar, M., & Vermersh, P. : Action/Cognition située et assistance à la coopération. In J. Charlet (Ed.), Ingénierie des connaissances IC2001. Grenoble: PUG (2001).
11. Sperber, D., & Wilson, D.: Relevance. Communication and cognition (2nd edition ed.). Oxford: Basil Blackwell (première édition 1986, Cambridge, MA: Harvard University Press) (2001).

Penguin Quart - Slovak Digit Speech Recognition Game Based on HMM[1]

Marek Nagy

Department of Applied Informatics,
Faculty of Mathematics, Physics and Informatics, Comenius University
Mlynska dolina, 842 48 Bratislava, Slovak Republic
mnagy@ii.fmph.uniba.sk
http://www.ii.fmph.uniba.sk/~mnagy

Abstract. In this article I focus on a simple education game Penguin Quart which is designed to use a speech dialogue. A genesis of it was motivated by effort to try a digit speech recognition in a real environment. The game was developed universally not only to educate but also to collect digit speech samples and to improve its recognition accuracy.

1 Introduction

A speech recognition is a very interesting area. Applications which use speech dialogue are more user friendly than other ones. Natural language communication with a computer adds to applications a new dimension.

A communication with computer by natural language was spontaneously divided into two main streams - a speech recognition and a speech synthesis. Approaches which try to solve the problem of a speech synthesis are the most popular and widely used because a human hearing is more flexible and can adapt to a worse computer synthesized speech. But the problem of a speech recognition is more difficult. A computer is strictly mathematically founded and cannot be very good adapted to a speech from different people. The main stream of the speech recognition is divided to the next three groups: a speaker independent (SI), a speaker depend (SD) and a speaker adaptable (SA) speech recognition. It is divided according to amount of speakers who are using the application. SI means that an application will be used by any one and SD means that it will be used by users who are selected beforehand. SA approaches try to adapt a recognition process to an actual speaking man.

---

[1] Partially supported by national grants VEGA 1/0131/03, VEGA 1/1055/04 and UK/379/2005.

Please use the following format when citing this chapter:

Nagy, Marek, 2006, in IFIP International Federation for Information Processing, Volume 204, Artificial Intelligence Applications and Innovations, eds. Maglogiannis, I., Karpouzis, K., Bramer, M., (Boston: Springer), pp. 179–186

I suggest an application - a game which introduces a speech dialogue into an education environment [5, 8]. The game is suggested with a goal to teach small children digits and with a side effect to collect speech samples of digits (zero, one, ... nine) [1]. This application also helps to explain speech recognition problems to master degree students at the university and motivate them to develop similar applications on my lectures.

2 Penguin Quart game

Penguin Quart is a simple game. It is motivated by the very popular kids card game. The real game is played by two or more players in generally. Every player obtains few cards at beginning. Of course, cards are signed by pictures, numbers or words. In the game every card is duplicated four times. Cards are mixed up before dealing out. How many cards player obtains depends on a mutual agreement. All remain cards are stored in a card packet. After it somebody starts the game. He queries one card from his ones. The player must point at somebody from who queries the card. If a determined player has such a card he must hand it over to the asking player and the player continues, otherwise the asking player takes one card from the packet and the next one continues. The aim of the game is to collect quartets of same cards. The game finishes when all quartets are collected. Who collects the most quartets evidently wins.

Fig. 1. Every kid has own record where is a name, gender and score

Penguin Quart has simplified rules. It is played by two players (like motivational game [9]). One is a computer (represented by a penguin) and the second is a child. They are alternating. While the first one is listening the second one makes query. The request is made by a voice. The child must say a word into a computer microphone. Possible words are digits: zero, one, ... nine. The game is localized in the Slovak language therefore it recognizes Slovak digits only. The penguin always starts a game. He welcomes a child and prompts him to choose his name from a list.[2] See figure 1.

Cards are dealt out after the child choice. Both obtain one card which is placed before the child and the penguin. Now, the penguin really starts and asks for a card (a number). The number is showed in a bubble.[3] (see figure 2). The child must click on either the same numbered card or the packet.[4]

Fig. 2. The game in a progress. It is a penguin turn

The Penguin comments and prompts the child to ask a card. Now he must say a number (of a card) into a computer microphone. Kids have 3 seconds to speak a number. A child bubble appears either with the recognized number or empty after an recognition process.[5] The child can correct the number in the bubble by clicking on his cards. It has reason because the recognition process may do mistakes or the time limit expires. (See figure 3) At the end of a turn the child must confirm a choice by clicking on the bubble.[6]

The game continues this way. Players change one another. At the game end, when cards run out, collected quartets are counted up. The penguin presents the result and determines the winner and then the game can start again from the beginning.

---

[2] This was inserted due to a Slovak language specific feature - a grammatical gender. When was used bare masculine gender girls were disturbed by it. The list of players, besides gender, includes names with scores. It makes the game more familiar and score exhort children to mutually compete.

[3] This is important from a pedagogical perspective. Kids listen to sounds of numbers and simultaneously look at their symbols. It can be signed as a teaching phase.

[4] Children are looking for same number symbol as they have heard and seen. This is a pedagogical training phase.

[5] The time limit was introduced after experiments with a silence/speech detector. Because the game was used in a noisy classroom it happened that the speech detector was not capable to finish a recognition process in reasonable time.

[6] From a pedagogical point of view this is an important moment of the game. Children must speak numbers correctly and they see feedback immediately. In other words they see what they say. And at this moment they check if what they have sad (have showed in the bubble) is same symbol as they want to say. This can be signed as an examine phase.

3   Data collecting and dividing

Increasing a successfulness of the recognition requires an adequate training time. It is not acceptable for a perspective user to extend time which he will spend with an application. A solution of the problem may be in an automatic adaptation or training. Users can work with the application without any restriction.[7] While the user is working the application makes moves which lead to increasing the recognition accuracy. It makes changes immediately or postpone them to the future background training. The application would have to utilize so many input informations as obtains from users. It is difficult because the application must not leave a line of its usual usage.

Fig. 3. The game in a progress. It is a child turn. Just click on the bubble

Trained Hidden Markov Models (HMM) of digits are used in the application Penguin Quart (PQ). Their accuracy was not so good and the problem was to increase it. Every word what children say into a microphone during a game is used in a recognition process and saved hierarchically on a computer disc. Sounds are saved at the 16kHz sample rate and with the 16bits precision. A low cost headset microphone was used.

The first version of the game was used on a day summer camp in 2001 [10]. I assisted children how to play the game and I helped a computer (the penguin) with recognition mistakes. After the mission I adapt collected data. I labeled every sound by a word from a set {zero, one, two, ..., nine}. It was a long-winded work. Samples must be heard and then labeled. It turned out that it is a good idea to save samples and their classifications together. Then the label process reduce itself and it is sufficient to check and to correct only bad automatic classifications. Labels also span short initial and final silence.

The computer with the game was placed in the hall together with other 24 children working on computers and therefore a respective background noise was presented. Speakers was 9-14 years old children and about 20 years old students. A Bratislava language dialect was presented. (But children from Poprad and other places have occurred too.) Approximately 150 speakers are covered by the dataset. It is important to notice that collected patterns are spontaneous spoken words (not

---

[7]   If we don't consider an accuracy of recognition to be a restriction.

read). I made dataset named DS_1 from these data. Collected and processed data were divided into two groups: training and testing data. Data for testing were chosen from Wednesday of each week. (The camp last for 4 weeks and children were changed every week.) By this decision, the training set contains patterns of all speakers. A word accuracy, which is computed on this set, can be considered as speaker depend (SD). Totally DS_1 contains 6448 training patterns and 1494 testing patterns.

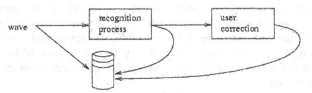

Fig. 4. Wave samples are passed through a recognition process and are simultaneously saved with their classification together. The user adjusting decision is saved too

Next mission on the day camp was repeated in 2003. Data were collected by same manner but a name and a sex of speaker were attached to saved sound patterns. Children, which had been recorded before, did not take part in the camp in 2001. These data (recorded in 2003) represent testing patterns in the dataset named DS_2. Training data of DS_2 are represented by all data from the dataset DS_1 (training + testing). A word accuracy, which is computed on DS_2 testing patterns, can be considered as speaker independent (SI). Totally dataset DS_2 contains 7942 training patterns and 1731 testing patterns.

Table 1. SNR decomposition of the sound patterns for the both datasets DS_1 and DS_2

SNR:	5-10dB	10-15dB	15-20dB	>20dB	Total
DS_1-train	296	1630	1607	2915	6448
DS_1-test	64	459	406	565	1494
DS_2-train	360	2089	2013	3480	7942
DS_2-test	68	477	460	726	1731

Naturally, an application cannot rely on 100% recognition accuracy (like keyboard typing or mouse clicking) or it happens that the user makes a mistake and therefore it is needed make the correction of a classification to be possible. The correction is also saved together with wave files.[8] So saved data contain sound samples, classifications and user corrections (see figure 4).

As it was mentioned the background noise is presented. The HTK [6] library computes the SNR (signal noise ratio) automatically and I categorize the patterns into four groups 5-10dB, 10-15dB, 15-20dB and more than 20 dB. See Table 1 which contains quantities of the sound patterns belonging to the SNR groups.

---

[8] These "user" labels are useful during sample labeling of letters that sometime sounds such similarly.

4 Digit recognition.

The recognition engine uses statistical approach to classify a newly spoken word. It is based on Hidden Markov Models (HMM). Every word has own statistical model. The classification algorithm computes and measures a new sound probability against all models and the best one is taken as the recognition result [4].

The recognition module utilizes the HTK toolkit library [6]. (The API documentation does not exist but source codes are available. In the game, HVite.c [6] was adopted and changed.) The recognition process uses a very small vocabulary - ten words of numbers. One, two, three, four, five, six, seven, eight, nine, zero are binded in a simply grammar. See figure 5. Every word is represented by one HMM. These models are off line trained from patterns and into recognition process enter through HTK library.

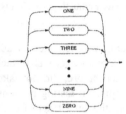

Fig. 5. Grammar for digit recognition

Number of states in models is chosen according to the longest word. (For example Slovak digit sedem [s e d e m @]). For shorter Slovak words (päť, tri, ...) a phoneme will be modeled by two states. These models of "phonema" are chained together. Special states are added at the start and at the end of the phoneme chain. This states model initial and final silence. The HTK toolkit requires two additional states: initial and final states. These states serve for linking models together and they have no significance for the isolated words recognition where one model represents one word from a vocabulary. See [6] for a closer explanation. As it can be seen on figure 6, the whole final model has 10 states but only the 8 ones are active. A topology of transitions among states is adopted from [4].

If it is needed, the silence states are automatically omitted by the appropriate transition as can be seen on figure 6. A probability of some transitions were zeroed in training process and the transitions disappeared because probability became subliminal for the HTK mathematical unit. An observation is composed of 3 streams. The first stream contains 12 Mel-Frequency Cepstral Coefficients (MFCC) and energy factor. The second stream contains deltas of the first one and the third contains deltas of second one. It can be imagine that these streams are modeled with tree topological identical models which are strictly synchronized.

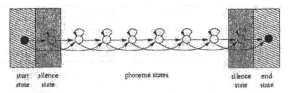

Fig. 6. The Hidden Markov model topology of digits

12 MFCC are computed from 12 cepstral coefficients which are computed from 40 frequency filter banks. As it can be read in [6], probability functions, which model observations in states, are more important than probability of transitions. The output probability is commonly represented by Gaussian Mixture Densities for this purpose. But how many mixture components use in the density? I made an experiment which results are showed on the figure 7. The graphs represent a word accuracy at appropriate number of mixture components.

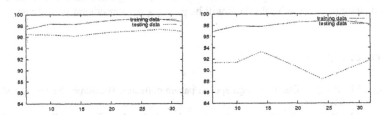

Fig. 7. A word accuracy on the datasets DS_1 (left) and DS_2 (right)

As it can be seen on the figure 7, a word accuracy on training data is very close to 99%. But the best SD accuracy (dataset DS_1) is 97.33% and the best SI accuracy (dataset DS_2) is only 93.30%. For the SD case, the best number of mixture components is 28 what is in contrast with the best SI case. It needs only 14 components. The word accuracy decomposition by SNR is showed in Table 2. The decomposition is computed for the case where each state contains 14 mixture components in stream. A total accuracy is also showed for a comparison.

To determine when speech starting and when finishing speech/silence detector is used in HTK. But as I mention earlier the time limit was introduced because the game was used in noisy classroom and it happened that the speech detector was not capable to finish a recognition process in reasonable time. The detector uses an actual energy of a frame. The energy is tested if exceeds a silence detector threshold. An appropriate number of exceeded energies in the energy sequence (a limited size window of energies) begins and ends the recognition.

Table 2. The SNR decomposition of a word accuracy for 14 Gaussian components per a state

SNR:	5-10dB	10-15dB	15-20dB	>20dB	Total
DS_1-train	97.97%	98.53%	99.25%	97.43%	98.17%

SNR:	5-10dB	10-15dB	15-20dB	>20dB	Total
DS_1-test	93.75%	97.17%	97.04%	95.22%	96.19%
DS_2-train	96.67%	98.37%	98.51%	96.98%	97.70%
DS_2-test	95.59%	93.08%	94.13%	93.25%	**93.30%**

5 Conclusion

The game presented in this paper was used on summer day camp for children [10] where achieves a success. A little children was captured by speech dialogue so that they talked to the penguin about various things. I took the penguin at an elementary school [2]. Of course every mission brings a new sound pattern data which can be used to train the HMM set of digits. The best recognition reach a accuracy of 93.30% for the SI case and 97.33% for the SD case. In a real environment it works fine thanks to various training data which are recorded at all SNR bands. In my future work, I will focus on expanding a recognition vocabulary to cover whole the Slovak alphabet. I am also going to organize an experiment in 1st grade at an elementary school which will be part of a regular education process.

References

1. Nagy, M.: Penguin Quart - a digit speech pattern collector, Bratislava, Slovak republic, Slovko 2003 (2003)
2. Nagy, M.: Penguin Quart - hlasom ovládaná edukačná hra, Trenčín, Slovak republic, INFOVEK 2004 (2005) (in Slovak)
3. Nagy, M.: Utilizing an education game Penguin Quart to develop a speech recognition of Slovak digits, Bratislava, Slovak republic, Informatics 2005 (2005)
4. Psutka, J.: Komunikace s počítačemem mluvenou řečí, ACADEMIA, Praha, Czech republic (1995) (in Czech)
5. Schalkwyk, J., Hosom, P., Kaiser, E., Shobaki, K.: CSLU-HMM: The CSLU hidden markov modeling environment (2000)
6. Young, S., Evermann, G., Kershaw, D., Moore, G., Odell, J., Ollason, D., Povey, D., Valtchev, V., Woodland, P.: The HTK Book 3.2. (2002)
7. Young, S.: Probabilistic methods in spoken dialogue systems, England, Cambridge University Engineering Dept. (2000)
8. Project LISTEN - A Reading Tutor that Listens, Carnegie Mellon University, USA: http://www.cs.cmu.edu/~listen/
9. Reading Games - Roxie's Reading Fish: http://www.latticeworksw.com/roxread.htm
10. Summer Day Camp for children, Comenius University, Slovakia: http://www.edi.fmph.uniba.sk/tabor

Impact of Face Registration Errors on Recognition

E. Rentzeperis, A. Stergiou, A. Pnevmatikakis and L. Polymenakos

Athens Information Technology, Autonomic and Grid Computing,
Markopoulou Ave., 19002 Peania, Greece
{eren, aste, apne, lcp}@ait.edu.gr
http://www.ait.edu.gr/research/RG1/overview.asp

Abstract. Face recognition systems detect faces in moving or still images and then recognize them. However, face detection is not an error-free process, especially when designed for real-time systems. Thus the face recognition algorithms have to operate on faces that are not ideally framed. In this paper we analyze quantitatively the impact of face detection errors on six different face recognition algorithms. Hence, we propose a matching of face recognition algorithms with face detector performance, which can be used for a system based on the expected performance of the face detector.

1   Introduction

Face recognition has many applications in security and human-machine interfaces. It can be applied either like other biometric recognition approaches, by requiring the person to pose in a very controlled way, or unobtrusively, on still or moving images of the person. In the first approach, the face is manually extracted and, if necessary, normalized, prior to the application of any face recognition algorithm. The second approach is much more interesting, but poses a serious problem: the automatic detection and normalization of the face.

Many different face recognition algorithms have been reported in the literature [1-8] and have been tested on different face databases [8-11], adhering or not to a standard evaluation methodology [11-13]. In most of these reports, the performance of the different algorithms is assessed on manually extracted and normalized faces. Comparisons, when attempted with a common database and methodology, only assess which method performs best under a particular type of impairment (pose, illumination or expression variation) [13,14].

When all these algorithms are used in the context of a fully-automatic face recognition system, then the faces presented to the recognizer are not manually extracted. The automatic face detection process involves finding the face, locating in

Please use the following format when citing this chapter:

Rentzeperis, Elias, Stergiou, Andreas, Pnevmatikakis, Arstodemos, Polymenakos, Lazaros, 2006, in IFIP International Federation for Information Processing, Volume 204, Artificial Intelligence Applications and Innovations, eds. Maglogiannis, I., Karpouzis, K., Bramer, M., (Boston: Springer), pp. 187–194

it some features and based on these, geometrically normalizing the face to match some template [15-17]. This is the face registration process. Face detection on still images given ample processing time is a problem more or less solved [16], resulting to small registration errors. For real-time operation and under unconstrained lighting and pose conditions, face registration becomes very difficult [15], and the registration errors can grow significantly.

Hence there is a need to compare the different face recognition algorithms in terms of their robustness to face registration errors. Here we address this need by assessing the impact of face registration errors on six different face recognition algorithms. We use the evaluation methodology in [13] to obtain the performance of the algorithms, and then perform statistical analysis of the results to obtain the optimum method for different face detection accuracy ranges.

This paper is organized as follows: In Section 2, the face recognition algorithms to be compared are outlined. Then, in Section 3 the evaluation methodology and the experimental results are presented. Finally, in Section 4 the conclusions are drawn.

2   Face recognition methods

The impact of face registration errors on six face recognition algorithms is compared. The algorithms are the Eigenfaces [1], Fisherfaces [3], Elastic Bunch Graph Matching (EBGM) [4], pseudo Two-Dimensional Hidden Markov Models (2D-HMM) [2], correlation filters [5] and Laplacianfaces [6]. These algorithms have been implemented and extensively tested by the authors [18-20] on a variety of standard face databases and on a novel video database [13]. They have been incorporated into a real-time face recognition system [15] operating in the SMART lab [21], allowing us to determine the best algorithm for the system according to the performance of the detection system. In the rest of this section, these algorithms are briefly introduced.

2.1   Eigenfaces

Eigenfaces [1] is a linear subspace projection algorithm that uses Principal Component Analysis (PCA). As no class label information is used in PCA, the projection is estimated in an unsupervised manner. After linear projection, the resulting recognition space is of much lower dimension. The PCA feature vectors are robust to noise and minor head rotations, but not to illumination changes [3,18].

Since its introduction in 1991, the eigenface technique has seen many modifications [3]. In [3,18] the influence of distance metrics and eigenvector selection on PCA performance is analysed. Eigenvector selection consists of discarding a few eigenvectors with larger eigenvalues and/or some of those with the smallest. This is attributed to the empirical observation that the discarded eigenvectors with the larger eigenvalues encode direction-of-illumination changes. Discarding three such eigenvectors is shown in [3,18] to greatly enhance PCA performance.

2.2 Fisherfaces

PCA maximizes the total scatter of the training vectors while reducing their dimensions. It is optimum in the mean-squared error sense for representation in the resulting subspace, but offers no guarantee of optimality for classification. Linear Discriminant Analysis (LDA) on the other hand does take into account class labels and maximizes the between-class scatter under the constraint that the within-class scatter is minimized. This results to compact clusters for each class, as far as possible from each other. This projection is optimum for classification and is supervised. A PCA+LDA combination, termed Fisherfaces, was introduced in [3] and was proven robust to illumination changes [3,18].

2.3 Elastic Bunch Graph Matching

EBGM [4] assumes that the positions of certain facial features are known for each training image. The image regions around these features are convolved with 40 complex 2D Gabor kernels. The resulting 80 coefficients constitute the Gabor jet for each facial feature. The Gabor jets for all facial features are grouped in a graph, the Face Graph, where each jet is a node and the distances between facial features are the weights on the corresponding vertices. The information in the Face Graph is all that is needed for recognition; the image itself is discarded. All Face Graphs from the training images are combined in a stack-like structure called the Face Bunch Graph (FBG). Each node of the FBG contains a list of Gabor jets for the corresponding facial feature from all training images, and the vertices are now weighted with the average distances across the training set. The positions of the facial features in the testing images are unknown; EBGM estimates them based on the FBG. Then a Face Graph can be constructed for each testing image based on the estimated positions. The Face Graph of each testing image is compared with the FBG to determine the training image it is most similar to, according to some jet-based metric. In [4], a number of such metrics is proposed, most of which can also be used for the feature estimation step. Our results in [19] indicate that Displacement Estimation Local Search is the best choice for facial feature localization; for the actual identification stage, Displacement Estimation Grid Search yields the best recognition rate.

2.4 Pseudo Two-Dimensional Hidden Markov Models

Face recognition using HMM is based on approximating blocks from the face image with a chain of states of a stochastic model [2]. For the pseudo 2D HMM the image blocks are extracted by scanning the face from left to right, top to bottom with an overlap both in horizontal and vertical direction. Pixel intensities do not lead to robust features, as they are susceptible to illumination changes and other detrimental effects. A transformation like the 2D Discrete Cosine Transform attenuates those distorting effects, leading to better performance. A pseudo 2D HMM model of hidden states is obtained by linking left-right 1D HMM models with vertical super-states. For the training of each class the Baum-Welch algorithm is used. In the recognition phase the class that gives the highest value for the probability of the observation sequence of the testing image, given the class model, is considered the most likely to be the true identity of the testing face. Our results in [20] indicate that close cropping the faces and using mixture of three Gaussians for the states enhance performance.

2.5 Correlation Filters

Face recognition can be performed by cross correlating a face image with a suitable filter and processing the output. Many correlation filters have been proposed [5]; amongst them, the Minimum Average Correlation Energy filter (MACE) is reported to perform best. It reduces the large sidelobes by minimizing the average correlation energy plane while at the same time satisfying the correlation peak constraints at the origin. These constraints result in the correlation plane close to zero everywhere except at a location of a trained object, where a sharp peak appears. For recognition, the output plane is searched for the highest point and that value, as well as the values of its surrounding points, is used to determine the class that the face belongs to. We have implemented and tested the MACE correlation filter algorithm in [20].

2.6 Laplacianfaces

The Eigenfaces and Fisherfaces algorithms both use linear projection to a subspace aiming to preserve the global structure of the face. Laplacianfaces [6] on the other hand, is an algorithm that uses optimal linear approximations to the eigenfunctions of the Laplace-Beltrami operator. By aiming to preserve the local structure of the face, Laplacianfaces attempts to attenuate the unwanted variations resulting from changes in lighting, facial expression and pose. In that, Laplacianfaces shares many of the properties of nonlinear projection algorithms. We have implemented and tested the Laplacianfaces algorithm in [20].

3   Experimental results

The evaluation methodology proposed in [13] is followed to assess the performance of the face recognition algorithms outlined in the previous section. In particular, the HumanScan database [22] is utilized. This database offers 20 feature points on each face; including the two eye centers. The eye centers are used to register the faces, whereas all the rest are utilized in the training images for EBGM. To introduce the needed registration errors, Gaussian noise is added to the co-ordinates of the eye centers. Then the noisy co-ordinates are used in the face normalization process.

The variance of the added noise in each co-ordinate is controlled so that the RMS error is a given percentage of the eye distance. This way, different versions of the normalized database are obtained, with the RMS eye perturbation ranging from zero (ideal normalization) to 7% of the eye distance. To get a feeling of the meaning of eye perturbation range selected for the comparison of the algorithms, the RMS eye perturbation that results form the face detection scheme presented in [15] is between 4.7% (full scale HumanScan faces) and 7.2% (HumanScan faces decimated to 10 pixels eye distance). Hence, depending on the resolution, state-of-the-art face detection systems are expected to have an RMS eye perturbation in the upper half of the selected testing range.

The effect of the eye perturbation on the faces is to shift, scale and rotate them in a random manner. Examples of the erroneously registered faces are shown in Fig. 1. While some of them are registered moderately well, there are others where the registration errors have caused only a tilted part of the face to lie in the template or significant background portion to enter the template.

Fig. 1. Effect of 4% RMS eye perturbation on 21 randomly selected HumanScan faces from a single person

The algorithms are tested with 5 training faces per person. This is a moderate number for face recognition systems that are intended for smart room or human-machine interfaces, but a rather large one for security applications. The 400 runs described in [13] are carried out, for each of the six algorithms and each of the eight different degrees of eye perturbation, allowing for a statistically sound analysis of the results. The median value for each group of 400 runs is reported in Fig. 2. Note that two variants of the eigenfaces algorithm are tried: the classic one and that without the three eigenvectors that correspond to the largest eigenvalues (PCAw/o3).

From the results depicted in Fig. 2, the correlation filters algorithm is the most sensitive to face registration errors, followed by the Laplacianfaces. The rest of the methods are close up to 2% RMS eye perturbation, a value that is very optimistic for real-time face detectors. This is indicated in the boxplots [23] of Fig. 3, where a test of the statistical significance of the different median values is performed. The PCA variants and pseudo-2D HMM have statistically similar performance; LDA and EBGM are somewhat better, with LDA being the winner at 5% significance level. At 3% RMS eye perturbation, the subspace projection methods start deteriorating. Of these, the first to deteriorate is the PCAw/o3. This is to be expected, since the first few eigenvectors encode only illumination changes (hence unwanted within class variation) only if the registration is ideal. This is also the reason that PCAw/o3 performs badly in face databases without ideal face registration, with pose variations and with pronounced expression changes [13]. At large RMS eye perturbations, above 5% RMS, such as those expected in real-time detectors operating on low resolution faces, the performance of supervised and unsupervised subspace projection becomes comparable; Eigenfaces even exceed Fisherfaces in performance at 7% RMS, indicating ill-training. This is again to be expected; five training images are not able to capture the within class variation introduced by the large registration errors.

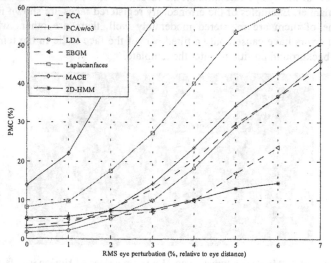

Fig. 2. Probability of misclassification of the face recognition algorithms under varying percentage of RMS eye perturbation and 5 training faces per person

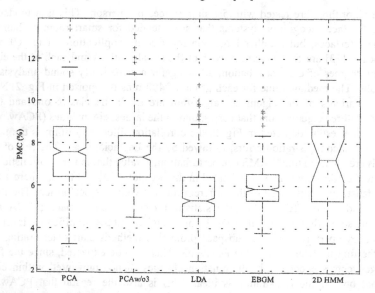

Fig. 3. Boxplots of the PMC of the linear subspace projection algorithms, the pseudo-2D HMM and the EBGM for 2% RMS eye perturbation and 5 training faces per person. The difference in the median values (horizontal lines) is statistically significant at the 5% significance level only if the notches of the boxes do not overlap

The pseudo-2D HMM and EBGM algorithms perform noticeably better than the rest at 3% RMS or higher eye perturbation. Both deteriorate only minimally up to 3% RMS, with EBGM being marginally better up to 4% RMS. After that EBGM deteriorates fast, while pseudo-2D HMM retains its performance remarkably well. The robustness of EBGM up to 4% RMS is due to the search for the feature points inherent to the recognition algorithm. This search can compensate for medium displacements of the features from the expected positions. As for the exceptional robustness of the pseudo-2D HMM algorithm to face registration errors, it is due to the stochastic nature of the model of the face. The transitions between the states (overlapping blocks of the face image) are probabilistic, and can account for the perturbation of the feature locations. This is the reason for the success of the pseudo-2D HMM algorithm in the ORL database [2] it was tested when introduced, where no particular care has been taken in registering the ORL faces.

4   Conclusions

Since in most applications, face recognition algorithms do not perform stand-alone but within detection and recognition systems, the face registration errors resulting from imperfect face detections become important. In this paper we have quantitatively analyzed the impact of face registration errors on six face recognition algorithms and one of their variants, to establish ranges of face detection accuracy where some of them are optimal. These are summarized in Table 1. The experimentally established robustness of the various face recognition algorithms is also backed-up by an analysis of the features of the algorithms.

Table 1. Optimum face recognition algorithms depending on face registration accuracy

Face registration accuracy (% of eye distance, RMS)	Optimum algorithm
[0,2]	LDA
(2,4]	EBGM
> 4	2D HMM

References

1. Turk, M., Pentland, A.: Eigenfaces for Recognition. J. Cognitive Neuroscience. (1991) 71-86
2. Samaria, F., Harter, A.: Parametrisation of a Stochastic Model for Human Face Identification. 2nd IEEE Workshop on Applications of Computer Vision. (1994) 138-142
3. Belhumeur, P., Hespanha, J., Kriegman, D.: Eigenfaces vs. Fisherfaces: Recognition Using Class Specific Linear Projection. IEEE Trans. Pattern Analysis and Machine Intelligence. 7 (1997) 711-720
4. Wiskott, L., Fellous, J-M., Krueger, N., Malsburg, C.: Face Recognition by Elastic Bunch Graph Matching. In: Jain, L.C. et al. (eds.) Intelligent Biometric Techniques in Fingerprint and Face Recognition. CRC Press (1999) 355-396

5. Xie, C., Vijaya Kumar, B. V. K. , Palanivel, S., Yegnanarayana, B.:A Still-to-Video Face Verification System Using Advanced Correlation Filters. International Conference on Biometric Authentication. (2004) 102-108
6. He, X., Yan, S., Hu, Y., Niyogi, P., Zhang, H.-J.: Face Recognition Using Laplacianfaces. IEEE Trans. Pattern Analysis and Machine Intelligence. 3 (2005) 328-340
7. Bartlett, M., Movellan, J., Sejnowski, T.: Face Recognition by Independent Component Analysis. IEEE Trans. Neural Networks. 6 (2002) 1450-1464
8. Yang, J., Frangi, A., Yang, J.-Y., Zhang, D., Jin, Z.: KPCA Plus LDA: A Complete Kernel Fisher Discriminant Framework for Feature Extraction and Recognition. IEEE Trans. Pattern Analysis and Machine Intelligence. 2 (2005) 230-244
9. Georghiades, A., Belhumeur, P., Kriegman, D.: From Few to Many: Illumination Cone Models for Face Recognition under Variable Lighting and Pose. IEEE Trans. Pattern Analysis and Machine Intelligence. 6 (2001) 643-660
10. Liu, X., Chen, T., Vijaya Kumar, B.V.K.: On Modeling Variations For Face Authentication. International Conference on Automatic Face and Gesture Recognition, (2002) 369-374
11. Philips, P., Moon, H., Rizvi, S., Rauss, P.: The FERET Evaluation Methodology for Face-Recognition Algorithms. IEEE Trans. Pattern Analysis and Machine Intelligence. 10 (2000) 1090-1104
12. Phillips, P. et al.: Overview of the Face Recognition Grand Challenge. CVPR. (2005) 947-954
13. Pnevmatikakis, A., Polymenakos, L.: A Testing Methodology for Face Recognition Algorithms. 2nd Joint Workshop on Multimodal Interaction and Related Machine Learning Algorithms. Edinburgh. (2005)
14. Li, S. Z., Lu, J.: Face Detection, Alignment and Recognition. In Medioni, G., Kang, S. (eds.) Emerging Topics in Computer Vision. Prentice-Hall (2004) 455
15. Pnevmatikakis, A., Polymenakos, L.: An Automatic Face Detection and Recognition System for Video Streams. 2nd Joint Workshop on Multimodal Interaction and Related Machine Learning Algorithms. Edinburgh. (2005)
16. Hsu, R.-L., Abdel-Mottaleb, M., Jain, A. K.: Face Detection in Color Images. IEEE Trans. Pattern Analysis and Machine Intelligence. 5 (2002) 696-706
17. Stiefelhagen, R., Yang, J., Waibel, A.: Tracking eyes and monitoring eye gaze. Workshop on Perceptual User Interfaces. Banff, Canada. (1997)
18. Pnevmatikakis, A., Polymenakos, L.: Comparison of Eigenface-Based Feature Vectors under Different Impairments. Int. Conf. Pattern Recognition. (2004) 296-300
19. Stergiou, A.: Elastic Bunch Graph Matching Face Recognition: Performance and Comparison with Subspace Projection Methods. MSc Thesis, Athens Information Technology. (2004)
20. Rentzeperis, E.: A Comparative Analysis of Face Recognition Algorithms: Hidden Markov Models, Correlation Filters and Laplacianfaces vs. Linear subspace projection and Elastic Bunch Graph Matching. MSc Thesis, Athens Information Technology. (2005)
21. Soldatos, J., Polymenakos, L., Pnevmatikakis, A., Talantzis, F., Stamatis, K., Carras, M.: Perceptual Interfaces and Distributed Agents supporting Ubiquitous Computing Services. Eurescom. (2005)
22. Jesorsky, O., Kirchberg, K., Frischholz, R.: Robust Face Detection Using the Hausdorff Distance. in Bigun, J., Smeraldi, F. (eds.): Audio and Video based Person Authentication. Springer (2001) 90-95
23. McGill, R., Tukey, J. W., Larsen, W. A.: Variations of Boxplots. The American Statistician. (1978) 12-16

Unsupervised Segmentation of Meeting Configurations and Activities using Speech Activity Detection

Oliver Brdiczka, Dominique Vaufreydaz, Jérôme Maisonnasse, Patrick Reignier

INRIA Rhône-Alpes
655 Av. de l'Europe
38330 Montbonnot, France
{brdiczka, vaufreydaz, maisonnasse, reignier} @inrialpes.fr

Abstract. This paper addresses the problem of segmenting small group meetings in order to detect different group configurations and activities in an intelligent environment. Our approach takes speech activity detection of individuals attending a meeting as input. The goal is to separate distinct distributions of speech activity observation corresponding to distinct group configurations and activities. We propose an unsupervised method based on the calculation of the Jeffrey divergence between histograms of speech activity observations. These histograms are generated from adjacent windows of variable size slid from the beginning to the end of a meeting recording. The peaks of the resulting Jeffrey divergence curves are detected using successive robust mean estimation. After a merging and filtering process, the retained peaks are used to select the best model, i.e. the best speech activity distribution allocation for a given meeting recording. These distinct distributions can be interpreted as distinct segments of group configuration and activity. To evaluate, we recorded 6 small group meetings. We measured the correspondence between detected segments and labeled group configurations and activities. The obtained results are promising, in particular as our method is completely unsupervised.

1   Introduction

Ubiquitous computing [14] integrates computation into all-day environments. People are enabled to move around and interact with computers more and more naturally. One of the goals of ubiquitous computing is to enable devices to sense changes in the environment and to automatically adapt and act based on these changes. A main focus is laid on sensing and responding to human activity. Human actors need to be identified in order to perceive correctly their activity. In order that

Please use the following format when citing this chapter:

Brdiczka, Oliver, Vaufreydaz, Dominique, Maisonnasse, Jerome, Reignier, Patrick, 2006, in IFIP International Federation for Information Processing, Volume204, Artificial Intelligence Applications and Innovations, eds. Maglogiannis, I., Karpouzis, K., Bramer, M., (Boston: Springer), pp. 195–203

ubiquitous computer devices act and interact correctly with users, addressing the right user at the correct moment and perceiving his correct activity is essential. Thus we need to detect potential users and their connection while they are doing an activity.

The focus of this work is analyzing human (inter)action in meeting environments. In these environments, users are collaborating in order to achieve a common goal. Several individuals can form one group working on the same task, or they can split into subgroups doing independent tasks in parallel. The dynamics of group configuration and activity need to be tracked in order to supply reactions or interactions at the most appropriate moment. Changes in group configuration need to be detected to identify main actors, while changes in activity within a group need to be detected to identify activities.

This paper proposes an unsupervised method for detecting changes in group configuration and group activity based on measuring the Jeffrey divergence between adjacent histograms. These histograms are calculated for a window sliding from the beginning to the end of the meeting and contain the frequency of (human) activity events. The peaks of the Jeffrey divergence curve are used to segment distinct distributions of activity events and to find the best model of activity event distributions for the given meeting. The method has been tested on speech activity detection events as sensor information for interacting individuals. We focus thus on verbal interaction. The evaluation has been done with speech activity recordings of 6 meetings.

2   Previous and Related Work

Many approaches for the recognition of human activities in meetings have been proposed in recent years. Most work uses supervised learning methods [2], [5], [7], [11]. Some projects focus on supplying appropriate services to the user [11], while others focus on the correct classification of meeting activities [5] or individual availability [7]. Less work has been conducted on unsupervised learning of meeting activities [15]. The recognition of human activity based on speech events is often used in the context of group analysis. In general, the group and its members are defined in advance. The objective is then to use frequency and duration of speech contributions to recognize particular key actions executed by group members [5] or to analyse the type of meeting in a global manner [3]. However, the detection of dependencies between individuals and their membership in one or several groups is not considered. The automatic detection of conversations using mutual information [1], in order to determine who speaks and when, needs an important duration of each conversation. To our knowledge, little work has been done on the analysis of changing small group configuration *and* activity. In [2] a real-time detector for changing small group configurations has been proposed. This detector is based on speech activity detection and either trained with recorded meetings or defined by hand based on conversational hypotheses. In [2], the authors showed that different meeting activities, and especially different group configurations, have particular distributions of speech activity. Detecting group configuration or activity [2], [5], [7] requires, however, a predefined set of activities or group configurations. New activities or group configurations with a different number of individuals cannot be detected and distinguished with these approaches. Our approach focuses on an unsupervised method segmenting small group meetings into consecutive group configurations and activities. These configurations and activities are distinguished by their distributions, but not labelled or compared. The method can thus be seen as a first step within a classification process identifying (unseen) group configurations and activities in meetings.

3   Approach

3.1   Speech Activity Detector: A Multi-Agent System

Our approach is based on speech activity detection (SAD) of individuals attending a meeting. We are recording the speech of each individual using lapel microphones. We admit the use of lapel microphones in order to minimize detection errors. An automatic speech detector parses the audio channels of the different lapel microphones and detects which individual stops and starts speaking.

Our speech activity detector is composed of several sub-systems: an energy detector, a basic classifier and a neural net trained to recognize voiced segments like vowels for example. At each time, i.e. for each frame, each sub-system gives an answer indicating whether the input signal is speech or not. A hand-crafted rule based automaton then determines the final result: speech activity or not. The complete system is shown in Fig. 1.

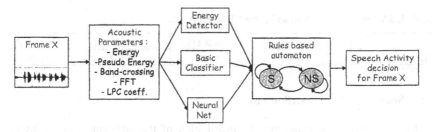

Fig. 1 Diagram of our SAD system.

This speech activity detector is designed to be light-weight; it can be run efficiently on more than 50 channels at the same time. The output is a vector containing a binary value (speaking, not speaking) for each individual that is recorded. This vector is transformed to a 1-dimensional discrete code used for further treatment. The automatic speech activity detector generates an output observation every 16 milliseconds.

Energy detector

The energy detector uses pseudo energy computation in order to detect variations of the input signal energy. Its answer can be START_SPEAKING, STILL_SPEAK, STOP_SPEAK or SILENCE. The detection is based on couples of time delays and thresholds: *TimeOn/EnergyOn* and *TimeOff/EnergyOff*. The initial values for time delays and thresholds were the ones used during the NESPOLE! Project [6]. The energy detector is then able to adapt dynamically *EnergyOn* and *EnergyOff*, given the final SAD answer to retrain itself. *TimeOn* et *TimeOff* were set to 100 ms and 800 ms respectively.

Basic Classifier

This classifier is dedicated to recognize and to tag three specific sound classes: fricatives, low frequency sounds like computer or air conditioning fans, and all other sounds. The classifier computes the energy for 5 identical sub-frequency bands on the spectrum from 1 to 8000 hertz (higher frequencies are not considered). Given the 5 energy values, the module classifies the audio signal.

Neural Net

The neural net is a multi-layer perceptron with 2 hidden layers. It uses advanced coefficients computed on the input frames as input: *band-crossing* [12], *Energy and* 16 *predictor coefficients* extracted from a speech analysis method called Linear Predictive Coding (LPC) [10]. This module is the only sub-system that needs to be trained. The training was made on 1 hour of French speech extracted from the BREF corpus [3]. The phonetic labels used during the training phase are not the original BREF ones but were computed with RAPHAEL [13], a French recognizer.

Precision/Recall

In the following table, we summarize our SAD accuracy using the annotated evaluation data from the CHIL project [11] in the same experimental conditions.

Table 1. SAD results calculated within the CHIL evaluations.

	Recall [%]	Precision [%]	Fallout [%]	Error [%]
Lapel micropone	96.45	89.10	37.72	11.46

3.2   Speech Activity Distributions

In [2], the authors stated that the distribution of the different speech activity observations is discriminating for group configurations in small group meetings. Thus we assume that in small group meetings distinct group configurations and activities have distinct distributions of speech activity observations. The objective of our approach is hence to separate these distinct distributions, in order to identify distinct small meeting configurations and activities.

The observations of the speech activity detector are an unordered 1-dimensional discrete code indicating who is currently speaking (e.g. for four lapel microphones, the code is between 0 (no speech) and 15 (everybody is speaking)). As we do not want to admit any a priori distribution, we use histograms to represent speech activity distributions. A histogram is calculated for an observation window (i.e. the observations between two distinct time points in the meeting recording) and contains the frequency of each observation code within this window.

To separate different speech activity distributions, we calculate the Jeffrey divergence [8] between the histograms of two adjacent observation windows. The Jeffrey divergence is a numerically stable and symmetric form of the Kullback-Leibler divergence between histograms. We slide two adjacent observation windows from the beginning to the end of the recorded meetings, while constantly calculating the Jeffrey divergence between these windows. The result is a divergence curve of adjacent histograms (Fig. 2).

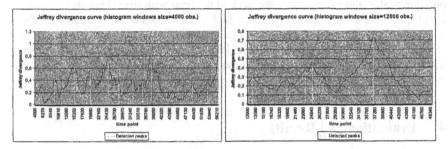

Fig. 2. Meeting 5: Jeffrey divergence between histograms of sliding adjacent windows of 4000, and 12000 observations (64sec and 3min 12sec)

The peaks of the curves indicate high divergence values, i.e. a big difference between the adjacent histograms at that time point. The size of the adjacent windows determines the exactitude of the divergence measurement. The larger the window size, the less peaks has the curve. However, peaks of larger window sizes are less precise than those of smaller window sizes. Thus we parse the meeting recordings with different window sizes (sizes of 4000, 6000, 8000, 10000, 12000, 14000 and 16000 observations, which corresponds to a duration between 64sec and 4min 16sec for each window). The peaks of the Jeffrey divergence curve can then be used to detect changes in the speech activity distribution of the small meeting recording.

3.3 Peak Detection

To detect the peaks of the Jeffrey divergence curve, we use successive robust mean estimation. Robust mean estimation has been used in [9] to locate the center position of a dominant face in skin color filtered images. Mean and standard deviation are calculated repeatedly in order to isolate a dominant peak. To detect all peaks of the Jeffrey divergence curve, we apply the robust mean estimation process successively to the Jeffrey divergence values.

3.4 Merging and Filtering Peaks from different Window Sizes

Peak detection using successive robust mean estimation is conducted for Jeffrey curves with histogram window sizes of 4000, 6000, 8000, 10000, 12000, 14000 and

16000 observations. A global peak list is maintained containing the peaks of different window sizes. Peaks in this list are merged and filtered with respect to their window size and peak height.

The small number of peaks resulting from merging and filtering is used to search for the best allocation of speech activity distributions, i.e. to search for the best model for a given meeting.

3.5 Model Selection

To search for the best model for a given meeting recording, we examine all possible peak combinations, i.e. each peak of the final peak list is both included and excluded to the (final) model. For each such peak combination, we calculate the average Jeffrey divergence of the histograms between the peaks. As we want to separate most distinct speech activity distributions, we accept the peak combination that maximizes the average divergence between the peak histograms as the best model for the given meeting.

4   Evaluation and Results

The result of our approach is the peak combination separating best the speech activity distributions of a given meeting recording. As we admit that distinct distributions of speech activity are discriminating for group configurations and activities in small group meetings [2], we interpret the intervals between the peaks as segments of distinct group configuration and activity. To evaluate our approach, we recorded 6 small group meetings. The group configurations and activities of these meetings have been labeled. For the evaluation of the detected segments, we use the *asp*, *aap* and *Q* measures proposed in [15].

4.1   Experiments

To evaluate our approach, we recorded 6 small group meetings (between 4 and 5 individuals). The number and order of group configurations, i.e. who will speak with whom, and of group activities, e.g. presentation/questions/discussion etc., were fixed in advance for the experiments. The timestamps and durations of the group configurations and activities were, however, not predefined and changed spontaneously. The individuals were free to move and to discuss any topic.

4.2   Evaluation measures

To evaluate, we dispose of the timestamps and durations of the (correct) group configurations and activities. However, classical evaluation measures like confusion matrices can not be used here because the unsupervised segmentation process does not assign any labels to the found segments.

$$asp = \frac{1}{N} \sum_{i=1}^{N_s} p_{i\bullet} \times n_{i\bullet} \quad, \quad aap = \frac{1}{N} \sum_{j=1}^{N_a} p_{\bullet j} \times n_{\bullet j} \quad, \quad Q = \sqrt{asp \times aap}$$

with

n_{ij} = *total number of observations* N_a = *total number of activities*
    in segment i by activity j

$n_{i\bullet}$ = *total number of observations* N_s = *total number of segments*
    in segment i

$n_{\bullet j}$ = *total number of observations* N = *total number of observations*

Fig. 3. Average segment purity (*asp*), average activity purity (*aap*) and the overall criterion Q

Instead, we use three measures proposed in [15] to evaluate the detection results: average segment purity (*asp*), average activity purity (*aap*) and the overall criterion Q (Fig. 3). The *asp* is a measure of how well a segment is limited to only one activity, while the *aap* is a measure of how well one activity is limited to only one segment. The Q criterion is an overall evaluation criterion combining *asp* and *aap*, where larger Q indicates better overall performance.

4.3   Results

Figure 4 shows the labeled group configurations/activities for each small group meeting as well as the segments detected by our approach. Table 2 indicates the *asp*, *aap* and Q values for each meeting as well as the average of these values for all meetings. Unlike meeting recordings 1, 4, 5 and 6, recordings 2 and 3 contain numerous wrong speech activity detections caused by correlation errors and microphone malfunctions. However, our approach worked well for meeting recording 2, while the segmentation of meeting recording 3 is mediocre. The overall results of our approach are very good; the average Q value is 0.82. By excluding meeting 3, we even obtain a Q value of 0.88.

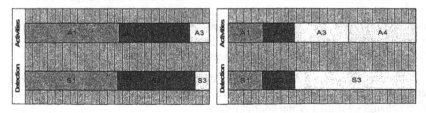

Meeting 1 (Q=0.93, duration=9min 14sec) Meeting 2 (Q=0.81, duration=10min 14sec)

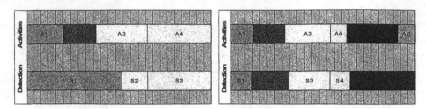

Meeting 3 (Q=0.51, duration=16min 11sec)   Meeting 4 (Q=0.84, duration=14min 47sec)

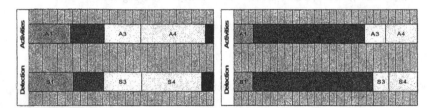

Meeting 5 (Q=0.92, duration=16min 12sec)   Meeting 6 (Q=0.90, duration=25min 2sec)
Figure 4. Group Configurations/Activities and their detection for meetings 1-6.

Table 2. *asp*, *aap* and *Q* values for the recorded meetings.

	asp	aap	Q
Meeting 1	0.93	0.92	0.93
Meeting 2	0.67	0.99	0.81
Meeting 3	0.42	0.62	0.51
Meeting 4	0.78	0.91	0.84
Meeting 5	0.92	0.91	0.92
Meeting 6	0.88	0.91	0.90
Average	0.77	0.88	0.82

5 Conclusion

We proposed an unsupervised method for segmenting small group meeting configurations and activities. This method is based on the calculation of the Jeffrey divergence between histograms of observations of speech activity. The peaks of the Jeffrey divergence curve are used to separate distinct distributions of speech activity observations. These distinct distributions can be interpreted as distinct segments of group configuration and activity. We measured the correspondence between the detected segments and labeled group configurations and activities. The obtained results are promising, in particular as our method is completely unsupervised.

Further meeting recordings need to be done in order to apply and evaluate our method on more and subtler meeting activities. These meeting activities will include activity changes within a group configuration.

Our method can help obtaining a first segmentation of a meeting. The detected segments can then be used as input for further classification tasks like meeting comparison, meeting activity recognition etc.

Future work will concern the test of our method on further meeting information. Speech activity detection is not sufficient to disambiguate all situations. Further information like head orientation, pointing gestures or interpersonal distances seem to be good indicators. Thus a multimodal approach needs to be envisaged. The method can easily be extended to such an approach as we only need to upgrade the observation codes used for the generation of the histograms.

References

1. Basu S., *Conversational Scene Analysis*, Ph.D. Thesis. MIT Department of EECS. September, 2002.
2. Brdiczka, O., Maisonnasse, J., and Reignier, P., *Automatic Detection of Interaction Groups*, Proc. Int'l Conf. Multimodal Interfaces, 2005 (to appear).
3. Burger, S., MacLaren, V., and Yu, H., *The ISL Meeting Corpus: The Impact of Meeting Type on Speech Style*, Proc. of ICSLP 2002, Denver, CO, USA, 2002.
4. Lamel L., Gauvain J.L., Eskenazi M., *BREF, a large vocabulary spoken corpus for French*, Eurospeech'91, Gênes (Italie), 1991.
5. McCowan, I., Gatica-Perez, D., Bengio, S., Lathoud, G., Barnard, M., and Zhang, D., *Automatic Analysis of Multimodal Group Actions in Meetings*, IEEE Trans. on Pattern Analysis and Machine Intelligence, vol. 27, no. 3, pp. 305-317, March 2005.
6. Metze, F., Mc Donough, J., Soltau, H., Waibel, A., Lavie, A., Burger, S., Langley, C., Levin, L., Schultz, T., Pianesi, F., Cattoni, R., Lazzari, G., Mana, N., Pianta, E., Besacier, L., Blanchon, H., Vaufreydaz, D., Taddei, L., *The Nespole! Speech-to-Speech Translation System*, Human Language Technologies 2002, San Diego, California (USA), March 2002.
7. Muehlenbrock, M., Brdiczka, O., Snowdon, D., and Meunier, J.-L., *Learning to Detect User Activity and Availability from a Variety of Sensor Data*, Proc. IEEE Int'l Conference on Pervasive Computing and Communications, March 2004.
8. Puzicha, J., Hofmann, Th., and Buhmann, J., *Non-parametric Similarity Measures for Unsupervised Texture Segmentation and Image Retrieval*. Proc. Int'l Conf. Computer Vision and Pattern Recognition, 1997.
9. Qian, R. J., Sezan, M. I., and Mathews, K. E., *Face Tracking Using Robust Statistical Estimation*, Proc. Workshop on Perceptual User Interfaces, San Francisco, 1998.
10. Rabiner L., Juang B.H., *Fundamentals of Speech Recognition*, Prentice Hall PTR, ISBN 0-130-15157-2, 1993.
11. Stiefelhagen, R., Steusloff, H., and Waibel, A., *CHIL - Computers in the Human Interaction Loop*, Proc. Int'l Workshop on Image Analysis for Multimedia Interactive Services, 2004.
12. Taboada J., Feijoo S., Balsa R., Hernandez C., *Explicit estimation of speech boundaries*, IEEE Proc. Sci. Meas. Technol., vol. 141, pp. 153-159, 1994.
13. Vaufreydaz, D., *Modélisation statistique du langage à partir d'Internet pour la reconnaissance automatique de la parole continue*, Ph.D. thesis in Computer Sciences, University Joseph Fourier, Grenoble (France), 226 pages, January 2002.
14. Weiser, M., *Ubiquitous Computing: Definition 1*, http://www.ubiq.com/hypertext/weiser/UbiHome.html, March 1996.
15. Zhang, D., Gatica-Perez, D., Bengio, S., McCowan, I., and Lathoud, G., *Multimodal Group Action Clustering in Meetings*, Proc. Int'l Workshop on Video Surveillance & Sensor Networks, 2004.

A Model of Real-Time Indoor Surveillance System using Behavior Detection

M.W. Lin and J.R. Tapamo
School of Computer Science, University of KwaZulu-Natal
Desmond Clarence Building, Durban 4041, South Africa
{limn, tapamoj}@ukzn.ac.za

Abstract. In this paper, we present a real-time surveillance system that is suitable for the indoor environment. The system is designed to detect, track and recognize the behavior of humans, using a single static camera. Background subtraction is applied to extract moving objects; these objects are tracked using linear approximation. Shadow regions are detected and removed using linear dependence and spatial connectivity properties of the shadow regions. Pattern matching and TDL (Two Dimensional Logarithmic) search approach are used to solve the problem of the occlusion of objects and depth reasoning. Behaviors of moving objects are detected by examining the sequence of shapes extracted from the scene. Shapes of moving objects are interpreted as characters of an alphabet. Each character represents a class of similar blob shapes classified using K-Means clustering. The model is used to recognize behaviors in an office with promising results.

1. Introduction

To automate surveillance solutions, a visual surveillance system using computer vision algorithms to detect actions of interest in real-time and gathering of data for events reasoning, is the current trend that is driving the shift from traditional surveillance systems that require important human resources in numbers and competencies to provide a real-time response. In general, visual surveillance systems are categorized into indoor or outdoor applications due to different environments and requirements. These requirements affect the low level implementation. On one hand outdoor environments may include the problems of unstable background, caused by situations ranging from tree waving to weather conditions like rain or snow. On the other hand indoor environments may get multi-lighting sources with shadow effects

Please use the following format when citing this chapter:

Lin, Ming-Wei, Tapamo, Jules-Raymond, 2006, in IFIP International Federation for Information Processing, Volume 204, Artificial Intelligence Applications and Innovations, eds. Maglogiannis, I., Karpouzis, K., Bramer, M., (Boston: Springer), pp. 204–211

which also increase the difficulties of surveillance.

Using computer vision to gather data and provide real-time event detection has been studied for both indoor and outdoor applications. To track objects, Masoud *et al.* [1] has built a system that is able to track and count pedestrians in real-time; this system proceeds at 3 levels: raw image, blobs and pedestrians. Blobs are obtained from raw image and one pedestrian is represented by one or many blobs; spatio-temporal coordinates of the pedestrians are recorded and tracking is done by using extended Kaman filtering. The system built by Koller *et al.* [2] extracts contour and tracks vehicles on highways using cubic splines combined with Kalman filter. Affine motion of the moving objects is also estimated using Kalman filter.

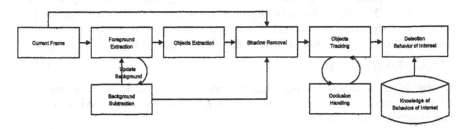

Fig. 1. Flowchart of the system.

To detect behaviors of interest, Cucchiara *et al.* [3] built an indoor system that is able to detect postures such as standing, crouching, sitting and lying by analyzing the vertical and horizontal projected histograms.

Haritaoglu *et al.* [4] and Wren *et al.* [5] designed systems that identified and tracked human using models of head, hands, feet and torso; gestures, postures and interactions between objects can be defined and detected.

The rest of the paper is organized as follows: in section 2 we describe the model of the system; some experiments are done and results are discussed in section 3; the conclusion and future work are presented in the last section.

2. System Model Overview

Foreground is extracted by taking the difference between the current frame and the background frame; background is updated using Gaussian model. Blobs are extracted by performing connected components finding. Candidate shadow regions are selected and used as a mask to filter out noising shadow from the moving objects. Each object is represented by one blob and tracked using linear approximation. TDL searching method combined with texture matching approach is used to solve the occlusion problem. Each behavior of interest is modelled as a sequence of characters; each character represents a set of shapes that has similar seven invariant moments [9]. A behavior is detected by the system if the sequence of the shapes extracted from the detected moving object is similar to a behavior of interest. The processes are detailed in following subsections. The flowchart of the system is shown in Fig. 1.

2.1 Background Subtraction

Background subtraction [6] is an approach to extract moving objects by taking the difference of the gray levels pixel by pixel of the current frame and the maintained background frame. A pixel is set as foreground if the difference of current frame and the background frame is larger than a threshold as shown in equation (1). In this system unimodal background model is used where each pixel in the background frame is modelled as a Gaussian distribution. For each pixel $(x^c y)$ of the background, two values are maintained: mean μ and variance σ. From frame to frame the background model is updated by Infinite Impulse Response filtering. Mean is the actual value of the pixel while the value of pixels in background frame is updated as in equation (2). The variance of the pixel is used to control the threshold in order to determine if a pixel from the current image belongs to the foreground or the background, it is updated as in equation (3).

$$| I_t(x,y) - B_t(x,y) | > \sigma_t(x,y) \tag{1}$$

where $I_t(x^c y)$ and $B_t(x^c y)$ represent the value of the pixel at $(x^c y)$ for the frame and maintained background at time t,   is a real value used to adjust the system for better performance.

$$B_{t+1}(x,y) = (1-\alpha)\mu_t + \alpha| B_t(x,y) - I_t(x,y) | \tag{2}$$

$$\sigma_{t+1}(x,y) = (1-\alpha)\sigma_t + \alpha(B_t(x,y) - I_t(x,y))^2 \tag{3}$$

where   is a constant used for the system to control the speed of the updated rate of the background.

2.2 Shadow Region Detection

In our system, we try to identify the behavior of the objects based on the stream of the shapes extracted from moving objects. Hence, it is important to filter out the regions of the shadow that may distort the shape of the moving objects. To detect the shadow we use an approach similar to the one proposed by Cucchiara *et al.* [8]. This method makes use of two properties of the shadows:

- *Linear dependence* shadow regions are linear dependant on the covered background region.
- *Spatial connectivity* shadow usually appears as a region.

For the first property, the shadow region is usually darker than the background region that is covered by it, and this can be expressed mathematically as in equation (4). For the second property of the shadow, morphology operation can be used to filter out the regions and pixels that are not large enough as a region of the shadow.

$$\frac{I_t(x,y)}{B_t(x,y)} = \lambda \text{ , for all pixel (x,y) in the shadow region, where } \lambda \in \Re \qquad (4)$$

Candidate shadow regions are used as a mask to filter out the shadow region. Shadow regions are removed by setting pixels as background if these belong both to foreground and shadow regions. Shadow candidate regions are extracted by applying algorithms as shown in equations (5), (6) and (7). Foreground with shadow removed is obtained using equation (8). Default mask size of the dilation and erosion in this system is set to 5 *by* 5. Experimental results show that shadow regions can be detected and removed. It is important to mention that shadow was not removed entirely. In most of the cases it shows sufficient performance. Some results are shown in *Fig.* 2.

$$SM1(x,y) = \begin{cases} 1, & if \ \eta \le \frac{I_t(x,y)}{B_t(x,y)} \le \theta \\ 0, & otherwise \end{cases} \qquad (5)$$

$$SM2(x,y) = \begin{cases} 1, & if \ SM1(x,y) \oplus Erosion(u,v) \\ 0, & otherwise \end{cases} \qquad (6)$$

$$SM3(x,y) = \begin{cases} 1, & if \ SM2(x,y) \ominus Dilation(u,v) \\ 0, & otherwise \end{cases} \qquad (7)$$

$$newFG(x,y) = \begin{cases} fg(x,y), & if \ fg(x,y) \ne 0 \ AND \ SM3(x,y) = 0 \\ 0, & otherwise \end{cases} \qquad (8)$$

where *newFG* is the new foreground with shadow removed, *fg*(*x,y*) is the value of the pixel (*x,y*) of the initial foreground obtained from background subtraction.

2.3 Extraction of Moving Objects

After the foreground has been extracted using background subtraction, connected components operation is performed to merge all the foreground pixels that are connected into homogenous blobs. To avoid one object appearing in two or more separated blob components, morphology operations are performed after the connected components detection. Opening morphology operation with mask size 3 × 3 is used to remove the small noise and merge the closely situated yet separated components into one. Each blob is thereby represented as one object and after the shadow is removed, information about the blobs is then calculated. For each extracted blob, we maintain the following attributes: *Center*, *Area*, *Bounding Box*, *Density*, *Velocity*, and the *seven Invariant Moments*.

2.4 Objects Tracking

A linear approximation approach is used to track detected moving objects. For each frame, blobs from the previous frame are matched to the blobs extracted from the current frame. Blobs from the previous frame are first shifted to the estimated new location on the current frame; after the shifting of blobs to the estimated location, if the bounding box of the blob B^i_{t-1} from the previous frame t-1 overlaps the bounding box of the blob B^j_t from the current frame t, it is then a potential match for the blob B^i_{t-1} to the blob B^j_t. We refer to blob B^i_{t-1} as the parent of the blob B^j_t and blob B^j_t as the child of the blob B^i_{t-1}. For each blob from the previous frame, a new location is estimated by shifting the location of the blob by the velocity of the blob. The velocity of the blob is a linear approximation by taking the displacement of the blob between its current location and its location in the previous frame. As a result of using such parent-child relationship, five different following conditions could be encountered:

1) 1 parent blob matched to 1 child blob
2) 1 parent blob matched to 0 child blob
3) 0 parent blob matched to 1 child blob
4) 1 parent blob matched to more than 1 child blob
5) more than 1 parent blob matched to 1 child blob

For 1) the blob is traced successfully from the previous frame to the current frame, the same object still appears in the scene with a predicable movement; if a parent blob ends up with no child blob as in 2), a search is performed around the estimated location, if there are blobs around the search region, a parent-child relationship is assigned to these blobs, otherwise the object is assumed to have exited from the surveillance scene and tracking of this object is terminated; if a blob from the current frame has no parent blob as in 3), it is marked as a new object, new tracking is initiated for it; if a parent blob has more than 1 child blob, similarity function that makes use of the information of size, location and density of the blob is measured, the parent blob will retain the child relationship to the most similar child blob, parent-child relationship to all other child blobs with lower similarity is unset. If more than 1 parent blob assigned child relation to the same blob, object occlusion has occurred; details for solving the occlusion are described in the next section.

2.5 Occlusion Handling

Occlusion occurs when two or more parent blobs are referenced to the same child blob. In this system, occlusions are solved by estimating new location for the parent blobs that give the maximum coverage rate to the occluded child blob and texture matching is used to find depth order of the parent blobs. To estimate the location of the parent blobs, the TDL (Two Dimensional Logarithmic) searching approach combined with the hit function is used. The best location for parent blobs is the location that maximizes the sum of the hit functions. The TDL searching approach is a suboptimal searching solution proposed by Jain *et al.* [7]; it gives efficient computation time with sufficient accuracy. Hit function is the function that returns the number of pixels that the parent blob covers to the occluded child blob after the shifting of the parent blob with TDL searching displacement. The initial TDL search location is the position plus the velocity of the parent blob. Once the best location for each of the parent blobs is estimated, texture matching is then performed to solve the depth order of the occluded objects. The shape and texture of parent blobs from the previous frame shifted with the best estimated displacement found using TDL earlier on is used to match the texture of the occluded blob. The parent blob that gives the lowest cost will be the object that is closest to the camera. The MAD (Mean Absolute Difference) is used as the distance function for texture matching. Experiments conducted using pattern matching to solve short time occlusion give promising result, see Fig. 3.

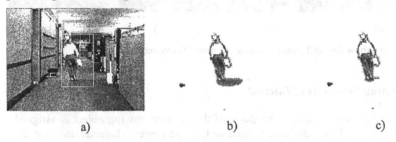

Fig. 2. Figure a) shows original hall monitor frame at index 70, b) and c) show detected and extracted moving objects from this system without and with shadow detection.

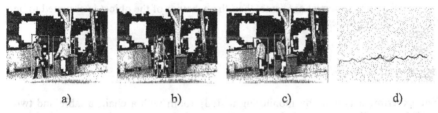

Fig. 3. Figures a) b) c) show an example of the occlusion event, d) shows trajectories of the detected moving objects.

2.6 Characters and Behaviors Learning

Behaviors of interest are modelled as streams of characters and saved in a knowledge base. Each character represents a set of shapes that share 7 similar invariant moment features. Learning of the characters is by extracting 7 invariant moments from the shapes of the detected moving objects from a training data set. Based on 7 invariant moments, K-Means clustering is then performed to separate these shapes into K different classes; each class is then represented by a unique character. The centroid value for each class is then the features of the character. After the character learning, each character is considered as a unique pattern. Invariant moments are appropriate to model shapes of the moving objects because they conserve invariance by translation, rotation and scaling of objects. More detail about invariant moments can be found in [9, 10]. This set of characters is then used to represent any possible shape of the moving objects that the system can detect.

The learning of behaviors of interest is done by extracting each behavior of interest from a sequence of frames. From each frame the extracted shape of the blob is then assigned to a character by comparing 7 invariant moments of the blob to the characters. The nearest Euclidian distance is used to find the best matched character. Each behavior of interest is then represented as a stream of characters.

a)   b)   c)   d)

Fig. 4. Figures show four different behaviors of interest the system aims to detect.

2.7 Detecting Behaviors of Interest

To detect behaviors of interest, the shape of the detected moving object is assigned to a character. Euclidian distance is used to find the nearest character amongst the character set and the shape of the object. For an object that is traced by the system, a stream of characters representing a sequence of the shape captured from the system will be maintained. If the end piece of substring from the traced object and the string of the behavior of interest are same, then the behavior of the object is assumed to be the behavior of interest.

3. Experiments

The experiment is done by monitoring a study room with a chair, a table and two bookshelves. There are four behaviors of interest for the system to monitor wherein a human is positioned as follows: seated facing away from the table, seated facing the table, touching bookshelf-1, touching bookshelf-2. Fig. 4 shows four different behaviors which the system aims to detect. A character set is obtained by first collecting 862 different shapes of the human posture in the room environment; these shapes are then clustered into 29 different classes, centroid values for each class are then represented as a unique character from A to Z and @,#,$.

The capture speed of the system is set to 5 frames per second, each behavior of interest is represented by 5 characters, by doing this, the system examines the behavior of moving objects by matching 5 key characters to the 5 shapes of the detected moving objects extracted in the last 1 second.

With just one training sequence for each behavior of interest, the system is able to detect 4 distinct behaviors of interest; each behavior of interest gives unique character streams: seated facing away from the table - AAAAA, seated facing the table - HHHHH, touching bookshelf-1 - NNNNN, touching bookshelf-2 - VVVVV. Through the 50 testing behaviors within about 3200 frame sequences: results show 36 behaviors recognized correctly in an appropriate time, the system missed detection of 11 behaviors and 3 behaviors are detected as wrong behavior of interest.

4. Future Work and Conclusions

We have designed and presented a model of real-time surveillance system. For our future works, we intend to explore further this modelling approach of behavior of moving object using character representation; character modelling is suitable for the movements that require regular posture and cadence as in aerobic exercise and Chinese martial art. This approach combined with Edit Distance has been used successfully to model and detect the movements of Chinese martial art. We also want to interpret the behavior of the detected human at higher levels by combining several short time behaviors.

Acknowledgments

The authors would like to thank the National Research Foundation of South Africa for their support of this work. The authors would like also thank to Cathy and Mei-Zhu for making available testing data.

References

1. U. Masoud and N.ikolaos P. Papanikolopoulos, "A Novel Method for Tracking and Counting Pedestrains in Real-Time Using a Single Camera," IEEE Trans. On Vehicular Tech. Vol. 50, No. 5 Sep 2001.
2. D. Koller, J. Weber and J. Malik, "Robust Multiple Car Tracking with Occlusion Reasoning," In Proceedings of Third European Conference on Computer Vision, Stockholm, Sweden, May 2-6, 1994, pp. 189-196, LNCS 800, Springer-Verlag, 1994.
3. R. Cucchiara, C. Grana, A. Prati and R. Vezzani, "Computer vision system for in-house video surveillance," In IEE Proceedings of Visual Image Signal Process. Vol. 152, No. 2, April 2005.
4. I. Haritaoglu, Larry S. Davis and D. Harwood. w4 who? when? where? what? a real time system for detecing and tracking people," IEEE Trans. on Pattern Analysis and Machine Intelligence, Vol.22 Aug 2000.
5. C. Wren, A. Azarbayejani, T. Darrell and A. Pentland, "Pfinder: Real-time Tracking of the human body," IEEE Trans. on Pattern Analysis and Machine Intell., 19(7):780-785, 1997.
6. S.Y. Chien, S.Y. Ma and L.G. Chen, "Efficient Moving Object Segmentation Algorithm Using Background Registration Technique," IEEE Trans. on Circuits and Systems for Video Tech. Vol. 12 No. 7 July 2002.
7. Jaswant R. Jain, Anil K. Jain, "Displacement measurement and its application in interframe image coding," IEEE Transactions on Communications, Volume COM-29, Number 12, p 1799 - 1808, December 1981
8. R. Cucchiara, C. Grana, M. Piccardi, A. Prati and S. Sirotti, "Detecting Moving Objects, Ghosts, and Shadows in Video Streams," IEEE Trans. on Pattern Analysis and Machine Intelligence, Vol. 25, pp. 1337-1342, 2003.
9. M-K. Hu, "Visual pattern recognition by moment invariants," IRE Trans. on Information Theory, IT-8:pp. 179-187, 1962.
10. A. Khotanzad and Y. H. Hongs, "Invariant image recognition by Zernike moments," IEEE Trans. on Pattern Analysis and Machine Intelligence, 12(5):pp. 489-497, 1990

A Filter Module Used in Pedestrian Detection System

Gengxin Miao, Yupin Luo, Qiming Tian, Jingxin Tang
Department of Automation, Tsinghua University, Beijing, 100084,
P.R.China
mgx03@mails.tsinghua.edu.cn, luo@tsinghua.edu.cn,
tianqm00@mails.tsinghua.edu.cn, tangjx@mail.tsinghua.edu.cn

Abstract. Most pedestrian detection systems are built based on computer vision technology and usually are composed of two basic modules: object detection module, and recognition module. This paper presents an efficient filtering module, which works between the two basic modules, based on extracting the 3-dimensional information from single frame images. The filter module removes the noisy objects extracted by object detection module and thus reduces the burden of the recognition module. 3-D information, such as height, width and distance are extracted from single frame images. Using this information, a Bayesian classifier is employed to implement the filter. The main contribution of this filter module is that it removed about 30% noisy objects detected by the object detection module. The total computing cost and error detection rate is reduced when this filter module is used in the pedestrian detection system.

1 Introduction

According to the report [9], there are, every year, lots of pedestrians killed in traffic crashes in the US. Also, the pedestrian security problem is very serious all over the world. Considering this, the demand for computer vision based pedestrian detection systems arises.

The hardware of the pedestrian detection system is composed of a camera mounted on the front part of vehicle and a computer processing the video signals captured by the camera. Most of the existing computer vision based systems used a two-stepped algorithm: detection module and recognition module. Objects in the video are detected in the detection phase, and then these objects are classified with

Please use the following format when citing this chapter:

Miao, Gengxin, Luo, Yupin, Tian, Qiming, Tang, Jingxin, 2006, in IFIP International Federation for Information Processing, Volume 204, Artificial Intelligence Applications and Innovations, eds. Maglogiannis, I., Karpouzis, K., Bramer, M., (Boston: Springer), pp. 212–220

various pattern recognition techniques in the recognition phase. Example systems can be found in other researchers' studies [4][5][7].

The simple two-phased systems may lead to heavy computing burden since the detection module marked too many image candidates for the classification module. Tian et al. [6] have made some rigid rules to filter the objects extracted by the detection module according to the position of the candidate images. Broggi et al. [1] concerned the projection process from a real world to a 2-dimensional image. Both of the methods recognized that the height of the candidates is crucial information for removing the noisy candidates. Neither of them, however, calculated the 3D information online. On one hand, the filtering rate is low; on the other hand, there are lots of candidates being filtered by mistake.

This paper focuses on a filter model which works between the object detection module and the recognition module used in a computer vision based pedestrian detection system. In figure 1, an example image from the video can illustrate the problem encountered in the existing system.

Fig 1. An example image from the video

In figure 1, the yellow rectangles show the results extracted by the detection module, and the red rectangles represent the output of classification module which are expected to be pedestrians. In fact, the smaller red rectangle is not an image of a pedestrian, and just because its scale is too small so that based on the image information the classifier cannot recognize it from the pedestrian objects. In this image, too many yellow rectangles influence both the efficiency and the effectiveness of the recognition module.

In this filter module, the camera is primarily calculated with mature techniques [8]; since the camera is fixed on the vehicle, its parameters can be regarded as constant when the vehicle is operating on the road after the coordinate systems are finely established. In the calculation, the image information is totally ignored since that is the task of recognition module; the 3-dimensional information is calculated just based on the position where the candidate objects exist. Similar approach can be found in [2]. After that, a Bayesian classifier is employed to accomplish the filter task.

The rest of the paper is organized as follows. Section 2 presents the camera module used in this module; Section 3 describes the detail of this filter module; the experimental results are shown in Section 4; and, at last, Section 5 draws the conclusion and proposes some future work.

2   Camera Model and Definition of Coordinate System

A camera consists of optical elements and an image surface. By varying the optics of the camera, many different projection of a given scene can be obtained. Among this set of projection models, the pinhole model [3] is the simplest projection model, as shown in formula (1)

$$
s\begin{bmatrix} u \\ v \\ 1 \end{bmatrix} = A\begin{bmatrix} r_1 & r_2 & r_3 & t \end{bmatrix}\begin{bmatrix} X \\ Y \\ Z \\ 1 \end{bmatrix}
\tag{1}
$$

where   s = coefficient related to the object distance
              [u, v]' = image coordinates
              A = the camera's intrinsic parameter
              $[r_1, r_2, r_3, t]'$ = the camera's extrinsic parameter
              [X, Y, Z]' = object coordinates in the world coordinate system

The definition of these symbols will not be described again for the space limitation.

For intrinsic parameter calibration, lots of researchers have developed a variety of methods to implement the calibration. Among them, Zhang, Z. [8] proposed a flexible technique to easily calibrate the intrinsic parameters. For its convenience and precision, we implemented Zhang's method in our experiment.

The camera is fixed on the vehicle, and, thus, the relative position of the two coordinate systems is invariable; in other words, the external parameter of the camera can be fixed via a convenient definition of the camera coordinate system and the real world coordinate system. To simplify the problem, the image coordinate system and the world coordinate system are established as shown in figure 2.

As shown in figure 2, both of the two coordinate systems have the constantly parallel direction. Therefore, the extrinsic parameter matrix should be like this:

$$
B = \begin{bmatrix} 1 & 0 & 0 & 0 \\ 0 & 1 & 0 & -h_c \\ 0 & 0 & 1 & 0 \end{bmatrix} \quad h_c \text{ is the camera's height}
\tag{2}
$$

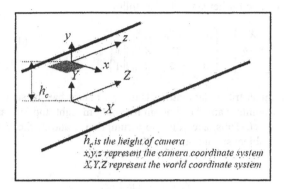

Fig 2. Camera and world coordinate systems

3 Our Approach

This section will mainly present two problems. 1) What are the data that the filter module will use to calculate the real size; and 2) What is the real size estimation process.

3.1 Online Size Estimation

The online size estimation algorithm is designed based on single frame images. To make this process feasible, some assumptions are proposed.

3.1.1 Assumptions: After estimating the camera parameters, the real size of the objects can be estimated based on some assumptions.

Assumption 1: Both the intrinsic and extrinsic parameters of the camera are invariable since the camera is fixed on the vehicle.

Assumption 2: The input objects are standing on the road plane. (Since the target of the module is pedestrian who are definitely standing on the ground)

Assumption 3: The road is planar.

3.1.2 Equations used for 3-dimensional information Estimation: Based on the camera module and the assumptions described above, the 3-dimensional information can be calculated from the single frame images.

Put the extrinsic parameter matrix (B described in Section 3.1) in formula 1. Thus:

$$\begin{bmatrix} u \\ v \\ 1 \end{bmatrix} = \frac{A}{s} \begin{bmatrix} X \\ Y - h_c \\ Z \end{bmatrix} \qquad (3)$$

The formula can be further simplified as follows:

$$\begin{bmatrix} X \\ Y-h_c \\ Z \end{bmatrix} = s\begin{bmatrix} A^{-1}_{11} & A^{-1}_{12} & A^{-1}_{13} \\ 0 & A^{-1}_{22} & A^{-1}_{23} \\ 0 & 0 & A^{-1}_{33} \end{bmatrix}\begin{bmatrix} u \\ v \\ 1 \end{bmatrix} \qquad (4)$$

Since A is an upper triangular matrix, its inverse matrix has the same character.

There are four points (named as bottom left, bottom right, top left, and top right) to present each object. Thus, according to assumption 2 and 3, the Y value of the bottom edge of the object should be zero. Thus:

$$\text{Equation 1:} \quad \begin{bmatrix} X_l \\ -h_c \\ Z \end{bmatrix} = sA^{-1}\begin{bmatrix} u_l \\ v_b \\ 1 \end{bmatrix} \qquad (5)$$

Furthermore, when examining the top and right edges of the object and the image, another equation can be achieved:

$$\text{Equation 2:} \quad \begin{bmatrix} X_r \\ Y_t-h_c \\ Z \end{bmatrix} = sA^{-1}\begin{bmatrix} u_r \\ v_t \\ 1 \end{bmatrix} \qquad (6)$$

Combining the two equations, the following real size related information can be calculated:

$$\begin{aligned}
Dis = Z &= -h_c \frac{A^{-1}_{33}}{A^{-1}_{22}v_b + A^{-1}_{23}} \\
Height = Y_t &= h_c \frac{A^{-1}_{22}v_t - A^{-1}_{22}v_t}{A^{-1}_{22}v_b + A^{-1}_{23}} \\
Width = X_r - X_l &= -h \frac{A^{-1}_{11}u_r - A^{-1}_{11}u_l}{A^{-1}_{22}v_b + A^{-1}_{23}}
\end{aligned} \qquad (7)$$

3.3 Classifier

Three attributes (the distance, the height, and the width) can be computed to represent each object. Among of the three, the height is the most crucial cue to filter those non-pedestrian objects. Since the height to width ratio is constant (the objects are extracted based on template matching algorithm), the width information is omitted in the further calculation. The pedestrians can stand at any distance from the vehicle; in light of this, the distance information seems to be of less use either. However, when the distance increases, the estimation of height will be involved with a larger error. Therefore, the two dimensional information of both height and distance are used as the input of the Bayesian classifier.

To assure the formula has an analytical solution, a Gaussian function is used to approximate the probability density function of the distribution of real height and distance of the candidate objects. All the samples should be firstly divided into two categories, the positive and the negative (which means the pedestrian objects and the non-pedestrian objects). Then the estimation of the mean value and the variance of the height and distance corresponding to each category can be achieved.

Thus, the discriminant functions and the decision surface can be expressed as follows.

$$g_p(x) = -\frac{1}{2}\begin{bmatrix} Dis - \mu_{dp} \\ Height - \mu_{hp} \end{bmatrix}^T \begin{bmatrix} \Sigma_{dp} & 0 \\ 0 & \Sigma_{hp} \end{bmatrix}^{-1} \begin{bmatrix} Dis - \mu_{dp} \\ Height - \mu_{hp} \end{bmatrix} - \frac{1}{2}\ln\begin{vmatrix} \Sigma_{dp} & 0 \\ 0 & \Sigma_{hp} \end{vmatrix} \quad (8)$$

$$g_{np}(x) = -\frac{1}{2}\begin{bmatrix} Dis - \mu_{dnp} \\ Height - \mu_{hnp} \end{bmatrix}^T \begin{bmatrix} \Sigma_{dnp} & 0 \\ 0 & \Sigma_{hnp} \end{bmatrix}^{-1} \begin{bmatrix} Dis - \mu_{dnp} \\ Height - \mu_{hnp} \end{bmatrix} - \frac{1}{2}\ln\begin{vmatrix} \Sigma_{dnp} & 0 \\ 0 & \Sigma_{hnp} \end{vmatrix}$$

According to formulae (7) and (8), the decision surface should be decided below:

$$f(x) = g_p(x) - g_{np}(x) = \frac{1}{2}\left(\left(x - \mu_{np}\right)^T \Sigma_{np}^{-1}\left(x - \mu_{np}\right) - \left(x - \mu_p\right)^T \Sigma_p^{-1}\left(x - \mu_p\right)\right) + C \quad (9)$$

4 Experimental Results

Our experiment is implemented based on a tape record derived from the real scenery in the streets during nighttimes. In the whole video file, there are 1,144,323 candidate objects extracted. Firstly, the video data are divided into two parts: some data for training and the other for test. There are 500,000 objects used for training and the rest for testing. In all the object samples, there are 9,333 positive objects and the others are negative ones.

4.4 Parameter Tuning

4.1.1 Probability Density Function Estimation: In order to design a classifier based on the height and distance information of the objects, the different distribution characters on these features of the two categories of objects should be examined first. In this section, the probability density function of the height and distance of both groups of objects is estimated.

As mentioned above (see Section 3.3), this section uses Gaussian function to estimate the probability density function of the height and distance of both positive and negative objects. The results are shown in the following table.

Table1. Results of probability density function estimation

	Mean value μ	Variance Σ
Positive objects, distance	52.6m	4556.25
Positive objects, height	1.109m	1.9
Negative objects, distance	111m	77952.6
Negative objects, height	2.75m	51.7

4.1.2 Decision Surface Estimation: Theoretically, the height of object is independent to its distance from the vehicle. However, when the objects go farther from the camera, the image will be blurred and, consequently, the error in estimating its distance and height will be greater. Therefore, both the height and the distance information are useful to establish the Bayesian classifier.

Figure 3 shows the parameter tuning process in which the curve labeled as *positive* shows the retain rate of pedestrian objects when the parameter of the decision surface varies; and the *negative* curve shows the filter rate of non-pedestrian objects when the parameter of the decision surface varies.

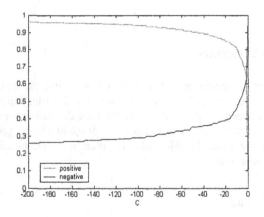

Fig 3. Parameter tuning graph

The parameters should be chosen based on this principle: the most of the negative objects should be filtered and most of the positive ones should be retained. However, there is not a clearly optimal value shown in this figure, since when the negative objects' curve increases (which means the filter rate is growing), the positive objects' curve drops (which means the loss of pedestrian objects is also growing). As shown in figure 3, -100 is chosen as a decision surface.

5   Test Results

Once the decision surface is determined, it can be used to classify the test data collection. The result of the filter is shown below.

In figure 4, the vertical axis represents the number of candidate objects for both categories. The horizontal axis represents the parameter of the decision surface.

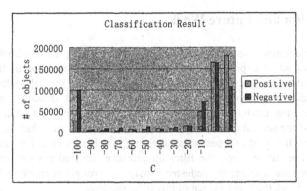

Fig 4. Test results

Because the pedestrian samples are too few to be comparable with the non-pedestrian samples, to amplify the result, this figure magnifies the number of pedestrian objects by 500 times. To make it clearer, the two ratio values (the two-ratio values, or the values of the two ratios) are calculated as follows.

$$\frac{\text{Left samples}}{\text{Total samples}} = 71.4\%$$

$$\frac{\text{Left positive samples}}{\text{Total positive samples}} = 94.1\%$$

(10)

In formula 10, the test results are shown clearly. The filter module finally removed 28.6 percents of the candidate objects, among which there are only 5.9 percents of the positive objects which are removed by mistake. This result is very satisfying for the further process. On one hand, by removing a lot of candidates, the following modules can save lots of time in processing them. On the other hand, most of the removed objects (326,716 among 327,276, almost 98.8%) are non-pedestrian objects. Thus, as a result, the wrong detection ratio of the following modules can be decreased.

5.1 Discussion

The wrong detection is mainly produced in two ways: 1) the approximated camera parameters import errors in calculating the real size information especially when the objects are in long distances. And 2) the mistaken segmentation of objects offered by former detection module brings an ineffaceable error in the following calculation. These two kinds of errors weakened the power of the filter module. To reduce the effect of the first type of error, the classification algorithm also had the distance information as an input; in this way, the results are improved remarkably. For the limitation of space, the former experimental results without considering the distance information are not included in this paper.

6 Conclusion and Future Work

To further improve the performance of this filter module, the two kinds of errors should be studied in depth. For the first type of error, the error of the camera parameters can be estimated, and consequently the error of the calculated real size information can be estimated as well as the height and distance information. Currently, the filter module avoided processing the raw image information, thus it can't get rid of the second type of error. Most of the time, the mistaken segmentation contains only a half part of a pedestrian dressing in different colors for the coat and the trousers. For future work, the filter module can detected a small range in the image and examine whether the pedestrian image is wrongly segmented. These will potentially improve the performance of this filter module.

References

1. Broggi, A. Fascioli, A. Carletti, M. Graf, T. Meinecke, M.: A multi-resolution approach for infrared vision-based pedestrian detection. 2004 IEEE intelligent vehicles symposium. Parma, Italy, (2004) Pages: 7-12
2. Criminisi, A.; Reid, I.; Zisserman, A.: Single view metrology. Computer Vision, 1999. The Proceedings of the Seventh IEEE International Conference on Volume 1, 20-27, 1999.9 Pages:434-441 vol.1
3. David, A.: Computer Vision: a modern approach, ISBN:0130851981. Chapter 2
4. Gavrila, D.: Pedestrian detection from a moving vehicle. European Conference on Computer Vision. Trinity College Dublin, Ireland. (2000) Pages: 37-49
5. Nanda, H.: Probabilistic template based pedestrian detection in infrared videos. 2002 IEEE intelligent vehicles symposium. EPFL, Switzerland (2000) Pages: 15-20 vol.1
6. Qiming Tian, Yupin Luo, Dongcheng Hu: Pedestrian detection in nighttime driving. ICIG'04 Hongkong China (2004) Pages:116-119
7. Bin Zhang, Qiming Tian, Yupin Luo: A multi-layer classifiers framework for pedestrian detection in cluttered nighttime background Visual Communications and Image Processing Beijing, China (2005) Pages: 143-148
8. Zhengyou Zhang: Flexible Camera Calibration by Viewing a Plane from Unknown Orientations. ICCV 1999 Kerkyra, Greece, (1999) Pages: 666-673 vol.1
9. http://www-nrd.nhtsa.dot.gov/departments/nrd-30/ncsa/ National center for statistics and analysis of the national highway traffic safety administration (accessed 12. May, 2005)

User Localization for Intelligent Crisis Management

Ondrej Krejcar

VSB Technical University of Ostrava, Centre for Applied Cybernetics,
Department of Measurement and Control, 17. listopadu 15,
708 33 Ostrava, Czech Republic
ondrej.krejcar@vsb.cz
http://cak.vsb.cz

Abstract. The proliferation of mobile computing devices and local-area wireless networks has fostered a growing interest in location-aware systems and services. Additionally, the ability to let a mobile device determine its location in an indoor environment at a fine-grained level supports the creation of a new range of mobile control system applications. Main area of interest is in model of radio-frequency (RF) based system enhancement for locating and tracking users of control system inside buildings. The locating and tracking of users is useful for rescue people to find closer way in unknown building. The software can navigate these people through the unknown space to accident place. The experimental framework prototype uses a WiFi network infrastructure to let a mobile device determine its indoor position as well as to deliver IP connectivity. Experiments show that location determination can be realized with a room level granularity.

1 Introduction

The usage of various wireless technologies that enable convenient continuous IP-level (packet switched) connectivity for mobile devices has increased dramatically and will continue to do so for the coming years. This will lead to the rise of new application domains each with their own specific features and needs. Also, these new domains will undoubtedly apply and reuse existing (software) paradigms, components and applications. Today, this is easily recognized in the miniaturized applications on network-connected PDAs that provide more or less the same functionality as their desktop application equivalents. The web browser application is such an example of reuse. Next to this, it is very likely that these new mobile application domains adapt new paradigms that specifically target the mobile environment. We believe that an important paradigm is context-awareness. Context is relevant to the mobile user, because in a mobile environment the context is often

Please use the following format when citing this chapter:

Krejcar, Ondrej, 2006, in IFIP International Federation for Information Processing, Volume 204, Artificial Intelligence Applications and Innovations, eds. Maglogiannis, I., Karpouzis, K., Bramer, M., (Boston: Springer), pp. 221–227

very dynamic and the user interacts differently with the applications on his mobile device when the context is different. While a desktop machine usually is in a fixed context, a mobile device goes from work, to on the road, to work in-a-meeting, to home, etc. Context is not limited to the physical world around the user, but also incorporates the user's behavior, and terminal and network characteristics.

Context-awareness concepts can be found as basic principles in long-term strategic research for mobile and wireless systems such as formulated in [6]. The majority of context-aware computing to date has been restricted to location-aware computing for mobile applications (location-based services). However, position or location information is a relatively simple form of contextual information. To name a few other indicators of context awareness that make up the parametric context space: identity, spatial information (location, speed), environmental information (temperature), resources that are nearby (accessible devices, hosts), availability of resources (battery, display, network, bandwidth), physiological measurements (blood pressure, hart rate), activity (walking, running), schedules and agenda settings. Context-awareness means that one is able to use context information.

We consider location as prime form of context information. Our focus here is on position determination in an indoor environment. Location information is used to determine an actual user position and his future position. We have performed a number of experiments with the control system, focusing on position determination, and are encouraged by the results. The remainder of this paper describes the conceptual and technical details of this.

2   Basic Concepts and Technologies of User Localization

The proliferation of mobile computing devices and local-area wireless networks has fostered a growing interest in location-aware systems and services. A key distinguishing feature of such systems is that the application information and/or interface presented to the user is, in general, a function of his physical location. The granularity of location information needed could vary from one application to another. For example, locating a nearby printer requires fairly coarse-grained location information whereas locating a book in a library would require fine-grained information.

While much research has been focused on development of services architectures for location-aware systems, less attention has been paid to the fundamental and challenging problem of locating and tracking mobile users, especially in in-building environments. We focus mainly on RF wireless networks in our research. Our goal is to complement the data networking capabilities of RF wireless LANs with accurate user location and tracking capabilities for user needed data pre-buffering. This property we use as information ground for extension of control system.

2.1   Location-Based Services

Location-based services (LBS) are touted as 'killer apps' for mobile systems. An important difference between fixed and mobile systems is that the latter operate in a particular context, and may behave differently or offer different information and interaction possibilities depending on this context. Location is often the principal aspect determining the context. Many different technologies are used to provide location information. Very common is the GPS system, which uses a network of satellites and provides position information accurate within 10–20 m. However, due to its satellite based nature, it is not suited for indoor positioning. In cellular telecommunication networks such as GSM, the cell ID gives coarse-grained position information with an accuracy of about 200 m to 10 km. For fine-grained indoor location information, various technologies are available, based on infrared, RF, or ultrasonic technologies often using some type of beacon or active badge. Given the ubiquity of mobile devices like PDAs, however, active badges will probably be superseded by location technologies incorporated in these devices.

In the context of our experimental setup, we need indoor position information accurate enough to determine the room in which the user is located. We must deploy a separate location technology, where we use the information available from a WiFi network infrastructure to determine the location with room-level accuracy. By this information possible user track is estimate.

2.2 WiFi - IEEE 802.11

The Institute of Electrical and Electronics Engineers (IEEE) develops and approves standards for a wide variety of computer technologies. IEEE designates networking standards with the number 802. Wireless networking standards are designated by the number 11. Hence, IEEE wireless standards fall under the 802.11 umbrella. Ethernet, by the way, is called 802.3 [1].

802.11b is an updated and improved version of the original IEEE 802.11 standard. Most wireless networking products today are based on 802.11b. 802.11b networks operate at a maximum speed of 11 Mbps, slightly faster than 10-BASE-T Ethernet, providing a more than fivefold increase over the original 802.11 spec. The 802.11 standard provided for the use of DSSS and FHSS spread-spectrum methods. In 802.11b, DSSS is used. We use only 802.11b infrastructure (PDA has 802.11b standard) so other standards (802.11a or g) is not needed to describe. However, it can be possible to develop a PDPT framework with it.

2.3 Data Collection

A key step in the proposed research methodology is the data collection phase. We record information about the radio signal as a function of a user's location. The signal information is used to construct and validate models for signal propagation. Among other information, the WaveLAN NIC makes available the signal strength (SS) and the signal-to-noise ratio (SNR). SS is reported in units of dBm and SNR is expressed in dB. A signal strength of s Watts is equivalent to $10*\log10(s/0.001)$ dBm. A signal strength of s Watts and a noise power of n Watts yields an SNR of $10*\log10(s/n)$ dB. For example, signal strength of 1 Watt is equivalent to 30 dBm. Furthermore, if the noise power is 0.1 Watt, the SNR would be 10 dB. The WaveLAN driver extracts the SS and the SNR information from the WaveLAN firmware each time a broadcast packet is received. It then makes the information available to user-level applications via system calls. It uses the *wlconfig* utility, which provides a wrapper around the calls, to extract the signal information.

2.4 Localization Methodology

The general principle is that if a WiFi-enabled mobile device is close to such a stationary device – Access Point (AP), it can "ask" the location provider's position by setting up a WiFi connection. If the mobile device knows the position of the stationary device, it also knows that its own position is within a 100-meter range of this location provider. Granularity of location can improve by triangulation of two or several visible WiFi APs as described on figure [Fig. 1].

The PDA client will support the application in automatically retrieving location information from nearby location providers, and in interacting with the server. Naturally, this principle can be applied to other wireless technologies.

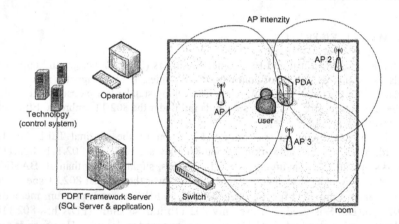

Fig. 1. Localization principle - triangulation.

The application (locator) based on .NET language is now created for testing. It is implemented in C# using the MS Visual Studio .NET 2003 with compact framework and a special OpenNETCF library enhancement [3] and [7]. Current application [Fig. 2] records just one set of signal strength measurements. By this set of value the actual user position is determined.

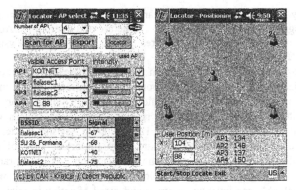

Fig. 2.PDA Locator – AP intensity & Positioning.

2.5 WiFi Middleware

The WiFi middleware implements the client's side of location determination mechanism on the Windows CE 3.0 PocketPC operating system and is part of the PDA client application. The libraries used to manage WiFi middleware are: AccessPoint, AccessPointCollection, Adapter, AdapterCollection, AdapterType, ConnectionStatus, Networking, NetworkType, and SignalStrength. Methods from the Net library are used for example to display Visible WiFi AP. See figure [Fig. 3].

```
dtVisibleAP = new DataTable("Visible AP");
DataRow drDataRow;
adptrColection = Networking.GetAdapters();
foreach (Adapter adptr in adptrColection)
{
  Application.DoEvents();
  if (adptr.Type==AdapterType.Ethernet)
  {
    foreach (AccessPoint ap in
             adptr.NearbyAccessPoints)
    {
      drDataRow = dtVisibleAP.NewRow();
      drDataRow["BSSID"] =
        (ap.Name.ToString());
      drDataRow["Signal [%]"] =
    ((ap.SignalStrength.Decibels).ToString());
      dtVisibleAP.Rows.Add(drDataRow);
    }
  }
}
```
Fig. 3 Sample code – signal strength from AP.

3 User Localization in Intelligent Crisis Management

Many people define crisis management as emergency response or business continuity, while other people will only consider the public relations aspect [8]. They are all partially correct, but true crisis management has many facets. It must be thoroughly integrated into the organization's structure and operations. Achieving an effective level of crisis management requires a thorough internal analysis, strategic thinking and sufficient discussion.

Crisis Management is the umbrella term that encompasses all activities involved when an organization prepares for and responds to a significant critical incident. An effective crisis management program should be consistent with the organization's mission and integrate plans such as Emergency Response, Business Continuity, Crisis Communications, Disaster Recovery, Humanitarian Assistance, etc.

Fireman, police and rescue service are very important part of this crisis management. Management and coordination of this people is now practicable by shortwave communication (radio, transmitter), but new mobile communication technologies as PDA's can level up potential and speed of action in crisis situations. As discussed before, we can locate any people with PDA running client software. But how localization of these people can help them? Advantage is in tracking of these people. For example when fireman arrive to crisis place, his PDA will make an interconnection to crisis management system of building which fireman arrive and the software on PDA will guide the fireman by shortest safe way directly to the centre of problem in the crisis building. In this case function, the PDA has of navigator and it can help people to make a good orientation around unknown building.

4   Conclusion

The main objective of this paper is in the enhancement of control system for locating and tracking of users inside a building. It is possible to locate and track the users with high degree of accuracy.

In this paper, we presented the control system framework enhancement that uses and handles location information. The framework provides a model that deals with location. Furthermore, a mechanism for location determination is a part of the framework. The indoor location of a mobile user is obtained through an infrastructure of WiFi access points. This mechanism measures the link quality of nearby location provider access points to determine actual user position. User location is used in core of server application of PDPT framework.

The experiments show that the location determination mechanism provides a good indication of the actual location of the user in most cases. The median resolution of the system is approximately five meters, about the size of a typical office room. Some inaccuracy is inherent to the way location information is obtained using the WiFi infrastructure. For the framework application this was not found to be a big limitation.

The experiments also show that the current state of the basic technology used for the localization (mobile device hardware, PDA operating system, wireless network technology) is now at the level of a high usability of the localization applications.

Acknowledgement

This work was supported by the Ministry of Education of the Czech Republic under Project 1M0567

References

1. Reynolds, J.: Going Wi-Fi : A Practical Guide to Planning and Building an 802.11 Network, CMP Books, 2003. ISBN 1578203015
2. Wigley, A., Roxburgh, P.: ASP.NET applications for Mobile Devices, Microsoft Press, Redmond, 2003. ISBN 073561914X
3. Tiffany, R.: SQL Server CE Database Development with the .NET Compact Framework, Apress, 2003. ISBN 1590591194
4. Thilmany, Ch.: A .Net Patterns: Architecture, Design, and Process, Addison-Wesley Professional, 2003. ISBN 0321130022
5. The Internet Engineering Task Force RADIUS Working Group: http://www.ietf.org/
6. The Wireless World Research Forum (WWRF): http://www.wireless-world-research.org/
7. OpenNETCF - Smart Device Framework: http://www.opennetcf.org/
8. Crisis Management International: http:// http://www.cmiatl.com

An Intrusion Detection System for Network-Initiated Attacks Using a Hybrid Neural Network

Stefanos Koutsoutos, Ioannis T. Christou, Sofoklis Efremidis

Athens Information Technology, 19km Markopoulou Ave. Paiania 19002
Greece

skou@ait.edu.gr, ichr@ait.edu.gr, sefr@ait.edu.gr

Abstract. We present a hybrid system based on a combination of Neural Networks and rule-based matching systems that is capable of detecting network-initiated intrusion attacks on web servers. The system has a strong learning component allowing it to recognize even novel attacks (i.e. attacks it has never seen before) and categorize them as such. The performance of the Neural Network in detecting attacks is very good with success rates of more than 78% in recognizing new attacks. However, because of an alarmingly high false alarm rate that measures more than 90% on normal HTTP traffic carrying image uploads we had to combine the original ANN with a rule-based component that monitors the server's system calls for detecting unusual activity. A final component combines the two systems to make the final decision on whether to raise an intrusion alarm or not. We report on the results we got from our approach and future directions for this research.

1 Introduction

Intrusion Detection is a major issue that every administrator has to deal with effectively so as to maintain proper operation of their Internet-connected servers. Network security and Intrusion Detection was studied as early as 40 years ago [6], but with the current growth of the Internet and the number of attackers, it has taken on a very prominent role in the fields of computer and communications security ([7, 12, 18, 21]). For this reason, the problem has been widely studied from a number of different perspectives. Data Mining approaches have been used to detect unusual activities on the servers ([8,10]). System calls are monitored in [9] to discover patterns that are characteristic of an intrusion. Actual Intrusions (when another person actually takes over in an unauthorized way someone else's workstation) have

Please use the following format when citing this chapter:

Koutsoutos, Stefanos, Christou, Ioannis, Efremidis, Sofoklis, 2006, in IFIP International Federation for Information Processing, Volume 204, Artificial Intelligence Applications and Innovations, eds. Maglogiannis, I., Karpouzis, K., Bramer, M., (Boston: Springer), pp. 228–235

also been studied in [16,17,20] and dealt with a number of different approaches, many times utilizing Artificial Intelligence techniques.

The idea of using Artifical Neural Networks or ANNs ([3, 22]) for finding novel attacks is not new ([1, 2, 4, 13, 14]). The usual approach is to train a neural network with the behavior of the system and let it recognize any behavior which substantially differs from the one considered as normal. The behavior is described to a neural network with a number of features, like system calls invocation, rates of system call invocation, etc. In this paper *we explore the possibility of using a hybrid system based on neural networks which will be trained and accept data directly from the data network and try to identify attacks using this data, in real time, by continually monitoring the network as well as the server state.*

The ultimate goal is to be able to identify both known and unseen attacks, on the fly, mainly using their binary signature, as this travels through the network. There are numerous kinds of attacks, each of which has a completely different structure of signature. Because different applications may use different protocols, network traffic may substantially differ from one case to another. This variety renders the task of building a neural network, which will be able to respond to every possible attack, essentially infeasible. In order to overcome this kind of problem, *we chose to fix the target application/protocol used as well as the kind of attacks we are targeting. The application chosen is an Apache web server (Linux/i386), and the kind of attacks we are targeting is remote code injection attacks, exploiting stack or heap overflows, etc*

2   Detecting Attacks in the Network Traffic of a Web Server

One of the first issues in the design of a Neural Network is the type of inputs it will accept, or the features to be used in the representation. Supplying raw network data to the ANN is not a good idea, because of their size, but even more importantly because it is then really hard for the neural network to learn classifying patterns in this kind of data. Finally the ANN input's layer size must be large enough to be able to accept an amount of data that will enable it to judge correctly whether an attack is included in the network packet or not. Having an "aggregator function" that does not essentially loose any important features in our network data for classification purposes (operating on the packets right before they enter the ANN) may both minimize their size and keep their "structure" intact. The aggregator function we used was:

$$f(m) = \frac{\sum_{i=0}^{w} m_i \cdot m_i}{w \cdot 255^2}$$

In the above formula, the parameter m_i refers to the i'th byte of the incoming packet.. The window, 'w', is a system parameter, which specifies the amount of bytes "grouped" together in one number. The denominator normalizes the output in the interval [0,1]. This function's main goal is to minimize the data load passed on to the

ANN. The feature extractor's output for the same data, but different window values keeps on the same levels, although as the window grows, the output graph tends to attenuate

2.1   Training the ANN

A component which listens to any inbound web server traffic, will face the HTTP protocol, and mainly page requests (HTTP GET requests), but some requests may well be file upload requests or other form-handling requests (HTTP POST requests). These are also included in the traffic that can be seen. Using the feature extractor introduced above, we can verify that pure text (ASCII) won't ever cause the ANN to give an output larger that 0.22. This of course means that the task of differentiating between text and binary data is an easy task. The HTTP protocol is a text based protocol, but of course not all binary traffic is malicious. File uploading, (such as the uploading of multimedia material) supported by many sites, may result in the ANN seeing images or other kinds of binary files. So, in order to differentiate between this category and malicious code, we trained an ANN with jpeg image file parts for one class and actual code for the other. The library which we used for taking the code exemplars was libc because it's the one closer to the system that any other, so it's more probable to look like code to be injected in an application.

In the general case of measuring the ability of the neural network to distinguish between the two classes, we found out that the ANN can indeed classify code as such, but it's difficult for it to correctly identify image binary data from potentially harmful code. In our tests, we trained several neural networks, using standard BackPropagation [22]. The input layer sizes selected were 10 and 20. The hidden layer sizes ranged from half the input layer size to its double. The epochs each ANN had gone through were 1000, 5000 and 10000. In total we trained 30 ANNs with 800 exemplars per group. Figure 1 shows the performance graph of all those ANNs. The line marked 't/set-1' refers to the train-set data which should be classified as malicious traffic, while 't/set-0' refers to normal traffic. The line 'class-1' refers to the NN performance on real malicious traffic, which has not been seen by the NN during its training. Accordingly, 'class-0' is normal traffic, which the NN has not seen during its training.

The correct classification of real malicious traffic (class-1) doesn't exceed 80%, for any of the NNs trained. This means that 80% of completely novel attacks are correctly identified as such. We can also see that the percentage of correct classification of real normal traffic (class-0) is always below that of class-1, for all the case where the performance for class-1 is above 50%.

By augmenting a few the training set with more code (t/set-1) and less image data (t/set-0), we got an interesting outcome, for the same NN architectures. The train set had 300 exemplars of (artificial) normal traffic (t/set-0) and 500 ones of code (t/set-1). The results are shown in Figure 2.

What is important to notice in these two graphs, is that although the correct classification percentage for malicious traffic (class-1) has improved substantially, the one for normal traffic remained at the same levels. Nevertheless, although the ANN can correctly classify potentially malicious code as such, it is also often mislead when presented with jpeg images, giving false alarms at an unacceptably high rate.

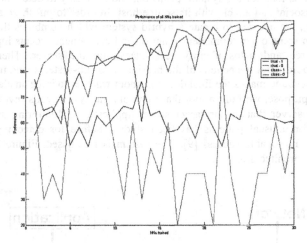

Fig. 1. ANN Performance using 800 exemplars per category

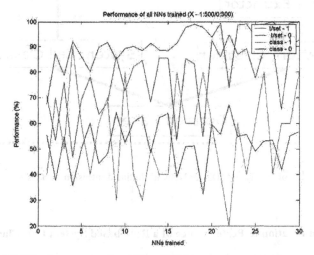

Fig. 2. ANN Performance using 500 and 300 exemplars per category

3 Architecture of a Hybrid Intrusion Detection System

As mentioned above, using the trained ANN alone as an IDS would suffer serious performance problems with normal traffic. Essentially, because of the very high false alarms rates, the system would be useless as any system administrator would quickly decide to ignore all alarms raised by the ANN, including of course the real ones. Nevertheless, the system has a lot of advantages, including its minimal size, which is translated to less load for the system it runs on, and its ability to detect new attacks. It can also associate an attack with its source host. In order to put these advantages into good use, we decided to create a hybrid system which combines this network classifier with some other component. That second component accepts input from a different source and helps identify real attacks on the server. Then, a third component coordinates the actions of the previous two sub-systems, and taking their outputs into account, makes the final decision about whether to issue an alarm or not.

For this purpose, we built a tool that monitors the system calls invoked by the Apache web server that is our target server application. Monitoring system call invocations for unusual patterns has been studied before for detecting intrusion attempts with reasonable success [9]. The system is rule-based. Figure 3 shows a schema of our architecture.

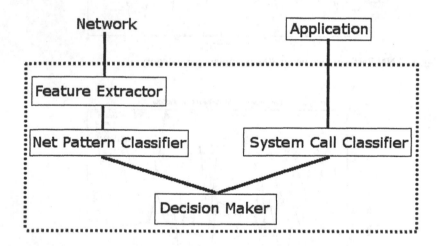

Fig. 3. Architecture of the Hybrid IDS for Network-initiated Intrusion Attacks

3.1   Implementation & Performance of a Rule-based System Call Classifier

In order to successfully create and test a Rule-based system-call classifier, we needed a training set containing some patterns of misbehavior as well as the usual patterns of normal system call invocations under normal circumstances. For this reason, we created a web application as a CGI program in C with two exploitable buffer overflows and installed it on our Apache test server running under Linux. Afterwards, a number of attacks, together with normal requests were created. In total each test set contained 100 requests carrying no attack and no file upload, 100 requests carrying an attack but no file upload, 100 with file upload but no attack, and 100 requests carrying an attack with a file upload

The Decision Maker component works by continuously listening to the output of the network classifier, and when this output exceeds a certain threshold (set empirically to 0.8), the Decision Maker asks the opinion of the System-Call Classifier. If the output of the second component also exceeds a certain threshold, then an alarm is raised. We monitored the Apache system calls under normal conditions (no attacks), and produced a series of "acceptable" system calls stored in a configuration file. In the first version of this Rule-based subsystem, the system call classifier monitors the server and all its children processes for any invocation that is not described in the configuration file. If a call not matching any of the ones in the configuration file is detected the subsystem raises an alarm. The output of this rule-based classifier is always binary in nature (giving always a 0 or a 1). The results for the overall system are shown in table 1. In the first column of the table, NF/NA means „requests containing No File uploads and No Attack", NF/WA means „request containing No File uploads but containing an Attack", „WF/NA" means „request containing File upload, No Attack", and finally „WF/WA" means „request containing File upload, With Attack". The columns heading „Min" and „Max" indicate what was the minimum or maximum number of alarms raised per request in each test-set, and „Total" describes the total number of alarms raised for the whole test-set. Each test-set, as mentioned previously, comprised of 100 requests.

Table 1. Performance of the Hybrid IDS using a Rule-based system call classifier.

Reqsts:	NetClassifier Alarms:			Decision Maker:		
	Total	Min.	Max	Total	Min	Max
NF/NA	0	0	0	0	0	0
NF/WA	73	1	3	65	1	2
WF/NA	98	2	5	0	0	0
WF/WA	97	1	5	58	1	2

As can be seen from the above table, the false alarms rate of the overall system is essentially reduced to zero. The IDS is now capable of detecting approximately 60% of new -never before seen- attacks. Another benefit of this approach is that it is independent of the nature of new attacks. The system administrator only needs to update the rule-based subsystem's configuration file when a new web application or web service is installed on the server, by gathering some data on what constitutes normal system call invocations with the new application, an operation that can be very easily automated.

So, the system performance while being essentially usable, still leaves room for improvement. In the next and final section we describe the directions we are currently taking to improve upon the current system implementation.

4   Future Directions

Because it was noted that often the false alarms raised by the network classifier had a lower than many of the real attacks output level, an easy modification to the Decision Maker is to assume the following strategy: when the network classifier's output is above a certain very high threshold TH, always raise an alarm without even consulting the system call classifier; when the network classifier's output is above a certain threshold TL, but below TH, then consult the system call classifier and combine their results.

Yet another line of research we are actively pursuing is that of detecting „long-lasting" attacks by better monitoring system-calls; in particular, having a larger time window to work with, a rule-based induction system such as ID3 and derivatives, or SLIPPER2 [23] can be used to classify *system call sequences* which should likely give good indications on whether an attack is in progress.

Finally, we are in the process of investigating the effectiveness of alternatives to BackPropagation as the learning-from-errors mechanism such as the GeneRec algorithm, that also happens to have a more plausible biological basis [11], even though it seems to require more computing power.

References

1. W.Lee, S.Stolfo, K.Mok: "A Data Mining Framework for Building Intrusion Detection Models" - Proceedings of the 1999 IEEE Symposium on Security and Privacy (May 1999)
2. H.Debar, M. Becker, D. Siboni: "A Neural Network Component for an Intrusion Detection System" - Proceedings of the 1998 National Information Systems Security Conference (NISSC'98) October 5-8 1998. Arlington, VA.
3. LiMin Fu: "A Neural Network Model for Learning Rule-Based Systems" - Proceedings of the 1992 International Joint Conference on Neural Networks, I-343:I- 348. [R, L].
4. H. Teng, K. Chen, S. Lu: "Adaptive Real-time Anomaly Detection Using Inductively Generated Sequential Patterns" - Proceedings of the IEEE Symposium on Research in Security and Privacy, pages 278-284, Oakland CA, May 1990.
5. T. Lane, C. Brodley: "Approaches to Online Learning and Concept Drift for User Identification in Computer Security" - Proceedings of the Fourth International Conference on Knowledge Discovery and Data Mining, pp. 259-263 (1998).
6. J.Anderson: "Computer Security Threat Monitoring and Surveillance" - Tech. Rep., James P Anderson Co., Fort Washington, PA, Apr. 1980.
7. A. Lazarevic, P. Dokas, L. Ertoz, V. Kumar, J. Srivastava, P. Tan: "Cyber Threat Analysis – A Key Enabling Technology for the Objective Force (A case study in Network Intrusion Detection)" - Proceedings 23rd Army Science Conference, Orlando, FL, December 2002.
8. P. Dokas, L. Ertoz, V. Kumar, A. Lazarevic, J. Srivastava, P. Tan: "Data Mining for Network Intrusion Detection" - Tutorial at the Pacific-Asia Conference on Knowledge Discovery in Databases, Seoul, April 30, 2003.

9. C. Warrender, S. Forrest, B. Pearlmutter: "Detecting Intrusions using System Calls – Alternative Data Models" - IEEE Symposium on Security and Privacy (1998).
10. L. Ertoz, E. Eilertson, A. Lazarevic, P. Tan, P. Dokas, V. Kumar, J. Srivastava: "Detection and Summarization of Novel Network Attacks Using Data Mining" – Minnesota INtrusion Detection System (MINDS) Technical Report, 2003.
11. R. C. O'Reilly, and Y. Munakata: "Computational Explorations in Cognitive Neuroscience: Understanding the Mind by Simulating the Brain", MIT Press, Boston, MA, 2000.
12. T. Lunt: "Real-Time Intrusion Detection" - Technical report, Computer Science Laboratory, SRI international, Menlo Park, CA, February 1992.
13. J. Frank: "Artificial Intelligence and Intrusion Detection – Current and Future Directions" - Technical Report, Division of Comp. Science, University of California at Davis, 1994.
14. J. Ryan, M. Lin, R. Miikkulainen: "Intrusion Detection with Neural Networks" - AI Approaches to Fraud Detection and Risk Management: Papers from the 1997 AAAI Workshop (Providence, Rhode Island), pp. 72-79. Menlo Park, CA: AAAI.
15. M. Mahoney, P. Chan: "Learning Rules for Anomaly Detection of Hostile Network Traffic" - Proceedings of the Third IEEE International Conference on Data Mining, p.601, November 19-22, 2003
16. A. Ghosh, A. Schwartzbard, M. Schatz: "Learning Program Behavior Profiles for Intrusion Detection" - Reliable Software Technologies Corporation, 1999.
17. J. Cannady: "Artificial Neural Networks for Misuse Detection" - National Information Systems Security Conference (1998).
18. L. Ertoz, A. Lazarevic, E. Eilertson, P. Tan, P. Dokas, V. Kumar, J. Srivastava: "Protecting Against Cyber Threats in Networked Information Systems" - SPIE Annual Symposium on AeroSense, Battlespace Digitization and Network Centric Systems III, Orlando, FL (2003)
19. L. Lankewicz, M. Benard: "Real-time Anomaly Detection Using a Nonparametric Pattern Recognition Approach" - Proceedings of the of 7th Computer Security Applications conf., San Antonio, TX, 1991.
20. J. Shavlik, M. Shavlik. "Selection, Combination and Evaluation of Effective Software Sensors for Detecting Abnormal Usage on Computers Running Windows NT/2000" – Shavlik Technologies Apr. 2002.
21. K. Ilgun: "USTAT: A Real-time Intrusion Detection System for UNIX" Proceedings of the IEEE Symposium on Security and Privacy,Oak-land, CA, May 1993.
22. N. Bose, P. Liang: "Neural Network Fundamentals with Graphs, Algorithms, and Applications" – McGraw-Hill, 1996.
23. W. W. Cohen, and Y. Singer, "Simple Fast & Effective Rule Learner", AAAI/IAAI 1999, pp. 335-3

Which Adequate Trust Model for Trust Networks?

Dimitri Melaye[1], Yves Demazeau[1], and Thierry Bouron[2]

[1] IMAG - Laboratoire Leibniz,
46, avenue Felix Viallet, 38031 Grenoble Cedex, France,
dimitri.melaye@imag.fr, yves.demazeau@imag.fr
[2] FTR&D,
38-40 rue du Général Leclerc 92794,
Issy les Moulineaux cedex 9 PARIS, France,
thierry.bouron@francetelecom.com

Abstract. This article deals with the choice of individual trust models adapted to networks. We consider trust as a social and effective multi-agent process. We introduce the notion of trust networks viewed as a set of one-to-one trust relationships, we wonder which trust model should be chosen to build and exploit it. We extract five criteria for comparison of trust models. We then evaluate two trust models and discuss what could be a relevant trust model in a multi-agent setting.

1 Introduction

The expansion of the distributed systems such as electronic trade or services for citizens highlights new problematics where trust plays a crucial role [1] . Trust has been recently identified as an essential notion in the business to business applications where the relationship are supported electronically in an open environment. It is viewed as "the subjective probability by which an agent expects that another agent performs a given action on which its welfare depends" [2].

Following Castelfranchi and Falcone's work [3] and Demazeau's VOWELS methodology [4], a trust process can be based on three of the four vowels of the VOWELS methodology: A (Agent), I (Interaction), E (Environment) and O (Organisation). We distinguish the trust model and the decision-taking. The trust model computes a trust level between two agents, and is function of I and E. The decision-taking is agent-centered (A) and is grounded on the *trust level* and on the *risk* taken by relying (typically, a decision-taking with a high risk requires a high trust level).

The aim of our work is to consider trust as a social process and to pass from individual trust to social networks. Thus, an agent will be able to take into account its social and organizational resources. It necessitates to consider the fourth vowel of [4], the organization (O). For this purpose, we introduce reasoning about the other agents' trust in the previous trust process. Reasoning is based on a *trust network* that can be viewed as a set of trust one-to-one models. To build and exploit the *trust networks*, the choice of the one-to-one trust model is crucial for the implementation of the trust networks. In [5], we have exhibited several characteristics of a trust model, among which the number of the considered relationships (one-to-one, n-to-one and n-to-p). In

Please use the following format when citing this chapter:

Melaye, Dimitri, Demazeau, Yves, Bouron, Thierry, 2006, in IFIP International Federation for Information Processing, Volume 204, Artificial Intelligence Applications and Innovations, eds. Maglogiannis, I., Karpouzis, K., Bramer, M., (Boston: Springer), pp. 236–244.

this paper, we propose a focus on the comparison of one-to-one models for the trust networks. We concentrate on the relation between the trust model, the trust network, and the decision-taking.

First we introduce the notion of trust networks inspired by Sichman's networks [6]. We assume a trust network is built from one-to-one models. We then derive and formalize five criteria for its building and its exploitation: observability, understandability, handlability, social exploitability, and context-scalability. We finally evaluate two trust models regarding these criteria, and discuss what could be a relevant trust model.

1.1 Motivation and principles

A multi-agent system cannot be reduced to the simple sum of its agents: social reasoning and environment have a crucial role in the coordination and the interactions between cognitive agents. Indeed, it is necessary to evaluate the agents' social resources. Thus, trust should be considered as a network of relationships rather than independent one-to-one relationships. But usually, MAS contribution only consider one-to-one trust models.

In order to pass from individual trust to social networks, we have taken an inspiration from Sichman's dependence networks [6], where we have replaced dependence with trust. Each agent can compute the supposed trust relationship between the other agents. The set of these relationships makes up *its trust network*. We assume these trust relationships are. As an agent's trust network is its *subjective* representation of the trust relationships, it generally different of the "objective" trust network that emerges from the effective trust relationships between the agents of the system.

1.2 Formalization

Formally, an agent is characterized by an external description: each agent has structured information about the other agents' trust. These information are private and own.

Definition 1. *The agent's trust network is the set of the trust model considered by it between the other agents. Formally, let N_i be the number of agents considered by an agent i. Let T_i be its trust network. We have $T_i = \{M_{ijk} \mid 1 \leqslant j \leqslant N_i, 1 \leqslant k \leqslant N_i, j \neq k\}$, where M_{ijk} is the trust model considered by the agent i between the agent j and k.*

T_i can be viewed as the oriented graph $G_i(X_i, E_i)$ where X_i is the set of the N_i nodes (agents known by i), and E_i is the set of the edges (relationships between these agents). Each edge e_{ijk} of this graph is valuated by the trust model considered by the agent i between the agent j and the agent k. The update of the trust models and the update of the graph are independent: the latter is updated only at the time of its use.

Such a net synthesizes the supposed trust relationships between the agents. In the framework of a social multi-agent system, the agents do not always interact each other directly. So some intermediary agents are often necessary to satisfy their goals. For instance, concerning the bottom-up coalition formation, even if an agent must consider the trusted agents, it should also consider the agents that trust in itself and that can rely on other agents. Thus, it is not sufficient to take into account trust only at an agent-centered level, and it is necessary to consider the others' trust.

1.3 Which one-to-one trust model do we need?

We have assumed that an agent's trust network can be viewed as a set of one-to-one models of trust connecting every agents. Therefore, technically, which trust model to choose to derive the agent's trust and to take some decisions? In the remainder of this article, we precise the necessary properties of each M_{ijk} trust model. We propose five criteria to compare one-to-one trust models: observability, understandability, handlability, social exploitability, and context-scalability. These criteria are based on three of the four vowels of the VOWELS methodology [4]: A (Agent), I (Interaction), and E (Environment). The I vowel corresponds to the building of the trust network from the trust models. The A vowel corresponds to the social exploitability of the trust models by the agents. The E vowel corresponds to the problem of scalability of our model: it is linked up with the property of context-sensitivity of trust. The fourth vowel, the organization (O), is supported by the trust networks themselves, and is not used actually yet.

Interaction: observability, understandability and handlability As trust is built from interactions and observations [7], the interaction vowel is used for to the building of the trust networks. For this purpose, we distinguish three criteria: observability, understandability and handlability.

Observability In order to build its trust network, an agent should be able to derive the trust relationships that exist between the other agents. On the contrary of Fullam and Barber's evaluation [8], the important thing is not that an agent i is able to determine the target agent k's objective trustworthiness, but that it is able to determine the agent j's trust in k. For this purpose, either the agent must be able to use the observations of the interactions between the agent j and the agent k (direct observation or indirect observation if it does not take part in ones), or the agent must be able to use other agents' opinion. These both sources of trust correspond to the Observer role and to the Evaluator role in Mulller's work [9]. Let us notice the observations should respect the privacy of the interactions: they can be only some "clues".

Proposition 1. *Let A_i the set of the agents knwon by the agent i. Let M_{ijk} be the trust model built by the agent i between the agent j and the agent k. The criterion of observability is fulfilled iff M_{ijk} is equipped with a function $observability_{ijk}$:*

$$observability_{ijk} : \{O_{njk}\}_{n,j,k \in A_i} \times \{E_{njk}\}_{n,j,k \in A_i} \rightarrow T$$

where

- *T is the set of the final trust levels.*

- $\{O_{njk}\}_{n,j,k \in A_i}$ is the set of the observations reported by the agents n about the relationship between j and k. When $n = j$, it corresponds to a direct observation. When $n \neq i$, it corresponds to an indirect observation.
- $\{E_{njk}\}_{n,j,k \in A_i}$ is the set of the final trust values between j and k according to n. In other words, it is n's evaluation about agent j's trust in the agent k. If $n = j$, the agent n corresponds to a trust third party.

Understandability and handlability The model should not be reduced to a final trust level obtained by an obscure mechanism. Since trust consists in *beliefs* [3], trust should be broken up into beliefs corresponding to the different components of trust (e.g. personal, reputation, generalization or competence dimension). The aim of this breaking up is to be able to have different computable components to reason about them at the network level. Indeed, these components correspond to orthogonal networks: for instance, let us consider the framework of online auctions of specialized objects. Non-specialized occasional buyer's trust is based on the generalization and/or reputation dimension. What is more, these agents trust in specialists' opinions easily. However, it is not the case of the specialized agents: they belong to the same dense network of specialists, and do not trust in other specialists blindly. In fact, their trust is supported by the personal dimension. Thus, according to the agents, the basis of trust is not the same and is supported by different dimensions. Moreover, if a non-specialized agent specializes, trust between it and the other specialized agents switches from generalized trust to personal trust.

Proposition 2. *Let be B_i the set of the possible states of agent i's beliefs. The criterion of understandability is fulfilled iff the function $observability_{ijk}$ is the composition of two function g_{ijk} and $understand_{ijk} : \{O_{njk}\}_{n,j,k \in A_i} \times \{E_{njk}\}_{n,j,k \in A_i} \rightarrow B_i$ such that:*

$$observability_{ijk} = g_{ijk} \circ understand_{ijk}$$

Proposition 3. *Let be B_i the set of the possible states of agent i's beliefs. The criterion of handlability is fulfilled iff the function $observability_{ijk}$ is the composition of two function $handle_{ijk} : B_i \rightarrow T$ and h_{ijk} such that:*

$$observability_{ijk} = handle_{ijk} \circ h_{ijk}$$

We can notice the criteria of understandability and handlability are satisfied both iff $observability_{ijk}$ is the composition of $understand_{ijk}$ and $handle_{ijk}$.

Agent: social exploitability The final aim of a trust network is to take a decision by taking into account the other agents, and not only one. This trust decision, called "reliance", should end in a social action [6] based on several other agents.

Proposition 4. *Let T_i^n be the set of the trust levels of the n agents known by the agent i and A_i be the set of the agent i's possible actions. The criterion of social exploitability is fulfilled iff it exists the function $social\_exploitability_i$ such that:*

$$social\_exploitability_i : T_i^n \rightarrow A_i \text{ with } |n > 1|.$$

Environment: context-scalability Trust is a contextual notion. It refers to a given context. Thus, in a naïve approach, an agent should have one trust network per context. However, it can lead to a too heavy system, since the potential number of models used by an agent's trust network increases quadratically with the number of the considered agents. The contexts should be handled in a way not to have one model per context. In this purpose, we should have a mechanism to derive a model for a given context from a model for another context . It permits to reduce the number of model and to define their interdependences.

Proposition 5. *Let $\mathcal{W}$ be the set of the possible contexts, and M_{ijk}^{ω} be the trust model of the agent i concerning j's trust in k for a context $\omega \in \mathcal{W}$. The criterion of context-scalability is fulfilled iff it exists the function $context\_scalability_i$ permitting to pass from some known n contexts to another context:*

$$context\_scalability_i : \mathcal{M}_i^n \rightarrow \mathcal{M}_i$$
$$context\_scalability_i(M_{ijk}^{\omega_1}, M_{ijk}^{\omega_2}, ..., M_{ijk}^{\omega_n}) = M_{ijk}^{\omega_{n+1}}$$

We have described the five criteria permitting to evaluate one-to-one trust models adapted to social networks. They must account for their relevance in an effective multi-agent context. In the remainder of this article, we put them into practice by examining and discussing three trust models.

2 Model examination

We have chosen two trust models for evaluation: Sabater and Sierra's ReGreT system [10], and Castelfranchi and Falcone's model [3]. They permit an agent to determine trust in another agent, so that they are good candidates for the building of a trust network. According to our social view of trust, we have deliberately avoided the game theory-oriented systems to concentrate on more socio-cognitive and reputation trust models. The choice has been fixed on a set of models that are representative of different views of trust and that are completed enough to be evaluated and implemented actually. Due to lack of space, we evaluate only two models and we do not detail them to concentrate on the relevant points for our evaluation. In the following sections, we evaluate these models according to the previous criteria. We summarize te result of each evaluation in a table.

2.1 The model by Sabater and Sierra [10]

The ReGreT system may be one of the most complete systems. The model is based on three dimensions of trust that are integrated numerically by weighting to obtain a reputation measure: the individual dimension, the social dimension (witness, neighbourhood, and system reputation) and the ontological dimension. The individual dimension deals with direct interactions. The social dimension uses other agents' information. The ontological dimension supports the context notion.

Observability. Although nothing is evoked about the exterior observability of the interactions, the function $observability_{ijk}$ is implementable (observations and evaluations). However, the strong restriction is that the agents can exchange information only coming from their own direct observations or interactions: formally, the sets $\{O_{njk}\}_{n,j,k \in \mathcal{A}_i}$ and $\{E_{njk}\}_{n,j,k \in \mathcal{A}_i}$ are defined with the restriction $n = j$.

Understandability and handlability. With this model, the function $observability_{ijk}$ is decomposable: $understand_{ijk}$ breaks up trust into three dimensions (individual, social, ontological) and $handle_{ijk}$ is implemented by a simple numerical combination of the values of these dimensions.

Social exploitability. The model is exploited with a negotiation model in a one-to-one framework: the decision-taking is based on a function $rely$ that takes into account only one agent ($social\_exploitability_i : T_i^1 \to A_i$)

Context-scalability. With its ontological dimension, this model proposes a naïve implementation of the function $context\_scalability_i$: the reputation in a given context is obtained by the numerical combination of the reputation of the less general context, according to a ontological structure.

Table 1. Summary of the examination of Sabater and Sierra's model [10].

	Observ.	Underst.	Handl.	Social expl.	Context-scal.
Evaluation	+	++	+	-	+

The examination is summarized in the table 2. This model is relevant for three criteria: understandability, handlability, and context-scalability. It is interesting for the observability criterion too.

2.2 The model by Castelfranchi and Falcone [3]

This model contrasts with the previous models, because it assumes the agents can be irrational, that is to say they had not to maximize their utility. Moreover, on the contrary of the previous models based on quantitative approaches, this cognitive model is based on the BDI approach, and highlights the importance of the intention in the trust process.

Observability. In this model, the observability is not evoked.

Understandability and handlability. Based on a cognitive structure of trust, [3] implementes this model with cognitive fuzzy map. Indeed, the function $understand_{ijk}$ is implemented: the model computes a set of belief values (ability, willingness, dependence) derived from the sources of trust. The function $handle_{ijk}$ is implemented too by computing a trust level from these beliefs.

Social exploitability. The decision-taking is based on a function $social\_exploitability_i$ that takes into account only one one agent ($social\_exploitability_i : T_i^1 \to A_i$)

Context-scalability. The problem is not asked.

The examination is summarized in the table 3. This model is relevant for two criteria: understandability and handlability.

Table 2. Summary of the examination of Castelfranchi and Falcone's model [3].

	Observ.	Underst.	Handl.	Social expl.	Context-scal.
Evaluation	-	++	++	-	-

3 Discussion

As we have seen in the previous section, the recent research in trust for MAS lead to many interesting and different models. The common characteristic of the examined models is their decentralized approach. It seems it is established that the centralized systems of trust are not relevant in a multi-agent context: the experience showed these systems such as the Ebay system where the opinions are centralized are perfectible. According to our criteria, the results of our examination are quite disappointing. No model is really adapted to pass from individual trust to social networks. In fact, all these trust models are not thought out as a multi-agent mechanism. They correspond to an agent-centered mechanism above all, even if some multi-agent aspects (like reputation) are plugged.

3.1 About the measures

Observability. The models do not fulfil the criteria of observability. It is not surprising since their purpose is only to provide an agent with a way to determine the true trustworthiness of other agents (on the contrary of our need: a model that can determine the subjective agent's trust in a target agent). It is a drawback, because observability is necessary to build the trust networks. Sabater and Sierra proposes a similar mechanism to communicate the evaluations. But they are limited to the agents' own experiences too: it is a drawback for our trust networks, because it limits the sources of trust (it would be as if there would be no reputation mechanism in an agent-centered approach).

Understandability and handlability. These both criteria are fulfilled by the ReGreT system[10] and Castelfranchi and Falcone's model [3]. However, there is a difference in their implementation: the computed beliefs in Sabater and Sierra's model correspond to the sources of trust in Falcone and Castelfranchi's. Indeed, the computed beliefs in [3] correspond to a more abstract concept. We show the main difference between these both models: Falcone and Castelfranchi's model is based on a cognitive approach, whereas Sabater and Sierra is not. In the next section, we will precise our interest for such a model.

Social exploitability. The criteria is the less fulfilled one. The models exploit trust only for one target agent. One more time, they are not thought out as a multi-agent mechanism.

Context-scalability. Only Sabater and Sierra's model proposes a relevant mechanism for the management of the context. Generally, the context aspects are not studied in the one-to-one trust model, since they do not correspond to a need of scalability: the scalability is easier in an agent-centered framework.

3.2 Choosing individual trust model for networks

According to our examination, there is no trust model which we can use as it is for our purpose. However, we can extract two avenues of research in order to have a model fulfilled the criteria.

First the model should be based on a symbolic approach. Indeed, these latter are more relevant for our trust networks, since they support reasoning and explicit handling of trust components. Thus, they are more adapted to the fulfilment of the criteria of understandability and context-scalability. Liau's model [11] have proposed a trust model based on modal logic that formalizes the internal components of trust. Although this model does not include social aspects and does not seem have been implemented, the modal logic approach is an interesting avenue to fulfil the criteria of understandability and context-scalability.

Secondly we are interested in a Castelfranchi-inspired model [3]. The breaking up of trust and the social approach of this model is adapted to our real multi-agent view. We think the fulfilment of the observability and social exploitability criteria necessitates such an approach, since the "others" are taken into account. The main critic about this socio-cognitive model deals with the problem of the rationality of the agents [12]: Castelfranchi's model would be motivated from humans and would not adapted to a rational approach. Although this critic is pertinent in a pure artificial system, it is not relevant in a multi-agent system that could include the user. Now, as we evoked in introduction, we are interested in such systems and we need a model that is generic enough to support the potential irrationality of the user.

4 Conclusion

This article has presented a study of trust models for *trust networks*. By regarding trust as a social and effective multi-agent process, we have introduced the notion of trust networks. An agent's trust network is its subjective representation of the trust relationships between the agents of the system. It can be considered as a set of one-to-one trust relationships, so we have wondered which trust model to choose. We have derived from the notion of trust networks five criteria for comparison of trust models: observability, understandability and handlability, social exploitability, and context-scalability. We have then evaluated three trust models regarding these criteria.

The results of our examination show that no model is really adapted to our need. However, we think a more symbolic approach like modal logic is relevant. Thus, in the future, our work will deal with the building of a trust model inspired by Castelfranchi and Falcone's work and formalized by such a tool. It will address as much as possible the criteria that are not fulfilled.

Acknowledgements We thank France Telecom R&D for supporting the research reported in this paper (CRE 46128855 France Telecom - CNRS).

References

1. Urban, G.: Building an internet trust generator: Adaptive experimentation on the internet to improve site trust and sales. Technical report, MIT (2003)

2. Gambetta, D.: Can we trust trust? In Gambetta, D., ed.: Trust: Making and Breaking Cooperative Relations. Department of Sociology, University of Oxford (2000) 213–237

3. Castelfranchi, C., Falcone, R., Pezzulo, G.: Trust in information sources as a source for trust: a fuzzy approach. In: Proceedings of AAMAS'03, ACM Press (2003) 89–96

4. Demazeau, Y.: Steps towards multi-agent oriented programming. In: IWMAS'97. (1997)

5. Melaye, D., Demazeau, Y.: Modles et rseaux de confiance, analyse bibliographique. Cahiers du Leibniz 142 (2005)

6. Sichman, J., Conte, R., Castelfranchi, C., Demazeau, Y.: A social reasoning mechanism based on dependence networks. In Cohn, A.G., ed.: Proceedings of ECAI'94, Chichester, John Wiley & Sons (1994) 188–192

7. Jonker, C.M., Treur, J.: Formal analysis of models for the dynamics of trust based on experiences. In Garijo, F.J., Boman, M., eds.: Proceedings of MAAMAW'99. Volume 1647., Berlin, Springer-Verlag: Heidelberg, Germany (1999) 221–231

8. Fullam, K.K., Barber, K.S.: Evaluating approaches for trust and reputation research: Exploring a competition testbed. In: Proceedings of The Workshop on Reputation in Agent Societies at Intelligent Agent Technology, Beijing (2004)

9. Muller, G., Vercouter, L., Boissier, O.: Towards a general definition of trust and its application to openness in mas. In: Sixth International Workshop on Trust, Privacy, Deception, and Fraud in Agent Societies, Melbourne (2003)

10. Sabater, J., Sierra, C.: Social regret, a reputation model based on social relations. SIGecom Exch. 3 (2002) 44–56

11. Liau, C.: Belief, information acquisition, and trust in multi-agent systems- a modal logic formulation. Artificial Intelligence 149 (2003) 31–60

12. Ramchurn, S.D., Huynh, D., Jennings, N.R.: Trust in multi-agent systems. The Knowledge Engineering Review 19 (2004)

XML Systems for Intelligent Management of Pervasive Computing Resources

Dimitris Alexopoulos[1], George Kormentzas[2] and John Soldatos[3]

1 National Technical University of Athens, School of Electrical &
Computer Engineering., 9 Heroon Polytechneiou Str., GR-15773 Zografou,
Greece, dalexo@telecom.ntua.gr
WWW home page: http://www.telecom.ntua.gr
2 University of the Aegean, Dept. of Information & Communication
Systems Engineering, Karlovasi, Samos, 83200, Greece, gkorm@aegean.gr
WWW home page: http://www.samos. aegean.gr
3 Athens Information Technology, 19,5 km Markopoulou Peania, Ave.,
jsol@ait.edu.gr
WWW home page: http://www.ait.edu.gr

Abstract. XML technologies have been recently extensively used in IP based
network management, where they have been proven capable of alleviating the
SNMP shortcomings in configuration management. Our XMLNET system
described in [1] has demonstrated that XML systems can greatly facilitate the
development of network management applications even in complex
heterogeneous multi-vendor networks. In this paper, we present extensions to
the XMLNET architecture, with a view to managing not only network devices,
but also middleware and hardware resources used in the scope of ubiquitous
computing. Ubiquitous computing services are supported by a highly
distributed and heterogeneous infrastructures comprising a wide range of
sensors (e.g., cameras, microphones, motion sensors, temperature sensor), a
well as middleware components (e.g., recognition algorithms, perceptual
components). The introduced extensions to XMLNET for ubiquitous
computing environments, aim at lever-aging the merits of XMLNET for the
inherently complex configuration management operations entailed in
pervasive and ubiquitous computing applications.

1 Introduction

Recently, we have witnessed the development of a number of network management
solutions (see for example [1-8]), based on the Extensible Markup Language (XML).
XML is a standardized meta-markup language by W3C, which features several
benefits that can facilitate management tasks. In particular:

Please use the following format when citing this chapter:

Alexopoulos, Dimitris, Kormentzas, George, Soldatos, John, 2006, in IFIP International Federation
for Information Processing, Volume 204, Artificial Intelligence Applications and Innovations, eds.
Maglogiannis, I., Karpouzis, K., Bramer, M., (Boston: Springer), pp. 245–253

- XML is easy to generate, parse and process, which provides flexibility in handing XML representations of management information.
- XML supports sophisticated data structuring, and can therefore handle complex organizations of management information.
- XML DTD (Document Type Definitions) and XML Schemas specify and validate the structure of XML documents, thus alleviating developers from tedious tasks.
- XML comes with numerous W3C technologies (http://www.w3c.org) supporting rapid development of XML based network management applications. Characteristic examples are the Extensible Stylesheet Transformations (XSLT), which transform XML documents to other XML formats and XPath/XQuery discovering XML elements subject to criteria.
- XML operations can be transformed to SOAP operations allowing management functions to be exported as web services. This allows for loose integration of heterogeneous distributed management systems based on the Web Services paradigm. Similarly, integration can be supported with other types of systems (e.g., Operations Sup-port Systems (OSS)).
- XML has high-level semantics, and is therefore appropriate for performing bulk configuration operations.

In the area of IP based network management XML based solutions have been adopted to alleviate the limitations of the Simple Network Management Protocol (SNMP) [9]. This is manifested in research (e.g., [1-8], [10]), standards (e.g., [11]), as well as industrial initiatives (e.g., [12-14]). Configuration management of composite heterogeneous networks is one particular area where XML management technologies add value to conventional network management approaches. This is mainly due to the high-level semantics of XML, and the wide range of technologies and tools that can easily and flexibly process XML documents. The XML high level semantics can be used to express complex high level configuration commands that impact the status of multiple heterogeneous devices. Note that the power of XML based configuration mechanisms can be exploited not only in the area of network management, but possibly in other fields dealing with heterogeneous systems. The latter are likely to rely on complex configuration processes for their operation.

In this paper, we argue that XML based configuration mechanisms are applicable to configuration management processes entailed in the scope of pervasive and ubiquitous computing (Ubicomp) systems and services. Ubicomp systems exploit the full range of sensors, devices and networks available to transparently provide services, regard-less of time and user's location [15]. Ubicomp services are essentially context-aware services that acquire and process information about their surrounding environment. Ubicomp infrastructures typically include [16]:

- A transparent sensing infrastructure, which is as non-intrusive as possible.
- Middleware for controlling sensors and actuating devices.
- Collection of perceptual components gaining elementary context cues from the various sensor streams.
- Information fusion components combining elementary context cues towards deriving more sophisticated context.

It is therefore evident that Ubicomp infrastructures comprise numerous hardware, software and middleware components, which make them extremely diverse and heterogeneous. Configuring a Ubicomp infrastructure entails therefore several operations on a variety of components and devices. Given the complexity of the associated management operations, we suggest the use of XML based management mechanisms to-wards flexibly configuring the wide range of components comprising a ubiquitous computing environment. In this paper we extend our XMLNET architecture for net-work management [1], to account for ubiquitous computing devices and components. XMLNET extensions are required towards dealing with an augmenting set of devices comprising not only network elements, but also sensors, actuating devices, middle-ware components and services. Moreover, XMLNET has to be augmented to handle not only network related information (e.g., Element level Management Information Bases (MIB)), but also information relating to sensors, actuators and middleware elements such as perceptual components. The paper describes these extensions and outlines applications that manifest the benefits of the XML based approach.

The rest of this paper is structured as follows: Section 2 provides a brief yet comprehensive description of the XMLNET architecture, to allow readers understand its key functionalities. Section 3 discusses extensions to XMLNET towards managing resource and services within an heterogeneous pervasive computing environment. Section 4 describes potential applications of the proposed XML based architecture for managing pervasive computing resource. Finally, Section 5 concludes the paper.

2   Overview of the XMLNET architecture

The XMLNET architecture [1] provides the means for structuring complex management operations (at the Element Management Layer (EML) and at the Network Management Layer (NML)) as XML documents. EML composite operations consist of several atomic management operations each one affecting or querying a single MIB object. NML composite operations are structured as a set of composite EML operations. Authoring specifications (XML schemas) guide the development of XML documents, according to a composition language. This composition language reflects the core programmability of the system, since it makes provisions for aggregating primitive SNMP (get / set operations) into higher level operations. Moreover, the composition language supports additional features such as allowing for repeatedly executing operations (i.e. looping), processing information elements and enforcing actions when particular conditions are met. Based on the XML schemas specifying this composition language, network managers define composite management operations as XML based APIs at both the EML and the NML levels. XML management applications are authored through assembling API operations and defining parameter values. Note that the composition language is a key element of the architecture, since it specifies how atomic operations are combined into composite ones, as well as how composite ELM operations are combined to composite NML operations. The composition language realizes the programmability of the architecture, since it transforms XML documents to simple network management programs that can be parsed and executed by the run-time environment. The XML schemas defining the structure of application and API documents reflect the constructs and capabilities of the composition language.

The architecture specifies also a runtime environment that parses and executes XML based applications. This environment renders application development a matter of XML authoring. This approach results in cost effective application development, while increasing authoring flexibility and boosting the programmability of management operations. Also, a potential standardization of APIs can allow third parties (e.g., vendors, NMS providers) to produce network management applications. Based on this architecture we have implemented a network management system enabling authoring and execution of XML management documents comprising EML and NML management applications. This system [17] makes use of a rich set of XML technologies and XML based programming techniques.

As far as the presentation and visualization of the network management applications is concerned, a rendering subsystem presents XML results to a console. This subsystem fulfills visualization requirements relating to the application and/or user preferences. XML technologies (e.g., XSL) can be exploited towards developing presentation mechanisms. XSL can be used to filter XML documents returned by XML applications. Thus, XSL presentation templates are required, along with (EML or NML) XML application documents. XSL templates can be stored in a repository and retrieved based on application requirements. Overall, the major benefit of this architecture is that application development becomes a matter of XML authoring, which is more cost effective than conventional SNMP programming or scripts (e.g., in Perl, Tcl) authoring [18]. Moreover, the XML APIs constitute XML protocols allowing execution of NML and EML operations. These protocols expose an interface to potential management applications. A standardization of this interface can make network management operations open and programmable. Openness hinges on that third party vendors and/or network managers can use the APIs to develop applications. Programmability allows different network management applications to be authored through writing and assembling XML documents. Note that the XML based interfaces (i.e. APIs) to the XMLNET system are accessible in a distributed fashion through conventional distributed programming mechanisms (e.g., XML-RPC, RMI (Remote Method Invocation), Simple Object Access Protocol).

3 XMLNET for Intelligent Management of Ubicomp Resources

Following paragraphs list the extensions required to exploit the XMLNET architecture for managing pervasive & ubiquitous computing resources. Moreover, they describe the required modifications to existing XMLNET sub-systems.

Adapters

XMLNET relies on the low element level network management protocols with a view to interfacing to network elements. Pervasive computing environments comprise however a much richer collection of sensors, actuators, devices, as well as middleware components (e.g., perceptual components). Towards conveying management commands to these components, implementation of device specific adapters is required. These adapters transform commands expressed in XML protocols (e.g., SOAP, XML-RPC) to the devices based on protocols that can access the proprietary low-level capabilities of each device. In the case of Firewire cameras for example, an adapter constitutes a bridge from XML to IEEE1394 commands. Similarly, a perceptual component (e.g., tracker) maps XML commands to the proprietary API provided by the component developer. Figure 1, depicts an enhanced version of the XMLNET architecture, including the additional element level adapters and parsing engines.

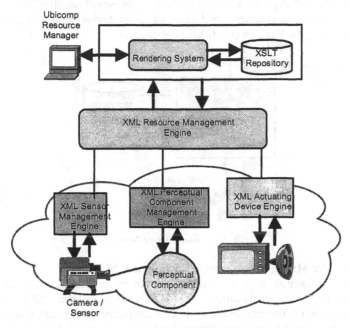

Fig. 1. Overview of the XMLNET architecture for managing Ubicomp Resources

XML Information Bases

XMLNET leverages XML representations of network management information. Towards targeting a wider pervasive computing, there is a need to represent in an XML format. Formatting information about pervasive computing devices and components as XML documents has the distinct advantage of facilitating access to this information from the wide range of heterogeneous components of a ubiquitous computing environment. These components are likely to run on different platforms and/or to be written in a variety of different languages. Thus, a neutral format (such as XML) eases information fusion and exchange in a pervasive environment. Moreover, it can ease the portability of components across different pervasive environments (e.g., different smart spaces). Indeed, installing a middleware component for pervasive computing in a different operational environment demands a clear specification of input, output and configuration parameters.

Element Level Managers

XMLNET incorporates special ELM parsers that process XML commands targeting network elements. In a pervasive computing environment, additional parsers need to be implemented for all sensors, devices and other components comprising a pervasive computing environment. These parsers along with the corresponding adapters can be classified as Element Level Managers including:

- An XML based interface for accessing the element, device or component.
- An interface to the XML representation of the information pertaining to the element.
- The adapter enabling access to the low-level capabilities of the element.

Figure 2 depicts an Element Level Manager for an engine pertaining to a sensor (specifically a digital Firewire (i.e. IEEE.1394 camera).

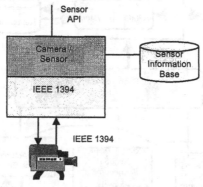

Fig. 2. XML based Sensor Manager

XML Resource Managers - Pervasive Environment Managers

The core intelligence of the XMLNET enhanced architecture for pervasive computing resources management lies in the higher level XML resource management engine, depicted in Figure 1. This component parses higher-level XML document comprising a variety of element-level operations pertaining however to the whole range of elements available in a pervasive environment. Towards combining these element-level XML operations a composition language is required, driving the combination of element-level operations towards intelligent added-value operation. Note that the scope of such a composition language is unlimited; however the XML based composition language of XMLNET [1] can serve as a starting point. This language supports:

- Serial combination of element-level operations, which is particularly useful for composing complex configuration operations impacting several elements and components.
- Automatic extraction of derivatives on quantities relating to the operation of the components (e.g., actual frame-rates for a camera, recognition accuracy for recognition/identification algorithms etc.).
- Event triggering upon occurrence of specific conditions (e.g., when some threshold is exceeded).

- Looping, allowing for repeatedly executing the same operation or batch of operations.

Note however that the composition language of the pervasive environment manager can be significantly extended to include information about component combinations such as combination of perceptive components according to particular situation models [19]. In such a case, a situation modeling component can dynamically define the perceptual components that support it and reflect this combination in a certain composition construct.

4 Prototype Applications

Having a number of element level interfaces at hand, along with a composition language to combine them, we may build a large number of innovative applications, utilities and services. Characteristic examples include:
- A Smart Space Resource Manager (SSRM), as a utility enabling monitoring and control of perceptual components, sensors and actuating services available in a smart space (e.g., smart room). Administrators of a smart space may use the SSRM utility to manage a variety of heterogeneous distributed entities from a single entry point. Such a resource manager has been already built [20], [21], based however only on element level operations. The combination of element level operations ac-cording to the XMLNET composition language can allow for the automation of more complex operations in the scope of a smart space. Such complex operation may for example include the automatic configuration of all sensors and perceptual components of a smart space for a particular application.
- Service development and deployment utilities, that automatically start, configure the components entailed within a service, while also auditing their interrelation-ships and interoperation. For example, a utility may audit the integrity of a situation modeling component (e.g., a situation recognition engine) by setting appropriate thresholds relating to the operation of all the components supporting the situation model. Accordingly, the administrator of the pervasive environment or service will get notifications on the appropriate operation of the situation model as a whole.

5 Conclusions

Configuring Ubicomp services is a particularly tedious task, given the numerous hardware, software and middleware components comprising a Ubicomp service. XML based protocols feature high-level semantics and come with a large number of ready-to-use tools for parsing and processing meta-data. Therefore, XML base architectures are appropriate to automating configuration management tasks in the scope of large scale, diverse and heterogeneous pervasive computing environments. The XMLNET system (originally designed for network management) provides a conceptual architecture that can be applied in ubiquitous computing management. This architecture needs however to be augmented with:

- Interfaces to the low-level capabilities of the whole range of elements and devices entailed in ubiquitous computing. While XMLNET relies on SNMP based interfaces to network elements, the augmented system should also offer interfaces to sensors, actuators and middleware components.
- Element level XML Parsers, processing high-level management commands and translating them into element level operations on sensors, devices and perceptual components.
- A Pervasive Resource Manager, combining element level operations into higher level added value operations for the pervasive environment at hand. Key to this combination is a composition language specifying how to compose added value operation based on the API interfaces provided by the element level components.

The augmented architecture can serve as a basis for a number of useful tools and applications, facilitating management of pervasive computing infrastructures, as well as development, deployment and integration of ubiquitous computing services.

Acknowledgment

The work reported in this paper is supported in part by 'Pythagoras II – Research Group Support of the University of the Aegean'.

References

1. Dimitris Alexopoulos and John Soldatos, 'XMLNET: A Cost Effective Network Management Architecture based on XML technologies', Journal of Systems and Network Management (Kluwer), Vol. 13, No. 4, December 2005.
2. Jeong-Hyuk Yoon, Hong-Taek Ju and James W. Hong, 'Development of SNMP-XML Translator and Gateway for XML-based Integrated Network Management', in the International Journal of Network Management (IJNM), Vol. 13, No. 4, July-August 2003, pp. 259-276.
4. J. Schönwälder, A. Pras and J.P. Martin-Flatin: 'On the Future of Internet Management Technologies', in IEEE Communications Magazine, Vol. 41, No. 10, October 2003.
5. George Pavlou, Paris Flegkas, Stelios Gouveris, and Antonio Liotta, 'On Management Technologies and the Potential of Web Services', IEEE Communications Magazine, special issue 'XML based Management of Networks and Services', vol.42, No.7, July 2004.
6. Vladimir Tosic, Wei Ma, Bernard Pagurek, Babak Esfandiari, 'Web Service Offerings Infrastructure (WSOI) - A Management Infrastructure for XML Web Services', in the Proc. of the NOMS 2004 conference.
7. Raouf Boutaba, Wojciech Golab, and Youssef Iraqi, 'Lightpaths on Demand: A Web-Services-Based Management System', IEEE Communications Magazine, special issue 'XML based Management of Networks and Services', vol.42, No.7, July 2004.
8. O'Connell, P.; McCrindle, R.., "Using SOAP to clean up configuration management", Computer Software and Applications Conference, 2001. pp. 555–560.
9. W. Stallings, "SNMP, SNMPv2, SNMPv3, and RMON 1 and 2" Third edition, Addison-Wesley, Reading, MA, USA, 1999.
10. Network Management Research Group, http://www.ibr.cs.tu-bs.de/projects/nmrg/
11. IETF Network Configuration Working group, http://www.ietf.org/html.charters/netconf-charter.html

12. 'XML based Network Management', Juniper Networks White Paper, http://www.juniper.net/solutions/literature/white_papers/
13 Cisco CNS family of Products, http://www.cisco.com/en/US/products/sw/netmgtsw/index.html
14. NextHop, GATED software, http://www.nexthop.com/products/gated.shtml
15. Weiser M., The Computer for the 21st Century. Scientific American, vol. 265, no. 3, 1991, pp. 66–75.
16. Soldatos J., Pandis I., Stamatis K., Polymenakos L., Crowley J., 'A Middleware Infrastructure for Autonomous Context-Aware Computing Services', accepted for publication to the Computer Communications Magazine, special Issue on Emerging Middleware for Next Generation Networks (2005).
17. The XMLNET network management system, http://www.telecom.ntua.gr/xmlnet (2005).
18. John Soldatos and Dimitris Alexopoulos, 'Cost effective IP networks Management based on XML Authoring', in the Proc. of the Terena Network Conference, TNC 2004, Rhodes, Greece, June, 7-10, 2004.
19. Soldatos, J., Polymenakos, L., Pnevmatikakis, A., Talantzis, F., Stamatis, K., Carras, M.: Perceptual Interfaces and Distributed Agents supporting Ubiquitous Computing Services. In: The Proc. of the Eurescom Summit 2005 (2005) 43–50.
20. Pandis I., Soldatos J., Paar A., Reuter J., Carras M., Polymenakos L., 'An Ontology-based Framework for Dynamic Resource Management in Ubiquitous Computing Environments', in the Proc. of the 2nd International Conference on Embedded Software and Systems, Northwestern Polytechnical University of Xian, P.R.China, December 16-18. (2005).
21. John Soldatos, Kostas Stamatis, Siamak Azodolmolky, Ippokratis Pandis and Lazaros Polymenakos 'Semantic Web Technologies for Ubiquitous Computing Resource Management in Smart Spaces', submitted for publication in the International Journal of Web Engineering and Technology (IJWET).

A constraint based approach for aiding heat treatment operation design and distortion evaluation

M. Aldanondo[1], E. Vareilles[1], K. Hadj-Hamou [2] and Paul Gaborit [1]

1 Centre de Génie Industriel - Ecole des Mines d'Albi-Carmaux
Campus Jarlard - 81013 Albi CT Cedex 09 - France
{aldanondo , vareilles, gaborit}@enstimac.fr
2 GILCO - ENSGI – INP Grenoble - France
hamou@gilco.inpg.fr

Abstract. This paper presents an interactive constraint based system that simultaneously assist design and evaluation. This work is driven by an industrial case dealing with heat treatment operation. The first part presents the problem and provide ideas of the solution. Then the knowledge model mixing discrete and numerical constraints is presented. The third section provides filtering elements in order to permit interactive assistance. The last one discusses the designed system. The originality of the proposition lies in the gathering of classical discrete constraints filtering techniques with numerical constraint 2B consistence filtering mechanisms that were necessary to respond to the industrial need.

1 Introduction

The goal of this communication is to present an interactive constraint based system that simultaneously allows interactive design of a heat treatment operation and qualitative distortion evaluation. This problem originates from a European project called VHT for "Virtual Heat Treatment" (project No G1RD-CT-2002-00835).

A heat treatment operation consists in raising the temperature of a steel part until a certain temperature, keeping at this temperature for a while, then cooling down rapidly. The expected effect is an improvement of the mechanical properties of the part. But, simultaneously, a negative effect corresponding with part distortions occurs most of the time.

A heat treatment operation can be defined according to :
- the material of the part, characterized by parameters relevant to the chemical composition and the mechanical/thermal/structural behaviours,

Please use the following format when citing this chapter:

Aldanondo, Michel, Vareilles, Elise, Hadj-Hamou, Khaled, Gaborit, Paul, 2006, in IFIP International Federation for Information Processing, Volume 204, Artificial Intelligence Applications and Innovations, eds. Maglogiannis, I., Karpouzis, K., Bramer, M., (Boston: Springer), pp. 254–261

- the geometry of the part, characterized by parameters relevant to the shape, massivity, symmetry of the part, hole existence...,
- the heat treatment conditions, characterized by parameters describing the heating device, the cooling system, the parts layout during heating and quenching and various tuning (duration, temperature, flow-rate...).

Classical heat treatment knowledge gathers relations between previous parameters permiting the definition of a heat treatment operation which improves the mechanical properties of the part. In order to estimate distortion, some specific knowledge can be added in order to give some kind of a qualitative score.

The goal of this paper is to show that these two kinds of knowledge can be formalized as a constraint satisfaction problem (CSP) and permit to provide an interactive assistance tool for defining heat treatment operations and evaluating relevant distortion. The rest of the paper is organized as follows.

The second section presents the knowledge model gathering a design part and an evaluation part. It will be shown that three kinds of constraints are necessary: discrete constraints, numerical constraints and mixed constraints. As we target an interactive assistance, the filtering elements for each kind of constraints will be described in section three. Then some interests and limits of the system will be discussed in the last section.

2   The knowledge model

The goal of this section is to present an overview of the knowledge model. This section is divided in two parts. The first one describes the model piece relevant to design while the second deals with the evaluation part. The last one shows how the two model pieces fit together.

For each sub section, the model is described as a constraint satisfaction problem (CSP) [1] and outlines the kind of variables and the kind of constraints that are necessary. Various models were designed with heat treatment experts, coming both from academia and industry, through a dozen of meetings planed during the past18 months [2]. The most advance one concerns parts that belong to a part family "axis" (one dimension much longer than the two others) and is considered in this paper.

2.1   Piece of model relevant to heat treatment design

Around 50 parameters have been identified by the experts. Each parameter is associated with a design variable {vp} upon which the user can input a domain restriction. These variables are either symbolic or numerical. Two kinds of constraints where used.

2.1.1 Compatibility constraints
Most of the constraints relevant to heat treatment design are compatibility constraints expressing restrictions on combinations of variable values. As variables are either symbolic or numerical, three kinds of compatibility constraints are present, but all of

them can be represented thanks to compatibility tables. The three kinds of constraints are :
- discrete : when all constraint variables are symbolic. In this case constraints represents allowed combinations of symbolic values.
- continuous : when all constraints variables are numerical. In this case constraints represents allowed combinations of intervals,
- mixed : when constraint variables are symbolic and numerical. In this case constraints represents allowed combinations of intervals and symbolic values.

2.1.2 Activity constraints

In order to be able to modulate the existence of some parameters, it is necessary to be able to express some variable existence conditions. This kind of constraints, called activity constraint in the dynamic extension of CSP [3], have the following shape, X = "x" => Y exists, meaning if variable "X" equal the value "x" then variable "Y" exists. They have been mainly used to describe geometric parameters of the part as for example :
- hole_existence = "yes" => Variable_hole_diameter exists,
- part_thickness $\in$ [10 , 20] => Variable_part_area exists.

2.2 Piece of model relevant to the evaluation of distortion

As part distortion is geometrically very complicated to describe, heat treatment experts have proposed to quantify five basic distortion components for the part family "axis": (i) "spool/barrel", (ii) "banana", (iii) "ovalization", (iv) "spacing/tightening" and (v) "umbrella". It can be noted that "spacing/tightening" distortion can exist, only if the part has got a hole and "umbrella" distortion can exist if shoulder shapes are present. Previous activity constraints are necessary to model this two conditions.

In the CSP framework, a way to compute the evaluation of a solution is to assign weights to each parameter values and to each allowed combinations of parameter values relevant to constraints. Because the goodness of a solution is usually influenced by both the quality of the values chosen and the resulting associations of values. The evaluation of a solution is defined as the sum of the weights of all the values and pairs of values involved in the solution [4]. The main interest of this approach lies in its simplicity and its optimisation possibilities. But in an interactive design process, this approach does not easily allow the user to input some constraint on the resulting score and to see the consequences on the parameter values. In our case, the possibility to input a maximum value on a distortion component and to input parameter values with respect to this constraint is a necessity. Therefore, it was decided to use a simple formulae to compute the distortion score relevant to each distortion component. Next sub sections present necessary evaluation variables and evaluation constraints.

2.2.1 Evaluation variables

In order to calculate such a score, heat treatment experts propose the following approach based on three kinds of distortion attributes:

- a first small subset (15 parameters) of heat treatment parameters, vp, allows a first quantification of each distortion component, named potential distortion attribute, vd_pot,
- a second larger subset (45 parameters) of heat treatment parameters, vp, permits to quantify intermediate distortion attributes, vd_int. These attributes modulate each potential distortion component in a similar way. 26 intermediate distortion attributes have been identified.
- the resulting score of each distortion component, named final distortion attribute vd_fin, is computed as a product of the relevant potential distortion attribute and the set of intermediate distortion attributes.

Each distortion attribute is associated with an evaluation variable. These variables are all numerical and defined within intervals. In order to compare and to normalize solutions, heat treatment experts decided that (i) each final distortion component (vd_fin) is quantified into an interval [1, 1000] , where "1" means no distortion and "1000" means maximum distortion, (ii) each potential distortion component (vd_pot) is quantified into an interval [1, 20] while (iii) each intermediate distortion attribute (vd_int$_k$) is quantified into intervals [1, α_k] such their product belongs to an interval [1, 50].

2.2.2 Evaluation constraints
As potential and intermediate distortion attributes are all numerical and parameters either symbolic or numerical, constraints linking these distortion attributes with parameters are either mixed or numerical. All these constraints are expressed thanks to compatibility tables : (i) 5 constraints for the quantification of the 5 components of potential distortion (vp, vd_pot) and (ii) 26 constraints for the quantification of the 26 intermediate distortion attributes (vp, vd_int).

As each final distortion component is obtained with the computation of the product of the relevant potential distortion component and the set of intermediate distortion attributes, the following numerical constraint : vd_fin = vd_pot*$\Pi_{k=1 \text{ to } 26}$(vd_int$_k$) must be defined for each of the five distortion components.

2.3 Gathering the two model pieces in a single model

The two model pieces are gathered in a single design/evaluation model as shown in figure 1 with two distortion components. This model shows :
- two kinds of variable (represented with circles on figure 1) associated with :
  - parameters (vp), symbolic or numerical variables,
  - distortion attributes (vd_pot, vd_int, vd_fin), numerical variables,
- three kinds of constraints between :
  - parameters (vp), these constraints gathers activity and compatibility constraints, they can be symbolic, numerical or mixed constraints, they are mainly expressed thanks to compatibility tables (solid lines on figure 1), they correspond with the knowledge relevant to heat treatment operation,
  - parameter (vp) and distortion attributes (vd_pot, vd_int), these constraints are compatibility constraints, they can be numerical or mixed constraints, they are described with compatibility tables, (doted lines on figure 1), they correspond

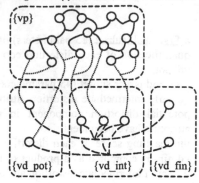

with the knowledge relevant to the distortion evaluation of heat treatment operation,

- distortion attributes (vd_pot, vd_int, vd_fin), these constraints are compatibility constraints, they are numerical constraints, they are defined with the "product" mathematical operation (broken lines on figure 1).

Fig.1   Architecture of the model

The object of the next section is to study how this model can be used to interactively and simultaneously allows design and evaluation of a heat treatment operation.

3   Filtering techniques

The object of this section is to present the various filtering techniques that are necessary and to show how they are gathered in a single filtering engine.

3.1   Compatibility constraints

For discrete constraints, the simple arc consistency technique (AC-3) is used to propagate this kind of constraints. As some constraints have an arity larger than two, AC-3 has been adapted.

For mixed and numerical constraints expressed with compatibility tables including intervals, the association of a label with each interval permits to consider them as discrete constraints [5]. The previous filtering means can be used except that when the definition domain of a numerical variable is reduced, it is necessary to reconstruct the definition domain of the variable with classical set operations (union, intersection). Filtering therefore goes as follows:

1 - Input on variable var-x
2 - Put var-x in list-var-1
3 - While list-var-1 non empty :
4 - Take variable var-i of list-var-1
5 - Put constraint including var-i in list-cst-1
6 - While list-cst-1 non empty :
    7 - Take cst-j of list-cst-1
    8 - Filter cst-j with var-i
    9 - If a reduced var is numerical : Reconstruct definition domain of the reduced var
    10 - Put var, with a reduced domain, in list-var-1

When the variables are all numerical and constraints written with a mathematical formula, $f(x_1, x_2...x_n) = 0$, 2B-Consistency, proposed by [6] and based on interval arithmetic [7], proposes filtering techniques that operate fine if :

(i) $f(x_1, x_2...x_n) = 0$ can be projected on any variable x_i , meaning that a function f_i exists as : $x_i = f_i(x_1, x_2....x_{i-1}, x_{i+1},...x_n)$

(ii) any projection f_i is continuous and monotonous.

(iii) only one constraint expressed as a formula acts on a same variable subset. 2B-Consistency is weak when more than one constraint acts on a same sub-set of variables (corresponding to some constraint intersection). It is shown in [8] that a simple problem gathering two variables and three constraints cannot be fully filtered.

(iv) each variable occurs only one time in a formula. In the opposite case, for example: $x_1^2 - x_1 - x_2 = 0$, it has been shown that the way to express the mathematical expression, for example : $x_1^2 - x_1 - x_2 = 0$ or $x_{1*}(x_1 - 1) - x_2 = 0$, influences the quality of the filtering operation [8].

As this kind of constraints is only present in our model for computing the product quantifying the final distortion attribute (vd_fin = vd_pot * $\Pi_{1\ to\ 26}$(vd_int)), the previous restrictions are not present and 2B-Consistency can be used. For a single continuous constraint, filtering is done as follows :

1- Input on variable var-x
2- Put var-x in list-var-1
3- While list-var-1 non empty :
4- Take variable var-i of list-var-1
5- Put all constraint projections including var-i in list-cst-1 except the one relevant to var-i
6- While list-cst-1 non empty :
    7- Take constraint projections of list-cst-1
    8- Compute the resulting domain of the projected variable
    9- Intersect resulting domain with initial domain of the projected variable
    10-If domain is reduced, put projected variable in list-var-1

3.2 Activity constraints

In order to deal with activity constraints, we only need to use the "Require Variable" activity constraint (var-x = "x" => var-y exists) among the four categories (Require, Require not, Always require, Always require not) proposed by [3] Resulting filtering goes as follows :

1- Input on variable var-x
2- Put var-x in list-var-1
3- While list-var-1 non empty :
    4- Take variable var-i of list-var-1
    5- Put activity constraint including var-i in its premise (left part of =>) in list-a-cst-1
    6- While list-a-cst-1 non empty :
        7- Take a-cst-j of list-a-cst-1
        8- Evaluate the premise of a-cst-j
        9- If true, add triggered var-y (right part of =>) in the current problem and put
        this variable in list-var-1

3.3   Gathering the filtering techniques in a single engine

The three filtering techniques have been gathered in a single engine. It was decided to first filter activity constraints, then constraint expressed with compatibility tables to finish by constraints defined by formulae. The architecture of the global filtering is therefore as follows:

> Input on var
> var in list-var-1
> While list-var-1 non empty
>   Take variable var-i of list-var-1
>   *Filter activity constraint (section 3.2)*
>   Result : can add variables to the current problem and put them in list-var-1
>   *Filter discrete, mixed, continuous constraints defined with compatibility tables (section 3.1)*
>   Result : put variables with a reduced domain in list-var-1
>   *Filter Continuous constraints defined with formulae(section 3.1)*
>   Result : put variables with a reduced domain in list-var-1

4   Interest and limits of the proposed approach

All these elements have been set up in a software mock-up that can be seen on the web at : http://iena.enstimac.fr:20000/cgi-bin/vht.pl. Two modes to use the system have been identified in the beginning of section 2.2. The first one, consisting in interactively inputting restrictions only on parameters and see the computation of the relevant distortion, raises an interesting point. While the other, inputting parameter restrictions (that are not negotiable) and some threshold on the maximum value of the distortion in order to get domain restrictions (on negotiable parameters), points out a limit of the approach.

For the first mode, at the beginning of the design process, each final distortion attribute has a definition domain equal to the interval [1, 1000] meaning that no information about distortion level is available. As filtering is launched after each user input, each final distortion domain is progressively reduced during the design process. Even if sometime this definition interval is split in different intervals, this allows the user to see the progressive effects of his selections on each final distortion component. This interesting behaviour is allowed by 2B-Consistency that operates with interval arithmetic. At the end of the design process, each final distortion attribute has a domain corresponding with a reduced interval. An average between the lower and upper interval bounds can be calculated for solution comparison.

The previous good point has a drawback while dealing with the second mode. If the user inputs restrictions that affect variables corresponding with parameters (vp) and final distortion attributes (vd_fin), the proposed filtering approach can lead to an inconsistent problem. This problem comes from the arc consistence filtering techniques that consider sequentially only one constraint at a time and check only the consistence of pair of variables. Filtering with a stronger consistency could avoid this problem but would be too much time consuming.

5 Conclusions

The goal of this communication was to present an interactive constraint based system that simultaneously allows interactive design and qualitative evaluation of heat treatment operations.

A knowledge model gathering a design model piece and an evaluation model piece was designed. The corresponding constraint satisfaction problem uses discrete and numerical variables, discrete, mixed and numerical constraints. Classical filtering techniques, for discrete constraints (compatibility tables), have been embedded with 2B-consistence, for numerical constraints (formulae), in a single filtering engine.

The resulting configuration software allows the user to input restrictions either on the parameters defining the operation to design or on the attributes that characterize the evaluation score.

The model and aiding design software are now in a validation step performed by end users. In spite of the aiding decision tool, users underline the fact that they better understand heat treatment process. The drawback, discussed in section 4, is avoided during design by progressively reducing final distortion attributes with a "try and error" procedure.

In terms of knowledge modelling, it can be pointed out that heat treatment experts succeeded rather quickly to deal with the formalism variable/domain/constraint. This confirms, as frequently reported in other papers, that the natural and easy to understand concept of the CSP approach makes it a good candidate for domain knowledge representation.

References

1. Tsang E.: Foundations of constraints satisfaction. Academic Press London (1993).
2. David Ph, Veaux M., Vareilles E., Maury J.:Virtual Heat Treatment Tool for Monitoring and Optimising Heat Treatment Process. 2e International Conference on Thermal Process Modelling and Computer Simulation, Nancy, (2003).
3. Mittal S., Falkenhainer B.: Dynamic Constraint Satisfaction Problems. AAAI ConferenceBoston USA, (1990) 25-32.
4. Hulubei T., Freuder E.C., Wallace R.J.:. The Goldilocks problem. AI EDAM, Volume 17, Number 1, (2003) 3-11.
5. Faltings B.: Arc consistency for continuous variables. Artificial Intelligence, volume 65, (1994) 363-376.
6. Lhomme O. : Consistency techniques for numerical CSPs. IJCAI conference, Chambéry, France, (1993).
7. Moore R.E.: Intervals Analysis. Prentice Hall, (1966).
8. Lhomme O., Rueher M. : Application des techniques CSP au raisonnement sur les intervalles. Revue d'intelligence artificielle, Dunod, Vol. 11, (1997) 283-311.

Applying AI to Cooperating Agricultural Robots

Kurt Nielsen[1], Jakob Appel[1], and Yves Demazeau[2]

[1] The Maersk Mc-Kinney Moller Institute for Production Technology, University of
Southern Denmark Campusvej 55 DK-5230 Odense M DENMARK
{kurtn, appel}@mip.sdu.dk,
[2] Laboratoire Leibniz, Institut IMAG 46, avenue Félix Viallet F-38031 Grenoble
Cédex FRANCE
Yves.Demazeau@imag.fr

Abstract. We consider the experimental development of collaborating
robots able to work within fields of crops. Specifically we investigate
how AI principles can be applied to this agricultural domain and how
the user should be involved in such a system. To support collaboration
between agents a representation of responsibilities and dependencies
is necessary. This is done by introducing groups and roles, from MAS
theory, that the agent must adhere to, formalised by the Agent-Group-
Role (AGR) model. To enable a human user to influence the system
we adopt the principles declared by the VOWELS paradigm. We then
show that the AGR model and the VOWELS paradigm, enable us to
solve two practical agricultural problems, and lastly we argue that the
obtained results can be transferred to other domains, such as pervasive
computing.

1 Introduction

The AgroBots project[1] deals with various advanced technologies for agriculture, mainly the development of prototypical robots able to establish, maintain,
monitor, and harvest fields of crops. In [2] Ferentinos et al. propose a solution
for the path planning problem of agricultural robots and in [3] Han et al. propose how agricultural robots can be guided by a vision system. In this paper
we investigate how we can obtain collaboration between the robots, by focusing on the "Explorer-Transporter Paradigm", introduced by the authors in [4].
Essentially this paradigm consists of two types of robots, namely explorers who
traverse the field(s), exploring weed and crop type and collaborate to build up
a precise map of the field and transporters who are holders of different types of
fertiliser or pesticides and spray the field(s) based on the information gathered
from the explorers. Furthermore, the farmer must be able to intervene with the
robots, such that they at all time behave according to his needs and desires.

The remainder of this section is structured as follows: Subsection 1.1 introduces MAS, which were chosen as the analytical approach, as it, to a high
degree, captures the characteristics of intelligent robots in an agricultural domain. Subsection 1.2 introduces two practical agricultural problems that we

Please use the following format when citing this chapter:

Demazeau, Yves, Nielsen, Kurt, Appel, Jakob, 2006, in IFIP International Federation for Information
Processing, Volume 204, Artificial Intelligence Applications and Innovations, eds. Maglogiannis, I.,
Karpouzis, K., Bramer, M., (Boston: Springer), pp. 262–270

have chosen to focus on in this paper. Subsection 1.3 describes the structure of the remainder of the paper.

1.1 MAS

In AI research biology, human behaviour and mind are often used as sources of inspiration, and they all serve as the ultimate, but so far unreachable, abstraction for researchers. MAS(MAS) are seen as an abstraction, resembling biology and human behaviour, where an agent is an autonomous proactive entity, that collaborates with its fellow agents and the environment, in order to reach its goals. MAS encapsulate and capture the agents' flexible, autonomous and problem-solving behaviour, the richness of agents interactions, and the organisational structures and social capabilities into one entity. This powerful abstraction is a promising, but so far, a research oriented approach for developing a range of complex, typically, distributed computer systems. In [5] Jennings et al. argue, among others, that MAS provide the ability to solve problems in a natural and efficient way in domains characterised by unpredictability, complexity and distribution. So far, this is more based on assumptions than on practical experiences.

1.2 Two Agricultural Problems

There is a great amount of design challenges in connection with the Explorer-Transporter paradigm and consequently we need to narrow down which problems we will focus on. In collaboration with industrial partners[6], we have identified the two following problems that are of both research and corporative interest: (i) Tool Changing: an agricultural robot should be much like a tractor that is able to dynamically change its tool and adapt to new problem domains, (ii) Human Intervention: the user should be able to change and influence the system according to his current and future needs.

1.3 Structure of the Paper

Section 2 introduces organisational theory from MAS and adduces how this can help to solve the Tool Changing problem. Section 3 introduces user interaction theory and state the usability of this for the Human Intervention problem. Section 4 summarises the developed system and how the Tool Changing and Human Intervention problems were actually implemented. Section 5 concludes on the work and puts the paper into perspective.

2 Solving Tool Changing using Organisational Theory

An agricultural robot should be able to change its working tool dynamically through its lifetime. This entails a change regarding which robots it should and can collaborate with, and hence tool changing equals a change of the organisation as will be deduced in the following.

Just as with human organisations, agent organisations provide a description of how the members of the population interact with one another [7]. Agent organisations have properties, norms and authority relationship structures which transcend individual agents and help them to coordinate their actions. The set of properties, norms and structures form the organisational setting, which contains communication lines, authority lines, interactions patterns and descriptions of expected behaviour [8]. In [9], Demazeau makes a more formal description:

$$Organisation(MAS) = Roles + Links$$

that is, the organisation is a set consisting of all the roles that exist in the system, and of all the links among the agents that connect the roles one to another, and show the mutual connectivity between roles. The roles and interactions are typically expected to be relatively stable and change slowly over time [10].

2.1 The Role of Roles

If we were to decompose organisations we would at some stage end up in the building block called *role* [11]. Roles are an inherent part of organisations, and are a way of describing behaviour, responsibility and interaction [12]. The following constraints are general in MAS when an agent takes on a role: (i) Obligations and responsibilities: A role is inherently connected with certain duties, and a role, therefore, has responsibilities, (ii) Requirements and abilities: Not all agents can take on a role, they often require physical and/or logical abilities.

From the work represented by Masolo et al. in [12] we adopt the following dynamic properties of roles: (i) An agent can play different roles simultaneously, (ii) An agent can change a role, (iii) An agent can play the same role several times simultaneously, meaning that an agent might be acting different specialisations of the same role at a time, (iv) A role can be played by different agents, simultaneously or at different times.

The above properties means that roles can be assigned to agents in at least two ways: endogenously (emergent self-organisation as the system runs) or exogenously (by the designer when the system is initialised) [10]. Note that an agent can play multiple roles, as long as they do not coincide in their responsibility area, which would result in a conflict and a dysfunctional organisation.

In the next subsection we introduce the AGR model, which is an effective tool to model an organisation and to help limit irrelevant information processing.

2.2 AGR

In [13] the notion "Organisation Centered MAS" is introduced. It is built on the concept of "groups" and "roles", where groups refer to an overall partitioning of the organisation, which may be overlapping. Groups and roles were combined by Ferber and Gutknecht in [14] that proposed an organisational based modelling scheme, called AGR for AGR, to describe MAS in organisational terms. Only agents that are members of the same group may communicate, but agents can be members of several groups simultaneously. Thereby groups can be used to regulate, foster, or support the interaction of those agents within the group [15]. By complying to the AGR model we propose the agent architecture depicted in figure 1. For simplicity we have replaced the representation of the internal

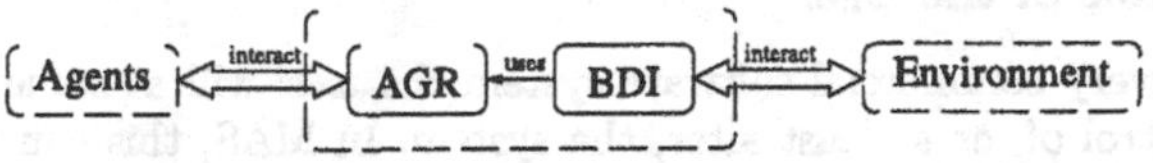

Fig. 1. The agent architecture with the addition of the AGR model.

Belief-Desire-Intention(BDI) architecture with a box called BDI. There has been many approaches in the AI community for an agent architecture, but as BDI is far the most notorious and respected agent model it was selected. For an introduction to BDI see [16] and for a more elaborated explanation of how we specifically implemented the BDI box see [4].

2.3 Tool Changing Design

If we decompose the result of a tool change we get the following results: (i) Change of obligations and responsibilities: a tool is a physical representation of a certain capability. Inherently an agent's capability is connected to a number of obligations and responsibilities which the agent should attend to with the certain capability, (ii) Change of mutual dependencies: when changing tool an agent should also change its surroundings expectations towards the agent and its own mutual dependencies.

By implementing an AGR structure, we can model the change of obligations and responsibilities as a change of role. The other result of a tool change, change of mutual dependencies, can be modelled as a change of group, since a group is defined as a clustering of activity dependent and interacting agents. Hence, by letting an agent dynamically change which roles it play and which groups it participate in, it is able to change its tool throughout its lifetime and still maintain the proper collaborative links.

3 Solving Human Intervention using User Interaction Theory

So far, decisions that have to be made within the agricultural establishment have, to a high degree, been taken by the individual farmer. Hence, it is highly unlikely that he overnight wants to assign full control to the robots, and not at some point wish to overrule a robots decision or rework its strategies.

The notion of a user has been remarkably absent in the MAS literature. One of the reasons for this is probably that MAS are still far from having their true breakthrough both research and industry wise and, therefore, the need to represent the user has so far been minimal[17]. In this system, however, we can not ignore the user's perspective, as we see it as an inherent part in any agricultural process, independently of whether the robots are autonomous or controlled directly by a user.

3.1 The Role of the User

In almost every commercial software system the user will at some point wish to take control of, or at least alter, the system. In MAS, this can be done by enabling the user to change an agent's beliefs, desires, intentions and capabilities, both via normal agent interactions, but also due to other entry points to the agent, that only exist for the user. This enables the user to modify or replace work processes, both directly by updating the intentions and capabilities, but also by affecting beliefs and desires. In the next subsection we present the VOWELS paradigm, which recognises the user as an essential part of a MAS.

3.2 The VOWELS Paradigm

The VOWELS paradigm is a popular decomposition model that breaks down MAS into its constituent parts. The four basic bricks of the VOWELS paradigm, initially introduced by one of the coauthors in [18], are the Agents, the Environment, the Interactions and the Organisations (A, E, I, O). In [19], the lack of a user representation is discussed as the user can hardly be described with the same terms as an agent, which result in the addition of a user(U). In addition to these bricks, the VOWELS paradigm is guided by a *declarative* principle, which states that a MAS will be composed of agents, environments, interactions, organisations and users:

$$MAS = A + E + I + O + U \tag{1}$$

3.3 Human Intervention Design

In order to model an agent in a realistic MAS we have to take into account the effects that the user can have upon an agent's beliefs, desires, capabilities, groups and roles. This leads to an extension of the agent architecture diagram, presented in figure 1, which by the addition of the VOWELS gives us the model depicted in figure 2. By enabling the user to modify an agent's role and/or membership of a group, the user is able to e.g. make a tool change and by modifying an agent's capabilities, beliefs and/or desires a new behaviour can be obtained. Thus, by complying to the VOWELS paradigm and acknowledge the user's part in a MAS, we obtain a system that provides the desired flexibility with respect to the intervention of a human user, and thereby we achieve a solution for the Human Intervention problem. In the next section we will explain how we implemented the two agricultural problems.

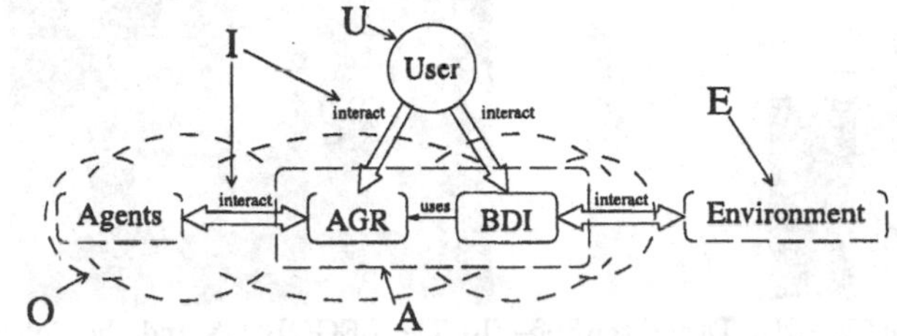

Fig. 2. The agent architecture with the addition of the user. The VOWELS bricks, including the new U, are added to show them in a more practical context.

4 Implementation

To verify and experiment with the proposed solutions from section 2 and 3 for the Tool Changing and Human Intervention problem, three prototype platforms have been used. The software kernels used are the same on each of the platforms facilitating three different levels of realism: (i) AgroBOT: an advanced robotic platform developed by Bygholm[20], consisting of physical robots that can navigate in an agricultural field, (ii) LEGOBOT: a laboratory set-up developed by the Maersk Institute [21], that apply simple physical robots for simulation, (iii) SoftBOT: a virtual robot platform that is used as an abstraction of the two above listed robots and, therefore, allows for fast developing.

The overall goal of the considered part of the AgroBots project is to develop the AgroBOT platform itself. However, in order to speed up development time and to facilitate experiments with alternative designs of strategies and techniques, the LEGOBOT and SoftBOT platforms were introduced, which is the focus of this paper.

4.1 The Setup

The developed system provides an overview window that depicts the field and the agents within it, as visualised in figure 3(a). The agents are represented as squares with different colours according to their role and the agents' unique identification numbers are printed upon the squares, so that the user can identify the agents. The LEGOBOTs physically move upon a restricted area, whereas the SoftBOTs are projected upon the restricted area as squares with their unique Id number depicted in the middle. This construction is shown in figure 3(b).

4.2 Experimenting with Tool Changing and Human Intervention

The AGR model has been implemented providing the agents with the organisational properties listed in section 2. Furthermore, the user is able to interact with the agents, through interaction agents(IA), both as an observer that is

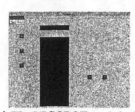 

(a) The LEGOBOTs and the Soft- (b) The LEGOBOTs and the SoftBOTs
BOTs in the overview window.   in their physical environment.

Fig. 3. The virtual and physical environment, both containing black box-shaped obstacles.

able to monitor the agent's internal state, but also as an active player that can change the agent's roles and exchange plans dynamically. Plans are an inherently part of the BDI model, introduced in subsection 2.2, and can be thought of as a recipe for achieving a goal.

The interaction agents are activated by clicking on an agent icon on the overview window and are so far able to do the following: (i) Show roles: the IA is capable of showing all roles that an agent has the potential to be. That is both its active and none-active roles, (ii) Activ ate and deactivate role: the IA activates and deactivates roles, (iii) Show plans: the IA shows the current plans that an agent currently possesses, (iv) Exchange plan: the IA dynamically exchanges plans to another agent.

4.3 Last Words Regarding the System

The developed system uses concepts from MAS frameworks such as JACK[22] (capabilities and plans) and MadKit[23] (AGR model), but also concepts which, to our knowledge, can not be found in any MAS framework today such as dynamic exchange of plans and direct user interaction with agents' mutual dependencies and responsibilities, which makes the system unique in MAS context.

5 Conclusion

In this paper we have advocated the applicability of group-based role definitions for intelligent agricultural robots. Furthermore a representation of an user was introduced as an indispensable part of an agricultural system and MAS in general. To substantiate these claims two real world agricultural problems were implemented, namely Tool Changing and Human Intervention. This proved the AGR model to not only be of theoretical interest and that user interaction is of vital importance within AI applications. Allowing agents to change their roles and group memberships dynamically gives the agents the opportunity to adapt to changes in their environment, or even to change their application domain, whereby the system is not only applicable for agricultural robots or alike, but also within areas with other characteristics.

Most computer researchers agree that computer systems are going to be everywhere and will always be connected and active, referred to as pervasive computer systems. The MAS approach has relevance to pervasive computing as they both rely on situatedness, openness, locality in control and locality in interactions. However, the MAS approach suffers from the absence of the human input and interaction, which is a core aspect of pervasive computing. We have proposed the VOWELS paradigm as a start and we believe that the aspect of human interaction with MAS will become a major research area in the future.

References

1. http://www.agrobots.dk.
2. Ferentinos, K.P., Arvanitis, K.G., Sigrimis, N.: Heuristic optimization methods for motion planning of autonomous agricultural vehicles. J. of Global Optimization **23** (2002) 155–170
3. Han, S., Zhang, Q., Ni, B., Reid, J.: A guidance directrix approach to vision-based vehicle guidance systems. In: COMPUTERS AND ELECTRONICS IN AGRICULTURE 43 (3). (2004) 179–195
4. Appel, J., Nielsen, K.: Applied multi-agent systems principles to cooperating robots in tomorrow's agricultural environment. Master's thesis, University of Southern Denmark Campusvej 55 DK-5230 Odense M DENMARK (2005)
5. Jennings, N.R., Wooldridge, M.: Applying agent technology. Applied Artificial Intelligence **9** (1995) 351–361
6. http://www.agrobots.dk/deltagere.htm.
7. Horling, B., Lesser, V.: A Survey of Multi-Agent Organizational Paradigms. Computer Science Technical Report 04-45, University of Massachusetts (2004)
8. Karageorgos, A., Mehandjiev, N., Thompson, S.: Ramasd: a semi-automatic method for designing agent organisations. Knowl. Eng. Rev. **17** (2002) 331–358
9. Demazeau, Y., Costa, A.C.R.: Populations and organizations in open multi-agent systems (1996)
10. Odell, J., Parunak, H., Fleischer, M.: The role of roles in designing effective agent organizations (2003)
11. Gasser, L.: Perspectives on organizations in multi-agens systems (2001)
12. Masolo, C., Vieu, L., Bottazzi, E., Catenacci, C., Ferrario, R., Gangemi, A., Guarino, N.: Social roles and their descriptions (2004)
13. Ferber, J., Gutknecht, O., Michel, F.: From agents to organizations: An organizational view of multi-agent systems. In Paolo Giorgini, Jrg P. Mller, J.O., ed.: Agent-Oriented Software Engineering IV. Springer-Verlag (2003) 214–230
14. Ferber, J., Gutknecht, O.: A meta-model for the analysis and design of organizations in multi-agent systems (1998)
15. Odell, J., Nodine, M., Levy, R.: A metamodel for agents, roles, and groups (2005)
16. Nagi, K.: Transactional Agents. Springer-Verlag (2001)
17. Albert, P., Demazeau, Y., Elfallah-Seghrouchni, A.: Incitations et freins à la mise en oeuvre de sma. In: Systèmes Multi-Agents. (2004) 261–289 (In France).

18. Demazeau, Y.: From interactions to collective behaviour in agent-based systems (1995)
19. Demazeau, Y.: Créativité émergente centrée utilisateur. In: 11èmes Journées Francophones sur les Systèmes Multi-Agents. (2003) 31–36 (In France).
20. The Danish Agricultural Research Centre of Horsens, http://www.agrsci.dk/jbt.
21. The Maersk Mc-Kinney Moller Institute for Production Technology, University of Southern Denmark, http://www.mip.sdu.dk/.
22. http://www.agent-software.com/.
23. http://www.madkit.org/.

Capacity Evaluation of an Indoor Smart Antenna System at 60 GHz

Nektarios Moraitis[1] and Demosthenes Vouyioukas[2]
[1]Mobile Radiocommunications Laboratory, National Technical
University of Athens
9 Heroon Polytechniou str. 15773, Zografou, Athens, Greece
morai@mobile.ntua.gr
[2]Dept. of Information and Communication Systems Engineering,
University of the Aegean
Karlovasi 83200 Samos, Greece
dvouyiou@aegean.gr

Abstract. In this paper, a study for indoor channel modeling is presented for the millimeter frequency band, by using various configurations of multiple element antenna systems. A multi-ray model is proposed and verified through simulation process for capacity prediction of a high data rate wireless system. The proposed model utilizes the geometric characteristics of the environment, the angle of arrival and angle of departure of each one of the propagation paths, the antenna elements and their spacing. The results showed that the system capacity increases significantly if two or four elements are used at both terminal antennas instead of the basic SISO configuration. In order to accomplish major improvement in the data rates, a MIMO system at 60 GHz should operate within a range of 10 to 20 m in an indoor environment with the view of obtaining sufficient Signal to Noise Ratios.

1 Introduction

Multiple antenna systems and in general multiple input-multiple output (MIMO) systems are an optimistic technique for future wireless communications, valuable for overcoming the effects of multipath interference and thus giving capacity and spectrum efficiency. Over the last years, the force for wireless systems and in particular for mobile communications to deal with new services requires high capacity, robustness against interferences, privacy and accurate prediction of the reception signals, thus modeling of the propagation channel. The demand for data rates greater than 2 Mb/s up to 155 Mb/s are enormous and Wireless Broadband Systems (WBSs) are emerging rapidly.

Please use the following format when citing this chapter:

Moraitis, Nektarios, Vouyioukas, Demosthenes, 2006, in IFIP International Federation for Information Processing, Volume 204, Artificial Intelligence Applications and Innovations, eds. Maglogiannis, I., Karpouzis, K., Bramer, M., (Boston: Springer), pp. 271–280

In millimeter wave frequencies the propagation modeling, apart from the known empirical models, can be realized based on geometrical optics using ray-tracing theory. In the 60 GHz region the diffraction phenomenon can be neglected, and the sum of the direct ray and the reflected rays is enough to describe the behavior of the propagation channel with great accuracy [1]. The modeling in extremely high frequencies poses the problem of the accurate description of the propagation scenarios at the wavelength scale (5 mm at 60 GHz). Hence the main target is to describe the main obstructions and the surfaces that affect the signal propagation. The description is not only in terms of the geometric characteristics of the propagation environment, but also in terms of the surface electromagnetic parameters (relative dielectric constant, losses etc) in order to extract the surface reflection coefficients.

In this paper we present a multi-ray model in order to describe the signal propagation at 60 GHz in an indoor environment and to calculate further the capacity of the proposed MIMO system. In order to predict the performance of multiple array systems, the angle of arrival and angle of departure of each one of the propagation paths, jointly with the antenna elements and their spacing, were considered. The presented channel model is based on the assumption, that there are few dominant reflections of the signal - four single reflected plus four double reflected rays plus the direct component - consisting of a total of 9 rays. The propagation mechanisms are explained analytically whereas channel parameters, such as propagation paths and the corresponding gains of each path arriving at the receive antenna, are calculated.

This paper is organized as follows; section 2 deals with the channel modeling and the proposed multi-ray model and explaining the mechanisms and the behavior of the signal propagation. In Section 3 an analytically description of the geometry of the environment under consideration is presented along with the simulation procedure of the proposed channel model, dealing with two different geometry scenarios. In Section 4, the results of the space-time channel model are presented taking into consideration the accomplishment of the capacity improvement (C > 1 b/s/Hz), in order to evaluate the total throughput of the MIMO system. Finally, Section 5 is devoted to discussion and conclusions derived by the entire simulation procedure.

2 Channel Model

In order to calculate the capacity of a system with one antenna element at both terminals, the channel impulse response, $h(\tau)$, between the transmit and receive antenna is a prerequisite. In case of a multiple input-multiple output (MIMO) configuration, which has N_{TX} transmit antennas and M_{RX} receive antennas the channel matrix has to be calculated [2]. The $N_{TX} \times M_{RX}$ channel matrix $H(\tau)$ for a MIMO system denotes the impulse response $h_{ij}(\tau)$, between the j-th (j = 1, 2, ..., N_{TX}) transmit antenna and the i-th (i = 1, 2, ..., M_{RX}) receive antenna. One of the most widely used physical models to calculate the channel matrix $H(\tau)$ is [3]:

$$H(\tau) = \sum_{l=1}^{L} \beta_l a_R(\phi_{R,l}, \theta_{R,l}) a_T^*(\phi_{T,l}, \theta_{T,l}) \tag{1}$$

where L is the number of propagation paths, β_l are the corresponding gains of each path arriving at the receive antenna, $\phi_{R,l}$ and $\theta_{R,l}$ are the azimuth and elevation angles of a propagation path arriving at the receiver antenna, whereas $\phi_{T,l}$ and $\theta_{T,l}$ are the azimuth and elevation angles of a path departing from the transmit antenna. The symbol $*$ denotes conjugate transpose. Furthermore, $a_R(\phi_R, \theta_R)$ is the array response vector for a plane wave arriving from direction ϕ_R, θ_R and $a_T(\phi_T, \theta_T)$ represents the transmitter steering vector for the direction ϕ_T, θ_T. The model given by (1) is based on the assumption that there are few spatially well separated dominant reflectors in the far-field. For each dominant reflector one significant multipath is assumed. In the case of uniform linear arrays (ULAs) with spacing Δx at both transmitter and receiver antennas, and the elements placed along the x-axis of the propagation plane (shown in Fig. 1), the array steering and response vectors are given by:

$$a_T(\phi_T, \theta_T) = \begin{bmatrix} 1 & e^{-j\frac{2\pi}{\lambda}\Delta x \cos(\phi_T)\sin(\theta_T)} & \cdots & e^{-j\frac{2\pi}{\lambda}\Delta x (N_{TX}-1)\cos(\phi_T)\sin(\theta_T)} \end{bmatrix}^t \tag{2a}$$

$$a_R(\phi_R, \theta_R) = \begin{bmatrix} 1 & e^{-j\frac{2\pi}{\lambda}\Delta x \cos(\phi_R)\sin(\theta_R)} & \cdots & e^{-j\frac{2\pi}{\lambda}\Delta x (M_{RX}-1)\cos(\phi_R)\sin(\theta_R)} \end{bmatrix}^t \tag{2b}$$

where t denotes transpose, N_{TX} and M_{RX} are the number of the elements at the transmit and receive antenna respectively and λ is the wavelength (5 mm at 60 GHz). Equation (1) has also a matrix representation and is given by [3]:

$$H(\tau) = A_R(\phi_R, \theta_R) H_P A_T^*(\phi_T, \theta_T) \tag{3}$$

where $A_R(\phi_R, \theta_R)$ is an $M_{RX} \times L$, and $A_T(\phi_T, \theta_T)$ is an $N_{TX} \times L$ matrix respectively and both are given by:

$$A_R(\phi_R, \theta_R) = \begin{bmatrix} a_R(\phi_{R,1}, \theta_{R,1}) & a_R(\phi_{R,2}, \theta_{R,2}) & \cdots & a_R(\phi_{R,L}, \theta_{R,L}) \end{bmatrix} \tag{4a}$$

$$A_T(\phi_T, \theta_T) = \begin{bmatrix} a_T(\phi_{T,1}, \theta_{T,1}) & a_T(\phi_{T,2}, \theta_{T,2}) & \cdots & a_T(\phi_{T,L}, \theta_{T,L}) \end{bmatrix} \tag{4b}$$

where L is the number of propagation paths. In (3) $H_P = diag(\beta_1, \beta_2, \ldots, \beta_L)$ is a $L \times L$ matrix that contains the gain of the each propagation path. Hence by using (3) we can calculate the $N_{TX} \times M_{RX}$ channel matrix $H(\tau)$, if we know the angle of arrival (AoA) and angle of departure (AoD) of each one of the L propagation paths, the antenna elements and their spacing. The power gains β_l (received amplitude) of each path can be calculated by using a multi-ray model which describes the signal propagation at a desired frequency.

The multi-ray model is a general case of the two-ray model for more than two reflected components. The reflected components may exhibit single or double reflection from a plane surface. The reflection geometry can be described in the horizontal as well as in the vertical plane as shown in Fig. 1. Hence, if we know the geometry of the environment where the signal propagates (length, width, height) and the surface reflection coefficients, the received power of each reflected ray could be determined as well as the AoAs and AoDs of each ray. The total received power can be calculated by the summation of N single reflected and M double reflected rays given by [4], [5]:

$$\beta = \sqrt{K} \left| \frac{1}{d_0} + \sum_{i=1}^{N} \frac{R_i}{d_i} e^{j\Delta\phi_i} + \sum_{j=1}^{M} \frac{R_{ja} \cdot R_{jb}}{d_j} e^{j\Delta\phi_j} \right| \qquad (5)$$

where d is the horizontal separation between the transmitter and receiver, d_0 is the path length of the direct component and d_i, d_j are the path lengths each of the i single and j double reflected rays. Moreover, R_i is the reflection coefficient of i single reflected ray whereas R_{ja}, R_{jb} are the reflection coefficients of the j double reflected rays on a and b reflecting surfaces respectively. Finally $\Delta\phi_i = 2\pi\Delta l_i / \lambda$ and $\Delta\phi_j = 2\pi\Delta l_j / \lambda$ are the phase differentials between the direct and the reflected rays with Δl_i and Δl_j the differential path lengths between the direct and the i single and j double reflected rays, and λ is the wavelength. The factor K is a constant that incorporates the transmitted power, antenna gains etc. From (5) the total received power β at a given distance d between the transmitter and receiver can be calculated. The power of each one of the reflected arrays β_l can be easily calculated and the total number of paths $L=M+N+1$. Hence, knowing the path gains the AoDs and the AoAs of the reflected rays from (5), we can determine the $N_{TX} \times M_{RX}$ channel matrix $H(\tau)$ by substituting (2a), (2b), (4a) and (4b) in (3).

Finally after calculating the channel matrix of a $N_{TX} \times M_{RX}$ system, its capacity, assuming a channel unknown to the transmitter, can be easily obtained as a function of the signal to noise ratio (SNR), according to the relationship [2]:

$$C = \log_2 \det \left(I_{MR_X} + \frac{E_s}{N_{TX} N_0} HH^* \right) \qquad (6)$$

where I_{MR_X} is a unitary $M_{RX} \times M_{RX}$ matrix, E_s / N_0 is the SNR, N_{TX} stands for the transmitter antenna elements and $*$ denotes conjugate transpose. The capacity is referred as the error free spectral efficiency, or the data rate per unit bandwidth that can be sustained reliably over the MIMO link. Thus given a bandwidth W Hz, the maximum achievable data rate over this bandwidth using the MIMO channel will be WC b/s.

3   Simulation Procedure

The simulation environment is a corridor with dimensions $30 \times 1.75 \times 2.80$ m^3 as shown in Fig. 1. The left and right wall surface is made of brick and plasterboard with wooden doors every 3 m but in order to simplify the simulation procedure we assume the surface as a uniform wall, made of brick and plasterboard with its dielectric characteristics given in Fig. 1. The floor is made of concrete and covered with marble, whereas the suspended ceiling is made of aluminium sheets, holding the fluorescent light tubes. Furthermore, all the material characteristics are provided as well as the propagation geometry and the terminal positions. Each terminal it is assumed to have one, two or four elements with Δx spacing orientated along the x-axis of the propagation plane as illustrated in Fig. 1.

In order to simplify the simulation procedure and reduce the calculation time we use in (5) four single reflected ($N=4$), plus four double reflected ($M=4$) rays plus the direct component (9 reflected rays in total). Hence, H_P will be a 9×9 matrix, $A_R(\phi_R, \theta_R)$, a $M_{RX} \times 9$ matrix, and $A_T(\phi_T, \theta_T)$, a $N_{TX} \times 9$ matrix respectively.

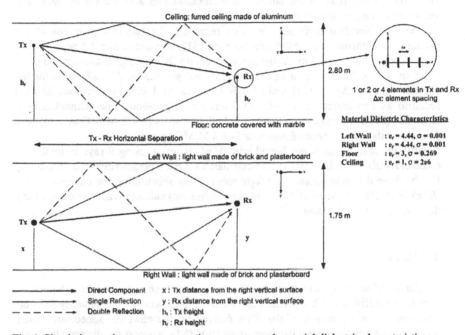

Fig. 1. Simulation environment, propagation geometry and material dielectric characteristics.

Some additional assumptions are:

- The diffraction is not taken into account, since at 60 GHz the phenomenon is almost negligible and the diffracted power does not contribute to the total received power.
- The non-uniformities of the surface materials in indoor environments are such that the produced scattering has not a substantial contribution to the received power.
- The most significant contribution is from the 9 rays previously reported. Further reflected rays are not taken into account since their contribution to the total received power is insignificant. It has been shown [4], [5] that 9 rays in total can describe with great accuracy the signal propagation in the specific environment.
- Only second order reflections are taken into account, since third or fourth order reflections, especially at 60 GHz, are negligible contributors to the average power.

- Atmospheric propagation losses are not taken into account since in indoor environments the attenuation is very small (11.6 dB/km) [6].

During the entire simulation procedure vertical polarization is assumed. Hence, for the rays reflected from vertical walls we use the perpendicular reflection coefficient ($R_{s\perp}$), whereas for the rays from floor and ceiling surfaces we use the parallel reflection coefficient ($R_{s\parallel}$). Both reflection coefficients are given in [7]. In the reflection coefficient equations the complex dielectric constant [7] is given by $\varepsilon = \varepsilon_r - j60\sigma\lambda$ where ε_r is the relative dielectric constant of the reflecting surface, σ is the conductivity of the surface in Siemens/m and λ is the wavelength. The values of ε_r and σ are given in Fig. 1 [8], [9].

We consider two different scenarios regarding the terminal positions at the propagation environment. At the first scenario (S1) we assume h_t = 1.5 m, h_r = 1.35 m, x = 1.25 m and y = 0.5 m. At the second scenario (S2) the inputs are h_t = 2.5 m, h_r = 1.5 m, x = 0.875 m (center of the corridor) and y = 0.5 m. At both scenarios the element spacing Δx in (2a) and (2b) is taken 2λ or 1 cm. Furthermore, at each scenario we considered three different antenna configurations; one element at both terminals (SISO system), two elements at both terminals (2 × 2, MIMO system), and four elements at both terminal antennas (4 × 4 MIMO system).

Finally, the simulation is conducted with MatLab script, using 9 rays in total. The channel matrix described by (3) was calculated for each predetermined scenario and for the three different antenna configurations. Then substituting the channel matrix $H(\tau)$ in (6), the capacity of the channel in b/s/Hz was calculated as a function of the desired signal to noise ratio.

4   Results

For an efficient system that operates with more than one element antennas, is required to fulfill C > 1 b/s per unit bandwidth. Fig. 2 presents the capacity for a 60 GHz system as a function of the SNR derived by the aforementioned simulation procedure. The first scenario has been considered (S1), whereas the distance between the transmitter and receiver has been selected 10 m and 20 m. It is clear that the capacity increases if the antenna elements are increased for a given value of SNR. For example if we select 10 dB SNR and 10 m distance, the capacity increases from 3.5 b/s/Hz for a SISO system to 8.4 b/s/Hz for a 2 × 2 MIMO and up to 26.6 b/s/Hz for a 4 × 4 MIMO system. In other words by using four elements at both terminals we can almost multiply by eight the data rate per unit bandwidth relative to SISO system at the frequency of 60 GHz. If we increase the distance (20 m) from Fig. 2b we observe that for a 10 dB SNR the capacity is 3.5 b/s/Hz for a SISO system, 8.8 b/s/Hz for a 2 × 2 MIMO and 14.6 b/s/Hz for a 4 × 4 MIMO system. The efficiency of the system is lower at greater distances since the propagation losses at 60 GHz are significant.

Fig. 3 presents the capacity for a 60 GHz system as a function of the SNR for the second scenario (S2). For a 10 m distance, and a 4 × 4 MIMO system with 10 dB SNR the capacity drops from 26.6 b/s/Hz to 14.6 b/s/Hz. In average, the capacity increases 3.4 b/s/Hz if we lower the transmitter, regarding all the antenna configurations.

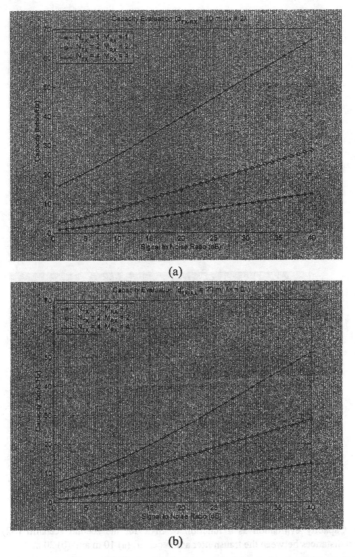

(a)

(b)

Fig. 2. Capacity as a function of SNR for the first scenario (S1) and two different distances between the transmitter and receiver, (a) 10 m and (b) 20 m

According to [10] the systems that operate at 60 GHz will be a part of fourth generation systems (4G) and may feature transmission rates up to 155 Mb/s especially in an indoor environment. In Europe two frequency segments having a bandwidth of 1 GHz have been allocated around 60 GHz. This will give the capability to allocate channels up to 100 MHz for the users [11].

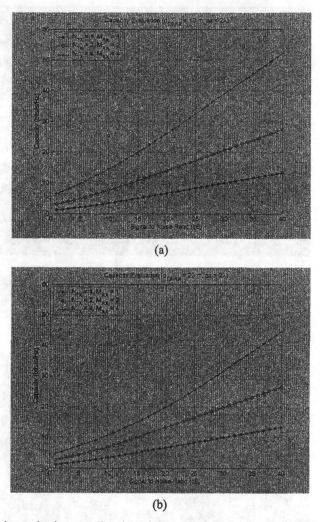

(a)

(b)

Fig. 3. Capacity evaluation as a function of SNR for the second scenario (S2) and two different distances between the transmitter and receiver, (a) 10 m and (b) 20 m.

According to this, having a 100 MHz bandwidth available and combining the results derived by the simulation procedure, we can achieve an explicit transmission rate of 2.7 Gb/s for a 4×4 MIMO system with 10 dB SNR at a distance of 10 m from the transmitter for the first scenario (S1). For a 20 m distance the rate will be 1.5 Gb/s. For the second scenario (S2) the achievable rates are 1.5 Gb/s at 10 m and 1.1 Gb/s at 20 m from the transmitter respectively. It is evident that in order to realize a major improvement in the data rates, a MIMO system at 60 GHz should operate within a range of 10 to 20 m maintaining low SNR (10 dB at least in order to double the data rate per unit bandwidth relative to SISO system).

In [12] wideband channel measurements were performed in the same corridor, transmitting a bandwidth of 100 MHz. The results revealed that the channel exhibits frequency selective characteristics. The coherence bandwidth that determines the performance of a digital system was found 22.48 MHz for 90% correlation and 54.11 MHz for 75% correlation respectively. This is the useful bandwidth that one can achieve the maximum potential data rate without coding (22.48 Mb/s or 54.11 Mb/s). Based on this if we apply a 4×4 MIMO system with 10 dB SNR at a distance of 10 m from the transmitter for the second scenario (S2), the feasible rates will be 327 Mb/s (for 90% correlation) and 788 Mb/s (for 75% correlation). The data rate is increased significantly. For a 20 m distance the rates become 241 Mb/s and 581 Mb/s respectively.

5 Conclusions

This paper presented a simulation procedure in an indoor environment at 60 GHz in order to evaluate the capacity by using multiple element antennas. Different scenarios were evaluated and compared. It was found, that the system capacity increases significantly if two or four elements are used at both terminal antennas instead of the basic SISO configuration. Furthermore, it was observed that in order to realize a major improvement in the data rates, a MIMO system at 60 GHz should operate within a range of 10 to 20 m with the view of maintaining low Signal to Noise Ratios. Efficient capacities, that would at least double the data rates per unit bandwidth relative to a SISO system, can be obtained while the volume of SNR maintaining equal and over 10 dB.

The main target as a future work is to extent the channel model and thus the simulation procedure in different environment types, applying different antenna configurations. Also, SIMO and MISO configurations will be investigated, incorporating different element number, positions and spacing.

References

1. Correia L.M, Prasad R., An overview of wireless broadband communications, IEEE Commun. Mag. (1997) 28-33.
2. Paulraj A., Nabar R., Gore D., Introduction to space-time wireless communications, Cambridge University Press (2003).
3. Sayeed A. M., Modeling and Capacity of Realistic Spatial MIMO Channels, IEEE Int. Conf. on Acoustics, Speech, and Sig. Proc., Vol.4 (2001) 2489-2492.
4. Moraitis N., Constantinou P.: Indoor channel modeling at 60 GHz for wireless LAN applications, Proc. PIMRC '02, Vol. 3 (2002) 1203-1207.
5. Moraitis N., Indoor radio channel characterization at millimeter wave frequencies for the development of wireless broadband systems, Ph.D. thesis, National Technical University of Athens (2004).

6. Moraitis N., P. Constantinou, Indoor channel measurements and characterization at 60 GHz for wireless local area network applications, IEEE Trans. on Antennas and Propagation, Vol. 52 no. 12 (2004) 3180-3189.
7. Rappaport T.S., Wireless Communications, Upper Saddle River, NJ: Prentice Hall (1996).
8. Sato K. et al, Measurements of the complex refractive index of concrete at 57.5 GHz, IEEE Trans. Antennas Propagation, Vol. 44 no. 1 (1996) 35-39.
9. Sato K. et al., Measurements of reflection and transmission characteristics of interior structures of office building in the 60-GHz band, IEEE Trans. Antennas Propagation., Vol. 45 no. 12 (1997) 1783-1792.
10. Smulders P., Exploiting the 60 GHz band for local wireless multimedia access: prospects and future directions, IEEE Commun. Mag., Vol. 40 no. 1 (2002) 140-147.
11. Prasad R., Overview of wireless communications: Microwave perspectives, IEEE Commun. Mag., (1997) 104-108.
12. Moraitis N., Constantinou P., Millimeter Wave Propagation Measurements and Characterization in an Indoor Environment for Wireless 4G Systems, Proc. PIMRC '05 (2005).

Steady State Contingency analysis of electrical networks using machine learning techniques

Dimitrios Semitekos and Nikolaos Avouris
Electrical and Computer Engineering Dep. HCI Group
University of Patras, 26 500 Rio Patras, Greece.
dsem@ee.upatras.gr, avouris@upatras.gr

Abstract. Steady state contingency analysis aims at the assessment of the risk certain contingencies may pose to an electrical network. This is a particularly important task of network operators, especially as network stability issues become of prime importance in the current era of electricity deregulation. The article focuses on the analysis of experimental data that are produced through operating point simulation, contingency application, machine- learning cross validation (based on pre-contingency network index selection algorithms) to point out the "nature" of given contingencies. Experimental statistical results of contingency prediction and selected network state indicators are translated to electric network data in an effort to further interpret the "nature" of each contingency and produce effective predicting algorithms that support operators.

1 Introduction

Application of machine learning techniques to security assessment of electrical networks has been proposed by many researchers [1]. In this paper we discuss the process of simulating many different operating points (*OPs*) of a network through the variation of three parameters: the load level, the unit commitment and the network topology [2]. The idea of training of machine learning algorithm on a per contingency basis for subsequent contingency predictions using a preclassified learning set (*LS*) of operating states or operating points (*OPs*) is described in detail in [3].

In this paper, a more extended contingency analysis study is presented, where the contingencies examined can be classified in groups of interest. Experimental data demonstrate that combinations of contingencies tend to produce behavior of incremental nature in what concerns their predictability when machine learning tools are used. It can also be assumed that the consequences a contingency may entail to a

Please use the following format when citing this chapter:

Semitekos, Dimitrios, Avouris, Nikolaos, 2006, in IFIP International Federation for Information Processing, Volume 204, Artificial Intelligence Applications and Innovations, eds. Maglogiannis, I., Karpouzis, K., Bramer, M., (Boston: Springer), pp. 281–289

network may be reflected on the information value of the active or reactive power network indices calculated at pre-contingency times. Sensitivity analysis results about various machine learning algorithms implemented as well as various training to testing split quotas, also lead to interesting results, showing a per contingency consistency in predictions. Experimental results also show that for every contingency to a certain extent the predictive powers of the machine learning tools are influenced by the distribution of the prediction classes in the training data set.

2   The experimental environment

For the needs of our study the electric network of the Greek island of Crete has been used. fig. 1(a).

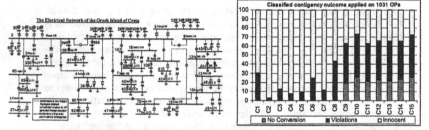

Fig. 1. (a) The electrical network of Crete. (b) The effect of the 15 contingencies studied on the 1031 Operating Points of the network of Crete.

Screened simulated variations in network connectivity, load level and generation plan lead to diversified Operating Points (*OPs*) that are representative of possible states of the electric network. The experimental environment of the simulated *OPs* considered 22 scenarios of line outages. 10 load levels were considered during *OP* simulation ranging from full load scenario to 70% of it. Also 6 different generation scenarios were applied. Thus 22x10x6=1320 *OP* scenarios were simulated, 1031 of which were violations free and were saved in the *OP* repository. Subsequently, 15 line outage events, defined as contingencies under study, were applied on the 1031 simulated *OPs*.

The effect of contingencies on the *OPs* was classified in three discreet categories "innocent", "non-conversion" and "violations". The classification of the contingency outcome for all *OPs* is depicted in fig. 1(b), which demonstrates that there are potentially dangerous (C_8 to C_{15}) and harmless (C_2, C_4, C_5 C_7) contingencies. The contingency effect distribution to classes varies. The questions set focus on the predictability of the effect of these contingencies in relation to selected network characteristics, automatic learning algorithms used and training to testing data split quotas.

3   A study on feature selection

For most machine learning algorithms that are insensitive to feature redundancy, the selection of additional features will always lead to improvement (even marginal) of the performance achieved, no matter the computational overhead. For instance C4.5 deals remarkably well with irrelevant and redundant information, which is why feature selection has generally resulted in little if any improvement in its accuracy.

In the paper we assume that feature selection algorithms can be applied on the contingencies we study in a "reverse engineering" way, outlining the electrical behavior of the contingencies. For our study, we combined results out of five different feature selection algorithms and searching methods, included in [4]: The *CfsSubsetEval* algorithm selects a number of the most prevalent features while the *WrapperSubsetEval*, the *InfoGainAttributeEval* and the *GainRatioAttributeEval* algorithms rank all available features according to their predicting powers.

In our study, from a total of 19 candidate features the most prevalent features of the selection algorithms were split into two sets of importance marked in common with "1" and "2" (the most significant ones – selected by both *BestFirst* and *RandomSearch CfsSubSetEval* algorithms). Corollary, the eight most significant features were selected using these algorithms and marked with "1" and "2" (the most significant features). The results from all algorithms were marked in an aggregate table on a scale 1 to 4.

Typical examples of the features of this table (that refer to pre - contingency application saved *OPs* network indices) are:

- *PMargin1,2,4*: Active power margins. Calculated over $PI = \sum_{i=1}^{L} W_i \left(\frac{P_i}{\hat{P}_i} \right)^{2n}$, for

  values of n equal to 0.5, 1 and 2. [3], [5], [6], [7], [8]

- *QMargin1,2,4*: Reactive power margins. Calculated over $QI = \sum_{i=1}^{NG} W_{Q_i} \left(\frac{Q_i}{Q_i^{Max}} \right)^{2n}$,

  for values of n equal to 0.5, 1 and 2 respectively [9], [4]. An extensive discussion of indices that can be used for this problem is included in [10].

Table 1. Results from all features selections algorithms used marked in a scale of 1 to 4 (the most significant ones)

Features	C1	C2	C3	C4	C5	C6	C7	C8	C9	C10	C11	C12	C13	C14	C15
RedLoad%															
Lines															
TotalRating															
TotalPLoad															
TotalPGen	1														
TotalQLoad	1														
TotalQGen	1	3	1		2	3	2	2	1	1		1		1	2
VoltStabIdx		3	1	1		2			1				1	1	
MVAFlow			2			3									
MVAFlDivRat	1	1			1	2		2							
P%Losses															
PVIndex		2		2	3		2		2	1	2	2	2	2	
QVIndex		1		3											
PMargin1	1		2	2		2		2					1		2
PMargin2	3	2	3	1		1			1	1	1	1	1	1	1
PMargin4		1	2			1		1	2	2					
QMargin1		1	1			1	1		2	1			1		
QMargin2	2		2	2	1		1	1	1		1	1	1		1
QMargin4					2			1		1	3			1	

This way, for every contingency, four significant sets of features are formed. Features marked with "*4*" named "*red*" areas (the most significant ones), with "*3*" - "*orange*" areas, with "*2*" - "*green*" areas and with "*1*", "*grey*" areas (the less significant ones). In our study, the following sets of features were considered for cross validation contingency analysis:

- "*Red*" features.
- "*Red*" and "*orange*" features.
- "*Red*", "*orange*" and "*green*" features.
- "*Red*", "*orange*", "*green*" and "*grey*" features.
- *All* available features.

So, our proposed strategy consists of experimenting with the "most significant" sets of features, gradually enriching them with the "less and less significant" ones, ending up using all available features, no matter the redundancy. The proposed technique is useful for assessing the trade off of the enlarging set of features to the computational overhead. Like this, a "threshold" of features can be set for every examined contingency.

4 Experimental results

For all planned experiments and contingencies applied on the simulated *OPs*, the data were split in 70% - 30 % machine learning training and testing sets respectively and 40-fold cross validations were carried out, considered enough for avoiding bias.

The following machine learning algorithms were implemented: *J48* (C4.5 Decision Trees) [11], *NNge* (Nearest Neighbor with Generalization) [12], *BayesNet*

(K2, B Bayes networks) [13], *MLP - MultilayerPerceptron* [14]. The main conclusions of the study are:

- The *NNge* algorithm for all chromatic areas achieves the best predictions and exhibits the least diversions per chromatic area. Best predictions are then attained by the *J48*, the *MLP* and the *BayesNet* algorithms. (fig. 2(b)) After *NNge*, the *BayesNet* and the *J48* algorithms also exhibit smaller diversions per chromatic area than the *MLP* algorithm. (fig. 2(a))
- Fig. 5(b) shows that for the *BayesNet*, the *J48* and the *NNge* algorithms the orange area can be considered as a significant *threshold* set of features combining a relatively high predictability with a rather restricted set of features.

    The *MLP* algorithm exhibits a rather "greedy" behavior in what concerns extending chromatic areas of features (fig. 2(b)).

    On the contrary, the *BayesNet* algorithm for the orange area reaches its highest predictability further addition of features deteriorates its predictability (especially when all features are used). Langley and Sage [15], elucidate this behavior of the Bayesian algorithm mentioning that the predictability of the Bayesian algorithm is improved when redundant features are removed. This property of the Bayesian algorithm shown in fig. 2(b), supports our assumption of considering the orange area of features as a *threshold* set of features.

- It was also found that on a per contingency basis, for all chromatic areas and machine learning algorithms applied, the predictability of each contingency, when compared to the predictability of another contingency, it tends to fluctuate in a similar way. Thus, contingencies C_1 to C_8 tend to exhibit higher prediction rates and lower percentile correct prediction spread rates, while this does not seem the case for contingencies C_9 to C_{15}.

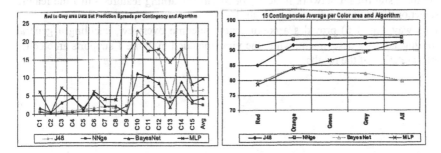

Fig. 2. (a) Maximal averaged percentile correct prediction spread rates among all chromatic areas for the *ML* algorithms (b) 15 Contingency *averaged* percentile correct prediction rates per chromatic area of data (including *all* available features) for the *ML* algorithms

We assume that these permanent fluctuations in the predictability of all contingencies depend on the "*nature*" of each contingency. Attempting to further interpret the role of the "nature" of a contingency, we presume that it can be explained in statistical and electrical terms.

In statistical terms, we suppose that the distribution of the outcome of the application of a contingency for all 1031 OPs to the classes ("Innocent", "Operating violations" and "Non conversion of the power flow algorithm") is related to the predictive powers of the machine learning algorithms. This relation is investigated next.

For this reason, we calculate the standard deviations of the class distribution outcomes of each contingency (fig. 1(b)). Provided that the standard deviations of all contingencies fluctuate between the values 93.11 to 566.91, dividing them by 6, we transform them in a percentile scale. Considering the best prediction curves for the *NNge* and the *J48* algorithms, we also transform the data on a percentile scale using the transformations $J48'(i) = (J48(i) - Min\{J48(1) .. J48(15)\})*10+2$ and $NNge' = (NNge(i) - Min\{NNge(1) .. NNge(15)\}) *10+5$, where the index i refers to any of the 15 contingencies. Then, the average of the *J48'* and *NNge'* prediction is considered. All transformations are depicted in fig. 3.

Comparing the *Std* and the *AVG* curves of fig. 3 for all 15 contingencies, we observe that the initial distribution of the effect of the contingencies to the network is related to the achieved prediction rates of the machine learning algorithms. This can be considered the *statistical* explanation to the *nature* of a contingency. Statistical analysis correlation coefficient ρ was found equal to 0.9605, demonstrating a strong correlation between these two curves.

5   Discussion of the Results

A rough electric profile of a contingency can be easily outlined through the contingency application outcome class distribution, as well as through the ranking of the most significant network indices - or machine learning features - that the feature selection algorithms indicate, see Table 1.

This way, fig. 1(b) provides a contingency outcome overview, enabling a general contingency risk assessment; while the view included in Table 1 supports an electric interpretation of the results.

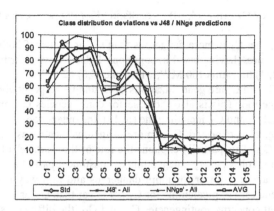

Fig. 3. 15 Contingency linear transformations of the class distribution outcomes standard deviations (fig. 2), versus the transformed *J48'* and *NNge'*, all features predictions.

Indeed, the most significant features can characterize a contingency as potentially harmful to the active power level, or the reactive power level / voltage profile, or both. So, when most significant network indices such as the "*MVAFlow*", "*MVAFlowDivRat*", the "*PVIndex*" or the "*Pmargin1,2,4*", are selected, then the contingency can be considered as potentially harmful at the active power level. When indices such as the "*VoltStabIdx*", the "*QVIndex*", or the "*QMargin1,2,4*" are selected as the most significant ones, then the contingency can be considered as potentially harmful to the reactive power / voltage profile level. When mixed indices are selected, then we can suppose the contingency exhibits a mixed behavior.

If we try to provide an electrical explanation of results such as prediction rates, most significant selected features and contingency distributions, we have to refer to the contingency definitions themselves.

Useful conclusions can come out of such an approach:

Contingencies C_9 to C_{15} include the *MVAFlow* and *MVAFlDivRat* features in the red area (containing the most significant features), while *PMargin1* and *PMargin4* features are included to subsequent orange and green areas. We can so consider these contingencies as potentially harmful to the active power level. From fig. 2, we can also observe similar contingency output distributions. If we refer to the contingency definitions, (fig. 1) we can conclude that the line (6,11) outage, that is common to all C_9 to C_{15} contingencies leads to active power level problems.

Corollary, contingencies like the C2, C5 and C7 indicating more significant features such as the *TotalQGen*, *VoltStabIdx*, *QMargin1* and *Qmargin4* can be considered as contingencies potentially harmful to the reactive power / voltage profile level. Contingencies as C_1 and C_4 exhibit a rather mixed behavior.

Experimental results indicate an incremental effect in what concerns the behavior of certain line outages (contained in certain contingency definitions). Thus, certain contingencies can be characterized by the cumulative effects of the line outages they contain.

For instance contingency C_1, that is a one-line outage contingency - (line (2, 4)) - causes "*Violations*" for 31% of *OP* cases. (fig. 2). On the contrary, the one line outage contingency C_2 - (line (4, 6)) – results in "*Violations*" for less than 4% of the cases.

We can suppose that C_1 is more dangerous than C_2, no matter if both contingencies are neighboring ones, (having bus 4 in common). Indeed, if we refer to the base case scenario, line (2, 4) transmits 100 MW, while line (4,6) 42 MW.

Contingencies C_8 and C_7 are generalizations of C_1 and C_2 respectively, including the (6, 7) line outage too. This is also the case for contingencies C_{10} and C_{11} that are generalizations of C_1 and C_2, including the (6, 11) line outage too.

According to fig. 2, as expected, C_8 is more dangerous than C_7 as well as C_{10} more dangerous than C_{11}. This partially explains the role of the "*nature*" of a contingency that also lies in the role of every outaged line as constituent part of a contingency.

Prediction rates are also lower for more dangerous and in a way more difficult to predict contingencies. So, predictions for C_1 are lower than C_2, as C_8 are lower than C_7, while in what concerns contingencies C_{10} and C_{11}, the differences in predictions are rather small.

6   Conclusions

Experimental results discussed in this article lead to interesting conclusions:

Graphical visualization of populations of features shows aggregation of outcome classes to Gaussian regions of interest and proves very helpful for contingency analysis. This applies to the distributions of the outcome of contingencies (fig. 2), as well as to the outcome per network index used.

Best *feature selection algorithms* tend to point out to the most significant power transmission indices and / or voltage profile indices, automatically sketching out the nature of a contingency.

The role of the *nature* of a contingency has been investigated. This is partially explained in statistical terms such as the contingency application outcome class distributions, the selected sets of features (chromatic areas) and the machine learning algorithms used. In electrical terms the role of constituent elements of each contingency has been analyzed, such as single line outages contained in contingency definitions, and the incremental effect of multiple components outage.

Experimental results lead to different sets of features that are suitable for predictions of each contingency. A threshold can be set between the number of features and the improved predictions trade-off. Machine learning tools and feature selection tools can be helpful at such a quest, also outlining the expected performance of classes of contingencies from a machine learning perspective.

The predictions have been checked against various training to testing data split quotas and exhibited high prediction rates for all cases, as well as common behaviors on a per contingency basis. Similar behaviors have been identified during data set feature selection analysis, machine learning tool selection analysis and data set split quota analysis. An optimization of all these factors on a per contingency basis can lead to improved predictions for steady state machine learning contingency analysis.

For the majority of the experiments carried out the nearest neighbor algorithm seems to achieve the best results. Generalizing, we can conclude that the application of instance based learning algorithms to static electric contingency analysis problems presents advantages.

The reported study combined machine learning techniques with statistical modeling, proving that such approaches are suitable for hard engineering applications in such fields like electrical networks analysis and operation.

References

1. Wehenkel L.A., "Automatic Learning Techniques in Power Systems", Kluwer Academic Publ., 1998
2. Cholley P., C. Lebrevelec, S. Vitet, M. de Pasquale, "A Statistical Approach to Assess Voltage Stability Limits", Bulk Power System Dynamics, and Control IV – Restructuring, August 24-28 1998, Santorini, Greece,
3. Hatziargyriou N.D., Contaxis G.C., Sideris N.C., "A decision tree method for on-line steady state security assessment", IEEE Trans. on Power Systems, Vol. 9, Nr. 2, May 1994, p. 1052
4. Ian H. Witten, Eibe Frank, "Practical Machine Learning Tools and Techniques with Java Implementations", Morgan Kaufmann Publishers, 2000
5. Albuyeh F., Bose A., Heath B., "Reactive power considerations in automatic contingency selection", IEEE Trans. on Power Apparatus and Systems, Vol.PAS-101, (1) 1982, p. 107
6. Mikolinnas T.A., Wollenberg B.F., "An advanced contingency selection algorithm", IEEE Transactions on Power Apparatus and Systems, Vol.PAS-100, No.2. February 1981, p.p. 608-611
7. Lauby M.G., Mikolinnas T.A., Reppen N.D., "Contingency selection of branch outages causing voltage problems", IEEE Transactions on Power Apparatus and Systems, Vol.PAS-102, No.12, December 1983, p.p. 3899-3904
8. Yuan-Yih Hsu, Han-Ching Kuo, "Fuzzy-set based contingency ranking", Transactions on Power Systems, Vol. 7, No. 3, August 1992
9. Ejebe G.C., Wollenberg B.F., "Automatic contingency selection", IEEE Transactions on Power Apparatus and Systems, Vol.PAS-98, No.1. Jan/Feb 1979, p.p. 97-109
10. Semitekos D., N. M. Avouris, "A Toolkit for Power systems Security Assessment Based on Hybrid Machine-Learning Techniques", International Journal of Engineering Intelligent Systems, EIS 358, 2004
11. Quinlan J.R., C4.5: Programs for Machine Learning, San Mateo, Morgan Kaufmann, 1993
12. Martin B., "Instance-Based learning: Nearest Neighbor With Generalization", Master Thesis, University of Waikato, Hamilton, New Zealand, 1995
13. Cooper G. and E. Herskovits, "A Bayesian method for the induction of probabilistic networks from data", Machine Learning, 9, 309-347, 1992
14. Minsky M. and S. Papert, "Perceptrons", Cambridge MA, MIT Press, 1969
15. Langley P. and S. Sage, "Induction of selective Bayesian classifiers", Proc. 10th Conference on Uncertainty in Artificial Intelligence, Seattle, W.A, 1994. Morgan Kaufmann.

Robust Multimodal Audio-Visual Processing for Advanced Context Awareness in Smart Spaces

Aristodemos Pnevmatikakis, John Soldatos, Fotios Talantzis
and Lazaros Polymenakos
Athens Information Technology
19,5 km Markopoulou Peania, Ave.
{apne, jsol, fota, lcp}@ait.edu.gr
http://www.ait.edu.gr

Abstract. Identifying people and tracking their locations is a key prerequisite to achieving context-awareness in smart spaces. Moreover, in realistic context-aware applications, these tasks have to be carried out in a non-obtrusive fashion. In this paper we present a set of robust person identification and tracking algorithms, based on audio and visual processing. A main characteristic of these algorithms is that they operate on far-field and un-constraint audio-visual streams, which ensures that they are non-intrusive. We also illustrate that the combination of their outputs can lead to composite multimodal tracking components, which are suitable for supporting a broad range of context-aware services. In combining audio-visual processing results, we exploit a context-modeling approach based on a graph of situations. Accordingly, we discuss the implementation of realistic prototype applications that make use of the full range of audio, visual and multimodal algorithms.

1 Introduction

The emerging Ubiquitous Computing paradigm aims at exploiting casually accessible sensors, devices and networks to transparently provide computing services, regardless of time and location of the user [1]. A core characteristic of ubiquitous computing environments is context sensitivity, which refers to the ability of ubiquitous devices/systems to react to their environment and adapt their behavior accordingly [2]. To this end, ubiquitous computing services are essentially context-aware, since they acquire and process information about their surrounding environment. This information is derived implicitly, without requiring end-users to provide explicit input. There are several approaches to derive implicit information. As a prominent example there are tag-based approaches, where tags are read to track

Please use the following format when citing this chapter:

Pnevmatikakis, Aristodemos, Soldatos, John, Talantzis, Fotios, Polymenakos Lazaros, 2006, in IFIP International Federation for Information Processing, Volume 204, Artificial Intelligence Applications and Innovations, eds. Maglogiannis, I., Karpouzis, K., Bramer, M., (Boston: Springer), pp. 290–301

objects and infer context [3]. Another approach is the wearable computing paradigm, where sensors and customized input-output operations are used to instrument humans [4]. Context-awareness can be also realized in smart spaces [5], which leverage sensors and effectors to achieve natural interaction between the humans and the environment.

In this paper we emphasize context-awareness in smart spaces. Context derivation in smart spaces relies on sophisticated audio-visual processing algorithms, which leverage audio and video sensors to derive context. For example, audio processing may be used to derive the location of speakers (i.e. acoustic localization). Similarly, processing of video streams can be used to track people location (i.e. visual person tracking), to detect faces (i.e. face detection), as well as recognize people (i.e. face recognition). A key challenge for these audio-visual processing algorithms is that they should be as non-intrusive as possible, which is in-line with the unobtrusive human-centric nature of context-aware applications in smart spaces. The audio and visual processing techniques introduced in this paper are aligned to this requirement, as they operate on far-field and un-constraint audio-visual streams. Hence the operation of the proposed algorithms does not require that human actors are under specific lighting conditions or have a particular orientation.

Another challenge is to combine context cues from both audio and video signal processing towards identifying more complex contextual states. Non-trivial context-aware applications need to identify composite situations based on combinations of elementary context cues about people identity and location, as well as context from other sources (e.g., sensors, other perceptual components). Along with the audiovisual processing algorithms, we also illustrate a context modeling approach for fusing context from these algorithms. This modeling approach is based on a graph of situations defining the situation of interest and the allowed transitions between them. While this approach is quite static, it can enable a wide range of context-aware applications, for example, relating to support for meeting and conferences, as well as security and surveillance. As prominent examples, we illustrate the implementation of context-aware actuating services, group activities recognition and memory aids in the scope of lectures, meeting and conferences. The rest of the paper is structured as follows: section 2 presents algorithms for deriving context based on far-field visual processing, while section 3 elaborates on audio processing algorithms for speaker localization and tracking. Section 4 illustrates our context modeling approach based on the network of situations techniques. Section 5 discusses some real-life prototype applications that leverage both the presented algorithms and the introduced situation modeling technique. Finally section 6 concludes the paper.

2 Visual Processing

The block diagram of the visual system is shown in Fig. 1. It comprises a detector that operates on video streams and a recognizer that provides the identity of the faces detected over a time interval. The detector begins with a tracker that segments the bodies from the video streams. This is based on Stauffer's [6] adaptive background estimation. Compared to a static background, the adaptive approach fades into the background lighting variations and furniture movements. This is coupled with a shadow detector [7] to get rid of shadows that deform the extracted body shapes and cause false alarms of target collisions. In order not to fade the bodies into the background when the people remain stationery, the gated approach of [8] is used to treat the found bodies as targets and the region around a target in a frame as a gate, i.e. as the region where it is expected to find the target in the next frame. Should the background adaptation fade an immobile body by diminishing the foreground pixels inside the gate, the target is not lost; the estimated body position and the gate remain the same as in the previous frame.

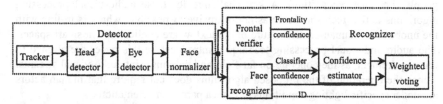

Fig. 1. Block diagram of the complete face detection and recognition system

Target collisions are handled both while they occur, and after they finish. The former is important for smart room applications, where people can be collaborating for some time and have their targets overlapping. At collisions, the involved targets are merged into a super-gate, in which the known number of bodies is sought. Handling during collision is the attempt to keep the targets approximately separated using k-means. When a collision finishes, it is important not to swap the tracks, since face recognition is based on each track. This is done by matching the 2D histogram of normalized red and green color components of each of the post-collision targets to those of the pre-collision targets.

Heads are detected by processing the outline of the body. The derivative of the width of the body as a function of its height at shoulder level increases significantly, indicating the beginning of the head. This approach fails at profile views and at bent-over bodies; in those cases just a fixed percentage of the body height over width is passed as head, usually resulting to overestimated head regions. This degrades both the speed and the accuracy of the eye detector that follows. The latter is not very troublesome, as profile faces are useless for recognition.

The eye detector operates inside the head region. The approach followed is based on vector quantization of the colors and face geometry constraints. Since thick, raised hair with highlights deteriorates detection performance, the face region inside the head is estimated by processing the edge image of the head region (Fig. 2.a). The vertical and horizontal sums of pixels in the edge image drop rapidly outside the face region and the face is finally confined within sums that are above 85% of the sum means across every direction. The colors of the pixels of the face are vector-quantized to 6 colors, to identify distinct regions inside the face (Fig. 2.b). Properties of the regions are used to identify eye candidates. The properties related to color are brightness and resemblance to human skin. The latter is evaluated using the human skin color histogram of [9]. Both these quantities should be low, since, at the targeted resolution, eyes usually are a blur. The properties related to shape are the extent and the roundness of the regions. Finally, the properties related to face geometry are the center locations of the regions, which are mildly constrained inside the head region. These constraints can lead to misses at profile views, but this is not troublesome, since profiles are not useful for recognition. The eye positions are estimated by searching for the darkest spots near the candidate region centers. Based on them, the faces are normalized to standard size. Eye detection errors of more than 10% of the eye distance usually result to misclassifications. Only smaller errors are regarded a hit. The hit rate as a function of eye distance increases abruptly in the 16 to 18 pixels range. Hit rates below 30% for eye distances close to 10 pixels are not unexpected; one pixel of error is not unusual for human annotators! As expected, the RMS eye detection error relative to the eye distance drops as the face resolution increases.

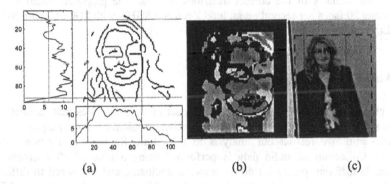

(a)   (b)   (c)

Fig. 2. Eye detector. (a) Estimation of the face inside the head region. (b) Regions after vector quantization. (c) Body, head and eyes

The recognizer is based on the PCA+LDA combination [10]. Even though there are methods less sensitive to eye detection [11], these are much slower and hence not suitable for real-time operation. The system is trained to recognize 16 people. This is a reasonable number for smart room applications. Although intensity preprocessing helps under illumination changes [10], it is destructive under pose and expression changes [10], so it is not used. To account for the effect of imperfect eye detection [11], the manually annotated eye positions of the ten training faces per person are deliberately perturbed to every one of their eight neighbors, in total creating 81 training faces form every original one [8]. This produces an RMS eye perturbation of 2% of the eye distance, effectively matching the training and testing conditions.

After recognition, each detected face is associated with an identity *ID* and two confidence values *W* and *D*. *W* is the confidence the classifier has about the decision that person k_1 is the best-matching, compared to the second-best, k_2. This can be expressed as the ratio of the distance d_2 of the testing face from the center of k_2, over its distance d_1 from the center of k_1:

$$W = d_2/d_1 \qquad (1)$$

D is related to the certainty of the system that the face is frontal. This can be expressed as the Distance From Face Space (DFFS) [12] when the projection is done on 12.5% of the eigenfaces with the largest eigenvalues. W and D are combined into a single confidence value C as:

$$C = W^6 \cdot 2^{-D/3277} \qquad (2)$$

As the detector is not perfect and suitable faces are not always available, the system accumulates identities and confidences over some time interval T and fuses them into a single identity using the sum rule [13]. This decision fusion scheme renders the system very robust to eye misalignments and pose changes. The system is tested two months after training, with three videos per person, using three different camera zoom settings. As a result the eye distances are between 8 and 28 pixels. Even though 57.8% of the individual recognitions failed, the system always yields the correct identity from on average the 2nd frame onwards, as the average of the sum of the confidences of the correct decisions is 72%. The proposed visual system processes 20 faces per second on an Intel Zeon at 2.8GHz, with 2Gb of RAM, SUSE 9.3 Linux and using the Intel IPP libraries.

3 Audio Processing

The processing of audio streams provides a set of functionalities that facilitate the localization, recognition and context interpretation problems. For the purposes of the present work we restrict our analysis to the Audio Source Localization (ASL) system. Collection of audio data is performed using a total of 80 microphones located in different places inside the acoustic enclosure and organized in different topologies. More analytically, there is a 64 channel linear microphone array and four smaller clusters of microphones, each containing four microphones. Each of the microphone clusters has the microphones organized in an inverted T topology.

A dominant requirement in the dynamic environments in which the microphones are employed is the localization of speakers. This is generally dealt with the estimation of the direction of arrival (DOA) of the acoustic source by means of time delay estimation (TDE) algorithms. Estimation of DOA essentially provides us with the direction from which sound is arriving from. Typically, audio data is collected in frames so that the current TDE estimate can be provided. Combination of several DOAs can then provide us with the actual source position.

The practical and, in many ways, severely restricting disadvantage of traditional methods for TDE [14] is that if the system is used in reverberant environments, the returned estimate could be a spurious delay created by the ensuing reflections. For the purposes of our system, we have proposed [15] a new mathematical framework that resolves to great amount the reverberation issues and generates robust estimations. It is thus of interest to briefly investigate the used model.

Consider two of the microphones with a distance d between them. The sound source is assumed to be in the far field of the array. For the case in which the environment is non-reverberant, the assumption of a single source leads to the following discrete-time signal being recorded at the mth microphone (where $m=1, 2$):

$$x_m(k) = s_m(k - \tau_m) + n_m(k) \tag{3}$$

where τ_m denotes the time in samples that it takes for the source signal to reach the mth microphone, and n_m is the respective additive noise (assumed to be zero mean and uncorrelated with the source signal). The overall geometry of the corresponding system can be seen in Fig. 3. Without loss of generality, this considers m_1 to be the reference microphone, i.e., $\tau_1=0$. The delay at m_2 is then the relative delay between the two recorded signals, and thus, the relationship is reduced to $x_1(k)=x_2(k-\tau_2)$. The DOA is defined with respect to the broadside of the array as a function of any delay τ as:

$$\theta = \arcsin\left[\frac{\tau c}{f_s d}\right] \tag{4}$$

where f_s is the sampling frequency, and c is the speed of sound (typically defined as 343 m/s). Thus, DOA estimation methods rely on successful estimation of τ. However, in a real reverberant environment, each of the microphone recordings are a result of a convolution operator between the speech signal and a reverberant impulse response of significant length (depending on the reverberation level).

In order to overcome the problems introduced by reverberation we make use of the concept of mutual information (MI) by tailoring it appropriately to the tracking of an acoustic source. A review of the concept can be found in the work of Bell et al. [16].

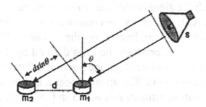

Fig. 3. Geometry of the recording system

Most of the DOA estimation techniques are required to operate in real time. We must, therefore, assume that data at each sensor m are collected over t frames $x_m=[x_m(tL), x_m(tL+1),..., x_m(tL+L-1)]$ of L samples. Since the analysis will be independent of the data frame, we can drop t to express frames simply as x_m for any t. In the context of our model, and for any set of frames, we may then write

$$x_1 = x_2(\tau) \tag{5}$$

where $x_m(\tau)$ denotes a delayed version of x_m by τ samples. Thus, the problem is to estimate the correct value of and the DOA by processing two frames x_1 and $x_2(\tau)$ only.

If we were to neglect reverberation, only a single delay is present in the microphone signals. Thus, the measurement of information contained in a sample l of x_1 is only dependent on the information contained in sample l-τ of $x_2(\tau)$. In the case of the reverberant model, though, information contained in a sample l of x_1 is also contained in neighboring samples of sample l-τ of $x_2(\tau)$ due to the fact that the model is now convolutive. The same logical argument applies to the samples of $x_2(\tau)$. In order to estimate the information between the microphone signals, we use the marginal MI that considers jointly N neighboring samples and can be formulated as follows [17] for the case where the recordings exhibit Gaussian behavior

$$I_N = -\frac{1}{2}\ln\frac{\det[C(\tau)]}{\det[C_{11}]\det[C_{22}]} \tag{6}$$

with the joint covariance matrix $C(\tau)$ given as

$$C(\tau) \approx \begin{bmatrix} x_1 \\ x_1(1) \\ \vdots \\ x_1(N) \\ x_2(\tau) \\ x_2(\tau+1) \\ \vdots \\ x_2(\tau+N) \end{bmatrix}\begin{bmatrix} x_1 \\ x_1(1) \\ \vdots \\ x_1(N) \\ x_2(\tau) \\ x_2(\tau+1) \\ \vdots \\ x_2(\tau+N) \end{bmatrix}^T = \begin{bmatrix} C_{11} & C_{12}(\tau) \\ C_{21}(\tau) & C_{22} \end{bmatrix} \tag{7}$$

If N is chosen to be greater than zero, the elements of $C(\tau)$ are themselves matrices. In fact, for any value of τ, the size of $C(\tau)$ is always $2(N+1)\times2(N+1)$. For the purposes of the present letter, we call N the *order* of the tracking system. When $C(\tau)$ reaches a maximum as a function of at a specific time shift τ, then there is at this point a joint process with a maximum transport of information between x_1 and $x_2(\tau)$. According to the presented information-theoretical criterion, this is the delay that synchronizes the two recordings. In the context of DOA, this delay returns the correct angle θ, at which the signal coincides with the microphone array.

The last step in the ASL process is the combination of several DOA estimates, in order to get the actual 3D coordinates of the speaker. This is performed by calculating the crossing points between the lines defined by the estimated DOAs. In most cases these lines cross in more than one point and thus, the speaker lies within some area defined by these points. The speaker position is found by, employment of a closed-form source location estimator as found in [18]. This estimator represents a tremendous computational saving over other exhaustive search methods.

The DOAs that feed the estimation of the 3D coordinates are provided by considering a series of microphone pairs in the enclosure. The system is able to provide coordinates in space because as discussed earlier, the inverted T arrays have microphones in different planes.

4 Context Modeling

Our context modeling approach relies on the network of situations paradigm [19,20]. According to this paradigm the contextual states of interest are structured into a graph where the nodes denote the target states ST and the arcs ed the possible transitions between contextual states. Specifically, edge ed_{ij} denotes that it is possible to reach state ST_j from state ST_i.

Contextual states may be arbitrarily complex in terms of their defining cues. The situation model is accompanied by a truth table, which depicts the underlying combination of audio or visual processing component outputs that trigger each one of the composite contextual states. To formally specify how the situation transitions occur, assume that the smart space is supported by m components having $k_1, k_2, \ldots, k_m$ outputs respectively and let $k = \max(k_1, k_2, \ldots, k_m)$. Without any loss of generality we can represent the observed outputs of all perceptual components at a given time instant t using the matrix:

$$P_{out}(t) = \{p_{ij}(t)\}, \text{ where } 1<i<m \text{ and } 1<j<k \qquad (8)$$

where $p_{ij}(t)=0$ for $j>k_i$, since there are perceptual components providing less than k outputs. As a result, $P_{out}(t)$ contains the observations of the perceptual components outputs at time instant t.

For each situation ST_l ($1<l<m$) targeted by a situation model we define a matrix S_l comprising the target values of the perceptual components that according to the situation modeling lead to ST_l, as follows:

$$S_l = \{s_{ij}\}, 1<i<m, 1<j<k \qquad (9)$$

where $s_{ij} \neq 0$ if the j-th output of the i-th perceptual component contributes in the triggering the state ST_l and $s_{ij} = 0$ otherwise. Towards associating with the non-zero s_{ij} values with the observed outputs $p_{ij}(t)$, we perform an element-wise multiplication of $P_{out}(t)$, with the following matrix:

$$A_l = \{a_{ij}\}, 1<i<m, 1<j<k \qquad (10)$$

where $a_{ij}=1$ if $s_{ij} \neq 0$ and $a_{ij}=0$ otherwise. The result of the element-wise multiplication is a P_l matrix filtering the observed outputs in a way that only values defining the state ST_l are retained:

$$P_l = \{a_{ij} \cdot p_{ij}(t)\}, 1<i<m \text{ and } 1<j<k \qquad (11)$$

ST_l occurs when all the elements of the matrices P_l and S_l coincide i.e.:

$$S_l - P_l = \{s_{ij} - a_{ij}\, p_{ij}\} = O_{mk} \qquad (12)$$

where O_{mk} corresponds to the matrix having all its elements equal to zero. In practice, due to perceptual component inaccuracies (i.e. measurement errors) it is rare to achieve a total agreement between target and observed values. Therefore, the triggering of the situation may be defined as the case when the elements of the two matrices almost coincide, thus allowing the observed outputs to somewhat deviate from the target values:

$$S_l - P_l = \{s_{ij} - a_{ij}\, p_{ij}\} = E_l \{e_{ij}\} \qquad (13)$$

where $|e_{ij}|<thr$. In order for situation ST_l to be triggered, (13) has to be fulfilled, while at the same time the situation model has to be on a state ST_p that allows transition to ST_l. Therefore:

$$ST_p \rightarrow ST_l \text{ occurs whenever } |s_{ij} - a_{ij}\, p_{ij}| <thr \text{ and } ed_{pl}=1 \qquad (14)$$

Note that this network of situations approach is general and applicable not only to audio-visual processing outputs but also to more general class of observations, which may include any sensor signals. In practice the matrix S_l is likely to be very sparse, which can greatly simplify (13). It is also noteworthy that (8)-(13) assume numeric values for perceptual components. While this may sound limiting, it is in general possible to encode several other domains as numbers.

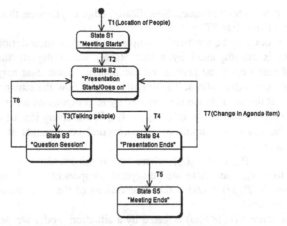

Fig. 4. Situation Model tracking different states within a meeting

Fig. 4 depicts a sample situation model for tracking activities in a meeting. The situation model consists of five states corresponding to the commencement of a meeting, the start of a presentation during the meeting, a question on the presentation, the end of a presentation and the end of a meeting. The arcs in Fig. 4 denote the possible transitions. For example a question can only occur, while a presentation is in progress, since there is no means to reach state ST_3 unless the model is in ST_2. Table 1 illustrates how particular situation states are triggered based on underlying perceptual components. NIL denotes the starting state. As an example the start of the meeting (i.e. the transition NIL$\rightarrow ST_1$) occurs when an expected number of people are speaking very close to the table. Given a number of perceptual components (i.e. TablePeopleCount (based on Face Detection), WhiteBoardPeopleCount (based on Face Detection), Speech Activity Detection, Acoustic Localization) and their APIs, Table 1 can be mapped to equation (13) in a straightforward way. Nevertheless, the mapping is in general service specific since the elements of the matrices $E_1, E_2,..., E_5$ (see equation (13)) are likely to be defined based on the problem at hand.

Table 1. Mapping Perceptual Component Outputs to Situation Transitions

Situation Transition	Combinations of Perceptual Components Outputs
NIL → S1	*TablePeopleCount=N (N people in table area), Speech Activity Detection=1*
S1 → S2	*WhiteBoardPeopleCount=1 (1 in board area), TablePeopleCount=N-1 (N-1 in table area), Acoustic Localization = (X, Y) within the board Area*
S2 → S3	*Acoustic Localization = (X, Y) within the Table Area*
S3 → S2	*Acoustic Localization = (X, Y) within the board Area*
S2 → S4	*TablePeopleCount=N, WhiteBoardPeopleCount=0*
S4 → S2	*WhiteBoardPeopleCount=1, TablePeopleCount=N-1 Acoustic Localization = (X, Y) within the board Area*
S4 → S5	*TablePeopleCount=0 (everybody has left)*

5 Prototype Applications

A number of prototype context-aware applications have been developed based on the algorithms and the context modeling approach illustrated above. These applications are fully functional within our prototype smart space, which consists of a variety of sensors, devices and perceptual components.

The intelligent display service selects the optimal display device according the location of the target person(s) within a smart room. A smart space may have more than one means to display information. The service selects the device that is more convenient for the room participants. This is accomplished through examining display requests it in relation to the current users' context. The context of interest includes the location and orientation of participants, which are tracked based on the audio/visual processing techniques detailed above. The algorithm attempts to provide a satisfactory view for as many participants as possible.

The intelligent meeting recorder is a recording service, which can be instantiated for any of the cameras within the smart space. A realistic meeting recording service is expected to operate like an automated intelligent camera-man. In particular, an ambient recording selects the optimal camera view based on the location and orientation of the participants, as well as based on their activities and role within the group interaction. A thorough description of this service can be found in [21].

The memory jog pervasive service aims at providing non-obtrusive assistance to humans during meetings, lectures and presentations in the smart space [22]. The service identifies participants and tracks their locations within the smart room. It also keeps track of meeting progress based on a known agenda. Moreover, it records the event based on the best-camera selection mechanism. The recording is tagged with meta-data from the situation model of the service, to allow selective retrieval of the recording. The memory jog can also provide context-aware assistance through displaying relevant information from past meetings. The memory jog relies on all the audio-visual perceptual components presented above and exploits the situation model of Fig. 4 to follow higher level situations such as agenda tracking, questions tracking, meeting commencement and meeting finish.

6 Conclusions

In this paper we presented a set of robust audiovisual processing systems able to support the emerging wave of ubiquitous computing services. These systems acquire information implicitly and unobtrusively; further processing provides context-awareness. Thus the audio-visual streams are processed in order to answer the questions who, where and what. With the systems presented we can robustly identify people, find their location, track their movement and activities in an in-door multi-sensor environment. Situation modeling based on the audiovisual information acquired supplies the middleware foundation for advanced ubiquitous computing services. We presented 3 such services - the intelligent display, the intelligent meeting recorder and the memory jog. Future work will investigate more dynamic situation modeling, scalability (more participants and sensors), extendibility (more perceptual components) and the enhancement of user experience in the smart spaces.

Acknowledgements

This work is sponsored by the European Union under the integrated project CHIL, contract number 506909.

References

1. M. Weiser, "The Computer for the 21st Century" Scientific American, vol. 265, no. 3, 1991, pp. 66–75.
2. D. Anind, D. Salber and G. Abowd, 'A conceptual framework and a toolkit for supporting the rapid prototyping of context-aware applications', Human-Computer Interaction, 16,. 2001.
3. R. Want, A. Hopper, V. Falcao and J. Gibbons, 'The Active Badge location System', ACM Transactions on Information Systems 10(1), pp. 91-102, January 1992.
4. A. Smailagic, D.P. Siewiorek "Application Design for Wearable and Context-Aware Computers", IEEE Pervasive Computing Vol. 1 No. 4 Dec. 2002 pp. 20-29.
5. B. Johanson, A. Fox and T. Winograd. 'The Interactive Workspaces Project: Experiences with Ubiquitous Computing Rooms', IEEE Pervasive Computing Magazine Vol. 1 No. 2, April-June 2002.
6. C. Stauffer and W. Grimson, "Adaptive background mixture models for real-time tracking", CVPR, pp. 246–252, 1999
7. L-Q. Xu, J. Landabaso and M. Pardàs, "Shadow Removal with Blob-Based Morphological Reconstruction for Error Correction", ICASSP 2005
8. A. Pnevmatikakis and L. Polymenakos, "An Automatic Face Detection and Recognition System for Video Streams", *2nd Joint Workshop on Multimodal Interaction and Related Machine Learning Algorithms*, Edinburgh, July 2005
9. M. Jones and J. Rehg. "Statistical color models with application to skin detection", *Computer Vision and Pattern Recognition*, pp. 274–280, 1999
10. E. Rentzeperis, A. Stergiou, A. Pnevmatikakis and L. Polymenakos, "Impact of Face Registration Errors on Recognition", AIAI 2006, accepted for publication
11. A. Pnevmatikakis and L. Polymenakos, "A Testing Methodology for Face Recognition Algorithms", *Lecture Notes in Computer Science*, Vol. 3869, 2005
12. M. Turk and A. Pentland, "Eigenfaces for Recognition", *J. Cognitive Neuroscience*, pp. 71-86, March 1991
13. J. Kittler, M. Hatef, R.P.W. Duin and J. Matas, "On combining classifiers", *IEEE Trans. Pattern Anal. Mach. Intell.*, Vol. 20, No. 3 pp. 226–239, March 1998
14. C. H. Knapp and G. C. Carter, "The generalized correlation method for estimation of time delay," IEEE Trans. Acoust., Speech, Signal Process., vol. ASSP-24, no. 4, pp. 320–327, Aug. 1976.
15. F. Talantzis, A. G. Constantinides, and L. Polymenakos, "Estimation of Direction of Arrival Using Information Theory," IEEE Signal Processing, vol. 12, no. 8, pp. 561-564, Aug. 2005.
16. A. Bell and T. Sejnowski, "An information maximization approach to blind separation and blind deconvolution," Neural Comput., vol. 7, pp. 1129–1159, 1995.
17. T. M. Cover and J. A. Thomas, Elements of Information Theory. New York: Wiley, 1991.

18.J. Smith and J. Abel, "Closed-form least-squares source location estimation from range-difference measurements," IEEE Trans. Acoust., Speech, Signal Processing, vol. ASSP-35, pp. 1661–1669, Dec. 1987.
19.J. L. Crowley, 'Context Driven Observation of Human Activity', in the Proc. of the European Symposium on Ambient Intelligence, Oct. 2003.
20.J. Soldatos, I. Pandis, K. Stamatis, L. Polymenakos, J. Crowley, 'A Middleware Infrastructure for Autonomous Context-Aware Computing Services', Computer Communications Magazine, special Issue on Emerging Middleware for Next Generation Networks, to appear 2006.
21.S. Azodolmolky, N. Dimakis, V. Mylonakis, G. Souretis, J. Soldatos, A. Pnevmatikakis, L. Polymenakos, 'Middleware for In-door AmbientIntelligence: The PolyOmaton System', in the Proc. of the 2nd NGNM workshop, Networking 2005, Waterloo, Canada, May 2005.
22.J. Soldatos, L. Polymenakos, A. Pnevmatikakis, F. Talantzis, K. Stamatis and M. Carras, 'Perceptual Interfaces and Distributed Agents supporting Ubiquitous Computing Services', in the Proc. of the Eurescom Summit 2005, April 2005, pp. 43-50.

Toward supporting group dynamics

Fabio Pianesi, Massimo Zancanaro, Vera Falcon, Elena Not
ITC-irst
Via Sommarive, 18
38050 Povo Trento Italy
{pianesi,zancana,falcon,not}@itc.it

Abstract. The complexity of group dynamics occurring in small group interactions often hinders the performance of teams. The availability of rich multimodal information about what is going on in meetings makes it possible to explore ways of providing support to dysfunctional teams from facilitation to training sessions, addressing both the individuals and the group as a whole. A necessary step in this direction is that of capturing and understanding group dynamics. In this paper, we discuss a particular scenario, in which meeting participants receive a multimedia feedback on their relational behavior, as a first step towards increasing self-awareness. We describe the background and the motivation for a coding scheme partially inspired by the Bales' Interaction Process Analysis aimed at identifying suitable observable behavioral sequences and an experimental investigation on the acceptability of such a service.

1 Introduction

Most of the current research work in using multimodality to support group interaction is aimed toward providing easy access to computerized services for the group to efficiently accomplish its tasks [12]. For example, in the CHIL project, most of the services provided are aimed at offering better ways of connecting people (the Connector service) and supporting human memory (the Memory Jog) [32]. The research in the AMI project mostly focuses on off-line multimedia retrieval and multimedia browsing of information obtained from meetings [26]. The DARPA-funded project CALO supports a group in creating a project schedule by automatically interpreting gestures and speech, including the learning of new words [21].

In the field of CSCW where the focus is often in distributed meetings, the social relationships among the participants of a meeting has been recognized as a

Please use the following format when citing this chapter:

Pianesi, Fabio, Zancanaro, Massimo, Falcon, Vera, Not, Elena, 2006, in IFIP International Federation for Information Processing, Volume 204, Artificial Intelligence Applications and Innovations, eds. Maglogiannis, I., Karpouzis, K., Bramer, M., (Boston: Springer), pp. 302–311

fundamental aspect of the meetings' efficacy since the seminal work of Tang [30]. Although in face to face interactions visibility and awareness of others' behaviour is not a problem, the success of a meeting is often hindered by how participants behave. According to a survey in [14] professionals agree that as much as 50% of meeting time is unproductive and that up to 25% of meeting time is spent discussing irrelevant issues. In order to improve meetings performance, external interventions such as facilitators and training experiences are commonly employed. Facilitators are neutral and non-evaluating servants of the meeting group. Their role is to help participants maintain a fair and focused behavior during the meeting, directing and setting the pace of the discussion. They help and solicit the group agreement about content to be analyzed and about the correct process to adopt to reach a viable solution. They protect individuals from personal attacks and are responsible for maintaining an open and balanced conversational flow (preventing monologues and assuring everyone gets a change to express their ideas).

Ideally, systems for CSCW in co-located settings should include virtual facilitators who "observe" and analyze the behavior of meeting participants, by means of audio/visual sensory devices, and intervene to mediate the discussion. Obviously, this is an extremely challenging design- and implementation-task, requiring incremental steps of problem dissection and solving. First and foremost, the acceptability of suggestions and directives based on social observations coming from a virtual facilitator need to be assessed. Would a meeting participant consider as reliable and acceptable suggestions like: "Bob, you're sure doing a lot of talking. Let's hear from some of the other people[1]", when coming from a virtual facilitator? Would he be willing to change his behavior after that, therefore impacting on the group dynamics? And, more in general: would he be willing to be observed and analyzed in his social behavior? Indeed, the shift of focus from task-based functionalities commonly supported in CSCW systems to functionalities targeting the social behavior is not only difficult from a technical point of view but also challenging from a design point of view since it can be expected that these types of services trigger complex, and possibly negative, reactions from the users. The problem is too rich of complex facets to be addressed as a whole.

To take a step at a time, our research is currently focusing on the latter two questions above: would meeting participants accept to work in an augmented environment whose task is not merely to provide technological support but also that of deliberately keeping trace of their behavior and understanding their role in the discussion? To better isolate the variables to be evaluated, we decided to shift from the facilitator-scenario, where high interactivity and human-computer dialogue is involved, to a simplified scenario where the meeting participant is confronted with the external, virtual, observer just at the end of the meeting. We therefore investigated the feasibility, the usefulness and the acceptability of a functionality inspired by *coaching*; it consists of a report about the social behaviour of individual participants that is generated from multimodal information, and privately delivered to them. The underlining idea is that the individual, the group(s) they are parts of, and the whole organization might benefit from an increased awareness of participants about their own behavior during meetings.

[1] This sample sentence has been taken from [14], page 101.

The main goal of this paper is to discuss the users' response to such a multimodal system. In order to investigate the grounds of our approach, we also present a coding scheme for annotating observed group dynamics as a prerequisite for the actual realization of social-aware services (of which the relational report is one example).

2 Supporting Group Efficacy by Relational Reports

In social psychology, the "Ringelmann effect" or "social loafing" postulates that the individuals' performances decrease with the size of the group [23; 20]. Indeed, there is evidence that this effect has a lesser impact when the amount of contribution of each participant can be compared to the contribution of the others [18]. The usefulness of an external feedback has also been considered in the multimodal coaching field [7; 25], based on the support provided to users by embodied conversational agents.

In discussing the role of collaboration for teachers, Andersen [1] suggests that peer coaching sessions among teachers provide a scheduled opportunity to step out of the reflexive mode and think reflectively, and that the coaching process allows the externalization of both tough contents and processes that are normally internal, making them available to examination. Reflective thinking is fundamental in the development of meta-strategic knowledge [24]. That is, the kind of knowledge that experts possess about their own thinking and that includes information about the effectiveness and applicability of various strategies. There are three stages in the reflective process [10]: (i) the return to experience (what happened?); (ii) attending to feelings (how did I feel, why did I act or react this way?); and (iii) the re-evaluation of the experience (what does it mean?). Reflective thinking, as noted by Andersen [2], can be effectively fostered in coaching relationship. The coach is a "different observer" than the coachee; by bringing a different perspective to the relationship, the coach can see both circumstances and possibilities that the coachee can't [9].

In our work we propose a multimodal system that monitors the group behavior and generates individual reports about the participants' behavior. The system observes the meeting as a coach would do, and not as a recorder. This means that the system does not keep trace of exactly what people said and what they did as the meeting goes by. The generated reports are not minutes, but represent a more qualitative, meta-level interpretation of what happened in the social dynamics of the group. They do not contain information like "in the first part of the meeting you have talked for ten minutes about machine learning techniques useful to solve the problem" but rather "in the first part of the meeting you have provided the group with background information" or "you have prevented others from intervening in the discussion". The reports are delivered privately to each participant after the meeting, with the purpose of informing them about their behavior rather than evaluate it. Hence, the system acts as a coach for the individual group participants. Since the coaching relationship is based upon trust and permission [13], we may expect problems regarding acceptability to arise.

2.1 A Sample Multimedia Relational Report

The technological plausibility and feasibility of the automatic generation of these *relational reports* is supported by the fast growing results gained in the field of multimodal multiparty meeting processing [25], which make more reliable the multimodal perception and understanding of a wide array of information sources (speech, voice tone and prosody, gestures, handwriting, sketches and other manual activity, body and head posture, eye gaze, ...).

The relational reports are generated by a rule-based system starting from a "social" annotation of the meeting according to the coding scheme described in the next section. The report is built according to the task and socio-emotional roles simultaneously assumed by the speaker during the interaction. Each final relational report has the form of a multimedia presentation where a talking head describes the behavior of the participant in an informative rather than normative way. The presentation is enriched with short audio-video clips from the actual meeting that exemplify the information presented. An example of the relational reports we are considering is the following: "You have actively contributed to the meeting." while showing a neutral expression. Then, the talking head changes into an happy expression, and continues "You've helped to focus the discussion on the relevant topics and have provided useful information and opinions to clarify some of the issues. At the beginning and at the end of the meeting, you have kept records of various aspects of group progress." Finally, moving to a sad expression she adds: "You have profitably cooperated with your colleagues, even though a contrast with R.Z. emerged during the first part of the meeting."

3 Observing Group Behavior

A coding scheme for annotating group behaviour should, in the first place, be usable by human annotators. This is needed both for exploratory research aiming at understanding relevant social phenomena and assessing the coding scheme, and to provide data bases that can be used to train systems. Then, the categories of coding scheme must be capable of mapping onto constellations of low-level patterns that can be detected through vision and speech.

Among the available notions of group members' roles [22], that defining them in terms of behaviour enacted in a particular context was of particular interest to us. Indeed, that notion moves away from a strictly organizational perspective in which roles are defined by the social positions within the group, and it differs from approaches defining roles according to the social expectation associated with a given position [22]. In other words, functional roles allow exploiting information about what actually happened in the course of the interaction, while reducing the necessity for knowledge about the group' structure, history, position in the organization, etc.

Benne and Sheats [6] provided a list of "functional roles" recognizable in working groups, according to which interest is predominant in the behaviour: task-oriented, maintenance-oriented or individual-oriented. The first two kinds of roles are directed toward the group's need: *task-oriented roles* provide facilitation and coordination, while *maintenance roles* contribute to structure and preserve interpersonal relations, in order to reduce tensions and maintain smooth group functioning. The third type of roles, the *individual roles*, is "individual-centred" and performed in order to reach individual need rather than group's goals. During the interaction, each person can enact more than one role. Even if a definite answer to the quest for "optimal" group productivity is not provided, the authors emphasise the threat due to a strong presence of individual roles, and the importance of achieving the task and maintaining the relationship between members.

Similarly, Bales [4] proposed the Interaction Process Analysis, a framework to study small group interaction, by classifying roles in face-to-face interaction in a two-dimensional space.

Building on Benne and Sheats's functional roles and on Bales' two dimensional approach, and drawing on observations performed on a set of face-to-face meetings, a coding scheme was produces consisting of five labels for the Task Area and five labels for the Socio Emotional Area. The *Task Area* includes functional roles related to facilitation and coordination tasks as well as to technical experience of members, while *Socio Emotional Area* concerns the relationships between group members and the functional roles oriented toward the functioning of the group.

The Task Area roles are the following.

Orienteer: is the person orienting the group. S/He introduces the items on the agenda, defining the position of the group relative to the goals and helps keeping the group focused and on track. S/He summarizes the main ideas of the group, recording the most important arguments in the discussion, the minutes, and the group decisions. S/He spells out suggestions in terms of examples or develops meanings, offers a rationale for suggestions previously made and tries to deduce how an idea would work out if adopted by the group.

Giver (Information, Opinion, Suggestion): is the person providing factual information and answering to questions: s/he often has expertise on a given topic. S/He states his/her beliefs and attitudes about an idea: expresses personal values as opposed to factual information; shows or clarifies the relationship or linkage among various ideas and suggestions, trying to pull them together.

Seeker (Information, Opinion, Suggestion): S/He requests suggestions and information to promote effective group decisions. S/He can also ask for clarification of values and opinions expressed by other members of the group.

Procedural technician is the person who does something for the group. S\He uses the material resources available to the group, managing them for the sake of the group.

Follower: S/He listens, does not participate actively to the interaction.

The roles pertaining to the Socio Emotional Area are the following.

Attacker: S/He may work in many ways – deflating the status of others, expressing disapproval of the values, acts or feelings of others, attacking the group or the problem it is working on, joking aggressively, showing envy toward another's contribution by trying to take credit for it. S/He consistently reacts negatively to other's ideas: makes very critical comments, usually indirectly using humor.

Gate-keeper: S/He is the moderator within the group, who mediates the communicative relations: s/he attempts to keep communication channels open by encouraging or facilitating the participation or by proposing regulation of the flow of communication. S/He mediates the differences between other members, attempts to reconcile disagreements, relieves tension in conflict situations.

Protagonist: S/He takes the floor without need to be consulted driving the conversation. S/he assumes a personal perspective asserting his/her authority or superiority because of his/her status or because of the particular task she/he is performing.

Supporter: S/He shows a cooperative attitude indicating understanding, attention and acceptance as well as providing technical and relational support to other members of the group. S/He also keeps a collaborative climate sharing the common objects and trying to make them available to each member.

Neutral: Going along with the group, s/he passively accepts the idea of others, serving as an audience in group discussion.

Assessing the coding scheme

In order to assess our coding scheme, two independent judges have manually annotated four hours and half of video recorded meetings. In particular, three hours and half have been considered for the Socio Emotional Area and one hour for the Task Area.

Video snippets are annotated with t-uples like <task; p; o; start:1.796; end:170.066; duration:168.269> where the various elements in the tuple respectively indicate: (1) the type of occurring role (whether in the Task Area or Socio Emotional Area); (ii) an id code identifying the observed participant; (iii) an id code identifying the observed role (e.g. "o" for observer); (iv) the start time of the observed role; (v) the end time of the observed role; (vi) its duration. The annotators' agreement has been assessed using the K of coefficient [11], considering the number of seconds as measure. The mean score was 0.88 for the Task Area and 0.8 for the Socio Emotional Area. The coding scheme can therefore be considered reliable [see Falcon et al. 2005] .

The assessment of a reliable coding scheme is a vital step before proceeding to define procedures for the automatic perception, fusion, interpretation and annotation of the multimodal input coming from sensory devices which monitor the meeting. Within CHIL, we are currently investigating which verbal and non-verbal multimodal patterns can be used to automatically identify the social roles.

3.1 From coding to reports

The example presented in section 2.1 was manually built from the annotations of a real meeting. For each participant, a table was compiled showing the distribution of his/her roles. For each role, we took into consideration the total number of seconds the relevant participant played that role, as well as the role's distribution during the meeting (for the sake of simplicity, we considered the meeting as divided into quarters).

A number of patterns were then elicited and mapped to verbal statements that describe the behaviour. The pattern "high Protagonist+Orieenteer held for XY part of the meeting" is mapped onto the sentence "You have actively contributed to the XY part of the meeting". Similar patterns were then used to build the rest of the example above.

More elaborate strategies involve reasoning about the behaviour of various participants at a time. For example, should the participant for whom the report is prepared have maintained high percentages of "orienteer" role especially at the beginning and at the end of the meeting with the others being silent or neutral, the report could include a statement like "at the beginning of the meeting you have helped define the agenda and initiate the discussion, summing up the outcome of the meeting at the end". At the opposite, should the considered participant have maintained significant percentages of "orienteer" and "seeker" roles for the most part of the meeting, a statement as the following could be included: "During the meeting you have played a leading role, defining discussion topics and soliciting your colleagues' participation." In case sequences of seeker-(recorder)-attacker are observed, the report could be complemented with: "in some cases, however, you have displayed a critical and aggressive behaviour as a response to your colleagues' contribution".

Within CHIL, there is an on-going effort aimed at the automatic generation of relational reports starting from meeting annotations. The system is based on an existing strategic text planner which accesses a repository of declaratively defined discourse schemata based on the pattern rules described above. The linguistic realization of sentences is currently template-based. Notwithstanding the limitations of the current, preliminary, implementation of the generator, a positive response to the technological feasibility of the system has emerged. An example of brief report actually automatically generated from real data is the following: "You have actively contributed to the meeting, supporting the discussion with your knowledge, helping here and there to focus the discussion on the relevant topics, taking notes. You've had a particular involvement especially at the end of the discussion."

4 An initial evaluation of the relational reports

In this section we present and discuss a study we conducted to understand the way people would react to the very idea of the relational report. In particular, we were interested in investigating four different dimensions: the perceived usefulness of such a service; its reliability — that is, whether people think that an automatic system can reliably provide a report on such a delicate matter as individual behaviour in group situations; its intrusiveness — that is, the perceived degree of intrusiveness of a service that monitors group and individual behaviour to provide reports on their relational behaviour; and its acceptability — what affects the acceptance of the report by addressees?

4.2 The experiment

Eleven groups of four people each were requested to enter in a structured discussion of about half an hour following the Mission Survival Task[2].

All the groups were video-recorded using four fixed omni-directional cameras, closed-talk microphones and seven T-shaped microphone arrays, each consisting of four omni directional microphones. There was no attempt to hide the recording devices since one of the purposes of the experiment was to evaluate the acceptability of being recorded. All the participants were non-technical persons and they had been told that the purpose of the experiment was data collection for the development of a multimodal system.

Few days after, the participants received an individual report elaborated by a social psychologist. Each report described the behaviour of the participant in terms of the functional roles played during the meeting. The psychologist took the roles of the coding scheme as a reference, adopting a descriptive style and without mentioning explicitly the role labels (for example, the "Orienteer/Protagonist" label was paraphrased as "[...] She initiates the discussion by proposing an importance order, justifying it and using a quiet tone of voice [...]"). In writing the reports, the psychologist considered only behavioural aspects of the participants, such as the posture and the tone of voice, and not aspects related to content such as the individual contributions to the discussion.

Half of the participants were told that their report was automatically elaborated by an intelligent system able to monitor the groups' behaviour, while the other half (i.e. the control group) were told that the report was written by a psychologist.

The attitude toward the report was tested by a seven item questionnaire aimed at assessing the perceived usefulness, its reliability, the perceived degree of intrusiveness and its acceptability. A semantic differential aimed at assessing the appropriateness, the completeness and the clarity of the report (the semantic differential was part of the 6-scale questionnaire proposed by Garrison, 2003 with a Cronbach alpha of 0.9482) was also used.

4.1 Results

The answers to the questionnaire were analyzed with a two-tailed multivariate ANOVA (p=.05), considering 42 questionnaires: half for the "expert source" of the report and half for the (pretended) "system source" of the report. The independent variable was the source of the report, in order to monitor how it affects the dimensions investigated in the questionnaires items (dependent variables). Generally, there were no statistically significant differences among the questionnaire's responses in the two groups. The subjects' attitudes were more positive toward the system source (though not is a significant way) in regard to: (i) the perceived usefulness of the report for improving their own relational behaviour $(F(1,40)=$ .366), (ii) the perceived usefulness for improving interactions in meetings $(F(1,40)=$

---

[2] This task consists in having the group discussing how to survive in a disaster scenario, like moon landing or a plane crashing in Canada. This kind of test has often been used in experimental and social psychology to elicit discussions in groups.

.143), and (iii) the willingness to remember the report observations $(F(1,40)= .175)$. Vice versa, the subjects' attitudes were more positive toward the human expert in regard to: (i) the usefulness of the report for stimulating reflection on behavioural aspects not considered in the past $(F(1,40)= 2.138)$, (ii) the completeness of the report in catching relevant behavioural aspects $(F(1,40)= .293$ for caught and $F(1,40)=.518$ for not caught aspects), and (iii) the analysis ability of the expert $(F(1,40)= 1.675)$.

Regarding the subscales of the semantic differential, they were analyzed with a two-tailed multivariate ANOVA with p=.05. In this analysis, a more positive attitude toward the human expert emerges, but not at a statistical significant level. The more relevant difference emerged in the appropriateness sub-scale $(F_{(1,40)}= 4,007, p=.05,$ only marginally significant), less evident in completeness $(F_{(1,40)}= 2.079)$ and clarity $(F_{(1,40)}= .901)$ sub-scales.

5 Conclusion

In supporting co-located groups, multimodality is generally used to help the group in getting easier access to computerized services. In this paper, we proposed that it can be employed to provide meta-level services that are meant to impact on the group dynamics. This shift of focus from task-based functionalities to functionalities targeting the social behaviour is not only difficult from a technical point of view but also challenging from a design point of view since it can be expected that these types of services trigger complex, and possibly negative, reactions from the users.

As a case study of such a typology of services, we investigate a functionality inspired by coaching: it consists of a report about the social behaviour of individual participants that is generated from multimodal information, and privately delivered to them. We provide a motivation for this functionality by drawing from studies on the so-called "reflective process" and by discussing the benefit of coaching provided by humans to other humans. The underlining idea is that the individual, the group(s) they are parts of, and the whole organization might benefit from an increased awareness of participants about their own behaviors during meetings. Since the coaching relationship is based upon trust, we expected problems regarding acceptability to arise when an automatic system enters into play. Yet, the initial evaluation conducted in a controlled experiment where the experimental group was told that the report was prepared by an automatic system did not show any statistical difference in acceptability with respect to the control group that received a report prepared by a human expert.

References

1. P. R. Cohen, R. Coulston, , and K. Krout, Multimodal Interaction During Multiparty Dialogues: Initial Results. In *Proceedings of the 4th IEEE International Conference on Multimodal Interfaces*, October 14-16, Pittsburgh, PA, 2002, pp.448-453.

2. A. Waibel, H. Steusloff, and R. Stiefelhagen, CHIL: Computer in the Human Interaction Loop. In NIST ICASSP Meeting Recognition Workshop, Montreal, Canada, 2004.
3. I. McCowan, D. Gatica-Perez, S. Bengio, D. Moore and H. Bourlard Towards Computer Understanding of Human Interactions. In: Ambient Intelligence, E. Aarts, R. Collier, E. van Loenen & B. de Ruyter (eds.), Lecture Notes in Computer Science, Springer-Verlag Heidelberg, 2004, pp. 235-251.
4. E. Kaiser, D. Demirdjian, A. Gruenstein, X. Li, J. Niekrasz, M. Wesson, and S. Kumar, A Multimodal Learning Interface for Sketch, Speak and Point Creation of a Schedule Chart. In *Proceedings of the Sixth International Conference on Multimodal Interfaces (ICMI 2004)*, October 14-15, State College, Pennsylvania, USA, 2004, pp.329-330.
5. J.C. Tang, Findings from observational studies of collaborative work, *International Journal of Man-Machine Studies*, **34**, 143-160 (1991).
6. M. Doyle, and D. Straus, *How To Make Meetings Work* (The Berkley Publishing Group, New York, NY. 1993).
7. D.A. Kravitz, and B. Martin,. Ringelmann rediscovered: The original article, *Journal of Personality and Social Psychology*, **50** (May 1986), 936-941 (1986).
8. J.M. Jackson, and S.G. Harkins, Equity in effort: an explanation of the social loafing effect. *Journal of Personality and Social Psychology*, **49**, 1199-1206 (1985).
9. S.G. Harkins and M, Jackson. The Role of Evaluation in Eliminating Social Loafing, *Personality and Social Psychology Bulletin* **11**(4), 457-465 (1985).
10. T. Bickmore, and R, Picard, Subtle Expressivity by Relational Agents. In *Proceedings of the CHI 2003 Workshop on Subtle Expressivity for Characters and Robots*, April 7h, Fort Lauderdale, FL, 2003.
11. Y. Liu, and Y.S. Chee, Intelligent Pedagogical Agents with Multiparty Interaction Support. In *Proceeedings of IEEE/WIC/ACM International Conference on Intellingent Agent Technology, IAT 2004*, Los Alamitos, CA: IEEE Computer Society, 2004, pp. 134-40.
12. C. Andersen, A Theoretical Framework for Examining Peer Collaboration in Preservice Teacher Education. In *Proceedings of the 2000 Annual International Conference of the Association for the Education of Teachers in Science,* January 6-9, Akron, Ohio, 2000.
13. D. Kuhn, M.Garcia-Milà, A. Zohar, and C. Andersen, Strategies of knowledge acquisition. *Monographs of the Society for Research in Child Development*, **60**(4), 1995.
14. D. Boud, , R. Keogh, and D. Walker, *Reflection: Turning experience into learning*.(Kogan Page, London, 1988).
15. C. Andersen, *A microgenetic study of science reasoning in social context*. Unpublished doctoral dissertation, Columbia University, MO, (1998).
16. G. Bloom, C. Castagna, and B.Warren, More than mentors: Principal coaching. *Leadership*. May/June (2003).
17. A.L. Costa, and R.J. Garmston,. *Cognitive Coaching: A Foundation for Renaissance Schools*. (Christopher-Gordon Publishers, Norwood, MA, 2002).
18. D. Katz, and R.L. Kahn, *The social psychology of organizations* (2nd ed.). (John Wiley, New York, 1978).
19. K.D. Benne, and P. Sheats, Functional Roles of Group Members, *Journal of Social Issues* **4**, 41-49 (1948).
20. R.F. Bales, *Personality and interpersonal behavior*. (Holt, Rinehart and Winston, New York, 1970).
21. V. Falcon, C. Leonardi, F. Pianesi, and M.Zancanaro, Annotation of Group Behaviour: a Proposal for a Coding Scheme. In *Proceedings of Workshop on Multimodal Multiparty Multimodal Processing (MMMP)* at ICMI, October 7, Trento, Italy, 2005, pp. 39-46.
22. Garrison, B. The perceived of Electronic Mail in Newspaper Newsgathering. In *Proceedings of Communication Technology and Policy Division, Association for Educational in Journalism and Mass Communication Midwinter Conference*, March 1, Boulder, Colorado, 2003.

Multimodal Integration of Sensor Network

Joachim Neumann, Josep R. Casas, Dušan Macho, Javier Ruiz Hidalgo

Signal Theory and Communications Department

UPC – Technical University of Catalonia

Campus Nord edifici D5 Jordi Girona 1-3, 08034 Barcelona, SPAIN

{joachim,josep,dusan,jrh}@gps.tsc.upc.edu

Abstract. At the Universitat Politècnica de Catalunya (UPC), a Smart Room has been equipped with 85 microphones and 8 cameras. This paper describes the setup of the sensors, gives an overview of the underlying hardware and software infrastructure and indicates possibilities for high- and low-level multi-modal interaction. An example of usage of the information collected from the distributed sensor network is explained in detail: the system supports a group of students that have to solve a lab assignment related problem.

1 Introduction and Motivation

The smart room at UPC has been designed to hold group meetings, presentations and undergraduate courses in small groups. The multimodal integration of the sensors in distributed sensor network aims at providing services to the participants in the smart room, which go beyond the computing capabilities of non-integrated computer and sensor-networks.

The UPC smart room permits implementation and testing of a large variety of audio technologies, such as Automatic Speech Recognition (ASR), Speaker Identification (SID), Speech Activity Detection (SAD), Speaker Localization & Tracking (SLT), Acoustic Event Detection (AED), etc. At UPC we are currently active in SID, SAD, SLT, and AED audio technologies.

For video technologies, the multicamera setup in the smart room allows experimenting with visual analysis technologies that strongly rely in exploiting the available redundancy when the same scene is seen from up to 8 different cameras. Not only 3D visual analysis is possible in the smart room, but also any 2D visual analysis approach can be improved by selecting at any time the best camera for a given analysis task. The list of video technologies currently being developed in the smart room are Person Localization and Tracking (PLT), Face Detection (FD), Face

Please use the following format when citing this chapter:

Neumann, Joachim, Casas, Josep, Macho, Dusan, Hidalgo, Javier Ruiz, 2006, in IFIP International Federation for Information Processing, Volume 204, Artificial Intelligence Applications and Innovations, eds. Maglogiannis, I., Karpouzis, K., Bramer, M., (Boston: Springer), pp. 312–323

ID (FID), Body Analysis (BA), Gesture Recognition (GR), Object Detection (OD) and Analysis (ODA) and Text Detection (TD).

In addition, multi-modal approaches (audio + video) are being currently investigated for the Person Identification and Person Localization & Tracking technologies.

2 Sensor setup

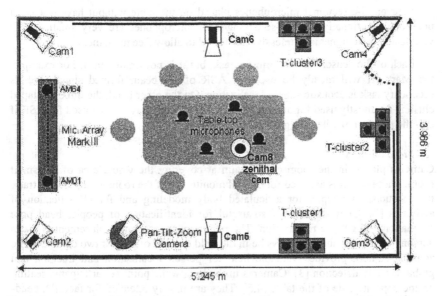

Fig. 1. Sensor set-up of the Smart Room at UPC: the multi-sensor system consists of various audio and video sensors

In order to provide the services to the group of students, the distributed sensor network needs to identify the participants in the room, track their positions over time as well as detect speech and identify voices. The system is capable of continuous monitoring of the UPC smart room [1]. It provides the necessary infrastructure to perform an audio-visual scene analysis as well as a basic modeling of room scenarios. The multi-sensor system is also be used for data collection during technology development.

Audio Sensors
The multi-microphone network should provide audio data for analysis of the acoustic scene in the smart-room by allowing detection and localization of multiple acoustic events, speech activity detection and speech recognition, speaker localization and tracking, etc.

A NIST Mark III 64 microphone array provides audio signal sampled at 44.1 kHz with 24-bit sample representation with all channels sample synchronized. The array is connected to the acquiring computer via Ethernet cable and it is placed close to the wall and approximately 4 m from the main talker area (see Figure1).

Three T-shaped microphone clusters consisting of 4 microphones are positioned on three walls except the wall with Mark III (see Figure 1) at the height of about 2 m. Similarly to Mark III, the clusters provide sample synchronized signals sampled at 44.1 kHz with 24-bit resolution.

Four omni-directional microphones placed on the table without having a fixed position. Additionally, fife close-talking/lapel microphones are very small, barely visible and their signal is wirelessly transferred to allow free movement.

Each of the sensors has its primary task, but it is not limited to it. For example, the Mark III will mostly be used for ASR of the beam formed signal, but its secondary task is acoustic source localization. On the other hand, the three T-shaped clusters are mostly used for audio localization, but they may also be used for ASR if e.g. the position of talker suggests it.

Video Sensors

Cameras placed in the room corners aim at covering the whole area of the smart room. These cameras are used for overall monitoring of the room, to detect and track the locations of people, for articulated body modeling and for classification of activities [2]. They might be also useful for identification of people, head pose estimation and gesture recognition. The requirement for camera placement is that a person in the room should always be in the field of view of at least two cameras. The zenithal camera provides valuable help for person localization and tracking and global activity detection [3]. Cameras in the long walls point at participants seating on the opposite side of the table [4,5]. They are mostly intended for face ID, head-pose and hand gesture recognition and multimodal speaker detection. Finally, the active pan-tilt-zoom camera is primarily aimed at the presenter or the person speaking. It also points at the door when idle, so that a shot of the face of any newcomer is obtained for face ID.

3   Applied Analysis Technologies

Table 1. List of technologies implemented in UPC's smartroom

Technology	Description
Tracker3D	Multi-camera perceptual component that detects foreground objects such as persons or chairs, laptops, etc. The module tracks these objects over time. Foreground (FG) detection is carried out separately over each one of the camera video sequences. The binary masks obtained from this process are input for a particular

Technology	Description
	application of the ShapeFrom Silhouette algorithm [6,7], which results in a) 3D voxelized representation of the foreground objects in the room, and b) improved robustness and consistency in the original 2D FG regions detected from the camera images. A 3D object tracker is then applied for the tracking of the 3D FG labeled objects/persons of interest.
Blob Analysis	Deeper analysis of the abovementioned 3D foreground objects: distinguishes chairs from people, detects body posture (standing, sitting, etc) and gestures (raising hand). A standard model of the human body is aligned to the detected 3D objects. The positions of joints and nodes of the human model are updated over time to track the object, always considering the restrictions of the human body model.
FaceDetector	Detects faces in a camera image and creates a mask containing the face. For 3D FG blobs identified as persons, we resort to the camera providing the best available image or to the PTZ camera (cf. Fig. 1). On this image, and taking into account the foreground region, the contour of the face is traced and input to the next module.
Face ID	Based on the analysis of the Face Detector, this module identifies a face from a face-database A frontal face view is choosen whenever available. If not, the database considers also side and profile views. The ID of the face is assigned to the 3D object, which, now can be tracked over time until a confirmation/refresh of the ID can be performed.
Object detector	Certain 3D FG blobs not detected as persons are further analyzed by this module. A model-based classification algorithm, classifies them (e.g. "laptop") and analyses their state (lid open / close, on / off).
Teacher GUI	Graphical user interface (GUI) that provides a service to the teacher: it allows the teacher to browse through highlights (snapshot from one of the cameras and a text describing the situation). Also the teacher GUI informs the teacher if one of the students has called him (raising hand) and informs the Memory Jog service, if the teacher acknowledges the student's call.
Highlights	Service provided to the students: allows the memory Jog to give the students a hint, e.g. highlights of the work done by a previous group.
Question (cf. Fig 6)	A GUI that allows to directly interacting with the Memory Jog. It also controls the Selection of the assignment, the selection of the tower and the entry of the solution.
Answer[1]	Question and answering engine. This perceptual component

[1] This technology has been provided by the Natural language processing Group at UPC. However, since this paper is on multimodal integration, we do not go into details here.

Technology	Description
	consists of a front-end that knows about the topic (e.g. the selected tower) and a back-end that generates the answer from a database.
Recorder	Perceptual component that records highlights for the Teacher GUI, which are automatically generated from a snapshot of the scene from one of the cameras and an explaining text.
RoomStatus	A simple foreground pixel-counter that detects activity in predefined areas of the room (e.g. door open / door closed).
SpeechDetector	The output of speech activity detection contains the information about whether there is anybody speaking in the room or not. The UPC SAD system 9], similarly to the SID system, employs frequency filtering features. The original dimension of the feature vector (49) is reduced to 1 by applying linear discriminant analysis (LDA). Then, a decision tree classifier is used to obtain the final speech/non-speech decision. Both the LDA transformation matrix and the decision tree parameters are estimated during the training phase. In the main far-field microphone task of the CHIL evaluations our SAD system achieved 11.78% detection error rate 10]. Due to low computational requirements of the system, nearly a hundred of such systems can be running simultaneously real-time in our smart-room. SAD system is part of the yearly CHIL service demonstrations together with other UPC technologies.
Speaker identification	Speaker identification provides information about the identity of the active speaker. Our SID system is based on Gaussian mixture modeling. As acoustic features we use Mel-frequency cepstral coefficients and frequency filtering features. During the training phase, a Gaussian mixture model (GMM) for the training feature vectors corresponding to the given speaker is estimated; one GMM is estimated for each speaker, and a silence model is also built. During testing, the likelihood that a sequence of feature vectors was produced by the given GMM is calculated for each speaker model and the speaker ID is chosen as the model with the largest likelihood. In the regular evaluations performed within the CHIL project, we achieved a performance of 98.3% correct identifications in the task where only 5 seconds of signal from a far-field microphone is available and the identities of 11 lecturers are needed to be differentiated.
AcousticLocalzator	The speaker localization and tracking technology offers at each timestamp a 3-dimmensional position of the active acoustic source or several sources; it can be a speaking person, but also a ringing phone or moving chair. The UPC

Technology	Description
	SLT system is based on the cross-power spectrum phase approach [11], which we showed is quite robust to the speaker head orientation 12] if using an appropriate distribution of microphone arrays. We use three T-shaped microphone arrays and one linear array (Mark III), so that there is a microphone array at each wall in the room. When evaluating out SLT technology within the CHIL evaluations 10, we achieved 80% of correct localizations, where the localization is considered as a correct if the distance between the system's output and the reference is lower than 50cm. Our SLT system is running real-time in UPC's smart-room and it is being regularly shown in the CHIL service demonstrations complementing the other UPC technologies.
Acoustic event classification	The objective of acoustic event detection is to detect and classify various acoustic events that may occur in a smart-room, such as door opening/closing, phone ringing, chair moving, and also vocal tract produced non-speech sounds such as cough, laugh, etc. AED is a relatively new area and at UPC we currently focus on the investigation of appropriate features and classification/detection methods. In our publications 13-15], we compare and combine ASR features and acoustic features. Also, we showed that the support vector machine approach provides a good classifier alternative to the more common approaches such as Gaussian mixture models.
Wavplayer	The wavplayer is the voice of the Memory Jog service. This perceptual component can synthesize speech and play pre-recorded messages in a polite way.

The following figure shows the cross-connection between a subset of the abovementioned analysis technologies in a smartflow map (see the following section on Software Architecture for an explanation of the distributed data flows)

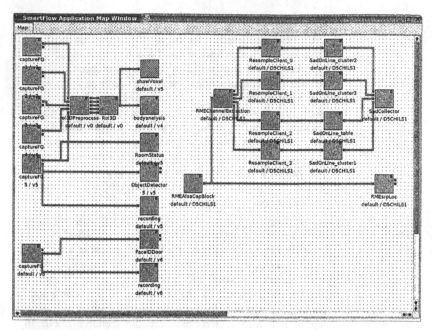

Fig. 2. Smartflow map of the client programs that were running simultaneously on 10 computers

4   Software Architecture

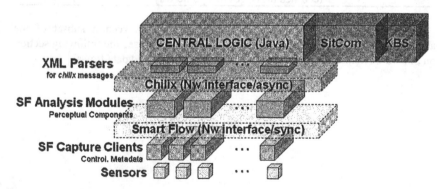

Fig. 3. Block diagram of the software architecture

The distributed computing environment smartflow allows to create and to run different algorithms transparently into a network of different computers. For the UPC Smart Room the NIST Smart Space [8] system has been adopted as the infrastructure for distributed computing. Smart Space provides a client-server mechanism to configure a network of computers. This means that audiovisual modules can be run from any computer (allowing the distribution the complexity of algorithms) and that data communication between modules is handled by the Smart Space server.

The output of each of these smartflow (SF) analysis stages is fed asynchronously into the common central logic framework. This framework guarantees that multimodal audiovisual algorithms can seamlessly access the data captured by audio and video sensors. All analysis data is sent as XML message to a central logic.

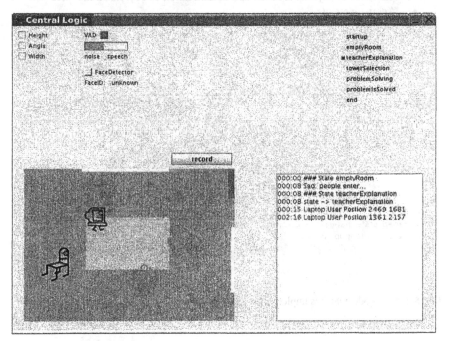

Fig. 4. : GUI of the central logic software that receives the information of all perceptual components.

Although the software architecture has been designed with real-time applications in mind, it provides a mechanism to use audiovisual technology modules in both real time and in non-real time situations. Non-real time scenarios allow capturing data from the room and processing it at a later time. This allows developing audiovisual algorithms or to test non-real time or slow algorithms. The software architecture also provides modules to read and write all captured or processed data into disk and to reproduce the data at a later time at, for instance, different rates. The audiovisual modules do not need to be modified to adapt to these situations.

Based on the output of the sensors, mono- and multi-modal analysis technologies carry out scene-analysis tasks. This knowledge is fed into a situation model in the central logic in order to understand what is going on in the room. Knowledge about the status of the situation model and the collected data allow services to be provided to the participants of a meeting taking place in the Smart Room. The situation model contains information about:

- The state of the meeting: empty room, Teacher explanation, Tower selection, Problem solving, Solution found.
- The state of each participant: ID information, speaking / non-speaking, position changes, gestures.
- The state of objects: location and classification of objects on the table
- Acoustic events.

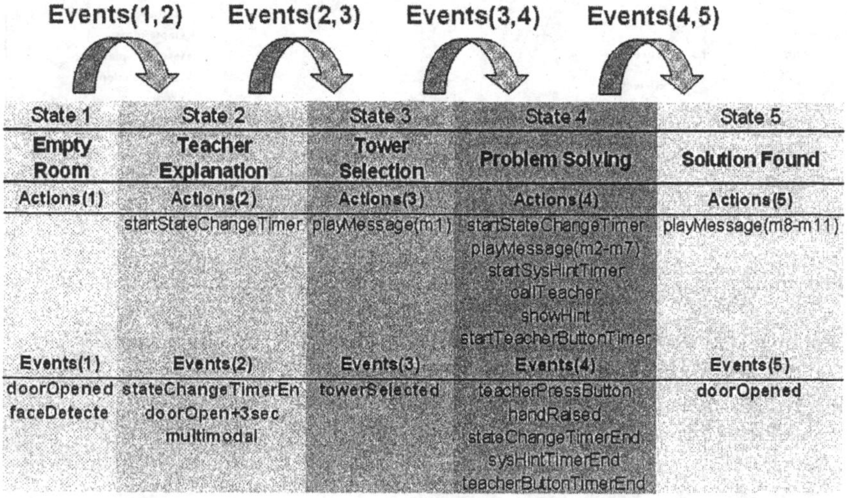

Events(1,2)   Events(2,3)   Events(3,4)   Events(4,5)

State 1	State 2	State 3	State 4	State 5
Empty Room	**Teacher Explanation**	**Tower Selection**	**Problem Solving**	**Solution Found**
Actions(1)	Actions(2)	Actions(3)	Actions(4)	Actions(5)
	startStateChangeTimer	playMessage(m1)	startStateChangeTimer playMessage(m2-m7) startSysHintTimer callTeacher showHint startTeacherButtonTimer	playMessage(m8-m11)
Events(1)	Events(2)	Events(3)	Events(4)	Events(5)
doorOpened faceDetecte	stateChangeTimerEn doorOpen+3sec multimodal	towerSelected	teacherPressButton handRaised stateChangeTimerEnd sysHintTimerEnd teacherButtonTimerEnd	doorOpened

Fig. 5. : State model which is implemented in the central logic.

5 The Memory Jog Service

Service provided by the system is called "Memory Jog", because it helps participants in the Smart Room by providing background information and memory assistance. The basic concept of the Memory Jog is based on information shift in time and space. For example, the Memory Jog seeks, finds and retrieves information on demand using the Question & Answering technology. The Memory Jog can also translate requests/notice/advice from one user to another user (information shift). This information is not only provided unobtrusively, it can be provided reactively (on request) or proactively (automatically). To achieve this, the service needs to be context- and content-aware. The implementation of the service further strives at providing the correct information in a polite manner. The following table illustrates the various moments in which the Memory Jog service can be active in a typical situation:

Table 2. List of events that are noticed by the system (in parenthesis its explained how the system learns about the event). The right column shows the action taken by the system.

Event noticed... (how detected?)	...and react
Start of lab session (multimodal detection)	starts perception & analysis
Teacher selects and explains the task (interaction with GUI)	Stores information in database, initialized internal timers (for Q&A)
Teacher leaves (multimodal detection)	starts interacting w/students through its voice (a pre-recorded message is played)
A questions is asked (interaction with GUI)	The system answers and notes down if a relevant information has been requested
An assumptions about the task is made(interaction with GUI)	The system notes down the assumption (highlight for Teacher GUI, cf. Table 1)
Someone raises his hand (video technologies)	The system calls teacher through the Teacher GUI (cf. Table 1)
The teacher responds to the student's request or he does not respond to the students request (timeouts in the Teacher GUI)	The system informs students about the teachers arrival or it hives a pre-recorded hint.
The progress of the students is slow	The system sends a pre-recorded hint (Highlight, cf. Table 1). This service is proactive.
The students have reached a solution (interaction with GUI)	The system notes down (highlight for Teacher GUI, cf. Table 1)
The students are leaving the room (multimodal detection)	The system plays a goodbye message and gives further instructions

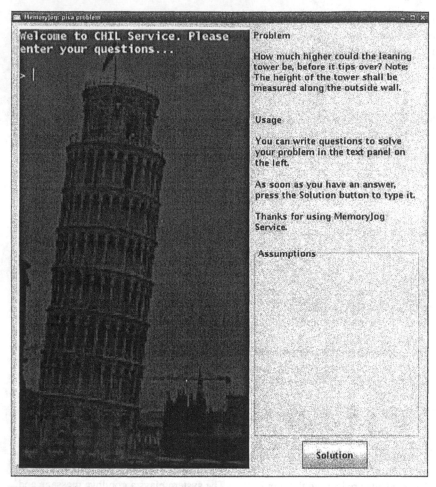

Fig. 6. : Graphical user interface of the Memory Jog service.

6   Conclusion

The application of the multiple sensors and analysis modules in a combined set-up demonstrates that multi-modal integration can be utilized beneficial in a service given to humans (in our case students) in a unobtrusive service that is only possible in a multimodal integration of sensor networks.

References

1. Josep R. Casas, R. Stiefelhagen, et al, "Multi-camera/multi-microphone system design for continuous room monitoring," CHIL-WP4-D4.1-V2.1-2004-07-08-CO, CHIL Consortium Deliverable D4.1, July 2004.
2. J-L. Landabaso, L-O. Xu, M. Pardas, Robust Tracking and Object Classification Towards Automated Video Surveillance, Proc. of International Conference on Image Analysis and Recognition ICIAR 2004, Porto, Portugal, September 29 - October 1, 2004, Proceedings, Part II, p. 463–470
3. J. L. Landabaso, M. Pardàs, L.-Q. Xu, Hierarchical Representation of Scenes using Activity Information, Proc of ICASSP 2005, March 18-23, Philadelphia, USA.
4. Josep R. Casas, O. Garcia, et al, "Initial multi-sensor selection strategy to get the best camera/microphone at any time," CHIL-WP4-D4.2-V2.0-2004-10-18-CO, CHIL Deliverable D4.2, October 2004.
5. O. Garcia, J.R. Casas, "Functionalities for mapping 2D images and 3D world objects in a Multicamera Environment," 6th International Workshop on Image Analysis for Multimedia Interactive Services (WIAMIS), Montreux, Switzerland, April, 2005.
6. A. Laurentini, "The visual hull concept for silhouette-based image understanding," IEEE Trans, Pattern Anal. Mach. Intell., 16(2):150–162, 1994.
7. J.L. Landabaso, M. Pardas, "Foreground regions extraction and characterization towards real-time object tracking," In Proceedings of Joint Workshop on Multimodal Interaction and Related Machine Learning Algorithms (MLMI '05), 2005. 3
8. NIST smart space system, http://www.nist.gov/smartspace
9. Padrell J., Macho D., Nadeu C., "Robust Speech Activity Detection Using LDA Applied to FF Parameters", Proc. ICASSP'05, Philadelphia, PA, USA, March 2005.
10. Macho D., Padrell J., Abad A., Nadeu C., Hernando J., McDonough J., Wölfel M., Klee U., Omologo M., Brutti A., Svaizer P., Potamianos G., Chu S.M., "Automatic Speech Activity Detection, Source Localization, and Speech Recognition on the CHIL Seminar Corpus", Proc. ICME 2005, Amsterdam, The Netherlands, July 2005.
11. Omologo M., Svaizer P., "Acoustic event localization using a crosspower-spectrum phase based technique," in Proc. ICASSP'94, Adelaide, 1994.
12. Abad A., Macho D., Segura C., Hernando J., Nadeu C., "Effect of Head Orientation on the Speaker Localization Performance in Smart-room Environment", Proc. INTERSPEECH – EUROSPEECH 2005, Lisbon, Portugal, September 2005.
13. Temko A., Macho D., Nadeu C., "Selection of features and combination of classifiers using a fuzzy approach for acoustic event classification", Proc. of 9th European Conference on Speech Communication and Technology, Interspeech 2005, Lisbon, Portugal, September 2005.
14. Temko A., Macho D., Nadeu C., "Improving the performance of acoustic event classification by selecting and combining information sources using the fuzzy integral", Lecture Notes in Computer Science (LNCS), vol. 3869, February 2006
15. Temko A., Nadeu C., "Classification of Acoustic Events using SVM-based Clustering Schemes", Pattern Recognition, in press, Elsevier, 2006

Multimodal Identity Tracking in a Smartroom

Keni Bernardin[1], Hazim Kemal Ekenel[1], and Rainer Stiefelhagen[1]

Universität Karlsruhe, ITI,
76131 Karlsruhe, Germany
{keni, ekenel, stiefel}@ira.uka.de

Abstract. The automatic detection, tracking, and identification of multiple people in intelligent environments is an important building block on which smart interaction systems can be designed. Those could be, e.g. gesture recognizers, head pose estimators or far field speech recognizers and dialog systems.

In this paper, we present a system which is capable of tracking multiple people in a smartroom environment while infering their identities in a completely automatic and unobtrusive way. It relies on a set of fixed and active cameras to track the users and get closeups of their faces for identification, and on several microphone arrays to determine active speakers and steer the attention of the system. Information coming asynchronously from several sources, such as position updates from audio or visual trackers and identification events from identification modules, is fused at higher level to gradually refine the room's situation model. The system has been trained on a small set of users and showed good performance at acquiring and keeping their identities in a smart room environment.

1 Introduction and Related Work

In recent years, there has been a growing interest in intelligent systems for indoor scene analysis. Various research projects, such as the European CHIL or AMI projects [16, 17] aim at developing smart room environments, at facilitating human-machine and human-human interaction, or at analyzing meeting or conference situations. To this effect, multimodal approaches that utilize a variety of far-field sensors, video cameras and microphones, to gain rich scene information and achieve robust, unobtrusive and detailed scene understanding gain more and more popularity. Related research has focused, for example, on understanding the actions of individuals or the interactions between groups of persons in the room [4, 5], estimating their head pose [6], their body posture, analyzing their speech, to infer higher level knowledge, produce meeting summaries [8], offer useful proactive services, etc. An essential task on the way to realizing these goals is the location and identification of humans in the scene.

While much research has been done on indoor tracking or on person identification in the past, work has only begun on building integrated, online systems that tackle all the related subtasks without severe restrictions on the scenario

---

Please use the following format when citing this chapter:

Bernardin, Keni, Ekenel, Hazim Kemal, Stiefelhagen, Rainer, 2006, in IFIP International Federation for Information Processing, Volume 204, Artificial Intelligence Applications and Innovations, eds. Maglogiannis, I., Karpouzis, K., Bramer, M., (Boston: Springer), pp. 324–336

or application environment. Choudhury et al. [7] present a person identification system based on the fusion of multimodal cues. It is however limited to a single user required to stand closely in front of the identifiying sensors. Another approach, shown by Yang et al. [8], tackles more complex scenarios including multiple users. A framework including color-based person and face tracking, speech detection, localization and segmentation, and audio-visual ID is presented. The integration is, however, still made conceptually on a frame level, assuming most cues for fusion are accessible at every point in time. This restricts the application to scenarios such as e.g. a small meeting around a table.

The problem when dealing with general, unconstrained environments involving several users is that information gained from passive sensors is either too coarse or noisy to allow correct identification, or too focused and narrow to keep track of all users or capture good identification features at the right time. This is why several approaches resort to a combination of sensors, using wide-view fixed cameras or microphone arrays to keep track of users in the room, and pan-tilt-zoom (PTZ) cameras to actively seek high resolution images for identification.

Tsuruoka et al. [9] present a system that tracks a lecturer in a classroom using foreground segmentation on images from a fixed camera and uses a fuzzy control scheme to steer an active camera and deliver closeup views. It is however limited to a single user standing in front of a clean background. Peixoto et al. [10] use one fixed camera and a binocular active camera system, and implement a target seletion strategy based on state transitions to deal with scenarios involving several users. Hampapur et al. [11] perform 2D and 3D blob tracking on images from two fixed cameras and locate head regions by analyzing the silhouettes of tracked persons. They discuss several strategies for target selection and active camera assignment to capture good facial views. Like the previous two approaches, they do not, however, address the problem of recognizing users in the closeup views or of fusing identification results over time. Similarly, Stillman et al. [12] achieve tracking, face detection and recognition of multiple users using a combination of fixed and PTZ cameras, but they do not offer a framework for camera/target selection or for fusion of the identification results.

In a real, dynamic environment, face recognition accuracy on single frames is highly dependent on lighting conditions, head orientations, face alignment precision, and so forth, and using the information from several frames for identification can bring a substantial improvement. Moreover, limitations in the number of available cameras for active scanning, delays between the time of image capture and the availability of recognition results, etc, force us to deal with incomplete information coming sporadically from several sources with variable confidence.

Our system deals with these issues by remapping ID results to person tracks, accumulating confidences, and deciding on the most probable ID for a track dynamically. Moreover, our fusion scheme allows us to implement a simple procedure for detection of unknown persons, although the recognition modules themselves were not designed for this purpose. Our system uses a fixed camera for tracking, several T-shaped microphone arrays for speech localization and two active cameras for person identification, and realizes an online, incremental identification of multiple persons in our smartroom.

In the following section, we present a detailed description of the tracking and identification system and of its various components. Section 3 then explains the developed camera selection and data fusion technique. Section 4 shows a sample recognition scenario and section 5 gives a short summary and an outlook.

2 Multimodal Identity Tracking System

This section describes our developed system for simultaneous person tracking and identification in our smartroom. It is designed to acquire the identities of several persons on the fly, i.e. without requiring them to pass through designated areas or to specifically interact with identification devices. It also keeps track of all identified persons and refines its confidence with time.

It is composed of several components, distributed over a network of computers, which seamlessly work together while dealing with latency and synchronization issues. For each of these components, which will be described in the following, fast and effective techniques had to be adopted to allow for realtime application. The first of these components is a multiperson tracker which analyzes the scene from a ceiling-mounted camera and delivers the positions of all persons present in the room. These are compared with the output of a speech detection and source localization module which uses the input from several microphone arrays to pinpoint the active speaker and provide a focus of attention for subsequent components. The person of interest is then actively focused on by a set of pan-tilt-zoom cameras which deliver high resolution images of his or her head from several different views. On these images, a two-stage algorithm is applied to detect and align near frontal faces, which are sent to the face identification module. The recognized identities are tagged with an identification time and confidence and sent to a fusion module, where the information coming asynchronously from all other modules is merged: Visual and audio tracks are compared, identity tags from several sources are spatially and temporally matched to tracks, and confidences are accumulated in order to gain a gradually refined view of all identities in the room.

Both the acquisition and the processing of information are distributed over a network of computers. A total of four Pentium IV, 3GHz machines is used: One for the visual and acoustic tracking each and two more for the control of active cameras and the analysis of closeup views.

Fig. 1 gives an overview of the system and of the interaction between its components.

2.1 Multiple Person Tracking in Wide Angle Views

The multiple person tracking module was designed to work on wide angle images captured from the top of the room. The advantage of such views is that they

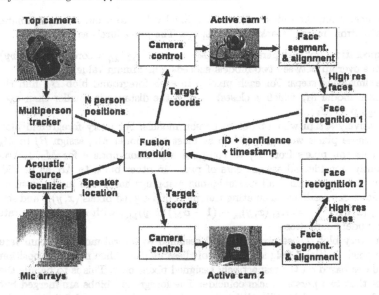

Fig. 1. Overview of the multimodal identity tracking system components

reduce the chance of occlusion by objects or overlap between persons. The drawback is that detailed analysis of the tracked persons is difficult as a top view offers only few good features for identification. This is why, in our system, a combined approach is followed.

The person tracker module processes images captured by a SCORPION SCOR-03NSC firewire color camera equipped with a 180° fisheye lens at 15fps with a resolution of 640x480 pixels.

The tracking algorithm is essentially composed of a simple but fast algorithm for foreground blob segmentation followed by a more complex EM algorithm based on person models:

First, foreground patches are extracted from the images by using a dynamic background model. The background model is created on a few images of the (preferably empty) room and is constantly adapted with each new image with an adaptation factor α. Background subtraction and thresholding yield an initial foreground map, which is morphologically filtered. A connected component analysis provides the foreground blobs for tracking. Blobs below a certain size are rejected as segmentation errors.

The subsequent EM tracking algorithm tries to find an optimal assignment of the detected blobs to a set of active person models, instantiating new models or deleting unnecessary ones if need be. A person model, in our case is composed of a position (x, y), a velocity (vx, vy), a radius r and a track ID. In our implementation, the radius was set to a fixed value, to avoid wrong estimates resulting from merged tracks, shadows, etc. The procedureis as follows:

- Expectation: For each person model M_i, update $(x, y)_{M_i}$ according to $(vx, vy)_{M_i}$. If the overlap between two models exceeds a maximum value, fuse them.
- Maximization steps: For each pixel p in each foreground blob B_j, find the person model M_k which is closest to p. If the distance is smaller than r_{M_k}, assign p to M_k.
- Iteratively assign whole blobs to person models: For every foreground blob B_j whose pixels were assigned to at most one model M_k, assign B_j to M_k and use all pixels from B_j to compute a position update for M_k. Subsequently, consider all assignments of pixels in other blobs to M_k as invalid. Repeat this step until all unambiguous mappings have been made. Position updates are made by calculating the mean of assigned pixels $(x, y)_m$ and setting $(x, y)_{M_{k,new}} = \alpha_M (x, y)_m + (1 - \alpha_M) (x, y)_{M_k}$, with α_M the learnrate for model adaptation.
- For every blob whose pixels are still assigned to several models, accumulate the pixel positions assigned to each of these models. Then make the position updates based on the respectively assigned pixels only. This is to handle the case that two person tracks coincide: The foreground blobs are merged but both person models still subsist as long as they do not overlap too greatly, and can keep track of their respective persons when they part again.
- For each remaining unassigned foreground blob, initialize a new person model, setting its (x, y) position to the blob center. On the other hand, if a model stays unassigned for a certain period of latency, delete it.
- Using the updated model positions, calculate new velocity estimates (vx, vy).
- Repeat the procedure from step 1.

The two stage approach results in a fast tracking algorithm that is able to initialize and maintain several person tracks, even in the event of moderate overlap. Relying solely on foreground maps as features, however, makes the system relatively sensitive to situations with heavy overlap. This could be improved by including color information, or with e.g. temporal templates, as proposed in [1].

By assuming an average height of 1m for a person's body center, and using calibration information for the top camera, the positions in the world coordinate frame of all N tracked persons are calculated and output.

2.2 Speech Detection and Localization

In parallel to the visual tracking of all room occupants, acoustic source localization is performed on a separate machine to estimate the position of the active speaker. For this, the system relies on the input from four T-shaped microphone clusters installed on the room walls. They allow a precise localization in the horizontal plane, as well as a rough height estimation. Two subtasks are accomplished:

- Speech detection and segmentation. This is currently done by thresholding in the power spectrum, but techniques more robust to non-speech noise and cross-talk are already being experimented with.
- Speaker localization and tracking. This is done by estimating time delays of arrival between microphone pairs using the Generalized Cross Correlation function (GCC):

$$R_{12}(\tau) = \frac{1}{2\Pi} \int_{-\infty}^{\infty} \frac{X_1(e^{j\omega\tau} X_2^*(e^{j\omega\tau})}{|X_1(e^{j\omega\tau} X_2^*(e^{j\omega\tau})|} e^{j\omega\tau} d\omega$$

where $X_1(\omega)$ and $X_2(\omega)$ are the Fourier transforms of the signals of a microphone pair in a microphone array.

As opposed to other approaches, where speaker positions are first calculated for microphone pairs, and the resulting positions later combined, this approach uses a Kalman filter that directly receives as input the correlation results from the various microphone pairs, and performs the tracking in a unified probabilistic way, thereby achieving more robust and accurate results. The details of the source localizer can be found in [13].

The output of the speaker localization module is the tracked position of the active speaker in the world coordinate frame. This position is compared in the fusion module to those of all visually tracked persons in the room and the person closest to the speech source is chosen as focus of interest.

2.3 Acquisition of High Quality Face Images for Identification

Once a person of interest has been determined, several parallel processes are launched to acquire frontal views of his or her face for identification. For this, two subtasks are accomplished: The automatic control of active cameras for the acquisition of closeup views and the detection and alignment of frontal faces in the captured images.

The first part is accomplished by two SONY EVI-D70P cameras mounted on the room walls. They are placed such as to offer best views of a presenter as he is talking to the audience or facing the projection board, but also offer good coverage of the rest of the room. Each camera is connected to a separate machine running dedicated components for automatic camera control and for detection, alignment and identification of faces in its images.

The second part is done by a two stage algorithm using appearance based object detectors. Because of the dynamic nature of the images, algorithms that require a static background, such as foreground segmenters, or complex initialization and slow object movement, such as contour trackers, are not applicable. The detectors used here are cascades of classifiers built on haar-like features, as described in [2, 3]. They offer fairly good detection rates and are fast enough for realtime use.

In a first pass, a face detector is used to find occurences of nearly frontal faces in the image. The image is scanned at several scales and bounding rectangles for face candidates are returned. In our implementation, the generally available frontal face classifier cascade included in the OpenCV [18] library was used. Its advantage is that it was not tuned to a specific environment and is fairly robust to lighting and background changes. It does however deliver a moderate amount of false detections or tilted faces, which are not suitable for identification.

This is why the inside of the detected rectangle is again scanned in a second pass with specially trained classifiers to recognize eye regions. These dedicated "eye cascades" have been trained on face images recorded in our smartroom. Only if both tests are passed, and two eyes can be detected, reasonably situated inside the face rectangle, the thereby aligned face is passed on for recognition. This two stage approach guarantees an extremely high precision rate with practically 0% false detections. Fig. 2 shows the face detection and alignment process.

Fig. 2. Face detection and alignment in active camera images. In a first pass, the face area is found by a frontal face detector. In a second pass, the region inside the detected rectangle is scanned with a specialized eye detector. If two eyes can be found, the face is aligned and passed on for recognition. The procedure guarantees extremely low false alarm rates

2.4 Face Recognition

The recognition is made using a local appearance based face representation approach. A detailed description of the technique can be found in [14, 15]. A detected and normalized face image is divided into blocks of 8x8 pixels. Each block is then represented by its DCT coefficients. The top-left DCT coefficient is removed from the representation since it only represents the average intensity value of the block. From the remaining DCT coefficients, the ones containing the highest information are extracted via zig-zag scan. the DCT coefficients obtained from each block are concatenated to construct the feature vector which is used by a nearest neighbor classifier with the normalized correlation d as distance metric:

$$d = \frac{f_{training} \cdot f_{test}}{\|f_{training}\| * \|f_{test}\|}$$

The distance of the feature vector to its assigned class is subsequently also used to derive a confidence measure for the identification.

The class representative vectors for the nearest neighbor algorithm were obtained by applying the same decomposition technique described above on a set of training images. The images were captured automatically by the active cameras at different points in the room, using the detection and alignment technique described in section 2.3, and training was done offline. Currently, nine users, mostly students and members of our lab were trained in, using approximately 70 training images per person. The biggest challenge to the recognition algorithm is the completely unconstrained nature of our scenario, as variations in lighting, in head orientation, in face sizes, and in the daily appearance of users have to be coped with. The recognizer is also not able to distinguish between unknown users and known but poorly recognizable ones. While this can lead to faulty recognition results for single images, these errors are corrected later on by the fusion module which accumulates the ID tags and confidences for a person to produce a combined hypothesis.

3 Asynchronous Fusion and Identity Tracking

The main goal of our system is to realize an unobtrusive identification and tracking of all room occupants by actively seeking and fusing the best cues for recognition whenever they become available. As good facial shots are not easy to acquire, this raises the need for a fusion technique that deals with incomplete information coming in an irregular way.

The fusion module analyzes tracks from the multiperson tracker and position estimates from the source localizer and, using a selection strategy, decides which camera to point at which user to achieve quick identification. It also sporadically receives ID tags from several modules which it must map back to person tracks.

The currently implemented selection strategy is quite simple: Whenever available, the acoustic localization estimates are compared to the visual tracks, and if necessary an attention switch is made and both cameras are focused on the active speaker. This strategy assumes speakers are the most important actors and tries to achieve high recognition rates for them first. However, other strategies are also thinkable:

- Achieve accurate recognition for all room occupants as fast as possible. This would prioritize participants that have not been identified yet.
- Try to refresh all identities of all participants as regularly as possible. This is a good strategy if e.g. our confidence in the tracker's accuracy is low.
- Focusing two cameras on one person increases the chances to get a frontal face. Alternatively, split cameras among users, possibly choosing the best camera for a user e.g. using head orientation estimates.

– In situations where one person often speaks, keep one camera on the speaker and use the other to examine the audience.
– Define regions of high priority in the room, e.g. the door, to quickly identify new persons entering the room, etc.

Once the cameras were steered and face images captured, the fusion module waits to receive ID tags coming from the different identification modules and matches them to their respective tracks. As delays resulting from processing steps and network latency can cause ID tags for a track to come at a sensitively late time, a temporal matching has to be made also. This is currently done by keeping a history of the selected foci of attention and resynchronizing with the received ID tags based on image time stamps.

By doing this, the ID tags and their confidences can be accumulated for every track to improve recognition accuracy. Currently, the last 10 ID tags for a track are considered. The confidence scores for every hypothesized identity are accumulated, normalized and the identity with the highest score is chosen if this score surpasses 50%.

This procedure also serves to recognize unknown persons. When an un-trained face is repeatedly presented to the ID module, it typically outputs a hypothesis with low confidence or a series of different hypotheses. Therefore, the accumulated confidence never reaches 50% for any identity and the track ID is marked as unknown. Note that in this way, the ID tracker system only outputs track identities in which it is confident, and can in time recover from initial wrongful decisions. Fig. 3 shows an example output of the ID tracking system.

Fig. 3. The output of the identity tracking system. The colored circles represent the person models. The identities for recognized persons are printed on top of the respective tracks. The yellow line points at the actual focus of attention of the active cameras

4 Example Scenario

Figures 4 and 5 shows an example run of our identity tracker for a short scenario involving 3 users. The users enter the room and engage in conversation before they sit down together at the table. Upon entrance, they are automatically tracked by the person tracker module. User A is targeted by the active cameras and immediately recognized as "Ken". Then, user B starts to talk and the focus of attention is switched to him. The system can not, however capture a clean face shot for recognition, the identifiaction confidence is low and he is marked as "unknown". After a while, user C goes to the presentation area and starts to talk. The active cameras focus on his face, but the first identification attempts wrongfully classify him as "Kai". As frontal face shots keep getting captured, though, the confidence for the correct ID, namely "Toby", rises. The system output gradually passes from "Kai" to "unknown", to "Toby". Finally, user B speaks again. The system focuses on his face and acquires a few good facial views, definitely classifying him as "Kai". Once all users are identified, the system keeps tracking them and updates their identities everytime they take turns speaking.

Fig. 4. Example scenario involving 3 users in our smartroom

5 Conclusion and Outlook

In this paper, a system for the simultaneous tracking and incremental identification of multiple users in a smartroom scenario is presented. The system relies on a variety of sensors and processing units distributed over a network of computers. Visual tracks gained from a wide angle top view camera and speaker localization cues delivered by a combination of microphone arrays are used to sequentially select persons of interest. Active cameras mounted on the

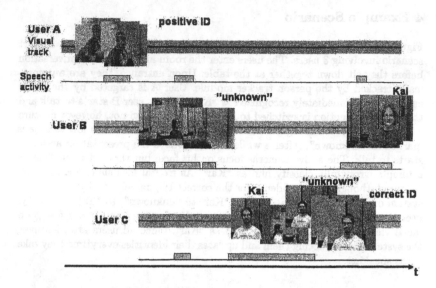

Fig. 5. Example identification scenario. The colored bars represent the visual person tracks in time. Below them, the speech activity for the respective users is depicted. The system immediately recognizes user A from a series of high quality face shots. As user B speaks, attention switches, but the system cannot capture good enough images for definite identification. Confidence is low and the user is marked as unknown until, later on, better views can be obtained. User C is first misrecognized as "Kai". As correct ID results eventually come in, though, the fusion module revises its confidence for user C, labeling him as unknown, until good enough confidence can be reached to make a definite and correct ID

room walls are used to focus in on the speakers and gain high quality closeup views. A two stage algorithm detects frontal faces in the captured images and aligns them with respect to the eye positions. Parallel processes recognize the cropped faces through a local appearance based method using DCT coefficients. The resulting IDs are sent back to a fusion module, which realizes spatial and temporal alignment, accumulates confidences for person tracks, recognizes unknown persons and gradually updates all known person identities. The system actively seeks good cues for identification in an unobtrusive way, requires no specific interaction with the users and functions in realtime at a framerate of 15fps.

Future efforts will go into improving the performance of the various system components: Adding more features to the person tracking module to increase robustness; improving the smoothness of camera control and the hit rate of the face detectors; extending the face ID modules to recognize profile views; etc.

Another planned improvement is the inclusion of acoustic speaker identification cues. This would allow to recognize speakers even if no good facial view can be acquired for long periods of time.

It should also be worthwhile to experiment with other priority management and camera selection strategies, e.g. decoupling cameras or providing feedback from the active camera images to steer the selection and control process.

Finally, complementing the system to allow it to automatically recognize, cluster, and train in unknown faces in an unsupervised way will be the next big step towards making it generally usable for a wide range of real life applications.

References

1. Rania Y. Khalaf and Stephen S. Intille, *"Improving Multiple People Tracking using Temporal Consistency"*, Massachusetts Institute of Technology, Cambridge, MA, MIT Dept. of Architecture House_n Project Technical Report, 2001.
2. Rainer Lienhart and Jochen Maydt, *"An Extended Set of Haar-like Features for Rapid Object Detection"*. IEEE ICIP 2002, Vol. 1, pp. 900–903, Sep. 2002.
3. Paul Viola and Michael Jones, *"Rapid Object Detection using a Boosted Cascade of Simple Features"*. Accepted Conference On Computer Vision And Pattern Recognition, 2001.
4. Iain McCowan, Daniel Gatica-Perez, Samy Bengio, Guillaume Lathoud, Mark Barnard, Dong Zhang, *"Automatic Analysis of Multimodal Group Actions in Meetings"*. IEEE Transactions on Pattern Analysis and Machine Intelligence, vol. 27, no. 3, pp. 305-317, March, 2005.
5. R. Stiefelhagen, *"Tracking Focus of Attention in Meetings"*. IEEE International Conference on Multimodal Interfaces - ICMI 2002, pp. 273-280, Pittsburgh, 2002.
6. M. Voit, K. Nickel, R. Stiefelhagen, *"Multi-view Head Pose Estimation using Neural Networks"*. Second Workshop on Face Processing in Video (FPiV'05), in association with IEEE Second Canadian Conference on Computer and Robot Vision (CRV 2005), 9-11 May 2005, Victoria, BC, Canada.
7. Tanzeem Choudhury, Brian Clarkson, Tony Jebara and Alex Pentland, *"Multimodal Person Recognition using Unconstrained Audio and Video"*. Second Conference on Audio- and Video-based Biometric Person Authentication '99 (AVBPA '99), pages 176-181, Washington DC
8. Jie Yang, Xiaojin Zhu, Ralph Gross, John Kominek, Yue Pan, Alex Waibel, *"Multimodal people ID for a multimedia meeting browser"*. Proceedings of the 7th ACM International Conference on Multimedia '99, Orlando, FL
9. Shinji Tsuruoka, Toru Yamaguchi, Kenji Kato, Tomohiro Yoshikawa, Tsuyoshi Shinogi, *"A Camera Control Based Fuzzy Behaviour Recognition of Lecturer for Distance Lecture"*. Proceedings of the 10th IEEE International Conference on Fuzzy Systems, December 2001, Melbourne, Australia.
10. P. Peixoto, J. Batista, H. Araujo, *"A surveillance system combining peripheral and foveated motion tracking"*. Proceedings of the Fourteenth International Conference on Pattern Recognition. Volume 1, 16-20 Aug. 1998 Page(s):574 - 577 vol.1

11. Arun Hampapur, Sharath Pankanti, Andrew W. Senior, Ying-li Tian, Lisa Brown, Ruud M. Bolle, *"Face Cataloger: Multi-Scale Imaging for Relating Identity to Location"*. IEEE Conference on Advanced Video and Signal Based Surveillance (AVSS 2003), July 2003, Miami, FL.
12. S. Stillman, R. Tanawongsuwan, and I. Essa, *"A system for tracking and recognizing multiple people with multiple cameras"*. Technical Report GIT-GVU-98-25, Georgia Institute of Technology, Graphics, Visualization, and Usability Center, 1998.
13. T. Gehrig, K. Nickel, H. K. Ekenel, U. Klee, and J. McDonough, *"Kalman Filters for Audio-Video Source Localization"*. IEEE Workshop on Applications of Signal Processing to Audio and Acoustics, Oct. 2005.
14. H.K.Ekenel, R. Stiefelhagen, *"Local Appearance based Face Recognition Using Discrete Cosine Transform"*. 13th European Signal Processing Conference (EUSIPCO), Antalya Turkey, September 2005.
15. H.K.Ekenel, R. Stiefelhagen, *"A Generic Face Representation Approach for Local Appearance based Face Verification"*. CVPR IEEE Workshop on Face Recognition Grand Challenge Experiments, San Diego, CA, USA, June 2005.
16. CHIL - Computers In the Human Interaction Loop, http://chil.server.de
17. AMI - Augmented Multiparty Interaction, http://www.amiproject.org
18. OpenCV - Open Computer Vision Library, http://sourceforge.net/projects/opencvlibrary

Multimodal Focus Attention and Stress Detection and feedback in an Augmented Driver Simulator

Alexandre Benoit, Laurent Bonnaud, Alice Caplier, Phillipe Ngo, Lionel Lawson, Daniela G. Trevisan, Vjekoslav Levacic, Céline Mancas, Guillaume Chanel
Laboratoire des Images et des Signaux, INPG Grenoble, France
www.similar.cc

Abstract. This paper presents a driver simulator, which takes into account information about the user's state of mind (level of attention, fatigue state, stress state). The user's state of mind analysis is based on video data and biological signals. Facial movements such as eyes blinking, yawning, head rotations... are detected on video data: they are used in order to evaluate the fatigue and attention level of the driver. The user's electrocardiogram and galvanic skin response are recorded and analyzed in order to evaluate the stress level of the driver. A driver simulator software is modified so that the system is able to appropriately react to these critical situations of fatigue and stress: some audio and visual messages are sent to the driver, wheel vibrations are generated and the driver is supposed to react to the alert messages. A multi threaded system is proposed to support multi messages sent by different modalities. Strategies for data fusion and fission are also provided.

1. Introduction

The main goal of this project is to use multimodal signal and video processing to provide an augmented user's interface for driving. In ths aper, we are focusing on passive modalities. The term augmented here can be understood as an attentive interface supporting the user interaction. So far at most basic level, the system should contain at least five components: (1) sensors for determining the user's state of mind; (2) modules for features or data extraction; (3) a fusion process to evaluate incoming sensor information; (4) an adaptive user interface based on the results of step 3 and (5) an underlying computational architecture to integrate these components.

In this paper, we address the following issues:

Please use the following format when citing this chapter:

Benoit, Alexandre, Bonnaud, Laurent, Caplier, Alice, Ngo, Phillipe, Lawson, Lionel, Trevisan, Daniela, Levacic, Vjekoslav, Mancas, Celine, Chanel, Guillaume, 2006, in IFIP International Federation for Information Processing, Volume 204, Artificial Intelligence Applications and Innovations, eds. Maglogiannis, I., Karpouzis, K., Bramer, M., (Boston: Springer), pp. 337–344

- Which driver simulator to use?
- How to characterize a user's state of fatigue or stress?
- Which biological signals to take into account?
- What kind of alarms to send to the user?
- How to integrate all these pieces – data fusion and fission mechanism?
- Which software architecture is more appropriate to support such kind of integration?

A software architecture supporting real time processing is the first requirement of the project because the system has to be interactive. A distributed approach supporting multi threaded server can address such needs.

We are focusing on stress and fatigue detection. The detection is based on video information and/or on biological information. From video data we extract relevant information to detect fatigue state while the biological signals provide data for stress detection. The following step is the definition of the alarms to provide to the user. Textual and vocal messages and force feedback are considered to alert the user.

The rest of the paper is organized as follows: section 2 present the global architecture of the demonstrator, section 2.1 describes how we detect driver's hypo-vigilance states by the analysis of video data, section 3 presents how to detect driver's stress states by the analysis of some biological signal, sections 4 describes the data fusion and fission strategies and section 5 gives details about the demonstrator implementation.

2. Conceptual architecture

The diagram of **Fig 1** presents the conceptual architecture of our attentive driver simulator. We propose a distributed approach to integrate our components. On one PC under Linux we have integrated all video data based detection and analysis as well as the fusion and fission components. Another PC under Windows is used to run the driver simulator and a third PC is used for biological signals acquisition and analysis. Communication between all the PCs is done by exchanging XML messages. For that the Dialog Controller included in the driver Simulator software should be able to receive multi messages (i.e. from biological signals station and from video based station). A multi threaded server approach is developed and included in the driver simulator.

2.1. Hypo-vigilance detection based on video data

The state of hypo-vigilance (either related to fatigue or inattention) is detected by the analysis of video data. The required sensor is a camera facing the driver. Three indices are considered as hypo-vigilance signs: yawning, head rotations and eyes closing for more than 1s.

Face detection: In this paper, we are not focusing on face localization. The face detector should be robust (no error in face localization) and should work in real time. We chose to use the free toolbox MPT [5]. This face detector extracts a square-bounding box around each face in the processed image. The MPT face detector works nearly at 30 frames per second for pictures of size (320x200 pixels), which is not the case of other face detectors such as OpenCV [13] for example.

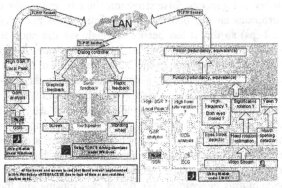

Fig 1: Overview of the system architecture

Head motion analysis: Once a bounding box around the driver's face has been detected, head motion such as head rotations, eyes closing and yawning are detected by using an algorithm working in a way close to the human visual system. In a first step, a filter coming from the modeling of the human retina is applied. This filter enhances moving contours and cancel static ones. In a second step, the FFT of the filtered image is computed in the log polar domain as a modeling of the primary visual cortex. The detail of the proposed method is described in [1].

Fig 2: OPL filtering results for eyes and mouth.

As a result of retinal filterings, noise and luminance variations are attenuated and moving contours are enhanced.

The modeling of the primary visual cortex consists in a frequency analysis of the spectrum of the retina filters outputs in each region of interest of the face: global head, eyes and mouth (see in sequel for the description of eyes and mouth region of interest extraction).

In order to estimate the rigid head rotations [3], the proposed method analyses the spectrum of the retina filters output in the log polar domain. It detects head motion events and is able to extract its orientation.

For the detection of yawning or eyes closing, three identical processes are done independently [4]. On each region of interest (each eye and the mouth), a spectrum analysis is also carried out: we are looking for vertical motion related to eyes closing or to yawning.

Eyes and mouth detection: The mouth can be easily extracted in the lower half of the detected bounding box of the face.

Concerning the eyes, the spectrum analysis in the region of interest is accurate only if each eye is correctly localized. Indeed around the eyes, several vertical or horizontal contours can generate false detection (hair boundary for example). The MPT toolbox proposes an eye detector but it requires too much computing time (frame rate of 22 fps) so that it has been discarded. We use another solution: eye region is supposed to be the area in which there is the most energized contours. Assuming that the eyes are localized in the 2 upper quarters of the detected face, we use the retina output. The retina output gives the contours in these areas and due to the fact that the eye region (containing iris and eyelid) is the only area in which there are horizontal and vertical contours, the eye detection can be achieved easily. We use two oriented low pass filters: one horizontal low pass filter and a vertical low pass filter and we multiply their response. The maximum answer is obtained in the area with the most horizontal and vertical contours: the eye regions. The eye area detection is performed at 30 frames per second.

Hypo-vigilance alarms generation: We detect eyes closing and then generate an alarm.We detect mouth yawning: when a yawn occurs, the mouth is wide open. This generates a very high-energy increase on the log-polar spectrum that can be easily extracted. The global head motion events are detected with the global head spectrum analysis. We only extract the fact that a head motion has occurred.

Fusion strategy: After the video analysis, Boolean information about yawning or not, about eyes closing or not and about head moving or not are available. A simple fusion strategy based on the three index is proposed:

if head motion is detected
  send an alarm to the user
  hypo-vigilance value=100
else
  if both eyes are closed during 1s
    send an alarm to the user
    hypo-vigilance value = 50
  if the driver is yawning
    send an alarm to the user
    hypo-vigilance value = 50+hypovigilence value
end

The variable hypo-vigilance associated to each index is set to 50 or 100. The highest the value, the highest the hypo-vigilance.

Note that in this very simple fusion strategy, information about head motion kind of rotation is not taken into account. A more sophisticated fusion strategy has been tested and is described in section 4.

3. Stress detection based on Biological signals analysis

The application consists of the following three main parts: a) initialization part, b) haptic loop and c) visual loop. The initialization part establishes connection with the hardware devices, reads the scene, initializes the collision detection algorithm and starts the haptic and visual loops. The haptic loop updates the scene using data from the devices, checks for collisions between the hand and scene objects, sets the new position of the hand and objects, triggers feedback forces and enables sound playback. The visual loop reads the current position of scene objects and renders the scene.

Biological signals are used in order to detect stress situation. ECG (Electrocardiogram) and GSR (Galvanic Skin Response) are announced by literature as very promising to detect driver stress in real situations [11, 12]. In a stressful time, the GSR signal and the heart rate signal (extracted from the ECG) are supposed to increase. Two different experiments have been considered; they aim at detecting either driver stress over a long time period or punctual driver stress.

The main drawback of the data acquisition system is that for the moment, on line analysis is not possible. For that reason, the study on biological signal for stress detection has not yet been implemented in the current demonstrator.

4 Fusion strategy

In this section, we describe and test a data fusion based on Bayesian Network. It is used for the purpose of hypo-vigilance detection but it also represents a global fusion method for the integration of additional information in the detection process. Note that this fusion process is not integrated in the final demonstrator for the moment due to the lack of significant data.

Human fatigue generation is a very complicated process. First, fatigue is not observable and it can only be inferred from the available information. In fact, fatigue can be regarded as the result of many contextual variables such as working environments, health and sleep history. Also, it is the cause of many symptoms, e.g. the visual cues, such as irregular eyelid movements, yawning and frequent head tilts. Second, human's visual characteristics vary significantly with age, height, health and shape of face. To effectively monitor fatigue, a system that integrates evidences from multiple sources into one representative format is needed. Naturally, a Bayesian Networks (BN) model is a good option to deal with such an issue.

A BN provides a mechanism for graphical representation of uncertain knowledge and for inferring high-level activities from the observed data. Specifically, a BN consists of nodes and arcs connected together forming a directed acyclic graph. Each node can be viewed as a domain variable that can take a set of discrete values or a continuous value. An arc represents a probabilistic dependency between the parent node and the child node.

Some contextual information such as temperature, time of day, sleep history, etc can be used to build a prior probability for the fatigue node. For that we use the parameters proposed in [7]. For the face data fusion we have considered a very preliminary version where the network evidences change when: eyes closed more than 1 sec; yawning occurs; down head motion are detected simultaneously or not. As result we got the level of fatigue, which is sent to the data fission component.

Data fission duty is to collect the data from data fusion and to generate an alert XML message that is sent to the driver simulator. Data fission function is called at the rate the driver's state detection is progressing. Generated messages are in XML format. We decided for XML because it is extendable and messages are sent only when the driver's state changes. Driver's state may be defined by a fatigue value (either coming from the Bayesian Network result or from the simple fusion process) that is an output variable of data fusion. Table 1 and Table 2 present the fusion strategy for the simple method and for the Bayesian network based method respectively.

Data fission only creates the message if the driver's state has changed and is different than the previous one. If the user's state is the same as in previous call, data fission generates 'NOT_CHANGED' message. In that way the XML message does not need to be sent to the driver simulator after each call of the data fission function.

Table 1: Fission strategy with the simple fusion process

Fatigue range	50	50	100
Message	Open the eyes	Yawning: be careful	Stop moving the head
Shaking power	'100'	'100'	'100'

Table 2: fission strategy with the BN based method

Fatigue range	[0,33]	[33,66]	[66,100]
Message	"	'Tired'	'Asleep'
Message color	"	'Green'	'Red'
Shaking power	'0'	'0'	'100'

Once the alert message has been sent, the driver is supposed to acknowledge to the system that the message has been understood. For example, in the case of the simple fusion process, each time an alert is detected, wheel vibrations are triggered. The driver has to stop these vibrations by pushing a button. The reaction time is also recorded, this time being correlated with the hypo-vigilance or fatigue user's state.

5 Demonstrator

5.1 Overview of the global system

The developed demonstrator is made of 2 PCs: one under Windows for the driver simulator and one under Linux for hypo-vigilance states detection, 1 SONY digital camera, 1 LOGITECH force feed back wheel, 1 projection screen, 1 video-projector and 2 loudspeakers.

5.2 Driver Simulator

Around ten driver simulators have been studied. The choice of the driver simulator has to take into account some features such as: open source software, "First person view": (i.e. cockpit view with wheel) and dashboard, source code easy to modify and possible use of a vibration feedback wheel.

The chosen driver simulator is TORCS [9] because it is a well architectured GPL program with well structured source code and a well designed user interface.

This simulator is working under Linux and windows platforms. The main sources are written in C++ with the OpenGL library. The graphics quality of the simulator is correct and it has a first person view. Fig.3 presents an illustration of TORCS simulator.

We integrate an interaction from the Data Analysis Kernel to our driving Simulator.

The main work consisted in

- Allowing a Text Message to be displayed within the game graphical interface.
- Creating a multi-threaded Server within the application whose purpose is accepting different clients connexions.
- Integrating a force Feedback wheel in order to warn the user with another modality than the visual one.
- Allowing the user to make a feedback on the message displayed by stopping it.
- Parsing XML messages from the multimodal analysis of the driver. Indeed, it is possible to change the color, the string of the sent message and the feedback power.

Fig 3: Global views of the demonstrator, Torcs driver simulator illustration and alert message example

5.3 Implementation of hypo-vigilance detection

Due to the fact that ECG and GSR signals cannot be processed on line with the data acquisition station we used, the detection of stress state has not been implemented in real time.

5.4 Alert message generation

The Display Changes: Three different visual or audio messages depending on the index of hypo-vigilance can be displayed on the first view of the driver simulator (see Table 1 for the considered visual messages and Fig. 3 for an example of message incrustation during the game). In order to show the message, we need to change all the graphical classes within the source code. The communication between the main program and all the libraries is created by using some global variables and also by creating new links between several libraries.

Force Feedback implementation: Force Feedback is used to make the wheel shaking when hypo-vigilance is detected. Shaking power is defined by XML message of data fission. Shaking becomes stronger and gradually reaches its maximum value. Force Feedback uses the DirectInput library, a part of the Microsoft DirectX SDK. The library is based on "The Force Feedback Direct Input Library (DIL)" made by Bryan Warren and Alex Koch. This library can be loaded at [8]. Here, this library has been altered from functions to class. In class we can set the time period that shaking needs to reach the maximum vibration time, vibration activation threshold and to modify the shaking of the wheel dynamically. We also use the class to check whether the button is pressed, and if pressed stops the wheel shaking.

Message parsing and controlling the input devices of driver simulator: After the XML message arrives through the socket connection it is parsed. We use Microsoft

XML parser to parse the message. You can download the MSXML parser from Microsoft web site. After the parsing, controller class activates the screen display message or starts the wheel shaking.

The Server Side: We choose to implement a Server side for the interaction between the multimodal devices and the user. The network protocol used is TCP/IP. We implement this socket by using threads. Those threads access global variables under mutual exclusion. We use a "GPL" library called Openthreads for this implementation.

6. Future Works and Conclusion

We have developed an augmented driver simulator based on video analysis for driver's attention controlling. First promising studies about physiological data have to be improved and integrated in the global system. This will induce the development of an appropriate data fusion method in order to control both the driver's attention level and the driver's stress.

Once the driver has been alerted, it will be necessary to perform some specific tests in order to control that driver's stress or fatigue has actually decreased.

For the moment, the global system is running almost 10 frames per second. It will be necessary to optimize video data analysis algorithms in order to speed up the frame rate.

References

1. Benoit A., Caplier A. –Motion Estimator Inspired from Biological Model for Head Motion Interpretation – WIAMIS05, Montreux, Suisse, avril 2005.
2. Torralba A. B., Herault J. "An efficient neuromorphic analog network for motion estimation." IEEE Transactions on Circuits and Systems-I: Special Issue on Bio-Inspired Processors and CNNs for Vision. Vol 46, No. 2, February 1999.
3. Benoit A. , Caplier A. "Head nods analysis : interpretation of non verbal communication gestures " IEEE ICIP, Genova, Italy, 2005.
4. Benoit A. , Caplier A. "Hypovigilence Analysis: Open or Closed Eye or Mouth ? Blinking or Yawning Frequency ?" IEEE AVSS, Como, Italy, 2005.
5. Machine Perception Toolbox (MPT) http://mplab.ucsd.edu/grants/project1/free-software/MPTWebSite/API/.
6. Bayes Net Toolbox for MatLab http://www.cs.ubc.ca/~murphyk/Software/BNT/bnt.html
7. Qiang Ji, Zhiwei Zhu and Peilin Lan, Real-Time Nonintrusive Monitoring and Prediction of Driver Fatigue, IEEE Transactions on Vehicular Technology, Vol. 53, No. 4, July, p1052-1068, 2004.
8. Force Feedback Direct Input Library http://courses.washington.edu/css450/Fall2003/web_contents/direct_input_lib/DirectInput.html
9. TORCS Driver Simulator: http://torcs.sourceforge.net/
10. Similar Network of Excellence: www.similar.cc
11. S. K. Lal, A. Craig, "Driver fatigue: electroencephalography and psychological assessment", Psychophysiology, 39, 3, May 2002.
12. J.Healey, J.Seger, R.Picard, "Quantifying driver stress: developing a system for collecting and processing bio-metric signals in natural situation", MIT technical report n°483.
13. OpenCV : www.intel.com/technology/computing/opencv

A Fuzzy Expert System for the Early Warning of Accidents Due to Driver Hypo-Vigilance

I. G. Damousis, D. Tzovaras and M. G. Strintzis
Informatics & Telematics Institute
1st Km Thermi-Panorama Road, PO Box 361,
GR-57001 Thermi-Thessaloniki, Greece
{damousis, tzovaras}@iti.gr

Abstract. In this paper a Fuzzy Expert System for the prediction of Hypovigilance-related accidents is presented. The system uses physiological modalities in order to detect signs of extreme hypovigilance. An advantage of such a system is its extensibility regarding the physiological modalities and features that it can use as inputs. In that way, even though currently only eyelid-related features are exploited, in the future and for prototypes designed for professionals other physiological modalities, such as EEG can be easily integrated in the existing system in order to make it more robust and reliable.

1 Introduction

The loss or the disruptions of sleep result in sleepiness during periods when the person should usually be fully awake. The loss of even one night's sleep can lead to extreme short-term sleepiness. The effects of sleep loss are cumulative and regularly losing one or two hours of sleep a night can result to chronic sleepiness over time

Sleep deprivation and related phenomena of excessive fatigue, prolonged inattention, hypovigilance and stress are among the key causes of serious industrial accidents such as nuclear accidents, chemical and environmental disasters, as well as fatal accidents [1].

An automated sleepiness monitoring system could watch over people to make sure the alertness and attention levels are high and warn or even take predefined measures when extreme hypovigilance is detected, in order to prevent an accident. This kind of system could increase the level of safety for everyone since it can be applied on a wide range or users, from regular drivers to sensitive equipment operators.

Several monitoring systems for the automatic hypovigilance detection have been developed over the past years [references]. The majority of those systems focus on

Please use the following format when citing this chapter:

Damousis, Ioannis, Tzovaras, Dimitrios, Strintzis, Michael, 2006, in IFIP International Federation for Information Processing, Volume 204, Artificial Intelligence Applications and Innovations, eds. Maglogiannis, I., Karpouzis, K., Bramer, M., (Boston: Springer), pp. 345–352

the diagnosis of the physiological demonstration of sleepiness, by recording and analyzing features that in most cases are related to the driver's blinking behavior.

Even though blink-related features intuitively and experimentally [2] seem to be the most suitable candidates for hypovigilance detection, studies show that these features are not enough accurate and reliable enough since they exhibit strong interpersonal (between persons) and intrapersonal (same person different times) variability. Aiming to address the limitations of the current hypovigilance detection and accident warning systems, we develop a new multimodal sleep prediction algorithm, which will be integrated in an automatic accident warning and sleep prediction prototype for drivers within the Integrated Project SENSATION.

The major objective of SENSATION is the development of new, unobtrusive sensors, capable of providing measurements that allow the online extraction of advanced physiological features that are not currently available in the existing warning systems. These features will potentially allow more accurate hypovigilance detection and the development of more reliable sleep prediction systems (less false warnings).

In this paper we describe the framework for such a multimodal physiological sleep prediction system, which is based on fuzzy logic expertise and trained with the use of real-coded Genetic algorithms. Also some preliminary results from the analysis of the training data, concerning the accident prediction effectiveness of blink-related features are reported.

2 The Fuzzy Expert System in general (FES)

Fuzzy logic is a research area based on the principles of approximate reasoning and computational intelligence. It departs from classical sets, logic and strict Boolean (True or False) decisions and assignments. Instead, it uses soft linguistic variables (e.g. small, medium, large), and a continuous range of truth-values in the interval [0, 1]. Fuzzy models are employed in cases where a system is difficult to model exactly (but an inexact model is available), or ambiguity and vagueness is encountered in the problem formulation.

A typical fuzzy system comprises the following key parts:
* A rule base containing a number of IF-THEN rules,
* A fuzzy inference unit, which performs the inference operations of the rules
* The fuzzification interface which transforms crisp inputs into fuzzy variables that are processed by the fuzzy inference unit,
* The defuzzification interface that transforms the fuzzy output into a crisp number.

Expert knowledge can be "stored" in a fuzzy system's IF-THEN rules. This transfusion of knowledge in the system can take place either by the manual definition of the fuzzy rules, or by the training of the system using training cases or patterns. After the fuzzy rules are defined, the system is capable of making inferences and its output or decision simulates the one of an expert's. In that way the system is called Fuzzy Expert System.

Recently, the fuzzy inference system suggested by Takagi, Sugeno and Kang (TSK fuzzy model) has gained a great interest in several applications in fuzzy modelling and control. The TSK fuzzy models consist of linguistic fuzzy rules represented in the following form:

$$R^{(j)}: \quad IF\ (x_{p,1}\ is\ A_1^j\ )\ AND\ ...\ AND\ (x_{p,NPI}\ is\ A_{NPI}^j)$$
$$THEN\ y_j = F_j\ (x_{c,1},\ x_{c,2},\ ...,\ x_{c,NCI})\quad j=1,...,NR \tag{1}$$

where NR is the number of fuzzy rules.

The *"IF"* precondition statements define the premise part while the *"THEN"* rule functions constitute the consequent part of the fuzzy model.

- $\overline{X}_p = [x_{p,1},\ ...,\ x_{p,NPI}\ ]^T$ is the input vector to the premise part comprising NPI input variables.

- A_i^j are labels of fuzzy sets describing linguistically the input component $x_{p,i}$ $i = 1,\ ...,\ NPI$. (e.g. "low", "medium", "high").

- $\overline{X}_c = [x_{c,1},\ ...,\ x_{c,NCI}\ ]^T$ denotes the input vector to the consequent part of $R^{(j)}$ containing NCI input variables.

Finally, $y_j = F(\overline{X}_c)$ represents the *j-th* rule output which is a function of the consequence part input components $x_{c,i}$, $i = 1,...,\ NCI$. A special case of particular importance is encountered when the rule functions are linear polynomials of the consequent inputs:

$$y_j = F(\overline{X}_c) = \lambda_0^j + \sum_{i=1}^{NCI} \lambda_i^j x_{c,i} \tag{2}$$

where λ_i^j are weight coefficients and λ_0^j is a bias term.

Each linguistic label A_i^j is associated with a membership function $\mu_i^j(x_{p,i})$. These are usually unimodal functions (triangular, Gaussian, bell shaped, etc.), taking values in the interval $[0, 1]$. Gaussian type memberships are employed described by

$$\mu_i^j(x_{p,i}) = \exp\left[-\frac{1}{2}\frac{\left(x_{p,i} - m_i^j\right)^2}{\left(\sigma_i^j\right)^2} \right] \tag{3}$$

where m_i^j and σ_i^j are the mean value and the standard deviation of the membership function, respectively (Fig. 1 (a)).

The firing strength of the rule $R^{(j)}$, representing the degree to which $R^{(j)}$ is excited by a particular premise input vector $\overline{X}_p$, is determined by

$$\mu_j(\overline{X}_c) = \prod_{i=1}^{NPI} \mu_i^j(x_{p,i}). \tag{4}$$

The antecedent fuzzy sets pertaining to a rule $R^{(J)}$ define a fuzzy region within the premise space (Fig.1 (b))

$$\mathbf{A}^{(J)} = A_1^j \times A_2^j \times \cdots \times A_{NPI}^j. \tag{5}$$

Essentially, $\mathbf{A}^{(J)}$ represents a multidimensional fuzzy set with a membership distribution defined by (4).

Using this notation, the TSK rule can be brought in the following compact form:

$$R^{(j)}: \quad IF \quad \overline{X}_p \quad is \quad A^{(j)} \quad THEN \quad y_j = F_j\left(\overline{X}_c\right) \qquad (6)$$

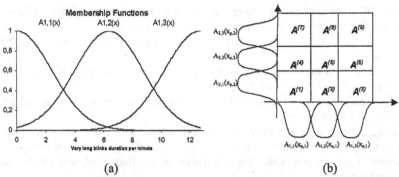

(a)   (b)

Fig.1. (a) Assuming the "very long blinks duration per minute" feature is a premise input, $x_{p,1}$, three fuzzy sets $A_{1,1}$, $A_{1,2}$ and $A_{1,3}$ can express the linguistic propositions that the measured "very long blinks duration per minute" is "Low", "Medium" or "High", respectively. Thus, for a specific sample $x_{p,1} = 4\ sec$ the memberships for each of the fuzzy sets are 0.2, 0.62, 0.0 respectively and the measured "very long blinks duration" is linguistically described as "medium to low". (b) Three membership functions $A_{i,1}(x_{p,i})$, $A_{i,2}(x_{p,i})$, and $A_{i,3}(x_{p,i})$ are used for each premise input i, to express linguistic properties of the inputs, forming nine fuzzy regions that define the boundaries of the system's fuzzy rules.

Given the input vectors $\overline{X}_p$ and $\overline{X}_c$, the final output of the fuzzy model is inferred using the weighted average defuzzification method [12] as follows

$$y = \frac{\sum_{j=1}^{NR} \mu_j(\overline{X}_p) \cdot F_j(\overline{X}_c)}{\sum_{j=1}^{NR} \mu_j(\overline{X}_p)} \qquad (7)$$

From the above description, it can be seen that the basic philosophy of the TSK model is to decompose the premise space into fuzzy regions $\mathbf{A}^{(j)}$ and approximate the system's behaviour in every region by a simple submodel $F(\overline{X}_c)$. Thus, the overall model can be regarded as a fuzzy blending of linear submodels with simpler structure.

3. Accident Prediction Fuzzy Expert System

Our objective is to develop a TSK fuzzy model that provides early warnings for accidents that are due to driver's hypovigilance or sleep onset, based on physiological features. The fuzzy decomposition of the premise space should allow the discrimination between different physiological demonstrations of extreme sleepiness and address the inter-personal variability. In order though for such a system to be efficient and to model (in order to detect) all the different ways that people exhibit extreme hypovigilance just before the sleep onset, we have to select the appropriate physiological features that describe adequately these ways.

3.1 Selection of the physiological inputs

To construct the fuzzy model structure, a number of premise inputs $x_{p,1}, ..., x_{p,NPI}$ should be properly selected. These are the decision variables that constitute the premise space and will allow the formulation of rules (discrete cases). Each premise variable will then partitioned by a certain number of fuzzy sets that cover adequately its universe of discourse as shown in Fig.1(a).

The number of premise inputs should be as small as possible. A reasonable choice is to select one or two inputs. This is dictated by our requirement to keep the number of rules to an acceptably low level. However the great inter-personal variability of the physiological signs that characterize the phase prior to sleep onset may require the use of several features that will serve as FES premise inputs in order to define as accurately as possible all the different classes of physiological behaviours prior to falling asleep. There are several studies in the literature that aim to determine the appropriate physiological signals that allow hypovigilance diagnosis from a broad set of candidate inputs [5], [6], however most of them are inconclusive and there seems to be no golden standard in feature selection or combination of features that can lead to a full proof prediction system.

The physiological features that are related to hypovigilance are EEG features such as alpha and theta waves, eyelid activity features such as long blinks, eye activity related features such as slow eye movements (SEM) and pupillography.

However, since EEG and SEM data can only be acquired via electrodes, they cannot be used for online predictions due to restrictions stemming from user unobtrusiveness requirements. Because of this, EEG analysis is only used as a reference and we can only utilize eyelid activity features (blinks) that can be recorded unobtrusively with CMOS cameras.

For the proposed FES, the decision on the blink-related features selection was taken following a two-steps process:

1) Literature review study in order to pinpoint the most promising features for the discrimination of the various behaviours prior to sleep [5],[6] and also following the guidelines over the use of various physiological for hypovigilance diagnosis and sleep prediction provided by [7],[9].

2) Experimental parametric analysis of the above features using real driving data from 37 subjects [3], in order to select the features with the highest correlation to accidents (Fig.2).

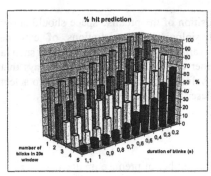 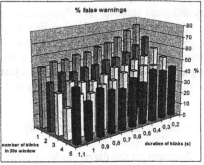

Fig. 2. Parametric analysis of the "number of long blinks" feature. The variables are the duration of a "long blink" and the number of long blinks during a 20 second window that slides every five seconds. Even though the sensitivity of the feature is good (e.g. when 5 detected blinks with duration over 0,2 s around 70% of the hits are predicted within the next 2 minutes), the specificity of the system is not acceptable (more than 40% of the warnings are inaccurate).

4. Genetic Algorithm (GA) training of the FES parameters

The objective of the FES training is to set the values of the premise and consequence part variables in such way as to predict as accurately as possible the accidents, based on the eyelid-related features that are used as inputs. The training patterns have the following structure:

$$\left[\overline{X}_p \middle| \ \overline{X}_c \middle| \ Y_{ACCIDENT} \right]$$

where $\overline{X}_p$ and $\overline{X}_c$ are the input vectors to the premise and the consequent part respectively (blink-related features) and $Y_{ACCIDENT}$ is a binary value that indicates whether an accident happened at that moment ("1") or not ("0"). We must note here that the accidents are filtered based on EEG and EOG analysis in order to take into considerations only those accidents that are due to hypovigilance [4].

For the training of the accident prediction FES a real-coded GA is used. For this GA implementation the parameters of the premise and the consequence parts are concatenated in order to form a *genotype* or *chromosome* which is a consolidated representation of a FES. The premise parameters are the mean values and standard deviations of the membership functions that partition the premise inputs. These variables define fully the membership functions and also set the boundaries of the fuzzy rules (the *IF* part of the rules).

The consequence part parameters are the λ_i^j, $i = 0, ..., NCI$, $j = 1, ..., NR$ coefficients that define the output of each fuzzy rule as shown in (7).

All training parameters, as well as the training patterns' data are normalized in the [0, 1] space. An obvious advantage of the real-coded GA over binary-coded GAs is that with the direct encoding of floating-point numbers in the chromosomes we achieve absolute precision, overcoming the critical decision of the number of bits to be used for the encoding of8each FES parameter.

The training process of the FES using GA begins with the random generation of an initial population of m genotypes. The quality of the solution that a specific genotype represents is measured by calculating its fitness following the next steps:

a) *Decomposition of the chromosome into FES premise and consequence parameters*

b) *Calculation of FES output for each training pattern*

Equation (3) provides the memberships of the training pattern to the fuzzy sets that partition the premise inputs. Then the pattern's firing strength for each fuzzy rule is calculated (4). Each rule has an output that corresponds to the specific pattern as is shown in (2). The overall output of the FES for the specific pattern is the weighted average of the fuzzy rules' outputs as shown in (7). Each rule's contribution to the final solution is analogous to the degree that the pattern triggers the specific rule.

c) *Calculation of the chromosome's fitness*

The FES output is compared with a threshold. The threshold is also part of the chromosome, hence trainable as well. If the output of the FES is larger than the threshold then the expert system produces an accident warning ("1"). If not, the system's output is "0". The outputs of the system are compared to the actual accidents and a measure of accuracy is calculated:

$$FitnessFunction = \frac{1 + shp(\%)}{1 + far(\%)} \qquad (8)$$

Where *shp(%)* is the successful hit prediction ratio, defined as the percentage of hits that were predicted and *far(%)* is the false alarms ratio which is defined as the percentage of FES warnings that did not correspond to an accident up to 2 minutes ahead. As it can be seen from (8) this fitness function promotes the sensitivity (promoting accurate predictions) and the specificity of the system (false alarms).

The GA is allowed to evolve for a number of generations. The evolution takes place using the well-known genetic operators of selection, crossover [9] and mutation [8]. The final FES derives from the elite solution of the GA at the final generation. Upon termination of the training process, the quality of the obtained model is verified with the testing data set. While GA training lasts from minutes to some hours, depending on the size of the measurements database, the on-line predictions that are based on real time measurements are attained instantly.

5. Experimental results and Conclusions

A FES was developed as described in Sections 2, 3 and 4. However because the feature extraction process is currently not concluded, only blink-related features that are available by conventional low frame rate cameras were used. As it was mentioned in section 3.1, the only blink-related feature that exhibited adequate sensitivity and specificity was the number of long-blinks feature. In order to present this feature as a fuzzy premise input, we used the duration of the "long blinks" that were detected during the previous 20 second window. Based on the findings of section 3.1 we defined the duration that characterizes a long blink, using the sensitivity/specificity ratio as criterion. In that special case that we only use one feature to create our system, the FES can only be considered as a fine-tuning method based on AI techniques, aiming to maximize sensitivity (prediction accuracy) and specificity (false alarms minimization). This process led to 72% accuracy in hit prediction accompanied by 32% false alarms. Future work includes the study and integration of new more advanced eyelid-activity related features when they are available, in order to develop a more reliable accident prediction system. These features include PERCLOS [2], amplitude and peak closing velocity as well as lid closure and opening speed [6]. Eye gaze features are also being extracted in order to provide information about fixations that usually accompany extreme hypovigilance. A second step will be the integration of EEG features such as alpha and theta waves for the development of a sleep prediction system for professionals, where sensor unobtrusiveness is less important than reliability.

These new features can be easily integrated due to the open structure of the FES and the flexibility of the GA training as opposed to the various mathematical models.

References

[1]   Akerstedt et al., "Work organisation and unintentional sleep: results from the WOLF study" *Occup Environ Med* 2002;59:595-600.

[2]   Dinges, Mallis, et al.: Evaluation of techniques for ocular measurement as an index of fatigue and the basis for alertness management. Final report for the USDOT, NHTSA, 104pp, Report No. DOT HS 808 762, 1998

[3]   Björn Peters, Anna Anund, Joakim Östlund and Magnus Hjälmdahl, Results of Sensation Pilot 2.5 – WP1.7 (Alertness Monitoring Database), SENSATION internal deliverable, Nov. 2005.

[4]   Rechtschaffen, A., & Kales, A. (1968). A manual of standardized terminology, techniques and scoring system for sleep stages of human subjects. Bethesda: US Department of Health, Education and Welfare, Public Health Service.

[5]   N.Galley, R.Schleicher, L.Galley, "Blink parameter for sleepiness detection" and other works by the same authors.

[6]   Caffier, P.P., Erdmann, U., Ullsperger, P. Experimental evaluation of eye-blink parameters as a drowsiness measure. Eur J Appl Physiol, 89: 319-325, 2003.

[7]   Yannis Damousis, Dimitrios Tzovaras: Correlation between SP1 data and parameters and WP 4.4.2 algorithms, Sensation Internal Report (Draft Nov2004)

[8]   Z. Michalewicz, Genetic Algorithms + Data Structures = Evolution Programs, New York / USA, Springer-Verlag, 1996.

[9]   F. Herrera, M. Lozano, J.L. Verdegay, Tuning fuzzy controllers by genetic algorithms, Internat. J. Approx. Reasoning 12 (1995) 299-315.

[10] Alex H. Bullinger et al "Criteria and algorithms for physiological states and their transitions, SENSATION_Del_1_1_1.doc", SENSATION Deliverable 1.1.1, August 2004.

Mixed Reality Cane Simulation

D. Tzovaras[1], K. Moustakas[1,2], G. Nikolakis[1], M.G. Strintzis[1,2]
[1] Informatics & Telematics Institute
1st Km Thermi-Panorama Road, PO Box 361,
GR-57001 Thermi-Thessaloniki, Greece
{tzovaras, moustak, gniko}@iti.gr
[2] Electrical and Computer Engineering Department
Aristotle University of Thessaloniki
GR-54006 Thessaloniki, Greece
strintzi@eng.auth.gr

Abstract. In the present paper a mixed reality cane simulation environment is presented that allows blind people to navigate in virtual worlds. The application is based on the combination of a real cane with a haptic force feedback system. The users can therefore handle the cane in a natural way and perceive realistic force feedback from virtual objects. Experimental results demonstrate the advantages of the MR approach when compared to the VR one.

1. Introduction

Virtual Reality (VR) and Mixed Reality (MR) systems are generally based on the use of advanced displays in order to provide an immersive visual interface. However VR and MR applications are not limited to visual feedback [1]. Audio feedback as well as haptic feedback can be used for the creation of immersive applications. These modalities are also suitable for the creation of applications for the blind and the visually impaired.

The HOMERE system presented in [2] is a multimodal system designed so as to aid the visually impaired people to explore and navigate inside virtual environments. The system provides the user with different sensations when navigating inside a virtual world: a force feedback corresponding to the manipulation of a virtual blind cane, a thermal feedback corresponding to the simulation of a virtual sun, and an auditory feedback in spatialized conditions corresponding to the ambient atmosphere and specific events in the simulation. A visual feedback of the scene is also provided to enable sighted people to follow the navigation of the main user.

Please use the following format when citing this chapter:

Tzovaras, Dimitrios, Moustakas, Konstantinos, Nikolakis, Georgios, Strintzis Michael, 2006, in IFIP International Federation for Information Processing, Volume204, Artificial Intelligence Applications and Innovations, eds. Maglogiannis, I., Karpouzis, K., Bramer, M., (Boston: Springer), pp. 353–360

In [3,4] a haptic virtual reality tool developed for the training of the visually impaired is presented. The proposed approach focuses on the development of a highly interactive and extensible Haptic Virtual Reality training system that allows visually impaired, to study and interact with various virtual objects in specially designed virtual environments, while allowing designers to produce and customize these configurations. The training scenarios include cane simulation, used for performing realistic navigation tasks.

The purpose of this paper is to develop a mixed reality cane simulation environment based on the existing VR cane simulation application [3,4] and to conduct tests with blind users in order to obtain measurable results and derive qualitative and quantitative conclusions on the added value of the mixed reality system. The CyberGrasp haptic device was selected, based on its commercial availability and maturity of technology. In this paper we have developed a mixed reality environment for cane simulation and performed comparative tests with end users in order to identify the advantages of the mixed reality cane simulation. Moreover a novel superquadric based collision detection algorithm was integrated and tested with the system.

The paper is organized as follows. Section 2 describes an overview of the cane simulation system, including a general flow chart and features available in both the VR and MR systems. Section 3 describes the existing VR cane simulation system and including details of the hardware setup as well as information concerning the force feedback calculation. Section 4 describes the novel mixed reality cane simulation application. Section 5 describes the usability evaluation of the system. Finally, Section 6 draws the conclusions.

2. System Overview

This section describes the hardware setup used for the cane simulation applications (both VR and MR) as well as the software components that compose the cane simulation platform.

2.1 Hardware setup

The cane simulation hardware prototype consists of the CyberGrasp™ haptic device, a powerful workstation with specialized 3D graphics acceleration, input devices (primarily mouse and keyboard) and speakers (Figure 1).

The prototype handles both human-hand movement input and haptic force-feedback using Immersion's CyberGlove® and CyberGrasp™ haptic devices [5]. CyberGlove® is a widely used human-hand motion-tracking device of proven quality. CyberGrasp™ is currently one of the very few force-feedback devices that are offered commercially, providing high quality of construction, operation and performance. The 350g CyberGrasp™ exoskeleton is capable of applying a maximum of 12N per finger force-feedback at interactive rates and with precise control. Both devices are supported by the VHS™ software developer kit, which allows straightforward integration with custom virtual reality software.

An important component of the cane simulation system is the motion tracking hardware and software, required for tracking the position and orientation of the hand of the user. The system prototype utilizes Ascension's MotionStar Wireless™ [6] motion tracker to accomplish this task. Other motion trackers, offering similar or better accuracy and responsiveness and a similar way of communication via local network, can easily be plugged into the system.

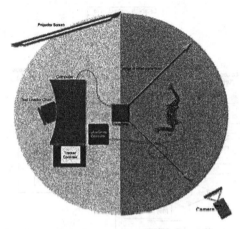

Fig 1. Cane Simulation Setup

2.2 Application core

The application consists of the following three main parts: a) initialization part, b) haptic loop and c) visual loop. The initialization part establishes connection with the hardware devices, reads the scene, initializes the collision detection algorithm and starts the haptic and visual loops. The haptic loop updates the scene using data from the devices, checks for collisions between the hand and scene objects, sets the new position of the hand and objects, triggers feedback forces and enables sound playback. The visual loop reads the current position of scene objects and renders the scene.

Figure 2 presents the general flow chart for the mixed reality cane simulation system. It is similar to the flow chart of the original VR application and includes the tracking of the real cane and a new module for force feedback calculation.

Collision detection is performed between the virtual cane and the VR scene using an SQ based collision detection algorithm presented in [7]. In order to check for collision between an object and the cane, the implicit formulae of the superquadrics is calculated for each point of the scene object. If the result is less than one at least for a point of the object, collision is reported.

If $F_i(x, y, z)$, 1 $\forall SQ_i$; the point (x, y, z) lies outside the cane.

else the point (x, y, z) lies inside the cane.

The cost of executing collision detection tests only for the vertices composing a 3D mesh, and not for the elementary surfaces as most traditional collision detection methods do, is that in cases, where the mesh is coarse and the triangles are relatively large, the superquadric may penetrate a triangle or even pass through it without collision report. In order to solve this problem additional control points are inserted inside each triangle so that the distance between adjacent points is constant, i.e. a 2D grid is applied onto the triangle. In this way the collision tests are performed for the control points for each segment of the virtual hand.

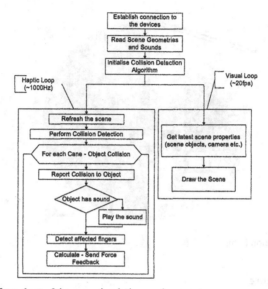

Fig 2. General flow chart of the cane simulation environment

The system supports also 3D sound using the OpenAL (www.openal.org)library in order to create realistic audio feedback.

3. VR Cane Simulation

Cane simulation, has been used for performing realistic navigation tasks with the use of CyberGrasp, which in combination with the Ascension MotionStar wireless tracker leads to a significant workspace (up to 7 meters). These simulations include indoor and outdoor environments such as navigation in the interior of a bank or a public building, traffic light crossing, etc.

The cane was simulated to be an "extension" of the users index finger. The relative position between the index finger and the top of the cane is illustrated in Figure 3.

The force feedback applied to the hand of the user depends on the collision of the cane and the scene objects. When the cane hits on the ground, force feedback is send to the index finger of the user (shown in Figure 3). Force feedback is applied to the thumb when the cane collides with an object laying on its right side (shown in Figure 3). Force feedback is applied to the middle ring and pinky fingers when the cane collides with an object being on its left side (Figure 3).

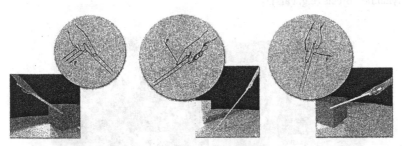

Fig. 4. Cane collision with the ground, an object on the left hand side of the user and an object on the right hand side of the user.

The forces applied to the user are: a constant continuous force that emulates the force provided by grasping a real cane, a cosine force effect (buzzing) provided to the user when the cane is penetrating an object and a Jolt force effect is send to the user when the cane hits an object or the ground. Cosine force effect is described by the equation

$$F=a(1+\cos(2\pi\omega t))\ (1)$$

the Jolt force effect by the equation

$$F=ae^{-kt}.\qquad(2)$$

where, a is the amplitude of the force and k is the attenuation factor. The cane simulation application is adjustable in terms of:
- the cane length,
- the grasping force, the floor hit force and the wall hit force and
- the level of buzzing (force when cane is penetrating an object),

in order to make the test leader able to modify the simulation parameters online, based on the user requirements.

4. MR Cane Simulation

The MR interface is an extension of the interface described in the VR cane simulation application. The user wears the CyberGrasp and a waistcoat for carrying the Force Control Unit (FCU) for the CyberGrasp and the Motionstar control unit to connect the magnetic sensors. The first sensor is attached to CyberGrasp device and the second sensor is attached to the real white cane. Sound and haptic feedback are provided by the system upon collision of the cane with the virtual objects with respect to the position of the objects in the scene and the orientation and position of the users head. The parameters of the virtual cane (size, collision forces) are adjusted so that it fits to the real cane and the user can perceive the contacts similarly as with the real one. Environmental sounds are assigned to static objects in the scene (e.g. realistic traffic lights sound is assigned to traffic lights in the virtual scene) as well as to dynamic objects (e.g. cars).

Fig. 4. Users practicing in the cane simulation environment

Force Feedback calculation in the case of the MR application is more complex than in the VR case. The grasping force is deactivated since the user grasps the real cane. A simplified dynamics model is used to calculate the force feedback applied to the fingers. The proposed model takes into account that Cybergrasp can apply forces approximately perpendicular to the users fingertips. In order to detect fingers that should perceive force the relative position of the user's digits and the cane is calculated along side with the moving direction of the cane. Force effect amplitude is multiplied by the cosine of the angle between the cane direction vector and a vector perpendicular to the finger digit (Figure 5).

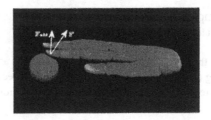

Fig. 5. Force feedback for the CyberGrasp

The main advantage of the MR cane simulation over the VR system is that the user can handle the cane as in real world conditions without any restrictions in the grasping way. This cannot be implemented in the VR system because grasping an object (i.e. the cane) in the desired way without using any visual feedback is a difficult task and could cause inconsistence between the actual position of the VR cane and the position imagined by the user.

5. Usability Evaluation

Initial versions of the applications have been evaluated with blind and visually impaired users. Specifically, the white cane simulation has been tested with blind and visually impaired users from the Thessaloniki Blind School and the Pan-Hellenic Blind association.

Twenty-six persons participated in the tests from the Central Macedonia Local Union of the Panhellenic Association for the Blind in Greece. The users were selected so as to represent the following groups: blind from birth, blind at a later age, adults, and children. The evaluation consisted of three phases. In the first phase the users were introduced to the system and were allowed to use it for a while in order to get used to the device and to calculate the most comfortable parameters for the cane (i.e. length, force amplitude).

In the second phase the users performed the tasks. The total time to complete the task, users comments and success or failure in performing the task were recorded for each user. In the third face the users answered questionnaire, about the performance and the usability of the system.

According to the comments of the users during the tests and their response to the questionnaires, the following conclusions can be drawn: It was deemed very important to utilize both acoustic and haptic feedback, as they are indispensable for the orientation. It is also important to note that a percentage ranging from 96% of the users have characterized the tests as useful or very useful.

An initial comparative test has been performed to estimate the importance of using a mixed reality system over a virtual reality system as well as the significance of each modality to users navigation. Specifically, the system was evaluated for the following cases

* MR with haptic feedback, without audio feedback
* MR without haptic feedback, with audio feedback
* VR with multimodal feedback (both haptic and audio)
* MR with multimodal feedback.

The evaluation was based on psychophysical criteria and was performed using questionnaires. The results showed that the users preferred in terms of usability the MR simulation with multimodal feedback. The second choice was the VR with multimodal feedback. Third was the MR using only audio feedback and last was the MR using only haptic feedback. The ranking shows the importance of the multimodal feedback.

6. Conclusions

The evaluation results on the initial version of the system were promising. The fact that blind persons use different ways to grasp the cane led to the decision of creating an application that can simulate various ways of grasping and using the cane. This led to the design of the MR cane simulation system, which tracks the position of the users hand and the real white cane.

In the cases of the cane simulation, technical limitations constrain its applicability. Specifically, the system cannot prevent the user from penetrating objects in the virtual environment. The maximum workspace is limited to a 7 m - diameter hemisphere around the tracker transmitter (the 1 m limitation, caused by the CyberGrasp™ device is solved by using a backpack so that the user can carry the CyberGrasp™ actuator enclosure). The maximum force that can be applied is limited to 12N per finger and the feedback update rate is 1KHz.

Concluding, the usability evaluation results demonstrate that the proposed mixed reality application was considered as an improvement of the original work [3,4], whereas it still leaves a lot of room for improvement and supplement. Provided that further development is carried out, the system has the fundamental characteristics and capabilities to incorporate many requests of the users for the creation of a more realistic training environment.

The approach chosen, fully describes the belief of blind people to facilitate and improve training practices. It represents an improvement of life for the blind and the visually impaired people when connected to reality training. These facts are evident from the participants' statements.

Except from the direct benefits of the proposed system, as many of the users mentioned, the technology based on virtual environments can eventually provide new training and job opportunities to people with visual disabilities.

Acknowledgment This work has been conducted in conjunction with the "SIMILAR" European Network of Excellence on Multimodal Interfaces of the IST Programme of the European Union (www.similar.cc).

References

1. Burdea G.C. and Coiffet P. Virtual Reality Technology (2nd ed.). Wiley-IEEE Press (2003).
2. Lecuyer A., Mobuchon P., Megard Ch., Perret J., Andriot C., Colinot J.P.: HOMERE: a Multimodal System for Visually Impaired People to Explore Virtual Environments, IEEE Virtual Reality Conference 2003 (VR'03), (2003) 251.
3. D. Tzovaras, G. Nikolakis, G. Fergadis, S. Malasiotis and M. Stavrakis.: Design and Implementation of Haptic Virtual Environments for the Training of Visually Impaired, IEEE Trans. on Neural Systems and Rehabilitation Engineering, Vol. 12, No. 2, (2004) 266-278.
4. D. Tzovaras, G. Nikolakis, G. Fergadis, S. Malassiotis and M. Stavrakis: Virtual Environments for the Training of Visually Impaired, CUWATTS Conference, Cambridge, (2002).
5. Immersion Technologies Inc.: Virtual Hand Suite 2000: User & Programmer Guides, http://www.immersion.com/3d/products/virtualhand_sdk.php.
6. Ascension Technology Corporation: MotionStar Wireless, http://www.ascension-tech.com/.
7. K. Moustakas, G. Nikolakis, D. Tzovaras and M.G. Strintzis, "Haptic Feedback Using an Efficient Superquadric Based Collision Detection Method", in First Joint Eurohaptics Conference and Symposium on Haptic Interfaces for Virtual Environment and Teleoperator Systems, Pisa (2005).

3D content-based search using sketches

K. Moustakas[1,2], G. Nikolakis[1], D. Tzovaras[1], S. Carbini[3], O. Bernier[3]
and J.E. Viallet[3]

[1] Informatics & Telematics Institute
1st Km Thermi-Panorama Road, PO Box 361,
GR-57001 Thermi-Thessaloniki, Greece
{tzovaras, moustak, gniko}@iti.gr
[2] Electrical and Computer Engineering Department
Aristotle University of Thessaloniki
GR-54006 Thessaloniki, Greece
[3] France Telecom R&D, Lannion, France
{sebastien.carbine, olivier.bernier,
jeanemmanuel.viallet}@rd.francetelecom.com

Abstract. The present work presents a novel framework for 3D content-based search and retrieval. On contrary to most state-of-the-art approaches, the query model can be not only an existing object from a database but also a model manually generated by the user using sketches. In the context of the proposed framework, three interfaces to the sketch-based 3D search application were tested and comparative results were extracted according to usability and efficiency criteria.

1. Introduction

Search and retrieval of 3D objects is nowadays a very challenging research topic and has application branches in numerous areas like recognition in computer vision and mechanical engineering, content-based search in e-commerce and edutainment applications etc. [1]. These application fields will expand in the near future, since the 3D model databases grow rapidly due to the improved scanning hardware and modeling software that have been recently developed.

The difficulties of expressing multimedia and especially 3D content via text-based descriptors, reduces the performance of the text-based search engines to retrieve the desired multimedia content. To resolve this problem, 3D content-based search and retrieval (S&R) has drawn a lot of attention in the recent years.

However, the visualization and processing of 3D models are much more complicated than those of simple multimedia data [2]. The major difference lies in

Please use the following format when citing this chapter:

Moustakas, Konstantinos, Nikolakis, Georgios, Tzovaras, Dimitrios, Carbini, Sebastien, Bernier, Olivier, Viallet, Jean Emmanuel, 2006, in IFIP International Federation for Information Processing, Volume 204, Artificial Intelligence Applications and Innovations, eds. Maglogiannis, I., Karpouzis, K., Bramer, M., (Boston: Springer), pp. 361–368

the fact that 3D models can have arbitrary topologies and cannot be easily parameterized using a standard template, which is the case for images. Moreover, there can be many different models of representing them, i.e. indexed facets, voxel models etc. Finally, processing 3D data is much more computationally intensive, than processing media of lower dimension, and often requires very large amounts of memory.

Many researchers worldwide are currently developing 3D model recognition schemes. A number of approaches exist in which 3D models are compared by means of measures of similarity of their 2D views [3]. More direct 3D model search methods focus on registration, recognition, and pairwise matching of surface meshes [4]. However, these methods require a computational costly search to find pairwise correspondences during matching. Significant work has also been done in matching 3D models using geometric characteristics, where initial configurations are derived from conceptual knowledge about the setup of the acquisition of the 3D scene [5] or found automatically by extracting features such as curvature or edges [6].

A typical S&R system, like the aforementioned ones, evaluates the similarities between query and target objects according to low-level geometric features. However, the requirement of a query model to search by example often reduces the applicability of an S&R platform, since in many cases the user knows what kind of object he wants to retrieve but does not have a 3D model to use as query.

Imagine the following use case: The user of a virtual assembly application is trying to assemble an engine of its spare parts. He inserts some rigid parts into the virtual scene and places them in the correct position. At one point he needs to find a piston and assemble it to the engine. In this case, he has to manually search in the database to find the piston. It would be faster and much more easier if the user had the capability of sketching the outline of the piston using specific gestures combined with speech in order to perform the search. In the context of this project the integration of speech and gestures for the generation of the query model is addressed. Speech commands are used for performing specific actions, while gesture recognition is used to draw a sketch of the object and to manipulate the scene objects in the 3D space. The system is also capable to assemble the built objects so as to generate complex structures. The sketch-based 3D search engine has been tested using three interfaces. Comparative results on the usability and efficiency of the interfaces are presented in the experimental results section.

2. 3D content-based search

For each 3D model, rotation invariant geometrical descriptors are extracted. In particular, the object is initially normalized in terms of translation and scaling, i.e. it is translated to the center of the coordinate system, and is scaled uniformly so that the coordinates of all its vertices lie in the interval [0,1]. Next, N concentric spheres are built centered at the origin of the coordinate system. Each sphere is built using tessellation of a normal icosahedron so that the vertices over its surface are uniformly distributed. In the experiments 20 concentric spheres of 16002 vertices are used. For each sphere the discrete 3D signal $F(r_S, \theta_i, \phi_i)$ is assumed, where i is the index of the sphere vertices. The values of function $F(r_S, \theta_i, \phi_i)$ are calculated using the Spherical Trace Transform (STT) [7].

The extraction of the final descriptor vectors, which will be used for the matching algorithm, is achieved by applying the spherical functionals "T", as described in [7], to the initial features $F(r_S, \theta_i, \phi_i)$ generated from the STT. The spherical functionals for each concentric sphere "ρ" are summarized below:

$$T_1(F) = \max\{F(r_S, \theta_i, \phi_i)\} \tag{1}$$

$$T_2(F) = \sum_{j=1}^{N_S} |F'(r_S, \theta_i, \phi_i)| \tag{2}$$

$$T_3(F) = \sum_{j=1}^{N_S} F(r_S, \theta_i, \phi_i) \tag{3}$$

$$T_4(F) = \max\{F(r_S, \theta_i, \phi_i)\} - \min\{F(r_S, \theta_i, \phi_i)\} \tag{4}$$

$$T_l(F) = A_l^2 = \sum_m a_{lm} \tag{5}$$

where N_S is the total number of sampled points $(\eta_j, j = 1, \ldots, N_S)$ at each concentric sphere, $l = 0, \ldots, L$ and $-l < m < l$. The values of a_{lm} are the expansion coefficients of the Spherical Fourier Transform [8]:

$$a_{lm} = \sum_{i=1}^{N_S} F(r_S, \theta_i, \phi_i) \cdot Y_{lm}(\eta_i) \frac{4\pi}{N_S} \tag{6}$$

where $Y_{lm}(\eta_i)$ corresponds to the spherical harmonic function, which is defined through:

$$Y_{lm}(\theta, \phi) = k_{l,m} P_l^m(\cos\theta) e^{jm\phi} \tag{7}$$

where P_l^m is the associated Legendre polynomial of degree l and order m, $k_{l,m}$ a normalization constant and j the imaginary unit.

The quantities A_l^2 are invariant to any rotation of the 3D model. Choosing a sufficiently large number of L coefficients of the Spherical Fourier Transform, a total number of $L + 4$ spherical functionals is used for each concentric sphere.

Finally, the descriptor vectors $D(l)$ are created, where $l = 0, \ldots, (L+4)N_C$ is the total number of descriptors and N_C is the number of concentric spheres. In the experiments described in the sequel, $L = 26$ and $N_C = 20$ were chosen.

Now, let A, B, be two 3D part models, and D_A, D_B, their descriptor vectors respectively. The two parts are compared in terms of similarity according to the following formula:

$$D_{dissimilarity} = \sqrt{\sum_{l=1}^{(L+4)N_C} |D_A(l) - D_B(l)|} \tag{8}$$

Fig. 1 depicts the retrieved objects using as input the first model of each column.

Fig. 1. 3D search results using as query the models of the first row.

3. Sketching the query model

The sketch-based query model generation algorithm aims to provide the sufficient means for the easy and fast design of an approximation of the target model using primitive objects. It consists of the following steps:

1. Sketching the 2D contour of the desired primitive object.
2. Choosing among the corresponding 3D shapes using speech commands [9] (e.g. for a circle choose between sphere, cylinder and cone) and define its height, which cannot be drawn in 2D.
3. If a new primitive is desired go to Step 1, otherwise proceed to Step 4.
4. Assemble the primitives to form the final shape

The user initially sketches, using one of the sketching interfaces that will be described in the sequel, the 2D contour of the primitive to be inserted, e.g. circle for a sphere, a cylinder or a cone, rectangle for parallelepipeds, cubes and triangles for a pyramid or a prisma. These shapes are recognized using least squares minimization with the Levenberg-Marquardt algorithm [10][11] and a sample primitive is automatically inserted in the scene. Next, the degrees of freedom that cannot be defined just from the 2D sketch are defined and the primitive is manipulated. In other words the user defines the height of the object and translates, scales, rotates it until it reaches its target position. After inserting all the primitives they are assembled to the final target query model that is used as input to the 3D content based search procedure described in Section 2. An example of the sketching procedure is illustrated in Fig. 2.

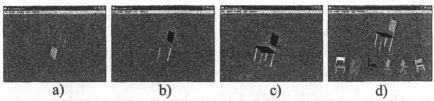

a)   b)   c)   d)

Fig. 2. a,b,c) Sketching procedure and d) 3D search results

4. Query interfaces

The query interface to the 3D search engine is a multimodal gesture-speech interface. The following table describes, the actions that are controlled with gestures and with speech.

Table 1. Speech-Gesture controlled actions

Speech controlled actions	Actions performed using gestures or automatically by the system
No speech	The 3D pointer follows the motion of the user's hand
Selection	Point at the object to be selected
Translation	Move the hand until the object reaches the target 3D position
Rotation	Rotate the hands like grabbing and rotating a sphere
Scaling	Increase decrease the distance between the hands
Sketching	Freehand sketching
Search	Use the selected object as query and search for similar content
Select group	Initiate grouping the primitives and call the selection command for each primitive
Retrieve	Retrieve the objects from the database starting with the most similar
Next	Retrieve next object
Delete	Delete selected object
Clone	Clone selected object
Stop action	Stop currently performed action

Speech recognition is performed as described in [9][10] and pointing gestures are extracted using one of the following interfaces:

4.1. Unobtrusive interface

The first interface is totally unobtrusive. The head and hands of the user are captured using a stereo camera and are efficiently tracked [10] using a statistical model composed of a color histogram and a 3D spatial Gaussian function [12], while the user sketches or performs specific actions.

4.2. Virtual reality haptic interface

The backbone of this interface is a haptic glove that is used as input to the application, as it is capable of identifying hand gestures, and as output since it provides tactile or force feedback. It handles both human-hand movement input and haptic force-feedback for the fingers using Immersion's CyberGlove® (Fig. 3a) and CyberGrasp™ (Fig. 3b) haptic devices [13]. CyberGlove® is a widely used human-hand motion-tracking device of proven quality. CyberGrasp™ is currently one of the very few force-feedback devices that are offered commercially, providing high quality of construction, operation and performance. The 350g CyberGrasp™ exoskeleton is capable of applying a maximum of 12N per finger force-feedback at interactive rates and with precise control. The direction of the force feedback is approximately perpendicular to the fingertips.

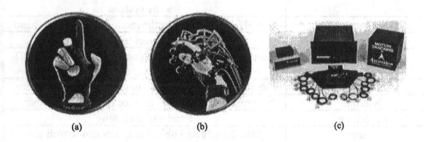

(a) (b) (c)

Fig. 3. a) CyberGlove, b) CyberGrasp, c) Motionstar wireless tracker

Additionally to the haptic devices a position tracker device for providing information on the accurate position of the hand is used. Based on the requirements of the proposed application, the MotionStar Wireless Tracker of Ascension Technologies Inc. has been selected as the appropriate device, mainly due to its wireless nature (Fig. 3c). Combining CyberGrasp with the motion tracker can create a workspace of six meters diameter hemisphere where the user can move and interact with the virtual model, in contrary with the usual systems that limit the user workspace to be less than half a meter (just in the front of a personal computer).

4.3. Air-mouse interface

The third interface consists of a wireless air-mouse [14] that has the exact functionalities of a typical 2D mouse and can additionally by operated in the air since it utilizes a gyroscope sensor to identify changes in its orientation. Notice that, despite the fact that it can be operated in the 3D space, it is not a 3D mouse.

5. Experimental results

The developed sketch-based 3D search platform was evaluated in many scenarios where the user had to sketch the query object in order to search for similar content. The aim of the evaluation was to test and compare the three different interfaces with respect to several parameters, which are:

- – User immersion
- – Usability
- – 3D manipulation efficiency
- – Mobility
- – Robustness
- – Computational efficiency
- – Device intrusiveness
- – Cost

Fig. 4 illustrates three snapshots, while using the sketch-based 3D search platform, while Table 2 presents the comparative results of their evaluation.

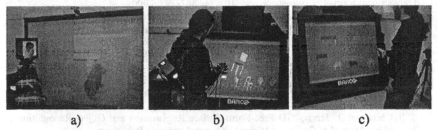

a)   b)   c)

Fig. 4. a) Unobtrusive interface, b) Haptic interface, c) Air-mouse interface

Table 2. Comparison of the interfaces

	Unobtrusive	Haptic VR	Air-mouse
User Immersion	Very high	High	Very low
Usability	Very high	Very high	Moderate
3D manipulation efficiency	Very high	Very high	Very low
Mobility	Very low	Very low	Very high
Robustness	High	Very high	Very high
Computational efficiency	Moderate	High	Very high
Cost	High	Very high	Very Low
Device intrusiveness	Very low	High	Low

6. Conclusions

In the present paper a sketch-based 3D search system was presented. The user is capable of creating the query object using speech and gesture instead of using an existing model to search for similar 3D content. Three different interfaces for human computer interaction were tested and comparative results were extracted that indicate that each interface has its advantages and disadvantages. Which one to use? It depends absolutely on the context of the application to be developed.

Acknowledgment. This work has been supported by the EU funded SIMILAR Network of Excellence.

References

1. S. Berchtold and H.P. Kriegel, "S3: Similarity Search in CAD Database Systems", Proc. of SIGMOD, J. Peckham, Ed. ACM, pp. 564-567, 1997.
2. E. Paquet and M. Rioux, "Nefertiti: A Tool for 3-D Shape Databases Management", SAE Transactions: Journal of Aerospace, vol. 108, pp. 387-393, 2000.
3. J. Loffler, "Content-based Retrieval of 3D models in Distributed Web Databases by Visual Shape Information", Proc. of Int. Conf. on Information Visualisation (IV2000), 2000.
4. A. E. Johnson and M. Hebert, "Using Spin-images for Efficient Multiple Model Recognition in Cluttered 3-D Scenes", IEEE Trans. on Pattern Analysis and Machine Intelligence, vol. 21, no. 5, pp. 433-449, 1999.
5. G. Blais and M. Levine, "Registering Multiview Range Data to Create 3D Computer Objects", IEEE Trans. on Pattern Analysis and Machine Intelligence, vol. 17, no.8, pp. 820-824.
6. C. S. Chua and R. Jarvis, "3D Free-Form Surface Registration and Object Recognition", Proc. of Int. Journal of Computer Vision}, Kluwer Academic Publishers.
7. P.Daras, D.Zarpalas, D.Tzovaras and M.G.Strintzis, "3D Model Search and Retrieval based on the Spherical Trace Transform", IEEE Intl Workshop on Multimedia Signal Processing, Sienna, Italy, 2004.
8. D.V. Vranic and D. Saupe, "Description of 3D-shape using a complex function on the sphere", Proc. IEEE International Conference on Multimedia and Expo, pp. 177-180, 2002.
9. R. Schwartz and Y.L. Chow, "The N-Best Algorithm: an Efficient and Exact Procedure for Finding the N Most Likely Sentence Hypothesis", ICASSP 1990, pp. 81-84, 1990.
10. K. Moustakas, D. Tzovaras, S. Carbini, O. Bernier, J.E. Viallet, S. Raidt, M. Mancas, M. Dimiccoli, E. Yagci, S. Balci and E.I. Leon, "MASTER-PIECE: A Multimodal (Gesture+Speech) Interface for 3D Model Search and Retrieval Integrated in a Virtual Assembly Application", Proceedings of the eNTERFACE 2005, pp. 62-75, August 2005.
11. D.W. Marquardt, "An Algorithm for the Least-Squares Estimation of Nonlinear Parameters", SIAM Journal of Applied Mathematics, vol. 11, no. 2, pp. 431-441, 1963.
12. S. Carbini, J. E. Viallet and L. Delphin-Poulat, "Context dependent interpretation of multimodal speech-pointing gesture interface", International Conference on Multimodal Interfaces, Trento, Italy, 2005.
13. Immersion Technologies Inc., "Virtual Hand Suite 2000: User & Programmer Guides", http://www.immersion.com/3d/products/virtualhand_sdk.php.
14. Gyration Inc., http://www.gyration.com/go24airmouse.htm.

Manual Annotation and Automatic Image Processing of Multimodal Emotional Behaviors in TV Interviews

Jean-Claude Martin[1], George Caridakis[2], Laurence Devillers[1],
Kostas Karpouzis[2], Sarkis Abrilian[1]

1 LIMSI-CNRS, BP 133, 91403 Orsay Cedex, France
{martin, devil, abrilian}@limsi.fr
2 Image, Video and Multimedia Systems Lab, National Technical
University of Athens, Iroon Polytechniou 9, GR-157 80 Athens, Greece,
{kkarpou, gcari}@image.ece.ntua.gr

Abstract. Designing affective Human Computer-Interfaces such as Embodied Conversational Agents requires modeling the relations between spontaneous emotions and behaviors in several modalities. There have been a lot of psychological researches on emotion and nonverbal communication. Yet, these studies were based mostly on acted basic emotions. This paper explores how manual annotation and image processing might cooperate towards the representation of spontaneous emotional behavior in low resolution videos from TV. We describe a corpus of TV interviews and the manual annotations that have been defined. We explain the image processing algorithms that have been designed for the automatic estimation of movement quantity. Finally, we explore several ways to compare the manual annotations and the cues extracted by image processing.

1 Introduction

Designing affective Human Computer-Interfaces such as Embodied Conversational Agents requires modeling the relations between spontaneous emotions and behaviors in several modalities. There has been a lot of psychological researches on emotion and nonverbal communication of facial expressions of emotions [8], and on expressive body movements [2, 5, 17, 18]. Yet, these psychological studies were based mostly on acted basic emotions: anger, disgust, fear, joy, sadness, surprise. In the area of affective computing, recent studies of non-verbal behavior during emotions are also limited with respect to the number of modalities or the spontaneity of the emotion. For example, cameras are used by [13] to capture markers placed on

Please use the following format when citing this chapter:

Martin, Jean-Claude, Caridakis, George, Devillers, Laurence, Karpouzis, Kostas, Abrilian, Sarkis, 2006, in IFIP International Federation for Information Processing, Volume 204, Artificial Intelligence Applications and Innovations, eds. Maglogiannis, I., Karpouzis, K., Bramer, M., (Boston: Springer), pp. 369–377

various points of the whole body in order to recognize four acted basic emotions (sadness, joy, anger, fear).

With respect to other modalities than facial expressions, static postures were recorded by De Silva et al. [4] using a motion capture system during acted emotions (two nuances for each of four basic emotions; e.g. upset and angry as nuances of anger). In Gunes et al. [11] the video processing of facial expressions and upper body gestures are fused in order to recognize six acted emotional behaviors (anxiety, anger, disgust, fear, happiness, uncertainty). A vision based system that infers acted mental states (agreeing, concentrating, disagreeing, interested, thinking, and unsure) from head movements and facial expressions is described in el Kaliouby et al. [10]. Choi et al. [3] describe how video processing of facial expressions and gaze are mapped onto combinations of emotions (neutral, surprise, fear, sadness, anger, disgust, happiness).

These studies are dealing with basic acted emotions, and real-life multimodal corpora are very few despite the general agreement that it is necessary to collect audio-visual databases that highlight naturalistic expressions of emotions [7].

Indeed, building a multimodal corpus of real-life emotions is challenging since it involves subjective perception and requires time consuming manual annotations of emotion at several levels. This manual annotation might benefit from image processing via the automatic detection of emotionally relevant video segments. Estimation of movement quantity by automatic image processing might validate the manual annotations of movements during the time-based annotation of the video, and also of emotional activation at the level of the whole video. Automatic processing might provide finer numerical values which are not possible with manual annotations. Finally automatic annotation might ease the manual annotation process by providing movement segmentation and precise values of expressive parameters such as the speed, the spatial expansion or the fluidity of a gesture. Manual annotation and image processing provide information at different levels of abstraction and their integration is not straightforward. Furthermore, most of the work in image processing of emotional behavior has been done on high quality videos recorded in laboratory situations where emotions might be less spontaneous than during non staged TV interviews.

The goals of this paper are 1) to explore the applicability of image processing techniques for low resolution videos from TV, and 2) explore how manual annotation and image processing might cooperate towards the representation of spontaneous emotional behavior. Section 2 describes the corpus of TV interviews that has been collected and the manual annotations that have been defined. Section 3 explains the image processing algorithms that have been designed for the automatic estimation of movement quantity. Section 3 explores several ways to compare the manual annotations and the results of image processing with the illustration of three video samples.

2   Manual annotation of multimodal emotional behaviors

The EmoTV corpus features 50 video samples of emotional TV interviews [1]. The videos are encoded in Cinepak Codec by CTi (720x576, 25 images/sec). The goal of the EmoTV corpus is to provide knowledge on the coordination between modalities during non-acted emotionally rich behaviors. A multilevel coding scheme has been designed and enables the representation of emotion at several levels of temporality and abstraction [6]. At the global level there is the annotation of emotion (categorical and dimensional including global activation). Similar annotations are available at the level of emotional segments of the video. At the level of multimodal behaviors [15] there are tracks for each visible modality: torso, head, shoulders, facial expressions, gaze, and hand gestures. The head, torso and hand tracks contain a description of the pose and the movement of these modalities. Pose and movement annotations thus alternate. Regarding the annotation of movements, we inspired our annotation scheme of the expressivity model proposed by [12] which describes expressivity by a set of six dimensions: spatial extent, temporal extent, power, fluidity, repetition, overall activity. Movement quality is thus annotated for torso, head, shoulders, and hand gestures.

For gestures annotation, we have kept the classical attributes used for gesture annotation [14, 16] but focused on repetitive and manipulator gestures which occur frequently in EmoTV. Our coding scheme thus enables not only the annotation of movement expressivity but also the annotation of the structural descriptions ("phases") of gestures as their temporal patterns might be related to emotion: preparation (bringing arm and hand into stroke position), stroke (the most energetic part of the gesture), sequence of strokes (a number of successive strokes), hold (a phase of stillness just before or just after the stroke), and retract (movement back to rest position). We have selected the following set of gestures functions ("phrase") as they revealed to be observed in our corpus: manipulator (contact with body or object), beat (synchronized with the emphasis of the speech), deictic (arm or hand is used to point at an existing or imaginary object), illustrator (represents attributes, actions, relationships about objects and characters), emblem (movement with a precise, culturally defined meaning). Currently, the hand shape is not annotated since it is not considered as a main feature of emotional behavior in our survey of experimental studies nor in our videos.

Whereas the annotations of emotions have been done by 3 coders and lead to computation of agreement [6], the current protocol used for the validation of the annotations of multimodal behaviors is to have a 2nd coder check the annotations followed by discussions. We are considering the validation of the annotations by the automatic computation of inter-coder agreements from the annotations by several coders.

3 Automatic processing of videos of emotional behaviors

Image processing is used to provide estimations of head and hand movements by combining 1) location of skin areas and 2) the estimation of movement (Fig. 1). The task of head and hand localization in image sequences is based on detecting continuous areas of skin color. For the given application, a very coarse model is sufficient, since there is no need for recognition of hand shape. As mentioned before the examined corpus is based on real-life situations and therefore the person's original posture is arbitrary and not subject to spatial constraints such as "right hand on the right side of the head" when the person's hands are crossed. In addition to this some skin-like regions may mislead the automatic detection and tracking algorithm. To tackle the above problems a user-assisted initialization process is required as the starting point for the tracking algorithm. During this process the user confirms the regions suggested by the system as the hands and head of the person participating in the multimodal corpora ; after that, since lighting and color conditions do not usually change within the clip, detection and tracking are performed automatically. Another usual impediment to image processing of TV videos is the fact that camera movement can be uncontrolled and may result in skin regions moving abruptly within a clip without the subject showing the relevant activity. In our approach, this can be tackled by taking into account the change of the relevant positions of the skin regions, since they will not change in the event of sudden camera movement.

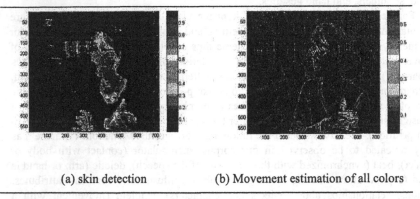

| (a) skin detection | (b) Movement estimation of all colors |

Fig. 1. Steps in image processing for automatic estimation of movement quantity: (a) skin detection, (b) movement estimation of all colors. The next step is to compute the intersection of (a) and (b) for estimating movement of skin areas

The measure of movement in subsequent frames is calculated as the sum of the moving pixels in the moving skin masks, normalized over the area of the skin regions. Normalization is performed in order to discard the camera zoom factor, which may make moving skin regions appear larger without actually showing more vivid activity. Possible moving areas are found by thresholding the difference pixels between the current frame and the next, resulting to the possible motion mask. This mask does not contain information about the direction or the magnitude of the movement, but is only indicative of the motion and is used to accelerate the algorithm by concentrating further tracking only in moving image areas. Both color and motion masks contain a large number of small objects due to the presence of noise and objects with color similar to the skin. To overcome this, morphological filtering is employed on both masks to remove small objects. In the following, the moving skin mask is created by fusing the processed skin and motion masks, through the morphological reconstruction of the color mask using the motion mask as marker.

Overall activation is considered as the quantity of movement during a conversational turn. In our case it is computed as the sum of the motion vectors' norm (Eq. 1).

$$OA = \sum_{i=0}^{n} |r(i)| + |l(i)| \tag{1}$$

Spatial extent is modeled by expanding or condensing the entire space in front of the agent that is used for gesturing and is calculated as the maximum Euclidean distance of the position of the two hands (Eq. 2). The average spatial extent is also calculated for normalization reasons. The temporal parameter of the gesture determines the speed of the arm movement of a gesture's meaning carrying stroke phase and also signifies the duration of movements (e.g., quick versus sustained actions). Fluidity differentiates smooth/graceful from sudden/jerky ones. This concept seeks to capture the continuity between movements, as such, it seems appropriate to modify the continuity of the arms' trajectory paths as well as the acceleration and deceleration of the limbs. To extract this feature from the input image sequences we calculate the sum of the variance of the norms of the motion vectors. The power actually is identical with the first derivative of the motion vectors calculated in the first steps.

$$SE = \max(|d(r(i) - l(i))|) \tag{2}$$

We illustrate our approach on the combination of image processing and manual annotation on a video of the EmoTV corpus (duration 29 seconds, frame rate 25 fps, 722 frames). The image processing module provides information related to emotional behavior at two levels: 1) a global level of the whole video clip, and 2) a local level (e.g. between two frames). At the global level of the whole video, an estimation of the overall activation is computed. For the video 3, this overall activation (Eq. 1) normalized by the number of frames is 1340. It was compared with the results obtained with two laboratory recorded videos with different behaviors but similar viewpoint. The overall activation for a video with fewer movements (showing a single gesture) was smaller (44). For a video with more activation (showing several repetitive gestures), this value was higher (2167).

After the user-assisted initialization step the tracking algorithm is responsible for classifying the skin regions in the following frames of the examined video. Skin region size, distance wrt the previous classified position of the region, flow alignment and spatial constraints. These criteria ensure that the next region selected to replace the current one is approximately the same size, close to the last position and moves along the same direction as the previous one as long as the instantaneous speed is above a certain threshold. As a result each candidate region is being awarded a bonus for satisfying these criteria or is being penalized for failing to comply with the restrictions applied. The winner region, the one that collects the most points during this process, is appointed as the reference region for the next frame. The criteria don't have an eliminating effect, meaning that if a region fails to satisfy one of them is not being excluded from the process, and the bonus or penalty given to the region is relative to the score achieved in every criterion test. The finally selected region's score is thresholded so that poor scoring winning regions are excluded. In this case the position of the body part is unchanged wrt that in the previous frame. This feature is especially useful in occlusion cases when the position of the body part remains the same as just before occlusion occurs. After a certain number of frames the whole process is reinitialized so that a possible misclassification is not propagated.

4   Comparing manual annotations and automatic processing

In this section we illustrate the comparison of manual and automatic processing on three videos from the EmoTV corpus. These three investigated videos have different profiles. Video 41 which includes only head movement. Video 3 includes torso and hand movements. Video 36 includes movements of other people in the background.

4.1   Global activation of behaviors in each video

The values obtained for 1) the manual annotation of emotional activation, 2) the automatic estimation of movement quantity at the level of the whole video clip, 3) the % of seconds of each video for which there is at least one manual annotation of movement (either head, hand or torso) are given in Table 1.

Video #	41	3	36
(1) Emotional activation (manual annotation) 1:low activation, 5: high activation	3	4,33	4,66
(2) Estimation of movement quantity (automatic image processing)	959,60	1132,80	2240,50
(3) % of sec. for which there is at least one manual annotation of movement (head, hand or torso)	73,6	92,6	94,4

Table 1. Values of three manual and automatic measures of emotional activation in three videos

These three values provide different estimations of the quantity of multimodal activity related to the emotions. These values are consistent with the different profiles of these videos. The correlation analysis suggests that measures (1) and (3) may be correlated ($r = 0,97$). This might reveal a consistency in the manual annotation process. The correlation analysis also suggests that (1) and (2) may be correlated ($r = 0.74$). This shows that the automatic processing of videos might be useful for validating the manual annotation of activation at the global level of each video. Finally, the correlation analysis suggests that (2) and (3) may be correlated ($r = 0,58$). However, due to the small sample size, these three values do not reach statistical significance. More data are needed to confirm such a result.

4.2   Time-based estimation and annotation of movement

At the local time-based level, we were willing to compare the manual annotations (of the movements of the head, hands and torso) with the automatic estimation of movements. The current state of the image processing module enables to provide an estimation of the movement between each frame for the whole image. The current image processing module does not provide separate estimations of movement for the different body parts (e.g. image areas). Thus, we compared the union of the manual annotations of movements in the head, hands and torso modalities with the automatic estimation of movements. When the image processing module detected a movement, we decided that there would be an agreement with the manual annotations if a movement had been manually annotated in at least one of the three modalities.

The continuous values of motion estimation provided by the image processing module need to be thresholded in order to provide a Boolean automatic annotation of movements that can be compared with the manual annotations. Setting different values to this threshold for automatic movement detection leads to different values of agreement between the manual annotations and the automatic detection of movement. The value of the amplitude threshold above which the image processing module decides that a movement has been detected should be the minimal value at which a movement should have been perceived and annotated. We evaluated the agreement between the union of the manual annotations of movements and the estimation of movement with several values of this amplitude threshold above which the image processing module decides that a movement has been detected. The tested values for this threshold were between 0.1% and 40% of the maximal value of estimation of movement quantity. We use a 0,04 s. interval for computing the agreement between manual and automatic annotations since it is the interval between 2 frames used by the automatic processing.

The resulting confusion matrix is provided in Table 2. The agreement is the highest for video 3 which features many movements of the head, hand and the upper area of the torso where the skin is visible. The lowest agreement is obtained with video 36 which features people moving in the background, the movement of whom have not been manually annotated since we focus on interviewed people. An intermediate value is obtained for video 41 which only features slight movements of the head and a few movements of the torso. These three videos from EmoTV are rich in annotation of movements of either hand, torso or head. The % of frames for which there is no manual annotation of movements are 26% for video 41, 7% for video 3, and 5% for video 36.

Table 2. Confusion matrix between manual annotation of movement and automatic estimation of movement quantity (for example the column "Auto 0 – Manual 0" describes the agreements no manual annotation of movements / no automatic detection of movement)

Video #	Agreements			Disagreements		
	Auto 0 Manual 0	Auto 1 Manual 1	Total	Auto 0 Manual 1	Auto 1 Manual 0	Total
3	1%	89%	90%	3,5%	6,5%	10%
41	19%	48%	67%	25%	8%	26%
36	4%	45%	49%	49%	2%	51%

In order to compute statistical measures of the agreement between manual and automatic annotations, we balanced the number of frames with and without manual annotation by 1) computing the number of frames without any manual annotation of movement, and 2) by a random selection of the same number of frames with a manual annotation of movement. For video 3, a threshold for motion detection of 8% of maximum movement quantity, leads to a maximum kappa (0,71). For video 36, the maximum kappa is 0,6 (threshold 9%). For video 41, the maximum kappa is 0,425 (threshold 0.6%). For the three videos the kappa is very low when the threshold is too low (the system considers that there is always a movement from automatic processing, and when compared to the manual annotation, the agreement is lower). Then the kappa increases until reaching its highest value (e.g. the values described above), and then decreases as the threshold becomes higher.

5 Conclusions and future directions

In this paper we have described an exploratory approach aiming at computing various relations between manual and automatic annotations of videos of multimodal emotional behaviors. We observed that some dimensions of manual annotations and results of automatic might be correlated. A next step is to consider other videos in order to reach statistical significance in the comparison of manual annotation of activation and the automatic estimation of movement quantity. We will consider videos with very few movements in order to be able to compare the manual and the automatic annotations with classical kappa measures for all the annotations.

Future direction also include the use of temporal filters for improving the automatic detection of movements, the separate estimation of movement quantity for different body parts of the image (including tracking of these areas), the automatic extraction of values for the expressive parameters such the spatial extent (Eq. 2), the validation of the manual annotation of activation at the level of emotional segment, the relations between the estimation of movement quantity and gesture phases (preparation, stroke, retraction), the inclusion of torso annotation in the union of movement annotation only if it includes a skin area.

Acknowledgments

This research is partly supported by the EC Project HUMAINE (IST-507422).

References

1. Abrilian, S., Devillers, L., Buisine, S., Martin, J.-C.: EmoTV1: Annotation of Real-life Emotions for the Specification of Multimodal Affective Interfaces. 11th International Conference on Human-Computer Interaction (HCII'2005) (2005a) Las Vegas, Nevada, USA

2. Boone, R. T., Cunningham, J. G.: Children's decoding of emotion in expressive body movement: The development of cue attunement. Developmental Psychology 34 5 (1998)
3. Choi, S. M., Kim, Y. G.: An Affective User Interface Based on Facial Expression Recognition and Eye Gaze Tracking. 1st International Conference on Affective Computing and Intelligent Interaction (ACII'2005) (2005) Beijing, China 907-915
4. De Silva, P. R., Kleinsmith, A., Bianchi-Berthouze, N.: Towards unsupervised detection of affective body posture nuances. 1st International Conference on Affective Computing and Intelligent Interaction (ACII'2005) (2005) Beijing, China 32-40
5. DeMeijer, M.: The contribution of general features of body movement to the attribution of emotions. Journal of Nonverbal Behavior 13 (1989)
6. Devillers, L., Abrilian, S., Martin, J.-C.: Representing real life emotions in audiovisual data with non basic emotional patterns and context features. First International Conference on Affective Computing & Intelligent Interaction (ACII'2005) (2005) Beijing, China 519-526
7. Douglas-Cowie, E., Campbell, N., Cowie, R., Roach, P.: Emotional speech; Towards a new generation of databases. Speech Communication 40 (2003)
8. Ekman, P.: Basic emotions. Handbook of Cognition & Emotion. J. Wiley (1999)
9. Ekman, P., Walla, F.: Facial Action Coding System (FACS). (1978)
10. el Kaliouby, R., Robinson, P.: Generalization of a Vision based Computational Model of Mind Reading. 1st International Conference on Affective Computing and Intelligent Interaction (ACII'2005) (2005) Beijing, China 582-590
11. Gunes, H., Piccardi, M.: Fusing Face and Body Display for Bi-modal Emotion Recognition: Single Frame Analysis and Multi-Frame Post Integration. 1st International Conference on Affective Computing and Intelligent Interaction (ACII'2005) (2005) Beijing, China 102-110
12. Hartmann, B., Mancini, M., Pelachaud, C.: Implementing Expressive Gesture Synthesis for Embodied Conversational Agents. Gesture Workshop (GW'2005) (2005) Vannes, France
13. Kapur, A., Kapur, A., Virji-Babul, N., Tzanetakis, G., Driessen, P. F.: Gesture Based Affective Computing on Motion Capture Data. 1st International Conference on Affective Computing and Intelligent Interaction (ACII'2005) (2005) Beijing, China 1-8
14. Kipp, M.: Gesture Generation by Imitation. From Human Behavior to Computer Character Animation. Boca Raton, Dissertation.com Florida (2004)
15. Martin, J.-C., Abrilian, S., Devillers, L.: Annotating Multimodal Behaviors Occurring during Non Basic Emotions. 1st International Conference on Affective Computing & Intelligent Interaction (ACII'2005) (2005) Beijing, China 550-557
16. McNeill, D.: Hand and mind - what gestures reveal about thoughts. University of Chicago Press, IL (1992)
17. Newlove, J.: Laban for actors and dancers. Routledge New York (1993)
18. Wallbott, H. G.: Bodily expression of emotion. European Journal of Social Psychology 28 (1998)

MPEG-4 Facial Expression Synthesis
based on Appraisal Theory

Lori Malatesta, Amaryllis Raouzaiou and Stefanos Kollias
Image, Video and Multimedia Systems Laboratory,
National Technical University of Athens,
9, Heroon Politechniou str., Zografou 15780, Greece
{lori, araouz}@image.ece.ntua.gr
stefanos@cs.ntua.gr

Abstract. MPEG-4 facial animation parameters are used in order to evaluate theoretical predictions for intermediate expressions of a given emotion episode, based on Scherer's appraisal theory. MPEG-4 FAPs and action units are combined in modelling the effects of appraisal checks on facial expressions and temporal evolution issues of facial expressions are investigated. The results of the synthesis process can then be applied to Embodied Conversational Agents (ECAs), rendering their interaction with humans, or other ECAs, more affective.

1. Introduction

Affective computing dictates the importance of creating interfaces which are not solely limited to the synthetic representation of the face and the human body, but which also expresses feelings through facial expressions, gestures and the body pose. The most significant challenge is the compatibility of an ECA with MPEG-4 standard and its use in various applications. The use of affective avatars can be applied in many sectors – culture, gaming, e-learning, while their compatibility with the MPEG-4 standard makes it possible for avatars to interact with synthetic objects and to be seamlessly integrated in different scenes.

Scherer's appraisal theory investigates the link between the elicitation of an emotion and the response patterning in facial expression [6]. It predicts intermediate expressions based on sequential appraisal checks and postulates a cumulative effect on the final expression.

The current work aims to investigate this cumulative effect through the synthesis of the temporal evolution of facial expressions during emotion elicitation based on the mapping of Ekman's Action Units [9] to MPEG-4 FAPs.

Please use the following format when citing this chapter:

Malatesta, Lori, Raouzaiou, Amaryllis, Kollias, Stefanos, 2006, in IFIP International Federation for Information Processing, Volume 204, Artificial Intelligence Applications and Innovations, eds. Maglogiannis, I., Karpouzis, K., Bramer, M., (Boston: Springer), pp. 378–384

2. ECA's facial expression and the component process model

The processes of emotion elicitation and emotion expression constitute central issues in rendering an ECA more affective. Emotion theory offers a variety of models each aspiring to capture the emotion expression process. One would expect that the choice of the modelling approach would be irrelevant of the task at hand and would aim to capture global patterns. Contrary to this intuition, relevant research has shown that the choice of the modelling approach is strongly correlated to the task the agent will be asked to carry out. For example the dimensional approach [10] to emotion modelling is more fitting for the case of emotion recognition i.e. anger detection. It remains a challenge to identify the emotion model for an ECA that will not be dependant of specific action examples.

By studying the requirements for a naturalistic interaction with an ECA, a very central issue in the approach each model adopts is the temporal evolution of an expression and how it is affected by surrounding stimuli. Scherer's component process model provides predictions for intermediate expressions as well as a prediction for the final emotion expression based on appraisal checks preformed on various specifically defined components. In the current work we are interested in evaluating this theoretical model and in investigating ways in which appraisal check results and the accompanying predictions can become a behaviour metric for ECAs in a dynamic environment.

According to cognitive theories of emotion, emotions are closely related to the situation that is being experienced (or, indeed, imagined) by the agent. Specifically, emotions are connected to mental representations that emphasize key elements of a situation and identify them as being either positive or negative. These representations have generally been called appraisals. An appraisal can be thought of as a model which is selective and valenced – i.e., highlights key elements of a situation and their values for good or ill [1]. Early examples of this approach can be found in [3], [4]. Appraisals are not necessary conscious, thus the evaluation processes can occur also by an unconscious way as demonstrated by an important corpus of study in cognitive neuroscience, with different methods as subliminal presentations of stimuli or by clinical neuropsychology (e.g. [5]).

Scherer has developed an appraisal model of emotion in which emotions are conceptualized as the outcome of a fixed sequence of checks [6], [7]. According to Scherer's view, emotion serves an important function as "...an evolved phylogenetically continuous mechanism that allows increasingly flexible adaptation to environmental contingencies by decoupling stimulus and response and thus creating a latency time for response optimization" [6].

The appraisal is the sequence of Stimulus Evaluation checks (SECs), which represent the smallest set of criteria necessary to account for the differentiation of main groups of emotional states. These checks are not necessarily binary and are subjective (i.e. they depend on both the appraising individual's perception of and inference about the specific characteristics of the event [6].

The individual SECs can be grouped together in terms of what are called Appraisal Objectives, of which there are four: 1) Relevance Detection: comprising Novelty Check, Intrinsic Pleasantness Check, and Goal Relevance Check; 2)

Implication Assessment: comprising Causal Attribution Check, Discrepancy from Expectation Check, Goal/Need Conduciveness Check, and Urgency Check; 3) Coping Potential Determination: comprising Control Check, Power Check, and Adjustment Check (can the event be controlled, if so by how much power do I have to exert control, and if not can I adjust?); 4) Normative Significance Evaluation: comprising Internal Standards Check, and External Standards Check. A major assumption of Scherer's SEC Theory is that the sequence of the checks and of the groups is fixed. However, this does not rule out parallel processing as, in theory, all of the SECs are processed simultaneously.

Representations of emotional states using this model of emotion are explained in terms of cognitive appraisals of the antecedent situation, and these appraisals account for the differentiated nature of emotional responses, individual and temporal differences in emotional responses, and for the range of situations that evoke the same response. Appraisals also make appropriate emotional responses likely, and conflict between automatic, unconscious appraisals and more consciously deliberated ones may explain some of the more irrational aspects of emotions [3].

3. MPEG-4 based representation and the Facial Action Coding System

In the framework of MPEG-4 standard [8], parameters have been specified for Face and Body Animation (FBA) by defining specific Face and Body nodes in the scene graph. MPEG-4 specifies 84 feature points on the neutral face, which provide spatial reference for FAPs definition. The FAP set contains two high-level parameters, visemes and expressions. Most of the techniques for facial animation are based on a well-known system for describing "all visually distinguishable facial movements" called the Facial Action Coding System (FACS). FACS is an anatomically oriented coding system, based on the definition of "Action Units" (AU) of a face that cause facial movements and tries to distinguish the visually distinguishable facial movements using the knowledge of facial anatomy. An Action Unit could combine the movement of two muscles or work in the reverse way, i.e., split into several muscle movements. MPEG-4 FAPs are strongly related to the AU [11]. Description of archetypal expressions by means of muscle movements and AUs has been the starting point for setting the archetypal expression description through FAPs.

In particular, the Facial Definition Parameter (FDP) and the Facial Animation Parameter (FAP) set were designed in the MPEG-4 framework to allow the definition of a facial shape and texture, eliminating the need for specifying the topology of the underlying geometry, through FDPs, and the animation of faces reproducing expressions, emotions and speech pronunciation, through FAPs. Viseme definition has been included in the standard for synchronizing movements of the mouth related to phonemes with facial animation. By monitoring facial gestures corresponding to FDP and/or FAP movements over time, it is possible to derive cues about user's expressions and emotions. Various results have been presented regarding classification of archetypal expressions of faces, mainly based on features or points mainly extracted from the mouth and eyes areas of the faces. These results indicate that facial expressions, possibly combined with gestures and speech, when the latter is available, provide cues that can be used to perceive a person's emotional state.

4. Facial expression synthesis based on Appraisal Theory predictions

Based on the predictions of Scherer's appraisal theory for the intermediate expressions of hot anger and fear, videos animating the transition between the predicted expressions were generated using the GretaPlayer MPEG-4 decoder. The process was based on the mapping of Ekman's Action Units to MPEG-4 FAPs [11]. This approach aims to be the beginning of an attempt to model the effects of appraisal checks on facial expressions, taking advantage of the flexibility and the expressivity the GretaPlayer engine has to offer.

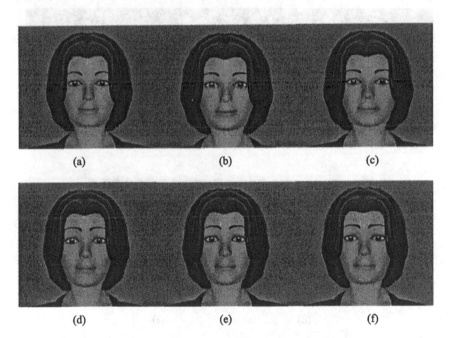

(a)   (b)   (c)

(d)   (e)   (f)

Fig. 1. Intermediate predictions of facial expressions according to Scherer's appraisal theory for the case of fear-(a) neutral, (b) novelty-sudden, (c) unpleasant, (d) discrepant, (e) goal obstructive, (f) low control-final expression –fear. Each expression is derived from the "addition" of the previous expression's AUs and those of the current one.

Until recently, most of our work had to do with static images of the apex of an expression, since no videos with satisfactory resolution that would allow the tracking of the evolution of a FAP in successive frames were available. In contrast to a display of static images of the intermediate predictions, in the process of video synthesis, the temporal evolution of the expressions poses various issues on the synthesis procedure. Lacking the information about the track each facial animation parameter follows through time; various methods of transition between the intermediate expressions were investigated.

The appraisal theory predicts a *cumulative effect* of intermediate predictions on the final expression of an emotion. This effect needs empirical investigation in order to determine the appropriate method of animation of the effect. We have identified two major ways of treating the evolution of an expression between the intermediate expression predictions provided by the appraisal checks, an additive animation and a sequential one. They are methods based on principles of computer graphics that require further empirical testing on the naturalness of their outcome. In this preliminary research both approaches were tested in depth, the sequential presentation of intermediate expressions was used in the case of hot anger and the additive presentation of the intermediate expressions was used in the case of fear. Results on a frame level can be seen in Figures 1 and 2.

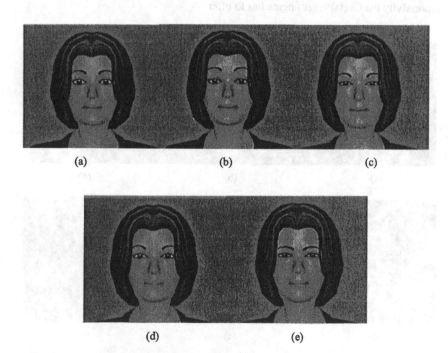

(a)   (b)   (c)

(d)   (e)

Fig. 2. Intermediate predictions of facial expressions according to Scherer's appraisal theory for the case of hot anger-(a) neutral, (b) novelty-high, (c) goal obstructive, (d) control high/power high, (e) final expression –hot anger.

In the case of additive animation –as seen in the fear example, each intermediate expression is derived by the addition of the AUs of the current expression to the AUs of the previous appraisal check AUs.

This approach was found to be problematic in the cases when subsequent expressions are constituted of conflicting animations. For example in the case of hot anger the "novelty high" intermediate expression, according to the appraisal theory predictions ([2]) is includes raised eyebrows among others. The next intermediate prediction is "goal obstructive" and predicts lowered eyebrows. This conflict renders the animation problematic and the outcome of a sequential representation is confusing.

In the case of sequential animation – as adopted in the hot anger example, all intermediate expressions are animated in sequence. This could be realized either by interposing the neutral expression between the predictions or by "tweening" from one expression to the other keeping the common deformations as the common denominator. The approach containing the neutral expressions between predicted expressions renders the outcome counterintuitive. Overall the tweening approach is friendlier to the eye but is still not perceived as a realistic expression generation. Such conclusions demand further investigation in order to empirically prove such hypotheses. Both expert and simple user evaluation is needed.

5. Conclusion-Future Work

The synthesis of emotional facial expressions should be used to systematically address the questions of the underlying mechanisms of the emotion elicitation process, as well as the temporal unfolding emotional expression. The results presented in this paper aim to constitute the basis of future research and interdisciplinary collaboration between relevant research groups. Expert opinions as well as specific hypothesis testing are required to back or falsify the current preliminary conclusions. Future work will be comprised of in depth investigation of the temporal evolution issues that arose. More emotional expressions need to be synthesized in order to obtain substantial empirical evidence on the veracity of the appraisal theory predictions in expression synthesis.

Acknowledgments

This research is partly supported by the EC Project HUMAINE (IST-507422).

References

[1]   Picard, R. W.: *Affective Computing*. MIT Press, Cambridge, MA, (1997)

[2]   Wehrle, T., Kaiser, S., Schmidt, S. & Scherer, K. R.: Studying the dynamics of emotional expression using synthesized facial muscle movements. *Journal of Personality and Social Psychology, 78* (1) (2000) 105-119

[3]   Roseman I.J. and Smith, C.A.: Appraisal Theory: Overview, Assumptions, Varieties, Controversies. In Scherer, K.R., Schorr, A., & Johnstone, T., (Eds) Appraisal Processes

in Emotion: Theory Methods, Research. Oxford, New York: Oxford University Press, 3-19 (2001)

[4]   Ortony, A., Clore, G.L. and Collins, A.: The Cognitive Structure of Emotions, Cambridge, UK: Cambridge University Press (1988)

[5]   Pegna, A. J., Khateb, A., Lazeyras, F., & Seghier, M. L.: Discriminating emotional faces without primary visual cortices involves the right amygdala. *Nature Neuroscience*, *8*(1), 24–25 (2004)

[6]   Scherer, K.R.: Appraisal Considered as a Process of Multilevel Sequential Checking. In Scherer, K.R., Schorr, A., & Johnstone, T., (Eds) Appraisal Processes in Emotion: Theory Methods, Research. Oxford, New York: Oxford University Press, 92-129 (2001)

[7]   Scherer, K.R.: On the Nature and Function of Emotion: A Component Process Approach. In Scherer, K.R., & Ekman, P., (Eds) Approaches to Emotion. Hillsdale, New Jersey, London: Lawrence Erlbaum Associates, Publishers. 293-318 (1984)

[8]   Tekalp, M., Ostermann, J.: Face and 2-D mesh animation in MPEG-4. Image Communication Journal, Vol.15, Nos. 4-5 (2000) 387-421

[9]   Ekman, P.: "Facial expression and Emotion," *Am. Psychologist*, vol. 48 pp.384-392 (1993)

[10]   Raouzaiou, A., Tsapatsoulis, N., Karpouzis, K., Kollias, S.: Parameterized facial expression synthesis based on MPEG-4. EURASIP Journal on Applied Signal Processing, Vol. 2002, No. 10. Hindawi Publishing Corporation (2002) 1021-1038.

[11]   Raouzaiou, A., Caridakis, G., Malatesta, L., Karpouzis, K., Grandjean, D., Burkhardt, F., Kollias, S.: "Emotion Theory and multimodal Synthesis of Affective ECAs", submitted for publication to *Achieving Human-Like Qualities in Interactive Virtual and Physical Humanoids*, Special Issue of the International Journal of Humanoid Robotics, Catherine Pelachaud and Lola Cañamero (eds.)

Towards On- and Off-line Search, Browse and Replay of Home Activities

Anton Nijholt

Human Media Interaction, University of Twente
PO Box 217, 75000 AE Enschede
The Netherlands
anijholt@cs.utwente.nl,
WWW home page: http://hmi.ewi.utwente.nl/~anijholt

Abstract. Ambient Intelligence research is about ubiquitous computing and about social and intelligent characteristics of computer-supported environments. These characteristics aim at providing inhabitants or visitors of these environments with support in their activities. Activities include interactions between inhabitants and between inhabitants and (semi-) autonomous agents, including mobile robots, virtual humans and other smart objects in the environment. To provide real-time support requires understanding of behavior and activities. Clearly, being able to provide real-time support also allows us to provide off-line support, that is, intelligent off-line retrieval, summarizing, browsing and even replay, possibly in a transformed way, of stored information. Real-time remote access to these computer-supported environments also allows participation in activities and such participation as well can profit from the real-time capturing and interpretation of behavior and activities performed supported by ambient intelligence technology. In this paper we illustrate and support these observations by looking at results obtained in several European and US projects on meeting technology. In particular we look at the Augmented Multiparty Interaction (AMI) project in which we are involved.

1 Introduction

Environments equipped with Ambient Intelligence technology provide social and intelligent support to its inhabitants. The majority of ambient intelligence research is on providing support to individuals living or working in these smart environments. However, in home and office environments we have also people interacting with each other and interacting with smart objects (e.g., a mobile robot, furniture, intelligent devices, and virtual humans on ambient displays). Cameras, microphones and other sensors can be used to detect and capture such activities. Can the

Please use the following format when citing this chapter:

Nijholt, Anton, 2006, in IFIP International Federation for Information Processing, Volume 204, Artificial Intelligence Applications and Innovations, eds. Maglogiannis, I., Karpouzis, K., Bramer, M., (Boston: Springer), pp. 385–392

environment, using this sensorial input, support this multi-party interaction, e.g. in a home environment, as well?

Looking at smart environments from the point of view of supporting multi-party interaction adds some interesting research issues to the area of ambient intelligence research. Firstly, in order to be able to provide support, the environment is asked to understand the interactions between its inhabitants and between inhabitants and the environment or smart and maybe mobile objects available in the environment. Although we see the development of theories of interaction and behavior, these theories are rather poor from a computational point of view and therefore they hardly contribute to the design of tools and environments that support activities of human inhabitants. Hence, the need for computational theories of behavior and interactions needs to be emphasized. A second research issue that needs to be mentioned is the real-time monitoring of activities, the on-line access to information about activities taking place and also the on-line remote participation in activities or influencing activities in smart environments. The third research issue concerns the off-line access to stored information about activities in smart environments. This latter issue may involve retrieval, summarization, replay and browsing.

Certainly, not all three research issues need to be considered for every type of smart environment. Sometimes we are only interested in providing real-time support to an individual entering an ambient intelligence environment. Sometimes we just want to monitor what is happening and having an alert when something unusual occurs. Sometimes we want to know what activities were there when we were not present. Sometimes we need to retrieve, browse or replay previously stored information about activities in the past in order to support current activities.

There is one important domain of application of ambient intelligence technology where all these research issues play an important role. This is the domain of meetings supported by smart environment technology. In this domain it is useful to provide support during the meeting, it is useful to allow people who can not be present to view what is going on, it is useful to allow people to remotely participate and it is useful to provide access to captured multimedia information about a previous meeting, both for people who were present and want to recall part of a meeting and for people who could not attend.

The aim of this paper is to look at the way results from research and development done in the context of some large research projects on the design and development of meeting support technology (smart meeting rooms, remote meeting participation, distributed meetings, distributed collaborative work spaces, etc.) can be explained and explored in the context of smart home environments.

In section 2 of this paper we look at ambient intelligence in home environments and extend existing views in order to include multi-party interaction support and replay of events. In section 3 of this paper we discuss the research issues in several projects dealing with the development of meeting support technology. We explain and review the research approaches from a point of view that allows exportation to other research and application areas. In section 4 we extend these views and approaches to (remote) meeting support such that it becomes clear that topics such as visualization, virtual reality and embodied agents (virtual humans).can play important roles in providing not only meeting support, but also, with appropriately equipped smart home environments, to support (1) multi-party interaction and joint activities of family members (including virtual pets and virtual humans), (2) real-time monitoring and participation in such activities, and (3) retrieving, browsing, and replaying of previously captured and stored information about activities that took place in a particular environment. Section 5 contains conclusions and has observations about future research.

2 Social and Intelligent Home Environments

Whatever kind of situation we are in, when 'ambient intelligence' in one or other way is able to support our activities we can be happy with it. Maybe the activities can be done more efficiently due to this support or they can become more enjoyable. Do we want to look back at activities, do we want to retrieve information about previous activities or do we want to experience these activities again, maybe from an other view point or being in an other's person skin?

Our viewpoint is that there are lots of reasons to want to look back on a previous activity in which we or our friends and relatives were involved. This is certainly obvious when looking at a meeting event. We always do, trying to remember what happened, what was said and what decisions were taken for what reasons. Traditionally there are minutes of a meeting, participants have their own notes and there is other material that can be consulted (agenda, list of participants, documents, presentations). More and more we see audio and video recordings of meetings appear in order to be able to back to a certain moment during a meeting. This makes clear that meetings differ from spontaneous gatherings, from family gatherings and, generally, meetings and joint activities between friends, relatives and family members. Meetings are structured and certain goals are defined in advance.

Hence, a meeting differs from joint activities in a home environment, but also in home environments meeting support technology that is now developed in some large European projects can play useful roles. The home environment can ask for real-time support for activities that take place, sometimes it can be useful or enjoyable to remotely take part in home activities and sometimes we would like to experience in some or other way an important moment again. Presently this is done with diaries, photo albums and video collections. Web providers make it already possible to share these collections with others. Personal archives are made accessible for others and personal notes and thoughts appear in blogs on the web. This can be considered as a first step to a continuous registration of events in social environments [1] and at the same time to technology that makes it possible to search, browse and replay such information or allow to get immersed in this information (see also [2]).

Currently, most ambient intelligence technology that is being developed concerns applications as home environment control and automation. Personal entertainment, health care and security are other application areas. In our view we should also look at events that involve multi-party interaction for which real-time support is useful and where support requires some high-level interpretation (in contrast with turning on the lights when someone enters the room). This interpretation allows also for off-line intelligent search in the stored information, the development of intelligent browsing tools and multimedia presentation of the information. Among the possibilities for multimedia presentation we include ways of replaying, probably in a transformed and manipulated way of home activities (family meetings, visits of relatives, playing with children, a birthday party, a wedding, just an evening at home with everyone doing usual things, preparing a dinner in the kitchen, et cetera). Being able to interpret, search, browse and replay recorded meeting data is part of the European AMI (Augmented Multi-party Interaction) project. Having a (mixed reality) 'album' of important events is one of the streams (*My Life Album*) of the *IntoMyWorld* candidate Presence II project [3]. Among the examples that are mentioned is the possibility to allow people to re-immerse themselves in their own weddings. In this paper an attempt is presented to bring these approaches together.

3 The AMI (Augmented Multi-party Interaction) Project

3.1 General Background and Introduction

By looking at the earlier mentioned AMI project we want to make clear that technology obtained in multi-party interaction research as is now becoming available, can be usefully employed in the context of other smart environments. The AMI[1] project builds on the earlier M4 project (Multi-Modal Meeting Manager). Both projects are concerned with the design of a demonstration system that enables structuring, browsing and querying of archives of automatically analyzed meetings. The meetings take place in a room equipped with multimodal sensors. Multimedia information captured from microphones and cameras are translated into annotated multimedia meeting minutes that allow for retrieval, summarization and browsing. The result of the M4 project was an off-line meeting browser.

More than in M4, in the recently started AMI project attention is on multimodal events. Apart from the verbal and nonverbal interaction between participants, many events take place that are relevant for the interaction and that therefore have impact on their communication content and form. For example, someone enters the room, someone distributes a paper, a person opens or closes the meeting, ends a discussion or asks for a vote, a participants asks or is invited to present ideas on the whiteboard, a data projector presentation is given with the help of laser pointing and later discussed, someone has to leave early and the order of the agenda is changed, etc. Participants make references in their utterances to what is happening, to presentations that have been shown, to behavior of other participants, etc. They look at each other, to the person they address, to the others, to the chairman, to their notes and to the presentation on the screen, etc. Participants have facial expressions, gestures and body posture that support, emphasize or contradict their opinion, etc.

To study and collect multimodal data smart meeting rooms are maintained by the different research partners. They are equipped with cameras, circular microphone arrays and, recently introduced, capture of whiteboard pen writing and drawing and note taking by participants on 'electronic paper'. Participants also have lapel microphones and cameras in front of them to capture facial expressions.

---

[1] AMI started on 1 January 2004 and has duration of three years. It is supported by the EU 6th FP IST Programme (IST IP project FP6-506811).

3.2 AMI: From Signal Processing to Interpretation

The meeting support application researched in the AMI project [4] requires the development of tools that take into account the meeting context. Rather than zooming in on constraining general methods of detecting and interpreting events in physical environments, we have a bottom-up approach starting with observed events in meeting environments and attempting to model and explain them using more general observations on theories of verbal and nonverbal communication.

Models are needed for the integration of the multimodal streams in order to be able to interpret events and interactions. These models include statistical models to integrate asynchronous multiple streams and semantic representation formalisms that allow reasoning and cross-modal reference resolution. Apart from the recognition of joint behavior, i.e., the recognition of group actions during a meeting, there is also the recognition of the actions of individuals, and the information fusion at a higher level for further recognition and interpretation of the interactions.

When looking at the actions of the individuals during a meeting several useful pieces of information can be collected. First of all, there can be person identification using face recognition. Current speaker recognition using multimodal information (e.g., speech and gestures) and speaker tracking (e.g., while the speaker rises from his chair and walks to the whiteboard) are similar issues. Other, more detailed but nevertheless relevant meeting acts can be distinguished: for example, recognition of individual meeting actions by video sequence processing.

Presently models, annotation tools and mark-up languages are being developed in the project. They allow the description of the relevant issues during a meeting, including temporal aspects and including low-level fusion of media streams. In our part of the project we are interested in high-level fusion, where semantic/pragmatic (tuned to particular applications) knowledge is taken into account (see e.g. [5]). I.e., we try to explore different aspects of the interpretation point of view. We hope to integrate recent research in the area of traditional multimodal dialogue modeling. These issues will become more and more important since models, methods and tools that need to be developed in order to make this possible can be used for other events taken place in smart and ambient intelligence environments as well.

4   Towards Virtual Reality Representations and Replay

In our research we have looked at capturing meeting activities from an image processing point of view and at capturing meeting activities from a higher-level point of view, that is, a point of view that allows, among others, observations about dominance, focus of attention, addressee identification, and emotion display. We studied posture and gesture activity, using our vision software package. A flock-of-birds package was used to track head orientation of some of our 4-party meetings. It allowed us to display animated representations of meeting participants in a (3D) virtual reality environment [6]. In this environment visualized events can be augmented with meta-observations provided by support agents and displayed in the virtual environment. This is illustrated in Fig. 1.

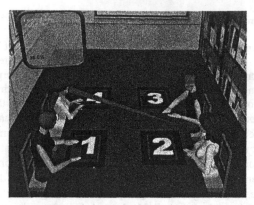

Fig. 1. The virtual meeting room showing gestures, head movements, speech transcript, addressee(s) and the percentage a person has spoken until that moment

Even more attractive is it to have meetings represented in a virtual meeting room (VMR), where participants do not all share the same physical space. We introduced a prototype version of a distributed meeting room set-up. This set-up [7] allows the connection of several inhabited smart meeting rooms and the representation of the participants and their activities in a shared virtual environment, made accessible for participants (and observers) in real-time. It allows the participants to take part in the meeting, perceiving the verbal and nonverbal communication by other participants through their avatars, from their assigned position around the meeting table. As shown in Fig. 2, also in this distributed version we can add meta-information about the meeting and its progress to the visualization of the virtual room.

The technology used within the DVMR experiment differs substantially from normal video conferencing technology. Rather than sending video data as such, this data is transformed in a format that enables analysis and transformation. For the DVMR experiment the focus was on representing poses and gestures, rather than, for example, facial expressions. Poses of the human body are easily represented in the form of skeleton poses [8], essentially in the same format as being used for applications in the field of virtual reality and computer games. Such skeleton poses are also more appropriate as input data for classification algorithms for gestures.

Another advantage for remote meetings, especially when relying on small handheld devices, using wireless connections, is that communicating skeleton data requires substantially less bandwidth than video data. A more abstract representation of human body data is also vital for combining different input channels, possibly using different input modalities. Here we rely on two different input modalities: one for body posture estimation based upon a video camera, and a second input channel using a head tracker device. Although the image recognition data for body postures also makes some estimation of the head position, it turned out that using a separate head tracker was much more reliable in this case.

The general conclusion is, not so much that everyone should use a head tracker device, but rather that the setup as a whole should be capable of fusing a wide variety of input modalities. This will allow one to adapt to a lot of different and often difficult situations. In the long run, we expect to see two types of environment for remote meetings: specialized meeting rooms, fully equipped with whatever hardware is needed and available for meetings on the one hand side, and far more basic single user environments based upon equipment that happens to be available. The capability to exploit whatever equipment is available might be an important factor for the acceptance of the technology. In this respect, we expect a lot from improved speech recognition and especially from natural language analysis. The current version of the virtual meeting room requires manual control, using classical input devices like keyboard or mouse, in order to look around, interact with objects etcetera. It seems unlikely that in a more realistic setting people that are participating in a real meeting would like to do that. Simpler interaction, based upon gaze detection but also on speech recognition should replace this situation

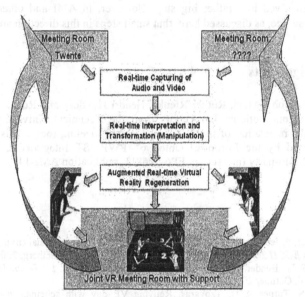

Fig. 2. Capturing, manipulation and re-generation of activities in remote locations in a joint virtual meeting room

5   Conclusions

Home automation is important, but providing real-time support to inhabitants during their activities is important as well. This real-time support requires interpretation of home activities. In many of these activities we have to deal with multi-party interaction. That is, there are verbal and nonverbal interactions between the human inhabitants of the environment. Moreover, with the introduction of mobile robots, smart objects and virtual embodied agents displayed on walls and objects, the multi-party members will also include these artificial and pro-active agents. The environment needs some understanding of such interactions and therefore we need to look for models for multi-party verbal and nonverbal interaction.

Meetings are rather controlled events and therefore they are a more acceptable target for preliminary research in this direction. We looked at the approaches and preliminary results obtained in the European AMI project on smart meeting environments. In this project real-time support is only one of the objectives. Rather the emphasis is on querying and browsing the multimedia information that is captured using various types of sensors. Being able to replay in one or other form of a meeting is an interesting objective. These additions to real-time support are useful in home environments as well. Apart from real-time support to home inhabitants and real-time remote access from other smart environments, it also allows intelligent querying, browsing and replay of previous interesting events. From detecting rather straightforward events as entering a room, being in the proximity of a certain object or identifying a person in the room, to the interpretation of events in which more persons are involved is a rather big step. However, in AMI and other large EU projects we now see, as discussed here, that small steps in this direction are taken.

Acknowledgements

I want to thank Job Zwiers, Rutger Rienks, Hendri Hondorp and Ronald Poppe for their research contributions. Jan Peciva from the Technical University of Brno helped with the realization of the distributed virtual meeting room. This work was partly supported by the European Union 6th FWP IST Integrated Project AMI (Augmented Multi-party Interaction, FP6-506811, publication AMI-147).

References

1. M. Deutscher, P. Jeffrey & N. Siu. Information capture devices for social environments. In: Proceedings *EUSAI 2004*, LNCS 3295, Springer-Verlag Berlin Heidelberg, 2004, 267-270.
2. S. Vemuri & W. Bender. Next-generation personal memory aids. *BT Technology Journal*, Vol. 22, No 4, October 2004, 125-138.
3. P. Turner, S. Turner & D. Tzovaras. Reliving VE day with schemata activation. In: Proceedings *8th International Workshop on Presence: Presence 2005*. M. Slater (ed.), London, 2005, 33-38.
4. I. McCowan, D. Gatica-Perez, S. Bengio, D. Moore, H. Bourlard. Towards Computer Understanding of Human Interactions. In: *Ambient Intelligence*, E. Aarts et al. (Eds.), LNCS, Springer-Verlag Heidelberg, 235 - 251.
5. A. Nijholt. Multimodality and Ambient Intelligence. In: *Algorithms in Ambient Intelligence*. W.F.J. Verhaegh, E.H.L. Aarts & J. Korst (eds.), Kluwer, Boston, 2003.
6. A. Nijholt, J. Zwiers & J. Peciva. The Distributed Virtual Meeting Room Exercise. In: Proceedings ICMI 2005 Workshop on Multimodal multiparty meeting processing, A. Vinciarelli & J-M. Odobez (eds.), Trento, Italy, October 2005, 93-99.
7. A. Nijholt. Meetings in the Virtuality Continuum: Send Your Avatar. In: Proceedings 2005 International Conference on CYBERWORLDS, T.L. Kunii, S.H. Soon & A. Sourin (eds.), IEEE Computer Society Press, Los Alamitos, USA, November 2005, Singapore, 75-82.
8. R. Poppe, D. Heylen, A. Nijholt, & M. Poel. Towards real-time body pose estimation for presenters in meeting environments. *Proc. 13th Intern. Conference in Central Europe on Computer Graphics, Visualization and Computer Vision*. V. Skala (Ed.), Plzen, Czech Republic, 2005, 41-44.

Engineering an interoperable adaptive hypermedia testing tool supporting user adaptable strategies

Fotis Lazarinis, Simeon Retalis
University of Piraeus
Department of Technology Education and Digital Systems
80 Karaoli & Dimitriou
185 34 Piraeus, Greece
lazarinf@unipi.gr, retal@unipi.gr

Abstract. In this paper we present a web based tool for authoring adaptive assessments based on IMS QTI, IMS LIP and IEEE PAPI learning standards. The tool allows authors of assessments to customize the applied adaptation strategies to meet their own teaching experiences and goals. During the assessment procedure the system accumulates knowledge about learners and adapts the exposure of items based on this knowledge and on the adaptable rule model. Design decisions and the employed user, domain and rule models are analyzed and discussed. Results from a usability evaluation are discussed at the end of the paper.

1 Introduction

Adaptive Educational Hypermedia Systems provide a learning environment adapted to the individual characteristics and goals of the learners [1]. Adaptive Educational Hypermedia Systems can be used both for assessment and self-assessment providing a tailored testing environment which results to a shorter and less demanding assessment.

Most of the current adaptive testing systems rely on the Computerized Adaptive Testing technique [2] and the Item Response Theory [3] and depending on the learner's performance they pose easier or more complex questions. This unique adaptation criterion limits the capabilities offered to educators for identifying the learning difficulties and misconceptions of their students. The majority of these systems represent their data in a custom way, i.e. in a custom made database or XML structure, preventing knowledge sharing between applications [4, 5].

CosyQTI has been designed taking into account two very important factors. Firstly, that the data models employed should comply with established learning

Please use the following format when citing this chapter:

Lazarinis, Fotis, Retalis, Simeon, 2006, in IFIP International Federation for Processing, Volume 204, Artificial Intelligence Applications and Information Innovations, eds. Maglogiannis, I., Karpouzis, K., Bramer, M., (Boston: Springer), pp. 393–400

standards to support interoperability among e-learning systems. Secondly, adaptive decisions should not be fixed and thus pedagogically limited. Instead, the adaptivity decisions should be left to educators who could then integrate their own teaching experiences and intelligence into the system. This can be achieved through the customization of a broad set of predefined adaptive rules.

The paper is organized as follows. In section 2, a brief introduction to adaptation in assessment systems is provided. Section 3 presents the basic modules of CosyQTI and discusses the factors that influenced their design. Section 4 presents the results of usability experiments and section 5 summarizes and gives directions for further research.

2 Adaptation in Assessment Systems

The most well known adaptation technique is Computer Adaptive Testing (CAT). This involves a computer-administered test in which, the selection/presentation of each question and the decision to end the process are dynamically adapted to the learner's performance in the test [2]. Computer Adaptive Testing is based on Item Response Theory [3]. In the adaptive testing procedure, depending on the learner's answers to questions, easier or questions of increased difficulty are posed. The criterion for selecting questions is to match the question's difficulty level with the learner's estimated knowledge level. It has been shown that these questions are more "informative" in terms of conclusions that can be drawn on the learner's knowledge. The goal is to accurately estimate the learner's knowledge. Several approaches exploit the idea of adaptive testing. Huang in [6] describes the CBAT-2 adaptive testing algorithm that generates content-balanced questions and SIETTE [7] is an adaptive assessment authoring tool that employs this technique.

Another adaptation technique, which is however mainly used in computer-assisted surveys, is Adaptive Questions, as defined by Pitkow and Recker in [8]. This method causes the generation of a dynamic sequence of questions depending on learner's responses. In this case, questions are divided in categories based on whether they do not cause any adaptation at all, trigger one follow-up question, or trigger more than one follow-up question. It has been shown that web-based adaptive questionnaires can reduce the number and complexity of questions presented to users. Adaptive questionnaires have been used to assess web users' attitudes in CATES [9].

3 Overview of CosyQTI

CosyQTI is a web based tool allowing authors to create both adaptive and non-adaptive web based assessments. The component based architecture of the system, depicted in figure 1 using UML notation, consists of a learner model, a domain model and a rule model. The item selection engine is implicitly created based on these models. The learner model contains information such as the goals, preferences, qualifications, knowledge estimations and usage data of each learner. The domain model follows the IEEE/ACM Computing Curricula structure [10] and additional domains can be easily integrated. The rule model is user adaptable meaning that educators adapt a set of predefined rules to meet their own pedagogical goals and beliefs.

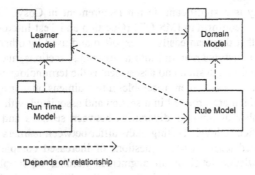

'Depends on' relationship

Fig. 1. High level component architecture of CosyQTI

3.1 Assessment authoring

After authentication educators select the domain of the assessment and create a new assessment or edit an existing one through a homogeneous interface (see figure 2). Educators can create or re-use items (questions) of various types and group them to sections. Each section is associated with a concept which in turn is associated with a domain.

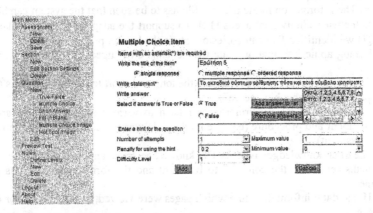

Fig. 2. Creation of multiple choice questions

For each assessment item the educator may alter the default values of the additional data which are difficulty level, hints, number of attempts, penalty for using the hint, and minimum and maximum score (see figure 2). The different types

of items supported are:
(i) True/False
(ii) Multiple choice (single, multiple or ordered response)
(iii) Fill-in-the-blanks
(iv) Multiple Image choice
(v) Image hot spot.

Interoperability is a significant design requirement in CosyQTI. Therefore the created assessments conform to IMS QTI (Question and Test Interoperability) XML standard [11], so that they can easily be exported and used by other IMS compliant applications. QTI structures material into assessments, sections, and items. An item is the formal name for a question and assessment is the terminology used for a test.

The structure of an assessment resembles a two dimensional array. Each row is a set of questions which are grouped in a section and associated with a concept of the domain. The number of items is diversified between sections and they are sorted based on their difficulty level. Testing paths differ between learners as in real world classes. Experienced teachers pose questions of increased complexity to students with a high knowledge level or an augmented number of simpler questions to students with lower performance. In both cases the ultimate goal of educators is to encourage all the students to actively participate in the learning procedure. Similarly in CosyQTI the testing path of a new learner may initiate in question 1 of section 1, while in other learners the assessment procedure may start in question 1 of section 2 or in a question of increased difficulty level of section 1.

3.2 Learner model

The adaptivity of the system relies primarily on the learner model which contains the goals, preferences, knowledge and usage data of each learner. This information is crucial as the adaptive rules are based on these data as we will see in the next sections. The information in the user profile has to be such that the system can better adapt to the user's individual needs [12]. To support the adaptive approach taken in CosyQTI we identified five categories of data in the learner profile:

(i) Demographic information: data that remains unchanged, such as age, gender, etc.
(ii) Learner goals: which are related to the long and short term learning goals (e.g. "to pass test X with a high score").
(iii) Learner preferences: preferences related to various aspects of the learning environment and procedure (e.g. the mode of delivery, accessibility requirements, or assessment).
(iv) Learner knowledge: records the knowledge level and the weaknesses and strengths related to the concepts to be learnt and the formal qualifications of a learner.
(v) Usage data: information like which pages were viewed, in what order, for how long, etc.

For satisfying the interoperability design principle we structured the data using learning standards. More specifically, the attributes that compose a learner's profile have resulted from a selection and combination of elements from IMS LIP [13] and IEEE PAPI [14] standards. This combination of elements serves our key objective for interoperability without compromising the attributes and services required [15].

3.3 Domain model

Domain model is a set of associated concepts which form hierarchies of concepts. Concepts of the domain model may be atomic or composite containing other atomic or composite concepts. The IEEE/ACM vocabulary [10] is utilized for testing purposes in the current implementation of CosyQTI. However CosyQTI is an open domain web testing tool, meaning that a mechanism has been developed which allows automatic integration of domains following the IEEE/ACM vocabulary structure. Thus educators of various disciplines are able to utilize the system.

The domain model contains additionally a series of learning objectives such as 'learn concept X', 'describe the common characteristics of concept X', etc. Learning objectives are high level abstract learning goals which are associated with concepts at run time. Educators define learning objectives for each section or item of an assessment and the system automatically determines, based on the learner's performance, whether these learning goals are satisfied or not. The domain model is overlaid [16] in the learner model based on the concepts and learning objectives of an assessment.

3.4 Rule model

Adaptation decisions are set by the educators during the authoring phase. An educator is able to adapt the assessment to the requirements of an individual or to the aims of a class by adapting a set of *IF* <condition> *THEN* <action> rules. During the creation stage trigger points are set and actions are specified based on the learning preferences and pedagogical aims of the teacher (see figure 3). Rules are applicable either to new users or to existing users for whom the system, based on their previous interactions, has a complete learner profile. Adaptation rules may be combined with the aid of Boolean operators.

Events relate to the previous knowledge on the assessed subject, formal qualifications, previously estimated knowledge level or performance during the execution of an assessment. Conditions are set by the educators and are thresholds which should a learner pass an action is realised. Actions may be section advancement, knowledge level increase or decrease, assessment ending, ascent or descent of the difficulty level. For example an educator may impose section advancement and knowledge level increase if the score of a learner during the first five questions of a section is greater or equal to 75%.

3.5 Run time model

When learners log in to the system they are identified and described by their personal model. The user model has to form an accurate image of the learner so it needs to be updated frequently to include any changes. The learner's knowledge is updated in our system, based on the section topics a learner is assessed on. The algorithm used to update the user's knowledge is implicitly formed based on the author's rules. Learners get immediate feedback and help on their choices.

System keeps the learner's usage data which includes historical information about the learner's performance in the test as well. It is very useful to keep track of the learner's actions and the sequence of sections and items visited. This information is required in cases where an author wants to apply advanced rules such as "If the user performed very well in section A but performed poorly in section B, then present a new section with intermediate difficulty level". This type of rule condition is currently under development. Also usage data can be used for opening the learner model during or at the end of an assessment [17].

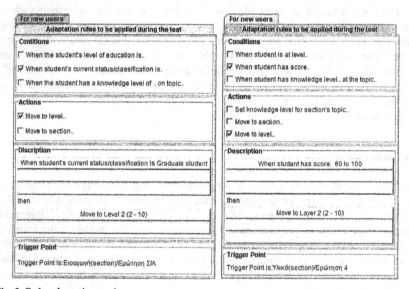

Fig. 3. Rule adaptation options

5 Evaluation

CosyQTI is a web based adaptive assessment tool which can be used for self-assessment as well. Its main goal is to support learning by adapting the testing procedure to the performance, goals and preferences of learners and to the teaching experiences and intelligence of educators. Thorough evaluation of such a system is a complex and time consuming procedure involving compound criteria, several users and different approaches.

The initial evaluation performed regarded the system's added value offered to educators. The system's authoring capabilities and features were explained and exhibited to five experienced IT instructors. Then we asked them to create a 4 section assessment consisting of 10 questions each. We asked the participants to supply their own queries and should they judge it appropriate and necessary to adjust some of the available adaptive rules.

During the test authoring phase we recorded their adaptation decisions. As seen in table 1 most of the educators defined section advancement if a learner achieves a specific score in the first 5 or 7 questions. However two of them created more specialised compound rules applied either at the start or at the end of each section. These rules depend on the estimated knowledge level of learners. If it is high then force the system to increase the knowledge level and thus the difficulty level of the subsequent questions.

Table 1. Adaptive rules created from the educators

Educator	Trigger point	Condition	Action
1	Question 5 of each section	Score > 75%	Move on to the next section
2	Question 7 of each section	Score >= 90%	Move on to the next section
3	1. Test initiation	1. Degree in computer science or certificate in IT	1. Pose questions of increased difficulty level
	2. Question 5 of each section	2. Score >= 100%	2. Move on to the next section
4	End of first section	Score >= 80%	Increase knowledge level and difficulty level of posed questions
5	Start and end of each section	High or low knowledge level in the domain	Increase/decrease difficulty level of posed questions

This short evaluation revealed that such a system is quite useful because it grants educators with freedom to apply their own intelligence and teaching philosophy. However enrichment of the rule model is necessary and possibly a mechanism for defining new rules instead of simply adjusting the predefined ones is necessary as well. In any case more exhaustive evaluation experiments are needed to realize the full potential of the system and to recognize design weaknesses.

5 Discussion and Future Work

This paper presents the basic components and design decisions of a web based adaptive assessment authoring tool. Data models conform to international standards making the system interoperable with other e-learning tools. Educators have the ability to tailor multiple criteria to their goals and to the individual needs of their learners. The authoring environment makes the addition and modification of learning content straightforward and allows the educators to efficiently customize the execution of the assessment and assign various learning objectives to items and sections. Learners get immediate feedback on each question and an analytical explanation at the end of the assessment.

The usability experiment revealed that the capabilities and the non restrictive nature of the system are very useful to educators. Different educators applied different pedagogical approaches to test the knowledge of their students on the same domain. The evaluation produced new research directions with respect to the adaptation model. More adaptive rules and more adaptability freedom needed to simulate real teacher/student classes.

References

1. Brusilovsky, P: Adaptive hypermedia. User Modeling and User-Adapted Interaction 11 (2001) 87-110.
2. van der Linden, W. J., Glas, C. A. W.: Computerized Adaptive Testing: Theory and Practice. Netherlands: Kluwer Academic Publishers (2000)
3. Hambleton, R. K., Swamination, H., Rogers, H. J.: Fundamentals of Item Response Theory. Newbury Park: Sage Publications (1991)
4. De Bra, P., Aroyo, L., Chepegin, V.: The Next Big Thing: Adaptive Web-Based Systems. Journal of Digital Information, 5(1) (2004) http://jodi.tamu.edu
5. Retalis, S.: Usable and Interoperable E-Learning Resources Repositories. In: Sanjaya Mishra & Ramesh C. Sharma (eds): Interactive Multimedia in Education and Training, Idea Group Inc. 249-269 (2004)
6. Huang, S.: A Content-Balanced Adaptive Testing Algorithm for Computer-Based Training Systems. In: Frasson, C., Gauthier, G., Lesgold, A. (eds.): Intelligent Tutoring Systems, Third International Conference, Springer (1996) 306-314
7. Guzmán, E., Conejo, R., García-Hervás, E.: An Authoring Environment for Adaptive Testing Educational Technology & Society 8 (3) (2005) 66-76
8. Pitkow, J., Recker, M.: Using the Web as a Survey Tool: Results from the Second WWW User Survey. Computer Networks ISDN Systems 27(6) (1995) 809-822
9. Chou, C.: Constructing a Computer-Assisted Testing and Evaluation System on the World Wide Web – the CATES experience. IEEE Transactions on Education 43(3) (2000) 266-272
10. IEEE/ACM Computing Curricula 2001 – CS Body of Knowledge, http://www.computer.org/education/cc2001/final/appa.htm
11. IMS Question and Test Interoperability Specification, http://www.imsglobal.org/question/
12. Kobsa, A.: Generic User Modeling Systems. User Modeling and User-Adapted Interaction 11 (2001) 49–63
13. IMS Learner Information Package Specification, http://www.imsproject.org/profiles/
14. IEEE PAPI Learner http://edutool.com/papi/
15. Dolog, P., Gavriloaie, R., Nejdl, W., Brase, J.: Integrating Adaptive Hypermedia Techniques and Open RDF-based Environments. In: Proc. of 12th International World Wide Web Conference, Budapest, Hungary (2003)
16. De Bra, P., Aroyo, L., Cristea, A.: Adaptive Web-Based Educational Hypermedia. Web Dynamics, (2004) 387-410
17. Bull, S., Pain, H.: Did I say what I think I said, and do you agree with me? Inspecting and Questioning the Student Model. In: J. Greer (ed): Proceedings of World Conference on Artificial Intelligence in Education, AACE: Charlottesville, VA (1995) 501-508

Teaching a Computer Science Course using Adaptable Instructional Images

Stavros K. Filippidis[1], and Ioannis A. Tsoukalas[2]

[1] Multimedia Lab, Department of Informatics, Aristotle University of
Thessaloniki,
GR-54124 Thessaloniki, Greece
sfilippi@csd.auth.gr

[2] Multimedia Lab, Department of Informatics, Aristotle University of
Thessaloniki,
GR-54124 Thessaloniki, Greece
tsoukala@csd.auth.gr

Abstract. In this paper, we use adaptable instructional digital images. The images used are the result of screen capture. These images illustrate the specific use of a spreadsheet software package in order to complete a given task. This task consists from several parts, and for these parts the corresponding images are given in different versions. Each version is using a different amount of details for the same part of the task. The task is accessible to the students through a single html file hosted on a web site, available through an Intranet. Via this web site students choose their preferable "knowledge path" (that is: the choice of image files they make in order to view the whole task). In the experimental course set, there are 3 steps where students choose between 2 versions for each, giving altogether 8 different choices (knowledge paths) that a student can choose from.

1 Introduction and Theoretical Analysis

Research has been performed in many aspects of using animation, multimedia and video for instruction, as well as relative issues of pedagogy and didactics on children [1-12]. Research has also been performed in many aspects of adaptive and adaptable hypertext, hypermedia and multimedia [13-18]. In this paper, we use adaptable instructional images (that is: in this system students adapt to the system themselves while using it). The approach we use here makes the assumption that the adaptation has to be performed without changing the media used to present a certain knowledge item. For example, a concept we found out that is best to be taught using instructional images, will not be presented as well if we choose to teach it using digital audio (e.g.: aural instructions). So, in order to use adaptation to give different knowledge paths to each student, we do not change the used media itself; we prefer

Please use the following format when citing this chapter:

Filippidis, Stavros, Tsoukalas, Ioannis, 2006, in IFIP International Federation for Information Processing, Volume 204, Artificial Intelligence Applications and Innovations, eds. Maglogiannis, I., Karpouzis, K., Bramer, M., (Boston: Springer), pp. 401–408

to change the content of the certain media. This assumption and approach was followed by [14] (where it was used for the case of adaptable instructional video). In the case of this experiment, we change the content of the instructional images. By the term "knowledge path" we are referring to the 8 different choices a student can make: Considering that there are 3 steps where students choose between 2 versions for each, there are altogether 2*2*2=8 different choices.

By making different versions of instructional images for the same part of the course, we provide different levels of detail to students: Students can either choose the non – detailed images (they only view the result of the certain part of the task) or the detailed version of the images.

Students can choose a sequence of instructional images all based on the same approach, or they can choose images using each time the appropriate alternative version.

The method of instruction uses adaptation (alternative images for the same part of the task) and gives the student more flexibility in order to adapt this method to his/her personal needs. So, the students can create their own knowledge path and they can use it to complete the given task taking all the time they need. This method is similar to the method used by [14] (where it was used for the case of adaptable instructional video).

2 The experiment

We used the described method in order to teach a course on spreadsheets to high school students. In this course, students have to calculate the remaining amount of euros to be paid, from someone who got a loan from a bank, at the end of a given period. We divided this exercise into ten (10) steps, and some of the steps had different approaches (and different versions of images).

The goals of the experiment are to examine the following: Did students find the applied method useful, easy to use, and easy to learn and did they feel satisfied using it? Are the results of the students relevant among these categories (usefulness, ease of use, ease of learning, and satisfaction)? Is there any difference in terms of using the detailed version of images or not?

The steps and approaches are as follows.

2.1 The Steps of the Given Task

For the first step, students have to create the initial spreadsheet (table) and enter headings and data to it. This step has a limited number of special actions to be performed in the spreadsheet: Merging cells, formatting cells and enter initial data of the task. For this first step, two different versions of images were used.

In the first approach, we presented an image containing the completed screenshot of the spreadsheet for this step. In the second approach, we presented a series of 15 images that presented, in detail, what the students had to do in order to complete the first step.

For steps 2-6, students have to calculate the result of some cells by typing the proper types (e.g.: =C1+D2). For these steps, two different versions of images were used.

In the first approach, we presented images (one for each step) containing the completed screenshot of the spreadsheet for these steps. In the second approach, we presented a series of 10 images (two for each step) that presented, in detail, what the students had to do in order to complete these steps.

For steps 7-10, students have to calculate the rest of the cells by using the completion method. For these steps, two different versions of images were used.

In the first approach, we presented images (one for each step) containing the completed screenshot of the spreadsheet for these steps. In the second approach, we presented a series of 6 images that presented, in detail, what the students had to do in order to complete these steps.

2.2 Experimental Setup

The experimental setup is similar to the experimental setup used by [14] (where it was used for the case of adaptable instructional video). We used all the above images to create our experiment: We created a single (and very simple to use) web page (html file). Please note that in this experiment we didn't use any special authoring environment. In this html file, we gave instructions to the students (subjects of the experiment) about the steps they had to follow in order to complete the given task. For each step, simple (text) instructions were given: These instructions were about the contents of each of the images (alternative versions) available on every step, so that the students could choose the proper version of the images they would like to view for each of the steps. This html file and the corresponding image files were available to the students through an intranet. Each of the students completed the given task by following the instructions and viewing the image files (available through the html file).

The method was applied to 43 high school students. After completing the given task, each student completed a questionnaire about how he/she evaluated the method of instruction. We used the USE questionnaire [20]. We used all statements from this questionnaire [20], except one that did not fit our case of study. The word "it" in the USE questionnaire [20] was changed to "this method" (the use of adaptable digital images for instruction).

In this questionnaire, the students had to rate their agreement with the given statements about how they felt using this method of instruction. For each statement, they had to circle or X out the level of agreement that applied (where 1 means strongly disagree, 4 means neither disagree nor agree, and 7 means strongly agree; and NA means it doesn't apply). Finally, the option of not rating a statement was given (by cycling nothing or by cycling the "NA" option).

Also, in each questionnaire the students completed yes or no to the question "did you use the detailed version of the images?", and also their sex (male or female).

This type of questionnaire had been used by [14] and [19].

3 Statistical Analysis and Results

3.1 Grouping Initial Statements of the Questionnaire into Categories

In order to group these statements into categories for further statistical analysis, we grouped them into four categories, using the categories as they appear in [20]:

Category 1: Usefulness
Category 2: Ease of Use
Category 3: Ease of Learning
Category 4: Satisfaction

For each of these categories, we calculated the mean value of all the statements of the category, and we used this mean value as the value of the category.

So, further statistical analysis was performed using these four categories, and not the 29 initial statements. In fact, we transformed the 29 discrete variables we initially had (from the questionnaires) into 4 non-discrete variables.

This kind of transformation had also been performed to the questionnaire used by [14] and [19].

Please note that for some of the statistics that follow, we recoded these 4 non-discrete variables into discrete variables for statistical purposes.

3.2 Statistical Results and Correlations between Categories

The boxplots for the four categories are given in figure 1. Statistical facts for the four categories are given in table 1. In table 2 we see correlations between the categories (in pairs of two). We see that they are (in pairs of two) related with correlations significant at the 0.01 level (2-tailed).

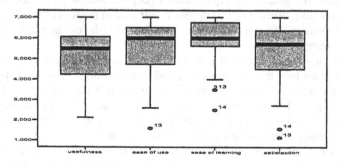

Fig. 1. Boxplots for the four categories

Table 1. Statistical facts for the four categories

		Usefulness	Ease of use	Ease of learning	Satisfaction
N	Valid	43	43	43	43
	Missing	0	0	0	0
Mean		5.19	5.56	5.86	5.28
Std. Error of Mean		0.86	0.177	0.190	0.222
Std. Deviation		1.220	1.161	1.246	1.453
Skewness		-0.786	-0.962	-1.352	-1.052
Std. Error of Skewness		0.361	0.361	0.361	0.361
Kurtosis		0.462	0.925	1.566	0.710
Std. Error of Kurtosis		0.709	0.709	0.709	0.709
Percentiles	10	4.00	4.00	4.00	3.00
	25	4.00	5.00	5.00	4.00
	50	5.00	6.00	6.00	6.00
	75	6.00	6.00	7.00	6.00
	90	6.60	7.00	7.00	7.00

Table 2. Correlations between the categories

		usefulness	ease of use	ease of learning	satisfaction
usefulness	Pearson Correlation	1	0.828(**)	0.757(**)	0.921(**)
	Sig. (2-tailed)	.	0.000	0.000	0.000
	N	43	43	43	43
ease of use	Pearson Correlation	0.828(**)	1	0.902(**)	0.929(**)
	Sig. (2-tailed)	0.000	.	0.000	0.000
	N	43	43	43	43
ease of learning	Pearson Correlation	0.757(**)	0.902(**)	1	0.839(**)
	Sig. (2-tailed)	0.000	0.000	.	0.000
	N	43	43	43	43
satisfaction	Pearson Correlation	0.921(**)	0.929(**)	0.839(**)	1
	Sig. (2-tailed)	0.000	0.000	0.000	.
	N	43	43	43	43

** Correlation is significant at the 0.01 level (2-tailed).

3.3 Independent Samples Test

We made independent samples t-test to check whether the mean values of the four categories differ significantly in terms of using detailed version of images or not. In table 3 we see group statistics using the details as grouping variable.

Table 3. Grouping statistics (grouping variable: details used)

	details used	N	Mean	Std. Deviation	Std. Error Mean
usefulness	detailed	29	5.06158	1.190709	0.221109
	simple	13	5.65385	1.092295	0.302948
ease of use	detailed	29	5.45517	1.324157	0.245890
	simple	13	5.87350	0.932766	0.258703
ease of learning	detailed	29	5.80172	1.263109	0.234553
	simple	13	6.21154	0.518875	0.143910
satisfaction	detailed	29	5.14778	1.486324	0.276003
	simple	13	5.60440	1.293829	0.358844

In table 4, we see results for Levene's test for equality of variances.

Table 4. Levene's test for equality of variances (Equal variances assumed)

	F	Sig.
usefulness	0.014	0.905
ease of use	1.269	0.267
ease of learning	6.228	0.017
satisfaction	0.192	0.664

We can see that sig>0.10 for categories usefulness, ease of use and satisfaction, so we can assume equal variances for these categories. Also, we can see that sig<0.10 for category ease of learning, so we can not assume equal variances for this category.

So, the independent samples t-test for our case is given in table 5.

Table 5. Independent samples t-test

		t	df	Sig. (2-tailed)	Mean Difference	Std. Error Difference
usefulness	Equal variances assumed	-1.527	40	0.135	-0.592270	0.387867
ease of use	Equal variances assumed	-1.027	40	0.310	-0.418332	0.407204
ease of learning	Equal variances not assumed	-1.489	39.867	0.144	-0.409814	0.275182
satisfaction	Equal variances assumed	-0.956	40	0.345	-0.456612	0.477731

We can see that sig(2-tailed)>0.05 so the mean values of the four categories do not differ significantly in terms of using the detailed version of images or not.

4 Conclusions

To begin with, as we can see in table 1 the mean values for the four categories usefulness, ease of use, ease of learning and satisfaction are, respectively, 5.19, 5.56, 5.86, and 5.28. So, considering that these values are >4, we can say that students found the applied method useful, easy to use, easy to learn and they felt satisfied using it.

As we can see from table 2, correlation is significant between the four categories (in pairs of two). So, the results of the students are relevant among the categories. So, we can say – for example – that if a student is satisfied with the applied method, then we expect that he/she would find it useful as well.

Finally, from table 5 we conclude that the mean values of the four categories (usefulness, ease of use, ease of learning, and satisfaction) do not differ significantly in terms of using the detailed version of images or not.

References

1. Bolhuis, S., Voeten, M. J. M.: Toward self-directed learning in secondary schools: what do teachers do? *Teaching and Teacher Education*, 17 (2001) 837-855.
2. Crawford, R.: Teaching and learning IT in secondary schools: towards a new pedagogy? *Education and Information Technologies*, 4, IFIP (1999) 49-63.
3. Downes, T.: Children's Participation in Evaluating the Role of New Information and Communication Technologies in Schools. *Education and Information Technologies*, 4:3 (1999) 331-341.
4. Furr, P. F., Ragsdale, R. G.: Desktop Video Conferencing. How to Avoid Teacher and Student Frustration. *Education and Information Technologies*, 7:4 (2002) 295-302.
5. Knezek, G., Christensen, R.: Impact of New Information Technologies on Teachers and Students. *Education and Information Technologies*, 7:4 (2002) 369-376.
6. Mayer, R. E., Moreno R.: Animation as an Aid to Multimedia Learning. *Educational Psychology Review*, Vol. 14, No. 1 (2002) 87-99.
7. Mumtaz, S.: Children's Conceptions of Information Communications Technology. *Education and Information Technologies*, 7:2 (2002) 155-168.
8. Passig, D., Levin, H.: The Interaction between Gender, Age, and Multimedia Interface Design. *Education and Information Technologies*, 6:4 (2001) 241-250.
9. Schraw, G., Flowerday, T., Lehman, S.: Increasing Situational Interest in the Classroom. *Educational Psychology Review*, Vol. 13, No. 3 (2001) 211-224.
10. Selwyn, N.: Students' attitudes towards computers in sixteen to nineteen education. *Education and Information Technologies*, 4:2 (1999) 129-141.
11. Watson, D. M.: Pedagogy before Technology: Re-thinking the Relationship between ICT and Teaching. *Education and Information Technologies*, 6:4 (2001) 251-266.
12. Webb, M. E.: Pedagogical Reasoning: Issues and Solutions for the Teaching and Learning of ICT in Secondary Schools. *Education and Information Technologies*, 7:3 (2002) 237-255.
13. Cristea, A. I.: What can the Semantic Web do for Adaptive Educational Hypermedia? *Educational Technology & Society*, 7(4) (2004) 40-58.

14. Filippidis, S. K., Tsoukalas, I. A.: Adaptable Instructional Video: Using Instructional Video with Adaptable Content to Teach a Computer Science Course. *In Proceedings of IADIS International Conference "Cognition and Exploratory Learning in Digital Age" (CELDA2005)*, (2005) accepted for publication.
15. Lin, C.-B., Young, S. S.-C., Chan, T.-W., Chen, Y.-H.: Teacher-oriented adaptive Web-based environment for supporting practical teaching models: a case study of "school for all". *Computers & Education*, 44 (2005) 155 – 172.
16. Papanikolaou, K. A., Grigoriadou, M., Magoulas, G. D., Kornilakis, H.: Towards new forms of knowledge communication: the adaptive dimension of a web-based learning environment. *Computers & Education*, 39 (2002) 333 – 360.
17. Papasalouros, A., Retalis, S., Papaspyrou, N.: Semantic Description of Educational Adaptive Hypermedia based on a Conceptual Model, *Educational Technology & Society*, 7(4) (2004) 129 – 142.
18. Triantafillou, E. Pomportsis, A., Demetriadis, S.: The design and the formative evaluation of an adaptive educational system based on cognitive styles. *Computers & Education*, 41 (2003) 87 – 103.
19. Filippidis, S., Tsoukalas, I.: Using Digital Video as an Asynchronous Method of Instruction. *In Proceedings of The 3rd IEEE International Conference on Advanced Learning Technologies (ICALT'03)* (Athens, Greece, July 09 - 11, 2003) 130 – 134.
20. Lund, A. M.: Measuring Usability with the USE Questionnaire. *Usability Interface*, STC Usability and User Experience Community, Vol.8, No. 2 – Success Stories (October 2001), http://www.stcsig.org/usability/newsletter/0110_measuring_with_use.html

e-Class Personalized: Design and Evaluation of an Adaptive Learning Content Management System

Evelthon G.Prodromou and Nikolaos Avouris
Human-Computer Interaction Group,
Electrical and Computer Engineering Dept., University of Patras
GR-26500, Patras, Greece
eprodromou@upnet.gr, avouris@upatras.gr

Abstract. This paper presents e-Class Personalized (e-CP), a new extension of the widely available open source Learning Content Management System e-Class. e-CP monitors interaction of the users of e-Class with its content and services and adapts the services to better suite the users' interests and tasks. E-CP has been tested for over a year at the University of Patras e-Class server with over 20,000 users. It drew positive response by the user population that were exposed to this version of the leaning Content Management System. In this paper we discuss architectural decisions and evaluation results of e-CP.

1 Introduction

Learning Management Systems (LMS) are software applications based on internet technologies that support management and delivery of distance learning content and services. LMSs need to be usable, reliable, affordable for their users and educationally relevant. The use of LMS in education offers definite advantages. More specifically they overcome time and space constraints, they offer flexibility in learning methods, they support extensive interaction between teachers and students whilst simultaneously allowing for inexpensive management and modification of learning resources.

The main functionality that a typical LMS needs to provide to its end users, students, teaching staff and administrators, includes: (a) *Course Management* which concerns tools that deal with the creation, administration, adaptation and supervision of courses. (b) *Classroom Administration* which includes tools that deal with handling of students and trainees, the creation of study groups, assignments etc. (c) *Communication tools* that supporting real time and asynchronous interaction between students and tutors. Such tools include email, chat rooms, voice and image conferencing, announcements and agenda management. Advanced LMS offer even

Please use the following format when citing this chapter:

Prodromou, Evelthon, Avouris, Nikolaos, 2006, in IFIP International Federation for Information Processing, Volume 204, Artificial Intelligence Applications and Innovations, eds. Maglogiannis, I., Karpouzis, K., Bramer, M., (Boston: Springer), pp. 409–416

more possibilities for cooperative learning such as sharing of archives and applications, sharing of workspaces and the whiteboard, while often more advanced services like synchronous design and modeling tools may be supported, e.g. see [1]. (d) *Students' Tools* facilitate students' access, administrate and study of the available material. Examples of such tools are private and public notes on text, indexes, personal histories, offline study, search engines etc. (e) Content management which deals with the tools that create, store and distribute learning material, the administration of archives, addition and extraction of learning material etc. (f) *Evaluation tools* deal with the administration of assignments on the internet, delivery of activities, self evaluation tests, student participation statistics etc. (g) *School administration* deals with the tools that handle student presence control, student performance, student registration, personal data of the students, financial matters, timetables etc.

Each one of these services is desirable to have an interface which adapts to the user's needs and requirements. In addition, the adaptable content of each service may affect the main system interface so that the user has overall control of the system the moment he/she connects to the system. These are some of the requirements for adaptivity of LMSs which have been tackled in the research reported in this paper. In the following we discuss general issues and state of the art of adaptive web applications and in particular adaptive LMSs and subsequently we focus in a specific case of design, development and evaluation of such a system, the e-Class Personalized, which permits adaptation of interaction according to the history of system usage by each individual user.

2 On Adaptive Learning Management Systems

The rapid development and wide use of the internet has influenced the way we access information in general and on-line learning services in particular. An internet application or an internet portal may provide large amounts of information which can meet the preferences and expectations of many different users. Most Universities and educational establishments have added such technological support to their users, facilitating and enhancing the face-to-face everyday teaching and other educational activities.

Users of such establishments are usually a heterogeneous group with widely different needs. Therefore the great quantities of information available may cause confusion and disorientation. This is what the development of web personalization services aim to solve. This approach deals with adaptation of interaction between the user and the internet application in order to serve these widely diverging users' needs and preferences.

A learning management system assumes the existence of distinct user roles (teacher, trainee, administrator). The selection of information presented to the end-user is based on these roles. The administrator has full access to the learning management system, the teachers manages content of the courses he/she is responsible for and the student has the appropriate information for the courses he/she is registered for. So the adaptive user interface deals with different needs of each group of end-users.

In order to be useful to individual learners, LMS, must be adaptive, since when learning from a Web-tutor there is often no availability of supporting colleagues to provide assistance as in a normal classroom situation. Minimum adaptivity of a Web- based educational application, according to [2] includes collecting, some data about the student working with the system and creating, the Student Model. This Model can be then used to adapt the presentation, of the course material, e.g. ranking content according to the user's interests, adapting navigation through it, sequencing, and annotation, to the student. Further possible levels of adaptivity are discussed in [3], while there are a number of examples of such systems and architectures, as in [4], [5]. In the rest of the paper we describe our experience with development and evaluation of an adaptive LMS for a widely available open source management system, e-Class.

3 Design of e-Class Persolized (e-CP), an adaptive open source Learning Management System

e-Class (www.eclass.gr) is an open source learning management system. The development of this software has been the result of an initiative of *GU Net* the organization that supervises the Greek Universities backbone network and provides value added services to its members. e-Class has been spawned from the Claroline project, a European open source LMS (www.claroline.net). Currently e-Class and Claroline development follows different tracks, resulting in two different platforms, despite the common origin. e-Class has been used by all major Greek Universities with many hundreds of thousands of users. Contribution to the development of this platform has been made by many developers in Greece. The University of Patras HCI lab has contributed with the e-Class Personalized (e-CP) which is discussed here. This is currently under consideration to be included in one of the forthcoming major releases of the e-Class platform. The main considerations of e-CP design are discussed first. These will provide the adaptive behavior pattern of the system. Taking these into account we then decide ono issues like the user interface to be developed as well as key architectural decisions, like the development of a user modeling system, based on users' interaction data.

3.1 Overview of requirements

One of the main aspects of e-CP is related to the navigation support and design of the user-centered interface design. The key design issue was related to the redesign of the end user *home page*. Analysis of the previous design of e-Class demonstrated that it was heavily course-centered, instead of user-centered. The user entering the system was faced with a list of courses, like in most such platforms. So any changes in a course content, for which a user is registered, are not immediately clear to the user upon entering the system. The user has to check on a daily basis for any changes in all the courses content he/she is registered for, a tedious process, requiring a long sequence of clicks.

It is also clear that the system needs to provide a greater degree of adaptivity. The home page, central to users' interaction and conceptualization of such a system, needs to have a more meaningful content. This has to adapt to the needs of each user and user group, depending on the user and his/her role on the platform. In addition, the user needs to continue having access to the services provided by the current home page. At the same time a study needs to be carried out to identify the services to which the user should have access to directly from this home page and to identify how these services should be presented to facilitate the search and selection of information.

Considering the current system, the user should continue to have access to the list of courses he is registered for as well as the navigation menu. In addition he/she needs instant access to all important course tools and information, while a special attention focusing mechanism should be devised that permit immediate attention drawing on any changes which might have occurred, since the previous visit.

So an Adaptive Subsystem was designed and developed as a module, to meet these requirements. This subsystem, in effect takes over the control from the central system of e-class when a user logs in and adapts the user interface according to the specific characteristics of the user, found in the User Model. The most prominent characteristic of this module is to provide all relevant and timely information grouped in the same page, using a ranking mechanism to allow for the most relevant information to appear at the top of the list, taking in consideration historical data of interaction.

In addition technical considerations have to be met. An adaptive system has as its primary goal the reformulation of the content and services in order to meet the characteristics of different users. This has to occur through an automated and fast procedure.

The adaptive system has to be easy to use and further maintain and support. It must provide the capacity to add new functionality without major changes in the source code, especially in the context of an open source project, where maintainability of the application is one of the main considerations. To achieve these objectives, a modular architecture was defined. In addition, one of the main technical challenges was to interface to the existing system and take care not to burden the service, deteriorating performance.

The user interface of the adaptive system needs to be significantly richer to the initial one. This is a result of the fact that the user is now provided with greater amounts of information and expanded interaction possibilities. However special care needs to be taken so that there is continuity between the new and the old user interface, since such systems have large numbers of users who do not wish to be faced with major discontinuity of their already developed mental models of the application. At the same time the additional information and services in the interface has to be properly organized and provide coherent instructions.

In the following section we describe how the developed module has met these requirements. This is done through a number of evaluation tests.

4 Formative evaluation of interaction– Keystroke Level Analysis

An analytical method called Keystroke Level Analysis (KLM) [6] was initially used for testing the developed concept of the adaptive system interface. This is a technique used during the requirements development and initial planning phase in order to assess the efficiency of a system. This is part of the GOMS knowledge model. This model is based on the assumption that the user is experienced and makes no mistakes while using the system. This is a laborious method if it is to be used on extensive parts of the interface. It may though offer quite accurate results. It is particularly for comparative studies among suggested alternative designs.

For the system we used the adaptive interface which provides access to services like announcements, deadlines, schedule and a discussion forum. In addition we have menu options and the user's list of courses. The analysis method was applied on these items using the KLM model. The results are shown on table 1.

As seen from the results in table 1 there is significant access improvement (61% in average) for each tool. What is important is that the time needed (in the personalized version) may even be decreased to zero if there is no other change and if this is notified to the user.

Table 1. Results of the KLM evaluation model on the tools used for the personalization interface. T1 is the time the user needs to check the specific tool, and T2 is the same time through the personalized interface

Tool	eClass (sec)	eClass personalized (sec)
Announcements	$T_1=a(5,86)$	$T_2=b(4,48)$
Assignments	$T_1=a\ (8,59)$	$T_2=d(4,48)$
Agenda	$T_1=a\ (5,86)$	$T_2=f(4,48)$
Forum	$T_1=a\ (11,32)$	$T_2=h(4,48)$

As an example we can show a part of the personalized interface which regards the assignments tool.

In figure 1 we see the reason behind the significant access time improvement to the tool. Using the personalized interface the steps required to check or submit an assignment are decreased to one from three initially.

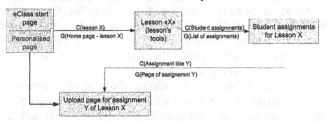

Fig. 1. The STD diagram of the the task "Deliver Assignment" when using the existing system (black path) and the personalized system (red path)

In figure 2 we see the structure of the assignments tool in the personalized module. There is clear distinction between columns and rows, clearly indicating the course, the assignment and the deadline. At the same time the second column indicates that it is active, a link to the assignments upload tool. This is made possible by clicking on the assignment title. At the same time we are provided with delivery confirmation for the assignment. The message "delivered" appears next to the assignment title. This is based on the existing system use which allows resubmission of an assignment within the deadline.

Therefore, in planning an adaptive interface one must take care to provide the functionalities already offered by the system for each tool that need to personalize to user needs.

ΟΙ ΔΙΟΡΙΕΣ ΜΟΥ		
Μάθημα	Εργασία (Κάντε κλικ για παράδοση)	Λήξη Διορίας
22C901 ΒΑΣΕΙΣ ΔΕΔΟΜΕΝΩΝ ΚΑΙ ΓΝΩΣΕΩΣ	Φροντιστηριακή Άσκηση 1 - 2005 [ΠΑΡΑΔΟΘΗΚΕ]	12-10-2005
Εισαγωγή στα Συστήματα Ηλεκτρικής Ενέργειας	Να γίνει η εικονική εργαστηριακή άσκηση 1	31-10-2005
Εισαγωγή στα Συστήματα Ηλεκτρικής Ενέργειας	Να γίνει η εικονική εργαστηριακή άσκηση 2	10-11-2005

Fig. 2. The assignments block when the user has assignments to deliver. There are three columns. The first column is the Course column. The second column is the Assignment column that informs us of the title of our assignment due. The third column is the Deadline column that informs us when the assignment will expire.

5. Design and performance of the Adaptive Component

In this section we discuss implementation problems and performance testing of the Adaptive CLM system developed.

The e-class environment structures data per course. This data model is reflected in the user interaction. So a new user-centered interaction model needs to be based on a transformation of this data model, without however imposing high computational load at run time, caused by the necessary queries in multiple databases. Our aim here is the construction of an algorithm which present in an efficient and timely way relevant data taking into account the user preferences. The system keeps records of user access, such as date and time of accessing a course and the user ID. The information in the log file is processed at regular intervals and are then placed in a scoreboard. Each user-course combination is a distinct entry on the board. An adaptive system needs to maintain a record of user's access and accordingly rank courses in order of importance for the user. This way, courses of high importance are easily accessible as can be found at the top of the courses list. The same principle is also applied to other services, like agenda items, assignments, scheduled events etc.

Let us consider a course classification index $ERA \in [0,1]$, where 0 (zero) indicates that the user has never visited the course and 1 that the user continually visits this course, without visiting any other.

Let us discuss the algorithm for calculating ERA for all courses of a student. Suppose that after processing the data from the logging table we are provided with the following information for a student: Total course hits:100 and Hits on the specific course: 35

A first estimation could be: $ERA = \dfrac{35}{100} = 0,35$, which is a good initial estimate.

Suppose that the scoring algorithm is executed each week. If for a course we have 35 ± 3 hits, the position of a course on the course list will not be significantly changed.

But what happens if the course is visited 35 ± 3 times per week and for one week the user needs to access it far less or far more often? In this case the position of the course on the list will change even though the particular week is an exception to the usual usage pattern. This is not a desirable change. To compensate for this we add "memory" to the system. The algorithm will be executed once a week but will "remember" user preferences. This "memory" will register the ranking of each course for the whole month (one registration per week). Each registration includes all the measurements from the time of the activation of the algorithm using an overlay between registrations. So, we now have:

$ERA_{TOT} = (ERA_{N-3} + ERA_{N-2} + ERA_{N-1} + ERA_N) \div 4$, where:

$ERAi$ takes value i=N for the period $\{-\infty < t \leq t_0\}$, N-1 for

$\{-\infty < t \leq t_{0-1}\}$, N-2 for $\{-\infty < t \leq t_{0-2}\}$ and N-3 for $\{-\infty < t \leq t_{0-3}\}$

So we now have a balanced method of calculation of the scoring algorithm which disallows abrupt variations in cases of a typical interaction between user and system.

The implementation of the usage data collection system is done through the central parser of the application. This parser provides for the transfer of the user from the personalization interface to the course environment selected.

At the same time it collects usage data which can be analyzed by the algorithm. Specifically it stores dates, time, user id and course id in its own space on the database of the e-Class system. Therefore usage data tells us which user accessed which course.

We evaluated the algorithm by using 21298 events from the logging table of the database. The algorithm was programmed in java and used threads to control the program run time and CPU usage. Our purpose was to create a light algorithm that has minimum CPU and memory requirements of the web server. The algorithm has an initial peak when it fetches the logs for processing. After this, it is hardly noticeable. This was made possible since the algorithm is not time-critical and more logs can be added to the logging table as the algorithm is active.

A benchmarking experiment was conducted of this algorithm, using simulations of server balances in the form of eight different thread sleep times ranging from 5ms up to 40ms with a step of 5ms. For each thread sleep-time we performed 10 simulations and received the average duration. In figure 3 the results of the simulation are shown. The algorithm is almost linear and gives good performance results for the amount data processed.

6. Conclusions

In this paper the e-Class Personalized prototype has been presented. The prototype was tested for performance at the keystroke level, simulating improvement of user keystroke activity. An average improvement of 61% was measured according to this test. In addition, the ranking algorithm that adapts content presentation to the users' usage patterns was tested for performance A linear behavior of the algorithm in terms of server load, simulated through a thread sleep was demonstrated, while the absolute load was not found noticeable in typical server conditions. After the reported tests, the new version of the e-class software was installed on the Network Centre of the University[1] serving over 20,000 users. In the first phase a limited number of users was exposed to this software. Through a focus group we measured their reaction to the new system and the first findings have been very positive. As we approach the end of the first year of operation of the prototype, we plan a more systematic evaluation using the logfiles of the system itself.

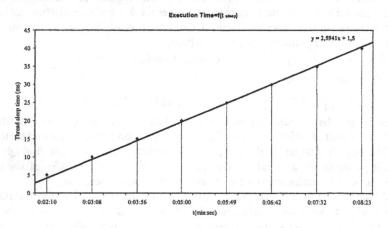

Fig. 3. Ranking algorithm execution time vs thread sleep time

References

1. Avouris N., Margaritis M., and Komis V., Modelling interaction during small-group synchronous problem-solving activities: The Synergo approach, 2nd International Workshop on Designing Computational Models of Collaborative Learning Interaction, ITS2004, 7th Conference on Intelligent Tutoring Systems, Maceio, Brasil, Sept. 2004.
2. Devedzic V. B., Key Issues in Next-Generation Web-Based Education, IEEE Trans. On Systems, Man and Cybernetics-Part C, Vol 33 (3), August 2003, pp. 339-349.
3. Brusilovsky P., "Adaptive and intelligent technologies for web-based education," Künstliche Intell., no. 4, pp. 19–25, 1999.
4. Virvou M. Automatic reasoning and help about human errors in using an operating system. Interacting with Computers, 11, pp. 545 – 573, 1999.
5. Avgeriou, A. Papasalouros and S. Retalis: Learning Technology Systems: issues, trends, challenges, proceedings of the 1st IOSTE symposium in Southern Europe, Science and Technology Education, Paralimni, Cyprus (2001)
6. Card S.K., Moran T.P., Newell A., The keystroke-level model for user performance with interactive systems, Com. of ACM, vol 23, pp. 396-410, 1980.

[1] Special thanks are due to the Network and Computing Center of the University of Patras for their support and in particular to Dr. V. Daskalou and A.G. Voyiatzis

The Use of Psychophysiological Measures for Designing Adaptive Learning Systems

Stamos T. Karamouzis
Loyola University New Orleans,
Computer Information Science Department
6363 St. Charles Ave., New Orleans, LA 70185, USA
stamos@loyno.edu

Abstract. When we trace the history of mind and learning theories we clearly see a transitioning course that traverses Cartesianism, Behaviorism, and finally Functionalism. Current advances in computer scanning technologies reinforce the view that learning should also be examined under the prism of brain-centered materialist theories. Adaptive learning systems are instructional technologies that try to minimize the mismatch between learner needs and the learning environment. Currently, they try to elicit the learner needs with performance measures but they ignore learner differences at the brain level. This paper offers a shift of viewpoint in thinking about future adaptive learning systems. If we want education to be precisely tailored to the needs of learners then instructional technologies must take advantage of known individual differences in brain processing. The paper offers the justification of such an approach, analyzes its implications, proposes an implementation model, reviews related work, and outlines future challenges.

1 Introduction

The history of computer-based learning systems can be traced back as far as the beginning of computing. Since the early computing days an effort was made to create learning systems that adapt their functionality based on the learner needs and capabilities thus giving birth to the class of adaptive learning systems. The most notable early work in adaptive learning systems was done by B. F. Skinner in the 1960s. Skinner and his colleagues developed the concept of programmed learning where a teaching machine engages a learner in a task, and uses a comparison of the learner's performance to a model of how the task should be performed in order to provide the learner with advice to successfully complete the task [27, 28].

Through the years, evolutionary forces resulted in the development of learning systems that represent a leap beyond the earlier Skinnerian work in terms of their capacity to detect learner abilities and deficiencies as well as to provide insightful

Please use the following format when citing this chapter:

Karamouzis, Stamos, 2006, in IFIP International Federation for Information Processing, Volume 204, Artificial Intelligence Applications and Innovations, eds. Maglogiannis, I., Karpouzis, K., Bramer, M., (Boston: Springer), pp. 417–424

remediation. In the traditional mode of operation adaptive learning systems maintain the domain knowledge that needs to be conveyed to the learner (domain module), the learner's existing knowledge (learner's module), and the pedagogical methods that can be used in order to convey the domain knowledge (methods module). Through the interaction of these modules the learning systems are able to make judgments about the student's knowledge, skills, and progress. The methods module tailors the learning experience to the student's needs, automatically, without the intervention of a human instructor [1, 3].

Today's adaptive learning systems are capable of modifying any individual student's learning experience as a function of information obtained through their performance on situated tasks or assessments [12]. Situated tasks can be any dynamic learning challenge that requires a measurable response on the part of the learner. These can include problem sets, learning task challenges, a Socratic dialogue, or experiences in simulated environments. In a nutshell, the adaptation is done based only on performance measurements.

When we trace the history of mind and learning theories we clearly see a transitioning course that traverses Cartesianism, behaviorism, and finally functionalism [13]. Current advances in computer scanning technologies reinforce the view that learning should also be examined under the prism of brain-centered materialist theories.

Nowadays, advances in psychophysiological techniques, such as brain scanning, make it possible to identify differences in human brain processing that correspond to differences in learning styles and capabilities. The knowledge of such differences is valuable in every educational setting because teaching methods that may work well for a large majority of learners may be counterproductive when used with learners that their brain processing deviates from the majority. Additionally the same psychophysiological techniques may reveal, in real time, the learner's cognitive state.

Therefore, with this article, I propose the design of adaptive learning systems that incorporate the use of psychophysiological measurements, in addition to performance measurements, in modifying the student's learning experience. I assert that such systems will be more effective and I hope to stimulate new ideas and research in this direction.

In particular, I give a brief overview of the relevant psychophysiological techniques, I explain how such techniques may benefit learning theories, I propose a new implementation model for adaptive learning systems, and I outline future challenges.

2 Psychophysiology

Psychophysiology research and practice deals with the interactions between the mind and body by recording how the body is functioning and relating the functions recorded to behavior. The field is based on the premise that changes in the body's functioning cause changes in behavior and vice versa [9]. Psychophysiological recording techniques are generally non-invasive. That is, they record from the body's surface and nothing goes into the person being recorded.

Nowadays, the filed of Psychophysiology is employing a number of techniques that help elicit data about the function and structure of the brain. They can be divided into those that provide functional information and those that provide structural information about the brain [5].

2.1 Structural Measures

The magnetic resonance imaging (MRI), magnetic resonance spectroscopy (MRS), and diffusion tensor imaging (DTI) are methods used to measure brain structure and chemistry. For example, magnetic resonance imaging (MRI) can be used to measure gross size or volume differences in brain regions while magnetic resonance spectroscopy (MRS) can be used to measure the concentration of cerebral metabolites that have been related to neuronal loss or damage. Thus MRS can provide additional insight as to why an MRI-based measure of a brain structure may be smaller. Finally, diffusion tensor imaging (DTI) allows for measures of the regularity and myelination of fiber tracts and provides a more precise measure of myelination of fibers than traditional MRI measures of white matter volume. All three of these structural imaging methods can be correlated with behavior, but none involves simultaneous collection of behavior or the capability of measuring brain changes associated with trial-by-trial behavior.

2.2 Functional Measures

In contrast, Electroencephalography (EEG), event related potentials (ERP), single photon emission computed tomography (SPECT), positron emission tomography (PET), functional magnetic resonance imaging (fMRI), near infrared spectroscopy/optimal imaging (NIRS), and magnetoencephalography (MEG) are classified as functional imaging methods because they measure changes in brain activity associated with simultaneous changes in behavior.

In particular, Electroencephalography (EEG) is a method for capturing and measuring brain waves and as such provides evidence of how the brain functions over time. It is commonly used for detecting and observing certain conditions, such as seizures, by observing changes in the normal pattern of the brain's electrical activity [8, 30]. The output from an EEG is recorded as a graph of brainwaves on a time scale and simply reveals rough brainwave frequency and amplitude. Measuring Event Related Potentials (ERP) involves correlating the EEG brainwave response with a stimulus (event) and averaging the result of dozens to thousands of stimulus expositions together to get a clear picture of what electrical activity takes place upon presentation of that specific stimulus [2]

A Single Photon Emission Computed Tomography (SPECT) scan is a type of nuclear imaging test that shows how blood flows to tissues and organs. This is done by ejecting the body with a radioactive chemical that emits gamma rays and can be detected by a scanner. SPECT scans are relatively inexpensive and readily available. [14]

Positron emission tomography (PET) is a technique that produces a three-dimensional image or map of functional processes in the body based on the detection of radiation from the emission of positrons. This is achieved by injecting into the body a short-lived radioactive tracer isotope that decays by emitting the detected positrons [4]. This technique differs from a SPECT scan in that the chemical is being absorbed by surrounding tissues rather than staying in the blood stream, therefore the images are not limited to areas where blood flows.

Functional magnetic resonance imaging (fMRI) is a technique that exposes the brain with a high static magnetic field and a small alternating radiofrequency field. Thus is capable of visualizing changes in chemical composition of brain areas or changes in the flow of fluids that occur over time periods of seconds to minutes. It can be used to find out what the brain is doing when subjects perform specific tasks or are exposed to specific stimuli [6]. There are three advantages to fMRI scaning over PET scanning 1) It is not invasive since the signal does not require injections of radioactive isotopes, 2) the total scan time required can be very short, i.e., on the order of 1.5 to 2.0 min per run, and 3) it is capable of fine resolutions in the order of 1.5 x 1.5 mm or even less.

Near infrared spectroscopy (NIRS) offers a safe, non-invasive means of monitoring cerebral function without the use of radioisotopes or other contrast agents. NIRS systems measure the oxygenated blood flow through the brain by shining light in the near infrared (NIR) range of the spectrum through the scalp [31].

Magnetoencephalography (MEG) is noninvasive technology for functional brain mapping that is based on the measurement of intercellular currents of the neurons in the brain, spontaneously or to a given stimulus [19]. MEG combines many of the advantages of PET and fMRI scanning but MEG's temporal resolution of 1 ms is far superior while having an equivalent spatial resolution.

3 Psychophysiology & Learning

Functional imaging techniques are capable of measuring subtle task-induced changes in signals from the brain and as such they can be of particular interest in formulating learning theories and constructing learning environments. In general, they can be useful in the filed of learning for three reasons. First they can shed light into understanding how learning occurs. Second they can identify differences in learning styles and capabilities. Third they can monitor in real time and reveal an individual's cognitive state.

3.1 Understanding Learning

Through the years a number of learning theories have been developed usually aligned along the philosophical theories of the time. Nowadays, the advances in brain scanning technologies allow us to develop a better understanding and insight of how learning occurs and thus piece-by-piece either validate or refute existing theories. For example imaging studies using fMRI of the prefrontal cortex helped identify how humans focus attention on the task at hand while ignoring distractions [7, 16]. Those studies are significant because, contrary to current learning theories, prove that attention control is achieved by amplifying task-relevant information, rather than by inhibiting distracting stimuli.

3.2 Identifying Differences

Over the past two decades researchers from various labs were able to use structural and functional brain imaging techniques in identifying learner differences such as learners with dyslexia and attention deficit disorder [10, 20, 25, 26].

For example, Richards and Berninger [21, 25] used functional magnetic resonance spectroscopy and fMRI to show that there are chemical differences between the brains of learners with dyslexia and those of other learners. Their work is based on monitoring metabolic activity of the brain. When the brain is at work, it uses energy. One by-product of energy use in the brain is lactate. By measuring where lactate is being produced, they were able to see which part of the brain was active.

Identifying learner abilities is crucial in an educational setting in order to choose the pedagogical methodology that matches best the learner's abilities. For example in teaching reading, pedagogical methods based on intensive or systematic drill in phonemic awareness or phonetic decoding strategies may actually be harmful to dyslexic learners. Such teaching might simply emphasize reliance on mental strategies that are as likely to diminish reading ability for dyslexics, instead of improve it.

3.3 Revealing Cognitive States

Since the early 90's researches proposed the use of Psychophysiology for eliciting cognitive states. In 1995, Pope, Bogart, and Bartolome developed a system that used EEG in airplane simulators to monitor when pilots are engaged and when they're disengaged during a typical flight. The pilot's level of engagement was then used by a system that adapted the airplane's level of automation. When pilots became disengaged, the airplane became less automated and the additional work required pulled the pilots back into the process of flying the aircraft [17, 18].

Expanding upon the work of Pope and his colleagues, St. John, Kobus, Morrison, and Schmorrow have described a new DARPA program aimed at developing systems that can detect an individual's cognitive state and then manipulate task parameters to overcome four primary "bottlenecks" in cognitive performance: attention, executive functioning, sensory input, and working memory [29].

Although Pope's and St. John's work aimed at developing adaptive automation systems that enhance an operator's effectiveness the same principles and finding are applicable in learning systems that can adapt to better fit learner needs. In fact, one of Pope's striking findings was the similarity between the brain waves of disengaged pilots and the brain waves of learners with Attention Deficit Disorder.

4 A Model for Adaptive Learning Systems

The power that psychophysiological measures give us in understanding how learning occurs, in identifying individual learning differences, and in revealing cognitive states can be invaluable for every educational setting.

In particular, for designing an adaptive learning system I propose that such measures should be integral part of the learner's module in order to transform the domain and the instructional methods modules. In all of the existing systems the learner's module is exclusively comprised of the learner's motives and knowledge as it is being assessed by performance measures. The incorporation of psychophysiological findings can greatly improve the accuracy of the learner's module. This can be done at two distinct collection levels.

First, a battery of psychophysiological tests should be administered to assess the student's learning style and abilities. This will create an individualized profile, diagnostic in style, which gives answers to the questions: Is the learner an auditory personality? visual? tactile/kinesthetic? dyslexic? etc. This psychophysiological profile should be incorporated into the learner's module along with the information from the performance measurements thus resulting in an augmented learner's module. At the second collection level real-time information about the learner's cognitive state should be collected. The psychophysiological monitoring should match specific learning materials and tasks with constructs such as effort, arousal, attention, and workload.

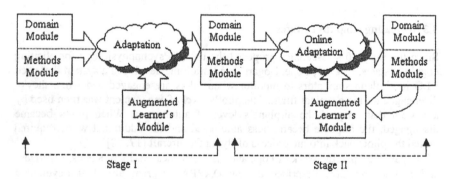

Fig. 1. Model for an Adaptive Learning System

In traditional adaptive learning systems Artificial Intelligence (AI) techniques have been instrumental in providing the adaptation of the domain and methods modules. Based on this model AI techniques should also be applied for interpreting the psychophysiological findings. To this day only limited work has been done in this direction [22, 23].

The existence of those two levels of collecting psychophysiological measurements leads us into a two-stage model for adaptive learning systems (figure 1). At Stage I, the initialization stage, the domain knowledge and the set of available pedagogical methodologies get customized based on the initial learner's module that includes the psychophysiological profile from the first collection level. Stage II, the real-time stage, further adapts the domain and methods modules in a dynamic way as the second level collection occurs. Such adaptation may include reprioritizing or rescheduling tasks, changing the level of difficulty, or switching between verbal and spatial information formats.

5 Discussion

The notion of using psychophysiology for explaining learning processes was first introduced by Tom Mulholland in 1974 but since no work has been achieved [15]. Nowadays, the impressive advances in psychophysiological techniques progressed our abilities to understand how learning occurs, identify individual learning differences, and reveal cognitive states. Despite the isolated successes many significant challenges must be overcome if the proposed model for adaptive learning systems is to move out of the laboratory.

First of all, more experimentation needs to be done. Today, the work done in augmented cognition does not have learning in mind [24]. Future experimentation needs to focus on learning, learning differences, and cognitive states as they specifically relate to learning tasks. Second, researchers in this area need to establish the validity of the approach through systematic controlled tests and replication.

Additionally, serious effort needs to be invested in order to achieve remote psychophysiological monitoring [11]. Only when we eliminate the wiring and physical contact between machine and humans we'll be able to truly develop applications outside the laboratory.

Also, numerous other issues such as determining the frequency of adaptive changes, adaptive algorithms, types of interfaces, improving the signal-to-noise ratio of psychophysiological measures, extracting useful signals from within dynamic environments, etc. need to be addressed. Nonetheless, the proposed model poses as a starting point in an exciting direction that holds enormous promise for the future of adaptive learning systems.

References

1. Alberink, M. & Veenstra, M. *A framework for adaptable hypermedia authoring*. TI/RS/2001/067 Enschede, Telematica Instituut (2001)
2. Brandeis, D., Lehmann, D.: Event-related potentials of the brain and cognitive processes: approaches and applications. *Neuropsychologia* **24** (1986) 151-68
3. Brusilovsky, P., Peylo, P.: Adaptive and Intelligent Web-based Educational Systems. *International Journal of Artificial Intelligence in Education* **13** (2003) 156–169
4. Carson, R., Herscovitch, P., Daube-Witherspoon, M.: *Quantitative Functional Brain Imaging With Positron Emission Tomography*. Elsevier (1998)
5. Casey, B.J., de Haan, M.: New methods in developmental science. *Developmental Science* **5** (2002) 265–267
6. Cohen, M.S., Bookheimer, S.Y.: Localization of brain function using magnetic resonance imaging. Techniques in Neuroscience **17** (1994) 268-277
7. Egner T., Hirsch, J.: Cognitive control mechanisms resolve conflict through cortical amplification of task-relevant information. *Nature Neuroscience* **8** (2005) 1784 - 1790
8. Emerson, R. G., Pedley, T.A.: Electroencephalography and evoked potentials. In: *Neurology in Clinical Practice*. Vol. 1, Butterworth-Heinemann (2000) 473-485

9. Frank, Y., Pavlakis, S.G.: Brain imaging in neurobehavioral disorders. *Pediatric Neurology* 25 (2001) 278-287
10. Giedd, J.N., Blumenthal, J., Molloy, E., Castellanos, F.X.: Brain Imaging of Attention Deficit/Hyperactivity Disorder. *Annals of the New York Academy of Sciences* 931 (2001) 33-49
11. Jemison, M., Mandavilli, R., Wang, S., Morgan-Reynolds, R.: Using Remote Psychophysiological Monitoring for Human Performance T&E. *ITEA Journal* March/April (2004) 15-16
12. Jones, M., Winne, P.H.: *Foundations and Frontiers of Adaptive Learning Environments*. Springer Verlag (1992)
13. Lyons, W.: *Matters of the Mind*. Edinburgh University Press (2001)
14. Masdeu, J.C., Brass, L.M., Holman, B.L., et al.: Special review: Brain single photon emission tomography. *Neurology* 44 (1994) 1970-1977
15. Mulholland, T.B.: Training visual attention. *Academic Therapy* 10 (1974) 5-17
16. Nieuwenhuis, S., Yeung, N.: Neural mechanisms of attention and control: losing our inhibitions? *Nature Neuroscience* 8 (2005) 1631 – 1633
17. Pope, A.T., Bogart, E.H., Bartolome, D.: Biocybernetic system evaluates indices of operator engagement. *Biological Psychology*, 40 (1995) 187-196
18. Prinzel, L.J., Pope, A.T., Freeman, F.G., Scerbo, M.W., Mikulka P.J.: Empirical Analysis of EEG and ERPs for Psychophysiological Adaptive Task Allocation. *NASA/TM-2001-211016*, National Aeronautics and Space Administration (2001)
19. Ribary, U., Mogilner, A., Joliot, M., Volkman, J., Rusinek, H., Llinas, R.: The use of magnetoencephalography (MEG) and magnetic resonance imaging (MRI) to localize normal and pathological human brain function. *Radiology* (1992) 185-199
20. Richards, T.L.: Functional Magnetic Resonance Imaging and Spectroscopic Imaging of the Brain: Application of fMRI and fMRS to Reading Disabilities and Education. *Learning Disabilities Quarterly* 24 (2001) 189 - 203
21. Richards, T.L., Berninger, V.W., Aylward, E.H., et al.: Reproducibility of proton MR spectroscopic imaging (PEPSI): comparison of dyslexic and normal-reading children and effects of treatment on brain lactate levels during language tasks. *American Journal of Neuroradiology* 23 (2002) 1678-85
22. Russell, C., Wilson, G.: Feature Saliency Analysis for Operator State Estimation. *Proceedings of the 11th International Conference on Human-Computer Interaction* (2005)
23. Russell, C., Wilson, G.: Comparing Classifiers for Real Time Estimation of Cognitive Workload. *Proceedings of the 11th International Conference on Human-Computer Interaction* (2005)
24. Scerbo, M.W.: Biocybernetic Systems: Information Processing Challenges that Lie Ahead. *Proceedings of the 11th International Conference on Human-Computer Interaction* (2005)
25. Serafini, S., Steury, K., Richards, T.D, Abbott, R., Berninger, V.: Comparison of fMRI and PEPSI during language processing in children. *Magn Reson Med* 45 (2001) 217-225
26. Shaywitz, S.: Overcoming Dyslexia. Random House (2005)
27. Skinner, B.F.: Why we need teaching machines. *Harvard Educational Review* 31 (1961) 377-98
28. Skinner, B.F., Holland, J.G.: The use of teaching machines in college instruction (Parts II-IV). In A. A. Lumsdaine & R. Glaser (Eds.), *Teaching machines and programmed learning: A source book*. Washington, DC: Department of Audio-Visual Instruction, National Education Association (1960) 159-172
29. St. John, M., Kobus, D.A., Morrison, J.G., Schmorrow, D.: Overview of the DARPA Augmented Cognition technical integration experiment. *International Journal of Human-Computer Interaction* (2004) 131-149.
30. Tyner, F.S., Knott, J.R., Meyer, W.B.: *Electroencephalography*. New York: Raven Press; (1983)
31. Villringer, A., Chance, B.: Non-invasive optical spectroscopy and imaging of human brain function. *Trends in Neurosciences* 20 (1997) 435-442.

Developing Personalized E-Books:
A Multi-Layered Approach

Konstantina Chatzara, Athanasios Mpantsos, Demosthenes Stamatis
and Athanasios Tsadiras
Department of Informatics
Technological Educational Institute of Thessaloniki
P.O.BOX 14561, 54101 Thessaloniki, Greece
Email: tsadiras@it.teithe.gr

Abstract. Users of hypermedia systems are heterogeneous, came from different backgrounds and have different level of knowledge in the use of information systems. This paper discusses a multi-layered approach for developing personalized e-books. The layers regard both Human Computer Interaction/Navigation level and the Content of the e-book. These layers are defined and described in detail. The tei-Book architecture is also presented in the paper and it is proposed as suitable for providing personalized e-book views to the various e-book readers. This is done by an E-Book manager that manage to provide the appropriate e-book view according to the User Profiles and Book Profile Components that dynamically are developed by the tei-Book. Future work includes the evaluation of the personalized e-book views and also the evaluation of system's usability.

1 Introduction

Adapting books to electronic form in order to be readable by users in a computer system is a concept that motivated research very early. The book metaphor has acted as the primary way of presenting e-learning systems in a book like lay out [1]. Electronic browsing systems as SuperBook [2] and the Book Emulator [3], as well as recent commercial offerings of hand held devices of book size [4] are a few of the examples of the research into the e-book domain.

The demands and expectations of diverse users have grown fast. A recent study reports that even for experienced users of common personal computers, approximately 45% of their time is wasted with frustrating experiences tied to confusing menus, indecipherable dialog boxes, and hard to find functions [5]. The users find themselves disorientated, feeling stressed out and disappointed, end up giving up the learning procedure to avoid further annoyance.

Please use the following format when citing this chapter:

Chatzara, Konstantina, Mpantsos, Athanasios, Stamatis, Demosthenes, Tsadiras, Athanasios, 2006, in IFIP International Federation for Information Processing, Volume204, Artificial Intelligence Applications and Innovations, eds. Maglogiannis, I., Karpouzis, K., Bramer, M., (Boston: Springer), pp. 425–432

The e-book as a learning platform should be able to accommodate for all users but usually it is designed in a unified way, cutters for the middle line of users, excluding the novice ones or makes the application unattractive for the experienced users. The inequity of access to hypermedia products, often called the digital divide [6] addresses the need of adapting the way the user accesses an e learning system to cater for each individual separately.

In order to cater to different user needs, information systems can be tailored manually by the user or automatically by the system. Systems that allow the user to change certain system parameters, and adapt their behavior accordingly, are called adaptable. Systems that adapt to users automatically based on their assumptions about them are called adaptive [7]. Whereas the first group of adaptations aims at enabling and improving the overall access to the information system, the second group of adaptations aims at individualizing one specific hypermedia system.

Personalization of the e learning systems is increasingly important. Research has shown that most users prefer the control afforded by an adaptable approach to personalization rather than a system-controlled adaptive approach. No study, however, has compared the efficiency of the two approaches.

Multi layers have been introduced in order to divide the interface of an application into sections and make each section accessible by the user separately [8,9,10]. Instead of presenting all features at once it is proposed to allow the user to choose the features he prefers according to his skills and personal needs. An example of a multi-layered application has been illustrated in the search engines on the Internet in which the novice users just type a keyword in a search box and the results are presented in a certain sequence. Users are usually satisfied with the whole procedure, which is easily accessed. Experienced users might use a more advanced interface, which allows them to use more criteria (country they are seeking information from, time depended results, order of the results when presented). The above approach gives users control over the sets of features available at any moment but a clear separation between the different functions is incorporated. The two layers of accessing the information is presented clearly leaving the user in control.

Each level can be designed separately; nevertheless all layers have to share common aesthetics. Distinct goals that will be achieved in each level have to be clarified. It is vital for the user to navigate through the system without the notion of disorientation. Confusion between switching between layers has to be avoided.

Cognitive learning models have to be incorporated in order to define the principles of the design of a multi layered e-learning application and usability testing as well as user feedback will be essential. Facilities as help menu that clarifies the use and scope of each level have to be examined and the interaction between interface layers and layers of the content presentation also have to be addressed.

By adding to this debate the issue of not only adapting the navigation but adapting the content of the subject the e-learning application is designed for, we are presented with a much more complex system. In the following chapter the layers structure of presentation of the content and the navigation will be described, incorporating both the adaptive and the adaptable approach.

2. E-Book layers definition

This paper discusses a multi-layer approach to developing personalized e-books [11]. A system for supporting this personalization process, **tei-Book** (transformable electronic and intelligent **Book**) was developed at the Department of Informatics of the Technological Educational Institute (TEI) of Thessaloniki. As it is shown in figure 1, our layered approach, proposes the existence of layers both to the HCI (human-computer interaction/navigation level) of the e-book and to the content of the e-book.

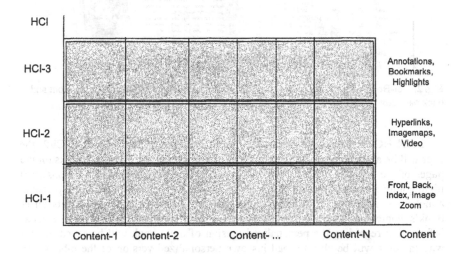

Fig. 1. Layers concerning both to the HCI of the e-book and the content of the e-book.

According to the proposed design, there are three different layers/levels of HCI. These are the following:

Level HCI-1. This layer is designed for first-time and novice users of computer systems, having no experience of how to use hypermedia. In this layer, only a static menu will be presented, having simple functions such as return to index, go to next and previous page and exit (see figure 2). Additional to these, images can zoom-in to reveal details of various initially small images in the e-book. The user of this layer will use the book metaphor and he will be able to navigate through e-book contents without feeling disoriented.

Level HCI-2. In this level, users that have some experience in hypermedia, additionally to the features of level HCI-1, will be able to find in the e-book, (a) hyperlinks, (b) imagemaps (images are separate in different areas, each area having a link to a corresponding e-book position) and (c) videos with the necessary navigation buttons (play, pause, stop, fast forward, rewind). The user of this level will feel free to navigate more flexibly to the whole book in a much faster manner.

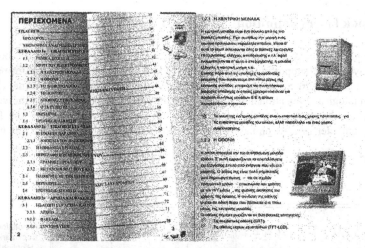

Fig. 2. Tei-Book with book like layout, page turning simulation, table of contents, front and back page cover

Level HCI-3. In this top level, additionally to the features of level HCI-2, the user will be able to personalize the e-book, by (a) adding his own bookmarks on the pages of the e-books, (these work as hyperlinks to specific e-book positions), (b) highlighting sentences that he considers important for him, and (c) adding personal annotations on the pages of the e-book, that can be his personal comments on e-book's content (Figure 3). Every time the user of level 3 exits the e-book, information regarding the personalized version of the e-book will be saved. In this way the user will be able to load his own personalized version of the e-book and continue his study from the point he stopped studying the e-book, viewing also his past annotations, highlights and bookmarks.

Separating out the HCI-layers enable users to learn HCI features in a meaningful sequence, while help screens are avoided. Nevertheless help menu can be added to explain the functions of each HCI level. E-book readers can gain confidence and after mastering layer HCI-1 move on to higher layers, when needed or when they had time to experiment with.

The e-book can also have different levels of content. The e-book domain expert can identify different levels of users according to their past knowledge on the e-book subject, their age and the depth of the knowledge they are looking for in the e-book. In this way, level Content-1 will correspond to the simplest content version which will suitable for the absolute beginner of the e-book subject, having no prerequisites. In the same manner, highest content level, level Content-N, will correspond to the most advanced content version of the e-book that will be suitable for the most experienced on the subject and concerned reader of the e-book. The number of different content levels is not defined, since it depends on the subject and the scope of the readers the e-book's authors want to reach.

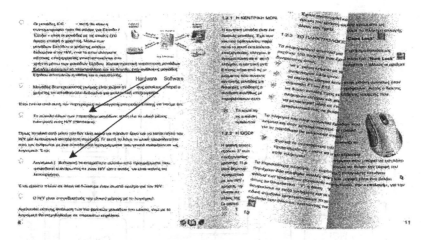

Fig. 3. Tei-Book with user's personal annotations and highlighted content.

According the above and figure 1, an e-book reader who is novice to the use of hypermedia but very experienced on the e-book subject, should use the e-book tuned to levels HCI-1 & Content-N, whereas an experienced hypermedia user with no background knowledge on the subject of the e-book, should use the e-book tuned to levels HCI-3 & Content-1.

3. The tei-Book Architecture

The personalization supported by the tei-Book system that we propose, is orthogonal in the sense that HCI layered based personalization and content based personalization could be applied as two separated processes. These processes can then be combined to provide the final view of personalized e-book to its users.

Figure 4 shows the architecture of the tei-Book system. The content material constituting a specific e-book is stored in the e-book Content Base.

The HCI Adaptation module is the one responsible to decide for the HCI layer adaptation pertinent to each user. In order to do so it keeps a data base of user profiles. These profiles are updated when the user initiates a reading session, either based on his direct will or by following an interactive questionnaire approach in order to diagnose his level. In such a way the e-book is functioning as an adaptable hypermedia system. The profiles could also be updated automatically by the system which monitors the user interaction through a microadaptation submodule (HCI Monitor) in order to allow for dynamic HCI layer switching. In such a way the e-book could be considered as an adaptable hypermedia system.

The Content Adaptation module is responsible to decide for the content layer adaptation which provides different views to different users. In order to do so it keeps a data base of book profile components. These book profile components are updated:

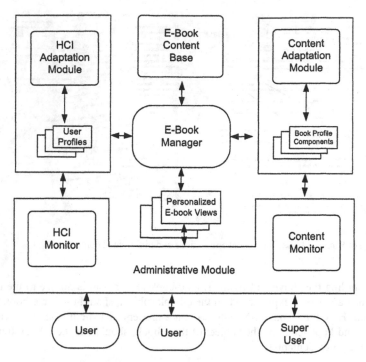

Fig. 4. The tei-Book architecture

(a)   When a user initiates a reading session at HCI level 3, where content
        adaptations tools (for bookmarking, annotation, paragraph hide et.c.) are
        provided. In this case, a book profile consisting of a single book profile
        component is created which governs content personalization for the user in
        question.

(b)   When a special user (e.g. author of the e-book or experienced teacher using
        the e-book as e-learning material for its students) initiates a reading session
        in order to transform the e-book content. In this case, a discrete number of
        book profile components could be generated corresponding to different
        levels of content adaptation. The special user then has the possibility of
        assigning these levels to specific user groups. Based on these content
        profile components the content adaptation module can produce one or
        more book profiles to be assigned to final users.

In both cases, user's actions regarding content change are controlled through the
Content Monitor Module. In the second case content based personalization acts as a
tool to a teacher to annotate and transform the e-book in order to enhance a specific
strategy for reading to be followed by the students.

The e-book Manager subsystem is responsible for producing the personalized e-
book views for the specific users. It does so by using the e-book content base and by
collaborating with the HCI and Content Adaptation modules. By providing sufficient
redundancy and separation of content from HCI layout, the system ensures through

the e-book Manager module that for any given situation adaptation is possible without involving the complete content management chain.

The Administrative module apart from accommodating the HCI and Content Monitors is responsible for controlling the whole user interface to the e-book and for keeping user accounts. The system works as a web based client server application and users need to go through a login authentication procedure in order to work with their personalized version of the e-book. Additionally when a personalized e-book view is finalized it can be compiled and used off-line by its user as a stand alone hypermedia document.

4. Conclusions – Future Work

This paper suggested a multi-layer approach to developing personalized e-books. Two types of personalization are possible: HCI based layers of personalization and content based layers of personalization. These two types could either be applied separately or could be combined. The layers were defined and the architecture of the tei-Book system, which is used as a framework for developing personalized e-books, was presented. A first version of the tei-Book was implemented together with a complete e-book case study, an e-book containing an introduction to Computer Systems. This case study will be used in order to evaluate the personalized e-book views that are produced during the interaction between users (both readers and teacher) and the tei-book system. Based on the evaluation results a more complete version of the suggested architecture will be implemented. Usability testing is also essential and comparison between the adaptable and the adaptive aspects of personalization has to be examined in the future.

References

1. Golovchinsky, G., Marshall, C.: Designing Electronic Books, ACM Transactions on Computer-Human Interaction, Vol. 7, No. 2, (2000)
2. Egan, D. E., Remde, J.R., Gomez, J.M., Landauer, T.K., Eberhardt, J., and Lochbaum, C.C. Formative designevaluation of SuperBook. ACM Transactions on Information Systems, (1989)
3. Benest, I.D. A hypertext system with controlled hype. In McAleese, R. and Green, C. (eds.). Hypertext: State of the Art. Intellect Books, Oxford, 1990.
4. D. Berleant, : Models for reader interaction systems , Ninth International Conference on Information and Knowledge Management (CIKM), Washington, D.C., ACM Press, (2000), pp127-133.
5. Ceaparu, I., Lazar, J., Bessiere, K., Robinson, J., and Shneiderman, B., Determining causes and severity of end-user frustration, International Journal of Human-Computer Interaction, (2004).
6. Shneiderman, B., Promoting universal usability with multi-layer interface design, ACM Conference on Universal Usability, ACM Press, New York (2003)
7. Fink, J., Kobsa, A., Schreck, J.: Personalized Hypermedia Information Provision through

Adaptive and Adaptable System Features: User Modeling, Privacy and Security Issues, Proc. of the Workshop Adaptive Systems and User Modeling on the World Wide Web of the 6th Int. Conf. on User Modeling, Chia Laguna, Sardinia (1997)

8. Plaisant, C., Kang, H., and Shneiderman, B., Helping users get started with visual interfaces: multi-layered interfaces, integrated initial guidance and video demonstrations, Proc.Human-Computer Interaction International, Lawrence Erlbaum Associates,

9. Kang, H., Plaisant, C., and Shneiderman, B., New approaches to help users get started with visual interfaces: Multi-layered interfaces and Integrated Initial Guidance, Proc. of the Digital Government Research Conference, Boston, MA (May 2003).

10. Dunlop, MD, Johnson, CW, Reid, J.: Exploring the Layers of Information Retrieval Evaluation. In Interacting with Computers, 10 (3), (1998), p. 225-236

11. Chi, E. H.; Hong, L.; Heiser, J.; Card, S. K.: eBooks with indexes that reorganize conceptually. Extended Abstracts of the ACM International Conference on Human Factors in Computing Systems (CHI 2004); Austria, (2004), 1223-1226.

Designing a Solver for Arithmetic Constraints to Support Education in Mathematics*

Ana Paula Tomás, Nelma Moreira, and Nuno Pereira

DCC-FC & LIACC
University of Porto, Portugal
\{apt,nam,nfp\}@dcc.fc.up.pt

Abstract. We present a conditional rewrite system for arithmetic and membership univariate constraints over real numbers, designed for computer assisted learning (CAL) in elementary math. Two fundamental principles guided the design of the proposed rewrite rules: *cognitive fidelity* (emulating steps students should take) and *correctness*, aiming that step-by-step solutions to problems look like ones carried out by students. In order to gain more flexibility to modify rules, add new ones and customize solvers, the rules are written in a specification language and then compiled to Prolog. The rewrite system is complete for a relevant subset of problems found in high-school math textbooks.

1 Introduction

To understand what people do when they do mathematics and write programs emulating that process is a continuous research topic in Artificial Intelligence, Automated Reasoning, and Symbolic Computation [3, 8]. Computer Mathematics is by now an established, although developing, subject. The challenge is to make the systems, including Computer Algebra systems and Proof Assistants, more (mathematician-)friendly [1]. Symbolic computation systems, like the commercial packages Maple and Mathematica, are widely used, though they can produce unexpected or wrong answers [1, 2, 5]. Nevertheless, in order to reduce the effort of writing solvers, some web-based learning environments and e-learning authoring tools support (unsafe) interaction with them [7, 10]. Those packages were not developed specifically for education, which makes it difficult to get them generate step-by-step solutions that are *cognitive faithful*, i.e. that emulate the steps a student should take. In [2] a discussion about design criteria of software for mathematics education is given. AG-ILMAT – *Automatic Generation of Interactive Drills for Mathematics Learning* (www.ncc.up.pt/AGILMAT/) – aims at the design and implementation of a system to automatically create and solve math exercises, continuing research work reported in [9]. There, we introduced a prototype, called DEMOMATH, that also

---

* Partially funded by FCT and POSI, co-financed by EC fund FEDER, under project AGILMAT (contract POSI/CHS/48565/2002).

Please use the following format when citing this chapter:

Tomas, Ana Paula, Moreira, Nelma, Pereira, Nuno, 2006, in IFIP International Federation for Information Processing, Volume 204, Artificial Intelligence Applications and Innovations, eds. Maglogiannis, I., Karpouzis, K., Bramer, M., (Boston: Springer), pp. 433–441

yields one-line solutions for some exercises. Its solver is fairly ad-hoc, and cannot be easily adapted to present step-by-step solutions with pedagogic interest, which motivated our current work. We propose a conditional rewrite system for arithmetic and membership univariate constraints over real numbers. To gain flexibility, the rules are written in a specification language and then compiled to Prolog. In the next section we recall basic notions of real-valued functions and give examples of problems we want to automate. In Section 3 we introduce our representation for problems and constraints and show how to convert membership to arithmetic constraints, and reciprocally. Section 4 is devoted to the presentation of the proposed rewriting system, which was designed to be complete for the problems that can be solved by analyzing the sign variation of functions created by DEMOMATH.

2 Some Mathematical Background and Examples

We start with some notions about real-valued functions. $\mathbb{R}$ stands for the set of the real numbers, a, b, c, k for real constants, f, g, h for generic real-valued functions over $\mathbb{R}$, and x, y, z for real valued variables. As usual, $\mathcal{D}_f$ is the domain of the function f, and its image (a.k.a., range) is $f(\mathcal{D}_f) = \{f(x) : x \in \mathcal{D}_f\}$. We represent the restriction of f to $D \subseteq \mathcal{D}_f$ by $f|_D$ and the inverse function by f^{-1}, if it exists. If f is strictly monotonic over D, then $f|_D$ is invertible. The following table shows the basic functions studied in math at high school and some of their properties, if we exclude the trigonometric functions and generic polynomial functions $pol_{a_n,...,a_0} : x \mapsto \sum_{i=0}^{n} a_i x^i$.

f	$\mathcal{D}_f$	$f(\mathcal{D}_f)$	Behavior in $\mathcal{D}_f$	Inverse function
$id : x \mapsto x$	$\mathbb{R}$	$\mathbb{R}$	strictly increases, odd	$id^{-1} = id$
$c_k : x \mapsto k$	$\mathbb{R}$	$\{k\}$	constant, even	—
$p_k : x \mapsto kx,\ k \neq 0$	$\mathbb{R}$	$\mathbb{R}$	strictly increases if $k > 0$ strictly decreases if $k < 0$ odd	$p_k^{-1} : x \mapsto \frac{1}{k}x$
$pol_{a,b} : x \mapsto ax + b$	$\mathbb{R}$	$\mathbb{R}$	strictly increases if $a > 0$ strictly decreases if $a < 0$ odd if $b = 0$	$pol_{a,b}^{-1} : x \mapsto \frac{1}{a}x - \frac{b}{a}$
$pow_{2n+1} : x \mapsto x^{2n+1}$	$\mathbb{R}$	$\mathbb{R}$	strictly increases, odd	$pow_{2n+1}^{-1} = rad_{2n+1}$
$pow_{2n} : x \mapsto x^{2n}$	$\mathbb{R}$	$\mathbb{R}_0^+$	symmetric w.r.t. $x = 0$ $pow_{2n}|_{\mathbb{R}_0^+}$ strictly increases even	$(pow_{2n}|_{\mathbb{R}_0^+})^{-1} = rad_{2n}$
$rad_{2n+1} : x \mapsto {}^{2n+1}\!\sqrt{x}$	$\mathbb{R}$	$\mathbb{R}$	strictly increases, odd	$rad_{2n+1}^{-1} = pow_{2n+1}$
$rad_{2n} : x \mapsto {}^{2n}\!\sqrt{x}$	$\mathbb{R}_0^+$	$\mathbb{R}_0^+$	strictly increases	$rad_{2n}^{-1} = pow_{2n}|_{\mathbb{R}_0^+}$
$abs : x \mapsto |x|$	$\mathbb{R}$	$\mathbb{R}_0^+$	symmetric w.r.t. $x = 0$ $abs|_{\mathbb{R}_0^+}$ strictly increases even	$(abs|_{\mathbb{R}_0^+})^{-1} = id|_{\mathbb{R}_0^+}$
$exp_a : x \mapsto a^x$	$\mathbb{R}$	$\mathbb{R}^+$	strictly increases if $a > 1$ strictly decreases if $0 < a < 1$	$exp_a^{-1} = log_a$
$log_a : x \mapsto log_a x$	$\mathbb{R}^+$	$\mathbb{R}$	strictly increases if $a > 1$ strictly decreases if $0 < a < 1$	$log_a^{-1} = exp_a$

Composition, sum, difference, product and quotient of functions are represented by $\circ$, $+$, $-$, $\times$ and $/$. We have $\mathcal{D}_{f \circ g} = \mathcal{D}_g \cap \{x : g(x) \in \mathcal{D}_f\}$, $\mathcal{D}_{f \odot g} = \mathcal{D}_f \cap \mathcal{D}_g$ for $\odot \in \{+, -, \times\}$ and $\mathcal{D}_{f/g} = \mathcal{D}_f \cap \mathcal{D}_g \setminus \{x : g(x) = 0\}$. A piecewise function f is of form $(f_i, D_i)_{i=1}^n$, with $n \geq 2$, being $f(x)$ given by $f_i(x)$ if $x \in D_i$.

Drills and practice We now give some examples of exercises we are interested in automating. The first ones are from a high school math textbook (grade 11). To create the two last ones and get their solution we have used AGILMAT (available at www.ncc.up.pt:8080/Agilmat/).

- Find the domain of $f(x) = \frac{\sqrt[3]{1-x^2}}{4-x+\sqrt{x+2}}$.
- Express $g(x) = |x-1| + |x+1| + x$ without using the absolute value function. Solve $g(x) < |x+3|$.
- Study the sign variation of $-\sqrt{\frac{2|2x^2+2x|}{-3x-1}} - 1$ for $x \in \mathbb{R}$. (Solution: Negative in $]-\infty, -\frac{1}{3}] \cup \{0\}$ (the domain of the expression)).
- Solve $\left(2\,|-x^2 - 2x + 1|\right)^2 \left(2x^4 - x^2 - 3\right) \neq 0$ for $x \in \mathbb{R}$. (Solution: $]-\infty, \infty[\setminus \{-1 - \sqrt{2}, -\frac{1}{2}\sqrt{6}, -1 + \sqrt{2}, \frac{1}{2}\sqrt{6}\}$)

3 Constraints and Problems

We would like to solve problems that may involve arithmetic and membership constraints, because both types coexist in some math problems. We define *atomic* and *complex* constraints as follows.

The *atomic arithmetic constraints* are either of the form $f(x) \lhd g(x)$ and $f(x) \lhd k$ with $\lhd \in \{=, \neq, >, <, \leq, \geq\}$, f and g are real valued functions on reals and k is a ground arithmetic-term. The *atomic membership constraints* are of form $f(x) \lhd S$ with $\lhd \in \{\in, \notin\}$ and S is a ground set-term. The conjunction and disjunction of a finite number of constraints in the variable x is *a (complex) constraint* $C(x)$.

We often write C instead of $C(x)$, since we will address only problems that involve a unique variable. We use $\lhd^{-1}$ to denote the inverse of the binary relation $\lhd$, for $\lhd \in \{=, \neq, \leq, \geq, >, <\}$. We inductively define *the domain of constraint* C (denoted by $\mathcal{D}_C$) by $\mathcal{D}_{f(x) \lhd g(x)} = \mathcal{D}_f \cap \mathcal{D}_g$, $\mathcal{D}_{f(x) \lhd k} = \mathcal{D}_{f(x) \lhd S} = \mathcal{D}_f$, $\mathcal{D}_{\wedge_{i=1}^n C_i} = \cap_{i=1}^n \mathcal{D}_{C_i}$ and $\mathcal{D}_{\vee_{i=1}^n C_i} = \cup_{i=1}^n \mathcal{D}_{C_i}$.

The *problem* P of finding all $x \in D$ that satisfy the constraint C is denoted by a tuple $\langle C, x, D \rangle$. A problem is in *solved form* iff it is $\langle id(x) \in D, x, D \rangle$ and D is then called *the solution set* of the problem. (For short, we shall write $\langle x \in D, x, D \rangle$ instead.)

3.1 Membership versus Arithmetic Constraints

It is important to be able to convert membership to arithmetic constraints and reciprocally. For that we define two representations for sets. A set is in a *standard form* if it is either $\emptyset$ or the union of a finite sequence $S_1, \ldots, S_n$ of non-empty intervals and/or finite sets of $\mathbb{R}$, that are pairwise disjoint and such that $\sup(S_i) \leq \inf(S_{i+1})$ for all $1 \leq i < n$ and if $\sup(S_i) = \inf(S_{i+1})$ then $\sup(S_i) \notin S_i$ and $\inf(S_{i+1}) \notin S_{i+1}$. The infimum and supremum of each set may be $-\infty$ and $+\infty$. A *constraining set* is a subset of $\mathbb{R}$ that may be written in standard form.

Although the *constraining sets* do not fully represent all subsets of $\mathbb{R}$, they cater for the most frequent types of sets that occur in math drills, if trigonometry is excluded. This standard form is like a picture of the set in the real axis.

Example 1. The set $([-3, -1[\cup\{2, 17\} \cup [8, 11[\cup]11, 14[) \setminus \{10\}$ is a constraining set and it standard form is $[-3, -1[\cup\{2\} \cup [8, 10[\cup]10, 11[\cup]11, 14[\cup\{17\}$.

We now introduce *the reduced normal form* which gives a more compact *arithmetic* representation of each constraining set, being thus relevant for CAL. The reduced normal form is unique. A constraining set is *in reduced normal form* (**rnf**) iff it is given in one of the following forms: $\mathbb{R}$, $\emptyset$, a finite non-empty set, $\cup_{i=1}^n S_i$, $\mathbb{R} \setminus S_{n+1}$, $(\cup_{i=1}^n S_i) \setminus S_{n+1}$, $((\cup_{i=1}^n S_i) \setminus S_{n+1}) \cup S_{n+2}$, or $(\cup_{i=1}^n S_i) \cup S_{n+2}$, for a finite sequence of non-empty and non-universal intervals $S_1, \ldots, S_n$ with $\sup(S_i) < \inf(S_{i+1})$, for $1 \leq i < n$ and S_{n+1}, S_{n+2} non-empty disjoint finite sets such that $S_{n+1} \subset \cup_{i=1}^{n} S_i$ and $S_{n+2} \cap (S_i \cup \{\inf(S_i), \sup(S_i)\}) = \emptyset$, for every $i \leq n$.

Example 2. $\mathrm{rnf}([-3, -1[\cup\{2, 17\}\cup[8, 11[\cup]11, 14[)\setminus\{10\}) = (([-3, -1[\cup[8, 14[)\setminus \{10, 11\}) \cup \{2, 17\}$.

Let $\mathcal{S}_{\lhd}^{k}$ denote the set $\{x \in \mathbb{R} : x \lhd k\}$, for $k \in \mathbb{R}$ and $\lhd \in \{=, \neq, >, <, \leq, \geq\}$. E.g., $\mathcal{S}_{\geq}^{-3}$ is $[-3, +\infty[$, and $\mathcal{S}_{<}^{5}$ and $\mathcal{S}_{\neq}^{2}$ are $]-\infty, 5[$ and $\mathbb{R}\setminus\{2\}$. To help transform membership constraints into arithmetic constraints we introduce τ_1 that writes sets given in reduced normal form in terms of $\mathcal{S}_{\lhd}^{k}$'s, for suitable k's and $\lhd$'s and is defined as follows.

The map τ_1 is given by: $\tau_1(\mathbb{R}) = \mathbb{R}$, $\tau_1(\emptyset) = \emptyset$, $\tau_1(\{a_1, \ldots, a_n\}) = \cup_{i=1}^{n} \mathcal{S}_{=}^{a_i}$, $\tau_1([a, +\infty[) = \mathcal{S}_{\geq}^{a}$, $\tau_1(]-\infty, a]) = \mathcal{S}_{\leq}^{a}$, $\tau_1(]a, +\infty[) = \mathcal{S}_{>}^{a}$, $\tau_1(]-\infty, a[) = \mathcal{S}_{<}^{a}$, $\tau_1([a, b]) = \mathcal{S}_{\geq}^{a} \cap \mathcal{S}_{\leq}^{b}$, $\tau_1([a, b[) = \mathcal{S}_{\geq}^{a} \cap \mathcal{S}_{<}^{b}$, $\tau_1(]a, b]) = \mathcal{S}_{>}^{a} \cap \mathcal{S}_{\leq}^{b}$, $\tau_1(]a, b[) = \mathcal{S}_{>}^{a} \cap \mathcal{S}_{<}^{b}$, for $a, b \in \mathbb{R}$, and, $\tau_1(\mathbb{R}\setminus\{a_1 \ldots, a_n\}) = \cap_{i=1}^{n} \mathcal{S}_{\neq}^{a_i}$, $\tau_1(A\setminus\{a_1 \ldots, a_n\}) = \tau_1(A) \cap (\cap_{i=1}^{n} \mathcal{S}_{\neq}^{a_i})$, for $A \neq \mathbb{R}$, and $\tau_1(\cup_{i=1}^{n} A_i) = \cup_{i=1}^{n} \tau_1(A_i)$.

This transformation τ_1 is quite convenient to convert $f(x) \in S$ into an arithmetic constraint, for $\emptyset \neq S \neq \mathbb{R}$.

The transformation τ_2 acts on membership constraints $f(x) \in S$, for S presented in terms of $\mathcal{S}_{\lhd}^{k}$'s, being inductively given by: $\tau_2(f(x) \in \mathbb{R}) = (f(x) \in \mathbb{R})$, $\tau_2(f(x) \in \emptyset) = (f(x) \in \emptyset)$, $\tau_2(f(x) \in \mathcal{S}_{\lhd}^{k}) = (f(x) \lhd k)$, $\tau_2(f(x) \in \cup_{i=1}^{n} S_i) = (\vee_{i=1}^{n} \tau_2(f(x) \in S_i))$ and $\tau_2(f(x) \in \cap_{i=1}^{n} S_i) = (\wedge_{i=1}^{n} \tau_2(f(x) \in S_i))$. Each of these reductions between different set representations was implemented in Prolog. We reused a module developed for DEMOMATH for operating constraining sets in standard form [9]. Union, intersection and set difference are translated by cup, cap and setminus. Some symbolic representations were introduced for $\mathcal{S}_{\lhd}^{k}$, e.g., s(real), s([]), s(K,eq), s(K,lt), s(K,leq). Exact arithmetic for a subset of $\mathbb{R}$ is supported also by a module defined for DEMOMATH, that uses CLP($\mathbb{Q}$) for some computations [6].

For every given constraining set S (s.t. $\emptyset \neq S \neq \mathbb{R}$) and function f, we shall write $\Gamma(f(x) \in S)$ as an abbreviation of $\tau_2(f(x) \in \tau_1(\mathrm{rnf}(S)))$. Clearly, $\tau_2(f(x) \in \tau_1(\mathrm{rnf}(S)))$ is an arithmetic constraint that is equivalent to $f(x) \in S$. Because we consider that $x \in S$ is simpler than $\Gamma(x \in S)$, we introduce yet another transformation $\tilde{\Gamma}$ defining it by $\tilde{\Gamma}(id(x) \in S) = (id(x) \in \mathrm{rnf}(S))$ and $\tilde{\Gamma}(f(x) \in S) = \Gamma(f(x) \in S)$, for $f \neq id$.

Proposition 1. *For all constraining sets S, $\langle f(x) \in S, x, D \rangle$ is equivalent to $\langle \tilde{\Gamma}(f(x) \in S), x, D \rangle$.*

Example 3. If $S = [-3, -1[\cup[8, 11[\cup]11, +\infty[)$, we may rewrite, $\Gamma(f(x) \in S)$ as

$$\Gamma(f(x) \in S) = \tau_2(f(x) \in \tau_1(([-3, -1[\cup[8, +\infty[) \setminus \{11\}))) =$$
$$= \tau_2(f(x) \in ((\mathcal{S}_{\geq}^{-3} \cap \mathcal{S}_{<}^{-1}) \cup \mathcal{S}_{\geq}^{8}) \cap \mathcal{S}_{\neq}^{11}) =$$
$$= ((f(x) \geq -3 \wedge f(x) < -1) \vee f(x) \geq 8) \wedge f(x) \neq 11$$

If f is $rad_3 \circ pol_{2,-7}$, i.e., $f(x) = \sqrt[3]{2x - 7}$, for solving $\langle f(x) \in S, x, \mathbb{R} \rangle$, students transform the membership constraint to arithmetic constraints. Our solver does the same thing.

Each atomic constraint $C = (f(x) \lessgtr k)$ or $C = (f(x) \lessgtr S)$, is equivalent to $(f(x) \in \text{ctrSet}(C))$, for $\text{ctrSet}(C)$ given by $\text{ctrSet}(f(x) \in S) = S$, $\text{ctrSet}(f(x) \notin S) = \mathbb{R} \setminus S$ and $\text{ctrSet}(f(x) \lessgtr k) = S^k_\lessgtr$. So, $\text{ctrSet}(C)$ is a constraining set that contains $f(x)$ if C holds. We also introduce a partial function nf that writes some constraints to a standard form: $\text{nf}(f(x) \lessgtr \beta) = (\tilde{\Gamma}(f(x) \in \text{ctrSet}(f(x) \lessgtr \beta)))$ for ground β and $\text{nf}(\bigotimes_{i \in I}(f(x) \lessgtr_i \beta_i)) = (\tilde{\Gamma}(f(x) \in \tilde{\bigotimes}_{i \in I} \text{ctrSet}(f(x) \lessgtr_i \beta_i)))$ for ground β_i. Here $\tilde{\vee} = \cup$ and $\tilde{\wedge} = \cap$.

4 Solving Problems

To design pedagogically relevant solvers we cannot manipulate problems and constraints in an arbitrary way. The *rewrite rules* we propose use some extra mathematical knowledge, e.g. about functions behavior, and, if applicable, transform a problem into an equivalent one, under some specific conditions. For instance, the rule BOUNDRANGE checks whether an atomic constraint is valid or inconsistent based on functions range. It states that: *for any generic functions f and g, $f \neq id$, and any ground set-term or arithmetic-term β, if $D \subseteq \mathcal{D}_{f \circ g}$ and $\mathcal{E}$ is such that $f(\mathcal{D}_f) \subseteq \mathcal{E}$ then*

$$\langle (f \circ g)(x) \lessgtr \beta, x, D \rangle \to \langle x \in D, x, D \rangle \text{ if } \text{ctrSet}((f \circ g)(x) \lessgtr \beta) \supseteq \mathcal{E};$$
$$\langle (f \circ g)(x) \lessgtr \beta, x, D \rangle \to \langle x \in \emptyset, x, \emptyset \rangle \text{ if } \text{ctrSet}((f \circ g)(x) \lessgtr \beta) \cap \mathcal{E} = \emptyset;$$
$$\langle (f \circ g)(x) \lessgtr \beta, x, D \rangle \to \langle \tilde{\Gamma}((f \circ g)(x) \in S \cap \mathcal{E}), x, D \rangle$$
$$\text{if } \lessgtr \notin \{=, \neq\}, \emptyset \neq S \cap \mathcal{E} \neq S \text{ and } S \not\supseteq \mathcal{E}, \text{ where } S = \text{ctrSet}((f \circ g)(x) \lessgtr \beta).$$

The rewrite rules look like $P \to P'$ *if condition* although some preconditions were stated in a global head. This kind of mathematical representation does not make clear the intended operational reading of each rule. Implicit meta-knowledge should be made explicit in order to be able to explain solution steps. Because of that, and to gain also more flexibility to modify rules, add new ones and customize solvers to different users or curricula, we developed a language for specification of rewrite rules. The corresponding formulation of BOUNDRANGE looks as follows. Relevant conditions for writing explanations are annotated with (#).

```
BOUNDRANGE(P)
  begin
    is_atomic(P:ctr), is_ground(P:ctr:rhs),
    subseteq(func_dom(P:ctr:lhs:func),P:dom),
    (#)P:ctr:lhs:func =? F o G, !F =? id,
    E := (#)boundImage(F,func_dom(F)),
    S := (#)ctrSet(P:ctr)
    if (#)supseteq(S,E), (#)note("valid %", P:ctr)
      rewrite_to sfprob(P:var,inset,P:dom)
    elif (#)seteq(S cap E,s([])), (#)note("inconsistent %", P:ctr)
      rewrite_to sfprob(P:var,inset,s([]))
    else !inlist(P:ctr:op,[eq,neq]),
      (#)note("necessarily %", ctr(P:ctr:lhs:func,P:var,inset,E cap S)),
```

!seteq(($\#$)rnf(E cap S),S) rewrite_to
    prob(tgm(ctr(P:ctr:lhs:func,P:var,inset,E cap S)),P:var,P:dom)
  endif
end

The specification language is a functional language with implicit types. Primitive (data)types are **boolean, real, set, function, constraint** and **problem**. All built-in constructs are typed and every rule definition must be type checked. Due to space limitations we can not describe its details in this paper. The definition of a rule consists of a name, a parameter (of type **problem**) and a sequence of conditions followed either by a nested if_block or by a **rewrite_to** exp, where **exp** corresponds to the resulting problem, if no condition is *false*. Atomic conditions will allow the specification and the verification of mathematical knowledge as relations between functions, sets and real numbers; equality of problems or constraints; properties of functions; transformations and computations, etc. Each rule is compiled to a Prolog predicate. The if-block is translated to an auxiliary predicate, whose clauses correspond to the branches of the if-block. A single branch may succeed. Besides defining the rewrite rules, we need to specify how they are applied for solving problems. For that we use the notion of strategy [4]. A trivial strategy is to try to apply all available rules until either a solved form or an upper bound on the number of steps (rule applications) is reached. But other strategies may be defined.

4.1 Cognitive faithful rewriting rules

We now present some of the rewrite rules, that contribute to the novelty of this work. The whole set is complete for a set of problems arising in high-school math curricula and that can be generated by DEMOMATH. The grammar that describes the arithmetic expressions involved in them is presented in [9]. For space reasons, we omit their formal definition, except for a few, presenting their aim instead. We start by REDUCEPROBDOMAIN, that says that solutions must be in $D \cap \mathcal{D}_C$. Then, we give four rules for handling complex constraints and the rules for atomic constraints, omitting BOUNDRANGE.

ReduceProbDomain To guarantee that solutions are in $D \cap \mathcal{D}_C$.
SplitConstraints To rewrite several top level conjuncts (or disjuncts).
AggregateNormalize To rewrite several atomic constraints $f(x) \lessgtr_i \beta_i$, that
    occur at top level, to a simpler form (may detect inconsistency/validity).
Conjunctive To rewrite a single conjunct at top level.
Disjunctive To rewrite a single disjunct at top level.
ArithNormalize To convert a single membership constraint to an arithmetic
    constraint if the latter is simpler.
DefRealValuedFunc To rewrite membership constraints $f(x) \in S$ or $f(x) \notin S$
    for $S = \emptyset$ or $S = \mathbb{R}$, to solved form.
DomainAtomConstr To rewrite a constraint $(x \lessgtr \beta)$ to solved form.

ConstantFunc To rewrite a constraint involving the constant function to a constraint $f(x) \lessdot k$ or to a solved form.

StrictMonotonic To rewrite $(f \circ g)(x) \lessdot k$ to a simpler form when f is strictly monotonic.

AxialSymMonotonicBranch To rewrite $(f \circ g)(x) \lessdot k$ to a simpler form when f is symmetric w.r.t. $x = a$, strictly monotonic on $\mathcal{D}_f^{\geq a}$ (i.e., the set of points in $\mathcal{D}_f$ that are greater than or equal to a).

We also introduce five specific rules **AffineTransf**, **Power**, **Absolute-Value**, **Quadratic**, **Radix** to rewrite $(f \circ g)(x) \lessdot k$ to a simpler form, when f is $pol_{a,b}$, pow_n, abs, $pol_{a,b,c}$ and rad_n. Although they are instances of the **Strict-Monotonic** and **AxialSymMonotonicBranch**, these more advanced rules are best suited for handling generic functions, once students have already studied their behavior. For all but $pol_{a,b}$ and pow_{2n+1} (whose range is $\mathbb{R}$), conditions are imposed to disallow their application if it can be trivially deduced that the constraint is inconsistent (by using **BoundRange**). For example, **Absolute-Value** is defined by $\langle (abs \circ f)(x) \lessdot k, x, D \rangle \to \langle \widetilde{\Gamma}(f(x) \in \mathcal{B}_{0,\lessdot}^k), x, D \rangle$ if $k \in \mathbb{R}$ and $k \geq 0$, where $\mathcal{B}_{a,\lessdot}^\delta$ is $\{x \in \mathbb{R} : |x - a| \lessdot \delta\}$. That is, $\mathcal{B}_{a,\lessdot}^\delta = S_\lessdot^{a+\delta} \cup S_{\lessdot-1}^{a-\delta}$, if $\delta > 0$, and $\lessdot \in \{\geq, >\}$, $\mathcal{B}_{a,\lessdot}^\delta = S_\lessdot^{a+\delta} \cap S_{\lessdot-1}^{a-\delta}$, if $\delta > 0$ and $\lessdot \in \{\leq, <\}$, and so forth. The following rules handle constraints involving sum, product, difference and quotient of functions and also the piecewise function.

Piecewise To replace a constraint that involves a piecewise function f, given by $f \equiv (f_i, D_i)_{i=1}^n$, by a disjunctive constraint induced by the relevant branches f_i's.

ProductByConstant To rewrite $(c_k \times f)(x) \lessdot k'$ to a simpler form.

DiffSquare To factorize a difference of two squares $(pow_N \circ g - pow_M \circ h)(x) \lessdot 0$, for N and M even.

NullProduct To simplify a constraint by applying the rules for null product and sign of a product.

FactMonotonic To simplify constraints $(f \circ g)(x) \lessdot (f \circ h)(x)$ when $f \neq id$ is strictly monotonic. It is useful for solving $rad_n(X) \leq rad_n(Y)$ for instance.

FactOdd To simplify $(f \circ g)(x) \lessdot ((-f) \circ h)(x)$ when $f \neq id$ is odd. It states that: $\langle (f \circ g)(x) \lessdot ((-f) \circ h)(x), x, D \rangle \to \langle (f \circ g)(x) \lessdot (f \circ (-h))(x), x, D \rangle$ if $f \neq id$ is an odd function and $g \neq h$.

ToHomQuotient To rewrite $(f/g)(x) \lessdot k$ to $(f - c_k \times g)/g)(x) \lessdot 0$.

DiffMono To rewrite $(f \circ g - f \circ h)(x) \lessdot 0$ to $(f \circ g)(x) \lessdot (f \circ h)(x)$ when f is strictly monotonic.

SignDiff To rewrite $f(x) \lessdot g(x)$ to $(f - g)(x) \lessdot 0$.

SumNull To simplify $(f + g)(x) = 0$ and $(f + g)(x) \neq 0$ when the ranges of f and g are both in $\mathbb{R}_0^-$ or $\mathbb{R}_0^+$.

SquarePol To simplify constraints of form $(rad_2 \circ f - g)(x) \lessdot 0$ and $(rad_2 \circ f)(x) \lessdot g(x)$.

We need the last rules to guarantee the solvers completeness for the expressions that DEMOMATH creates. The solvers will not support user-defined expressions

$f(x)$, unless they may be *recognized* by the system. Simple algebraic manipulations may be carried out to express f in terms of a different combination of primitive functions.

Applications of CAL to math education require a careful analysis of procedures that students usually apply to solve math drills to design generic solvers with pedagogic relevance. We claim that solvers based on the proposed rewrite rules set fulfills this requirement. The system is being implemented in Prolog.

References

1. H. Barendregt. Towards an Interactive Mathematical Proof Language. in F. Kamareddine (ed.), *Thirty Five Years of Automath*, Kluwer (2003) 25-36.
2. M. Beeson. Design Principles of Mathpert: Software to support education in algebra and calculus. In N. Kajler (ed.), *Computer-Human Interaction in Symbolic Computation*, Texts and Monographs in Symbolic Computation, Springer-Verlag (1998), 89-115.
3. A. Bundy. *The Computer Modelling of Mathematical Reasoning*. A. Press (1983).
4. H. Cirstea, C. Kirchner, L. Liquori, and B. Wack. Rewrite strategies in the rewriting calculus. *Electr. Notes Theor. Comput. Sci.*, 86:4 (2003).
5. H. Gottliebsen, T. Kelsey, U. Martin. Hidden Verification for Computational Mathematics. *J. Symbolic Computation* 39 (2005) 539-567.
6. C. Holzbaur. OFAI clp(q,r) Manual, Edition 1.3.3. Austrian Research Institute for Artificial Intelligence, TR-95-09, Vienna (1995).
7. E. Melis, E. Andrés, J. Büdenbender, A. Frischauf, G. Goguadze, P. Libbrecht, M. Pollet, C. Ullrich. ActiveMath: A Generic and Adaptive Web-Based Learning Environment, *Int. J. of AI in Education* 12:4 (2001) 385-407.
8. A. Robinson, A. Voronkoy (Eds). *Handbook of Automated Reasoning*, Elsevier Science (2001).
9. A. P. Tomás, J. P. Leal. A CLP-Based Tool for Computer Aided Generation and Solving of Maths Exercises. In V. Dahl, P. Wadler (Eds), *Practical Aspects of Declarative Languages, 5th Int. Symposium PADL 2003*, LNCS 2562, Springer-Verlag (2003) 223-240.
10. G. Xiao. WIMS – An Interactive Mathematics Server, *Journal of Online Mathematics and its Applications* 1, MAA (2001).

A Tutoring System Discovering Gaps in the Current Body of Students' Knowledge

Sylvia Encheva[1] and Sharil Tumin[2]

[1] Stord/Haugesund University College, Bjørnsonsg. 45, 5528 Haugesund, Norway
sbe@hsh.no
[2] University of Bergen, IT-Dept., P. O. Box 7800, 5020 Bergen, Norway
edpst@it.uib.no

1 Introduction

Most learning management systems do not support a flexible navigational structure and an open assessment mechanism allowing incorporation of new pedagogical ideas. These learning management systems do not allow server side scripting for dynamic presentation of content either. Our idea is to develop a tool follows and supports each student's learning process by modelling a tutoring system based on classroom teaching.

This paper focuses on a tutoring system discovering gaps in the current body of students' knowledge. A framework for building new courses or updating existing ones by choosing learning objects developed at universities that are members of a federated learning system is also provided. The aim of this framework is twofold. First assisting a lecturer in collecting learning objects closest to the lecturer's vision on what a subject should contain and how the content should be presented. Secondly, present a student with content, tailored according to student's individual learning preferences.

Let us consider a lecturer affiliated with an educational institution that is member of a federated learning system. Suppose the system is able to provide a large number of learning objects (LOs) upon the lecturer request. A lot of time and efforts can be spared if the system can first filter and rank those LOs according to the lecturer's preferences. Another important issue is how to build a course supporting student's individual learning preferences. The system can help both the lecturer and the students by presenting each student with a LO chosen from the related set of selected LOs but tailored according to the student's individual learning styles and preferences. Identifying a student's style and then providing instruction consistent with that style contributes to more effective learning [3].

2 Related Work

Expert and theoretical knowledge about the use of technology for assessment is offered in [2].

Please use the following format when citing this chapter:
Encheva, Sylvia, Tumin, Sharil, 2006, in IFIP International Federation forInformation Processing, Volume 204, Artificial Intelligence Applications and Innovations, eds. Maglogiannis, I., Karpouzis, K., Bramer, M., (Boston: Springer), pp. 442–449

An intelligent system for assisting a user in solving a problem was developed in [7]. A personalized intelligent computer assisted training system is presented in [8]. A model for detecting student misuse of help in intelligent tutoring systems is presented in [1]. An investigation of whether a cognitive tutor can be made more effective by extending it to help students acquire help-seeking skills can be found in [5]. Evidence that when used appropriately, on-demand help can have a positive impact on learning was found in [9].

We focus on a different aspect of use of intelligent tutoring systems which is an attempt to first detect lack of prior knowledge of each student and then fill in the gaps.

3 Tutoring System

A course work is made of a set of subjects. Each subject contains an ordered set of related topics. Each topic contains a set of definitions, statements, examples, hints and tests. The tests within a topic are grouped into levels of difficulties and are used to asses students' level of knowledge about a particular topic.

For each topic, a student is initially presented with a Web page containing theory (definitions and statements) and supporting examples, where it is explicitly stated which part is required and which part is recommended for additional reading, to the current curriculum. The student is expected to study the presented material.

The student is then asked to take a test in the form of multiple choice question tests and provide a level of confidence in each answer. This test assumed that the student has learned and understood the presented materials in that particular topic.

From the result of the test, the system will guide the student through an automatic tutoring session if the student fails the test or presents the student with the next topic. The automatic tutoring session guides the student downwards (lower level of difficulties) according to the student mistakes and upwards again using the same path without a human tutor within the current topic.

Suppose the current topic was designed with three levels (A,B,C) in descending order of difficulties 1. After failing the test on level A, the automatic tutoring session brings the student to level B for reading suitable theory, hints and solving new examples. A new multiple choice question test for level B is then presented to the student. The automatic tutoring session checks the result of the level B test. If the student fails the test B then the automatic tutoring session brings the student down to the next (easier) level (level C). If the student passed the test B then the automatic tutoring session brings the student up again to next (more difficult) level (level A).

These iterations of tests between levels terminate when the student passes the multiple choice question test at the top most level (level A) or the student chooses to break out of the current automatic tutoring session. The materials and the multiple choice question tests presented at each level are dynamically produced depending on student's responses to the given tests. At any level the automatic tutoring session distinguishes wrong answers caused by miscalculation, lack of knowledge, and misconception. By automatically tracking the students' paths in response to theirs tests results, the automatic tutoring session helps the students to learn from their mistakes.

The automatic tutoring session keeps a record of all students' interactions with the system, providing data about level of knowledge of each student. This information can be used to compare the performance of each student against the whole class, compare the overall performance of different classes against each other, and to keep statistics of usage of particular learning units (statement, problems, hints, and examples). This helps content developers (teachers, lecturers, tutors) to improve on certain aspect of learning units by including new materials.

The automatic tutoring session is the heart of our tutoring system employing several intelligent agents working in concert which respond to students real time interactions to the system Web based interface. The agents interact with each other, record students' knowledge states and status and based on rules stored in the database provide students with personalized adaptive learning experience.

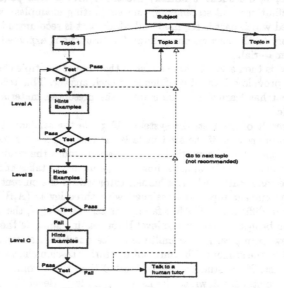

Fig. 1. Automated tutoring session

4 System Architecture

The system framework is composed of three main components: Web server, database and agents implemented on a Linux server.

Web server: Apache Web server with mod_python (Python interpreter). Dynamic HTML pages are created by server-side scripts (SSS) written in Python in response to students' interactions with the system using a Web browser. Having Python interpreter embedded in the Web server improves performance and reduces response time thus increases user satisfaction. Python is used to program the whole system including database connectivity and the agents.

Database : SQLite is used as a relational database. SQLite is a small *C* library that implements a self-contained, embeddable, zero-configuration Structured Query Language (SQL) database engine. SQLite is small and fast compare to other open source database engines for example PostgreSQL and MySQL. A complete database is stored in a single disk file that supports databases up to 2 terabytes (241 bytes) in size. Database files can be freely shared between machines with different byte orders. It is easy to set up a distributive multi-databases system using SQLite. A Python module pysqlite is used as a DB-API 2.0-compliant database interface for SQLite databases from within Python program.

Each subject meta-data is stored in its own database. Each student's automatic tutoring session data has its own database. We used native file system file structure to structure subjects and students' classes. One database is used for user administration and global references to others operational databases. This provides us with a flexible and expendable multi-databases system.

Agents: Independent agents written in Python provide the system support for students' automatic tutoring session. The Web server scripts and agents communicate with each other using XML-RPC (remote procedure call) over HTTP. The communication sub-system is also implemented in Python using xmlrpclib module. The system is supported by user, test and diagnostic agents that will be discussed later on in this paper.

By using three open source software - Apache, SQLite and Python we are able to implement a machine based tutoring system for teaching mathematical courses for higher education.

4.1 Agents

Agents are free running programs, capable of mutual interaction. The interaction can be in the form of message passing (XML-RPC) or producing changes in their common environment (data saved into or fetched from databases).

User agent: In order to use service provided by the system a person must register as a user to the system. A registered user will be given identity (user identification and password) and authority (student or teacher) within the system. The user agent is responsible in providing users' authentication and authorization data to other agents and keeping track of user current session, knowledge state

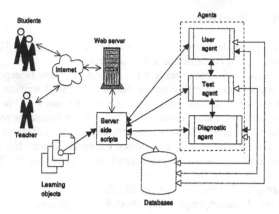

Fig. 2. System architecture

and working profiles. The user agent records students learning progress through the system. All learning material subscriptions and test results for a particular student are saved into the student personal database. Data saved in this database is used for the student's automatic tutoring session. These data also provides the student's audit-trail. Such audit-trail data can be used for billing purposes and course planning.

Test agent: This agent is equipped with a pedagogically crafted scheme with a set of questions and answers for each topics and levels. The agent responds to a particular student test results and his/her audit-trail to provide the student with personalized automatic tutoring session. The student can then subscribe to those learning materials suggested by his/her automatic tutoring session. The agent also calculates scores, show result status and keeps track of assessments taken by each student. After each assessment the test agent sends summarized information to diagnostic agent.

Diagnostic agent: Each automatic tutoring session is determined by pedagogical requirements. Each automatic tutoring session is structured using dependencies among learning materials, level and relationships between tests options, and inference rules triggered by a particular student interaction with the system. These requirements, relations and rules are crucial to the effectiveness of the system as a learning aid. Expert tutors experienced in the subject of learning are employed to define the pedagogical requirements of the diagnostic agent. This agent is the most difficult to implement and the success of the system depends on its implementation.

In order to support an adaptive learning environment these agents need a large collection of LOs, in particular - hints, examples and tests. A federation of organizations sharing LOs can in principal provide such collection.

5 Framework for Building New Courses

Suppose universities $U_1, U_2, ..., U_n$ are members of a federated learning system. A lecturer, affiliated with university U_j is developing a new course.

What is known for this course is the following - students will obtain degree (D) in for example engineering, mathematics, statistics or physics; it is at bachelor, master or Ph.D. level (L); it is an introductory, intermediate or advanced course level (C); table of contents of the subject (S).

Let us assume that it is an advanced course in differential equations for engineering students on a master program in fire safety.

Figure3 illustrates how an automated system for building courses using LOs in a federated learning system can assist a lecturer. A lecturer sends a quarry to the system about existing LOs in an advanced (C) course in differential equations (S) for engineering students (D) on a master program (L).

(1) Select universities (U_D) offering degree in engineering.
(2) Select universities (U_L) offering master degree in engineering, (U_L $\subseteq$ U_D).
(3) Select universities (U_C) offering advanced courses, (U_C $\subseteq$ U_L).
(4) Select universities (U_S) offering courses in the desired subject, (U_S $\subseteq$ U_C).
(5) Select universities (U_LOs) offering courses that contain LOs, wanted by the lecturer, (U_LOs $\subseteq$ U_S).
(6) Collect the wanted LOs that belong to the universities in the set U_LOs.
(7) Choose the most suitable LOs.
(8) Consider whether the course is complete.

If one of the sets U_D, U_L, U_C, U_S, U_LOs is empty or the list of obtained LOs is incomplete, the lecturer will be asked to send a new quarry. In our example it could be a degree in physics, mathematics or statistics. If the system search exhausts all possibilities in this federated system the lecturer is advised to consider other options like search among other systems or develop the missing LOs.

Intelligent Diagnostics- It is based on each individual's learning styles and preferences. An intelligent agent will choose the most appropriate LOs for the course. An agent is first checking whether all definitions and statements required are included in the suggested LOs. Another agent determines whether the level of difficulties assumed for the new LOs corresponds to the level of difficulties of the suggested LOs. The unfolding model (shortest distance) is used while comparing different LOs. The level of difficulties is judged based on the included theory, examples and assessment tests. A questionnaire is put to the students for determining their individual learning preferences.

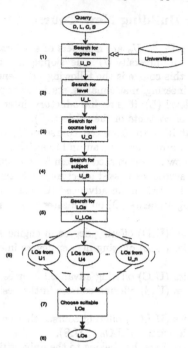

Fig. 3. Search process for LOs among federated universities

Stack Profiler - In the recommendation on how to proceed, a student can choose to subscribe to one or more suggested LOs. The student's LO subscriptions are placed in a stack-like structure in the student profile data. Initially, the profile stack contains a sequential ordering of LOs in a given subject. A student can choose to skip any presented LOs and go to the next one at any time.

Policy - The curriculum of each subject at every university should be described using a set of agreed upon metadata presented in a standard structure in a database.

LO Caching - If LOs in a course are connected with hyperlinks, the course builder risks to end up with some dead links during the semester. If all LOs in a course are cached on a local server, the course builder is sure that all LOs are going to be available to the students through the entire semester. The owners of the LOs have no control over the amount of students and number of times those LOs are used. However, the owners of the LOs can include f. ex. 1 ×1 pixel gif picture in every LO. Thus the owners will get information from log files for the number of times a LO has been used and by how many different users.

6 Conclusion

The system is designed to enhance the specific features of each user, without increasing the differences between users in what concerns the level of understanding or the ability to creatively use the acquired knowledge.

The paper describes also a framework for building new courses or updating existing ones by choosing learning objects developed at universities that are members a federated learning system. The aim of is to assisting a lecturer in collecting learning objects closest to the lecturer's vision on what a subject should contain and how the content should be presented, and to present a student with contents, tailored according to student's individual learning preferences.

References

1. Baker R S, Corbett A T, Koedinger K R (2004) Detecting student misuse of intelligent tutoring systems. Lecture Notes in Computer Science, Springer-Verlag, Berlin Heidelberg New Jork 3220: 531–540
2. Conole G, Crewe E, Oliver M, Harvey J (2001) A toolkit for supporting evaluation. The Association for Learning Technology Journal 9: 38–49
3. Jonassen D H , Grabowski B L (1993) Handbook of Individual Differences, Learning, and Instruction. Mahwah, N.J. Erlbaum.
4. Hron A, Friedrich H F (2003) A review of web-based collaborative learning: factors beyond technology. Journal of Computer assisted Learning 19: 70–79
5. Koedinger K R , McLaren B M, Roll I (2004) A help-seeking tutor agent. Proceedings of the Seventh International Conference on Intelligent Tutoring Systems, ITS 2004, Springer-Verlag, Berlin 227–239
6. Lepper M R, Woolverton M, Mumme D, Gurther G (1993) Motivational techniques of expert human tutors: Lessons for the design of computer-based tutors. In S.P. Lajoie, S.J. Derry (Eds.): Computers as cognitive tools. LEA, Hillsdale, NJ 75–105
7. Liu C, Zheng L, Ji J, Yang C , Li J, Yang W (2001) Electronic homework on the WWW. First Asia- Pacific Conference on Web Intelligence 540–547
8. Pecheanu E, Segal C, Stefanescu D (2003) Content modeling in Intelligent Instructional Environment. Lecture Notes in Artificial Intelligence, Springer-Verlag, Berlin Heidelberg New Jork 3190: 1229–1234
9. Renkl A (2002) Learning from worked-out examples: Instructional explanations supplement self- explanations. Learning and Instruction 12: 529–556

Sequencing Parametric Exercises for an Operating System Course

Pilar Prieto Linillos, Sergio Gutiérrez, Abelardo Pardo,
and Carlos Delgado Kloos

Department of Telematic Engineering
Carlos III University of Madrid, Spain
{pilar_pl,sergut,abel,cdk}@it.uc3m.es

Abstract. An adaptive tutoring system for an Operating System course is presented. The architecture, based on sequencing graphs, that supports an adaptive sequencing of the learning units is described. The content structure is presented as well. The system is now in use in regular university courses and results of this experience will be published in the future.

1 Introduction

Web based education (henceforth WBE) has seen in recent years a significant increase in both in its functionality as well as possible scenarios. E-learning systems are now present in an ever growing number of companies as well as educational institutions of all levels. After a first stage in which these systems offered mainly content management and course management capabilities, systems now offer solutions that cover pedagogical aspects such as activity sequencing.

When users of an e-learning platform are simply given access to a set of documents for each course, there is a high risk of being "lost in cyberspace" [1]. As important as having access to the proper documents, course activities and how they are organized within a course have a direct impact on the overall effect of the learning experience. Adaptive Hypermedia is a research area that focus on how hypermedia can be changed according to the user needs. When applied to e-learning, these techniques are generally known as "personalized learning" or "adaptive educational hypermedia". The idea is to customize learning material and activities and provided a personal environment for each learning [2].

This paper presents how a sequence of parametric exercises has been deployed in the context of a course on Operating Systems. Parametric exercises are those with content suitable to be instantiated an unlimited number of times with different data [3]. A set of exercises are initially designed and hierarchically organized by topics. A transition structure similar to a state machine is defined.

The presented framework allowed the teaching staff to organize a significant set of exercises from different operating system topics such as process scheduling, memory management, disk organization, and file system techniques. As a result a web based tutor offers the students a personalized exercise sequence based on the previously given answers. The system has been implemented and

Please use the following format when citing this chapter:

Linillos, Pilar Prieto, Santos, Sergio Gutierrez, Pardo, Abelardo, Kloos, Carlos Delgado, 2006, in IFIP International Federation for Information Processing, Volume 204, Artificial Intelligence Applications and Innovations, eds. Maglogiannis, I., Karpouzis, K., Bramer, M., (Boston: Springer), pp. 450–458

tested in a reduced environment and is now being used in regular university courses.

The rest of the document is organized as follows. Section 2 presents related work in the area of tutoring systems and e-learning content sequencing. Section 3 describes how the material is organized to cope with its complexity as well as the conditions to describe the transitions. Design of the tutor on operating systems is described in 4. An example of exercises covering a concrete topic of the course is shown in 5. The document terminates with a brief outline of future work in 6

2 Related Work

There is a wide variety of strategies proposed for sequencing educational material even before the appearance of e-learning platforms. In the area of computer assisted learning, intelligent tutoring systems [4] typically include a "tutoring model" that decides which information to be shown to the user. Techniques such as bayesian networks or neural networks (to mention a few) are used to deduce such information. The common characteristic of these systems is that designers do not specify directly this sequence but an algorithm to compute it.

The ideas included in this paper asume that a the designer specifies such sequence (or set of possible sequences). In this scenario several languages have been proposed to define these sequences. They are usually referred to as "Educational Modelling Languages" or EMLs (see [5] for a survey). Other techniques use already existing languages. As an example, in [6] UML (Unified Modelling Language) is used to define the sequences emphasizing in the use of ontologies to guide the student.

Two more initiatives that seem to capture the interest of the e-learning comunity are Simple Sequencing [7] and Learning Design [8]. Both of them are specifications proposed by the IMS Global Consortium and have become part of SCORM [9]. Simple Sequencing assumes the material is organized as a tree and provides conditions to modify an in-order traversal of the nodes. Learning Design tackles a wider problem because it allows the possibility of specifying arbitrarily complex activities such as discussions, collaborative tasks, etc.

The main problem with these techniques is that require the designer to learn an additional notation to formally describe a learning experience. The proposed approach can be considered as a tradeoff between expressive power and simplicity. The goal is to capture the experience teaching staff has about how material should be sequenced with the most intuitive formalism possible, a graph.

In [10], Collet et al. propose using a graph to describe a sequence of problems in a way similar to the one propose in this document. Transitions are initially defined by a user and later modified depending on the probabilities associated with the transtions. The algorithm used to modify these probabilities follows an ant colony optimization strategy.

In the proposed approach, the designer is in charge of providing a transition structure with a set of conditions that consider different scenarios when solving the exercises. Instead of dinamically adjusting the graph structure, the conditions attached to the transitions allow for a large number of possible paths along the graphs. The main challenge when deploying this paradigm has been taking a concrete course on operating systems and designing the transition graph with concrete exercises.

Sequencing graphs, presented in the next section, specify how to sequence learning activities in our system. They are powerful enough to allow arbitrary sequencing in a simple and intuitive manner, yet they can cope with big amounts of activities without becoming unmanageable due to their inherent hierarchy. This hierarchy allows to store small amounts of connected activities (a plain graph) in nodes that are part of a higher level organisation (another plain graph, but with graphs inside).

3 Sequencing Graphs

In our system, Sequencing Graphs define the sequencing of learning units. In the following definition, a *learning unit* is any digital learning content to be delivered to the user of an elearning platform including, but not limiting to, an exercise, its solution, a page with formulae and explanatory text, a commented photograph, etc.

3.1 Plain graph

A Sequencing Graph is defined recursively. In this subsection the plain graph with no hierarchy is presented. The hierarchy is explained in 3.2. A plain graph is defined as follows:

A *plain transition graph* G is a tuple (V, E) where V is a set of nodes each of them a learning unit and E is a set of directed arcs connecting nodes in V.

An *environment* Π is a set of pairs variable-value, where information about the student and its relation to the graph can be stored. Attribute values are divided into two types: strings and integers. Changes in the environment are made after each unit is delivered (any output data is stored in it) and, more importantly, by the *actions*.

An *action a* determines a change in the environment. This can be the addition of a new pair to the environment, the change of an existing one or the deletion of it (PUT actions and DEL actions).

A *condition c* specifies a boolean expression. Operators allowed for integer comparison are $=$, $<$, $\leq$, $>$, $\geq$. Strings (including booleans) can only be checked for equality. The allowed boolean connectives are ! , &, | for negation, conjunction and disjunction respectively.

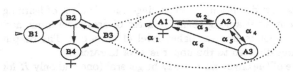

Fig. 1. Sequential graph hierarchy example.

An arc $\alpha \in$ E is a tuple (v_1, v_2, c, A) where $v_1, v_2 \in$ V. When condition c evaluates to true, the corresponding transition is suitable to be taken. Should the arc be followed, the corresponding set of actions A would be executed, modifying the environment.

At this point it can be seen that given a set of activities and a transition graph, the effectiveness of the system is captured in how transitions are enabled and how each activity modifies attribute values (thus collecting user data) altering the traversing of the graph. The proposed system assumes these functionalities to be created by a tutor or designer and provides a user friendly environment to develop the transition structure, allowing for a solid student supervision using the collected data.

It should be noted that the proposed architecture is generic enough to encompass a wide range of sequencing techniques. On one end linear sequencing of a set of conventional activities is implemented by a set of units with no parameters and a transition function returning always the next activity. At the other end, a non trivial set of highly customizable activities are interconnected through a large number of arcs labeled with conditions referring to different aspects such as scores, solution time, level of expertise, etc.

3.2 Hierarchy. Sequencing graphs.

Although plain graphs provide a powerful and flexible mecanism to express sequencing of learning units, they may become too complex for a large number of units. In this situation defining or maintaining a large transition structure can become infeasible.

A possible solution to overcome this is the use of hierarchy. Diferent kinds of *hierarchical graphs* have been already proposed and used with good results in other scientific fields [11]. The main idea is to consider smaller graphs defining sequencing of small sets of learning units as a node of another graph (which defines a sequencing itself) of a higher level of abstraction.

A sequencing graph is thus defined recursively as follows:

A *sequencing graph* SG $= (V,$ E, $V_i,$ $V_o)$ is a tuple where elements in V are either learning units or sequencing graphs, E is a set of arcs, $V_i \subset$ V is its set of input nodes and $V_o \subset$ V is its set of output nodes.

With this new definition, a sequencing graph is a set of learning units and subgraphs connected among them by a set of arcs. The input nodes are the possible entry points from a higher level of hierarchy. The output node are those with arcs directed to the upper level of hierarchy.

The scope of the environment may be general (one and only Π for the whole SG) or there could be a different environment for each level (Π_l) of hierarchy, with a mechanism to copy variables from one level to the upper ones. We have selected the latter approach, in order to make the implementation easier to use, and defined a SAVE action that copies a variable from the current environment to the upper level one (see section 5 for an example).

The possible sequencings defined by a sequencing graph are very intuitive to see. Nevertheless, in [12] the traversing algorithm is formally expressed. As we have not made any change to that, we do not repeat it here for the sake of space.

An example of a sequencing graph is given in Figure 1, with two levels of hierarchy which nodes are labeled with letters A and B. Input nodes at each level are marked with a white incoming arrow. Output nodes are marked with a cross, representing an arc going to the parent level. Output nodes could have a number of outgoing arcs going to the "parent", each one with a different condition and a different set of actions, if this fits the pedagogical purpose of the graph.

4 Tutor Structure

The course considered in this work is included in the fall semester of a fourth year in Telecommunication Engineering Degree. The course material is a subset of what is usually covered on a course on this topic in most universities. The reference book is "Operating Systems Concepts" [13]. The course objective is for the students to become familiar with the types of problems present in any operating system as well as a sample of techniques used to solve them.

The first decision to design the tutor was to select those areas that would be covered. The selected concepts were: process management, cache memory, memory management, disk management and file systems. In principle, any topic included in the course was suitable to be included in the tutor. However, these topics were selected because they were identified as those that posed a greater difficulty for the students to assimilate and where exercise solving would most likely had a positive effect. Despite of being a topic more suitable for a computer architecture course, cache memory is part of the course material due to dependencies derived from the entire degree.

The design process for the tutor followed a hierarchical approach to benefit from the architecture discussed on Section 3. The first level sequencing structure is trivial. Topics are covered sequentially as explained in the course lectures. The reason why no other possibility was allowed at this level is concept dependency.

Module	Learning Units	Exercises	Documents
Process Management	Scheduling Policies	5	6
	Scheduling Policy Analysis	2	1
	Performance Analysis	2	1
Cache Memory	Memory Access Time	1	1
	Direct Mapping	5	1
	Associative Mapping	2	1
	Set Associative Mapping	4	1
Memory Management	Contiguous Assignment	2	4
	Paging. Access Time	1	1
	Paging. Address Space	3	1
	Paging. Page Tables	2	2
	Paging. Process Allocation	1	1
	Paging. Page Replacement	2	3
Disk Management	Disk Access Scheduling	2	6
File Systems	Access Permissions	2	1
	Inodes	1	1
	Sector Allocation	3	2
Total		40	34

Table 1. Learning Units, Exercises and Documents for each Module

Concepts covered in one module make use of the ones previously covered. All sequence adaptation is then contained in each module separately.

Within each module, the material was divided into "learning units". In the context of this work, a learning unit is informally defined as a set of topics containing a set of exercises and a set of documents explaining the concepts required to solve these exercises.

The learning units present in the tutor as well as the number of exercises and auxiliary documents are shown in Table 1. As it can be seen, for each module, a subset of topics were selected. Again, each topic can be arbitrarily extended to cover more learning units, but the presented selection was based on the difficulty perceived by the students as well as how feasible was to design a set of effective exercises.

5 An Example

The tutor is composed of many graphs and subgraphs. The smallest ones are composed of only two elements, with an arc connecting both: one corresponds to the question and the other one with the grading of a particular parametric exercise. The biggest ones have almost ten elements, and up to twenty arcs conecting them (figure 2 is an example).

In this section we will explain in some detail one of the graphs (the right half of figure 1), the one corresponding to the section about 'Access permission' section of the tutor.

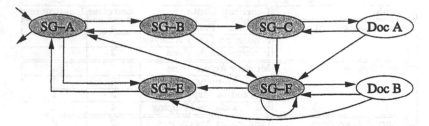

Fig. 2. Example of Graph for Learning Unit

The objective of this section of the tutor (graph) is to assess the knowledge of the student about file permissions in UNIX. First, it shows the student an exercise. If the students shows a great expertise on the matter, the section is finished. If not, another exercise of lower difficulty is delivered. If the student fails on the easy exercise, it is assumed that he knows nothing on the topic, so an auxiliary document is delivered and the student is advised to read it. More exercises are delivered then: good answers will lead to more difficult problems and bad answers will move the student in the opposite direction. The cycle is repeated until the student answers correctly all the questions of the hard exercise or has tried a number of times. At that moment, the section is finished (the sequencing goes up a level) and the tutor selects another section. The marks of the student are saved so that the tutor knows if this section should be revisited.

The graph has three nodes. Nodes A1 and A2 are sub-graphs and node A3 is an activity itself. Nodes A1 and A2 are graphs containing the exercises and node A3 links to the theory web page. Node A1 is both the only entry node and the only exit node. The complete set of conditions and actions is shown in table 2.

When the user comes to this level (graph) from an upper level of hierarchy, a new environment is set for him at an *init* phase, and it is initialised with only one new pair: *penalization_acc_perm = 0.*

The variable *penalization_acc_perm* acts like a counter to ensure that the student does not get stucked in this graph. Every time the student fails in one of the two exercises (nodes A1 and A2), condition in arcs 2 and 4 are evaluated to *true* and the arc is followed. The corresponding actions increase the value of *penalization_acc_perm* by 250, with a maximum of 1000. Conditions in arcs 1 and 6 ensure that after four or five (depending on the spacific path of the student) failed attempts, as the value of *penalization_acc_perm* will have reached 1000, the student will go up to the upper level. There he will be redirected to another part of the tutor and come back here later to cover this part.

It can be seen that variables can be put into the environment at the *init* phase or by the actions when an arc is followed. This is the case with *grade_acc_perm*, which is created and introduced when arc 1 is followed to the

Arc	Condition	Action(s)
1	all_evaluation=correct OR penalization_acc_perm=1000	[1] PUT grade_acc_perm = = 1000 - penalization_acc_perm; [2] SAVE grade_acc_perm
2	all_evaluation=incorrect AND penalization_acc_perm < 1000	[1] PUT penalization_acc_perm = = min(1000,penalization_acc_perm + 250); [2] DEL all_evaluation
3	all_evaluation=correct	[1] DEL all_evaluation
4	all_evaluation=incorrect	[1] PUT penalization_acc_perm = = min(1000,penalization_acc_perm + 250); [2] DEL all_evaluation
5	penalization_acc_perm < 1000	—
6	penalization_acc_perm=1000	—

Table 2. Conditions and actions for 'Access permission' graph

parent node. Furthermore, as this variable will be needed for the sequencing at the upper level and the level's environment is erased as the student goes up, a SAVE action is needed so its value is not lost.

The third way in which the environment can be modified is by the learning units themselves, or by lower level graphs, using SAVE actions. This is the case of variable *all_evaluation*. This variable is the result of a SAVE action from the lower level, either from node A1 or A2. As children of these nodes are exercises, they set several variables in the environment (the lower level's one). When the output arc is taken, a PUT and a SAVE action on it set this *all_evaluation* variable in this level. Its value determines whether arcs 1 or 2, or 3 or 4 must be followed. Note that, when the corresponding arc is followed, a DEL action erases *all_evaluation*. This is necessary so the result of the exercise under A1 does not affect the sequencing after A2, and viceversa.

6 Conclusions and Future Work

An application for sequencing parametric exercises about operating system topics has been presented. Using sequencing graphs to define the transitions between exercises, a web-based tutoring system has been designed that adapts the sequence of exercises to the capabilities and needs of the students. The system is now in use in regular university courses. Results of this experience will be published in the future.

There are two main lines for future work, both in relation with the sequencing graphs that the tutor is based on. First, they have been developed based on the past experience of the teachers of the target courses, in an ad-hoc fashion. Further research and application of these ideas should lead to some best practices that will make it easier to apply them by other educators, much in the way that design patterns [14] can be useful. On the other hand, a graphical editing tool is necessary to make the design process easier and faster, and it is now in development.

References

1. Brusilovsky, P.: Adaptive educational hypermedia. In: International PEG Conference. (2001) 8–12
2. Cristea, A.: Authoring of adaptive and adaptable educational hypermedia: Where are we now and where are we going? In: IASTED International Conference in Web-Based Education. (2004)
3. Brusilovsky, P., Miller, P.: Course delivery systems for the virtual university. In Tschang, F.T., Santa, T.D., eds.: Access to Knowledge: New Information Technologies and the Emergence of the Virtual University. Elsevier Science (2001) 167–206
4. Murray, T.: Authoring intelligent tutoring systems: An analysis fo the state of the art. Int. J. of Artificial Intelligence in Education **10** (1999) 98–129
5. Rawlings, A., Rosmalen, P.V., Koper, R., Rodrguez-Artacho, M., Lefrere, P.: Survey of educational modelling languages (EMLs). Technical report, CEN/ISSS WS/LT Learning Techonologies Workshop (2002)
6. Dolog, P.: Model-driven navigation design for semantic web applications with the uml-guide. Engineering Advanced Web Applications (2004)
7. IMS Global Learning Consortium: IMS Simple Sequencing specification (2003) v.1.0.
8. IMS Global Learning Consortium: IMS Learning Desing specification (2003) v.1.0.
9. Learning, A.D.: SCORM 2004 (sharable content object reference model). Specification (2004)
10. Semet, Y., Lutton, E., Collet, P.: Ant colony optimisation for e-learning: Observing the emergence of pedagogical suggestions. In: IEEE Swarm Intelligence Symposium. (2003)
11. Harel, D.: Statecharts: A visual formalism for complex systems. Science of Computer Programming **8** (1987)
12. Rioja, R.M.G., Santos, S.G., Pardo, A., Kloos, C.D.: A parametric exercise based tutoring system. In: Frontiers in Education Conference. (2003)
13. Silberschatz, A., Galvin, P.: Operating Systems Concepts. 7th edn. Addison-Wesley (2004)
14. Avgeriou, P., Vogiatzis, D., Tzanavari, A., Retalis, S.: Design patterns in adaptive web-based educational systems: An overview. Advanced Technology for Learning (2004)

A gene expression analysis system for medical diagnosis

Dimitris Maroulis[1], Dimitris Iakovidis[1], Stavros Karkanis[2], Ilias Flaounas[1]

1 University of Athens, Dept. of Informatics and Telecommunications,
Panepistimiopolis, 15784 Ilisia, Greece
2 Lamia Institute of Technology, Dept. of Informatics and Computer
Technology, 35100 Lamia, Greece
rtsimage@di.uoa.gr

Abstract. In this paper we present a novel system that utilizes molecular-level information for medical diagnosis. It accepts high dimensional vectors of gene expressions, quantified by means of microarray image analysis, as input. The proposed system incorporates various data pre-processing methods, such as missing values estimation and data normalization. A novel approach to the classification of gene expression vectors in multiple classes that embodies vari-ous gene selection methods has been adopted for diagnostic purposes. The pro-posed system has been extensively tested on various, publicly available data-sets. We demonstrate its performance for prostate cancer diagnosis and com-pare its performance with a well established multiclass classification scheme. The results show that the proposed system could be proved a valuable diagnostic aid in medicine.

1 Introduction

Microarray analysis has yet to be widely accepted for diagnosis and classification of diseases, despite the exponential increase in microarray studies reported in the literature. In the last decade a variety of software systems dedicated to microarray analysis have been developed. Do et al. [1] proposed the GeneClust software for microarray data analysis which implements hierarchical clustering and gene shaving algorithms [2]. Li and Wong [3] proposed the dChip software which implements a model-based expression analysis of oligonucleotide arrays and several high-level analysis procedures, including comparative analysis and hierarchical clustering. Peterson [4] proposed Clusfavor, a software package oriented in unsupervised analysis of microarrays. A powerful software suite named Genesis has been developed by Sturn et al. [5] for large-scale gene expression analysis. It includes filters, normalization and visualization tools, distance measures as well as clustering and classification algorithms such as hierarchical clustering, self-organizing maps, k-

Please use the following format when citing this chapter:

Maroulis, Dimitris, Iakovidis, Dimitris, Karkanis, Stavros, Flaounas, Ilias, 2006, in IFIP International Federation for Information Processing, Volume 204, Artificial Intelligence Applications and Innovations, eds. Maglogiannis, I., Karpouzis, K., Bramer, M., (Boston: Springer), pp. 459–466

means, principal component analysis, and Support Vector Machines (SVMs). Colantuoni et al. [6] developed a web-based tool named Snomad for the standardization and normalization of microarray data, using two non-linear transformations which correct both bias and variance of microarray element signal intensities. Saal et al. [7] developed Base, a software system for the management of biomaterial information, raw data and images, which provides integrated and "plug-in"-able normalization, data viewing and analysis tools. An open source suite of tools named TM4 has been developed by Saeed et al. [8]. It consists of four major applications, namely Microarray Data Manager (MADAM) which is a data entry and management tool for microarray experiments, TIGR_Spotfinder which is a semi-automated image analysis software, Microarray Data Analysis System (MIDAS) which is used for data normalization and filtering, and Multiexperiment Viewer (MeV) which is a data mining tool that implements a variety of clustering algorithms. Another software suite provided in open source is Bioconductor. It comprises of several packages that provide innovative tools for the analysis and comprehension of genomic data [9]. Su et al. developed RankGene, a software system which integrates a variety of popular ranking criteria, ranging from the traditional t-statistic to the one-dimensional SVMs [10]. A minimum spanning tree representation of gene expression data is being exploited by Excavator, a software system for microarray data clustering [11]. Toyoda and Konagaya [12] developed KnowledgeEditor, a graphical aid for biologists on biomolecular network modelling. Recently Pieler et al. proposed ArrayNorm a versatile and platform-independent application for the visualization, normalization and statistical identification of genes with significant changes in expression [13].

Most of the available software systems require technical skills and knowledge of complicated operations with which, physicians and biologists are not usually familiar. In this paper we present a novel, user friendly microarray data analysis software system which utilizes gene expression data for medical diagnosis. The proposed system does not require any technical knowledge by its users. It implements various pre-processing methods, and features a novel SVM-based architecture that embodies various gene selection methods in its structure and allows for the discrimination of multiple diseases or subtypes of a disease. Moreover, it handles the adjustment of its parameters automatically.

The rest of this paper is organized in four sections. Section 2 provides an overview of the proposed system and describes the methods it embodies. Experimental results from its application for prostate cancer diagnosis are presented in Section 3. Finally, in the last section the conclusions of this study are summarized.

2 System's Overview

The proposed system is capable of "learning" to recognize the pathology of samples provided to its input through a supervised training procedure. It embodies a Pre-processing and a Diagnostic Unit. The Pre-processing Unit prepares the gene expression data to passing into the Diagnostic Unit, which is the main processing unit of the proposed system.

The system's graphical user interface (Fig. 1) allows the user to switch between two modes of operation: the training and the diagnostic mode. The training mode of operation requires a gene expression matrix of pathologically characterized samples as input. The system automatically determines the best parameter settings for a particular diagnostic problem by grid search. After training, the system is capable of performing medical diagnosis based on a patient's gene expression data.

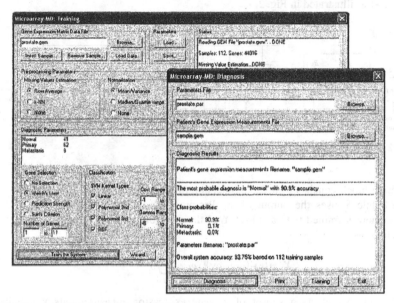

Fig. 1. The system's graphical user interface.

2.1 Pre-processing Unit

The Pre-processing Unit handles the management of missing values as well as the normalization of the gene expression levels. Poor quality in the preparation of the cDNA targets contributes to low quality gene expression measurements, as it affects the mean values and the standard deviation of the spots' intensities, their size and their contrast to the local background areas [14]. Such low quality measurements are usually discarded and missing values appear.

In the Pre-processing Unit of the proposed system we have included a) the row-average method, as it is simple and effective [14] and b) the k-nearest neighbours method (k-NN) which is more robust than the row-average method but requires more computations [15].

2.2 Diagnostic Unit

The Diagnostic Unit handles medical diagnosis as a multi-class classification problem. It is capable of classifying the input gene expression vectors to N classes noted as ω_i, $i = 1, 2... N$. Each class corresponds to samples acquired from healthy patients, from patients suffering from the same disease or from patients suffering from a subtype of a particular disease. It comprises of N-1 cascading blocks B_j, $j = 1$, 2, ... N-1 as illustrated in Fig. 2.

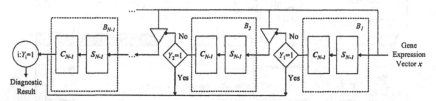

Fig. 2. The Diagnostic Unit.

Each block consists of a Gene Selection Module S_j and a Classification Module C_j. Module S_j uses the output of the Pre-processing Unit as input. Module C_j is autonomously trained with a subset X_j of the available training samples X, where X_j is defined as

$$X_j = \left\{ x \in \left(\omega_j \cup \omega_h \right) \right\}, \ \omega_h = \bigcup_{p=j+1}^{N} \omega_p \tag{1}$$

Module S_j selects a subset of τ_j gene expression measurements which best discriminates class ω_j from class ω_h and maximizes the classification performance of the module C_j. Given a test vector x, the module C_j is fed with τ_j gene expression measurements and outputs 1, if $x \in \omega_j$, or -1, if $x \notin \omega_j$. If $x \notin \omega_j$, the next block B_{j+1} will be activated to classify the test vector using the corresponding τ_{j+1} gene expression measurements. Otherwise the classification task terminates and x is assigned to class ω_j. The last block B_{N-1} decides whether $x \in \omega_{N-1}$ or $x \in \omega_N$.

The gene selection modules of the Diagnostic Unit integrate three ranking criteria for the selection of differentially expressed genes (Eqs. 2-4) [16-18] have shown that these criteria can be efficiently used for the identification of differentially expressed genes. These criteria suggest that the genes are ranked in descending order based on the absolute value of the $Z(g)$ statistic for each gene g.

$$Z(g) = \frac{m_g^j - m_g^h}{\sigma_g^j + \sigma_g^h} \tag{2}$$

$$Z(g) = \frac{m_g^j - m_g^h}{\sqrt{\dfrac{(\sigma_g^j)^2}{n_j} + \dfrac{(\sigma_g^h)^2}{n_h}}} \tag{3}$$

$$Z(g) = \frac{n_j(m_g^j - m_g)^2 + n_h(m_g^h - m_g)^2}{\sum_{i \in \omega_j}(x_{gi} - m_g^j)^2 + \sum_{i \in \omega_h}(x_{gi} - m_g^h)^2} \tag{4}$$

The (m_g^j, σ_g^j) and (m_g^h, σ_g^h) correspond to the mean and standard deviation of the expression levels of the gene g for the training samples that belong to ω_j and ω_h classes respectively and m_g is the mean expression level of gene g for the entire training set. The x_{gi} is the (g, i) element of the gene expression matrix that corresponds to the expression level of gene g for the sample i. The number of samples belonging to each of the above classes is denoted by n_j and n_h. The τ_j top-ranked genes are selected as they lead to a large between-class distance and a small within-class variance.

The classification module of each block of the Diagnostic Unit implements a binary SVM classifier. SVM training involves a quadratic programming optimization procedure which aims to the identification of a subset of vectors from the available set of training vectors x_i, $i=1,2,...n$ called *support vectors*. These vectors are utilized in the derivation of a separating hypersurface that separates the two classes $y_i \in \{-1, 1\}$, according to the following equation

$$\sum_{\forall i: 0 < \lambda_i \leq c} \lambda_i y_i K(x_i, x) + w_0 = 0 \tag{5}$$

where $0 < \lambda_i < c$ are Lagrange multipliers that correspond to the support vector solutions, c is a positive cost parameter, and $K(x_i, x_j)$ is a kernel function that maps the input space into a high dimensional Hilbert space [19].

In the diagnostic mode of operation, given a test vector x_i, the trained SVM outputs a label Y in accordance with the following formula

$$Y = sign\left(\sum_{\forall i: 0 < \lambda_i \leq c} \lambda_i y_i K(x_i, x) + w_0\right) \tag{6}$$

which designates the class in which an unknown vector x_i belongs to. This information is subsequently used for the derivation of the final diagnostic result.

3 Results

Experiments were conducted on publicly available datasets to evaluate the performance of the proposed system for the diagnosis of diseases. We summarize the results of the application of the proposed system for prostate cancer diagnosis. The prostate cancer dataset used was first studied by Lapointe et al. [20] and it is available from the Stanford Microarray Database [21]. It consists of 112 samples with 44,016 gene expressions spanning three classes, namely 62 primary prostate tumors, 41 normal prostate samples and 9 pelvic lymph node metastases.

The gene expression matrix data file of the prostate cancer dataset was loaded to the system and the structure of the diagnostic unit was determined to two blocks. The first block was assigned to the discrimination of the normal from the joint primary and metastatic samples, while the second block was assigned to the discrimination of primary from metastatic samples.

Comparative classification results were obtained by running the experiments also using the well established one-vs-one SVM combination scheme [22]. During the training mode of the SVM-based classification schemes (Cascading and one-vs-one) the kernel functions tested were the linear, the 2nd and 3rd order polynomial and the RBF [19]. The ranges of the training parameters considered were 2^{-5} to 2^{15} for the cost parameter c and 2^{-15} to 2^3 for the γ parameter. The best parameters that maximize the performance for the cascading and the one-vs-one schemes were determined automatically using grid search. The order of the blocks in the cascading model was determined based on the histopathological sub-classification of carcinomas [20]. A range of one to 11 genes was considered in the gene selection process.

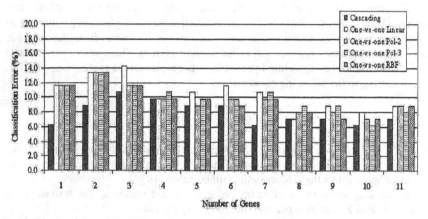

Fig. 3. Diagnostic accuracy of the proposed system (cascading SVM architecture) compared with the standard one-vs-one SVM combination scheme, for various numbers of input genes.

In all cases, the proposed architecture results in lower or comparable classification error rates with the one-vs-one scheme. The minimum classification error obtained for the prostate cancer dataset reached 6.3% in three cases using one, seven or ten genes. The same classification error rate was obtained by one-vs-one scheme using 3rd order polynomial kernel and ten genes. So, the proposed architecture has an advantage over these schemes as it is capable of providing a better or comparable performance using fewer genes. The upper classification error bound of the cascading SVMs architecture is 10.7%, whereas this bound increases to 14.3% for the one-vs-one scheme.

The results are presented in Fig. 3. The diagram shows that the proposed architecture leads to lower classification error rates compared to the one-vs-one classifier using one to five genes. The one-vs-one SVM combination scheme with linear kernel resulted in the lowest classification error using six input genes.

The classification errors achieved by the proposed system on other publicly available datasets were also low. These include colon cancer (9.7%), and lung cancer (1.5%) datasets [23][24].

4 Conclusions

We presented a biomedical software system capable of supporting medical diagnosis using gene expression data produced by microarray experiments. The major contribution of the proposed system in the process of medical diagnosis is that it offers to the physicians substantial molecular-level information by exploiting gene expressions. The gene expression measurements are pre-processed and subsequently used for the classification of the corresponding samples in two or more categories depending on their pathology.

The proposed system has been tested on various publicly available microarray datasets, including those provided by Stanford Microarray Database [21]. In most cases the overall diagnostic accuracy it provides, exceeds 90%. Its high accuracy was avouched in this paper by demonstrating its application for prostate cancer diagnosis. It can be concluded that the proposed system can be used as a valuable diagnostic aid by physicians and with the decreasing cost of microarrays it could potentially be used in everyday medical practice.

Moreover the cascading SVM combination scheme provides low classification error rates which are comparable and in most cases lower than the rates obtained by the one-vs-one SVM combination scheme especially when a small number of genes is involved. The proposed architecture utilizes N-1 classifiers whereas the one-vs-one SVM combination scheme utilizes $N(N-1)/2$ classifiers and the one-vs-one SVM combination scheme utilizes N classifiers.

Currently, the approach followed for the system to learn from new training data involves discarding the existing classifier, combining the old and the new data and training a new classifier from scratch using the aggregate data. Within our prospects is the enhancement of the proposed system by incorporating an incremental approach to SVM learning that will allow efficient on-line training without losing prior knowledge from additional datasets that will later become available.

Acknowledgment

This research was funded by the Operational Program for Education and Vocational Training (EPEAEK II) under the framework of the project "Pythagoras - Support of University Re-search Groups" co-funded by 75% from the European Social Fund and by 25% from national funds. We would also like to thank the anonymous reviewers for their helpful comments and suggestions.

References

1. Do, K.-A., Nikolova, R., Roebuck, P., Broom, B.: GeneClust, http://odin.mdacc.tmc.edu /~kim/geneclust/, accessed Nov. 2004
2. Hastie, T., Tibshirani, R., Eisen, M. B, Alizadeh, A., Levy, R., Staudt, L., Chan, W.C., Botstein D., and Brown, P.: 'Gene shaving' as a method for identifying distinct sets of genes with similar expression patterns. Gen. Biol. 1 (2000) 0003.1-0003.21
3. Li, C., Wong, W. H.: Model-based analysis of oligonucleotide arrays: Expression index computation and outlier detection. PNAS 98 (2001) 31-36
4. Peterson, L.E.: CLUSFAVOR 5.0: hierarchical cluster and principal-component analysis of microarray-based transcriptional profiles. Gen. Biol. 3 (2002) 0002.1-0002.8

5.   Sturn, J. Quackenbush, Z. Trajanoski: Genesis: cluster analysis of microarray data. Bioinformatics 18 (2002) 207-208
6.   Colantuoni, C., Henry, G., Zeger, S., Pevsner, J.: SNOMAD (Standardization and NOrmalization of MicroArray Data): web-accessible gene expression data analysis, Bioinformatics 18 (2002) 1540-1541
7.   Saal, L. H., Troein, C., Vallon-Christersson, J., Gruvberger, S., Borg, Å., Peterson, C.: BioArray Software Environment: A Platform for Comprehensive Management and Analysis of MicroarrayData. Gen. Biol. 3 (2002) 0003.1-0003.6
8.   Saeed, A.I., Sharov, V., White, J., Li, J., Liang, W., Bhagabati, N., Braisted, J., Klapa, M., Currier, T., Thiagarajan, M., Sturn, A., Snuffin, M., Rezantsev, A., Popov, D., Ryltsov, A., Kostukovich, E., Borisovsky, I., Liu, Z., Vinsavich, A., Trush, V., Quackenbush, J.: TM4: a free, open-source system for microarray data management and analysis. Biotechniques 34 (2003) 374-378
9.   Gentleman, R., Rossini, R., Dudoit S., Hornik K.: The Bioconductor FAQ, (2003) official URL. http://www.bioconductor.org/
10. Yang, S., Murali, T. M., Pavlovic, V., Schaffer, M., Kasif, S.: RankGene: identification of diagnostic genes based on expression data. Bioinformatics. 19 (2003) 1578-1579
11. Xu, D., Olman, V., Wang, L., Xu, Y.: EXCAVATOR: a computer program for efficiently mining gene expression data. Nucleic Acids Research 31 (2003) 5582-5589
12. Toyoda T., Konagaya, A.: KnowledgeEditor: a new tool for interactive modeling and analyzing biological pathways based on microarray data. Bioinformatics. 19 (2003) 433-434
13. Pieler, R., Sanchez-Cabo, F., Hackl, H., Thallinger G.G., Trajanoski, Z.: ArrayNorm: comprehensive normalization and analysis of microarray data. Bioinformatics. 20 (2004) 1971-1973
14. Zhang, W., Shmulevich, I., (ed.), Computation and Statistical Approaches to Genomics, Kluwer Academic Publishers, Boston, (2002)
15. Troyanskaya, O., Cantor, M., Sherlock, G., Brown, P., Hastie, T., Tibshiran, R., Botstein D., Altman, R.B., Missing value estimation methods for DNA microarrays. Bioinformatics 17 (2001) 520-525
16. Pan, W., A comparative review of statistical methods for discovering differentially expressed genes in replicated microarray experiments. Bioinformatics. 18 (2002) 546-554
17. Golub, T.R. et al.: Molecular Classification of Cancer: Class Discovery and Class Prediction by Gene Expression Monitoring. Science. 286 (1999), 531-537
18. Sun, M., Xiong, M.: A mathematical programming approach for gene selection and tissue classification. Bioinformatics 19 (2003) 1243-1251
19. Vapnik, V.: Statistical Learning Theory, John Will and Sons, New York, (1998)
20. Lapointe, J., Li, C., Higgins, J.P., Van de Rijn, M., Bair, E., Montgomery, K. et al. : Gene expression profiling identifies clinically relevant subtypes of prostate cancer. Proc. Nat. Acad. Sci. 101 (2004) 811-816
21. Stanford Microarray Database, http://genome-www5.stanford.edu., accessed Nov. 2004.
22. Hsu C.W., Lin, C.J., A comparison of Methods for Multiclass Support Vector Machines, IEEE Trans. Neural Networks, 13 (2002), 415–425
23. Alon, U., Barkai, N., Notterman, D.A., Gish, K., Ybarra, S., Mack, D., Levine, A. J.: Broad patterns of gene expression revealed by clustering analysis of tumor and normal colon tissues probed by oligonucleotide arrays, Proc. Nat. Acad. Sci. 96 (1999) 6745–6750.
24. Bhattacharjee, A., Richards, W.G., Staunton, J., Li, C., Monti, S., Vasa P., et al.: Classification of human lung carcinomas by mRNA expression profiling reveals distinct adenocarcinoma subclasses. Proc. Nat. Acad. Sci. 98 (24) (2001) 13790-13795

Recording, Monitoring and Interrelating Changes of Invivo Bio-cells from Video (*Biosignatures*)

Nikolaos Bourbakis

ITRI, WSU, College of Engineering, Dayton, OH 45435
AIIS Inc. , nbourbakis@woh.rr.com

Abstract. This paper presents a synergistic methodology for automatically recording, monitoring and interrelating changes occurred in invivo bio-cells without any user's assistance. The methodology presented here combines several techniques, such as projection functions, registration, segmentation with region synthesis, local-global graphs and stochastic Petrinets. Each of these techniques produces complementary results and the synergistic combination of them generates a methodology that produces the bio-signatures of bio-cells in sequences of images. Illustrative results are also provided.

1 Introduction

Detecting and recording changes in different images captured from the same scene at different time and orientation is a subject of important interest in the area of medical imaging. Several methodologies have been proposed with good results [1-10]. Most of these methods use quantitative difference measures and a wide list of quantitative image difference measures can be found in [1]. The measures come mainly from signal processing area and do not take into account an image interpretation. Let we name at least some of them. Given two images I, J, both of size $M \times N$, the following measures were defined [1].

Maximum Difference $\quad MD = max \ |I_{ij} - J_{ij}|$;

Normalized Average Difference $\quad NAD = (1/\sum|I_{ij}|)[\sum |I_{ij} - J_{ij}|]$;

Average Difference $\quad AD = (1/MN) \sum |I_{ij} - J_{ij}|$;

Mean Square Error $\quad MSE = (1/MN) \sum (I_{ij} - J_{ij})^2$;

Normalized Mean Square Error $\quad NMSE = [1/\sum(I_{ij})^2][\sum (I_{ij} - J_{ij})^2]$;

Peak Signal to Noise Ratio $\quad PSNR = 10log_{10} (I^2max/MSE)$;

$\qquad$ *where I_{max} is a maximum possible pixel value.*

There also methods for detecting changes in images and they are related to the human visual system (HVS), where its sensitivity depends on viewing conditions, namely on image illumination, background illumination, viewing distance, color fidelity. Those conditions must be usually fixed while evaluating an image distance

---

Please use the following format when citing this chapter:

Bourbakis, Nikolaos, 2006, in IFIP International Federation for Information Processing, Volume 204, Artificial Intelligence Applications and Innovations, eds. Maglogiannis, I., Karpouzis, K., Bramer, M., (Boston: Springer), pp. 467–475

measure. An interesting approach is proposed in [2]. They choose the viewing distance adaptively for every image so that the image of an object appears at the peak of the HVS sensitivity curve, or about 8 cycles per degree. The quality measure is then based on the background illumination level sensitivity and the spatial frequency nonlinear models. Moreover, a simple and in some degree valuable model to insure that image changes produced in their process of embedding a piece of information into an image is visually transparent is used in [3]. The S-CIELAB standard is followed to transform each image into an opponent-color representation. Then apply low-pass filtering to each of the 3 bands and the result transform into CIE XYZ-tristimulus coordinates. Finally, the CIELAB formula for color differences ΔE is evaluated (its definition can be found in [4]. A value of ΔE less than 1 implies that the differences are not detectable by humans. S-CIELAB requires some calibration parameters like viewing distance (angle), white point, and the mapping between the digital representation of the color images and the spectral reflectance of the displayed images.

In addition, a method based on local global (L-G) graphs for efficiently representing the cell's structural features (shape, size, color, texture, regions) and to some degree the changes occurred in different consecutive images has been presented in [10]. Thus, the new contribution in this paper is the correlation and interrelation of the detected changes for automatically generating bio-signatures or contributing to an interpretation of the events or actions that took place in the sequence of images [9].

2. The Bio-signature based Method

This method is based on the synergistic combination of several techniques, such as pixels projections [7], registration [8], region-grown segmentation with region synthesis [6], local-global graphs [5], Stochastic Petri nets (SPN) [9]. In particular, the pixels projection functions offer an efficient capability for detecting changes in 2D images captured from the same altitude and the same direction. The image registration is offering the capability for matching same regions in images taken from different scale, translation and rotation. The image segmentation contributes the clustering of different regions with certain characteristics, such as same of similar color, texture and the synthesis of regions composes regions with similar features into larger regions that serve the goals of the criteria selected by the user or a particular application. The L-G graphs provide an accurate representation of the regions structural features. Finally the SPN model offers to the synergy operational features, such as timing, synchronization, parallelism, concurrence of events that occurred in consecutive images captured by a video camera [9].

2.1. Pixels Projection Functions

The pixels projection functions are based on the Radon transformation:

$$T(\rho,\theta) = R_\theta[f(x,y)] =$$
$$\int\int f(x,y) \cdot \delta(\rho - x\cos\theta, \rho - y\sin\theta)dxdy.$$

ρ,θ are the spatial variables in the radial coordinates, ρ is the radium and θ the angle, and δ is the Kronecer's delta function defined as: $\delta_{ij} = 1$ if i=j, and $\delta_{ij} = 0$ if i≠j. Then the Radon transformation is expressed as

$$T_{0^{\circ}}(y) = \sum_{x}^{Nr} I(x,y) \qquad\qquad T_{0^{\circ}}(y) = \sum_{x}^{Nr} I(x,y)$$

The result of this process is the decomposition of the initial 2-D signal into two 1-D signal.

2.2. Registration

Image registration is the process of geometrically or topologically aligning two images of the same scene that have been taken under varying conditions. It is usually employed as the first stage in medical imaging. For the case of change detection, the objective is to find the differences between two images of the same scene that have been taken from variable viewpoints, at different times, using different cameras. Figure 1 illustrates the image registration process in two bio-images.

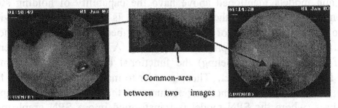

Figure 1: It shows two WCE images taken from different directions and different time and the 91% mapping of a possible common areas after registration.

2.3. Region Growing Image Segmentation

Here, we use the Fuzzy-like Reasoning Segmentation (*FRS*) method with Region Synthesis that adds light model as one of the segmentation factors. Its result is more accurate in terms of perception and more suitable for later reconstructing work. The FRS method has three stages (smoothing, edge detection and segmentation). The initial smoothing operation is intended to remove noise. The smoother and edge detector algorithms are also included in this processing step [6]. The segmentation algorithm uses edge information and the smoothed image to find segments present within the image. Figure 2 shows a segmented image and the synthesis of regions based on predefined recognition criteria.

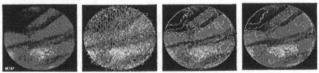

Fig. 2: It illustrates the results from an image segmentation and the synthesis of regions with similar features generating the desirable region-object

2.4. L-G Graphs

The *Local-Global* (*L-G*) graph method combines local-regional information with global topological representation of information distributed in an image [7]. The graph is a more accurate representation of an object. Thus, we avoid using a nonlinear graph matching function. By combining the *FRS* method and the *L-G* graph method, we can improve object recognition accuracy without increasing computation complexity. Thus, here the L-G graph is capable of describing with adjustable accuracy and robustness the features contained in an image. The main components of the L-G graph are: (i) the local graph that represents the information related with color, texture, shape, size, (ii) the skeleton graph that provides in formation about the internal shape of each segmented region, and the global graph that represents the relationships among the segmented regions for the entire image. Thus, the basic idea behind this graph based method is the local and global geometric representation of the image features and their relationships. The selection of the graph structure for representing the information extracted from an image is important for two reasons: 1) it is a generic and very flexible information representation scheme; 2) it is very robust and computationally not very expensive.

2.5. Stochastic Petri-net Graphs

The graph models mentioned above have the capability of holding structural information for objects. Thus, the missing element is the functional behavior of a object. The functional behavior of an object is described by the states that the object could be transferred after an appropriate triggering. A successful and power model capable of describing (or modeling) the functional behavior of a system is the Stochastic Petri-net (SPN) model. Thus, in order to maintain the structural features of the graph model and the functional features of the SPN model, a mapping is presented here, where the SPN model is transformed into a SPN graph model as follows [9]:

$$m : G \rightarrow SPNG$$

where, {Ni} → {Pi}, graph-nodes correspond into SPN places, and {aij} → {tij}, relationships corresponds into SPN transitions.

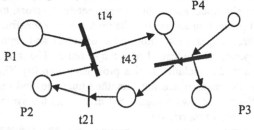

The SPNG above illustrates an object that has four different states (Places Pi, i=1,2,3,4). Each place Pi has its own structural features transferred from the corresponding graph node Ni. The transitions t14 and t43 represent relationships among the same parts of an object and a stochastic distribution of time required to fire that transition. The transition t21 requires no time to fire.

2.6. Illustrative Examples

In this section we present illustrative examples of bio-images taken from a sequence of images (especially two at a time) for showing the results of the changes detection methods. The examples 1 and 2 show results for detecting changes in two images using the Radon transformation with horizontal, vertical and diagonal projections.

The changes were detected by combining the horizontal, vertical and diagonal projections. This methods alone is good for images where rotation and scaling don't occurred. The example-3 presents the structural and the functional parts of the bio-signatures extracted from the changes occurred in invivo cells from a sequence of images.

Example-1: Two images taken from the same region with differences

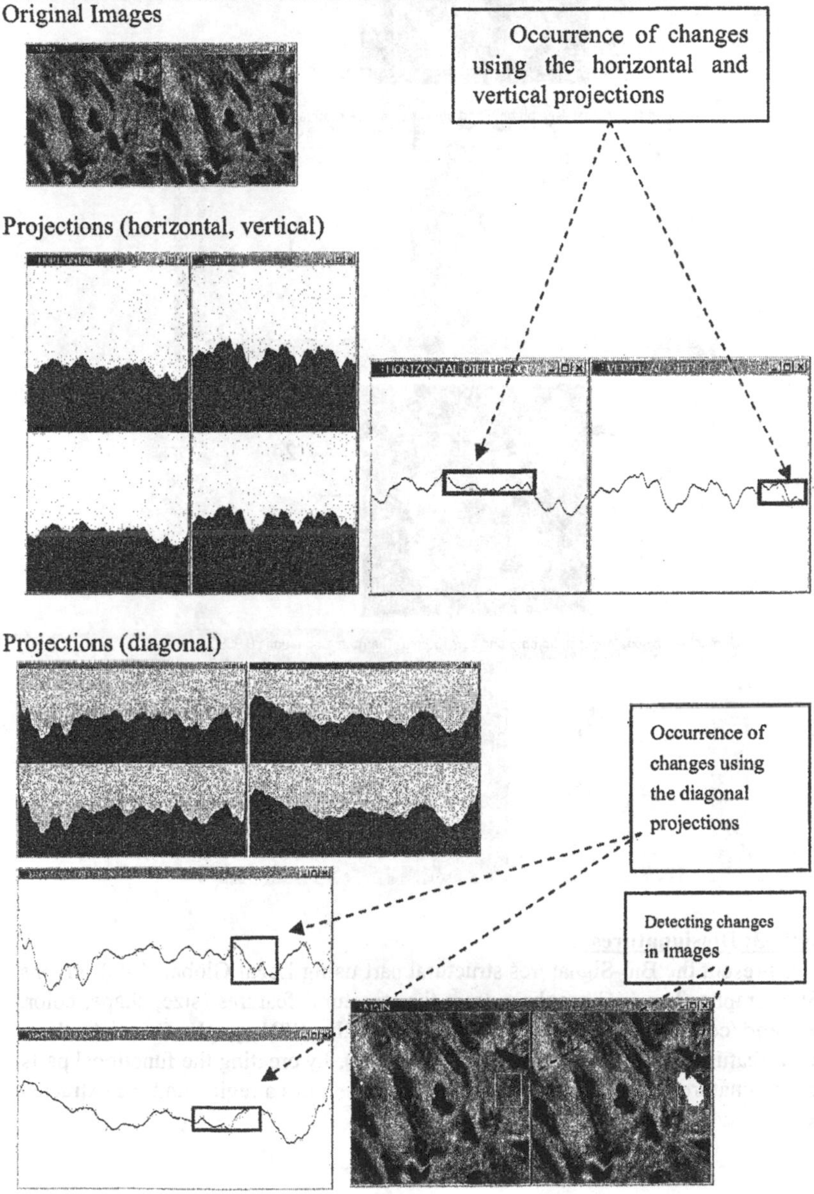

Original Images

Occurrence of changes using the horizontal and vertical projections

Projections (horizontal, vertical)

Projections (diagonal)

Occurrence of changes using the diagonal projections

Detecting changes in images

Example-2: Changes detected in images taken from the same region but in different times

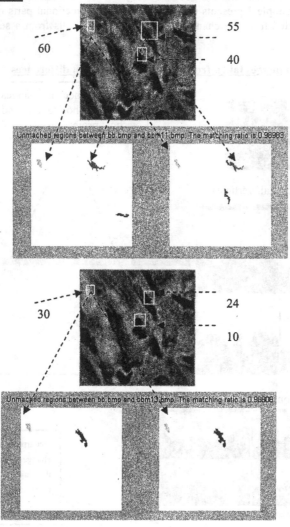

Example-3: Biosignatures.

Here we present the Bio-Signatures structural part using Local Global (L-G) graphs and SPN graphs. The L-G graphs extract the structural features (size, shape, color, texture, and centroid) of each cell's region and the SPN graphs associate these structural features with their changes in time (states), by creating the functional parts of the biosignatures. The illustrative example below shows a region and the extracted featues.

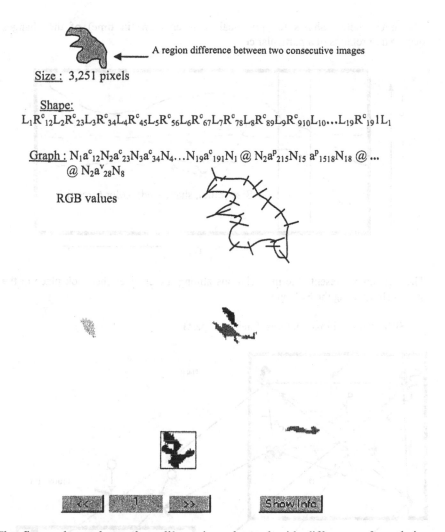

A region difference between two consecutive images

Size : 3,251 pixels

Shape:
$L_1R^c{}_{12}L_2R^c{}_{23}L_3R^c{}_{34}L_4R^c{}_{45}L_5R^c{}_{56}L_6R^c{}_{67}L_7R^c{}_{78}L_8R^c{}_{89}L_9R^c{}_{910}L_{10}...L_{19}R^c{}_{19}1L_1$

Graph : $N_1a^c{}_{12}N_2a^c{}_{23}N_3a^c{}_{34}N_4...N_{19}a^c{}_{191}N_1$ @ $N_2a^p{}_{215}N_{15}$ $a^p{}_{1518}N_{18}$ @ ...
@ $N_2a^v{}_{28}N_8$

RGB values

The figure above shows the cell's regions detected with differences from their previous status by using software tool's. One region was then selected and frame for extracting its features. Also the features extracted from two region are shown below.

Region (1) info	Region (2) info
RGB value: R = 41 G = 41 B = 41	RGB value: R = 132 G = 132 B = 132
Region size is 518	Region size is 314
Region centroid (193.8641 99.9691)	Region centroid (52.293 152.2707)

Region (1~) info	Region (2~) info
RGB value: R = 87 G = 87 B = 87	RGB value: R = 139 G = 139 B = 139
Region size is 535	Region size is 278
Region centroid (120.0879 123.9925)	Region centroid (51.4187 152.5507)

The figure below shows the graphical representation (in time) of the changes occurred in regions of a particular cell.

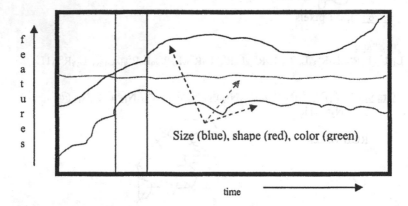

The last figure presents the interrelations among the changes that took place in the same cell by using the SPN graphs.

SPN graphs (bio-signatures, functional part)

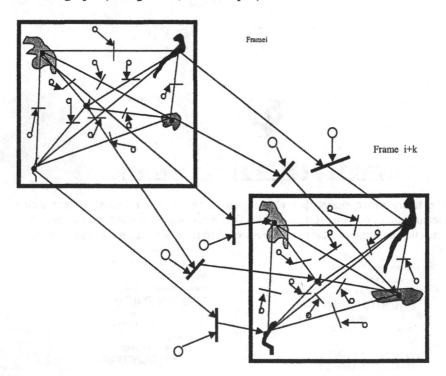

3. Conclusions

The extraction of bio-signatures (structural, functional) was the subject described in this paper. The bio-images were captured by a microscope/video camera. This methodology is used for the Bio-signatures project sponsored by AIIS Inc. for recoding and interrelating the behavior (changes) of cancerous cells.

References

1. M. Kutter and F. A. P. Petitcolas, "A fair benchmark for image watermarking systems", Electronic Imaging '99. Security and Watermarking of Multimedia Contents, ISOE, Vol. 3657, San Jose, CA, Jan 1999.
2. J. A. Saghri, P. S. Cheatham, a. Habibi, "Image Quality Measure Based on Human Visual System Model", Optical Engineering,Vol. 28, No. 7, July 1989
3. D. J. Fleet and D. J. Heeger, "Embedding Invisible Information in Color Images", Proc. of the ICIP, pp. 532–535, Santa Barbara, California, Oct 1997
4. Mark D. Fairchild, Color Appearance Models, Addison Wesley Longman, Inc., 1998
5. N. Bourbakis, Emulating human visual perception for measuring differences in images using an SPN graph approach, IEEE T-SMC, 32, 2, 191-201, 2002
6. A.Moghaddamzadeh and N.Bourbakis, "A Fuzzy Region Growing Approach For Segmentation of Color Images", Pattern Recognition, Vol. 30, No. 6, pp. 867-881, 1997
7. N.Bourbakis, Detecting differences in sequences of images using PFF and LGG, IEEE Conf. TAI-2002, Nov. 2002, VA, pp. 355-362.
8. S.Makrogiannis and N.Bourbakis, Stochastic optimization scheme for automatic registration of aerial images, IEEE TAI-2004, FL, Nov.15-17, 2004, pp. 328-336.
9. N.Bourbakis, J.Gattiker and G.Bebis Representing and interpreting human activity and events from video, Int. JAIT, vol.12,1,2003.
10. N.Bourbakis, Emulating human visual perception for measuring differences in images using an SPN graph approach, IEEE T-SMC, 32, 2, 191-201, 2002.

An Archetype for MRI guided Tele-interventions

Menelaos Karanikolas[1,4], Eftychios Christoforou[2,3], Erbil Akbudak[2],
Paul E. Eisenbeis[2], and Nikolaos V. Tsekos[2,*]

[1]Department of Anesthesiology, [2]Mallinckrodt Institute of Radiology,
[3]Department of Electrical and System Engineering Washington University,
CB 8225, 4525 Scott Avenue, St. Louis, MO 63110, USA
[4]Department of Anaesthesiology and Critical Care Medicine, Faculty of
Medicine University of Patras, Rion 26500, Greece
tsekosn@mir.wustl.edu
WWW home page: http://www.cvil.wustl.edu/Staff/Tsekos/

Abstract. The aim of this work is to evaluate a robotic system for remote performance of minimally invasive procedures with real-time magnetic resonance imaging (MRI) guidance inside clinical cylindrical scanners. In these studies, the operator had no physical access to the subject and used MR images and video from the observation camera in the scanner to control the robot. The control software allowed manual and semi-automated control modes and included components for collision avoidance, with the subject or the gantry of the scanner, and on-the-fly adjustment of the MR imagine plane to visualize the procedure. Studies were performed initially on phantoms and lastly on a pig inside a standard clinical cylindrical 1.5 Tesla MR scanner.

1 Introduction

1. 1 MRI Guided Interventions

Magnetic Resonance Imaging (MRI) is one of several imaging modalities available for performing diagnostic and therapeutic image guided interventions (IGI). Compared to other competing modalities, MRI offers several advantages (1,2). (A) MRI offers a plethora of soft-tissue contrast mechanisms (e.g. perfusion, angiography and diffusion) which allow the assessment of both morphology and function. In addition MRI allows for monitoring the effects of procedures, such as thermal and cryo-ablations, which alter tissue properties. (B) MRI is the only true three-dimensional (3D) modality that allows oblique 3D or multislice imaging. (C) Compared to X-rays, it does not use ionizing radiation and therefore is safer for the patient and medical staff. When cylindrical MR scanners are used, a major limitation is the extreme magnetic environment and limited access to the patient. While open scanners offer direct access to the patient, these systems are limited by their

Please use the following format when citing this chapter:

Karanikolas, Menelaos, Christoforou, Eftychios, Akbudak, Erbil, Eisenbeis, Paul, Tsekos, Nikolaos, 2006, in IFIP International Federation for Information Processing, Volume 204, Artificial Intelligence Applications and Innovations, eds. Maglogiannis, I., Karpouzis, K., Bramer, M., (Boston: Springer), pp. 476–483

suboptimal image quality and low speed of image acquisition. To address the patient accessibility limitation of cylindrical scanners, remotely actuated and controlled robotic manipulators have been introduced. Several examples of such MR-compatible manipulators have been demonstrated, for brain biopsies (3), breast interventions (4-6), and general purpose (7,8).

1.2 Tele-Interventions based on MRI Guidance

As imaging modalities improve, and communication capabilities are becoming faster and more reliable, there may be potential for physicians to provide specialized diagnostic services, or even therapeutic procedures from a distance. As physician and equipment resources are distributed unevenly geographically, patients sometimes have to travel great distances to reach facilities with capability and expertise to provide specialized care. Traveling in order to receive care is not only a great inconvenience and expense for the patient, but may even contribute to deterioration of the disease. In addition, when time is of importance, the capability to provide treatment from a distance may allow for timely diagnosis and intervention.

Recently, the possibility of conducting interventions from a remote location is receiving attention (9,10). Performance of remote operations is a very complex and challenging task, from the technical and clinical point of view. Our work in this area focuses mainly on one aspect of this undertaking. Specifically, we are investigating whether a physician can perform an intervention based primarily on MR images without physical access to the subject. This paper describes an interventional system based on an MR-compatible manipulator and examines the feasibility of conducting spinal diagnostic and stereotactic procedures from a distance, i.e. with the physician in a location physically separate from the location of the patient. This is a pilot project, and should be looked at only as a feasibility study.

2 Overview of the Manipulator

Figure 1a reviews the overall layout of the interventional system, which is described in detail in (8). The system is composed of a seven degree-of-freedom (DOF) MR-compatible robot, hardware and software for its control. The manipulator has a Cartesian positioner, which resides in-front of the scanner (Fig. 1) and provides three orthogonal DOF (X, Y and Z), and an articulated arm with four DOF, which is deployed inside the gantry (Fig. 2). Two of these DOF are rotational (θ_1 and θ_2), resembling a dual "elbow" in-tandem, to set the Euler angle (ϕ) on the vertical plane. The third rotational DOF (θ_3) resembles a "wrist", orthogonal to the axis of θ_2 axis to set the other Euler angle (θ). These six DOF are actuated with ultrasonic motors. The seventh DOF is on the end-effector of the manipulator and sets the depth of insertion (Δ) with a manual cable-driven mechanism. The control software, reviewed in Fig. 4, was developed in the Simulink (The Mathworks Inc., Natick, MA) based xPC Target real-time environment and utilizes two dedicated personal computers (PC) (Fig. 1). The "Host PC" provides means for manual control, through a graphical user interface (GUI) or a master/slave device. It also generates and sends instructions to the "Target PC", for real-time control of the manipulator, and to the MR scanner, for adjustment of the position and orientation on of the imaging plane.

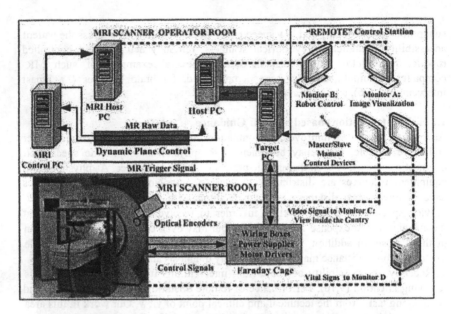

Fig. 1: The main components of the system and their connections.

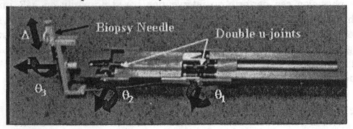

Fig. 2: Photograph of the distal end of the arm depicting its four DOF

Table 1: Characteristics of the Degrees of Freedom

DOF	Transmission	Operation	Backlash	Rigidity
X	Rack & Pinion	± 15 cm	~ 0 cm	~ 0 cm/Nm
Y	Lead Screw	± 9 cm	~ 0 cm	~ 0 cm/Nm
Z	Rack & Pinion	± 20 cm	~ 0 cm	~ 0 cm/Nm
θ1	Shaft and Bevel Gear	± 45 deg	± 2 deg	1.2 deg/Nm
θ2	Shaft, u-joints, Bevel Gear	± 45 deg	± 1.25 deg	2.6 deg/Nm
θ3	Shaft & u-joints	± 180 deg	± 3 deg	11.5 deg/Nm
Δ	Cable	8 cm	~ 0 cm	~ 0 cm/Nm

3 Control Environment

Control of the manipulator is based on four elements which operate in synergy *(Fig. 3)*. (a) A safety component which checks continuously to prevent collision of the manipulator with the gantry or the subject. (b) A procedure to register the position of the manipulator relative to the coordinate system of the MR scanner. (c) A GUI human-machine interface for entering control commands. *(d) Software which performs calculations for controlling the manipulator and updates the position and orientation of the imaging plane using the* forward kinematics solutions.

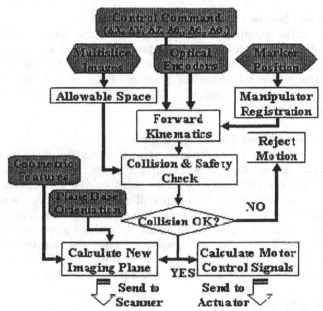

Fig. 3: Block diagram of the main processes of the control software. The input parameters are shaded in gray.

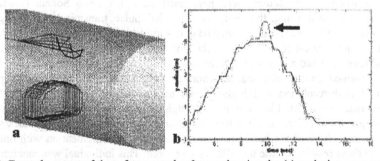

Fig 4: Example output of the safety control software showing the (a) exclusion zone and (b).example of a commanded (red dashed) and executed motion (black continuous line).

3.1 Safety Controls

The safety component uses a set of transverse slices to extract the boundaries of the subject, with an edge-detection (Canny-based) algorithm to generate the subject-defined maneuvering exclusion zone (Fig. 4a). The safety component reads the solution of the forward kinematics and continuously checks whether the current position and any commanded motion are within the allowable maneuvering zone. Figure 4b shows example of the actuation of the Y (vertical) DOF. When the commanded motion causes the robot to enter in the exclusion zone, the safety routine prevents its execution and the robot remains idle (black arrow).

3.2 Human-Machine Interface

Manual control of the manipulator was performed with a simple GUI with user-defined motion steps of 0.1 mm to 5 mm for the linear DOF and 1° to 5° for the rotational DOF. The motion instructions are then fed to the forward kinematics routine which calculates the position of the end-effector at the conclusion of the commanded motion. This solution is then sent to the safety component.

3.3 Manipulator-driven Control of the MR scanner

For manipulator-driven control of the position and orientation of the imaging plane, the control software calculates the current position and orientation of the plane on which the interventional tool loaded on the end-effector will reside at the end of each step. Two types of manipulator-driven scanner control are available. With the computer-managed type, the Target PC continuously updates the imaging plane on-the-fly without any involvement by the operator. With the operator-managed type, the orientation of a slice remains unchanged during the actuation of a certain DOF to always image the end-effector during to actuation of this particular DOF.

4 Experimental Studies

4.1 Set Up

All experimental MR studies were performed on a 1.5 Tesla Sonata (Siemens Medical Solutions) using the body coil for RF pulse transmission and signal reception. To evaluate whether a physician can guide a procedure remotely without direct physical access to the subject, the interventionalist was located at the MR control room and had access to the following information and tools (fig. 1a). (a) MR images viewed on the MR scanner monitor and included windows shown pre-operation high-resolution and high-contrast images, and a window dedicated in viewing real-time updated low-contrast and high speed images. (b) Continuous video streaming on a dedicated monitor from a stationary camera located at the back side of the scanner (toward the head). (c) Continuous audio communication with one of the co-authors residing inside the MR scanner room. This individual was monitoring the system performance and, in particular, checking whether the needle appeared to bend or deviate for any other reason from its predefined path. This was deemed necessary since the black and white camera did not give a very clear depiction of the needle before it entered in the animal. (d) Robot control using a GUI on the monitor of the Host PC. In the operator room there is also a monitor which displays the main vital signs (EKG, blood pressure, respiratory rate and arterial oxygen saturation). Since the animal was euthanized in our experiments, we did not use this monitor.

4.2 Phantom Studies

Registration of the manipulator to the scanner coordinate system was performed by measuring the coordinates of the center of a cross shaped MR-visible marker (made of 3% Gd-filled 3.1 mm diameter tubes), attached to a specific position on the end-effector). Computer-managed manipulator-driven dynamic imaging studies were performed on a phantom composed of a piece of beef with embedded two Gd-filled tubes (same as above) and a 500 cc saline bag rested on its side. Imaging was conducted with a true fast imaging with steady precession (TrueFISP) sequence (TR/TE/α = 4.3 ms/2.15 ms/30°; slice = 8 mm; matrix = 128x256; FOV = 260x260mm^2; pixel size = 1.5x1.5 mm^2). Two 3.1 mm diameter Gd-filled tubes were attached to the end-effector for viewing the otherwise MR-invisible manipulator.

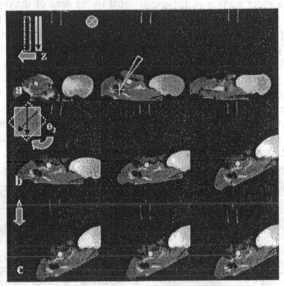

Fig. 5: Selected frames from an image-guided procedure monitored with the computer-managed manipulator-driven dynamically controlled TrueFISP.

Figure 5 shows a study with the computer-managed manipulator-driven dynamic update of the imaging plane. Initially, panel 4a, the operator moved the manipulator over the phantom, to select a target (cross) and a direction of insertion, approximately within the dashed-line triangle. Maneuvers were then performed as example rotating the wrist joint (3b) to align the needle with the planned strategy of target acquisition. All the specified targets were reached with an accuracy of 3.2 mm, relative to the center of structures ranging in size from between 1 cm and 1.4 cm diameter. The in-plane orientation accuracy of the path was within 2.5° for each one of the two Euler angles.

4.3 Spinal procedure

The system was tested for the performance of a spinal procedure on a euthanized pig. Scout images were obtained with a spin-echo (SE) sequence (TR/TE = 500ms/15ms;

slice thickness = 4 mm, acquisition matrix 384 x 512 and a pixel size 1.3x1.3 mm^2) for preliminary localization of the target tissue, which, in this particular experiment was the spinal canal in the lumbar area. Once the area of intervention was defined, the arm of the robot was advanced into the cylindrical MRI scanner.

The desired trajectory of the MRI-compatible 20 G needle followed a slightly paramedian approach, so that the needle could avoid the spinous processes of the lumbar vertebral bodies, and could advance towards the spinal canal without encountering any bony structures in its projected path. The selected trajectory was defined by two points: (a) the entry point, which was marked by the interventional physician on the transverse MR image at skin depth, and (b) the destination point, located in the outer portion of the spinal canal in the area of the posterior epidural space. After the trajectory was defined on the images, the physician maneuvered the remote manipulator until the long axis of the needle was aligned with the indicated trajectory as confirmed by MR imaging, the needle was gradually advanced, under intermittent MRI imaging,. Once the needle advanced approximately 2 mm short off the total length of advancement, MR images were collected to confirm proximity of the tip of the needle to the target tissue. Based on these images, the needle was further advanced to reach the targeted spinal canal (Fig. 5). The entire procedure, including initial scouting images, definition of the needle trajectory, manipulator alignment and, finally, needle advancement until it reached the target took approximately 45 minutes.

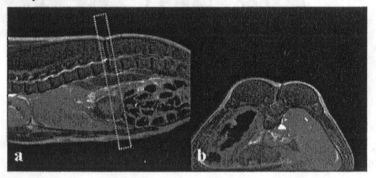

Fig. 6: Selected slices showing (a) an oblique sagittal view of the pig's abdomen and (b) an oblique transverse. The white box in (a) indicates the position of the slice shown in (b). Note the MR compatible needle as it enters and reaches the spinal canal.

5 Discussion and Conclusions

A prototype system is presented for performing minimally invasive interventions with real-time MR guidance inside a cylindrical MR scanner using a seven DOF robotic manipulator. Experiments were performed to assess whether an interventionalist can perform a procedure just by using MR images and position information from the robot control software but without physical access to the subject. At this early stage, the project is focused on the procedural aspect and the work-load of combining robotics with MR imaging to perform a procedure without physical presence in the operating suite. Therefore, certain technical aspects critical for a clinical implementation of the system, such as the technology used for remote connection, were not addressed (9,10).

This pilot project pointed to certain improvements of this system including additional cameras \for better visualization of the area inside the gantry of the scanner and improved voice communication since; the latter is important since the MR room is extremely noisy during data acquisition. The system should also have a mechanism to compensate for patient movement, regardless of whether this movement is smooth and predictable (e.g. respiratory movement) or unpredictable to ensure accuracy of needle tip position and patient safety.

Acknowledgments: This work was supported in part (MR pulse sequences and real-time reconstruction hardware/software) by the NIH grant RO1HL067924. NVT also thanks the Special Secretary General of the Secretariat of Operational Programs, Ministry of Health, Greece.

References

1. Debatin-G.Adam JF, editor. Interventional Magnetic Resonance Imaging: Springer; 1998.
2. Jolesz F, Kahn T, Lufkin R. Genesis of interventional MRI. J Magn Reson Imaging 1998;8(1):2.
3. Masamune K, Kobayashi E, Masutani Y, Suzuki M, Dohi T, Iseki H, Takakura K. Development of an MRI-compatible needle insertion manipulator for stereotactic neurosurgery. J Image Guid Surg 1995;1(4):242-248.
4. Kaiser WA, Fischer H, Vagner J, Selig M. Robotic system for biopsy and therapy of breast lesions in a high-field whole-body magnetic resonance tomography unit. Invest Radiol 2000;35(8):513-519.
5. Felden A, Vagner J, Hinz A, Fischer H, Pfleiderer SO, Reichenbach JR, Kaiser WA. ROBITOM-robot for biopsy and therapy of the mamma. Biomed Tech (Berl) 2002;47(Suppl 1 Pt 1):2-5.
6. Larson BT, Erdman AG, Tsekos NV, Yacoub E, Tsekos PV, Koutlas IG. Design of an MRI-compatible robotic stereotactic device for minimally invasive interventions in the breast. J Biomech Eng 2004;126(4):458-465.
7. Hempel E, Fischer H, Gumb L, Hohn T, Krause H, Voges U, Breitwieser H, Gutmann B, Durke J, Bock M, Melzer A. An MRI-compatible surgical robot for precise radiological interventions. Comput Aided Surg 2003;8(4):180-191.
8. Tsekos NV, Ozcan A, Christoforou E. A Prototype Manipulator for MR-guided Interventions Inside Standard Cylindrical MRI Scanners. J Biomech Eng 2005;127:972-980.
9. Seibel RM, Melzer A, Schmidt A, Plabetamann J. Computed Tomography- and Magnetic Resonance Imaging: Guided Microtherapy. Semin Laparosc Surg 1997;4(2):61-73.
10. Marescaux J, Leroy J, Gagner M, Rubino F, Mutter D, Vix M, Butner SE, Smith MK. Transatlantic robot-assisted telesurgery. Nature 2001;413(6854):379-380.

Differential Evolution Algorithms for Finding Predictive Gene Subsets in Microarray Data

D.K. Tasoulis, V.P. Plagianakos, and M.N. Vrahatis

Computational Intelligence Laboratory, Department of Mathematics
University of Patras, GR–26110 Patras, Greece
University of Patras Artificial Intelligence Research Center
{vpp,dtas,vrahatis}@math.upatras.gr

Abstract. The selection of gene subsets that retain high predictive accuracy for certain cell-type classification, poses a central problem in microarray data analysis. The application and combination of various computational intelligence methods holds a great promise for automated feature selection and classification. In this paper, we present a new approach based on evolutionary algorithms that addresses the problem of very high dimensionality of the data, by automatically selecting subsets of the most informative genes. The evolutionary algorithm is driven by a neural network classifier. Extensive experiments indicate that the proposed approach is both effective and reliable.

1 Introduction

In modern clinical practice, the correct and accurate treatment of patients heavily depends on diagnoses that incorporate complex clinical and histopathological data. In some cases this task is difficult or even impossible due to the large amount of data and the limited time and/or resources. To this end, fully automated techniques that can assist in the correct diagnoses are of great value. Moreover, as the number of microarray experiments increases constantly, these techniques are becoming more and more a part of personalized healthcare. Thus, robust computational methods to support this expansion are needed.

To understand a biological processes that a living cell undergoes, one has to measure the *gene expression levels* in different developmental phases, different body tissues, and different clinical conditions. Although this kind of information can aid in the characterization of gene function, the determination of experimental treatment effects, and the understanding of other molecular biological processes [4], it also presents new challenges for researchers. Compared to the traditional approach to genomic research, which has been to examine and collect data for a single gene locally, DNA microarray technologies have rendered possible the simultaneous monitoring of the expression pattern of thousands of genes. Unfortunately, the original gene expression data are contaminated with noise, missing values and systematic variations due to the experimental procedure. Several methodologies can be employed to alleviate these problems, such

Please use the following format when citing this chapter:

Tasoulis, Dimitris, Plagianakos, Vassilis, Vrahatis, Michael, 2006, in IFIP International Federation for Information Processing, Volume 204, Artificial Intelligence Applications and Innovations, eds. Maglogiannis, I., Karpouzis, K., Bramer, M., (Boston: Springer), pp. 484–491

as Singular Value Decomposition based methods, weighted k–nearest neighbors, row averages, replication of the experiments to model the noise, and/or normalization, which is the process of identifying and removing systematic sources of variation.

Discovering the patterns hidden in the gene expression microarray data and subsequently using them to classify the various conditions is a tremendous opportunity and a challenge for functional genomics and proteomics [4]. A promising approach to address this task is to utilize computational intelligence techniques, such as Evolutionary Algorithms (EAs) and Feedforward Neural Networks (FNNs).

EAs refer to stochastic optimization algorithms which employ computational models of evolutionary processes. They share the common conceptual base of simulating the evolution of the individuals that form the population using a predefined set of operators. Commonly two types of operators are used: *selection* and *search* operators. The most widely used search operators are *mutation* and *recombination*. The selection operator mainly depends on the perceived measure of *fitness* of each individual and promotes natural selection in the form of the survival of the fittest. The recombination and the mutation operators stochastically perturb the individuals providing efficient exploration of the search space. This perturbation is primarily controlled by the user defined recombination and mutation rates. Although simplistic from a biologist's viewpoint, these algorithms are sufficiently complex to yield robust and powerful search mechanisms, and have shown their strength in solving hard real world optimization problems.

FNNs are parallel computational models comprised of densely interconnected, simple, adaptive processing units, characterized by an inherent proponsity for storing experiential knowledge and rendering it available for use. FNNs have been successfully applied in numerous application areas. To train an FNN, supervised training is probably the most frequently employed technique. The training process is an incremental adaptation of connection weights that propagate information between neurons. Unfortunately, employing FNNs (or any other classifier) directly to classify the samples is almost infeasible due to the *curse of dimensionality* (limited number of samples coupled with very high feature dimensionality). One solution is to preprocess the expression matrix using a dimension reduction technique [6, 14].

In this paper, we follow a different approach. EAs and FNNs are employed to discover subsets of informative genes that accurately characterize all the samples. Generally, the aim is to reduce the initial gene pool from several thousand genes (5,000–10,000 or more) to 50–100. Several gene selection methods based on statistical analysis have been developed to select these predictive genes and perform dimension reduction. Those methods include t-statistics, information gain theory, and principal component analysis (PCA) [5]. It is evident that the choice of feature selection is difficult and bears a significant effect on the overall classification accuracy. Typically, accuracy on the training data can be quite high, but not replicated on the testing data.

The rest of the paper is organized as follows. In Section 2 the proposed approach is presented. In Section 3 is devoted to the presentation and the discussion of the experimental results. The paper ends with concluding remarks and some issues for future work.

2 Algorithms and Methodology

To classify samples using microarray data, it is necessary to decide which genes, from the ones assayed, should be included in the classifier. Including too few genes and the test data will be incorrectly classified. On the other hand, having too many genes is not desirable either, as many of the genes will be irrelevant, mostly adding noise. This is particularly severe with a noisy data set and few subjects, as is the case with microarray data.

In the literature, both supervised and unsupervised classifiers have been used to build classification models from microarray data. This study addresses the supervised classification task where data samples belong to a known class. EAs are applied to microarray classification to determine the optimal, or near optimal, subset of predictive genes on complex and large spaces of possible gene sets. Although a vast number of gene subsets are evaluated by the EA, selecting the most informative genes is a non trivial task. Common problems include the existence of: a) relevant genes that are not included in the final subset, because of the insufficient exploration of the gene pool, b) significantly different subsets of genes being the most informative as the evolution progresses, and c) many subsets that perform equally well, as they all predict the test data satisfactorily. From a practical point of view, the lack of a unique solution does not seem to present a problem.

The EA approach we propose maintains a population of trial gene subsets; imposes random changes on the genes that compose those subsets; and incorporates selection (driven by a neural network classifier) to determine which are the most informative ones. Only those genes are maintained in successive generations; the rest are removed from the trial pool. At each iteration, every subset is given as input to an FNN classifier and the effectiveness of the FNN determines the fitness of the subset of genes. The size of the population and the number of features in each subset are parameters that we explore experimentally.

2.1 The Differential Evolutionary Algorithm

Differential Evolution [11] is an optimization method, capable of handling non-differentiable, nonlinear and multimodal objective functions. To fulfill this requirement, DE has been designed as a stochastic parallel direct search method, which utilizes concepts borrowed from the broad class of evolutionary algorithms. The method typically requires few, easily chosen, control parameters. Experimental results have shown that DE has good convergence properties and outperforms other well known evolutionary algorithms [11]. DE has been applied on numerous optimization tasks. It has successfully solved many artificial benchmark problems, as well as, hard real–world problems. In [3] DE has been applied to train neural networks and in [7, 8] we have proposed a method to efficiently train neural networks having arbitrary, as well as, constrained integer weights. The DE algorithm has also been implemented on parallel and distributed computers [12, 9].

DE is a population–based stochastic algorithm that exploits a population of potential solutions, *individuals*, to effectively probe the search space. The population of the individuals is randomly initialized in the optimization domain with *NP*, n–dimensional vectors, following a uniform probability distribution and is evolved over time to explore the search space. *NP* is fixed throughout the training process. At each iteration, called *generation*, new vectors are generated by the combination of randomly chosen vectors from the current population. This operation in our context is referred to as *mutation*. The outcoming vectors are then mixed with another predetermined vector – the *target* vector – and this operation is called *recombination*. This operation yields the so–called *trial* vector. The trial vector is accepted for the next generation depending on the value of the fitness function. Otherwise, the target vector is retained in the next generation. This last operator is referred to as *selection*.

2.2 Search Operators

The search operators efficiently shuffle information among the individuals, enabling the search for an optimum to focus on the most promising regions of the solution space. The first operator considered is mutation. For each individual x_g^i, $i = 1, \ldots, NP$, where g denotes the current generation, a new individual v_{g+1}^i (mutant vector) is generated according to one of the following equations:

$$v_{g+1}^i = x_g^{\text{best}} + \mu(x_g^{r1} - x_g^{r2}), \tag{1}$$

$$v_{g+1}^i = x_g^{r1} + \mu(x_g^{r2} - x_g^{r3}), \tag{2}$$

$$v_{g+1}^i = x_g^i + \mu(x_g^{\text{best}} - x_g^i) + \mu(x_g^{r1} - x_g^{r2}), \tag{3}$$

$$v_{g+1}^i = x_g^{\text{best}} + \mu(x_g^{r1} - x_g^{r2}) + \mu(x_g^{r3} - x_g^{r4}), \tag{4}$$

$$v_{g+1}^i = x_g^{r1} + \mu(x_g^{r2} - x_g^{r3}) + \mu(x_g^{r4} - x_g^{r5}), \tag{5}$$

where x_g^{best} is the best member of the previous generation; $\mu > 0$ is a real parameter, called *mutation constant*, which controls the amplification of the difference between two individuals so as to avoid the stagnation of the search process; and $r_1, r_2, r_3, r_4, r_5 \in \{1, 2, \ldots, i - 1, i + 1, \ldots, NP\}$, are random integers mutually different. Trying to rationalize the above equations, we observe that Equation (2) is similar to the crossover operator used by some Genetic Algorithms and Equation (1) derives from it, when the best member of the previous generation is employed. Equations (3), (4) and (5) are modifications obtained by the combination of Equations (1) and (2). It is clear that more such relations can be generated using the above ones as building blocks.

The recombination operator is subsequently applied to further increase the diversity of the mutant individuals. To this end, the resulting individuals are combined with other predetermined individuals, called the target individuals. Specifically, for each component l ($l = 1, 2, \ldots, n$) of the mutant individual v^i_{g+1}, we choose randomly a real number r in the interval $[0, 1]$. We then compare this number with the *recombination constant*, ρ. If $r \leqslant \rho$, we select, as the l-th component of the trial individual u^i_{g+1}, the l-th component of the mutant individual v^i_{g+1}. Otherwise, the l-th component of the target vector x^i_{g+1} becomes the l-th component of the trial vector. This operation yields the trial individual. Finally, the trial individual is accepted for the next generation only if it reduces the value of the objective function.

One problem when applying EAs, in general, is to find a set of control parameters which optimally balances the exploration and exploitation capabilities of the algorithm. There is always a trade off between the efficient exploration of the search space and its effective exploitation. In [13] a detailed study and experimental results on exploration vs. exploitation issues are presented. In this paper we employed the Equation (1) as a search operator.

2.3 Fitness Function

For the proposed system, each population member represents a subset of genes, so a special representation must be designed. When seeking subsets containing n genes, each individual consists of n integers. The first integer is the index of the first gene to be included in the subset, the second integer denotes the number of genes to skip until the second gene to be included is reached, the third integer component denotes the number of genes to skip until the third included gene, and so on. This representation was necessary in order to avoid multiple inclusion of the same gene. Moreover, a version of DE that uses integer vectors has been proposed and thoroughly studied in previous studies [7, 8, 9].

FNNs were used as a classifier to evaluate the fitness of each gene subset. One third of the data set is used as a training set for the FNN and one third is used to measure the classification accuracy of the FNN classifier. The remaining patterns of the data set are kept to estimate the classification capability of the final gene subset. All the FNNs were trained using the well known and widely used Resilient backpropagation (Rprop) [10] training algorithm. Rprop is a fast local adaptive learning scheme, performing supervised training. To update each weight of the FNN, Rprop exploits information concerning the sign of the partial derivative of the error function.

In our experiments, the five parameters of the Rprop method were initialized using values commonly employed in the literature. In particular, the increase factor was set to $\eta^+ = 1.2$; the decrease factor was set to $\eta^- = 0.5$; the initial update value is set to $\Delta_0 = 0.1$; the maximum step, which prevents the weights from becoming too large, was $\Delta_{max} = 50$; and the minimum step, which is used to avoid too small weight updates, was constantly fixed to $\Delta_{min} = 10^{-6}$ [10].

3 Presentation of Experiments

In this section we report the experimental results. We have tested and compared the performance of the proposed system on many publicly available microarray data sets. Here we report results from the following two data sets:

- The COLON data set [1] consists of 40 tumor and 22 normal colon tissues. For each sample there exist 2000 gene expression level measurements. The data set is available at http://microarray.princeton.edu/oncology.
- The PROSTATE data set [2] contains 52 prostate tumor samples and 50 nontumor prostate samples. For each sample there exist 6033 gene expression level measurements. It is available at http://www.broad.mit.edu/cgi-bin/cancer/datasets.cgi.

Since the appropriate size of the most predictive gene set is unknown, DE was employed for various gene set sizes ranging from 10 to 100 with a step of 10. The FNN used at the fitness function consisted of 2 hidden layers with eight and seven neurons, respectively. The input layer contained as many neurons as the size of the gene set. One output neuron was used at the output layer whose value for each sample determined the network classification decision. Since both problems had two different classes for the patterns, a value lower than 0.5 regarded the pattern to belong to class 1 otherwise regarded it to belong to class 2.

For each different gene set size the data was partitioned randomly into a learning set consisting of two-thirds of the whole set and a test set consisting of the remaining one third, as already mentioned. The one third of the training set was used by the Rprop algorithm to train the FNNs, and the performance of the respective gene set was measured in the other one third. The test set was only used to evaluate the classification accuracy that can be obtained using the final gene set discovered by the DE algorithm. To reduce the variability, the splitting was repeated 10 times and 10 independent runs were performed each time, resulting in a total of 100 experiments, for gene set size.

The classification accuracy of the proposed system is illustrated using boxplots in Figure 1. Each boxplot depicts the obtained values for the classification accuracy, in the 100 experiments. The box has lines at the lower quartile, median, and upper quartile values. The lines extending from each end of the box (whiskers) indicate the range covered by the remaining data. The outliers, i.e. the values that lie beyond the ends of the whiskers, are denoted by crosses. Notches represent a robust estimate of the uncertainty about the median.

As demonstrated, using a gene set size of 50–80 for the COLON dataset the algorithm managed to achieve the best results; comparable to those obtained by other approaches [6, 15]. The same is achieved for the PROSTATE dataset for a gene set size ranging from 40 to 60.

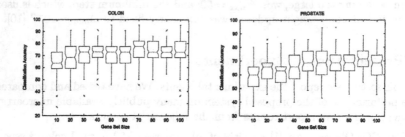

Fig. 1. Classification accuracy obtained by FNNs trained using the DE selected gene set for the COLON (left) and PROSTATE (right) datasets.

4 Concluding Remarks

In this article we propose an Evolutionary Algorithm that maintains a population of trial gene subsets and evolves them to determine which are the most informative ones. At each iteration, every subset is given as input to a Feedforward Neural Network and the effectiveness of the Network determines the subsets that will be maintained in future generations. Experiments on microarray datasets indicate that the proposed approach is effective and reliable. The advantages of the proposed approach include its completely automatic operation. Moreover, the result of the algorithm differs from PCA-like reduction techniques since it does not transform the input space but rather directly detects informative genes. Additionally, the use of Neural Networks as a classifier allows the discovery of non-linear relationships between the input and output. On the other hand, the whole procedure is quite time consuming. However, considering the slow experimental nature of the complete microarray experiments, the required time seems negligible.

In a future correspondence, we will investigate the performance of the proposed approach when different evolutionary algorithms are employed. We also intend to incorporate unsupervised clustering algorithms in an attempt to implement a system capable of clustering the genes and simultaneously finding the most informative subsets.

Acknowledgment

The authors would like to thank the European Social Fund, Operational Program for Educational and Vocational Training II (EPEAEK II), and particularly the Program "Pythagoras" for funding this work. This work was also partially supported by the University of Patras Research Committee through a "Karatheodoris" research grant.

References

1. U. Alon, N. Barkai, D.A. Notterman, K.Gish, S. Ybarra, D. Mack, and A.J. Levine. Broad patterns of gene expression revealed by clustering analysis of tumor and normal colon tissues probed by oligonucleotide array. *Proc. Natl. Acad. Sci. USA*, 96(12):6745–6750, 1999.
2. D. Singh et al. Gene expression correlates of clinical prostate cancer behavior. *Cancer Cell*, 1:203–209, 2002.
3. J. Ilonen, J.-K. Kamarainen, and J. Lampinen. Differential evolution training algorithm for feed forward neural networks. *Neural Processing Letters*, 17(1):93–105, 2003.
4. D. Jiang, C. Tang, and A. Zhangi. Cluster analysis for gene expression data: A survey. *IEEE Transactions on Knowledge and Data Engineering*, to appear.
5. T. Li, C. Zhang, and M.Ogihara. A comparative study of feature selection and multiclass classification methods for tissue classification based on gene expression. *Bioinformatics*, 20(15):2429–2437, 2004.
6. V.P. Plagianakos, D.K. Tasoulis, and M.N. Vrahatis. Hybrid dimension reduction approach for gene expression data classification. In *International Joint Conference on Neural Networks 2005, Post-Conference Workshop on Computational Intelligence Approaches for the Analysis of Bioinformatics Data*, 2005.
7. V.P. Plagianakos and M.N. Vrahatis. Neural network training with constrained integer weights. In P.J. Angeline, Z. Michalewicz, M. Schoenauer, X. Yao, and A. Zalzala, editors, *Proceedings of the Congress of Evolutionary Computation (CEC'99)*, pages 2007–2013. IEEE Press, 1999.
8. V.P. Plagianakos and M.N. Vrahatis. Training neural networks with 3–bit integer weights. In W. Banzhaf, J. Daida, A.E. Eiben, M.H. Garzon, V. Honavar, M. Jakiela, and R.E. Smith, editors, *Proceedings of the Genetic and Evolutionary Computation Conference (GECCO'99)*, pages 910–915. Morgan Kaufmann, 1999.
9. V.P. Plagianakos and M.N. Vrahatis. Parallel evolutionary training algorithms for 'hardware-friendly' neural networks. *Natural Computing*, 1:307–322, 2002.
10. M. Riedmiller and H. Braun. A direct adaptive method for faster backpropagation learning: The Rprop algorithm. In *Proceedings of the IEEE International Conference on Neural Networks, San Francisco, CA*, pages 586–591, 1993.
11. R. Storn and K. Pricc. Differential evolution – a simple and efficient adaptive scheme for global optimization over continuous spaces. *Journal of Global Optimization*, 11:341–359, 1997.
12. D.K. Tasoulis, N.G. Pavlidis, V.P. Plagianakos, and M.N. Vrahatis. Parallel differential evolution. In *IEEE Congress on Evolutionary Computation (CEC 2004)*, volume 2, pages 2023–2029, 2004.
13. D.K. Tasoulis, V.P. Plagianakos, and M.N. Vrahatis. Clustering in evolutionary algorithms to efficiently compute simultaneously local and global minima. In *IEEE Congress on Evolutionary Computation*, volume 2, pages 1847–1854, Edinburgh, UK, 2005.
14. M.E. Wall, A. Rechtsteiner, and L.M. Rocha. Singular value decomposition and principal component analysis. In *A Practical Approach to Microarray Data Analysis*, pages 91–109. Kluwer, 2003.
15. J. Ye, T. Li, T. Xiong, and R. Janardan. Using uncorrelated discriminant analysis for tissue classification with gene expression data. *IEEE/ACM Transactions on Computational Biology and Bioinformatics*, 1(4):181–190, 2004.

Feature Selection for Microarray Data Analysis Using Mutual Information and Rough Set Theory

Wengang Zhou, Chunguang Zhou, Guixia Liu, Hong Zhu
College of Computer Science and Technology, Jilin University,
Changchun 130012, P. R. China
wgzhou@email.jlu.edu.cn

Abstract. Cancer classification is one major application of microarray data analysis. Due to the ultra high dimension of gene expression data, efficient feature selection methods are in great needs for selecting a small number of informative genes. In this paper, we propose a novel feature selection method based on mutual information and rough set (MIRS). First, we select some top-ranked features which have higher mutual information with the target class to predict. Then rough set theory is applied to remove the redundancy among these selected genes. Binary particle swarm optimization (BPSO) is first proposed for attribute reduction in rough set. Finally, the effectiveness of the proposed method is evaluated by the classification accuracy of SVM classifier. Experi-ment results show that MIRS is superior to some other classical feature selec-tion methods and can get higher prediction accuracy with small number of fea-tures. Generally, the results are highly promising.

1 Introduction

The development of microarray technology has made it easy to monitor the expression pattern of thousands of genes simultaneously and a huge amount of gene expression data has been produced during microarray experiments. These data has widely been applied to accurate prediction and diagnosis of cancer. Especially cancer classification [1] is an important issue because it can identify many genes relevant to cancer. The results reported in the literature have confirmed the effectiveness of mining cancer information from gene expression data. But microarray data often consists of small number of samples and large number of genes. The ultra high dimension of gene expression data makes it necessary to develop effective feature selection methods in order to reduce the computation cost and improve the classification accuracy.

Please use the following format when citing this chapter:

Zhou, Wengang, Zhou, Chunguang, Liu, Guixia, Wang, Yan, 2006, in IFIP International Federation for Information Processing, Volume 204, Artificial Intelligence Applications and Innovations, eds. Maglogiannis, I., Karpouzis, K., Bramer, M., (Boston: Springer), pp. 492–499

There are two general approaches to feature selection: filters [2] and wrappers [3]. In a filter method, features are selected based on the intrinsic characteristics which determine their relevance with the target classes. In wrapper type methods, the usefulness of a feature is directly judged by the estimated accuracy of a learning method and typically requires huge computational effort. Thus, it is difficult for wrappers to deal with large feature sets such as gene expression data. We mainly focus on the selection of a few tens features among several thousands by developing an efficient filter methods for cancer classification. When a small number of informative genes are selected, their biological relationship with the target disease can easily be identified.

Mutual information [4] has recently been proposed for feature selection. One common practice to use this method is to simply select the top-ranked genes with higher mutual information. But a deficiency of this simple ranking approach is that the features can be correlated among themselves. If gene g_i is ranked high for classification task, other genes highly correlated with gene g_i are also likely to be selected. This raises the issue of redundancy in feature set. Rough sets theory provides a feasible way to deal with redundancy [5]. An important concept is reduct in rough sets theory. Reduct is those minimal attribute sets of information system, which keep the same classify capability with original attribute set. The aim of reduction is to find out a minimum set of relevant attributes (features) that describe the dataset as well as all the original attributes do. Thus finding reduct can select the most relevant genes with the target class to predict and remove the redundancy among the selected features.

In this paper, we propose a novel feature selection method so called MIRS by integrating mutual information and rough set theory. First, mutual information is used to select some top-ranked genes which have higher mutual information from each data set. Then rough set theory is applied to remove the redundancy among these selected genes. Binary particle swarm optimization (BPSO) is first suggested as an attribute reduction algorithm for rough sets. Finally, the effectiveness of MIRS is evaluated by the classification accuracy of SVM classifiers. Experiment results show that the pro-posed method is superior to some other classical feature selection methods and can always get higher classification accuracy with fewer features.

2 Mutual Information for Feature Selection

In accordance with Shannon's information theory [6], the uncertainty of a random variable Y can be measured by the entropy $H(Y)$. For two variables X and Y, the conditional entropy $H(Y\,|\,X)$ measures the remaining uncertainty of Y when X is known. The mutual information (MI) $I(X;Y)$ measures the certainty about Y that is resolved by X. Apparently, the relation of $H(Y), H(Y\,|\,X)$ and $I(X;Y)$ is as follows:

$$I(X;Y) = H(Y) - H(Y\,|\,X) \tag{1}$$

The objective of training a classification model is to minimize the uncertainty about predictions on class labels Y for the known observations X. Thus, it is equivalent to increase the MI $I(X;Y)$ as much as possible for training a classifier. The goal of feature selection process for classification is naturally to achieve the smallest subset of possible features which have higher values of $I(X;Y)$. With the entropy defined by Shannon, the prior entropy of Y is expressed as follows:

$$H(Y) = -\sum_{y \in Y} P(y) \log P(y) \qquad (2)$$

where $P(y)$ represents the probability of Y. The conditional entropy $H(Y|X)$ is computed according to the following formula:

$$H(Y|X) = -\int P(x)(\sum_{y \in Y} P(y|x) \log P(y|x)) dx \qquad (3)$$

The mutual information MI between X and Y is presented formally as follows:

$$I(X;Y) = \sum_{y \in Y} \int P(y|x) \log \frac{P(y,x)}{P(y)P(x)} dx \qquad (4)$$

The estimation of probability density is based on the distribution of mutual information [7] in a Bayesian framework by a second-order Dirichlet prior distribution. Beta approximation of the distribution is adopted in this paper. The top-ranked 700 genes and 500 genes with higher mutual information for the leukemia data set and the colon data set discussed in section 5 are selected respectively.

If too many genes are selected, there must be much noise retained in the data. On the other hand, if we select very few genes, some information contained in the data set for classification may be lost. The number of genes we select for the two data sets is determined with respect to the observation from classification experiments. Subsequently the redundancy among these selected genes will be removed in section 4.

3   Background on Rough Set Theory

Rough set theory is first introduced by Pawlak [8] in the 1980s as a mathematical tool to deal with uncertainty. In this section, we will introduce the principal concepts of rough sets theory related to our attribute reduction approach.

Information System: In rough sets theory, an information system S is denoted as $S = \{U, A, V, f\}$, where U is a finite set of instances $U = \{x_1, x_2, \cdots, x_n\}$. A is a finite set of attributes (features) and consists of condition attribute set C and decision attribute set D. $f : U \times A \rightarrow V$ is a function that $f(x_i, q) \in V_p$ for every $q \in A, x_i \in U$.

Indiscernibility Relation: Let $P \subseteq A, x_i, x_j \in U$, a binary relation IND called indiscernibility relation is defined as follows:

$$IND(P) = \{(x_i, x_j) \,|\, (x_i, x_j) \in U \times U, a \in P, f(x_i, a) = f(x_j, a)\} \qquad (5)$$

Let $U / IND(P)$ denote the family of all equivalence classes of the relation $IND(P)$. For simplicity notation $U / IND(P)$ will be written as U / P.

Lower Approximation: Let $R \subseteq C$ and $X \subseteq U$, the R-lower approximation set of X is the set of all elements of U which can be certainly classified as elements of X according to knowledge R. It can be presented formally as follows:

$$\underline{R}X = \bigcup \{Y \in U/R : Y \subseteq X\} \qquad (6)$$

Positive Region: The positive region of decision attribute set D with respect to R is the set of all objects from universe U that can be classified with certainty to classes of U/D employing attributes from R. It can be defined as follows:

$$POS_R(D) = \bigcup_{X \in U/D} \underline{R}X \qquad (7)$$

4 BPSO for Attribute Reduction in Rough Set

Particle swarm optimization (PSO) is an evolutionary computation technique first introduced for use in real number space by Kennedy and Eberhart in 1995. It has been shown to be a powerful optimization method in many practical applications. In 1997, a binary version of particle swarm optimization (BPSO) is proposed and its performance has been tested on five benchmark functions [9]. But it has not been widely used and still need much further research.

Rough set can be used to find out all possible feature subsets. However, examining exhaustively all subsets of features for selecting the optimal one has been proved to be NP-hard [10]. Heuristic algorithms provide a new way to solve this NP-hard optimization problem. In this section, we suggest binary particle swarm optimization as an attribute reduction algorithm in rough set and apply it to find minimal reduct by removing the redundancy among the genes selected by mutual information.

4.1 Data Preprocessing

The values of gene expression level are continuous. But rough set can only handle discrete attribute value. Hence in order to use the attribute reduction algorithm, all the express level values of selected genes must be discretized firstly. The Entropy/MDL discretization algorithm of Rosetta [11] is used in our experiments. During the entire procedure of attribute discretization and attribute reduction, we combine the training samples with the testing samples together for each data set.

4.2 Population Initialization

Let n be the number of selected features (genes) by mutual information from the original data set. The velocity of i_{th} particle is initialized as a n-dimensional vector with the following form: $V_i = (v_{i1}, v_{i2}, \cdots, v_{in})$. Then the initial position of the i_{th}

particle $X_i = (x_{i1}, x_{i2}, \cdots, x_{in})$ can be computed according to Eq. (11). Where $v_{ij} \in [-6,6], x_{ij} \in \{0,1\}, j \in \{1,2,\cdots,n\}$. x_{ij} is equal to 1 or 0 which indicates the corresponding feature is selected or not. We put all the selected features of the i_{th} particle into the attribute set P_i.

4.3 Fitness Evaluation

The goal of reduction is to use fewer features to achieve the same or better performance compared with that obtained using the complete feature set. Hence, individual evaluation contains the following two objectives: (1) Minimization of the feature numbers; (2) Maximization of the classification capability. We have to make some tradeoffs between the two objectives. In this paper, classification capability is always have higher priority. If two individuals have the same classification capability, the individual with fewer features will have higher fitness. A simple weighting method is adopted to define the fitness of particles as follows:

$$f(i) = w_1 \times fc(i) + w_2 \times (1 - fn(i)) \tag{8}$$

$$fc(i) = card(POS_{P_i}(D)) / card(U) \tag{9}$$

where w_1 and w_2 are weight coefficients, $fc(i)$ is the classification capability we can get by using the feature set P_i, $fn(i)$ is the number of features contained in P_i, $card(U)$ represents the cardinality of the set U.

4.4 Update Velocity and Position

Each particle represents a candidate solution with four state variables: v_i, x_i, p_i, p_g. These variables present the current velocity, current position, previous best position and current global best position of the i_{th} particle respectively. The velocity and position vector are updated according to the following equations:

$$V_{ij} = w \times V_{ij} + c_1 \times rand() \times (P_{ij} - X_{ij}) + c_2 \times rand() \times (P_{gj} - X_{ij}) \tag{10}$$

$$X_{ij} = \begin{cases} 0, if \ \rho \ge sig(V_{ij}) \\ 1, if \ \rho < sig(V_{ij}) \end{cases} \tag{11}$$

where c_1 and c_2 are known as acceleration coefficients, X_{ij} represents the j_{th} element of the n-dimensional vector X_i. *Rand* () produces a random number between 0 and 1. ρ is a random number selected from the uniform distribution in [0, 1]. The function $sig(V_{ij})$ is a sigmoid limiting transformation.

5 Gene Expression Data Sets

There are several microarray data sets published from cancer gene expression studies. Two data sets of them are used to test the effectiveness of our proposed method. Because the benchmark data sets have been studied in many papers, we can compare the results of our method with others conveniently.

Leukemia data set [12] consists of 72 samples: 25 samples of acute myeloid leukemia (AML) and 47 samples of acute lymphoblastic leukemia (ALL). Each sample contains the expression levels of 7129 genes measured using high density oligonucleotide microarrays. In our experiments, 38 samples are used as training data and the remaining 34 samples are used as test data.

Colon data set consists of 62 samples of colon epithelial cells taken from cancer patients [13]. Each sample contains 2000 gene expression levels. 20 out of 62 samples are normal samples and the remaining are cancer samples. In our different experiments, 31 or 44 samples are used as training data and the remaining 31 or 18 samples are used as test data.

6 Experiment Results

In all the experiments, BPSO is run with a population size of 30 and it is terminated when the maximum generation of 600 is arrived. The five parameters in the Eq. (8) and Eq. (10) are set to as follows: $w = 1, c_1 = c_2 = 2, w_1 = 100, w_2 = 0.06$. All the algorithms are implemented in matlab 6.5. The features selected by BPSO are used for testing the classification accuracy by support vector machine (SVM) [14]. The classification accuracy is measured by the number of correct predictions made by the classifier over the test set.

In table 1, experiment results are displayed by using different feature selection methods (No indicates no feature selection). The classification accuracy is obtained by using linear SVM. For the colon data set, 44 samples are used as training data and 18 samples as testing data in this experiment. We can observe that our proposed feature selection method MIRS can always obtain higher classification accuracy with fewer features compared with using MI only. The effectiveness of MIRS is also verified by the remarkable improvement of classification accuracy compared with not using feature selection.

Table 1. The comparison results on feature number and classification accuracy

Dataset	Original No.	FS method	Selected No.	Accuracy
Leukemia	7129	No	7129	58.8%

Dataset	Original No.	FS method	Selected No.	Accuracy
	7129	MI	700	94.1%
	7129	MIRS	48	97.1%
Colon	2000	No	2000	50.0%
	2000	MI	500	66.7%
	2000	MIRS	32	94.4%

Table 2. Comparison of classification accuracy between MIRS and other methods

Data set	Feature selection	Linear SVM	Rbf SVM
Leukemia	MIRS	97.1%	97.1%
	PC	79.4%	79.4%
	CC	85.3%	85.3%
Colon	MIRS	80.7%	83.9%
	PC	64.5%	64.5%
	CC	64.5%	64.5%

We have also compared the performance of MIRS with some other classical feature selection techniques on the two real gene expression data sets. The comparison results are shown in table 2. The results of other techniques are extracted from a survey re-ported by Sung [15]. These feature selection techniques being compared include principal components (PC) and correlational coefficient (CC).

In this experiment, we use 31 samples as training data and the other 31 samples as testing data for the colon data set so that we can compare with the results of Sung directly. We try the following two kinds of support vector machines: (1) Linear SVM (no kernel); (2) Radial basis function SVM (RBF kernel). It is obvious that our pro-posed method is consistently better than the above methods in all the two data sets.

7　Conclusions

In this paper, we propose a novel feature selection method based on mutual informa-tion and rough set (MIRS). First, we select some top-ranked features which have higher mutual information with the target class to predict from two public available real gene expression data sets. Then rough set theory is applied to remove the redun-dancy among these selected genes. Binary particle swarm optimization (BPSO) is first proposed for attribute reduction in rough set. Finally, the effectiveness of the proposed method is evaluated by the classification accuracy of SVM classifier. Ex-periment results show that MIRS can always get higher prediction accuracy with small number of features compared with using MI only and is superior to some other classical feature selection methods. Generally, the results are highly promising.

Acknowledgments

This work is supported by the National Natural Science Foundation of China under Grant No. 60433020 and the Key Laboratory of Symbol Computation and Knowledge Engineering of the Ministry of Education.

References

1. Furey T., Cristianini N., Duffy N.: Support Vector Machine Classification and Validation of Cancer Tissue Samples Using Microarray Expression Data. Bioinformatics, 16 (2000) 909-914
2. Model F., Adorjan P., Olek A., Piepenbrock C.: Feature Selection for DNA Methylation Based Cancer Classification. Bioinformatics, 17 (2001) 157-164
3. Kohavi R., John G.: Wrapper for Feature Subset Selection. Artificial Intelligence, 97 (1997) 273-324
4. Chow T., Huang D.: Estimating Optimal Feature Subsets Using Efficient Estimation of High-Dimensional Mutual Information. IEEE Transactions on Neural Networks, 16 (2005) 213-224
5. Zhong N., Dong J.Z.: Using Rough Sets with Heuristics for Feature Selection. Journal of Intelligent Information System, 16 (2001) 199-214
6. Cover T., Thomas J.: Elements of Information Theory. Wiley Series in Telecommunications, New York (1991)
7. Zaffalon M., Hutter M.: Robust Feature Selection by Mutual Information Distributions. Proceedings of the 14th International Conference on Uncertainty in Artificial Intelligence, (2002) 577-584
8. Pawlak Z.: Rough Sets. International Journal of Computer Information Science, 11 (1982) 341-356
9. Kennedy J., Eberhart R.C.: A Discrete Binary Version of the Particle Swarm Algorithm. Proceedings of the 1997 Conference on Systems, Man, and Cybernetics. Piscata-way NJ, IEEE Press (1997) 4104-4109
10. Skowron A., Rauszer C.: The Discernibility Matrices and Functions in Information Systems. Intelligent decision support: Handbook of applications and advances of rough set theory, 11 (1992) 331-362
11. Aleksander Øhrn: Institute of Mathematics, University of Warsaw, Poland. http://rosetta.lcb.uu.se/
12. Golub T.R., Slonim K.D., Tamayo P. et al.: Molecular Classification of Cancer: Class Discovery and Class Prediction by Gene Expression Monitoring. Science, 286 (1999) 531-537
13. Alon U., Barkai N. et al.: Broad Patterns of Gene Expression Revealed by Clustering Analysis of Tumor and Normal Colon Cancer Tissues Probed by Oligonucleotide Arrays. PNAS, 96 (1999) 6745-6750
14. Vapnik V.: The Nature of Statistical Learning Theory. Springer-Verlag, Berlin Heidel-berg New York (1995)
15. Sung-Bae Cho, Hong-hee Won: Machine Learning in DNA Microarray Analysis for Cancer Classification. Proceedings of the First Asia-Pacific bioinformatics conference on Bioinformatics, 19 (2003) 189-198

A Support Vector Machine Approach to Breast Cancer Diagnosis and Prognosis

Elias Zafiropoulos, Ilias Maglogiannis, Ioannis Anagnostopoulos [1]

1   Department of Information and Communication Systems Engineering,
University of the Aegean,
GR 83200 Karlovasi, Samos, Greece

Abstract. In recent years, computational diagnostic tools and artificial intelligence techniques provide automated procedures for objective judgments by making use of quantitative measures and machine learning. The paper presents a Support Vector Machine (SVM) approach for the prognosis and diagnosis of breast cancer implemented on the Wisconsin Diagnostic Breast Cancer (WDBC) and the Wisconsin Prognostic Breast Cancer (WPBC) datasets found in literature. The SVM algorithm performs excellently in both problems for the case study datasets, exhibiting high accuracy, sensitivity and specificity indices.

1   Introduction

The implementation of training algorithms in the prognosis and diagnosis of cancer is a research area of great interest, while significant research work has been published in literature, basically in the area of neural networks [1], [2], [3], [4]. In the present re-search work, a SVM model is implemented for the breast cancer diagnosis and prognosis problem using the Wisconsin Diagnostic Breast Cancer (WDBC) as well as the Wisconsin Prognostic Breast Cancer (WPBC) datasets, which are publicly available at http://ftp.ics.uci.edu/pub/machine-learning-databases/breast-cancer-wisconsin/. These datasets involve measurements taken according the Fine Needle Aspirate (FNA) test. The role of diagnosis is to provide a distinction between the malignant and benign breast masses. In case that a patient is diagnosed with breast cancer, the malignant mass must be excised. After this or a different post-operative procedure, a prediction of the expected course of the disease must be determined. However, prognostic pre-diction does not belong either on the classic learning paradigms of function approximation or classification. This is due to a patient can be classified as a "recur" case (instance) if the disease is observed, while there is not a threshold point at which the patient can be considered as a "non-recur" case. The data are therefore censored since a time to recur for only a subset of

Please use the following format when citing this chapter:

Zafiropoulos, Elias, Maglogiannis, Ilias, Anagnostopoulos, Ioannis, 2006, in IFIP International Federation for Information Processing, Volume 204, Artificial Intelligence Applications and Innovations, eds. Maglogiannis, I., Karpouzis, K., Bramer, M., (Boston: Springer), pp. 500–507

patients is known. For the other patients, the length of time after treatment during which malignant masses are not found is known. This time interval is the disease free survival (DFS) time, which can be reported for an individual patient or for a study population. In particular, the right endpoints of the recurrence time intervals are right censored, as some patients will inevitably change hospital, doctors or die of other unrelated with the cancer causes. The prognosis of the specific time interval is considered a difficult problem since the training data are right censored [1], [2], [3], [4].

In the present paper, the Support Vector Machines (SVM) algorithm is implemented for the breast cancer diagnosis and prognosis problem and the WPBC – WDBC data are used as a case study [5], [6], [7], [8]. The SVM algorithm performed excellently in both prognosis and diagnosis problems for the WPBC/WDBC datasets exhibiting high accuracy, sensitivity and specificity indices. In Section 2, all the details concerning the medical data characteristics and the problem formulation for each dataset in the cases of prognosis and diagnosis are presented. Section 3 contains the basic principles of the SVM algorithm for data classification. Section 4 presents the proposed approach for prognosis and diagnosis of the case study datasets and all the corresponding results, while in Section 5 the paper is concluded.

2. Medical Data Characteristics and Problem Formulation

The WDBC and WPBC datasets are the results of the efforts made at the University of Wisconsin Hospital for the diagnosis and prognosis of breast tumours solely based on FNA test. This test involves fluid extraction from a breast mass using a small-gauge needle and then visual inspection of the fluid under a microscope. Figure 1 depicts two images, which were taken from fine needle biopsies of breast as appeared in [9].

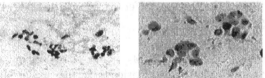

Fig. 1. Images taken using the FNA test: (a) Benign, (b) Malignant

The WDBC dataset consist of 569 instances (357 benign – 212 malignant), where each one represents FNA test measurements for one diagnosis case. For this dataset each instance has 32 attributes, where the first two attributes correspond to a unique identification number and the diagnosis status (benign / malignant). The rest 30 features are computations for ten real-valued features, along with their mean, standard error and the mean of the three largest values ("worst" value) for each cell nucleus respectively. These ten real values, which are depicted at Table 1, are computed from a digitized image of a fine needle aspirate (FNA) of breast tumour, describing characteristics of the cell nuclei present in the image and are recorded with four significant digits.

The WPBC dataset consists of 198 instances (151 non-recur - 47 recur), where each one represents follow-up data for one breast cancer case. Each instance has 35 attributes, where the first three attributes correspond to a unique identification number and to the prognosis status (recur / non-recur) following by the recurrence time (Time to Recur - TTR) or the DFS time respectively. Then they follow the above-mentioned 30 features, while the last two attributes are the diameter of the excised tumour (in cm) and the number of positive axillary lymph nodes observed at time of surgery. Four instances were not included in the training/testing set since the Lymph node values were missing. For the addressed problem, both WDBC and WPBC datasets were used in several publications in the medical literature [10], [11], [12], [13]. In addition, due to their consistency and robust creation, these datasets are also used for verification purposes over the classification or prediction performance of information systems in other scientific areas [14], [15].

Table 1. WDBC/WPBC cell nuclei characteristics attributes.

Cell Nuclei Characteristics
1. radius [mean of distances from centre to points on the perimeter],
2. texture [standard deviation of grey-scale values],
3. perimeter,
4. area,
5. smoothness [local variation in radius lengths],
6. compactness [((perimeter)2 / area) - 1],
7. concavity [severity of concave portions of the contour],
8. concave points [number of concave portions of the contour],
9. symmetry,
10. fractal dimension ["coastline approximation" – 1]

3   Principles of the Support Vector Machines Algorithm for Data Classification

The Support Vector Machines (SVMs) is a novel algorithm for data classification and regression which allows the expansion of the information provided by a training dataset as a linear combination of a subset of the data in the training set (support vectors) [5], [6]. These vectors locate a hypersurface that separates the input data with a very good degree of generalization. The SVM algorithm is a learning machine; there-fore it is based on training, testing and performance evaluation, which are common steps in every learning procedure. Training involves optimization of a convex cost function where there are no local minima to complicate the learning process. Testing is based on the model evaluation using the support vectors to classify a test dataset. Performance is based on error rate determination as test dataset size tends to infinity.

The mathematical formulation of the Support Vector Machine algorithm for data classification and regression is presented extensively in literature [5], [6], [7]. A critical issue is the selection of a suitable kernel function that will transform the initially non-separable data in a new feature space where they are separable. Several kernel functions can be used, such as the following:

$$k(X_i, X_j) = e^{-|X_i-X_j|^2/2\sigma^2} \qquad \text{(Gaussian RBF kernel) (1)}$$
$$k(X_i, X_j) = (X_i \cdot X_j + m)^p \qquad \text{(polynomial kernel) (2)}$$

4 The proposed approach of the SVM Algorithm Classification Problem for Prognosis and Diagnosis of Breast Cancer

4.1 Classification of the WPBC patient data based on the Disease Free or Recurrence Time (prognosis)

The SVM algorithm has been implemented in the case of the WPBC instances for data classification according to the recurrence or the DFS time. The WPBC instances were divided over four classes, namely C1, C2, C3 and C4, according to the value of the recurrence or the DFS time. In other words, C1 corresponds to the instances, in which the DFS time or the recurrence time was between 1 and 12 months, while C2, C3 and C4 correspond to intervals between 1-3 years, 3-6 years and more than 6 years. Table 2 depicts the amount of the WPBC dataset instances in respect to the above-mentioned categorization. The first column indicates the time interval class, while the second and the third columns present the amount of instances, when the tumour recurred (NR) and the amount of instances when the tumour did not recur (NN).

Table 2. WPBC instances according to the categorized interval time and prognosis status

Class	Interval time	N_R	N_N	Total
C_1	Less than 1 year	20	23	43
C_2	1 year – 3 years	14	34	48
C_3	3 years – 6 years	7	48	55
C_4	More than 6 years	5	43	48
			Total	194

Based on the categorization of the WPBC instances in the four intervals depicted in Table 2, the SVM algorithm has been applied for the corresponding two-class classification problem of each time interval. The training set and test set originated from the WPBC instances, while the attributes used were the ones depicted in Table 1, together with the "tumour size" and "lymph node status" features found only in the WPBC dataset. Several kernel functions were tried in order to find the least complex function that results in low number of support vectors comparing to the training set and exhibits satisfactory performance in data classification. The top results are depicted in Table 3. The Gaussian Radial Base function (RBF) with sigma=1 exhibits the best performance with accuracy varying from 96.91% to 94.84% for the four time intervals. The SVM algorithm was implemented in Matlab using a Pentium PC at 2.6GHz with 512 MB RAM. The execution time for calculating the support vectors using the Gaussian RBF with sigma=1 as a kernel function was approximately 12 seconds, while for the rest of the cases with different kernel functions varied for 11 to 14 seconds.

Apart from the accuracy indices presented in Table 3, the performance of a binary classifier can be further evaluated using the sensitivity and specificity indices. Assuming that if an instance belongs to the time interval it is classified positive, otherwise it is classified negative, the sensitivity and specificity indices can be defined as follows:

$$\text{Sensitivity} = TP/(TP+FN) \tag{3}$$
$$\text{Specificity} = TN/(TN+FP) \tag{4}$$

where:

TP (TN) =Number of True Positive (True Negative) classified instances; i.e. instances that the learning machine classifies correctly

FP (FN) =Number of False Positive (False Negative) classified instances; i.e. the learning machine labels the instance as positive (negative) while it is negative (positive)

Table 3: Results of the SVM algorithm using alternative kernel functions for the classification of WPBC cases in each time interval

		Kernel functions				
		Polynomial		Gaussian RBF		
		p=2	p=3	σ=1	σ=2	σ=3
C1	No of SVs	74	91	104	93	104
	Errors	152	42	10	27	39
	Accuracy (%)	21.65	78.35	94.84	86.08	79.90
C2	No of SVs	77	106	122	103	112
	Errors	46	46	9	20	31
	Accuracy (%)	76.29	76.29	95.36	89.69	84.02
C3	No of SVs	192	97	108	99	109
	Errors	55	55	6	31	43
	Accuracy (%)	71.65	71.65	96.91	84.02	77.84
C4	No of SVs	177	78	100	93	95
	Errors	143	51	9	19	33
	Accuracy (%)	26.29	73.71	95.36	90.21	82.99

These indices have been calculated for the SVM learning machine using the Gaussian RBF with σ=1 (sigma=1) and the corresponding results are presented in Table 4. The presented performance indices have been also calculated for the various kernel functions examined in Table 3 and the corresponding results for the kernel functions with the top performance are presented in Figures 3 and 4. In these figures, the specificity and sensitivity indices for the Gaussian RBF (sigma=1) are higher comparing to other kernel functions in all cases of classification in the four time intervals. This fact together with the high total accuracy depicted in Table 3 indicate the proposed SVM learning algorithm with the Gaussian RBF (sigma =1) kernel function as a superior binary classifier of the WPBC instances in the selected time intervals of recurrence or the DFS time.

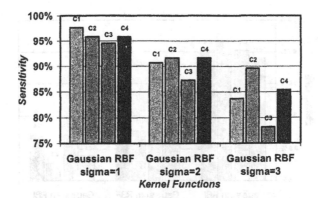

Fig. 3: Sensitivity indices for the SVM learning machine using alternative kernel functions for the classification according to the recurrence or the disease-free time survival (DFS) time.

Table 4: Sensitivity and specificity indexes for the SVM algorithm implementation using the Gaussian radial base function with $\sigma=1$ as kernel function

	Time Intervals			
	C1	C2	C3	C4
Positive	43	48	55	48
Negative	151	146	139	146
True Positive Classified	42	46	52	46
True Negative Classified	142	139	136	139
False Positive Classified	9	7	3	7
False Negative Classified	1	2	3	2
SENSITIVITY (%)	97.67	95.83	94.55	95.83
SPECIFICITY (%)	94.04	95.21	97.84	95.21

4.2. Automated Diagnosis of Breast Cancer Based on the WDBC Patient Data

Furthermore, the SVM algorithm has been implemented for the successful automated diagnosis of benign vs. malignant melanoma instances in the case of the WDBC patient data. The training set was constructed by randomly selecting 350 cases out of the WDBC instances, while the complete dataset was used for test set. In this way, the efficiency of the SVM algorithm has been examined using data that have not been used in the train set. Several kernel functions were tried in order to find the least complex function that results in low number of support vectors comparing to the training set and exhibit satisfactory performance in data classification. The best results are presented in Table 5. The Gaussian RBF with $\sigma=0.6$ exhibits the best performance with accuracy approximately 90%. Accordingly, the SVM algorithm for the WDBC case was also implemented in Matlab using a Pentium PC at 2.6GHz with 512 MB RAM. The execution time for calculating the support vectors based on the kernel functions of varied from 70 to 74 seconds.

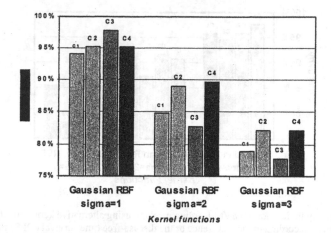

Fig 4: Specificity indices for the SVM learning machine using alternative kernel functions for the classification according to the recurrence or the disease-free time survival (DFS) time.

Table 5: Results of the SVM algorithm for the diagnosis of benign / malignant melanoma for the WDBC cases

Kernel functions	No of SVs	Errors	Accuracy (%)
Gaussian RBF (σ=3)	45	112	80.32%
Gaussian RBF (σ=2)	42	109	80.84%
Gaussian RBF (σ=1)	48	83	85.41%
Gaussian RBF (σ=0.8)	54	73	87.17%
Gaussian RBF (σ=0.6)	*67*	*61*	*89.28%*

The sensitivity and specificity indices, as they have been defined in Eq 12 and 13, have been calculated for all kernel functions presented in Table 5 and the corresponding results are presented in Figure 5, together with the accuracy of each kernel function.

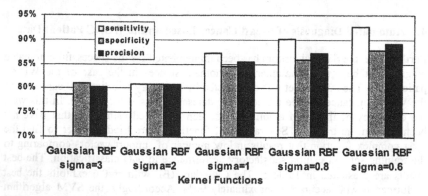

Fig. 5: Sensitivity, specificity and accuracy for the top performance kernel functions in the SVM learning machine for diagnosis of the WDBC instances

5. Conclusions

This paper focuses on the implementation of the SVM algorithm for the diagnosis and prognosis of breast cancer. Firstly, the methodology was implemented for the prognosis problem based on Wisconsin Prognostic Breast Cancer datasets. The SVM algorithm performed excellently, exhibiting high values of accuracy (96.91%), specificity and sensitivity indices. Similarly, automated diagnosis using SVM was implemented for the Wisconsin Diagnostic Breast Cancer datasets and the accuracy was approximately 90%, while sensitivity and specificity indices were also satisfactory.

References

1. Burke H. B., Goodman P.H., et al, Artificial neural networks improve the accuracy of cancer survival prediction, Cancer, Vol. 79, pp. 857-862, 1997.
2. Choong P.L, deSilva C.J.S et al., Entropy maximization networks, An application to breast cancer prognosis, IEEE Transactions on Neural Networks, 1996, 7(3):568-577.
3. Mangasarian et al, "Breast cancer diagnosis and prognosis via linear programming", Operations Research, 43(4), pp. 570-577, July-August 1995.
4. Street W. N., "A neural network model for prognostic prediction", Proceedings of theFifteenth International Conference on Machine Learning, Madison, Wisconsin, Morgan Kaufmann, 1998.
5. Burges C.: A tutorial on support vector machines for pattern recognition [http://www.kernel-machines.org/].
6. Schölkopf B.: Statistical learning and kernel methods [http://research.Microsoft.com/~bsc].
7. Campbell C.: Kernel methods: a survey of current techniques, [http://www.kernel-machines.org/].
8. Maglogiannis I. G., Zafiropoulos E. P. Characterization of digital medical images utilizing support vector machines. BMC Medical Informatics and Decision Making 2004; 4:4.
9. Wolberg W.H., Street W.N., Heisey D.M., and Mangasarian O.L., Computer-derived nuclear features distinguish malignant from benign breast cytology, Human Pathology, 26:792--796, 1995.
10. Tourassi G.D., Markey M.K., Lo J.Y., Floyd Jr. C.E., A neural network approach to breast cancer diagnosis as a constraint satisfaction problem, Med. Phys. Vol.28, pp. 804–811, 2001.
11. Wolberg W.H., Street W.N., Heisey D.M., and Mangasarian O.L., Computer-derived nuclear features distinguish malignant from benign breast cytology, Human Pathology, 26:792--796, 1995.
12. Wolberg W.H., Street W.N., and Mangasarian O.L., Machine learning techniques to diagnose breast cancer from fine-needle aspirates, Cancer Letters 77 (1994) 163-171.
13. Wolberg W.H., Street W.N., and Mangasarian O.L., Image analysis and machine learning applied to breast cancer diagnosis and prognosis, Analytical and Quantitative Cytology and Histology, Vol. 17, No. 2, pages 77-87, April 1995.
14. Hoya T. and Chambers J. A., "Heuristic pattern correction scheme using adaptively trained generalized regression neural networks", IEEE Trans. Neural Networks, vol.12, no.1, pp. 91-100, 2001.
15. Kaban A., Girolami M., Initialized and guided EM-clustering of sparse binary data with application to text based documents, 15th International Conference on Pattern Recognition, Vol.2 pp.744-747, Sept. 2000.

Source Code Author Identification Based on N-gram Author Profiles

Georgia Frantzeskou, Efstathios Stamatatos, Stefanos Gritzalis,
Sokratis Katsikas
Laboratory of Information and Communication Systems Security
Department of Information and Communication Systems Engineering
University of the Aegean, Karlovasi, Samos, 83200, Greece
{gfran, stamatatos, sgritz, ska)@aegean.gr

Abstract. Source code author identification deals with the task of identifying the most likely author of a computer program, given a set of predefined author candidates. This is usually .based on the analysis of other program samples of undisputed authorship by the same programmer. There are several cases where the application of such a method could be of a major benefit, such as authorship disputes, proof of authorship in court, tracing the source of code left in the system after a cyber attack, etc. We present a new approach, called the SCAP (Source Code Author Profiles) approach, based on byte-level n-gram profiles in order to represent a source code author's style. Experiments on data sets of different programming language (Java or C++) and varying difficulty (6 to 30 candidate authors) demonstrate the effectiveness of the proposed approach. A comparison with a previous source code authorship identification study based on more complicated information shows that the SCAP approach is language independent and that n-gram author profiles are better able to capture the idiosyncrasies of the source code authors. Moreover the SCAP approach is able to deal surprisingly well with cases where only a limited amount of very short programs per programmer is available for training. It is also demonstrated that the effectiveness of the proposed model is not affected by the absence of comments in the source code, a condition usually met in cyber-crime cases.

1 Introduction

Nowadays, in a wide variety of cases it is important to identify the author of a (usually limited) piece of code. Such situations include authorship disputes, proof of authorship in court, cyber attacks in the form of viruses, trojan horses, logic bombs, fraud, and credit card cloning etc. Although source code is much more formal and restrictive than spoken or written languages, there is still a large degree of flexibility

Please use the following format when citing this chapter:

Frantzeskou, Georgia, Stamatatos, Efstathios, Gritzalis, Stefanos, Katsikas, Sokratis, 2006, in IFIP International Federation for Information Processing, Volume204, Artificial Intelligence Applications and Innovations, eds. Maglogiannis, I., Karpouzis, K., Bramer, M., (Boston: Springer), pp. 508–515

when writing a program [6]. Source code author identification is much harder than natural language authorship attribution or writer identification (of handwriting) or even speaker recognition. The traditional methodology that has been followed in this area of research is divided into two main steps ([5, 7, 1]). The first step is the extraction of software metrics representing the author's style and the second step is using these metrics to develop models that are capable of discriminating between several authors, using a classification algorithm.

However, there are some disadvantages in this traditional approach. The first is that software metrics used are programming language dependant. For example metrics used in Java cannot be used in C or Pascal. The second is that metrics selection is not a trivial process and usually involves setting thresholds to eliminate those metrics that contribute little to the classification model. As a result, the focus in a lot of the previous research efforts, such as [1] and [5] was into the metrics selection process rather than into improving the effectiveness and the efficiency of the proposed models.

In this paper we present an approach to source code author identification we call the SCAP (Source Code Author Profiles) approach, which is an extension of a method that has been applied to natural language text authorship identification [3]. In the SCAP method, byte-level n-grams are utilised together with author profiles. We propose a new simplified profile and a less complicated similarity measure that proved to be quite effective even in cases where only limited training set is available for each author. Our methodology is programming language independent since it is based on low-level information and has been tested to data sets from two different programming languages Java and C++. Special attention is paid to the evaluation methodology. Disjoint training and test sets of equal size were used in all the experiments in order to ensure the reliability of the presented results. Moreover, the significance of the comments in the source code is examined. It is demonstrated that the effectiveness of the SCAP model is not affected by the absence of comments, a condition usually met in cyber-crime cases.

The rest of this paper is organized as follows. Section 2 describes our approach and section 3 includes the source code author identification experiments. Finally, section 4 contains conclusions and future work.

2 The SCAP Approach

In this paper, we present the SCAP (Source Code Author Profiles) approach, which is an extension of a method that has been successfully applied to text authorship identification [3]. It is based on byte level n-grams and the utilization of a similarity measure used to classify a program to an author. Therefore, this method does not use any language-dependent information.

An n-gram is an n-contiguous sequence and can be defined on the byte, character, or word level. Byte, character and word n-grams have been used in a variety of applications such as text authorship attribution, speech recognition, language modelling, context sensitive spelling correction, optical character recognition etc. In our approach, the Perl package Text::N-grams [4] has been used to produce n-gram tables for each file or set of files that is required. The n-gram table contains the n-grams found in a source code file and their corresponding frequency of occurrence.

The algorithm used, computes n-gram based profiles that represent each of the author category. First, for each author the available training source code samples are concatenated to form a big file. Then, the set of the L most frequent n-grams of this file is extracted. The profile of an author is, then, the ordered set of pairs $\{(x_1; f_1);$ $(x_2; f_2),...,(x_L; f_L)\}$ of the L most frequent n-grams x_i and their normalized frequencies f_i. Similarly, a profile is constructed for each test case (a simple source code file). In order to classify a test case in to an author, the profile of the test file is compared with the profiles of all the candidate authors based on a similarity measure. The most likely author corresponds to the least dissimilar profile (in essence, a nearest-neighbour classification model).

The original similarity measure (i.e. dissimilarity more precisely) used by Keselj [3] in text authorship attribution is a form of relative distance:

$$\sum_{n \in profile} \left(\frac{f1(n) - f2(n)}{\frac{f1(n) + f2(n)}{2}} \right)^2 = \sum_{n \in profile} \left(\frac{2(f1(n) - f2(n))}{f1(n) + f2(n)} \right)^2 \quad (1)$$

where $f_1(n)$ and $f_2(n)$ are the normalized frequencies of an n-gram n in the author and the program profile, respectively, or 0 if the n-gram does not exist in the profile. A program is classified to the author, whose profile has the minimal distance from the program profile, using this measure. Hereafter, this distance measure will be called Relative Distance (RD).

One of the inherent advantages of this approach is that it is language independent since it is based on low-level information. As a result, it can be applied with no additional cost to data sets where programs are written in C++, Java, perl etc. Moreover, it does not require multiple training examples from each author, since it is based on one profile per author. The more source code programs available for each author, the more reliable the author profile. On the other hand, this similarity measure is not suitable for cases where only a limited training set is available for each author. In that case, for low values of n, the possible profile length for some authors is also limited, and as a consequence, these authors have an advantage over the others. Note that this is especially the case in many source code author identification problems, where only a few short source code samples are available for each author.

In order to handle this situation, we introduce the SCAP approach. It includes a new similarity measure that does not use the normalized frequencies f_i of the n-grams. Hence the profile we propose is a Simplified Profile (SP) and is the set of the L most frequent n-grams $\{x_1, x_2,..., x_L\}$. If SP_A and SP_P are the Author and Program Simplified Profiles, respectively, then the similarity distance is given by the size of the intersection of the two profiles:

$$\left| SP_A \cap SP_P \right| \quad (2)$$

where |X| is the size of X. In other words, the similarity measure we propose is the amount of common n-grams in the profiles of the test case and the author. The program is classified to the author with whom we achieved the biggest size of intersection. Hereafter, this similarity measure will be called Simplified Profile Intersection (SPI). We have developed a number of perl scripts in order to create the sets of n-gram tables for the different values of n (i.e., n-gram length), L (i.e., profile length) and for the classification of the program file to the author with the smallest distance.

Table 1. The data sets used in this study. Program sample length is expressed by means of Lines Of Code (LOC)

	MacDonellC++	OSJava1	NoComJava	OnlyComJava	OSJava2
No Authors	6	8	8	6	30
Min-Max Samples per Author	5-114	4-29	4-29	9-25	4-29
Total Samples	268	107	107	92	333
Training Set Samples	134	56	56	46	170
Testing Set Samples	133	51	51	43	163
Size of smallest sample (LOC)	19	23	10	6	20
Size of biggest sample (LOC)	1449	760	639	332	980
Mean LOC in Training Set	206.4	155.48	122.28	64.58	170.84
Mean LOC in Test Set	213	134.17	95.92	56.48	173.03
Mean LOC/sample	210	145	109.1	60.53	172

3 Experiments

3.1 Comparison with a previous method

Our purpose during this phase was to check that the presented approach works at least equally well as the previous methodologies for source code author identification. For this reason, we run this experiment with a data set that has been initially used by Mac Donell [7] for evaluating a system for automatic discrimination of source code author based on more complicated, programming language-dependent measures. All the source code samples were written in C++. The source code for programmers one, two, and three were from programming books and programmers four, five, and six were experienced commercial programmers. Detailed information for the C++ data set is given in Table 1. The best reported result by Mac Donell [7] on the test set was 88% using the case-based reasoning (that is, a memory-based learning) algorithm. Table 2 includes the classification accuracy results for various combinations of n (n-gram size) and L (profile size). In most cases, classification accuracy reaches 100%, much better than the best reported ([7]) accuracy for this data set (88% on the test set). This proves that the presented methodology can cope effectively with the source code author identification problem based on low-level information.

More importantly, RD performs much worse than SPI in all cases where at least one author profile is shorter than L. This occurs because the RD similarity measure (1) is affected by the size of the author profile. When the size of an author profile is lower than L, some programs are wrongly classified to that author. In summary, we can conclude that the RD similarity measure is not as accurate for those n, L combinations where L exceeds the size of even one author profile in the dataset. In all cases, the accuracy using the SPI similarity measure is better than (or equal to) that of RD. This indicates that this new and simpler similarity measure included in SCAP approach is not affected by cases where L is greater than the smaller author profile.

Table 2. Classification accuracy (%) on the MacDonellC++ data set for different values of n-gram size and profile size using RD and SPI similarity measures

Pro file Size	n-gram Size											
	3		4		5		6		7		8	
	RD	SPI	RD	SPI	RD	SPI	RD	SPI	RD	SPI	RD	SPI
1000	100	100	100	100	100	100	100	100	100	100	99	99
1500	100	100	100	100	100	100	100	100	99	99	99	100
2000	98	100	100	100	100	100	100	100	100	100	100	100
2500	99	100	100	100	100	100	100	100	100	100	100	100
3000	56	100	100	100	100	100	100	100	100	100	100	100

Table 3. Classification accuracy (%) on the OSJava1 data set

Pro file Size	n-gram Size											
	3		4		5		6		7		8	
	RD	SPI	RD	SPI	RD	SPI	RD	SPI	RD	SPI	RD	SPI
1500	88	100	100	100	100	100	100	100	100	100	100	100
2000	35	100	80	100	100	100	100	100	100	100	100	100

Table 4. Classification accuracy (%) on the NoComJava set

Pro file Size	n-gram Size											
	3		4		5		6		7		8	
	RD	SPI	RD	SPI	RD	SPI	RD	SPI	RD	SPI	RD	SPI
500	94	94	94	94	94	94	94	94	92	94	92	92
1500	35	98	47	90	80	98	96	98	98	98	98	98
2000	33	92	14	98	20	100	31	100	61	100	78	100

Table 5. C Classification accuracy (%) on the OnlyComJava data set

Pro file Size					n-gram Size						
	3		4		5		6		7		8
	RD	SPI	RD	SPI	RD	SPI	RD	SPI	RD	SPI	RD	SPI
1500	98	98	98	98	98	100	95	95	95	95	95	98
2000	23	91	98	100	98	100	95	100	95	98	95	98

3.2 The role of comments

The experiments described in this section are based on a data set of open source programs written in Java. In more detail, source code samples by 8 different authors were downloaded from freshmeat.net. The amount of programs per programmer is highly unbalanced, ranging from 4 to 30 programs per author. The source code sample size was between 23-760 lines of code. In many cases, source code samples by the same programmer have common comment lines at the beginning of the program. Such comment lines were manually removed since they could (positively) influence the classification accuracy. The total number of programs was 107 and they were split into equally-sized training and test sets. Hereafter, this data set will be called OS-Java1.

This data set provides a more realistic case of source code author identification than student programs that have been used in similar studies ([2], [5]). Open source code is similar to commercial programs which usually have comments and they are usually well structured. Most of the open source programs are longer than the student programs. More importantly, this data set enables us to examine the role comments play in the classification model. We have decided to perform three different experiments on this data set. For this reason, we first filtered out any comments from the OSJava1 data set, resulting a new data set (hereafter, called NoComJava). Then, another data set was constructed using only the comments from each source code sample (hereafter, called OnlyComJava). Note that in the latter case, the resulting data set includes fewer programs than the original because any source code files with no comments were removed. The OnlyComJava data set includes samples by 6 different authors with 9 – 25 files per author. Detailed information for OSJava1, NoComJava, and OnlyComJava data sets is shown in Table 1.

The application of the proposed methodology to the OSJava1, NoComJava, and OnlyComJava data sets is described in Tables 3, 4, and 5, respectively. Notice that two different profile sizes are indicated (1500 and 2000) since they provide the best results (as has been demonstrated in previous study [2]). The classification results for the OSJava1 data set are perfect for any n-gram size and similarity measure. This is mainly because the source code samples of this data set are relatively long. Moreover, for many candidate authors there is a sufficient amount of training samples. Interestingly, the accuracy remains at the top level when removing the comment lines of these samples (NoComJava data set). However, this stands only for the SPI similarity measure. RD fails to retain such performance in most cases. In more detail, for L=500, RD and SPI have (almost) identical performance. When L increases to 1500, the accuracy of RD drops for low values of n (n<6). When L increases to 2000, the accuracy of RD drops for all values of n. This happens because at least one author has author profile shorter than the predefined value of L. RD is not able to handle effectively such cases. Note that the accuracy of SPI increases with L. This is a strong indication that the proposed SPI similarity measure better suits the source code author identification problem. On the other hand, when examining only the comments of each source code sample (OnlyComJava dataset), the RD similarity measure is more competitive, which indicates that it better suits natural language.

Table 6. Classification accuracy (%) on the OSJava2 data set

| Pro file | n-gram Size | | | | | | | | | | | |
| | 3 | | 4 | | 5 | | 6 | | 7 | | 8 | |
Size	RD	SPI	RD	SPI	RD	SPI	RD	SPI	RD	SPI	RD	SPI
1000	93	93	93	94	95	95	94	94	96	95	94	94
1500	92	92	94	94	95	95	96	96	96	97	95	95
2000	31	92	72	94	95	95	95	94	95	96	96	96
2500	13	93	37	94	54	95	79	94	94	94	95	95
3000	14	89	13	94	24	95	38	95	58	95	75	95

Again, the best results are obtained using the SPI measure. Probably, this is explained by the extremely short samples that constitute the OnlyComJava data set.

3.3 Dealing with many authors

The previous experiments have shown that our approach is quite reliable is quite reliable when dealing with a limited number of candidate authors (6 to 8). In this section we present an experiment that demonstrates the effectiveness of the proposed method when dealing with dozens of candidate authors. For that purpose a data set was created by downloading open-source code samples by 30 different authors from freshmeat.net. Hereafter, this data set will be called OSJava2. Details on this data set can be found in Table 1. Note that the available texts per author ranges from 4 to 29. Moreover, in average the samples of this data set are longer in comparison to the OSJava1. This data set includes programs on the same application domain written by different authors. In addition the samples of many authors are written over a long time period and therefore there might be programming style changes of certain authors.

The samples were split into equally-sized training and test set. Note that the training set was highly unbalanced (as OSJava1). The best accuracy result was 96.9% and has been achieved using the SPI similarity measure as can be seen in Table 6. Again, RD fails to deal with cases where at least one author profile is shorter than L. In most cases, accuracy exceeds 95%, using the SPI similarity measure indicating that the SCAP approach can reliably identify the author of a source code sample even when there are multiple candidate authors. The best result corresponds to profile size of 1500.

4 Conclusions

In this paper, the SCAP approach to source code authorship analysis has been presented. It is based on byte-level n-gram profiles, a technique successfully applied to natural language author identification problems. This method was applied to data sets of varying difficulty demonstrating surprising effectiveness. The SCAP approach includes a new simplified profile and a less-complicated similarity measure that better suit the characteristics of the source code authorship analysis problem. In particular the SCAP approach can deal with cases where very limited training data per author is available (especially, when at least one author profile is shorter than the predefined profile size) or there are multiple candidate authors, conditions usually met in source code authorship analysis problems (e.g. source code authorship disputes, etc.) with no significant compromise in performance.

More significantly, the role of comments in the source code is examined. The SCAP method can reliably identify the most likely author when there are no comments in the available source code samples, a condition usually met in cyber-attacks. However, it is demonstrated that the comments provide quite useful information and can significantly assist the classification model to achieve quasi-perfect results. Actually, the comments alone can be used to identify the most likely author in open-source code samples where there are detailed comments in each program sample.

A useful direction for further work would be the discrimination of different programming styles in collaborative projects. In addition, cases where all the available source code programs are dealing with the same task should be tested. Finally, the visualization of the stylistic properties of each author could be of major benefit in order to explain the differences between candidate source code authors.

References

1. B Ding, H., Samadzadeh, M., H., Extraction of Java program fingerprints for software authorship identification, The Journal of Systems and Software, Volume 72, Issue 1, Pages 49-57 June 2004.
2. Frantzeskou, G., Stamatatos, E., Gritzalis, S., Supporting the cybercrime investigation process: Effective discrimination of source code based on byte level information, in Proc. 2nd International Conference on e-business and Telecommunications Networks (ICETE05), 2005.
3. Keselj, V., Peng, F., Cercone, N., Thomas, C., N-gram based author profiles for authorship attribution, In Proc. Pacific Association for Computational Linguistics 2003.
4. Keselj, V.,. Perl package Text::N-grams http://www.cs.dal.ca/~vlado/srcperl/N-grams or http://search.cpan.org/author/VLADO/Text-N-grams-0.03/N-grams.pm, 2003.
5. Krsul, I., and Spafford, E. H, Authorship analysis: Identifying the author of a program, In Proc. 8th National Information Systems Security Conference, pages 514-524, National Institute of Standards and Technology, 1995.
6. Krsul, I., and Spafford, E. H., 1996, Authorship analysis: Identifying the author of a program, Technical Report TR-96-052, 1996.
7. MacDonell, S.G, and Gray, A.R. Software forensics applied to the task of discriminating between program authors. Journal of Systems Research and Information Systems 10: 113-127 (2001).

AJA – Tool for Programming Adaptable Agents

Mihal Badjonski[1], Mirjana Ivanović[1], Zoran Budimac[2]
1 Datenknecht GmbH, Frankfurt am Main, Germany
mbadjonski@yahoo.com

2 Department of Mathematics and Informatics, Faculty of Science,
University of Novi Sad,
Trg D. Obradovića 4, 21000 Novi Sad, Serbia & Montenegro
{mira,zjb}@im.ns.ac.yu

Abstract. Agent-building tools have an important role in popularizing and application of agent technology. This paper describes a new agent-programming tool AJA. AJA consists of two programming languages: HADL for defining of higher-level agent constructs and Java+ for low-level programming of these constructs. Among other interesting features AJA presents an original approach of incorporating artificial neural nets, into a programming language.

1 Introduction

Agent programs are usually relatively complex ones. To design and implement agents from scratch, especially the ones in a multi-agent system, is a time-consuming proc-ess. Beside the implementation issues, e.g. network communication among agents, there are many design and higher-level problems to be solved.

One way to facilitate agent transition from research laboratories to mainstream programming is to build and provide agent-oriented programming tools such as agent-oriented programming languages, agent-oriented integrated development environ-ments, (IDEs) and agent-oriented design tools.

This paper presents AJA – a tool for programming of multi-agent systems based on adaptable java agents (AJA). Using an original approach, AJA combines Java with higher-level agent-constructs and with AI-components and thus provides an effective environment for the programming of multi-agent systems.

Please use the following format when citing this chapter:

Badjonski, Mihal, Ivanovic, Mirjana, Budimac, Zoran, 2006, in IFIP International Federation for Information Processing, Volume 204, Artificial Intelligence Applications and Innovations, eds. Maglogiannis, I., Karpouzis, K., Bramer, M., (Boston: Springer), pp. 516–523

2   AJA features

The design of AJA is based upon the positive and negative experience obtained in de-signing and implementing the agent-oriented language LASS ([1], [2], [3], [4]) as well as upon the analyses of the existing agent building tools and environments. AJA tool is based on the following ideas.

Agent-Programming Language is used together with Java - a few agent-oriented languages have been created so far, mainly as the results of agent-research projects. The purpose of these languages, such as AGENT0, PLACA, Concurrent MetateM, AgentSpeak, is to introduce a new programming paradigm, to show new agent-oriented programming concepts and language constructs. However, these languages are not well suited for the commercial projects, because they miss the conventional features, such as database programming support, GUI programming support, etc.

The goal of our work was to create an agent-development tool that can be used in the implementation of the enterprise-scaled real-world multi-agent systems. In other words, the tool introduces new language, but at the same time it should be powerful enough to support all standard features (e.g. database access, windows-based GUI, etc.) that can be found in popular programming languages, such as Java.

The existing programming languages, first of all Java, already support many fea-tures: database programming, network programming, security, multimedia, etc. It would make no sense to implement everything again in an agent-oriented language. Instead, two languages can be used together: an agent-programming language to spec-ify high-level agent parts and Java can be used to implement these components.

2.1 AJA Agent Architecture

AJA agents can be classified as: software, static, middle-sized and big-sized agents, agents that can learn agents with hybrid architecture, and agents for both cooperative and competitive systems. An AJA agent consists of the following parts:

- Beliefs – primitive values, data structures, and the values generated by AI compo-nents.
- Actions – blocks of code that can be seen as atomic agent actions. AJA provides the synchronization mechanism for the parallel actions execution.
- Reflexes – condition-action(s) pairs. Reflex is a reactive component.
- Negotiations – represent the inter-agent communication as automaton. There are three types of negotiations in AJA: requesting negotiation – used when agent initi-ates the communication; responding negotiation – used when agent responses to the request; WWW negotiation – used for user-agent communication via Internet.
- Initialization part – actions that execute after agent has been activated.
  Two languages are used for the programming of AJA agents:
- HADL (Higher Agent Definition Language) – provides constructs for the higher-level declaration of agent beliefs, actions, negotiations, reflexes, and initialization.
- Java+ - is used for the implementation of higher-level agent parts defined in HADL. Java+ extends Java with the constructs for accessing agent beliefs,

actions, negotiations, reflexes, and GUI. Java+ makes the agent integration with the legacy Java software straightforward.

Agent program written in HADL and Java+ is translated into Java.

2.1.1 Beliefs

Beliefs of an AJA agent represent the information it has about the world. Beliefs define agent's internal state. There are three types of beliefs in AJA: Java values (both primitive and compound); Adaptable parameters; Dependant values.

Java Values - resembles global variables in traditional programming languages. They store primitive or compound values.

Adaptable Parameters - An agent program usually contains constants whose optimal values are not known in advance, because they depend on user preferences or some other unpredictable values. One possibility is to use adaptable parameters (real num-bers) instead of constants. Adaptable parameter adjusts its value at run-time according to the feedback received. Adaptable parameter in AJA has two optional attributes: lower bound, upper bound. The Listing 2. shows an example of adaptable parameter declaration.

Listing 1.

```
BELIEFS
...
    eventAlertTime : ADAPTABLE LBOUND << 0 >> = << 15 >>;
...
```

Dependant Values - are implemented using artificial neural network (ANN). A pro-grammer uses dependant values in AJA program without the need to understand how exactly an ANN learns and computes the output value from its input values. The de-pendant values (i.e. ANNs) can be, with no doubt, very useful in programming of in-telligent agents. Dependant values are declared as shown in the Listing 3.

Listing 2.

```
BELIEFS
...
consultationDuration :
            DEPENDS_ON
                    numOfStudents MIN << 1 >> MAX << 30 >>,
                    daysBefore MIN << 0 >> MAX << 50 >>
                    MIN_VAL << 1 >>  MAX_VAL << 240 >>
                    EXAMPLES_FILE "nnsamples.txt"
                    HIDDEN_LAYERS 5;
...
```

There are two input values for this dependant belief:
- numOfStudents with the lower bound 1 and the upper bound 30,
- daysBefore with the lower bound 0 and the upper bound 50.

The minimal output value is 1 and the maximal is 240. The examples for the ANN are in the file nnsamples.txt. The ANN has one hidden layer with five nodes.

2.1.2 Actions

An AJA action consists of a block of Java+ code, return value type, and parameters. In the declaration of AJA action it can also be specified which actions are not compatible with the action being declared. The AJA run-time system blocks the action execution until any of the incompatible actions is executed. In the Listing 4. declarations of an AJA action are given.

Listing 3.

```
ACTION void eventAlertAct()
  <<AlertDialog ad =
     new AlertDialog($AG_JFRAME, $GET_BEL(engToAlert));
     ad.show();
     if (ad.earlier()){$AP_HIGHER(eventAlertTime); }
     else if (ad.later()){$AP_LOWER(eventAlertTime);} >>
```

The action eventAlertAct does pop-ups a dialog window that alerts user about the incoming engagement. The class AlertDialog extends javax.swing.JDialog. $AG_JFRAME is the reference of the agent window (subclass of javax.swing.JFrame). If user gives negative reinforcement regarding the event alerting time, then the corresponding adaptable parameter will receive it. The action eventAlertAct has no incompatible ac-tions.

AJA action can be started explicitly using one of the three Java+ constructs. Further-more, an AJA action can also be started as a result of reflex triggering.

2.1.3 Reflexes

The first part of AJA reflex is activation condition, whose value determines whether the second part of the reflex should be executed or not. Reflex activation condition is checked periodically. Each reflex executes in separate thread. If there are more than one reflexes being executed at the same time, then they execute concurrently in paral-lel threads of execution. There is only one Java+ construct used with reflexes.

2.1.4 Negotiations

Requesting and responding negotiations are the construct an agent uses in order to communicate with other agents. Agent initiates the communication with a requesting negotiation. In the opposite situation, when other agent has initiated the communica-tion, the agent uses a responding negotiation to respond. There can be more than one instances of the same negotiation executed at the same time. Both types of negotia-tions are represented as automata and usually consist of several message sending and message receiving between two agents or among more agents. Each message contains a speech act string and optionally an array of serializable Java objects. Due to the dif-ferent ways the requesting and the responding negotiations are started, they have slightly different syntax. Each requesting negotiation consists of its name, return type, parameters, initialization part, and negotiation states. The first state in the negotiation is always called START. The negotiation ends, when a final state (FINAL) is reached.

3   A PDA implemented in AJA

Personal digital assistant (PDA) agent is a computer program aimed at performing simple and tasks on behalf of its user: handle e-mail of its user or it may monitor or find interesting newsgroups or web sites on the Internet and filter 'interesting' information [12]. A PDA may maintain the appointment schedule of its user and independently make or cancel appointments [12], [13]. A PDA communicates with other PDAs and performs some tasks that would otherwise have to be performed by the user. The implemented MAS using AJA tool consists of agents that act like personal digital assistants (PDAs). Each PDA belongs to one lecturer at University. The main purpose of a PDA agent is:

- to maintain the timetable of its owner,
- to alert the owner to the approaching engagements registered in the timetable such as appointments with colleagues and consultations with students,
- to alert the owner when a colleague has a birthday,
- to be helpful in creating new engagements (where other colleagues participate),
- to enable students to register themselves online for the consultations.

The implemented MAS is fully scalable, hence the number of agents in the system is irrelevant for the system performance. For implementation of the PDA new concepts introduced in AJA (dependable values and adaptable parameters.) are used.

3.1 Beliefs

The AJA code defining PDA agent beliefs is given in Listing 7.

timeTable - one instance of the class **TimeTable** stores and maintains all engage-ments, colleagues-data and available times of the agent owner. **eventAlertTime** - is an adaptable parameter and represents how many minutes before the next event should be the lecturer reminded. The value of this belief determines the alert time for engagements in the timetable. **eventAlertTimeToBackup** - belief has a boolean value. It is used in the activation condition of the reflex that stores the belief **eventAlertTime** into a file. **engToAlert** - belief stores the first engagement to which the agent owner should be alerted. **birthdaysTomorrowToAlert** and **birthdaysTodayToAlert** - These two beliefs store the persons having birthdays tomorrow and today respectively. **consultationDuration** - this belief is a dependant value. It is used for the estimation of the expected duration of consultations with students. It was empiri-cally found out, that the duration of a consultation depends on the number of ap-pointed students and the time remaining to the next exams. The analytical function however is not available; hence a dependant value belief (i.e. a neural net) is used.

The neural net nested in this belief has two input nodes. The first one represents the number of students appointed for the consultation (between one and thirty) and the second one specifies the number of days before the next exams (between zero and fifty). The value of the belief is the expected duration of the consultation in minutes. The examples for the supervised learning are stored in the file nnsamples.txt, which can be found in the current directory. The example file stores one example at a line. The first line in the file is: '1 24 8', meaning that if only one student comes to the consultations, 24 days before the exams, the consultation duration is 8 minutes.

Listing 4.

```
BELIEFS
    //schedule of the lecturer's engagements
    timeTable :  TimeTable;
    //how many minutes before the next event
    //the lecturer be reminded
    eventAlertTime : ADAPTABLE LBOUND << 0 >> = << 15 >>;
    eventAlertTimeToBackup : boolean = << false >>;
                    //used in backupEventAlertTimeReflex
    engToAlert : Engagement; // used in eventAlertReflex
    birthdaysTomorrowToAlert : Vector ; //used in
birthdayAlertReflex
    birthdaysTodayToAlert : Vector ; //used in
birthdayAlertReflex;
        //expected duration of the consultation with students
    consultationDuration : DEPENDS_ON
                    numOfStudents MIN << 1 >> MAX << 30 >>,
                    daysBefore MIN << 0 >> MAX << 50 >>
                MIN_VAL << 1 >> MAX_VAL << 240 >>
                EXAMPLES_FILE "nnsamples.txt"
                HIDDEN_LAYERS 5;
                    //one hidden layer with five nodes
    consultationDurationToBackup : boolean = << false >>;
                    //used in backupConsultationDurationReflex
```

3.2 Actions

The actions declaration part in the PDA agent program contains thirty-eight actions. The actions declared can be logically grouped into the following five groups: actions manipulating the timetable; actions alerting the user; actions performing backup of important beliefs; actions implementing GUI.

Timetable Manipulation - The actions that modify the **timeTable** belief are rela-tively simple ones. For example the action **removeOldEngagementsAct** removes old entries from the timetable.

Alerting the User - There are two actions that alert the user to the incoming events. The first one is the action **eventAlertAct**, and the second alerting action is the action **birthdayAlertAct**. Backup - Theoretically, an AJA agent runs all the time. However, in praxis this is not the case, so, the important agent be-liefs have to be saved in the files periodically. When the agent starts, it should check if the backup files exist and to initialize its beliefs from the files if they are found.

GUI - At last, but not at least, there are several actions implementing GUI communi-cation with the user. The action that implements the main menu is the action **doGUIAct**.

3.3 Reflexes

A PDA agent in MAS has six reflexes divided into three groups: a) reflexes invoking the actions that alert the user about incoming events; b) reflexes invoking actions per-forming backup of important beliefs; c) reflexes maintaining the timetable.

4   Related work

AJA presents an original approach to integrating artificial intelligence technologies with a programming language. Our research was influenced by different sources during several last years.

In AJA there are two programming levels. This concept of two languages is adopted from HOMAGE [14]. In HOMAGE the lower level is object oriented and it is used for the definition of objects in languages C++, Common Lisp and/or Java. Ob-jects defined at lower level are used in a higher, agent-oriented level. The higher pro-gramming level in AJA consists of the programming language HADL, which is used for the description of the main agent parts. The lower level Java+ consists of the pro-gramming language Java extended with the constructs for the accessing agent parts defined in HADL, like in HOMAGE. Because of the fact that Java+ language extends Java, it is possible to use all useful Java features in the implementation of AJA agents (e.g. JDBC for the database access).

JACK [10], [11] is an agent-oriented development environment, which extends Java with new, agent-oriented constructs. In AJA, namely in Java+, Java is also ex-tended with the new language constructs. However, JACK and AJA have nothing more in common.

The experience gained in the design and implementation of the Java package for agent programming LASSMachine [1] was very helpful in the creation of AJA.

A negotiation construct in AJA corresponds to a conversation in COOL [4]. AJA ne-gotiation is also represented as automaton. In AJA however a state in automaton has slightly different semantic that it has in COOL. In AJA a state in the negotiation automaton is not strictly bound to message receiving and message sending like it is in COOL. AJA negotiation states are more flexible. They simply divide the negotiation into the logical parts that correspond to various states in the negotiation process.

Subsumption architecture [6], [7], [8] gave surprisingly good results in robotics. It consists of hierarchically organized behaviors, which are the only components con-trolling the robot. AJA reflexes are similar to behaviors, but there are some important differences: a) AJA reflexes are triggered by boolean conditions; b) AJA agents have beliefs, which store their world models; c) AJA reflexes and AJA negotiations jointly control AJA agents.

In papers [15] and [16] intelligent agents were seen as a vehicle for AI-related tech-nologies in the mainstream programming. It also was the inspiration for including AI components into the AJA tool: dependant values (i.e. neural networks), and adaptable parameters.

5 Conclusions

The paper presented a tool for programming of multi-agent systems named AJA. AJA consists of two programming languages: HADL and Java+. Higher-level components of an agent are specified using HADL. The low-level implementation of HADL com-ponents is done using Java+.

One of the most interesting and original features of AJA is the integration of artificial intelligence techniques, such as artificial neural nets, with a programming language. Other advantages of AJA include: grouping of individual communicative acts into negotiations, proactive and/or reactive nature of AJA agents, secure inter-agent communication using SSL and digital signatures, accessibility via Internet, unrestricted use of Java platform in AJA programs, etc.

References

1. M. Badjonski, "Implementation of Multi-Agent Systems using Java", Master thesis, Institute of Mathematics, Faculty of Science, University of Novi Sad, Yugoslavia, 1998.
2. M. Badjonski, M. Ivanović "LASS - A language for Agent-Oriented Software Specification", Proceedings of VIII Conference on Logic and Computer Science LIRA, Novi Sad, Septem-ber, 1997, pp. 9-18.
3. M. Badjonski, M. Ivanović, Z. Budimac, "Software Specification Using LASS", Proceedings of Asian'97, Lecture Notes in Computer Science Vol 1345, Springer-Verlag, Kathmandu, Nepal, December, 1997, pp. 375-376.
4. M. Badjonski, M. Ivanović, Z., Budimac, "Agent Oriented Programming Language LASS", Computer Science and Electronic Eng., Horwood Publishing Ltd., 1999.
6. R. A. Brooks, "A Robust Layered Control System for a Mobile Robot", IEEE Journal of Ro-botics and Automation, 2(1):14-23, 1986.
7. R. A. Brooks, "Intelligence without Reason", Proceedings of the Twelfth International Joint Conference on Artificial Intelligence (IJCAI-91), Sydney, Australia, 1991, pp 569-595.
8. R. A. Brooks, "Intelligence without Representation", Artificial Intelligence, 47:139-159, 1991.
10. P. Busetta, R. Rönnquist, A. Hodgson, A. Lucas, "Jack intelligent agents - Components for Intelligent Agents in Java", AgentLink News Letter, January 1999, pp. 2-5.
11. http://www.agent-software.com.au/
12. P. Maes, "Agent that Reduce Work and Information Overload", Communications of the ACM, 37(7):31-40, July 1994.
13. T. M. Michell, R. Caruana, D. Freitag, J. McDermott, D. Zabowski, "Experience with a Learning Personal Assistant", Communication of the ACM, 37(7):80-91, July 1994.
14. A. Poggi, G. Adorni, "A Multi Language Environment to Develop Multi Agent Applications", Working Notes of the Third International Workshop on Agent Theories, Architectures and Languages, ECAI '96, Budapest, Hungary, pp. 249-261.
15. S. Schoepke, "Facilitating the Deployment of Intelligent Agents in the Application Development Mainstream", AgentLink News Letter, July 1999, pp. 10-12.
16. S. Schoepke, "Intelligent Agents will be a Vehicle for other AI-related Technologies", Posi-tion Paper, International Workshop on Agent-Oriented Information Systems (AOIS'99), 1999, available at http://www.aois.org/99/schoepke.html .

Investigating the Predictability of Empirical Software Failure Data with Artificial Neural Networks and Hybrid Models

Andreas S. Andreou, Alexandros Koutsimpelas
Department of Computer Science, University of Cyprus,
75 Kallipoleos Str., P.O. Box 20537, CY1678, Nicosia, Cyprus
aandreou@ucy.ac.cy, cs99ak2@ucy.ac.cy

Abstract. Software failure and software reliability are strongly related concepts. Introducing a model that would perform successful failure prediction could provide the means for achieving higher software reliability and quality. In this context, we have employed artificial neural networks and genetic algorithms to investigate whether software failure can be accurately modeled and forecasted based on empirical data of real systems.

1 Introduction

One of the major demands in Software Engineering is reliability. Non-reliable systems lead to dissatisfied customers and system users, extra human hours devoted on testing and difficulties through the maintenance phase. High reliability ensures that there is a small failure probability during the execution of a program [8] [9]. The term failure defines the inability of the program to respond to user requests correctly, that is, as prescribed in its requirements [9], caused by a programming error during the implementation or an ill-defined user need during the analysis of the system. Measuring the occurrences of failures in a system provides a way to determine its reliability. These measurements reflect the system quality and can be used in decision-making and problem solving processes. Essentially, there are four ways to record failure occurrences [9]:

- Time of failure
- Time of interval between failures
- Cumulative failures expressed up to a give time t
- Failures experienced in a time interval Δt

Software failure data is a reliability measurement but suffers many disadvantages mainly because of its dependence to the simulation environment and user knowledge. A system being tested in a controlled environment produces different failure data if tested under real use and there is always an issue for the ability of the

Please use the following format when citing this chapter:

Andreou, Andreas, Koutsimpelas, Alexandros, 2006, in IFIP International Federation for Information Processing, Volume 204, Artificial Intelligence Applications and Innovations, eds. Maglogiannis, I., Karpouzis, K., Bramer, M., (Boston: Springer), pp. 524–532

tester. People tend to use software differently and failure data recorded from expert users differ dramatically from failure data of naive users. This partially explains the difficulties in modeling the behavior of software failures.

Having a model that predicts the occurrences of software failures may help software analysts and developers produce quality and reliable systems. Knowing a priori that a failure may occur in a specific time and monitoring thoroughly the problematic system at that moment increases the probability of successful error discovery. One way to achieve this is to study the behavior of empirical failure occurrence data and investigate its predictability, building upon a previous research that investigated the nature of software failures using a non-parametric analysis [2]. The findings of that study were quite interesting as they support a random explanation of the behavior of empirical software failures, which resembles that of pink noise. We will attempt to question or support those findings by utilizing several forms of neural networks, including hybrid models (i.e. combined with genetic algorithms) trained with the same data series to investigate their predictability level.

The rest of the paper is organized as follows: Section 2 provides an overview on neural networks and genetic algorithms, while section 3 describes the models proposed to produce the failure predictions. Finally, section 4 draws the concluding remarks.

2 Theoretical Background

2.1 Artificial Neural Networks

Artificial neural networks are based on the model of the human brain neuron cells and try to mimic their functions. The human brain contains billions of neuron cells connected to each other through synapses. The input signals of each cell are added in the body cell and the summation is provided to other cells through the axon. Based on this, an artificial neuron is a mathematical model, which tries to duplicate this function. The neuron input vector x is multiplied with the input weights vector w and an adder sums those products. The result is passed to an activation function φ and its output becomes the neuron's output. The mathematical representation of an artificial neuron is [6]:

$$u_k = \sum_{j=1}^{m} x_j w_{kj} \qquad (1)$$

$$y_k = \phi(u_k) \qquad (2)$$

where x is the input vector of neuron k, w_k the weighs vector and u_k the dot product of those two. The neuron output y_k is defined as the result of the activation function φ given the dot product u_k.

Combining several artificial neurons and organizing them into layers sets up an artificial neural network. By imitating the job of neuron cells the artificial neural networks inherit advantages such as generalization, input-output mapping fault tolerance and adaptability. When the neuron outputs of a layer are provided as inputs to the neurons of the next layer, the neural networks are called fully connected. The outputs of the last layer are the network's outputs. The number of network inputs, the number of neurons per layer, their activation function and the number of layers define the network's architecture. The most popular network architecture is the Multi Layer Feed Forward Perceptrons [6]. Networks belonging in the category are composed of many layers, more than one and their neurons are fully connected with the neurons of the next layer.

Another category of neural network architecture is the Recurrent Networks. Observations of the human brain show that the output of a neuron cell is often redirected as an input to the same cell [6]. This kind of loop is implemented in the model of the recurrent neuron. Using this type of neurons produces networks that can solve more difficult problems. Typical examples of recurrent networks are the Elman networks, the Hopfield networks and the Kalman Filtering [5].

In order to be able to solve a problem, neural networks have to go through a training phase. In most cases, this training is supervised meaning that the networks try to learn by applying changes to there synaptic weights according to the errors computed on their outputs. The errors are the differences of the network output for a specific input pattern from the actual values provided. There are many training algorithms that implement this process, the most popular being the back propagation algorithm [6] and its variations. After the training phase the network generalizes its knowledge; it can provide satisfactory responses to unknown input patterns.

2.2   Genetic Algorithms

Genetic algorithms are stochastic, probabilistic algorithms that model natural phenomena such as inheritance and Darwinian strife for survival [7]. They are used to search a space of possible solutions through a process of evolving and evaluating individuals representing solutions and selecting the best one. The evolution works by encoding the possible solutions in a chromosome-like format, usually bit strings of specific length. A population of these chromosomes is randomly initialized and an evaluating loop begins. A fitness function selects the individuals with the highest fitness values. The selected atoms are undergone genetic operators like crossover (mating two individuals by exchanging their parts at a random position) and mutation (flipping bits from 0 to 1 and vice versa), which alter their values and hence their fitness [7].

3   Empirical Findings

This paper presents three attempts to find suitable neural networks for software failure occurrence predictions. The first one combines feed-forward neural networks trained with various algorithms and evolved by a genetic algorithm in terms of architecture. The second one utilizes recurrent networks and the third is a variation of the first one where the training data have been preprocessed.

3.1 Musa Dataset

In the 70s J. Musa created a dataset of software failures while working for the Bell Telephone Laboratories. The purpose of this work was to verify the ability of SRGM to simulate the occurrences of failures. Sixteen systems where monitored, such as operation system, word processors and real time systems, creating datasets that provided information about system code, day of failure and time intervals between failures in seconds. Three of these datasets were used in this work to train neural networks: Project 5 with 831 samples, SS1B with 375 samples and SS3 with 278 samples.

Previous research in this field [8] [9] have shown that the nature of the software failure data is non-deterministic and random. As seen in fig. 1, time intervals may vary as execution proceeds and it's very difficult to locate a pattern in this series especially with the presence of spikes adding more complexity. Furthermore, R/S analysis performed by Andreou and Leonidou [1] concluded that the characteristics of software failure data in Musa's datasets are similar to that of pink noise.

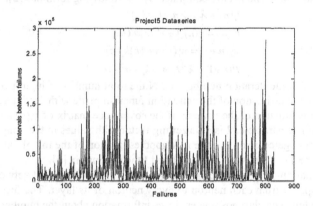

Fig. 1. Musa Dataset, Bell Laboratories, Project 5 interval between failures (seconds)

3.2 Feed Forward Neural Networks and Genetic Algorithms

The first attempt to locate an artificial neural network architecture that performs software failure data prediction was made using multi-layer feed-forward perceptrons that are trained with the Project 5, SS1B and SS1 data series. For the investigation part of the experiment, a dedicated genetic algorithm was designed and implemented according to the theory of evolutionary algorithms [7].

Each chromosome of the genetic algorithm represents a feed-forward neural network. The genes of the chromosome include information about the number of inputs, the number of nodes per layer and the activation functions per layer. Limits were set to the number of inputs, sixteen per networks, and the number of neurons, thirty-two per layer. The output layer is consisted of one neuron with a linear activation function. Each network has two hidden layers by default.

Apart from information on the number of neurons and the activation function, an extra gene is used to specify the training algorithm used to train the network represented by the chromosome. The back propagation algorithm is used and its variations (back propagation with momentum, back propagation with adaptive learning rate) [5]. Furthermore, optimized algorithms that use Jacobian and Hessian matrices were utilized to perform weight corrections, such as the Levenberg-Marquardt back-propagation [4], the Quasi-Newton BFGS [3] and the Bayesian regularization back-propagation [4].

3.3   Recurrent Networks and Genetic Algorithms

In the case of recurrent neural networks the chromosomes were altered to accommodate the Multiple Extended Kalman filtering Algorithm (MEKA) [1], which is an alternation of the Extended Kalman Filtering Algorithm [5]. The synaptic weights wi of node i are computed by the following formulas [2]:

$$r_i(n) = \lambda^{-1} P_i(n-1) q_i(n) \tag{3}$$

$$k_i(n) = r_i(n)[1 + r_i^T(n) q_i(n)]^{-1} \tag{4}$$

$$w_i(n+1) = w_i(n) + e_i(n) k_i(n) \tag{5}$$

$$P_i(n+1) = \lambda^{-1} P_i(n) - k_i(n) r_i^T(n) \tag{6}$$

where, n = 1...N the iteration number and N the total number of input patterns. The vector $q_i(n)$ is the estimation of the activation function made with Taylor series. $P_i(n)$ is the current estimation of the inverse of the covariance matrix of $q_i(n)$ and $k_i(n)$ the kalman gain. The parameter λ is a forgetting factor with values in the range $[0,1]$ and $e_i(n)$ is the propagated error to node i. A good estimation of the initial values of P is $e^{-1}I$, where e real in the range $[10^{-6}, 10^{-2}]$ and I the eye matrix [5].

The population of the genetic algorithm is consisted by recurrent networks where feedback loops go from each neuron to every neuron of its layer. The feedback time delay is one step. The chromosome encloses information about the number of inputs, the number of neurons per layer and the activation function of each layer (tansig and logsig).

3.4   SRGM Datasets

In order to compare the findings of real datasets with SRGMs, two artificial dataset were created based on the formulas of the Musa Basic and the logarithmic Musa-Okumoto models [2]. Those datasets, MB and MO respectively, were used in the same manner as real datasets searching for a network that would perform their prediction. The idea is that by succeeding to find a neural network that perform prediction on those artificial data and failing on real data one may argue their ability to model real software failures occurrences.

These data set were created by solving the mean value function $\mu(t)$ for t_i for each of the two models. The mean value function represents the number of failures expected to occur up to time moment t. Those functions are [8]:

$$MO: \mu(t) = [1 - e^{-fKBt}]N \tag{7}$$
$$MB: \mu(t) = N\ln(1 + \phi t) \tag{8}$$

where N is the expected number of failure in infinite time, φ is the failure rate per fault, K is the fault exposure ratio, B is the fault reduction factor and f a factor calculated as the average object instruction execution rate of the computer r divided by the number of source code instructions of the application under testing I_S times the average number of object instruction per source code instruction Q_s [8].

Assuming discreet time, replacing $\mu(t)$ with an integer positive variable i and setting [2]:

$$MO: i = N\ln(1 + \phi t) \tag{9}$$
$$MB: i = (1 - e^{-fKBt})N \tag{10}$$

we get:

$$MO: t_i = \frac{1}{\phi}\left(e^{i/N} - 1\right) \tag{11}$$

$$MB: t_i = -\frac{1}{fKB}\ln\left(1 - \frac{i}{N}\right) \tag{12}$$

Using the above formulas the times of failure occurrences were computed for each SRGM using the values suggested by [8]: (φ, f, K, B) = (7.8, 7.4 10^{-8}, 4.2 10^{-7}, 0.955).

3.5 Preprocessed Datasets

It is common practice to preprocess the data prior to training neural networks so as to remove possible biases and achieve better results. During the experiments of this study three different preprocessing methods were used; logarithms, difference of sequential logarithms (log (t_{n+1})-log (t_n), where t_n the nth time interval of the software failure series) and logarithms with spikes threshold. The new data were used for training the different networks described in section 3.1. For this experiment only the Project 5 dataset was used because is the one with the most samples.

3.6 Results

The experiments were conducted with a population of 50 feed-forward neural networks and a limit of 20 epochs, and a population of 100 recurrent networks and a limit of 50 epochs for the genetic algorithm. During the evolution process the fitness evaluation was done with the Mean Relative Error (MRE) [2] and the fitness function:

$$fitness = \frac{1}{1 + MRE} \tag{13}$$

For each experiment two sets were created. The first one, the training set, consisted of the first 75% of the dataset under investigation. The second set, the remaining data of the dataset under investigation, were used to validate the neural network with data that did not participate in the training. The optimum networks, defined as I-H_1-H_2-1 (I: number of inputs, H_1: number of neurons in first hidden layer, H_2: number of neurons in second hidden layer) were simulated taking as inputs the training and testing sets, and their responses were used for statistical analysis. The results of this analysis are presented in Table 1.

The Mean Squared Error (MSE) and the Mean Absolute Error (MAE), being data depended criteria, may provide a view on the success to predict the time series but for large input values they don't supply substantial information. On the other hand, the Mean Relative Error (MRE), by not being data depended, may offer a good criterion about the success to predict effectively future software failure intervals. The Normalized Root Mean Squared Error (NRMSE) examines the ability of a network to predict compared to a mean predictor. NRMSE values greater or equal to 1 imply that the network under verification doesn't curry out predictions but instead computes the mean value of its inputs. Finally, the Correlation Coefficient assess the ability of the network to follow the trend of the time series inspected.

Table 1. Statistical results for each dataset

Dataset	Algorithm	Network	Type	NRMSE	CC	MSE	MRE	MAE
Project5	traingdm	7-15-23-1	Train	1.2080	-0.0855	2.04×10^9	0.9834	2.54×10^4
			Test	1.1733	-0.2076	2.47×10^9	0.9624	2.62×10^4
	MEKA	16-32-32-1	Train	1.2061	-0.0196	2.06×10^9	0.9967	2.54×10^4
			Test	1.1746	-0.0067	2.45×10^9	0.9949	2.61×10^4
SS1B	trainbfg	16-17-24-1	Train	2.103	0.2395	6.23×10^{10}	0.9984	1.49×10^5
			Test	1.7328	0.1856	3.67×10^{10}	0.9992	1.08×10^5
	MEKA	15-16-24-1	Train	1.2425	-0.088	6.19×10^{10}	0.9323	1.48×10^5
			Test	1.1969	-0.0598	3.76×10^{10}	0.9285	1.08×10^5
SS3	trainbfg	16-24-7-1	Train	1.2286	0.1933	7.22×10^{10}	0.9949	1.57×10^5
			Test	1.2751	0.1257	2.4×10^{11}	0.9998	3.08×10^5
	MEKA	16-22-27-1	Train	1.2065	-0.074	7.19×10^{10}	9.2633	1.57×10^5
			Test	1.2709	-0.0751	3.14×10^{11}	1.2036	3.5×10^5
MB	trainbr	4-9-29-1	Train	9.67×10^{-9}	1	5.01×10^{-5}	2.03×10^{-11}	0.0069
			Test	2.91×10^{-8}	1	5.08×10^{-5}	2.03×10^{-11}	0.0069
MO	trainbr	15-20-30-1	Train	0.002	1	2.87×10^7	3.54×10^{-6}	4.56×10^{-4}
			Test	0.0854	1	5.69×10^{-5}	5.21×10^{-5}	0.0067
log (P5) no spikes	trainlm	6-28-28-1	Train	7.35×10^{-4}	1	2.13×10^{-6}	1.11×10^{-4}	8.45×10^{-4}
			Test	1.8568	0.017	19.7321	0.7552	3.4748
diff. log (P5)	trainbr	16-4-12-1	Train	0.9992	Inf[1]	32.2626	Inf	3.3908
			Test	0.974	Inf	77.6024	Inf	3.9268
log (P5)	trainlm	13-23-27-1	Train	0.0368	0.9993	0.0308	0.0085	0.077
			Test	1.6545	-0.0048	118.77	0.7896	7.2237

Even though there were cases where the statistical criteria showed that a network succeeded in predicting the training data set (preprocessed datasets), there was no success in predicting the testing data. This results in the failure of the networks to generalize and expand their knowledge. The NRMSE with values near and above 1 indicate that essentially only the mean values were actually computed. On the other hand, feed-forward neural networks managed to predict with high accuracy the artificial datasets created from equations (11) and (12).

---

[1] Division with zero

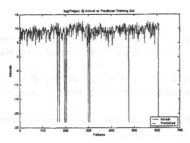 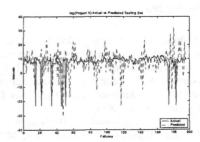

Fig. 2. Log values for Project 5: Training set (left) and testing set (right), with the response of the optimum network (actual samples are presented in solid line and predictions in dashed)

4 Conclusions

The predictability of software failure data was investigated using artificial neural networks and hybrid modeling in an attempt to understand the nature of software failure data with non linear (neural networks), probabilistic and stochastic (genetic algorithms) models.

Our research focused on utilizing neural networks (feed forward and recurrent networks) to predict empirical failure samples recorded by J. Musa for Bell Telephone Laboratories in the '70s for software reliability verification. The findings of our analysis come to support previous work [2] [9] on the subject stating that software failure data are non-deterministic in nature, resembling a random series and more specifically pink noise.

Examining the results in Table 1 and Fig. 3 it is clear that none of the networks investigated managed to produce accurate predictions. The statistical error between actual series values and network-simulated values exceeded the standards and the correlation coefficient showed that the predicted data series suffer from trend capturing and present the inability to reproduce accurate values. What the neural networks managed to do is provide a mean value computation of their inputs, as supported by the NRMSE, with results equal or greater than unity. On the other hand, artificially generated failure data created using known SRGM formulas were successfully predicted. This questions the ability of SRGMs to effectively capture and model the behavior of software failure and hence reliability.

Future work will focus on preprocessed data and advanced recurrent neural networks. The statistics gathered for preprocessed data indicated that the networks used presented better results, achieving higher prediction ability. Advanced recurrent neural networks having scaling time delays greater than one on their feedback loops will be examined to test whether prediction accuracy may be improved. Finally, new software failure data need to be recorded that would express failure tendency of today's software so as to examine possible changes in the reliability behavior of modern software.

References

1. Andreas, A., S., Georgopoulos, E., F., Likothanassis S., D.: Exchange-Rates Forecasting: A Hybrid Algorithm Based on Genetically Optimized Adaptive Neural Networks, Computational Economics (2002), 191-210
2. Andreas, A., S., Leonidou, C.: Nonparametric Analysis of Software Reliability. Revealing the Nature of Software Failure Dataseries. Department of Computer Science, University of Cyprus, Cyprus (2003)
3. Dennis, J., E., Schnabel, R., B.: Numerical Methods for Unconstrained Optimization and Nonlinear Equations, Englewood Cliffs, NJ Prentice-Hall (1983)
4. Hagan, M., T., Demuth, H., B., Beale, M., H.: Neural Network Design, Boston, MA: PWS Publishing (1996)
5. Haykin, S.: Kalman Filtering and Neural Networks, Wiley-Interscience (2001)
6. Haykin, S.: Neural Networks: A Comprehensive Foundation, Prentice-Hall, Second Edition (1999)
7. Michalewicz, Z.: Genetic Algorithms + Data Structures = Evolution Programs, Third Edition, Springer-Verlag Berlin Heidelberg New York (1996)
8. Musa, J., D.: A Theory of Software Reliability and its Application, IEEE Trans. Software Eng. 1(3) (1975), 312-327
9. Musa, J., D.: Software Reliability Engineering, McGraw-Hill (1999)
10. Patra, S.: A neural network approach for long-term software MTTF prediction, Fast abstracts of 14th IEEE International Symposium on Software Reliability Engineering (ISSRE2003), Chillarege Press (2003).

Selecting the Appropriate Machine Learning Techniques for the Prediction of Software Development Costs

Stamatia Bibi, Ioannis Stamelos

Aristotle University of Thessaloniki, Department of Informatics, 54124, Greece, {sbibi,stamelos}@csd.auth.gr

WWW home page: http://sweng.csd.auth.gr

Abstract. This paper suggests several estimation guidelines for the choice of a suitable machine learning technique for software development effort estimation. Initially, the paper presents a review of relevant published studies, pointing out pros and cons of specific machine learning methods. The techniques considered are Association Rules, Classification and Regression Trees, Bayesian Belief Networks, Neural Networks and Clustering, and they are compared in terms of accuracy, comprehensibility, applicability, causality and sensitivity. Finally the study proposes guidelines for choosing the appropriate technique, based on the size of the training data and the desirable features of the extracted estimation model.

1 Introduction

Cost estimation refers to the prediction of the human effort (typically measured in man-months) and time needed to develop a software artifact [5]. The estimation is based on various attributes of the software project, such as language type, personnel skills, computer platform, project constraints, etc. Such information is found in historical cost data bases that may be small data sets coming from the estimating software organization or large multi-organizational data bases. Although commercial cost estimation models are available, ad hoc models, based on selected past project data are considered the best approach.

Many studies have been published so far regarding the applicability of machine learning approaches to software cost estimation. Due to the different parameters of the experiments, the different data sets used and the varying evaluation methods no general conclusions can be directly drawn concerning the suitability of each method. Target of this study is to examine the compiled knowledge and experience coming from the application of machine learning techniques. The final result is the extraction

Please use the following format when citing this chapter:

Bibi, Stamatia, Stamelos, Ioannis, 2006, in IFIP International Federation for Information Processing, Volume 204, Artificial Intelligence Applications and Innovations, eds. Maglogiannis, I., Karpouzis, K., Bramer, M., (Boston: Springer), pp. 533–540

of a set of guidelines that will help an estimator select the appropriate method based on the environment in the context of which the estimation is performed.

In the following, the basic criteria for judging a cost estimation technique are presented as research questions:

How **comprehensible** is the extracted model? This is important in a problem domain such as project effort prediction since the estimator must trust the model's output, otherwise the prediction may be rejected by management.

How **applicable** is the method? The cost, effort and time needed to learn and extract an estimation model may be crucial for estimation environments that lack human experts, time or money to devote to such activities. It is important to possess effective tools that will support method application.

Does the model address **causality**? When a software project is less productive compared to others it is important to have a clue of the main reasons that caused this. Estimation should include causality, in a way that it is easily interpreted. A simple cost estimate is not enough any more, it should be accompanied with supporting evidence justifying the reasons for this estimate.

Does the method handle **missing values**? In software engineering data sets noise is a usual phenomenon. If a method can ignore missing values without excluding projects or independent variables then it has an advantage compared to a method that can handle only complete data. This is an important feature for software data sets that are usually small and incomplete.

Is **uncertainty** considered in the models? In every estimation process, uncertainty is an inevitable element that should be well managed. This element is even more important in software cost estimation models, where money, time, resources and customer relationships depend on this estimation.

What is the **accuracy** of the models? The accuracy of an estimation model is among the most important features of a method. Due to the fact that each study has different parameters direct comparison of the accuracy of the models cannot be performed. Though, several conclusions can be drawn about the situations under which each method outperforms the rest.

Does the method support a **dynamic approach** to the problem? For estimation problems that evolve over time, such as software cost estimation, techniques that can deal with updated information have an advantage over static techniques.

What is the **sensitivity** of the method? The sensitivity of a method involves its ability to produce accurate estimations even when several parameters change.

The paper is structured as follows: Section 2 shows how machine learning techniques are applied for estimating software development cost. Section 3 reports the results of published research studies and compares techniques. Section 4 compiles estimation guidelines for determining the appropriate technique(s) according to the data in hand. Section 5 concludes the paper and provides research directions.

2 Machine Learning Techniques in Software Cost Estimation

In this section we will demonstrate how the five machine learning methods can be used for softeware cost estimation.

An AR [1] coming from the domain of software cost estimation will have as Rule Body certain software project attribute values and as a Rule Head a productivity (or cost, or effort) value. A simple example of an AR is presented in table 1.

Table 1. Association Rule for Software Productivity Estimation

If language used = cobol and development type= enhancement
then 40<productivity ≤60   support=5% confidence= 85%

This rule is interpreted as following: If the language that will be used for the development of new project is COBOL and the development type of the project is enhancement then there is 85% (confidence value) probability that the productivity value of the project will be between 40 and 60 lines of code per hour. This rule is classifies correctly 5% of the instances in the training data set.

Bayesian Belief Networks [13] in software cost estimation are directed acyclic graphs with each node representing a software project variable, or software development effort. A simple Bayes Network estimating software effort is the one presented in figure 1.

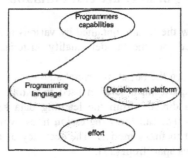

Fig. 1. A BBN for software effort estimation

Attached to the node of effort there is a node probability table that provides possible values of the effort based on the combination of values that the programming language and the development platform nodes take.

CART is a widely used statistical procedure for producing classification and regression models with a tree-based structure in predictive modeling [2]. The CART tree model of figure 2 for software cost estimation consists of an hierarchy of univariate binary decisions that leads to the prediction of software productivity.

Clustering [9] is the process of decomposing or partitioning a data set into groups so that the points in one group are similar to each other and are as different as possible from the points in other groups. In software cost estimation to our knowledge clustering have been used mainly for selecting similar groups of project in which another estimation technique will be used to provide a prediction.

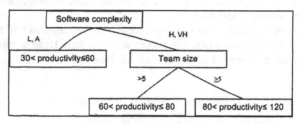

Fig. 2. CART for software productivity estimation

NNs [11] are massively parallel systems comprising simple interconnected units, artificial neurons. The neuron computes a weighted sum of its inputs and generates an output if the sum exceeds a certain threshold. This output then becomes an excitatory or inhibitory input to other neurons in the network. The process continues until one or more outputs are generated. In software cost estimation the inputs are the project attribute values, the output is the estimation of productivity.

3 Machine learning in software cost estimation

In this section we review the results obtained by various researchers and provide a comparative table based on the model quality criteria we proposed in the Introduction.

Rule induction has been the target of several studies [1], [2], [6], [11], [15]. The studies are differentiated by the algorithm used to extract rules. Studies [1], [2] extract association rules directly from the learning data set. Study [11] extracts mutually exclusive rules that can form regression trees, while studies [6] and [15] utilize rules as a support to fuzzy models. The accuracy of the method is a central theme to almost all studies apart from [11].

The studies considered identify comprehensibility of the results as a clear advantage of the method. Rules are among the most representative forms of human notion, they are transparent and therefore easily read and understood. Rule representation style helps the estimator understand the prediction and any underlying assumptions upon which it is based. Rules may be rephrased and provided to offer a clearer explanation as to how a prediction has been made and the evidence on which the prediction is based. Additionally, rules have the ability to include uncertainty in the prediction as each rule is accompanied by two probabilities that show the statistical validity and strength of the rule in the learning data set.

The accuracy of AR as an estimation method depends mainly on the number of rules extracted and whether AR has support from other methods. For example in study [11] when the pruned set of rules is evaluated the accuracy is decreased. In studies [1], [2] the number of rules extracted is large and therefore the estimation accuracy increased. The main problem of the method is that when rule induction is used, estimation accuracy is relatively low. On the other hand when association rules are used accuracy is higher but it cannot be guaranteed that the model will be able to classify all new projects. Another problem of the method is its sensitivity to parameter selection (number of rules, independent variables participating in the model, size of the training set). Changing one of the parameters may cause large model output fluctuation and reduce the accuracy of the estimates.

Bayesian Belief Networks is a relatively new approach to the problem of software cost estimation. Direct application of BBN on software cost estimation is found in two studies [3], [13], while [4] utilized Bayesian analysis for calibrating the well-known COCOMO II model. Bayesian analysis is a well-defined and rigorous process of inductive reasoning. A distinctive feature of the Bayesian approach is that it permits the investigator to use both sample (data) and prior (expert-judgment) information in a logically consistent manner in making inferences [4]. This is done by using Bayes' theorem to produce a 'postdata' or posterior distribution for the model parameters. Using Bayes' theorem, prior (or initial) values are transformed to postdata views.

Among the other advantages of the method is its ability to represent domains that evolve over time. BBN can offer a dynamic approach to the problem of software cost estimation as they are able to update their estimates when more information is included in the model. In general, using BBN estimation uncertainty is captured elegantly in the node probability tables that accompany each model and causality is addressed by pointing out the variables that mainly affect cost. Among the disadvantages of the method is that in small data sets BBN can be inaccurate, when particular combination of values of the independent variables are excluded from the learning set. Also the method cannot handle missing values, and though BBN support visual representation of the results the estimator has to be knowledgeable of the method in order to interpret the quantitative results as well.

Classification and Regression Trees are explored and applied in the comparative studies [2], [4], [7], [8]. In these studies the accuracy of the method usually is average to low and it is a fact that CART has never achieved the best performance among the compared methods. The main advantage of the method is that it is easily applied and produces comprehensible models. Additionally CART has the ability to classify all potential projects to a cost value even if the attributes of the project under estimation have not appeared in the training data set. CART can also handle missing values but the performance of the method increases when there is no noise in the learning data. Among the problems of the method is that the splitting of the data in each node sometimes seam unreasonable, as the method cannot deal with scale variables. Also due to the automated pruning of the tree that CART tools support, in order to avoid over-fitting to the data, several cost values that are loosely represented in the data tend to be omitted, resulting in the misclassification of projects belonging to minor cost intervals.

Neural networks have been often applied and compared in the domain of software cost estimation [6], [9], [11], [12], [14]. Most studies concerned with the use of NNs to predict software development effort have focused on comparing their accuracy with that of algorithmic models, rather than on the suitability of the approach for building software effort prediction models. In most studies where NN have been utilized the technique has relatively high accuracy and usually outperforms the rest of the techniques. We note, however, that other factors such as explanatory value and configurability are poorly addressed by the method. NN produce results in the form of a "black box" and therefore it is difficult for an estimator to understand the rationale under which the prediction has been made. Also the application of NN is a difficult, time consuming procedure. Among the main drawbacks of the method is its sensitivity to the data. Overfitting of the models to the training data is another reported problem.

Clustering has been applied on software cost estimation in combination with other methods [9]. First data are split into homogeneous clusters and then another method is applied. Clustering provides important information when the initial estimation models from the training data set are not satisfying and the models have to be re-generated using a part of the data. Clustering is useful for selecting data that will be in the same set for extracting estimation models.

Table 2 summarizes the results of the examined studies and provides a tool for comparing the various machine learning techniques.

Table 2. Comparison of machine learning methods in terms of quality criteria

Methods/ Criteria	AR	BBN	CART	CLUSTERING	NN
comprehensibility	high	medium	high	medium	low
applicability	medium	medium	high	high	low
causality	high	high	medium	medium	low
missing values	yes	no	yes	yes	no
uncertainty	medium	high	medium	medium	low
accuracy	depends	medium	low	NA	high
dynamic update	NA	high	NA	NA	high
sensitivity	high	medium	Medium	low	high

4 Choosing the appropriate technique

A standard approach in practical software cost estimation is to apply more than one technique [10], in order to avoid biased estimates. Based on the above assumptions we suggest a decision tree for selecting the appropriate technique according to the size of the data set and the importance that the estimator assigns to each model criterion. The overall approach is presented in the form of a decision tree presented in figure 3.

When the number of training data is relatively large (e.g. a large multi-organization data base or a rich local cost data base is used) the suggested method is BBN. BBN have the ability to represent various aspects of the cost estimation problem and when applied to large data sets potential disadvantages of the method are handled. In case the estimator is interested only in high accuracy of the estimates, and has the available resources to apply the method then the use of NN is suggested.

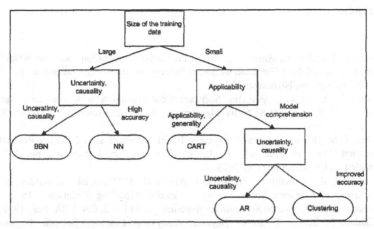

Fig. 3. Decision tree for selecting software cost estimation method

In small data sets (typically local software cost data bases) the selection of the method varies based on the situation of the estimation. When there is little time or the available tools and the estimation model must classify all possible projects then the use of CART is suggested, although accuracy may be a problem. On the other hand if uncertainty and causality of the model play important role in managerial decisions such as selection of tools, staff and platform for the project, the use of AR is proposed. AR will show which attributes affect the effort of a software project and the level they influence it. Finally if none of the previous hypotheses is valid and the models extracted directly from one machine learning technique are not satisfactory, the use of clustering is suggested along with re-application of the first technique.

5 Conclusions and future work

In this paper we examined five machine learning techniques in terms of accuracy, comprehensibility, causality, applicability, sensitivity, uncertainty, handling of missing values and dynamic update. Several advantages and disadvantages of AR, BBN, CART, clustering and NN have been indicated. Based on the assumptions coming from current literature regarding machine learning techniques, we suggested a number of guidelines for selecting the appropriate estimation methods based on the needs and the resources of the estimator.

It is obvious that for more detailed analysis of the above issues further research has to be done applying and comparing directly the above methods under the same estimation situation. Future work may also involve the application of the methods in large data sets, with missing values and noise. Also possible combination of machine learning methods for software cost estimation is definitely an interesting approach for solving the problems each method has alone.

References

1. S. Bibi, I. Stamelos, L. Angelis: Software Productivity estimation based on Association Rules, In Proc. of 11th European Software Process Improvement Conference, pp. 13A1, Trondheim, Norway, November 2004.
2. S. Bibi, I. Stamelos, L. Angelis: Software Cost Prediction with Predefined Interval Estimates, In Proc. of 1st Software Measurement European Forum, pp. 237-246, Rome, Italy, January 2004.
3. S. Bibi, I. Stamelos, L. Angelis: Bayesian Belief Networks as a Software Productivity Estimation Tool, In Proc. of 1st Balkan Conference in Informatics, pp. 585-596, Thessaloniki, Greece, November 2003.
4. L.C. Briand, K.E. Emam, D. Surmann, I. Wieczorek, K. Maxwell, An Assessment and Comparison of Common Software Cost Estimation Modeling Techniques, In Proc. of International Conference on Software Enginnering, pp. 313-322, CA, USA, May 1999
5. S. Chulani, B. Boehm, B. Steece, Bayesian Analysis of Empirical Software Engineering Cost Models, IEEE Transactions on Software Engineering, 25(4), pp. 573-583, 1999.
6. X. Huang, L. Capretz, J. Ren, D. Ho, A Neuro-Fuzzy Model for Software Cost Estimation, In Proc. of 3d International Conference on Quality Software, pp. 126- 133, Texas, USA, November, 2003.
7. R. Jeffery, M. Ruhe, I. Wieczorek, Using Public Domain Metrics to Estimate Software Development Effort, In Proc. of International Software Metrics Symposium, pp. 16-27, California, USA, April, 2001.
8. B. Kitchenham, A procedure for analyzing unbalanced datasets, IEEE Transactions on Software Engineering, 24(4), pp. 278-301, 1998.
9. A. Lee, C. Cheng, J. Blakrishnan, Software development cost estimation: Integrating neural network with cluster analysis, Information and Management, 34 (1), pp. 1-9, 1998.
10. S. MacDonell, M. Shepperd, Combining techniques to optimize effort predictions in software project management, Journal of Systems and Software , 66 (2), pp. 91-98, 2003.
11. C. Mair, G. Kadoda, M. Lefley, K. Phalp, C. Schofield, M. Shepperd, S. Webster, An Investigation of Machine Learning Based Prediction Systems, Journal of Systems and Software, 53, pp. 23-29, 2000.
12. K. Srinivasan, D. Fisher, Machine Learning Approaches to Estimating Software Development Effort, IEEE Transactions on Software Engineering, 21(2), pp. 126-137, 1995.
13. I. Stamelos, P. Dimou, L. Angelis, E. Sakellaris, On the Use of Bayesian Belief Networks for the Prediction of Software Development Productivity, Information & Software Technology, 45, pp. 51-60, 2003.
14. N. Tadayon, Neural Network Approach for Software Cost Estimation, In Proc of International Conference on Information Technology, pp. 815-818, 2, LA, USA, April, 2005.
15. Z. Xu, T. Khoshgoftaar: Identification of fuzzy models of software cost estimation, Fuzzy Sets and Systems, pp. 141-163, 145(1), 2004.

On the Idea of Using Nature-Inspired Metaphors to Improve Software Testing*

Francisca Emanuelle Vieira[1], Francisco Martins[1], Rafael Silva[1]
Ronaldo Menezes[2,1]**, and Márcio Braga[3,1]

[1] NATUS Project, IVIA
Fortaleza, Ceará, Brazil
{martins.filho,rafael.silva,emanuelle.vieira}@ivia.com.br
[2] Computer Sciences, Florida Tech
Melbourne, Florida, USA
rmenezes@cs.fit.edu
[3] Software Engineering, IVIA
Fortaleza, Ceará, Brazil
marcio.braga@ivia.com.br

Abstract. The number of software defects found in software applications today costs users and companies billions of dollars annually. In general, these defects occur due to an inadequate software development process that does not give the necessary importance to testing. Another contributor to these costs is the lack of adequate automated tools that can find "bugs" that would not otherwise be verified by experts. This paper looks at the combinatorial characteristics of the problem of testing – tools essentially search among all test cases for those that are promising (find existing bugs in the application) – and the effect that abstractions inspired by nature, such as genetic algorithms and swarm intelligence, may have in the construction of more "intelligent" testing tools. The paper argues that these abstractions may be used to construct automated tools that are more powerful, less biased, and able to incorporate expert knowledge while maintaining the ability to discover new, never-thought-of software defects.

1 Introduction

Software applications consist of a sequence of well defined instructions intended for execution in a computer. The exact sequence of instructions that is executed depends on several factors but primarily on the input values and the order these values are presented to the application. The majority of software testing tools (and programmers) perform functionality testing where the test cases are generated from real data. This approach is necessary but not sufficient. The choice of test cases is generally driven by the experts' concept of what is important to be tested. Still, software testers struggle to

---

* This research is funded by the Conselho Nacional de Desenvolvimento Científico e Tecnológico (CNPq), Brazil, under grant number 551761/2005-9

** Corresponding Author

Please use the following format when citing this chapter:

Vieira, Francisca Emanuelle, Martins, Francisco, Silva, Rafael, Menezes, Ronaldo, Braga, Marcio, 2006, in IFIP International Federation for Information Processing, Volume 204, Artificial Intelligence Applications and Innovations, eds. Maglogiannis, I., Karpouzis, K., Bramer, M., (Boston: Springer), pp. 541–548

answer questions such as: *what test cases should be executed?* and *What sequence of operations should be placed in a test case?* What we all would like to answer is: *all of them*. However, this is an impossibility for medium to large systems for the number of possible sequences is very large, making the problem intractable -- and humans have a limited capability in understanding complex systems [1]. To make matters worse, Dijkstra [6] observed that the number of bugs in an application has a direct relation to the logic implemented rather than just the input values. He also stated that software testing can be used to show the presence of bugs but never the absence.

What is true is that the discipline of practical software testing suffers from a lack of respect from other computer science fields. It is important to make sure that what is meant by *practical* software testing. In general there are two basic approaches to test software. The first, more accepted in the academia, consists of using formal specification to design an application and then use theorem provers to demonstrate the application's properties. This approach is very strict but not often used given that the majority of software developers and designers are not prepared to deal with the strictness of formal specifications. As if this was not sufficient, the breadth of formal specification methods do not encompass all the functionality needed in today's applications.

The second approach consists of the traditional software engineering models (eg. waterfall, spiral, prototyping) that have a specific phase for testing that generally occurs after the application has been implemented. Granted: modifications to these traditional models have been proposed to incorporate testing in every phase of the software development, or for instance to minimize mistakes while developing with methodologies such as extreme programming [2]. However, despite all the claims of these techniques being effective, the truth here is that current approaches are insufficient to appropriately test software, thus causing the current status of the field which clearly seems to be loosing the battle of providing users with reliable software.

The point to be made is not that software testing is a non-scientific, not-deserving-attention field but rather that current approaches are not sufficient to convince academics and practitioners that the field needs to be taken seriously. From a financial point of view, it only makes sense to look at software testing with more attention given that low estimates, put the cost of software testing at around 40% of the overall cost of development [11]. Ergo what is needed is a scientific method that allows testing to be carried out effectively without the need for the rigorous approach that exist in formal methods. This paper discusses the use of nature-inspired metaphors in a process to improve the *status quo* of automated software testing.

2 Software Testing

Software testing is a main area of research in the Software Engineering community and is even subject of independent study in many universities. The process of software development is far from being trivial. The complexity of the new applications asks for a development process with strict quality control at every phase of the process.

2.1 Automation of Testing Procedures

In the last years, software testing has been considered one of the most important procedures to assure software quality. Software engineering has created many techniques to derive a set of test cases. However, a main theme to many researchers and practitioners in the area has been the creation of automated testing tools that are reasonably autonomous with the objective of assuring that software budgets remain within the estimates.

An automated testing tool, would execute the work of a tester, but with an advantage, it is cheaper – most of the cost of testing comes from personnel and the longer working hours they require to test the applications. Research in technologies such as the ones inspired in Artificial Intelligence and their integration in software testing appears to be the correct way to move forward. Artificial Intelligence can naturally aid the the process of testing by augmenting the ability of a software to discover defects that would not likely to be found by experts due to their bias.

2.2 Testing as an Optimization Problem

It is fair to say that applications will never be free of defects – problems exist even if all the development steps are taken correctly and the requirement analysis done thoroughly. Software testing aims at eliminating the majority of these problems via a systematic process that identifies components of the software prone to errors.

The identification of components with defects is not trivial given the size of the search space: all the possible execution sequences of the software. This is an unbounded space; there is no systematic process that can explore all the search space in a finite amount of time. As Dijkstra [6] said

> *Program testing can be used to show the presence of bugs, but never to show their absence.*

Hence, the discussion whether software testing can be used as a verification tool is subject of discussion in the testing community since the publications of the seminal work on verification edited by Boyer and Strother-Moore [4]. Independently of the answer to the discussion about the validity of testing as verification, and the arguments in favor software testing such as [7], the truth is that software testing is the *de facto* industry standard for validation and verification of software.

The development of automated testing tools is in unison with the industry standard. Industry has a growing need for tools that are efficient (in their execution) and effective (in finding bugs). Nature has provided us with several models that that when implemented are efficient and effective in dealing with complex problems. This paper discusses the direction that can be followed in a research that combines nature-inspired algorithms, namely genetic algorithms and swarm intelligence, in the design of automated tools for software testing.

3 Nature-Inspired Models in Software Testing

Our argument that software testing can be seen as an optimization problem gives us the opportunity to look at techniques that have been successfully used in the optimization arena and their usefulness to software testing.

3.1 Genetic Algorithms

Genetic Algorithms (GAs) was proposed by Holland in 1975 [8] as a metaheuristic to combinatorial problems. It was inspired by the process of natural selection as proposed by Darwin [5]. GAs have been successfully used in a plethora of practical applications. The main steps involved in using GAs are:

Codification: Solutions for problems need to be coded as a genotype that can evaluated based on some fitness value. There must be a total order on the fitness values to allow solutions to be compared against each other.

Population Creation: A group of (normally) random-generated individuals are created to compose a population of fixed size. As part of this step, one needs to look at the issue of diversity in the population. The more diverse the population, the more likely it is that good genetic sequences (part of the genotype) are present in the population.

Individual Selection: Given the fitness of each individual, as calculated by the fitness function, the algorithm can stochastically select candidates of the population to be used in the next step (mating).

Mating: Mating requires the selection of two or more individuals. Mating can occur in various ways but the most common is point-crossover in which a "cut" point is randomly selected and new individuals are generated from combinations of the genotypes' parts. For instance, with a 1-point-crossover and two individuals, one can generate 2 new individuals combining the first part one parent with the second part of the other, and vice-versa. The decision to mate is also stochastic – individuals may be selected and not mate.

Mutation: Mutation is a process that allows the introduction of new genetic material in the population. Although mutation is an important step, it is normally desirable with less frequency. Hence GAs set the mutation rate of algorithms to very low probabilities. A larger than necessary mutation rate may had a undesirable side-effect to the algorithm convergence.

Understanding the steps above are essential in understanding what GAs can offer to software testing. As explained earlier, software testing consists of a difficult search for solutions in an open search-space. GA is a mechanism to explore this space in a consist, impartial, and systematic way. A GA approach may remove the partiality of currently software testing techniques that rely on the knowledge of a software-testing expert. Section 4 describes the use of GAs in testing.

3.2 Swarm Intelligence

In nature, we find examples of intelligence being revealed at the group level in species with limited cognitive capacity, such as ants, bees and termites. This type of intelligence is called Swarm Intelligence (SI) and it has been extensively studied [3, 9]. SI is an area of research that has shown efficiency in dealing with distributed problems where the solution space of the problem is large. In SI, agents are not aware of the entire problem but are only programmed to do simple actions that (maybe) contribute to the solution of the problem. The joint action of these agents and their interactions causes the emergence of a solution to the problem.

In insects colonies, the indirect communication through stigmergy is very common. In this type of communication, the agent behavior modifies the environment, which, in a feedback loop, influences the behavior of the insects. For example, ants use pheromone to indicate paths to food sources while other ants use this information to stochastically decide their own paths.

There are several metaphors in swarm intelligence that may be used to improve the automation of software testing. In particular, we could use an approach based on alarm pheromone [10] to ensure that a set of test cases is tested by distributed tools. This could take the form of ants (representing testing tools) that explore a terrain (space of test cases to be executed) making test cases already tested less attractive to the ants. The emergent behavior of such action is that ants would be spread across the space of cases. At the same time, one can apply a negative feedback in test cases that have been executed a long time ago so that they gradually become more attractive to the ants.

4 Nature-Inspired Test Automation

The obvious question is whether the approaches described above can yield good test cases and good testing tools. In this section we discuss the use of the ideas and how they can be combined for form an interesting automated tool.

The occurrence of a defect in a software application is directly proportional to the level of inconsistency the state of the application is in. This means that when an error occurs in an application it was not necessarily the last operation, ℓ, executed in the application that caused the defect; it may have been a sequence of previously executed operations that caused the application to be in an inconsistent state by the time ℓ was executed. Our premise is that an application has a state of inconsistency ϕ_i which is non-decreasing as operations $,\ell_i,$ are executed. Or in other words, for any sequence of operations, $\phi_i \leq \phi_{i+1}$. This means that every transition t from operation ℓ_i to ℓ_{i+1}, written as $t(\ell_i \rightarrow \ell_{i+1})$, adds to the state of inconsistency of the application. In these lines, the goal of software testing is to minimize $t(\ell_j \rightarrow \ell_k), \forall j, k$.

Given the definition above, we can assign values to each possible transition in a software system to represent the contribution of that transition to the degree of inconsistency of the application. Clearly, this is a biased approach that should be avoided in practice – we require an expert to define how problematic a particular transition is. Still, we are using this here because the bias does not affect what we are trying to demonstrate: that approaches such as GA can be used to evolve good test cases. Table 1 shows the representation of the transition values.

Table 1. Representation of the assigned values for inconsistency added by each transition. For instance $t(\ell_2 \to \ell_3) = v_{3,2}$.

	ℓ_1	ℓ_2	ℓ_3	$\cdots$	ℓ_n
ℓ_1	$v_{1,1}$	$v_{1,2}$	$v_{1,3}$	$\cdots$	$v_{1,n}$
ℓ_2	$v_{2,1}$	$v_{2,2}$	$v_{2,3}$	$\cdots$	$v_{2,n}$
ℓ_3	$v_{3,1}$	$v_{3,2}$	$v_{3,3}$	$\cdots$	$v_{3,n}$
$\vdots$	$\vdots$	$\vdots$	$\vdots$	$\ddots$	$\vdots$
ℓ_n	$v_{n,1}$	$v_{n,2}$	$v_{n,3}$	$\cdots$	$v_{n,n}$

Given a transition table as the one in Table 1 we can define a fitness function, f_s, for a test case (sequence of instructions) $s = \ell_1, \ell_2, ..., \ell_k$ as $f_s = \sum_i^{k-1} t(\ell_i \to \ell_{i+1})$. This indicates that the larger the value of f_s the better the sequence is considered given that it is more likely to take the application to an inconsistent state. GA can now be used to evolve a population of sequences of a fixed size into an individual that is close to a maximum value for f_s. The resulting sequence is generated as part of an automated process in which experts do not play a role in the sequence (except for the definition of the transition table).

What is important here is that this is just a (perhaps naïve) example of a fitness function. Functions based on other factors may be used to generate a test case. In fact, in a more elaborate use of GAs, the transition table itself can be updated in a feedback loop based on the result of the execution of the test case (as described later in Figure 1). That is, it may be possible to initialize the transition table with the same value for all cells (or random values for each cell) and upon the execution of a sequence that did not cause problem the values for all transitions that are part of the sequence can be decreased by a certain percentage causing the table to slowly converge to a configuration where the values do really indicate the contribution each transition is adding to the inconsistency of the application.

SI (as described in Section 3.2) may also be used to generate test sequences based on a structure similar to Table 1. Ants (agents) may be programmed to traverse a transition table. The agents would make transitions less important (via negative feedback) each time a transition from one operation to another is traversed. Similarly, each time a transition presents problem, its value may be positively reinforced to influence agents to generate test cases including that transition.

The NATUS project explores SI for a different purpose. Once good test cases are generated using GAs, one still have to prioritize their execution. Note that this is not a question of just listing the cases and testing from the beginning of the list to the end because this may not give us a diverse list of cases being tested (assuming that not all cases can be tested in the time frame available for testing). Basically, a space of test cases generated by the GA can be explored by ants (testing tools) where the higher the fitness value of the sequence the more likely it is to be executed. In a process opposite to ant foraging and inspired in alarm pheromones [10], the ants can make locations in the environment (test-cases) less desirable as they select the cases. This makes the ants (testing tools) more inclined to choose tests that have not yet been executed. The obvious question here is why not choose from the list of test cases deterministically? This approach is possible and should be done if the number of test cases is small or one has enough time to execute all test cases. However, when testing large applications, it is not necessarily true that the execution based on a deterministic order will provide us with a subset of test cases that is diverse enough (cover most transitions). Also, one need to understand that important test cases (according to the fitness value) may be executed and indeed cause problems in the application. This test continues to be open for re-test and should continue to be considered according to its fitness value (or even with an increased fitness value). The use of positive feedback can be used to reinforce the fitness value of such test cases, thus attracting more ants to explore that case again.

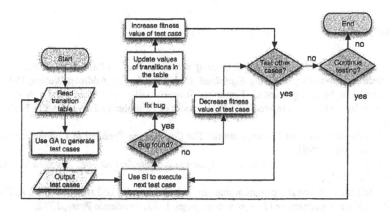

Fig. 1. A flow of a testing tool that utilizes the GA and SI approaches described earlier

5 Conclusion

This paper discussed automation in software testing and explored the idea that testing can be seen as an optimization problem. The paper argues that an efficient and effective software testing tool can be devised from GAs and SI. These are scientific approaches that have already been proved to work in problems where solutions need to be found in a large space of candidates.

Figure 1 summarizes all the automation process this paper proposed. In a nutshell, *(i)* a transition table is created (as in Table 1) which indicates a degree of inconsistency added by pairwise operations; *(ii)* a GA uses the table to generate test cases (sequence of operations) according to a fitness function; *(iii)* a SI algorithm explores the set of test cases (by executing them) and updates the transition table and the fitness value of the executed test depending on the occurrence of a bug in the test case – if a bug is found and the problem fixed, the transition which caused the problem has its degree of inconsistency decreased and the test case itself has its fitness value increased (as it is still attractive to testing tools). The execution of this process yields a fully automated testing process.

As part of the NATUS project, we are currently working on a prototype of a tool as described in Figure 1 – preliminary results look promising. The current results are for the GA part of the algorithm and are based on non-real-world values for the transition table. Our future work we propose to explore a real-world application and implement the SI part of the proposed automated process. On the SI front we are developing a model for the alarm pheromone which we intend to use as part of our proposed automation process.

References

1. A.-L. Barabási. *Linked: The New Science of Networks*. Perseus Publishing, 2002.
2. K. Beck. *Extreme Programming Explained: Embrace Change*. Addison-Wesley, 1999.
3. E. Bonabeau, M. Dorigo, and G. Theraulaz. *Swarm Intelligence: From Natural to Artificial Systems*. Santa Fe Institute Studies in the Sciences of Complexity Series. Oxford Press, July 1999.
4. R. Boyer and J. Strother-Moore, editors. *The Correctness Problem in Computer Science*. Academic Press, 1981.
5. C. Darwin. *On the Origin of Species: A facsimile of the first edition*. Harvard University Press, July 1975.
6. E. W. Dijkstra. Structured programming. In O.-J. Dahl, E. W. Dijkstra, and C. A. R. Hoare, editors, *Notes on Structured Programming*, pages 1–82. Academic Press, 1972.
7. J. B. Goodenough and S. L. Gerhart. Toward a theory of test data selection. In *Proceedings of the international conference on Reliable software*, pages 493–510, 1975.
8. J. H. Holland. *Adpatation in Natural and Artificial Systems*. University of Michigan Press, Ann Arbor, MI, 1975.
9. J. Kennedy and R. C. Eberhart. *Swarm Intelligence*. Morgan Kaufmann, 2001.
10. C. Lloyd. The alarm pheronones of social insects: A review. Technical report, Colorado State University, 2003.
11. C. E. Williams. Software testing and uml. In *Proceedings of the 10th International Symposium on Software Reliability Engineering*, Boca Raton, Florida, Nov. 1999. IEEE Press.

Fast Video Object Tracking using Affine Invariant Normalization

Paraskevi Tzouveli, Yannis Avrithis and Stefanos Kollias

National Technical University of Athens
Electrical and Computer Engineering Department
Iroon Polytexneiou 9, 15780, Athens, Greece
email: (tpar,kntal)@image.ntua.gr

Abstract. One of the most common problems in computer vision and image processing applications is the localization of object boundaries in a video frame and its tracking in the next frames. In this paper, a fully automatic method for fast tracking of video objects in a video sequence using affine invariant normalization is proposed. Initially, the detection of a video object is achieved using a GVF snake. Next, a vector of the affine parameters of each contour of the extracted video object in two successive frames is computed using affine-invariant normalization. Under the hypothesis that these contours are similar, the affine transformation between the two contours is computed in a very fast way. Using this transformation to predict the position of the contour in the next frame allows initialization of the GVF snake very close to the real position. Applying this technique to the following frames, a very fast tracking technique is achieved. Moreover, this technique can be applied on sequences with very fast moving objects where traditional trackers usually fail. Results on synthetic sequences are presented which illustrate the theoretical developments.

1 Introduction

Object tracking is a very common problem in computer vision and image processing applications. The localization of object boundaries in a video frame and its tracking in the next frames [1],[2],[8]-[13] is a crucial issue in the materialization of a tracking method. It is therefore important and challenging to develop an approach to track objects under geometric transformations. Such an approach can allow the tracking of fast moving objects.

In this paper, a fully automatic method for fast tracking of video objects in a video sequence using affine invariant normalization is proposed. Initially, the detection of a video object is achieved using a GVF snake [3], [5]. Next, a vector of the affine parameters of each contour of the extracted video object in two successive

Please use the following format when citing this chapter:

Tzouveli, Paraskevi, Avrithis, Yannis, Kollias, Stefanos, 2006, in IFIP International Federation for Information Processing, Volume 204, Artificial Intelligence Applications and Innovations, eds. Maglogiannis, I., Karpouzis, K., Bramer, M., (Boston: Springer), pp. 549–556

frames is computed using affine-invariant normalization [6]. Under the hypothesis that these contours are similar, the affine transformation between the two contours is computed in a very fast way.

Using this transformation to predict the position of the contour in the next frame allows initialization of the GVF snake very close to the real position. Applying this technique to the following frames, a very fast tracking technique is achieved. Moreover, this technique can be applied on sequences with very fast moving objects where traditional trackers usually fail. Results on synthetic sequences are presented which illustrate the theoretical developments.

2 Problem Statement

The basic idea in active contour models or snakes is to evolve a curve, subject to constraints from a given image, in order to detect objects in that image [4]. For instance, starting with a curve around the object to be detected, the curve moves toward its interior normal and has to stop on the boundary of the object. Usually, using the contour of the previous frame, we can estimate the contour of the object of the next frame.

However, the main drawback of the active contours methods is the position estimation of the object contour if it is moved very fast. If the object is fast the contour can not be estimated and can be lost for the rest frames of the sequence. In addition, active contours methods still suffer from the sensitive of initial parameters while the computation is an expensive process which makes difficult the implementation of active contours in real time applications.

On the other hand, the active contours can also be initialized across the object boundary and if the initialization is closed to the real boundary, the object boundary is quickly localised. Our method uses this feature of active contours, having an initialization contour very close to the object boundary. The initialization contour can be acquired applying the proposed affine normalization transformation (Section 5) to the previous contour of a video sequence, in order to compute the initialization of the next contour. The initialization of the next contour can be applied very quickly, providing an accurate estimation of the object contour of the next frame.

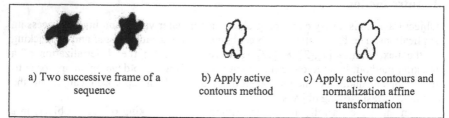

| a) Two successive frame of a sequence | b) Apply active contours method | c) Apply active contours and normalization affine transformation |

Figure 1: Finding the contour of next frame knowing the previous contour

Figure 1a depicts two successive frames of a fast moving object of a video sequence. The contour is shown as dash line in Figure 1b and 1c image depicts the estimation of the next contour knowing the previous contour. It is obvious (Figure 1b) that using only an active contour method taking as input the contour of the previous frame, the estimation of the object is not accurate. Figure 1c represents the estimation of the contour according to affine normalization transformation and it is very close to the real contour of the object. This simple example proves that the proposed method can be used for very fast moving video objects tracking.

3 Active Contours and Gradient Vector Flow

The automatic localization of objects of interest in an image or video sequence is a challenging task. Objects of interest are presented in many techniques with active contours [3]-[5]. In the proposed method, we use the GVF snake [5] in order to extract the objects of interest from a video sequence (Video Object) and accelerate the proposed VO tracking procedure.

The basic idea in active contour models is to evolve a curve, subject to constraints from a given image, in order to detect objects in it. Starting with this curve within the image domain and moving it under the influence of internal and external forces derived from image data, we can acquire the boundaries of the objects of interest.

A new external force for active contours, called Gradient Vector Flow, has been proposed in [5], trying to tackle problems that are associated, with initialization and poor convergence, to boundary concavities. The GVF snake begins with the calculation of a field of forces, called the GVF forces, over the image domain. The GVF forces are used to drive the snake, modeled as a physical object having a resistance to both stretching and bending, toward the boundaries of the object.

The GVF forces are calculated by applying generalized diffusion equations to both components of the gradient of an image edge map. Because the GVF forces are derived from a diffusion operation, they tend to extend very far away from the object so that snakes can find objects that are quite far away from the snake's initial position. This same diffusion creates forces which can pull active contours into concave regions.

4 Affine invariant normalization

Normalization is a procedure that enables comparison between different images of the same object, as well as of different objects, since distances are always measured in a normalized frame [7],[7] and [12]. In the proposed method, affine-invariant normalization is applied to the object curves in order to make them affine invariant, and thus appropriate for curves matching. For this purpose, a set of transformations is applied to each point of the contour composing the object curve.

For the sake of simplicity, let us assume a synthetic video sequence, the first frame of which is depicted in Figure 2. Figure 1 also illustrates its contour which has been extracted using GVF snake (section 2).

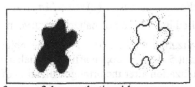

Figure 2: First frame of the synthetic video sequence and its contour

Firstly, the obtained contour is re-sampled in order to be constituted of a fixed number of equidistant points without losing its original shape. Equation 1 represents the N points of the contour of the kth frame of the synthetic sequence:

$$c_k = [x_i, y_i]^T, \quad i = 0,1,\dots N-1, \quad k = 1,2\dots K \quad \text{(Eq.1)}$$

For each contour, the (p-q) order moments are given by Eq. 2:

$$m_{pq}(c) = \frac{1}{N} \sum_{i=0}^{N-1} (x_i^p y_j^q) \quad \text{(Eq. 2)}$$

Moments of order up to two are used for the construction of the normalized curve. The orthogonalization procedure comprises a set of linear operations (translation, scaling, and rotation) that do not depend on the selected starting point of the closed curve. The orthogonalization of the curve can be acquired:

$$n_a(c) = R_2 \cdot B \cdot R_1 \cdot A \cdot (c-T) \quad \text{(Eq. 3)}$$

where $T = \begin{bmatrix} \mu_x \\ \mu_y \end{bmatrix} = \begin{bmatrix} m_{10}(c) \\ m_{01}(c) \end{bmatrix}$ is the translation of the initial resample curve,

$A = \begin{bmatrix} \sigma_{1x} & 0 \\ 0 & \sigma_{1y} \end{bmatrix} = \begin{bmatrix} 1/m_{20}(c_I)^{1/2} & 0 \\ 0 & 1/m_{02}(c_I)^{1/2} \end{bmatrix}$ is the scaling factor which is

applied to the translated curve, while $R_1 = \begin{bmatrix} \sin(r_{1x_2}) & -\cos(r_{1y_2}) \\ \cos(r_{1x_2}) & \sin(r_{1y_2}) \end{bmatrix}$ is the rotation

factor applied to the curve, already scaled using factor σ_1. In the proposed method,

$r_1 = \pi/4$. The matrix $B = \begin{bmatrix} \sigma_{2x} & 0 \\ 0 & \sigma_{2y} \end{bmatrix} = \begin{bmatrix} 1/m_{20}(c_{II})^{1/2} & 0 \\ 0 & 1/m_{02}(c_{II})^{1/2} \end{bmatrix}$ denotes

the second scaling factor, applied in the curve after the counterclockwise by $\pi/4$

rotation while $R_2 = \begin{bmatrix} \sin(r_{2x_4}) & -\cos(r_{2y_4}) \\ \cos(r_{2x_4}) & \sin(r_{2y_4}) \end{bmatrix}$ is the rotation matrix, applied to the

curve, already scaled using the factor σ_2 with $r_2 = [(a_1 + a_{N-1})/2] \mod \pi$ (where $a_1 = (x_1, y_1)$ and $a_{N-1} = (x_{N-1}, y_{N-1})$ the average value of Fourier phases).

At this point we have achieved the reduction of affine transformations to orthogonal ones and we need a transformation invariant to rotation and reflection. The overall normalization (orthogonalization and normalization) is now affine invariant and the starting point normalization is necessary since the rotation normalization depends on the starting point. Thus, a standard circular shift is defined using the first and last Fourier phases: $p(z) = [(N/4\pi) \cdot (a_1 - a_{N-1})] \mod (N/2)$ and the opposite shift is applied in order to normalize the curve $n_p(z) = S_{-p(z)}(z)$.

The presented normalization method transforms the object contours in order to make them affine invariant 5. To sum up, an affine normalization of a contour can be achieved applying normalization after the orthogonalization of the contour:

$$n_p(n_a(c)) = S_{-p}(R_2 \cdot B \cdot R_1 \cdot A \cdot (c-T)) = S(R_2 \cdot B \cdot R_1 \cdot A \cdot (c-T), -p) \quad \text{(Eq. 4)}$$

5   Tracking VO using normalization affine transformation

The tracking method that we propose in this section provides a fully automatic affine invariant method for fast tracking video object in a video sequence. Initially, a GVF snake is implemented in the first frame of the sequence in order to provide an initial estimation of the video object contours (c_1). Having as pattern for the GVF snake the contour of first frame of the video sequence, the contour c_2, of the second frame can then be acquired.

In the next step, applying affine normalization (Eq. 4) to each contour, the $a_1(c_1) = n_p(n_a(c_1))$ and $a_2(c_2) = n_p(n_a(c_2))$ for contour c_1 and c_2 respectively, is obtained. Now, we can define the vector of normalized affine parameters which can be represented as $P = \{D, g, s\}$ where $D = R_2 \cdot B \cdot R_1 \cdot A$ is the rotation-scaling deformation matrix while parameter $g = -D \cdot T$ represents the video object translation and $s = -p$ is a shifting parameter. The overall normalization affine is:

$$a(c) = n_p(n_a(c)) = S((Dc + g), -s) \quad \text{(Eq.5)}$$

After normalization of each contour of the first two sequential video objects, accepting that these contours are almost equal, we can assume that

$$a_1(c_1) = a_2(c_2) \xrightarrow{\text{Eq.5}} S(D_1c_1 + g_1), -s_1) = S(D_2c_2 + g_2), -s_2)$$

$$\Rightarrow D_2c_2 + g_2 = S(S(D_1c_1 + g_1), s_1 - s_2)$$

$$\Rightarrow c_2 = D_2^{-1} \cdot (S((D_1c_1 + g_1), s_1 - s_2) - D_2^{-1}g_2) \text{ with } D_2 \neq 0$$

$$\Rightarrow c_2 = \cdot S((D_2^{-1}D_1c_1 - D_2^{-1}(g_1 - g_2)), s_1 - s_2)) \quad \text{(Eq.6)}$$

Now, we can define the transformation:

$$a_2^{-1} \circ a_1 = \left\{ D_2^{-1}D_1, \ g_1 - g_2, \ s_1 - s_2 \right\} = a_{1 \to 2} \quad \text{(Eq. 7)}$$

Eq.7 will be examined in order to verify that knowing the previous contour, the computation of the next contour of the video object is possible by applying this transformation. For this purpose, the steps of our algorithm are presented.

The algorithm requires, as input, the contours of the video object contained in the first and second frame. It can be computed applying a GVF snake to the first and second frame of the video sequence.

Then, the affine normalization (Eq. 4) is applied to the first and second frame contour, taking $a_1(c_1) = n_p(n_a(c_1))$ and $a_2(c_2) = n_p(n_a(c_2))$ respectively. The vectors of normalized affine parameters of the video object from first and second frame can now be computed: $P_1 = \{D_1, g_1, s_1\}$ and $P_2 = \{D_2, g_2, s_2\}$.

Having the vectors P_1, P_2 of normalized affine parameters, the transformation $a_2^{-1} \circ a_1$ can be computed using Eq. 7.

Supposing that the contour of the video object of the third frame, follows approximately the same transformation ($a_{1 \to 2}$) as the first and second contour, the application of this transformation places the contour of the third video object close enough to the real position. Then, applying a GVF snake which takes as input the contour that has been achieved applying the transformation to the second contour, the right estimation of the third contour can be achieved very quickly:

$c_3 \approx s(a_{1\rightarrow2}(c_2))$ (Eq.8)

Having the next contour c_3 the transformation $a_{2\rightarrow3}(c_3)$ is computed. Then, applying the GVF snake to the next video frame a very close estimation of the video object boundary that the fourth frame included can be achieved $c_4 \approx s(a_{2\rightarrow3}(c_3))$.

Following the same procedure for the next frame c_i, the transformation $a_{i-1\rightarrow i}(c_i)$ for the video object of next frame is computed and estimation of the position of the next video object is calculated applying the GVF snake $s(a_{i-1\rightarrow i}(c_i))$.

Applying the proposed method to the following frames, a fast tracking technique can be achieved. The method discussed in this paper was tested on several video sequences with very fast moving objects and a series of experiments has been performed. Firstly, the accuracy of the affine normalization method is examined using a synthetic video sequence.

Figure 3 illustrates the first five successive frames of a synthetic video sequence. The video object of the second frame has been rotated by $\varphi = 30°$ while in third frame it has been translated. In fourth frame the video object has been scaled by 5% and in the last frame it has been rotated by $\varphi' = -30°$ and translated.

Figure 3: Synthetic video sequence

According to the proposed method, using the GVF snake method, the contours of the first two frames can be extracted. Then, we compute the vectors P_1, P_2 of normalized affine parameters as well as the transformation $a_{1\rightarrow2} = a_2^{-1} \circ a_1$. In order to measure the similarity between curves $c_i = s(a_{i-2\rightarrow i-1}(c_{i-1}))$ $i \geq 3$ and c_{real_i}, we use the Euclidean distance is used. The value of similarity of the contours approaches 97%.

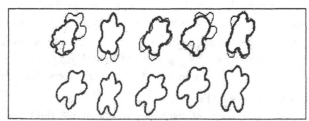

Figure 4: Fast video object tracking with or without affine invariant normalization

In Figure 4, $c_i = s(c_{i-1})$ is depicted with a dash-line in first line using only GVF snake while the estimation of $c_i = s(a_{i-2 \to i-1}(c_{i-1}))$ is depicted in the second line with a dash-line contour too. It is obvious that the estimation of the contours which uses GVF snake and affine normalization is closer to thin-line c_{real_i} that uses only GVF snake.

The result that the comparison between the proposed method and the GVF snake method gives is depicted in Figure 5. It can be seen that our algorithm reduces the number of GVF snake iteration more than 60%. In this experiment are used twenty successive frames of the synthetic video sequence.

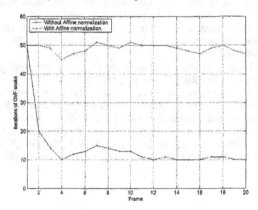

Figure 5: Iterations of GVF snake with and without affine normalization

6   Conclusion

In this paper, we have proposed a method for tracking using affine invariant normalization for very fast moving objects. The video object detection for the two first successive frames is achieved using a GVF snake. Next, using affine-invariant normalization, a vector of the affine parameters of each extracted video object is computed. Assuming that these contours are similar, we compute the affine transformation between these contours. Using this transformation to predict the position of the contour in the next frame allows initialization of the GVF snake very close to the real position. Experimental results suggest that our algorithm have great potential for tracking video objects with very fast moving objects where traditional trackers usually fail.

References

1. J. Guo, J. Kim, and C. Kuo, "An interactive object segmentation system for MPEG video," IEEE Proceedings of International Conference on Image Processing, Kobe, Japan, 1999.
2. C. Gu and M. Lee, "Semiautomatic segmentation and tracking of semantic video objects," IEEE Trans. Circuits and Systems for Video Technology, Vol. 8, No. 5, pp.574-584, September, 1998.
3. M. Kass, A. Witkin, and D. Terzopoulos, "Snakes: Active Contour models," Int'l J. Computer Vision, vol. 1, pp. 312-333, 1988.

4. H. S. Ip and S. Dinggang, "An Affine-Invariant Active Contour Model (AI-Snake) for Model-Based Segmentation," Image and Vision Computing, 16(2), pp. 135-146, 1998.
5. C. Xu and J.L.Prince, "Gradient Vector Flow: A New External Force for Snakes" IEEE Proceedings Conference on Computer Vision and Pattern Recognition, pp 66-71, 1997
6. Y. Avrithis, Y.Xirouhakis, S. Kollias, "Affine-invariant curve normalization for object shape representation, classification, and retrieval," Machine Vision and Applications, 13, pp. 80-94, 2001.
7. Y.S. Abu-Mostafa and D. Psaltis, "Image Normalization by Complex Moments," IEEE Trans. Pattern Analysis and Machine Intelligence vol. 7, pp. 46-55, Jan. 1985.
8. F. Leymarie and M. D. Levine, "Tracking deformable objects in the plane using an active contour model," IEEE Trans. Pattern Anal. Machine Intell., vol. 15, pp. 617–634, 1993
9. A. Blake, M. Isard and D. Reynard, "Learning to track the visual motion of contours", Journal of Artificial Intelligence, vol. 10, pp. 323-380, 1997
10. C. Tomasi T. Kanade "Shape and Motion from Image Streams: a Factorization Method", Full Report on the Orthographic Case, March 1992, Cornell TR 92-1270 and Carnegie Mellon CMU-CS-92-104A.
11. J. Shi and C. Tomasi, "Good features to track", IEEE Proceedings Conference on Computer Vision and Pattern Recognition, pp 593-600, 1994.
12. Y. Avrithis, Y. Xirouhakis and S. Kollias, "Affine-Invariant Curve Normalization for Shape-Based Retrieval, " in Proc. of 15th International Conference on Pattern Recognition (ICPR '00), Barcelona, Spain, September 2000, pp. 1015-1018.
13. Y. Xirouhakis, Y. Avrithis and S. Kollias, "Image Retrieval and Classification Using Affine Invariant B-Spline Representation and Neural Networks," in Proc. of IEE Colloquium on Neural Nets and Multimedia, London, UK, October 1998, pp. 4/1-4/4.

Knowledge Acquisition from Multimedia Content using an Evolution Framework

D. Kosmopoulos, S. Petridis, I. Pratikakis, V. Gatos, S. Perantonis,
V. Karkaletsis, G. Paliouras

Computational Intelligence Laboratory,
Institute of Informatics and Telecommunications
National Centre for Scientific Research "Demokritos",
15310 Aghia Paraskevi Attikis, Athens, Greece
{dkosmo,petridis,ipratika,bgat,sper,vangelis,paliourg}@iit.demokritos.gr

Abstract. We propose an approach to knowledge acquisition, which uses multimedia ontologies for fused extraction of semantics from multiple modalities, and feeds back the extracted information, aiming to evolve knowledge representation. This paper presents the basic components of the proposed approach and discusses the open research issues focusing on the fused information extraction that will enable the development of scalable and precise knowledge acquisition technology.

1 Introduction

The main goal of multimedia content analysis is the automated extraction of indices describing the document content. The high complexity that characterises the multimedia content along with the currently prevailing dearth of precise modelling for multimedia concepts makes automatic semantics extraction a very difficult and challenging task. Although latest advances in multimedia content analysis have improved capabilities for effective searching and filtering, a gap still remains between low-level feature descriptions that can be automatically extracted such as colours, textures, shapes, motions, and so forth, and high-level semantic descriptions of concepts like objects, scenes and events that set the basis for meaningful multimedia content description. A suitable approach to bridge this gap is to use a semantic model in the extraction process. Moreover, the analysis of single modalities, in particular of visual content alone, is inadequate in all but a small number of restricted cases. The effort required to provide problem-specific extraction tools makes single-media solutions non-scalable, while their precision is also rarely adequate.

The proposed approach, which is envisaged in the framework of the IST project BOEMIE, is unique in that it links multimedia extraction with ontology evolution, creating a synergy of enormous yet unrealized potential. Driven by domain-specific

Please use the following format when citing this chapter:

Kosmopoulos, Dimitrios, Petridis, Sergios, Pratikakis, Ioannis, Gatos, Vassileios, Perantonis, Stavros, Karkaletsis, Vangelis, Paliouras, Georgios, 2006, in IFIP International Federation for Information Processing, Volume 204, Artificial Intelligence Applications and Innovations, eds. Maglogiannis, I., Karpouzis, K., Bramer, M., (Boston: Springer), pp. 557–565

multimedia ontologies, the information extraction systems implementing the proposed approach will be able to identify high-level semantic features in image, video, audio and text, and fuse these features for optimal extraction. The ontologies will be continuously populated and enriched using the extracted semantic content. This is a bootstrapping process, since the enriched ontologies will in turn be used to drive the multimedia information extraction system.

This work provides the key ideas involved in the whole system and then focuses on the semantics extraction from multimodal features. Section 2 highlights the related research. Section 3 presents the main aspects of the proposed approach, the architecture designed for its implementation and the basic components of the architecture. Section 4 outlines the semantic extraction approach and section 5 provides an application scenario we are currently examining for the evaluation of the proposed approach. Section 5 discusses some of the issues that arise under this bootstrapping framework and need to be searched. The paper concludes by presenting our next steps.

2   State of the art

The proposed approach towards the automation of knowledge acquisition from multimedia content, through ontology evolution, is based on the synergy of various technologies. This section highlights the state of the art of the technologies involved.

2.1   Semantics extraction from multimedia content

Semantics extraction from multimedia content is the process of assigning conceptual labels to either complete multimedia documents or entities identified therein. In general, extraction can be performed at three different levels:

- Layout: the syntactic structure an author uses for multimedia documents (camera shots, audio segments, text syntax).
- Content: relates layout segments to elements that an author uses to create in a multimedia document (e.g. setting, objects, humans …).
- Semantics: expresses the intended meaning of the author.

In the case where content is available in multiple related modalities, these can be combined for the extraction of semantics. The combination of modalities may serve as a verification method, a method compensating for inaccuracies, or as an additional information source [5]. The processing cycle of combination methods may be iterated allowing for incremental use of context. The major open issues in the combination approaches concern the efficient utilization of prior knowledge, the specification of open architecture for the integration of information from multiple sources and the use of inference tools for efficient retrieval.

Most of the multimedia extraction approaches encountered in the literature are based on learning methods, e.g. naive Bayes classifiers, decision tree induction, k-Nearest neighbor, Hidden Markov model [9], [12].

2.2   Multimedia Ontologies

Ontologies can play a major role in multimedia content interpretation because they can provide high-level semantic information that helps disambiguating the

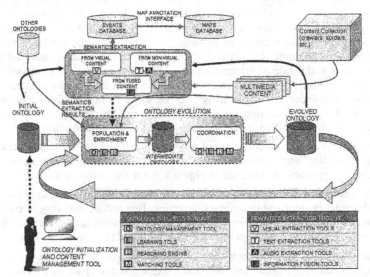

Figure 1. Architecture of the integrated system

labels assigned to multimedia objects. Indicative approaches for constructing multimedia ontologies are the ones presented in [7], [11] [13]. The major open issues here concern the automatic mapping between low level audio-visual features and high level domain concepts, the automated population from unconstrained content and when there are no metadata attached to the content. In cases of complex domains, multiple ontologies may be present and ontology coordination techniques [4], [8], [6] have to be employed.

2.3 Synergy between information extraction and ontologies

The interaction between information extraction and ontology learning has also been modelled at a methodological level as a bootstrapping process that aims to improve both the conceptual model and the extraction system through iterative refinement, but it is limited to textual content so far and is not fully automated [10], [3].

3 Methodology and architecture

We advocate an ontology-driven multimedia content analysis (semantics extraction from images, video, text, audio/speech) through a novel synergistic method that combines multimedia extraction and ontology evolution in a bootstrapping fashion. This method involving on the one hand, the continuous extraction of knowledge from multimedia content sources in order to populate and enrich the ontologies and, on the other hand, the deployment of these ontologies to enhance the robustness of the multimedia information extraction system.

On the side of ontology evolution, we propose (a) a unified representation for multimedia ontologies and related knowledge, which will link domain-specific concepts with low-level features and structural descriptions and (b) a methodology and a toolkit for ontology evolution to support ontology learning, ontology merging and alignment, semantic inference for consistency maintenance, and ontology management. On the side of information extraction, we propose (a) a methodology and an open architecture for information extraction from multimedia content using data fusion techniques and (b) A toolkit for semantic extraction from multimedia content. Within the extraction architecture, tools will be developed to support extraction from image, audio, video and text, as well as information fusion.

We also propose an open architecture of a system that integrates the components for ontology evolution and semantics extraction in order to realise the synergistic bootstrapping approach. As depicted in Figure 1, the major components are:

- The multimedia ontology which links domain-specific ontologies with multimedia content and descriptor ontologies. This will be evolving through the ontology evolution component. An ontology initialization tool will be developed to provide a friendly user interface for the creation of the initial ontology.

- The semantics extraction component which will provide tools for the analysis of single modalities (visual, text and audio extraction tools) as well as tools for fusing information from multiple media sources (information fusion tools). The whole extraction process will be ontology driven in the sense that the ontology will provide the initial knowledge to the extraction process and will also be used to disambiguate the extraction.

- The ontology evolution component which will use the results of the extraction process to populate the multimedia ontology with instances of the various concepts, to enrich the ontology with new concepts and relations, as well as to coordinate the ontologies composing the multimedia ontology.

4 Semantics extraction toolkit

The semantics extraction toolkit is composed of subsystems that process separate modalities and namely visual (still images or image sequences) and non-visual content (audio and text). The results are fused using ontology-based or probabilistic framework and the results are used for content annotation and ontology evolution.

4.1 Semantics extraction from visual content

Our effort concentrates on the development of a semantics extraction toolkit from visual content including tools for:

- *Scene categorisation,* i.e., to categorize the depicted content into various high level classes, e.g. indoor/outdoor city/landscape, office, corridor, street, etc.). Features to be used are color histograms, color coherence vectors, DCT coefficients, edge direction histograms, edge direction coherence vectors, and motion vectors. Sub-blocks analysis can be employed for independent initial classification of blocks, which will be combined next using reasoning.

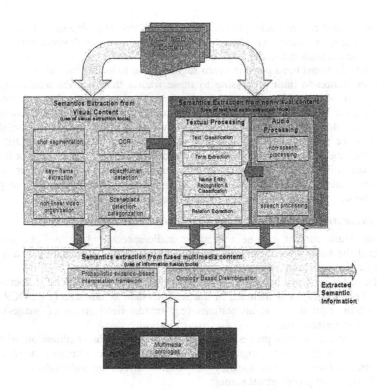

Figure 2 Architecture of the semantics extraction subsystem

- *Video-OCR*, in order to extract as much information as possible about the depicted settings, objects, persons through appropriate name/noun/verb identification.
- *Object detection, recognition and tracking*, mainly through motion analysis and matching with related patterns to differentiate solid objects from deformable ones, e.g., vehicles from humans. Other features used may include skin color or facial features for humans. For tracking, the particle filtering technique may be employed or the MPEG moving object descriptors may be exploited if available. The expected found objects can be significantly reduced by the previous steps.
- *Place recognition*, i.e., recognition of known places based on features that are unique for each place (e.g., landmarks) and based on the results of the previous processing steps.

It is critical to be able to spot independent visual entities either in single images or image sequences. Furthermore, we provide support to the ontological description which will require expressing relations (structural, spatial, temporal) between the visual objects. In light of this need, our methodology focuses on research of tools for automatic image segmentation and video segmentation, which will enable us to partition an image or a sequence of images into meaningful spatial or spatiotemporal objects. In this perspective, all mid-level feature identification are treated in a region-based fashion. Moreover, we use advanced machine learning techniques for recognition and categorization, in order to address various problems that are related to the use case. Semantics are extracted by matching/linking with visual information included in the multimedia ontologies.

Some additional tools perform video segmentation to isolate the video shots, key-frame extraction to limit processing to those frames that describe adequately the content and video organization (in a non-linear fashion) to find similar shots through clustering and to limit processing to shot representatives and to assist user browsing.

To provide a qualitative measure for the visual detectors involved, confidence measures are employed. These measures will be taken into account in BOEMIE's reasoning engine, which will be able to modify the visual detector's confidence scores according to a set of contextual rules and supplementary rules expressed by the corresponding semantic model that determines how likely it is for the given object (or scene) to appear in the given visual content.

4.2 Semantics Extraction from non-visual content

Non-visual content can be textual or audio/speech, which will be used to construct the basis for a meaningful contextual knowledge culminating at a toolkit for semantics extraction from non-visual content.

The text is provided by unstructured (e.g. raw text) or semi-structured documents (e.g. HTML pages) or is included in image/video data as raw data (e.g., OCR text, speech transcriptions) or as annotations (e.g. textual descriptions of images). The effort is concentrated on:

- using available text processing tools and resources in combination with the domain-specific and geographic ontologies of the multimedia ontology to extract information that "localises" the content directly or indirectly, e.g., names of exhibition places, street names;
- extracting semantic information, e.g., in the vehicle exhibition case, extract information such as the event name, event dates, event organisers, exhibitors (vehicle brand names), exhibits (vehicle models) and multimedia related to it.

On the other hand, audio processing is used to extract features from both speech and non-speech audio. The effort here is concentrated on the detection of:

- Environmental sounds for the detection of setting
- Names in speech data to infer references to places of interest

Methodologically, the audio channel is separated into speech and non-speech segments using BIC segmentation and speaker detection. As regards non-speech environmental sounds, a state-of-the-art classification method, based on machine learning, is to be used for the generic automatic construction of (possibly nested) sequences of data transformations (tree-like features). The sound classifier deploys acoustic models of sounds and permits differentiation of different sound sources (applause, laughter) and environments (traffic vs. quiet museum). The speech segments are recognized using a syllable-based speech recognizer for the English language. Since the ontologies providing the basis for feature derivation are evolved throughout the content extraction process, it is critical that the vocabulary of words which are identified by the speech recognition component is dynamic.

4.3 Semantics Extraction from Multimedia Content

Single modalities are not always powerful enough to encompass all aspects of the content and identify concepts precisely. Fusing information from multiple media sources [1] is expected, on one hand, to improve the validity of indices extracted independently from each modality and, on the other, to provide a unifying framework promoting the complementarity of the modalities in respect to different aspects and/or different levels of granularity of the underlying concepts encompassed in the ontology of a (possibly evolving) domain. At the same time, a cross-modality fusion architecture is also expected to naturally bridge the gap between low level mode-specific features and higher level concepts, by facilitating the identification and separation of mode-independent and mode-specific features necessary to capture the ontology concepts.

In particular, fusion techniques are investigated based on:

- Ontology-based disambiguation: The results of the extraction process are used to build hypotheses. These are then matched to information included in the multimedia ontology to build more precise higher-level hypotheses. During this process, conflicts or inconsistencies may be found, prompting the revision of intermediate results, and, possibly, the adjustment of parameters for low-level processing modules to achieve more precise results at higher levels. This is implemented as a closed-loop extraction process.

- Probabilistic evidence-based interpretation framework: The evidence in this case is provided by low-level features and the extracted semantics may belong to intermediate abstraction levels. This thread of thought has been particularly studied in the context of synchronous or quasi-synchronous information streams for audio-visual speech recognition, modelled as variants of HMM [2].

The semantic data is input into the multimedia ontology, which is divided into (a) Multimedia content ontology, which represents content structure (b) Multimedia descriptor ontology, which models concepts and properties that describe visual characteristics of objects including MPEG-7 standard features and (c) Domain-specific ontologies, which contain concepts and properties related to the knowledge of the domain of interest (related application scenario). The multimedia ontology will be then evolved through the mechanisms described in the previous section.

4. Application scenario

The application concerns the enrichment of digital maps with semantic information. The process involves an automatic collection and annotation service for public events in a number of major cities from the Web and proprietary sources. The domain of public events include commercial exhibitions, sport events, concerts etc. The results of the annotation process, i.e., the identified entities and their properties, will be linked to geographical locations and stored in a content server. The user will be provided with immediate access to the annotated content base, through the user-friendly interface of digital maps, which will also provide immediate navigation guidance to the place of interest. The domain-dependent semantic model will be used by the extraction architecture to identify multimedia information related to the concepts in the ontologies. Further, from the extracted information, new concepts will be generated to extend the ontologies, using the evolution architecture.

As a concrete example of the application scenario, consider the domain of vehicle exhibitions, an application that has significant commercial and social interest, while at the same time it is associated with a wealth of complementary multimedia content that is evolving over time. Given such a domain, the following stages will be followed to customize and use the envisaged system (see Fig. 1):

- Initialization: Forming of the initial multimedia semantic model for the domain by collecting and merging existing ontologies for sub-domains, referring for example to car, and motorcycle exhibitions and linking them to multimedia descriptor ontologies, using the ontology initialization and content annotation tool.

- Training: Training of the various semantics extraction and ontology evolution tools to the domain. To that end, a training dataset containing representative and annotated multimedia content will be constructed using the ontology initialization and content annotation tool.

- Information gathering: After customization, the first step of its run-time use is to collect content from various Web and proprietary sources. In the case of car exhibitions, such sources will include TV and news programmes, on-line magazines, the sites or proprietary databases of car suppliers and dealers, specialized discussion fora and Weblogs, as well as generic content sources. Different sources will provide different types of content, which when fused semantics can lead to a rich description of concepts and their instances.

- Semantics extraction: The trained semantics extraction tools will be applied at regular intervals to the incoming stream of multimedia content, performing two parallel tasks: (a) Extracting the relevant information from each piece of content, such as event venue, event dates, event organisers, exhibits and multimedia related to it, exhibitors, etc. Single modalities will be processed separately and then will be fused (b) associating the information to concepts of the ontologies, by identifying their characteristic elements in multimedia content, e.g., terms in the text and audio, objects in visual content, crowd density, indoor/outdoor, etc.

- Ontology evolution: Population of the ontologies with instances of the various concepts, together with their properties (accompanied by annotation). The concept modelling task, performed by the extraction methods, will lead to suggestions for the enrichment of the ontologies, through novelty detection.

- Information positioning and retrieval: The concept instances annotated on the multimedia content will be linked to the map data in the digital maps server. The user will be able to browse content and issue queries about exhibits, events, etc. The results will always be associated to places on the digital map also considering time.

5   Concluding remarks

We proposed a new approach towards automation of knowledge acquisition from multimedia content, by introducing the notion of evolving multimedia ontologies which will be used for the extraction of information from multimedia content. This is a synergistic approach, combining multimedia extraction and ontology evolution in a bootstrapping process involving, on the one hand, the continuous extraction of semantic information from multimedia content in order to populate and enrich the ontologies and, on the other hand, the deployment of these ontologies to improve significantly the performance of existing single-modality approaches in terms of scalability and precision.

In terms of semantics extraction from multimedia content, we propose the integration of an ontology-based approach with a probabilistic inference scheme. We need to examine carefully the role of the ontology in fusing information extracted from multiple media. We will also examine ways to learn optimal multimedia-based feature combinations. Synchronization and alignment of the different modalities is another issue, since all modalities must refer to a common timeline.

Ontologies must be sufficiently expressive in order to describe the construction space for possible interpretations in general and for specific interpretation results in terms of a particular piece of media. Multimedia applications have highlighted the need to extend representation languages with capabilities which allow for the treatment of the inherent imprecision in multimedia object representation, matching, detection and retrieval. Since existing standard web languages do not provide such capabilities, research effort needs to be directed towards representation and management of uncertainty, imprecision that exists in real life applications.

In terms of ontology population and enrichment, we will exploit the multimedia semantic model as well as current research on learning and aiming to develop a generic framework for ontology learning and inference from multimedia content.

References

1. Belur V. Dasarathy, Elucidative fusion systems - an exposition, Information Fusion, Vol 1, pp 5-15, 2000.
2. Samy Bengio, Multimodal speech processing using asynchronous Hidden Markov Models, Information Fusion, Volume 5, pp 81-89, 2004
3. Brewster, F. Ciravegna, and Y. Wilks. User-centred ontology learning for knowledge management. In B. Andersson, M. Bergholtz, and P. Johannesson, editors, NLDB, volume 2553 of Lecture Notes in Computer Science, pages 203–207. Springer, 2002.
4. S. Castano, A. Ferrara, S. Montanelli, and G. Racca, "Matching Techniques for Resource Discovery in Distributed Systems Using Heterogeneous Ontology Descriptions", IEEE Proc. of the International Conference on Coding and Computing, Las Vegas, USA, 2004
5. Cees G.M. Snoek, M. Worring Multimodal Video Indexing: A Review of the State-of-the-art Multimedia Tools and Applications, 25, 5–35, 2005
6. OntoWeb. Deliverable D1.3. A survey on ontology tools, 2002 (ed. Gómez Pérez)
7. J. Hunter, "Adding Multimedia to the Semantic Web - Building an MPEG-7 Ontology", International Semantic Web Working Symposium (SWWS), Stanford, 2001
8. K. Kotis, G. Vouros. HCONE approach to Ontology Merging. ESWS'04. The Semantic Web: Research and Applications, LNCS, Vol. 3053, Springer-Verlag, (2004)
9. C.D. Manning and H. Schutze, Foundations of Statistical Natural Language Processing. The MIT Press, Cambridge, USA, 1999.
10. A Maedche and S. Staab. Mining ontologies from text. In R.Dieng and O.Corby, editors, EKAW, vol. 1937, Lecture Notes in Computer Science, pp. 189–202. Springer, 2000.
11. V.Mezaris, I.Kompatsiaris, N.V.Boulgouris and M.G.Strintzis: "Real-time compressed domain spatiotemporal segmentation and ontologies for video indexing and retrieval", IEEE Transactions on Circuits and Systems for Video Technology, Special Issue on Audio and Video Analysis for Multimedia Interactive Services, vol. 14, pp. 606-621, May 2004.
12. L.R. Rabiner, A tutorial on hidden markov models and selected applications in speech recognition, Proceedings of the IEEE, Vol. 77, No. 2, pp. 257–286, 1989.
13. R. Troncy, "Integrating Structure and Semantics into Audio-Visual Documents", In the second International Semantic Web Conference, LNCS 2870, pp. 566-581, 2003.

Exploratory Search: Image Retrieval without Deep Semantics

John I. Tait

School of Computing and Technology, University of Sunderland, St. Peter's
Campus, Sunderland Sr6 0DD, UK
John.Tait@sunderland.ac.uk

Abstract. This paper relates semantics as it is used in linguistics and natural
language processing to the operational requirements of image retrieval
systems. This is done in the context of a model of exploratory search and
image annotation or indexing. The paper concludes this operational context
requires the use of a restricted form of semantics compared with the usual one
from linguistics or natural language processing, focussing on words rather
sentences.

1 Introduction

Semantics is a notoriously difficult topic. Within Linguistics, on which most work in
computerised Natural Language Processing (NLP) rests, it is often all but impossible
to draw clear distinctions between syntax, semantic, and pragmatics let alone define
the content of semantics alone.

However, this is not a doctrine of despair: in this paper I want to show how
within a given operational context the general problems of semantics can be avoided,
or at least restricted to the extent they are solvable in the medium term.

More generally I want to look at the task of retrieving still images from
databases. I will attempt to show how restricting ourselves to this task allows us to
avoid such general and difficult questions as "what does this image mean?" which I
believe are the root of much of the difficulty with the notion of semantics.

By both recognising that the real issues relate to operations involving humans
(not abstract ones involving computers alone) and recognising that at some point this
allows a human understanding (or subjective semantics if you will) to be brought to
bear on the operational task at hand, one can focus on much more tractable questions
like "Is this image relevant to the ends of this person at this time?". This can be
explored in a framework of exploratory search

Please use the following format when citing this chapter:

Tait, John, 2006, in IFIP International Federation for Information Processing, Volume 204, Artificial
Intelligence Applications and Innovations, eds. Maglogiannis, I., Karpouzis, K., Bramer, M., (Boston:
Springer), pp. 566–574

The paper begins with a brief overview of the use of the term semantics in Linguistics and NLP. The idea of exploratory search is then introduced, developed using a model and related to recent developments in image annotation. The paper concludes with an attempt to bring together the implicit notions of *semantics* inherent in exploratory search and image annotation with the linguistic notion of semantics previously introduced.

2. Semantics in Linguistics and NLP

Semantics is of course the study of meaning.

James Allen in his classic text book [1] identified seven kinds of knowledge relevant to natural language understanding (including speech): phonetic and phonological; morphological; syntactic; semantic; pragmatic; discourse; and world knowledge. Syntactic knowledge:

"concerns how words can be put together to form correct sentences and determines what structural role each word plays in the sentence and what phrases are subparts of what other phrases" (p10)

whereas semantic knowledge:

"concerns what words mean and how these meanings combine in sentences to form sentence meanings. This is the study of context-independent meaning – the meaning a sentence has regardless of the context in which it is used." (p10)

Note the emphasis Allen places on word meaning and the way they combine presumably constrained and driven through the syntactic constructions in which they appear.

Even within this constrained notion of (linguistic) semantics there are further complications. Leech [17] within an essentially compatible framework identifies (oddly) seven types of meaning, in essentially three groups: Conceptual, Associative and Thematic. Lyons [18] effectively identifies ten types of meaning, through the rather recursive device of looking at the meanings of the noun "meaning" and the verb "to mean".

Allen, and Leech (the latter less clearly) are committed to the idea that words have distinct senses or meaning[1]. But even this is controversial: see Kilgarriff [16] for a discussion. The English word "bank" with its two homonyms ("financial institution" and "river bank") is well known. More difficult examples are not hard to find. Consider the word "drug". Are sentences in which it is used interchangeably with "narcotic" using a different sense from those which in which it is used interchangeably with "medicine"?

The reason for this short discussion of semantics as the term is understood by the natural language understanding and linguistics communities is to contrast this with the way it used in the multi-media and image retrieval communities. Jörgensen [13] (p167ff) and more recently, for example, Koskela and Laaksonen [15] and Heesch and Rüger [11] use the term with a much narrower meaning: semantic in the context

---

[1] Lyons position is somewhat more sophisticated considering, for example the notion of "linguistic fields".

of image retrieval is understood to be confined to assigning conceptual labels from some sort of fixed vocabulary to the whole or parts of a region, possibly with some sort of spatial relations between regions identified.

This is much more restricted notion of semantics than is commonly employed in natural language processing. There is nothing wrong with it (especially given the state-of-the art in multimedia retrieval and how far multimedia retrieval has come in the past ten years or so): but a failure to recognise the differences in the ways the term is being used is likely to lead to confusion.

It might be better to recognise that what is adopted in the multimedia field is an *operational semantics*, in which meaning is defined in terms of specific operations and tasks, with no claim to deal with the general meaning of multimedia data. Indeed many would claim that adopting restrictions in terms of task and domain is precisely where progress has been made in both natural language processing and the semantic web.

3. Exploratory Search

The real focus of the paper is a new way of looking at the process of multimedia retrieval: **exploratory search**.

Exploratory search is a notion which applies to all forms of information seeking, but is especially applicable to multimedia retrieval. It focuses on situations where the searcher has an ill specified information need. It cuts across the commonly used searching characterisation of *information discovery* [14] versus *previously seen information retrieval* (e.g. Dumais et al [9]) in which the primary characterisation is whether the search system is mainly intended to support the retrieval of items previously not seen by the searcher (information discovery) versus those previously seen but whose virtually whereabouts are presumably currently unknown.

Most current or proposed exploratory search systems have some sort of topological metaphor underlying both their indexing structures and their interfaces. A typical system might involve some sort of categorisation or clustering step which is used to identify key examples or summaries, an associated similarity space or spaces which allow the topological space to be projected onto a two or two-an-a-half dimensional display space and some form of analytical query to allow users to "parachute" in to suitable areas of the topological space without considering the whole of it [6,28].

Some systems focus more on guided interaction and the process of negotiating the search, but the common theme is the metaphor of exploring an underlying space.

I don't want to claim that exploratory search is anything new or radical: indeed many of the ideas can be traced back to Belkin and others [5] and the notion of Anomalous States of Knowledge, if not before.

Neither do I want to pretend the term is my own[2].

Digital Still Image Retrieval provides an interesting challenge for emerging exploratory image search systems. This is for three reasons. First, the content of

---

[2] See http://www.umiacs.umd.edu/~ryen/xsi/

images is rich, multi-facetted and complex (an image is worth a thousand words). Second, user needs are highly subjective (even compared to text) and difficult to define (browsing for the pleasure of browsing, my grandchildren give me joy, whereas yours are merely children). Third it is possible to attend to and take in many images more or less simultaneously, in a way which is not possible with text and music for example.

This has is leading to the emergence of a new field which I think is best called Semantic Content Based Image Retrieval (SCBIR) in contrast to Content Based Image Retrieval based on low-level features [23].

Before moving on to a more detailed discussion of SCBIR and Exploratory Search I want to look more carefully at the term semantics and way it is understood in natural language processing and linguistics.

4. A Model for Exploratory Image Search

As with most interactive information retrieval systems the first step is to split the retrieval into two: an indexing process which can take place (slowly) offline and an interactive retrieval process which of necessity must operate rapidly and be focussed on effective and "comfortable" use by real people undertaking searches.

The indexing process then takes on a subsidiary role in which data is selected and organised to allow rapid and effective organisation of the interactive retrieval engine. Although the indexing process is in fact technically more demanding, since it is logically subsidiary I want to consider first the exploratory search process.

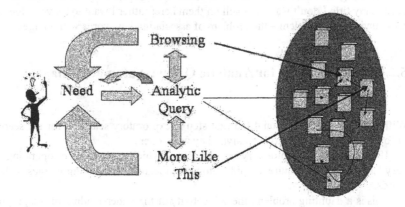

Fig. 1. A Model for Exploratory Image Retrieval

Figure 1 presents a model for exploratory image retrieval. In it a searcher first comes to the system with some sort of need or requirement for an image. This they express as an analytic query, for example as a list of key words.

This will produce an initial retrieved set of images. These may well change the searchers idea of their need. The retrieved set may also act as a starting point for other forms of retrieval: for example requests for more images in some sense similar to one of the retrieved set: or less directed browsing. The images seen during these subsequent search operations may in themselves change or refine the searchers idea of their need. Eventually, presumably, the searcher will find a satisfactory image set of images or give up.

Now I make no great claims for this model. It is very similar in outline to ones presented, for example, in Belew (2000) Chapter 1. Compared to Belew, following Belkin, Oddy and Brooks (1982) there is perhaps, a little more emphasis on the impact of the results of retrieval on the searchers perception of their own need, but this is a matter of detail.

More to the point is the reliance of the model, on the one hand, on comprehensible notions of semantic similarity, and on the other on an effective and efficient means of indexing the images to support analytic query.

Indexing to support analytic query is primarily a process of assigning appropriate key words to images. I will return to this point later.

Semantic similarity is needed to support both browsing and relevance feedback or more-like-this access. Human notions of image similarity are complex (see [13], Chapter 2 for a review). Browsing often also requires some notion of directionality or scent [8] so that the user can browse successive image sets which have more or less of some property.

Current systems operate with similarity computed using low-level features: in particular colour (see for example [19], [20]), and this is an impoverished notion of image semantics.

Browsing and search are essential features of exploratory search systems, but despite my title I don't want to dwell on them here: rather I want to move to look at a more underlying problem – the problem of associating key words with images.

5. SCBIR Indexing for Analytic Query: Automatic Image Annotation

Within the model of Section 4 the first step in exploratory search is for the searcher to formulate their need into an analytic key word query.

If we are to build exploratory search systems which are capable of operating on a very large scale, we require a rapid, automatic, means of annotating images with key words.

This is a daunting problem: the subjectivity of the understanding of images, their complexity and the semantic gap caused by the differences between the low-level features of images used in computerised processing of digital images and human understanding, all contribute to the significant progress which has been made with this problem in recent years.

The semantic gap also occurs in other forms of non-textual image retrieval (like video and music) but the problems it poses and the ways to overcome them are distinctive in still image searching partially because of some technical problems posed by still images (meaningful segmentation of still images is especially hard) but equally, as noted above, still image perception has some special properties which may be exploited in the interface.

In particular it appears possible for searchers to rapidly or simultaneously scan very large numbers of still images in result sets. This contrasts with text, where, seemingly fuller attention needs to be applied to results viewed, and consequently the useful size of result sets presented. Video appear to present related problems, with distraction by non-relevant results being a greater problem.

However, it must be pointed out there is a need for mush more extensive ecologically valid, human centred studies is this area before firm conclusions can be drawn. Markkula and Sormunen [21], for example, report their searchers frequently adopted what they perceived to be the best or easiest search strategy. It is unclear whether their perceptions were in fact correct.

However, there appears to have been real progress with bridging the semantic gap in the past few years. The successes have in common the use of various forms of supervised and semi-supervised machine learning. For clarity, in supervised machine learning the learning system builds a model on a hand analysed set of data called the training set. In this case this will be a set of images which have been manually annotated. Semi-supervised systems will either have some form of manual assessment or correction on additional unseen data or combine the use of entirely automatic, unsupervised learning with supervised learning.

The most successful of these early attempts employed models from machine translation, [2,3] although more recently there have been suggestions the relationship between the task and Machine Translation is more indirect [27]. Other forms of machine learning and adaptive computing have also proved successful [7, 10, 12, 24, 25, 26].

There are three main observations to be made about these pieces of work.

First, they generally focus on the assignment of unordered sets of key words to the whole of an image, since this is really what is required for indexing. Where they do not, they are not reliant on accurate, meaningful segmentation of the image. They have models which combine both the relationship between areas of the image and words and the corrections for the likely errors in those relationships.

Second, all have vocabularies which are much too small for practical applications. Current systems have vocabularies of a few hundred terms in contrast to the 20,000 plus terms in the Art and Architecture Thesaurus [13], for example.

Third, for the forseeable future they are relatively errorful, in the sense that they will often assign words to images which would not seem relevant to a human being. However, in the context of exploratory search this is not a real problem. The human searcher can overcome the errors made by the indexing systems by using the browsing and relevance feedback mechanisms, provided of course, those errors are not so severe and numerous that the searcher see no relevant images in the early phases of their search.

6. The Relationship between Linguistic Semantics and Image Semantic for Exploratory Search

In Section 2 I overviewed the use of the word "semantics" as it is used in Natural Language Processing and Image Retrieval. I also introduced the term *operational semantics* to describe a situation in which no claim is made about the generality of the semantics without a task.

I now want to weave together the two threads of this paper: exploratory search and semantics.

The first observation I want to make is that there is a critical element in Allen's definition of semantics discussed in Section 2 which is missing from all the subsequent discussion of exploratory search and image retrieval. Allen's definition focuses on sentence meaning, rather than the meaning of words, which has been the focus in the subsequent discussion.

One might argue that this focus on the sentence is a weakness of most conventional NLP and linguistic work. However most work in NLP takes the sentence as the important unit of meaning.

However, operationally, in the context of exploratory search, few searchers wish to express their needs through well formed sentences.

Conversely, considering the image annotation or indexing process, there seems to be little utility in annotating images with long sentences rather than a bag of key words. (I accept it is plausible some phrases might be useful: e..g "ducks on water".) Indeed annotating images with sentences opens up a real Pandora's box: which are the important concepts/words to include in the sentence (depends on the context of use): if we use several sentences when to stop; and so on. These matters are only on the research agenda in the longest term.

My purpose here is to point out that within Natural Language Processing or Linguistics a focus on the meaning of words seems a very narrow use of the term semantics, Yet in moving to a specific operational task: like exploratory search; in order give an attainable scope and definition to our enterprises in multimedia we may need to focus on this narrow use at least in the short term.

7. Conclusions

In this paper I have attempted to do three things.

First I have attempted to overview the way the term "semantics" is used in Natural Language Processing.

Second, I introduced the idea of exploratory search and model for its use in image retrieval, including the use of automatic image annotation.

Third I attempted to relate the notion of semantics as it is used in NLP and Linguistics to the operational context of exploratory image search.

Semantics as the term is used in NLP and Linguistics implies a very deep and complex notion of meaning. By focussing on a specific, practical operational context (like exploratory search) we can avoid the possibly intractable problems posed for multimedia processing by these deep semantics.

Acknowledgements

I would like to thank Peter Enser for originally introducing me to Corinne Jörgensen's excellent and comprehensive book. I would also like to thank Ryen White for introducing me to the idea of Exploratory Search and for making very useful comments on an earlier draft of this paper.

References

1. Allen, J. Natural Language Understanding (2nd Ed.). Benjamin/Cummings, Redwood City, CA, USA. 1995.
2. Barnard, K. P. Duygulu and D. Forsyth, "Recognition as Translating Images into Text" Internet Imaging IV, Electronic Imaging 2003 (Invited paper). IS&T/SPIE 2003.
3. Barnard, K., Duygulu, P., Forsyth, D., de Freitas, N., Blei, D., and Jordan, M.I. (2003) Matching words and pictures. Journal of Machine Learning Research, vol. 3, pp. 1107-1135.
4. Belew, R.K. Finding Out About. Cambridge University Press, 2000.
5. Belkin, N.J., R.N. Oddy and H.M. Brooks. ASK for Information Retrieval: Part I: Background and Theory. Journal of Documentation 38(2), 1982. Reproduced in Reading in Information Retrieval. K. Sparck Jones and P. Willett (Eds). Morgan Kaufman, San Francisco, CA, USA. 1997.
6. Cai, D. He, X, Z. Li, Ma, W.-Y. and J.-R. Wen "Hierarchical Clustering of WWW Image Search Results Using Visual, textual and Link Information" Proceeding of the 12th Annual ACM International Conference on Multimedia (MM '04), ACM Press, 2004. 952-959.
7. Carneiro, G., Vasconcelos N. "A Database Centric View of Semantic Image Annotation and Retrieval" Proceeding of the 28th Annual International ACM SIGIR Conference on Rsearch and Development in Information Retrieval (SIGIR 2005), Salvador, Brazil. ACM Press. 2005. 559-566.
8. Chi, E.H. P. Pirolli, J. Pitkow "The scent of a site: a system for analyzing and predicting information scent, usage, and usability of a Web site" Proceedings of the SIGCHI conference on human factors in computing systems, The Hague, The Netherlands, ACM Press 2000 161-168
9. Dumais, S. E. Cutrell, J.J. Cadiz, G. Jancke, R. Saran, D.C. Roberts "Stuff I've Seen: A System for Personal Information Retrieval and Re-use" . Proceedings of the 26th Annual International ACM SIGIR Conference on Research and Development in Information Retrieval (SIGIR-2003), Toronto, Canada. 2003.
10. Ghostal, A., P. Ircing, S. Khidanpu. "Hidden Markov Models for Automatic Annotation and Content-based Retrieval of Images and Video" Proceeding of the 28th Annual International ACM SIGIR Conference on Research and Development in Information Retrieval (SIGIR 2005), Salvador, Brazil. ACM Press. 2005. 544-551.
11. Heesch, D. and S. Rüger, "Image Browsing: Semantic Analysis of NNk Networks" Image and Video Retrieval, Proceeding of the 4th International Conference, CIVR 2005.LNCS 3568 Springer 2005. 609-618.
12. Jeon, J. and R. Manmatha. (2004). "Using Maximum Entropy for Automatic Image Annotation". 3rd International Conference on Image and Video Retrieval (CIVR 2004), 24-32.

13. Jörgensen, C. Image Retrieval: theory and Research. Scarecrow Press, Oxford, UK. 2003.
14. Kearn, A and S.M. Smith "The Information Discovery Framework" Symposium on Designing Interactive Systems (DIS 2004), Cambridge, Mass. USA. 2004.
15. Koskella, M. and J. Laaksonen "Semantic Annotation of Image Groups with Self-organizing Maps", Image and Video Retrieval, Proceeding of the 4th International Conference, CIVR 2005.LNCS 3568 Springer 2005. 518-527.
16. Kilgarriff, A. I Don't Believe in Word Sense. Computers and the Humanities 31(2), March 1997. pp 91-113.
17. Leech, G. Semantics. Penguin. Harmondsworth, Middlesex, UK. 1974.
18. Lyons, J. Semantics. Cambridge University Press.1977
19. McDonald, S.. T.-Sh. Lai and J.I.. Tait, "Evaluating a Content Based Image Retrieval System" Proceedings of the 24th ACM SIGIR Conference on Research and Development in Information Retrieval (SIGIR 2001), New Orleans, September 2001. W.B. Croft, D.J. Harper, D.H. Kraft, and J. Zobel (Eds).
20. McDonald S. and J.I. Tait "Search Strategies in Content-Based Image Retrieval" Proceedings of the 26th ACM SIGIR Conference on Research and Development in Information Retrieval (SIGIR 2003), Toronto, July, 2003. pp 80-87.
21. Markkula, M. and E. Sormunen "Searching for Photos: Journalists Practices in Pictorial IR". The Challenge of Image Retrieval, a Workshop and Symposium on Pictorial IR. Newcastle-upon-Tyne, UK. 1998.
22. Pulman, S.G. "Lexical Decomposition" in Charting a new Course: Natural Language Processing and Information Retrieval – Essays in Honour of Karen Spärck Jones. J.I. Tait (Ed.) Springer 2005.
23. Smeulders, A.W.M., Worring, M., Santini, S. Gupta, A., and Jain, R. (2000) Content-based image retrieval at the end of the early years. IEEE Transactions on Pattern Analysis and Machine Intelligence, vol. 22, no. 12, pp. 1349-1380.
24. Srikanth, M., J. Varner, M. Bowden, D. Moldovan "Exploiting Ontologies for Automatic Image Annotation" Proceeding of the 28th Annual International ACM SIGIR Conference on Research and Development in Information Retrieval (SIGIR 2005), Salvador, Brazil. ACM Press. 2005. 552-558.
25. Tsai, C.F. K. McGarry and J.I. Tait "Automatic Metadata Annotation of Images via a Two-level Learning Framework" ACM SIGIR Semantic Web Workshop, Sheffield, July 2004. pp 32-42
26. Tsai, C.F., K. McGarry and J.I. Tait "Qualitative Evaluation of Automatic Assignment of Keywords to Images". Information Processing and Management, Volume 42 Issue 1, January, 2006. pp 136-154.
27. Virga, P., P. Duygulu "Systematic Evaluation of Machine Translation methods for Image and Video Annotation," Image and Video Retrieval, Proceeding of the 4th International Conference, CIVR 2005.LNCS 3568 Springer 2005.174-183.
28. Yee, K.-P., K. Swearingen, K. Li, M. Hearst. "Faceted Metadata for Image Search and Browsing" Proceedings of the SIGCHI conference on Human factors in computing systems, Ft. Lauderdale, Florida (CHI 2003). ACM Press. 2003 401-408.

Word Senses: The Stepping Stones in Semantic-Based Natural Language Processing

Dan Tufiş

Institute for Artificial Intelligence, 13, Calea 13 Septembrie, 050711,
Bucharest 5, Romania
Faculty of Informatics, University "A.I. Cuza", 16, Gral. Berthelot, Iaşi,
6600, Romania
tufis@racai.ro

Abstract. Most of the successful commercial applications in language processing (text and/or speech) dispense of any explicit concern on semantics, with the usual motivations stemming from the computational high costs required by dealing with semantics in case of large volumes of data. With recent advances in corpus linguistics and statistical-based methods in NLP, revealing useful semantic features of linguistic data is becoming cheaper and cheaper and the accuracy of this process is steadily improving. Lately, there seems to be a growing acceptance of the idea that multilingual lexical ontologies might be the key towards aligning different views on the semantic atomic units to be used in characterizing the general meaning of various and multilingual documents. Depending on the granularity at which semantic distinctions are necessary, the accuracy of the basic semantic processing (such as word sense disambiguation) can be very high with relatively low complexity computing. The paper substantiates this statement by presenting a statistical/based system for word alignment (WA) and word sense disambiguation (WSD) in parallel corpora.

1 Introduction

Most difficult problems in natural language processing stem from the inherent ambiguous nature of the human languages. Ambiguity is present at all levels of traditional structuring of a language system (phonology, morphology, lexicon, syntax, semantics) and not dealing with it at the proper level, exponentially increases the complexity of the problem solving. Currently, the state of the art taggers (combining various models, strategies and processing tiers) ensure no less than 97-

Please use the following format when citing this chapter:

Tufis, Dan, 2006, in IFIP International Federation for Information Processing, Volume 204, Artificial Intelligence Applications and Innovations, eds. Maglogiannis, I., Karpouzis, K., Bramer, M., (Boston: Springer), pp. 575–582

98% accuracy in the process of morpho-lexical full disambiguation. For such taggers a 2-best tagging[1] is practically 100% accurate.

One further step is the word sense disambiguation (WSD) process. In the fregean compositional semantics, the meaning of a complex expression is supposed to be derivable from the meanings of its parts, and the way in which those parts are combined. Depending on the representation formalisms for the word-meaning representation, various calculi may be considered for computing the meaning of a complex expression from the atomic representations of the word senses. Obviously, one should be able, before hand, to decide for each word in a text which of its possible meanings is the contextually right one.

Therefore, it is a generally accepted idea that the WSD task is highly instrumental (if not indispensable) in semantic processing of natural language documents.

Considering the word senses, one calls upon an informal concept, namely the *context* of a word. The definition of *NLP context* is rarely made independent of an intended application and thus, it is very hard to find a generally acceptable formalization for this concept. The context of a targeted word is its vicinity. This vicinity can be a sequence (ordered or not) of orthographic words in a limited window (not very well linguistically motivated), a typographical unit (sentence, paragraph, section, chapter, or even the entire document), a sequence of linguistically interpreted (morphology, syntax, semantics) atoms making a coherent unit (phrase, sentence, chain of sentences). In the case of multilingual environments or, more precisely, parallel corpora (as is the case in this paper), the context is defined as the pair of the sentences which are mutual translations.

The WSD problem can be stated as being able to associate to an ambiguous word (w) in a text or discourse, the sense (s_k) which is distinguishable from other senses ($s_1, ..., s_{k-1}, s_{k+1}, ..., s_n$) prescribed for that word by a reference semantic lexicon. One such semantic lexicon (actually a lexical ontology) is Princeton WordNet [1] version 2.0[2] (henceforth PWN). PWN is a very fine-grained semantic lexicon currently containing 203,147 sense distinctions, clustered in 115,424 equivalence classes (synsets). Out of the 145,627 distinct words, 119,528 have only one single sense. However, the remaining 26,099 words are those that one would frequently meet in a regular text and their ambiguity ranges from two senses up to 36. Several authors considered that sense granularity in PWN is too fine-grained for the computer use, arguing that even for a human (native speaker of English) the sense differences of some words are very hard to be reliably (and systematically) distinguished. There are several attempts to group the senses of the words in PWN in coarser grained senses – *hyper-senses* – so that clear-cut distinction among them is always possible for humans and (especially) computers. We will refer in this paper to two hyper-sense inventories used in the BalkaNet project [2]. A comprehensive review of the WSD state-of the art at the end of 90's can be found in [3]. Stevenson and Wilks [4] review several WSD systems that combined various knowledge

---

[1] In k-best tagging, instead of assigning each word exactly one tag (the most probable in the given context), it is allowed to have occasionally at most k-best tags attached to a word and if the correct tag is among the k-best tags, the annotation is considered to be correct.

[2] http://www.cogsci.princeton.edu/~wn/

sources to improve the disambiguation accuracy and address the issue of different granularities of the sense inventories. SENSEVAL[3] series of evaluation competitions on WSD is a very good source on learning how WSD evolved in the last 6-7 years and where is it nowadays.

We describe a multilingual environment, containing several monolingual wordnets, aligned to PWN used as an interlingual index (ILI). The word-sense disambiguation method combines word alignment technologies, and interlingual equivalence relations in multilingual wordnets [5]. Irrespective of the languages in the multilingual documents, the words of interest are disambiguated by using the same sense-inventory labels. The aligned wordnets were constructed in the context of the European project BalkaNet. The consortium developed monolingual wordnets for five Balkan languages (Bulgarian, Greek, Romanian Serbian, and Turkish) and extended the Czech wordnet initially developed in the EuroWordNet project [5]. The wordnets are aligned to PWN, taken as an interlingual index, following the principles established by the EuroWordNet consortium. The version of the PWN used as ILI is an enhanced XML version where each synset is mapped onto one or more SUMO [6] conceptual categories and is classified under one of the IRST domains [7]. In the present version of the BalkaNet ILI there are used 2066 SUMO distinct categories and 163 domain labels. Therefore, for our WSD experiments we had at our disposal three sense-inventories, with very different granularities: PWN senses, SUMO categories and IRST Domains.

2 Word Alignment

The word alignment is the first step (the hardest) in our approach for the identification of word senses. In order to reduce the search space and to filter out significant information noise, the context is reduced to the level of sentence. Therefore, a parallel text $<T_{L1} T_{L2}>$ is represented as a sequence of pairs of one or more sentences in language L1 ($S_{L1}^1 S_{L1}^2...S_{L1}^k$) and one or more sentences in language L2 ($S_{L2}^1 S_{L2}^2...S_{L2}^m$) so that the two ordered sets of sentences represent reciprocal translations. Such a pair is called a translation alignment unit (or translation unit). The word alignment of a bitext is an explicit representation of the pairs of words $<w_{L1} w_{L2}>$ (called translation equivalence pairs) co-occurring in the same translation units and representing mutual translations. The general word alignment problem includes the cases where words in one part of the bitext are not translated in the other part (these are called *null alignments*) and the cases where multiple words in one part of the bitext are translated as one or more words in the other part (these are called expression alignments).

The input format is obtained from two raw texts that represent reciprocal translations. If not already sentence aligned, the two texts are aligned by a sentence aligner, similar to Moore's aligner [8] but which unlike it, is able to recover the non-one-to-one sentence alignments. The texts in each language are then tokenized, tagged and lemmatized. Frequently, the translation equivalents have the same part-of

[3] http://www.cs.unt.edu/~rada/senseval

speech, but relying on such a restriction would seriously affect the alignment recall. However, when the translation equivalents have different parts of speech, this difference is not arbitrary. *POS affinities,* $\{p(POS_m^{RO}|POS_n^{EN})\}$ and $p(POS_n^{EN}|POS_m^{RO})\}$, are easy to estimate and we use them to filter out improbable translation equivalents pairs.

The next pre-processing step is represented by the sentence chunking in both languages. The chunks are recognized by a set of regular expressions defined over the tagsets and they correspond to (non-recursive) noun phrases, adjectival phrases, prepositional phrases and verb complexes (analytical realization of tense, aspect mood and diathesis and phrasal verbs). The texts are further processed by a statistical dependency linking parser. Finally, the bitext is assembled as an XML document (XCES[4] compliant format), which is the standard input for most of our tools.

The proper word alignment process is achieved by a statistics-based module, named *COWAL* [9]. The alignment model considers a link between two candidate words as an object that is described by a feature-values structure which we call the *reification* of the link. The program starts building the most probable links *(anchor links)*: cognates, numbers, dates, and translation pairs with high translation probabilities. Then, it iteratively aligns content words (open class categories) in the immediate vicinity of the anchor links. The links to be added at any later step are supported or restricted by the links created in the previous iterations. The aligner has different weights and different significance thresholds on each feature and iteration. Each of the iterations can be configured to align different categories of tokens (named entities, dates and numbers, content words, functional words, punctuation) in decreasing order of statistical evidence.

A link between two tokens is characterized by a set of features with values in the [0,1] interval. The score of a candidate link (LS) between a source token i and a target token j is computed by a linear function of several features scores:

$$LS(i,j) = \sum_{i=1}^{n} \lambda_i * ScoreFeat_i \; ; \sum_{i=1}^{n} \lambda_i = 1$$

Although far from being perfect, the accuracy of word alignments and of the translation lexicons extracted from parallel corpora is rapidly improving. In the shared task evaluations of different word aligners, organized on the occasion of the 2003 Conference of the North American Association for Computational Linguistics and the 2005 Conference of the Association for Computational Linguistics, our winning systems[5] TREQ-AL[10] and COWAL produced wordnet-relevant translation lexicons[6] with an F-measure as high as 84.26% and respectively 89.92%.

The major features used by the COWAL aligner are briefly discussed below.

Translation equivalence. The word aligner invokes GIZA++ [11] to build translation probability lists for either lemmas or the occurrence forms of the bitext. The considered token for the translation model build by GIZA++ is the respective

---

[4] http://www.cs.vassar.edu/XCES/
[5] We participated only in the Romanian-English track (some other pairs of languages were French-English (in 2003) and Hindi-English and Inuktitut-English (in 2005).
[6] wordnet-relevant dictionaries are restricted only to translation pairs of the same major POS (nouns, verbs, adjectives and adverbs).

lexical item (lemma or wordform) trailed by its POS tag (eg. plane_N, plane_V plane_A). In this way we avoid data sparseness and filter noisy data. A further way of removing the noise created by GIZA++ is to filter out all the translation pairs below a LL-threshold. We made various experiments and empirically set the value of this threshold to 6. All the probability losses by this filtering were redistributed proportionally to their initial probabilities to the surviving translation equivalence candidates.

Translation equivalence entropy score. The translation equivalence entropy score is a favouring parameter for the words which have few high probability translations. Since this feature is definitely sensitive to the order of the lexical items, we compute an average value for the link: $\alpha ES(A)+\beta ES(B)$. Currently we use $\alpha=\beta=0.5$, but it might be interesting to see, depending on different language pairs, how the performance of the aligner would be affected by a different settings of these parameters.

$$ES(W) = 1 - \frac{-\sum_{i=1}^{N} p(W,TR_i)*\log p(W,TR_i)}{\log N}$$

Part-of-speech affinity. In faithful translations the translated words tend to be translated by words of the same part-of-speech. When this is not the case, the different POSes, are not arbitrary. The part of speech affinity, $P(cat(A)|cat(B))$, can be easily computed from a gold standard alignment. Obviously, this is a directional feature, so an averaging operation is necessary in order to ascribe this feature to a link: $PA=\alpha P(cat(A)|cat(B)) + \beta P(cat(B)|cat(A))$. Again, we used $\alpha=\beta=0.5$ but different values of these weights might be worthwhile investigating.

Cognates. The similarity measure, $COGN(T_S, T_T)$, is implemented as a Levenstein metric. Using the COGN test as a filtering device is a heuristic based on the *cognate conjecture* which says that when the two tokens of a translation pair are orthographically similar, they are very likely to have similar meanings (i.e. they are cognates).

Obliqueness. Each token in both sides of a bi-text is characterized by a position index, computed as the ratio between the relative position in the sentence and the length of the sentence. The absolute value of the difference between tokens' position indexes, subtracted from 1 gives the link's "obliqueness".

$$OBL(SW_i,TW_j) = 1 - \left| \frac{i}{length(Sent_S)} - \frac{j}{length(Sent_T)} \right|$$

Locality. Locality is a feature that estimates the degree to which the links are sticking together. There are three features to account for locality: (i) *weak locality*, (ii) *chunk-based locality* and (iii) *dependency-based* locality.

The value of the *weak locality* feature is derived from the already existing alignments in a window of N tokens centred on the focused token. The window size is variable, proportional to the sentence length. If in the window there exist k linked tokens and the indexes of their links are $<i_1 j_1>, ...<i_k j_k>$ then the locality feature of the new link $<i_{k+1}, j_{k+1}>$ is defined by the equation below:

$$LOC = 1 - \min(1, \frac{1}{k}\sum_{m=1}^{k}\frac{|i_{k+1} - i_m|}{|j_{k+1} - j_m|})$$

In the case of *chunk-based locality* the window span is given by the indexes of the first and last tokens of the chunk.

Dependency-based locality uses the set of the dependency links of the tokens in a candidate link for the computation of the feature value. In this case, the LOC feature of a candidate link $<i_{k+1}, j_{k+1}>$ is set to 1 or 0 according to the following rule:

if between i_{k+1} and i_α there is a (source language) dependency and if between j_{k+1} and j_β there is also a (target language) dependency then LOC is 1 if i_α and j_β are aligned, and 0 otherwise. Please note that in case $j_{k+1} \equiv j_\beta$ a trivial dependency (identity) is considered and the LOC attribute of the link $<i_{k+1}, j_{k+1}>$ is set to always to 1 (thus enabling a many to one word alignment).

Collocation. Bi-gram lists (only content words) were built from each monolingual part of the training corpus, using the log-likelihood score (threshold of 10) and minimal occurrence frequency (3) for candidates filtering.

We used the bi-grams list to annotate the chains of lexical dependencies among the contents words. Then, the value of the collocation feature is computed similar to the dependency-based locality feature. The algorithm searches for the links of the lexical dependencies around the candidate link.

3   Wordnet-based Sense Disambiguation

Once the translation equivalents identified, it is reasonable to expect that the words of a translation pair $<w^i_{L1}, w^j_{L2}>$ share at least one conceptual meaning stored in an interlingual sense inventory. As we mentioned in the introduction, the most generally used sense inventory is represented by the set of unique identifiers of the synsets in Princeton Wordnet. When interlingually aligned wordnets are available (as is our case), obtaining the sense labels for the words in a translation pair is straightforward: one has to identify for w^i_{L1} the synset S^i_{L1} and for w^j_{L2} the synset S^j_{L2} so that S^i_{L1} and S^j_{L2} are projected over the same interlingual concept. The index of this common interlingual concept (ILI) is the sense label of the two words w^i_{L1} and w^j_{L2}. However, it is possible that no common interlingual projection will be found for the synsets to which w^i_{L1} and w^j_{L2} belong. In this case, the senses of the two words will be given by the indexes of the most similar interlingual concepts corresponding to the synsets of the two words. Our measure of interlingual concepts semantic similarity is based on PWN structure. We compute the semantic-similarity[7] score by the formula $SYM(ILI_1, ILI_2) = \frac{1}{1+k}$ where k is the number of links from ILI_1 to ILI_2 or from both ILI_1 and ILI_2 to the nearest common ancestor.

---

[7] For a detailed discussion and an in-depth analysis of several other measures see [12]

4   Evaluation

The BalkaNet version of the "1984" corpus is encoded as a sequence of uniquely identified translation units. For the evaluation purposes, we selected a set of frequent English words (123 nouns and 88 verbs) the meanings of which were also encoded in the Romanian wordnet. The selection considered only polysemous words (at least two senses per part of speech) since the POS-ambiguous words are irrelevant as this distinction is solved with high accuracy (more than 99%) by our tiered-tagger [13]. All the occurrences of the target words were disambiguated by three independent experts who negotiated the disagreements and thus created a gold-standard annotation for the evaluation of precision and recall of the WSD algorithm. The table below summarizes the results.

Table 1. WSD precision, recall and F-measure

Precision	Recall	F-measure
76.12%	76.12%	76.12%

With the PWN senses identified (synset unique identifiers), sense labeling with either SUMO and/or IRST domains inventories is trivial: as we said in section 1, the synset unique identifiers of PWN are already mapped (clustered) onto these two sense inventories. The Table 2 shows a great variation in terms of Precision, Recall and F-measure when different granularity sense inventories are considered for the WSD problem. Therefore, it is important to make the right choice on the sense inventory to be used with respect to a given application. In case of a document classification problem, it is very likely that the IRST domain labels (or a similar granularity sense inventory) would suffice. The rationale is that IRST domains are directly derived from the Universal Decimal Classification as used by most libraries and librarians. The SUMO sense labeling will be definitely more useful in an ontology based intelligent system interacting through a natural language interface. Finally, the most refined sense inventory of PWN will be extremely useful in Natural Language Understanding Systems, which would require a deep processing. Such a fine inventory would be highly beneficial in lexicographic and lexicological studies.

Table 2. Evaluation of the WSD in terms of three different sense inventories.

Sense Inventory	Precision	Recall	F-measure
PWN 115424 categories	76.12%	76.12%	76.12%
SUMO 2066 categories	82.64%	82.64%	82.64%
DOMAINS 163 categories	91.90%	91.90%	91.90%

Similar findings on sense granularity for the WSD task are discussed in [4] where for some coarser grained inventories even higher precisions are reported. However, we are not aware of better results in WSD exercises where the PWN sense inventory was used. The major explanation for this is that unlike the majority work in WSD that is based on monolingual environments, we use for the definition of sense contexts the cross-lingual translations of the occurrences of the target words. The way one word in context is translated into one or more other languages is a very accurate and highly discriminative knowledge source for the decision-making.

5. Conclusions

The results in Table 2 show that although we used the same WSD algorithm on the same text, the performance scores (precision, recall, f-measure) significantly varied, with more than 15% difference between the best (DOMAINS) and the worst (PWN) f-measures. This is not surprising, but it shows that it is extremely difficult to objectively compare and rate WSD systems working with different sense inventories.

The potential drawback of this approach is that it relies on the existence of parallel data and at least two aligned wordnets that might not be available yet. Nevertheless, parallel resources are becoming increasingly available, in particular on the World Wide Web, and aligned wordnets are being produced for more and more languages (currently there are more than 40 ongoing wordnets projects for 37 languages). In the near future it should be possible to apply our and similar methods to large amounts of parallel data and a wide spectrum of languages.

References

1. Fellbaum, Ch. (ed.) WordNet: An Electronic Lexical Database, MIT Press (1998).
2. Tufiş, D. (ed): Special Issue on BalkaNet. Romanian Journal on Science and Technology of Information, Vol. 7 no. 3-4 (2004) 9-44.
3. Ide, N., Veronis, J., Introduction to the special issue on word sense disambiguation. The state of the art. Computational Linguistics, Vol. 27, no. 3, (2001) 1-40.
4. Stevenson, M., Wilks, Y., The interaction of Knowledge Sources in Word Sense Disambiguation. Computational Linguistics, Vol. 24, no. 1, (1998) 321-350.
5. Vossen P. (ed.) A Multilingual Database with Lexical Semantic Networks, Kluwer Academic Publishers, Dordrecht, 1998
6. Niles, I., and Pease, A., Towards a Standard Upper Ontology. In Proceedings of the 2nd International Conference on Formal Ontology in Information Systems (FOIS-2001), Ogunquit, Maine, (2001) 17-19.
7. Magnini B. Cavaglià G., Integrating Subject Field Codes into WordNet. In Proceedings of LREC2000, Athens, Greece (2000) 1413-1418.
8. Moore, R. 2002. Fast and Accurate Sentence Alignment of Bilingual Corpora in Machine Translation: From Research to Real Users. In Proceedings of the 5th Conference of the Association for Machine Translation in the Americas, Tiburon, California), Springer-Verlag, Heidelberg, Germany: 135-244.
9. Tufiş, D., Ion, R. Ceauşu, Al., Stefănescu, D.: Combined Aligners. In *Proceeding of the ACL2005 Workshop on "Building and Using Parallel Corpora: Data-driven Machine Translation and Beyond"*. June, 2005, *Ann Arbor, Michigan, June,* Association for Computational Linguistics, pp. 107-110.
10. Tufiş, D., Barbu, A., M., Ion, R. A word-alignment system with limited language resources. In Proceedings of the NAACL 2003 Workshop on Building and Using Parallel Texts; Romanian-English Shared Task, Edmonton (2003) 36-39.
11. Och, F., J., Ney, H., Improved Statistical Alignment Models, *Proceedings of ACL2000*, Hong Kong, China, 440-447, 2000.
12. Budanitsky, A., Hirst, G., Semantic distance in WordNet: An experimental, application-oriented evaluation of five measures. Proceedings of the Workshop on WordNet and Other Lexical Resources, NAACL, Pittsburgh, June, (2001) 29-34.
13. Tufiş, D., Tiered Tagging and Combined Classifiers, in F. Jelinek, E. Nöth (eds) Text, Speech and Dialogue, Lecture Notes in Artificial Intelligence, Vol. 1692. Springer-Verlag, Berlin Heidelberg New-York (1999) 28-33.

Space-Time Tubes and Motion Representation

Christos Diou, Anastasia Manta, and Anastasios Delopoulos

Multimedia Understanding Group,
Department of Electrical and Computer Engineering,
Aristotle University of Thessaloniki - Greece
diou@olympus.ee.auth.gr, manta@auth.gr, adelo@eng.auth.gr

Abstract. Space-time tubes, a feature that can be used for analysis of motion based on the observed moving points in a scene is introduced. Information provided by sensors is used to detect moving points and based on their connectivity, tubes enable a structured approach towards identifying moving objects and high level events. It is shown that using tubes in conjunction with domain knowledge can overcome errors caused by the inaccuracy or inadequacy of the original motion information. The detected high level events can then be mapped to small natural language descriptions of object motion in the scene.

1 Introduction

While video motion analysis is a broad subject that has been extensively studied, most of the established approaches appear to be insufficient when it comes to semantic analysis of video data. They either provide low level information that is primarily useful for coding purposes, or are highly dependent on image processing results that lack the accuracy required for identification of natural objects or events. Mobile object detection and tracking techniques have demonstrated satisfactory results (e.g., [5]), but often heavily rely on the robustness and effectiveness of the image processing algorithms applied; the use of common sense rules and domain knowledge is usually limited and implicit, integrated in the tracking algorithm.

In this paper we introduce space-time tubes as a general concept and discuss the ways they can be used to identify high level events related to natural object motion. One of the most important benefits is that low level processing is abandoned early in the event detection process, while results are mainly obtained using reasoning that can accomodate domain knowledge.

Since tubes have certain properties that can be directly mapped to events such as "Two objects meet", it is also possible to construct simple natural langugage descriptions of the events detected in a scene (see section 3).

2 Space-Time Tubes

Assume that sensors detect motion in a scene, so that a binary motion mask $I_b(x, y, t)$ is provided:

Please use the following format when citing this chapter:

Diou, Christos, Manta, Anastasia, Delopoulos, Anastasios, 2006, in IFIP International Federation for Information Processing, Volume 204, Artificial Intelligence Applications and Innovations, eds. Maglogiannis, I., Karpouzis, K., Bramer, M., (Boston: Springer), pp. 583–590

$$I_b(x, y, t) = \begin{cases} 1 & \text{if motion is detected at point } (x, y) \text{ at time } t \\ 0 & \text{otherwise} \end{cases} \qquad (1)$$

Note that moving points given by I_b correspond to the projection of moving objects on the sensor plane. When using a camera for example, the detected points result from processing frames that correspond to perspective projection at the camera projection plane and using the foreground extraction technique presented in [2] at a specific time (frame) is given in Figure 1(b).

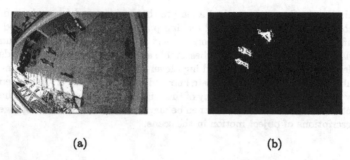

(a)   (b)

Fig. 1. A video scene and the corresponding binary mask for the moving points. The original image comes from the EC funded CAVIAR project [1].

The subset $S \subseteq \mathbb{R}^3$ of the moving points forms a topological space such that the function I_b defined above is the characteristic function of S. Moreover, every cross-section $S(t_0) \subseteq \mathbb{R}^2$ of S at time t_0 also defines a topological space, and the corresponding characteristic function is $I_b(x, y, t_0)$. An example is given in Figure 2, as obtained from a video sequence.

Any subset T of S that is connected and its cross-section $T \cap S(t_0)$ at t_0 is also connected for any t_0 is called a *tube*. A single connected component of S is called a *composite tube*, in the sense that it is formed by union of tubes. Note that for composite tubes and tubes, connectivity refers to $x - y - t$ space, while for their intersections at a specific time t, it refers to the $x - y$ space. Moreover, the above definitions allow tubes to have common elements. There are four main events that can be observed on tubes forming a composite tube:

1. *Start.* A tube starts at time t_0 if for every point $(x, y, t) \in T$, $t \geq t_0$. If tubes are maximal sets, i.e., they are the maximal sets that are connected and their cross-section $T \cap S(t_0)$ forms a connected component in $S(t_0)$, then their start points are the start points of the corresponding composite tube.
2. *Stop.* A tube stops at time t_0 if for every point $(x, y, t) \in T$, $t \leq t_0$. As with start points, if tubes are maximal sets, then their stop points are the stop points of the corresponding composite tube.
3. *Merge.* Two tubes T_1 and T_2 merge at point t_0 if their cross sections $T_1 \cap S(t)$ and $T_2 \cap S(t)$ are not connected for $t < t_0$ and are connected at t_0.

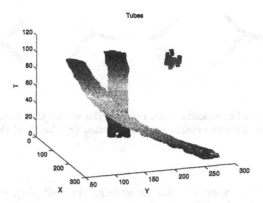

Fig. 2. The points detected in the $x-y-t$ space, as obtained by applying a foreground detection algorithm on a video sequence.

4. *Split.* Similar to merge, two tubes T_1 and T_2 split at point t_0 if their cross sections $T_1 \cap S(t)$ and $T_2 \cap S(t)$ are connected for $t < t_0$ and are not connected at t_0.

Merge and split points of tubes that are maximal sets are also merge and split points of the corresponding composite tube.

Tube segments are tubes that form a partition of a composite tube such that each one of them starts at a start, merge or just after a split event and stops at a stop, split or just before a merge event. Moreover, their cross section $T_s \cap S(t)$ at any time t forms a connected component of $S(t)$ (hence two tube segments can only be connected at their start or stop points). Given a composite tube, a number of possible tubes can be constructed. If we allow tubes to start or stop at any point (i.e., not restrict tubes to start or stop whenever a tube event occurs), there are infinite possibilities. However only one partition of tube segments can be constructed.

All of the above can be better explained using Figure 3, that shows sketches of what a projection of a composite tube on the $x - t$ plane might look like.

The above definitions depend on the topological properties of a given set of points S, however tubes also have certain geometric properties that are of interest, namely tube *centroid, area, velocity* and *duration*. For a tube T these four properties are functions of time.

The centroid can provide an approximation of the trajectory that the tube followed and for each time t equals the centroid of the set $S(t) \cap T$ of points. A similar property would be the tube *skeleton* that can be extracted via the use of a skeletonization algorithm, however this tends to be a computationally intensive process, compared to centroid calculation. A tube's area at time t is simply the area the tube occupies at that time. As far as velocity is concerned, both x and y axis velocity components v_x and v_y are the same for all points of a tube for a specific time t and are given by the tube's gradients $v_x(t) = \frac{dx}{dt}$

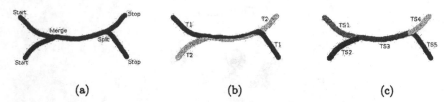

(a)	(b)	(c)

Fig. 3. (a) Sketch of composite tube, marking the events that occur. (b) Sketch of two possible tubes for the original composite tube, (c) Sketch of the corresponding tube segments.

and $v_y(t) = \frac{dy}{dt}$ for a specific point (x, y) (e.g., the centroid). Finally, a tube's duration is given by the difference $d = t_f - t_0$ of the stop and start times of the tube.

All the definitions above can easily be extended in the discrete case, if the sensor signal obtained is digital.

3 Mapping Natural Objects to Tubes

Tubes, or certain tube properties can be used to describe motion of natural objects in the observed scene i.e., find their trajectories and velocities and even lead to verbal descriptions of natural events such as "An object A entered the scene and moves fast" or "objects A and B meet".

Consider the ideal case, with sensor information provided being completely accurate and the binary mask I_b free of errors. Then, we can make the assumption that each moving natural object generates exactly one tube. A composite tube is generated when more than one objects move and their projections at the sensor plane meet at least once. Hence, given a composite tube that has a single tube segment (no merge or split) we can unambiguously determine the motion of the corresponding moving object. This is not the case in general, however: In Figure 3(a) there are multiple tubes that can form the initial composite tube and one example is given in Figure 3(b). If no restrictions are posed on the start/stop points and the area a tube can occupy, there is an infinity of possible natural events that would produce the same composite tube.

In most cases of practical interest a tube starts at an event of the corresponding composite tube i.e., a start, merge or split and stops at a stop, merge or split. We can therefore find a finite number of possible tubes for a given composite tube, a problem similar to finding all the connected subgraphs of a graph where each node will correspond to a tube event and each link to a tube segment. Additionally, subgraphs that are mapped to temporally concurrent tube segments are rejected e.g., TS_1 and TS_2 of Figure 3(c) cannot form a single tube (the corresponding natural object would be at two places at the same time).

Hence, for a given error-free composite tube this approach leads to a number of possible events. Tube features such as area or velocity may be used to determine the event that is most likely to have happened, but in general more features such as color or texture will need to be obtained in order to rank these events while the result will also depend on the application domain. This approach has the following advantages: (i) Tubes are used as a feature that can be employed by definitions of natural events in a knowledge base [3]. (ii) The possible events that are examined are restricted in number and identified. (iii) Processing with other features is optional but can greatly increase the accuracy of the inference process and enable balancing between complexity and validity of the results as developed in [3, 4] (iv) If other feature extraction algorithms are applied, tubes can provide the region of interest.

By assigning verbs to events (e.g., "meet" for merge, "part" for split), and designating each natural object with an alphanumeric label, it is possible to map the detected natural events to natural language descriptions as described in [6]. If objects are known or identified then their labels are replaced by their name or property.

4 Ambiguities due to Errors

In real-life applications sensor information will often be inaccurate and will lead to errors, due to imperfections of the devices and algorithms used. Additionally, there exist certain errors that are introduced when dealing with two-dimensional signals that describe three-dimensional scenes (e.g., occlusion). Certainly, the assumption that each moving object generates exactly one tube is not valid in that case and a tube preprocessing stage must be introduced before proceeding to examination of natural events.

There are three main errors that can be observed in tubes with respect to natural objects:

1. *Temporal discontinuity.* A single natural object may generate more than one tubes due to occlusion or other factors. An example is given in Figure 4(b), where two tubes are generated and correspond to a single tube given in Figure 4(a).
2. *Spatial discontinuity.* A single natural object generates two or more concurrent tubes, because parts of the object were detected as different moving objects. An example of the combination of this and the previous error is given in Figure 4(c).
3. *Noise.* A tube is generated where no moving object exists. This is common in algorithms that determine the motion mask of a video sequence, where sudden changes in the lighting conditions lead to detection of regions that do not correspond to moving objects in the original scene.

A tube preprocessing stage can be introduced to compensate for these errors based on how objects are expected to behave in the given application domain.

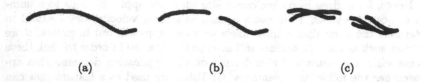

(a)   (b)   (c)

Fig. 4. Tube errors. (a) Correct tube. (b) Temporal discontinuity (c) Spatial and temporal discontinuity.

Generally, each composite tube or set of neighboring composite tubes is transformed into composite tubes that have "lower resolutions". A weight is assigned to each of them, designating the degree up to which they approximate the ideal scenario of section 3. Its value is determined using a set of metrics on tubes e.g., the distance or displacement vector between a stop and a consequtive start event (so as to identify temporal discontinuities) and a correpsonding fuzzy membership function [7]. For example, the tubes of Figure 4(c) can be transformed into the tubes of Figures 4(b) and 4(a).

For each transformed composite tube, there exists a different set of natural events, as in section 3. Based on the weight of each transformed composite tube a certainty value is assigned to each of the natural events, denoting our degree of belief that this event is what actually happened. Additional features can then be used to increase or reduce this certainty value and rank the possible outcomes.

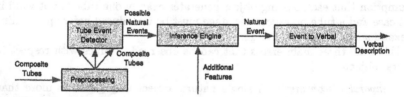

Fig. 5. The stages of identifying and assigning verbal descriptions to natural events using tubes.

Figure 5 presents a simplified block diagram that summarizes the use of tubes in extracting verbal descriptions based on motion in a scene. Note that there are two main sources of ambiguity in this process: (i) Image processing errors that are dealt with in the preprocessing stage and (ii) the one-to-many mapping of a composite tube to natural events. In the latter case the inference engine uses domain information as well as additional features to reason about the event that is most likely to have occurred.

5 Experiments

In order to evaluate the use of tubes in motion analysis and detection of natural events, a number of experiments were conducted using video sequences obtained from a static camera, mainly based on the datasets provided by [1]. The foreground mask is extracted using two techniques, the first one [8] is fast but rather error prone when there are sudden changes in the lighting conditions while the second [2] is more accurate but computationally intensive. In both cases filtering and morphological operations served as an initial processing stage.

A simple set of rules was used to transform and remove errors from the extracted composite tubes. These rules were based on the tube segments' duration and area as well as the distance between successive stop and start events. Tube segments with small duration or very small area were removed or merged with other tube segments depending on whether they formed a composite tube on their own. If such a tube segment was also a composite tube it was considered noise and was removed, otherwise it was merged with a tube segment with longer duration or larger area to avoid spatial discontinuities. Furthermore, composite tubes that were very close to each other were united to avoid temporal discontinuities.

Figure 6 shows an example taken from a 300-frame video sequence. Note that using rules to transform the original tubes removes the errors caused by inaccurate information obtained through image processing operations. In most experiments, the results from both foreground extraction algorithms were similar, even though the foreground mask provided by [2] was far more accurate.

6 Conclusions

Space-time tubes, a novel feature that can be used to analyze motion information, was presented and the stages required to obtain semantic-level natural language descriptions regarding events in the observed scene were outlined. Experiments that were carried out demonstrated how the use of tubes and tube processing can overcome image processing errors that would otherwise lead to false conclusions in event detection within video sequences. The main benefits of using tubes lie on the fact that information about natural events is obtained through knowledge based reasoning and rules, not based on raw sensor information or low level processing results that tend to be inaccurate. Furthermore, tubes can be used in conjunction with other features independently, thus allowing for smooth integration to a general reasoning framework.

References

1. EC Funded CAVIAR project/IST 2001 37540 http://homepages.inf.ed.ac.uk/rbf/CAVIAR/.

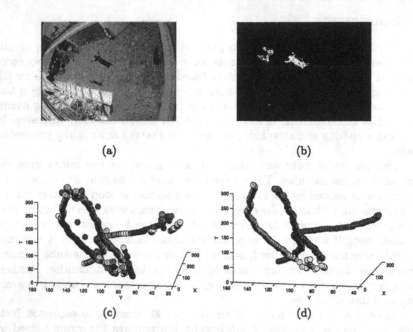

Fig. 6. (a) Original image (b) Foreground mask (c) Centroids of the tubes before processing. Different colors indicate tube segments. (d) Centroids of processed tubes.

2. Ahmed Elgammal, David Harwood, and Larry Davis. Non-parametric model for background subtraction. In *Proceedings of the 6th European Conference on Computer Vision*, pages 751–767, 2000.
3. M. Falelakis, C. Diou, A. Valsamidis, and A. Delopoulos. Complexity control in semantic identification. In *IEEE International Conference on Fuzzy Systems, Reno, Nevada, USA*, May 2005.
4. M. Falelakis, C. Diou, A. Valsamidis, and A. Delopoulos. Dynamic semantic identification with complexity constraints as a knapsack problem. In *IEEE International Conference on Fuzzy Systems, Reno, Nevada, USA*, May 2005.
5. Ismail Haritaoglu, David Harwood, and Larry Davis. w^4: Real-time surveillance of people and their activities. *IEEE Transactions on pattern analysis and machnine intelligence*, 22(8), August 2000.
6. Gerd Herzog and Peter Wazinski. Visual translator: Linking perceptions and natural language descriptions. *Artificial Intelligence Review*, 8(2-3):175–187, March 1994.
7. George J. Klir and Bo Yuan. *Fuzzy Sets and Fuzzy Logic; Theory and Applications*. Prentice Hall, 1995.
8. Christopher Richard Wren, Ali Azarbayejani, Trevor Darrell, and Alex Paul Pentland. Pfinder: Real-time tracking of the human body. *IEEE Transactions on pattern analysis and machnine intelligence*, 19(7):780–785, July 1997.

Semantic Concept Detection from News Videos with Self-Organizing Maps*

Markus Koskela[1] and Jorma Laaksonen[2]

[1] Centre for Digital Video Processing, Dublin City University, Ireland
markus.koskela@computing.dcu.ie
[2] Adaptive Informatics Research Centre, Helsinki University of
Technology, Finland
jorma.laaksonen@hut.fi

Abstract. In this paper, we consider the automatic identification of video shots that are relevant to a given semantic concept from large video databases. We apply a method of representing semantic concepts as class models on a set of parallel Self-Organizing Maps trained with multimodal low-level features. The presented experiments were conducted using a set of 170 hours of video containing recorded television news programs.

1 Introduction

Matching semantic concepts and visual data has attracted a lot of research attention recently in order to facilitate semantic indexing and concept-based retrieval of multimedia content. Traditional example-based retrieval via relevance feedback or other methods can be enriched with semantic concept models that have been trained off-line with considerably more positive and negative examples than what are available on-line for an ordinary image or video query. For producing large-scale semantic concept models of visual data, the predominant approach is to treat the problem as a generic learning problem in which existing sets of training data is used to learn models of different concepts over low-level feature distributions. This is due to scalability requirements, as a comprehensive visual lexicon needs models for hundreds or thousands of concepts.

In this paper, we study the problem of general semantic concept detection from news videos by utilizing a hierarchical approach to indexing video and by extracting multiple parallel features from the different data modalities. A set of Self-Organizing Maps (SOMs) is then trained on these features to provide a common indexing structure across the different modalities. The rest of the paper is organized as follows. The use of SOMs for indexing video and the used multimodal features are briefly described in Section 2. In Section 3 we discuss the use of parallel low-level SOM indices in modeling semantic concepts. A set of

* This work was supported by the Academy of Finland in the projects *Neural methods in information retrieval based on automatic content analysis and relevance feedback* and *Finnish Centre of Excellence in Adaptive Informatics Research*.

Please use the following format when citing this chapter:

Koskela, Markus, Laaksonen, Jorma, 2006, in IFIP International Federation forInformation Processing, Volume 204, Artificial Intelligence Applications and Innovations, eds. Maglogiannis, I., Karpouzis, K., Bramer, M., (Boston: Springer), pp. 591–599

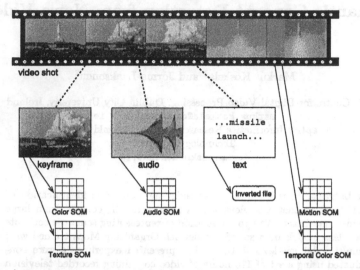

Fig. 1. A hierarchical view on video data and associated multimodal feature indices.

experiments in high-level concept detection on the TRECVID 2005 news video data are described in Section 4, and conclusions are presented in Section 5.

2 Indexing Video Shots with Self-Organizing Maps

The Self-Organizing Map (SOM) [1] is a powerful tool for exploring huge amounts of high-dimensional data. It defines an elastic, topology-preserving grid of points that is fitted to the input space. In a typical data mining, visualization, or information retrieval application, a SOM is trained in a fully unsupervised mode, using a large batch of training data. Yet, it is often known that the data contain some semantically related object groupings or classes, and there are available subsets of vectors belonging to such user-defined classes. Such a set of vectors can be mapped on a trained SOM by finding the best matching unit (BMU) for each vector in the set. These "hits" over the units of the SOM surface form a discrete probability distribution which characterizes the object class. Different distributions can be obtained by using different feature extraction techniques, leading to different representations of the same data items.

2.1 Indexing Hierarchical Objects

The PicSOM system [2] is a general framework for research on content-based indexing and retrieval of visual objects. An extension to PicSOM for indexing any multi-part and multimodal objects having a natural hierarchy with multiple SOMs was presented in [3]. Such object hierarchies can be found e.g. in web pages, e-mail and MMS messages, and digital video. The multi-part hierarchy used for indexing video shots in this paper is illustrated in Fig. 1. The video shot itself is considered as the main or parent object. The keyframes (i.e. representative still images captured within the shot), audio track, and automatic speech recognition (ASR) text data are linked as children of the parent object. This hierarchy could also be extended further, e.g. the keyframe objects could have image segments as subobjects, the original full video is the video shot's parent, etc. All object modalities may have one or more SOMs or other feature indices, and thus all objects in the hierarchy may have links to a set of associated indices.

In this setting, the relevance of each object in the tree structure can be considered as a property of not only the object itself, but to some extent also of the other objects in the same structure. The ground-truth assessments are propagated from the parent, i.e. video shot, object to all children objects, which are then mapped to their corresponding SOMs, as described in more detail in Section 3. Finally, before deciding on the most likely shots associated with a semantic concept, the subobject scores are propagated back to the corresponding video shots.

2.2 Multimodal Features

In indexing video data with SOMs, we used in total four video features, six still image features, and one audio feature. A separate 256×256-sized SOM was trained for each of these eleven features. For the ASR text data, we used two alternative conceptwise text features based on an inverted file. These features are only briefly listed below, see [4] for more details.

Video features. On the video shot level, we used the MPEG-7 [5] *Motion Activity* (MA) descriptor and temporal versions of three still image features: *Average Color* (AC), *Color Moments* (CM) and *Texture Neighborhood* (TN). The temporal image features are calculated by dividing the shot into five equal parts and extracting averaged feature vectors for each part. The feature vector of the shot is then obtained by concatenating these five vectors.

Image features. For the keyframe indices we used a set of six standard MPEG-7 [5] descriptors, viz. *Color Layout* (CL), *Color Structure* (CS), *Dominant Color* (DC), *Scalable Color* (SC), *Edge Histogram* (EH), and *Homogeneous Texture* (HT). The descriptors were extracted globally from every keyframe in the collection, i.e. no segmentation or zoning was used.

Audio features. The Mel-scaled cepstral coefficient, or shortly *Mel Cepstrum* (CE) is the discrete cosine transform applied to the logarithm of the mel-scaled filter bank energies, appended with the total power of the signal.

Text features. Unlike the other features, an inverted file instead of a SOM index was used for the ASR output. The text features were constructed by gathering concept-dependent lists of 10 and 100 most informative terms.

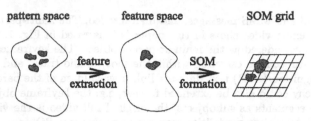

Fig. 2. Stages in creating a class model from the very-high-dimensional pattern space through the high-dimensional feature space to the two-dimensional SOM grid.

3 Semantic Concepts as SOM Class Models

Assume that we have trained a SOM in an unsupervised fashion, using a large set of high-dimensional vectors. Let us choose a subset of vectors, which may be included in the original training set or be a new sample of similar data. The subset contains objects that are semantically related, as defined by a human user. Such a subset is standardly *mapped* on the trained SOM by finding the BMU for each vector and counting the number of hits for each map unit. Normalized to unit sum, the hit frequencies give a discrete histogram which is a sample estimate of a probability distribution of the class on the SOM surface [6].

The shape of the distribution on the SOM surface depends on several factors:

– The distribution of the *original data* in the very-high-dimensional pattern space is generally given and cannot be controlled.
– The *feature extraction* technique in use affects the metrics and thus the distribution of all the generated feature vectors.
– The *overall shape* of the training set, after it has been mapped from the original data space to the feature vector space, determines the overall organization of the SOM.
– The *class distribution* of the studied object subset or class, relative to the overall shape of the feature vector distribution, specifies the layout of the class on the formed SOM.

Figure 2 visualizes how the pattern space is projected to feature space, the vectors of which are then used in training the SOM. The areas occupied by objects of a particular class are shown with gray shades.

In the very-high-dimensional pattern space the distribution of any nontrivial object class is most certainly sparse. As a consequence, in most cases it is meaningless to talk about the uni- or multimodality of class distributions in the pattern space. On the other hand, if the feature extraction stage is working properly, semantically similar patterns will in the feature space be mapped nearer to each other than semantically dissimilar ones. In the most advantageous situation, the pattern classes match clusters in the feature space, i.e. there exists a one-to-one correspondence between feature vector clusters and pattern classes. The relative distances between the feature vectors of a class

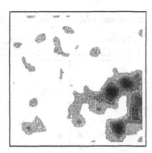

Fig. 3. An example class model (concept *explosion/fire* on the Color Layout SOM). Areas occupied by objects of the concept are shown with gray shades.

compared to the overall distribution of the feature space data determine how well the class is concentrated on nearby SOM units. This can also be measured quantitatively [6].

Due to the topology preservation property of the SOM, one may now force the neighboring SOM units to interact by *low-pass filtering* or *convolving* the hit distributions on the SOM surface. When the surface is convolved, the one-to-one relationship between input vectors' SOM indices and hits on the SOM surface is broken. Instead, each hit results in a spread point response around the BMU. These class-conditional distributions or *class models* can be considered as estimates of the true distributions of the semantic concepts in question, not on the original feature spaces, but on the discrete two-dimensional grids defined by the used SOMs (see Fig. 3 for an example). Thereby, instead of modeling the probability density function in the high-dimensional feature spaces, we are essentially performing kernel-based estimation of class densities at the discrete distributions over the SOM surface. Depending on the variance of the kernel function, these kernels will overlap and weight vectors close to each other will partially share each other's probability mass.

For example, the most representative objects of a given semantic concept can be obtained by locating the SOM units, and the objects mapped to these units, that have the highest responses on the estimated class distribution. And, as the response values of the parallel indices are mutually comparable, we can determine a global ordering and the overall best candidate objects also when using multiple SOMs. By locating the corresponding objects in all SOM indices, we get their scores with respect to different features. The total scores for the candidate objects are then obtained by summing up the mapwise values. Furthermore, the shortcomings of different features with certain semantic concepts can be examined by studying the objects that yield a strong response on the class distributions but do not share the semantic content in question.

The responses invoked by different class models on the SOMs can also be directly used in automatic annotation of new objects. For this purpose, there are two distinct approaches. First, we can enumerate over all concepts and annotate those new objects that have the overall highest responses on the class models

Table 1. Features used in the experiments for each concept to be detected.

semantic concept	video				image						audio	text	
	MA	AC	CM	TN	CL	CS	DC	SC	EH	HT	CE	10	100
walking/running	×	×							×				
explosion/fire			×		×				×			×	
maps		×	×				×	×	×	×		×	
flag-us	×		×	×					×		×		
building		×	×				×	×	×			×	
waterscape/waterfront	×	×	×	×	×				×			×	
mountain	×	×	×						×	×	×		
prisoner									×				
sports	×	×	×		×				×			×	
car	×	×	×	×	×				×	×	×	×	

with the corresponding concept or annotation [7]. Alternatively, the input objects we want to annotate can be used to construct a new class distribution which is then compared to the existing models of semantic concepts using some distance measure suitable for probability distributions [8]. The latter approach is suited for the annotation of object groups sharing a semantic concept in a natural way; with more reference objects of a given concept available, the estimate of the corresponding distribution can be expected to become more accurate.

4 Experiments

For associating specific semantic concepts with visual objects by using a generative approach, a method is needed for estimating the distribution of the concept over the feature representations of the training data. For this purpose, we use an existing lexicon for the development set of the TRECVID 2005 corpus and construct class models for the concepts to be detected (listed in Table 1; for the full definitions see [9, 10]), as described in Section 3. Thus, in these experiments, we do not use specialized detectors, but instead, all concepts are detected using the same procedure based on the ground-truth annotation of that concept.

The main video data for TRECVID 2005 [9] evaluations consists of about 170 hours of TV news in three languages (English, Chinese, Arabic) recorded in November 2004. In addition to the original videos transcoded to MPEG-1 format, a master shot reference [11], common keyframes for each shot, and automatic speech recognition output followed by automatic machine translation for the non-English news programs are provided. The data is split into development and test sets, with 43 907 and 45 766 shots in them, respectively. Furthermore, a joint effort to the participants to annotate the whole development set for 39 concepts (including the 10 concepts in the evaluation and 29 others) was organized. For this purpose, a downloadable tool for Windows platform provided by Carnegie Mellon University and a web-based tool [10] from IBM were available. In the end, most of the development set was in fact annotated twice, so we

Table 2. Detection results for each concept.

semantic concept	average precision			precision at depth			a priori prec.	
	PicSOM	median	max	100	1000	2000	devel.	test
walking/running	0.166	0.145	0.346	0.860	0.395	0.298	0.084	0.079
explosion/fire	0.026	0.037	0.129	0.160	0.055	0.037	0.010	0.009
maps	0.415	0.185	0.526	1.000	0.754	0.465	0.019	0.044
flag-us	0.064	0.071	0.253	0.280	0.091	0.065	0.007	0.011
building	0.226	0.236	0.511	0.970	0.465	0.350	0.073	0.076
waterscape/waterfront	0.344	0.187	0.493	0.970	0.340	0.218	0.026	0.019
mountain	0.305	0.155	0.458	0.920	0.282	0.180	0.013	0.016
prisoner	0.001	0.001	0.056	0.000	0.004	0.005	0.002	0.002
sports	0.210	0.231	0.521	0.560	0.234	0.143	0.040	0.013
car	0.200	0.181	0.369	0.960	0.441	0.297	0.067	0.045
mean	0.196	0.143	0.366	0.668	0.306	0.201	0.034	0.031

adopted a rule that a shot is considered relevant if either one of the annotators had accepted it.

In the high-level feature (concept) extraction task of TRECVID 2005, the purpose was to evaluate different detection methods for semantic concepts. Based on the annotation effort on the development set, the task was to return an ordered list of at most 2000 shots ranked according to the possibility of detecting the presence of the given concept in the shot. Due to the size of the test set, it was not evaluated in full for each concept. Instead, a pool of possibly relevant shots was first obtained by gathering sets of shots returned by the participating groups. These sets were then merged, duplicates removed, and the relevance of this subset is assessed manually. There were 22 participating groups submitting a total of 110 runs, all of which were pooled and judged to depth of 250 shots.

Instead of using a fixed set of features, we selected the set of used features for each concept separately. For this purpose, we applied a SFS-type feature selection scheme, in which we begin with an empty set and compute a criterion value for each of the potential features. If adding the feature with the highest value improves the overall result, that feature is added to the set of used features for that concept and the process is continued. Otherwise we stop the selection process. As the optimization criterion we used the average precision at 2000 returned items with two-fold cross validation on the development set.

The eleven features with SOM indices described in Section 2.2 along with the two concept-dependent text features were always included as potential features. The text features were alternative to each other, so only one of them could be selected. The conceptwise sets of selected features are listed in Table 1 (the feature abbreviations are listed in Section 2.2). As can be seen, the selection process typically resulted in 4–7 parallel features. The *prisoner* concept was a notable exception as adding any second feature, including the text features, beside Homogeneous Texture resulted in performance degradation.

The conceptwise results of detection performance are listed in Table 2. The (non-interpolated) average precision values are obtained by first determining and summing the precision at each location where a relevant shot is found and then dividing the result with the minimum of the total number of relevant shots or the maximum number of returned shots allowed (i.e. 2000). The maximum and median average precisions in Table 2 are also conceptwise, and do not therefore correspond to any single submission. The best single submission had a mean average precision of 0.336. It can be seen that the success of detecting different concepts varies considerably. Some concepts, such as *maps*, *building*, *waterscape/waterfront*, and *car* produce rather good results, especially in the beginning of the result list as can be seen from the "precision at depth 100" column, whereas detecting shots of the concept *prisoner* fails completely.

5 Conclusions

Statistical modeling of mid-level semantic concepts can be a very useful step in supporting high-level querying on visual data. In this paper, we described a method for applying multiple SOMs trained with multimodal features in semantic concept representation and detection. The class models for different semantic concepts were produced using a manually annotated video shot collection as the ground truth. For indexing video shots, we utilized a recently proposed method to support general hierarchical multimodal objects. The video shot, audio track, keyframes and ASR text data are all indexed separately and the ground-truth information and detection scores are propagated intrinsically.

The experiments reported in this paper were a part of our first time participation [4] in the annual TRECVID evaluation, and so we faced a lot of system development and other non-recurring work in order to be able to run the experiments. Therefore, we had limited time to study the effects of different setups and parameter values on the overall performance. Still, the results of the experiments are promising and can be seen to validate that SOM-based class models can be successfully used for detecting semantic concepts from multimodal data.

References

1. Kohonen, T.: Self-Organizing Maps. Third edn. Springer-Verlag (2001)
2. Laaksonen, J., Koskela, M., Oja, E.: PicSOM—Self-organizing image retrieval with MPEG-7 content descriptions. IEEE Transactions on Neural Networks, Special Issue on Intelligent Multimedia Processing 13 (2002) 841–853
3. Sjöberg, M., Laaksonen, J.: Content-based retrieval of web pages and other hierarchical objects with Self-Organizing Maps. In: Proceedings of 15th International Conference on Artificial Neural Networks (ICANN 2005), Warsaw, Poland (2005)
4. Koskela, M., Laaksonen, J., Sjöberg, M., Muurinen, H.: PicSOM experiments in TRECVID 2005. In: TREC Video Retrieval Evaluation Online Proceedings, TRECVID (2005)

5. ISO/IEC: Information technology - Multimedia content description interface - Part 3: Visual (2002) 15938-3:2002(E).
6. Laaksonen, J., Koskela, M., Oja, E.: Class distributions on SOM surfaces for feature extraction and object retrieval. Neural Networks **17** (2004) 1121–1133
7. Viitaniemi, V., Laaksonen, J.: Keyword-detection approach to automatic image annotation. In: Proceedings of 2nd European Workshop on the Integration of Knowledge, Semantic and Digital Media Technologies, London, UK (2005)
8. Koskela, M., Laaksonen, J.: Semantic annotation of image groups with Self-Organizing Maps. In: Proceedings of 4th International Conference on Image and Video Retrieval (CIVR 2005), Singapore (2005) 518–527
9. Over, P., Ianeva, T., Kraaij, W., Smeaton, A.F.: TRECVID 2005 - an introduction. In: TREC Video Retrieval Evaluation Online Proceedings, TRECVID (2005)
10. Volkmer, T., Smith, J.R., Natsev, A.P., Campbell, M., Naphade, M.: A web-based system for collaborative annotation of large image and video collections. In: Proc. 13th ACM International Conference on Multimedia, Singapore (2005)
11. Petersohn, C.: Fraunhofer HHI at TRECVID 2004: Shot boundary detection system. In: TREC Video Retrieval Evaluation Online Proceedings, TRECVID (2004)

Analysis of Semantic Information Available in an Image Collection Augmented with Auxiliary Data*

Mats Sjöberg, Ville Viitaniemi, Jorma Laaksonen, and Timo Honkela

Adaptive Informatics Research Centre,
Helsinki University of Technology
P.O.BOX 5400, FI-02015 TKK, Finland
{mats.sjoberg,ville.viitaniemi,jorma.laaksonen,timo.honkela}@hut.fi

Abstract. An art installation was on display in the Centre Pompidou National Museum of Modern Art in Paris, where visitors could contribute with their own personal objects, adding keyword descriptions and quantified semantic features such as *age* or *hardness*. The data was projected in real-time onto a Self-Organizing Map (SOM) which was shown in the gallery. In this paper we analyze the same data by extracting visual features from the images and organize the image collection with multiple SOMs. We show how this mapping facilitates the emergence of semantic associations between visual, textual and metadata modalities by studying the distributions of the different feature vectors on the SOMs.

1 Introduction

In this paper we conduct an analysis on an image collection that has been augmented with descriptive features and keywords. The image collection consists of a database collected during an interactive museum installation. This installation, "Pockets Full of Memories" was on display in the Centre Pompidou National Museum of Modern Art, Paris, France from April 10 to September 3, 2001 [1]. The visitors contributed over 3300 objects digitally scanning and describing them. This information was stored in a database and organized by the Self-Organizing Map (SOM) algorithm [2] that positioned objects of similar descriptions near each other in a two-dimensional map. The map of objects was updated online and projected on a wall in the gallery [1].

The self-organizing algorithm was the basic method used to create the "wall of objects". The SOM organized the input items into an ordered display, a planar map. In this exhibition, the input features consisted of attributes and keywords given by the exhibition visitors together with the objects. The attribute values and keywords were transformed into numerical form that could

---

* This work was supported by the Academy of Finland in the projects *Neural methods in information retrieval based on automatic content analysis and relevance feedback* and *Finnish Centre of Excellence in Adaptive Informatics Research*.

Please use the following format when citing this chapter:

Sjoberg, Mats, Viitaniemi, Ville, Laaksonen, Jorma, Honkela, Timo, 2006, in IFIP International Federation for Information Processing, Volume 204, Artificial Intelligence Applications and Innovations, eds. Maglogiannis, I., Karpouzis, K., Bramer, M., (Boston: Springer), pp. 600–608

serve as inputs to the SOM algorithm. Close to each item on the map there were items that had been given similar attribute values, items that had similar keywords, or both. Thus, all the items with a particular keyword were not necessarily next to each other if the other features varied. The ordering of the final map is a consequence of all the inputs. The phenomenon is called emergence: the order of the objects is not determined beforehand, but emerges through the audience contributions. The classification system is merely created through the large number of local interactions on the map, rather than specified by hand.

In the exhibition, even if the visual qualities of two different images were very similar, their respective owners may have evaluated their attributes very differently based on their subjective points of view. In this paper, we take a step further: we aim at correlating the visual features from the images themselves and the given metadata in order to extract semantic information. In the following, we describe the image segmentation process, how class distributions are analyzed and what features were used. After that, we present the experiment results and draw some conclusions.

2 Methods for Finding Semantic Associations

In this section, we describe the methodological steps needed in finding semantic associations, i.e. associations between the automatically computed multimodal features and the separate metadata. We outline the method for image segmentation and then provide details of the semantic association process. Finally we shortly present the different feature extraction methods used. The described processing stages have been implemented in our PicSOM[2] content-based image retrieval (CBIR) system [3].

2.1 Segmentation

The purpose of image segmentation is to partition images into segments that can be analyzed separately. Individual segments are often easier to analyze and interpret than the image as a whole, e.g. when the segments correspond to distinct objects in the physical world. Analysis of the individual segments also facilitates the interpretation of the whole image in terms of its constituent segments and their relationships. In the current application, the image segmentation algorithm is used to separate the objects of interest from image backgrounds. The subsequent image analysis is thus more accurately focused on the properties of the relevant objects, not on the properties of the different backgrounds against which the objects happen to be scanned.

The segmentation proceeds in two steps. First, a generic color image segmentation partitions the images into eight regions. The generic segmentation method first radically oversegments the image. This is achieved by applying

---

[2] http://www.cis.hut.fi/picsom

Fig. 1. Two images from the collection and their segmentations. In the left "watch" image the background is dark whereas it is light in the right "lipsalve" image.

the k-means algorithm [4] to the CIE L*a*b* color space [5] representations of the image pixels. After this process, the resulting regions are merged until eight regions are left. The merging criterion is based on the combination of the average color of the regions and a multi-scale edge strength measure.

The second step of segmentation exploits the special image structure with centrally located objects against nearly constant-colored backgrounds. Here a straightforward set of inference rules is applied to tag some of the regions as background. The remaining regions are interpreted to represent the objects of interest. The tagging begins by identifying the likely background color by considering those regions that are homogenous in color and form a significant part of the peripheral image area. Having the background color identified, similarly colored homogeneous regions are tagged as background if they are adjacent to either the image borders or already tagged background regions.

The image segmentation results are good in most cases. Some exceptions result from the background color seamlessly penetrating the object. An example can be seen in Fig. 1 where the dark background color can not be separated from the dark areas of the band of the wrist watch. Also objects that stand out poorly from the background and disconnected objects (e.g. transparent plastic bags and thin necklaces) often result in deficient segmentations. Fortunately, even when the segmentation results are strictly speaking erroneous, they are still often adequate for the subsequent image analysis as similar objects are segmented in a qualitatively similar manner. For instance, as the wrist bands of watches are often regarded partly as background, the image analysis concentrates on the clock-faces for most wrist watches. For the current experiments the segmentations are at least adequate in focusing the image analysis to the relevant parts of the images. It does not seem likely that the experiment results would be significantly compromised by faulty segmentations.

2.2 Analysis of Class Distributions

In a typical application of the Self-Organizing Map (SOM) in data mining, visualization or information retrieval, a SOM is trained in a fully unsupervised mode, using a large batch of training data vectors. Yet, the data often contains some semantically related object groupings or classes, and sets of objects belonging to such user-defined classes are known. Such a set of vectors can be mapped on a trained SOM by finding the best matching unit for each vector in the set. These "hits" over the map units form a discrete probability distribution over the two-dimensional SOM surface which characterizes the object class. Qualitatively different distributions can be obtained from the same data by using different feature extraction techniques, leading to different numerical representations of the data items.

The mapping of a semantic class on a specific SOM gives insight into how well the corresponding feature can cluster the vectors of that class. The sparse value fields on the maps are low-pass filtered to spread the information. This also helps visual inspection as the marked areas become larger and more uniform.

In our study, we map the user-given keywords on the SOM surfaces along with the images themselves to see which keywords, numerical attributes and visual features correlate the best. This in turn will reveal the semantic characteristics of the objects from their visual appearances and associated metadata.

2.3 Extraction of Multimodal Features

We used in total three different image features, the user-provided attribute values and keywords. A 64×64-sized SOM was trained for each of these five features. In the following, the features are described in some detail.

Visual Features: The visual features were extracted only from the area of the image which the segmentation algorithm had identified as belonging to the object (i.e. not the background). The standard MPEG-7 [6] *Edge Histogram* feature measures the distribution of edge directions within the object and thus describes the texture and local shapes. *Zernike moments* [7] describe the overall shape of the object's segmentation mask. The *color moment* feature characterizes the color distribution within the object with the three first central moments.

Value Features: For each image, eight values were given by the owner of the object, quantifying its properties with regard to specific attributes as shown in Fig. 2. The property pairs were old—new, soft—hard, natural—synthetic, disposable—long use, personal—nonpersonal, fashionable—not fashionable, useful—useless, and functional—symbolic. The quantifications were given using a touch sensitive screen. We have scaled the resulting values to the range [−1, 1] and collected them as components of an 8-dimensional *values* vector.

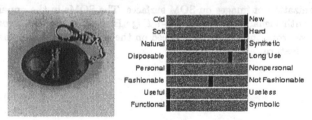

Fig. 2. An "attackalarm" and the property values given by its owner.

Keyword Features: The keyword text data was primarily used as such to annotate the images and to define per-keyword image classes. In addition, we also created an *n-gram* statistical feature made of character triplets extracted from the keywords.

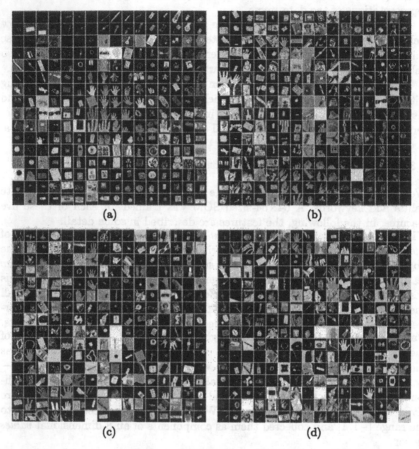

(a)   (b)

(c)   (d)

Fig. 3. Organization of images on SOM surfaces. The SOMs in the upper row have been trained with visual features MPEG-7 *Edge Histogram* (a) and *color moments* (b). In the lower row, the SOM (c) is based on the *values* feature and the SOM (d) on the *n-gram* feature.

3 Experiments and Results

3.1 Creation of Visually Organized Maps

Fig. 3 shows four SOMs created with different features. Each SOM unit is represented by a visual label which is the most similar image of the database in that feature space. The SOM surface in Fig. 3(a) is organized according to the *Edge Histogram* feature. Objects with similar shapes and orientations form clusters. Within the clusters the object shapes change continuously, thus retaining to topographical ordering of the shape feature space. In subfigure (b) another visual feature, *color moments*, has been used, and a color-based organization is evident.

The SOM of Fig. 3(c) is organized according to the *values* feature. Some clear clusters are formed, for example to the left of the center we find many plush toys and teddy bears with values that reveal softness and very personal items. Additionally, for example, in the upper right corner there are many watches and mobile phones with values indicating items that are useful, functional, new and synthetic. The organization produced by the *n-gram* feature in the bottom-right SOM (d) is not that evident, but one can see that e.g. shoes appear in nearby locations.

3.2 Correlations of Visual Maps and Semantic Concepts

¿From the different attribute quantifications given by the owners of the objects we generated a set of semantic classes. The value ranges $[-1, 1]$ are divided into three equal parts, where the low-end and high-end parts correspond to the semantic extremes. For example, for the *hardness* property, objects with values in the range $[-1, -\frac{1}{3}]$ belong to the semantic class *soft* and those with values in the range $[\frac{1}{3}, 1]$ belong to the class *hard*.

In Fig. 4 we have the distributions of three different semantic classes mapped onto the *Edge Histogram* SOM: *soft*, *natural* and *fashionable*. The dark areas represent map units to which many objects from that semantic class have been mapped to. One immediately notes a clear correlation between the *soft* and *natural* classes. There seems to be a large set of objects that are both soft and natural, roughly in the middle of the *Edge Histogram* SOM. Visual inspection of the SOM labels in Fig. 3(a) indicate that these are mostly human hands. In addition, the two distributions cluster quite cleanly, indicating that the feature is very discriminative when evaluating these semantic properties.

The observed correlation is intuitively easy to understand as many natural objects are also soft. Besides, the *Edge Histogram*, being a texture feature sensitive to local edges in the image, should be good at discriminating soft edges from hard ones. The distribution of *fashionable* items shows an example where *Edge Histogram* does not discriminate well as the distribution is relatively disperse.

In Fig. 5 the class *disposable* has been mapped on three different SOMs: *Edge Histogram*, *Zernike moment* and *color moment*. All three maps show good or very good clustering, with the disposable objects cleanly mapped into contiguous areas of the SOMs. Upon inspection of the visual labels on the SOM of the rotation-invariant *Zernike moment* shape descriptor (not shown here), we notice that the positively-marked upper-right corner of the map shows mostly rectangular objects like candy boxes and pieces of paper like bus tickets. A similar analysis of the visual labels of the *color moments* SOM in Fig. 3(b) shows mostly items with white or light colors.

3.3 Matching of English and French Words

One interesting aspect of the keyword collection is that it consists of both English and French words. One typical class of objects in the database is referred to as *pen* or *pencil* in English and *crayon* in French. In the collection, there are 11 images keyworded as *pen*, 9 as *pencil* and 33 as *crayon*. The distributions of these sets on the *Zernike moment* SOM are plotted in Fig. 6. One can see that the areas of densest object distributions are mostly located in the bottom part of the SOM surface. This result supports our working hypothesis that meaningful relationships between both intra-lingual synonyms and inter-lingual word translations can emerge based on auxiliary, non-textual data modalities.

4 Conclusions

The self-organization of objects is an effective method for detecting inherent structures, patterns and clusters in complex collections of data. With it, one is able to automatically find different kinds of associations between the items when different data modalities and features are considered in parallel. We are ascertained that these phenomena will prove to be useful in semantic analysis of multimodal data collections. Potential application areas include emergent semantic representations useful in the contexts of the semantic web, machine translation, visual data mining, and creation of pictorial dictionaries.

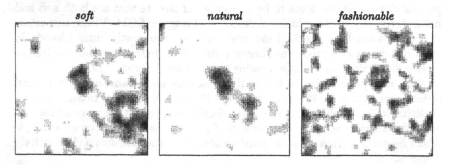

Fig. 4. The class models of *soft*, *natural* and *disposable* on the *Edge Histogram* SOM.

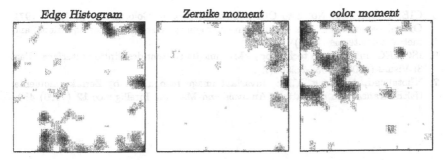

Fig. 5. The class models of *disposable* objects on the MPEG-7 *Edge Histogram*, *Zernike moment* and *color moment* SOMs.

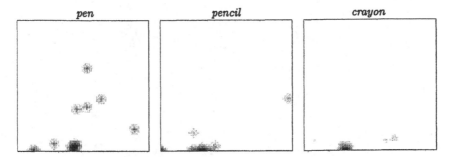

Fig. 6. Distributions of *pen*, *pencil* and *crayon* classes on the *Zernike moment* SOM.

The described procedure also demonstrates the use of automatic image segmentation to focus the processing on relevant parts of the images. In the light of the presented example, it is evident that segmentation does not need to be exactly correct in order to be helpful in processing visually-grounded semantic information. In general, autonomous machine learning from large multimodal databases in a statistical manner seems to provide an efficient and robust method for modeling grounded semantic relationships.

References

1. Legrady, G., Honkela, T.: Pockets full of memories: an interactive museum installation. Visual Communication **1** (2002) 163–169
2. Kohonen, T.: Self-Organizing Maps. Third edn. Volume 30 of Springer Series in Information Sciences. Springer-Verlag (2001)
3. Laaksonen, J., Koskela, M., Oja, E.: PicSOM—Self-organizing image retrieval with MPEG-7 content descriptions. IEEE Transactions on Neural Networks, Special Issue on Intelligent Multimedia Processing **13** (2002) 841–853
4. Schalkoff, R.J.: Pattern Recognition: Statistical, Structural and Neural Approaches. John Wiley & Sons, Ltd. (1992)

5. CIE: Supplement No. 2 to CIE publication No. 15 Colorimetry (E-1.3.1) 1971: Official recommendations on uniform color spaces, color-difference equations, and metric color terms (1976)
6. ISO/IEC: Information technology - Multimedia content description interface - Part 3: Visual (2002) 15938-3:2002(E).
7. Khotanzad, A., Hong, Y.H.: Invariant image recognition by Zernike moments. IEEE Transaction on Pattern Analysis and Machine Intelligence 12 (1990) 489–497

Supporting Semi-Automatic Semantic Annotation of Multimedia Resources

Jeff Z. Pan and Chris Mellish

Dept. of Computing Science, University of Aberdeen, Aberdeen AB24 3UE, UK
{jpan,cmellish}@csd.abdn.ac.uk

Abstract. Ontologies provide an attractive basis for the representation of semantic information to be attached to multimedia information. However, the flexibility available to develop one's own ontology or partially reuse an existing ontology means that human input is unavoidable in the process of creating the annotations. We address the issue of how to use ontology reasoning services and natural language generation to provide presentations of relevant ontology structures for human use.

1 Capturing Intended Meanings with Ontologies

Multimedia resources are complex spatio-temporal signals providing information at several levels of abstraction. How to make the huge amount of multimedia information more easily accessible to automatic processing of multimedia resources by programs is an important issue. One possible solution is to associate multimedia resources with some annotations, with the help of which automatic processes have better understanding of the contents of multimedia resources. However, annotations alone do not establish the semantics of the vocabulary used in the annotations.[1]

One way of giving meaning to annotations is to provide some external agreement on the meaning of a set of information properties. For example, the Dublin Core Metadata Element Set [4] provides 15 'core' information properties, such as 'Title', 'Creator', 'Date', with descriptive semantic definitions (in natural language). One can use these information properties in, e.g., RDF or META tags of HTML. The limitation of the 'external agreement' approach is its inflexibility, i.e., only a limited range of pre-defined information properties can be expressed.

An alternative approach is to use ontologies to specify the meaning of Web resources. *Ontology* is a term borrowed from philosophy that refers to the science of describing the kinds of entities in the world and how they are related. In computer science, ontology is, in general, a 'representation of a shared conceptualisation' of a specific domain [6, 13]. It provides a shared and common *vocabulary*, including important concepts, properties and their definitions, and *constraints*, sometimes referred to as background assumptions regarding the intended meaning of the vocabulary, used in a domain that can be communicated between people and heterogeneous, distributed application systems. The ontology approach is more flexible than the external agreement approach because users can customise vocabulary and constraints in ontologies.

---

[1] For example, an annotation asserting that the object in an image is an elephant does not explain what elephants are.

Please use the following format when citing this chapter:

Pan, Jeff, Mellish, Chris, 2006, in IFIP International Federation for Information Processing, Volume 204, Artificial Intelligence Applications and Innovations, eds. Maglogiannis, I., Karpouzis, K., Bramer, M., (Boston: Springer), pp. 609–617.

Example 1. The meaning of a user-defined concept 'adults' can be specified as 'persons whose age are at least 18', where 'persons' can be an atomic concept in an ontology:[2]

$$\text{Adult} \equiv \text{Person} \sqcap \exists age.\texttt{atleast18}.$$

In general, there are at least two advantages of the ontology approach in creating multimedia annotations: (i) It is more flexible; uses can define the vocabulary needed in their domain. (ii) Aspects of the intended meaning of these vocabulary can be explicitly represented. However, while the above advantage (ii) makes it possible for ontology experts to check the intended meaning of terms defined in an ontology, it is usually too hard for ordinary users to check such intended meaning by themselves.

In this paper, we address the issue of how to use ontology reasoning services and natural language generation to provide human-readable presentation of parts of ontologies. We claim this is an important way to support human users who have to create multimedia annotations. The rest of the paper is organised as follows. After a brief introduction of ontology languages (Section 2), we argue that the human beings play an important role in creating multimedia annotations. Based on this observation, we discuss techniques on how to generate natural language to represent axioms in ontologies, with the help of classification (Section 4). We provide a worked example (Section 5) to illustrate our approach before we conclude the paper.

2 Ontology Languages

The technique presented is not restricted to any specific ontology language. As the OWL Web Ontology Language is based on Description Logic, here we will assume that we will use a Description Logic as the ontology language.

Description Logics (DLs) [1] are a family of class-based knowledge representation formalisms, equipped with well-defined model-theoretic semantics [2]. A Description Logic $\mathcal{L}$ consists of an alphabet of distinct concept names (C), role names (R) and individual (object) names (I); together with a set of constructors to construct concept and role descriptions (also called $\mathcal{L}$-*concepts* and $\mathcal{L}$-*roles*, respectively). DLs have a model theoretic semantics, which is defined in terms of interpretations. An *interpretation* (written as $\mathcal{I}$) consists of a *domain* (written as $\Delta^{\mathcal{I}}$) and an *interpretation function* (written as $\cdot^{\mathcal{I}}$), where the domain is a nonempty set of objects and the interpretation function maps each individual name a $\in$ I to an element $a^{\mathcal{I}} \in \Delta^{\mathcal{I}}$, each concept name CN $\in$ C to a subset $CN^{\mathcal{I}} \subseteq \Delta^{\mathcal{I}}$, and each role name $RN \in$ R to a binary relation $RN^{\mathcal{I}} \subseteq \Delta^{\mathcal{I}} \times \Delta^{\mathcal{I}}$. The interpretation function can be extended to give semantics to $\mathcal{L}$-concepts and $\mathcal{L}$-roles (see table 1 for the semantics of concept and role descriptions of OWL DL). Let C, D be $\mathcal{L}$-concepts, C is *satisfiable* iff there exist an interpretation $\mathcal{I}$ s.t. $C^{\mathcal{I}} \neq \emptyset$; C *subsumes* D iff for every interpretation $\mathcal{I}$ we have $C^{\mathcal{I}} \subseteq D^{\mathcal{I}}$. A DL knowledge base consists of a set of axioms. Due to the limitation of space, here

---

[2] Please refer to Section 2 for details of the following Description Logics syntax. Note that the Semantic Web standard ontology language does not support customised datatype, such as atleast18, which is supported by a datatype extension of OWL DL, called OWL-Eu [10].

Abstract Syntax	DL Syntax	Semantics
Class(A)	A	$A^{\mathcal{I}} \subseteq \Delta^{\mathcal{I}}$
Class(owl:Thing)	$\top$	$\top^{\mathcal{I}} = \Delta^{\mathcal{I}}$
Class(owl:Nothing)	$\bot$	$\bot^{\mathcal{I}} = \emptyset$
intersectionOf($C_1, C_2, \ldots$)	$C_1 \sqcap C_2$	$(C_1 \sqcap C_2)^{\mathcal{I}} = C_1^{\mathcal{I}} \cap C_2^{\mathcal{I}}$
unionOf($C_1, C_2, \ldots$)	$C_1 \sqcup C_2$	$(C_1 \sqcup C_2)^{\mathcal{I}} = C_1^{\mathcal{I}} \cup C_2^{\mathcal{I}}$
complementOf(C)	$\neg C$	$(\neg C)^{\mathcal{I}} = \Delta^{\mathcal{I}} \setminus C^{\mathcal{I}}$
oneOf($o_1, o_2, \ldots$)	$\{o_1\} \sqcup \{o_2\}$	$(\{o_1\} \sqcup \{o_2\})^{\mathcal{I}} = \{o_1^{\mathcal{I}}, o_2^{\mathcal{I}}\}$
restriction(R someValuesFrom(C))	$\exists R.C$	$(\exists R.C)^{\mathcal{I}} = \{x \mid \exists y.\langle x, y \rangle \in R^{\mathcal{I}} \wedge y \in C^{\mathcal{I}}\}$
restriction(R allValuesFrom(C))	$\forall R.C$	$(\forall R.C)^{\mathcal{I}} = \{x \mid \forall y.\langle x, y \rangle \in R^{\mathcal{I}} \to y \in C^{\mathcal{I}}\}$
restriction(R hasValue(o))	$\exists R.\{o\}$	$(\exists R.\{o\})^{\mathcal{I}} = \{x \mid \langle x, o^{\mathcal{I}} \rangle \in R^{\mathcal{I}}\}$
restriction(R minCardinality(m))	$\geqslant mR$	$(\geqslant mR)^{\mathcal{I}} = \{x \mid \#\{y.\langle x, y \rangle \in R^{\mathcal{I}}\} \geq m\}$
restriction(R maxCardinality(m))	$\leqslant mR$	$(\leqslant mR)^{\mathcal{I}} = \{x \mid \#\{y.\langle x, y \rangle \in R^{\mathcal{I}}\} \leq m\}$
restriction(T someValuesFrom(u))	$\exists T.u$	$(\exists T.u)^{\mathcal{I}} = \{x \mid \exists t.\langle x, t \rangle \in T^{\mathcal{I}} \wedge t \in u^{\mathrm{D}}\}$
restriction(T allValuesFrom(u))	$\forall T.u$	$(\forall T.u)^{\mathcal{I}} = \{x \mid \exists t.\langle x, t \rangle \in T^{\mathcal{I}} \to t \in u^{\mathrm{D}}\}$
restriction(T hasValue(w))	$\exists T.\{w\}$	$(\exists T.\{w\})^{\mathcal{I}} = \{x \mid \langle x, w^{\mathrm{D}} \rangle \in T^{\mathcal{I}}\}$
restriction(T minCardinality(m))	$\geqslant mT$	$(\geqslant mT)^{\mathcal{I}} = \{x \mid \#\{t \mid \langle x, t \rangle \in T^{\mathcal{I}}\} \geq m\}$
restriction(T maxCardinality(m))	$\leqslant mT$	$(\leqslant mT)^{\mathcal{I}} = \{x \mid \#\{t \mid \langle x, t \rangle \in T^{\mathcal{I}}\} \leq m\}$
ObjectProperty(S)	S	$S^{\mathcal{I}} \subseteq \Delta^{\mathcal{I}} \times \Delta^{\mathcal{I}}$
ObjectProperty(S' inverseOf(S))	S^-	$(S^-)^{\mathcal{I}} \subseteq \Delta^{\mathcal{I}} \times \Delta^{\mathcal{I}}$
DatatypeProperty(T)	T	$T^{\mathcal{I}} \subseteq \Delta^{\mathcal{I}} \times \Delta_{\mathrm{D}}$

Table 1. OWL concept and property descriptions

we only introduce concept inclusion axioms. A concept inclusion axiom is of the form $C \sqsubseteq D$, where C, D are $\mathcal{L}$-concepts. An interpretation $\mathcal{I}$ satisfies $C \sqsubseteq D$ if $C^{\mathcal{I}} \subseteq D^{\mathcal{I}}$.

In this paper, we use a well known DL reasoning service called *classification*, which is puts *concept names* in their proper place in a taxonomic hierarchy (according to subsumption). As a result of classification, we can obtain the following for a named concept X:

1. the named concepts that are *equivalent* to it;[3]
2. the named concepts that it *covers* (minimally subsumes);[4]
3. the named concepts that it *is covered by* (is minimally subsumed by).[5]

If necessary, the basic subsumption relation can be recovered from this information.

3 The Human Element in Annotation

A number of research projects have investigated how annotations for the Semantic Web can be semi-automatically derived for existing Web documents, and these could

---

[3] X is equivalent to Y iff X subsumes Y and Y subsumes X.

[4] X covers Y iff X subsumes Y, Y is not equivalent to X, and whenever X subsumes Z and Z subsumes Y then Z is equivalent to X or Y.

[5] X is covered by Y iff Y subsumes X, Y is not equivalent to X, and whenever Y subsumes Z and Z subsumes X then Z is equivalent to X or Y.

be adapted for textual documents in general. Techniques include using information extraction (IE) systems that exploit information in particular ontologies [5], providing special user interfaces that facilitate human markup of text [14] and using machine learning to infer general extraction patterns from texts that have already been marked up by humans [3]. However, these approaches all assume at least one of the following:

- Ontology terms always map in a straightforward way onto words in a document and vice versa. Yet it is clear that subtle aspects of content are not always signalled in a simple way by specific keywords.
- Generic patterns suffice to detect in natural language relationships from all specific ontologies. This ignores the fact that specific domains can have their own sublanguages and domain-dependent forms of expression (beyond single words).
- Information extraction expertise is available to create specific patterns for every ontology. This is unrealistic, given the specialised nature of IE expertise.
- Human involvement is required, to augment and edit any annotations that can be automatically created and/or create a training corpus for machine learning.

It is clear that, at present, significant human involvement is required for constructing document annotations for *textual* documents. For multimedia resources that are not textual, human involvement is indispensible. In addition, domain experts must make a significant contribution not only to creating annotations, but also to choosing an ontology in the first place (from among possibly a number of existing options) and also tailoring an existing ontology to meet the needs of the new application. But how will these people acquire the expertise to reliably understand and use the distinctions provided by the ontologies they need to work with? A number of tools have been built to enable a user to visualise the structure of an ontology (using mainly graphical approaches), but these tools are mainly designed for knowledge engineers, rather than domain experts or casual ontology users.

4 Natural Language Presentation of Ontologies

We believe that natural language is an important medium to exploit in presenting ontologies (or parts of them) to their users. To understand natural language, a user does not require any specialised training. Natural language is also well equipped to express the complex logical structures that arise in modern ontologies. Thus our research is trying to find ways of exploiting this medium. An ontology takes the form of a set of logical axioms, and so the challenge is to present the material of these axioms in comprehensible way using a language such as English. However, it is important to take on board the fact that the axioms may not come in a form ready for direct realisation in English. The axioms represent one possible way that the material could have been expressed, but there are many other possible ways that this could have been done equally well. For the ontology writer, the choice is arbitrary – because one can rely on reasoning services for ontologies, it is not necessary to worry about which of the many logically equivalent methods of expression to use. This means however that reasoning services must also be be used in natural language generation. The most relevant things to say may not be explicitly stated, but nevertheless may follow from the axioms. So determining the content to be expressed can be seen as a kind of *inference* from the axioms [8].

We now consider how the *classification* reasoning service can be used to provide the basic elements of a natural language answer to two types of questions that people ask when they are familiarising themselves with an ontology or seeking to use it for making distinctions.

4.1 Answering *What is X?*

To answer this question, we first of all classify all concepts, including X. The following can then be used to extract the key things to be expressed in an answer:

- Find Z such that X is equivalent to Z (to say "Xs are Zs"). In addition, if there is an axiom directly stating $X \equiv Z$, for some possibly complex concept Z, then this axiom can be stated.
- Find Z such that X is covered by Z (to say "an X is a kind of Z").
- Find Z such that X covers Z (to say "Xs include Zs").

The facts retrieved by these steps are closely related to the "identification", "attributive" and "constituency" rhetorical predicates used in McKeown's "identification schema" [7], and the overall answer could be constructed using the pattern of that schema. It would also be possible to recurse through the Z's introduced in the final step, this giving the effect of the "constituency schema".

4.2 Answering *What is the difference between X and Y?*

For this question, again all concepts should initially be classified, and in addition the concepts $X \sqcup Y, X \sqcap \neg Y$ and $Y \sqcap \neg X$ should be named and classified. Useful information for an answer can then be read from the classification results as follows: [6]

- Find Z such that $X \sqcup Y$ is covered by Z (to say "Xs and Ys are both Zs").
- Find minimal Z such that Z subsumes X and it is not the case that Z subsumes Y (to say "Although Xs are Zs, Ys are not necessarily so"). [7]
- Find minimal Z such that Z subsumes Y and it is not the case that Z subsumes X (to say "Although Ys are Zs, Xs are not necessarily so").
- Find maximal Z such that X subsumes Z and it is not the case that Y subsumes Z (to say "Whereas Zs are a kind of X, they are not necessarily a kind of Y").

---

[6] If negations of named concepts are also classified, other possibilities not discussed here include finding Z such that Z subsumes X and $\neg Z$ subsumes Y (to say "Although Xs are Zs, Ys are never Zs").

[7] A good way to find minimal Z subsuming or subsumed by something, and satisfying another condition, is to search through increasingly long paths of the transitive closure of the "covers" relation terminating when the condition is met. Similarly for maximal Z.

- Find maximal Z such that Y subsumes Z and it is not the case that X subsumes Z (to say "Whereas Zs are a kind of Y, they are not necessarily a kind of X").
- Find Z such that $X \sqcap \neg Y$ subsumes Z (to say "Whereas Zs are a kind of X, they are never a kind of Y").
- Find Z such that $Y \sqcap \neg X$ subsumes Z (to say "Whereas Zs are a kind of Y, they are never a kind of X").

Again, ways to organise this material as a coherent text can be found in the natural language generation literature, e.g. McKeown's "compare and contrast" schema and the work of Milosavljevic [9].

5 Worked Example

In this section, we apply our approach to a slightly revised version (for the sake of presentation) of the well know pizza ontology (http://www.co-ode.org/ontologies/pizza/).

$$\text{SpicyPizza} \equiv \text{Pizza} \sqcap \exists has.\text{SpicyTopping} \quad (1)$$
$$\text{VegPizza} \equiv \text{Pizza} \sqcap \forall has.\text{VegTopping} \quad (2)$$
$$\text{AmericanHot} \equiv \text{Pizza} \sqcap \exists has.\text{HopGreenPepperTopping} \sqcap \exists has.\text{DairyTopping} \quad (3)$$
$$\text{HopGreenPepperTopping} \sqsubseteq \text{SpicyTopping} \quad (4)$$
$$\text{Caprina} \equiv \text{Pizza} \sqcap \exists has.\text{TomatoTopping} \quad (5)$$
$$\text{TomatoTopping} \sqsubseteq \text{VegTopping} \quad (6)$$
$$\text{VegTopping} \sqsubseteq \neg(\text{FishTopping} \sqcup \text{MeatTopping} \sqcup \text{DairyTopping}) \quad (7)$$
$$\text{SpicyPizza} \sqsubseteq \text{ForeignPizza} \quad (8)$$
$$\text{VegPizza} \sqsubseteq \text{HealthyPizza} \quad (9)$$
$$\text{SpicyButNotVegPizza} \equiv \text{SpicyPizza} \sqcap \neg\text{VegPizza} \quad (10)$$
$$\text{VegButNotSpicyPizza} \equiv \text{VegPizza} \sqcap \neg\text{SpicyPizza} \quad (11)$$
$$\text{SpicyOrVegPizza} \equiv \text{SpicyPizza} \sqcup \text{VegPizza} \quad (12)$$

Note that, following our approach described in the previous section, we introduce axioms (10)–(12) into the ontology only for the second question below.

What is AmericanHot?

The classification service tells us that AmericanHot is covered by SpicyPizza, and there are no named concepts that AmericanHot is equivalent to or covers. There is also one axiom directly stating a complex concept equivalent to AmericanHot. Therefore, our explanation of AmericanHot is as follows: "AmericanHot is a kind of SpicyPizza. AmericanHots are Pizzas that *have* HopGreenPepperTopping and *have* DairyTopping".

What is the difference between SpicyPizza and VegPizza?

Axioms (10)–(12) are now added to the ontology, but (since they are not concepts in the original ontology) the concepts defined in these axioms are ignored in the selection of concepts to be used in the natural language explanation. The classification service tells us the following:

i SpicyOrVegPizza is covered by Pizza,
ii SpicyPizza is covered by ForeignPizza, which does not subsume VegPizza,
iii VegPizza is covered by HealthyPizza, which does not subsume SpicyPizza,
iv VegPizza covers Caprina, but SpicyPizza does not subsume Caprina,
v SpicyButNotVegPizza covers AmericanHot.

There are also two axioms directly defining SpicyPizza and VegPizza. Therefore, our explanation of the difference between SpicyPizza and VegPizza is as follows:

"SpicyPizzas are Pizzas that *have* SpicyTopping. VegPizzas are Pizzas that *have* VegTopping. (i) SpicyPizzas and VegPizzas are both Pizzas. (ii) Although SpicyPizzas are ForeignPizzas, VegPizzas are not necessarily so. (iii) Although VegPizzas are HealthyPizzas, SpicyPizzas are not necessarily so. (iv) Whereas Caprinas are a kind of VegPizza, they are not necessarily a kind of SpicyPizza (v) Whereas AmericanHots are a kind of SpicyPizza, they are never a kind of VegPizza."

6 Conclusion and Outlook

It has been argued that ontologies can be very helpful for multimedia annotations. With the fast development of the research and applications of ontologies, users will soon face a serious issue: given a set of ontologies about the same topic, which one suits their multimedia application best? In this paper, we have addressed the issue of how to use ontology classification reasoning service and natural language generation to provide presentations of relevant ontology structures for ontology users. The motivation of this research is illustrated in the example presented in Section 5. Axioms (1)-(9) are hard to understand for users without a logical background to understand. Although ontology editors can help organising axioms in ontologies and providing graphic representations of axioms to some extent, natural language explanations of the structure underlying the axioms are still necessary. In this paper, we have discussed how to provide explanations for the two questions: "What is X" and "What is the difference between X and Y", which are two useful questions potential users of ontologies would like to ask.

More complex questions (e.g. *What kinds of people have supervisors?*) can be answered by constructing and naming the appropriate complex concept descriptions (here, X≡ Person ⊓ ∃*supervisor*) and answering one of the above questions for that concept. Such concepts introduce more complex natural language realisation issues than simple named concepts. However, whereas previous work does not address the problem of selecting which facts to present, there are appropriate natural language generation techniques for handling the realisation of complex concepts, as used for instance in the Protégé OWL plugin [11] and older work with DLs [15].

Because there are an infinite number of possible concepts expressible with a given set of atomic concept and property names, it would be impossible to compute subsumption relationships beween all possible pairs of concepts. Thus the classification reasoning service only considers the relationships between named concepts. This means that, for instance, when answering a question *What is a student?* the above approach might be able to say *A student is a kind of person* but it would not be able to respond with *A student has an academic supervisor*, unless the concept ∃*supervisor*.Academic happens to have been named (and this expansion of the name can be retrieved). In the above, we have artificially named certain extra concepts to be classified, but we cannot know in advance all complex concepts that might be informative in the answer to a question. Further work will address this problem, possibly using approaches from approximate reasoning [12] to generate candidate plausible concepts.

References

[1] F. Baader and W. Nutt. Basic description logics. In Franz Baader, Diego Calvanese, Deborah McGuinness, Daniele Nardi, and Peter F. Patel-Schneider, editors, *The Description Logic Handbook: Theory, Implementation, and Applications*, pages 43–95. Cambridge University Press, 2003.

[2] F. Baader, D. L. McGuiness, D. Nardi, and P. Patel-Schneider, editors. *Description Logic Handbook: Theory, implementation and applications*. Cambridge University Press, 2002.

[3] Fabio Ciravegna and Yorick Wilks. Designing adaptive information extraction for the semantic web in amilcare. In S. Handschuh and S. Staab, editors, *Annotation for the Semantic Web*. IOS Press, Amsterdam, 2003.

[4] DCMI. Dublin Core Metadata Element Set, Version 1.1: Reference Description. DCMI Recommendation, URL http://dublincore.org/documents/dces/, June 2003.

[5] John Domingue, Martin Dzbor, and Enrico Motta. Magpie: Supporting browsing and navigation on the semantic web. In *Procs of IUI 2004*, 2004.

[6] T. R. Gruber. Towards Principles for the Design of Ontologies Used for Knowledge Sharing. In N. Guarino and R. Poli, editors, *Formal Ontology in Conceptual Analysis and Knowledge Representation*, Deventer, The Netherlands, 1993. Kluwer Academic Publishers.

[7] Kathleen R. McKeown. *Text Generation: Using Discourse Strategies and Focus Constraints to Generate Natural Language Text*. Cambridge University Press, Cambridge, 1985.

[8] C. Mellish and X. Sun. Natural language directed inference in the presentation of ontologies. In *Procs of the Tenth European Workshop on Natural Language Geeration*, Aberdeen, Scotland, 2005.

[9] M. Milosavljevic. *Maximising the Coherence of Descriptions via Comparison*. PhD thesis, Macquarie University, 1999.

[10] Jeff Z. Pan and Ian Horrocks. OWL-Eu: Adding Customised Datatypes into OWL. In *Journal of Web Semantics*, 2005. To appear.

[11] Alan Rector, Nick Drummond, Matthew Horridge, Jeremy Rogers, Holger Knoblauch, Robert Stevens, Hai Wang, and Chris Wroe. Owl pizzas: Practi-

cal experience of teaching owl-dl: Common errors and common patterns. In E. Motta, editor, *Procs of ECAW 2004*, pages 63–81. Springer LNCS 3257, 2004.

[12] Marco Schaerf and Marco Cadoli. Tractable reasoning via approximation. *Artificial Intelligence*, 74:249–310, 1995.

[13] M. Uschold and M. Gruninger. Ontologies: Principles, Methods and Applications. *The Knowledge Engineering Review*, 1996.

[14] Maria Varges-Vera, Enrico Motta, John Domingue, Mattia Lanzoni, Arthur Stutt, and Fabio Ciravegna. Mnm: Ontology driven semantic sem-automatic and automatic support for semantic markup. In *Procs EKAW2002*. Springer Verlag, 2002.

[15] J. Wagner, J. Rogers, R. Baud, and J-R. Scherrer. Natural language generation of surgical procedures. *Medical Informatics*, 53:175–192, 1999.

A Simulation Tool for Modelling Pedestrian Dynamics during Evacuation of Large Areas

Ioakeim G. Georgoudas, Georgios Ch. Sirakoulis,
and Ioannis Th. Andreadis

Democritus University of Thrace, Department of Electrical and Computer
Engineering,
Laboratory of Electronics,
GR 67100 Xanthi, Greece
{igeorg, gsirak, iandread}@ee.duth.gr
http://www.ee.duth.gr/people/frame.htm

Abstract. The movement of large numbers of people is important in many situations, such as the evacuation of a building in an emergency. In this paper, pedestrian dynamics during the evacuation of large areas is simulated using a computational intelligent technique, based on Cellular Automata. The characteristic feature of the proposed model is that the crowd consists of independent parts rather than treated as homogeneous mass. The crowd behaviour is artificially formatted by the response of each of these parts to the rule according to which each pedestrian reaches one of the possible exits. Furthermore, an efficient graphical user interface has been developed, in order to study various hypotheses concerning the pedestrians' activity features. Collisions among pedestrians have been encountered while collective effects prominent at crowd behaviour have been also realised during simulation. Finally, the presence of fixed as well as user-defined moveable obstacles has been taken into account.

1 Introduction

When we are at a major sporting event or travelling on public transport or shopping around in shopping precincts, our safety and comfort depend crucially on our fellow crowd members and on the design and operation of the facility we are in. Thus it is unnerving to realize that the modelling currently used to design and operate these venues has more in common with the design of water-pipe networks than anything with a human dimension. As a result the need for a different and potentially far more realistic crowd behaviour modelling approach is of great importance.

Please use the following format when citing this chapter:

Georgoudas, Ioakeim, Sirakoulis, Georgios, Andreadis, Ioannis, 2006, in IFIP International Federation for Information Processing, Volume 204, Artificial Intelligence Applications and Innovations, eds. Maglogiannis, I., Karpouzis, K., Bramer, M., (Boston: Springer), pp. 618–626

During the last decade, it has been adopted the approach of modelling a crowd composed of discrete individuals rather than being faced as a homogeneous mass that behaves like a flowing fluid [1]. In the past, one of the main constraints for such an approach was the enormous number of calculations required to be solved for each crowd member. Fortunately, modern computer power has changed this situation. An additional step towards further simplification of modelling such processes can be the introduction of computational intelligent techniques such as Cellular Automata (CA) [2-3].

As far as it concerns particularly the simulation of pedestrian dynamics, CA models of generally two-dimensional (2-d) nature have been reported in literature [4-5]. Some of them treat pedestrians as particles subject to long-range forces [5] and others use walkers leaving a trace by modifying the underground on their paths [4]. More-over, generalisations of the city traffic model have been proposed mainly focusing on the occurrence of a jamming transition as the density of pedestrians is increased [4, 6]. The majority of the models reported, adopted as the most suitable update procedure the parallel update.

In this paper a user-friendly parameterized model attempts at further and more detailed investigation of pedestrian dynamics focusing on specific rather than generalised behaviour under certain conditions. To this direction, the user is provided with the ability to predefine distinguishing features of the evacuated area, incorporating both topological-oriented parameters and parameters that describe the crowd formation. In particular, the extent of the area, the presence as well as the exact location of obstacles, the number and the allocation of the exits are easily defined. Moreover, as far as it concerns crowd features, there are options regarding the population, crowd behaviour, velocity as well as the existence or not of different types of individuals (children or elderly and middle-aged). It should be reminded that all crowd characteristics are individual dependent. Consequently, the existence of several, externally defined parameters enhances the surveillance perspectives of a certain area. General characteristics are confined, indicating thus certain characteristics allowing the implementation of more effective monitoring techniques. Finally, data obtainable by video monitoring can be also supplied to the model in order to realize in what extent is the model capable of reproducing various observed phenomena under panic circumstances.

2 Mathematical definition of the proposed technique

In this section a more formal definition of a CA will be presented [7]. In general, a CA requires:
1. A regular lattice of cells covering a portion of a d-dimensional space;
2. A set $C(\vec{r}, t) = \{C_1(\vec{r}, t), C_2(\vec{r}, t), ..., C_m(\vec{r}, t)\}$ of variables attached to each site r of the lattice giving the local state of each cell at the time $t = 0, 1, ...$;
3. A rule $R = \{R_1, R_2, ..., R_m\}$ which specifies the time evolution of the states $C(\vec{r}, t)$ in the following way:

$$C_j(\vec{r}, t+1) = R_j\left(C(\vec{r}, t), C(\vec{r} + \vec{\delta}_1, t), C(\vec{r} + \vec{\delta}_2, t), ..., C(\vec{r} + \vec{\delta}_q, t)\right) \tag{1}$$

where $\vec{r} + \vec{\delta}_k$ designates the cells belonging to a given neighbourhood of cell $\vec{r}$.

In the above definition, the rule R is identical for all sites, and it is applied simultaneously to each of them, leading to a synchronous dynamics. It is important to notice that the rule is homogeneous, i.e. it does not depend explicitly on the cell position r. However, spatial (or even temporal) inhomogeneities can be introduced by ascribing definite and permanent values for some states $C_j(\vec{r})$ in some given locations of the lattice. In the above definition, the new state at time $t+1$ is only a function of the previous state at time t. It is sometimes necessary to have a longer memory and introduce a dependence on the states at time t-1, t-2, ..., t-k. Such a situation is already included in the definition, if one keeps a copy of the previous state in the current state.

The neighbourhood of cell $\vec{r}$ is the spatial region in which a cell needs to search in its vicinity. In principle, there is no restriction on the size of the neighbourhood, except that it is the same for all cells. However, in practice, it is often made up of adjacent cells only. For 2-d CA, two neighbourhoods are often considered [7]: The von Neumann, which consists of a central cell (the one which is to be updated) and its four geographical neighbours north, west, south and east. The Moore neighbourhood contains, in addition, second nearest neighbours northeast, northwest, southeast and southwest that is a total of nine cells. Extending the neighbourhood leads to various types of boundary conditions such as periodic (or cyclic), fixed, adiabatic or reflection [7].

CA can sufficiently represent phenomena of arbitrary complexity and at the same time can be simulated exactly by digital computers, because of their intrinsic discreteness, i.e. the topology of the simulated object is reproduced in the simulating device [8]. The CA approach is consistent with the modern notion of unified space–time. In computer science, space corresponds to memory and time to processing unit [9]. In CA, memory (CA cell state) and processing unit (CA local rule) are inseparably related to a CA cell [10]. In addition, algorithms based on CA run quickly on digital computers [9]. Models based on CA lead to algorithms which are fast when implemented on serial computers, because they exploit the inherent parallelism of the CA structure [8-10].

3 The Proposed Model

The proposed model is a 2-d CA and aims at the simulation of crowd dynamics during the evacuation of a large area. The whole area under test is divided into a 2-d matrix of identical square cells, with side length a, represented by a CA, assuming that each cell of the area is a CA cell. The grid of the CA is considered as homogeneous and isotropic, thus defining major model's features. Furthermore, CA cells are being able to exist in two possible states; either free or occupied by exactly one particle. Moreover, every cell covers an extent of approximately 40x40 cm^2 [4], thus including even the situation of a dense crowd. In any case the value of a is user defined and should be a compromise between accuracy and computer time and memory.

As far at it concerns the update process, it should be mentioned that it takes place in parallel for all particles. During each time step, an individual chooses to move in one of the eight possible directions of its neighbourhood. However in some cases it is not possible to move at all due to the occupation of cells by other particles. In any case, a particle cannot overcome more than one cell at a time step, meaning that in case that it moves, it does it with a maximum velocity of one cell per time step. Two more assumptions regarding velocity have been also considered. The first one defines that acceleration as well as braking time are negligible while the second one following the attributes of homogeneous and isotropic grid demands stable and common velocity for all particles of the same type. Consequently, a model of maximum velocity equal to unity is formed, meaning that movements are only performed towards the closest neighbours.

A brief description of the local CA rule follows. The general scheme is that each particle moves towards the direction which is closer to exit. In order to implement the appropriate movement, the transition matrix of each occupied cell, depending on the CA cell itself and its neighbours, is updated at every time step. Each matrix element represents a possible updated spatial state of the occupied cell, placed at the centre of the matrix, at the next time step, $t+1$. As far as it concerns the elements' values, these indicate the distances from the escape point of the occupied cell and its eight closest neighbours, respectively. The distance is defined as the minimum number of cells needed to be covered in order to reach the exit, moving strictly either in longitudinal (vertical) or in latitudinal (horizontal) direction. This way, the shortest path towards the exit is scouted.

In Fig. 1 is illustrated an example of a transition matrix. The occupied cell at time step t (dashed cell), placed at the centre of the array, is referred as (i,j). Consequently, each cell is described by its relative position to the central one. The number found at the top of each cell represents the distance of the possible new position from the exit. For instance, a particle placed at cell $(i-1,j-1)$ needs 5 steps to reach the exit, i.e. 4 steps vertically and 1 horizontally. The minimum distant cell, e.g. cell $(i+1,j)$ placed just 2 steps away from the exit (bold line), becomes the choice of the new particle's position at the next time step, $t+1$.

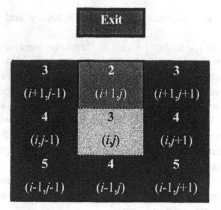

Fig. 1. An example of a transition matrix.

As soon as all possible routes have been detected, the shortest prevails and the particle moves this way at the next time step. This process takes place in parallel for all occupied cells. In case of multiple exits, the whole procedure is repeated for each one separately. In case of collisions the following scheme has been adopted; the particle does not move towards the target unless it is not occupied and it is free to move if no other particle targets at the same cell. In the latter, the cell that fronts the exit proceeds.

The flowchart of the model is illustrated in Fig. 2 while the aforementioned procedure can be summarized as follows:

When all the external parameters (population, noise percentage, type of individuals' percentages, area extent, number of obstacles and obstacles coordinates, number of exits and exits coordinates) have been defined and as a result the evacuation area has been thoroughly defined it is time for the CA to start its evolution. For each occupied cell in the CA grid the corresponding transition matrix is calculated. This process takes place in parallel for all particles. The location of the array's minimum value element represents the target cell of the central reference particle (i,j) for the next update step. If the target cell is occupied, the particle remains to its prior position after update step, while in the case that the target cell is free and no other particle targets it, the move takes place. Finally, provided that the target cell is free and more than one particles target it, then the one that fronts the exit proceeds.

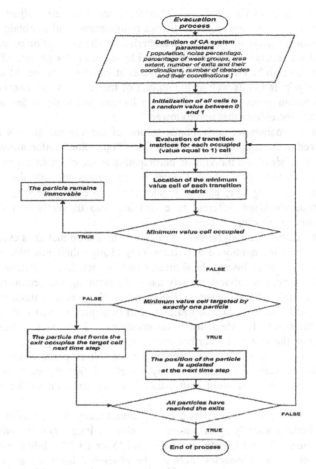

Fig. 2. Flowchart of the evacuation process algorithm.

4 Description of the Graphical User Interface

A graphical user interface (GUI) based on Matlab® has been developed. The simulator can be used as a computer tool for the study of the room evacuation process. No previous knowledge of CA or computer programming is necessary to use the simulator, because of the user-friendly graphical user interface that has been developed.

The GUI is equipped with various parameter options, in such an extent that it can provide an adequate level of prominent features of the area under test. It is oriented to elevate the space characteristics of the evacuated area as well as distinctive properties of the crowd's synthesis. Therefore, the user can adjust the basic parameters of the system according to her/his requirements and to obtain an optical visualisation for a variety of system's characteristics. The evacuation process can be demonstrated for several exit locations defined by the user, for an area of a defined extent which can also be enriched with obstacles at various locations. Moreover, the density of the population as well as the motion of the particles can also be adjusted and the simulation process can be further enhanced including different types of individuals, e.g. the elderly that move slower.

Every system parameter corresponds to one of the various buttons and all of them are placed at the right side of the GUI. The 'Population' button allows the user to define the number of the individuals participating at the evacuation process. Each of them is presented by a coloured point which moves towards the closer exit location. The following one, called 'Weak groups percent', introduces a certain amount of individuals of different type that are also distinctively coloured for reasons of better monitoring.

During the demonstration, for each particle the transition matrix is evaluated and according to the aforementioned algorithm, they change their position in order to reach the escape point following the shortest route. In fact, all evaluations have been made for Moore neighbourhood, namely using 9 (including the central cell) active neighbours. As rationally expected, collisions delay the process without blocking it; already occupied positions are not available and multiple targeted cells are finally occupied by these particles which are preferentially placed relative to the exit.

Furthermore, the graphical interface provides the option to supply in some extent additional delay to the particles' motion using the 'Noise percent' edit button. It represents the movement's obstruction by undefined factors, such as panic or hysteria, resulting in a left-right drift parallel to the direction of the population motion.

The extent of the area under test can be parametrically defined using the 'Area Extent' edit buttons specifying in number of cells the length and the width of the area. The number of exits is defined in the field 'Max Exits' while the number of obstacles is set in the 'Obstacles' button. The obstacles' locations as well as the exits' exact locations are defined by setting their x, y − coordinates at the corresponding fields.

After setting all the simulation parameters, the simulator is activated by clicking the button 'Start' on the top-right of the interface. 'Stop' button freezes the evacuation process demonstration, allowing the user to capture certain phases of the procedure aiming at closer surveillance. 'Info' button provides a short description of the aforementioned algorithm as well as access to the code itself while the 'Close' button closes the demonstration window.

In Fig. 3 four different successive snapshots of the simulation process are presented for different time steps.

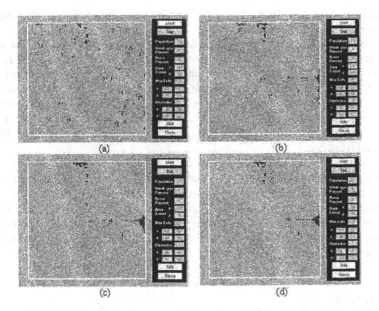

Fig. 3. Four different successive snapshots of the proposed model's GUI for different time steps. Middle aged individuals are coloured red, while the elderly individuals as well as children are coloured green. Black dots correspond to the obstacles' locations.

5 Conclusions

The presented pedestrian dynamics model is a computational technique based on the principles of a 2-d CA. Although a simplified version due to assumptions concerning velocity and negligible acceleration and braking time, certain attributes of crowd behaviour, such as collective effects, collisions and delaying factors have been successfully encountered during simulation process. Several important phenomena of crowd dynamics, meaning transition to incoordination (arching) due to clogging as well as mass behaviour, have become pronounced.

The user-friendly interface provides the ability for observing various situations of room evacuation process, thus drawing useful conclusions. Room arrangement, regarding the number and the location of exits as well as the obstacles' ordering can be defined in a user-friendly manner. The fact that the model is parameter-enriched in quite a remarkable extent offers the option of an easy, external adjustment of various significant features of the evacuated area, concerning both topological as well as crowd formation aspects. Consequently, the existence of several, externally defined parameters enhances the surveillance perspectives of a certain area. General characteristics are confined, thus indicating certain characteristics allowing the implementation of more effective monitoring techniques.

Based on the flexibility of the proposed model, it could be possible that video sequences related to crowd escaping to be used in order to calibrate the CA model. Furthermore, this possibility could elucidate the response of the model to real data. In other words, data from video monitoring can be supplied to the model in order to realize in what extent is the model capable of reproducing various observed phenomena under panic circumstances. Such an upgrade would certainly increase its level of credibility, in order to be used to test gathering areas for their suitability to emergent situations.

Finally, due to the fact that in terms of circuit design and layout, ease of mask generation, silicon-area utilization and maximization of clock speed, CA are perhaps one of the most suitable computational structures for VLSI realization, the VLSI implementation of the proposed CA algorithm is straightforward with no silicon overhead. As a result it is feasible the perspective of an integrated surveillance system, with camera based monitoring algorithms that would be able to provide the necessary video data.

References

1. Helbing, D., Farkas, I. Vicsek, T.: Simulating dynamical features of escape panic. Nature. 407 (2000) 487–490
2. von Neumann, J.: Theory of Self-Reproducing Automata. University of Illinois Press, Urbana IL (1996)
3. Wolfram, S.: Theory and Applications of Cellular Automata. World Scientific, Singapore (1986)
4. Burstedde, C., Klauck, K., Schadschneider, A., Zittartz, J.: Simulation of pedestrian dynamics using a two-dimensional cellular automaton. Physica A. 295 (2001) 507–525
5. Aubé, F., Shield, R.: Modeling the Effect of Leadership on Crowd Flow Dynamics. Lecture Notes in Computer Science. 3305 (2004) 601–611
6. Klüpfel, H., Meyer-König, T., Wahle, J., Schreckenberg, M., in: S. Bandini, T. Worsch (Eds.), Theory and Practical Issues on Cellular Automata, Springer, Berlin, 2000.
7. Chopard, B., Droz, M.: Cellular Automata Modeling of Physical systems. Cambridge University Press, Cambridge (1998)
8. Karafyllidis, I., Andreadis, I., Tzionas, P., Tsalides Ph., Thanailakis, A.: A Cellular Automaton for the Determination of the Mean Velocity of Moving Objects and its VLSI Implementation. Pattern Recognition. 29 (1996) 689-699
9. Sirakoulis, G.Ch.: A TCAD system for VLSI implementation of the CVD process using VHDL. Integration, the VLSI Journal. 37 (2004) 63-81
10. Sirakoulis, G.Ch., Karafyllidis, I., Thanailakis, A.: A Cellular Automaton for the propagation of circular fronts and its applications. Engineering Applications in Artificial Intelligence. 18 (2005) 731-744

Radar Imaging by Range Density Functions

Askin Demirkol[1] and Erol Emre[2]

[1] Department of Electrical and Computer Engineering,University of Missouri, Rolla,MO
65409-0040 USA
demirkol@umr.edu
[2] Department of Computer Engineering, Sakarya University, Sakarya-Turkey
emre@sakarya.edu.tr

Abstract. In this paper, as an active sensor imaging technique, a new target density function in form of the range density function(RDF) is developed by Gabor transform which is called short time Fourier transform (STFT). It is shown that Gabor theory, (STFT) can be used as approach to imaging by active sensors by transmitting a waveform which is a kernel for this transform. Then an alternative signal dimension reduction approach is proposed to the developed technique by taking advantage of Walsh functions.
Keywords: active sensor imaging, SAR-ISAR, target density function, range density function, Gabor transform, Short time Fourier transform (STFT), Walsh function.

1 Introduction

Imaging is a mapping process from three dimensional object to two dimensional image [1, 2, 3, 4, 5]. This transformation is obtained by using signal transforms such as Fourier and Wavelet transforms [1, 6, 7, 2, 3, 4, 5]. Radar imaging is based on a multi-sensor image fusion technique, which is in the form of multiple-apertures and arrays [8, 9, 10, 11, 12, 13].

Target density function(TDF) is the reflectivity of spatially, continuously distributed targets and it is an important characteristic of radar imaging. TDF is known by different names such as ambiguity function, density function, target density function, object(target), object reflectivity function, doubly-spread reflectivity function, and reflection coefficient [8, 9, 10, 11, 12, 13].

There are two well known approaches on TDF. First one considers the integration of all point scatterers off the target scatterer centers. is able to obtain the whole object. This radar imaging technique is based on inverse Fourier transform(IFT) and used mostly in inverse synthetic aperture radar(SAR) studies [1, 16, 2, 3, 4, 5].

Second method on TDF is a dense target environment approach by Fowle and Naparst [14, 15]. This takes into consideration the existence of densities of the targets in a high dense target environment. It is based on the ambiguity functions with two variables as range and velocity[17, 18, 19]. Especially, the advanced function in the dense target environment by Naparst is developed in a novel way. Rather than typical radar imaging, this is an approach to measure the closeness of the targets to each other

Please use the following format when citing this chapter:

Demirkol, Askin, Emre, Erol, 2006, in IFIP International Federation forInformation Processing, Volume 204, Artificial Intelligence Applications and Innovations, eds. Maglogiannis, I., Karpouzis, K., Bramer, M., (Boston: Springer), pp. 627–634

in the dense target environment. However, in this work is inspired partly by Naparst model.

In this study, a new TDF is produced as a range density function considering a range-scanning angle plane different from the early approaches. This technique is developed based on Gabor theory which is called short term Fourier transform (STFT).

2 Walsh Functions

Walsh functions are orthogonal functions and composed of square waves with (0-1) amplitudes. Unlike the Rademacher functions, Walsh functions are complete. Mathematical theory of Walsh functions corresponds to Fourier analysis-based sine-cosine functions [20, 21, 22, 23].

Walsh functions are defined in a limited time interval, T, known as the time-base. Like the sine-cosine functions, two entities are required for a complete definition. These are a time period, t, which is normalized to the time base as t/T, and an ordering number, n, which is related to frequency. A Walsh basis function is represented by $Wal(n, t)$. A general Walsh function with pulse basis functions can be written as [20, 21, 22, 23]

$$Wal(n, t) = sign[(sin2\pi t)^{b_0} \prod_{k=1}^{m} (cos2^k \pi t)^{b_k}] \tag{1}$$

where n and m are related to each other. If u is a binary value of the decimal, n, and $g(u)$ is a number of digits, then m is represented as

$$m = g(u) - 1 \tag{2}$$

b_0 and b_k in Equation 1 are either 0 or 1.

A set of Walsh functions derived from Equation 1 is given in Figure 1 [20, 21, 22, 23]. These sets of Walsh functions are in form of typical radar pulse train.

While behavior of both Fourier and Walsh series are similar, basis functions have different forms. Walsh function can be expressed as a time series similar to the Fourier theory:

$$f(t) = \sum_{k=0}^{\infty} F_k Wal(k, t) \tag{3}$$

If this is compared with Fourier series, $p(t) = \sum_{k=-\infty}^{\infty} \alpha_k e^{jk\omega_0 t}$, their basis functions become important separators. The basis functions are infinite in Fourier series($-\infty \leq k \leq \infty$), while finite in Walsh series($0 \leq k \leq \infty$). The finite basis functions provide important advantage in signal processing in terms of dimension reduction.

Two new functions, **sal** and **cal**, which are analogues of **sine** and **cosine** functions in Fourier series, are defined by Walsh functions [20, 21, 22, 23].

$$f(t) = a_0 Wal(0, t) + \sum_{k=1}^{\infty} [a_k cal(k, t) + b_k sal(k, t)] \tag{4}$$

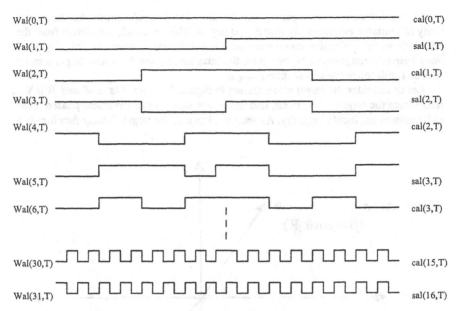

Fig. 1. A set of Walsh functions.

where

$$a_0 = \int_{-1/2}^{1/2} f(t)Wal(0,t)dt, \ a_k = \int_{-1/2}^{1/2} f(t)cal(k,t)dt, \ b_k = \int_{-1/2}^{1/2} f(t)sal(k,t)dt$$

(5)

3 Imaging by Gabor Theory

In this paper, an active sensor imaging is studied by an alternative target density function(TDF), which is based on a linear phased array radar system and the range-scanning angle. New target density function, $g(R, \beta)$ is composed of two variables, which are the range R, and the scanning angle β. Definition of $g(R, \beta)$ in developed here is given as the following.

Definition 1. Target Density Function is the limit of the ratio of the amplitude of the signal reflected from an infinitesimally neighborhood about the point (R, β) to the amplitude of the incoming signal.

By this definition, the new target density function $g(R, \beta)$ is;

$$g(R, \beta) = \lim_{d(\Omega) \to 0} \frac{A_r}{A_t}$$

(6)

where $d(\Omega)$ is the diameter of the disc about the point $(R, \beta) \in \Omega$, A_r and A_t are the amplitudes of the reflected and the transmitted signals, respectively.

In this definition, the target density function(TDF) is relevant to the the reflectivity of spatially, continuously distributed targets. This approach is different from the conventional target density function definitions stated early. Instead of ambiguity functions based on range-velocity variables, the imaging is taken by a new target density function with the range and scanning angle.

Let us consider the target plane shown in Figure 2, where β is $cos\theta$ and R is the range from the target to the radar, and the sensor elements in the linear phased array radar system are located equally. As seen in Figure 2, the target density function is a

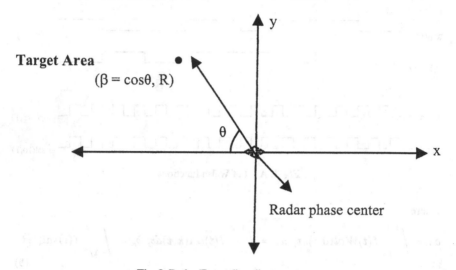

Fig. 2. Radar-Target Coordinate system.

function of the spatial coordinates (R, β) in the upper semi-plane.

Now, let us obtain the target density function. Let $P(t)$ be any periodic function of time, such as a train of pulses,where

$$p(t) = \sum_{k=-\infty}^{\infty} \alpha_k \, e^{jk\omega_0 t} \qquad (7)$$

$$\omega_0 = 2\pi \times \text{PRF}, \qquad (8)$$

where PRF is the pulse repetition frequency.

$$W(t) = e^{j\omega_c t} \qquad (9)$$

Where $W(t)$ is the carrier signal.

$$s_m(t) = p(t)W(t) \qquad (10)$$

Where $s_m(t)$ is the modulated signal transmitted in the fixed direction β, which can be done by a directed single antenna or a phased array using beamforming.

The reflectivity of one point at $g(R, \beta)$

$$y(t, \omega) = s_m(t - 2R/c - \beta x/c)g(R, \beta) \tag{11}$$

Let us generalize Equation 11 for the whole radar-target semi upper plane by superpositioning principle considering all point scatterers related to the range-angle.

If $g(R, \beta)$ is the reflectivity of the point (R, β), and R_1 is the maximum range of interest target area; then the total reflected incoming signal to the phase center will be

$$y(t, \omega) = \int_{-1}^{1} \int_{0}^{R_1} s_m(t - (\frac{2R + \beta x}{c}))g(R, \beta)dRd\beta$$

$$= \int_{-1}^{1} \int_{0}^{R_1} p(t - (\frac{2R + \beta x}{c}))W(t - (\frac{2R + \beta x}{c}))g(R, \beta)dRd\beta \tag{12}$$

where $y(t, \omega)$ is the output of the sensor located at center (the feature space), and c is the speed of light.

If Equation 7 substitutes in Equation 12, the total reflected incoming signal to the phase center will be,

$$y(t, \omega_0) = \int_{-1}^{1} \int_{0}^{R_1} \sum_{k=-\infty}^{\infty} \alpha_k e^{jk\omega_0(t-(\frac{2R+\beta x}{c}))} W(t - (\frac{2R + \beta x}{c}))g(R, \beta)dRd\beta \tag{13}$$

Now a new target density function is defined by utilizing Definition 1 and Figure 2. This function is the *range density function (RDF)*.

In a linear phased array of point sensor system, if R is the range from the sensor in a fixed direction (β), which is direction cosine of the line joining the point and the phase center, as a new target density function, the new range density function (RDF) is defined as follows.

Definition 2. Range Density Function, $f(R)$ is the reflectivity of the point at range R.

By this definition, $f(R)$ represents the image along the range or the distance to the sensor.

Let us formulate this definition. The range density function function $f(R)$ or $g_\beta(R)$ at a fixed angle, β,

$$f(R) \equiv g_\beta(R) \equiv g(\beta, R) \tag{14}$$

By the definition of the point at a fixed angle, β and Equation 14, Equation 13 will be

$$y(t, \omega_0) = \int_{0}^{\infty} \sum_{k=-\infty}^{\infty} \alpha_k e^{jk\omega_0(t-\frac{2R}{c})} W(t - 2R/c)f(R)dR \tag{15}$$

Let's define

$$t_\perp = \frac{2R}{c} \quad and \tag{16}$$

$$W(t) = W_\perp(-t) \tag{17}$$

and uniquely define h to be the function such that

$$f(R) = h(t_\perp) \tag{18}$$

Then Equation 15 can be rewritten as

$$y(t, \omega_0) = \frac{c}{2} \sum_{k=-\infty}^{\infty} \alpha_k e^{jk\omega_0 t} \int_0^\infty e^{-jk\omega_0 t_\perp} W(t_\perp - t) h(t_\perp) dt_\perp \tag{19}$$

If Equation 19 is demodulated by $\frac{2}{c}\frac{1}{\alpha}e^{-jk\omega_0 t}$

$$y_k(t, \omega_0) = \int_0^\infty e^{-jk\omega_0 t_\perp} W(t_\perp - t) h(t_\perp) dt_\perp \tag{20}$$

Extend the domain of definition of $h(t_\perp)$ to $(-\infty, \infty)$ by defining $h(t_\perp) \equiv 0$ for $t_\perp < 0$. Then, it is seen that Equation 20 is the Gabor transform, which is known short-time Fourier transform, STFT of $h(t_\perp)$, that is $y_k(t, \omega_0)$ evaluated at the frequency ω_0.

The inverse Gabor (STFT) transform yields $h(t_\perp)$ as

$$h(t_\perp) = \frac{1}{2\pi||W||^2} \int_{-\infty}^\infty \int_{-\infty}^\infty y_k(t, \omega_0) e^{jk\omega_0 t_\perp} W^*(t_\perp - t) d\omega_0 dt \tag{21}$$

which is desired result. One can obtain the reflectivity of a target area at angle β, by transmitting $e^{jk\omega_0 t}W(t)$ with varying ω_0, and observing the reflected signal for all time. In theory, if the Gabor window function is chosen plausible as a band-limited function, $y_k(t, \omega_0)$ can be determined from its values over any finite length time interval, and the target density function $h(t_\perp)$, can be recovered[24]. Thus, by using a novel target density function $f(R)$ or $g_\beta(R)$, the radar targets can be imaged by utilizing Short Time Fourier Transform.

Infinity of k in Equation 21 can be optimized by some filtration, compressing or estimation methods. However, an alternative way may be proposed to reduce k dimension and smooth the new TDF;

- **Walsh Approach:** While the new TDF is developed, at the beginning, the basis functions of the modulating signal had infinite dimensions. In contrast to infinite basis functions($-\infty \leq k \leq \infty$) in the Equation 7, Walsh functions are expressed in finite pulse basis functions in Equation 3. They have an essential advantage to the radar imaging in terms of basis dimension reduction.

In case of using Walsh functions with pulse form, this function in the Equation (3) will replace the Equation 7 in the new algorithm as a modulating Walsh function with finite dimensions. The Walsh function in question is a modulating signal in the form of a pulse train. After Walsh function is chosen with respect to some parameters like PRF in Equation (7), the new algorithm can resume the remaining steps after Equation (8) in a similar manner.

4 Summary and Conclusion

In this paper, an alternative target density function(TDF) is obtained by a new algorithm and technique differently from the conventional approaches. Main contributions of this study ;

- *A proposed target density function algorithm:* The target density function (TDF) is represented in form of the range density function considering a novel range and scanning angle plane. It is produced by a new technique based on Gabor or short time fourier transform (STFT). It is shown that Gabor theory (STFT) can be used as approach to imaging by active sensors by transmitting a waveform which is a kernel for this transform such as a window function.

The present TDF is generated partly by analogy to Fowle-Naparst and SAR-ISAR approaches.

- *Comparing to Fowle-Naparst:* As an advanced work of Fowle, Naparst target density function is developed for a high dense target environment with multiple targets, whose velocities are close to each other. This TDF acts like a separator rather than an imaging function for the targets at the distance with a given velocity.

TDF proposed here is obtained by a scanning angle and range in a high dense target environment. The main difference is in the imaging approach, which is capable of sensor imaging the targets in a dense target environment via phased array radar system.

- *Comparing to ISAR:* While ISAR imaging is based on multi-aperture principle, the present imaging method is a multi-sensor image fusion technique based on the phased array radar system. On the contrary, the proposed target density function is produced by the integration of scanning angles at a fixed range.

References

1. Chen, V.C., Ling, H.: Time-Frequency transforms for radar imaging and signal analysis,(2002)
2. Gupta, I.J.: "High-Resolution radar imaging using 2-D linear prediction," IEEE Transactions on antennas and propagation, 42 January (1994) 31–37
3. Odendaal, J.W.: "2-D Radar Imaging," Communications and Signal Processing, 1994. COMSIG-94., Proceedings of the 1994 IEEE South African Symposium on, 4 October (1994) 146–151
4. Prickett, M.J.: "Principles of inverse synthetic aperture radar(ISAR) imaging," IEEE EASCON, (1980), 340–344
5. Ausherman, D.A., Kozma, A., Walker, J., Jones, H.M., Poggio, E.C.: "Developments in radar imaging," IEEE Transactions on Aerospace and Electronic Systems 20 no.4 (1984) 363–400
6. Chen, V.C. Qian, S.: "Time frequency transform vs. fourier transform for radar imaging," Time-Frequency and Time-Scale Analysis, 1996., Proceedings of the IEEE-SP International Symposium on, 18-21 June (1996) 389–392

7. Krone, A.W., Munson, D.C.: "A Fourier model of ISAR imaging of approaching targets," Acoustics, Speech, and Signal Processing, 1992. ICASSP-92., 1992 IEEE International Conference on, **3** 23-26 March (1992) 13–16

8. Wald, L.: "Some terms of reference in data fusion" IEEE Transactions on geoscience and remote sensing, **37**, no.3, May (1999) 1190–1193

9. Sarma, V.V.S., Raju, S.: "Multi-sensor data fusion and decision support for airborne target identification," IEEE Transactions on systems, man, and cybernetics, **21** no.5 (1991)

10. Zhou, Y.T.: "Multi-sensor image fusion," Image Processing, 1994. Proceedings. ICIP-94., IEEE International Conference, **1** 13-16 November (1994) 193–197,.

11. Durrant-Whyte, H.F.: "elements of sensor fusion," Intelligent Control, IEE Colloquium on, 19 Febuary (1991) 5/1–5/2

12. Varshney, P.K.: "multi-sensor data fusion," electronics and communication engineering journal, December (1997)

13. Hall, D.L., Llinas, J.: "An Introduction to multi-sensor data fusion," Proceedings of the IEEE , **85** Issue.1, January (1997) 6–23

14. Fowle, E.N., Kelly, E.J., Sheehan, J.A.: "Radar system performance in a dense-target environment," IRE Int.Convention record, no.4 (1961) 136–145

15. Naparst, H.: "Dense target signal processing," IEEE Transactions on information theory **37** no.2 March (1991)

16. Siebert, W.McC.: "A radar detection philosophy," IEEE Transactions on Information Theory, **2** Issue.3 September (1956) 204–221

17. Woodward, P.M.: Probability and information theory with applications to radar,(1957).

18. Blahut, R.E., Wilcox, C.H., Miller, W.: "The synthesis problem for radar ambiguity functions," Springer-Verlag, Mathematics subject classifications:78A45,22E70,43A80,(1991) 229–260

19. Auslander, L., Tolimeri, R.: "Radar ambiguity functions and group theory," SIAM,J.Math.Anal. **16** (1985) 577–601

20. Walsh, J.L.: A closed set of normal orthogonal functions. Amer. J. Math. **45** (1923) 5–24

21. Beauchamp, K.G.: Walsh functions and their applications. Academic press, (1975)

22. Tzafestas, S.G.: Walsh functions in signal and systems analysis and design. A Hutchinson Ross Publication (1985).

23. Harmuth, H.F.: Applications of Walsh functions in communications. IEEE Spectrum November (1969) 8-2-91

24. Papoulis, A.: "A new algorithm in spectra analysis and band-limited extrapolation," IEEE Transactions in Circuits and Systems, v.CAS-22, September (1975) 735–742

A Method for Incremental Data Fusion in Distributed Sensor Networks

Damianos Gavalas[1], Grammati Pantziou[2], Charalampos Konstantopoulos[3], Basilis Mamalis[2]

[1] Department of Cultural Technology and Communication, University of the Aegean, Mytilini, Lesvos Island, Greece
dgavalas@aegean.gr

[2] Department of Informatics, Technological Education Institute of Athens, Athens, Greece
{pantziou, vmamalis}@teiath.gr

[3] Research Academic Computer Technology Institute, Patras, Greece
konstant@cti.gr

Abstract. The use of mobile agents for data fusion in wireless sensor networks has been recently proposed in the literature to answer the scalability problem of client/server model. In this article, we consider the problem of calculating a near-optimal route for a mobile agent that incrementally fuses the data as it vis-its the nodes in a distributed sensor network. The order of visited nodes affects not only the quality but also the overall cost of data fusion. Our proposed heu-ristic algorithm adapts methods usually applied in network design problems in the specific requirements of sensor networks. It suggests the optimal number of MAs that minimizes the overall data fusion cost and constructs near-optimal itineraries for each of them. The performance gain of our algorithm over alter-native approaches is demonstrated by a quantitative evaluation..

1 Introduction

Multiple sensor data fusion is an evolving technology, concerning the problem of how to fuse data from multiple sensors in order to make a more accurate estimation of the environment [6]. It improves reliability while offering the opportunity to minimize the data retained. Applications of data fusion cross a wide spectrum, including environment monitoring, automatic target detection and tracking, battlefield surveillance, remote sensing, global awareness, etc [1]. They are usually time-critical, cover a large geographical area, and require reliable delivery of accurate information for their completion. Most energy-efficient proposals are based on the traditional client/server computing model to handle multisensor data fusion in

Please use the following format when citing this chapter:

Gavalas, Damianos, Pantziou, Grammati, Konstantopoulos, Charalampos, Mamalis, Basilis, 2006, in IFIP International Federation for Information Processing, Volume 204, Artificial Intelligence Applications and Innovations, eds. Maglogiannis, I., Karpouzis, K., Bramer, M., (Boston: Springer), pp. 635–642

Distributed Sensor Networks (DSNs); in that model, each sensor sends its sensory data to a back-end processing element (PE) or sink. However, as advances in sensor technology and computer networking allow the deployment of large amount of smaller and cheaper sensors, huge volumes of data need to be processed in real-time. In this paper, we propose the usage of mobile agents in DSNs for data fusion tasks as an alternative to the traditional client/server model.

The remainder of the paper is organized as follows: Section 2 reviews works related to our research. Section 3 discusses the design and functionality of our heuristic algorithm for designing near-optimal itineraries for mobile agents performing data fusion tasks in DSNs. A quantitative evaluation is presented in Section 4, while Section 5 concludes the paper and presents future directions of our work.

2. Related Work

Mobile agent (MA) technology has been proposed as an answer to the scalability problems of centralized models. The term MA refers to an autonomous program with the ability to move from host to host and act on behalf of users towards the completion of a given task [5]. MAs have been proposed in a variety of applications in traditional networks, including e-commerce, network management, information retrieval, etc [5]. DSN environments form a promising application area for MAs; yet, they pose new challenges as the link bandwidth is typically much lower than that of a wired network and sensory data traffic may even exceed the network capacity.

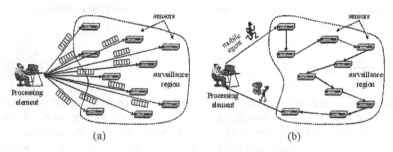

Fig. 1. Centralized vs. Mobile Agents-based data fusion in Distributed Sensor Networks.

To solve the problem of the overwhelming data traffic, [6] and [7] proposed the use of MAs for scalable and energy-efficient data aggregation. By transmitting the software code (MA) to sensor nodes, a large amount of sensory data may be filtered at the source by eliminating the redundancy. MAs may visit a number of sensors and progressively fuse retrieved sensory data, prior to returning to the PE to deliver the data. This scheme proves more efficient than traditional client/server model, wherein row sensory data are transmitted to the PE where data fusion takes place (see Fig. 1).

A number of research articles propose ways for the efficient usage of MAs in the context of DSNs. In particular, MAs have been proposed for enabling dynamically reconfigurable DSNs [8], in multi-resolution data integration and fusion [6], etc. These applications involve the usage of multi-hop MAs visiting large numbers of sensors. The order in which those sensors are visited (i.e. MAs itinerary) is a critical issue, seriously affecting the overall performance. Randomly selected routes may even result in performance worse than that of the conventional client/server model; yet, that issue is not addressed in these works.

To the best of our knowledge, only [7] and [9] deal with the problem of designing optimal MA itineraries in the context of DSNs. In [7], Qi and Wang proposed two heuristic algorithms to optimize the itinerary of MAs performing data fusion tasks. In Local Closest First (LCF) algorithm, each MA starts its route from the PE and searches for the next destination with the shortest distance to its current location. In Global Closest First (GCF) algorithm, MAs also start their itinerary from the PE node and select the node closest to the center of the surveillance region as the next-hop destination.

The output of LCF-like algorithms highly depends on the MAs original location, while the nodes left to be visited last are associated with high migration cost [4] (see, for instance, the last two hops in Fig. 2a); the reason for this is that they search for the next destination among the nodes adjacent to the MA's current location, instead of looking at the 'global' network distance matrix. On the other hand, GCF produces in most cases messier routes than LCF and repetitive MA oscillations around the region center, resulting in long route paths and undesirable performance [7][9].

Wu et al proposed a genetic algorithm-based solution for computing routes for an MA that incrementally fuses the data as it visits the nodes in a DSN [9]. Although providing superior performance (lower cost) than LCF and GCF algorithms, this approach implies a time-expensive optimal itinerary calculation (genetic algorithms typically start their execution with a random solution 'vector' which is improved as the execution progresses), which is unacceptable for time-critical applications, e.g. in target location and tracking. Also, in such applications, the group of visited sensor nodes (i.e. those with maximum detected signal level) is frequently changed over time depending on target's movement; hence, a method that guarantees fast adaptation of MAs itinerary is needed.

Most importantly, both the approaches proposed in [7] and [9] involve the use of a single MA object launched from the PE station that sequentially visits all sensors, regardless of their physical location on the plane. Their performance is satisfactory for small DSNs; however, it deteriorates as the network size grows and the sensor distributions become more complicated. This is because the MA's roundtrip delay increases linearly with network size, while the overall migration cost increases exponentially as the traveling MA accumulates into its state data from visited sensors [3]. The growing MA's state size not only results in increased consumption of the limited wireless bandwidth, but also consumes the limited energy supplies of sensor nodes.

Our algorithm has been designed on the basis of thee objectives: (a) MA itineraries should be derived as fast as possible and adapt quickly to changing networking conditions (hence, an efficient heuristic is needed), (b) MA itineraries should include only sensors with sufficient energy availability and exclude those with low energy level, (c) The number of MAs involved in the data fusion process should depend on the number and the physical location of the sensors to be visited; the order an MA visits its assigned nodes should be computed in such a way as to minimize the overall migration cost.

3. The Near – Optimal Itinerary Design (NOID) Algorithm

The problem of designing optimal itineraries is similar to traditional network design problems such as the Constrained Minimum Spanning Trees (CMST) problems [4]. In such problems, the objective is the optimal selection of the links connecting terminals to concentrators or directly to the network center, resulting in the minimum possible total cost. The output of CMST algorithms typically comprises topologies partitioned on several multi-point lines (or tree branches), where groups of terminals share a sub-tree to a specific node (center). Since the objective of itinerary planning in DSN environments is to connect groups of sensors with multi-lines (itineraries) all originated at the PE node (center), the similarity with CMST problems becomes evident. Hence, it is reasonable to use algorithms originally devised for CMST problems in the application area of MA itinerary planning. Our NOID (Near – Optimal Itinerary Design) algorithm adapts some basic ideas of Esau-Williams (E-W) algorithm [2] in the requirements of itinerary planning problem.

The cost function used in E-W algorithm considers selected links cost as the only contributing factor to the total itinerary cost. This is certainly not adequate metric to evaluate the cost of agents itineraries c_{total}. A key factor also affecting c_{total} is the agent size; more importantly, the agent size increment rate [3], which depends on the amount of data collected by the MA on every sensor. Let us assume that a set of itineraries $I = \{I_0, I_1, \ldots, I_{k-1}\}$ is constructed, each assigned to an individual MA object i. Each itinerary I_m includes a set of sensors to be sequentially visited by a single MA: $I_m = \{S_0, S_1, \ldots, S_n, S_0\}$. Note that all itineraries originate and terminate at the PE node S_0. The total cost per polling interval over all itineraries $|I|$ becomes:

$$c_{total} = \sum_{i=0}^{|I|-1} \sum_{j=0}^{|I_i|-1} \left(d_{ij} + s_i \right) \cdot c_{ij} \tag{1}$$

where d_{ij} is the amount of data collected by the ith MA on the first j visited sensors, s_i the MA initial size and c_{ij} the cost of utilizing the link traversed by the MA i on its jth hop, i.e. the wireless link connecting sensors S_j and S_{j+1} (c_{ij} is given by the network cost matrix). In principle, NOID algorithm aims at constructing a set of itineraries I minimizing the cost function of equation (1).

A comparison among NOID and LCF, GCF heuristics is illustrated in Fig. 2. The algorithms' outputs for the particular DSN configuration of Fig. 2 are based on the cost matrix presented in Table 1. In our prototype implementation, the calculation of the DSN cost matrix entries is only based on the spatial distance between sensors. This decision approach has been taken because the transmission power (hence, energy) required to transmit data between pairs of sensors increases linearly with their physical distance [1][9]. However, as a future extension, we intend to incorporate sensor energy availability metric in the calculation of cost matrix values.

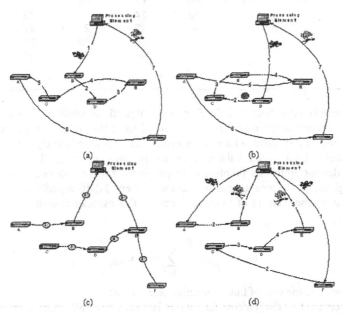

Fig. 2. (a) Output of LCF, (b) Output of GCF, (c) Output of NOID (the sequence numbers indicate the order in which the corresponding MA migrations are accepted, i.e. the algorithm's iteration sequence numbers), (d) MA itineraries derived from the NOID algorithm's output.

The itinerary design algorithm is executed at the PE node; this is a reasonable choice since an MA always starts its data collection journey from the PE node, which can usually be equipped with more powerful computing resources than regular sensor nodes. The PE node has the predetermined knowledge necessary for performing the global optimization, such as the geographical locations (through GPS interfaces) and transmitting/receiving parameters of sensor nodes.

Unlike LCF and GCF algorithms, NOID takes into account the amount of data accumulated by MAs at each visited sensor (without loss of generality, we shall assume this is a constant d). Namely, it recognizes that traveling MAs become 'heavier' while visiting sensors without returning back to the PE to 'unload' their collected data [3]. Therefore, NOID promotes small itineraries enabling the parallel employment of multiple cooperating MAs, each visiting a subset of sensors.

Specifically, the aim of NOID algorithm is, given a set of sensors $S = \{S_0, S_1, ..., S_{n-1}\}$, the PE node S_0 and the cost matrix C, to return a set of near-optimal itineraries $I = \{I_0, .., I_k\}$, all originated and terminated at the PE. Initially, we assume $|S|$ ($= n$) itineraries $I_0, .., I_{n-1}$, as many as the network nodes, each containing a single host (S_0, $S_1, ..., S_{n-1}$, respectively). On each algorithm step, two nodes i and j are 'connected' and, as a result, the itineraries $I(i)$ and $I(j)$ including these hosts respectively are merged into a single itinerary.

Table 1. Cost matrix of the DSN shown in Fig. 2.

	S_0	A	B	C	D	E	F
S_0	-	50	40	62	56	42	88
A		-	22	24	58	73	177
B			-	22	21	27	130
C				-	19	39	131
D					-	18	80
E						-	73
F							-

As mentioned in Section 2, LCF and GCF algorithms usually fail as they tend to leave hosts located far from the center stranded since they prioritize the inclusion of hosts closed to last selected host or the center. As a result, relatively expensive links are left last to be included in the solution, significantly increasing the overall cost. A way of dealing with this problem is to pay more attention to nodes far from the center, giving preference to links incident upon them. NOID algorithm accomplishes this by using the concept of 'tradeoff function' ti ,j associated with each link (i, j), defined by:

$$t_{i,j} = c_{i,j} + \sum_{k=1}^{|I(i)|+|I(j)|} d - C_{i,S_0} \qquad (2)$$

where $c_{i,j}$ is the cost of link connecting nodes i and j.

The concept of the tradeoff function is introduced in E-W algorithm, defined as follows: $t_{i,j} = c_{i,j} - C_{i,S_0}$. Equation (2) extends and adapts this function in the specific requirements of agent itinerary planning problem. In particular, the inclusion of a parameter representing the amount of data collected from each host (d) and also the number of hosts already included in the itineraries considered for merging, i.e. $|I(i)|$ and $|I(j)|$, obstructs the construction of large itineraries, thereby promoting the formation of multiple itineraries, assigned to separate MAs. Equation (2) implies that the more nodes an itinerary already includes, the more difficult for a new host to become part of that itinerary, especially when d is large.

In equation (2), C_{i,S_0} is the cost of connecting $I(i)$ to the PE S_0. Initially, this is simply the cost of connecting node i directly to the PE. As i becomes part of an itinerary containing other sensors, however, this changes to:

$$C_{i,S_0} = \min_{k \in I(i)} c_{k,S_0} \qquad (3)$$

On each algorithm's step, tradeoff function values $t_{i,j}$ are evaluated for all pairs (i,j), except of those where nodes i and j are already part of the same itinerary; the 'itineraries' including the nodes that produce the minimum $t_{i,j}$ value are merged. For instance, if the tradeoff function is minimized for the pair of nodes m and n, then $I(m)$ and $I(n)$ are merged into one itinerary. When NOID's execution finishes, one or more 'sub-trees' (groups of nodes) rooted at the PE node have been constructed; this is shown on Fig. 2c, where the sequence numbers enclosed within circles indicate the order in which individual links (or migrations) become accepted in the corresponding algorithm steps. It is then a trivial task to produce the itineraries (started and terminated at the PE node) for traversing the nodes of each sub-tree; these itineraries correspond to a post-order traversal of the sub-trees (shown in Fig. 2d).

4. Quantitative Evaluation

The total costs associated with LCF, GCF and NOID proposed solutions (shown in Fig. 2a, Fig. 2b and Fig. 2d, respectively) are calculated using the generic cost function of equation (1):

$$C_{LCF} = s * C_{0,B} + (s + d) * C_{B,D} + (s + 2d) * C_{D,E} + (s + 3d) * C_{E,C} + (s + 4d) * C_{C,A}$$
$$+ (s + 5d) * C_{A,F} + (s + 6d) * C_{F,0}$$

$$C_{GCF} = s * C_{0,D} + (s + d) * C_{D,C} + (s + 2d) * C_{C,B} + (s + 3d) * C_{B,E} + (s + 4d) * C_{E,A}$$
$$+ (s + 5d) * C_{A,F} + (s + 6d) * C_{F,0}$$

$$C_{NOID} = [s * C_{0,A} + (s + d) * C_{A,B} + (s + 2d) * C_{B,0}] + [s * C_{0,E} + (s + d) * C_{E,C} + (s + 2d) * C_{C,D} + (s + 3d) * C_{D,F} + (s + 4d) * C_{F,0}]$$

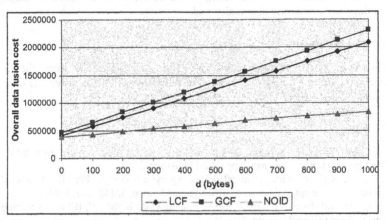

Fig. 3. The overall cost of performing data fusion tasks in the DSN of Fig. 2 by MAs with code size s = 1000 bytes and itineraries derived by LCF, GCF and NOID algorithms.

Assuming an MA of initial size $s=1000$ bytes that collects an amount of $d=100$ bytes from each sensor visited and after substituting various costs with the corresponding values found in the cost matrix of Table 1, we get: $C_{LCF} = 575300$, $C_{GCF} = 646900$ and $C_{NOID} = 430500$ cost units (see Fig. 3), i.e. NOID offers cost saving of 25.2% over LCF and 33.5% over GCF algorithm.

Note that unlike LCF and GCF algorithms, NOID proposes different number of itineraries (MAs employed in parallel) depending on the s/d ratio. In particular, as the s/d ratio decreases (the MA accumulates larger amounts of data), NOID algorithm proposes a large number of small itineraries (so that the corresponding MAs do not become too 'heavy') and its performance gain over LCF and GCF improves further. For instance, for $s=1000$ bytes and $d=700$ bytes, NOID proposes three itineraries: $I_1 = \{0,1,2,0\}$, $I_2 = \{0,3,4,0\}$, $I_3 = \{0,6,5,0\}$; in that scenario, the cost saving offered by NOID over LCF and GCF becomes 54,3% and 58,7% respectively.

5. Conclusions and Future Work

In this article we presented NOID, an efficient heuristic algorithm that derives near-optimal itineraries for MAs performing incremental data fusion in DSN environments. Our algorithm considers spatial distance among sensor nodes for constructing MA itineraries and is shown to outperform alternative existing approaches.

At the time these lines were written, NOID algorithm was under evaluation through simulation tests through a Java-based implementation. LCF and GCF will also be implemented for demonstration and comparison purposes. Simulation results will be analyzed to compare the performance of these algorithms in target tracking applications, in large-scale DSNs, in terms of: (a) the overall agents itinerary cost (total itinerary length), (b) mean energy level of the sensors visited by MAs, (c) overall time for completing data fusion tasks.

Acknowledgement

This work has been co-funded by 75% from EU and 25% from the Greek government under the framework of the Education and Initial Vocational Training II, Programme Archimedes.

References

1. F. Akyildiz, W. Su, Y. Sankarasubramaniam, E. Cayirci, "A survey on sensor networks", IEEE Communications Magazine, pp. 102-114, August 2002.
2. L.R. Esau, K.C. Williams, "On teleprocessing system design. Part II- A method for approximating the optimal network, IBM Systems Journal, 5, 142–147, 1966.
3. A. Fuggeta, G.P. Picco, G. Vigna, "Understanding Code Mobility", IEEE Transactions on Software Engineering 24(5), pp. 346–361, 1998.
4. A.Kershenbaum, "Telecommunications Network Design Algorithms", McGraw-Hill, 1993.
5. Milojicic D., "Mobile agent applications", IEEE Concurrency, 7(3), July-Sep. 1999.
6. H. Qi, S.S. Iyengar, K. Chakrabarty, "Multi-Resolution Data Integration Using Mobile Agents in Distributed Sensor Networks", IEEE Transactions on Systems, Man, and Cybernetics, Part C: Applications and Rev., 31(3), pp. 383-391, August 2001.
7. H. Qi, F. Wang, "Optimal itinerary analysis for mobile agents in ad hoc wireless sensor networks", Proceedings of the International Conference on Wireless Communications, pp.147-153, 2001.
8. T. Umezawa, I. Satoh, Y. Anzai, "A Mobile Agent-Based Framework for Configurable Sensor Networks", Proceedings of the 4th International Workshop on Mobile Agents for Telecommunications Applications (MATA'02), pp. 128-140, October 2002.
9. Q. Wu, N. Rao, J. Barhen, S. Iyengar, V. Vaishnavi, H. Qi, K. Chakrabarty, "On Computing Mobile Agent Routes for Data Fusion in Distributed Sensor Networks", IEEE Transactions on Knowledge and Data Engineering, 16(6), pp. 740-753, June 2004.

Information Society: the two faces of Janus

Michalis Vafopoulos
Department of Cultural Technology and Communication,
University of the Aegean, Faonos St., 81100 Mytilini, Greece.
vaf@aegean.gr

Abstract. Knowledge could be considered as the most critical dual factor – input and output – in production and scientific processes. Strategic and influential use of Information and Communication Technologies (ICTs) - the so called Information Society (IS) – reveals vast potential in knowledge production and economic development. In our point of view, two are the key issues in effective ICTs exploitation: (a) social consensus about quantity, quality and processing mechanisms of public information and (b) transformation process path between the general e-work model and the g-work paradigm. In this context, the knowledge-based development codifies the positive face of IS, in contrast to personal data abuse. The concept of the "new democratic deficit" is introduced in order to move into the foreground the significant dialectic relationship between ICTs and society.

1 Introduction

IS is a political and scientific concept, since ICTs affect in a horizontal way many aspects of our life. In the first section, the Data Information Knowledge and Wisdom Hierarchy (DIKW) is described. The origins and evolution of the IS concept are presented in the next section. Third section is devoted in the double face of Janus which characterizes the IS in practice. The positive aspect refers to the knowledge-based development as it is described by the g-work analytical framework. Personal data abuse by legal or illegal authorities constitutes the negative face of the IS.

2 Data – Information – Knowledge

The Data Information Knowledge and Wisdom Hierarchy (DIKW) – or the "Knowledge or Information Hierarchy" or the "Knowledge Pyramid" – was initiated by Milan Zeleny [1] and builds on the equation of Data, Information, Knowledge and Wisdom to "know-nothing", "know-what", "know-how" and "know-why", respectively. The mainstream view with few variations is that data is raw numbers

Please use the following format when citing this chapter:

Vafopoulos, Michalis, 2006, in IFIP International Federation for Information Processing, Volume 204, Artificial Intelligence Applications and Innovations, eds. Maglogiannis, I., Karpouzis, K., Bramer, M., (Boston: Springer), pp. 643–648

and facts, information is processed data, and knowledge is authenticated information [2,3,4]. Specifically, data is raw in any form, – functional or not – and has no meaning beyond its existence. Information is meaningfully interrelated data. A certain meaning can be - not necessarily – valuable. In computer and information sciences, relational databases and data interoperability technologies (mainly XML, RDF, OWL [12,14] and SKOS [13,14]) enable the data – information conversion. Knowledge is structured information for facts, procedures, concepts, interpretations, observations, and theories. Wisdom is considered to be a human process by which we evaluate right and wrong, good and bad knowledge.

Last decades, the evolution and wide dissemination of digital goods [5,6,33] triggered an information overload [7,8,9,10] since data, information and knowledge could be primarily analyzed as the most famous digital goods. Social consequences of the technological advances are commonly codified by the Information Society (IS) concept.

3 Information Society

According to Susan Crawford [30] scientists have systematically been considered the increase of publications in the seventeenth and nineteenth century [15,16], but the concept of "Information Society" was initiated by the economist Fritz Machlup in 1962. Machlup in his milestone book called "The Production and Distribution of Knowledge in the United States" [17] analyzed the imperfections of competition in a free society. The basic aspects of his study were the causal interrelation among the cost of copyrights and Research and Development (R&D) and knowledge production. His conceptualization for the knowledge process was consisted of (a) R&D, (b) Education, (c) Communication and its media and (d) Information machines and services. Based on this approach he studied the share of information as a component of the Gross National Product (GNP) of the United States and he found – among many interesting results – that the aggregate knowledge production made up 29% of the adjusted GNP and the total civilian labor force engaged in knowledge-producing activities in the United States was equal to 42.8% in 1969.

Machlup's ideas inspired a series of other authors, but profoundly Peter Drucker [18], which introduced the concept of "Knowledge Society" and predicted that by the late 1970s, the knowledge sector would account for one half of the GNP. The concept of Information Society (IS) was established in the annual meeting of American Society for Information Science in 1970, which was entitled as "The Information-Conscious Society" meeting [19].

Last decades, fast advances in the Information and Communication Technologies (ICTs) triggered wide research efforts about IS in economic studies and computer and social sciences. The disciplines of Knowledge Management [11] and Social Informatics [20] have emerged and Artificial Intelligence [42] and Knowledge Engineering [43] revitalized. The concept of IS enriched by traditional social theories, such as Marxist-inspired or post-Marxist theories, more or less critical theories of modernity and/or postmodernity, or theory of structuration [21,22]. Analysis of the informational network society initiated by Manuel Castells

[23,24,25,26,27] is shaping a new framework based on analytical resources developed in modern social theory and new political economy. Related terms to IS are considered to be Digital Society [31] and Virtual Society [28].

We are still far away from a general theory for the IS. In my point of view, IS needed to be addressed in a trans-disciplinary framework, a step further to inter-disciplinarity, based on an integrated view of different disciplinary epistemologies. According to Vafopoulos et al [29] "In trans-disciplinary research, the point is not just application of given methodologies but also implication, a result of imagining entirely new possibilities for what disciplines can do. The 'trans' in trans-disciplinarity is about recognizing the holistic approach of this process of investigation which trans-forms mainstream definitions of research".

In this context, the first step in the trans-disciplinary framework is considered to be the analysis of the positive and the negative consequences in the modern IS.

4 The two faces of Janus: Knowledge vs. Control

In the current analysis, the positive face of Janus is reflected in the knowledge-based development and the negative is referred to personal privacy violation issues.

4.1 Knowledge – based development and the g-work model

Knowledge is synchronously the most valuable input and output in the process of economic development. Despite the fact that nowadays knowledge is characterized by excess supply and is under – used, mainly because it can not be accumulated like an ordinary good [32]. Danny Quah [32] points out that "As humanity becomes more educated, and ideas, tastes, and beliefs integrate more closely, the greater become the potential social benefits from deploying all the different kinds of knowledge - those that increase our productivity, improve our health, and raise our quality of life".

In this context, ICTs can be viewed as an opportunity to obtain economies of scale in the knowledge production and dissemination process. Particularly, digital goods – including knowledge – are nonrival, infinitely expansible, indivisible, aspatial and recombinant [33], Semantic Web technologies [34] provide knowledge interoperability and reprocess, high tech collaborative working environment applications offer quasi face-to face almost costless meetings and Grid computing is releasing vast amounts of processing power [35].

A comprehensive analytical and practical framework for knowledge creation, reuse and exploitation in the personal, business and academic sector based on the Semantic Grid technologies [36] is considered to be g-work [14]. G-work is defined to be a step further to e-work [37]. G-work was introduced as a personal Grid e-workspace for every citizen and was defined to have four interconnected parts: (a) Digital Storage, (b) Network Traffic, (c) Processing Power and (d) One-stop Web Services. As Vafopoulos et al [14] argues, today business practice is compatible to g-work, web services for all citizens are being released everyday around the world and academia – specifically life, computer and information sciences – is adapting to this innovative operational model [38].

But in any case, it is not ICTs themselves but the way people use them that influences whether or not and how ICTs gets actually used. Furthermore, in case of social and economic reforms, it is not just the technology itself but the motivation for people to co-operate each other.

4.2   Control society, surveillance and personal data privacy

The development concept is concentrated in an opportunity: more and better input in every citizen's information set, and a threat: personal data privacy. The trade-off is not conspicuous but is fundamental: more personal data in a collaborative working environment means more chances to work, co-operate, interact, learn and develop your personality, but also increase possibilities for personal data abuse. In the above trade – off

the September 11 2001 terrorist attacks on New York and Washington are considered as a turning point since security and surveillance operations – including e-mail and Internet monitoring – [39] become first priority in public policies and funding. Before that key date, studies on the social impact of surveillance and monitoring systems were concentrated in the concept of centralized power [40]. According to David Lyon [39] "The increasingly automated discriminatory mechanisms for risk profiling and social categorizing represent a key means of reproducing and reinforcing social, economic, and cultural divisions in informational societies".

Hacking [41] and inventions in software systems poses the other major category of risks for personal data privacy. Widespread use of ICTs in everyday life drives a substantial increase in the value of legality which in turn follows a correspondent increase in the law-breaking activity. The major issue in this case is that benefits coming from the IS are divided into a vast and loosely – connected group of people with not necessarily common interest and action plan. On the contrary, benefits from law-breaking activity in the IS framework are exploited by small, flexible and well – organized teams. The above asymmetrical value function for the adaptation of information technologies partially explains observed time and technology lags in public compared to private Web Services technologies.

In the g-work framework [14], besides the technical aspect of data privacy (i.e. semantic firewalls and Community Authorization Service for Group Collaboration), an independent "third intermediator entity" run by representatives from local authorities is proposed.

5   Policy implications

Information Society is a political and scientific concept, since ICTs shaped by society and shape society. Society - ICTs dialectic relation until now has been given less attention. IS is becoming the major aspect in personal, social, business and scientific life.

5.1 Personal and social aspect

The key concept in the personal and social aspects of the IS is introduced to be "the new democratic deficit". The new democratic deficit is defined to have two dimensions:
1. the lack of free access to structured information and knowledge concerning public action for all citizens and
2. unauthorized and nonvoluntary access to personal data from third parties.

For instance, democratic deficits exist when a government service is not available for a group of citizens or a telephone call is recorded without legal authorization.

5.2 Research and business aspect

The research and business aspect of the IS is focused in the transition from the general e-work model to the g-work paradigm. Specifically, from e-work which is "including all information-processing work carried out away from the establishment using a computer and a telecommunications link to deliver the work" [37], nowadays, scientists and businessmen are trying to g-work, namely to semantically interoperate with people, knowledge, software and hardware.

In order to exploit the benefits of IS we should agree on specific standards on the:
- quality,
- quantity and
- knowledge formation tools and mechanisms of public information.

Quality refers to interoperability and reusability standards of information in order to solve everyday problems with minimum cost. Quantity mainly involves the discrimination between personal and public information. Knowledge formation tools include software and organizational structures capable to transform raw data and information to useful knowledge.

6 Conclusion

ICTs by augmenting human senses change and/or remove limits among social structures. Since this basic finding seems not to be fully appreciated by the majority of politicians, academia owes to guide the way through an efficient and fair IS exploitation. Social and technology scientists should work together without technological or social monolithic determinism in order to achieve sustainable development for human societies.

References

1. Zeleny, M.: Management Support Systems: Towards Integrated Knowledge Management, Human Systems Management, 71 (1987), 59-70
2. Dretske, F.: Knowledge and the Flow of Information, MIT Press, Cambridge, MA. (1981)

3. Machlup, F.: Knowledge: Its Creation, Distribution, and Economic Significance, Volume I, Princeton University Press, Princeton, NJ. (1980)
4. Vance, D.: Information, Knowledge and Wisdom: The Epistemic Hierarchy and Computer-Based Information System, in Proceedings of the Third Americas Conference on Information Systems, B. Perkins and I. Vessey (eds.), Indianapolis, IN, (1997)
5. Quah, D.: A weightless economy. UNESCO Courier (1998)
6. Quah, D.: Increasingly weightless economies. Bank of England Quarterly Bulletin, 37(1) (1997) 49–56
7. Berghel, H.: Cyberspace 2000: dealing with information overload, Communications of the ACM 40 (2) (1997) 19-24
8. Kirsh, D.: A few thoughts on cognitive overload. Intellectica (2000)
9. Lewis, D.: Dying for Information? London: Reuters Business Information (1996)
10. Feather, J.: In The information society: A study of continuity and change. London: Library Association (1998)
11. Alavi, M., Leidner, D.: Knowledge Management Systems: Emerging Views and Practices from the Field. Communications of the AIS (1999)
12. Gil, Y., Ratnakar V.: A Comparison of (Semantic) Markup Languages. Proceedings of the International FLAIRS Conference, Pensacola Beach, Florida, May 14-16 (2002) http://trellis.semanticweb.org/expect/web/semanticweb/comparison.html .
13. Simple Knowledge Organisation System (SKOS), W3C Semantic Web Activity (2005) http://www.w3.org/2004/02/skos/
14. Vafopoulos, M., Gravvanis, G., Platis, A.: The personal grid e-workspace, In: Grid Technologies: Emerging from Distributed Architectures to Virtual Organizations, M.P. Bekakos, G.A. Gravvanis and H.R. Arabnia, (eds) WIT Press, (2005)
15. Kronick, D.: A history of scientific and technical periodicals. Metuchen, NJ: Scarecrow Press (1962)
16. Billings, J. S.: Selected papers. Chicago: Medical Library Association (1965)
17. Machlup, F.: The production and distribution of knowledge in the United States. Princeton, NJ: Princeton University Press (1962)
18. Drucker, P.: The age of discontinuity. New York: Harper & Row (1968)
19. Proceedings of the American Society for Information Science. Washington, D.C.: ASIS, (1970)
20. Kling, R., Crawford, H., Rosenbaum, H., Sawyer, S., Weisband, S.: Learning from Social Informatics: Information and Communication Technologies in Human Contexts Centre for Social Informatics, Indiana University (2000)
21. Giddens, A.: The Constitution of Society. Outline of the Theory of Structuration. Polity Press, (1986)
22. Giddens, A.: The Consequences of Modernity. Polity Press, (1992)
23. Castells, M.: High Technology, Economic Restructuring, and the Urban-Regional Process in the United States. In Manuel Castells (ed.) High Technology, Space, and Society. Urban Affairs Annual Reviews, Volume 28. SAGE Publications. (1985)
24. Castells, M.: The Informational City. Information Technology, Economic Restructuring, and the Urban-Regional Process. Oxford: Basil Blackwell (1989)
25. Castells, M.: The Information Age. Economy, Society and Culture. Vol. I: The Rise of the Network Society. Oxford: Blackwell (1996)
26. Castells, M.: The Information Age. Economy, Society and Culture. Vol. II: The Power of Identity. Oxford: Blackwell (1997)

Ant Seeker: An algorithm for enhanced web search

Georgios Kouzas, Eleftherios Kayafas and Vassili Loumos
NTUA department of Electical, Electronic and Computer Engineering,
Multimedia Lab 11.26, Zografou Campus, 15773, Athens, Greece.
gkouzas@ece.ntua.gr, kayafas@cs.ntua. gr, loumos@cs.ntua.gr

Abstract. This paper proposes a web search algorithm, which aims to distinguish irrelevant information and to enhance the amount of the relevant information in respect to a user's query. The proposed algorithm is based on the Ant Colony Optimization algorithm (ACO), employing in parallel document similarity issues from the field of information retrieval. Ant Colony Optimization algorithms were inspired through the observation of ant colonies. In our approach, ants are used as agents through Internet, which are capable of collecting information, calculating the content similarity in each visited node and generating routing paths through the web.

1 Introduction

A rapid growth of Internet activity is observed in the last years, especially concerning web applications and information dissemination for many topics [1]. Unfortunately, the chaotic structure of the web makes the search of specific and categorized information ineffective [2]. Search engines, like Google, remarkably improved the web search but some weaknesses still remain unresolved. High percentage of irrelevant retuned results, or the information reproduction, is very frequent to a simple query based search, in the WEB. Our system proposes an alternative way to enhance information in terms of precision as well as to further categorize the search results. Ant colony algorithms were initially used to give solutions in combinatorial problems such as the well known "Traveling Salesman Problem" [3]. However, the usefulness of the ACO algorithms is expanded in other scientific areas like data mining [4] and, more recently, web search [5].

In our approach we suggest a modification over an ACO algorithm, which was firstly proposed by Dorigo and described in [6]. The similarity measurement, as defined in [7] and [8], will be used for the recognition of the duplicated information. The paper is organized as follows. The next section summarizes the related work in the field of web search in respect to the confronted problem, which must be

Please use the following format when citing this chapter:

Kouzas, Georgios, Kayafas, Eleftherios, Loumos, Vassili, 2006, in IFIP International Federation for Information Processing, Volume 204, Artificial Intelligence Applications and Innovations, eds. Maglogiannis, I., Karpouzis, K., Bramer, M., (Boston: Springer), pp. 649–656

surmounted. Section 3 describes our proposal among with all necessary algorithmic procedures and modules. In particular, we present the meta-search algorithm used for the initial result collection [9], defining in parallel, and the conception of similarity for content relevancy. Finally, we portray our modification over an ACO schema (Ant Seeker) explaining its functions analytically.

2   Related Work

With the phenomenal growth of the web, most of the search services have accepted the fact that it would be almost impossible to index the entire web. Instead, they concentrate on a specialized subset of the web and use ranking techniques to determine which of the web pages to index [10][11]. A web user is not aware of this problem and when a search service returns to him no relevant results, he will probably conclude that pertinent resources do not exist. In addition, during web search, the user must be aware of the query syntax of every search engine, a fact that renders the process even more consuming.

The evolution in the query-based web search became with the algorithm is used by Google, which looks at the links on a page and the links on pages linking to the current page. This can be used in two ways. If all the link descriptions of links to a given page could be found, then an accurate description of the given page could be created from them which do not rely on any one person's perspective or the biased perspective of a page author who includes his own meta-data. This is a potentially powerful tool in web mining [12], but to make a compendious description the whole web would have to be searched for links for the given page with obvious drawbacks. Meta-search engines became to solve the query-translation problem and the meta-results merging problems but the content-based search was still remained unsolved.

Other algorithms are focused to a content based search [4], [5], [8] and based on classification algorithms, but require a large sample set of web pages in order to be trained. Similarity factor as described in [7] and [8] provides a simple and effective approach for classifying content-relevant documents. However the content based search is still used in a small scale search.

In our approach, we are trying to combine these two different search techniques, the query based and the content based search. The first level of our search is the user filtered results of a meta-search engine in respect of a user defined query, enhanced with the second level content based search through similarity.

3   Description of the System

The proposed algorithmic procedure is based on the following concept. An information source (web page or site) should probably lead to another information source, with a similar content. A meta-search engine collects and ranks the results of more than one search engine in order to present the results in terms of relevance. Each web page that contains relevant information is set as a starting point. Ant Seeker algorithm is used to correlate the starting point with a destination point (another web page), linked in a close depth. In the beginning, starting points are defined as the initial query results derived from the meta-search engine. The algorithm is executed for each starting point. If a web page with similar or identical content is discovered, it is defined as destination point. When a destination point is reached, it is defined as a starting point and the algorithm is repeated. The similarity factor is used to assign a similarity weight in the content of different web pages. The basic functions of the proposed system are illustrated in figure 1 aiming at grouping similar information. The meta-search engine, the Similarity factor and the ant seeker algorithm are described bellow:

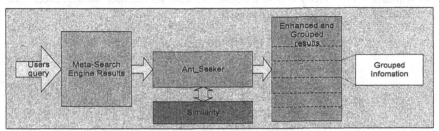

Fig. 1. The architecture of the proposed system

3.1 The meta-search algorithm

A meta-search engine is chosen for the query results instead of a typical search engine, like Google, because the meta-search engine utilizes more than one known search engine and the user gets enhanced amount of information, recording in parallel his search preferences. The meta-search engine chosen for our approach is a user-defined (UMSE) and it is described in [9]. UMSE uses a rank-based isolated merging method, since it uses information, which is readily available from search servers, without requiring any other server functionality [13],[14]. In other words the proposed method employs server-assigned ordinal ranks in order to generate the merged list of the meta-results. The UMSE 'extracts' the required information from all the submitted services combined with the meta-results and the user profile information. Then the duplicate information sources are removed. The problem of UMSE is addressed to have a search engine ranking $S = \langle R, r \rangle$, consisted of a set R of results and an ordering r. Given N ranking from N different search engines, the anticipated outcome is the generation of a single ranking $S_m = \langle R_m, r_m \rangle$, such that $R_m = R_1 \cup ... \cup R_N$ and r_m is the derived meta-results ranking. In other words, the merging algorithm compares whether the information source retrieved in the rth rank position of search engine with priority p, exists until the $(r-1)^{th}$ rank position of the other selected search engines. The duplicate fields in the above sequence are eliminated while the procedure ends with the assignment of the last meta-result. The number of the meta-results is the total returned results from all the involved search engines, having removed the duplicated fields. UMSE allows the user to adjust the number of the returned results from each used search service. This number has a large impact on the total number and the presentation time of the meta-results.

3.2   The similarity Factor

The similarity factor is used to recognize the content relevancy. For the respective investigation, we used the algorithm described in [7] and [8]. This similarity factor is based on syntactic properties of the document. In our approach the content of web pages is defined as the document.

Let's suppose that there is an N-word document. Every single word of the document is ordered to be the start of a k-word sequence. Consequently, the document is represented as a set of N-word subsequences and each subsequence is a set of k continuant words. Two identical documents have exactly the same set of subsequences. Two utterly different documents have no common subsequences. The similarity of two documents is defined as:

$$S_{1,2}^k = \frac{S_1^k \cap S_2^k}{S_1^k \cup S_2^k} \quad 0 \le S_{1,2}^k \le 1 \ (1)$$

Where S1 is the number of subsequences appearing in the first document, S2 is the number of subsequences appearing in the second document and k is the word length for every subsequence.

The k parameter controls the sensitivity of the similarity factor. The larger the value of parameter k, the bigger the sensitivity of similarity. For example, let's suppose that there are two N-word documents which differ in one single word. Each document has N subsequences and each subsequence has k words. Each single word appears in k subsequences. Thus, the number of subsequences appearing in both documents is equal to (N - k) and the total number of subsequences existing in both documents is (N + k). The value of similarity factor is $(N - k)/(N + k)$. If the value of parameter k is set equal to N then the value of similarity is equal to zero. On the other hand, if k=1 then s≈1 (N>>1), which means, that we have a word to word comparison between these documents.

3.3   The Ant Seeker algorithm

The basic concept of ant colony algorithms was inspired by the observation of swarm colonies, specifically ants [15]. Since most species of ants are blind, they deposit a chemical substance called pheromone to find their way to the food source and back to their colony [16], [17]. The pheromone evaporates over time. It has been shown experimentally that the pheromone trail leads to the detection of shortest paths [18]. For example, a set of ants, initially, create a path to the food source. An obstacle with two ends is placed in their way, with one end more distant than the other. In the beginning, equal numbers of ants spread around the two ends of the obstacle. The ants, which choose the path of the nearer end of the obstacle, return before the others. The pheromone deposited to the shortest path increases more rapidly than the pheromone deposited to the farther one. Finally, as more ants use the shortest path, the pheromone of the longest path evaporates and the path disappears. In artificial life, the Ant Colony Optimization (ACO) uses artificial ants, called agents, to find solutions to difficult combinatorial optimization problems [6], [3].

ACO algorithms are based on the following concept. Each path followed by an ant is associated with a candidate solution to a given problem. The amount of pheromone deposited on a path followed by an ant is proportional to the quality of the corresponding candidate solution for the target problem. Finally, when an ant has to choose between two or more paths, those with the larger amount of pheromone have a greater probability of being chosen by the ant.

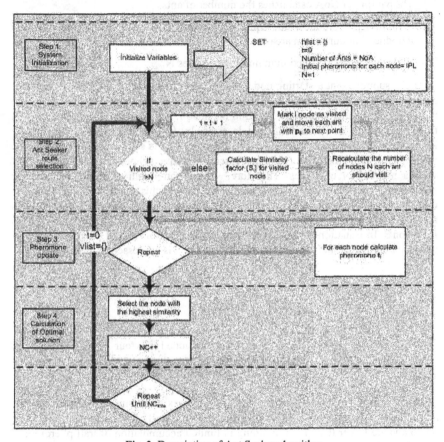

Fig. 2. Description of Ant Seeker algorithm

In our approach, we propose a modification of the ACO algorithm [6], which we call Ant_Seeker. In this algorithm each artificial ant employs the following properties:

- Each ant is capable of carrying memory (pheromone based)

- The node selection is based on pheromone level deposited in each node.

- Each ant has a maximum number of nodes that can visit before discovering a destination node.

- All ants start from a starting node

- Each ant uses the similarity factor to define (calculate) the document identity as mentioned above.

The following paragraph describes how the ant seeker algorithm is applied to the web search. The figure 2 illustrates the In order to initialize our model we introduce the following parameters:

➤ The parameter NoA establishes the number of ants.

➤ An initial pheromone value equal to IPV, is set in every new linked paged is introduced in our search area

➤ Each ant can visit a maximum number of nodes N_{max}

Let's suppose that a starting node is given by a meta-search engine. All ants are initially set to the starting point. Each time, every ant must move from a node i to node j which should be directly linked to the node i. The directly movement between node i and j is called accessibility and described by h_{ij} parameter. If node j is directly linked to node i, the parameter h_{ij} is set to 1 otherwise is set to zero. Let $\tau_i(t)$ be the pheromone amount on node i at time t. Each ant at time t chooses the next node until visit a number N of nodes. Therefore, we call an iteration of the Ant_Seeker algorithm the completion of route for each ant. At this point the pheromone is updated according to Equation 2, where ρ is a coefficient such that $(1 - \rho)$ represents the evaporation of trail between time t and $t+1$, while $\Delta\tau_i$ is given according to Equation 3. In Equation 3, $\Delta\tau_i^k$ is the quantity per unit of level of pheromone is laid on node i by the k_{th} ant between time t and $t+1$ and   is expressed by Equation 4.

$$\tau_i(t+1) = \rho \cdot \tau_i(t) + \Delta\tau_i \quad (2)$$

$$\Delta\tau_i = \sum_{k=1}^{m} \Delta\tau_i^k \quad (3)$$

$$\Delta\tau_i^k = \begin{cases} Q \cdot S_{MAX}^k & \text{if k ant visits node i in its tour} \\ 0 & \text{otherwise} \end{cases} \quad (4)$$

In Equation 4, Q is a constant and S_{MAX}^k is maximum similarity value the ant meets on its tour and is calculated according to Equation 1. The coefficient ρ must be set to a value lower than 1 for avoiding unlimited accumulation of trail pheromone. An initial pheromone value equal to IPV is set in every new node is added to the search area. In order to satisfy the constraint that an ant doesn't visit a visited node, each ant is associated with a data structure called the *vlist*, that saves the nodes already visited and forbids the ant to visit them again before a tour have been completed. When a tour is completed, the *vlist* is used to compute the ant's current solution (i.e., the node with the maximum value of Similarity factor). The *vlist* is then emptied and the ant is free to choose again.

The transition probability from node i to node j for the kth ant is defined at Equation 5, where allowedk = {Nodes can be visited - vlist}. Therefore the transition probability is a trade-off between accessibility (which states that only directly linked nodes should be chosen) and pheromone level at time t (which states that if this node was previously selected then this node highly desirable, thus implementing the autocatalytic process).

$$P_{ij} = \frac{\tau_j \cdot h_{ij}}{\sum\limits_{k \in allowed_k} \tau_k \cdot h_{kj}} \quad (5)$$

Where h_{ij} is the accessibility of node j from node i and is given by Equation 6.

$$h_{ij} = \begin{cases} 1 & \text{if } j \text{ node is directly linked from node i} \\ 0 & \text{otherwise} \end{cases} \quad (6)$$

$$N_a = \frac{\sum\limits_{n=1}^{Vn} (n \cdot S_n)}{\sum\limits_{n=1}^{Vn} n} \cdot N_{max} \quad (7)$$

Each ant has a specific number of nodes that can visit. This number defines the depth search of each ant. If an ant follows a path of links which contains nodes with high values of similarity, the ant has the ability to continue its search deeper. If an ant chooses a path of nodes with low values of similarity the search will stop shortly. The last visited nodes, are assigned with higher weights as far as their significance is concerned. The total number of visited nodes for each ant must not exceed a maximum value N_{max}. The expected number of nodes that each ant can visit is given by Equation 7 where Vn is the number of visited nodes and S_n is the similarity value of node n.

4 Conclusion

It is concluded that sustainable development for web search may be achieved with the conjunction of well known optimization algorithms and similarity metrics. The final assessment of the proposed method will be evaluated on a large set of web pages.

In addition, we undertake a research among other Artificial Intelligence methods in order to create a hybrid approach to provide an automatically adjustment of the number of the returned results from each search service used. The main scope is to achieve a successful combination of "query-based" and "semantic-based" operation in our system.

References

1　I. Anagnostopoulos, C. Anagnostopoulos, G. Kouzas and D. Vergados, "A Generalised Regression algorithm for web page categorisation", Neural Computing & Applications journal, Springer-Verlag, Vol. 13, no. 3, pp. 229 – 236, 2004.

2　I. Anagnostopoulos, C. Anagnostopoulos, Vassili Loumos, Eleftherios Kayafas, "Classifying Web Pages employing a Probabilistic Neural Network Classifier", IEE Proceedings – Software, vol. 151, no. 03, pp. 139-150, March 2004.

3　Bianchi, L., Gambardella L.M., Dorigo M., 2002, „An ant colony optimization approach to the probabilistic travelling salesman problem". In Proceedings of PPSN-VII, Seventh Inter17 national Conference on Parallel Problem Solving from Nature, Lecture Notes in Computer Science. Springer Verlag, Berlin, Germany.

4　R.S. Parpinelli, et al. Data Mining with an Ant Colony Optimization Algorithm. IEEE Trans. on Evolutionary Computation, special issue on Ant Colony algorithms, 6(4), pp. 321-332, Aug. 2002.

5　P.S. Szczepaniak et al. (Eds.): "Ants in Web Searching Process" AWIC 2005, LNAI 3528, pp. 57–62, 2005.c Springer-Verlag Berlin Heidelberg 2005

6　Dorigo M., and Maniezzo V., 1996, "The ant system: optimization by a colony of cooperating agents". IEEE Transactions on Systems, Man and Cybernetics, 26(1), 1-13.

7　Broder A, Glassman S, Manasse M, Zweig G. Syntactic clustering of the Web. Proceedings of the 6th International World Wide Web Conference, April 1997; 391–404.

8　Dennis Fetterly, et al. "A large-scale study of the evolution of Web pages" SOFTWARE— PRACTICE AND EXPERIENCE 2004; 34:213–237

9　Anagnostopoulos I., Psoroulas I., Loumos V. and Kayafas E., "Implementing a customized meta-search interface for user query personalization", , 24th International Conference on In-formation Technology Interfaces, ITI 2002, pp. 79-84, June 24-27, 2002, Cavtat/Dubrovnik, CROATIA.

10　Oyama S, Kokubo T, Ishida T (2004) Domain-specific Web search with keyword spices. IEEE Transactions on Knowledge and Data Engineering. 16(1):17–27

11　Pokorny J (2004) Web searching and information retrieval. Computing in Science & Engineering. 6(4):43-48

12　Soumen Chakrabartia, Byron Doma, Prabhakar Raghavana, Sridhar Rajagopalana, David Gibsonb, and Jon KleinbergcAutomatic. Automatic Resource compilation by analyzing hyperlink structure and associated text, 1998.

13　Craswell, Nick, Hawking, David and Thistlewaite, Paul. Merging Results from Isolated Search Engines. 10th Australasian Database Conference, Auckland, New Zealand, January 1999, Springer-Verlag, Singapore.

14　Yuwono, Budi and Lee, Dik L. Server ranking for distributed text retrieval systems on the internet. In Topor, Rodney and Tanaka, Katsumi, editors, DASFAA '97, pages 41-49, Melbourne. World Scientific, Singapore.

15　Bonabeau E., Dorigo M., & Theraulaz G. "Intelligence: From Natural to Artificial Systems", Oxford University Press.

16　Dorigo M. and Caro G.D., 1999, "The Ant Colony Optimization Meta-heuristic," in New Ideas in Optimization, D. Corne, M. Dorigo, and F. Glover, Eds. London: McGraw-Hill, pp. 11-32.

17　Dorigo M., and Caro G.D., 1999, "Ant Algorithms Optimization. Artificial Life", 5(3), 137-172.

18　Chen S., Smith. S., 1996, "Commonality and genetic algorithms". Technical Report CMU-RITR-96-27, The Robotic Institute, Carnegie Mellon University, Pittsburgh, PA, USA.

Increasing Intelligent Wireless Sensor Networks Survivability by Applying Energy-Efficient Schemes

Nikolaos A. Pantazis[1], Dimitrios J. Vergados[1,2], Dimitrios D. Vergados[1]

1 University of the Aegean, Department of Information and
Communication Systems Engineering
GR-83200, Karlovassi, Samos, Greece
{npantazis, vergados}@aegean.gr
2 National Technical University of Athens, School of Electrical and
Computer Engineering
Iroon Polytexneiou 9, GR-157 73, Zografou, Athens, Greece
djvergad@telecom.ntua.gr

Abstract. Intelligent Energy efficiency is an important research topic for ad-hoc Wireless Sensor Networks (WSN). Power saving makes it possible to guarantee basic levels of system performance, such as connectivity, throughput and delay, in the presence of both mobility-immobility and a large number of sensor nodes. A large variety of approaches for intelligent energy-efficient schemes have been proposed in the literature focusing on different performance metrics. This article presents a comprehensive survey of recent energy-efficient schemes in ad-hoc wireless sensor networks, the application of which increases nodes' lifetime and thus, network connectivity and survivability.

1 Introduction

Wireless Sensor Networks (WSNs) have been increased dramatically the recent years as they are used more and more in the daily life. Such ad-hoc wireless sensor networks find applications in medical, military, motion tracking, environmental control etc. Wireless Sensor Networks consist of a great number of small in size, inexpensive, low-power intelligent sensor nodes, which are densely and randomly distributed either inside the phenomenon or very close to it. Sensor nodes consist of sensing, processing and communicating components because their function is to collect and disseminate critical data while their position need not be predetermined [1]. Network lifetime is very important issue in the WSNs. The energy problem

Please use the following format when citing this chapter:

Pantazis, Nikolaos, Vergados, Dimitrios J., Vergados, Dimitrios D., 2006, in IFIP International Federation for Information Processing, Volume 204, Artificial Intelligence Applications and Innovations, eds. Maglogiannis, I., Karpouzis, K., Bramer, M., (Boston: Springer), pp. 657–664

becomes harder in ad-hoc wireless sensor networks; due to their limitations arising from their nature. In order to guarantee the WSNs survivability and increase network lifetime in such special purpose environments intelligently, various energy-efficient schemes have been proposed in the literature. This paper presents and evaluates recent energy-efficient schemes; where their efficient choice extends the nodes' lifetime and therefore the network data communication and survivability.

The rest of the paper is organized as follows: Section 2 discusses the survivability issues arising from the application of energy-efficient schemes. Section 3 proposes and analyzes various energy-efficient schemes in Ad-hoc intelligent wireless sensor networks and Section 4 presents a performance evaluation. Finally, Section 5 concludes the paper.

2   Survivability Issues by the Application of Energy-Efficient Schemes in Intelligent Wireless Sensors

The main performance issues of mobile ad-hoc sensor networks include the speed and ease of deployment, efficient data delivery and efficient use of device battery life. Data delivery is intimately related to the routing protocol used the aim of which is to maintain network connectivity in an efficient manner. Battery life is a major player in such networks and also an important limiting resource. Battery power is used to run local applications on a device as well as to send, receive and relay data. Conserving battery life is an important consideration in maintaining network connectivity. Such a network requires a lightweight energy-management framework that does not burden the resource-limited network nodes with undue processing needs. Thus, in order to guarantee the WSNs' survivability and increase network lifetime in various environments, many energy-efficient schemes have been proposed. In some cases, wireless sensors are expected to be able to operate for a long period of time in the idle mode, and transmit the gathered data, when required, as soon as possible. Under theses assumptions, most of the time the sensor nodes waste energy by listening continuously to the wireless channel, even though no useful information is being transmitted. Why are the energy-efficient schemes so important for the intelligent sensors?

Given the dynamic nature of most sensor networks, an efficient energy-management framework enhances the overall survivability of the network. For that reason, using stable communication links is crucial for establishing stable paths between sensor nodes. Rerouting is especially costly in these networks without infrastructure, since it usually results in (at least partly) flooding the network. The stability of a communication link is given by its probability to persist for a certain time span, which is not necessarily linked with its probability to reach a very high age. For example, consider a number of sensor nodes randomly spread over in a hostile area where the target of interest is moving. Consider also, that the sensors' density depends on operation scope (motion detection, tracking etc.) of the sensor as well as the land morphology. Also, the replacement frequency of the sensors or the sensors' battery is very rare, due to replacement cost. Moreover, the existence of alternative routing improves the survivability of communication. It minimizes failures and the packet delivery delays. It increases network complexity and the energy spent in each sensor node. In order to track the specific target intelligently, metrics from at least two nodes are required. In case that one sensor is out of battery, the system cannot come to the result and thus the intelligent system fails to attain its goal. Therefore, energy is a valuable commodity in wireless networks due to the limited battery of the portable devices. It does not only extend network communication but guarantees intelligent system's performance.

3 Energy-Efficient Schemes in Ad-hoc Intelligent Wireless Sensor Networks

Several Energy-Efficient Schemes have been proposed in the literature. The Energy-Efficient Scheme may be classified into two main categories: Active and Passive. Active refers to mechanisms that achieve energy conservation by utilizing energy-efficient network protocols, and Passive refers to mechanisms that save a node's power by turning-off the radio (transceiver) interface module [2]. However our research work considers only the Passive ones.

3.1 Power-Aware Multi-Access with Signaling (PAMAS)

PAMAS (Power-Aware Multi-Access with Signaling) is a new multi-access protocol for ad-hoc radio networks based on the original MACA protocol with the addition of a separate signaling channel [3]. It saves nodes' battery power, by turning-off the nodes which are not in active transmission or sending packets. In PAMAS protocol the receiving mobile nodes transmit a busy tone (in a separate control channel) when they start receiving frames so that other mobile nodes know when to turn-off. When a mobile node does not have data to transmit, it should power itself off if a neighbor begins transmitting to some other node. A node should turn-off even if it has data to transmit if at least one of its neighbor-pairs is communicating. A mobile node, which has been turned-off when one or more of its neighbor-pairs started communicating, can determine the length of time that it should be turned-off by using a probe protocol. In this protocol, the node performs a binary search to determine the time when the current transmission will end. However, the loss of probe frames may cause significant power wastage.

3.2 Sensor-MAC (S-MAC)

S-MAC (Sensor-MAC) is an intelligently distributed protocol, which gives the possibility to nodes to discover their neighbors and build sensor networks for communication without being obliged to have master nodes. [4]. There are no clusters or cluster heads here. The topology is flat. This solution, proposed by Wei Ye et al. [5], focuses mainly on the major energy wastage sources while achieving good scalability and collision avoidance capability. The major energy wastage sources may be classified into overhearing, idle listening, collisions and control packet overhead [6]. S-MAC introduces the following two techniques to achieve the reduction of energy consumption. Firstly, neighboring nodes are synchronized to go to sleep periodically so that they do not waste energy when a neighboring node is transmitting to another node or by listening to an empty channel. The overhearing problem is avoided this way. Secondly, the control packet overhead of the network is kept low because synchronized neighboring nodes form virtual clusters to synchronize their wake-up and sleep periods. Actually, there is no real clustering and no inter-cluster communication problem. Also, S-MAC consists of three components: Periodic Listen and Sleep, Collision and Overhearing Avoidance and Message Passing. In Periodic Listen and Sleep Neighboring nodes are synchronized in such a way as to listen together and sleep together. In Collision and Overhearing Avoidance, collision is avoided through the adoption of a contention-based scheme. In Message Passing, the indicated method is the fragmentation of long messages into smaller ones and their transmission in a burst.

3.3 Dynamic Voltage Scaling (DVS)

The application of turn-off techniques can produce substantial energy savings in idle system states; however, additional energy savings are possible through the optimization of the sensor node performance in the active state. Dynamic Voltage Scaling (DVS) is an effective tool for reducing to the minimum the CPU energy [7], [8]. If we recognize that peak performance is not always required, then we can achieve significant energy savings. This implies the dynamic adaptation of the processor's operating voltage and frequency based on instantaneous processing requirements. The main idea behind DVS is to adapt the power supply to the changes of the workload. In other words, this approach varies the processor voltage under software control to meet dynamically varying performance requirements. More analytically: DVS allows devices to dynamically change their speed and voltage, while in operation, and thus trade-off energy for delay. This allows the processor to provide the minimum required (necessary) clock frequency with the maximum possible energy efficiency. To do this, DVS requires intelligent algorithms, termed voltage schedulers, to determine the operating speed of the processor at run-time. The goal of DVS is to adapt the power supply and operating frequency to match the workload. This way, the visible performance losses are not of importance. The hard part of the problem lies in the fact that future workloads are often non-deterministic. So the efficiency depends on predicting the future workloads.

3.4 Dynamic Power Management (DPM) in Wireless Sensor Networks

An operating-system-directed power management technique, contributing to a dynamic increase of the lifetime of the sensor node, is proposed by Sinha et al. [9]. This model of sensor node deals with switching of node state in a power-efficient manner. Once the system has been designed, additional power savings can be obtained by using Dynamic Power Management (DPM). DPM is an effective tool in reducing system power consumption without significantly degrading performance. The basic idea behind this scheme is to turn sensor node components (sensor with A/D converter, Processor, Memory and Transceiver) OFF when not required (if no events occur) and get them back (wake them up) when necessary. Such event-driven power consumption is critical to maximum battery life. Although this power-saving method seemingly provides significant energy gains, we should not overlook the fact that sensor nodes communicate with each other using short data packets [4]. The shorter in length the packets are, the more the consumption of start-up energy is achieved. This is because the switching of a node, from one state to another, takes some finite time and resource. More analytically, sleep-state transitioning has the overhead of storing processor state and turning-off power. Waking-up also takes a finite amount of time. Therefore, if we keep turning the transceiver OFF during each idling slot, over a certain period of time, then we might end-up consuming more energy than if the transceiver had been left ON. So, the operation in a power-saving mode is energy-efficient only if the time spent in that mode is greater than a certain threshold. It is obvious that the implementation of the correct policy for sleep-state transitioning is critical for DPM success. The authors propose a workload prediction strategy based on adaptive filtering of the past workload profile and analyze several filtering schemes.

3.5 Energy-Efficient Communication Protocol for Wireless Micro-Sensor Networks (LEACH)

The authors [10] focus on communication protocols, which can have significant effect on the overall energy dissipation of these networks. The analysis of the advantages and disadvantages of the conventional routing protocols proved that these protocols of direct transmission, minimum transmission energy, multi-hop routing, and static clustering might not be optimal for wireless micro-sensor networks. LEACH (Low-Energy Adaptive Clustering Hierarchy) [10] is an intelligent self organizing, clustering-based protocol which minimizes energy dissipation in wireless micro-sensor networks by using randomized rotation of the high-energy cluster-head position in such a way as to rotate among the various sensors in order to distribute the energy load evenly among the sensors in the network. This rotation allows the energy requirements of the system to be distributed evenly among all the micro-sensors and thus, not draining the battery of a single sensor. LEACH randomly selects micro-sensor nodes as cluster heads, so the high energy dissipation in communicating with the base station is spread to all the sensor nodes in the micro-sensor network. Once all the nodes are organized into clusters, each cluster head creates a schedule for the nodes in its cluster. This allows the radio components of each non-cluster-head node to be turned-off at all times except during their transmit time, thus minimizing the energy dissipated in the individual sensors. In addition, LEACH is able to perform local computation in each cluster head to reduce the amount of data that must be transmitted to the base station. This achieves a large reduction in the energy dissipation, as computation is much cheaper than communication. LEACH can achieve as much as a factor of 8 reduction in energy dissipation compared with direct communication and a factor of 4 to 8 reduction in energy compared with MTE (Minimum Transmission Energy) routing. In addition to reducing energy dissipation, LEACH successfully distributes energy usage among the nodes in the network such that the nodes die randomly and at essentially the same rate.

3.6   Intra-Super-Frame Power Management for IEEE 802.15.3 WPAN

Since Power Management (PM) is an important issue for the battery-powered portable devices, the proposed scheme should satisfy the following objectives: To assist the devices to sleep and, to reduce the wakeup time as much as possible. There have been several works in literature on the MAC design for power management in wireless systems. Most of them were based on the MAC layer of 802.11 WLAN and there has been no work report on IEEE 802.15.3 systems so far. IEEE 802.15.3 [11] has gained much research attention recently and it is to enable a high-speed and low-power wireless connectivity among portable devices within a Wireless Personal Area Networks (WPAN). PM is critical for the portable devices in IEEE 802.15.3 WPAN. Due to the property of TDMA-based MAC of 802.15.3, one of the key issues for power management is to schedule the order of the multiple streams among multiple users to minimize the total wakeup times. Thus, it is revealed that this power management problem is in general a Hamilton path problem. Using the graph theory, the authors define the lower bounds and upper bounds for minimum wakeup times. An efficient Minimum-Degree Searching (MDS) Algorithm is proposed to find the suboptimal order.

3.7   TDMA Scheduling for Energy Efficiency in Wireless Sensor Networks

TDMA Scheduling Schemes can be used for energy-efficiency in WSNs. Sleep-mode synchronization schemes (like S-MAC) unavoidably introduce sleep-mode related delay that increases with the achieved power conservation. TDMA scheduling in ad-hoc wireless sensor networks is equivalent to the Broadcast Scheduling Problem (BSP), which is a well-known NP-Complete problem. Thus, intelligent algorithms are required for providing near-optimal solutions. Both distributed and centralized algorithms may be introduced to solve this problem of TDMA scheduling. Even though distributed algorithms are more suitable for wireless sensor networks, centralized TDMA scheduling allows more flexibility. In case the centralized approach is used, the gateway gathers the connectivity information between all the sensor nodes in the network, and uses existing energy-efficient routing algorithms to calculate the paths from every sensor node to the gateway. Then, the gateway constructs a TDMA frame that ensures collision avoidance. This schedule is broadcasted back to the sensor nodes, allowing them to know when they can transmit or receive a packet. On the other hand, if a distributed TDMA scheduling scheme is used, the TDMA frame is constructed locally based on information exchanged between neighbors. The basic concept of the proposed scheme is to optimize the operation of these schemes, in order to minimize the end-to-end delay. In the proposed scheme the sensor nodes are normally in sleep mode. Network connectivity is ensured by scheduling TDMA-based wakeup intervals, which are used for propagating WakeUp messages, prior to data transmissions. Appropriate scheduling of the WakeUp intervals allows the data packets to be delayed by only one sleep interval for the end-to-end transmission from the sensors to the gateway. More specifically, the proposed algorithm [12] can create a TDMA schedule appropriate for WU transmissions in wireless sensor networks. The TDMA scheduling algorithm assigns a transmission slot for every node in the sensor network, and a number of reception slots for every forwarding sensor node, one for each corresponding transmitting sensor node. Moreover, possible transmissions, to the same destination, should be assigned in different time slots. Sensor nodes, which are not one-hop neighbors, should receive at the same time, in order to achieve the reduction of the total frame length to the minimum possible.

4 Performance Evaluation

For both DPM and DVS schemes, the operation in a power-saving mode is energy-efficient only if the time spent in that mode is greater than a certain threshold. It is obvious that the implementation of the correct policy for sleep-state transitioning is critical for energy saving. However, the authors propose a workload prediction strategy based on adaptive filtering of the past workload profile and analyze several filtering schemes. On the other hand, sleep-wakeup strategies like PAMAS, S-MAC and TDMA do not require this kind of predictions, but the energy conservation is limited by other factors such as the access delay and/or hardware complexity. For the PAMAS scheme, simulation results showed that power saving in the range from 10% (for sparsely connected networks) to almost 70% (for fully connected networks) could be achieved without affecting the delay-throughput behavior. The main disadvantage of the PAMAS scheme is that it requires a separate signaling channel, and thus requiring more complicated hardware. In addition to that the power losses of the signaling channels should be taken seriously into account. However, since the PAMAS scheme does not affect the delay, it can be useful for delay-critical wireless sensor networks. On the other hand, the S-MAC algorithm is fully distributed, and relies on local exchange of neighboring information. The periodic listen and sleep of the S-MAC algorithm can achieve significant power saving, at the cost of the end-to-end delay that becomes excessive for multi-hop communications. Finally, the TDMA scheme is balanced between the two previous schemes, and can achieve the lowest end-to-end delay for a specific power conservation level in some wireless sensor network configurations (almost static topology, very low traffic load). These wireless sensor networks, that are typical in environmental monitoring and disaster WSNs are expected to have a longer lifetime and the application of the S-MAC scheme can be the best solution. For the other WSNs topologies, where the main problem is how to schedule the order of the multiple streams among multiple users to minimize the total wakeup times, the MDS algorithm can be a suboptimal solution. The simulation results for the MDS algorithm show that it is usually near-optimal (more than 95%) and it can actually achieve the lower bound for the minimum wakeup times in most cases, presenting remarkable performance.

5 Conclusions

Intelligent sensor system's efficiency is based on the data obtained by the sensors. Sometimes the information received by one sensor is not enough to perform a measurement correctly (e.g. track a moving object) and the simultaneous data receipt from two or more sensors is required. Also, in various application schemes, replacement of power resources might be impossible. Therefore, sensor node lifetime shows a strong dependence on battery lifetime and intelligent sensors' system performance, depending on the energy-efficient schemes, obtains additional significance. In this paper, several passive energy-efficient schemes were presented, analyzed and evaluated. Although each scheme is well-suited for certain scenarios, it is not guaranteed that any of them is the best for all situations. Intelligent energy-efficient algorithms can not only increase the lifetime of a specific node, but also intelligent scheduling can increase the network lifetime in relation to the required number of nodes for performing a measurement. Thus, the efficient choice of the proper energy-efficient scheme extends the nodes' lifetime, assures network survivability and connectivity and thus the overall system's performance for a specific measurement is accomplished.

References

1 Ian F. Akyildiz, Weilian Su, Yogesh Sankarasubramaniam, and Erdal Cayirci, "A survey on sensor networks", IEEE Communications Magazine, Aug. 2002, pp. 102-114.

2 Praveen Rentala, Ravi Musunui, Shashidhar Gandhar Gandham, and Udit Saxena, "Survey on Sensor Networks", in Proc. of Int. Conf. on Mobile Computing and Networking, 2001.

3 S. Singh, CS. Raghavendra, "PAMAS: Power-Aware Multi-Access Protocol with Signaling for Ad-Hoc Networks", Computer Comm. Review, 28 (3), 1998, pp. 5-26.

4 P. Rentala, R. Musunuri, S. Gandham and U. Saxena, "Survey on Sensor Networks", in Proc. of International Conference on Mobile Computing and Networking, 2001.

5 W. Ye, J. Heidemann and D. Estrin, "An Energy-Efficient MAC Protocol for Wireless Sensor Networks", in Proc. of the 21st IEEE INFOCOM, 2002.

6 Lodewijk Van Hoesel, Tim Nieberg, Jian Wu, and Paul J. M. Havinga, "Prolonging the Lifetime of Wireless Sensor Networks by Cross-Layer Interaction", IEEE Wireless Communications, Vol. 11, No. 6, Dec. 2004, pp. 78-86.

7 Trevor Pering, Tom Burd, and Robert Brodersen, "The Simulation and Evaluation of Dynamic Voltage Scaling Algorithms", in Proc. of International Symposium on Low Power Electronics and Design, 1998, pp. 76-81.

8 Vadim Gutnik and Anantha P. Chandrakasan, "Embedded Power Supply for Low-Power DSP", IEEE Trans. VLSI Systems, Vol. 5, No. 4, Dec. 1997, pp. 425-435.

9 Amit Sinha, Anantha Chandrakasan, "Dynamic Power Management in wireless sensor networks", IEEE Design and Test of Computer, Vol. 18, Iss. 2, 2001, pp. 62-74.

10 Wendi Rabiner Heinzelman, Anantha Chandrakasan and Hari Balakrishnan "Energy-Efficient Communication Protocol for Wireless Microsensor Networks", in Proc. of the 33rd Hawaii International Conference on System Sciences , 2000, pp. 3005- 3014.

11 Zihua Guo, Member, Richard Yao, Wenwu Zhu, Xin Wang, and Yong Ren, "Intra-Superframe Power Management for IEEE 802.15.3 WPAN", IEEE Communications Letters, Vol. 9, No. 3, Mar. 2005, pp. 228-230.

12 Dimitrios D. Vergados and Dimitrios J. Vergados and Christos Douligeris, "A new approach for TDMA scheduling in Ad-hoc networks", 10th IFIP International Conference on Personal Wireless Communications (PWC'05), Colmar, France, 2005, pp. 107-114.

Acknowledgment: This work has been supported by GSRT, Hellenic Ministry of Development, through the PENED 2003 Project: "Design and Development Models for QoS Provisioning in Wireless Broadband Networks".

A Review of Video Watermarking and a Benchmarking Framework

V. Moutselakis, S. Tsekeridou

Democritus Univ. of Thrace, Dept. of Electrical & Computer Engineering,
67100 Xanthi, Greece
{emoutsel,tsekerid}@ee.duth.gr

Abstract. The rapid use of Internet has led to the investigation of digital watermarking as a complementary technology to traditional protection mechanisms. Significant research efforts and review works presenting unifying characteristics of different methods have been reported for audio and image watermarking. In the context of video watermarking, though, there is a great deal of non-uniformity in presented approaches. The objective in this paper is to give an in-depth overview of different video watermarking techniques in order to single out the particularities of that field. Furthermore, the paper presents a benchmarking framework for objective video watermarking performance evaluation. We conclude that novel techniques need to be implemented and unexplored video-driven approaches have to be investigated.

1 Introduction

The rapid growth of Internet and networked multimedia systems in the past decade has raised concerns from the content designers, since multimedia data nowadays can be flawlessly copied and rapidly disseminated at large scale. Encryption and steganography were proved to be insufficient for digital media protection and thus digital watermarking emerged, aiming at embedding auxiliary information into a host digital signal by imposing secure, imperceptible signal changes (with the employment of a special constructed signal, called watermark that is embedded into original content such as image, video, or audio, producing a watermarked signal). Digital watermarking allows the user to manipulate the content.

We focus on digital video watermarking, where time enhances the flexibility of the solution space. Available data are greater than image data, a fact that during watermark design is useful both for the designer and the attacker as it supports reliable embedding of auxiliary data using sophisticated temporal masking, but also, allows the attacker to make greater use of correlators that lead to more effective watermark estimation and removal attacks.

There is a great academic and industrial interest on the design of a copyright protection system for MPEG-2 coded video distributed on Digital Versatile Disk (DVDs), employing the

Please use the following format when citing this chapter:

Moutselakis, Vangelis, Tsekeridou, Sofia, 2006, in IFIP International Federation for Information Processing, Volume 204, Artificial Intelligence Applications and Innovations, eds. Maglogiannis, I., Karpouzis, K., Bramer, M., (Boston: Springer), pp. 665–672

digital video watermarking technology [25]. A video watermarking system has also been designed by the Galaxy Group to complement the existing content scrambling system (CSS) that is part of the DVD standard; the technology is now called WaterCast and is being applied in the automatic monitoring of digital video broadcasts [9].

In Fig. 1 a general model is provided presenting the entire video watermarking process.

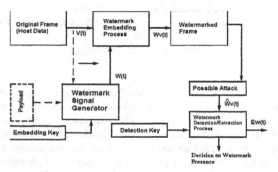

Fig. 1. Video watermarking process model

The video watermarking process consists of two main stages: Watermark Generation and Embedding and Watermark Detection and/or Extraction. At first, the watermark signal generator creates the watermark signal and is provided with an embedding key (the use of a secret such key, to create and embed the watermark is often required for security reasons) and possibly a payload (auxiliary information), and produces $W(t)$, the watermark, to be inserted into the video. Some watermarking techniques further use the original video frame sequence $V(t)$ to achieve more effective watermark embedding. Once the watermark is constructed, it is inserted into the original video frame to produce the watermarked video frame. The specific methods by which the watermark is constructed and embedded is dependent on the watermarking technique. The output of the embedder is the watermarked video $W_v(t)$.

In Fig. 1, $\hat{W}_v(t)$ denotes the watermarked video that is possibly attacked and is provided to the detector. If the video has not been attacked, then $W_v(t)$ is identical to $\hat{W}_v(t)$ for all t. The watermark detector examines the received video and determines if the watermark is present. In Fig. 1, $E_w(t)$ denotes the extracted watermark. The detector is also provided with a detection key necessary for the detection of the watermark. A symmetric (private key) watermark uses identical embedding and detection keys, whereas asymmetric (public key) watermarks use distinct but related such keys, similar in concept to public key cryptography.

In the sequel, a review of existing video watermarking techniques is given and a video watermarking benchmark framework is proposed.

2   Types of Attacks

An attack is any processing that aims at impairing watermark detection or communication of information conveyed by it [5]. An attack causes watermarked video to be altered, intending to remove the embedded watermark or make detection more difficult (*intentional attacks*).

Watermarked data on the other hand is often processed in some way prior to detection. This may include compression, signal enhancement, or digital-to-analog (D-A) and analog-to-digital (A-D) conversion. Thus, we should take into account the case that an embedded watermark is unintentionally impaired by such processing (*non-intentional attacks*).

In this section, we concentrate mainly on *intentional attacks*:

Simple or noise/waveform attacks: attempt to modify both host data and watermark without intending to trace and remove the watermark. Linear/non-linear, temporal/spatio-temporal filtering, waveform-based compression, noise addition are included in this category.

Geometric attacks (or *synchronization attacks*): are accomplished by geometrically transforming the data. For video data, this means frame spatial shift, frame rotating and temporal filtering attacks. The watermark is not ultimately removed by the data (as the goal of these attacks is to force the detector to confront a more difficult synchronization problem), so it is possible to successfully detect and recover it. Temporal synchronization attacks in video include frame dropping, insertion, transposition, averaging (temporal interpolation or scaling).

Removal attacks: are focused on detecting the watermark, isolating it from the host data and eventually removing it, without breaking the security of the watermarking algorithm (e.g., without the key used during watermark embedding, as in [4]). This category includes *denoising, quantization* (e.g., for compression), *remodulation*, and *collusion attacks* (these occur when an attacker obtains collections of video frames that are analyzed or combined with the purpose of producing a non watermarked copy of the original).

Forging attacks: attempt to sabotage the owner's watermark, that is, the attacker wants to forge the original watermark.

Statistical attacks: try to detect the embedded watermark by comparing and finding similarities among a number of watermarked signals that belong to the same owner (whereas collusion attacks involve many copies of a given data set, each signed with a different key).

Protocol attacks: attempt to subvert the security of the watermark, hence attack the entire concept of the watermarking application. They do not directly impact watermark detection.

Ambiguity attacks are based on the concept of invertible watermarks. The malicious forger knows that the data are watermarked. He tries to subtract his own watermark from the watermarked data to later claim to own them and therefore cause uncertainty regarding their true owner. It is essential for copyright protection applications to employ non-invertible watermarks to eliminate the possibility of ambiguity attacks.

Another attack in this category is the *copy attack*: it aims at estimating a watermark from the watermarked data and copies it to some other "target" data without ultimately destroying the watermark or hindering its detection [5].

3   Video Watermark Embedding Methodologies

The embedding process of a watermark into multimedia signals is divided in three categories regarding the entry domain:

1) The watermarks that are constructed in the *spatial/temporal domain*, commonly named as *spatial watermarks*.

[1] models a multi-stage watermarking process. The amount of watermarking imposed on a specific stage counterbalances the quality of the final result. Each selected stage is watermarked by selecting a set of "constraints" (that indicate the presence of the author's

signature), then using preprocessing of the stage's input and post processing of the stage's output to ensure that a disproportionate number of these constraints are satisfied.

In [2], the embedding process employs meaningful information bits in the luminance mean values of each frame. To deal frame removal attacks, synchronization bits are also integrated alternating with the watermark information bits (in both cases a pseudo random sequence (PRS) generator of different length is used). The watermark PRS values are per frame embedded by modifying the mean luminance value of individual frames.

In [10], a state machine key generator is used to produce time-invariant, time-independent, and time-periodic key schedules, to support temporal synchronization for blind video watermarking. The design of the watermark and its key schedule affect the ease of synchronization. The use of a feature vector allows the key sequence produced to be video-dependent. A video-dependent key schedule can increase the difficulty of inverting the watermark and make it more robust against ownership [26] and copy [27] attacks but may cause temporal synchronization loss due to attacks changing the feature vectors [10].

2)   The watermarks incorporated into the *frequency/transform domain*, commonly named as *spectral (or transform-based) watermarks.*

They are integrated within the related transform coefficients. In particular, they involve use of DCT, DWT and DFT or FFT within the embedding process. In video watermarking, significant research efforts are reported to employ 3D DCT, 3D DWT, 3D DFT [24], 3D TWT [12]. The *Temporal Wavelet Transform* (TWT) has scalable temporal resolution.

In [4] the Integer-to-Integer DWT (IIDWT) is used so that both the input and output data to DWT are characterized in integer values. The watermark data is embedded in high frequency regions [4], [6] to improve the watermark effectiveness. Embedding is done in only those coefficients whose norm is greater than a specified threshold in order to achieve perceptual invisibility and robustness against MPEG encoding and re-encoding.

3)   The watermarks inserted at the *compressed domain*.

The process of partial or full decompression of video files is skipped thus avoiding quality loss and extra computational cost. The watermarking process can be executed in real time.

In [8] the watermark is embedded directly in an MPEG-2 compressed bit stream by intentionally forcing bit errors. Thus, the error recovery option of a bidirectionally decodable packet (initially used to handle channel errors in [22]) is exploited so as to embed and retrieve the watermark. Reversible VLCs (RVLC) exhibiting error resiliency are implemented due to their two-way decoding directions capabilities. The watermark is encrypted prior to insertion to make it indistinguishable from randomly extracted bits.

4   Video Watermark Detection/Extraction Methodologies

A prevalent classification of watermark detection is based on whether the original data are used or not. Specifically, if the watermark detector does not require access to the original signal, the watermarking technique is called *blind*. Otherwise, it is known as *non-blind*.

A cryptographic system used in [1] based on public key encryption prevents the forger from discovering a set of constraints that match the original signature. A single metric, P_c is used, showing the probability of how many of the selected constraints (used to map an author's signature) are satisfied. Basically, P_c is the probability of a non-watermarked solution carrying the watermark. If the value of P_c is very low, the more effective the watermark scheme is. P_c is calculated as a sum of binomials, as shown in [1].

Table 4.1. Performance of method discussed in [1] under various attacks

Attack	Performance
Ambiguity Attacks	Brute-force attacks become computationally infeasible if the proof of authorship threshold is set sufficiently low (e.g., $P_c \leq 2^{-56}$)
Removal Attacks	Possible for an attacker to use tampering methods to remove a signature known to him, or to add an entirely new signature.
Forging Attacks	Successfully prevented when using a key encryption system

In [2], the detection process is based on the cross correlation of the embedded PRSs and the video frame mean luminance sequence. Each video frame has different luminance, so the use of an amplitude limiting filter followed by a whitening filter prior to correlation is proposed, in order to improve the detector performance.

Table 4.2. Performance of method discussed in [2] towards different kinds of attacks

Attack	Performance
Geometric Attacks: (frame *spatial shift* and frame *rotating* attacks)	Good performance against frame spatial shift attacks and frame rotating attacks.
Frame Removal Attacks and Temporal Filtering Attacks	Successfully prevented. Detection based on application of a low pass-filter on the luminance values and observation of the corresponding cross-correlation

In [4], the whole watermark extraction process occurs in the decoded video per frame based on a detection key. The averaged watermark obtained is compared to the embedded original watermark in order to ensure that it is exactly the same. Each frame is randomized prior to embedding of the watermark according to the value of a pair of keys, derived from the detection key, to successfully deal collusion and statistical attacks. In [4], it is proved that low values of PSNR (<34db) are obtained with quite big watermarks (> 25 bits).

Table 4.3. Performance of method in [4] under MPEG encoding and re-encoding

Attack	Performance
MPEG Encoding	Average BER ranges from 20-23% and increases steadily when the watermark length is 24 bits and over. Compared to the common DWT technique, the IIDWT one has a 4-8% better performance whatever the watermark length.
MPEG Re-encoding (2 MPEG encoding iterations)	Overall BER increased about 2-3% compared to single MPEG encoding. More robust than DWT, by an 8% difference in BER rate

In [8] the watermarked VLC must be identified the moment it is decoded. Therefore, the inserted watermark must immediately cause decoding failure in order to trigger reverse decoding that begins from the end-of-packet. To ensure forward detection failure right at the edge of a watermarked VLC, the decoded watermarked bit stream must begin with a sequence of so called *flag bits*, guaranteeing detection failure. If the packet length is known to the decoder, the last VLC to be recovered on reverse decoding is the same VLC that failed detection on forward decoding. At the end of this process, the watermark bits are extracted, whereas the stream is restored to its initial state. If the packet length is unknown to the decoder, another flag is used, a *reverse flag*, that causes detection failure on reverse decoding. The watermarking process of compressed media in the VLC domain is inherently fragile since the watermark is vulnerable to re-compression or transcoding. Errors during the detection process-when an incorrect watermark was decoded- are significantly low (they range from 0 - 0.15%) and they are not proportionally affected by the file size.

In [10] a model for symmetric blind video watermark detection is described using a detection key. The watermark detector applies a spatial de-correlating filter to reduce the host-signal interference, followed by a correlation detector and comparison with a threshold.

Table 4.4. Performance of method in [10] towards various synchronization attacks

Attack	Performance
Frame Dropping	Poor performance in cases of little temporal redundancy.
Frame Transposition	Performance similar to the frame dropping one.
Frame Insertion	Does not affect watermark detection. Method achieves a detection rate of 100%.

5 Performance Evaluation

One of the metrics widely used to evaluate watermarking schemes is the *False acceptance rate (FAR)*. FAR states the probability that an unknown individual will be falsely 'recognized' as the rightful owner of the reference video data upon presentation of his or her verification data. FAR is dependent on the selected tolerance limit within which the verification and reference data must match for there to be a successful authentication: the lower the tolerance limit, the lower the FAR and the higher the probability of FRR errors.

The *False rejection rate (FRR)* metric states the probability that the rightful owner of the reference data will be wrongly rejected. FRR is dependent on the tolerance limit within which the verification and reference data must match for there to be a successful authentication: the higher the tolerance limit, the lower the FRR and the higher the probability of FAR errors.

A quite simple metric used for evaluation is the *Bit Error Rate (BER)* that denotes the number of error bits divided by the watermark length (BER is calculated per frame).

6 Benchmarking Framework for Video Watermarking

Since the complete theoretical analysis of a watermarking algorithm performance with respect to different attacks is rather complicated, the developers of watermarking algorithms refer to the results of experimental testing performed in the scope of some benchmark. The benchmark combines the possible attacks into a common framework and weights the resulted performances depending on the possible application of the watermarking technology.

In image watermarking, several benchmarking tools have been developed to evaluate different methodologies, such as **stirmark, checkmark** and **optimark**. *Stirmark* is a generic tool provided with a watermarked input image, that generates a number of modified images used to verify watermark existence after a number of attacks. Stirmark proposes combination of different detection results and computation of an overall score. Stirmark has limited potentials for sophisticated image watermarking schemes as it does not properly model the watermarking process. *Optimark* is a benchmarking tool [32] that supports various attacks and employs differentiated performance metrics depending on the type of the detector used (and the output it produces) as well as on the characteristics of the watermarking algorithm.

Likewise, the main design challenges for a video benchmark framework are listed below:

- Detection performance evaluation using multiple trials employing different sets of data
  - o For watermarking schemes that follow frame-by-frame approaches where a different watermark is inserted in each video frame, the chosen set of data must include all the different watermarks used in order to evaluate their robustness,
  - o For watermarking schemes that also follow frame-by-frame approaches but embed the same watermark in all video frames, a much smaller set of frames need to be chosen,
  - o For more sophisticated watermarking methodologies based on a compression standard or embed a watermark in a three-dimensional (3-D) transform, the chosen set of data must be carefully chosen in order to ensure that all the possible watermarks used are evaluated and also the range of the testing data excludes the possibility of estimation errors (i.e. the case where the entire set of data is unwatermarked),
- Evaluation of the following detection/decoding performance metrics:,
  - o Bit error rate,
  - o Signal to Noise Ratio (SNR), and Peak Signal to Noise Ratio (PSNR) (as indirect measures for watermarked video quality estimation),
  - o False acceptance rate,
  - o False rejection rate,
- Evaluation of the mean embedding and detection time,
- Interface to input watermarking schemes and deploy watermark embedding and detection processes, thus weighing the outputs for certain attacks based on the target application
- Option for the user to choose any combination of attacks based on the target application.

Types of attack that could be included in such a benchmarking tool are: Copy attacks, Geometric attacks, Simple Waveform attacks (i.e. MPEG compression), Removal attacks (such as denoising, frame removal, frame linear transformations).

7 Conclusions and Future Prospects

Video watermarking is a recent area of exploration of digital watermarking. The increasing concern of multimedia owners for copyright protection motivates further research here. In this paper, we have reviewed a number of existing video watermarking schemes that cover a wide range of applications, varying from frame-based watermarking to more sophisticated video specific watermarking in a three-dimensional space. Furthermore, we compared a number of existing video watermarking techniques performance against attacks, and found that there is indeed room for improvement since all attacks cannot be completely dealt with. We further need to define detailed constraints based on the targeted application. We have also proposed a benchmarking framework for video watermarking presenting the main requirements to be met in order to objectively evaluate and rate a wide range of video watermarking methodologies.

Finally, we observe that there are only few video watermarking algorithms that meet the real-time or the three-dimensional constraint. These technical challenges remain unexplored and future research on these will play a decisive role in digital video watermarking.

References

1. B. Kahng et al., Watermarking Techniques for Intellectual Property Protection, *35th IEEE Design Automation Conf.*, San Francisco, USA, 1998, pp. 776 - 781
2. Yao Zhao, Reginald L. Lagendijk, Video Watermarking Scheme Resistant to Geometric Attacks, *IEEE Int. Conf. on Image Processing ICIP 2002*, 2002, pp. II-145- II-148 vol.2
3. A. Kejariwal, Watermarking, *Potentials IEEE Volume 22, Issue 4*, Oct-Nov 2003, pp. 37-40

4. S.N. Merchant et al., Watermarking of Video Data Using Integer-to-Integer Discrete Wavelet Transform, *Conf. on Convergent Technologies for Asia-Pacific Region TENCON 2003*, pp. 939- 943
5. S. Voloshynovskiy et al., Attacks on Digital Watermarks: Classification, Estimation-Based Attacks, and Benchmarks, *IEEE Communications Magazine*, August 2001, pp. 119-126
6. M. Kutter, Digital Image Watermarking: Hiding Information in Images, *PhD thesis*, EFPL, Lausanne, Switzerland, 1999
7. C. I. Podilchuk, E. J. Delp, Digital Watermarking: Algorithms and Applications, *IEEE Signal Processing Magazine*, July 2001, pp. 33-46
8. B. G. Mobasseri, D. Cinalli, Lossless watermarking of compressed media using reversibly decodable packets, *Elsevier Signal Processing, Article In Press, Corrected Proof*, Sept. 2005
9. K. Su; D. Kundur, D. Hatzinakos, Statistical invisibility for collusion-resistant digital video watermarking, *IEEE Trans. on Multimedia, Vol. 7, Issue 1*, Feb. 2005, pp. 43 - 51
10. E.T. Lin, E.J. Delp, Temporal synchronization in video watermarking, *IEEE Trans. on Signal Processing, Vol. 52, Issue 10, Part 2*, Oct. 2004, pp. 3007 - 3022
11. F. Deguillaume, G. Csurka, and T. Pun, Countermeasures for unintentional and intentional video watermarking attacks, *in Proc. SPIE, vol. 3971*, Jan. 2000, pp. 346–357
12. M. D. Swanson, B. Zhu, and A. T. Tewfik, Multiresolution scene-based video watermarking using perceptual models, *IEEE J. Select. Areas Commun., vol. 16, no. 4*, May 1998, pp. 540–550
13. C.-S. Lu, J.-R. Chen and K.-C. Fan, Real-time frame-dependent video watermarking in VLC domain, *Elsevier Signal Processing: Image Communication, Vol. 20, Issue 7*, Aug. 2005, pp. 624-642
14. S. H. Kwok, C. C. Yang, K. Y. Tam and Jason S. W. Wong, SDMI-based rights management systems, *Elsevier Decision Support Systems, Vol. 38, Issue 1*, Oct. 2004, pp. 33-46
15. X. Kong, Y. Liu, H. Liu and D. Yang, Object watermarks for digital images and video, *Elsevier Image and Vision Computing, Vol. 22, Issue 8*, Aug. 2004, pp. 583-595
16. G. Doërr and J.-L. Dugelay, A guide tour of video watermarking, *Elsevier Signal Processing: Image Communication, Vol. 18, Issue 4*, Apr. 2003, pp. 263-282
17. P. Judge and M. Ammar, WHIM: watermarking multicast video with a hierarchy of intermediaries, *Elsevier Computer Networks, Vol. 39, Issue 6, 21* Aug. 2002, pp. 699-712
18. M.P. Queluz, Authentication of digital images and video: Generic models and a new contribution, *Elsevier Signal Processing: Image Communication, Vol. 16, Issue 5*, Jan. 2001, pp. 461-475
19. F. Hartung and B. Girod, Watermarking of uncompressed and compressed video, *Elsevier Signal Processing, Vol. 66, Issue 3, 28 May 1998*, pp. 283-301
20. B.G. Mobasseri, M.P. Marcinak, Watermarking of MPEG-2 video in compressed domain using VLC mapping, *7th ACM Wor. on Multimedia and Security MM&Sec '05*, Aug. 2005
21. X. Zhang, S. Wang, A new watermarking scheme against inserter-based attacks suitable for digital media with moderate size, *3rd Int. ACM Conf. on Information Security InfoSecu '04*, Nov. 2004
22. M. Kutter and F. A. P. Petitcolas, A fair benchmark for image watermarking systems, *Security and Watermarking of Multimedia Contents*, *http://citeseer.ist.psu.edu/kutter99fair.html*, pp. 1-14
23. B. Girod, "Bidirectionally decodable streams of prefix ode-words", *IEEE Comm. Lett. Vol. 3, Issue 8*, Aug. 1999, pp. 245–247
24. F. Deguillaume et al., "Robust 3D DFT video watermarking,", *SPIE Conf. on Security and Watermarking of Multimedia Contents I, vol. 3657*, San Jose, USA, Jan. 25–27, 1999, pp. 113–124
25. J. A. Bloom et al., "Copy protection for DVD video", *Proc. of IEEE, vol. 87*, Jul. 1999, pp. 1267–1276
26. S. Craver et al., "Resolving rightful ownerships with invisible watermarking techniques: Limitations, attacks, and implications," *IEEE J. Select. Areas Commun., vol. 16*, May 1998, pp. 573–586
27. M. Kutter, S. Voloshynovskiy, and A. Herrigel, The watermark copy attack, *SPIE Security and Watermarking of Multimedia Contents II, vol. 3971*, San Jose, CA, Jan. 24–26, 2000, pp. 371–380
28. G. Doërr and J.-L. Dugelay, Security Pitfalls of Frame-by-Frame Approaches to Video Watermarking, *IEEE Trans. on Signal Processing, vol. 52, no. 10*, Oct. 2004 pp. 2955-2964
29. S. Pereira et al., Second generation benchmarking and application oriented evaluation, *Information Hiding Workshop III*, Pittsburgh, USA, April 2001
30. S. Voloshynovskiy et al., Attack modeling: Towards a second generation benchmark, *Signal Processing, Special Issue: Information Theoretic Issues in Digital Watermarking*, May, 2001
31. F. Petitcolas, R. Anderson, M. Kuhn, Attacks on copyright marking systems, *2nd Int. Wor. On Information Hiding*, IH'98, Portland, U.S.A., April 15-17, 1998
32. V. Solachidis, A. Tefas, N. Nikolaidis, S. Tsekeridou, A. Nikolaidis, I.Pitas, A benchmarking protocol for watermarking methods, *IEEE Int. Conf. on Image Processing*, Thessaloniki, Greece, 7-10 Oct., 2001, pp. 1023-1026

Chaotic Encryption Driven Watermarking
of Human Video Objects Based
on Hu Moments

Paraskevi K. Tzouveli, Klimis S. Ntalianis, Stefanos D. Kollias
National Technical University of Athens
Electrical and Computer Engineering Department
Iroon Polytexneiou 9, 15780, Athens, Greece
email: (tpar,kntal)@image.ntua.gr

Abstract. A novel human video object watermarking scheme is proposed in this paper, providing copyright protection of semantic content. The proposed method focuses on the existence of face and body regions within an initial image, however other cases can also be addressed. Initially detection of human video objects is achieved using two adaptive 2-D Gaussian models, one for skin color distribution modelling and the other for body localization modelling. A watermark is then designed using invariant Hu moments of each human video object, and the watermark insertion procedure is driven by an iterative encryption module based on chaotic functions. Performance of the proposed object based secure watermarking system is tested under various signal distortions and known cryptanalytic attacks.

1 Introduction

The copyright protection of digital images and video is an urgent issue of ownership identification. Many watermarking schemes [4]-[7] have been proposed for ownership protection, some of which providing significant resistance to image processing attacks. In this paper, a novel chaotic encryption driven watermarking scheme is proposed, based on Hu moments and applied to human video objects. The proposed system provides copyright protection of semantic content. In particular, the embedding method consists of two sub-modules: the automatic human video object detection sub-module and the watermark insertion sub-module, which is driven by chaotic encryption and modifies the Hu moments of the initial video object to provide the watermarked human video object.

Initially, human video object detection is performed for each candidate image, based on skin color distribution [1],[2]. Afterwards, an iterative cipher mechanism based on the logistic function is used in order to encrypt the pixel values of the human video object taking into consideration, in each iteration, the values of the previously encrypted pixels. As result, a chaotic "noise" is produced which is incorporated in producing the watermarked video object. This is achieved by modifying the Hu moments of the initial video object according to an additive scheme. In order to assure the robustness of the proposed watermarking method, the modification of moments is confined to a limited predefined interval. In the detection scheme a neural network classifier [3] is initially used in order to extract possible watermarked human video objects from each candidate image. Then, the watermark detection procedure is based on the comparison of Hu moments. Experimental results on real sequences further indicate the advantages of the proposed scheme.

2 Detection and Extraction of Human Video Object

The human face detection module that is used in the proposed method is based on the distribution of chrominance values corresponding to a human face [1], which occupy a very small region of the color space. The blocks of the image that are located at this small region can be considered as face block of the searching face class Ω_f. Using a Gaussian probability density function (pdf) [2], the histogram of chrominance values corresponding to the face class can be initially modelled as

$$P(x \mid \Omega_f) = \exp(-\frac{1}{2}(x-\mu_f)^T \cdot \Sigma_f^{-1} \cdot (x-\mu_f)) \Big/ 2\pi \cdot |\Sigma|^{1/2}$$ where $x=[u \ v]^T$ is a 2x1 vector

containing the mean chrominance components u and v of an examined block, μ_f is the 2x1 mean vector of a face class and Σ is the 2x2 variance matrix of the

probability density function: $\Sigma = \begin{bmatrix} \sigma_u^2 & \sigma_{u,v} \\ \sigma_{u,v} & \sigma_v^2 \end{bmatrix}$. σ_u^2 is the variance of the chrominance

component u, σ_v^2 is the variance of the chrominance component v and $\sigma_{u,v}$ corresponds to the covariance between u and v. Parameters μ_f and Σ are estimated based on a set of several face images and using the maximum likelihood algorithm. Each B_i block of the image is considered belong to the face class, if the respective $P(x(B_i)|\Omega_f)$ is high. The aspect ratio for face areas $R = H_f / W_f$ (where H_f is the height, while W_f is width of the head) was experimentally found to lie within the interval [1.4 1.6]. Using R and P, a binary mask, say M_f, is build containing the face area.

Detection of the body area can be achieved using geometric attributes that relate face and body areas. After the calculation of the geometric attributes (center $c_f = [c_x \ c_y]^T$, width w_f and height h_f) of the face region, the human body can be localized by incorporating a probabilistic model, the parameters of which are estimated according to c_f, w_f and h_f. The probability of each block B_i to belong to a human body class, say Ω_b can be computed by:

$$P(r(B_i) \mid \Omega_b) = \exp(-\frac{1}{2\sigma_x^2}(r_x(B_i)-\mu_x)^2)\exp(-\frac{1}{2\sigma_y}(r_y(B_i)-\mu_y)^2)\Big/(2\pi)\sigma_x\sigma_y$$

where $\mu_x = c_x$, $\mu_y = c_y + h_f$, $\sigma_x = w_f$, $\sigma_y = h_{f/2}$, are the parameters of the human body location proposed model and $r(B_i) = [r_x(B_i) \ r_y(B_i)]^T$ is the distance between the ith block and the origin. Similarly to human face detection, a block B_i belongs to the body class Ω_b, if the respective probability, $P(r(B_i)|\Omega_b)$ is high.

Finally the face and body masks are fused and human video objects are extracted. In Figure 1, the phases of the proposed method are illustrated. Firstly, the human video object region is detected within the initial image (Figure 1a) and an object mask is produced (Figure 1b). This mask is used for the extraction of human video object (Figure 1c) is extracted using the object mask. The human face and body detection modules provide an initial estimation of the human video object, forming the training set, say Df.

Then, in order to have a more reliable training set, a region of uncertainty is initially created around the selected foreground mask (face (Mf) and body (Mb)). Particularly, for each connected component (representing face or body region), the confidence interval of the Gaussian pdf model is selected to be 80%, meaning that only blocks falling into this interval are considered as candidate training blocks. Finally, as several blocks (8x8 regions of pixels) fall into this confidence interval, the PCA method is incorporated and a small set of training blocks is eventually selected for the training phase of the neural network.

| (a) Initial Image | (b) Object Mask | (c) Object Extraction |

Figure 1. Human Video Object Extraction Method

3 Moments invariants

In the literature, moment invariants have been used for object recognition in an image [2-7] regardless of their particular position, orientation, viewing angle, and gray-level variations. Central moment $m_{pq}^{(f)}$ of order $(p+q)$ of the image $f(x,y)$ are non-negative integers, and can be computed by $m_{pq} = \sum_x \sum_y (x-\bar{x})^p (y-\bar{y})^p f(x,y)$ where the coordinates $\bar{x} = m_{1,0}/m_{0,0}, \bar{y} = m_{0,1}/m_{0,0}$ denote the centroids of $f(x,y)$. The central moments of the image are invariant to translation as they are origin-independent. Scaling invariance can be achieved by normalizing the moments of the scaled image by the scaled energy $\eta_{pq} = m_{pq}/m_{00}^{\gamma}$ of the original (γ is the normalization factor $\gamma = (p+q/2)+1$). Hu [8] first introduced the mathematical foundation for two-dimensional moment invariants, based on methods of algebraic invariants, and demonstrated their application to shape recognition. Using nonlinear combinations of geometric moments, a set of seven invariant values, computed from central moments through order three, and independent of object translation, scale and orientation, can be calculated using the following equations:

$$\phi_1 = n_{20} + n_{02}, \quad \phi_2 = (n_{20} - n_{20})^2 + 4n_{11}^2$$
$$\phi_3 = (n_{30} - 3n_{12})^2 + (n_{03} - 3n_{21})^2, \quad \phi_4 = (n_{30} - n_{12})^2 + (n_{03} + n_{21})^2$$

$$\phi_5 = (3n_{30} - 3n_{12})(n_{30} + n_{12}) \cdot \left[(n_{30} + n_{12})^2 - 3(n_{21} + n_{03})^2\right]$$
$$+ (3n_{21} - n_{03})(n_{21} + n_{03}) \cdot \left[3(n_{30} + n_{12})^2 - (n_{21} + n_{03})^2\right]$$
$$\phi_6 = (n_{20} - n_{02}) \cdot \left[(n_{30} + n_{12})^2 - (n_{21} + n_{03})^2\right] + 4n_{11}(n_{30} + n_{12})(n_{21} + n_{03})$$
$$\phi_7 = (3n_{21} - n_{03})(n_{30} + n_{12}) \cdot \left[(n_{30} + n_{12})^2 - 3(n_{21} + n_{03})^2\right]$$
$$+ (3n_{12} - n_{03})(n_{21} + n_{03}) \cdot \left[3(n_{30} + n_{12})^2 - (n_{21} + n_{30})^2\right]$$

4 Logistic Map and Cryptography Scheme

Chaos theory is a set of ideas attempting to reveal structure in nonlinear dynamic systems [9]. Chaotic functions are very simple non-linear dynamical equations and can descript complex, chaotic behavior of a system [10]. Systems that present chaotic behavior are extremely sensitive to initial condition. Initializing a chaotic function by a key and after a number of iterations, this is able to generate random present different numerous [9], property that is very important for applications of cryptography. A great deal of chaotic behavior can be described by one, simple recursive function, the logistic map which is used in the proposed system. The logistic map function is expressed as: $x_{n+1} = r \cdot x_n(1 - x_n)$ where x takes values in the interval [0,1]. The remarkable features of the logistic map are the simplicity of its form (quadratic difference equation) and the complexity of its dynamics [9].

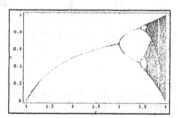

Figure 2.   Diagram of the Logistic Map

In Figure 2, a plot of the logistic map is shown versus r with values obtained after a number of iterations. When $r \geq 3.57$, periodicity gives way to complete chaos. Finally for r=3.9 to 4, the chaos values are generated in the complete range of 0 to 1. The secrecy of encrypted information is depended only on the encryption key. In the proposed system, the key size is 256-bit splitted into 32 subkeys of 8 bits each (session keys). The unprotected data which consist of the human video object that is extracted from the original image is called plaintext (denoted by p). Applying a key-depended encryption algorithm to the plaintext, the ciphertext (denoted by c) is produced.

5 The Embedding Module

An overview of the proposed system's embedding module is depicted in Figure 3 which contains two sub-modules: the automatic human video object detection sub-module and the watermark insertion sub-module. Initially the human video object is extracted by the video object detection module, as described in section 2.

Afterwards, the pixels of the human video object are scanned from top-left to the bottom-right providing the p_i pixels (plaintext pixels). The plaintext is an input to the mapping function which contains the logistic map. The robustness of the system is further reinforced by a feedback mechanism, which leads the cipher to acyclic behavior so that the encryption of each plain pixel depends on the key, the value of the previous cipher pixel and the output of the logistic map. In particular, the feedback mechanism includes four operations.

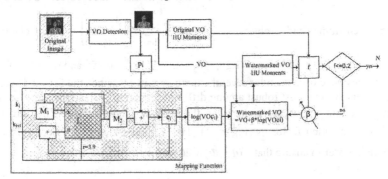

Figure 3. The Embedding Module

Firstly, the output value of the logistic map is input to box M1. The session key k_i is also input to M1 box. The box M_1 represents a mapping function from the input interval to the domain of the logistic map (real numbers in the interval [0, 1]) and fixes the initial value of x. The second operation interjects in the computation of the number of iterations the logistic map performs. Specifically, the cipher pixel is added to the k_{i+1} session key. The result of this addition provides the value of parameter x in order to serves control the number of iterations the logistic map performs. The box M2 serves with the purpose of normalizing the output of the logistic map. Normalization is performed by box M_2 which represents a fuzzy membership function mapping interval [0, 1] into the interval [0, 255]. Finally, the fourth operation is a summation of the plaintext and the normalized logistic map output which actually encrypts each plaintext p_i, producing the ciphertext c_i. Afterwards, the cipher video object (VOci) can be recomposed from the ciphertext. Eventually, the output of the mapping function is the modified video object *log(VOci)*. The watermarked video object $\tilde{O}$ is achieved adding the value *log(VOci)* multiplied by a weighed factor β to the video object which has been extracted from the original image (Figure 4).

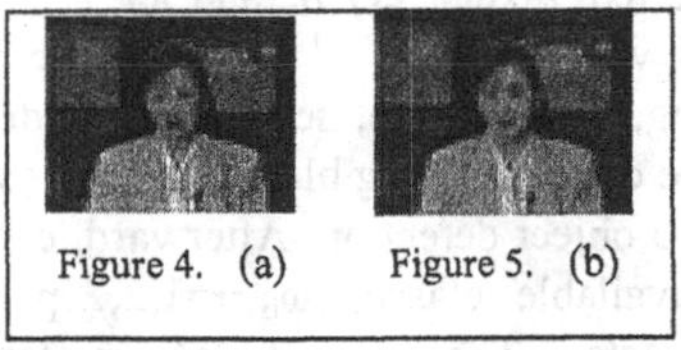

Figure 4. (a)   Figure 5. (b)

Figure 4. Original image (a) and image with watermarked video object (b)

Now let us consider that $\Phi = [\phi_1, \phi_2, \phi_3, \phi_4, \phi_5, \phi_6, \phi_7]^T$ is the invariant Hu moments of the original human video object O. Let also Φ^* be the invariant Hu moments of the watermarked human video object $\tilde{O}$. We can choose a function f, which can be any linear or non-linear combination of the invariant moments. In our case study, the function f is expressed as a sum value of the weighted average differences between Hu moments of the original human video object, ϕ, and the

watermarked human video object, ϕ^*: $f(\Phi^*, \Phi) = \sum_{i=1}^{7} w_i \left(\frac{\phi_i^* - \phi_i}{\phi_i} \right)$ where weights w_i

take the values $w_1 = 1.5$, $w_2 = 1.25$, $w_3 = 1$, $w_4, w_5 = 0.75$ and $w_6, w_7 = 0.50$. These values have been set after several experimental tests, since the first and second Hu moments are the most robust among different moments [10], so the values of the weighted factors w_1, w_2 are higher than the other weighted factors. The output of function f is called factor N (Figure 3). The weighted factor β is controlled by feedback in order to ensure that $f(\Phi^*, \Phi) \approx 20\%$.

6 The Detection Module

The detection module (Figure 5) includes two functions: the video object detector and the watermark detector. Firstly, when a candidate image is received, it passes through a neural network classifier [3] that detects video objects similar to the watermarked video objects.

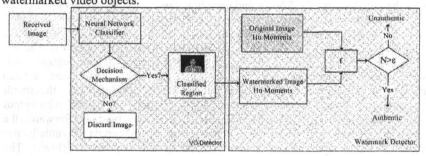

Figure 5. The Detection Module

Let us assume that the candidate image can be partitioned to a sequence of overlapping blocks of size 8x8 pixels, say B_i, and let b_i be a vector containing the lexicographically ordered values of the ith block of the image or a transformed version of it, by extracting, for example, several block descriptors, such as color, motion or texture. The case of overlapping blocks is adopted since pixel resolution is required for accurate video object detection. Afterward, each pixel of the candidate image is classified to available classes ω_i, i=1,2,...p, to one of p available watermarked video objects. The output of p-classification problem is $y(b_i) = [p_{\omega_1}^i, p_{\omega_2}^i \cdots p_{\omega_p}^i]^T$ where $p_{\omega_j}^i$ denotes the degree of coherence of b_i to class ω_j so each pixel is assigned to a class according to the highest degree of coherence. In order to efficiently perform the classification task, the neural network classifier is initially trained using blocks of each watermarked video object. Nevertheless, principal component analysis (PCA) is performed in order to reduce the number of similar training blocks in each watermarked video object. Finally, the classified pixels constitute the area of the respective video object.

In order to avoid a false detection, a decision mechanism is incorporated in order to calculate the ratio $R_i = \dfrac{N(\omega_i)}{F(vo_i)} \cdot 100$ (where $N(\omega_i)$, $i=1,2,\ldots,p$, is the number of pixels of each class and $F(vo_i)$, $i=1,2,\ldots,p$, is the number of pixels constituting each respective watermarked video object). If R_i is less than a threshold T then the candidate area is discarded, since it is considered too small for watermark detection. In other case, the watermark detection module is activated giving the classified region. Value of threshold T affects the false detection and false rejection rates and in the current work is selected by performing several experiments.

Having received a region that the neural network has classified as possible watermarked video object, the watermark detector module estimates the Hu moments of this region. In parallel, the seven values of the Hu moments of the respective original human video object are received as input. Afterwards, the value of function $f(\Phi^*,\Phi)$ can be computed and the value of N can be defined. Matching of the received human video object can be achieved by checking the validity of the equation $N \le \varepsilon$ where ε is the margin of acceptable error between the two video objects. Then, the detection procedure returns either 1, if the candidate video object is the watermarked video object, or 0, if the candidate video object is not watermarked.

7 Experimental Results

This section presents results that prove the robustness of the proposed system. To illustrate the security of the algorithm, a hacker's approach to crack a watermarked image is considered as a case. Since the 256-bit sequence of key is used as an input to the logistic map, this mean that the keyspace has 2^{256} different values. Additionally the number of iterations supported by the logistic map module is between 0 and 767, as cipher pixels take values in the interval [0, 512] and the session keys take values in the interval [0, 255].

So, the only way to break the proposed system is by brute–force attack scanning the whole keyspace that is to try 2^{256} different keys! Furthermore as the cipher of the proposed system is based on feedback mechanisms, periodicities in the encrypted data do not appear. The proposed system is suitable for real time applications as it spends less time in watermark insertion as only human video objects are considered and not the whole image Experimental results [3] have proved that the neural network classifier can sufficiently extract the human video object of an image which has passed the watermarking embedding procedure and has been attacked.

The watermarked video object can be detected under different attacks, (Table I), except from cropping where the attacked video object region is not similar to the watermarked one also and their moments are very different. The proposed watermarking scheme serves as a 1-bit watermarking system as it answers the yes/no question of authenticity. The threshold is set so as the attacked video object can be different from the watermarked object only by 1%. Robustness of the proposed scheme to geometric manipulations is guaranteed using invariant Hu moments. Only the value of the moments of the original video object is received from the detection module.

8 Conclusion

Nowadays, protection of digital media through networks is a crucial issue. Most watermarking systems are not taking into consideration regions of semantic information comprising the content that should be protected. Our proposed system takes as input images that contain human video objects. The human video objects are extracted by a face and body region detection module. Finally, each human video object is watermarked by modifying its Hu moments. The procedure is driven by a chaotic encryption module. Experimental results illustrate the robustness of the proposed scheme to attacks as well as noise addition, and image distortions.

Table I: Results of detecting the watermarked akiyo video object after several attacks

Attack		$f(\Phi^*, \Phi) = \frac{1}{7}\sum_{i=1}^{7} w_i \left(\frac{\phi_i^* - \phi_i}{\phi_i} \right)$		Watermark Detection	
Filtering	Gaussian	Median	0.004023	0.004023	Pass	Pass
JPEG	Q=50%	Q=10%	0.001229	0.004691	Pass	Pass
Rotation	5°	-1°	0.044546	0.000012	Pass	Pass
Scaling	50%	110%	0.002085	0.003790	Pass	Pass
Cropping 10%			0.40962		Fail	
Flipping			0.002162		Pass	

References

1. H. Wang and S-F Chang, "A Highly Efficient System for Automatic Face Region Detection in MPEG Video Sequences," IEEE Trans. CSVT, vol. 7, No. 4, pp. 615-628, August 1997.
2. N. Tsapatsoulis, Y Avrithis, S. Kollias "Facial Image Indexing in Multimedia Databases" in *Pattern Analysis & Applications*, vol. 4, pp. 93-107, 2001.
3. N. D. Doulamis, A. D. Doulamis, K. S. Ntalianis, and S. D. Kollias, "An Efficient Fully-Unsupervised Video Object Segmentation Scheme Using an Adaptive Neural Network Classifier" in *IEEE Transactions on Neural Networks*, Vol. 14(3), pp. 616-630, May 2003
4. F. A. P. Petitcolas, R. J. Anderson, and M. G. Kuhn, "Attacks on copyright watermarking systems," in *Proc. 2nd Int.Workshop Information Hiding*, pp. 218–238, 1998.
5. S. Pereira and T. Pun, "Robust template matching for affine resistant image watermarks" *IEEE Trans. Image Processing*, vol. 9, pp. 1123–1129, July 2000.
6. M. Kutter, S. K. Bhattacharjee and T. Ebrahimi, "Towards second generation watermarking schemes" in *Proc. IEEE Int. Conf. Image Processing* 1999, pp. 320–323.
7. C. Lin, M. Wu, J. Bloom, I. Cox, M. Miller, Y. Lui, "Rotation, scale, and translation resilient watermarking" *IEEE Trans. Image Processing*, vol. 10, pp. 767–782, May 2001.
8. M. K. Hu, "Visual pattern recognition by moment invariants," *IEEE Trans. Inform. Theory*, vol. 8, pp. 179–187, 1962.
9. G. Jakimoski and L. Kocarev, "Chaos and Cryptography: Block Encryption Ciphers Based on Chaotic Maps", *IEEE Trans.Circuits and Systems*, vol. 48, no. 2, Feb. 2001.
10. R. Devaney, "An Introduction to Chaotic Dynamical Systems", 2nd ed. *CA: Addison-Wesley*, 1989.

Semi-Fragile Watermarking Authentication with Local and Global Watermarks

Jinwei Wang[1,2], Shiguo Lian[2], Zhen Ren[2], Yuewei Dai[1] and Zhiquan Wang[1]

1   Department of Automation, Nanjing University of Sci. & Technol.
Nangjing 210094, P.R. China
wjwei_2004@163.com,
2   France Telecom R& D Beijing
Beijing 100080, P.R. China
shiguo.lian@francetelecom.com

Abstract. In this paper, a novel semi-fragile watermarking authentication scheme is proposed, which is based on two watermarks: the local watermark and the global watermark. The two watermarks complement each other. The local watermark is generated from the quantized ACs in 8×8 DCT block. The global watermark is produced by the lowest frequency subband in DWT-transformed image. In watermark embedding, the dither-modulation quantization rule is adopted to improve the scheme's security. In watermark detection and authentication, a novel authentication principle is proposed, which obtains good authentication performances. Experimental results prove that this scheme can exactly detect and verify the tampered location against JPEG compression and some other attacks.

1 Introduction

Till now, many authentication schemes have been proposed, which can be classified into two categories, i.e. fragile authentication [1] and semi-fragile authentication [2,3,4]. For the former, it can not tolerate any possible modification to the multimedia content, e.g., common signal processing operations (JPEG compression, filtering, noise, etc.). Differently, the semi-fragile authentication scheme is rapidly developed and widely used since almost all the applications allow the minor changes to multimedia works if their content could be proved authentic.

Being suitable for practical applications, many semi-fragile authentication schemes have been reported, which can be classified into two types, i.e. the content-independent scheme [5] and content-dependent scheme [4,6,7,8]. In the former scheme, the authentication data are the authentication sequences or logos independent of the multimedia content. For example, a random sequence is embedded into the DWT transform coefficients by quantizing them to integer

Please use the following format when citing this chapter:

Wang, Jinwei, Lian, Shiguo, Ren, Zhen, Dai, Yuewei, Wang, Zhiquan, 2006, in IFIP International Federation for Information Processing, Volume 204, Artificial Intelligence Applications and Innovations, eds. Maglogiannis, I., Karpouzis, K., Bramer, M., (Boston: Springer), pp. 681–688

multiples of a step size [5]. The drawback of this kind of scheme is that the security can not be guaranteed. For attackers, the unwatermarked coefficients can be modified to make authentication out of work, or the watermark can be estimated according to a watermarked image and then embedded into other images. In the content-dependent scheme, the authentication data are extracted from the multimedia content, which are then signed with digital signature or embedded into the multimedia content. This kind of scheme is emphasized in the following content.

The content-dependent scheme can be classified into signature-based scheme [7,8] and content-based watermarking scheme [4,6]. In [7], two labeling methods are proposed, which are based on the second-order image moments and image edges. In [8], the authentication information is formed based on the relationship of the DCT coefficients in 8×8 block pairs using a pre-determined secret mapping function. The clear drawback of a signature-based scheme is that authentication information's transmission or storing requires extra channels and this increases the scheme's danger. In [6], the authentication information described in [8] is inserted into DCT coefficients by the quantization method. As an improvement [4], the authentication information is inserted into DWT coefficients using random bias and non-uniform quantization. Compared with the signature-based scheme, the content-based watermarking scheme not only makes sure that the authentication information is exclusive but also saves extra channels. The drawback is that it changes images' content and degrades images' quality [8]. Generally, the semi-fragile content-based watermarking authentication scheme satisfies the following requirements [6,9]: imperceptibility, obliviousness, robustness, fragileness, location and security.

In this paper, a semi-fragile watermarking authentication scheme is proposed, which satisfies the general requirements. Two complementary feature watermarks, named the local watermark and the global watermark, are generated and embedded, which obtain good performances. The following content is arranged as follows. In Section 2, the architecture of the proposed authentication scheme is presented. The watermark generation is described in detail in Section 3. In Section 4, the embedding rule is proposed. In Section 5, the authentication process is designed. The security of the proposed scheme is analyzed in Section 6. In Section 7, experimental results are demonstrated. The conclusions are drawn and future work is presented in Section 8.

2   Architecture of the Authentication Scheme

The architecture of the proposed authentication scheme is depicted in Figure 1. In embedding process, two feature watermarks, named the local watermark and the global watermark, are generated and embedded into DCT coefficients. In the verification process, the authentication watermark extracted from the received image is compared with the one generated from the received image.

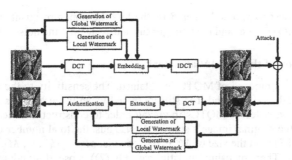

Figure 1. Architecture of the proposed scheme.

3 Generation of the Watermarks

The watermarks are composed of the local watermark and the global watermark. The local watermark is generated from the features of the quantized ACs in 8×8 DCT blocks. This watermark contains the detail information of images, which is sensitive to the changes of such detail components as textures or edges. The global watermark is produced by the features of the lowest frequency subband in the DWT-transformed image. This watermark contains the approximate information of images, which is sensitive to the changes of such approximate components as contours. Both of them will be presented in detail in the following content.

3.1 Extraction of the Local Feature

3.1.1 Pseudo-Random Sequence

Pseudo-random sequence X is generated from a chaotic map, i.e. Logistic map.

$$x_{n+1}=\lambda x_n(1-x_n) \tag{1}$$

The sequence is chaotic when λ is equal to 4. The initial value x_0 is considered as the secret key. Eq. 2 is used to generate the bi-value sequence Y (-1 or 1).

$$Y = \text{sign}(X-0.5) \tag{2}$$

Here, sign(x) is Sign function that gets 1 if x is no less than 0 and -1 if x is less than 0.

3.1.2 Quantization

The original image is transformed using blocked 8×8 DCT, and the transform coefficients are quantized by the quantization matrix Q. Q can adopt the given standard quantization matrix of JPEG, and the quantization and de-quantization rules are shown in Eq. 3 and Eq. 4, respectively.

$$M_k^Q = \text{Round}(\frac{F_k(u,v)}{\beta Q(u,v)}) \tag{3}$$

$$F_k^Q(u,v) = M_k^Q \cdot \beta Q(u,v) \tag{4}$$

Here $F_k(u,v)$ is the coefficient at position (u,v) in the k-th sub-image, $M_k^Q(u,v)$ is the multiple of quantizing $F_k(u,v)$ by $Q(u,v)$, $F_k^Q(u,v)$ is the quantized coefficient corresponding to $F_k(u,v)$, β is the modulation factor of Q, and Round($\cdot$) is to obtain the integer closest to x. The bigger β is, the less the non-zero quantized transform coefficients (MQTC) are, and the stronger the ability against the noise effect is.

3.2 Generation of the Local Watermark

By Eq. (3), M^Q composed of MQTC is obtained. The sensitivity to the noise can be changed by modulating β, and it is still increased when more MQTCs are selected. Consequently, we select n MQTCs in zigzag order to construct the vector M_k^Q. It is supposed that the original image's size is M×N. Thus, the total number of sub-image is L=(M/8)×(N/8), and the size of M^Q is n×L, that is, $M^Q = [M_0^Q, \cdots, M_k^Q, \cdots, M_{L-1}^Q]'$, k = 0, 1, $\cdots$, L-1. Then, by using Logistic map (Eq. (2)), a pseudo-random matrix Y = $[Y_0, \cdots, Y_k, \cdots, Y_{L-1}]$, k = 0, 1, $\cdots$, L-1, is generated. Next, the components in M^Q are multiplied by the corresponding one in Y and produce the product module 2, i.e. Eq. (5). Finally, the local watermark W^L is obtained, which is composed of the components W_k^L (k = 0, 1, $\cdots$, L-1).

$$W_k^L = (M_k^Q \cdot Y_k) \bmod 2 \tag{5}$$

Five 512×512 images are selected as examples to generate the local watermark. Here, let β and n be 10 and 5 respectively, which obtain strong robustness against the noise. The produced local watermarks of several sample images (Lena, Barbara, baboon, goldhill, and peppers) are shown in Figure 2.

Figure 2. Local watermarks generated from Lena, Barbara, baboon, goldhill and peppers. (from left to right)

3.3 Extraction of the Global Feature

3.3.1 Generation of Dither Quantization Matrix

By Logistic map (Eq. (2)), the integer dither matrix D with the size of M×N is generated, and is then partitioned into 8×8 sub-matrices. Next, every sub-matrix is added to the quantization matrix Q (the standard quantization matrix in JPEG) that is multiplied by α, i.e. a sensitivity factor. The bigger α is, the less sensitive it is to the noise. Finally, the dither quantization matrix Q^d with the size of M×N is obtained.

3.3.2 Extraction of the Global Feature

The original image is transformed using blocked 8×8 DCT, its transform coefficients are quantized by Eq. (3) with the dither quantization matrix Q^d, and the coefficients are then de-quantized by Eq. (4) with the same matrix Q^d. The produced image is named the quantized image. Then, the approximate data LL are extracted after the quantized image is transformed by DWT.

3.4 Generation of the Global Watermark

For most of the coefficients in the lowest frequency band are over 255, the LL coefficients are preprocessed. Then, the preprocessed LL is converted to a binary image by selecting the rational threshold. The ultimate binary image is taken as the global watermark W^G.

The five images mentioned above are taken as examples. Let α be 10, which achieves strong robustness against the noise. Figure 3 shows the produced global watermarks of the five images.

Fig. 3. Global watermarks generated from Lena, Barbara, baboon, goldhill and peppers. (from left to right)

4 Watermark Embedding

The adopted embedding rule is the quantization method [10] whose quantization step size Δ changing with the frequency difference in the embedding region. Here, Δ is a vector with its component as a part of the standard JPEG quantization matrix, and dither modulation (DM) is used to improve the security of watermark embedding.

5 Authentication

In most of the existing papers [5,7], only single feature watermark is embedded into the image. The feature watermark generated from the received image is compared with the one extracted from the received image. As shown in Figure 4, A_1 or A_2 is called verified authentication set, which denotes the set of all the covers that are verified on the basis of the feature watermark, while A is called attack authentication set, which denotes the set of the attacked watermarked covers under the condition of certain feature or some features. Thus, there exist the following questions in the single feature authentication scheme.

1) To obtain small false negative probability of A_1, the false positive probability of A_1 should be increased.
2) To obtain small false positive probability of A_2, the false negative probability of A_2 should be increased.

As can be seen, there are contradictions between the two false probabilities. To compromise between the false negative probability and the false positive probability, we use the multiple-features scheme. It is noted that the false negative probability becomes bigger although the intersection of A_1 and A_2 decreases the false positive probability. Additionally, the false positive probability becomes bigger although the union of A_1 and A_2 decreases the false negative probability. Consequently, the verified authentication set V of the proposed authentication scheme satisfies the following condition.

$$A_1 \cap A_2 < V < A_1 \cup A_2$$

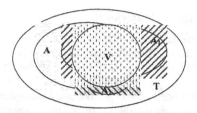

Figure 4. The proposed scheme's authentication set V. A is the ellipse region of horizontal line, A_1 is the ellipse region of backlash, A_2 is the ellipse region of oblique line, V is the circular region of vertical line, and T is the blank ellipse region.

The authentication process is described as follows. First, the local watermark $W^{L'}$ and global watermark $W^{G'}$ are generated from the received image to form a new watermark W'. Then, the watermark $\widehat{W}$ that is composed of $\widehat{W}^L$ and $\widehat{W}^G$ is extracted from the received image. Finally $\widehat{W}$ is compared with W' using XOR operation to implement the authentication, which produces the comparison results $W^{LL'}$ and $W^{GG'}$.

For the local watermark and the global watermark complement each other, the verification result depends on the two watermarks. When satisfying one of the following four conditions, the 8×8 sub-image is marked by 0, i.e. the gray region in Figure 5, which represents the tampered region. Here, $W^{LL'}(i, j)$ corresponds to the sub-image with size of 8×8 at position $(8i, 8j)$, and a gray part represents a sub-image with size of 8×8. Thus, the gray part in Figure 5(a) is marked when Condition (1) is satisfied, the gray part in Figure 5(b) is marked when Condition (2) is satisfied, and the gray part in Figure 5(c) is marked when one of Condition (3) and (4) is satisfied.

Condition (1): $W^{LL'}(i, j) = 1$ and $W^{GG'}(i, j+1) = 1$;
Condition (2): $W^{LL'}(i, j) = 1$ and $W^{GG'}(i+1, j) = 1$;
Condition (3): $W^{LL'}(i, j) = 1$ and $W^{GG'}(i+1, j+1) = 1$;
Condition (4): $W^{LL'}(i+1, j) = 1$ and $W^{GG'}(i, j+1) = 1$.

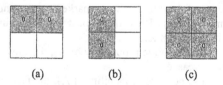

(a)   (b)   (c)

Figure 5. The marked sub-images. Here, a gray part represents a sub-image with size of 8×8.

6   Security Analysis

It is noted that a good authentication algorithm requires that the embedding process should not perturb the extraction of the feature watermarks, i.e. the exact extraction of the feature watermarks from the original watermarked image should be guaranteed. This property is satisfied in this paper, as shown in Eq. (8) [6,8], which makes the feature watermarks survive the embedding process.

$$((M \times \Delta_1) / \Delta_2) \times \Delta_1 = M \tag{8}$$

Here, M is a multiple of the quantization step Δ_1 and $\Delta_2 < \Delta_1$. The security represents not only that the watermark to be embedded is exclusive, but also that the watermark extracted from the received image can not be forged. The former emphasizes on the security of the algorithm to extract the feature watermarks, while the latter takes the embedding algorithm's security into consideration. In this paper, the local watermark and the global watermark are generated from the chaotic map controlled by the secret key. If the attacker has not the secret key, the watermark can not be forged. Additionally, the DM-quantization is adopted to embed watermarks, which uses the dither vector and makes it more difficult to extract the watermark from the watermarked image or forge it.

7   Experimental Results

First, we authenticate the modified watermarked images without attacks and check the location of the modified positions. Then, we authenticate the modified watermarked images after JPEG compression with a quality factor of 70 and check the location of the modified positions. Experimental results are shown in Figure 6.

To evaluate the performances of the proposed watermarking scheme, it is compared with the popular Chang's algorithm [6]. P_f denotes the probability that an image block gives an indication of modification but not malicious attacks. The comparative results are listed in Table 1. By observing the comparative results of signal processing attacks, our scheme obviously excels Chang's scheme.

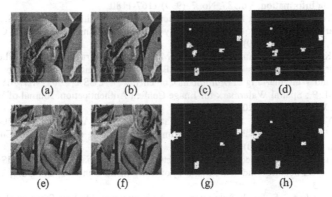

(a)   (b)   (c)   (d)

(e)   (f)   (g)   (h)

Figure 6. Experimental results. (a), (e): two original images, (b), (f): two modified watermarked image, (c), (g): two authentication results with no attacks, (d), (h): two authentication results after JPEG compression with a quality factor of 70.

Table 1. Comparisons of Two Schemes (Pf %)

Algorithms	No attack	JPEG (QF=70)	Gaussian noise(σ^2=30)	Lowpass filter	Salt-pepper	Sharpen	Histogram equalization
Our	0	0	0	8.5	34.6	58.3	57.4
Chang's	0.2	3.1	12.3	80.4	48.3	90.2	73.8

8   Conclusions

In this paper, a new semi-fragile authentication scheme with two novel feature watermarks is proposed. The local watermark and the global watermark are generated from the content of the image. The DM-quantization embedding rule guarantees the security of the watermarking scheme. The authentication process can prove that the modified content is exactly located. Simultaneously, experimental results show that the verification results of the proposed scheme are valid and satisfactory. In future work, our scheme will be further improved, including more simple and efficient extraction method of the feature watermark and the watermark embedding rule that is robust against more common signal processing attacks.

Acknowledgement

This work was supported by the National Natural Science Foundation of China through the grant number 60374066 and 60574082, and France Telecom R&D Beijing.

References

1. Lin,P.-L., Huang, P.-W., Peng, A.-W.: A Fragile Watermarking Scheme for Image Authentication with Localization and Recovery. Proceedings of the IEEE Sixth International Symposium on Multimedia Software Engineering, Washington, DC, USA, (2004) 146-153
2. Kundur, D., Hatzinakos, D.: Digital watermarking for telltale tamper-proofing and authentication. Proceedings of the IEEE Special Issue on Identification and Protection of Multimedia Information, Vol. 87, No. 7, (999) 1167-1180
3. Lin, E. T. Podilchuk, C. I., Delp, E. J.: Detection of Image Alterations Using Semi-fragile Watermarks. Proceedings of SPIE in Security and Watermarking of Multimedia Contents II, CA USA, Vol. 3971, (2000) 152-163
4. Maeno, K., Sun, Q., Chang, S.-F., Suto, M.: New Semi-Fragile Image Authentication Watermarking Techniques Using Random Bias and Non-Uniform Quantization. SPIE in Security and Watermarking of Multimedia Contents IV, CA USA, 2002, 4657: 659-670
5. Queluz, M. P.: Spatial Watermark for Image Content Authentication. Journal of Electronic Imaging, Vol. 11, No. 2, (2002) 275-285
6. Lin, C.-Y., Chang, S.-F.: Semi-Fragile Watermarking for Authenticating JPEG Visual Content. Proceedings of SPIE in Security and Watermarking of Multimedia Contents II, CA USA, Vol. 3971, (2000) 140-151
7. Queluz, M.P.: Content-Based Integrity Protection of Digital Images. Part of the IS&T/SPIE Conference on Security and Watermarking of Multimedia Contents, CA USA, Vol. 3657, (1999) 85-93
8. Lin, C.-Y., Chang, S.-F.: A Robust Image Authentication Method Distinguishing JPEG Compression from Malicious Manipulation. IEEE Transactions on Circuits and Systems of Video Technology, Vol. 11, No. 2, (2001) 153-168
9. Hu, Y.-P., Han, D.-Z.: Using Two Semi-Fragile Watermark for Image Authentication. Proceedings of the Fourth International Conference on Machine Learning and Cybernetics, Guangzhou China, Vol. 9, (2005) 5484-5489
10. Chen, B., Wornell, G. W.: Quantization Index Modulation: A Class of Provably Good Methods for Digital Watermarking and Information Embedding. IEEE Transaction on Information Theory, Vol. 47, No. 4, (2001) 1423-1443

Decentralising the Digital Rights Management Value Chain by means of Distributed License Catalogues

B. Vassiliadis, V. Fotopoulos, A.N. Skodras

Digital Systems & Media Computing Laboratory, School of Science and
Technology, Hellenic Open University,
13-15 Tsamadou st., GR-26222, Patras, Greece
{bb,vfotop1,skodras}@eap.gr

Abstract. Digital Rights Management (DRM) systems' interoperability is becoming one of the main obstacles for their wider adoption, especially from medium and small size users. Interoperability issues affect, among others, the management of content usage rules by third parties (authorities) and the automation of licensing procedures upon the purchase of digital content. The fundamental question of who is handling content licenses in the national or global DRM value chain is complex, with business, social and technological extensions. In this paper, we discuss current trends in DRM systems technology and business modelling and briefly present a proposal for handling digital content licensing, Distributed License Catalogues (DLCs). The DLC concept, borrowed from web engineering, makes available ("advertises") content or services concerning DRM functionalities, enabling multi-party DRM eco-systems.

1 Introduction

Digital Rights Management (DRM) systems appeared as a natural consequence of the need to electronically manage a wide range of IPR (Intellectual Property Rights) functionalities such as description, identification, trading, protection, monitoring and tracking. These functionalities should be able to be applied over both tangible and intangible assets including rights workflow and rights owner relationships [1].

DRMs are complex information systems in the sense that they highly involve technological, economical, business and most importantly, social factors. The first generation of DRM business models, as defined by the Imprimatur project [2] and later by Ianella's vision of their information architecture [3], was offering a full range of functionalities. The first DRM implementations showed the potential of the technology but also some pitfalls of the complex, full functionality approach.

Please use the following format when citing this chapter:

Vassiliadis, Vassileios, Fotopoulos, Vassileios, Skodras, Athanassios, 2006, in IFIP International Federation for Information Processing, Volume 204, Artificial Intelligence Applications and Innovations, eds. Maglogiannis, I., Karpouzis, K., Bramer, M., (Boston: Springer), pp. 689–696

Immature economics, lack of standards, potential misuse of user rights, prohibiting costs for small users, lack of appropriate legislation are some of the problems that need to be solved next. These primary issues naturally imposed an interoperability gap between different DRM implementations. This problem cannot be attributed solely to technology (e.g. lack of standards) but to other factors as well. For example, a social factor is that users are not satisfied with existing, strict usage rights policy of current DRM solutions [4,5]. The lack of relevant legislation, which is not matured in many countries, and usability are also drawbacks for DRM's wider adoption [6]. Most importantly, full functionality solutions are too costly for medium and small users

DRM is a relatively new technology, and as such it also faces a definition problem; there is no clear agreement of what DRM is "in the whole" [7]. The first days of the Internet saw a similar problem. The lack of standards caused a misuse of the term. Only when standards and architectures were placed, the Internet took the form we all know and use today.

DRM systems' interoperability is becoming one of the main obstacles for their wider adoption, especially from medium and small size users. Interoperability issues affect, among others, the management of content usage rules by third parties and the automation of licensing procedures upon the purchase of digital content. One of the fundamental questions in the DRM business model is "who is handling content licenses in the national or global DRM value chain?". Content usage rules are provided by the creators/owners. The classic business model does foresee many authorities who are responsible for supervising the proper use of usage rules, however technological, political, social, legislative issues are not dealt-with in such multi-authority environments. Does a single authority guarantees equal management of rights? Should all the functionalities of an authority (licensing, monitoring and reporting) be handled by one organization or could they be provided by many? Should the DRM community learn from other similar endeavours? For example, the most successful on-line, single-authority model is the DNS address system. It has been successful in managing Internet addresses for some time now, but the managing organization, a US-based institution, is getting increased criticism from abroad of the type: "why should a foreign institution manage our internet addresses?". Digital rights are equally important; governments would like at least some control over the management of the national content. Similarly, professional associations could also claim the role of authorities. The same goes for private organizations.

Having many authorities in the DRM value chain may possibly become a real need in the future, a need that will certainly create a whole lot of new questions of business, social and technological extensions. In this work, we examine a DRM business model where many authorities are handling digital content licensing. Discovery mechanisms are a critical factor to this distributed model. Its wider adoption requires addressing, among others, problems such as publication, description, discovery and security. We address the discovery issue by means of Distributed License Catalogues (DLCs). DLC is based on a web engineering concept, and more particularly UDDI (Universal Description, Discovery and Integration) catalogues, a standard for publishing and discovering web services [8]. We propose a new DRM business model where content providers or associations may act as authorities using thematically-oriented directories, to publish licenses and content rights. Although these catalogues are distributed, their architecture can be either client-server or Peer to Peer.

The rest of the paper is structured as follows: section 2 briefly describes current technology trends in DRM systems and presents the basic DRM business model. Section 3 introduces DLCs while section 4 briefly discusses possible implementation architectures. Finally, conclusions are drawn in section 5.

2 Digital Rights Management systems

Complete solutions to IPR protection and management such as DRM systems have been proposed for the management of licenses of media content throughout its lifecycle [9]. Technologically, the area of DRM is unique in the sense that it involves many diverse sub-areas: cryptography, signal processing and information theory, e-commerce, business modelling, legal and social aspects just to mention a few. Current DRM systems are complicated, expensive and inherit many of the shortcomings of the methods they use. They are considered however by many, a solution of great prospect.

A DRM system provides a complete set of functionalities for managing IPR [7]. DRMs can either be stand-alone systems or part of a larger on-line selling system relying on licenses which specify the content usage rules. Content is distributed with or without licenses but it cannot be used without them. Rules can be attached, embedded to the content or delivered independently [10]. It is important to note that DRM is about digitally managing rights and not managing digital rights; modern DRM systems cover the full range of IPR management including the description, identification, trading, protection, monitoring and tracking of all forms of rights' usage [3,11].

In [12] the authors discuss two definitions for DRM systems, the narrow and the broad. The narrow definition refers to systems that persistently protect content using mainly encryption techniques. The digital content is packaged (encrypted and metadata enriched) and then provided through distribution channels. Users need special controllers (client side s/w) in order to be authenticated and gain access through the decryption of content. License servers may be used to manage licenses describing access rights and conditions. The broad definition includes the above-mentioned functionalities and further extends rights management. It includes definition, management and tracking of rights (business rights, licensing, access tracking etc.).

Recent attempts to deploy DRM systems have shown that their success depends not only on technology but business issues as well. The underlying business model, that is the mechanism by which a business intends to generate revenue and profits, is of paramount importance. The business model defines the plans to serve customers involving both strategy and implementation. It greatly affects, and is affected by, the technology used. The creator produces the digital content and provides the usage rules to a third party (authority) which is responsible for supervising its proper use. Distributors receive the content from the creators and distribute it through the appropriate channels (e.g. e-shops) to the end-users (buyers). In order for the buyer to use the content, the appropriate license must be obtained by the authority. This happens after the appropriate request is sent to the authority by the buyer. The transaction is concluded when the authority pays royalties to the creator [2]. There is a plethora of DRM payment models: pay as you use, try-first buy-later, pay-per-view etc. Payment rules are closely connected to the way the content is supposed to be used and as such they are described by rules.

3 Supporting many Authorities with DLCs

Suppose that in the, not so distant, future the national or international legislation permits associations, companies or even single users to act as authorities for content they have created or they own. Although it is obvious that most of these authorities would not be able to provide the full functionality of an authority as described in the previous section, they could provide at least some kind of licensing services and accept payments (through integrated e-banking solutions). Overlooking the huge political, cultural and social implications which are not within the scope of this work to analyze, the question of the most efficient technology that will support such a model, naturally arises.

Traditionally, network applications have relied on client-server as their core technological model. Classic DRM designs of the past decade rely on such a model especially when dealing with Authority-related transactions. But what happens when authorities are dispersed in cyberspace and are heterogeneous in their interface configurations? In such a case users should be equipped with agents capable of performing Application-to Application (A2A) operations in order to ease interaction with different providers and authorities. Creators and distributors will be able to cooperate with different Authorities. The peers of such a network will be able to provide different services (functionalities) of a DRM system on-line. This model resembles more to the Service-Oriented [13] or, somewhat lesser, to the Peer to Peer [14] computing models than the client-server one (figure 1).

Service-Orientation supports the development of applications as if they were a connected network of functionalities (services) available, in a network-enabled environment, within and across different organizations. Services, the building blocks of Service-Oriented systems, may be made public, searched, reused and combined to form complex business processes while in the same time retaining a significant level of flexibility. This computing model will hopefully enable the transition of the software industry into a service industry.

Among the many technological questions that need to be answered in such a configuration is how to implement an efficient discovery mechanism, a critical factor to the overall utility of the scheme. Since there are many Authorities, Creators and Distributors on-line along with numerous digital content repositories, how can a user find the appropriate service/license/content? The same question was posed to the Web Engineering community when different software vendors made available on-line their web services. Web service registries are helping to narrow down the negotiation and searching time needed for service discovery. Their basic concept lays in the matching mechanism of the contractual and technical profile of the query to that of the services. In order for the searching procedure to be fast and more importantly automatic, information needs to be machine-processable. At present, Web services are mainly advertised in catalogues which are based on the Universal Description, Discovery and Integration standard - UDDI [8]. UDDI has become the predominant technological environment for service discovery. A large number of such centralized registry/repository implementations for intra-enterprise communication, each focusing on registering services of interest to respective groups, are anticipated. Besides UDDI, decentralized approaches based on Peer-to-Peer have been proposed in order to achieve increased fault-tolerance behaviour [15].

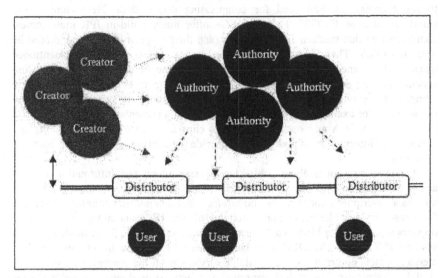

Fig. 1. A multi-party DRM eco-system

In this work we propose a similar conceptual approach. Among other services, digital content licensing is supported by Distributed License Catalogues (DLCs). DLCs are catalogues, actually registries or indexes that make available ("advertise") content or services concerning DRM functionalities, interfaces, creators, pricing etc. A DLC may be used by different nodes (creators and authorities alike) hosting a total DRM solution or providing a subset of DRM functionalities. New DRM business models can be supported where content providers or associations may act as authorities using centralized and thematically-oriented directories, to publish licenses and content rights. The structure of these registries should follow some kind of a standard following the example of UDDI.

4 The DLC Architecture

The problem facing the multi-party DRM eco-system is that each node (organisation) probably provides a different (or slightly different) set of monitoring and management services for its content. This diversity in services that actually provide the same core functionality (e.g. user tracking) is a natural consequence of the diversity between organisations. For example, different corporate culture and strategic goals may lead to different implementations of asset management services. Diversity stems from the diversity of media and metadata types used also; different representation of media artefacts include structured documents, still or moving images, audio and 3D or virtual reality objects. Representation is closely connected to the encoding method used for compressing digital data. New compression standards such as JPEG2000 and MPEG4 offer many build-in IPR management characteristics that modern DRM systems (and their respective services) should be able to exploit. Therefore, each node (or sets of nodes) in the aforementioned distributed scheme should provide a version of some of the core services. Core services can be coordinated using workflow management to build a larger, more complicated service. Services may also use digital artefacts from different repositories; for example, a user designs a multimedia presentation using digital still images from node A and small digital video clips from node B. DLCs publishing services and information of nodes should provide the starting point for such complex operations.

The DLC concept is about publishing service and artefact information and not about organisation and storage. For this reason it uses only semantics, that is metadata descriptions for services and artefacts and one multilayer ontology scheme for cross-searching like the one proposed in [16]. The DLC sits on top of the storage implementation giving birth to a 4-tier model, in contrast to the 3-tier models of web systems (figure 2). The DLC metadata are used to describe license information, media artefacts descriptions and available services from the current vendor using a UDDI-like structure. The multi-layer ontology scheme is used, on one hand for faster local searching and on the other, for facilitating service/content composition using information from other nodes. It can also be effectively used when a node is comprised by a set of sub-nodes (e.g. in the case of a portal). Similarly to the approach described in [16], our approach introduces a three layer semantic description of node contents (i.e. digital artefacts and services): the Upper Ontology layer, describes the basic concepts of the domains of knowledge of the content/services, a set of description ontologies (Domain layer) represents a more detailed description of each domain and the Semantic layer where the different semantic description of the cooperating nodes or sub-nodes lays. The proposed indexing scheme includes additional mapping information between the ontologies in the three layers providing the necessary information to search engines in order to navigate inside the ontology-based index.

Similar to web service discovery, we foresee two approaches for utilising the distributed DLC architecture: centralised and decentralised. In the centralised approach (actually the client-sever model) services, content or information about the content (usage rights) are registered in the DLC repository and clients are able to search it in order to find the appropriate solution. Unlike UDDI, the information in DLCs should not be made public; only authenticated users should gain access to information. A multi-level security scheme should provide different access rights to different users. In general, the client-server model suffers from performance bottlenecks when too many users search the same registry at the same time. The classic approach to add more servers or use load balancing techniques is not an efficient (or cost effective) solution. Decentralised approaches for service and information discovery have already been proposed by large software vendors. Approaches based on P2P infrastructures are gaining popularity in the Web Engineering field. For example, decentralized Web Services discovery uses either a structured or unstructured P2P infrastructure, although some hybrid solutions have appeared as well (e.g. super-peers). Unstructured P2P systems like Gnutella, define neighbours of peers in an ad-hoc manner and as such, they are appropriate for highly-transient peer populations communication [14]. Due to the lack of any structure, location mechanisms face significant problems relating to availability, scalability and persistence. Nevertheless, peers enjoy a large degree of autonomy. Similarly, discovery mechanisms in distributed DRM models may rely on P2P infrastructures reducing bottleneck problems.

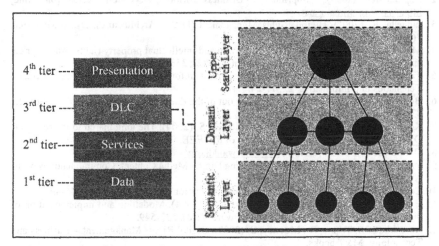

Fig. 2. 4-tier node architecture and a snapshot of a DLC multilayer ontology scheme.

5 Conclusions

The need for Digital Rights Management systems is greater than ever as copyright protection is becoming an important issue for organizations that create, use and distribute digital content through e-commerce channels. This work provided a general discussion of current DRM technological trends and pin-pointed some problems arising at a social, political and business level from their use. A new concept, namely DLCs were proposed as a solution for managing a highly distributed ecosystem of creators, authorities and users. DLCs were described here at a conceptual level and many details need to be determined even before deciding if they are a viable solution. However, the main idea behind this concept is to move beyond monolithic architectures that are inflexible and costly, towards Service-Oriented DRM systems.

Acknowledgements

This work was funded by the European Social Fund, Operational Programme for Educational and Vocational Training II (EPEAEK II), programme Pythagoras (contract no. 89188).

References

1. Eskicioglu, E.M. (2003). Protecting Intellectual Property in Digital Multimedia Networks. Computer, 36, 39-45.
2. Imprimatur (1999). Imprimatur Business Model, Version 2.1. [on line] http://www.imprimatur.net.
3. Iannella, R. (2001). Digital Rights Management (DRM) Architectures. D-Lib Magazine, 7(6).
4. McCalman, P. (2005). International diffusion and intellectual property rights: An empirical analysis. Journal of International Economics, 67(2), 353-372.
5. Towse, R. (2005). Economics and copyright reform: aspects of the EC directive. Telematics and Informatics, 22, 11-24.
6. Beute, B. (2005). Mobile DRM-usability out of the door?. Telematics and Informatics, 22, 83-96.
7. Koenen, R.H., Lacy, J., MacKay, M., Mitchell, S. (2004). The long march to interoperable Digital Rights Management. Proceedings of the IEEE, 92(6), 883-897.
8. OASIS (2005). UDDI [on line] http://www.uddi.org/
9. Memon, N., Wong, P.W. (1998). Protecting Digital Media Content. Communications of the ACM, 41(7), 34-43.
10. Cohen, J.E. (2003). DRM and Privacy. Communications of the ACM, 46(4), 46-49.
11. Hwang, S.O., Yoon, K.S., Jun, K.P., Lee, K.H. (2004). Modelling and implementation of digital rights. Journal of Systems and Software, 73(3), 533-549.
12. Rosenblatt, B., Trippe, B., Mooney, S. (2002). Digital Rights Management – Business and Technology. M&T books.
13. Singh, P.M., Huhns, M.N. (2005). Service Oriented Computing, Semantics, Processes, Agents. Wiley Press.
14. Androutsellis-Theotokis, S., Spinellis, D. (2004). A Survey of Peer-to-Peer Content Distribution Technologies. ACM Computing Surveys 36(4), 335–371.
15. Sakkopoulos E., Makris Ch., Sioutas S., Triantafillou P., Tsakalidis A., Vassiliadis B. (2005). NIPPERS: Network of InterPolated PeERS for Web Service Discovery. IEEE International Conference on Information Technology: Coding and Computing, 193-198.
16. Alexakos, Ch., Vassiliadis, B., Votis, K., Likothanassis, S. (2005), A Multilayer Ontology Scheme for Integrated Searching in Distributed Hypermedia. International Workshop on Adaptive and Personalized Semantic Web (in conjunction with ACM Hypertext 2006). [on line] www.ru5.cti.gr/HT05/files/likothanasis.pdf

AXMEDIS architectural solution for interoperable content and DRM on multichannel distribution

Pierfrancesco Bellini, Sauro Chellini, Tommaso Martini, Paolo Nesi,
Davide Rogai, Andrea Vallotti
Distributed System and Internet Technology Lab, Department of Systems
and Informatics, University of Florence
nesi@dsi.unifi.it
WWW home page: www.axmedis.org

Abstract. AXMEDIS project (Automating Production of Cross Media Content for Multi-channel Distribution) is partially funded by the European Commission to create an innovative technology framework for the automatic production, protection and distribution of digital cross-media contents over a range of different media channels including PC (on the internet), PDA, kiosk, mobile phones and i-TV (interactive-TV). The AXMEDIS project has proposed a set of integrated solutions and technologies that covers data model and DRM. This paper presents a brief introduction to the AXMEDIS IST FP6 EC project, while discussing the new functionalities enabled by the AXMEDIS architecture and solution in terms of interoperable content and DRM among different distribution channels. For further details on the AXMEDIS project, see the project website at www.axmedis.org.

1 Introduction

In the evolving scenario of the digital content market, final users are asking content distributors for more functionalities to be exploited on the acquired content. At present, the simple solutions already available on the market such as i-Tune or Microsoft Media based solutions are mainly related to business models and DRM (Digital Rights Management) mechanisms, allowing to exploit a number of limited rights on the acquired digital content. For instance, they could limit the content usage in the platform the content has been bought with or they could have a limited flexibility in porting the content on CDs (limited number of burnings, etc.), some limitations when it comes to copying the content (e.g., for a limited number of times) or other devices (e.g., from one i-Pod to another), etc. This is the beginning of a new era, when users are becoming more and more interested in acquiring digital content which can be really exploited on several different devices and tools, in comparison with what

Please use the following format when citing this chapter:

Bellini, Pierfrancesco, Chellini, Sauro, Martini, Tommaso, Nesi, Paolo, Rogal, Davide, Vallotti, Andrea, 2006, in IFIP International Federation for Information Processing, Volume 204, Artificial Intelligence Applications and Innovations, eds. Maglogiannis, I., Karpouzis, K., Bramer, M., (Boston: Springer), pp. 697–704

the users can do with the traditional physical media. A good analysis of the Traditional Rights Usage (TRU) has been carried out by DMP (Digital Media Project), http://www.dmpf.org/, see [1] for a comparison of DMP and AXMEDIS. In fact, consumers are setting out to acquire digital content that can be freely moved from one device to another at their homes, be passed into their children's hands when needed, be transferred on their mobile smartphones or into their cars, be collected in a house Media Center, etc.

In order to satisfy these needs, several challenges have to to be solved such as flexible Digital Rights Management, dynamic content adaptation, content modeling, content production on demand, content licensing, content interoperability, DRM interoperability, license processing, etc.

With this aim, AXMEDIS IST FP6 integrated project of the European Commission (Automating Production of Cross Media Content for Multi-channel Distribution) has been started up in September 2004. One of the main objectives of AXMEDIS is to create and exploit innovative technological framework for automatic production and distribution of cross-media contents over a number of different distribution channels (e.g., networked PC, PDA, kiosk, mobile phone, i-TV, etc) with DRM (Digital Rights Management). The AXMEDIS consortium consists of leading European digital content producers, integrators, aggregators, and distributors, together with information technology companies and research groups (http://www.axmedis.org, [2]).

2   AXMEDIS Main Features

In AXMEDIS a set of tools for content production, processing, protection and management has been produced. The main functionalities of the AXMEDIS tools include:

- Automated content gathering/crawling from legacy content management systems: ODBC, XML, ORCALE, MSSQL, MySQL, etc., [2].
- Content management database supporting the storage and access to AXMEDIS content (MPEG-21, any digital resource, etc., [2]) via a large set of metadata for each object called AXInfo, plus Dublin core, etc. Any other metadata format can be managed by the AXMEDIS metadata editors and tools. Different descriptors and metadata can be added into the AXMEDIS flexible model.
- Automated content processing, processing metadata and digital resources, extracting fingerprint, watermark, content synchronization, adaptation (change in resolution and format, Transcoding, etc.), coding/decoding, estimation of descriptors, license production and processing, content protection, publication, packaging, formatting, loading/saving, etc. These features are provided by means of AXMEDIS Editors and via the so-called AXMEDIS Content Processing GRID which is based on and a specific AXMEDIS extension of ECMA Script language [3]. It is a scalable solution for automating and accelerating all the phases of content processing, also integrated with Open Flow workflow.
- Editing AXMEDIS objects with a set of authoring tools. It is based on the AXMEDIS Object Model, called AXOM and extending MPEG-21 [5], and all the modules and tools to manipulate and create AXMEDIS objects and related information and digital resources such as: (i) a resource hierarchy viewer and editor, (ii) a visual and behavioral viewer and editor to show/manipulate visual and time aspects of digital resources, (iii) a DRM

viewer and editor, (iv) a protection information tools, (v) a set of plug-ins to use algorithms for content processing, (vi) a set of plug-ins to allow the integration of AXMEDIS Editor within other editing and viewing applications, (vii) a set of internal viewers and players for digital resources such as document, images, video, audio resources, etc., for more than 300 different file formats.

- Viewing and playing AXMEDIS objects with specific tools that support large set of possible digital resources, together with different business and transaction models. At present mainly on PC, while the same tools will be available on MAC, Linux, PDA, and maybe on mobiles. The current players are also usable as plug-in of Internet Explorer (ActiveX) and Mozilla.
- Automating distribution solutions at B2B level supporting both P2P and Client/Server models, automating publication and download of digital content from and to a P2P network for B2B distribution.
- Automating distribution solutions at B2C levels supporting both P2P and Client/Server models. Any third party distribution tool and solution can be used to distribute AXMEDIS content on their distribution channels. The usage of the AXMEDIS tools to realize different distribution channels and business models has already been tested: satellite data broadcast, Internet, cellular networks, wireless from kiosks, etc., to reach devices such as: i-TV PC, PC, PDA, mobiles, etc.
- Authentication, registration and certification of users and tools.
- Supervision and control of the exploitation of licensed rights by means of the AXMEDIS Certifier and Supervisor (AXCS) and the AXMEDIS Protection Manager Support (PMS).

All the above functionalities are available by means of a set of tools, libraries, solutions, guidelines, etc., that belong to the AXMEDIS Framework, AXFW (the specification is accessible on www.axmedis.org), [2]. The AXFW contains the necessary tools to set up distribution channels and make them interoperable. The AXFW includes: requirements, test cases, use cases, content for validations, general documentation of AXMEDIS tools and supports, source code, guidelines for source code production, state of the art analyses, market analyses, comparison with other technologies, guidelines on content production and distribution, tutorials on content protection, tutorial on AXMEDIS tools, etc. It is possible to get access to the AXMEDIS Framework by means of subscription/affiliation. Specific events are organised to present AXMEDIS technologies. Further information is available online at the project website, www.axmedis.org Furthermore, the AXMEDIS consortium will grant the sum of 1 Million Euro by means of a European competitive call to companies and research institutes interested in developing real solutions by exploiting AXMEDIS technologies.

3 AXMEDIS Model Flexibility

In order to guarantee interoperability of content and DRM, the most relevant aspect has to do with content model. In AXMEDIS several different content models can be adopted and the AXMEDIS tools may support all of them. As a general rule, the relevant elements of any protected digital content are digital resources, metadata, any kind of information needed to unprotect the objects and their related license. In AXMEDIS these elements may be managed in an independent way:

Metadata as AXMEDIS Information, **AXInfo**:

♦ Identification information, object unique ID, distributor ID, etc.

- ♦ Classification information also for indexing: Dublin core, etc.
- ♦ Descriptors, MPEG-7, for indexing, etc.
- ♦ References to content owner, to distributor, etc.
- ♦ Potential available rights, PAR, formalised in MPEG-21 REL.
- ♦ Etc.

Digital Resources:

- ♦ Any digital information: images, doc, txt, video, game, application, file, audio, etc.
- ♦ Hierarchy of digital resources according to MPEG-21 Digital Item model.

Protection Information, Prot.Info (IPMP information):

- ♦ What should be done to get access to a given information/resource.
- ♦ Tools used, their parameters, etc.
- ♦ extended version of MPEG-21 IPMP.

License:

- ♦ Which rights are provided, who is the recipient, which conditions, etc.
- ♦ MPEG-21 REL compliant, with some specific profile.

Usually, metadata and digital resources are combined in different ways, according to the production model used. In some cases, some metadata and/or digital resources are protected, whereas other ones may be left accessible, meaning unprotected. These combinations allow to create a complex content with promotional information and resources as well. The combination of metadata and digital resources is typically called the "Content".

In many DRM models, the content is protected and the specific Protection Information (which is called 'IPMP information' in some models like for istance MPEG) is stored to allow any opening of the object; the simpler solution is the key to decrypt the encrypted object. In AXMEDIS, the Protection Information can be both a complex set of instructions with the related protection tools to unprotect the object and also each single digital resource, beginning with the stream and/or the file on the disk.

The License is a sort of digital contract between the one who is selling the content (providing access to some specific set of rights) and the other party who is going to use/exploit them. It codes in some way the business model, and includes the rights which can be exploited by the users on a specific content, and it is formalized in some formal and consistent language such as ODRL (OMA), XrML, MPEG-21 REL, as in the AXMEDIS. The language is based on a dictionary of terms for defining the semantics of rights and related constraints (such as MPEG-21 RDD). In AXMEDIS, each license is assigned to a user, or to a group of them, or to a device or to a domain/set of devices. Any kind of business model can be implemented: pay per view, monthly rate subscription, all you can eat, pay per renting, pay per print, pay per stream, download, burning the CD, transcoding for migrating content on different devices or distributing them on different channels, etc. Supporting different constraints (number playing, temporal windows in which can be seen, expiration date, etc.) and additional features such as massing copies, building a collection, preview without paying, try and buy, etc. Before providing the Protection Information to open a given digital resource, the related Grant of the License has to be estimated to verify if the user has the right to get access to those content-related functionalities.

Each Grant of a given license may depend on the grants in other Licenses. For instance, a distributor may have received a License A for sublicensing (producing Licenses B) to its customers. On such grounds, each grant of License B is estimated if and only if the License A is accessible and can be positively processed, for instance on a License Server. This model produces a chain of Licenses that can be located in one or more servers.

In some solutions the Licenses and/or the Protection Information are cached on the device in some hidden location. This solution is a way to allow the exploitation of rights, when the device is not connected to the License Server, at the expenses of the security level.

The Protection Information and the License can be managed in different ways with respect to the metadata and digital resources. Mainly, three different models are possible:

Open Model: the Content is protected and the Protection Information is produced, while several different Licenses can be produced according to the business models and to the final users (see Fig.1). The Distributor has to produce a License for each final user or a group of them. Therefore, if the Distributor has O objects and U users, it may have O*U Licenses and only O Protection Information, one for each object. This model is suitable for P2P distribution, since the Objects can be freely distributed and when the user is interested in opening/playing one of them, he/she has to acquire a License which is the only way to obtain access to the Prot.Info.

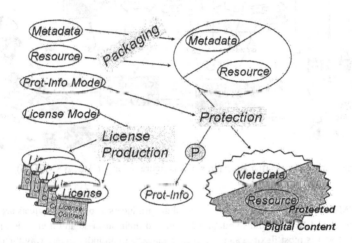

Fig. 1. Open Model (the copyrights of this figure belong to DSI AXMEDIS)

Governed Object: the Content is protected including the License inside. On such grounds, each object should be produced for each user. Therefore, if a Distributor has N objects and U users, it has to produce N*U Objects and Protection Information. This solution is very expensive to be realized, since the N*U Objects take a lot of space. In this case, for managing the same number of objects of the Open Model, a space larger U times is needed. If the needed number of objects is not produced the License is not associated with the User and it is larger and less precise, while the Objects can be passed on to other Users of the same group, or as a limit case the user in the License included is anonymous. This decreases the security level of the solution. This model is not suitable for P2P distribution, since the objects contain personal information about who bought them.

Augmented License: the Content is protected and the Protection Information is produced, while several different Licenses can be produced according to the business models and to the

final users .Each License contains the Protection Information. The Distributor produces a
License for each final user or for a group of them. Therefore, if the Distributor has O objects
and U users, it may have O*U Licenses. This model is suitable for P2P distribution since the
Objects can be freely distributed and when a user is interested in opening one of them, he has
to acquire the License. This model presents more risks than the Open Model since the License
contains the protection information and frequently the License has to be visible and accessible
to the final user.

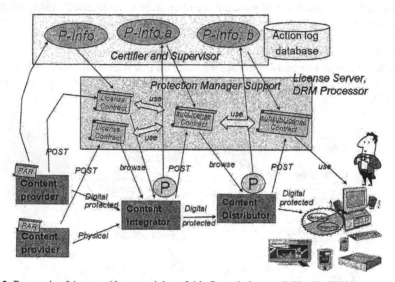

Fig. 2. Processing Licenses (the copyrights of this figure belong to DSI AXMEDIS)

   In AXMEDIS, the distributors and in general the producers of protected objects are free to
decide which model they prefer to adopt, according to their business and transaction models.
The Open Model is most flexible and it allows to manage in an independent way the chain of
licenses and the management of the Protection Information (see Fig.2). To this end, the
AXMEDIS Protection Manager Support (PMS) and the AXMEDIS Certifier and Supervisor
(AXCS) are provided.

   The AXCS collects and maintains the information regarding the registered objects, users,
devices, etc., and therefore it allows the management of black lists. It also stores the Protection
Information of each protected object, resource and the list of actions performed on them, the
so called Action Log database. Each Action describes an action performed on a given
content/resource, by a given user, on the basis of a given license, etc. The whole set of Action
Logs allows to produce the reporting to Distributors, to Content Providers, to Collecting
Societies, etc., and also the production of statistics on the use of digital content per area, per
device, per genre, per type, per sex, per device type, in a given period, etc.

   The PMS is a License Server that maintains the database of Licenses and it is capable of
processing chains of them for evaluating the Grants.

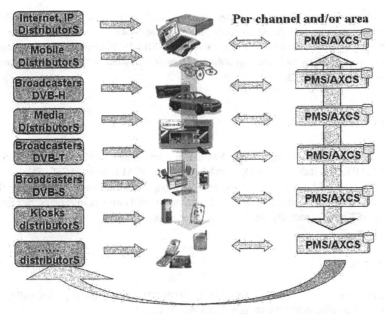

Fig. 3. AXMEDIS Multichannel (the copyrights of this figures is of DSI AXMEDIS)

The AXMEDIS architecture supports multichannel and interoperability by allowing the migration of content from different devices and among different channels. Such different channels may have their specific devices and business models and their specific DRM solutions. Each of them can be a customization of MPEG-21 REL or OMA ODRL. This means that the different PMS/AXCS managing the different geographic areas or channels have to communicate one another to exchange information about the: Actions Log, registered objects, Protection Information, Licenses, etc. In addition, the local AXCS has to provide access to the whole information stored in the Action Logs related to the usage of a given content or to a given content owner or distributor. The flow of this information is the most important problem concerning the interoperability of content and DRM. It has to put up with any possible failure of some PMSs or AXCSs.

4 Conclusions

AXMEDIS architecture and tools are a solution to automate, accelerate and restructure production and protection processes. This paper described a single aspect of the whole AXMEDIS architecture and framework design which is going to address many other problems and critical points. AXMEDIS framework can support data gathering from accessible Content Management Systems, transform legacy digital content in AXMEDIS objects, content authoring, and it can process them in the production, preserving security level along the whole value chain and therefore creating a perfect environment for content production, protection and distribution at both B2B and B2C levels. AXMEDIS solution is mainly based on MPEG-

21 model and it provides and stimulates the usage and the exploitation of the developed features for creating many AXMEDIS compliant tools and solutions, while making the core aspects and solution accessible in the form of AXMEDIS Framework. More technical information and/or how to make registration or submit affiliation to the AXMEDIS can be found on www.axmedis.org

Acknowledgements

The authors would like to thank all the AXMEDIS project partners (ANSC, AFI, EUTELSAT, Giunti ILABS, HP Italy, FHGIGD, DIPITA, CRS4, TISCALI, XIM, ACIT, FUPF, CPR, EXITECH, Univ of Leeds, etc.), the Expert-User-Group and all affiliated members for their contributions, supports and collaborations. The authors would also like to express their thanks to the EC IST FP6 for partially funding the AXMEDIS project.

References

1. AXMEDIS, "Comparing AXMEDIS, MPEG21 and DMP", accessible at www.chiarigllione.org and on WWW.AXMEDIS.org
2. AXMEDIS Use Cases, Official Deliverable of AXMEDIS project: www.axmedis.org.
3. P. Bellini, I. Bruno, P. Nesi, "A Distributed Environment for Automatic Multimedia Content Production based on GRID", Proc. of International Conference on Automated Production of Cross Media Content for Multi-channel Distribution, 30 November - 2 December 2005, Florence, Italy.
4. P. Bellini, P. Nesi, "An architecture of Automating Production of Cross Media Content for Multi-channel Distribution", Proc. of International Conference on Automated Production of Cross Media Content for Multi-channel Distribution, 30 November - 2 December 2005, Florence, Italy.
5. P. Bellini, P. Nesi, D. Rogai, A. Vallotti, "AXMEDIS Tool Core for MPEG-21 Authoring/Playing", Proc. of International Conference on Automated Production of Cross Media Content for Multi-channel Distribution, 30 November - 2 December 2005, Florence, Italy.

Computer Aided Diagnosis of CT Focal Liver Lesions based on Texture Features, Feature Selection and Ensembles of Classifiers

Stavroula G. Mougiakakou[1], Ioannis K. Valavanis[1], Alexandra Nikita[2],
Konstantina S. Nikita[1]

[1] National Technical University of Athens, Faculty of Electrical and
Computer Engineering, 9 Iroon Polytechniou Str., 15780 Zografou, Athens,
Greece
{smougia, knikita}@cc.ece.ntua.gr,
ivalavan@biosim.ntua.gr
[2] University of Athens, Medical School, Department of Radiology, 20
Papadiamantopoulou Str., 15228 Athens, Greece
anikita@cc.uoa.gr

Abstract A computer aided diagnosis system aiming to classify liver tissue from computed tomography images is presented. For each region of interest five distinct sets of texture features were extracted. Two different ensembles of classifiers were constructed and compared. The first one consists of five Neural Networks (NNs), each using as input either one of the computed texture feature sets or its reduced version after feature selection. The second ensemble of classifiers was generated by combining five different type of primary classifiers, two NNs, and three k-nearest neighbor classifiers. The primary classifiers of the second ensemble used identical input vectors, which resulted from the combination of the five texture feature sets, either directly or after proper feature selection. The decision of each ensemble of classifiers was extracted by applying voting schemes.

1 Introduction

Computer-Aided Diagnosis (CAD) systems, for the characterization of liver tissue, attract more and more attention, in order to assist clinicians in diagnosis, and reduce the number of required biopsies. Various approaches, most of them using ultrasound B-scan and Computed Tomography (CT) images, have been proposed based on different image characteristics, such as texture features, and fractal dimension estimators combined with various classifiers [1], [2], [3]. Texture analysis of liver

Please use the following format when citing this chapter:

Mougiakakou, Stavroula, Valavanis, Ioannis, Nikita, Alexandra, Nikita, Konstantina, 2006, in IFIP International Federation for Information Processing, Volume204, Artificial Intelligence Applications and Innovations, eds. Maglogiannis, I., Karpouzis, K., Bramer, M., (Boston: Springer), pp. 705–712

CT images based on Spatial Gray Level Dependence Matrix (SGLDM), Gray Level Run Length Method (GLRLM), and Gray Level Difference Method (GLDM) has been proposed in [4], in order to discriminate normal from malignant hepatic tissue. Texture features from SGLDM have been applied to a Probabilistic Neural Network (P-NN) in [5] for the characterization of hepatic tissue (hepatoma and hemangioma) from CT images. Additionally, SGLDM based texture features fed to a system of three sequentially placed Neural Networks (NNs) have been used in [6] for the classification of hepatic tissue into four categories.

The principal aim of the present paper is to assess the potential of ensembles of classifiers in the development of a CAD system able to discriminate four hepatic tissue types: normal liver (C1), hepatic cyst (C2), hemangioma (C3), and hepatocellular carcinoma (C4) from CT images.

2   Methodology

The generic design of a CAD system is presented in Fig. 1. Regions of Interest (ROIs) drawn by an experienced radiologist on CT images were driven to a feature extraction module, where five different texture feature sets were obtained. The full feature sets or their reduced versions obtained after proper feature selection in the feature selection module, were fed to two alternative ensembles of classifiers (EC). The primary classifiers of the first ensemble (EC1) were generated by applying a single learning algorithm to different data sets, while the classifiers of the second ensemble (EC2) were generated by using different learning algorithms on the same data set. The predictions of the primary classifiers of each ensemble were combined using appropriate voting schemes.

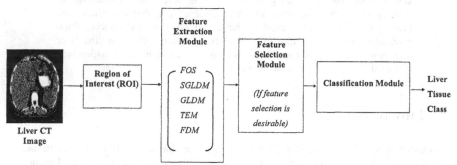

Fig. 1. Generic design of CAD1 ... CAD5

2.1   Image Acquisition

Abdominal non-enhanced CT images with a spatial resolution of 512×512 pixels and 8-bit gray-level at the W150+60 window taken from both patients and healthy controls were used. The diagnosed hepatic lesions from patients with C2, C3, and C4, were validated by needle biopsies, density measurements, and the typical pattern of enhancement after the intravenous injection of iodine contrast. The position, size and extent of the lesions were defined in CT images by an experienced radiologist. A total of 147 free-hand ROIs were sampled and distributed into three disjoint data sets (training, validation, and testing), as presented in Table 1.

2.2 Feature Extraction

In the feature extraction module, five sets of features were calculated for each ROI.

Table 1. Distribution of the available samples in training, validation, and testing set

	Training Set	Validation Set	Testing Set
Normal (C1)	42	17	17
Cyst (C2)	11	4	4
Hemangioma (C3)	16	6	6
Hepatocellular Carcinoma (C4)	14	5	5

2.2.1 First Order Statistics

Features from FOS [7] are easily computed from the intensity function of the image. In our study, six features were calculated for each ROI: average gray level (avg_{FOS}), standard deviation (std_{FOS}), entropy (ent_{FOS}), coefficient of variation (cv_{FOS}), skewness (sk_{FOS}), kurtness (kur_{FOS}).

2.2.2 Spatial Gray-Level Dependence Matrices

Texture characteristics can be derived from SGLDM of the ROI [7], [8]. The features calculated in our experiments are: angular second moment (asm_{SGLDM}), contrast (con_{SGLDM}), correlation (cor_{SGLDM}), variance (var_{SGLDM}), inverse difference moment (idm_{SGLDM}), entropy (ent_{SGLDM}), homogeneity (hg_{SGLDM}), cluster tendency (clt_{SGLDM}). The features were calculated for intersample spacing of 1, 2, 4, 6, 8, and 12 pixels. For each value of intersample spacing, the feature values are computed by averaging over four uniformly distributed angular directions, 0°, 45°, 90°, and 135°. Thus, a total of 48 texture characteristics were obtained through SGLDM for each ROI.

2.2.3 Gray-Level Difference Matrix

Application of the GLDM to each ROI results in a 20-dimensional feature vector. Five texture features, were extracted based on the gray level difference density function [9]: contrast (con_{GLDM}), mean value (mn_{GLDM}), entropy (ent_{GLDM}), inverse difference moment (idm_{GLDM}), angular second moment (asm_{GLDM}). These features were calculated for distances of 1, 2, 3, and 4 pixels. The final feature value for each distance was computed by averaging over the feature values corresponding to the four angular directions.

2.2.4 Laws' Texture Energy Measures

Laws' TEM are derived from three simple vectors of length three [10]. In our study, the following four Laws' zero-sum masks were used: $L5E5 = L5^{T}E5$, $E5S5 = -E5^{T}S5$, $L5S5 = L5^{T}S5$, $R5R5 = R5^{T}S5$. After convolving each ROI image with each of the four masks, the following measures were calculated: Sum of absolute values/# of pixels (as_{TEM}), *sum of squares/# of pixels (ss_{TEM})*, entropy (ent_{TEM}). Thus, twelve

Laws' energy measures (4 masks $\times$ 3 statistics per mask) are calculated for each ROI.

2.2.5 Fractal Dimension Texture Measurements

For each ROI, a 3-dimensional feature vector is estimated from the FDM. The components of the feature vector correspond to the parameters $H1_{FDM}$, $H2_{FDM}$, $H3_{FDM}$, of the multiresolution fractal feature vector [3].

2.3　Feature Selection

For the purpose of feature selection, a GA based on [11], was used in the present paper. The algorithm makes use of a randomly created initial population of N chromosomes. Each chromosome is a binary mask, with 1 indicating that the feature is selected, and 0 that the corresponding feature is omitted. The chromosomes are mated, with possibility depending on their fitness, in order to propagate their genetic material to their offspring. $N/2$ pairs of chromosomes are selected using the elitist selection method. The selected chromosomes are mated using the two-point crossover (crossover probability, P_c). The mutation genetic operator (mutation probability, P_m) is applied in order to switch the value of chromosome bits. Thus, a new chromosome is produced replacing the old one. The fitness function is estimated for the new population, and the best results are stored. The procedure is repeated for a number of N_G generations. The maximum squared Mahalanobis distance was used as fitness function [6]. Since the number of selected features is not taken into account in computing the fitness function, a "penalty" function for feature sets exceeding a given dimensionality threshold was applied. Thus, the corresponding individuals were assigned a fitness value equal to 50% of the average population fitness. The GA was run for a dimensionality threshold equal to ten [6]. The GA parameters were: $N = 200$, $N_G = 250$, $P_c = 0.8$, and $P_m = 0.008$.

2.4　Classification

The estimated texture features sets were applied to either of two different ensembles (EC1 and EC2) of classifiers. EC1 was constructed by combining five Multilayer Perceptron NNs (MLP-NN), each trained with one out of the five distinct texture feature sets, while EC2 was constructed by combining one MLP-NN, one Probabilistic NN (P-NN), and three Nearest Neighbor (k-NN) classifiers, each trained with the combination of the five computed texture feature sets. For each ensemble of classifiers the final decision was generated by combining the outputs of the corresponding primary classifiers through appropriate voting schemes.

2.4.1 Multilayer Perceptron Neural Network

The MLP-NN classifier [12] used in this study is based on a feed-forward NN consisting of one input layer with a number of input neurons equal to the number of features fed into the NN, one hidden layer with variable number of neurons, and one output layer consisting of two output neurons, encoding the different types of liver tissue (00=C1, 01=C2, 10=C3, and 11=C4). The MLP-NN was trained, using the training set, by the batched Back-Propagation (BP) algorithm with adaptive learning rate and momentum [12]. Moreover, the optimal number of hidden neurons, as well as the appropriate values of momentum and initial learning rate were estimated using a trial-and-error process, until no further improvement of classification accuracy in the validation set could be obtained.

2.4.2 Probabilistic Neural Network
The P-NN performs interpolation in multidimensional space [1]. The P-NN consists of one input layer, with number of neurons equal to the number of used features, a hidden layer, a summation unit layer, and an output layer. In order to classify a ROI the corresponding feature set is applied to the input layer and then into the hidden layer, followed by the summation layer. Finally, the neuron in the output layer classifies the ROI into the class with the highest probabilistic density function. The applied training procedure is the same as in the case of the MLP-NN classifier.

2.4.3 k-Nearest Neighbor Classifier
The k-NN classifier identifies the k nearest neighbors to the feature vector to be classified from the training set based on a distance measurement of the vectors. The feature vector is classified to the most frequent class occurring in the set of neighbors [13]. In this paper, a 1-NN classifier along with two mk-NN (modified k-NN, $k>1$, classifiers), mk_1-NN ($2 \le k_1 \le 5$) and mk_2-NN ($6 \le k_2 \le 9$), have been developed [13]. The mk-NN classifiers differs from the k-NN, in that the classification result is based both on the frequencies of the classes occurring in the set of neighbors, and on the distances of the neighbors from the feature vector.

2.4.4 Voting Scheme
A plurality and a weighted voting scheme were used to combine the predictions of the primary classifiers of EC1 and EC2 [14]. According to the plurality voting scheme, each primary classifier gives a vote for its prediction. The prediction receiving the most votes is the final prediction. According to the weighted voting scheme, the primary classifier predictions are averaged by taking into consideration a set of weights, with which the classifiers participate in the final prediction.

2.5   CAD System Architectures

Five alternative architectures (CAD1, …, CAD5) were developed based on the generic design of the CAD system presented in Fig. 1. CAD1 and CAD2 were constructed using EC1, while CAD3, CAD4, and CAD5 were based on EC2. In CAD1 (Fig. 3(a)), each of the full-dimensional FOS, SGLDM, GLDM, TEM, and FDM feature sets, estimated in the feature extraction module, is fed into one of the five primary classifiers of EC1. CAD2 (Fig. 3(b)) differs from CAD1 in that feature selection is applied to the feature vectors estimated from SGLDM, GLDM, and TEM, since they have high dimensionality. In CAD3 (Fig. 3(c)), each primary classifier uses as input the 89-dimensional feature set, which results from the combination of the full-dimensional FOS, SGLDM, GLDM, TEM, and FDM features sets. CAD4 (Fig. 3(d)) differs from CAD3 in that feature selection is applied

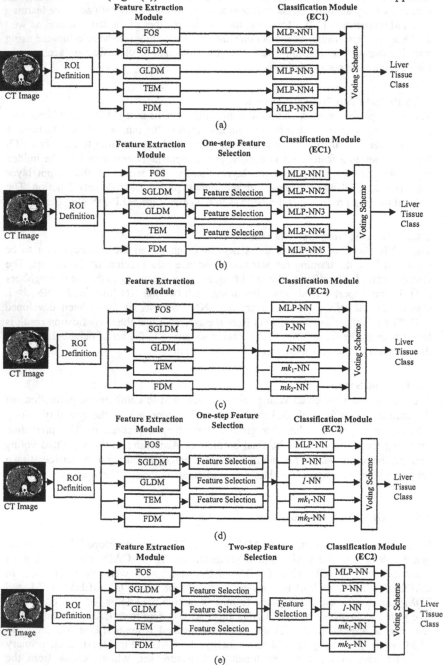

Fig. 2. Architecture of (a) CAD1, (b) CAD2, (c) CAD3, (d) CAD4, and (e) CAD5

to SGLDM, GLDM, and TEM feature sets prior to the combination with the full-dimensional FOS and FDM feature sets. The selected SGLDM, GLDM and TEM features are identical with the ones applied in CAD2. CAD5 (Fig. 3(e)) differs from CAD4 in that further feature selection is applied to the 30-dimensional feature set used by CAD4. The resulting 12-dimensional feature set provides input to each primary classifier of EC2 (CAD5). A plurality or weighted voting scheme extracts the final decision for each of EC1 and EC2.

3   Results and Discussion

In order to find the best performing CAD, the achieved classification rates of CAD1, ..., CAD5 in the testing set were comparatively assessed, along with their behavior to all the available datasets. All classification performances of the base classifiers and the ensembles of EC1 (CAD1 and CAD2) and EC2 (CAD3,..,CAD5) are presented in Tables 2 and 3, respectively. Based on Tables 2 and 3, it is observed that the primary classifiers of EC2 in CAD3, CAD4, and CAD5 classify better the liver regions, compared to the primary classifiers of EC1 in CAD1, and CAD2. CAD2, which uses EC1, and is the best of CAD1 and CAD2, achieved a classification performance in the testing set equal to 90.63%. This performance is slightly less than the best performance (93.75%) of CAD3, CAD4 and CAD5 which use EC2 and was achieved by CAD5. Furthermore, CAD2 with weighted voting scheme performs quite balanced in the datasets, while CAD5 had a quite unbalanced behavior. Thus the best architecture is CAD2 with weighted voting scheme.

Table 2. The individual and total classification performances of EC1 (CAD1, CAD2)

Classifier	Validation Set (%)		Testing Set (%)	
	CAD1	CAD2	CAD1	CAD2
MLP-NN1	90.63	(90.63)	87.50	(87.50)
MLP-NN2	65.63	71.88	62.50	56.25
MLP-NN3	65.63	65.63	53.13	43.75
MLP-NN4	87.50	84.38	81.25	90.63
MLP-NN5	65.63	(65.63)	59.38	(59.38)
Classifier Combination				
Plurality Voting Scheme	90.63	93.75	78.13	78.13
Weighted Voting Scheme	93.75	93.75	87.50	90.63

Table 3. The individual and total classification performances of EC2 (CAD3, CAD4, CAD5)

Classifier	Validation Set (%)			Testing Set (%)		
	CAD3	CAD4	CAD5	CAD3	CAD4	CAD5
MLP-NN	81.25	90.63	71.88	81.25	90.63	81.25
P-NN	93.75	96.88	90.63	81.25	81.25	90.63
1-NN	90.63	96.88	78.13	68.75	75.00	78.13
mk_1-NN	90.63	93.75	78.13	84.38	87.50	93.75
mk_2-NN	87.5	90.63	84.38	84.38	87.50	90.63
Classifier Combination						

| Plurality Voting Scheme | 90.63 | 96.88 | 81.25 | 84.38 | 84.38 | 93.75 |
| Weighted Voting Scheme | 90.63 | 96.88 | 84.38 | 84.38 | 84.38 | 93.75 |

In order to evaluate the classification ability of the proposed CAD architecture, to overcome problems encountered while assessing the various architectures, like the unusually better performances in the testing set compared to these on the validation set, and the fact that the ensembles did not outperformed all of the classifiers, it is under investigation the use of a larger image database, and more elaborate sampling schemes. Furthermore, the proposed system can be extended to other classes of liver lesions, and/or to liver images from other imaging devices.

4   Conclusion

The development of a CAD system aiming to discriminate four hepatic tissue types from non-enhanced CT images has been presented. An ensemble of classifiers has been constructed based on NN leading to a classification performance of 90.63%.

References

1. Kadah YM, Frag, AA, Zurada JM, Badawi AM, Youssef A-B M, Classification algorithms for quantitative tissue characterization of diffuse liver disease from ultrasound images, *IEEE Trans. Med. Imag.*, vol. 15, no. 4, (1996) 466-478.
2. Sun YN, Horng MH, Lin XZ, Wang JY, Ultrasonic image analysis for liver diagnosis, *IEEE Engin. Med. Biol.*, vol. 11-12, (1996) 93-101.
3. Wu Ch-M, Chen Y-Ch, Sheng Hsieh K, Texture features for classification of ultrasonic liver images, *IEEE Trans. Med. Imaging*, vol. 11, no. 2, (1992) 141-151.
4. Mir AH, Hanmandlu M, Tandon SN, Texture analysis of CT images, *IEEE Eng. Med. Biol. Mag.*, vol. 14, no. 6, (1995) 781-786.
5. Chen EL, Chung P-C, Chen CL, Tsa HM, Chang CI, An automatic diagnostic system for CT liver image classification, *IEEE Trans. Biomed. Eng.*, vol. 45, no. 6, (1998) 783-794.
6. Gletsos M, Mougiakakou SG, Matsopoulos GK, Nikita KS, Nikita A, Kelekis D, A computer-aided diagnostic system to characterize CT focal liver lesions: Design and optimization of a neural network classifier, *IEEE Trans. Inform. Techn. Biomed.*, vol. 7, no. 3, (2003) 153-162.
7. Haralick RM, Shaphiro LG, *Computer and Robot Vision*, vol. I. Addison-Wesley 1992.
8. Haralick RM, Shanmugan K, Dinstein I, Textural features for image classification, *IEEE Trans. Systems, Man, and Cybernetics*, vol. 3, no. 6, (1973) 610-622.
9. Weszka JS, Dryer CR, Rosenfeld A, A comparative study of texture measures for terrain classification, *IEEE Trans. System, Man, and Cybernetic*, vol. SMC-6, (1976) 269-285.
10. Laws KI, Rapid texture identification, *Proc. of the SPIE Conference for Missile Guidance*, vol. 238, (1980) 376-380.
11. Goldberg D, *Genetic algorithms in search, optimization and machine learning*, Addison-Wesley, (1989).
12. Haykin S, *Neural networks: A comprehensive foundation*, Prentice-Hall, (1999).
13. Wu Y, Ianakiev Kr, Govindaraju V, Improved k-nearest neighbor classification, *Pat. Recogn.*, vol. 35, (2002) 2311-2318.
14. Lam L, Suen Ch, Application of majority voting to pattern recognition: An analysis of its behavior and performance, *IEEE Trans. Systems, Man, and Cybernetics*, vol. 27, no. 5 (1997) 553-568.

Texture Analysis for Classification of Endometrial Tissue in Gray Scale Transvaginal Ultrasonography

Anna Karahaliou[1], Spyros Skiadopoulos[1], George Michail[2], Christina Kalogeropoulou[3], Ioannis Boniatis[1], George Kourounis[2], George Panayiotakis[1], and Lena Costaridou[1]

1 Department of Medical Physics, School of Medicine, University of Patras

2 Department of Obstetrics and Gynecology, School of Medicine, University of Patras

3 Department of Radiology, School of Medicine, University of Patras
costarid@upatras.gr

Abstract. Computer-aided classification of benign and malignant endometrial tissue, as depicted in 2D gray scale transvaginal ultrasonography (TVS), was attempted by computing texture-based features. 65 TVS endometrial images were collected (15 malignant, 50 benign) and processed with a wavelet based enhancement technique. Two regions of interest (ROIs) were identified (endometrium, endometrium margin) on each processed image. Thirty-two textural features were extracted from each ROI employing first and second order statistics texture analysis algorithms. Textural feature-based models were generated for differentiating benign from malignant endometrial tissue employing stepwise logistic regression analysis. Models' performance was evaluated by means of receiver operating characteristics (ROC) analysis. The best benign versus malignant classification was obtained from the model combining three textural features from endometrium and four textural features from endometrium margin, with corresponding area under ROC curve (Az) 0.956.

1 Introduction

Endometrial cancer is the fourth most prevalent malignant neoplasia among women [1]. The commonest presenting symptom of endometrial carcinoma is abnormal vaginal bleeding and thus is considered as indication for hysteroscopy and dilatation and curettage (D&C), which is the 'golden standard' for histological evaluation. However, given that more than 90% of postmenopausal and more than 98% of pre- and perimenopausal women with abnormal vaginal bleeding will have a benign

Please use the following format when citing this chapter:

Karahaliou, Anna, Skiadopoulos, Spyros, Michail, George, Kalogeropoulou, Christina, Boniatis, Ioannis, Kourounis, George, Panayiotakis, George, Costaridou, Lena, 2006, in IFIP International Federation for Information Processing, Volume 204, Artificial Intelligence Applications and Innovations, eds. Maglogiannis, I., Karpouzis, K., Bramer, M., (Boston: Springer), pp. 713–721

underlying cause, questions have arisen regarding the appropriateness of performing biopsies on all patients with bleeding [2].

Transvaginal sonographic assessment of the endometrium, which is usually based on endometrial thickness measurement, is a simple and non-invasive technique for excluding endometrial carcinoma. However, the cut-off values of endometrial thickness in literature vary considerably [3]. Most studies suggest the cut-off point of 4-5 mm endometrial thickness since it provides a high sensitivity, but specificity is reduced and thus resulting in many unnecessary biopsies.

Several approaches have been suggested in order to improve diagnostic accuracy of TVS. All of them focused on assessing qualitatively sonomorphological criteria (endometrial texture, regularity of endometrial-myometrial border, presence of central echo etc.) in addition to the sole measurement of endometrial thickness [4-6]. To the authors' knowledge, there are no reported studies assessing quantitatively endometrial texture for differentiating malignant from benign endometrial tissue. Computerized analysis of endometrial tissue (in terms of histogram based features) has only implemented in the context of ameliorating in vitro fertilization (IVF) outcome [7-9].

The aim of this study was to investigate the feasibility of computerized texture analysis in characterizing endometrial tissue as depicted in 2D gray scale TVS images. In particular, images were processed with a wavelet-based enhancement technique to facilitate delineation of two regions of interest (ROIs) corresponding to endometrium and to endometrium margin, respectively. First and second order textural features were extracted from the determined regions. Textural features-based models were generated for differentiating malignant from benign endometrial tissue, utilizing stepwise logistic regression analysis. Models' performance was evaluated by means of receiver operating characteristic (ROC) analysis.

2 Materials and Methods

2.1 Subjects and Image Acquisition

Eighty-two (82) perimenopausal and postmenopausal women with vaginal bleeding, scheduled for fractionated dilatation and curettage (D&C) or hysterectomy in the Gynecological Department of the University Hospital of Patras, were recruited. Seventeen (17) patients were excluded from the study due to hormonal replacement therapy or tamoxifen medication, suboptimal visualization of the endometrium attributed to medioverted or retroverted uterus, cancelled surgery and conservative surgery–myectomy resulting in 65 remaining patients. The average age of the patients was 57.2 years (range: 41-80 years). The histological diagnosis documented 15 malignant and 50 benign endometria.

All 65 patients underwent transvaginal scan on a single ATL HDI 3500 ultrasonic imager (Advanced Technology Laboratories, Bothell, WA, USA), with a multifrequency C 9-5 MHz transvaginal transducer, 48 hours or less before scheduled surgery. An experienced radiologist performed the examinations and obtained multiple representative transverse and longitudinal images documenting endometrial thickness for each patient. The digital 2D B-mode transvaginal ultrasonic endometrial images had 8 bits pixel depth and 768x576 pixels resolution. A dataset of 65 longitudinal images, in DICOM format, were selected under the concurrence of a radiologist and a gynecologist. The relationship between endometrial thickness and histological diagnosis is presented graphically in Fig. 1. As expected, the greater the endometrial thickness the higher the incidence of endometrial cancer.

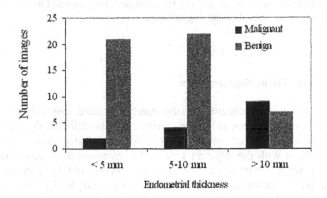

Fig. 1. Histogram illustrating the distribution of malignant and benign histological diagnosis with respect to endometrial thickness.

2.2 Image Processing with a Wavelet-based Algorithm

An image processing technique was employed to enhance the contrast of significant characteristics and to facilitate segmentation procedure. Each image of the dataset was processed with a locally adaptive wavelet based technique [10,11]. The method is based on local modification of multiscale gradient magnitude values provided by the redundant dyadic wavelet transform. Contrast enhancement is performed by applying a local linear mapping operator on multiscale gradient magnitude values. The first four frequency scales are used to enhance image characteristics of different size. Fig. 2(a) is an indicative image of the dataset, while Fig. 2(b) depicts the corresponding processed image acquired by application of the locally-adaptive wavelet technique.

An image visualization tool developed in our department [12,13] has been used for application of the processing technique and the segmentation procedure described in the following section. This tool is domain-specific to medical imaging and provides global and adaptive wavelet functionality, in addition to conventional visualization operations.

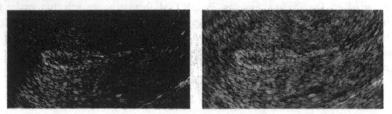

Fig. 2. (a) Indicative image of the dataset. (b) The corresponding processed image provided by application of the wavelet-based processing technique.

2.3 Endometrial Tissue Segmentation

A radiologist and a gynecologist, collaboratively, retraced manually a region of interest (ROI_1) corresponding to the endometrium without including endometrium border. A second region of interest (ROI_2) was delineated comprising of the endometrium along with the adjacent area of the myometrium (endometrium plus endometrium margin. To isolate the endometrium margin (ROI_3) a substraction of the two manually segmented ROIs was performed (ROI_2-ROI_1). The two ROIs corresponding to endometrium (ROI_1) and endometrium margin (ROI_3) were used for the subsequent texture analysis. Figure 3 depicts the identified endometrium (ROI_1) and endometrium margin (ROI_3) on the processed image depicted in fig. 2(b).

2.4 Feature Extraction

Thirty-two (32) textural features were extracted from the endometrium (ROI_1) and endometrium margin (ROI_3) of each processed image, employing first and second order statistics texture analysis algorithms.

2.4.1 First Order Statistics Textural Features

First order statistics measure the likelihood of observing a specific gray level value at a randomly chosen location of the image. They are computed from the histogram of the image, and depend only on individual pixel values and not on the interaction or co-occurrence of neighboring pixel values. In this study, four first order textural features corresponding to the four moments of each ROI's gray level histogram were calculated: Mean value (MEA), Standard Deviation (SD), Skewness (SKEW) and Kurtosis (KURT).

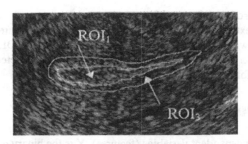

Fig. 3. Regions of interest corresponding to endometrium (ROI1) and to endometrium margin (ROI3).

2.4.2 Second Order Statistics Textural Features

The Gray Level Co-occurrence Matrix (GLCM) is a well-established robust statistical tool for extracting second order texture information from images [14,15]. The GLCM characterizes the spatial distribution of gray levels in the selected ROI. An element at location (i,j) of the GLCM signifies the joint probability density of the occurrence of gray levels i and j in a specified orientation θ and specified distance d from each other. In this study, four GLCMs corresponding to four different directions (θ=0°, 45°, 90° and 135°) and one distance (d=1 pixel), were computed for each selected ROI. Fourteen features were derived from each GLCM. Specifically, the features studied were: Angular Second Moment (ASM), Contrast (CON), Correlation (COR), Variance (VAR), Inverse Difference Moment (IDM), Sum Average (SUM_AV), Sum Variance (SUM_VAR), Sum Entropy (SUM_ENT), Entropy (ENT), Difference Entropy (DIF_ENT), Information Measure of Correlation 1 (IMCA1), Information Measure of Correlation 2 (IMCA2), Shade (SHA) and Promenance (PRO). Four values were obtained for each feature corresponding to the four matrices. The mean and range of these four values were calculated, comprising a total of twenty-eight second order textural features.

2.5 Classification

The 32 textural features extracted from endometrium (ROI$_1$) and endometrium margin (ROI$_3$) of the processed images were used as input variables for logistic regression analysis [16] to determine the subsets of features that can differentiate benign from malignant endometrial tissue. The histological findings regarding to benign or malignant diagnoses were considered as truth table. Specifically, the forward stepwise feature selection method of the logistic regression analysis was performed using a statistical software package (NCSS Statistical Software 2004, Kaysville, Utah, USA).

Two regression models were constructed, each one corresponding to endometrium (ROI$_1$) and to endometrium margin (ROI$_3$), respectively. Each model used as input variables the same 32 textural features extracted from ROI$_1$ and ROI$_3$, respectively. An additional regression model was constructed combining the 32 textural features extracted from ROI_1 and the 32 textural features extracted from ROI_3. This model will be referred as the one corresponding to (ROI_1/ROI_3).

The best model for ROI_1, ROI_3 and ROI_1/ROI_3 was constructed in the form of *logit(p)* values as follows:

$$log it(p) = log_e \left(\frac{Pr ob(Y = y_1)}{Pr ob(Y = y_2)} \right) = \beta_0 + \sum_{s=1}^{n} \beta_s X_s \qquad (1)$$

where Xs are the independent variables (features), Y is the binary dependent variable (pathology), which has two possible values, y1 (0: benign) and y2 (1: malignant), βo is the intercept and βs are the logistic regression coefficients. From these logit(p) values, the estimated probability of malignancy for a single case can be obtained from:

$$p = \frac{exp[log it(p)]}{1 + exp[log it(p)]} \qquad (2)$$

The leave-one-out validation methodology was performed for testing the logistic regression models. Their performance was evaluated by means of receiver operating characteristic (ROC) analysis, and classification accuracy was quantified by using the area under the ROC curve, A_z.

3 Results

Table 1. Best logistic regression models, as chosen by forward stepwise selection of textural features extracted from endometrium (ROI1), endometrium margin (ROI3), and combined endometrium/endometrium margin (ROI1/ROI3), in terms of logit(p) equations.

ROI	Best logistic regression model
ROI_1	-229.92 - 42.28 x M_CON -116.58 x M_COR + 455.80 x M_DIF_ENT + 247.35 x M_IDM + 0.08 x M_SUM_VAR -140.17 x R_DIF_ENT + 0.12 x R_PRO
ROI_3	-93.94 + 0.11 x MEA + 132.34 x M_ASM -33.23 x M_CON + 258.06 x M_DIF_ENT + 10.98 x R_CON -109.24 x R_IDM + 169.17 x R_SUM_ENT
ROI_1/ROI_3	-67.32 + 0.12 x MEA$_{ROI3}$ + 99.39 x M_ASM$_{ROI3}$ - 23.57 x M_CON$_{ROI1}$ + 179.09 x M_DIF_ENT$_{ROI1}$ + 9.11 x R_CON$_{ROI3}$ -123.40 x R_IDM$_{ROI3}$ + 0.03 x R_PRO$_{ROI1}$

M_ :mean of, R_ : range of

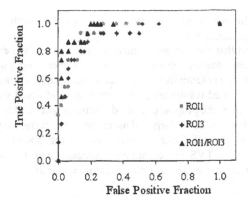

Fig. 4. ROC curves corresponding to the logistic regression feature-based models extracted from endometrium (ROI1), endometrium margin (ROI3) and combined endometrium/endometrium margin (ROI1/ROI3).

Table 1 provides the best logistic regression models, as chosen by forward stepwise selection of textural features extracted from ROI_1 and ROI_3, as well as for the model combining the features from ROI_1 and ROI_3 (ROI_1/ROI_3), in terms of *logit(p)* equations. All features entered in the regression models are statistically significant (Wald-test for each regression coefficient, $p<0.05$). As observed in Table 1, the features included in the regression models are differentiated with respect to the selected ROI.

The ROC curves corresponding to the three logistic regression models are presented in Fig. 4. The best performance is obtained by the model produced combining features from endometrium and endometrium margin (ROI_1/ROI_3) achieving an A_z value of 0.956. The models corresponding to ROI_1 and ROI_3 achieved A_z values of 0.937 and 0.909, respectively.

4 Discussion and Conclusion

The feasibility of implementing computer-aided analysis using textural features to characterize endometrial tissue as depicted in 2D gray scale TVS was reported. The computer extracted textural features were selected, due to their proven applicability to analyze texture in ultrasound images [17-20]. A wavelet-based processing technique was employed to enhance the contrast of significant features in the image, and to identify ROIs from which textural features were extracted. Forward stepwise logistic regression analysis was then implemented to determine the best combination of textural features and to characterize endometrial tissue.

Both endometrium and endometrium margin seem to possess significant textural information that can efficiently distinguish malignant from benign endometrium tissue. However, the combination of textural features from both regions yields the best classification performance.

It was suggested that the computer aided classification of the endometrial tissue, based on texture-based features, can contribute to a correct diagnosis of endometrial malignancy and thereby potentially help reduce unnecessary biopsies.

However, the reported results are preliminary and additional work is required to improve performance of the proposed method. Future efforts will focus on validating the proposed method using a larger dataset and by examining cases of blind histology. Future work will focus on investigating the potential increase in the diagnostic accuracy of TVS by combining computerized textural features with orientation features and by using other classification methods.

5 Acknowledgements

The authors would like to thank the staff of the Department of Radiology at the University Hospital of Patras for their contribution in this work.

References

1. S.L. Parker, T. Tong, S. Bolden, P.A. Wingo, Cancer Statistics, *CA Cancer J. Clin.* **46**, 5-27 (1996).
2. T.J. Dubinsky, Value of Sonography in the diagnosis of abnormal vaginal bleeding, *J. Clin. Ultras.* **32**, 348-353 (2004).
3. J.K. Gupta, P.F.W. Chien, D. Voit, T.J. Clark, K.S. Khan, Ultrasonographic endometrial thickness for diagnosing endometrial pathology in women with postmenopausal bleeding: a meta-analysis, *Acta Obstetr. et Gynec. Scand.* **81**, 799-816 (2002).
4. M. Weigel, K. Friese, F. Strittmatter, F. Melchert, Measuring the thickness-Is that all we have to do for sonographic assessment of endometrium in postmenopausal women? *Ultras. Obstet. Gynecol.* **6** 97–102 (1995).
5. G. Weber, E. Merz, F. Bahlmann, B. Rösch, Evaluation of different transvaginal sonographic diagnostic parameters in women with postmenopausal bleeding, *Ultras. Obstet. Gynecol.* **12**, 265-270 (1998).
6. B. Randelzhofer, H.J. Prompler, W. Sauerbrei, H. Madjar, G. Emons, Value of sonomorphologic criteria of the endometrium in women with postmenopausal bleeding: a multivariate analysis, *Ultrasound. Obstet. Gynecol.* **19**, 62-68 (2002).
7. Z. Leibovitz, S. Degani, R. Rabia, J. Tal, I. Eibchitz, I. Shapiro, Y. Paltieli, A. Aharoni, M. Steinkuler, G. Ohel, Endometrium-to-myometrium relative echogenicity coefficient. A new sonographic approach for the quantitative assessment of endometrial echogenicity. *Gynecol. Obstet. Invest.* **45**, 121-125 (1998).
8. R. Fanchin, C. Righini, J.M. Ayoubi, F. Olivennes, D. de Ziegler, R. Frydman, New look at the endometrial echogenicity: objective computer–assisted measurements predict endometrial receptivity in vitro fertilization – embryo transfer, *Fertil. Steril.* **74**, 274-280 (2000).
9. C.H. Yang, P.C. Chung, Y.C. Tsai, Endometrium estimation in a sequence of ultrasonic images, *Comput. Med. Imag. Graph.* **25**, 335-342 (2001).

10. P. Sakellaropoulos, L. Costaridou, G. Panayiotakis, A wavelet-based spatially adaptive method for mammographic contrast enhancement, *Phys. Med. Biol.* **48**, 787-803 (2003).
11. L. Costaridou, P. Sakellaropoulos, S. Skiadopoulos, G. Panayiotakis, Locally adaptive wavelet contrast enhancement. In: Medical Image Analysis Methods, edited by L. Costaridou (Taylor & Francis Group LCC, CRC Press: Boca Raton, FL, 2005), pp. 225-270.
12. P. Sakellaropoulos, L. Costaridou, G. Panayiotakis, An image visualization tool in mammography, *Med. Inform.* **24**, 53-73 (1999).
13. P. Sakellaropoulos, L. Costaridou, G. Panayiotakis, Using component technologies for web based wavelet enhanced mammographic image visualization, *Med. Inform.* **25**, 171-181 (2000).
14. R.M. Haralick, K. Shanmugam, I. Dinstein, Textural features for image classification, *IEEE Trans. Syst. Man. Cybern.* **3**, 610–621 (1973).
15. R.F. Walker, P. Jackway, I.D. Longstaff, Improving Co-occurrence Matrix Feature Discrimination, in: Proc. of the 3rd Conference on Digital Image Computing: Techniques and Applications, 643-648 (1995).
16. S. Menard, *Applied Logistic Regression Analysis* (Sage Publications, Thousand Oaks, CA, 2002).
17. H. Yoshida, D.D. Casalino, B. Keserci, A. Coskun, O. Ozturk, A. Savranlar, Wavelet-packet-based texture analysis for differentiation between benign and malignant liver tumours in ultrasound images, *Phys. Med. Biol.* **48**, 3735-3753 (2003).
18. R. Sivaramakrishna, K.A. Powell, M.L. Lieber, W.A. Chilcote, R. Shekhar, Texture analysis of lesions in breast ultrasound images, *Comput. Med. Imag. Graph.* **26**, 303-307 (2002).
19. D. Smutek, R. Sara, P. Sucharda, T. Tjahjadi, M. Svec, Image texture analysis of sonograms in chronic inflammations of thyroid gland, *Ultras. Med. Biol.* **29**, 1531-1543 (2003).
20. C.I. Christodoulou, C.S. Pattichis, E. Kyriacou, M.S. Pattichis, M. Pantziaris, A. Nicolaides, Texture and morphological analysis of ultrasound images of the carotid plaque for the assessment of stroke, in: Medical Image Analysis Methods, edited by L. Costaridou (Taylor & Francis Group LLC, CRC Press: Boca Raton, FL, 2005), pp. 87-135.

Wavelet-based Feature Analysis for Classification of Breast Masses from Normal Dense Tissue

Filippos Sakellaropoulos, Spyros Skiadopoulos, Anna Karahaliou, George Panayiotakis, and Lena Costaridou

Department of Medical Physics, School of Medicine, University of Patras, 265 00 Patras, Greece
costarid@upatras.gr

Abstract. Automated detection of masses on mammograms is challenged by the presence of dense breast parenchyma. The aim of this study was to investigate the feasibility of using wavelet-based feature analysis for differentiating masses, of varying sizes, from normal dense tissue on mammograms. The dataset analyzed consists of 166 regions of interest (ROIs) containing spiculated masses (60), circumscribed masses (40) and normal dense tissue (66). A set of ten multiscale features, based on intensity, texture and edge variations, were extracted from the ROIs subimages provided by the overcomplete wavelet transform. Logistic regression analysis was employed to determine the optimal multiscale features for differentiating masses from normal dense tissue. The classification accuracy in differentiating circumscribed masses from normal dense tissue is comparable with the corresponding accuracy in differentiating spiculated masses from normal dense tissue, achieving areas under the ROC curve 0.895 and 0.875, respectively.

1 Introduction

Breast cancer is the most prevalent cancer among women [1]. While screen/film mammography is currently the primary imaging technique for early detection and diagnosis of breast cancer, its high diagnostic performance is challenged by occult disease signs (masses and/or microcalcifications) due to the masking effect of dense breast parenchyma, often both characterized by quite similar radiographic densities [2,3]. While microcalcification clusters are indicative of early malignant processes, masses are the most important signs for detection of invasive breast cancer, with their extent being a very important prognostic factor. Masses can be described as more or less compact areas that appear brighter (radiopaque) than the parenchymal

Please use the following format when citing this chapter:

Sakellaropoulos, Filippos, Skiadopoulos, Spyros, Karahaliou, Anna, Panayiotakis, George, Costaridou, Lena, 2006, in IFIP International Federation for Information Processing, Volume 204, Artificial Intelligence Applications and Innovations, eds. Maglogiannis, I., Karpouzis, K., Bramer, M., (Boston: Springer), pp. 722–729

tissue. The major morphological categories of masses are spiculated and circumscribed [4].

Various features in combination with classification methods have been proposed for automated mass detection. Kegelmeyer et al. [5] have introduced edge orientation features based on local edge orientation histogram analysis as well as Laws' texture energy measures to identify spiculated mass containing areas. Chan et al. [6,7] proposed multiresolution texture analysis extracted from spatial Gray Level Dependence Matrices (GLDM) for differentiation of masses from normal tissue. Later on, Liu et al. [8] extended mass edge orientation analysis with a multiresolution scheme for the detection of spiculated masses. Linear phase non-separable 2D wavelet transform (WT) was used to extract features at each resolution on a pixel basis. Petrick et al [9] and Kobatake et al. [10] have utilized a combination of boundary (morphological) and multiresolution texture features (GLDM analysis) to identify and segment the extent of masses, respectively. Another approach in differentiating mass containing areas from normal tissue refers to area patterns constructed using principal component, independent component and factor analyses [11,12].

The performance of the proposed mass detection methods is characterized by high sensitivity (84-96%) and is challenged by the high number of false positive detections per image (1.0-4.4), especially in case of dense tissue [13,14].

The aim of this study is to investigate discriminant features for mass detection in a demanding mass dataset. To capture significant information from intensity, texture and edges of masses of various sizes and to differentiate them from normal dense tissue, histogram, texture and orientation-based features were extracted from the coefficients of an overcomplete wavelet transform. Stepwise forward logistic regression analysis was employed to determine the most discriminating subset of features in differentiating: (a) spiculated masses from normal dense tissue, (b) circumscribed masses from normal dense tissue and (c) both types of masses from normal dense tissue. The performance of the logistic regression models is evaluated by means of Receiver Operating Characteristic (ROC) analysis.

2 Materials and Methods

2.1 Case Sample

Mammographic images corresponding to extremely dense or heterogeneously dense (density 3 and 4, according to BIRADS lexicon) originating from the Digital Database for Screening Mammography (DDSM) of the University of South Florida [15] were selected. Images were digitized with Lumisys or Howtek scanner, at 12 bits pixel depth with spatial resolution of 50 μm and 43.5 μm, respectively. Regions of interest (ROIs) were selected with an image visualization tool developed in our department [16]. The sample consists of 166 ROIs, 60 ROIs containing spiculated masses, 40 ROIs containing circumscribed masses and 66 ROIs of normal dense tissue. The mean size (longest dimension) was 19 mm (range: 7-49 mm) and 12 mm (range: 6-31 mm) for spiculated and circumscribed masses, respectively. Histogram of mass subtlety (from 1=subtle to 5=obvious), according to DDSM database, is provided in Figure 1.

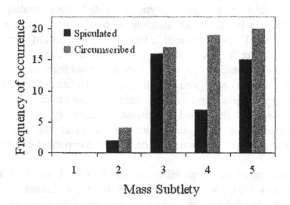

Fig. 1. Histogram of subtlety for spiculated and circumscribed masses of the sample.

2.2 Wavelet Transform

A fast, biorthogonal, Redundant Discrete Wavelet Transform (RDWT), originally used to derive multiscale edges from signals, is utilized in this work. It is based on a family of wavelet functions $\psi(x)$ with compact support, which are derivatives of corresponding Gaussian-like spline functions $\theta(x)$. The algorithm is implemented using a filter bank algorithm, called "algorithm a trous" [17,18], which does not involve subsampling. The discrete wavelet transform is a uniform sampling of the wavelet transform series, discretized over the scale parameter s at dyadic scales 2^j (wavelet transform series). [17,18]. The RDWT is calculated up to a coarse dyadic scale J. Therefore, the original image is decomposed into a multiresolution hierarchy of subband images, consisting of a coarse approximation image $S_{2^j}f(m,n)$ and a set of wavelet images $\left(W_{2^j}^1 f(m,n), W_{2^j}^2 f(m,n)\right)_{1 \leq j \leq J}$, which provide the details that are available in $S_1 f$ but have disappeared in $S_{2^j} f$. All subband images have the same number of pixels as the original, thus the representation is highly redundant. The RDWT computes the multiscale gradient vector. Coefficient subband images are proportional to the sampled horizontal and vertical components of the multiscale gradient vector, and thus they are related to local contrast [19]. The magnitude-orientation representation of the gradient vector, in the discrete case, is given by:

$$M_{2^j}(m,n) = \sqrt{\left|W_{2^j}^1(m,n)\right|^2 + \left|W_{2^j}^2(m,n)\right|^2} \ , \ A_{2^j}(m,n) = \arctan\left(\frac{W_{2^j}^2(m,n)}{W_{2^j}^1(m,n)}\right) \qquad (1)$$

2.3 Feature Extraction

The aim was to capture significant information from intensity, texture and edges of masses for their differentiation from normal dense tissue. Information from intensity, texture and edges from each ROI, containing spiculated or circumscribed mass, was extracted by means of histogram, texture and orientation features, respectively.

2.3.1 Histogram-based Features

Significant information from intensity variations was extracted by computing features based on histogram of low-frequency band (approximation image) for each ROI at three resolution scales (three to five). These features depend only on individual pixel values and not on the interaction or co-occurrence of neighboring pixel values. In this study, four features corresponding to the four moments of each ROI subimage histogram were calculated: Mean value, Standard Deviation, Skewness and Kurtosis.

2.3.2 Texture-based Features

Laws' texture energy features have been computed by first applying small convolution kernels to ROI subimages, and then performing a nonlinear windowing operation. In this study, the most discriminant set of convolution kernels [5] were used: L5*E5, E5*S5, L5*S5 and R5*R5, for texture discrimination between masses and normal dense tissue.

2.3.3 Orientation-based Features

To capture significant information from mass edges, two multiscale gradient-orientation features were extracted from each ROI:
- Standard Deviation of Gradient-Orientation [5,8]:

$$\sigma_{\text{hist}}(i,j) = \sqrt{\frac{1}{255}\sum_{n=0}^{255}\left(\text{hist}_{ij}(n) - \overline{\text{hist}_{ij}}\right)^2} \qquad (2)$$

where $hist_{ij}$ is the histogram of gradient orientations θ, calculated from high-frequency wavelet coefficients (detailed orientation image) for three scales (three to five), within $N(i,j)$ using 256 orientations (bins). Therefore, $hist_{ij}(n)$ is the number of pixels in $N(i,j)$ that have gradient orientations $\theta \in (-\pi/2 + n\pi/256, -\pi/2 + (n+1)\pi/256)$ where $n=0,1,2,...,255$. $\overline{\text{hist}_{ij}} = \frac{1}{256}\sum_{n=0}^{255}\text{hist}_{ij}(n)$ is the average bin height of $hist_{ij}$.

- Standard Deviation of Folded Gradient-Orientation [8]:

$$\sigma_\beta(i,j) = \sqrt{\frac{1}{K-1}\sum_{(m,n)\in N(i,j)}\left(\beta(m,n) - \overline{\beta(i,j)}\right)^2} \qquad (3)$$

where the folded gradient orientation $\beta\ (i,\ j)$ is defined as:

$$\beta(i,j) = \begin{cases} \theta(i,j) + \pi & \text{if } \overline{\theta_+}(i,j) - \theta(i,j) > \frac{\pi}{2} \text{ and } KP \geq KN \\ \theta(i,j) - \pi & \text{if } \theta(i,j) - \overline{\theta_-}(i,j) > \frac{\pi}{2} \text{ and } KP < KN \\ \theta(i,j) & \text{otherwise} \end{cases} \tag{4}$$

where

$$\overline{\theta_+(i,j)} = \frac{1}{KP} \sum_{\theta(m,n) \geq 0, (m,n) \in N(i,j)} \theta(m,n), \ \overline{\theta_-(i,j)} = \frac{1}{KN} \sum_{\theta(m,n) \leq 0, (m,n) \in N(i,j)} \theta(m,n) \tag{5}$$

are the mean values of positive and negative gradient orientations within $N(i,j)$, respectively. KP and KN are the number of positive and negative gradient orientations within $N(i,j)$, respectively.

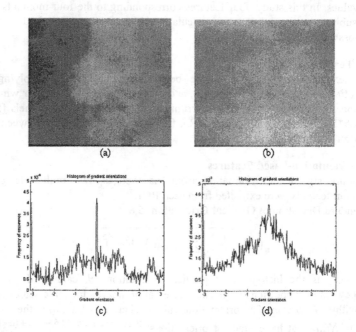

Fig. 2. Regions of a spiculated mass (B-3390_LCC) (a) and a normal dense tissue (C-0166_LCC) (b) as well as their gradient orientation histograms respectively (c and d).

Figure 2 provides two regions of mammograms, one with a spiculated mass (fig. 2a) and one with normal tissue (fig. 2b), along with their corresponding normalized gradient-orientation histograms (fig. 2c, 2d). The directions of spicules of the mass differ from the directions of normal tissue. Specifically, pixels at normal areas have gradient orientations pointing to a certain direction range, while pixels at spiculated masses tend to have gradient orientations distributed in more directions. Therefore, the standard deviation of gradient orientations in the neighborhood of a mass pixel will be larger than that in the neighborhood of a normal pixel. As a result, the gradient orientation histogram is flat near a mass area (fig. 2c), but has a peak in areas containing normal dense tissue (fig. 2d).

2.4 Mass vs. Normal Tissue Classification

Logistic regression analysis was employed to determine the optimal subset of features that can differentiate masses from normal dense tissue. Specifically, feature-based logistic regression model was constructed by means of the forward feature selection method based on the area under ROC curve (Az) as a feature performance metric. The feature with the best Az value is first entered in the logistic regression model. The second feature selected is the one that in conjunction with the first feature yields the highest Az value among the remaining features. This process continues until no significant increase in terms of Az value is offered by adding features. After logistic regression model construction the half-half training and testing methodology was applied. The performance of the logistic regression model was evaluated in terms of Az area and standard error.

To study the effect of mass type (spiculated and circumscribed) in classification accuracy, logistic regression models were constructed for three differentiation tasks: (a) spiculated masses from normal dense tissue (S-N), (b) circumscribed masses from normal dense tissue (C-N) and (c) both spiculated and circumscribed masses from normal dense tissue (B-N).

3 Results

The ROC curves produced from the feature-based logistic regression models for the three differentiation tasks are presented in Figure 3. The Az values are 0.895 0.036, 0.875 0.033 and 0.813 0.032 for the C-N, S-N and the B-N datasets, respectively.

The differences in Az values between C-N and B-N, as well as between S-N and B-N are statistically significant (two-tailed student's t-test, $p<0.05$), indicating the reduction in classification accuracy when all masses (spiculated and circumscribed) are considered in the differentiation task.

4 Discussion and Conclusion

Our preliminary results suggest that histogram, texture and orientation-based features extracted from the coefficients of an overcomplete wavelet transform in combination with logistic regression analysis can provide a successful classification scheme for the detection of spiculated and circumscribed masses in dense parenchyma, as proved by ROC analysis. The most discriminating features seem to be the Skewness, Standard Deviation of Gradient-Orientation and Standard Deviation of Folded

Gradient-Orientation. On the other hand, Laws' texture measures do not possess any significant information, although they have been used in similar classification tasks [5].

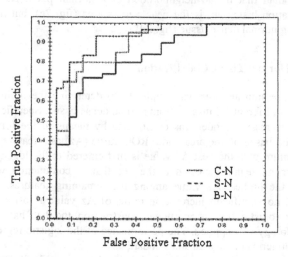

False Positive Fraction

Fig. 3. The ROC curves for mass classification in the three differentiation tasks.

The performances (Az values) achieved in the mass classification accuracy are higher than those reported in other studies for dense breast category [13,14]. These encouraging results are in support of further development of the proposed method into a fully automated mass detection method. Future efforts will focus on: (a) extraction of additional features (e.g. coherence, entropy), (b) use of other classification techniques and (c) validation using a larger dataset.

5 Acknowledgements

We would like to thank the European Social Fund (ESF), Operational Program for Educational and Vocational Training II (EPEAEK II), and particularly the Program PYTHAGORAS I (B.365.011), for funding the above work.

References

1. R.T., Greenlee, M.B. Hill-Harmon, T. Murray, M. Thun, Cancer statistics CA. Cancer J. Clin. 51, 15-36 (2001).
2. J. Heine, P. Malhotra, Mammographic tissue, breast cancer risk, serial image analysis and digital mammography, Acad. Radiol. 9, 298-316 (2002).
3. L. Costaridou, S. Skiadopoulos, P. Sakellaropoulos, C.P. Kalogeropoulou, E. Likaki, G. Panayiotakis, Evaluating the effect of a wavelet enhancement method in characterization of simulated lesions embedded in dense breast parenchyma, Eur. Radiol. 15, 1615-1622 (2005).

4. W. Dahnert, Breast, in: Radiology Review Manual, edited by W. Dahnert (Williams and Wilkins, Baltimore, 1996), pp. 402-418.
5. J. Kegelmeyer, J.M. Pruneda, P.D. Bourland, A. Hillis, M.W. Riggs, M.L. Nipper, Computer-aided mammographic screening for spiculated lesions, Radiology 191, 331–337 (1994).
6. D. Wei, H-P. Chan, M.A. Helvie, B. Sahiner, N. Petrick, D.D. Adler, M.M. Goodsitt, Classification of mass and normal breast tissue on digital mammograms: Multiresolution texture analysis, Med. Phys. 22, 1501-1513 (1995).
7. D. Wei, H-P. Chan, N. Petrick, B. Sahiner, M.A. Helvie, D.D. Adler, M.M. Goodsitt, False-positive reduction technique for detection of masses on digital mammograms: Global and local multiresolution texture analysis, Med. Phys. 24, 903-914 (1997).
8. S. Liu, C.F. Babbs, E.J. Delp, Multiresolution detection of spiculated lesions in digital mammograms, IEEE Trans. Image Proc. 10, 874-884 (2001).
9. N. Petrick, H-P. Chan, D. Wei, B. Sahiner, M.A. Helvie, D.D. Adler, Automated detection of breast masses on mammograms using adaptive contrast enhancement and texture classification, Med. Phys. 23, 1685-1696 (1996).
10. H. Kobatake, M. Murakami, H. Takeo, S. Nawano, Computerized detection of malignant tumors on digital mammograms, IEEE Trans. Med. Imaging 18, 369-378 (1999).
11. R. Zwiggelaar, T.C. Parr, J.E. Schumm, I.W. Hutt, C.J. Taylor, S.M. Astley, C.R.M. Boggis, Model-based detection of spiculated lesions in mammograms, Med. Im. Anal. 3, 39-62 (1999).
12. I. Christoyianni, A. Koutras, E. Dermatas, G. Kokkinakis, Computer aided diagnosis of breast cancers in digitized mammograms, Comp. Med. Im. Graph. 26, 309-319 (2002).
13. W.T. Ho, P.W.T. Lam, Clinical performance of computer-assisted detection (CAD) system in detecting carcinoma in breast of different densities, Clin. Radiol. 58, 133-136 (2003).
14. G.D. Tourassi, R. Vargas-Voracek, D.M. Catarious, C.E. Floyd, Computer-assisted detection of mammographic masses: A template matching scheme based on mutual information, Med. Phys. 30, 2123-2130 (2003).
15. M. Heath, K. Bowyer, D. Kopans, R. Moore, R. Kegelmeyer, The digital database for screening mammography. in: Proceedings of 5th International Workshop on Digital Mammography, edited by M.J. Yaffe (Medical Physics Publishing, Madison, WI, 2000), pp. 212-218.
16. P. Sakellaropoulos, L. Costaridou, G. Panayiotakis, An image visualization tool in mammography, Med. Inform. 24, 53-73 (1999).
17. P. Sakellaropoulos, L. Costaridou, G. Panayiotakis, A wavelet-based spatially adaptive method for mammographic contrast enhancement, Phys. Med. Biol. 48, 787-803 (2003).
18. L. Costaridou, P. Sakellaropoulos, S. Skiadopoulos, G. Panayiotakis, Locally adaptive wavelet contrast enhancement. In: Medical Image Analysis Methods, edited by L. Costaridou (Taylor & Francis Group LCC, CRC Press: Boca Raton, FL, 2005), pp. 225-270.
19. L. Costaridou, P. Sakellaropoulos, A. Stefanoyiannis, E. Ungureanu, G. Panayiotakis, Quantifying image quality at breast periphery vs. mammary gland in mammography using wavelet analysis, Br. J. Radiol. 74, 913-919 (2001).

Microcalcification Features Extracted from Principal Component Analysis in the Wavelet Domain

Nikolaos Arikidis, Spyros Skiadopoulos, Filippos Sakellaropoulos, George Panayiotakis, and Lena Costaridou

Department of Medical Physics, School of Medicine, University of Patras, Patras, Greece, 265 00 Patras, Greece

costarid@upatras.gr

Abstract. In presence of dense mammographic parenchyma, microcalcifications (MCs) are obscured by anatomical structures, resulting in missed or/and false detections. Image analysis methods applied to improve visualization, detection and/or characterization of MCs, are targeted to MC SNR improvement and are unavoidably accompanied by MC background over-enhancement or false positive (FP) detections. A set of new features is proposed, extracted statistically with Principal Component Analysis from the wavelet coefficients of real subtle MCs in dense parenchyma. Candidate MCs are segmented and classified with the proposed features, using Linear Discriminant Analysis. Our method achieved 69% true positive fraction of MC clusters with 0.2 FPs per image in a dataset with 54 subtle MC clusters in extremely dense parenchyma.

1 Introduction

Mammography is currently the technique with the highest sensitivity available for early detection of breast cancer on asymptomatic women [1]. Detecting the disease in its early stages increases the rate of survival and improves quality of patient's life [2]. Detection of early signs of disease, such as microcalcifications (MCs), with screening mammography, is a particularly demanding task for radiologists. This is attributed to the high-volume of images reviewed, as well as the MC low contrast resolution, limited by their size, especially in case of dense breast, accounting for about 25% of the younger female population [3]. Although many analysis methods are reported [4], capable of enhancing or identifying specific image details as MCs, the most promising ones based on the wavelet transform, they typically produce disturbing background over-enhancement or false positive (FP) detections.

Please use the following format when citing this chapter:

Arikidis, Nikolaos, Skiadopoulos, Spyros, Sakellaropoulos, Filippos, Panayiotakis, George, Costaridou, Lena, 2006, in IFIP International Federation for Information Processing, Volume 204, Artificial Intelligence Applications and Innovations, eds. Maglogiannis, I., Karpouzis, K., Bramer, M., (Boston: Springer), pp. 730–736

In the framework of the wavelet transform, MCs contain relatively large amounts of high spatial frequency information. However, a large component of the power in a mammogram at high spatial frequencies is also noise [5,6] (dense tissue structure and film artifacts). Netch *et al.* [7], based on the circularly symmetric Gaussian model, used a Laplacian kernel to detect MCs as local maxima at different frequency bands. Strickland et al. [8] have shown that the average 2D gray level profile of MCs is well described by a circularly symmetric Gaussian function. Since the optimum detector of Gaussian functions is the Laplacian of Gaussian, they used a wavelet filter close to the Laplacian of Gaussian to detect significant peak responses to objects of similar shape and of the same size as the Gaussian filter. Soft or hard thresholding was used to set to zero the low amplitude wavelet coefficients, mostly dominated by noise. Other researchers [9-11] used globally or locally adapted linear enhancement functions to enhance high amplitude coefficients, corresponding to MCs, at various frequency bands. These methods assume statistical properties for the anatomical structure, which acts as structure noise in visualization (detection and/or characterization) of abnormalities.

Structure noise, especially in dense parenchyma, is highly correlated with abnormalities, such as MCs, producing wavelet coefficients comparable with those corresponding to MCs [12,13]. A method to describe the correlated noise is Principal Component Analysis (PCA), which replaces unknown image patterns with the linear combination of known image patterns and it is used for compression, classification or noise reduction tasks [14-17].

An MC specific method is proposed that detects image regions with very low contrast and uses a local method, trained by real MCs, to separate MC regions from structure noise and film artifacts.

2 Materials and Methods

One of the most successful paradigms of medical image analysis in mammography is Computer-Aided Detection (CADetection) systems for MC clusters [18]. The typical architecture of such a system [19] consists of a preprocessing step to increase MC SNR and segmentation of candidate MCs. Following, features of candidate MC regions are extracted and a classifier is trained for differentiating MCs from other image components. In a last step, a criterion is used to find only MCs that form clusters. In our approach, new features are suggested based on PCA of the wavelet coefficients of real MCs, capable of identifying individual MCs.

2.1 MC Eigen-Image Features in the Wavelet Domain

PCA is a mathematical tool that can find principal components from a set of real MC regions. Those principal components can be thought of as a set of images [15], named MC eigen-images, which together characterize the variation of MC regions. Then, each MC region is represented by the linear combination of the MC eigen-images weights. For an unknown image, the segmented regions are replaced by the MC eigen-image weights and are classified.

Let a MC region $I(x,y)$ be a two-dimensional N by N array, considered as a one-dimensional vector with length N^2. Considering a horizontal vector $D=\{d_1,...,d_L\}$, of L images of dimension N^2 and denote $M=\{\mu_1,...,\mu_L\}$ the mean vector of the population D (μ_λ is the mean of the λth image d_λ, where $\lambda=1...L$).

The covariance matrix C of D is defined by:

$$C = (D - M)(D - M)^t \tag{1}$$

where $(D\text{-}M)^t$ is the transposed matrix of $(D\text{-}M)$ and its size is of order $N^2 \times N^2$. To all vectors $x_v=\{d_1(v),...,d_L(v)\}$ (where $v=1,...,N^2$) the following transform is applied:

$$y_{v,k} = (x_v - M) \cdot A_k \tag{2}$$

where A is a matrix whose columns $k=1...L$ are formed from the eigenvectors of C [20], named MC eigen-images, ordered following the monotonic decreasing order of eigenvalues.

The wavelet transform can be considered as a mathematical microscope that emphasizes on image details, where the scale defines the detail size. Wavelet analysis is performed with Mallat's dyadic wavelet transform [21]. When the wavelet filter $W_s f(x)$ is selected as the second derivative of the signal smoothed at scale j, high amplitude wavelet coefficients correlate with high curvatures. Gaussian functions, like MCs, are high curvature components at both vertical and horizontal direction and they can be differentiated from line-like structures. MCs have been highly correlated with the wavelet coefficients at scales 2 and 3 [10,22]. Thus, each MC region is replaced by four representations, which are the horizontal and vertical wavelet coefficients at the 2nd and 3rd scale (figure 1).

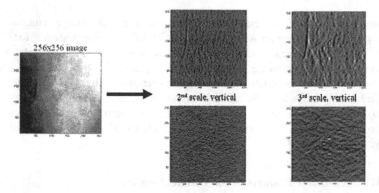

Fig. 1. The original image and its four (4) representations in the wavelet domain

When the wavelet transform is combined with PCA, the wavelet coefficients are used instead of using the pixel values to calculate the correlation matrix C [23]. The input data set d_v at the vth pixel is replaced by the wavelet coefficients $W_j^{(v)}$ for each scale j of the wavelet transform.

The correlation matrix $C^{(j)}$ is calculated relative to the horizontal vector:

$$x_j = \left\{ W_j^{(1)}, W_j^{(2)}, ..., W_j^{(N^2)} \right\}. \tag{3}$$

For each band j, the transform matrix A^j contains the eigenvectors of C^j, which are the wavelet-based MC eigen-images (figure 2). Applying the matrix A^j to the λth image, representing by the horizontal vector x_λ^j, the data are transformed to y_k^j:

$$y_k^j = (x_\lambda^j - M^j) \cdot A_k^j \tag{4}$$

where y_k^j is the projection of the wavelet coefficients x_λ^j to the kth principal component.

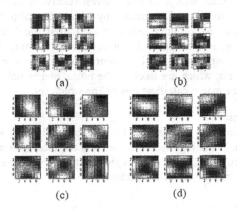

(a)   (b)

(c)   (d)

Fig. 2. Principal components (MC eigen-images) of the 2nd scale in the (a) horizontal and (b) vertical directions; and of the 3rd scale in the (c) horizontal and (d) vertical directions, respectively

Each MC eigen-image explains an amount of the variability of the MC regions, by the variance. The variability Vk is the variance of the kth MC eigen-image [24]:

$$V_k = \mathrm{var}\left(y_k^j\right) \tag{5}$$

and can be measured as a percentage of the total variability. Nine (9) MC eigen-images are selected at each scale and direction, which accounts about 98% of MC regions variability.

The processing steps for MC eigen-images extraction are the following:

• 41 MC regions with sizes below 0.5mm, random shapes and contrasts were selected from an experienced radiologist specialized in mammography, as the training dataset.

- The MC regions are represented at the wavelet domain by the vertical and horizontal wavelet coefficients. At the 2nd scale, the MC region has 5x5 pixels size and at the 3rd scale, the MC region has 9x9 pixels size.
- From each scale and direction, 9 eigen-images are selected to describe 98% of MC regions variation. A total of 36 eigen-images are used as features to recognize MC regions from other image components.

2.2 CADetection for MCs

2.2.1 Segmentation of Candidate MC Regions

MCs are very small structures, visible as small bright spots in the mammogram, because their mass attenuation coefficient is higher than any other structure in the breast. However, due to the growth of the MCs, there is no absolute lower bound to their contrast. Very small MCs have low contrast relative to the background, which is sometimes close to the noise caused by either the film granularity or the inhomogeneous tissue background. Morrow [25] used the Weber ratio (2%) to segment MC regions. In our approach, an even lower contrast threshold criterion (0.5%) is proposed pointing at very low contrast MCs. The size criterion excludes signals below 3 pixels, which are likely to be noise, and signals above 100 pixels, which are likely to be macro-calcifications or line structures.

2.2.2 Feature Extraction

Candidate MC regions are analyzed at the 2nd and 3rd scale, at the vertical and horizontal direction. Those regions are centered at the local maxima positions of the wavelet coefficients. Then, they are projected at the MC eigen-images and the resulting weights form a vector with 36 features.

2.2.3 Classification

Linear Discriminant Analysis was used to classify candidate MC feature vectors in three classes – individual MCs, film artifacts and structure noise. The training set consisted of the dataset used in MC eigen-image extraction, as well as 20 verified film artifact regions and a large number of noisy structures.

2.2.4 Clustering

Because isolated MCs are not clinically significant, the detection of clustered MCs is of paramount importance. Typically, at least 5 MCs per square centimeter are required to be considered a cluster, but three suspicious MCs could be enough to prompt a biopsy [26]. In our method, a cluster is defined and considered as a true positive (TP) when at least three candidate MCs have Euclidean distance less than 5mm.

3 Results

The method was tested on a dataset of 53 images. Specifically, 16 images were normal and 37 images contained 54 subtle MC clusters (46 malignant, 8 benign) in extremely dense parenchyma (density 4 of ACR BIRADS) with 12-bit pixel depth originating from Digital Database for Screen Mammography (DDSM) [27]. TP and FP clusters were counted for each mammogram and the number of FP clusters per image and the corresponding number of TP clusters are determined from an expert radiologist specialized in mammography. Our method achieved 69% TP fraction from 54 MC clusters with 0.2 FPs per image.

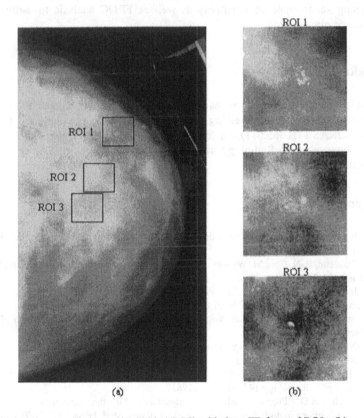

(a)   (b)

Fig. 3. (a) Mammographic image (A-1220_1.RCC) with three TP detected ROIs. (b) Magnified ROIs (176x178 pixels size) with an intensity windowing function applied.

A representative example with the detected MC clusters is presented in figure 3 (a). Figure 3 (b) provides the magnified image regions (176x178 pixels size), where a window intensity function has been applied to better visualize the detected MC clusters.

4 Discussion and Conclusion

New features for the detection of individual MCs, based on PCA in the wavelet domain, are proposed. PCA analyses the region statistics of real MCs to produce a new feature set, named MC eigen-images. Candidate MC regions are represented as weights of the MC eigen-images. The wavelet transform focuses on the analysis at scales 2 and 3, where the SNR of the MCs is increased.

The sensitivity of the detection algorithm is controlled by the dataset of real MC regions, used for principal component eigen images extraction. Compared to other studies [7,8], the achieved FP rate is extremely low, lending itself for further processing for detection or classification. A feature step is to add more subtle MCs in the training set to improve sensitivity as well as FROC analysis to estimate the performance optimization.

5 Acknowledgements

We would like to thank the European Social Fund (ESF), Operational Program for Educational and Vocational Training II (EPEAEK II), and particularly the Program PYTHAGORAS I (B.365.011), for funding the above work. We also thank the staff of the Department of Radiology at the University Hospital of Patras for their contribution in this work.

References

1. K. Smigel, Breast cancer death rates decline for white women, J. Nat. Cancer Inst. 87, 173 (1995).
2. L.A. Gaudette, R-N. Gao, M. Wysocki, F. Nault, Update on breast cancer mortality, Health Reports 9, 31-34 (1997).
3. V.P. Jackson, R.E. Hendrick, S.A. Feig, D.B. Kopans, Imaging of the radiographically dense breast, Radiology 188, 297-301 (1993).
4. R.N. Strickland, in: Image-Processing Techniques for Tumor Detection (Marcel Dekker Inc, New York, 2002)
5. R.M. Nishikawa, M.J. Yaffe, Signal-to-noise properties of mammographic film-screen systems, Med. Phys. 12, 32-39 (1985).
6. G.T. Barnes, D.P. Chakraborty, Radiographic mottle and patient exposure in mammography, Radiology 145, 815-821 (1982).
7. T. Netsch, H.O. Pitgen, Scale-space signatures for the detection of clustered microcalcifications in digital mammograms, IEEE Trans. Med. Imag. 18, 774-785 (1999).
8. R.N. Strickland, H.I. Hahn, Wavelet transforms for detecting microcalcifications in mammograms, IEEE Trans. Med. Imag. 15, 218-228 (1996).
9. P. Heinlein, J. Drexl, W. Schneider, Integrated wavelets for enhancement of microcalcifications in digital mammography, IEEE Trans. Med. Imag. 22, 402-413 (2003).
10.A.F. Laine, S. Schuler, J. Fan, W. Huda, Mammographic feature enhancement by multiscale analysis, IEEE Trans. Med. Imag. 13, 725-740 (1994).
11.P. Sakellaropoulos, L. Costaridou, G. Panayiotakis, A wavelet-based spatially adaptive method for mammographic contrast enhancement, Phys. Med. Biol. 48, 787-803 (2003).

Classification of Atherosclerotic Carotid Plaques Using Gray Level Morphological Analysis on Ultrasound images

E. Kyriacou [1,3], C.S. Pattichis [1], M.S. Pattichis [2], A. Mavrommatis[1],
S. Panagiotou[1], C.I. Christodoulou [1,3], S. Kakkos [4], A. Nicolaides [1,4,5]
[1]Department of Computer Science, University of Cyprus, 75 Kallipoleos
Str., P.O.Box 20578, 1678 Nicosia, Cyprus
ekyriac@ucy.ac.cy, pattichi@ucy.ac.cy,
Andreas.mavrommatis@itd.bankofcyprus.com, stavrpan@cytanet.com.cy,
cschr2@ucy.ac.cy, anicolai@cytanet.com.cy
[2]Department of Electrical and Computer Engineering, University of New
Mexico, Albuquerque, USA
pattichis@eece.unm.edu
[3]Cyprus Institute of Neurology and Genetics, Nicosia, Cyprus
[4]Department of Vascular Surgery, Faculty of Medicine, Imperial College,
University of London, London, UK
s.kakkos@imperial.ac.uk
[5]Vascular Screening and Diagnostic Centre, Nicosia, Cyprus

Abstract. The aim of this study was to investigate the usefulness of gray scale morphological analysis in the assessment of atherosclerotic carotid plagues. Ultrasound images were recorded from 137 asymptomatic and 137 symptomatic plaques (Stroke, Transient Ischaemic Attack -TIA, Amaurosis Fugax-AF). The morphological pattern spectra of gray scale images were computed and two different classifiers named the Probabilistic Neural Network (PNN) and the Support Vector Machine (SVM) were evaluated for classifying these spectra into two classes: asymptomatic or symptomatic. The highest percentage of correct classifications score was 66,8% and was achieved using the SVM classifier. This score is slightly lower than texture analysis carried out on the same data set.

1. Introduction

High-resolution ultrasound has made possible the noninvasive visualization of the carotid bifurcation and for that reason it has been extensively used in the study of arterial wall changes; these include measurement of the thickness of the intima

Please use the following format when citing this chapter:

Kyriacou, Efthyvoulos, Pattichis, Costas S., Pattichis, Marios S., Mavrommatis, Andreas, Panagiotou, Stavros, Christodoulou, Christodoulos, Kakkos, Stavros, Nicolaides, Andrew, 2006, in IFIP International Federation for Information Processing, Volume 204,Artificial Intelligence Applications and Innovations, eds. Maglogiannis, I., Karpouzis, K., Bramer, M., (Boston: Springer), pp. 737–744

media complex (IMT), estimation of the severity of stenosis due to atherosclerotic plaques and plaque characterization [1].

During the last decade, the introduction of computer aided methods and image standardization has improved the objective assessment of carotid plaque echogenicity, and heterogeneity [2], and has largely replaced subjective (visual) assessment [1], that had been criticized for its relatively poor reproducibility [3].

Previous studies investigated the usefulness of texture analysis [4-8], and more recently, multiscale morphological analysis was also used [6-9] towards the development of a Computer Aided Diagnostic (CAD) system for the classification of asymptomatic and symptomatic atherosclerotic plaques. These studies gave promising results.

Through this study we try to investigate gray scale morphological analysis in the aforementioned classification, and compare the findings with other studies.

The paper is structured as follows; section 2 describes the material, image acquisition, normalization and segmentation of plaque images. Sections 3 and 4 describe the gray scale morphological analysis and the classification algorithms, respectively. Section 5 gives the results and section 6 the concluding remarks.

2. Material, Image Acquisition, Normalization and Segmentation

A total of 274 carotid plaque ultrasound images (137 asymptomatic plaques and 137 symptomatic plaques associated with retinal or hemispheric symptoms (33 stroke, 60 TIA, and 44 AF). Patients with cardioembolic symptoms or distant symptoms (> 6 months) were excluded from the study. Asymptomatic plaques were truly asymptomatic if they had never been associated with symptoms in the past associated with retinal or hemispheric symptoms (Stroke, TIA or AF), i.e. unstable plaques.

The ultrasound images were collected in the Irvine Laboratory for Cardiovascular Investigation and Research, Saint Mary's Hospital, UK, using an ATL (model HDI 3000 - Advanced Technology Laboratories, Seattle, USA) duplex scanner with a linear broadband width 4-7 MHz (multifrequency) transducer, at approximately a resolution of 20 pixels/mm.

The images were normalized manually by adjusting the image linearly so that the median gray level value of blood was in the range of 0-5, and the median gray level of adventitia (artery wall) was in the range of 180-190 [10]. The scale of the gray level of the images ranged form 0 to 255. This normalization (i.e. using blood and adventitia as reference points) was necessary in order to extract comparable measurements in case of processing images obtained by different operators or different equipment [10].

The plaque identification and segmentation tasks are quite difficult and were carried out manually by a physician or vascular ultrasonographer who are experienced in scanning. The main difficulties are due to the fact that the plaque edges cannot be distinguished from blood based on brightness level difference, or using only texture features, or other measures. Also calcification and acoustic shadows make the problem more complex. Thus, acoustic shadows were excluded. A system for facilitating the automated segmentation of carotid plaque based on snakes is currently under development by our group [11].

3. Gray Scale Morphological Analysis

Morphological features are motivated from the need to study the basic structure of the plaque. In this study we used gray scale morphological analysis in order to identify morphological features of the plaques.

The morphological features of plaques are strongly associated with events. For example black (echolucent) plaques with white big blobs are considered to be very dangerous.

In morphological image processing, we proceed to characterize the size distributions of both the blob-components which appear white, and the hole-components which appear black. For describing these components, we consider a cross structural element ('+') that does not exhibit any directional selectivity. The size distribution measures the presence of blob components of radius proportional to the positive index of the Pattern Spectrum. Similarly, the size distribution of the presence of holes is proportional to the negative index of the Pattern Spectrum. We will next provide a mathematical description of the Pattern Spectrum.

We consider pattern spectra based on a flat '+' structural element B, made up of 5 pixels. The Pattern Spectrum is defined in terms of the Discrete Size Transform (DST). We define the DST [12-13] using the following equations:

$$f \to (d_0(f;B), d_1(f;B), \dots d_k(f;B)) \quad \text{where}$$

$$d_k(f;B) = f o k B - f o (k+1) B,$$

o denotes an open operation. The binary DST is a multi-resolution image decomposition scheme, which decomposes an image f into residual images $f \circ kB - f \circ (k+1)B$, for $k > 0$. The pattern spectrum of a binary image f, in terms of a structural element B, is given by:

$$P_{f;B}(k) = \|d_k(f;B)\| = \|f o k B - f o (k+1)B\|, k \ge 0 \quad \text{where}$$

$$\|f\| = \sum_{x,y} f(x,y), \quad f(x,y) \ge 0$$

We note that in the limit, as $k \to \infty$, we have that the resulting image $f \circ kB - f \circ (k+1)B$ converges to the zero image. Also, we note that with increasing values of k, $f \circ kB$ is a subset of the original image. For $k \ge 0$, we may thus normalize the Pattern Spectrum by dividing by the norm of the original image $\|f\|$. Similarly, as $k \to \infty$. Thus, to eliminate undesired variations, all the pattern spectra were normalized.

The pattern spectra were computed for gray scale images using a structural element of range 1 to 70. The probability density function *(pdf)* and the cumulative distribution function *(cdf)* were computed for each plaque. An example of an asymptomatic and a symptomatic plaque with the corresponding *pdf*s and *cdf*s is shown in Fig. 1.

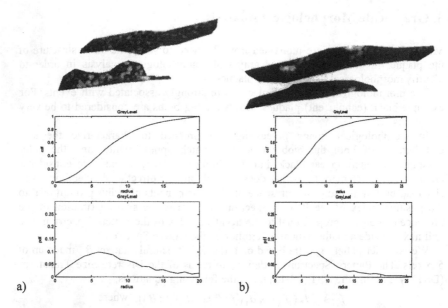

Fig. 1. a) Cumulative distribution function *(cdf)* plot and probability density function *(pdf)* for an asymptomatic carotid plaque. b) Cumulative distribution function *(cdf)* plot and probability density function *(pdf)* for a symptomatic (Stroke) carotid plaque.

4. Classification Models

The diagnostic performance of the morphological features was evaluated with two different classifiers: the Probabilistic Neural Network (PNN), and the Support Vector Machine (SVM). These classifiers were trained to classify the morphology features into two classes: i) asymptomatic plaques or ii) symptomatic plaques associated with retinal or hemispheric symptoms (Stroke, TIA or AF), i.e. unstable plaques.

The PNN [14] classifier basically is a kind of Radial Basis Function (RBF) network suitable for classification problems. This classifier was investigated for several spread radius in order to identify the best for the current problem. The SVM network was investigated using Gaussian Radial Basis Function (RBF) kernels; this was decided as the rest of the kernel functions could not achieve so good results. The SVM with RBF kernel was investigated using 10-fold cross validation in order to identify the best parameters such as spread of RBF [15].

The leave-one-out estimate was used for validating all the classification models. A total of 274 subsets of size 273 were used for training the classifiers, and the performance of the classifiers was evaluated on the remaining one subset.

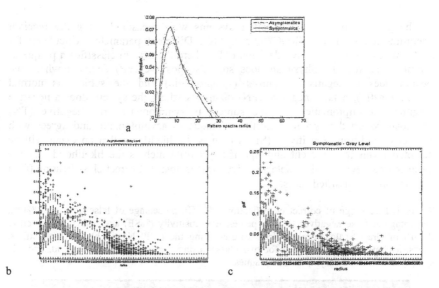

a

b   c

Fig. 2. a) Median probability density function *(pdf)* plots for the pattern spectra of gray scale images; symptomatic plot is plotted with a solid line while the asymptomatic one with a dotted line. b) Box plots of *pdf* for the asymptomatic carotid plaques. c) Box plots of *pdf* for the symptomatic carotid plaques. Box plots are described as follows: The notched box shows the median, lower and upper quartiles and confidence interval around the median for each feature. The dotted line connects the nearest observations within 1.5 of the inter-quartile range (IQR) of the lower and upper quartiles. Crosses (+) indicate possible outliers with values beyond the ends of the 1.5 x IQR.

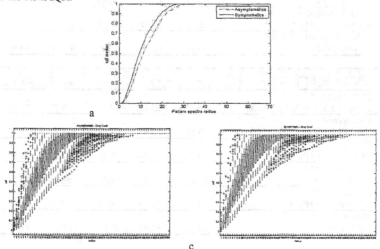

a

b   c

Fig. 3. a) Median cumulative distribution function *(cdf)* plots for the pattern spectra of gray scale images; symptomatic plot is plotted with a solid line while the asymptomatic one with a dotted line. b) Box plots of *cdf* for the asymptomatic carotid plaques. c) Box plots of *cdf* for the symptomatic carotid plaques.

The performance of the classifier systems were measured using the receiver operating characteristics (ROC) curves [16]. Different parameters calculated for ROC curves are true positive decision (TP) where the system classifies a plaque as symptomatic and the physician does so, false positive (FP) decision where the system does a negative diagnosis (symptomatic) and the subject is normal (asymptomatic), a false negative (FN) diagnosis where the system does a negative diagnosis (asymptomatic) and the subject is symptomatic, true negative (TN) diagnosis where the system identifies a plaque as asymptomatic and agrees with subject's condition. Sensitivity (SE) which is the likelihood that an event will be detected given it is present and Specificity (SP) which is the likelihood that the absence of an event will be detected given that is absent. Correct classification (CC) are the correct classified cases.

Table 1. Percentage of correct classifications (%CC), percentage of false positives (%FP), percentage of false negatives (%FN), percentage sensitivity (%SE) and percentage specifity (%SP) of Gray Scale morphological features using the a) PNN and b) SVM classifiers. Classification models developed for two classes using the leave one out method, and 137 symptomatic and 137 asymptomatic plaques.

SVM classifier	%CC	%FP	%FN	%SE	%SP
SVM rbf spread = 2.2627 *pdf* radii 2,3,5,10,21,23 +**PCA**	**66.79**	20.44	45.99	54.01	79.56
SVM rbf spread = 0.5657 *pdf* radii 2,3,5,10,21,23	65.33	28.47	40.88	59.12	71.53
SVM rbf spread = 2.2627 *cdf* radii 1-70 +**PCA**	63.14	42.34	31.39	68.61	57.66
SVM rbf spread = 2.2627 *cdf* radii 1-70	62.41	32.12	43.07	56.93	67.88
SVM rbf spread = 1.1314 *pdf* radii 1-70 +**PCA**	60.22	43.80	35.77	64.23	56.20
SVM rbf spread = 0.5657 *pdf* radii 1-70	**63.14**	**36.50**	**37.23**	**62.77**	**63.50**

PNN classifier	%CC	%FP	%FN	%SE	%SP
PNN spread =5 *pdf* radii 2,3,5,10,21,23 +**PCA**	56.57	22.63	64.23	35.77	77.37
PNN spread =5 *pdf* radii 2,3,5,10,21,23	56.57	22.63	64.23	35.77	77.37
PNN spread =5 *cdf* radii 1-70 +**PCA**	60.58	36.50	42.34	57.66	63.50
PNN spread =5 *cdf* radii 1-70	**62.04**	**35.77**	**40.15**	**59.85**	**64.23**
PNN spread =5 *pdf* radii 1-70 +**PCA**	58.76	42.34	40.15	59.85	57.66
PNN spread =5 *pdf* radii 1-70	60.22	48.91	30.66	69.34	51.09

5. Results

The median of the probability density function *(pdf)* extracted from the plaques can be seen in Fig. 2 while the median of the cumulative distribution function *(cdf)* can be seen in Fig. 3. Both are plotted against the radius of the pattern spectra used which is in the range of 1 to 70. According to the results we can observe that the symptomatic *cdf* is *stochastically* larger than the asymptomatic *cdf*. This implies that dark regions in the symptomatic cases were somewhat closer together, leaving smaller holes between the dark regions [17].

The *cdf*s and *pdf*s of different pattern spectra described in section 3 were used in order to classify the two classes of images using the PNN and SVM classifiers. Both classifiers were tested on both the *pdf* and *cdf* feature sets. The first set included features produced for the whole range of the radii investigated (1-70) while the second set included the pattern spectra of selected radii (2, 3, 5, 10, 21, and 23) [18]. In order to decide about the second set; the discriminatory power of the different pattern spectra radii was evaluated using the C4.5 decision trees algorithm [19]. The C4.5 was run and the pattern spectra radius with the highest discriminative score was computed. This pattern spectra was then removed and the C4.5 was run again to compute the next one discriminative feature. This procedure was carried out for 5 iterations and generated columns 2, 3, 5, 10, 21, 23. The dimensionality of the feature vectors from both sets was reduced using Principal Components Analysis (PCA) to account for 98% of the total variance.

Table 1 presents the results of the ROC analysis for the SVM and PNN classifiers for the different feature sets investigated. The highest percentage of correct classifications score was 66.7% and was achieved using the SVM classifier on the second set of data (*pdf* radii 2, 3, 5, 10, 21, and 23 + PCA). For PNN models, the highest percentage of corrects classifications score achieved was 62.04% for *cdf* radii 1-70.

6. Conclusions

Concluding, morphological features can help us understand the interrelations among different plaque intensity regions in ultrasound imaging of the carotid. In this study we have examined morphological results from gray scale images and we have found that there is significant overlap between pattern spectra coming from symptomatic and asymptomatic plaques. Most of the discriminating power was concentrated in the smaller components (with radii less than 30, as shown in Fig. 2). These results are comparable to results produced for multiscale morphological analysis of a similar dataset [5-8] as well as results produced by another group [4].

In previous work carried out by our group the highest percentage of correct classifications was 73% using texture features and the self-organising map (SOM) classifier [5]. Furthermore it was shown in [6-8] that multiscale morphological analysis features compare well with the most successful texture feature sets and provide additional information for the identification of individuals at risk of stroke. The combination of texture and morphology features slightly increased the correct classifications score [17].

Future work will include the investigation of the correct classification rate on larger and different data sets and the use of clinical factors.

Acknowledgment

This work was funded through the project Integrated System for the Evaluation of Ultrasound Imaging of the Carotid Artery (TALOS), of the Research Promotion Foundation of Cyprus.

References

1. G. Belcaro, A.N. Nicolaides, G. Laurora et al., Ultrasound morphology classification of the arterial wall and cardiovascular events in a 6-year follow-up study, *Arterioscler Thromb Vasc Biol* **16**, 851-6 (1996).
2. N. El-Barghouti, A.N. Nicolaides, T. Tegos et al., The relative effect of carotid plaque heterogeneity and echogenicity on ipsilateral cerebral infarction and symptoms of cerebrovascular disease, *Int Angiol* **15**, 300-6 (1996).
3. J.A.C Arnold, K.B. Modaresi, N. Thomas et al., Carotid plaque characterization by duplex scanning. Observer error may undermine current clinical trials, *Stroke* **30**, 61-5 (1999).
4. J.E. Wilhjelm, L.M. Gronholdt, B. Wiebe, S.K. Jespersen, L.K. Hansen, H. Sillesen, Quantitative Analysis of Ultrasound B-Mode Images of Carotid Atherosclerotic Plaque: Correlation with Visual Classification and Histological Examination, *IEEE Transactions on Medical Imaging*, **17**(6), 910-922 (1998).
5. C.I. Christodoulou, C.S. Pattichis, M. Pantziaris, A. Nicolaides, Texture Based Classification of Atherosclerotic Carotid Plaques, *IEEE Tr. on Med. Im.*, **22**, 902-912 (2003).
6. C.I Christodoulou, E. Kyriacou, M.S.Pattichis, C.S. Pattichis, A. Nicolaides, " A Comparative Study of Morphological and other Texture Features for the Characterization of Atherosclerotic Carotid Plaques", *Proc of CAIP 2003*, The Netherlands, 165-173, (2003).
7. C.I. Christodoulou, C.S. Pattichis, E. Kyriacou, M.S. Pattichis et. al., in:Applied Medical Image Analysis Methods. ed. by L. Costaridou, (CRC Press 2005), 87-135.
8. E. Kyriacou, M.S. Pattichis, C. Christodoulou, C.S. Pattichis, S. Kakkos, A. Nikolaides, in: Plaque Characterization using Multimodality Imaging: Pixel to Molecular, Ed. by J.S. Suri, C. Yuan, D.L. Wilson, S. Laxminarayan, (IOS Press, 2005), 241-275.
9. E. Kyriacou, M. Pattichis , C. Christodoulou , C. Pattichis, S. Kakkos , A. Nicolaides, Multiscale Morphological Analysis of the Atherosclerotic Carotid Plaque, *Proceedings of the 27th Annual Int. Conf. IEEE EMBS*, Shanghai, China (2005).
10.T.J. Tegos, M.M. Sametai, A.N. Nicolaides et al., Comparability of the ultrasonic tissue characteristics of carotid plaques, *J Ultrasound Med* **19**, 399-407 (2000).
11.C. Loizou, C. Pattichis, R. Istepanian, M. Pantziaris, A. Nicolaides, Atherosclerotic Carotid Plaque Segmentation, *Proceedings of the 26th Annual Int. IEEE EMBS conf.* USA, (2004).
12.E.R. Dougherty, *An Introduction to Morphological Image Processing*, (SPIE Optical Engineering Press 1992).
13.P. Maragos, Pattern spectrum and multiscale shape representation, *IEEE Trans. on Pattern Analysis and Machine Intelligence* **11**, 701 715 (1989).
14.D.F Specht, Probabilistic Neural Networks, *INNS Neural Networks* **3**(1), 109-118 (1990).
15.T. Joachims 11 in: Making large-Scale SVM Learning Practical. Advances in Kernel Methods - Support Vector Learning, B. Schölkopf and C. Burges and A. Smola (ed.) (MIT Press. 1999).
16.R.C. Ebrchart, R.W. Dobbins, *Neural Networks PC Tools A Practical Guide* (Academic Pr., 1990)
17.A. Mavrommatis, *Morphology of Carotid US Images*, MSc thesis, (Univ. of Cyprus 2006).
18.S. Panagiotou, *Classification of Plaques Using SVM Class.*, MSc thesis, (Univ. of Cyprus 2006).
19.J. Han, M. Kamber, *Data Mining: Concepts and Techniques* (Morgan Kaufmann, 2000).